Dictionary of
Pāli–Sanskrit–Hindi–English

Yogendra Singh

International Research
Institute of Buddhist Studies
Lucknow

D.K. Printworld (P) Ltd.
New Delhi

Cataloging in Publication Data — DK
[Courtesy: D.K. Agencies (P) Ltd. <docinfo@dkagencies.com>]

Singh, Yogendra, 1953-
    Dictionary of Pāli–Sanskrit–Hindi–English/
Yogendra Singh.
    p.   cm.
    English, Hindi, Pali and Sanskrit.
    ISBN 13: 9788124605240
    ISBN 10: 8124605246

    1. Buddhism — Dictionaries — Pali. 2. Buddhism —
Dictionaries — Sanskrit. 3. Pali language — Dictionaries —
Hindi. 4. Sanskrit language — Dictionaries — Hindi. 5. Pali
language — Dictionaries — English. 6. Sanskrit language —
Dictionaries — English. I. Tittle.

DDC 294.303   22

ISBN 13: 978-81-246-0524-0   ISBN 10: 81-246-0524-6
First Published in India in 2011
© International Research Institute of Buddhist Studies, Lucknow
First print run 1000 copies

Published by:
International Research Institute of Buddhist Studies
Vipin Khand, Gomti Nagar, Lucknow (U.P.)
Ph: (0522) 230 0504

and

D.K. Printworld (P) Ltd.
Regd. office : 'Srikunj,' F-52, Bali Nagar
Ramesh Nagar Metro Station
New Delhi - 110 015
Phones : (011) 2545 3975, 2546 6019; *Fax* : (011) 2546 5926
E-mail : indology@dkprintworld.com   *Web* : www.dkprintworld.com

Printed by: D.K. Printworld (P) Ltd. New Delhi.

THE DALAI LAMA

Preface

The teachings of the Buddha and their subsequent recording in Buddhist literature, both originated in India, giving rise to two streams of transmission: the Pali tradition and the Sanskrit tradition. While the Pali tradition flourished in southern countries like Sri Lanka, Burma, Thailand and Cambodia; the Sanskrit tradition prospered in northern lands such as China, Korea, Japan, Vietnam and Tibet. Thus, Pāli and Sanskrit are the original languages to which we may trace all the original Buddhist teachings. Both traditions thrived at the University of Nalanda, which I regard as the principle source of the Buddhist culture that came to Tibet. Therefore, I am delighted to know that the Interantional Research Institute of Buddhist Studies in Lucknow have completed the assembly of a *Pāli–Sanskrit–Hindi–English Dictionary* that will be of immense value to contemporary scholars in India who wish to study and unravel the original texts. My heartiest congratulations to all concerned.

8 September 2010

Prologue

THE teachings of the Buddha and the main Buddhist literature, in orginal, as well as in translation form, are contained mainly in Pāli, Sanskrit, Tibetan and Chinese, though the Buddhist texts were also translated into the languages of the other countries where Buddhism spread and became a popular religion during the later period. To study the core of the subject, the knowledge of the languages and the exact meaning of the words in proper context, situation and environment are essential. To provide a perfect study companion to the student of Buddhist studies, the idea of various comprehensive bilingual and polylingual dictionaries consisting of words of different languages floated in the minds of the members of the Executive Committee of Acharya Narendra Dev International Research Institute of Buddhist Studies, Lucknow, UP (previous name of the Institute) and a resolution was passed in the year 1989. The dream project was undertaken by the director of the Institute and in the first part of the planning the preparation of *Pāli–Sanskrit–Hindi–English Dictionary* was completed.

As a result of the above-mentioned project, we are much delighted to present the first part of the dictionary entitled *Pāli–Sanskrit–Hindi–English Dictionary*. The dictionary has been specially written to help those students who wish to carry on Buddhist studies and researches based on Pāli and Sanskrit languages. It has been one of the chief aims of the compiler to include in this dictionary all the words which are popularly used in the Buddhist Pāli and Sanskrit literature. To fulfil the purpose much stress has been laid on bringing out a really useful, enlarged and cheap edition.

The dictionary has been simplified as far as is humanly possible, giving easy assistance to the readers and researchers of Pāli canons. We have spared no effort to make the dictionary as useful as possible to a learner of the languages, but being the first work of its kind in the history of Buddhist literature, it has its own shortcomings and limitations. We hope that the learned people working in the field of lexicography would certainly make suggestions to improve it, and this dictionary will be a helping hand to the students, and the scholars will appreciate its utility. We have great pleasure in introducing it and wish all success to the furure projects of other bilingual dictionaries.

In the preparation of this dictionary the enormous help, guidance and advice provided by (late) Dr Jagdev Singh and (late) Prof. Bhikku Chandra Ratan was extraordinary. I express my deep sense of gratitude to them because without their sound effort this work would not have been completed.

Director   **Dr Yogendra Singh**
I.R.I.B.S

संकेत सूची (Abbreviations)

अ०	अव्यय	adjectival preposition
उप०	उपसर्ग	prefix
क्रि०	क्रिया	verb
क्रि० वि०	क्रिया विशेषण	adverb
कृ०	कृदन्त	an absolutive
चु०	चुरादिगण	verbs
जा० स०	जातक संख्या	noun (Buddha's previous birth stories)
दि०	दिवादिगण	verbs
न०	नपुंसक लिंग	neuter
पु०	पुल्लिंग	masculine
पू० क्रि०	पूर्वकालिक क्रिया	preterite verb
भूत०	भूतकाल	past tense
भू० क० कृ०	भूतकालिक कर्मणि कृदन्त (क्त)	praty-ay (implicit belief)
वि०	विशेषण	adjective
सर्व०	सर्वनाम	pronoun
स्त्री०	स्त्रीलिंग	feminine

अ

अ – (1) देवनागरी वर्णमाला का प्रथम अक्षर। the first letter of Devnāgarī script.

(2) एक उपसर्ग। पालि में संयुक्त वञ्जनों के पूर्व 'आ' उपसर्ग का ह्रस्व रूप। जैसे: आ+क्रोशति = अक्कोसति। a prefix. In Pāli prefix *ā* is shortened before a double consonant, e.g. *ā+kroṣati = akkosati.*

(3) नञ् तत्पुरुष समास में 'अ' का प्रयोग उपसर्गवत् होता है। इसका प्रयोग कुछ संज्ञा एवं विशेषण शब्दों के पूर्व निषेधात्मक अर्थ में किया जाता है। जैसे : न+कुसल = अकुसल। *a* is used as negative prefix to some nouns, adjectives and participles, e.g. *na+kusal = akusal.*

(4) भूतकाल (लङ् लकार) में धातु के पूर्व प्रयुक्त होने वाला उपसर्ग। जैसे अकासि = अकार्जीत (क्रिया)। the argument prefixed to some roots in the past-tense, e.g. *akāsi* — did.

अकट – भू० क्रि० (अकृत) अनिर्मित। not done, not artificial, natural.

अकत – देखें – 'अकट' see Akaṭa.

अकतं – न० (निर्वाणम्) निर्वाण, मुक्ति। liberation from existence.

अकतञ्ञु – वि० (अकृतज्ञ) कृतघ्न। ungrateful.

अकतञ्ञु-जातक (जा० सं० 10) – न० (अकृतज्ञ जातक) अकृतज्ञ व्यापारी की जातक कथा। the Jātaka tale of an ungrateful merchant.

अकनिट्ठदेव – पु० – (अकनिष्ठदेव) पाँच शुद्धावासों में से उच्चतम आवास में रहने वाले शीर्षस्थ देवगण। a class of superior gods living in the highest of the five *śuddhāvāsas.*

अकम्पियत्त – वि० – (अ+कम्पति) अकम्पित, स्थिर। the condition of not being shaken, stable.

अकलु – (अगरु) अगर नामक सुगन्धित काष्ठ से तैयार किया गया लेप। an ointment of black candana (sandalwood).

अकल्लं – न० – (अ+कल्यम्) व्याधि, रुग्णता। disease.

अकाच – वि० – (अ+काच) कच्चापन (अशुद्धता) रहित, निर्दोष, शुद्ध। pure, flawless.

अकारिय – वि० (कटु) कड़आ। bitter.

अकालरावी-जातक (जा० सं० 119) – असमय बांग देने वाले मुर्गे की जातक कथा। a Jātaka tale (No. 119) of a cock crowing at inappropriate time.

अकासीय – पु० – (अकाशीयः) जो काशीवासी न हो, राजस्व वसूलने वाले राज्य कर्मियों का एक वर्ग। not from the Kāśi-habitat, official name of certain tax collectors in king's service.

अकिच्चकार – पु० – (अ+कृत्य+कारः) अकरणीय कार्य करने वाला, कर्त्तव्य की अवहेलना करने वाला। not doing one's duty, doing what ought not to be done.

अकिंचन – वि० – (अकिञ्चनः) निर्धन, सम्पदाहीन। poor.

अकिरिय – वि० – (अ+क्रियः) निष्क्रिय, निठल्ला, अव्यावहारिक। not practical, unwise.

अकिलासु – वि० – (क्रियाशील) क्रियाशील, अप्रमादी। active, untiring, diligent.

अकुतोभय – वि० – (अकुतः+भय) जिसे कहीं या किसी से भय न हो, नितान्त भय रहित, निडर। fearless, one having no fear from any side, brave.

अकुप्प – वि० – (अ+कुप्प) स्थिर, अचंचल। immovable, steadfast, sure.

अकुप्पता-भाव – (अकम्पः) स्थिरता, अचंचलता। stability, steadi-ness, immovability.

अकुसल (अ + कुशलः) – जिसका परिणाम क्षेमकारी न हो गर्हित, पाप कर्म act of sin, demerit, bad action.

अकोविद – वि० – (अ + कोविदः) अनिपुण, दक्षतारहित। not clever, unskilful.

अक्क (1) – पु० – (अर्क) – अर्क-अक्का, अकौना, मदार नामक पौधा। a plant named *Galotropis Grigantis.*

अक्क (2) (अर्कः) – सूर्य। the sun.

अक्कन्त (अक्रान्तः) – जिस पर आक्रमण किया गया हो। पराभूत, आर्त। stepped upon, mount.

अवकन्दति (आ + √क्रन्द) – क्रन्दन करता है, विलाप करता है, चिल्लाता है। cries, laments, wails.

अक्कमन – न० – (आ + √क्रम = आक्रमण) हमला, धावा, चढ़ाई, चोट, वार। stepping upon, invasion, attack.

अक्कमति – क्रि० – (आ + √क्रम) आक्रमण करता है। attacks, steps upon, invades.

अक्कम्म – क्रि० – (आ + √क्रम +ल्यप् = आक्रम्य) आक्रमण करके, चढ़ाई करके। having attacked, invaded.

अक्कवन – न० – (अर्कवन) देखें 'अन्ध-वन'। see 'Andhavan.'

अक्कोस – (आ + क्रोशः) आक्रोश, चीख-पुकार, कुत्सा, कोसना, कटूक्ति। insult, abuse, reproach.

अक्कौन – न० – (अर्कवन) देखें 'अन्ध-वन'. see 'Andhavan'.

अक्ख (1) – पु० – (अक्षः) अक्ष, गाड़ी की धुरी। axle of cart or chariot.

अक्ख (2) – पु० – (अक्षः) जुए का पाँसा। dice for gambling.

अक्खक – न० – (अक्षकम्) गरदन के पास की हँसली नामक हड्डी। the collar-bone.

अक्खग्ग-कील – स्त्री० – (अक्षाग्र कीलकम्) धुरे पर आगे लगी कील। axis-bolt.

अक्खण – पु० – (अ + क्षणः) अनुपयुक्त बेला, अनुचित समय, दुर्भाग्य, बुरे दिन। inappropriate time, mis-fortune, misadventure, bad luck.

अक्खण वेधी – पु० – (अ + क्षण + वेधी) विद्युत गति से लक्ष्यवेध करने वाला धनुर्धर। an archer who shoots like lightning.

अक्खत – वि० – (अ + क्षत) अक्षत, जिसे चोट न लगी हो, अनाहत। unhurt, not wounded.

अक्खदस्स – पु॰ – (अक्ष + दर्शः) न्यायाधीश, निर्णायक। a judge, an umpire.

अक्खदेवी – पु॰ – (अक्ष + √ दिव्) जुआरी धूर्त्त। gambler, cunning.

अक्खधुत्त – पु॰ – (अक्ष + धूर्त्त) जुआरी। gambler.

अक्खय – वि॰ – (अ + क्षय) जिसका क्षय न हो, समाप्त न होने वाला। decayless, endless, eternal.

अक्खर – वि॰ सं॰ – (अ + क्षर) जिसका क्षरण न हो, वर्ण, हर्फ। a letter, a syllable, undecaying.

अक्खर फलक – न॰ (अक्षर + फलक) लिखने की पाटी, स्लेट, तख्ती। a board or slate to write on.

अक्खर समय – पु॰ (अक्ष + समय) लिखने-पढ़ने की कला। the art of reading and writing.

अक्खर माला – (अक्षर माला) पालि तथा सिंहली वर्णमाला के बारे में एक पदमयी रचना। a poetic book about Pāli and Simhalī syallables.

अक्खरिका – (अक्षरिका) एक मनोविनोद जिसमें उंगलियों से आकाश में संकेतित अक्षरो समूहों अथवा उंगली से पीठ पर संकेतित शब्दों को पढ़ना होता है। a game of recognizing syallables written in air or one's back.

अक्खात – क्रि॰ वि॰ – (आख्यात) कहा गया, व्याख्याकृत। announced, proclaimed.

अक्खातर – पु॰ – (आख्यातृ) आख्यान कर्ता, व्याख्याता, उपदेशक, मार्गद्रष्टा। speaker, preacher, story-teller.

अक्खाति – क्रि॰ – (आ + √ ख्या) कहता है, सुनाता है, समझाता है। says, declares, narrates.

अक्खान – नपु॰ – (आख्यानम्) आख्यान, कथा-वार्त्ता। story, legend, tale.

अक्खि – (अक्षि) आंख, नेत्र। the eye.

अक्खि-अंजन – (अक्षि अञ्जनम्) आंख में स्वास्थ्य अथवा सुन्दरता के लिए लगाया जाने वाला लेप। eye ointment, collyrium.

अक्खि-कूप – (अक्षि कूपम्) नेत्र गोलक। eyeball.

अक्खि-गण्ड – (अक्षिगण्ड) बरौनी। eye lashes.

अक्खि-गूथ – आंख का कीचड़। secretion from the eye.

अक्खि-छिद्द – (अक्षि छिद्रः) नेत्र का गड्ढा। socket of eye.

अक्खि-तारा-तारका – (अक्षितारकम्) आँख की पुतली, कनीनिका। pupil of eye.

अक्खि-दल – (अक्षिदल) आँख की पलक। the eyelid.

अक्खिपात – (अक्षिपात) दृष्टिपात। eye reach, glance.

अक्खिमल – (अक्षिमलः) आँख की मैल, कीचड़। dirt of eye.

अक्खिरोग – (अक्षि रोगः) नेत्र-रोग, दृष्टि-दोष। eye disease.

अक्खिक (1) – (अक्षिक) जाल रन्ध्र। the mesh of net.

अक्खिक (2) – (अक्षिकः) नेत्रवाला, दृष्टि सम्पन्न। having eye, with eyes.

अक्खिकाद्ध – वि॰ (अक्षिकार्द्ध) कनखियों से निहारने वाला। with half an eye, i.e. stealthily.

अक्खिकाण – (अक्षिकाणः) कानी आँख वाला। one-eyed man.

अक्खित्त (1) – (अ + क्षिप्त) जो फेंका न गया हो। not thrown aways.

अक्खित्त (2) – (आ + क्षिप्त) आक्षेपयुक्त, निष्कासित, फेंका हुआ। struck, exile, thrown.

अक्खोब्भ – (अ + √क्षुभ) अक्षोभ शान्त, अविचलित, निर्विकार। imperturbable, calm.

अक्खोबिनी – (अक्षौहिणी) सैन्य व्यूह की एक प्राचीन इकाई जिसमें 109350 पदाति, 65910 अश्वारोही, 21870 हाथी, और 21870 रथ सम्मिलित रहते थे। an army of 109350 soldiers, 65910 horses, 21870 elephants and 21870 chariots.

अक्खोभिनी – देखें अक्खोबिनी। see Akkhobinī.

अक्खोहिनी – देखें अक्खोबिनी। see Akkhobinī.

अक्खोहिणी – स्त्री॰ – (अक्षौहिणी) सम्पूर्ण सेना। total army.

अखेत्त – (अ + क्षेत्र) अक्षेत्र, अनुपयुक्त स्थान, बंजर भूमि। unsuitable place, barren soil, infertile.

अखात – न॰ – (आ + √खन = खात) गड्ढा, खाई। trench, pit.

अखिल – वि॰ – (अखिल) समस्त। the whole.

अग – वि॰ – (अ + ग = अग) अचल पर्वत, वृक्ष। immovable mountain, tree.

अगति – (अ + गति) दुर्गति, कुत्सित गति, कुपथ। evil practice, wrong doing.

अगद – (अ + गद) गद अर्थात् रोग की नाशक औषधि। medicine, drug.

अगरु (1) – वि॰ – (अ + गुरु) जो भारी न हो, हल्का। not heavy, not troublesome.

अगरु (2) – (अगरु) अगर नामक वृक्ष जिसका सुगंधित काष्ठ प्रसाधन में प्रयोग किया जाता है। aloewood.

अगलु – देखें अगरु (2)। see Agaru (2).

अगाध – वि॰ – (अगाध) अत्यधिक गहरा। very deep.

अगार – पु॰ – (आगार) घर, निवास-स्थान। house, dwelling place.

अगारिक-अगारिया – (आगारिक) गृही, गृहस्थ। layman, householder.

अग्ग – वि॰ – (अग्र) प्रथम, श्रेष्ठ। the highest, topmost, the superior one.

अग्गज – पु॰ – (अग्रज) बड़ा भाई। elder brother.

अग्गञ्ञ – वि॰ – (अग्रगण्य) श्रेष्ठ, अग्रतम। topmost.

अग्गता – स्त्री॰ – (अग्रता) श्रेष्ठता। superiority.

अग्गतो – अ॰ – (अग्रतः) आगे, सामने। in front of.

अग्गफल – (अग्र फलम्) फसल का प्रथम अन्नोत्पाद। the first harvest of a cultivation.

अग्गमग्ग – (अग्र मार्ग) निर्वाण प्राप्ति का श्रेष्ठ मार्ग। the superior path of salvation.

अग्गमहेसी – (अग्रमहिषी) पटरानी, प्रधान महिषी। the queen consort.

अगगञ्ञ – (अग्रगण्य) सत्कृतों मे प्रथम, यशस्वियों में श्रेष्ठ। known as the highest or foremost.

अग्गल – (अर्गल) अर्गला, किल्ली, सिटकनी। bolt, latch, sliding bar.

अग्गलत्थम्भ – पु० – (अर्गल स्तम्भ) अर्गला का खम्भा। pole fitted with sliding bar.

अग्गि – (अग्नि) अग्नि, आग। fire.

अग्गिक्खन्ध – पु० – (अग्नि स्कन्ध) लपटों का समूह, ज्वाला पुंज। a great mass of fire.

अग्गि जाल – न० (अग्निज्वाल) धव का फूल। flower of 'DHAVA' tree.

अग्गि परिचरण – (अग्नि परिचरण) अग्निचर्या, अग्निहोत्र। fire worship.

अग्गिसाला – (अग्निशाला) अग्निहोत्र कक्ष, यज्ञशाला। a room meant for fire worship.

अग्गि सिखा – (अग्नि-शिखा) लपट, ज्वाला। flame.

अग्गि हुत्त – (अग्निहोत्र) समिधाग्नि में होम पदार्थों की पूजाहुति। fire-sacrifice.

अग्गिक जातक (जा० स० 129) – ऐसे शृगाल की जातक कथा जिसके केश जंगल की आग से जल गये थे। a Jātaka tale (No. 129) of a jackal whose hair was burnt in a jungle fire.

√अग्घक्वादि – (√अर्घ) योग्य अथवा मूल्य का होना। worthy.

अग्घ (अर्घ) मूल्य, कीमत। price, worth, value.

अग्घक – (अर्घक) मूल्य निर्धारण करने वाला। an evaluator.

अग्घानक – देखें अग्घक। see Agghaka.

अग्घति – (अर्घति) मूल्योचित गुणवत्ता धारण करना। to deserve, to have the value of.

अग्घापन – (अर्घापण) मूल्य या अर्घता निर्धारित करना।. setting a price or valuation.

अग्घापनक – (अर्घापणक) मूल्य आँकने वाला, अर्घता निर्धारित करने वाला जौहरी। valuator.

अग्घापनीय – (अर्घापणीय) मूल्य आँकने योग्य वस्तु। that which is to be valued.

अग्घिक – पुष्पार्चन / माल्यार्पण द्वारा अभिवादन करना। to welcome with garland made of flowers, an obligation.

अग्घिय – किसी सम्पूज्य का, अभ्यागत का, पुष्पों से अभिवादन। garlanding of a guest, welcome with flowers.

अघ – (अघ) पाप, दुःख, विपत्ति, अशौच। grief, sin, pain, misfortune.

√अङ्क – (भ्वादि) – (√अङ्क) लक्षणे –– निशान बनाना, लिख लेना। to mark, to write.

अङ्क (1) – (अङ्कः) उत्संग, गोद, कोरा। the lap.

अङ्क (2) – (अङ्कः) लांछन, चिह्न। a mark, sign.

अङ्क (3) – (अङ्कः) संख्यावाची आकृति। a numerical figure.

अङ्कित – कृ० – (अङ्कित) अंकन किया हुआ, चिह्नित। marked.

अङ्कुर – (अङ्कुरः) अँखुआ, डाभ, कली। sprout, bud, shoot.

अङ्कुस – पु॰ – (अङ्कुशः) अंकुश, नियन्त्रक हाथी को वश में करने हेतु लौह-अस्त्र। good, an elephant-driver's hook.

अङ्कति – (√अङ्क लट् प्र॰ पन॰) अंकन करता है। marking something.

√अङ्ग – (भ्वादि) – (गमनार्थे) जाना। to go.

अङ्ग (1) (अङ्ग) बुद्धकालीन सोलह महाजन पदों में से एक। यह मगध के पूर्व स्थित था। चम्पा नदी इसे मगध से पृथक् करती थी। चम्पा नामक नगरी अंग की राजधानी थी। वर्तमान भागलपुर नगर प्राचीन चम्पा के सन्निकट बसा है। One of the great sixteen states mentioned in *pīṭhas*. It was situated east of Magadha, Champā was its capital, present-day Bhāgalpur is near ancient Champā city.

अङ्ग (2) – (अङ्ग) शरीर के अवयव, आंख, कान, हाथ, पांव, आदि। parts of body, elements of body, eye, ear, etc.

अङ्ग-राग – (अङ्ग-राग) सुगन्धित द्रव्यों से निर्मित चूर्ण जिसका प्रयोग अथवा उबटन आजकल के पाउडर की भांति शरीर प्रसाधन में होता था। fragrant powder for painting or applying on body talcum powder.

अङ्ग-जात – न॰ – (अङ्गजातम्) पुरुषेन्द्रिय अथवा जननेन्द्रिय। male or female organs.

अङ्गण – न॰ – (अङ्गणम्) आँगन। a courtyard, an open space.

अङ्गद – (अङ्गदम) बाजूबन्द-भुजवलय नामक आभूषण। ornament, bracelet for arm.

अङ्गना – (अङ्गना) नारी, कामिनी। woman.

अङ्ग-विज्जा – स्त्री॰ – (अङ्गविद्या) हस्त रेखाओं अथवा शरीर के अन्य अंगों के लक्षण के आधार पर भविष्य कथन की विद्या, सामुद्रिक शास्त्र। palmistry and other predictions from the marks on the body.

अङ्गार – (अङ्गारः) लकड़ी का दहकता हुआ कोयला। burning charcoal.

अङ्गिक – (अङ्गिक) अवयवों वाला। consisting of many parts.

अङ्गीरस – बुद्ध का समुज्जवल, दैदीप्यमान गुण बोधक नाम। the resplendent one, the Buddha.

अङ्गुट्ठ – (अङ्गुष्ठ) अँगूठा। thumb.

अङ्गुल – (अङ्गुल) अंगुल, एक गज का सोलहवां भाग। about an inch, a finger breadth.

अङ्गुलि – स्त्री॰ – (अङ्गुलि) अँगुली। finger.

अङ्गुलि-अट्ठि – (अङ्गुलि अस्थि) अंगुली की हड्डी। finger-bone.

अङ्गुलि-पब्ब – (अङ्गुलि पर्व) अंगुली की पोर। a knuckle, space between two joints of fingers.

अङ्गुलीयक – स्त्री॰ – (अङ्गुलीयक) अंगूठी। finger-ring.

अङ्गुलिमालसुत्त – (अङ्गुलिमाल-सूत्र) दस्युवृत्ति अङ्गुलिमाल के बुद्धानुभाव से हृदय परिवर्तन और स्थविर पद पाने का वृत्त (मज्झिम निकाय II.97)। the story of bandit Aṅgulimāla's conversion (Majjhima Nikāya II.97).

अङ्गुलि-मुद्धा – स्त्री॰ – (अङ्गुलि मुद्रिका) उंगली में धारण की जाने वाली अंगूठी। finger ornament, ring.

अंगुली – स्त्री० – (अङ्गुलि) उँगली। finger.

अंगुल्याभरण – न० – (अङ्गुलि + आभरणम्) अगूठी। finger-ring, ornament

अचल – वि० – (अचल) स्थिर, जो चलायमान न हो, अविचलित। immovable, steady, unshaken.

अचिर – (अ + चिर) सद्य नूतन, जो अभी-अभी हुआ हो। recent, new, nascent.

अचिरप्रभा – स्त्री० – (अचिरप्रभा) क्षणिदा, चंचला, बिजली। lightning.

अचिरवती – (अचिरवती) वर्तमान राप्ती नदी जो वर्तमान नेपाल देश के राप्ती अंचल से निकलकर उत्तर प्रदेश (भारत) के गोनर्द क्षेत्र में श्रावस्ती नगरी की उत्तरी सीमा पर बहती हुई घाघरा नदी में जाकर मिल जाती है। अचिरवती > अचिरावती > अजिरावती > ऐरावती > राप्ती। प्राचीन काल में मध्य देश में पंचमहानदियों में इनकी गणना होती थी। modern Rāptī river, running from Nepal to Uttar Pradesh. Also called Airawathi, counted in ancient times as one of the five great rivers.

अचेतन – वि० – (अचेतन) चेतना-रहित, बेहोश, जड़। senseless, inorganic.

अचेल – वि० पु० – (अ + चेल) निर्वस्त्र, नंगा। void of cloth, naked.

अचेलक – पु० – (अ + चेलकः) निर्वस्त्र रहने वाला साधु। naked ascetic, saint.

√अच्च – भ्वादि – (√अर्चपूजने) पूजा करना। to worship.

√अच्च (चु) – (√अर्च् = अर्चने) पूजा करना। to worship.

अच्चगा – (अति + √गम) अत्यगः। जो सबसे आगे निकल गया, सबको पार कर गया. one who surpassed, ahead of all.

अच्चङ्कुस – (अत्यङ्कुस) नियन्त्रण-शक्ति से बाहर। beyond control.

अच्चना – स्त्री० – (अर्चना) अर्चना, पूजा, वन्दना। worship, respect.

अच्चन्त – अ० – (अत्यन्त) अत्यन्त, निरन्तर। absolute, continuously.

अच्चय – (अत्ययः) अपराध, दोष। fault, guilt.

अच्चायिक – (अत्यायिक) तत्काल किया जाने वाला कार्य। urgent, immediate.

अच्चासन्न – (अत्यासन्न) अतिशय सन्निकट। very close, very near.

अच्चि – (अर्चि) अर्चि, ज्वाला। flame.

अच्चिमन्तु – (अर्चिमन्तृ) अग्नि। fire.

अच्चित – (अर्चित) पूजित, सम्मानित। esteemed, respected, honoured.

अच्चग्गत – (अत्युद्गत) अत्यधिक ऊँचा। extremely high.

अच्चुण्ह – (अत्युष्ण) अत्यन्त उष्ण। very hot.

अच्चुत – (अच्युत) शाश्वत, निर्विकार। everlasting, eternal.

अच्चुत-पद – (अच्युत पद) निर्वाण पद। eternal peace.

अच्चुस्सन्न – (अत्युसन्न) अत्यधिक भरा हुआ, अति घना। much abundant.

अच्चेति – (अति + √इ = अत्येति) गुजर जाता है। elapses, passes by.

अच्चोगाळह – (अत्यवगाद्) अत्यधिक प्रचुरता में गया हुआ । plunged into a great depth.

अच्चोदक – न॰ – (अत्यूदकम्) अत्यधिक जल । too much water.

अच्छ – वि॰ – (अच्छ) अच्छा, स्वच्छ, साफ । clear, pure.

अच्छक – (ऋक्षकः) भालू, रीछ । bear.

अच्छति – (√आस्) बैठता है, स्थित होता है । sits, remains.

अच्छम्भि – (निर्भीक) निर्भय, भयरहित । fearless, not frightened.

अच्छरा संघात – (अच्छरा संघात) चुटकी बजाना । snapping of fingers.

अच्छरा सद्द – (अच्छरा शब्द) चुटकी या ताली की आवाज । sound of snapping or clapping.

अच्छरिय – न॰ – (आश्चर्यम्) अचरज, अचम्भा । wonder.

अच्छादन – न॰ – (आच्छादन) वस्त्र, परिधान । garment, clothes.

अच्छादेति – (आ + √छद् = आच्छादयति) आच्छादित करता है, वस्त्र पहनाता है । covers with, clothes.

अच्छि – स्त्री॰ – (अक्षि) आँख । eye.

अच्छिन्दति – (आ + √छिन्द् = आछिन्दति) लूटता है, छीनता है । plunders, snatches.

अच्छेछि – (आ + √छिन्द्) भूतकालिक क्रिया । काट डाला, नष्ट करना । destroyed, broken away, cut out.

अच्छेज्ज – वि॰ – (अ + √छिद् + ल्यप् = अछेद्य) जो काटा न जा सके, अनश्वर । unbreakable, indestructible.

√अज – सम् उपसर्ग के साथ जाने के अर्थ में आता है । to go, it is used with prefix *sam*.

अज-अजा – (अजः, अजा) बकरा, बकरी । he-goat, she-goat.

अजपाल – (अजपालकः) बकरी चराने वाला । goat-herd, shepherd.

अजलण्डिका – (अजविष्ठा) बकरी की मेंगनी । goat's dung.

अजगर – (अजगरः) अजगर नामक सर्प । phython, boa constrictor.

अजञ्ञ – वि॰ – (अ + जन्य) दूषित, गन्दा । impure, dirty.

अजञ्ञ – न॰ – (अ + जन + ल्यप्) विजन में उद्भूत खतरा । danger.

अजातसत्रु (1) – पु॰ – (अ + जात + शत्रु) जिसका कोई शत्रु न हो । having no enemy.

अजातसत्तु (2) – पु॰ – (अजातशत्रु) मगध ा नरेश बिम्बिसार का पुत्र । the son of Magadha emperor, Bimbhisāra.

अजानन – न॰ – (अ √ज्ञा) अज्ञता, अज्ञान । ignorance.

अजिन – पु॰ – (अजिन) चीतल मृग के चर्म से बना हुआ बटुआ । the hide of the cheetal antelope used for sitting on.

अजिनपत्ता – (कन्दुकयष्टिः) गेंद खेलने का बल्ला, कन्दुकापहारक । a bat or playing stick.

अजिनि – क्रि॰ – (अ + √जि) अजिनि । भूतकालिक जीत लिया । conquered.

अजिम्ह – वि॰ – (अ + जिह्म) जो टेढ़ा न हो, सीधा, अकुटिल, सरल ।not crooked, straight.

अजिर – न॰ (अजिरम्) आँगन। courtyard.

अजी – स्त्री॰ – (अजा) बकरी। she-goat.

अजीरक – (अजीर्ण) बदहजमी, अपच। indigestion.

अजेय्य – (अ + √जि + ल्यप = अजेय्य) जिसे जीता न जा सके। unconquerable.

अज्ज – (अद्य) आज। today.

√अज्ज – (भू) – (गमने) जाना। to go.

√अज्ज – चुरादि – (मार्जने) साफ करना। to clean.

अज्जतगे – (अद्यताग्रे) आज से। henceforth.

अज्जतन – वि॰ – (अद्यतन) अधुनातन, वर्तमानकालिक। modern, referring to the present time.

अज्जव – (आर्जव) ऋजुता, सारल्य, सीधापन। straightness.

अज्जित – वि॰ (अर्जित) कमाया हुआ। earned.

अज्जुन – पु॰ (अर्जुन) (1) अर्जुन नामक वृक्ष जिसकी छाल हृदय रोग की अचूक औषधि है। (2) अर्जुन, मध्यम पान्डव, पार्थ। (1) The tree *Penta Patera* whose bark cures heart ailments. (2) the third brother among Pāṇḍavas.

अज्झक्ख – पु॰ (अध्यक्ष) अध्यक्ष। chair person, president.

अज्झगा – क्रि॰ (अधि + √गम = अधिगच्छति का भूतकालिक रुप) प्राप्त किया, अनुभव किया, जान लिया। experienced, came to, obtained.

अज्झत्त – वि॰ (अधि + आप्त = अध्याप्त) स्वकीय। personal, connected with self.

अज्झतिक – वि॰ (आध्यात्मिक) आत्म सम्बन्धी। connected with soul, inward.

अज्झयन – न॰ (अध्ययनम्) अध्ययन। study, learning.

अज्झाचार – (अधि + आ √चर = अध्याचारः) अतिक्रमण, सम्भोग क्रिया। transgression, sexual intercourse.

अज्झाचिण्ण – क्रि॰ वि॰ – (अध्याचीर्ण अध्याचरित का भूतकालिक रुप) अभ्यस्त। much practised, habitually done.

अज्झापन – न॰ (अध्यापनम्) पढ़ाना। to teach.

अज्झाय – पु॰ (अध्यायः) अध्याय, सर्ग। a chapter.

अज्झायक – पु॰ (अध्यापकः) अध्यापक, शिक्षक। a teacher, a tutor, instructor.

अज्झारुहति – क्रि॰ – (अधि + आ √रुह् - अध्यारोहति) चढ़ता है, ऊपर चढ़ता है। to climb, to rise up.

अज्झावसति – क्रि॰ – (अधि + आ + √वस् - अध्यावसति) वर्तमानकालिक निवास करता है, घर में वास करता है। inhabiting now, residing.

अज्झासय – पु॰ (अधि + आशयः = अध्याशयः) आशय, इरादा, मन्तव्य। intention, disposition.

अज्झुपगच्छति – क्रि॰ (अधि + उप + गच्छति) प्राप्त होता है, सहमत होता है। arrives, reaches, consents.

अज्झुपगमन – न॰ (अध्युपगमनम्) सहमति, पहुंच। arrival, agreement, approach.

अज्झुपेक्खति – क्रि॰ (अधि + उपक्षति) उपेक्षा करता है। neglects, remains indifferent.

अज्झुपेक्खन – भाव संज्ञा – (अध्युपेक्षणम्) उपेक्षा भाव अन्यमनस्कता। indifference.

अज्झुपेति – क्रि॰ (अध्युपेति) समीप पहुँचता है। comes near, approaches.

अज्झेन – न॰ – (अध्ययनम्) अध्ययन। study.

अज्झेसना – स्त्री॰ (अध्येषणा) प्रार्थना, आमन्त्रण। request, invitation.

अज्झेसित – कृ॰ (अध्येषित) अध्येसति का भूतकालिक कृदन्त रूप। पार्थिव, आमन्त्रित। requested, invited.

अज्झोकास – पु॰ (अध्याकाशः) खुला आकाश। the open sky.

अज्झोकिरति – क्रि॰ (अधि + अव √किर्) बिखेरता है। scatters over.

अज्झोगहाति – क्रि॰ (अधि + अव √गाह्) डूबता है, निलीन होता है, धँसता है। plunges into, enters, immerses.

अज्झोगाळह – भू॰ कृ॰ (अध्यवगाहति का भूतकालिक कृदन्त रूप) डूबा हुआ, निलीन, धँसा हुआ। plunged into, immersed.

अज्झोसान – न॰ (अध्यवसानम्) (1) समाप्ति, विश्रान्ति (2) आसक्ति। (1) completion, (2) attachment.

अज्झोहरण – न॰ (अधि + अव √ह = अध्यवहरणम्) निगलना, खा लेना। swallowing, eating.

अज्झोहरणीय – कृ॰ (अधि + अव + ह + अनीयर = अध्यवहरणीय) निगलने योग्य, खाने लायक। fit to be swallowed or eaten.

√अञ्च – भ्वादि (गमने) जाना। to go.

√अञ्छ – भ्वादि (आयामे) खींचना, निकालना। to pull.

√अञ्ज – भ्वादि (व्यक्ति म्रक्षण कान्ति व्यक्त करना) मालिश करना, सजना, आदर करना, जाना। anoint, smear, adorn onself with, to go.

अञ्जति – क्रि॰ (अञ्जति) अंजन लगाता है। applies collyrium to the eyes.

अञ्जन – न॰ (अञ्जनम्) अंजन, सुरमा। of the colour of collyrium, i.e., black.

अञ्जनवण्ण – वि॰ – (अञ्जन वर्ण) अंजन की भांति काला। of the colour of collyrium, i.e. black.

अञ्जन – पु॰ (अञ्जनः) शुद्धोदन की दोनों पत्नियों महामाया तथा महाप्रजापति गौतमी के पिता। father of Śuddhodana's two wives Mahāmāyā and Mahāprajāpati Gautami.

अञ्जलि – स्त्री॰ (अञ्जलिः) अंजलि, अँजुरी। lifting of folded hands as a token of reverence.

अञ्जलिपुट – न॰ (अञ्जलिपुटम्) कोई वस्तु लेने के लिए दोनों हथेलियों को सटाकर बनायी गयी दोने जैसी आकृति। folded and joined in order to retain something palm.

अञ्जस – क्रि॰ वि॰ (अञ्जस्) साक्षात् सीधे, सरलता से। straight, easily.

अञ्ञ – सर्व॰ (अन्य) दूसरा, अन्य। other, another one.

अञ्ञतम – वि॰ (अन्यतमः) बहुतों में से एक, कोई एक। one of many, some-one.

अञ्ञतर – वि॰ (अन्यतरः) कोई, जो सुपरिचित न हो। unfamiliar person.

अञ्ञतित्थिय – पु॰ – (अन्य तीर्थिकः) अन्य सम्प्रदाय का अनुयायी। an adherent of another faith or religion.

अञ्ञत्थ / अञ्ञत्र – अव्यय (अन्यत्र) अन्यत्र, कहीं और। elsewhere, somewhere else.

अञ्ञथत्त – न॰ (अन्यधात्व) मन का अन्यथा भाव को प्राप्त होना। alteration, change of mind.

अञ्ञथा – अव्यय (अन्यथा) दूसरी तरह, अन्यथा। otherwise, on the other hand.

अञ्ञदत्थु – अव्यय – (अन्यदस्तु) निश्चित् ही, चाहे जैसी, दूसरी तरह। surely, at any rate, on the other hand.

अञ्ञदा – अव्यय – (अन्य + दा) यदा (जब) तदा (कब) सर्वदा (सदैव) की भांति बना शब्द अन्य दा (किसी दूसरी बार)। on another day, at another time.

अञ्ञमञ्ञ / अञ्ञोञ्ञ – वि॰ – (अन्योन्म्) परस्पर। mutual.

अञ्ञा – स्त्री॰ (आ + √ज्ञा) पूर्णज्ञान, सर्वज्ञाता, अर्हत्व। perfect knowledge, arhantship.

अञ्ञाण – न॰ (अज्ञानम्) अज्ञान, अज्ञता। ignorance.

अञ्ञात (1) – वि॰ (आ + ज्ञात) सुविज्ञात। well known.

अञ्ञात (2) – वि॰ – (अ + ज्ञात) अज्ञात, अपरिचित। unknown, unfamiliar.

अञ्ञात कोण्डञ्ञ – पु॰ (अज्ञात कोण्डन्यः) भगवान बुद्ध का प्रथम प्रव्रजित शिष्य। the first disciple of Lord Buddha.

अञ्ञातक – वि॰ (अ + ज्ञातकः) जो सगा-सम्बन्धी न हो, अपरिचित। unknown, not related by blood.

अञ्ञातावी – वि॰ – (आ + ज्ञात + विद्य) सर्वज्ञ, अन्तर्दृष्टि सम्पन्न। one who knows everything or has insight.

अञ्ञातुकाम – वि॰ – (आ + ज्ञातुकामः) ज्ञानपिपासु, पूर्ण ज्ञान पाने का इच्छुक। desirous to obtain full knowledge.

अञ्ञोञ्ञ – अव्यय (अन्योन्य) एक-दूसरे से। one another.

√अट – (भू) (गमने) घूमना। to wander.

अटन – न॰ (अटनम) भ्रमण करना, घूमना। to roam about.

अटवि – स्त्री॰ – (अटवी) जंगल। forest.

अट्ट (1) – न॰ (अट्ट पन॰) मकान के ऊपर का कमरा, बुर्जी, अटारी। room on house top, a watch tower.

अट्ट (2) – (अर्थः) मुकदमा, वाद, अभियोग। lawsuit, case.

अट्टक – देखें अट्टालक। see Aṭṭālaka.

अट्टाल – देखें अट्टालक। see Aṭṭālaka.

अट्टालक – पु॰ – (स्त्री॰ अट्टालिका) अट्टालिका एक से अधिक छतों वाला मकान। house with more than one storey.

अट्ठ – वि॰ – (अष्ट) आठ। eight.

अट्ठक – वि॰ – (अष्टकम्) आठ-आठ वस्तुओं का समूह। a group of eight.

अट्ठम – वि॰ (अष्टमः) देखें अट्ठयक।
see Aṭṭhayaka.

अट्ठमक – वि॰ (अष्टमकः) आठवाँ। the
eighth.

अट्ठकथा – स्त्री॰ – (अर्थकथा) अर्थकथन,
व्याख्या। explanation, exposition,
a commentary.

अट्ठङ्गिक – पु॰ – (अष्टाङ्गिक) आठ अंगों
वाला, आठ भागों अथवा आठ अवयवों
वाला। having eight constituents.

अट्ठिकोमग्गो – पु॰ – (अष्टाङ्गिक मार्ग)
सिद्धार्थ ने चार आर्य सत्यों का साक्षात्कार
कर बुद्ध–प्रबुद्ध होकर दुःखों से आत्यन्तिक
निवृत्ति के लिए जिस मध्यम मार्ग
(मज्झिमा-पटिपदा) का उपदेश किया था
उसके आठ विभाग हैं अर्थात् यह मार्ग
अठपहला है। उक्त मार्ग पर चलने के
लिए जिन आठ साधनाओं का अभ्यास
अपेक्षित है वे हैं : सम्यक्-दृष्टि (सम्मादिट्ठि),
सम्यक्-संकल्प (सम्मा-संकप्पो), सम्यक्-
वाणी (सम्मावाचा), सम्यक्-कर्मान्त
(सम्मा-कम्मन्तो), सम्यग्जीव (सम्मा-
जीवो), सम्यक्-व्यायाम (सम्मावायामो),
सम्यक्-स्मृति (सम्मा-सति) और सम्यक्-
समाधि (सम्मा-समाधि)। eightfold
path-according to Buddha it is
essential to adopt the eightfold
noble path for attainment of
nirvāṇa.

अट्ठपद – पु॰ (अष्टपदः) अक्षफलक, शतरंज
खेलने का काष्ठ-फलक। chess board
or draught.

अट्ठापद – पु॰ (अष्टापद) शतरंज फलक।
chess board.

अट्ठसं – पु॰ (अष्टाशक) अष्टकोणिक,
अष्टभुज। eight-armed, octagonal.

अट्ठान – न॰ (अ + स्थानम्) अनुपयुक्त
स्थान, कुठौर। improper place.

अट्ठारस – वि॰ (अष्टादश) अट्ठारह।
eighteen.

अट्ठि – न॰ (अस्थि) हड्डी। bone.

अट्ठि-कङ्काल – पु॰ (अस्थि कङ्काल) मृत
शरीर की हड्डियों का ढाँचा। the
skeleton.

अट्ठि-कल्याण – न॰ (अस्थि कल्याणम्)
दन्त प्रभा। beauty of teeth.

अट्ठिमय – वि॰ – (अस्थिमय) हड्डी से
निर्मित। made of bone.

अट्ठि मिञ्जा – स्त्री॰ – (अस्थि मज्जा)
हड्डी के भीतर का नर्म गूदा। bone
marrow.

अट्ठिकत्त्वा – पूर्व का कृदन्त – (अस्थि +
कृत्वा) ध्यान देकर, रुचि लेकर। paying
much attention, being interested.

अट्ठित – क्रि॰ वि॰ – (अस्थित) अस्थित।
not steadfast.

अट्ठि संघाट – (अस्थि संघात) अस्थि पंजर,
कंकाल। the skeleton.

अट्ठिसेन-जातक (जा॰ सं॰ 403) –
राजोपवन में रहते हुए अयाचक तपस्वी
की जातक कथा। a Jātaka tale (No.
403) of a saint having no
demand in spite of dwelling in
the king's palace.

अड्ढ – वि॰ – (आढ्य) समृद्धिशाली,
धनाढ्य। opulent, wealthy,
prosperous.

अड्ढयोग – पु॰ – (आढ्य योगः) महल।
palace.

अड्ढता – स्त्री॰ – (आढ्यता) समृद्धि,
सम्पदा। prosperity, opulence.

अड्ढतिय – वि॰ – (सार्धद्वयम्) अढाई, ढाई, दो और आधा। two and a half.

अड्ढमास – पु॰ – (अर्द्धमासः) एक पाख, अर्धमास। fortnight.

अड्ढरत्त – स्त्री॰ – (अर्द्धरात्रिः) अर्द्धरात्रि, आधी रात, निशीथ। mid-night.

अड्ढुड्ढ – वि॰ – (सार्धत्रयम्) साढ़े तीन, हुण्ठ। three and a half.

अण – न॰ – (ऋणम्) ऋण। loan.

√अण – (भू॰) – (शब्दार्थे) शब्द करना। to utter.

अणु – पु॰ – (अणु) अत्यधिक बारीक कण, अणु। atom, molecule, very small size, tiny particle.

अणुमत्त – पु॰ – (अणुमात्रक) नितान्त नन्हे आकार वाला, अणुमात्र। very small, tiny sized.

अण्ड-अण्डक – पु॰ – (अण्डः-अण्डकः) (1) अण्डा (2) अण्डकोश। (1) an egg (2) the testicles.

अण्डज – न॰ – (अण्डज) अण्डे से उत्पन्न, पक्षी, सर्प। oviparous, born of an egg, a bird, a serpent.

अण्डभूत-जातक (जा॰ सं॰ 62) – स्त्रियों की स्वाभाविक चरित्रहीनता का ज्ञापन करने वाली जातक कथा। Jātaka tale (No. 62) on the profligacy of woman.

अण्डूपक – पु॰ – (अण्डूपक) बर्तन के नीचे रखने का कपड़े या रस्सी का बना इँडुआ। a cushion made of cloth or string to place under vessels.

अण्ण – पु॰ – (अर्ण) जल। water.

अण्णव – पु॰ – (अर्णव) जलधि, समुद्र। ocean.

अण्ह – पु॰ – (अह्) अह, अहनि, दिन। अह् रूप प्रायः सामासिक पदों में प्रयुक्त जैसेः पूर्वाह्, अपराह्। day, only in compounds, such as *pubbhaṇa*.

अतक्कित – क्रि॰ वि॰ – (अतर्कित) सहसा, औचक। suddenly.

अतसी – स्त्री॰ – (अतसी) अलसी व उसका पौधा। linseed, linseed plant.

अतच्छ – वि॰ – (अ + तथ्य) मिथ्या, अयथार्थ। false, falsehood.

अतन्दित – वि॰ – (अ + तन्द्रिन्) निरालस्य, अप्रमादी। not lazy, active.

अतप्पिय – वि॰ – (अतृप्य) परितोष न देने वाला, तृप्ति न दे सकने वाला। not satiable.

अति – उप॰ – (अति) अतिशयता, अधिकता का बोधक उपसर्ग। a prefix giving the meaning of over, excess.

अतिकड्ढति – क्रि॰ – (अति + √कड्ढ + व॰) भारी कष्ट से खींचता है, घोर श्रम करता है। pulls too hard, takes much labour, drudge.

अतिकर – वि॰ – (अतिकर) अत्यभिनय। overacting.

अतिक्कान्त – कृदन्त – (अति+ √क्रम) अतिक्रमण का शिकार। past participle of atikammati, suffering violation.

अतिक्कम – न॰ – (अति √क्रम) अतिक्रमण, उल्लंघन, सीमा को लाँघ जाना, गुजर जाना। going over, passing beyond, transgression.

अतिखिप्पं – वि॰ – (अति + क्षिप्रं) अति शीघ्र। too soon.

अतिखीण – वि॰ – (अति + क्षीण) अतिशय क्षीण, अतिकृश, दुर्बल। much exhausted, much wasted.

अतिगच्छति – क्रि॰ – (अति + √ गम् + व॰) अतिक्रमण करता है। overcomes, surpasses.

अतिगाळह – वि॰ – (अति + गाढ) अति सघन, अत्यधिक गाढ़ा, कठिन, अधिक कसा हुआ। intensive, very tight.

अतिघोर – वि॰ – (अति + घोर) अति भयानक, अति प्रचण्ड, भीषण। terrible, very fierce.

अतिचरित – क्रि॰ – (अति + √ चर + व॰) अतिक्रमण करता है, परगमन करता है। transgresses, commits adultery.

अतिचारिणी – स्त्री॰ – (अतिचारिणी) व्याभिचारिणी, कुलटा। unchaste woman.

अतिचारी – पु॰ – (अतिचारिन्) अतिक्रमणकारी, परस्त्रीगामी, जारकर्मी। transgressor, adulterer.

अतिण्ह – वि॰ – (अति + तृष्ण) अत्यधिक लोभी। too much greedy.

अतित्त – वि॰ – (अतृप्त) अतृप्त, असन्तुष्ट। unsatisfied.

अतित्थ – न॰ – (अ + तीर्थ) गलत तरीका, अनुचित समय, अनुपयुक्त ठौर, तीर्थाभाव। unsuitable place, way or manner.

अतिथि – पु॰ – (अतिथिः) मेहमान, पाहुन, आगन्तुक। a guest, stranger.

अतिदारुण – वि॰ – (अति दारुण) अति निर्मम, अति क्रूर, अति कठोर। horrible, very cruel, frightful.

अतिदिवा – अव्यय – (अति दिवा) दिन चढ़े। late in the day.

अतिदिसति – वि॰ – (अति + √ दिश + व) निर्देश करता है, स्पष्ट करता है। points out, indicates, explains.

अतिदूर – अव्यय – (अतिदूरम्) अत्यधिक दूरी, अतिशय दूर। great distance, too far.

अतिदेव – पु॰ – (अतिदेव) श्रेष्ठ देवता। superior god.

अतिधमति – क्रि॰ – (अति + √ धम + व॰) ढोल को बहुत जोर से या बार-बार बजाता है। beats a drum too loud or too often.

अतिधावति – क्रि॰ – (अति + √ धाव + व) बहुत तेज दौड़ता है, भारी दौड़धूप करता है, सीमा पार कर जाता है। runs fast, passes over the limits.

अतिधोनचारी – (अतिधावनचारिन) जीविका निर्वाह के लिए अहर्निश भागदौड़ करने वाला। one who indulges too much for livelihood.

अतिनामेति – क्रि॰ – (अति + नाम + एति) समय काटता है, दिन गुजारता है। kills the time, idles away time.

अतिनिगण्हाति – क्रि॰ – (अति + नि + √ ग्रह + व॰) अतिनिगृहणाति अधिक डाँटता-डपटता है। scolds excessively.

अतिपण्डित – पु॰ – (अ + पण्डितः) अति विचक्षण, अति चतुर। too clever.

अतिपपञ्च – न॰ – (अति प्रपञ्च) बहुत अधिक झमेला, अति व्यवधान। excessive, tarrying, too great delay.

अतिपात – पु॰ – (अतिपातः) वध, हत्या। slaughter, killing.

अतिपाती – पु॰ – (अतिपाती) हत्यारा, वधकर्ता। slaughterer.

अतिप्पगो – अव्यय – (अतिप्रग) बहुत जल्दी। at once.

अतिप्पसत्थ – पु॰ – (अति प्रसिद्ध) सुप्रसिद्ध। renowned.

अतिबहल – वि॰ (अति बहल) बहुत मोटा। very thick.

अतिबाळहं – क्रि॰ वि॰ – (अति बाढम्) अत्यधिक। too much.

अतिबाहेति – क्रि॰ – (अति + वाह्येति) भगा देता है, बाहर कर देता है। drives away, pulls out.

अतिभगिनी – स्त्री॰ – (अतिप्रिय भगिनी) अतिशय प्रिय बहन। too loving sister.

अतिभार – वि॰ – (अतिभारः) अतिशय भारी, अति गम्भीर। too heavy, a load.

अतिभारिय – देखें-अतिभार। see Aatibhāra.

अतिभोति – क्रि॰ – (अति + √भू + वा = अतिभवति) अतिक्रमण करता है। overcomes, tresspasses.

अतिमञ्जति – क्रि॰ – (अति + √मान + व = अतिमान्यते) तिरस्कार करता है, अपेक्षा करता है, अपमान करता है। slightens, neglects, despises.

अतिमनाप – वि॰ – अतिशय प्रिय। much beloved.

अतिमत्त – वि॰ – (अतिमात्र) अतिमात्र, अत्यधिक। too much.

अतिमान – पु॰ – (अतिमान) अभिमान, अहंकार। pride, arrogance.

अतिमुखर – वि॰ – (अतिमुखर) बातूनी, वाचाल। very talkative.

अतिमुत्तक – वि॰ – (अतिमुक्तक) मालती लता। the plant Guertenra Racemosa.

अतिमुदुक – वि॰ – (अतिमृदुक) अति मृदुल, सौम्य। very gentle.

अतियक्ख – पु॰ – (अति यक्ष) झाड़-फूँक करने वाला, ओझा। exorcist, one who cures by the magic of charms.

अतियाचना – स्त्री॰ – (अति + याचना) अत्यधिक याचना। begging too much.

अतियति – क्रि॰ – (अति + √इ + व) लांघ जाता है, पार कर जाता है। overcomes, excels.

अतियुव – त्रिलिङ्गी – (अतियुव) चिरतरूण। ever young.

अतिरिच्चति – क्रि॰ – (अतिरिच्यते) छूट जाता है, बचा रहता है। remains, left over.

अतिरित्त – वि॰ – (अतिरिक्त) अतिरिक्त। additional, extra.

अतिरित्ति – स्त्री॰ – (अतिरिक्ति) अतिरिक्त होने की स्थिति। remaining, state of excess.

अतिरेक – पु॰ – (अतिरेक) अधिकता, प्रचुरता। plenty, abundance, surplus.

अतिरोचित – क्रि॰ – (अति + √रुच् + व = अतिरोचते) अधिक चमकता है। outshines, surpasses, the splendour.

अतिलुद्ध – वि॰ – (अति + लुब्धः) अतिशय लोभी, कंजूस, महालालची। too greedy, miser, very miserly.

अतिवत्तति – क्रि॰ – (अति + √वर्त + व = अतिवत्तते) लांघ जाता है, पार कर जाता है। passes over, goes beyond.

अतिवस्सति – क्रि॰ – (अति वर्षति) अत्यधिक बरस रहा है। raining heavily.

अतिवाक्य – न॰ – (दुर्वचन) अपशब्द, दुर्वचन, पुरुष वचन। abuse, reproach, harsh word.

अतिवाहक – पु॰ – (अतिवाहक) अधिक भार ढ़ोने वाला। one who carries a heavy burden, a guide.

अतिविन्झति – क्रि॰ – (अति + विध्यति) पूरी तरह बींध देता है, आर-पार देख लेता है। sees through, pierces well, penetrates.

अतिविय – क्रि॰ वि॰ – (अतीव) अत्यन्त। veru much.

अतिविस्सट्ठ – वि॰ – (अतिभाषी) बहुत बक-बक करने वाला, बड़बड़िया। gossips too much, chatterbox.

अतिविस्सुत – पु॰ – (अति विश्रुत) सुप्रसिद्ध, प्रख्यात। very famous, renowned.

अतिवेलं – क्रि॰ वि॰ – (अतिवेलम्) अतिशय विलम्ब, अधिक देर हो जाना, बहुत समय बीत जाना। too late, takes too much time.

अतिसण्ह – वि॰ – (अतिश्लक्ष्ण) अति सूक्ष्म, अति चिकना। minute, subtle, too smooth, slippery.

अतिसम्बाध – वि॰ – (अति + सम्बाध) जहाँ बहुत अधिक भीड़-भाड़ हो, तंग रास्ता। too tight, crowded, narrow.

अतिसय – वि॰ – (अतिशय) आधिक्य, अतिशय। abundance.

अतिसार – पु॰ – (अतिसार) पुरानी पेचिश, अतिसार नामक रोग। chronic dysentery.

अतिसिथिल – वि॰ – (अतिशिथिल) बहुत ढीला, बहुत सुस्त। very loose, shaky or weak, too lazy.

अतिसीत – वि॰ – (अतिशीत) अतिशीतल, बहुत ठंडा। too cold.

अतिसीतल – वि॰ – (अतिशीतल) देखें 'अतिसीत'। same as Atisīta.

अतिसुण – (अति + शुनक) पागल कुत्ता। rabid dog.

अतिहट्ठ – वि॰ – (अतिहृष्ट) अत्यन्त प्रसन्नचित्त। very pleased.

अतिहरति – क्रि॰ (अति + √ हृ + व = अतिहरति) छीनता है, अपहरण करता है। snatches, abducts.

अतिहीन – वि॰ – (अतिहीन) अत्यन्त दरिद्र। very poor or destitute.

अतिहिलेति – क्रि॰ – (अतिहीलयति) घृणा करता है। hates too much.

अतीत – वि॰ – (अतीत) भूतकाल, पुराकालिक, प्राचीन काल। past, gone by.

अतीव – अव्यय – (अतीव) बहुत अधिक। very much, exceedingly.

अतो – अव्यय – (अतः) इसके बाद, इसलिए, अतएव। hence, now, therefore.

अत्त (1) – भू॰ कृदन्त – (आप्त) प्राप्त किया हुआ। that which had been taken up, assumed.

अत्त (2) – पु॰ – (आत्मन्) अपना, आप, आत्म। (1) ourself, yourself (2) soul.

अत्तकाम – पु॰ – (आत्म + काम) आत्म-प्रेम। love of self.

अत्तकिलमथ – पु॰ – (आत्मक्लेश) काय-क्लेश, आत्म-क्लेश। self-mortification.

अत्तगुत्ति – स्त्री॰ – (आत्म) आत्म-संयम। self-restrainment.

अत्तधञ्ञ – वि॰ – (आत्मघात्) आत्मघात। self-destruction, suicide.

अत्तदत्थ – पु॰ – (आत्मार्थ) आत्महित। one's own welfare.

अत्तदन्त – वि॰ – (आत्म + दान्त) आत्म-दमित। self-restrained.

अत्तदिट्ठि – स्त्री॰ – (आत्मदृष्टि) आत्म-दृष्टि, आत्मा का अस्तित्व मानना। speculation about the soul.

अत्तभाव – पु॰ – (आत्मभाव) व्यक्तित्व, आत्मभाव, आत्मीयता। personality, individuality.

अत्तवध – पु॰ – (आत्मवध) आत्म-विनाश। self-destruction, suicide.

अत्त-वाद – पु॰ – (आत्मवाद) आत्मा के अस्तित्व का पोषक सिद्धान्त। the theory of soul.

अत्त-हित – न॰ – (आत्महित) आत्महित। personal welfare.

अत्तज – पु॰ – (आत्मज) पुत्र, 'आत्मा वें जायते पुत्र'। the son.

अत्तजा – स्त्री॰ – (आत्मजा) पुत्री, दुहिता। daughter.

अत्तदीप – पु॰ – (आत्म-दीप) आत्मनिर्भर, स्वप्रकाशमान। self-reliance, self-dependent.

अत्तनीय – वि॰ – (आत्मीय) आ त र म -सम्बन्धी, नितान्त अपना। own, belonging to the self.

अत्तंतप – वि॰ – (आत्म-तपः) अपने आप को तपाने वाला। self-mortifying.

अत्तपच्चक्ख – वि॰ – (आत्म-प्रत्यक्ष) आत्म-साक्षी। self-witnessed.

अत्तपटिलाभ – पु॰ – (आत्म-प्रतिलाभ) निज अस्तित्व-ग्रहण, जन्म। acquisi-tion of a personality, birth.

अत्तमन – वि॰ – (आप्त + मन) प्रसन्न वदन। delighted.

अत्तसम्भव – वि॰ – (आत्म + सम्भव) आत्म-सम्भव, अपने आप से उत्पन्न। originated from one's self.

अत्तहेतु – अव्यय – (आत्महेतु) अपने आप के लिए, स्वनिर्मित, आत्महेतु। for one's own sake.

अत्ताण – वि॰ – (अत्राण) त्राण-रहित, बिना संरक्षण के। without protection.

√अत्थ – (चु॰) – (याचनार्थे) माँगना। to beg.

अत्थ – पु॰ – (अर्थ) धन, उपयोग, कल्याण, लाभ, माने, आवश्यकता, इच्छा, विनाश। wealth, welfare, gain, need, want, use, meaning, destruction.

अत्थक्खायी – वि॰ – (अर्थ+ख्यायी अर्थख्यायी) हितकर बात कहने वाला, हितवादी। showing or telling what is profitable.

अत्थकर – वि॰ – (अर्थकर) हितकर, लाभकारी। beneficial.

अत्थकाम – वि॰ – (अर्थकाम, अर्थकामी) हितचिन्तक। well-wisher.

अत्थकुसल – वि॰ – (अर्थकुशल) हित की बात समझने में दक्ष, अर्थ बताने में पटु। clever in finding what is beneficial, clever in exposition.

अत्थचर – वि॰ – (अर्थचर) हित की बात करने वाला उपकारी। doing good, busy in interest of others.

अत्थचरिया – स्त्री भाव वा॰ संज्ञा – (अर्थचर्या) हितचर्या, परोपकृति, परोपकार। doing good.

अत्थदस्सी – देखें – अत्थकाम। see Atthakāma.

अत्थभञ्जक – वि॰ – (अर्थभञ्जक) हितनाशक, अहितकारी। destroyer, evildoer.

अत्थवादी – पु॰ – (अर्थवादी) देखें – 'अत्थक्खायी'। see Atthakkhāyī.

अत्थकथा – स्त्री॰ – (अर्थकथा) अर्थ-विवृत्ति, भाष्य अर्थ की विस्तृत व्याख्या। commentary, explanation of meaning.

अत्थगम – पु॰ – (अस्तगमन) अस्तगत होना, छिप जाना, आँख से ओझल होना। setting down, hiding extinction.

अत्थञ्ञु – वि॰ – (अर्थज्ञ) अर्थ का ज्ञाता, कल्याणज्ञ। knowledgeable, benefactor.

अत्थना – स्त्री॰ – (अर्थना) याचना, प्रार्थना। begging, request.

अत्थर – पु॰ – (आस्तरण) बिछाने की चादर। bed-sheet.

अत्थरक – पु॰ – (आस्तरक) बिछाने वाला। one who spreads bed-sheet.

अत्थरत – क्रि॰ – (आ + √ स्तृ - आस्तरित का भूतकालिक रुप) बिछाया चादर से आच्छादित किया। spread over with.

अत्थरण – न॰ – (आस्तरणम्) बिछाने की चादर। bed-sheet.

अत्थवस – (अर्थवश – अर्थवशात्) कारण, कारणवश, उपयोग। reason, use.

अत्थसत्त – पु॰ – (अर्थशास्त्र) अर्थशास्त्र। economics.

अत्थाय – (अर्थ + चतुर्थी विभक्ति एकवचन अर्थाय) प्रयोजन के लिए जैसे किमर्थाय = किस मतलब से। for the sake of, meant for.

अत्थि – क्रि॰ – (अस्ति - √ अस् = व) है। exists.

अत्थिभाव – पु॰ – (अस्तिभाव) अस्तित्व। existence.

अत्थिक – (आर्थिकः) आर्थी, अर्थी, इच्छुक, किसी वस्तु की चाह रखने वाला जरुरतमन्द। desirous of, seeking for.

अत्थु – क्रि॰ – (अस्ति) इच्छार्थक, आज्ञार्थक शब्द हो जैसे : एवमस्तु – ऐसा हो। (imperative of अत्थि) be it so.

अत्र – अव्यय – (अत्र) यहाँ, इस ठौर। here.

अत्रज – पु॰ – (अत्रजः) आत्मज, पुत्र। male child born from oneself, son.

अत्रजा – स्त्री॰ – (अत्रजा) आत्मजा, पुत्री। female child born from oneself, daughter.

अत्रिच्छ – (वि॰) – (अतृप्य) अतिशय लोभी। very covetous.

अत्रिच्छा – (अतृप्ति) उद्दाम, आकांक्षा, उत्कट इच्छा। excess of greed.

अथ – अव्यय – (अथ) तब, यहाँ से, एत्पश्चात्, ग्रन्थारम्भ या आख्यान के आरम्भ करने के पूर्व का शब्द जैसे : अथ जातक कथा। hence, consequently.

अथब्बण – पु॰ – (अथर्ववेद) अथर्ववेद। the Atharvaveda.

अथा-निपात – (अथ) एत्पश्चात्, यहाँ से। and, also, further, likewise.

√ अद – (भू॰) – (भक्षणे) खाना। to eat.

अदक – पु॰ – (√ अद् + भक्षणे + क) खाने वाला, भक्षक। eater.

अदति – क्रि॰ – (√ अद् + व + अत्ति) खाता है। eats.

अदन – न॰ – (अदनम्) खाना, भोजन। food.

अदस्सन – न॰ – (अदर्शनम्) लोप, दिखाई न देना। absence, disappearance.

अदिट्ठ – वि॰ – (अदृष्ट) अदृष्ट जो दिखाई न पड़ा हो। not seen.

अदिन्न – वि॰ – (अदत्त) जो दिया न गया हो। not given.

अदिन्नादान – न॰ – (अदत्तादानम्) बिना अनुमति दूसरे की वस्तु ले लेना, चोरी। theft.

अदिस्समान – वि॰ – (अदृश्यमान) जो दिखाई न दे। invisible.

अदु – न॰ – (अमुक) फलाँ, अमुक। such and such.

अदुक्खमसुखा – स्त्री॰ – (अदुःख-सौख्यम्) न दुःख न सुख की स्थिति। state of neither grief nor pleasure.

अदूभक – वि॰ – (अविश्रम्भ-भञ्जक) जो विश्वासघाती नहीं। not treacherous.

अदूसक – वि॰ – (अदूषक) निर्दोष, निष्पाप, निरपराध। innocent.

अद्द – वि॰ – (आर्द्र) गीला, भीगा हुआ काई। moist, wet, algae, moss.

अद्दक – न॰ – (अद्रकम) अदरक। fresh ginger.

अद्दक्खि – भूतकालिक क्रिया – (√ दृश + लुङ् = अद्राक्षीत) देखा। saw.

अद्दसा – (भूतकालिक क्रिया) देखा। saw.

अद्दा – न॰ –(आर्द्रा नक्षत्र) आद्रा नक्षत्र। name of a *nakṣatra*.

अद्दि – पु॰ – (अद्रिः) पर्वत। mountain.

अद्दित – क्रि॰ वि॰ – (अद्रित) दबाया गया, दबाया हुआ। supressed, afflicted.

अद्ध (1) – पु॰ – (अर्द्धः) आधा। a half.

अद्ध (2) – पु॰ – (अध्व) मार्ग, पथ। way, track.

अद्धमास – पु॰ – (अद्धमास) एक पाख, पक्ष, आधा महीना। a fortnight.

अद्धगत – पु॰ – (अध्वगत) जिसने जीवनचर्या पूरी कर ली है। one who has traversed the span of life.

अद्धगु – पु॰ – (अध्वग) यात्री. traveller.

अद्धनिय – वि॰ – (अध्वनीय) यात्रा करने योग्य, चिरकाल तक बना रहने वाला। fit for travelling, lasting a long period.

अद्धा (1) – अव्यय – (अद्धा) निश्चयात्मक रूप से। indeed, certainly.

अद्धा (2) – पु॰ – (अध्व) मार्ग, पथ। path, way.

अद्धान – न॰ – (अध्वनम्) (1) लम्बा रास्ता, (2) दीर्घ समय। (1) long path, (2) long time or journey.

अद्धि – स्त्री॰ – (अध्वन) मार्ग। path.

अद्धिक – पु॰ – (अध्वक) यात्री। traveller, wayfarer.

अद्धुव – वि॰ – (अध्रुव) अस्थिर, अनिश्चित्। unstable, uncertain.

अद्वेज्झ – वि॰ – (असन्दिग्ध) असंदिग्ध। doubtless, uncontradictory.

अधम – (वि॰) – (अधम) नीच, पापी। mean, low, sinner.

अधम्म – पु॰ – (अधर्म) (1) कदाचरण, (2) मिथ्यामत। (1) misconduct, (2) false doctrines.

अधर – पु॰ – (अधर) (1) ओष्ठ, ओठ, (2) नीचे का। (1) the lip (2) lower.

अधि – उपसर्ग – (अधि) तक, पर। a preposition, up to, over, on, above.

अधिकत – वि॰ – (अधिकृत) अधिकृत, कारणीभूत। commissioned with, caused by.

अधिकतर – वि॰ – (अधिकतर) अधिकतर, दूसरे से अधिक। much exceeding.

अधिकरण – न॰ – (अधिकरण) (1) अधिष्ठान, (2) आधार, (3) सातवाँ कारक 'मुकदमा'। (1) ground, (2) substratum, (3) locative case, (4) a lawsuit.

अधिकरण-कारक – (अधिकरण कारक) वादी, विवादी। one who causes dispute, discussion or dissent.

अधिकरण-समथ – समर्थ, शमन (पु॰) (अधिकरण शपन) मुकदमे का निस्तारण। settling of law suit or a dispute.

अधिकरणिक – पु॰ – (अधिकरणिक) न्यायाधिष्ठाता, जज, न्यायाधीश। a judge.

अधिकरणी – स्त्री॰ – (अधिकरणी) लोहार की निहाई। a smith anvil.

अधिकार – पु॰ – (अधिकार) पद, आकांक्षा, प्रबन्धन। management, ambition, aspiration.

अधिकुट्टन – पु॰ – देखें अधिकोट्टन। see 'Adhikoṭṭana.'

अधिकोट्टन – न॰ – (अधिकुट्टन) काष्ठखंड जिस पर कसाई मांस के टुकड़े करता है। executioner's or butcher's block.

अधिकोधित – वि॰ – (अतिक्रुध) अत्यन्त क्रुद्ध। infuriated, enraged.

अधिगच्छति – क्रि॰ – (अधि + √गम् = अधिगच्छति) प्राप्त करता है, समझता है। obtains, understands, attains.

अधिगच्छि – भूतकालिक क्रिया – अधिगच्छति का भूतकालिक रूप प्राप्त किया। attained, obtained, understood.

अधिगण्हाति – क्रि॰ – (अधि + √ग्रह + व = अधिगृह्णाति) अधिग्रहण करता है, पार कर जाता है। surpasses, overpowers.

अधिगत – वि॰ – (अधिगत) प्राप्त। obtained.

अधिगम – पु॰ – (अधिगम्) प्राप्ति, ज्ञान। attainment, knowledge.

अधिगहीत – वि॰ – (अधि + ग्रह + ल = अधिगृहीत) अधिग्रहण किया हुआ। past participle.

अधिचित्त – न॰ – (अधि + चित्त) गम्भीर चिन्तन, उच्च चिन्तन, चित्त को एकाग्र करने की साधना। higher thought, concentration of mind.

अधिच्च – पूर्वकालिक क्रिया – (अधि + इ + √ल्यप् = अधीत्य) पढ़कर, अध्ययन करके। having learnt or grasped.

अधिच्चका – स्त्री॰ – (अधित्यका) उपत्यका, पहाड़ी की तलहटी। land lying at mountain's foot, foothill.

अधिठ्ठाति – क्रि॰ – (अधिष्ठाति) दृढ़ संकल्प करता है। stands firmly, takes dogged determination.

अधिट्ठान – न॰ – (अधिष्ठान) अधिष्ठान, निवास-स्थान। standing place, abode.

अधिट्ठातब्ब – कृदन्त – (अधिष्ठातव्य) अधिष्ठान करने योग्य, दृढ़ संकल्प योग्य। fit to be determined.

अधिट्ठान – न॰ – (अधिष्ठान) (1) स्थान, (2) संकल्प। (1) place, (2) resolution, determination.

अधिट्ठायक – पु॰ – (अधिष्ठायक) अधिष्ठाता, अधीक्षक। superintendent.

अधिप – पु॰ – (अधिप, अधिपति) स्वामी, संप्रभु। lord, ruler, master.

अधिपञ्ञ – पु॰ – (अधिप्रज्ञ) सुप्रज्ञ, प्रतिभावान। possessing higher wisdom.

अधिपञ्ञा – स्त्री॰ – (अधि प्रज्ञा) सुमेधा, उच्च प्रतिभा, श्रेष्ठ प्रज्ञा। higher wisdom.

अधिपतन – न॰ – (अधिपतन) ऊपर कूद पड़ना, आक्रमण। attack, falling upon.

अधिपन्न – वि॰ – (अधिपन्न) गृहीत। afflicted with, gone into.

अधिपात – पु॰ – (अधिपात) विनाश। destruction.

अधिपातक – पु॰ – (अधिपातक) अँख फोड़वा कीट, टिड्डा, फुदका। a grasshopper.

अधिपातेति – क्रि॰ – (अधिपातयति) नाशयति, नाश कर डालता है। demolishes, destroys.

अधिप्पाय – पु॰ – (अभिप्राय) अभिप्राय, इरादा। intention, opinion.

अधिप्पेत – भूतकालिक कृदन्त – (अभि+ प्र √ इ + ल = अभिप्रेत) वांछित, अभीष्ट। intended, desired.

अधिभवति – क्रि॰ – (अति भवति) दबा देता है, तिरस्कार करता है। contempts, overpowers.

अधिभू – पु॰ – (अधिभू) स्वामी। owner, master.

अधिमत्त – (वि॰) – (अधिमात्र) अत्यधिक मात्रा। exceeding too much.

अधिमन – पु॰ – (अधिमन) एकाग्रचित्त। concentrated.

अधिमणण – पु॰ – (अधर्मण) ऋणी, कर्जदार। borrower, indebted.

अधिमान – पु॰ – (अधिमान) 'अभिमान, अहङ्कार। undue estimate of oneself, egoism.

अधिमानिक – पु॰ – (अधिमानिक) ऐसा व्यक्ति जिसे सिद्धि पा लेने का गर्व मिथ्या हो। one who thinks that he has attained some supernatural knowledge though actually not being so.

अधिमुच्चति – क्रि॰ – (अधि + √ मूच + व = अधिगच्चति) झुकता है, अनुरक्त होता है। inclines towards.

अधिमुच्चन – न॰ – (अधि + मूर्च्छन) संकल्प करना, इरादा करना। making up one's mind, expressing intention.

अधिमुच्छित – कृदन्त – (अधिमूर्च्छित) सम्मोहित, मूर्च्छित। infatuated.

अधिमोक्ख – (अधिमोक्ष) दृढ़ निश्चय, अडिग संकल्प। firm resolve, firm determination.

अधिरोहनी – स्त्री॰ – (अधिरोहणी) सीढ़ी। a ladder, stairs.

अधिवचन – न॰ – (अधिवचन) नाम, पद, संज्ञा। a term, designation, noun.

अधिवत्तति – क्रि॰ – (अधि + √ वर्त्त + व = अधिवर्त्ते) अतिक्रमण कर जाता है, परास्त कर देता है। overpowers, encroaches.

अधिवत्थ – वि॰ – (अधिवासी) निवासी, निवास करने वाला। inhabiting, resident.

अधिवसति – क्रि॰ – (अधिवसति) रहता है, निवास करता है। inhabits, lives in.

अधिवासक – वि॰ – (अधिवासक) सहन करने वाला, झेलने वाला। patient, enduring.

अधिवासना – स्त्री॰ – (अधिवासना) सहनशीलता। endurance, forbearance.

अधिवासेति – क्रिया (अधिवासयति) सहन करता है। endures, waits for.

अधिसील – न॰ – (अधिशीलम्) उच्च कोटि का सदाचार। higher morality.

अधिसेति – क्रि॰ – (अधि + √ शी = अधिशेते) लेटता है। lies on.

अधीन – वि॰ – (अधीन) अधीन, वश में, आश्रित। dependent, belonging to.

अधीयति – वि॰ – (अधि + √ इ = अधीते) अध्ययन करता है। studies, learns by heart.

अधुना – अव्यय – वि॰ – (अधुना) जब, अचिर काल पूर्व, अद्यतन। now, recently.

अधो – अव्यय – (अधः) नीचे। under, below.

अधोकत – वि॰ – (अधःकृत) नीचे किया गया। lowered, turned down.

अधोगम – वि॰ – (अधोगामी) पतनोन्मुख। going downward.

अधोभाग – वि॰ – (अधोभागः) नीचे का हिस्सा। lower part.

अधोमुख – वि॰ – (अधोमुख) नीचे मुंह किये हुए। face down, cast down.

अनङ्गण – वि॰ – (अनङ्गण) राग-द्वेष रहित, वीतराग, निष्फल के। passionless, blameless.

√ अन – (भू) – पालने, जिलाना, रक्षा करना। to bring up, to protect.

अनच्छ – वि॰ – (अन् + अच्छ) मैला, अस्वच्छ। dirty.

अनण – वि॰ – (अनृण) ऋण / मुक्त। free of debt.

अनत्त – वि॰ – (अनात्म) अनात्म (सिद्धान्त)। soulless, unprincipled.

अनत्तमन – वि॰ – (अनात्ममन) असन्तुष्ट। displeased, dissatisfied.

अनत्थ – पु॰ – (अनर्थ) हानि, दुर्भाग्य, अकल्याण। loss, misfortune, misery.

अनधिवर – पु॰ – (अनधिवर) तथागत बुद्ध, समपूज्य। the blessed one.

अननुच्छविक – वि॰ – (अननुच्छविक) अनुपयुक्त, बेमेल, अयोग्य। improper, not befitting.

अननुसोचिय-जातक – (जा॰ सं॰ 328) – वाराणसी में धनिक ब्राह्मण रूप में जन्मे बोधिसत्व की जातक कथा। a Jātaka tale (No. 328) related to

Bodhisattva born as a rich brāhmaṇa in Varanasi.

अनन्त – वि॰ – (अनन्त) अन्त-रहित, सीमा-रहित, शाश्वत्। endless, unlimited, infinite.

अनन्तर – वि॰ – (अनन्तर) एतत्पश्चाद्, इसके बाद, बिना अन्तराल। next, adjoining, immediately following.

अनपेक्ख – वि॰ – (अनपेक्ष) अपेक्षा-रहित। without expectancy.

अनप्पक – वि॰ – (अनल्पक) जो अल्प न हो, प्रभूत, प्रचुर। much, abundant, not trifling.

अनभाव – पु॰ – (अनु + अभाव) जन्म-मरण का पूर्व अभाव। utter cessation.

अनभिरत – वि॰ – (अनभिरत) अन अनुरक्त, रस की अनुभूति न करता हुआ, अनासक्त। not taking delight in.

अनभिरति-जातक (1) – (जा॰ सं॰ 65) इस जातक कथा में स्त्रियों को निजी सम्पत्ति मानना अनुचित कहा गया। Jātaka tale (No. 65) which condemns the idea of treating a woman as personal property.

अनभिरति-जातक (2) – (जा॰ सं॰ 185) – जिसमें कहा गया है कि अच्छी स्मृति के लिए चित्त की स्थिरता आवश्यक है। Jātaka tale (No. 185) which indicates that the concentration of mind is essential for a good memory.

अनमतग्ग – वि॰ – (अन + मताग्र) जिसका आरम्भ और अन्त अज्ञात है। whose beginning and end are alike unthinkable.

अनय – पु॰ – (अनय) अनीति, दुर्भाग्य। injustice, misfortune.

अनरिय – वि॰ – (अनार्य) असभ्य, गँवार। ignoble, vulgar.

अनल – पु॰ – (अनल) अग्नि, पावक। fire.

अनलङ्कृत – वि॰ – (अन + अलम + कृत = अनलङ्कृत) (1) जो सन्तुष्ट न हुआ हो, (2) अलंकार-रहित। (1) dissatisfied, (2) not graceful.

अनवट्ठित – वि॰ – (अन् + अवस्थित) अनवस्थित, अस्थिर। unsettled, unsteady.

अनवय – वि॰ – (अन्यून) न्यून नहीं, सम्पूर्ण। not lacking, complete.

अनवरत – वि॰ – (अनवरत) निरन्तर, लगातार। constant.

अनवसेस – वि॰ – (अनवशेष) निरवशेष, सम्पूर्ण। without any remainder, complete.

अनवोसित – वि॰ – (अनवसित) जिसका अवसान न हुआ हो, असमाप्त, असम्पूर्ण। not complete, endless.

अनसन – न॰ – (अन + अशन = अनसन) उपवास, अनशन। fasting.

अनस्सासिक – वि॰ – (अनाश्वस्त) आश्वासन-रहित, निराश्वस्त। having no consolation.

अनाकुल – वि॰ (अन + आकुल) उलझन-रहित, शान्त। not confused, not entangled, calm.

अनागत – वि॰ – (अन + आगत) अप्राप्त, जो आया नहीं, भावी भविष्य। not come yet, the future.

अनागत-वसं – भावी मैत्रेय बुद्ध के बारे में काश्यप स्थविर द्वारा रचित एक ऐतिहासिक

कृति । a historical book about Maitreya Buddha written by Kāśyapa Sthavir.

अनागमन – न॰ – (**अनागमन**) आगमन का निषेध । not welcome.

अनागामी – पु॰ – (**अनागामी**) फिर इस संसार में लौटकर न आने वाला । the person who has attained *nirvāṇa*, who is not to return to this world again.

अनाचार – पु॰ – (**अनाचार**) दुराचार, कदाचार, दुर्व्यवहार । misconduct, immorality, misbehaviour.

अनाजानीय – वि॰ – (**अनाजानीय**) जो अच्छी नस्ल का न हो, निम्न रक्त का । of inferior race, not of pure blood.

अनाथ – वि॰ – (**अनाथ**) दुःखी, संरक्षक विहीन, असहाय । miserable, helpless, orphan.

अनाथपिण्डिक – पु॰ – (**अनाथपिण्डिक**) श्रावस्ती धन कुबेर श्रेष्ठि सुदत्त प्रसिद्ध उपाधि नाम । Sudatta, the rich merchant of Śrāvastī was famous as Anāthapiṇḍika, i.e., who feeds the poor.

अनादर – पु॰ – (**अनादर**) असम्मान, अपमान, तिरस्कार । disrespect, disregard.

अनादाय – पूर्व – (**अन + आदाय**) (**अन + आ + √दा + ल्यप्**) न लेकर, बिना लिये । without taking.

अनापाद – वि॰ – (**अन + आपाद**) अविवाहित पुरुष । unmarried man.

अनापादा – वि॰ – (**अन + आपादा**) अविवाहिता स्त्री । unmarried woman.

अनापुच्छा – स्त्री॰ – (**अन + आ + √पृच्छ् – अनापृच्छा**) न पूछना, जिससे पूछा न गया हो । without asking or unasked.

अनाबाध – वि॰ – (**अनाबाध**) बाधारहित । without hindrance.

अनामन्त – वि॰ – (**अनामन्त्रित**) अनिमन्त्रित, जिसे पूछा न गया हो । uninvited, unasked.

अनामय – वि॰ – (**अनामय**) नीरोग, व्याधि-रहित । free from illness.

अनामसित – वि॰ – (**अन + आ + √मृश = आमशने स्पर्श = अनामर्शित**) जो छुआ न गया हो, अस्पृष्ट । untouched.

अनामिका – स्त्री॰ – (**अनामिका**) मध्यमा व कनिष्ठा के बीच की उंगली । ring finger.

अनायतन – न॰ – (**अनायतनम्**) अयोग्य स्थान, अनुपयुक्त ठौर । improper place.

अनायास – वि॰ – (**अन + आयास**) बिना कष्ट के, आसानी से । without trouble, easily.

अनारत – क्रि॰ वि॰ – (**अनवरत**) निरन्तर, लगातार । continued, without end.

अनारम्भ – वि॰ – (**अनारम्भ**) बिना खटपट के । without turmoil.

अनालम्ब – वि॰ – (**अनालम्ब**) आधार-रहित । without support.

अनालय – वि॰ – (**अनालय**) आसक्ति-रहित । free from attachment.

अनावट – वि॰ वि॰ – (**अनावृत्त**) अनाच्छादित, खुला हुआ । open, not covered.

अनावत्ती – पु॰ – (**अनावत्री**) जिसकी पुनरावृत्ति न हो, न लौटने वाला । one who does not return.

अनावरण – वि॰ – (अनावरण) आवरण-रहित । without covering, without any obstacle.

अनाविल – वि॰ – (अनाविल) जो आबिल न हो, गन्दला न हो, स्वच्छ, शान्त । clean, undisturbed, peaceful.

अनावुत्थ – वि॰ – (अनावासित) जहाँ कोई न बसा हो, कोई न रहा हो । uninhabited, not dwelt in.

अनासक – वि॰ – (अन + √अश् = अनाशक) अशन न करने वाला, निराहार, उपवास करने वाला । without food, fasting.

अनासव – वि॰ – (अनासव) आसव या मदिरा-रहित । free from intoxicants, non-alchoholic.

अनासव – न॰ – (अनास्रव) निर्वाण । state of nirvāṇa.

अनालिहक – वि॰ – (अनाद्य) निर्धन । poor.

अनिक्कसाव – वि॰ – (अनिक्कषाय) काषाय अर्थात् चित्तमत्तों से युक्त । with impurity of mind.

अनिखात – वि॰ – (अनिखात) जो खोदा नहीं गया । un-dug part.

अनिघ – वि॰ – (अनघ) दुःखरहित । free from trouble.

अनिच्च – वि॰ – (अनित्य) अस्थिर, अनित्य, नश्वर । not stable, impermanent.

अनिच्छय – पु॰ – (अनिश्चय) निश्चयहीनता । lack of certainty.

अनिच्छा – (अन + इच्छा = अनिच्छा) अरुचि, इच्छा का अभाव । disliking, lack of desire.

अनिञ्जन – न॰ – (अन + √इ + इञ्जू = गतौ) गतिहीनता । immobility.

अनिट्ठ – (अनिष्ठ) जिसकी निष्ठा न हो, निष्ठाहीन । not agreeable.

अनिटि्ठत – वि॰ – (अनिष्ठित) अनिष्णात, अपरिपक्व, असमाप्त । inefficient, incomplete.

अनिन्दित – वि॰ – (अनिन्द्य) जो निन्दा के योग्य न हो । one who does not deserve contempt, deserving no contempt.

अनिमिस – वि॰ – (अनिमेष) निर्निमेष, बिना पलक झपके । unwinking, waking.

अनियत – वि॰ – (अनियत) अनिश्चित् । uncertain, not settled.

अनिदस्सना – स्त्री॰ – (अ + निदर्शना) निदर्शना या प्रतिबोध का अभाव, निर्वाण । liberation.

अनियमित – वि॰ – (अनियमित) नियम-रहित । indefinite, irregular.

अनिल – पु॰ – (वायु) अनिल, वायु । wind.

अनिल-पथ – पु॰ – (अनिल पथ) आकाश । sky.

अनिलोद्धुत – वि॰ – (अनिलोद्धृत) वायु-प्रकम्पित, हवा से झकझोरा हुआ । shaken by the wind.

अनिवत्तन – न॰ – (अ + निवर्त्तन) बिना रुकाव, बिना रुके .गमन । non-stoppage.

अनिसम्मकारी – वि॰ – (अ + निशाम्य + कारी = अविमृश्यकारी) बिना विचारे काम करने वाला, हड़बड़िया । hasty, not acting considerately.

अनिस्सर – वि॰ – (अनीश्वर) प्रभुता-रहित, प्रभावहीन, अकिंचन। having no power or influence.

अनिस्सित – क्रि॰ वि॰ – (अ + निः सृत) आसक्ति-रहित, अनासक्त। passionless, disinterested.

अनीक – न॰ – (अनीकम्) सेना। an army.

अनीकग्ग – वि॰ – (अनीकाग्र) सेना का अग्र भाग। front of the army

अनीकट्ठ – पु॰ – (अनीकस्थ) राजा का अङ्गरक्षक। a royal body-guard.

अनीघ – वि॰ – (अनघ) निष्पाप, निष्कलुष। free from sin or trouble.

अनीतिक – वि॰ – (अन् + ईति + क) हानिरहित, उपद्रव-रहित, इतिमुक्त। free from injury or harm.

अनीतिह – वि॰ – (अन् + ऐतिह्य) जो मात्र सुनी-सुनाई बात अर्थात् इतिहास कथन पर आधारित न हो। not based on hearsay, known by oneself.

अनुकंखी – नि॰ – (अनु + कांक्षी) आकांक्षा करने वाला। one who longs for.

अनुकन्तति – क्रि॰ – (अनु + √कृत्त + व = अनुकृत्तति) चीरता-फाड़ता है, काटता है। cuts into, shears.

अनुकम्पक – वि॰ – (अनुकम्पक) अनुकम्पा करने वाला, दयालु। one who has mercy, compassionate.

अनुकम्पति – क्रि॰ – (अनुकम्पति) अनुकम्पा करता है। shows pity on.

अनुकम्पन – न॰ – (अनुकम्पन) दया-भाव। compassion, pity, mercy.

अनुकम्पित – वि॰ – (अनुकम्पित) अनुकम्पा प्राप्त करना। pitied by.

अनुकम्पी – देखें – अनुकम्पक। see Anukampaka.

अनुकरोति – क्रि॰ – (अनु + √कृ = अनुकरोति) अनुकरण करता है, नकल करता है। imitates, repeats some action.

अनुकस्सति – क्रि॰ – (अनुकर्षति) खींचता है, दुहराता है। pulls on, repeats.

अनुकार – पु॰ – (अनुकार) अनुकृति, नकल। imitation.

अनुकारी – पु॰ – (अनुकारी) अनुकरण कर्त्ता। imitator.

अनुकिण्ण – क्रि॰ वि॰ – (अनु + कीर्ण) बिखेरा हुआ। scattered.

अनुकुब्बति – क्रि॰ – (अनुकरोति) देखें अनुकरोति। see Anukaroti.

अनुकूल – वि॰ – (अनुकूल) प्रतिकूल न होना। favourable, agreeable.

अनुक्कम – पु॰ – (अनुक्रम) सिलसिला, सूची, तरतबी। order, succession, list.

अनुखुद्दक – वि॰ – (अनु + क्षुद्रक) अल्प महत्त्व की वस्तु। minor, of less importance.

अनुग – वि॰ – (अनुग) पीछे चलने वाला, अनुगामी। follower, followed by.

अनुगच्छति – क्रि॰ – (अनु + √गम् + व) अनुगमन करता है, पीछे जाता है। followers, goes after.

अनुगत – क्रि॰ वि॰ – (अनुगत) जिसका कोई अनुगामी हो। accompanied by.

अनुगति – स्त्री॰ – (अनुगति) अनुगमन। following after.

अनुगामिक– वि॰ – (अनुगामिक) अनुगामी। follower.

अनुगामी – पु॰ – (अनुगामी) देखें अनुगामिक। see Anugāmika.

अनुगाहति – क्रि॰ – (अनु + √ गाह + व = अनुगाहति) डुबकी लगाता है। plunges.

अनुगिज्झति – क्रि॰ – (अनु + √ गृध् + व = अनुगृध्यति) लोभ करता है। covets.

अनुगिज्झ – वि॰ – (अनुगृद्ध) लालची, लोभी। covetous, greedy.

अनुगण्णहाति – क्रि॰ – (अनुगृह्णाति) अनुग्रह करता है। showers pity on, helps.

अनुगण्हन – न॰ – (अनुग्रहण) अनुग्रह। favour.

अनुगहित – वि॰ – (अनुगृहीत) अनुग्रहीत, अनुग्रह पाया। commiserated, helped.

अनुगाहक – पु॰ – (अनुग्रहकर्त्ता) अनुग्रह करने वाला, संरक्षक। helper, patron.

अनुगिरन्त – कृ॰ – (अनु + उद्गिरन्) न बोलते हुए। not uttering, not speaking.

अनुगघाटेति – क्रि॰ – (अनुद्घाटयति) उद्घाटन करता है। unfastens, opens.

अनुचंकमति – क्रि॰ – (अनुचङ्क्रमणकरोति) चक्रमण करने वाले के पीछे चलता है, छोटी सी दूरी तक बार-बार जाने-आने की क्रिया को चक्रमण कहते हैं। follows one who is walking up and down for a short distance.

अनुचर – पु॰ – (अनुचर) अनुगामी, सेवक। follower, attendant.

अनुचरण – न॰ – (अनुचरण) अभ्यास। practice.

अनुचरित – क्रि॰ वि॰ – (अनुचरित) अभ्यस्त। practised, attained.

अनुचिण्ण – भूतकालिक क्रि॰ – (अनुचीर्ण) अभ्यस्त। accompanied by, practised.

अनुचित – वि॰ – (अनुचित) अनुपयुक्त। improper.

अनुचिनाति – क्रि॰ – (अनु + चिनोति) संग्रह करता है। collects, practises.

अनुचिन्तेति – क्रि॰ – (अनु + चिन्तयति) बार-बार विचार करता है, चिन्तन करता है। thinks upon, considers.

अनुच्चारित – क्रि॰ वि॰ – (अनुच्चारित) उच्चारण न किया गया। unuttered.

अनुच्छिट्ठ – वि॰ – (अन् + उच्छिष्ट) ऐसा भोजन जो जूठा न हुआ हो। untouched (food), that is not polluted.

अनुच्छविक – वि॰ – (अनुच्छविक) अनुरूप, योग्य, समीचीन। suitable, befitting, proper.

अनुज – पु॰ – (अनुज) छोटा भाई। younger brother.

अनुजा – स्त्री॰ – (अनुजा) छोटी बहन। younger sister.

अनुजात – वि॰ – (अनुजात) तदन्तर उत्पन्न, पिता की समाकृति वाला। born after, resembling (one's father).

अनुजानाति – क्रि॰ – (अनुजानाति अनुज्ञापयति) अनुज्ञा अर्थात् अनुमति देता है। allows, gives permission.

अनुजीवति – क्रि॰ – (अनुजीवति) बना रहता है, जीवित रहता है। remains, subsists.

अनुजीवी – वि॰ – (अनुजीवी) दूसरे पर निर्भर जीवन वाला, उपजीवी, परोपकारी। dependent person.

अनुजु – वि॰ – (अन् + ऋजु) जो सीधा न हो, वक्र। not straight, crooked.

अनुज्ञा – स्त्री॰ – (अनुज्ञा) अनुमति, स्वीकृति। sanction, permission.

अनुज्ञात – वि॰ – (अनुज्ञात) अनुज्ञा प्राप्त, स्वीकृत। sanctioned, permitted.

अनुत्थान – न॰ – (अन् + उत्थान) उत्थान-हीनता, अक्रियशीलता। inactiveness.

अनुत्थित – (अनुत्थित) निश्चेष्ट। not risen up.

अनुडसति – क्रि॰ – (अनु + दंशति) डंक मारता है। stings.

अनुडहति – क्रि॰ – (अनु + दहति) जलाता है। burns over.

अनुडाहन – न॰ – (अनु + दाहन) जलाना, तप्यति। burning.

अनुतप्पति – क्रि॰ – (अनु + अतप्यति) अनुताप करता है, पछताता है। repents, regrets.

अनुताप – क्रि॰ – (अनुताप) परिताप, मनोव्यथा। anguish, remorse.

अनुतिट्ठति – क्रि॰ – (अनु + तिष्ठति) समीप खड़ा होता है, साथ देता है। stands by, agrees.

अनुतीर – न॰ – (अनुतीरम्) नदी कूल या समुद्र तट का समीप्य। river bank or seashore.

अनुत्तर – (अनुत्तर) जिससे बढ़कर कोई न हो, सर्वोत्तम, बेजोड़। incomparable, unsurpassed.

अनुत्तान – वि॰ – (अनुत्तान) जो उथला न हो, गहरा, गम्भीर। not shallow, deep.

अनुत्थुनाति – क्रि॰ – (क्रन्दति अनुतप्यते) चिल्लाता है, अनुताप करता है। moans, laments, bewails.

अनुत्रासी – वि॰ – (अत्रस्त) जो भयभीत नहीं है। one who does not fear, fearless.

अनुददाति – क्रि॰ – (अनुददाति) देता है। grants, concedes.

अनुदहति – देखें – अनुडहति। see Anuḍahati.

अनुदिसा – स्त्री॰ – (अनुदिशा) विदिशा, दो दिशाओं की मध्यवर्ती कोणीय दिशा। an intermediate direction.

अनुद्दया – स्त्री॰ – (अनुदया) अनुकम्पा. grace, pity.

अनुद्दिट्ठु – वि॰ – (अन + उदिद्दृष्ठ) अनिर्दिष्ट, असंकेतित, अकथित। not pointed out, not uttered.

अनुद्धत – वि॰ – (अन् + उद्धत) जो उद्धत न हो, निरंहकारी। not haughty.

अनुधम्म – (अनु + धर्म) धर्मानुमोदित, धर्मानुकूल। conformity with the law.

अनुधावति – (अनु + धावति) पीछा करता है, पीछे पीछे दौड़ता है। runs after.

अनुनय – पु॰ – (अनुनय) अनुनय, विनय, अभ्यर्थना, मैत्रीभाव। request, friendliness.

अनुनासिक – पु॰ – (अनुनासिक) नाक से उच्चरित होने वाले वर्ण। nasal.

अनुनेति – क्रि॰ – (अनु + नेति) सन्तुष्ट करता है, मना लेता है। appeases, conciliates.

अनुप – (अनूप) – पु॰ – (अनु + अप) जलमय धरती, गीली जमीन। wet land.

अनुपकुट्ठ – वि॰ – (अन + उपक्रुष्ट) उपक्रोश-रहित, अनवद्य, अनिन्द्य, निष्कलंक। blameless, irreproachable.

अनुपखज्जति – क्रि॰ – (हठात् + आक्षिपति) दखल देता है, बलात् प्रवेश करता है। intrudes.

अनुपगच्छति – क्रि॰ – (अनु + उपगच्छति) पास नहीं फटकता, निकट नहीं जाता है, वापस लौट आता है। does not approach, returns.

अनुपघात – पु॰ – (अन् + उपघात) चोट न पहुँचाना, अहिंसा। non-injury, nonviolence.

अनुपचित – वि॰ – (अन् + उपचित = असंचित) असंचित, असंगृहीत। not accumulated.

अनुपञ्ञाति – स्त्री॰ – (अनु + प्रज्ञप्ति) विज्ञप्ति का परिशिष्ट, उपनियम। supplementary regulation.

अनुपटियाति – स्त्री॰ – (अनु + प्रतिपाती) क्रम, क्रमानुसार। in order, successively.

अनुपट्ठित – वि॰ – (अनुपस्थित) गैर-हाजिर। absent, not present.

अनुपतित – वि॰ – (अनुपतित) ढकेला हुआ, गिरा हुआ। suppressed, fallen, pushed by.

अनुपत्ति – स्त्री॰ – (अनुपत्ति) प्राप्ति। attainment.

अनुपदं – अव्यय – (अनुपदम्) पीछे-पीछे, साथ-साथ शब्दशः। word by word, close behind.

अनुपद्दव – वि॰ – (अनुपद्रव) उपद्रव-शून्यता, शान्ति. free from turmoil, peaceful.

अनुपधारेति – क्रि॰ – (अनुपधारयति) विचार नहीं करता है। pays no consideration.

अनुपबज्जा – स्त्री॰ – (अनु + प्रव्रज्या) किसी दूसरे की देखा-देखी संन्यास लेना, किसी से प्रभावित होकर प्रव्रज्या ग्रहण करना। give up worldly life in imitation of another.

अनुपमेय – वि॰ – (अनुपमेय) अतुलनीय, जिसकी उपमा न मिले। incomparable.

अनुपरिगच्छति – क्रि॰ – (अनु + परि + + गच्छति) पीछे-पीछे या साथ-साथ परिक्रमा करता है। walks around with.

अनुपरिधावति – क्रि॰ – (अनु + परि + धावति) साथ-साथ पीछे दौड़ता है। runs around with.

अनुपरियाति – क्रि॰ – (अनुपरियाति) देखें – अनुपरिगच्छति। see Anupari-gacchati.

अनुपरिवत्तति – क्रि॰ – (अनुपरिवत्तति) लुढ़कता है। rolls about.

अनुपरिवेति – क्रि॰ – (अनु + परिवारयति) घेर लेता है। surrounds.

अनुपालित्त – वि॰ – (अन + उपलिप्त) जो किसी चीज में सना हुआ, लिबड़ा न हो। unstained, free from taint.

अनुपवज्ज – वि॰ – (अन् + उपवद्य) निरवद्य, निर्दोष, निष्कलंक। blameless.

अनुपविसति – क्रि॰ – (अनु + प्रविशति) प्रवेश करता है। enters, goes into.

अनुपसम्पन्न – वि॰ – (अन् + उपसम्पन्न) जिसने उपसम्पदा प्राप्त नहीं की है। one who has yet not received the full ordination or upsampadā.

अनुपस्सक – पु॰ – (अनुपश्यक) पर्यवेक्षक। an observer.

अनुपस्सना – स्त्री॰ – (अनुपश्यना) पुनर्विचार, गहन चिन्तन, पर्यवेक्षण। re-consideration, observation.

अनुपहच्च – कृ॰ – (अन् + उप + √हन + ल्यप् = अनुहत्य) बिना क्षति या आघात पहुँचाये। without wounding or hurting.

अनुपहत – क्रि॰ – (अन् + उपहत) जिसे चोट न पहुचाया गया हो। not spoilt, not damaged.

अनुपात – पु॰ – (अनुपात) कठोर शब्दों, कर्कश वाणी का प्रयोग। attack in speech.

अनुपाती – वि॰ – (अनुपाती) जो वाक्य प्रहार करता है। one who attacks in speech.

अनुपादाय – कृ॰ – (अन् + उप + आ + √दा + ल्यप् = अनुपादाय) बिना ग्रहण किये, बिना समझे। without grasping.

अनुपादान – वि॰ – (अनुपादान) अनासक्त, बिना ईंधन के। unattached, fuelless.

अनुपादिसेस – वि॰ – (अनुपादिशेष) अशेष उपाधि के निरोध वाली (निर्वाण धातु)। without any substratum.

अनुपःपुणाति – क्रि॰ – (अन् + उप + आपुणाति) प्राप्त करता है। reaches, attains.

अनुपापेति – क्रि॰ – (अनु + पापयति) प्राप्त कराता है। makes one acquire or receive.

अनुपाय – पु॰ – (कुत्सिय उपाय) अनुपयुक्त या अनुचित उपाय। wrong means.

अनुपायास – वि॰ – (अन् + उप + आयास) खेद रहित, चिन्ता रहित। sorrowless, serene.

अनुपालक – पु॰ – (अनुपालक) संरक्षण करने वाला, निर्देशों को यथावत् क्रियान्वयन करने वाला। guarding, protecting.

अनुपालेति – क्रि॰ – (अनुपालेति) पालन-पोषण करता है। one who guards or protects.

अनुपाहन – वि॰ – (अन् + उपानह) बिना जूते के। having no shoes.

अनुपुच्छति – क्रि॰ – (अन् + पृच्छ + व = अनुपृच्छति) पूछता है, जानकारी या प्रश्न करता है। inquires after.

अनुपुट्ठ – क्रि॰ वि॰ – (अनुपृष्ट) पूछा गया। being asked or questioned.

अनुपुब्ब – अव्यय – (अनुपूर्वम्) क्रमशः। successive, gradual.

अनुपेक्खति – क्रि॰ – (अन् + प्रे + ईक्षते) ध्यान देता है, विचार करता है। considers carefully.

अनुपेक्खना – स्त्री॰ – (अनुप्रेक्षणा) चिन्तन करना, ध्यानपूर्वक विचार करना। consideration (thorough).

अनुपेसति – क्रि॰ – (अनु + प्रेसयति) पीछे-पीछे भेजता है। sends after.

अनुपोसिय – वि॰ – (अनु + पोष्य) संरक्षण अथवा, पोषण के योग्य। fit to be nourished or fostered.

अनुप्पत्ति – स्त्री॰ – (अन् + उत्पत्ति) अप्राप्ति जन्म का प्राप्त न होना। unborn, cessation of rebirth.

अनुप्पदातु – पु॰ – (अनु + प्रदातृ) अनुप्रदान करने वाला दाता। a donor, one who bestows.

अनुप्पदान – न॰ – (अनुप्रदान) अर्पण, अर्पित किया जाना। giving, handing over.

अनुप्रदाति – क्रि॰ – (अनु + प्रदाति) अर्पित करता है, दे डालता है। gives out, hands over.

अनुप्पन्न – वि॰ – (अनुत्पन्न) अज्ञात, जिसका आविर्भाव न हुआ हो। not born, not risen.

अनुप्पबन्धन – न॰ – (अनुप्रबन्धन) चुस्त, निरन्तरता। continuance, being without end.

अनुप्फरण – न॰ – (अनुस्फरण) लगातार दमकना। flashing continuously.

अनुबद्ध – क्रि॰ वि॰ – (अनु + बद्ध) संलग्न, अनुलग्न, संयोजित। connected with, followed by.

अनुबन्धति – क्रि॰ – (अनुबन्धति) अनुबन्ध करता है, अक्षरशः अनुसरण करता है। pursues, follows.

अनुबन्धन – न॰ – (अनुबन्धन) संलग्नता, अनुसरण। follow-up, keep connected.

अनुबल – न॰ – (अनुबलम्) समर्थन, साहाय्य, प्रेरणा। help, stimulation.

अनुबुज्झति – क्रि॰ – (अनु + बुध्यति) बाध प्राप्त करता है, जानकारी प्राप्त करता है। conceives, understands.

अनुबुद्ध – वि॰ – (अनु + बुद्ध) अन्तः-प्रेरणा से बोधि अर्थात् जीवन के चर्या के रहस्यों का ज्ञान प्राप्त करने वाले अर्थात् सम्यक् सम्बुद्ध से उपदिष्ट होकर ज्ञान-सम्पन्न बनने वाला व्यक्ति। one who has attained enlightenment by the preaching of Buddha.

अनुबोध – पु॰ – (अनुबोध) समझ, ज्ञान। knowledge, understanding.

अनुव्यञ्जन – न॰ – (अनुव्यञ्जनम्) गौण लक्षण, छोटे-छोटे चिह्न। a secondary attribute.

अनुब्रूहेति – क्रि॰ – (अनु + बृह्यति) बढ़ाता है, अभ्यास करता है, सुधारता है। improves, practises.

अनुभवति – क्रि॰ – (अनुभवति) अनुभव करता है, चखता है। undergoes, partakes in.

अनुभवन – न॰ – (अनुभवन) अनुभव करना, चखना। experiencing of, understanding.

अनुभाव – पु॰ – (अनुभाव) प्रताप, प्रभाव, काव्य रस का अंग, मति निश्चय। splendour, influence, indication of feeling (in drama).

अनुभुत्त – देखें – अनुभूत। see Anubhūta.

अनुभूत – क्रि॰ वि॰ – (अनुभूत) अनुभव पाया हुआ, आस्वाद प्राप्त। enjoyed, undergone.

अनुभूयमान – क्रि॰ – (अनु + √भू + शानच् = अनुभयमान) अनुभव करता हुआ। being experienced.

अनुभोति – क्रि॰ – (अनुभवति) अनुभव कर रहा है। experiencing.

अनुमज्जति – क्रि॰ – (अनुमज्जति) थपथपाता है, डुबकी लगाता है। strokes, dives.

अनुमज्जन – न॰ – (अनुमज्जन) डुबकी लगाना, थपथपाना। stroking, diving.

अनुमञ्ञति – क्रि॰ – (अनुमन्यते) अनुमति देता है, समर्थन करता है। assents, approves.

अनुमत – क्रि॰ वि॰ – (अनुमत) अनुमति प्राप्त। approved.

अनुमति – स्त्री॰ – (अनुमति) अनुज्ञा, अनुमति, सहमति। permission, agreement.

अनुमान – पु॰ – (अनुमान) अनुमान, अन्दाजा। inference, assumption.

अनुमीयति – क्रि॰ – (अनुमीयते) अनुमान करता है। infers, assumes.

अनुमोदक – पु॰ – (अनुमोदक) प्रशंसा करने वाला, हाँ में हाँ मिलाने वाला। one who appreciates, thanksgiver.

अनुमोदति – क्रि॰ – (अनुमोदति) अनुमोदन प्राप्त = स्वीकृत। appreciates, rejoices in.

अनुयात – कृ॰ – (अनुयन्त) अनुगमन करता हुआ, अनुसरण करता हुआ। follows.

अनुयायी – पु॰ – (अनुयायी) अनुगमन करने वाला, पीछे चलने वाला। follower.

अनुयुञ्जति – क्रि॰ – (अनु + युञ्ज + व) किसी काम में जुटता है। engages in.

अनुयुत्त – क्रि॰ वि॰ – (अनुयुञ्जाति का भूतकालिक कृदन्त रुप) सन्नद्ध, किसी काम में जुटता हुआ। engaged in.

अनुयोग – पु॰ – (अनुयोग) साधना, तन्मयता। devotion, application.

अनुयोगी – पु॰ – (अनुयोगी) साधना-रत, भक्ति-रत। engaged in, one who is practising.

अनुरक्खक – वि॰ – (अनुरक्षक) प्रहरी, देखभाल या चौकसी रखने वाला। protector, guardian.

अनुरक्खण – न॰ – (अनुरक्षणम्) संरक्षण, देखभाल। protection, maintenance.

अनुरक्खति – क्रि॰ – (अनुरक्षति) देखभाल करता है। maintains, looks after.

अनुरक्खा – स्त्री॰ – (अनुरक्षा) संरक्षा, सुरक्षा। guarding, protecting.

अनुरक्खी – पु॰ – (अनुरक्षी) देखें अनुरक्खक। see Anurakkhaka.

अनुरक्खीय – वि॰ – (अनुरक्षीय) सुरक्षा योग्य, रक्षणीय। fit to be guarded.

अनुरज्जति – क्रि॰ – (अनुरज्जति = अनु + रज्जू + व) आकर्षित होता है, आनन्दित होता है। rejoices.

अनुरंजित – क्रि॰ वि॰ – (अनुरञ्जित) आह्लादित, आनन्दमग्न। rejoiced.

अनुरत्त – वि॰ – (अनुरक्त) प्रेमी, वफादार, आसक्त, प्रसन्न। fond of, attached to, faithful to.

अनुख – पु॰ – (अनु + ख) प्रतिध्वनि, गूंज। echo, resounding.

अनुरूप – वि॰ – (अनुरूप) समरूप, अनुसारी, अनुकूल। suitable, conforms with.

अनुरोदति – क्रि॰ – (अनु + √रूद् + व) विलाप करता है, चिल्लाता है। cries for, laments.

अनुरोध – पु॰ – (अनुरोध) (1) आग्रह (2) स्वीकृति, (3) अनुकूलता। (1) urge (2) consent, (3) favour.

अनुलाप – पु॰ – (अनुलाप) पुनर्कथन, अनुकथन। repetition, saying again.

अनुलिम्पति – क्रि॰ – (अनु + लेपयति) लीपता है, अस्तर चढ़ाता है। anoints, besmears.

अनुलिम्पयति – प्रेरणार्थक क्रिया (अनुलिम्पयति) अनुलेप कराता है। gets anointed, besmeared.

अनुलिम्पन – न॰ – (अनुलिम्पन) लीपना, अनुलेपन, अस्तर चढ़ाना। anointing, besmearing.

अनुलोम – बि॰ – (अनुलोम) सीधे क्रम में, अविलोम, जो विपरीत या उलटे क्रम में न हो। regular, not antagonistic.

अनुलोमेति – क्रि॰ – (अनुलोमेति) क्रम का अनुसरण करता है। remains in accordance with.

अनुवत्तति – पु॰ – (अनुवत्तते) अनुकूल आचरण करता है, अनुसरण करता है। agrees, follows, obeys.

अनुवत्तन – न॰ – (अनुवर्त्तन) अनुसरण, अनुपालन, अनुगमन। compliance, obedience.

अनुवत्तेति – क्रि॰ – (अनुवर्त्तयति) अनुकूल व्यवहार करता है, अनुकरण करता है, उत्तराधिकार बदलता है। agrees, imitates, follows.

अनुवदति – क्रि॰ – (अनुवदति) दोषारोपण करता है। blames.

अनुवसति – क्रि॰ – (अनुवसति) किसी के साथ वास करता है। resides with.

अनुवस्सं – अव्यय – (अनुवर्षम्) प्रतिवर्ष, वार्षिक, प्रत्येक वर्षा ऋतु में। in every rainy season, annually.

अनुवात – पु॰ – (अनुवात) अनुकूल पवन। favourable wind.

अनुवाद – पु॰ – (अनु + वाद) भाषान्तर करना। translation.

अनुवासन – न॰ – (अनुवासन) गन्ध से सुवासित करना। to perfume.

अनुवासित – क्रि॰ वि॰ – (अनुवासित) सुवासित किया हुआ। perfumed.

अनुवासेति – क्रि॰ – (अनुवासयति) सुवासित करता है। fill with a good smell, make it smell better.

अनुविचरति – क्रि॰ – (अनुविचरति) विचरण करता है। wanders about, roams about.

अनुविचारित – वि॰ – (अनुविचारित) सुविचारित। pondered over, reflected.

अनुविचारणा – स्त्री॰ – (अनुविचारण) (1) पुनर्विचारण (2) टहलना, चहलकदमी करना। (1) reconsidering (2) strolling.

अनुविचिनाति – क्रि॰ – (अनु + वि + √चिर + व = अनुविचिनेते) विचार करता है, चिन्तन करता है। ponders over, examines.

अनुविच्च – पूर्व का क्रि॰ – (अनु + वि + √च + ल्यप्) ज्ञात करके, विचार करके। having known or having considered.

अनुविञ्जक – पु॰ – (अनुविद्यक) परीक्षक, अनुसन्धानकर्ता। investigator, examiner.

अनुविज्जति – क्रि॰ – (अनु + √विद् + व) अनुसन्धान करता है, विश्लेषणात्मक ज्ञान अर्जित करता है। investigates, knows thoroughly.

अनुविब्ज्झति – क्रि॰ – (अनु + बिध्यति) बींधता है, परीक्षण करता है। pierces, examines thoroughly.

अनुवितक्केति – क्रि॰ – (अनुवितर्कयति) तर्क-वितर्क करता है, मनन करता है। ponders over, reflects.

अनुविदित – क्रि॰ वि॰ – (अनुविदित) अभिज्ञात, परिचयकृत, पहचान लिया गया, जान लिया गया। recognized, understood.

अनुविद्ध – क्रि॰ वि॰ – (अनु + विद्ध) बींधा हुआ। pierced.

अनुविधीयति – क्रि॰ – (अनु + वि + धीन्यते) विधि के अनुसार आचरण करता है। acts according to law, acts in conformity.

अनुविलोकेति – क्रि॰ – (अनुविलोकयति) निरीक्षण करता है, सम्परीक्षण करता है। looks over, surveys.

अनुवुद्ध – क्रि॰ वि॰ – (अनु + √विश् + क्त) रहता हुआ, वास करता हुआ। dwelt, lived.

अनुब्यञ्जन – न॰ – (अनुव्यञ्जन) उपलक्षण, गौण चिह्न। secondary, attribute.

अनुसक्कति – क्रि॰ – (अपसर्पति) सरकता है, एक ओर हट जाता है। moves back, moves aside.

अनुसंवच्छर – क्रि॰ वि॰ – (अनुसंवत्सरम्) प्रति वर्ष। every year.

अनुसंचरति – क्रि॰ – (अनुसञ्चरति) चलता फिरता है, घूमता है। walks along, goes around.

अनुसंचरण – न॰ – (अनुसञ्चरण) घूमना, इधर-उधर टहलना, चलना, फिरना। walking about, going around.

अनुसट – क्रि॰ वि॰ – (अनुसृष्ट) बिखेरा हुआ। scattered.

अनुसत्थर – पु॰ – (अनुशास्तृ) शिक्षक, उपदेशक। preacher, teacher.

अनुसत्थि – स्त्री॰ – (अनुशास्ति) निर्देश, नियम। rule, instruction.

अनुसन्दाति – क्रि॰ – (अनु + स्यन्दति) पीछे लगा रहता है। follows, accompanies.

अनुसन्धि – स्त्री॰ – (अनुसन्धि) मेल, परिणाम। connection, conclusion.

अनुसय – पु॰ – (अनुशयः) दूषित चित्तवृत्ति, चित्त का कुमार्गों के प्रति झुकाव। polluted attitude of mind, perverse disposition.

अनुसरति (1) – क्रि॰ – (अनु + √सृ + व = अनुसरति) अनुसरण करता है। follows, goes after.

अनुसरति (2) – क्रि॰ – (अनु + √स्मृः = अनुस्मरति) अनुस्मरण करता है, याद करता है। remembers.

अनुसवति – क्रि॰ – (अनु + √सु = अनुसवति) चूता है, टपकता है। flows or oozes continually.

अनुसयित – वि॰ – (अनुशयानः) सोया हुआ। dormant.

अनुसावक – पु॰ – (अनुश्रावकः) सुनाने वाला, उद्घोषक। one who announces.

अनुसावेति – क्रि॰ – (अनुश्रावयति) घोषणा करता है, सुनाता है। declares, announces.

अनुसासक – पु॰ – (अनुशासक) अनुशासन रखने वाला। preceptor, ruler.

अनुसासति – क्रि॰ – (अनुशासनं करोति) अनुशासन रखता है। keeps discipline, instructs.

अनुसासन – न॰ – (अनुशासन) मर्यादा-पालन। instruction, discipline.

अनुसासिक जातक – (जा॰ सं॰ 115) – एक पेटू भिक्षुणी की मर्यादा-हीनता सम्बन्धी जातक कथा। the Jātaka tale (No. 115) of a lady Bhikṣuṇī who was an excessive eater.

अनुसिक्खति – क्रि॰ – (अनु + √ शिक्षू) शिक्षा ग्रहण करता है। learns.

अनुसिक्खन – न॰ – (अनु + शिक्षण) किसी प्रसंग से सीख लेना। learning a lesson from.

अनुसिट्ठ – क्रि॰ वि॰ – (अनुशिष्ट) अनुशासित। disciplined.

अनुसिट्ठि – स्त्री॰ – (अनुशासित) उपदेश, अनुशासन। discipline, instruction.

अनुसूयक – वि॰ – (अन् + असूया + णवुल् = अनसूयकः) ईर्षा-रहित, not envious.

अनुसेति – क्रि॰ – (अनु + शेते) अनुशयन करता है, सोता है। sleeps, lies dormant.

अनुसोचति – क्रि॰ – (अनुशोचति) पछताता है, शोक करता है। bewails, mourns.

अनुसोचना – स्त्री॰ – (अनुशोचना) विलाप, क्रन्दन। bewail, mourn.

अनुसोत – पु॰ – (अनुस्रोतस्) धारा मुख। downstream.

अनुसोतगामी – पु॰ – (अनुस्रोतगामी) धारा प्रवाह का अनुसरण करने वाला। one who follows the stream.

अनुस्सति – स्त्री॰ – (अनुस्मृति) याद, स्मृति। memory, recollection, mindfulness.

अनुस्सरण – न॰ – (अनुस्मरण) याद, स्मरण। remembrance, memory.

अनुस्सरति – क्रि॰ – (अनुस्मरति) याद करता है। remembers.

अनुस्सव – पु॰ – (अनुश्रव) दन्तकथा, अनुश्रुति, किंवदन्ती। a hearsay tradition, a legend.

अनुस्सुक – वि॰ – (अन + उत्सुक) उत्सुकता-रहित, क्षीण मनोबल, सुस्त, उत्साह-रहित। coward, lazy unpleasant.

अनुहसति – क्रि॰ – (अनुहसति) परिहास करता है, मजाक उड़ाता है। mocks, jests.

अनून – वि॰ – (अन् + ऊनम्) न्यूनता-रहित, सम्पूर्ण। complete, not lacking.

अनूनक – पु॰ – (अनूनक = अन् + ऊन + क) जो न्यून न हो, सम्पूर्ण। not less, complete, full.

अनूनता – स्त्री॰ – (अनूनता) सम्पूर्णता। completeness.

अनूपम – वि॰ – (अनुपम) जिसकी उपमा न दी जा सके, अप्रतिम, अद्वितीय, अनन्य। incomparable, that which one without a second, has no comparison.

अनूप – पु॰ स्त्री॰ – (अनूप) जलबहुल भूमि, दलदल। marshy land.

अनूहत अनूहत – वि॰ – (अनूहत) जिसकी जड़ नहीं खुदी। not rooted out, not removed.

अनेक – वि॰ – (अनेक) एकाधिक कई। more than one, several, many.

अनेकत्थ – वि॰ – (अनेकार्थ) एक से अधिक अर्थ देने वाला। the word having more than one meaning.

अनेकप्पकारक – वि॰ – (अनेक प्रकारक) अनेक प्रकार वाला, अनेक रूपों, प्रजातियों, स्वरूपों वाला। multifarious, manifold, diverse.

अनेकविध – देखें – अनेकप्पकारक। see Anekappakāraka.

अनेज – वि॰ – (अन् + एजः) तृष्णा रहित। free from thirst, greed.

अनेघ – वि॰ – (अन् - इहम) इन्धन रहित।
fuel-less.

अनेळ – वि॰ – (अन् + एनस्) निर्दोष।
innocent.

अनेळक – (संस्कृत) देखें अनेळ। see
Anela.

अनेळगल – वि॰ – (निर्मूकः) जो गूंगा न
हो। not dumb.

अनेसना – स्त्री॰ – (अन् + एषणा) जीविका
की अनुचित तलाश। seeking evil path
for livelihood.

अनोक – न॰ – (अन् + ओकस) बेघर।
having no opportunity,
homeless.

अनोजा – स्त्री॰ – (अनुजा) नारंगी रंग के
फूलों वाला एक पौधा या उसका फूल।
a kind of shrub or tree with
orange flowers.

अनोतत्त – पु॰ –(अनुतप्त) हिमालय स्थित
झील मानसरोवर। Mānsarovara
lake in the Himālayas.

अनोतप्प – न॰ – (अनुत्ताप जघन्य) क्रूर
कर्म में जिसे दुःख न होता हो, क्रूर।
cruel, not afraid of sin.

अनोदक – वि॰ – (अन् + उदक) जल-
रहित, निर्जल। waterless.

अनोदिस्सक – वि॰ – (अन् + उद्देश्यक)
सर्वमान्य के लिए। which is meant
for all.

अनोनमति – क्रि॰ – (अन् + अवनयति) जो
झुकता नहीं है। which does not
stoop or bend down.

अनोम – वि॰ – (अनोमा) सर्वश्रेष्ठ।
superior.

अनोमा – कपिलवस्तु के पूर्व की एक नदी
जिसे गृहत्याग के अनन्तर सिद्धार्थ गौतम
ने सर्वप्रथम पार किया था। A river in
east Kapilvastu which was
crossed over by Siddhārtha
Gautama after he left the place
for good.

अनोमादस्सी – (अनोमा–दर्शी) विपश्चित,
सर्वद्रष्टा। one who has great
foresight.

अनोमज्जति – क्रि॰ – (अनु + मर्दति) शरीर
को हाथ से मलता है। massages the
body, rubs the body with his
hand.

अनोरपार – वि॰ – (अन + ओर + पारम्)
जिसका न ओर हो न पार, न इस ओर
तीर न उस ओर तीर। having (a
shore) neither on this side nor
the other side.

अनोवस्सक – वि॰ – (अनोवर्षक) वर्षा से
सुरक्षित। sheltered from the rains.

अन्त – पु॰ – (अन्त) अवसान, समाप्ति।
the end.

अन्तकर – वि॰ – (अन्ताकर) समापक, अन्त
करने वाला। putting an end.

अन्तकिरिया – स्त्री॰ – (अन्त-क्रिया) अवसान
क्रिया। ending, last rites.

अन्तगमन – न॰ – (अन्तगमन) अवसान को
प्राप्त करना, अन्त को पहुँचना। going
to an end.

अन्तगत – क्रि॰ वि॰ – (अन्तर्गत) सम्मिलित,
समाहित। inner, included.

अन्तगुण – न॰ – (आन्त्र) आँत। intestine.

अन्त-जातक – (जा॰ सं॰ 295) देवदत्त के
बारे में वेणुवन में उपदिष्ट जातक कथा।
Jātaka tale (No. 295) regarding
Devadatta.

अन्तक – पु॰ – (अन्तक) मृत्यु। death.

अन्तमसो – अव्यय – (अन्तमसो) अन्तिम दर्जे का। at last.

अन्तर – न॰ – (अन्तर) भेद, दूरी, भीतरी। difference, inside.

अन्तरे – न॰ – (अन्तरे) दो वस्तुओं या व्यक्तियों के बीच में। in between.

अन्तरकप्प – पु॰ – (अन्तरकल्प) दो कल्पों के बीच। intermediary *kalpa*.

अन्तरघर – न॰ – (अन्तरगृह) भीतर का घर। inner house.

अन्तरसाटक – न॰ – (अन्तः शाटकम्) भीतरी वस्त्र। undergarment, underwear.

अन्तरट्ठक – न॰ – (अन्तराष्टकम्) वर्षा के अतिशीत आठ दिवसों की अवधि। a group of eight days during rainy season having chill or dense snowfall.

अन्तरन्तरा – क्रि॰ वि॰ – (अन्तर-अन्तरा) जब-तब। now and then, occasionally.

अन्तरधान – न॰ – (अन्तर्धान) अदृश्य हो जाना, छिप जाना, दिखाई न पड़ना। disappear, vanish, invisible.

अन्तरवासक – पु॰ – (अन्तरवासक) (1) - अधोवस्त्र, (2) भीतरी वस्त्र, लुंगी या धोती की तरह पहना जाने वाला चीवर। inner garment.

अन्तरहित – क्रि॰ वि॰ – (अन्तरहित / अन्तर्निहित) भीतर छिपा हुआ, निलीन। disappeared, hidden.

अन्तरंस – पु॰ – (अन्तर + अंसं) दो कन्धों के बीच की दूरी। space between two shoulders.

अन्तरा – क्रि॰ वि॰ – (अन्तरा) बीच में। meanwhile, in between.

अन्तरा मग्गे – क्रि॰ वि॰ – (अन्तरमार्गे) बीच रास्ते में। on the way, on the road, enroute.

अन्तरापण – पु॰ – (अन्तरःआपण) दुकानों के बीच बाजार। market-place.

अन्तराय – पु॰ – (अन्तराय) विघ्न, बाधा। obstacle, danger.

अन्तरायिक – वि॰ – (अन्तरायिक) बाधक, विघ्न डालने वाला। forming an impediment, create trouble.

अन्तराल – न॰ – (अन्तराल) मध्यान्तर, बीच की स्थिति। interval.

अन्तरिक – वि॰ – (अन्तरिक) बाद वाला, दूसरा। next.

अन्तरीप – न॰ – (अन्तरीप) द्वीप, टापू। an island.

अन्तरीय – न॰ – (अन्तरीय) अधोवस्त्र लुँगी। inner garment.

अन्तलिक्ख – न॰ – (अन्तरिक्ष) आकाश और पृथ्वी के बीच का क्षेत्र। space, atmosphere.

अन्तवन्तु – वि॰ – (अन्तवान) अन्तवान, सान्त, जिसका अन्त हो। having an end.

अन्तरेन – वि॰ – (अन्तरेण) बिना। without.

अन्तिक – वि॰ – (अन्तिक) छोर पर स्थित, अन्तिम पड़ोसी। situated on the shore, final neighbour.

अन्तिम – वि॰ – (अन्तिम) आखिरी सबसे बाद वाला। last, final.

अन्तेपुर – न॰ – (अन्तःपुर) (1) महल का भीतरी भाग, (2) नगर का भीतरी हिस्सा। (1) inner portion of palace (for ladies), a harem, (2) inner portion of city.

अन्तेवासी – पु॰ – (अन्तेवासी) आचार्य के पास रहने वाला शिष्य। one who lives with his teacher, pupil.

अन्तो – अव्यय – (अन्तर) अन्दर। inside, within.

अन्तोकुच्छि – स्त्री॰ – (अन्तःकुक्षि) कोख। womb.

अन्तोगत – वि॰ – (अन्तर्गत) भीतर समाहित। included, contained.

अन्तोगब्भ – पु॰ – (अन्तर्गर्भ) अन्तःप्रकोष्ठ। inner chamber.

अन्तोगाम – पु॰ – (अन्तर्ग्राम) भीतर का गाँव। inner village.

अन्तोघर – न॰ – (अन्तर्गृह) भीतरी प्रकोष्ठ। inner room.

अन्तोजन – पु॰ – (अन्तर्जन) कुटुम्ब का सदस्य। people belonging to the family.

अन्तोजात – वि॰ – (अन्तर्जात) गुलाम। slave, born in a family of slaves.

अन्तोवस्स – न॰ – (अन्तर्वर्षम्) वर्षा काल के भीतर। in the rainy season.

अन्तोवुट्ठ – वि॰ – (अन्तः स्थ) भीतर स्थित। kept inside.

√ अन्द-भ्वादि – (बन्धने) बाँधना। to fasten, to tighten.

अन्दू – स्त्री॰ – (अन्दू) जंजीर, हाथ-पैर की जंजीर, बेड़ी। chain, irons, shackles.

अन्दुघर – न॰ – (अन्दुगृह) कारागार। prison.

अन्ध – वि॰ – (अन्ध) अन्धा, मूर्ख। blind, foolish.

अन्धकरण – वि॰ – (अन्धकरण) अन्धा करना, भ्रान्ति पैदा करना। confusing, blinding.

अन्धबाल – वि॰ – (अन्धबालः) निपट मूर्ख। very silly, foolish.

अन्धवन – न॰ – (अन्धवनम्) श्रावस्ती से दक्षिण-पश्चिम में एक गावुत (लगभग एक किलोमीटर) की दूरी पर अन्धवन (अन्धकवन) नामक एक महावन था। भगवान बुद्ध ने यहीं पर राहुल को 'चूल-राहुलोवाद सुत्तन्त' का उपदेश दिया था जिसका उल्लेख *मज्झिम निकाय* में हुआ है। एक अनुश्रुति के अनुसार यहाँ पाँच सौ अन्धों ने बुद्धानुभाव से चक्षु (दृष्टि) प्राप्त की थी। अन्धवन का उल्लेख अक्खिवन (अक्षिवन), अक्कवन (अर्कवन) तथा अकौन के नाम से भी मिलता है। वर्तमान समय मे यह स्थान अकौना के नाम से प्रसिद्ध है। Andhavana was a big forest, situated at a distance of a Gāvuta (about a kilometer) in south-west of Śrāvastī where Lord Buddha had delivered the sermon of 'Cūla Rāhulovād - Suttanta' to Rāhula as referred in the *Majjhima Nikāya*. We hear from tradition that five hundred blind persons had gained sight at this place by the grace of the Buddha. Andhavan has also been referred to as Akkhivana (Akṣivan), Akkavana (Arkavana) and Akaunā. Now it is known by the name of Akaunā.

अन्धभूत – वि॰ – (अन्धभूतः) नितान्त मूढ़। mentally blind.

अन्धक (1) – पु॰ – (अन्धक) मक्खी की एक प्रजाति। a type of fly.

अन्धक (2) – पु॰ – (अन्धक) आन्ध्र प्रदेश का निवासी। belonging to the Andhra Pradesh State.

अन्धक (3) – पु॰ – (अन्धक निकाय) स्थविरवाद से पृथक् हो जाने वाले भिक्षुओं का एक सम्प्रदाय। a sect of *bhikkhu*s spurned from Sthavira.

अन्धकार – पु॰ – (अन्धकार) अँधेरा। darkness, bewilderment.

अन्धतम – पु॰ न॰ – (अन्धतम) गूढ़तम अँधेरा, निबिडतम। deep darkness.

अन्न – न॰ – (अन्नम्) भोजन, भात। food, boiled rice.

अन्नद – पु॰ – (अन्नद) अन्न देने वाला, भोजन देने वाला। one who gives food.

अन्न-पान – न॰ – (अन्नपानम्) खान-पान, भोजन-पानी। food and drink.

अन्वग – वि॰ – (अन्वग) अनुगामी, पीछे चलने वाला। follower.

अन्वगा – क्रि॰ – (अनु + अगात्) अनुगमन किया। followed.

अन्वगु – क्रि॰ – (अन्वगच्छन्) उन लोगों ने अनुगमन किया। they followed.

अन्वड्ढमासं – अव्यय – (अनु + अर्द्धमासम्) हर पखवारे में। fortnightly, twice a month.

अन्वत्थ – वि॰ – (अन्वर्थ) अर्थानुसार। according to the sense.

अन्वदेव – अव्यय – (अन्वद् + एव) पीछे लगा हुआ। following behind.

अन्वय – पु॰ – (अन्वयः) मार्ग, क्रम, हेतु। course, conformity, tradition.

अन्वहं – क्रि॰ वि॰ – (अन्वहम्) अनुदिन, नित्य। daily.

अन्वागच्छति – क्रि॰ – (अनु + आगच्छति) पीछे-पीछे आता है। follows, comes behind.

अन्वाय – पूर्व॰ क्रि॰ – (अन्वाय) अनुभव करके, हो करके। attained, having undergone, experienced.

अन्वायिक – वि॰ – (अनुयायी) अनुगामी, सहचर। follower, companion.

अन्वाहत – वि॰ – (अनु + आहत) चोटिहल, मारा-पीटा हुआ। beaten, struck.

अन्वाहिण्डति – क्रि॰ – (अनु + आ + √हिण्ड = अन्वाहिण्डति) घूमता है। wanders.

अन्वेति – क्रि॰ – (अनु + एंति) अनुगमन करता है। approaches, follows.

अन्वेसक – क्रि॰ – (अन्वेषक) खोजने वाला, अन्वेषणकर्त्ता। searcher, seeker.

अन्वेसति – क्रि॰ – (अनु + इषति) अन्वेषण करता है, खोज करता है। seeks, looks for, searches.

अन्वेसणा – स्त्री॰ – (अन्वेषणा) गवेषणा, खोज। seeking, search, investigation.

अन्वेसी – पु॰ – (अन्वेषी) खोजकर्त्ता, खोजी। seeker, investigator, seeking after.

अन्ह – पु॰ – (अहन्) दिन, समस्त पदों में प्रयुक्त जैसे पूर्वाह्न, मध्याह्न, अपराह्न। day.

अपकड्ढति – क्रि॰ – (अप+कड्ढति) बाहर खींच ले जाता है, दूर खींच ले जाता है। draws away, takes away.

अपकरोति – क्रि॰ – (अपकरोति) अपकार करता है। hurts, offends, puts off.

अपकस्सति – क्रि॰ – (अपकर्षति) एक ओर खींच लेता है, हटा देता है। draws aside, removes.

अपकार – पु० – (अपकार) बुराई, हानि, दुष्कर्म । injury, misdeed, wrong.

अपक्क्रम – पु० – (अपक्रम) पलायन, भाग निकलना । escape, departure.

अपक्क्रमति – क्रि० – (अपक्रमति) पलायन करता है, भाग निकलता है । departs, goes away, escapes.

अपगच्छति – क्रि० – (अपगच्छति) हट जाता है, दूर चला जाता है । goes away, turns away.

अपगब्भ (1) – पु० – (अप + गर्भ) पुनः गर्भ में न आने वाला । not destined for another birth.

अपगब्भ (2) – वि० – (अप्रगल्य) अप्रगल्य, जो निडर, अभिमानी, प्रौढ़, निर्लज्ज न हो । not haughty.

अपगम – पु० – (अपगमन) चला जाना, ओझल हो जाना । moving aside, disappearance.

अपगम्य – पूर्व का क्रिया – (अपगम्य) दूर हटकर । having moved aside.

अपचय – पु० – (अप + $\sqrt{}$ चि + अच्) नाश, ह्रास, निरोध (जन्म का निरोध) । destruction, preventing birth.

अपचयगामी – पु० – (अपचयगामी) जन्म के निरोध के लिए यत्नशील । one who destroys, or prevents birth.

अपचयति – क्रि० – (अप + $\sqrt{}$ चय + व) सम्मान करता है । one who pays respect, honours.

अपचायी – पु० – (अपचायी) सम्मान करने वाला । one who pays respect.

अपचयन – न० – (अप + $\sqrt{}$ चय + ल्युट् = अपचयन) पूजा, श्रद्धा, सम्मान । worship, reverence.

अपचायक – देखें अपचायी । see Apacāyī.

अपचिनाति – क्रि० – (अप + $\sqrt{}$ चि + व) घटाता है, क्षीण करता है । diminishes, does away with, reduces.

अपचिति – स्त्री० – (अपचिति) सम्मान, प्रायश्चित । respect, expiate.

अपचिनन – न० – (अप + $\sqrt{}$ चि + क्तिन्) अधःपात, नाश, पाप का प्रायश्चित् । destruction, expiation.

अपच्च – न० – (अपत्य) सन्तान । offspring.

अपच्चकख – वि० – (अप्रत्यक्ष) जिसका प्रत्यक्ष नहीं हुआ । unseen, not realized.

अपजित – न० – (अपजितम्) हार, पराजय । defeat.

अपजित – वि० – (अप + $\sqrt{}$ जि + क्त) पराजित । defeated.

अपटु – वि० – (अपटु) अदक्ष, अनिपुण, अकुशल । unskilled.

अपणिडत – वि० – (अपण्डित) मूर्ख, अचतुर । fool, unwise.

अपण्णक – वि० – (अ + प्रश्नक / अप्रज्ञक) निर्दोष । innocent, faultless.

अपण्णक जातक – (जातक सं० 1) अनाथ-पिण्डिक तथा उसके पाँच सौ सहचरों को उपदिष्ट जातक कथा । the Jātaka tale (No. 1) related to Anāthapiṇḍika and his five hundred co-travellers.

अपत्थट – वि० – (अ + प्रसृत) जो फैला न हो । not spread out.

अपत्थद्ध – वि० – (अप + स्तब्ध) उत्तेजना-रहित । not haughty.

अपत्थिय – वि॰ – (अ + प्रार्थनीय) जिसकी इच्छा करना उचित नहीं। which ought not to be wished.

अपथ – पु॰ – (कुपथ / अपथ) गर्हित मार्ग, निन्दित पथ। condemned path, wrong way.

अपद – वि॰ – (अ + पद) पैर-रहित, बिना पाँव के। footless, lame, creeping insects.

अपदान (1) – न॰ – (अपदानम्) सदाचरण विशुद्ध आचरण, प्रशस्त कार्य। good conduct.

अपदान (2) – न॰ – जीवनचर्या, अनुश्रुति। routine of life, legend.

अपदान (3) – (अपदान) – खुद्दक निकाय के पन्द्रह ग्रन्थों में से एक। इसमें भगवान बुद्ध के समकालीन 547 भिक्षुओं तथा 40 भिक्षुणियों की जीवन कथायें संगृहीत हैं। one of the fifteen books from in *Khuddaka Nikāya.*

अपदिस – पु॰ – (अपदिश) साक्षी, गवाही। witness, testimony.

अपदिसति – क्रि॰ – (अप + √दिश = अपदिशति) साक्ष्य प्रस्तुत करता है। witnesses, quotes, testifies.

अपदेस – पु॰ – (अप + दिश् + घञ = अपदेश) कथन, वर्णन, बहाना। statement, explanation, excuse.

अपधारण – न॰ – (अपधारणम् अपिधानम्) ढक्कन। lid.

अपनामेति – क्रि॰ – (अपनयति) हटाता है, अलग करता है। removes, separates..

अपनिदहति – क्रि॰ – (अप + नि + √दह + व) छिपाता है। hides, conceals.

अपनिहित – क्रि॰ – (अपिहित) ढका- मुंदा, छिपा हुआ। hidden, covered.

अपनीत – क्रि॰ वि॰ – (अपनीत) हटाया हुआ, दूर कर दिया गया। taken away, removed.

अपनुदति – क्रि॰ – (अप + √नुद + व) हांक देता है, दूर भगा देता है। drives away, dispels.

अपनुदन – न॰ – (अपनुदितृ) हटाने वाला, अलग करने वाला। removal, dispelling.

अपनेति – क्रि॰ – (अपनयति) दूर करता है, हटाता है। dispeller of, remover of.

अपमार – पु॰ – (अपस्मार) मिरगी रोग। epilepsy.

अपर – वि॰ – (अपर) दूसरा, अन्य। another, other.

अपरज्जु – वि॰ – (अपरेद्युः) दूसरे दिन, बाद वाले दिन। on the following day, next day.

अपरज्झति – क्रि॰ – (अप + √राध + व) अपराध करता है। offends against, commits crime.

अपरण्ण – न॰ – (कदन्न) मोटा अनाज, निम्न कोटि का अन्न। coarse grain.

अपरद्ध – क्रि॰ वि॰ – (अपरद्ध) (1) दोषी, अपराधी, (2) असफल। (1) guilty, (2) failed.

अपरन्त (1) – (अपर + अन्त) दूसरा छोर। the other, next.

अपरन्त (2) – (तृतीय संगीति के उपरान्त धर्म प्रचार के लिए सम्राट् अशोक के जिन राज्यों में भिक्षु दल भेजा था उनमें से पश्चिमी भारत स्थित एक राज्य। name of a state in western India where king Aśoka sent *bhikkhu*s for preaching Buddhism.

अपरप्पच्चय – वि॰ – (अ + पर + प्रत्ययः) जो दूसरों के विश्वास पर निर्भर हो। not relying on others.

अपराजित – वि॰ – (अपराजित) जो पराजित न हुआ हो, अविजित। unconquered.

अपराध – पु॰ – (अपराध) दोष, कसूर। guilt, offence.

अपराधिक/अपराधी – पु॰ – (अपराधिक) दोषी, कसूरवार। guilty, criminal.

अपरापरिय – वि॰ – (अपरापरिय) निरन्तर, लगातार। ever following, successive.

अपरिग्गहित – वि॰ – (अपरिगृहीत) जिस पर अधिकार न किया गया हो। unoccupied, not in possession of.

अपरिच्छिन्न – वि॰ – (अपरिच्छिन्न) असीम, अविलग। limitless, infinite.

अपरिमाण – वि॰ – (अपरिमाण) परिमाण रहित, असीम। unlimited, measureless.

अपरिमित – वि॰ – (अपरिमित) असीमित। infinite.

अपलायी – वि॰ – (अ + पलायिन्) पलायन न करने वाला, निर्भिक। not running away, fearless.

अपलालेति – क्रि॰ – (अप + लालयति) दुलार करता है, लाड़-प्यार करता है। caresses, fondles.

अपलिबुद्ध – वि॰ – (अ + परि + बद्ध) बन्धन-मुक्त, बाधा रहित, स्वतन्त्र। unhindered, free.

अपलिखति – क्रि॰ – (अपिलिह्यति = अपि √लिह् + व) खुरचता है, चाटता है। scrapes, licks off.

अपालिखन – न॰ – (अपालिखन) खुरचना, चाटना। licking off, scraping.

अपलोकन – न॰ – (अवलोकन) सम्मति consent, permission.

अपवग्ग – पु॰ – (अपवर्ग) मुक्ति, निर्वाण, मोक्ष। salvation, release.

अपवज्जन – न॰ – (अपवर्जन) परित्याग। renunciation.

अपवत्तति – क्रि॰ – (अपवत्तते) निवर्त्तितया परावर्तित हो जाता है, घूम जाता है, लौट आता है। returns, goes back, turns back.

अपवदति – क्रि॰ – (अपवदति) अपवाद फैलाता है, दोषारोपण करता है, बदनामी करता है। reproaches, blames.

अपवहति – क्रि॰ – (अपवहति) ले जाता है, हाँकता है। drives away, drifts.

अपवाद – पु॰ – (अपवाद) निन्दा, बदनामी, अपकीर्ति। exception, slander, infamy.

अपविद्ध – क्रि॰ वि॰ – (अपविद्ध) फेंका गया, त्यागा गया। thrown away, rejected.

अपसक्कति – क्रि॰ – (अपक्रमेति = अपक्कमति), चला जाता है। goes aside.

अपसव्य – न॰ – (अपसव्य) दाहिना, उलटा, विरुद्ध। right side, opposite.

अपसादन – न॰ – (अपसादन) निग्रह। disparagement.

अपसादित – क्रि॰ वि॰ – (अपसादित) निग्रह किया हुआ, उपेक्षित, निन्दित। disparaged, condemned

अपसादेति – क्रि॰ – (अपसादयति) निग्रह करता है, निन्दा करता है। deprecates, declines.

अपस्मार – पु॰ – (अपस्मार) मिरगी रोग। epilepsy.

अपस्सय – (आश्रय) सहारा, तकिया, आश्रय। support, bolster.

अपस्सित – क्रि॰ वि॰ – (आश्रित) निर्भर, सहारे पर निर्भर। leaning against, depending on.

अपस्सयति – क्रि॰ – (अप + आश्रयते) आश्रय ग्रहण करता है, सहारा लेता है। depends on, leans against.

अपस्सेति – देखें – अपस्सयति। see Apassayati

अपस्सेन-फलक – न॰ – (अपाश्रय – फलक) सहारे का तख्ता। a bolster slab.

अपहन्तु – पु॰ – (अपहर्तृ) अपहरण करने वाला, हटाने वाला। one who removes/abducts.

अपहरति – क्रि॰ – (अपहरति) छीन लेता है, लूटता है। removes, takes away, plunders.

अपहरण – न॰ – (अपहरण) छीन लेना, लूटना। removal, stealing, abduction.

अपहार – देखें अपहरण। see Apaharana.

अपांग – पु॰ – (अपाङ्ग) लोचन, नेत्रकोर, अक्षिकोण। corner of eye.

अपाकट – वि॰ – (अप्रकट) अप्रकट, अज्ञात। unknown, unrevealed.

अपाकतिक – वि॰ – (अप्राकृतिक) अप्राकृतिक अस्वभाविक। unnatural.

अपाची – स्त्री॰ – (अ + प्राची) पश्चिम दिशा। western direction.

अपाचीन – (अ + प्राच्य) पाश्चात्य, पश्चिम दिशा का। western.

अपाद – वि॰ – (अ + पाद) पांव-रहित, पंगु। footless, lame, creeping inseats.

अपादक – देखें – अपाद। see Apāda.

अपान (1) – न॰ – (अपान) निःश्वास। breathing out.

अपान (2) – (अपान) पाँच प्राण वायु में से एक जिसका स्थान नाभि के नीचे है। Apāna Vāyu, wind passing through anus.

अपादान – न॰ – (अपादान) अलग करना, अलग होना, पृथक्करण, पाँचवी विभक्ति, अपादान कारक। separation, ablative case in grammer.

अपापक – वि॰ – (अ + पापकः) पाप-रहित, निर्दोष। without sin, innocent.

अपापुरण – न॰ – (अपापूरण) चाभी। key.

अपापुरति – क्रि॰ – (अप + आ + वृणीति) खोलता है। opens.

अपाय – पु॰ – (अपाय) यातना-लोक। the state of loss and woe, destruction.

अपायगामी – पु॰ – (अपायगामी) दुःखों की स्थिति में गमन। going to state of misery.

अपायमुख – न॰ – (अपायमुख) दुरवस्था का हेतु। cause of ruin.

अपायसहाय – पु॰ – (अपाय सहाय) अपव्ययी साथी, उड़ाऊ दोस्त। a spendthrift companion.

अपार – वि॰ – (अ + पार) असीम, बिना पार के, बिना छोर के। limitless, without any shore.

अपारनेय्य – वि॰ – (अपाय + नेय्य) दूसरे छोर पर न पहुँचने वाला, पहुँच से परे। unattainable, not leading to the other shore.

अपारुत – वि॰ – (अपावृत्त) जो आवृत्त न हो, खुला हो, आवरण-रहित। open.

अपालम्ब – पु॰ – (अपालम्ब) बैलगाड़ी के अगले भाग में सन्तुलन बनाये रखने का छोटा सा टेक, ऊँटरा। balancing board of a bullock cart.

अपि – अव्यय – (अपि) भी, ही, वाक्य के आरम्भ में प्रश्नवाची शब्द के रूप में भी प्रयुक्त। even then, as yet.

अपि- च – अव्यय – (अपि च) किन्तु। but, further, morever.

अपि- च खो – अव्यय – (अपि च खलु) तथापि, तब भी। and yet still.

अपि तु – अव्यय – (अपितु) किन्तु। but.

अपि नाम – अव्यय – (अपि नाम) यदि कहीं। if anywhere.

अपिस्सु – अव्यय – इतना-इतना। so much so.

अपिधान – न॰ – (अपिधान) पिहान, ढक्कन। a cover, lid, wrapper.

अपिलापन – न॰ – (पुनरालापन) दुहराना। counting again, repetition.

अपिहालु – वि॰ – (अप् + ईहालु) निर्लोभी। not greedy.

अपिहित – क्रि॰ वि॰ – (अपि + √धा + त) ढका हुआ, मुँदा हुआ। covered.

अपीहा – वि॰ – (अपीहा) देखें – अपिहालु। see Apihālu.

अपुच्छ – वि॰ – (पृच्छा) प्रश्न। question.

अपुञ्ज – न॰ – (अपुण्य) पाप। sin.

अपूप – न॰ – (अपूप) पुआ। sweet toast.

अपेक्खक – वि॰ – (आ + प्रेक्षक) प्रतीक्षा करने वाला। waiting for.

अपेक्खति – क्रि॰ – (अपेक्षते) अपेक्षा करता है, उम्मीद करता है। expects for, hopes for.

अपेक्खना – स्त्री॰ – (अपेक्षणा) आशा, उम्मीद। hope, expectation.

अपेक्खा – स्त्री॰ – (अपेक्षा) आशा, आसक्ति। hope, attachment.

अपेत – क्रि॰ वि॰ – (अप + √इ + त) चला गया। gone away.

अपेति – क्रि॰ – (अप + एति) चला जाता है। goes away.

अपत्तेयता – स्त्री॰ – (अ + पितृव्यता) पिता की अवज्ञा। irreverence towards father.

अपेय्य – वि॰ – (अ + पेय) जो पीने योग्य न हो। that should not be drunk, not drinkable.

अप्प – वि॰ – (अल्प) थोड़ा, कम, तुच्छ। small, little, insignificant.

अप्पक – देखें – अप्प। see Appa.

अप्पकसिरेण – क्रि॰ वि॰ – (अल्प + कृशेन) कुछ कठिनाई से। with little difficulty.

अप्पकिच्च – वि॰ – (अल्प + कृत्य) जिसे थोड़ा कार्य हो। one who has little or work or duties.

अप्पकिण्ण – वि॰ – (अ + प्रकीर्ण) न बिखरा हुआ। not scattered.

अप्पगब्भ – वि॰ – (अ + प्रगल्य) निरभिमानी। not proud, not impudent.

अप्पग्घ – वि॰ – (अल्पार्घ) अल्प मूल्य वाला। of little worth or value.

अप्पच्चय – पु॰ – (अ + प्रति + √ इ + अच् = अप्रत्यय) बिना हेतु के। without a cause.

अप्पटिरिवप्प – वि॰ – (अ + प्रतिक्षेष्य) प्रतिक्षेप करने के अयोग्य। not liable to be blamed.

अप्पटिघ – वि॰ – (अ + प्रतिन + √ घात = अप्रतिघ) बिना विरोध के, बिना क्रोध के। without anger/protest.

अप्पटिपुग्गल – पु॰ – (अप्रतिपुद्गल) अनन्य, अप्रतिम व्यक्ति, अद्वितीय व्यक्ति। matchless person, incomparable.

अप्पटिबद्ध – वि॰ – (अप्रतिबद्ध) अनासक्त। not committed.

अप्पटिभागी – वि॰ – (अप्रतिभागी) हिस्सेदार न होने वाला। non-contester, not being partner.

अप्पटिभाण – वि॰ – (अ + प्रति + भाण) अपरिविह्वलः, विमूढ, पलटकर उत्तर न देने वाला। unbewildered, not confused.

अप्पटिम – वि॰ – (अप्रतिम) अनुपमेय, अद्वितीय। incomparable.

अप्पटिवत्तिय – वि॰ – (अप्रतिवर्तनीय) जो उल्टा न घुमाया जा सके। not able to be rolled back.

अप्पटिवान – वि॰ – (अप्रतिवान) पीछे न हटने वाला, बाधक न बनने वाला। non-retreating, non-hindering.

अप्पटिवानी – वि॰ – (अप्रतिवादी) बाधक न बनने वाला, प्रतिवाद न करने वाला। non-opposing, non-rebutting.

अप्पटिबद्ध – वि॰ – (अ + प्रतिबिद्ध) अनबिंधा, जो बिंधा हुआ न हो। un-pierced.

अप्पटिसन्धिक – वि॰ – (अ + प्रति + सन्धिक) जो पुनः जोड़कर तैयार न किया जा सके, जिसके पुनर्जन्म की संभावना नहीं रही। irreparable, incapable of reunion/rebirth.

अप्पटिसम – वि॰ – (अ + प्रति + सम) जिसका समरूप न हो, अप्रतिम, अद्वितीय। incomparable, not having an equal.

अप्पणा – स्त्री॰ – (अर्पणा) किसी एक विषय या वस्तु पर ध्यान केन्द्रित करना, एकाग्रचित्तता प्राप्त करना। to concentrate.

अप्पणिहत – वि॰ – (अप्राणिहित) कामना-रहित। free from desire.

अप्पतिट्ठ – वि॰ – (अप्रतिष्ठ) असहाय। helpless, without a footing.

अप्पतिस्सव – वि॰ – (अप्पतिस्सव) विद्रोही। rebellious.

अप्पति(टी)हित – (अप्रतिहत) अनाक्रान्त, अबाधित। unsmitten, unobstructed.

अप्पतीत – वि॰ – (अप्रीत) अप्रसन्न। displeased, unhappy.

अप्पत्थ – वि॰ – (अल्पार्थ) अपर्याप्त अर्थ। insufficient meaning.

अप्पदुट्ठ – वि॰ – (अप्रदुष्ट) अक्रुद्ध, अदुष्ट। not angry, not corrupt.

अप्पधंसीय – वि॰ – (अ + प्रध्वंसीय) ध्वस्त न करने योग्य। not worthy of, demolition, being destroyed.

अप्पमञ्ञा – स्त्री॰ – (अप्रामाण्या) एक दार्शनिक शब्द। अप्रामाण्या अर्थात् स्वतः प्रमाण अस्तित्व वाली मानसिक स्थिति जिसमें चार गुणों का समावेश रहता है प्रेम, दया, करुणा और अनासक्ति। self-accomplished mental state, a technical term having four qualities – love, pity, compassion and disinterestedness.

अप्पमत्त – वि॰ – (अ + प्रमत्त) प्रमाद-रहित, कर्मठ, अप्रमादी, आलस्य-रहित। diligent, alert, languourless.

अप्पमाण – वि॰ – (अप्रमाण) प्रमाण-रहित। without proof, doubtful.

अप्पमाद – पु॰ – (अप्रमाद) निरालस्य, जागरूकता। vigilance, earnestness.

अप्पमेय्य – वि॰ – (अप्रमेय) जो मापा न जा सके। जो प्रमाण योग्य न हो, स्वतः सिद्ध हो। immeasurable, limitless.

अप्पवत्ति – स्त्री॰ – (अप्रवृत्ति) अविच्छिन्नता अथवा सातत्य का अभाव। non-continuance.

अप्पसाद – पु॰ – (अप्रसाद) प्रसन्नता का अभाव, असन्तोष। displeasure, dissatisfaction.

अप्पसत्थ (1) – वि॰ – (अल्पसार्थ) थोड़े साथियों वाला। having a few companions.

अप्पसत्थ (2) – वि॰ – (अ + प्रशस्त) अप्रशंसित। not being praised, unpraised.

अप्पसन्न – वि॰ – (अप्रसन्न) जो मुदित न हो। unhappy.

अप्पसमारंभ – वि॰ – (अल्प समारम्भ) जिसमें बहुत झंझट न हो, बहुत ताम-झाम न हो। of minor trouble/hindrance.

अप्पस्सक – वि॰ – (अल्पस्वक) बहुत थोड़ी सम्पत्ति वाला, निर्धन, दरिद्र। a pauper, possessing little, poor.

अप्पस्साद – वि॰ – (अल्प + आस्वाद्य) अल्प आस्वाद। not having much enjoyment/taste.

अप्पहीन – वि॰ – (अल्पहीन) सम्पूर्ण या विपुल क्षति से बचा हुआ। not completely removed or destroyed.

अप्पाणक – वि॰ – (अप्राणक) (1) प्राण-रहित, (2) कीड़ों मकोड़ों से रहित। (1) breathless (2) not containing insects.

अप्पातङ्क – वि॰ – (अल्पातङ्क) आतंक-रहित, रोग-रहित। free from illness or terror.

अप्पिच्छ – वि॰ – (अल्पेक्ष) अल्प इच्छा वाला। easily to be satisfied, desiring little.

अप्पिय – वि॰ – (अप्रिय) जो प्रिय न हो, अरूचिकर। unpleasent, disagreeable.

अप्पेकदा – क्रि॰ वि॰ – (अपि एकदा) किसी समय, कभी-कभी। sometimes, at any time.

अप्पेव – अव्यय – (अपि एव) अच्छा है, यदि ऐसा हो। it is good if so.

अप्पेवनाम – अव्यय – (अपि एव नाम) देखें – अप्पेव। see 'Appeva'.

अप्पेसक्क – वि॰ – (अल्पशक्य) अधिक प्रभावशाली नहीं। not very influential.

अप्पोसुक्क – वि॰ – (अल्प + औत्सुक्य) जिसमें उत्सुकता का अभाव है, अनुत्साही। inactive, unhappy.

अप्फुट – वि॰ – (अस्पृष्ट) जो छुआ न गया हो। untouched, pure.

अप्फोटेति – क्रि॰ – (आ + स्फोटयति) उँगलियाँ चटखाता (फोड़ता है)। cracks the fingers, claps the hands.

अफल – वि॰ – (अफल) निष्फल, फल रहित, व्यर्थ। fruitless, vain, useless.

अफस्सित – क्रि॰ वि॰ – (अस्पृष्ट) न छुआ हुआ, अनस्पृष्ट। untouched, pure.

अफासु – वि॰ – (दुस्साध्य) असुविधापूर्ण, कठिनाई वाला। uneasy, troublesome, difficult.

अफेग्गुक – वि॰ – (अ + फल्गु + क) सबल, मजबूत। strong, not weak, stout.

अबद्ध – वि॰ – (अबद्ध) न बँधा हुआ, स्वतन्त्र, मुक्त। free, not bound, unfettered.

अबन्धन – देखें अबद्ध। see Abaddha.

अबल – वि॰ – (अबल) दुर्बल, शक्तिहीन। weak, feeble.

अबला – स्त्री॰ – (अबला) नारी, स्त्री। the woman, having little strength.

अब्बण – क्रि॰ – (अ + ब्रण) घाव-रहित। woundless.

अब्बत – वि॰ – (अ + व्रत) व्रत-विहीन। having no fast, vow or pledge.

अब्बुद (1) – न॰ – (अर्बुद) गर्भाधान के पहले-दूसरे महीने की अवधि में भ्रूण की स्थिति। the condition of foetus between first-second month after conception.

अब्बुद (2) – (अर्बुद) ट्यूमर, कैंसर। a tumour, cancer.

अब्बूहति – क्रि॰ – (अ + व्यूहति) व्यूह-रचना का ध्वंस करता है। छिन्न-भिन्न करता है, छिपे को बाहर खींच निकालता है। disarrays, discloses, draws out.

अब्बूलह – क्रि॰ वि॰ – (अ + व्यूह) निर्व्यूहित, निर्व्यूहीकृत। devoid of military array, disarranged.

अब्बोकिण्ण – वि॰ – (अव्युतकीर्ण) सतत्, लगातार, बाधा-रहित, विघ्न-रहित। constant, ceaseless, without hurdle.

अब्बोच्छिन्न – वि॰ – (अ + व्युच्छिन्न) सतत्, विघ्न-रहित। uninterrupted.

अब्बोहारिक – वि॰ – (अ + व्यावहारिक) अव्यावहारिक, जो व्यवहार के अनुकूल न हो। negligible, impractical.

अब्भ – न॰ – (अभ्र) आकाश, बादल। sky, cloud.

अब्भकूट – न॰ – (अभ्र + कूट) मेघ, शिखर। the summit of a storm-cloud.

अब्भ-पटल – न॰ – (अभ्र + पटल) मेघ-समूह। mass of cloud.

अब्भक – न॰ – (अभ्रक) अबरक। mica.

अब्भक्खाति – क्रि॰ – (अभि + आ + √ ख्या + व) निन्दा करता है, विरुद्ध बोलता है। slanders, speaks ill of.

अब्भञ्जति – क्रि॰ – (अभि + √ अञ्ज + व) तेल मर्दन, तेल की मालिश करता है। anoints, lubricates.

अब्भञ्जन – न॰ – (अभि + √ अञ्ज् + ल्युट्) शरीर में मालिश करने का तेल, उबटन। massage oil, ointment.

अब्भतीत – वि॰ – (अभि + अतीत) जो व्यतीत हो गया। gone by, past.

अब्भनुमोदना – स्त्री॰ – (अभ्युनुमोदना) अत्यधिक सन्तोष व्यक्त करना। great appreciation, rejoicing after achieving merit.

अब्भन्तर – न॰ – (अभ्यन्तर) भीतर, अन्दर। interior, internal.

अब्भन्तर-जातक – पु॰ – (अभ्यन्तर जातक) (जा॰ सं॰ 281) बिम्बा देवी के लिए सारिपुत्र द्वारा आम्ररस प्राप्त किये जाने के सम्बन्ध में जातक कथा। Jātaka tale (No. 281) related to Sāriputra.

अब्भागत (1) – पु॰ – (अभ्यागत) पधारने वाला व्यक्ति, अतिथि। a guest, a stranger.

अब्भागत (2) – क्रि॰ वि॰ – (अभ्यागत) पधारा हुआ। one who has arrived.

अब्भागमन – न॰ – (अभ्यागमन) पदार्पण, आगमन। arrival, coming forward.

अब्भाघात – न॰ – (अभ्याघात) वध, हत्या। assasination, murder.

अब्भाचिक्खति – क्रि॰ – (अभि + आ + √चक्ख्) आक्षेप करता है, दोषारोपण करता है। accuses, blames, finds fault with.

अब्भाचिक्खन – न॰ – (अभि + आ + √चक्ष + ल्युट्) आक्षेप, दोषारोपण। accusation, slander, blame.

अब्भान – न॰ – (आह्वान) आह्वान, प्रायश्चित्त के उपरान्त भिक्षु की पुनः संघ में वापसी। purgation, return of a *bhikkhu* into the Sangha after atonement.

अब्भाहत – क्रि॰ वि॰ (अभ्याकृत) आक्रान्त, आक्रमित। attacked, afflicted.

अब्भुकिरण – न॰ – (अभि + उद् + किरण) बाहर खींचना, सींचना। drawing out, sprinkling.

अब्भुकिरति – क्रि॰ – (अभि + उद् + √किर्) बाहर खींचता है, सींचता है। pulls out, draws out.

अब्भुगच्छति – क्रि॰ – (अभ्युद्गच्छति) ऊपर जाता है, उभरता है, फैल जाता है। rises up, becomes diffused.

अब्भुगत – क्रि॰ वि॰ – (अभि + उद्गत) ऊपर उठा, उभरा हुआ, फैला हुआ। risen up, diffused, elevated.

अब्भुगमन – न॰ – (अभि + उद् + गमन) उभरना, उठना, ऊपर छा जाना। to rise up, to be diffused.

अब्भुग्गिरति – क्रि॰ – (अभि + उद् + गिरति) भाँजता है। raises up, brandishes something in a threatening manner.

अब्भुग्गिरण – न॰ – (अभि + उद् + √गृ ल्युट्) भांजना। brandishing.

अब्भुत्थान – न॰ – (अभ्युत्थान) उठना, समृद्ध होना, बढ़ना। to rise, to advance, to prosper.

अब्भुत (1) – वि॰ – (अद्भुत) आश्चर्यजनक, विस्मयकारी। wonderful, marvellous, astonishing.

अब्भुत (2) – न॰ – (अद्भुत) अचरज, आश्चर्य, विलक्षण। wonder, a marvel.

अब्भुदेति – क्रि॰ – (अभि + उदेति) उन्नति करता है, बढ़ता है, अभ्युदम को प्राप्त होता है। advances, rises, comes into existence.

अब्भुन्नता – स्त्री॰ – (अभि + उद् + नम + क्त + टाप्) अभ्युन्नता, समृद्धि, ऋद्धि की प्राप्ति। prosperity, achievement of mundane objects, success.

अब्भुम्मे – अव्यय – (वै॰ अब्भवम + मे) ओह। alas!

अब्भुय्याति – क्रि॰ – (अभि + उप + याति) चढ़ाई करता है। marches against.

अब्भुसूयक – वि॰ – (अभि + असूयक) उत्साही । enthusiastic, pushing.

अब्भेति – क्रि॰ – (अभि + एति) अवगाहन करता है । immerses, bathes, fathoms.

अब्भोकास – वि॰ – (अभ्यवकाशः) आकाश, अनाच्छादित स्थल, खुली जगह । uncovered place, unsheltered place, open air.

अब्भोकासिक – वि॰ – (अभ्यवकाशिक) खुली जगह रहने वाला, खुले आसमान के नीचे रहने वाला । one who lives under open sky.

अब्भोकिण्ण – वि॰ – (अभि + अवकीर्ण) संकुलित । crowded.

अब्भोकिरण – न॰ – (अभि + अव + √कृ + ल्युट् = अभ्यवकिरण) अभिसिंचन, अभिषेक । sprinkling, ablution.

अब्भोकिरति – क्रि॰ – (अभ्यवकिरति) अभिसिंचन करता है, अभिषेक करता है । sprinkles water over, performs ritual bathing.

अभब्बो – वि॰ – (अ + भव्यः) असुन्दर, अयोग्य, अनुपयुक्त । non-proficient, ugly, inauspicious.

अभय – वि॰ – (निर्भय, अभय) भय-रहित, भय का अभाव । fearless, safe.

अभया – स्त्री॰ – (हरीतकी) हरड़, हर्र, हर्रा । yellow myrobalan.

अभाव – पु॰ – (अभाव) लोप, अदर्शन । deficiency, non-availability, absence.

अभावित – वि॰ – (अभावित) अनभ्यस्त । not accustomed.

अभिकंखति – क्रि॰ – (अभिकांक्षित) इच्छा करता है, कामना करता है । aspires, longs.

अभिकंखन – न॰ – (अभिकांक्षण) इच्छा, कामना । aspiration, ambition.

अभिकिण्ण – क्रि॰ वि॰ – (अभिकीर्ण) बिखरा हुआ । scattered, spread over.

अभिकिरण – न॰ – (अभिकिरण) बिखराव । scattering.

अभिकिरति – क्रि॰ – (अभिकिरति) बिखेरता है । scatters, sprinkles.

अभिकीलति – क्रि॰ – (अभिक्रीडति) खेलता है । plays.

अभिकूजति – क्रि॰ – (अभि + √कूज + व) चहचहाता है, गुंजाता है । chatters, warbles.

अभिकूजन – न॰ – (अभिकूजन) गुंजन, चहकना । singing of birds, chattering.

अभिकूजित – क्रि॰ वि॰ – (अभिकूजित) अभिगुंजित, चहकील । chattered, warbled.

अभिक्कन्त – क्रि॰ वि॰ – (अभिक्रान्त) उन्नति करना, सुहावना (1) gone forward, past (2) most pleasant.

अभिक्कम – पु॰ – (अभिक्रम) आरम्भ, प्रयाण, धावा, अभियान । attack, begining, expedition, an undertaking.

अभिक्कमति – क्रि॰ – (अभिक्रमति) प्रयाण करता है, धावा बोलता है । approaches, travels, attacks.

अभिक्खण – वि॰ – (अभिक्षण) प्रतिक्षण, निरन्तर । continuous, uninterrupted.

अभिक्खणति – क्रि॰ – (अभि + √खन्) खोदता है । digs, excavates.

अभिक्खनन – न॰ – (अभिखनन) खोदना।
digging, excavation.

अभिगज्जति – क्रि॰ – (अभिक् + √गज्जं)
दहाड़ता है, गरजता है। roars,
thunders.

अभिगज्जन – न॰ – (अभिगर्जन) दहाड़,
गर्जना। roaring, thundering.

अभिगिज्झति – क्रि॰ – (अभि √गृध =
अभि-गृह्यति) तरसता है, लालच करता
है। craves for, pines for.

अभिगिज्झन – न॰ – (अभिगृध्यन) लालच,
अभीप्सा। greed, craving.

अभिघात – पु॰ – (अभिघात) हत्या, प्रहार
अभिसम्बन्ध। killing, stroke, blow.

अभिघातन – पु॰ – (अभिघात) प्रहार, हत्या।
slaying, murder, destroying.

अभिघाती – पु॰ – (अभिघाती) शत्रु विनाशक,
घात करने वाला। destroyer of enemy.

अभिजच्च – वि॰ – (अभिजात्य) कुलीनता।
nobleness of birth.

अभिजन – पु॰ – (अभिजन) सगे-सम्बन्धी।
blood-relation, family.

अभिजप्पति – न॰ – (अभि + √जल्प् =
अभिजल्पति) जाप करता है, आराधना
करता है। prays, mumbles.

अभिजात – वि॰ – (अभिजात) कुलीन, उच्च
कुलोत्पन्न। of noble birth, well-
born.

अभिजाति – स्त्री॰ – (अभिजाति) (1)
पुनर्जन्म, (2) प्रजाति। (1) rebirth (2)
species, breed.

अभिजानाति – (अभि + √ज्ञा = अभि-
जानाति = अभिज्ञाप्यते) भली-भांति
पहचानता है, पहचान लेता है। knows
fully, recognizes fully.

अभिजायति – क्रि॰ – (अभिजायते) उत्पन्न
होता है। is born or arises.

अभिजिगिंसति – क्रि॰ – जीतने की इच्छा
करता है। wishes to conquer.

अभिज्जमान – वि॰ – (अभिद्यमान) टूटने
या विलग करने के अयोग्य।
unbreakable, inseparable.

अभिज्झा – स्त्री॰ – (अभिध्या = अभि +
√ध्यौ + अङ् + टाप्) अतिशय लोभ,
अतिस्पृहा। covetousness, extreme
greed.

अभिज्झायति – क्रि॰ – (अभिध्यायते) दूसरों
की सम्पत्ति की प्रबल कामना करता है।
wishes for, covets eagerly.

अभिञ्ञ – वि॰ – (अभिज्ञ) पूर्णतया
जानकार। knowing well.

अभिञ्ञा – स्त्री॰ – (अभिज्ञा) स्मृति, पहचान,
विशिष्ट ज्ञान। remembrance,
recognition, specific knowledge.

अभिञ्ञाण – न॰ – (अभिज्ञान) पहचान
identification, a sign of
recognition.

अभिञ्ञाय – पूर्व क्रि॰ – (अभिज्ञाय) भली-
भाँति पहचान करके। having
recognized.

अभिञ्ञात – क्रि॰ वि॰ –(आभिज्ञात)
सुविदित। well known, identified.

अभिञ्ञेय – वि॰ – (अभिज्ञेय) पूरी पहचान
करने योग्य, सम्यक् ज्ञातव्य। which
should be well recognized.

अभिण्हजातक – (अभिन्न जातकम्) (जा॰
सं॰ 27) कुत्ते और हाथी के अभिन्न मित्र
बन जाने की जातक कथा। the Jātaka
tale (No. 27) of a dog and elephant
who were indispensable to each
other.

अभिणह – (अभिन्न) निरन्तर, लगातार, अविच्छिन्न। continuous, uninterrupted.

अभिणहं – देखें – अभिणह। see Abhiṇha.

अभिणहसो – अव्यय – (अभिन्नशः) अनवरत, निरन्तर। continuous, repeated by.

अभितत्त – वि॰ – (अभितप्त) अतिशय तपा हुआ। scorched by heat.

अभितपति – क्रि॰ – (अभिज्ञ + √ तप् + व) तपता है, चमकता है। shines.

अभिताप – पु॰ – (अभि + ताप) अत्यधिक उष्णता, प्रचण्ड ताप। extreme heat.

अभितालेति – क्रि॰ – (अभि + √ ताड्) पीटता है। beats, hammers.

अभितुण्ण – क्रि॰ वि॰ (अभि + तुद् + क्त = अभितुन्न) प्रहत, आहत किया हुआ, सताया हुआ। overwhelmed.

अभितुदति – क्रि॰ – (अभि + √ तुद्) आघात करता है, चुभोता है, पीड़ित करता है। incites, pricks, goads.

अभितो – अव्यय – (अभितः) चारों ओर। all around.

अभितोसेति – क्रि॰ – (अभि + √ तोष् = अभितोषयति) तुष्ट करता है, प्रसन्न करता है। pleases thoroughly.

अभित्थनति – क्रि॰ – (अभिस्तनति / अभिस्तनयति) गरजता है, दहाड़ता है। thunders, roar.

अभित्थरति – क्रि॰ – (अभिस्तरति) जल्दी करता है। makes haste, hurries.

अभित्थवति – क्रि॰ – (अभिस्तवति) प्रशंसा करता है, स्तुति करता है। praises, admires.

अभित्थवन – न॰ – (अभि + स्तवन) प्रशंसा, स्तुति। praise, admiration.

अभित्थुत – क्रि॰ – (अभि + स्तुत) प्रशंसित। praised, admired.

अभित्थुनाति – क्रि॰ – (अभिस्तुनाति) प्रशंसा करता है। praises.

अभिदोस – पु॰ – (अभिदोषः) गत सन्ध्या। last evening.

अभिदोसिका – स्त्री॰ – (अभिदोषिका) पूर्व-सन्ध्या सम्बन्धी, पूर्व सन्ध्याकालिक। belonging to previous evening.

अभिधमति – पु॰ – (अभि √ धम = अभि-धमति) बजाता है। blows, plays.

अभिधम्म – पु॰ – (अभिधर्म) अभिधम्म पिटक की विश्लेषणात्मक देशना। the analytic doctrine of the Buddhist canon.

अभिधम्म पिटक – पु॰ – (अभिधर्म पिटक) त्रिपिटक के तीन महाग्रन्थों में से एक-इसके अन्तर्गत सात ग्रन्थ हैं – *धम्म सङ्गनि, विभंग, कथावत्थु, पुग्गल-पञ्ञति, धातुकथा, यमक और पट्ठान*। the third division of Piṭakas. It consist of seven books *Dhammasaṅgani, Vibhaṅga, Kathāvatthu, Puggala-Pañati, Dhātukathā, Yamaka* and *Paṭṭhāna*.

अभिधम्मिक – पु॰ – (अभि धार्मिक) अभिधम्म के उपदेष्टा, अभिधम्म में निष्णात। one who teaches *Abhidhamma*.

अभिधा – स्त्री॰ – (अभिधा) नाम संज्ञा, अभिधान। name, appellation.

अभिधान – पु॰ – (अभिधान) देखें अभिधा। see Abhidhā.

अभिधानप्पदीपिका – स्त्री॰ – (अभिधान प्रदीपिका) बारहवीं शताब्दी में संस्कृत के अमरकोश के अनुरूप विरचित पालि-

कोश। a Pāli dictionary compiled in twelfth century.

अभिधावति – क्रि॰ – (अभि + √ धावू = अभिधावति) दौड़ता है, भागता है। runs towards.

अभिधेय्य (1) – वि॰ – (अभिधेय्य) नाम वाला। having the name of.

अभिधेय्य (2) – न॰ – (अभिधेय्य) अर्थ। meaning.

अभिनत – वि॰ – (अभिनत) प्रणत, विनत। having bowed down.

अभिनदति – क्रि॰ – (अभि + √ नद् = अभिनदति) आवाज करता है। makes sound.

अभिनन्दति – क्रि॰ – (अभि + √ नन्द् = अभिनन्दति) अभिनन्दन करता है। welcomes, greets.

अभिनन्दित – वि॰ – (अभिनन्दित) वेदित, प्रशंसित, जिसका अभिनन्दन किया गया हो। one who is welcome/ greeted/praised.

अभिनन्दन – न॰ – (अभिनन्दन) प्रहर्षण, अभिवादन, स्वागत। congratulation, welcome, greeting.

अभिनन्दी – पु॰ – (अभिनन्दी) आनन्द मनाने वाला। one who rejoices.

अभिनमति – क्रि॰ – (अभि √ नम्) प्रणाम करता है। bows down.

अभिनयन – न॰ – (अभिनयन) (1) लाना (2) पूछताछ। (1) the act of bringing (2) inquiry.

अभिनव – वि॰ – (अभिनव) नूतन, नवीन। new, fresh.

अभिनादित – वि॰ – (अभिनादित) निनादित, गुंजित। resounded with.

अभिनिकूजित – वि॰ – (अभिनिकूजित) चहचहाहट से गुंजायमान, कलरव-मंडित। resounded with the chirping of birds.

अभिनिक्खमति – क्रि॰ – (अभिनिष्कमति) अभिनिष्क्रमण करता है, गृह त्याग करता है। renounces, sacrifices family life.

अभिनिक्खमन – न॰ – (अभिनिष्क्रमण) परमार्थ के लिए गृह त्याग, चरम लक्ष्य की प्राप्ति हेतु प्रव्रज्या ग्रहण करना। renouncing the world for higher spiritual persuits.

अभिनिक्खिपति – क्रि॰ – (अभि + नि + √ क्षिप् = अभिनिक्षिपति) रख देता है। lays down.

अभिनिक्खिपन – न॰ – (अभि + निक्षेपण) रख देना। putting down.

अभिनिपज्जति – क्रि॰ – (अभिनिपद्यते) लेट जाता है। lies down on.

अभिनिपतति – क्रि॰ – (अभिनिपतति) नीचे गिरता है, टूट पड़ता है। falls down, breaks.

अभिनिपात – पु॰ – (अभिनिपात) उपागमन, चढ़ाई, आक्रमण। attack, invades.

अभिनिपातन – देखें अभिनिपात। see Abhinipāta.

अभिनिपाती – पु॰ – (अभिनिपाती) आक्रान्ता, हमलावर। aggressor, invader.

अभिनिप्पीलेति – क्रि॰ – (अभिनिपीडयति) पीड़ा देता है। oppresses or crushes.

अभिनिप्फज्जति – क्रि॰ – (अभि + निस + √ पद्) कार्यान्वित होता है, निष्पादित होता है, तत्पर होता है, पैदा होता है। accomplishes, produces.

अभिनिष्पत्ति – स्त्री॰ – (अभिनिष्पत्ति) कार्यान्वयन, उत्पत्ति, सम्पूर्ति। being brought about, accomplishment, production.

अभिनिष्फादित – क्रि॰ वि॰ (अभि + निष्पादित) निष्पन्न किया हुआ, क्रियान्वित। produced, accomplished.

अभिनिष्फादेति – क्रि॰ – (अभि + निष्पादयति) कार्यान्वयन करता है, पैदा करता है, तत्पर रहता है। produces, brings into existence.

अभिनिब्बत – क्रि॰ वि॰ (अभिनिवृत्त) पुनर्जन्मगृहीत, पुनरुद्भूत। reproduced, reborn.

अभिब्वत्ति – स्त्री॰ – (अभि + निवृत्ति) जन्मग्रहण, उत्पत्ति। birth, becoming.

अभिनिब्बत्तेति – क्रि॰ – (अभि + निर + √वृत्त) उत्पन्न करता है, जन्म ग्रहण कराता है। produces, brings into existence.

अभिनिब्बिदा – स्त्री॰ – (अभि + निर्वेद्य) वैराग्य। freedom from worldly desires.

अभिनिब्बत – वि॰ – (अभि + निवृत्त) पूर्णतया शान्त। perfectly calmed.

अभिनिमंतेति – क्रि॰ – (अभिनिमन्त्रयति) सादर निमन्त्रित करता है। cordially invites.

अभिनिम्मिणाति – क्रि॰ – (अभि + निर्मिमीते) उत्पन्न करता है, निर्माण करता है। creator, produces.

अभिनिरोपन – न॰ – (अभि + नि + रोपण) अपने चित्त को लगाना। fixing one's mind upon, application of mind.

अभिनिरोपेति – क्रि॰ – (अभि + नि + √रोप) अपने चित्त में स्थान देता है। fixes into one's mind, implants.

अभिनिविसति – क्रि॰ – (अभि + नि + √विश्) आसक्त होता है। clings to, adheres, attaches to.

अभिनिवेस – पु॰ – (अभिनिवेश) एकनिष्ठता, लगन, आसक्ति। inclination, tendency.

अभिनिसीदति – क्रि॰ – (अभि + निषीदति) समीप बैठता है। sits near.

अभिनिस्सट – क्रि॰ वि॰ – (अभि + निस्सृत) निकाल दिया गया, बाहर किया हुआ। expelled removed.

अभिनीत – क्रि॰ वि॰ – (अभि + नीत) ले आया गया। brought, fetched, carried.

अभिनीहट – क्रि॰ वि॰ – (अभि + निःसृत) बाहर लाया गया। taken out, removed.

अभिनीहरति – क्रि॰ – (अभि + नीहरति) बाहर लाता है। takes out.

अभिनीहार – पु॰ – (अभिनीहार) संकल्प। aspiration, resolution.

अभिपत्थित – क्रि॰ वि॰ – (अभि + पार्थित) वांछित, अभिप्रेत। longed for, hoped for.

अभिपत्थेति – क्रि॰ – (अभि + प्रार्थयति) अभ्यर्थना करता है, मांगता है, चाह प्रकट करता है। longs for, hopes for.

अभिपालेति – क्रि॰ (अभि + पाल्येति) लालन- पालन करता है, संरक्षण देता है। brings up, protects.

अभिपीडेति – क्रि॰ – (अभि + पीडयति) उत्पीड़न करता है, पीड़ा देता है, निचोड़ता है। oppresses, squeezes.

अभिपूरति – क्रि॰ – (अभि + पूरयति) पूर्णता प्रदान करता है। makes it perfect, completes.

अभिप्पकीरति – क्रि॰ – (अभिप्रकिरति) बिखेरता है। scatters, strews.

अभिप्पमोदति – क्रि॰ – (अभिप्रमोदते) आनन्दित होता है। rejoices.

अभिप्पसाद – पु॰ – (अभि + प्रसाद) श्रद्धा-भक्ति। faith, devotion.

अभिप्पसारेति – क्रि॰ – (अभिप्रसारयति) पसारता है, फैलाता है। stretches out, spreads.

अभिप्पसीदति – क्रि॰ – (अभिप्रसीदति) श्रद्धावान होता है। puts faith in, is devoted to.

अभिभवति – क्रि॰ – (अभिभवति) पराजित कर देता है। overcomes, defeats

अभिभवन – न॰ – (अभिभवन) विजय प्राप्ति। conquering, vanquishing.

अभिभवनीय – वि॰ – (अभिभवनीय) पराजित करने योग्य। that which should be defeated.

अभिभू – पु॰ – (अभिभू) विजेता। conqueror, overlord, winner.

अभिभूत – क्रि॰ वि॰ – (अभिभूत) विजित, पराजित। overpowered, vanquished.

अभिमङ्गल – वि॰ – (अभिमङ्गल) माङ्गलिक। auspicious.

अभिमण्डित – क्रि॰ वि॰ – (अभिमण्डित) सजाया गया। adorned.

अभिमत – वि॰ – (अभिमत) इच्छित। intented, wished for.

अभिमत्थति – क्रि॰ – (अभिमत्थति) मथता है। crushes, churns.

अभिमद्दति – क्रि॰ – (अभिमर्दति) मर्दन करता है। subdues, crushes.

अभिमद्दन – न॰ – (अभिमर्दन) मर्दन। crushing, subjugation.

अभिमान – पु॰ – (अभिमान) स्वाभिमान, गर्व। self-conceit, pride.

अभिमार – पु॰ – (अभिमारकः) डाकू, हत्यारा। a murderer, plunderer.

अभिमुख – वि॰ – (अभिमुख) उपस्थित, आमने-सामने। present, face to face.

अभियाचति – क्रि॰ – (अभियाचते) याचना करता है। begs, entreats.

अभियाचन – न॰ – (अभियाचन) अभ्यर्थना, याचना। request, entreaty.

अभियाचना – स्त्री॰ – (अभियाचना) देखें – अभियाचन। see Abhiyācana.

अभियाति – (क्रि॰) – (अभियाति) विरुद्ध जाता है। goes against.

अभियुञ्जति – (क्रि॰) – (अभियुज्यते) आरोप करता है, अभियोग लगाता है। accuses, blames, charges in lawsuit.

अभियुज्झति – क्रि॰ – (अभि + युध्यति) झगड़ा करता है, लड़ता है। quarrels, fights.

अभियुञ्जन – न॰ – (अभियुञ्जन) मुकदमा। trial, lawsuit

अभियोग – पु॰ – (अभियोग) वाद, मुकदमा, दोषारोपण। accusation, lawsuit allegation.

अभियोगी – पु॰ – (अभियोगी) दोषारोपण, मुकदमा दायर करने वाला। plaintiff; complainant.

अभिरक्खति – क्रि॰ – (अभिरक्षति) रक्षा करता है। protects, defends.

अभिरक्खन – न॰ – (अभिरक्षण) सुरक्षा, बचाव। protection.

अभिरति – स्त्री॰ – (अभिरति) प्रीति, आसक्ति। affection, love, intense-liking.

अभिरद्धि – स्त्री॰ – (अभिरद्धि = √ राध्) संतोष। full satisfaction.

अभिरमति – क्रि॰ – (अभिरमति) रमण करता है, भोग भोगता है। enjoys, takes pleasure in.

अभिरमन – न॰ – (अभिरमण) भोग। enjoyment.

अभिरमापेति – क्रि॰ – (अभिरमापयति) अभिरमण कराता है, सुख-भोग कराता है। causes one to take pleasure makes one enjoy.

अभिराम – वि॰ – (अभिराम) अनुकूल, मनोहर। favourable, charming, lovely.

अभिरुचि – स्त्री॰ – (अभिरुचि) इच्छा, कामना। longing, liking, ambition.

अभिरुचित – वि॰ – (अभिरुचित) अतिशय रुचिकर। most desirable.

अभिरुचिर – वि॰ – (अभिरुचिर) अत्यन्त सुन्दर। very pleasing, very delightful.

अभिरुद – वि॰ – (अभिरुद) गुंजन। resounding.

अभिरुप – वि॰ – (अभिरुप) अनुरुप, सुन्दर, सुखद। lovely, handsome, compatible with.

अभिरुहति – क्रि॰ – (अभि √ रुह + व) ऊपर चढ़ता है। ascends, goes up.

अभिरूळ्ह – क्रि॰ वि॰ – (अभिरूढ़) आरूढ़, सवार। ascended, risen up, mounted.

अभिरुहन – न॰ – (अभिरोहण) अधिरोहण, चढ़ाई। climbing, ascent.

अभिरोचेति – क्रि॰ – (अभि + √ रुच्) पसन्द करता है, रुचिकर लगता है। finds delight in, likes.

अभिरोपन – न॰ – (अभिरोपण) रोपना, चित्त को एकाग्र करना। concentration.

अभिरोपेति – क्रि॰ – (अभि + √ रोप्) रोपता है, चित्त को एकाग्र करता है। concentrates.

अभिलक्खित – क्रि॰ – (अभिलक्षित) चिह्नित। marked, designed.

अभिलक्खेति – क्रि॰ – (अभि + √ लक्ष् = अभिलक्षति, अभिलक्षयति, अभिलक्षयते) चिह्न लगाता है। marks, designs.

अभिलाप – पु॰ – (अभिलाप) संलाप, बोलना, बातचीत। talk, speech, dialogue.

अभिलासा – स्त्री॰ – (अभिलाषा) अभिलाषा। wish, desire.

अभिलाव – पु॰ – (अभि + √ लू = अभि-लणनम्) कटाई। cutting, harvesting.

अभिलेखेति – क्रि॰ – (अभिलेखयति) चिह्न लगवाता है। gets things marked, gets things designed.

अभिवञ्चन – न॰ – (अभिवञ्चन) वंचना, ठगी। robbery, deception, fraud.

अभिवट्ठ – क्रि॰ वि॰ – (अभिवृष्ट) जिस पर वर्षा हुई हो। rained upon.

अभिवड्ढति – क्रि॰ – (अभि √ वृध् = अभि-वद्धते) बढ़ता है, वृद्धि को प्राप्त होता है। grows, increases.

अभिवड्ढन – न॰ – (अभिवर्द्धन) वृद्धि, बढ़ोतरी, विकास। growth, increase.

अभिवण्णित – क्रि॰ वि॰ – (अभि $\sqrt{}$ वर्ण + क्त = अभिवर्णित) प्रशंसित। praised.

अभिवण्णेति – क्रि॰ – (अभि + वर्णयति) प्रशंसा करता है। praises.

अभिवदति – क्रि॰ – (अभि $\sqrt{}$ वद्) घोषणा करता है। declares.

अभिवंदति – क्रि॰ – (अभि $\sqrt{}$ वन्द् = अभि -वन्दयति) अभिवन्दना करता है, महिमागान करता है। bows down, honours.

अभिवंदितव्व – क्रि॰ – (अभिवन्दितव्य) वन्दनीय। deserving salutation, adorable.

अभिवस्सति – क्रि॰ – (अभिवर्षति) बरसाता है। rains over.

अभिवादन – न॰ – (अभिवादन) नमस्कार, प्रणाम, दण्डवत। salutation, bowing down.

अभिवादेति – क्रि॰ – (अभिवादयति) दण्डवत करता है, प्रणाम करता है। bows down, salutes.

अभिवादेतब्ब – कृदन्त – (अभिवादितव्य) अभिवादन के योग्य। deserving salutation, adorable.

अभिवायति – क्रि॰ – (अभि $\sqrt{}$ वा = अभि-वाति) हवा चलती है। (wind) blows.

अभिवारेति – क्रि॰ – (अभिवारयति) रोकता है, निवारण करता है। stops, cures.

अभिविजयति – क्रि॰ – (अभिविजयते) जीतता है। conquers, wins.

अभिविजनाति – क्रि॰ – (अभि + वि $\sqrt{}$ जि + नक = अभिविजनाति) जीतता है। conquers, wins.

अभिविञ्ञापेति – क्रि॰ – (अभि विज्ञापयति) प्रेरित करता है, विज्ञापित करता है। inspires, advertises.

अभिवितरति – क्रि॰ – (अभि + वितरति) बाँटता है, ध्यान देता है। distributes, donates, pays heed to.

अभिवितरण – न॰ – (अभिवितरण) दान। donation.

अभिवुट्ठ – देखें अभिवट्ठं। see Abhivaṭṭhaṁ.

अभिवुड्ढि – देखें अभिवड्ढि। see Abhivaddhi.

अभिविसिट्ठ – वि॰ – (अभि + विशिष्ट) अति विशेष, प्रमुख। excellent, most prominent.

अभिसंखत – क्रि॰ – (अभि + संस्कृत) सुसंस्कृत, सुसंस्कारित। cultured, well-prepared.

अभिसंखरोति – क्रि॰ – (अभि + संस्करोति) रचता है, संस्कार डालता है। decorates.

अभिसङ्खार – पु॰ – (अभि + संस्कार) सुसंस्कार, उच्च संस्कार। super culture.

अभिसङ्कारिक – वि॰ – (अभि + संस्कारिक) सुसंस्कारयुक्त, सुसंस्कृत। brought up in high culture, well cultured.

अभिसङ्ग – पु॰ – (अभिषङ्ग) आसक्ति, अत्य- धिक लगाव, मोह। craving, attachment, fascination.

अभिसज्ज – वि॰ – (अभिषज्जी) आसक्त, अनुरक्त। attached to, intent.

अभिसज्जति – क्रि॰ – (अभि + $\sqrt{}$ सज्जू) क्रोधित होता है। becomes angry, gets enraged.

अभिसज्जन – न॰ – (अभि √सज्ज् + ल्युट्) क्रोध। anger, fury.

अभिसञ्चेतेति –1 क्रि॰ – (अभि + सम + √चित् = अभि + सञ्चेतयति) विचार करता है। ponders over, thinks over.

अभिसट – क्रि॰ – (अभिसृत) सभागत। approached by, visited.

अभिसत्त – क्रि॰ – (अभिशप्त) अभिशप्त, शापित। cursed, accursed.

अभिसद्दहति – क्रि॰ – (अभिश्रद्दधते) श्रद्धा करता है। venerates.

अभिसंतापेति – क्रि॰ – (अभिसन्तापयति) जलाता है, संताप देता है। distresses, torments.

अभिसंद – पु॰ – (अभिष्यन्द) उतराना, प्रवाह। outflow.

अभिसंदन – न॰ – (अभिष्यन्दन) प्रवाह। flow.

अभिसंदहति – क्रि॰ – (अभि + सं √धा) जोड़ता है, मेल बिठाता है। joins, unites, connects.

अभिसंदेति – क्रि॰ – (अभिष्यन्दयति) प्रवाहित कराता है। reconciles.

अभिसंधि (1) – स्त्री॰ – (अभिसन्धि) अभिप्राय, मतलब। intention, purpose, opinion, meaning.

अभिसंधि (2) – स्त्री॰ – (अभिसन्धि) ठगी, षड्यन्त्र। cheating, conspiracy.

अभिसंदेति – क्रि॰ – (अभिष्यन्दयति) प्रवाहित करता है। makes to flow.

अभिसपति – क्रि॰ – (अभि √शप्) (1) शाप देता है, (2) शपथ लेता है। (1) curses (2) takes an oath.

अभिसपन – न॰ – (अभिशापन) (1) शाप (2) कसम। (1) curse (2) oath.

अभिसमय – पु॰ – (अभिसमय – बुद्ध का संस्कृत) स्पष्ट ज्ञान, स्थिरप्रज्ञता। realization, mental concentration, balanced state of mind.

अभिसमागच्छति – क्रि॰ – (अभि + सम + आ √गम्) पूर्ण रुप से समझ लेता है. realizes perfectly.

अभिसमाचारिक – वि॰ – (अभि + सम + आ √चर + ण्वुल्) सदाचारयुक्त। of good conduct.

अभिसमेच्च – पूर्व क्रि॰ – (अभि + समेत्य) भली प्रकार समझकर। having fully understood.

अभिसमेत – क्रि॰ – (अभिशयेति) हृदयंगम किया हुआ। completely realized, perfectly grasped.

अभिसमेति – क्रि॰ – (अभिशयेति) पूर्णतया हृदयंगम कर लेता है। grasps perfectly.

अभिसम्पराय – पु॰ – (अभि + सम् + परा √इ + अच्) भावी पुनर्जन्म, परलोक। rebirth, state after death.

अभिसम्बुज्झति – क्रि॰ – (अभि + सम् √बुध + य) सम्बोधि प्राप्त करता है, उच्चतम ज्ञान प्राप्त करता है। attains the highest wisdom.

अभिसम्बुद्ध – क्रि॰ – (अभि + सम्बुद्ध) सम्पूर्ण ज्ञानी। one who has attained the highest wisdom.

अभिसम्बोधि – स्त्री॰ – (अभि + सम्बोधि) पूर्ण ज्ञान। perfect knowledge.

अभिसम्भव – क्रि॰ – (अभि + सम्भव) दुःसम्भव, दुष्प्राप्य। hard to obtain, troublesome.

अभिसम्भवति – क्रि॰ (अभिसम्भवति) पाने, सामना करने या जीतने में समर्थ होता हैं। able to get, stand or overcome.

अभिसम्मति – क्रि॰ -- (अभिशाम्यति) रुकता है, शान्त होता है। is satiated, is pacified.

अभिसर – पु॰ – (अभि + √ सृ + अच्) साथी, अनुयायी। companion, follower.

अभिसाप – पु॰ – (अभिशाप) अभिशाप। curse.

अभिसारिका – स्त्री – (अभिसारिका) राज-सेविका, प्रिय से मिलने हेतु सज्जित युवती। a courtesan, a lady going stealthily to meet his lover.

अभिसिञ्चति – क्रि॰ - (अभिसिञ्चति) अभिषेक करता है, जल छिड़कता है। sprinkles water over, consecrates.

अभिसेक – पु॰ – (अभिषेक) अभिषेक, जल सिंचन। consecration, sprinkling, ablution.

अभिस्संग – पु॰ – (अभिष्वङ्ग = अभि √ स्वज्) लगाव। attachment.

अभिहट – क्रि॰ – (अभिहृत) हर लाया गया, ले आया गया, भेंट किया। usurped, won over fetched forcibly.

अभिहनति – क्रि॰ – (अभिहरति) लाता है, भेंट करता है। strikes, presents.

अभिहार – पु॰ – (अभिहार) उपहार, भेंट। gift, present, offering.

अभिहित – क्रि॰ वि॰ (अभिहित) जो कहा गया। spoken, uttered.

अभीत – वि॰ – (अ + भीत) निर्भय, निडर। fearless.

अभीरूक – वि॰ – (अ + भीरु + क) निर्भीक, भयमुक्त। brave, fearless.

अभूत – वि॰ – (अभूत) अयथार्थ, अस्तित्व-रहित। having no existence.

अभेज्ज – वि॰ – (अभेद्य) जिसे भेदा, काटा या बाँटा न जा सके। not to be split or divided.

अभोज्ज – वि॰ – (अभोज्य) अखाद्य, जो खाने योग्य न हो। inedible, not fit to be eaten.

अभ्यास – पु॰ – (अभ्याशः – अभि + √ अश्) सामीप्य। vicinity.

√ अम – भ्वादि – (गमने) जाना। to go.

अमच्च – पु॰ – (अमात्य) सचिव, अमात्य। secretary, minister.

अमज्ज – नपु॰ – (अ + मद्य) निरासव, मद-रहित, मदिरा-रहित। non-alcoholic.

अमज्जप – वि॰ – (अ + मद्यप) जो मद्यप नहीं, मदिरा-सेवन न करने वाला। abstaining from spirituous liquor.

अमत्त – वि॰ – (अ + मत्त) जो नशे में धुत्त न हो, अमत्त। not out of senses, one who is not intoxicated, sober.

अमत्तञ्जु – वि॰ – (अमात्रज्ञ) जिसे भोजन की उपयुक्त मात्रा का ज्ञान न हो, असंयत। immoderate eater.

अमत्तेय्य – वि॰ – (अमात्रेय) माता के प्रति अनादर-भाव रखने वाला। having no respect for one's mother.

अमनुस्स – पु॰ – (अमनुष्य) मानवेतर प्राणी, भूत-प्रेत, देवता। non-human, a demon, a ghost, a deity.

अमम – वि॰ – (अमम) ममताहीन, निर्लोभी। unselfish, free from greed.

अमर – वि०/पु० – (अमर) (1) जो मरे नहीं, (2) देवता। immortal, a deity.

अमरत्त – न० – (अमरत्व) अमरता। immortality.

अमरा – स्त्री० – (अमरा) फिसलनी मछली। an eel.

अमल – वि० (अमल) शुद्ध, निर्मल। pure, stainless.

अमस्सुक – वि० – (अश्मश्रुक) बिना दाढ़ी के। without beard.

अमातापितिक – वि० – (अमात्रपितृक) अनाथ, मातृ-पितृहीन। one who has lost one's parents, orphan.

अमातिक – वि० – (अमात्रिक) मातृहीन। one who has lost one's mother.

अमानुस – वि० – (अमानुष) अमनुष्य, मनुष्येतर। other than human being, non-human.

अमायावी – वि० – (अमायावी) जो मायावी नहीं, छल-कपट-रहित। not illusive, not deceptive.

अमावस – पु० – (अमावस) चाँद का सूर्य के साथ घर में रहना। new-moon night the day having a completely dark night due to moons conjunction with sun, Amāvasa comes once in thirty days.

अमावसी – स्त्री० – (अमावसी) अमावस्या। the night of Amāvasa, related to Amāvasa.

अमित – वि० – (अमित) असीम, अपरिमित, प्रचुर। boundless, immeasurable, abundant.

अमिताभ – वि० – (अमिताभ) अनन्त आभा वाले। of boundless lustre.

अमिता – स्त्री० – (अमिता) सिंहहनु की दो पुत्रियों में से एक देवदत्त की माँ। one of Sinhahanus two daughters who was the mother of Devadatta.

अमितोदन – (अमितोदन) सिंहहनु का पुत्र। शुद्धोदन का भाई महानाम तथा अनुरुद्ध का भाई। brother of Śuddhodana, son of Sinhahanu, and brother of Aniruddh.

अमित्त – पु० – (अमित्र) शत्रु। enemy, friendless.

अमिलात – वि० – (अम्लान) जो म्लान नहीं, जो मुरझाया नहीं। not withered, unfaded.

अमिस्स – वि० – (अमिश्र) अमिश्रित। unmingled, unmixed.

अमु – सर्वनाम – (अमु) अमुक, फलाँ-फलाँ। such and such, so and so.

अमुच्छित – वि० – (अमूढ) अमूढ, निर्लोभी, अमोहित। not bewildered or infatuated, non-confused.

अमुत्त – वि० – (अमुक्त) अमुक्त, बन्धनयुक्त। not free, bound.

अमुत्र – क्रि० वि० – (अमुत्र) अमुक स्थान पर। at/in such a place.

अमेज्झ/त्रिलिंगी – (अ + मेध्य) शुक्र, वीर्य। semen.

अमोघ – वि० – (अ + मोघ) जो मोघ अर्थात् निष्फल न हो, अचूक। sure, unfailing, unerring.

अमोह – पु० – (अ + मोह) अज्ञता का अभाव, प्रज्ञा। wisdom, free from delusion.

अम्ब – पु०/न० – (अम्ब) आम्र वृक्ष, आम का फल। a mango tree, a mango fruit.

अम्ब/अंकुर – पु॰ – (आम्राङ्कुर) आम का अंकुर। sprout of mango.

√ **अम्ब-भ्वादि** – (शब्दे) शब्द करना। to utter.

अम्ब-पक्क – न॰ – (पक्काम) पका आम। a ripe mango.

अम्ब-पान – न॰ –(आम्र-पानम्) आम का पन्ना, पके आम का रस। a syrup or juice made of mangoes.

अम्ब-पिण्डी – स्त्री॰ – (आम्र-पिण्डिका) आमों का गुच्छा। a bunch of mangoes.

अम्ब-वन – न॰ – (आम्र-वन) आम्र वन। a mango grove.

अम्ब-सण्ड – पु॰ – (आम्र-षण्ड) देखें – 'अम्ब वन'। see Amba vana.

अम्ब-लट्ठिका – स्त्री॰ – (आम्र-यष्टिका) आम का पौधा। a mango plant.

अम्ब-जातक (1) (जा॰ सं॰ 122) – न॰ – (आम्र-जातकम्) सूखे के समय हिमालय में रहने वाले एक तपस्वी ने जानवरों के लिए जल की व्यवस्था की थी। कृतज्ञ जानवर उसके लिए अनेक उपहार लाये थे। the Jātaka tale (No. 122) related to a hermit and beasts of Himālayan jungle.

अम्ब-जातक (2) (जा॰ सं॰ 474) – न॰ – (आम्र-जातकम्) बुद्धिमान चाण्डाल से शिल्प सीखने वाले ब्राह्मण की कथा। the Jātaka tale (No. 474) of a low-born (cāṇḍāla) architect, and his brāhmaṇa disciple.

अम्बचोर-जातक अम्बचोर-जातक (जा॰ सं॰ 344) – न॰ – (आम्र चोर जातकम्) आम्रवन में अपने लिए एक कुटी बनाकर रहने वाले दुष्ट तपस्वी सम्बन्धी जातक कथा (जा॰ सं॰ 344)। the Jātaka tale (No. 344) related to a fraudulent hermit.

अम्ब-पाली – स्त्री॰ – (आम्रपाली) वैशाली की प्रसिद्ध गणिका जिसने अपना आम्र वन बुद्ध-प्रमुख भिक्षु-संघ को दान दे दिया था। the famous prostitute of Vaiśālī who had donated her mango grove to the Lord Buddha's monastery.

अम्बर – न॰ – (अम्बर) (1) वस्त्र, (2) आकाश। (1) cloth, (2) sky.

अम्बा – स्त्री॰ – (अम्बा) जननी, माँ। mother.

अम्बिल – वि॰ – (आम्लिक) अम्लीय, खट्टा। sour, acidic, acid.

अम्बु – न॰ – (अम्बु) पानी। water.

अम्बुचारी – पु॰ – (अम्बुचारी) मछली आदि जलचर। aquatic animal.

अम्बुज – न॰ – (अम्बुज) कमल। lotus.

अम्बुधर – न॰ – (अम्बुधर) बादल। cloud.

अम्बुजिनी – स्त्री॰ – (अम्बुजिनी) पद्म-सर, पुष्करिणी, कमल सर। a lotus-lake, a lotus pond.

अम्भो – अव्यय – (अम्भो) अरे, हे! ओ! सम्बोधन। hail someone with words like arre, hē, ōh.

अम्म – स्त्री॰ – (अम्बे) माँ के लिए सम्बोधन। a loud calling to draw mother's attention.

अम्मण – नपुं॰ – (अम्मण) धान का माप विशेष (मन) तौल 14 किलोग्राम लगभग। a measure for food grains weighing about 14 kilograms.

अम्मा – स्त्री॰ – (अम्बा) माँ। mother.

अम्ह – सर्वनाम – (अस्मद्) मैं, हम। I, we.

अम्हि – क्रि॰ – (अस्मि) (मैं) हूँ। (I) am.

अम्ह-अम्हा – क्रि॰ – (स्म) हम हैं। (we) are.

√अय-भ्वादि – (गमनार्थे) जाना। to go.

अय – पु॰ – (आय) आय। income.

अय – न॰ – (अयस्) लोहा। iron.

अयकपाल – पु॰ – (अयस्कपाल) लौह-फलक। a lid or pan made of iron.

अयस – पु॰ / न॰ – (अयस्) लोहा। iron.

अय-कूट-जातक – (जा॰ सं॰ 340) पशुबलि प्रथा रोकने से सम्बन्धित जातक कथा। the Jātaka tale (No. 340) related to Bodhisattva's act of prohibiting animal sacrifice.

अयं – सर्वनाम – (अयम्) यह व्यक्ति। this (man, person).

अयथा – अव्यय – (अयथार्थ) अयथार्थ, मिथ्या। false (used in a compound word).

अयन – न॰ – (अयन) मार्ग, पथ। way, path.

अयस – पु॰ तथा न॰ – (अयश) अपयश, अपकीर्ति। ill repute, disgrace.

अयुत्त (1) – वि॰ – (अयुक्त) अयुक्त, अयोग्य, अनुपयुक्त। inappropriate.

अयुत्त (2) – न॰ – (अयुक्तम्) अनुचित, अन्याय। unjust, improper.

अयो-कूट – (अयोकूट) लोहे का हथौड़ा। iron-hammer.

अयो-खील – नपुं॰ – (अयस्कीलम्) लोहे का कीला। iron-stake, nail.

अयोगुळ – पु॰ – (अयोगुटिका) लोहे का गोला। iron-ball.

अयो-घन – न॰ – (अयोघन) लोहे का घन। iron-club.

अयो-मय – वि॰ – (अयोमय) लौह-निर्मित। made of iron.

अयो-संकु – पु॰ – (अयोशंकु) लोहे का नुकीला खूँटा। iron-spike.

अयो-घर-जातक – (अयोगृह जातकम्) (जा॰ सं॰ 510) बोधिसत्तव के लोहे के घर में जन्म ग्रहण की कथा। the Jātaka tale (No. 510) related to birth of Boddhisattva in an iron cage.

अयोग्य – वि॰ – (अयोग्य) अयोग्य। unable, unworthy.

अयोज्झ – वि॰ – (अयोध्य) जिसके विरुद्ध युद्ध न किया जा सके, अजेय। unconquerable.

अयोनिसो – क्रि॰ – (अयोनिशः) अनुचित तौर पर, अन्यायपूर्ण। improperly, injudiciously.

अय्य – पु॰ – (आर्य) आर्य, स्वामी। lord, master.

अय्यपुत्त – पु॰ – (आर्य-पुत्र) श्रेष्ठ, कुलीन, स्वामीपुत्र। noble, master's son.

अय्यक – वि॰ – (आर्यक) पितामह। grandfather.

अय्यका-अय्यिका – स्त्री॰ – (आर्यिका) पितामही। grandmother.

अय्या – स्त्री॰ – (आर्या) आर्या, स्वामिनी। mistress, lady.

√अर-भ्वादि – (√ऋ = गतौ) जाना। to go, to move.

अर – न॰ – (अर √ऋ = गतौ) पहिये की तीली या आर। spoke of a wheel.

अरक-जातक – (जा॰ सं॰ 169) – बोधिसत्व ने अपने शिष्यों को ब्रह्म-विहारों (मैत्री, करुणा, मुदिता तथा उपेक्षा) की शिक्षा दी। the preaching of Bodhisattva

(Jātaka No. 169) about four Brahma-vihāras.

अरक्खिय – वि॰ – (अरक्ष्य) जिसे सुरक्षित न रखा जा सकता हो। not able to be guarded.

अरक्खेय्य – वि॰ – (अरक्षणीय) जिसे आरक्षा की आवश्यकता न हो। which need not be guarded.

अरघट्ट – न॰ – (अरघट्ट) रहट। the wheel for drawing water from a well.

अरज – वि॰ – (अरज) रज-रहित, मल-रहित। free from dust or impurity.

अरञ्ञ – न॰ – (अरण्य) अरण्य, जंगली। forest, wild.

अरञ्ञक – वि॰ – (आरण्यक) अरण्य में रहने वाला। who lives in a forest.

अरञ्ञगत – वि॰ – (अरण्यगत) जंगल में गया हुआ। gone to a forest.

अरञ्ञवास – पु॰ – (अरण्यवास) आरण्य निवास। dwelling in a forest.

अरञ्ञ विहार पु॰ (अरण्य-विहार) वन-विहार। a forest hermitage.

अरञ्ञ-जातक – (अरण्य जातकम्) (जा॰ सं॰ 384) भार्या की मृत्यु के अनन्तर बोधिसत्त्व हिमालय में जाकर पुत्र सहित तपस्वी जीवन बिताने लगे वहाँ एक लड़की ने तरुण का शील भङ्ग किया। the Jātaka tale (No. 384) relating to violating the chastity of the hermit - Bodhisattva's son by a cunning girl.

अरञ्ञानी – स्त्री॰ – (अरण्यानी) एक बड़ा जंगल। a big forest.

अरण – वि॰ – (अरण) शान्तचित्त। peaceful, passionless.

अरणि – स्त्री॰ – (अरणि) शमी लकड़ी का टुकड़ा जिसे रगड़कर यज्ञीय अग्नि प्रज्वलित की जाती है। a piece of śamī wood for making fire by rubbing, with another piece.

अरणि-मथन – न॰ – (अरणि मंथन) आग पैदा करने के लिए लकड़ी के दो टुकड़ों को रगड़ना। rubbing of two wooden pieces of śamī to make fire.

अरति – स्त्री॰ – (अरति) अरुचि, अनासक्ति। non-attachment, aversion.

अरती – (अरती) मार की तीन कन्याओं में से एक। शेष दो हैं तण्हा (तृष्णा) तथा रगा (राग?)। one among the three daughters of Māra.

अरविन्द – न॰ तथा पु॰ – (अरविन्द) कमल। red lotus.

अरह – वि॰ – (अर्ह) योग्य। worthy, deserving.

√अरह – भ्वादि – (पूजने) पूजा करना, सम्मान करना। to pay respect or regard, to worship.

अरहद्धज – पु॰ – (अरहध्वज) अर्हताध्वज, भिक्षु का काषाय वस्त्र। monk's ochre-coloured, robe.

अरहति – क्रि॰ – (√अर्ह = अर्हति) योग्य होता है। deserves.

अरहत्त – पु॰ – (अर्हत्त्व) अर्हन्त बनने की क्षमता, मुक्ति पाने की स्थिति। state of an *arhanta*, final emancipation.

अरहत्त-फल – न॰ – (अर्हत्त्व-फल) अर्हत्त्व का फल, मोक्ष। final emancipation.

अरहत्तमग्ग – पु॰ – (अर्हत्त्व-मार्ग) अर्हत्त्व प्राप्ति का मार्ग। the path of emancipation.

अरहन्त – पु० – (अर्हन्त) जिसने अर्हत्त्व फल प्राप्त कर लिया है। one who has attained the final emancipation.

अरि – पु० – (अरि) शत्रु। an enemy.

अरिंदम – त्रिलिङ्गी – (अरिन्दम) विजेता, शत्रु का दमन करने वाला, रिपुञ्जय। tamer of enemies, a conquerer.

अरिञ्चमान – वि० – (अ + √रिच् + शानच् = अरिच्यमान) न छोड़ते हुए, प्रयास करते हुए। not giving up, pursuing earnestly.

अरिट्ठ (1) – वि० – (अरिष्टः = अ + रिष्ट) दुर्भाग्यशाली। unlucky.

अरिट्ठ (2) – पु० – (अरिष्ट) नीम का पेड़। a nīma (margosa) tree.

अरित्त – न० – (अरित्र) पतवार। a rudder.

अरित्त – वि० – (अ + रिक्त) जो थोथा या बेकार न हो। not empty, not futile.

अरिय (1) – वि० – (आर्य) श्रेष्ठ। noble.

अरिय (2) – पु० – (आर्य) श्रेष्ठ व्यक्ति। a noble man.

अरिय-कत्त – वि० – (आर्य-कत्त्व) आर्यजनों के अनुकूल। agreeable to noble persons (Āryas).

अरिय-धन – (आर्य-धनम्) आर्यों का श्रेष्ठ धन। sublime treasure of noble-persons (Āryas).

अरिय-धम्म – पु० – (आर्य-धर्म) श्रेष्ठ धर्म। noble religion.

अरिय-पुग्गल – पु० – (आर्य-पुद्गल) श्रेष्ठ व्यक्ति (जिसने आर्य ज्ञान प्राप्त कर लिया)। one who has attained the higher wisdom.

अरिय-मग्ग – पु० – (आर्य-मार्ग) श्रेष्ठ मार्ग। the path to attain higher wisdom.

अरिय-सच्च (1) – नपुं० – (आर्य-सत्य) आर्य सत्य, शाश्वत सत्य। the universal truth, eternal truth.

अरिय-सच्च (2) – पु० – (आर्यसत्य) चार आर्य सत्य जिनका साक्षात्कार कर राजकुमार सिद्धार्थ गौतम बुद्ध बने। वे हैं – दुःख, दुःख-समुदय, दुःख हेतु और दुःख निरोध। The four noble truths followed by Prince Siddhartha to become Buddha. They are *duḥkha, duḥkha-samudaya, duḥkha-hetu* and *duḥkha-nirodha.*

अरिय-सावक – पु० – (आर्य-श्रावक) श्रेष्ठ जनों का शिष्य। disciple of the noble ones.

अरियूपवाद – पु० – (अर्योपवाद) आर्यजनों के प्रति दुष्प्रचार। an act to insult a noble one.

अरिस – न० – (अर्शों) बवासीर। piles.

अरु – न० – (अरु) व्रण, घाव, नासूर। an old wound, fistula.

अरुकाय – पु० – (अरुकाय) व्रण, समूह।

अरुण – पु० – (अरुण) सूर्योदय के समय की ललाई। down, dark-red colour of the dawn.

अरूण-वण्ण – वि० – (अरुण वर्ण) लाल रंग का। of dark-red colour.

अरूप – वि० – (अरूप) आकार-रहित। formless, incorporeal.

अरूप-कायिक – वि० – (अरूप-कायिक) आकार-रहित जीवों से सम्बन्धित। belonging to the formless beings.

अरूप-भाव – पु॰ – (अरूप-भाव) आकार-रहित अस्तित्व। formless existence.

अरूप-लोक – पु॰ – (अरूप-लोक) आकार रहित लोक। the formless world.

अरूपावचर – वि॰ – (अरूपावचर) अरूपी से सम्बन्धित। belonging to the realm of formless.

अरूपी – पु॰ – (अरूपी) आकार-रहित जीव। the formless being.

अरे – अव्यय – (अरे) हे! अरे! आदि। he! hello!

अरोग – वि॰ – (अरोग) स्वस्थ, रोग-रहित। healthy, void of sickness.

अरोग-भाव – पु॰ – (आरोग्य-भाव) स्वास्थ्य। health, sicklessness.

अल – पु॰/न॰ – (अल) बिच्छु का डंक, केकड़े का पंजा। sting of a scorpion, claw of a crab.

अलं – अव्यय – (अलम्) पर्याप्त, अलम्। sufficient enough.

अलक्क – पु॰ – (अलर्क) पागल कुत्ता। a rabid dog.

अलकिखक – वि॰ – (अलक्ष्मीक) अभागा, दुर्भाग्यग्रस्त। unlucky, unfortunate.

अलक्खी – स्त्री॰ – (अलक्ष्मीः) दुर्भाग्य, निर्धनता। misfortune, poverty.

अलगद्द – पु॰ – (अलगर्दः) साँप की एक प्रजाति, मटियारी साँप, पनिहा साँप। a kind of water snake.

अलग्ग – वि॰ – (अलग्न) विलग, अनासक्त। not stuck or attached.

अलग्गन – न॰ – (अलग्नता) अनासक्ति। non-attachment.

अलङ्कत – (अलङ्कृत) अलंकृत, सजा हुआ। decorated.

अलङ्करण – न॰ – (अलङ्करण) सजावट। decoration.

अलङ्कार – पु॰ – (अलङ्कार) (1) सजावट (2) गहना, आभरण। (1) decoration (2) an ornament.

अलज्जी – वि॰ – (अलज्ज, निर्लज्ज) लज्जा-रहित, पाप-कर्म में ग्लानि अनुभव न करने वाला। shameless, not afraid of sin.

अलत्तक – न॰ – (आलक्तक) आलता, महावर, लाख का बना लाल द्रव। lacquered, varnish made of lac.

अलम्ब – वि॰ – (अलम्बित) जो लटकता न हो। not hanging, unsuspended.

अलम्बुस-जातक – (अलम्बु जातकम्) – (जा॰ सं॰ 523) अलम्बुषा नाम की अप्सरा द्वारा ऋषि-पुत्र भृंगी के लुभाये जाने की कथा। The Jātaka tale (No. 523) related to the temptation of ṛṣi Bhṛṅgī by the nymph Alambuṣā.

अलस – वि॰ – (अलस) आलसी। idle, lazy.

अलसता – स्त्री॰ – (अलसता) आलस्य। idleness, laziness.

अलसक – नपुं॰ – (अलस + कन = अलसक) अफारा रोग, बदहज्मी। indigestion.

अलहुक – वि॰ – (अ + लघु + क) भारी। heavy.

अलात – न॰/पु॰ – (अलात) लुआठी, अंगारयुक्त लकड़ी। fire-brand.

अलापु अलाबु – (अलाबु) लम्बी लौकी। long bottlegourd.

अलाभ – पु॰ – (अलाभ) मुनाफे का अभाव, हानि। loss, lack of profit.

अलाला – पु॰ – (अलाला) अमूकदर्शी। not deaf and dumb towards his duties.

अलि – पु॰ – (अलि) भौंरा, मधुप। black bee.

अलिक – न॰ – (अलीकम्) मिथ्या, झूठ। lie, falsehood

अलीन – वि॰ – (अलीन) अप्रमादी। not sluggish, active.

अलीन-चित्त-जातक – (जा॰ सं॰ 156) बोधिसत्त्व ने अलिनचित्त नामक वाराणसी नरेश का जन्म ग्रहण किया था। the Jātaka tale (no. 156) related to Alīnacitta, the king of Varanasi.

अलोभ – पु॰ – (अलोभ) निर्लोभ भाव। without greed.

अलोलुप – वि॰ – (अलोलुप) लोलुप नहीं, लालचहीन। not covetous, not distracted by desire.

अल्ल – वि॰ – (अल्ल) आर्द्र, गीला। wet, moist.

अल्लदारू – न॰ – (अल्ल–दारू) गीली लकड़ी, हरित काष्ठ। wet wood.

अल्लकप्प – पु॰ – (अल्लकप्प) मगध के समीप एक प्रदेश। अल्लकप्प के क्षत्रियों ने बुद्ध के शरीर के धातुओं पर अपना अधिकार जताया था। an ancient place near Magadha.

अल्लाप – पु॰ – (संलाप) बातचीत, संलाप। conversation.

अल्लीन – क्रि॰ वि॰ – (आलीन) आसक्त। stuck, clung, absorbed.

अल्लीयति – क्रि॰ – (आ + लीयते) आसक्त होता है। clings to, sticks to.

अल्लीयन – न॰ – (आलीयन) आसक्ति। attachment, sticking, clinging.

√अव-भ्वादि – (रक्षणे) रक्षा करना। to protect.

अवकड्ढति – क्रि॰ – (अवकर्षति/अपकर्षति) पीछे की ओर खींचता है। draws back, pulls back.

अवकड्ढन – न॰ – (अवकर्षण) पीछे की ओर खींचना। drawing back, detraction.

अवकड्ढित – क्रि॰ – (अवकर्षित) पीछे की ओर खींचा गया। dragged away, pulled down, detracted.

अवकन्तति – क्रि॰ – (अवकृन्तति) काट डालता है। cuts down.

अवकस्सति – क्रि॰ – (अवकर्षति) देखें 'अवकड्ढति'। see Avakaddhati.

अवकारक – वि॰ – (अवकारक) बिखेरने वाला। scatterer.

अवकास – (अवकाश) अवसर, स्थान, मौका। chance, room, opportunity.

अवकिरति – क्रि॰ – (अवकिरति) उड़ेलता है, बिखेरता है। pours down, scatters.

अवकिरिय – पूर्व क्रि॰ – (अवकीर्य) फेंक करके, बिखेर करके। having scattered.

अवकुज्ज – वि॰ – (अवकुब्ज) अधोमुख, औंधा। face downward, bent over.

अवववन्त – क्रि॰ वि॰ – (अवक्रान्त) पराभूत। overwhelmed.

अवक्कन्ति – स्त्री॰ – (अवक्रान्ति) प्रवेश। entry.

अवक्कमति – क्रि॰ – (अवक्रमति) प्रवेश करता है, पराभूत करता है। enters, overwhelms.

अवक्कम – पूर्व क्रि॰ – (अवक्रम्य) प्रविष्ट होकर। having entered.

अवक्कार – पु॰ – (अवस्कर) कूड़ा। refuse, dust.

अवक्कार-पाति – स्त्री॰ – (अवस्कर + पात्र) कूड़ा डालने का बर्तन। a dustbin.

अवक्खित्त – क्रि॰ वि॰ – (अवक्षिप्त) फेंका हुआ, निक्षिप्त। thrown, dropped, cast away.

अवक्खिपति – क्रि॰ – (अवक्षिपति) नीचे फेंकता है। throws down, drops.

अवक्खिपन – न॰ – (अवक्षेपण) फेंकना, नीचे गिराना। throwing down.

अवगच्छति – क्रि॰ – (अव + √गम् = अवगच्छति) प्राप्त करता है, समझता है। obtains, understands.

अवगण्डकार – पु॰ – (अवगण्डकार) मुँह फुलाना, भोजन ठूँसकर गाल फुलाने वाला। stuffing of the cheeks with food.

अवगणित – वि॰ – (अव + गणित) अपमानित। humiliated, belittled.

अवगत – क्रि॰ वि॰ – (अवगत) परिचित, ज्ञात। obtained, understood.

अवगाति – क्रि॰ – (अवगाहति) डुबकी लगाता है। प्रविष्ट होता है। dives into, plunges into, delves.

अवगाह – पु॰ – (अवगाह) देखें 'अवगाहन'। see Avagāhana.

अवगाहन – न॰ – (अवगाहन) डुबकी लगाना, घुसना। diving, plunging into.

अवगाही – पु॰ – (अवगाही) डुबकी लगाने वाला, diver.

अवगुण्ठन – वि॰ – (अवगुण्ठन) घूँघट। veil.

अवग्गह – पु॰ – (अवग्रह) बाधा। अनुग्रह का विलोम। hurdle, hindrance.

अवच (1) – अव्यय – (अवच) नीचे। प्रयोग केवल उच्चावच में। low (used in compound form as uccāvaca).

अवच (2) / अवोच – क्रि॰ – (अवोचत्) (उसने) कहा। (he) said.

अवचनीय – वि॰ – (अवचनीय) जो उच्चारण करने या कहने योग्य न हो। अशिष्ट या अश्लील भाषा। obscene, vulgar language.

अवचर – क्रि॰ वि॰ – (अव √चर) आवारागर्दी। loittering, loafing, vagrancy.

अवचरक – पु॰ – (अव + चारी) आवारा। vagabond, loafer, vagrant.

अवचरण – न॰ – (अवचरण) व्यवहार, बर्ताव। behaviour, occupation, dealing.

अवच्छिद – क्रि॰ वि॰ – (अवच्छिद्र) छिद्र-युक्त, दोष-युक्त। perforated, faulty.

अवजय – पु॰ – (अवजय) हार, पराजय। defeat.

अवजात – वि॰ – (अवजात) दोगला, हरामी। bastard, illegitimate.

अवजानन – न॰ – (अवज्ञा) अवहेलना। contempt.

अवजानाति – क्रि॰ – (अवज्ञापते) अज्ञा करता है, घृणा करता है। condemns, despises.

अवजिनाति – क्रि॰ – (पुनर्जयते) पुनः जीत लेता है। reconquers.

अवजित – वि॰ – (अव + √जि) पुनः जीत लिया गया। reconquered.

अवज्ज – वि॰ – (अवद्य) दोष-युक्त, त्याज्य निन्दनीय। discardable, condemnable.

अवज्झ – वि॰ – (अवध्य) अमारणीय, जो

वध करने योग्य न हो। not fit to be killed.

अवज्ञा – स्त्री॰ – (अवज्ञा) अनादर, उपेक्षा, घृणा। disregard, contempt.

अवज्ञात – क्रि॰ वि॰ – (अवज्ञात) उपेक्षित, तिरस्कृत। neglected, disregarded.

अवट्ठान – न॰ – (अवस्थान) स्थिति। situation, position.

अवड्ढि – स्त्री॰ – (अ + वृद्धि) अनुन्नति, क्षय, हानि। decline, loss, decay.

अवण्ण – पु॰ – (अवर्ण्य) दुर्गण, निन्दा, अपयश। censure, ill-fame.

अवतरण – न॰ – (अवतरण) अवरोहण, नीचे उतरना। descending.

अवतारी – पु॰ – (अवतारी) (1) नीचे उतरने वाला, (2) अवतार ग्रहण करने वाला। (1) descender (2) who incarnates superhuman.

अवतंस – पु॰ – (अवतंस) मुकुट-माल। crest, coronet.

अवतिण्ण – क्रि॰ वि॰ – (अवतीर्ण) पतित। degraded, wicked, corrupt.

अवत्थरति – क्रि॰ – (अवस्तरति) ढकता है, ऊ पर दबाता है। bounces, swoops down.

अवत्थु – वि॰ – (अ + वस्तु) निराधार। of no existence, non-existent.

अवदात – वि॰ – (अवदात) निर्मल, शुभ्र। white, clean, pure.

अवदान – (अवदान) योगदान, सहयोग। contribution.

अवदायति – क्रि॰ – (अवदानं क्रियते) अनुकम्पा करता है। bestows mercy, shows compassion.

अवधारण – न॰ – (अवधारण) selection, grasping, understanding.

अवधारेति – क्रि॰ – (अवधारयति) चयन करता है, ग्रहण करता है। selects, chooses, picks up.

अवधि – पु॰ – (अवधि) सीमा। limit.

अवनति – स्त्री॰ – (अवनति) गिरावट, पतन। downfall, decreasement.

अवनि – स्त्री॰ – (अवनि) पृथ्वी। earth.

अवपिबति – क्रि॰ – (अव + पिबति) पीता है। drinks.

अवबुज्झति – क्रि॰ – (अव + बुध्यति) पूरी तरह समझता है। comprehends, understands well.

अवबोध – पु॰ – (अवबोध) समझ, ज्ञान। knowledge, comprehension.

अवबोधेति – क्रि॰ – (अवबोधयति) समझा देता है, बोध करा देता है। makes one perceive.

अवभास – पु॰ – (अवभास) प्रकटन, चमक, प्रतीति। appearance, brightness, lustre.

अवभासति – क्रि॰ – (अवभासते) चमकता है, प्रतीत होता है। manifests, appears, shines.

अवभासित – वि॰ – (अवभासित) प्रकाशित, प्रतीत। manifested, resplendent.

अवभुञ्जति – क्रि॰ – (अव + √भुज = अवमुङ्क्ते) खा डालता है, भोग करता है। eats up, enjoys, rejoices.

अवमंगल – न॰ – (अव + मङ्गल) दुर्भाग्य, अपशकुन। misfortune, bad omen.

अवमंगल – वि॰ – (अव + मङ्गलः) दुर्भाग्यशाली। unlucky.

अवमञ्ञति – क्रि॰ – (अवमन्यते) अवमानना (तिरस्कार) करता है। discards, condemns.

अवमञ्जना – स्त्री॰ – (अवमञ्जता) अवमान, घृणा, निरादर। disregard, disrespect.

अवमानेति – क्रि॰ – (अवमन्यते) घृणा करता है, उपेक्षा करता है। condemns, despises, discards.

अवयव – पु॰ – (अवयव) अंग, भाग, हिस्सा। part, constituent.

अवरञ्झति – क्रि॰ – (अव + √राध = अवराध्यति) उपेक्षा करता है, चूक जाता है। despises, neglects, fails.

अवरोधक – पु॰ – (अवरोधक) रुकावट डालने वाला, बाधक। obstructor.

अवरोधन – न॰ – (अवरोधन) रुकावट, बाधा। obstruction.

अवलक्खण – वि॰ – (अव + लक्षण) कुरूप, कुलक्षणी। ugly, having unlucky signs.

अवलम्बति – क्रि॰ – (अवलम्बते) लटकता है, सहारा लेता है। hangs down, depends on.

अवलम्बन – न॰ – (अवलम्बन) (1) सहारा (2) लटकना (3) शरण। (1) hanging down (2) help (3) refuge.

अवलम्बित – क्रि॰ वि॰ – (अवलम्बित) hung, suspended.

अवलिखति – क्रि॰ – (अव + लिखति) काट-छाँट करता है, टुकड़े-टुकड़े कर डालता है। scrapes off, cuts into pieces.

अवलिम्पति – क्रि॰ – (अवलिम्पति) लीपता है, लेप करता है। smears with, plasters.

अवलेखन – न॰ – (अवलेखन) खुरचना। scraping off.

अवलेखन-कट्ठ – न॰ – (अवलेखन काष्ठम्) खुरचने हेतु बाँस की खपत्री। bamboo strips used for scraping.

अवलेपन – न॰ – (अवलेपन) लेप। smearing, plastering.

अवलेहन – न॰ – (अव + √लिह) चाटना। licking.

अवस – वि॰ – (अवश) शक्ति-हीन, अशक्त। frail, powerless.

अवसर – पु॰ – (अवसर) मौका। opportunity, chance.

अवसरति – क्रि॰ – (अव + √सृ = अवसरति) चल देता है, पहुँच जाता है। ventures, arrives.

अवसान – न॰ – (अवसान) अन्त, विराम, समाप्ति। the end, conclusion, cessation.

अवसिञ्चति – क्रि॰ – (अव + √सिञ्च्) सींचता है। waters, pours over, sprinkles.

अवसिट्ठ – क्रि॰ वि॰ – (अवशिष्ट) बचा हुआ, अवशेष। remaining, left over.

अवसिस्सति – क्रि॰ – (अवशिष्यते) बाकी बचता है। remains over.

अवसुस्सति – क्रि॰ – (अव शुष्यति) सूख जाता है। dries up, withers.

अवसुस्सन – न॰ – (अवशुष्यन) सूखना। drying up, withering.

अवसेस (1) – न॰ – (अवशेष) बाकी। remainder.

अवसेस (2) – वि॰ – (अवशेष) बचा हुआ। remaining.

अवसेसक – न॰ – (अवशेषक) बचा हुआ। that which is left-over, remainder.

अवस्सं – क्रि॰ वि॰ – (अवश्यम्) अनिवार्य तौर पर। inevitably, unavoidably.

अवस्सय – पु॰ – (उपाश्रय) आश्रय, सहारा। support, help.

अवस्सावन – न॰ – (अव + √सु = अवस्रावण) छानना। to filter, to sieve.

अवस्सित – क्रि॰ वि॰ – (आश्रित) आधारित। based, dependent.

अवस्सुत – क्रि॰ वि॰ – (अव + √स्रु + क्त) (1) चूने वाला, स्राव-युक्त (2) तृष्णा-युक्त। (1) leaking (2) lustful greedy.

अवहरण – न॰ – (अपहरण) चोरी, अपहरण। theft, abduction.

अवहरति – क्रि॰ – (अव + √हृ = अवहरति) चुराता है। steals, takes away.

अवहसति – (अवहसति) उपहास करता है, मुँह चिढ़ाता है। derides, laughs at.

अवहीयति – क्रि॰ –(अव + हीयते) पीछे छूट जाता है। stays behind.

अवन्ति – बुद्ध के समय के 16 जनपदों में से एक जिसकी राजधानी उज्जयिनी थी। one of the 16 states during Buddha's time, Ujjayinī was its capital.

आवाट – पु॰ – (अवटः) गर्त्त, गड्ढा, गड़ढ़ा। pit, cave.

अवापुरण – न॰ – (कुञ्चिका) चाबी, चाभी। key.

अवापुरति – क्रि॰ – (अव + आ √पूर्) (दरवाजा) खोलता है। opens the door.

अवारिय-जातक – (जा॰ सं॰ **379**) – बोधिसत्व द्वारा उपदिष्ट एक मूर्ख नाविक की कथा। the Jātaka tale (No. 379) relating to a foolish boatman.

अविकम्पी – पु॰ – (अ + वि + कम्पी) स्थिर चित्त, अविचलित मन वाला। calm, steady, composed.

अविक्खेप – पु॰ – (अ + विक्षेप) मानसिक सन्तुलन, शान्ति, विक्षेप का अभाव। calmness, balance of mind.

अविग्गह – पु॰ – (अविग्रह) अशरीरी, अनंग, कामदेव। bodyless, the god of love (in cupid mythology).

अविज्जमान – वि॰ – (अविद्य्‌मान) अविद्यमान। not existing.

अविज्जा – स्त्री॰ – (अविद्या) अविद्या। ignorance.

अविञ्ञाणक – वि॰ – (अ + संज्ञक) चेतना-रहित, संज्ञा-शून्य। senseless, unconscious.

अविञ्ञात – वि॰ – (अ + वि + ज्ञात) अज्ञात, अपरिचित। unknown, unfamiliar.

अवितथ – न॰ – (अवितथ) सत्य, यथार्थ। true, fact.

अविदित – वि॰ – (अविदित) अज्ञात। unknown.

अविदूर – वि॰ – (अ + वि + दूरे) समीप, बहुत दूर नहीं। not too far, near.

अविदूरे-निदान – तुषित देव-लोक से च्युत होकर बोधि-वृक्ष के नीचे बुद्धत्व प्राप्त करने तक का गौतम चरित्र अविदूरे-निदान कहलाता है। the story of Siddhārtha related to his descending from Tuṣita heaven up to his enlightenment.

अविद्दसु – पु॰ – (अविद्य्‌आसु) मूर्ख। a fool.

अविनासक – वि॰ – (अविनाशक) नाश न करने वाला। not causing destruction.

अविनासी – पु० – (अविनाशी) विनष्ट न होने वाला। imperishable.

अविनिब्भोग – वि० – (अ + वि + निर + भाज्य) अस्पष्ट, विभाजित या पृथक् करने के अयोग्य। indistinct, which cannot be separated.

अविनीत – वि० – (अ + विनीत) जो विनम्र नहीं। impolite, indisciplined.

अविप्पवास – पु० – (अ + वि + प्रवास) उपस्थिति, वियोग-शून्यता। non-separation.

अविभूत – वि० – (अविभूत) अस्पष्ट। indistinct.

अविरत – न० – (अविरत) लगातार। continuously, ceaselessly.

अविरुद्ध – वि० – (अविरुद्ध) अविरोधी, अनुकूल। non-contrary, favourable.

अविरूळिह – स्त्री० – (अविरूढ) वृद्धि का अभाव, पुनर्जन्म का अभाव। non-growth, cessation of rebirth.

अविरोध – पु० – (अविरोध) विरोध का अभाव। non-opposition.

अविलम्बितम् – क्रि० वि० – (अविलम्बितम्) द्रुत, सत्वर, शीघ्र। quickly, without delay, fast.

अविवाह्य – वि० – (अविवाह्य) जो विवाह योग्य न हो। unfit to be married.

अविसंवाद – पु० – (अविसंवाद) सत्य। truth.

अविसंवादक – वि० – (अविसंवादक) वंचना न करने वाला, झूठ न बोलने वाला। one who does not tell a lie, one who speeks truth.

अविसग्गता – स्त्री० – (अविसर्गता) चित्त की स्थिरता, शान्त-चित्त होना। calmness of mind.

अविस्सासनिय – वि० – (अविश्वसनीय) अविश्वसनीय। unfaithful, unreliable.

अविहित – वि० – (अविहित) अकृत, जो कभी किया नहीं गया हो। not performed before.

अविहिंसा – स्त्री० – (अ + वि + हिंसा) हिंसा का अभाव, दया। compassion, absence of cruelty.

अविहेठक – वि० – कष्ट न देने वाला, हैरान न करने वाला। not hurting or harassing.

अवीचि – वि० – (अ + वीचि) बिना लहर के। waveless.

अवीचि – स्त्री० – (अवीचि) नरक-विशेष। name of a hell.

अवीतिक्कम – पु० – (अ + व्यतिक्रम) नियम के व्यतिक्रम का अभाव, नियमों का अनुपालन। non-transgression.

अवीर – वि० – (अ + वीरः) कापुरुष, डरपोक, कायर। timid, a coward.

अबुट्ठिक – वि० – (अवृष्टिक) वर्षा का अभाव। rainless.

अवेक्खति – क्रिया – (अवेक्षते) देखता है, विचार करता है। looks at, considers, ponders over.

अवेच्च – पूर्व क्रि० – (अव + √इ + ल्यप्) जानकारी करके। having known.

अवेच्चपसाद – पु० –(अवेत्य + प्रसाद) दृढ़, श्रद्धा। perfect faith, intense reverence.

अवेभंगिक – वि० – (अविभजनीय) जो बाँटा न जा सके। which connot be distributed, indivisible.

अवेर – न॰ – (अवैर) अबैर, निर्बैरता। friendship, non-enmity.

अवेरी – वि॰ – (अ + वैरी) शत्रुता-रहित, मैत्रीपूर्ण। free from enmity, friendly.

अवेला – स्त्री॰ – (अ + वेला) अनुचित समय। improper time.

अव्यत्त – वि॰ – (अव्यक्त) (1) अव्यक्त (2) अपण्डित। (1) not manifest (2) not learned.

अव्यय – न॰ – (अव्यय) (1) सभी वचनों- विभक्तियों, पुरुषों में एकरूप रहने वाला शब्द (2) हानि का अभाव। (1) indeclinable particle, (2) imperishable, economical.

अव्ययेन – क्रि॰ वि॰ – (अव्ययेन) बिना किसी खर्च के। without any expenditure.

अव्ययी भाव – वह सामासिक पद जिसका पूर्व पद अव्यय हो। the compound (in grammar) the first part of which is indeclinable as its unit.

अव्याकत – वि॰ – (अव्याकृत) अव्याख्यात, जिसकी व्याख्या नहीं की गयी। unexplained, not designated.

अव्यापज्झ – वि॰ – (अ + व्यापाद्य) रोष- रहित, दुःख-रहित। free from oppression or suffering.

अव्यापाद – वि॰ – (अ + व्यापाद) ईर्ष्या- रहित, पर-द्रोह चिन्तन का अभाव। not thinking ill of others.

अव्यावट – वि॰ – (अ + व्यावृत) असंलग्न। not engaged.

अव्हय – पु॰ – (आह्वय) नाम। name, appellation.

अव्हयति – क्रि॰ – (आह्वयति) पुकारता, बुलाता है। calls.

अव्हात – क्रि॰ वि॰ – (आहूत) बुलाया गया। summoned, called-upon, invited.

अव्हान – न॰ – (आह्वान) आवाहन, बुलावा। call, invitation.

असंवर – न॰ – (अ + संवर) असंयम। unrestrainment, uncontrolled.

√ अस-ज्यादि – (खादने) खाना। to eat.

√ अस-दिवादि – (क्षेपणे) फेंकना। to throw.

√ अस-भ्वादि – (भुवि-विध्यर्थे) होना। to be.

असकिं – क्रि॰ वि॰ – (असकृत) एक बार से अधिक। more than once.

असक्क – वि॰ – (असक्य) असमर्थ। unable, incapable, incompetent.

असंकिण्ण – वि॰ – (असंकीर्ण) असंकीर्ण, बिना मिलावट के। unmixed, not crowded.

असंकिय-जातक – (जा॰ सं॰ 76) (अशङ्की जातक) बोधिसत्व की जागरूकता के कारण डाकू व्यापारियों को न लूट सकें। the Jātaka tale (No. 76) relating to an incident which prevented robbers from plundering merchants due to watchfulness of Bodhisattva.

असंकिलिट्ठ – वि॰ – (अ + सम् + क्लिष्ट) अलिप्त। non stained.

असंखत धातु – स्त्री॰ – (असंस्कृत धातु) असंस्कृत धातु। the unpurified state.

असंखेय्य – वि॰ – (असंख्य) अगणित। innumerable, incalculable.

असङ्ग – पु॰ – (असङ्ग) निरासक्त, आसक्ति-रहित। non-attached.

असच्च – पु॰ – (असत्य) असत्य। false, untrue.

असज्जमान – वि॰ – (असज्जमान) अनासक्त। non-clinging to.

असञ्ञी – वि॰ – (अ + संज्ञा) चेतना-रहित। unconscious.

असञ्ञत – वि॰ – (असंयत) संयम-रहित. unrestrained.

असठ – वि॰ – (अ + शठ) जो शठ नहीं, अदुष्ट। not fraudulent/wicked.

असण्ठित – वि॰ – (अ + संस्थित) चंचल, अस्थिर। not firm, unsettled.

असति – क्रि॰ – (अश्नाति) खाता है। eats.

असति-अधिकरण – (अ + सति) न होने पर। in the absence of.

असतिया -- क्रि॰ वि॰ – अनजाने। unintentionally, without knowledge.

असत्त – वि॰ – (अ + सक्त) अनासक्त। detached.

असत्थ – वि॰ – (अशस्त्र) शस्त्र-रहित। without weapons.

असदिस – वि॰ – (असदृश) असदृश, अनुपम। matchless, marvellous.

असदिस जातक – (जा॰ सं॰ 118) – असदिस राजकुमार की कथा। the Jātak tale (No. 118) related to the prince Asadisa.

असद्धम्म – पु॰ – (अ + सद्धर्म) (1) अधर्म (2) मैथुन। (1) misconduct, sin (2) sexual intercourse.

असन – नपुं॰ – (अशन) (1) भोजन (2) तीर (3) पत्थर। (1) food (2) an arrow (3) a stone.

असनि – स्त्री॰ – (अशनि) वज्र। thunderbolt.

असनि-पात – पु॰ – (अशनि–पात) व्रजपात। falling of thunderbolt.

असन्त – वि॰ – (असन्त) अस्तित्वहीन, दुष्ट। not existing, the wicked.

असन्तासी – वि॰ – (असन्तासी) निर्भय। fearless, unoppressed.

असंतुट्ठ – वि॰ – (असन्तुष्ट) असंतुष्ट, अप्रसन्न। unsatisfied, unhappy.

असंथव – नपु॰ – (अ + संस्तव) समाज से अलग रहना। separation from society.

असंतुट्टि – स्त्री॰ (असन्तुष्टि) असन्तोष, अप्रसन्नता। displeasure, unhappiness.

असंधिता – स्त्री॰ – (अ + सन्धिता) संधि का अभाव। disconnected state.

असंधिमित्ता – स्त्री॰ – (असन्धिमित्रा) अशोक की पटरानी। emperor Aśoka's principal queen.

असपत्त – वि॰ – (असपत्र) अजातशत्रु, शत्रु-विहीन। having no enemy.

असपपुरिस – पु॰ – (असत्पुरुष) दुष्ट व्यक्ति। wicked person.

असबल – वि॰ – (अ + शबल) बिना धब्बे या चित्ती के। spotless.

असब्भ – वि॰ – (असभ्य) असभ्य। जो सभा के योग्य न हो। uncivilized, vile.

असम – वि॰ – (असम) जो समतल नहीं, अप्रतिम। unequal, matchless.

असमान – वि॰ – (असमान) अप्रतिम। unequal.

असमाहित – वि॰ – (अ + समाहित) जिसका चित्त एकाग्र नहीं। not concentrated.

असमेक्खकारी – पु॰ – (असमीक्ष्यकारी)

जल्दबाज, बिना विचारे काम करने वाला। a hasty person.

असमोसरण – न॰ – (असमवसरण) न मिलना। lack of meetings.

असम्पकम्पिय – वि॰ – (असम् + प्रकम्य) कम्पन-रहित, भय-रहित। not to be shaken, fearless.

असम्पजञ्ञ – नपुं॰ – (असंप्रज्ञता) ज्ञान के अभाव की स्थिति। state of ignorance.

असम्पत्त – वि॰ – (अ + सम्प्राप्त) अप्राप्त। not arrived or gained.

असम्पदान-जातक – (जा॰ सं॰ 131) (असम्प्रदान जातकम्) अस्सी करोड़ के स्वामी संख नामक सेठ की कथा। the Jātaka tale related to Saṅkha-seṭṭhi having wealth of 80 crore.

असम्मूळ्ढ – वि॰ – (असंमूढ) जो मूढ़ नहीं। absence of confusion.

असम्मोस – पु॰ – (असंमोह) मोह या मूढ़ता का अभाव। one who is not self-restrained.

असयंवसी – वि॰ – (अस्वयंवशी) जिसका अपने आप पर वश न हो। one who is not self-restrained.

असय्ह – वि॰ – (असह्य) जो सहन न किया जा सके। unbearable.

असरण – वि॰ – (अशरण) जिसके लिए कोई शरण नहीं। helpless, having no shelter.

असहाय – वि॰ – (असहाय) अकेला, जिसका कोई सहायक नहीं। alone, having none to help.

असंवास – वि॰ – (अ + संवास) सहवास के अयोग्य। unfit to associate.

असंवुत – क्रि॰ वि॰ – (असंवृत्त)

आनाच्छादित, जो बन्द नहीं। not covered, unrestricted.

असंसट्ठ – वि॰ – (असंसृष्ट) मिलावट-रहित, अमिश्रित। unmixed.

असंहारिम – वि॰ – (असंहार्य) जिसे हिलाया न जा सके। immovable, unshakable.

असात – वि॰ – (असाध्य) प्रतिकूल। जिसे अनुकूल न किया जा सके। which cannot be favourable, against.

असात-मन्त्र-जातक – न॰ – (जा॰ सं॰ 61) माँ की आज्ञानुसार तरुण ब्राह्मण ने बोधिसत्त्व से अष्ट मंत्र सीखे। the Jātaka tale (No. 61) related to the story of a young brāhmaṇa who inspired by his mother learnt *aṣṭa mantra*.

असातरूप-जातक – (जा॰ सं॰ 100) – (असातरूप जातकम्) कोशल-नरेश तथा काशी-नरेश के परस्पर युद्ध करने की कथा। the Jātaka tale (No. 100) related to the war between kings of Kośal and Kāśī.

असाद – वि॰ – (अस्वादु) अस्वादिष्ट। unpalatable.

असार – वि॰ – (असार) सारहीन। worthless.

असारद्ध – वि॰ – (असंरब्ध) अनुत्तेजित। non-excited, cool.

असाहस – वि॰ – (अ + साहस) दुस्साहस का अभाव, कायर। not violent, timid, meek.

असि – पु॰ – (असि) तलवार। sword.

असिग्गाहक – (असि-ग्राहक) तलवारधारी, कृपाणधारी। sword-bearer.

असि-चम्म – न॰ – (असि-चर्म) ढाल। sword shield.

असि-धारा – स्त्री॰ – (असि धारा) तलवार की धार। the edge of a sword.

असि-पत्त – न॰ – (असिपत्र) तलवार की फाल। blade of sword.

असित – वि॰ – (अशित) भोजन। food.

असित – वि॰ – (असित) काला, अश्वेत। not white, black, wicked.

असित – पु॰ – (असित) शुद्धोदन का काल-देवल नामक राजगुरु। the royal priest of king Śuddhodana.

असिताभु-जातक – (जा॰ सं॰ 234) – (असिताभु जातकम्) राजा ने राजकुमार तथा उनकी भार्या असिताभु को देश निकाला दिया की जातक कथा। the jātaka tale(No. 234) in which the king expelled the prince and his wife Asitābhu, from the kingdom.

असिलक्खण-जातक – (जा॰ सं॰ 126) – (असिलक्षण जातक) तलवार को सूँघकर उसके भाग्य सम्पन्न होने न होने की बात बताने वाले ब्राह्मण की जातक कथा। the Jātaka tale (No. 126) of a brāhmaṇa who could tell by smelling swords whether they are lucky or unlucky.

असिथिल – वि॰ – (अशिथिल) जो ढीला नहीं, सुदृढ़। stiff, not loose.

असिनिद्ध – वि॰ – (अस्निग्ध) जो चिकना न हो, खुरदरा। having rough surface.

असीति – स्त्री॰ – (अशीति) अस्सी। eighty.

असीतिम – वि॰ – (अशीतितमः) अस्सीवां। eightieth.

असु – वि॰ – (असु) अमुक, फलां-फलां। such and such, any person referred to without naming.

असुचि – पु॰ – (अशुचि) गंदगी, वीर्य, विष्ठा। dirt, semen, dung, excreta.

असुद्ध – वि॰ – (अशुद्ध) अशुद्ध, अस्वच्छ। impure, unclean.

असुर – पु॰ – (असुर) देवताओं के विरोधी असुर। a demon.

असूर – वि॰ – (अ + शूर) कायर। a coward, a sluggish person.

असेख – वि॰ – (अशैक्ष्य) जिसे अब शिक्षा-दीक्षा की आवश्यकता नहीं, अर्हत्। one who does not need further education or training, an *arhanta*.

असेचनक – पु॰ – (आ + सेचनक) सन्तोष-प्रद, रूचिकर। delicious in itself.

असेवना – स्त्री॰ – (असेवना) नारी-संगति न करना। non-association with woman.

असेस – वि॰ – (अशेष) सम्पूर्ण। entire, complete.

असोक – वि॰ – (अशोक) शोक-रहित। free from sorrow.

असोक – पु॰ – (अशोक) वृक्ष-विशेष। a kind of tree, *Jonesia Asoka*.

असोक – पु॰ – (अशोक) बिन्दुसार नरेश का पुत्र मगध नरेश अशोक। Aśoka the great, the emperor of Magadha.

असोकाराम – पु॰ – (अशोकाराम) पाटलि-पुत्र, एक प्रसिद्ध विहार। a famous ancient monastery situated in Pāṭaliputra.

असोभन – वि॰ – (अशोभन) अशोभनीय, कुरूप। ugly, not befitting.

अस्नाति – क्रि॰ – (अश्नाति) खाता है। eats.

अस्मा – पु॰ – (अश्मन्) पत्थर। stone.

अस्मि – क्रि॰ – (अस्मि) (मैं) हूँ। (I) am.

अस्मिमान – पु॰ – (अस्मिमान) अहंकार। ego.

अस्स – पु॰ – (अश्व) घोड़ा। horse.

अस्सतर – पु॰ – (अश्वतर) खच्चर। mule.

अस्स-पोतक – पु॰ – (अश्वपोतक) बछेड़ा। a colt or foal.

अस्स-मण्डल – न॰ – (अश्वमण्डल) घुड़-दौड़ की भूमि। race-course for horse.

अस्स-मेध – पु॰ – (अश्वमेध) अश्वमेध यज्ञ। an ancient horse sacrifice.

अस्स-वाणिज – पु॰ – (अश्व-वाणिक्) घोड़ों का व्यापारी। horse dealers.

अस्स-सेना – स्त्री॰ – (अश्व-सेना) घुड़सवार सेना। cavalry.

अस्साजानिय – पु॰ – (अश्वाजानीय) अच्छी नस्ल का घोड़ा। a horse of good breed.

अस्सक – वि॰ – (अ + रचक) दरिद्र, जिसका अपना कुछ भी धन न हो। a penniless person, a pauper

अस्सक-जातक – (जा॰ सं॰ 207) – (अश्वक जातकम्) अस्सक नरेश की कथा। the Jātaka tale (No. 207) related to king Assaka.

अस्सकण्ण – पु॰ – (अश्व कर्ण) (1) साल वृक्ष, (2) पर्वत विशेष। (1) sāl tree (2) name of mountain.

अस्सत्थ – पु॰ – (अश्वत्थ) पीपल का पेड़, बोधि वृक्ष। the holy fig tree, Ficus religiosa.

अस्सद्ध – वि॰ – (अश्रद्ध) अश्रद्धावान्। faith-less, non-reverent.

अस्सम – पु॰ – (आश्रम) आश्रम। hermitage.

अस्समण – पु॰ – (अश्रमण) जो श्रमण नहीं, ढोंगी भिक्षु। a bogus monk.

अस्सयुज – पु॰ – (आश्विन) असौच, या क्वार का महीना। name of a month, i.e., Āśvina.

अस्सव – पु॰ – (आ + श्राव) मवाद। pus.

अस्सव – पु॰ – (आश्रवः) स्वामि-भक्त। loyal, a loyal person.

अस्सवणता – स्त्री॰ – (अश्रवणता) ध्यान न देना। paying no attention, careless.

अस्सवनीय – वि॰ – (अश्रवणीय) जिसे सुनना रुचिकर न लगे। not pleasant to hear.

अस्ससति – क्रि॰ – (आ + श्वसति) श्वास लेता है। breathes, inhales.

अस्साद – पु॰ – (आस्वाद) भोग, आस्वाद। taste, enjoyment.

अस्सादेति – क्रि॰ – (आस्वादयति) स्वाद लेता है। enjoys.

अस्सास – पु॰ – (आश्वास) (1) श्वास भरना (2) निश्चिन्तता। (1) inhalation (2) consolation.

अस्सासक – वि॰ – (आश्वासक) आश्वासन या सान्त्वना देने वाला। that which gives comforts or brings consolation.

अस्सासेति – क्रि॰ – (आश्वासयति) आश्वस्त करता है। consoles, assures.

अस्सु – न॰ – (अश्रु) अश्रु, आँसु। tears.

अस्सुत – वि॰ – (अश्रुतम) अश्रुत, जो सुना नहीं गया। unheard of.

अस्सुतवन्त – वि॰ – (अ + श्रुतवान) अज्ञानी। ignorant, one who is not learned.

अहन्न – (अहन्) दिन। day.

अहं – सर्वनाम – (अहम्) मैं। I.

अहंकार – पु॰ – (अहङ्कार) अभिमान। egotism.

अहारिय – वि॰ – (अ + हरणीय) अचल। immovable.

अहि – पु॰ -- (अहि) सर्प। snake, serpent.

अहि-गुण्ठिक – पु॰ – (अहि-गुण्ठिक) सँपेरा। snake-charmer.

अहिच्छत्रक – पु॰ – (अहिक्षत्रक) खुम्भी। mushroom.

अहि-फेण – न॰ – (अहि-फेन) अफीम। opium.

अहिगुण्डिक-जातक – (जा॰ सं॰ 365) – (अहिगुण्डिक जातकम्) बनारस के एक सँपेरे की जातक कथा। the Jātaka tale (No. 306) related to a snake-charmer of Vārānasī.

अहिरिक – वि॰ – (अ + ह्रीकः) लज्जा-रहित। shameless.

अहिवातक रोग – पु॰ – (अहिवातक व्याधिः) प्लेग नामक महामारी। buboenic plague.

अहीनिन्द्रिय – वि॰ – (अ + हीन + इन्द्रिय) जिसकी सभी इन्द्रियां सम्पूर्ण कार्यक्षम हों। one whose all sense-organs are functioning properly.

अहुहालिय – न॰ – (दन्ताविदंसक महाहसित) अतिशय ऊँची हँसी। loud laughter.

अहेतुक – वि॰ – (अहेतुक) बिना हेतु के। without any motive, causeless.

अहो – अव्यय – (अहो!) आश्चर्य-बोधक शब्द। An interjection signifying exclamation.

अहोगङ्ग – पु॰ – (अहोगङ्ग) उत्तर भारत का एक पर्वत। a mountain of north India.

अहोरत्त – न॰ – (अहोरात्रम्) दिन-रात। day-and-night.

अहोसि – क्रि॰ – (अभूत / आसीत्) वह था। he was.

अहोसिकम्म – न॰ – (निष्फलीभूत कर्म) वह विचार, कर्म, जो अब फलीभूत न होगा। an act or thought which has no longer any potential force.

अंस – पु॰ – (अंश) भाग, हिस्सा। part (of).

असं – न॰ – (असं) कन्धा, स्कन्ध। shoulder.

अंस-कूट – न॰ – (असं-कूट) कन्धा। shoulder.

असं-बन्धन – न॰ – (असं-बन्धन) कन्धे का पटुका। shoulder strap.

अंसु – पु॰ – (अंशु) किरण। ray of light.

अंसुक – न॰ – (अंशुक) वस्त्र। fine cloth.

अंसुमाली – पु॰ – (अंशुमाली) सूर्य। the sun.

आ

आ (1) – पालि एवं देवनागरी लिपि का दूसरा स्वर 'अ' का दीर्घ रूप। the second vowel of Devanāgarī and Pāli, long form of 'a' as in far.

आ (2) – उपसर्ग, संयुक्त व्यंजन के पूर्व आ ह्रस्व 'अ' हो जाता है। जैसे आ + क्रोशति – अक्कोसति। a prefix, ā is shortened before double consonant as ā + krośati = akkosati.

आकङ्क्षति – क्रि॰ – (आ + √काङ्क्ष = आकांक्षते) आकांक्षा या इच्छा करता है। longs for, desires.

आकङ्खा – स्त्री॰ – (आकांक्षा) आकांक्षा, इच्छा। longing, desires.

आकड्ढति – क्रि॰ – (आ + √कृष) खींचता है। pulls, draws.

आकड्ढन – न॰ – (आ + कर्षण) खींचना। pulling, dragging, drawing.

आकप्प – पु॰ – (आ + कल्प) (1) वेशभूषा, (2) चाल-ढाल (1) dress (2) deportment.

आकप्प-सम्पन्न – वि॰ – (आकल्प सम्पन्न) सदाचारयुक्त। of good conduct.

आकम्पित – कृद॰ – (आ + √कम्प् + त = आकम्पित) काँपता हुआ, भीत, त्रस्त। shaken, trembling.

आकर – पु॰ – (आकर) उत्पत्ति-स्थान, खान (सोने-चाँदी की)। a mine, a multitude.

आकस्सति – क्रि॰ – (आ + कर्षति) खींचता है, आकर्षित करता है। drags, pulls, draws, attracts.

आकार – पु॰ – (आकार) आकृति, स्थिति, शक्ल, बनावट। form, shape, figure, appearance.

आकास – पु॰ – (आकाश) आकाश। the sky.

आकास-गङ्गा – स्त्री॰ – (आकाश-गङ्गा) आकाश गङ्गा, क्षीरायण। milky-way, the celestial river.

आकास-चारी – वि॰ – (आकाश-चारी) आकाशचारिन्, आकाश में विचरण करने वाला। a sky wanderer, a wanderer in the sky, a celestial being.

आकासट्ठ – वि॰ – (आकास्थ) आकाश में विद्यमान, आकाश-स्थित। situated or living in sky, sky-borne.

आकासतल – न॰ – (आकाश-तल) किसी मकान की छत। flat roof of a building.

आकास-धातु – स्त्री॰ – (आकाश-धातु) ईथर। ether, shee beyond clouds.

आकिञ्चञ्ञ – न॰ – (अकिञ्चन्य) अकिंचनता, कुछ नहीं की अवस्था। nothingness, absence of any possession.

आकिण्ण – (आकीर्ण) प्रकीर्ण, भीड़ युक्त। strewed, crowded, full of.

आकिरति – क्रि॰ – (आ + √कृ = आकिरति) फैला देता है, बिखेर देता है। scatters, strews over.

आकुल – वि॰ – (आकुल) विक्षुब्ध, उलझा हुआ। agitated, confused.

आकोटन – न॰ – (आ + √ क्रुष्ट) चिल्लाना, खटखटाना। to shout, to knock, a harsh cry or sound.

आखु – पु॰ – (आखु) मूषक। rat, mouse.

आख्या – स्त्री॰ – (आख्या) नाम, संज्ञा। name.

आख्यात (1) – त्रिलिङ्गी – (आ + √ ख्या + क्त = आख्यात) कहा हुआ, बताया हुआ, प्रकटित। narrated, predicated.

आख्यात (2) – धातु। verb.

आख्यायिका – स्त्री॰ – (आख्यायिका) सत्य घटना पर आधारित कहानी। short narration, a true story.

आगच्छति – क्रि॰ – (आ + √ गम् = आगच्छति) आता है। comes to, approaches.

आगन्तु – वि॰ – (आगन्ता) आने वाला। one who is coming.

आगन्तुक – पु॰ – (आगन्तुक) अतिथि, पाहुन, अभ्यागत। guest, newcomer, stranger.

आगत -- कृदन्त – (आ + √ गम् + क्त = आगत) आया हुआ। come (past participle).

आगम – पु॰ – (आगम) (1) आना (2) धर्म, धर्म-ग्रन्थ (3) मित्र की तरह आकर दो अक्षरों के बीच में बैठ जाने वाला तीसरा व्यञ्जन (1) coming, approach (2) religion, scripture (3) an inserted consonant.

आगमन – न॰ – (आगमन) आना। coming, arrival.

आगमेति – क्रि॰ – (आ + गमयति) प्रतीक्षा करता है। expects, waits for.

आगम्म – पूर्व क्रि॰ – (आ + √ गम् + ल्यप् = आगम्य) पहुँचकर, आकर। having come, owing to.

आगामिक – (आगामिक) आने वाला। expected to come.

आगामी – वि॰ – (आगामी) आने वाला। coming in future, impending.

आगामीकाल – पु॰ – (आगामी काल) भविष्य। future.

आगारक-आगारिक – वि॰ – (आगारक / आगारिक) आगार अर्थात् घरवाला। {भण्डागारिक, खजानची}। storekeeper, treasurer.

आगाळह – वि॰ – (आ + गाढ) अत्यन्त गाढ, प्रगाढ, मजबूत, कठोर। strong, rough, tight, intense.

आगलायति – क्रि॰ – (आ + √ ग्ला = आग्लायति) पीड़ा देता है। gives troubles.

आगु – न॰ – (वैदिक संस्कृत – आगस्) दोष, अपराध। guilt, offence.

आगुचारी – पु॰ – (अघचारी) अपराधी। criminal, a villain.

आघात – पु॰ – (आघात) प्रहार, चोट, रगड़। striking, blow, stroke.

आघातन – न॰ – (आघातन) यातनागृह, कसाईखाना। a place of execution, a slaughter house, an abattoir.

आचमति – क्रि॰ – (आ + √ चम् = आचमति) आचमन करता है, कुल्ला करता है। ritually sips water, rinses mouth with water.

आचमन – न॰ – (आचमन) आचमन, कुल्ला। act of ritual sipping of water, rinsing.

आचमन-कुम्भी – स्त्री॰ – (आचमन-कुम्भी) आचमन पात्र, मुँह धोने का पात्र। used in pitcher for ritual sipping.

आचय – पु॰ – (आचय) संचय, संग्रह, बहुता-यत। collection, accumulation, plenty.

आचरति – क्रि॰ – (आ + चरति) आचरण करता है। practises, performs.

आचरिय – पु॰ – (आचार्य) सदाचार की शिक्षा देने वाला, आचार्य, शिक्षक। one who teaches the rules of conduct, preacher.

आचरिय-कुल – (आचार्य-कुल) गुरुकुल, आचार्य कुल। the family or the abode of teacher.

आचरिय-धन – न॰ – (आचार्य-धन) गुरु-दक्षिणा, आचार्य को दी जाने वाली फीस। fee given to a teacher.

आचरिय-मुट्ठि – स्त्री॰ – (आचार्य-मुष्टिः) आचार्य का ज्ञान-विशेष। unique specialization attained by a teacher in a particular branch of knowledge.

आचरिय-वाद – पु॰ – (आचार्य-वाद) परम्परागत मत। किसी आचार्य द्वारा प्रवर्तित विशिष्ट सिद्धान्त या सम्प्रदाय। a particular school of thought propounded by a teacher.

आचरियानी – स्त्री॰ – (आचार्यानी) आचार्या अथवा आचार्य की भार्या। a lady teacher or wife of a teacher.

आचाम – पु॰ – (आ + चम् = आचाम) उबलते चावलों का माण्ड या पिच्छा। the scum or impurities from boiling rice.

आचार – पु॰ – (आचार) व्यवहार, आचरण। conduct, behaviour.

आचार-कुसल – वि॰ – (आचार-कुशल) व्यवहार-कुशल, सदाचारयुक्त। well versed in good manners.

आचिक्खक – पु॰ – (आ + चक्ष् + ण्वुल) (आचक्षक) कहने वाला, बताने वाला। one who tells or informs.

आचिक्खति – क्रि॰ – (आचक्ष्यते) कहता है, बताता है। tells, informs.

आचिण्ण – कृदन्त – (आ + √चर् + क्त) आचरित, अभ्यस्त। practised or performed habitually.

आचिण्ण-कप्प – पु॰ – (आचीर्ण-कल्प) आचार-संहिता। code of conduct.

आचित – कृद॰ – (आ + √चि + क्त = आचित) संगृहीत, संकलित। accumulated, collected.

आचिनाति – क्रि॰ – (आ + √चि = अचिनाति) इकट्ठा करता है। accumulates.

आचीयति – क्रि॰ – (आ + √ची + चयने = अचीयति) एकत्रित हो जाता है, ढेर बन जाता है। collects, accumulates.

आचेर – पु॰ – (आचार्य) आचार्य (पालि आचरिय) का संक्षिप्त रूप अध्यापक। teacher who teaches the rules of good conduct.

आजञ्ञ – वि॰ – (आ + जञ्ञ) अच्छी नस्ल का। of good breed.

आजञ्ञ-जातक (1) – (जा॰ सं॰ 24) – बोधिसत्व के श्रेष्ठ नस्ल के घोड़े की योनि में उत्पन्न होने की कथा। the Jātaka tale (No. 24) related to Boddisattva's birth in the horse genus of superior breed.

आजानन – न॰ – (आ √ ज्ञा + ल्युट्) ज्ञान। knowledge.

आजानाति – क्रि॰ – (आ + जानाति) समझता है, जानता है। knows, understands.

आजानीय – पु॰ – (आजानीय) अच्छी नस्ल का घोड़ा। a horse of superior breed.

आजि – स्त्री॰ – (√ अज् - गतौ - आजि) संग्राम, दौड़-प्रतियोगिता, युद्ध। race, contest, fight.

आजीव – पु॰ – (आ + √ जीव् = प्राण धारणे) आजीविका, जीविका का साधन। livelihood.

आजीवक – पु॰ – (अजीवक) निर्वस्त्र रहने वाले तपस्वियों का एक सम्प्रदाय। a sect of non-Buddhist nude ascetics.

आजीवन (1) – न॰ – (आजीवन) आजीविका। livelihood.

आजीवन (2) – न॰ – (आ + जीवनम्) जीवनपर्यन्त। up to the whole life, life-long.

आट – पु॰ – (आटि) शराटि, कुररी, अथवा टिट्टिभ नामक पक्षी। osprey, a fish eating bird.

√ आण – (√ आ + ज्ञा = प्रेषणे) भेजना, आज्ञा देना। to send, to command.

आणा – स्त्री॰ – (आज्ञा) आज्ञा। order, command.

आणा-सम्पन्न – वि॰ – (आज्ञा-सम्पन्न) अधिकृत। authorised.

आणापक – पु॰ – (आज्ञायक) आज्ञा देने वाला। commander.

आणापेति – क्रि॰ – (आज्ञापयति) आज्ञा देता है। orders, commands.

आणि – पु॰ / स्त्री॰ – (आणिः) गाड़ी के धुरे की कील, अक्षकील। axis-bolt.

आणी – स्त्री॰ – (आणी) किल्ली, अर्गला। check-bar, sliding bar of the door.

आतङ्क – पु॰ – (आ + तङ्क + घञ्) व्याधि, वेदना, भय। illness, disease, fear, terror.

आतत – न॰ – (आतत) सँकरे मुँह वाला ढोल जिसमें एक ही ओर चमड़ा मढ़ा होता है। a drum leathered on one face.

आतत-वितत – न॰ – (आतत-वितत = क्षुद्रायतौ पटहौ) आतत-वितत नाम के दोनों प्रकार के ढोल। आतत एक ओर तथा वितत दोनों ओर मढ़ा हुआ ढोल। drum of both kinds.

आततायी – पु॰ – (आततायी) जो वध आदि अत्याचार करने के लिए उद्यत रहे। a murderer, a tyrant, person committing serious crimes.

आतत्त – कृदन्त – (आ + √ तप् + क्त) तप्त, तपाया हुआ। heated, scorched.

आतपत्त – न॰ – (आतप + त्र) आतप से त्राण करने वाला, छाता। an umbrella.

आतप – पु॰ – (आतप) धूप। sun-heat.

आतपाभाव – पु॰ – (आतप + अभाव) धूप का अभाव, छाँव। the lack of sun-heat.

आतपति – क्रि॰ – (आ + √ तप = आतपति) चमकता है। shines.

आतप्त – पु॰ – (आतप्य) प्रयत्न, प्रयास। ardour, exertion.

आताप – पु॰ – (आताप) चमक, गर्मी। glow, heat, ardour.

आतापन – न॰ – (आतापन) काय-क्लेश,

आत्म-पीड़ा। mortification, self-torture.

आतापी – वि० – (आतापी) कष्ट उठाने वाला, परिश्रमशील। ardent, strenuous.

आतापेति – क्रि० – (आ + तापयति) शारीरिक कष्ट देता है। scorches, torments.

आतुमा – पु० – (आतुमा) कुसीनारा तथा श्रावस्ती के बीच का एक नगर। a city between Kusīnārā and Śrāvastī.

आतुर – वि० – (आतुर) व्याधि-ग्रस्त, रोगी। sick, diseased.

आतोज्जं – न० – (आतोद्य - आ + √ तुद् + ल्यप्) बाजा। band, musical instrument.

आदर – पु० – (आदर) मान, गौरव।esteem, regard.

आदाति – क्रि० – (आ √ दा = आदाति) लेता है, ग्रहण करता है। takes, grasps.

आदान – न० – (आदान) ग्रहण करना। taking up, grasping.

आदायी – कृद० – (आदायी) आदाता, ग्रहण करने वाला। receiver, one who takes.

आदास – पु० – (आदर्श) दर्पण, मुँह देखने का शीशा।mirror.

आदास-तल – पु० – (आदर्श-तल) दर्पण-तल, शीशे का तल। surface of a mirror.

आदि – पु० – (आदि) सर्वप्रथम, आरम्भ। starting point, beginning.

आदि-कम्मिक – पु० – (आदि-कार्मिक) आरम्भ करने वाला। beginner.

आदि-कल्याण – वि० – (आदि कल्याणक्)

आरम्भ में कल्याणकारक। beautiful in the beginning.

आदिम – वि० – (आदिम) सर्वप्रथम, पहला। foremost.

आदिच्च – पु० – (आदित्य) सूर्य। the sun.

आदिच्च-पथ – पु० – (आदित्य-पथ) सूर्य-पथ, आकाश। the sky.

आदिच्च-बन्धु – पु० – (आदित्य-बन्धु) सूर्य कुलोत्पन्न, सूर्यवंशी।born in the solar race of kṣatriyas.

आदिच्चुपट्ठान-जातक – (जा० सं० 175) तपस्वियों के आश्रम को नष्ट-भ्रष्ट करने वाले बन्दर की कथा। the Jātaka tale (No. 175) related to a monkey who used to destroy the hermitage of some ascetics.

आदितो – अ० क्रि० वि० – (आदितः) आरम्भ से। from the beginning.

आदित्त – कृदन्त – (आदीप्त) जलता हुआ। burning, blazing.

आदित्त-जातक – (जा० सं० 424) – सोवीर राष्ट्र रोरुव के राजा भरत की कथा। the Jātaka tale (No. 424) related to king Bharat of Sauvīra.

आदिन्न – कृद० – (गृहीत) गृहीत। attained, grasped.

आदियति – क्रि० – (आददाति) ग्रहण करता है। takes, grasps.

आदिसति – क्रि० – (आदिशति) कहता है, घोषणा करता है। points out, announces.

आदिस्स – क्रि० – (आदिश्य) कहकर, घोषणा करके। having pointed out.

आदीनव – पु० – (आ + दीनवता) दुष्परिणाम, विपद। disadvantage, danger.

आदु – अव्यय – (आदु + तु) किन्तु 'या' लेकिन। but.

आदेति – क्रि॰ – (आददाति) लेता है, ग्रहण करता है। takes, grasps.

आदेय्य – वि॰ – (आदेय्य) ग्रहण करने योग्य। fit to be taken up, acceptable.

आदेय्य-वचन – न॰ – (आदेय्य-वचन) स्वागत-वचन। welcome address.

आदेवना – स्त्री॰ – (आदेवना) परिवेदना, रोना-पीटना। lamenting, crying.

आदेस (1) – पु॰ – (आदेश) आदेश। pointing out, order.

आदेस (2) – अक्षर-विशेष के स्थान पर किसी दूसरे व्यञ्जन का शत्रुवत आ बैठना। substitution of alphabets in grammar.

आदेसना – स्त्री॰ – (आदेशना) भविष्यवाणी करना, अनुमान लगाना। prophesying forecasting, guessing.

आधान – न॰ – (आ + √धा + ल्युट्) रखना, स्थापित करना, रखने की जगह। place where to lay or put.

आधान-गाही – पु॰ – (आधान-ग्राही) हठी, दुराग्रही। obstinate person.

आधार – पु॰ – (आधार) अवलम्ब, सहारा। basis, support, stand.

आधावति – क्रि॰ – (आधावति) दौड़ता है। runs towards.

आधावन – न॰ – (आधावन) दौड़। race, onrush.

आधिपच्च – न॰ – (आधिपत्य) स्वामित्व। ownership, lordship.

आधुनाति – क्रि॰– (आ + √धु = आधुनोति) धुन डालता है, हिला देता है। shakes, removes.

आधूत – कृद॰ – (आ + √धु + क्त) हिलाया गया। shaken.

आधेय्य – वि॰ – (आधेय) धारण करने योग्य। fit to be worn, wearable.

आन {आण} – न॰ – (आश्वास) ली गयी साँस, आश्वास। breathing, inhalation.

आनक – पु॰ – (आणक) पटह, भेरी नामक वाद्य। a kettledrum, a war drum.

आनण्य – न॰ – (आनृण्यम्) ऋण-मुक्ति। freedom from debt.

आनन – न॰ – (आनन) मुखड़ा, मुँह, चेहरा। face, mouth.

आनन्तरिक – वि॰ – (आनन्तरिक) ठीक बाद में घटने वाला, बिना किसी अन्तर के घटने वाला। immediately following.

आनन्द – पु॰ – (आनन्द) प्रीति, प्रसन्नता। joy, pleasure.

आनन्द – पु॰ – (आनन्द) भगवान् बुद्ध के प्रधान शिष्यों में से एक जिन्होंने अनन्य भाव से भगवान की सेवा की थी। one of the chief disciples of Buddha.

आनन्द-बोधि – पु॰ – (आनन्द बोधिः) जेतवन द्वार पर भिक्षु आनन्द द्वारा रोपा गया बोधि वृक्ष। name of the *pīpal* tree planted by disciple Ānand at the main gate of Jetavana.

आनयति – क्रि॰ – (आनयति) लाता है। brings to.

आनापान – न॰ – (आश्वास-प्रश्वास) भीतर की गयी और बाहर की गयी साँस, आश्वास-प्रश्वास। inhaled and exhaled breath.

आनाय – पु॰ – (आ + √नी + घञ = आनाय) जानवरों के पकड़ने का जाल। net for catching animals.

आनिसंस – वि॰ – (आ + नृशंस) मृदु, कृपालु, दयालु। kind, merciful.

आनिसद – न॰ – (आनिषद) नितम्ब, चूतड़। buttock, hip.

आनीत – कृद॰ – (आ √नी + क्त) लाया हुआ। brought.

आनीयमान – कृदन्त – (आ √नी + शानच्) आनीयमान, लाया जाता है। being brought.

आनुपुब्बी – स्त्री॰ – (आनुपूर्वी) क्रम, अनुक्रमणी। order, table of contents.

आनुभाव – पु॰ – (आनुभाव) प्रभाव, प्रताप, तेज। splendour, power, majesty.

आनेञ्ज – वि॰ – (आ + न √इञ्ज) न हिलने वाला, स्थिर, अचञ्चल। static, imperturbable, immobile.

आनेति – क्रि॰ – (आनयति) लाता है। brings.

आप – पु॰ तथा न॰ – (आपः) जल, पानी। water.

√आप – (√आप - व्याप्तौ) पहुँचना, पाना, जीतना। to reach, to obtain, to win.

आपगा – स्त्री॰ – (आपगा) नदी। river.

आपज्जति – क्रि॰ – (आ √पद् = आपद्यते) पास आता है, में पड़ता है, हो जाता है। approaches, falls into, happens.

आपण – पु॰ – (आपण) बाजार। market.

आपणिक – पु॰ – (आपणिक) व्यापारी, दुकानदार। merchant, shop-keeper.

आपतति – क्रि॰ – (आपतति) गिरता है। falls or rushes on.

आपतन – न॰ – (आपतन) गिरावट। fall.

आपत्ति – स्त्री॰ – (आपत्ति) आपदा, विनय के उल्लंघन का अपराध। getting into, an ecclesiastical offence.

आपदा – स्त्री॰ – (आपदा) दुःख, कष्ट, दुर्भाग्य। misfortune, distress, grief.

आपन्न – कृद॰ – (आ √पद + क्त) गृहीत, अनुप्राप्त, विपन्न। obtained, fallen into distress.

आपन्न-सत्ता – स्त्री॰ – (आपन्न - स्त्वा) प्राप्त सत्त्वा, गर्भिणी। a pregnant woman.

आपाण – न॰ – (आ + प्राण) साँस लेना व छोड़ना, श्वास-प्रश्वास। breathing, exhalation.

आपाण-कोटिक – वि॰ – (आ + प्राण + कोटिक) साँस चलने तक, प्राण रहने तक। up to the end of life.

आपाथ – पु॰ – (आ + पाथ) इन्द्रिय का गोचर क्षेत्र। sphere or range (of sense-organ).

आपाथ-गत – वि॰ – (आपाथ-गत) इन्द्रिय-गोचर होना। perceive through sense-organ.

आपादक – पु॰ – (आपादक) संरक्षक, बच्चे की देख-भाल करने वाला। one who takes care of a child, guardian.

आपादिका – स्त्री॰ – (आपादिका) धाय, धात्री, दाई। nurse, a foster mother.

आपादेति – क्रि॰ – (आपादयति) दूध पिलाती है। nurses.

आपान – न॰ – (आपान–गृह) मद्यपान, पेय-भवन। drinking-hall.

आपानक – वि॰ – (आपानक) पियक्कड़। drunkard.

आपानीय – वि॰ – (आ √पा + अनीयर्) पान करने या पीने योग्य। fit for drinking.

आपानीय-कंस – पु॰ – (आपान–चषक) सुरा-पात्र। drinking-bowl.

आपायिक – वि॰ – (आपायिक) नारकीय। born in or belonging to a state of misery.

आपुच्छति – क्रि॰ – (आ + पृच्छति) पूछता है, अनुज्ञा चाहता है। enquires after, asks permission.

आपुच्छा – स्त्री॰ – (आपृच्छा) अनुज्ञा। becomes full.

आपूरति – क्रि॰ – (आ + √ पूर = आपूर्यते) भरता है, सम्पूर्ण होता है। filling, becomes full.

आपूरण – न॰ – (आपूरण) पूर्ति। becoming full, filling.

आपोधातु – स्त्री॰ – (आपो-धातु) जलीय तत्त्व। the element of cohesion.

आफुसति – क्रि॰ – (आ + स्पृशति) स्पर्श प्राप्त करता है, साक्षात् करता है। feels, attains.

आबद्ध – कृदन्त – (आबद्ध) बँधा हुआ। fastened, bound.

आबन्धक – वि॰ – (आबन्धक) बाँधने वाला। trying, connecting, fixing element.

आबन्धति – क्रि॰ – (आ + बध्नाति) बाँधता है। binds, fastens.

आबाध – पु॰ – (आबाध) व्यथा, रोग। disease, affliction.

आबाधिक – वि॰ – (आबाधिक) पीड़ित रोगी। sick, affected with illness.

आबाधित – कृद॰ – (आबाधित) बाधित, दलित, दबाया हुआ। afflicted, oppressed.

आबाधेति – क्रि॰ – दबाता है, हैरान करता है। oppresses, harasses.

आभत – कृद॰ – (आ + भृत) लाया हुआ। brought, conveyed.

आभरण – न॰ – (आभरण) गहना, अलंकार। ornament, decoration.

आभरति – क्रि॰ – (आभरति) लाता है। brings, conveys.

आभस्सर – वि॰ – (आ + भास्वर) प्रकाशवान। radiant.

आभा – स्त्री॰ – (आभा) द्युति, कान्ति, प्रकाश। light, lustre, radiance.

आभाकर – पु॰ – (आभाकर) भास्कर, सूर्य। sun.

आभास – पु॰ – (आभास) रोशनी। light, lustre, radiance.

आभाति – क्रि॰ – (आभाति) चमकता है। shines, radiates.

आभावेति – क्रि॰ – (आ + भावयति) अभ्यास करता है। practises.

आभिदोसिक – वि॰ – (आभिदोषिक) गत रात्रि से सम्बन्धित। relating to the last evening.

आभिधम्मिक – वि॰ – (अभि + धार्मिकः) अभिधर्म का जानकार। versed in *abhidhamma*.

आभिन्दति – क्रि॰ – (आ + √ भिद् = विदारणे) काटता है। cuts, pierces.

आभिमुख्य – न॰ – (आभिमुख्य) साम्मुख्य, सामने होना। facing, turned towards.

आभिसमाचारिक – न॰ – (आभि + सामाचारिक) छोटे-मोटे कर्त्तव्य। minor duties.

आभिसेकिक – वि॰ – (अभिषेकिक) अभिषेक सम्बन्धी। related to ablution ceremony (ritual bathing).

आभुजति – क्रि॰ – (आ + √ भुज् = कौटिल्ये) झुकाता है। bends, coils.

आभुजन – न॰ – (√भुज् = कौटिल्ये) झुकाना। crouching, bending.

आभुजी – स्त्री॰ – (आभूर्जी, भूर्जिक) भोज-पत्र। birch leaf.

आभोग – पु॰ – (आभोगः) चिन्तन, विचार। ideation, thought.

आम (1) – अव्यय – (आम) स्वीकार बोधक अव्यय, हाँ। yes.

आम (2) – (आम्यके ईषत् पच्यते) जो देर से हज्म हो, मांस। hard in digestion, flesh.

आम/आमक – वि॰ – (आम/आमक) कच्चा, जो पका नहीं। raw.

आम-गन्ध – पु॰ – (आम-गन्ध) कृमिज गन्ध, कच्चे गोश्त की गन्ध, मांस। flesh, verminous odour.

आमगंधि – स्त्री॰ – (आम गंधिः) देखें – आमगन्ध। see Āma-gandha.

आमक-सुसान – न॰ – (आमक-श्मशान) अधजले शवों का श्मशान। grove where half-burnt corpses are thrown to be eaten by wild animals.

आमट्ठ – कृद॰– (आमृष्ट) स्पष्ट, छुआ हुआ, हाथ लगाया हुआ, माजा हुआ। wiped, rubbed.

आमण्ड – पु॰ – (आमण्डः) अंडी या एरण्ड का पौधा। castor plant.

आमण्डलीय – वि॰ – (आमण्डलीय) समूचे प्रशासनिक क्षेत्र अथवा अंचल से सम्बद्ध। belonging to the whole divison or region.

आमत्तिक – न॰ – (मृत्ति का पात्र) मिट्टी का बर्तन। earthernware, crockery.

आमद्दन – न॰ – (आ + मर्दन) पीसना, मीड़ना। crushing.

आमन्तन – न॰ – (आमन्त्रण) बुलावा, निमंत्रण। invitation.

आमन्तित् – कृद॰ – (आमन्त्रित) आहूत, निमंत्रित। called, invited.

आमन्तेति – क्रि॰ – (आ + √मन्तृ = आमन्त्रयति) बुलाता है, निमंत्रित करता है। invites, calls.

आमय – पु॰ – (आमय) व्याधि, रोग। illness.

आमलक – न॰ – (आमलक) आँवला का पेड़ व उसका फल। the tree and fruit of *Emblie Myrobalan*.

आमसति – क्रि॰ – (आमृशति) स्पर्श करता है। touches.

आमसन – न॰ – (आमृशन) स्पर्श करना, मलना। touching, pats.

आमा – स्त्री॰ – (भृत्या, चेटी) दासी। a slave woman.

आमासय – पु॰ – (अमाशय) पेट। stomach.

आमिस (1) – न॰ – (आमिष) शिकार किया गया जीव, माँस। meat, bait, flesh.

आमिस (2) – न॰ – (आमिष) उपयोग्य वस्तु, राज्य। territory.

आमुञ्चति – क्रि॰ – (आमुञ्चति) धारण करता है। puts on, wears.

आमुत्त – कृदन्त – (आमुक्त) सज्जित, आभरण धारण किये हुए। adorned.

आमेण्डन – न॰ – (आम्रेडन) बार-बार घोष करना। repeated announcement.

आमेण्डित – न॰ – (आम्रेडित) उद्घोषित, पुनः-पुनः उद्घोषित। repeatedly announced.

आमो – अव्यय – (आम) हाँ। yes.

आमोद – पु॰ – (आमोद) प्रसन्नता, हर्ष, आनन्द। enjoyment, pleasure.

आमोदति – क्रि॰ – (आ + √मुद्) प्रसन्न होता है, प्रमुदित होता है। enjoys, rejoices.

आमोदना – स्त्री॰ – (आमोदना) मुदित होने वाला अथवा हर्ष की स्थिति। the sense of pleasure, gladness.

आमोदमान – कृदन्त – (आमोदमान) आनन्दित या प्रमुदित होता हुआ। feeling pleasure or gladness.

आमोदेति – क्रि॰ – (आमोदयति) प्रमुदित करता है। entertains, delights, shows pleasure.

आय – पु॰ – (आय) आमदनी, लाभ। income.

आय-कम्मिक – पु॰ – (आय–कार्मिक) कर एकत्र करने वाला। tax collector.

आय-कोसल्ल – न॰ – (आय–कौशल्य) आय-वृद्धि के मामलों में निपुणता। skill in raising income.

आय-मुख – न॰ – (आय–मुख) आयस्रोत, आमदनी का साधन। means of income.

आयत – वि॰ – (आयत) लम्बा, विस्तृत। long, broad, extended.

आयतन – न॰ – (आयतन) क्षेत्र, इन्द्रिय, स्थिति। sphere, region, sense-organ, position.

आयतनिक – वि॰ – (आयतनिक) क्षेत्र-सम्बन्धी। belonging to a region.

आयति – स्त्री॰ – (आयति) उत्तर काल, दीर्घता, भविष्य। following time, length, future.

आयतिक – वि॰ – (आयतिक) भावी। belonging to the future.

आयतिका – स्त्री॰ – (आयतिका) द्रव प्रवाहित करने की नलिका। a tube, water-pipe.

आयत्त – वि॰ – (आयत्त) अधीन, निभृत। possessed, dependent.

आयत्त – न॰ – (आयत्त) स्वामित्व, मिल्कियत। possession.

आयस – वि॰ – (आयस) लोहे का, लौह निर्मित। made of iron.

आयसक्य – न॰ – अगौरव, अपमान। discard.

आयसमन्त – वि॰ – (आयुष्यमान) दीर्घजीवी, आयुष्यमान बुजुर्ग। blessed with longivity, venerable.

आयाग – पु॰ – (आयाग) यज्ञ-सम्बन्धी दान। donation connected with religious sacrifice.

आयाचक – वि॰ – (आयाचक) याची, याचना करने वाला। petitioner, applicant.

आयाचति – क्रि॰ – (आ + याचते) याचना करता है, प्रार्थना करता है। request, implores.

आयाचना – स्त्री॰ – (आयाचना) याचना, माँग, प्रार्थना। request, petition, application.

आयाचमान – कृदन्त – (आयाचमान) प्रार्थना करते हुए, याचना करते हुए। imploring.

आयाचिका – स्त्री॰ – (आयाचिका) याचना करने वाली स्त्री। lady petitioner, lady implorer.

आयाचितभत्त-जातक – (जा॰ सं॰ 19) वृक्ष देवता ने पशु हत्या की निन्दा की। the Jātaka tale (No. 19) related to the story of the deity of a banyan tree who condemend the slaughter of animals in religious sacrifice.

आयात – कृद॰ – (आयात) आगत। has/ have come.

आयाति – क्रि॰ – (आयाति) आता है। comes, approaches.

आयाम – पु॰ – (आयाम) फैलाव (लम्बाई-चौड़ाई-ऊँचाई)। dimension.

आयास – पु॰ – (आयास) कष्ट, परेशानी। trouble, sorrow.

आयु – न॰ –(आयु) जीने की अवधि, उम्र। age.

आयुक – वि॰ – (आयुक) लम्बी आयु वाला। blessed with longevity.

आयु-कप्प – पु॰ – (आयु–कल्प) आजीवन, जीवन भर। duration of life.

आयु-क्खय – पु॰ – (आयु–क्षय) आयु का क्षय। consumption of life.

आयु-सङ्खय – पु॰ – (आयु–संक्षय) आयु-समाप्ति। exhaustion of life, end of life.

आयु-सङ्खार – पु॰ – (आयु–संस्कार) जीवन में अर्जित संस्कार महत्॰। vital principles earned in life.

आयुत्त (1) – कृद॰ – (आयोजित्रत) जुटा हुआ। ploughed.

आयुत्तक (2) – पु॰ – (आयुक्त) आयुक्त, मंडलाधिकारी, कमिश्नर। the chief officer of a division, commissioner.

आयुध – न॰ – (आयुध) शस्त्रास्त्र, हथियार। weapon.

आयुवन्त – वि॰ – (आयुष्मान) दीर्घ आयु वाला। blessed with longevity.

आयुस्स – वि॰ – (आयुष्य) आयु-सम्बन्धी। related with age.

आयूहक – वि॰ – (आयुद्धक) संघर्षशील, क्रियाशील। active, one who strives for his aim.

आयूहति – क्रि॰ – (आ + युध्यति) प्रयत्न करता है, परिश्रम करता है। strives for his aim.

आयोग – पु॰ – (आयोग) (1) अनुरक्ति (2) प्रयत्न (3) बन्धन। devotion, exertion, bondage.

आयोधन – न॰ – (आयोधन) युद्ध। war, battle.

आर – पु॰/न॰ – (आर) सूजा, बड़ी सुई। shoemaker's awl, a ladle.

आरग्ग – न॰ – (आराग्र) सूजे की नोक, सुई का सिरा। the point of an awl.

आरपन्थ – पु॰ – (आरपन्थ) सिलाई की लाईन, सीवन। mark of awling, seam.

आरक्त्त – न॰ – (आरकत्त्व) दूरस्थ भाव। the state of being far from.

आरका – अव्यय – (आरका) दूरी। distance.

आरकूट – न॰ – (आरकूट) पीतल। brass.

आरक्खक – पु॰ – (आरक्षक) पहरेदार। guard, watchman.

आरक्खा – स्त्री॰ – (आरक्षा) पहरा, हिफाजत। protection, care, watch.

आरञ्ञक/आरञ्ञिक – वि॰ – (आरण्यक-आरणिक) आरण्यक, अरण्य (जंगल में) रहने वाला। belonging to or living in a forest.

आरञ्ञकत्त – न॰ – (आरण्यकत्त्व) अरण्य में रहने की शैली। the way of living in forest as a hermit.

आरञ्जित (1) – वि॰ – (आ + रञ्जित)

आरञ्जित

रक्तरंजित, खरोंच से युक्त। slashed, scratched.

आरञ्जित (2) – कृदन्त – (आरञ्जित) जुता हुआ। furrowed.

आरञ्जित (3) – न॰ – (आरञ्जितम्) तिल का चिह्न। sear, mark, symbol.

आरति – स्त्री॰ – (आ + रति) परित्याग, परिहार। abstinence, leaving of.

आरब्ध – कृद॰ – (आरब्ध) आरम्भ किया गया। begun, started.

आरब्ध-चित्त – वि॰ – (आरब्ध-चित्त) जिसने अपना चित्त जीत लिया हो। who has got full control over his senses.

आरब्ध-विरिय – वि॰ – (आरब्ध-वीर्य) प्रयत्नशील। dedicated, endeavouring.

आरब्भ – अव्यय – (आरम्य) (अमुक विषय) को लेकर के सम्बन्ध के बारे में। about someting, in reference to.

आरभति – क्रि॰ – (आरम्यते) (1) आरम्भ करता है, (2) वध करता है, (3) कष्ट पहुँचाता है। (1) begins (2) kills (3) tortures.

आरभन – न॰ – (आरभन) आरम्भ। start, begin.

आरम्भ – पु॰ – (आरम्भ) प्रयत्न, शुरु। begin.

आरम्मण – न॰ – (आ + रमण) रूप-रस आदि विषय जिनमें इन्द्रिय रमण करती हैं। object of senses.

आराव – पु॰ – (आ + √रु = आराव) शोर, चिल्लाहट, रोना। loud noise, chatter, wail.

आरा (1) – अव्यय – (आरात्) दूर से, पास से। from a distance.

आरा (2) – स्त्री॰ – (आर) मोची का सूजा। the awl of a shoemaker.

आराचारी – त्रिलिङ्गी – (आरातचारी) दूर रहने वाला। living far from.

आराधक – पु॰ – (आराधक) भक्ति-भाव से प्रसन्न करने वाला। one who propitiates.

आराधना – स्त्री॰ – (आराधना) उपासना, भक्ति-भाव से प्रसन्न करना। propitiation.

आराधेति – क्रि॰ – (आराधयति) भक्ति-भाव से प्रसन्न रखता है। propitiates.

आराधित – कृद॰ – (आराधित) भक्ति-भाव द्वारा प्रसन्नकृत। propitiated.

आराम – पु॰ – (आराम) (1) प्रसन्नता (2) उपवन (3) बगीचा। (1) delight (2) garden (3) a grove.

आराम-पाल – पु॰ – (आराम-पाल) उद्यान-पालक, माली। a gardener.

आराम-वत्थु – न॰ – (आराम-वस्तु) उद्यान भूमि। a site for a garden.

आरामिक – पु॰ – (आरामिक) विहार-सेवक। an attendant in a monastery.

आरामिक – वि॰ – (आरामिक) विहार से सम्बद्ध। related to Buddhist monastery.

आरामता – स्त्री॰ – (आसमता) आसक्ति। attachment.

आराम-दूसक-जातक – (जा॰ सं॰ 268) (आराम-दूषक जातकम्) जातक कथा बतलाती है हितेच्छु मूर्ख जनहानि ही पहुँचाते हैं। the Jātaka tale (No. 268) concludes that the foolish only does harm.

आरुण्ण – न॰ – (आ + रुदन) पश्चाताप,

विलाप, रोदन। lamenting, weeping, crying.

आरूप्प (1) – वि॰ – (अरूप) निराकार। an incorporeal being.

आरूप (2) – न॰ – (आरूप्य) अरूपता। formless state.

आरुहति – क्रि॰ – (आरोहति) चढ़ता है, सवार होता है, लसता है। ascends, mounts, climbs.

आरुहन – न॰ – (आरोहण) ऊर्ध्वगमन, चढ़ाई। ascending or climbing up.

आरुहन्त – कृद॰ – (आरोहमान) चढ़ता हुआ। who has climbed or evolved.

आरूळह – कृद॰ – (आरूढ) सवार, चढ़ा हुआ। mounted, ascended.

आरोग्य – न॰ – (आरोग्य) स्वास्थ्य। health.

आरोग्य-मद – पु॰ – (आरोग्य-मद) स्वास्थ्य का अहंकार। pride of health.

आरोग्य-साला – स्त्री॰ – (आरोग्य-शाला) चिकित्सालय। hospital.

आरोचना – स्त्री॰ – (आरोचना) मांगलिक सूचना। ceremonial announcement.

आरोचापन – न॰ – मांगलिक सूचना प्रसारित कराना। to spread or publish the ceremonial announcement.

आरोचापेति – क्रि॰ – (आरोचापयति) 'रोचना' भिजवाता है। मांगलिक सूचना करवाता है। gets the ceremonial announcement done.

आरोचित – कृद॰ – (आरोचित) प्रसारित, रोचना। announced.

आरोचेति – क्रि॰ – (आरोचयति) रोचना देता है। sends invitation (ceremonial).

आरोदना – स्त्री॰ – (आरोदन) रोना-धोना, विलाप करना। lamentation.

आरोपन – न॰ – (आरोपण) (1) (वृक्ष) रोपना, (2) आरोप लगाना। (1) plantation (2) accuse.

आरोपित – कृद॰ – (आरोपित) जिस पर दोष लगाया गया है। accused.

आरोपेति – क्रि॰ – (आरोपयति) दोषारोपण करता है। impeaches.

आरोह – पु॰ – (आरोहण) ऊपर चढ़ना, वृद्धि, ऊँचाई। climbing, growth, ascending.

आरोहक – पु॰ – (आरोहक) चढ़ने वाला। rider.

आरोहित – क्रि॰ – (आरोहति) सवार होता है, चढ़ता है। mounts, climbs, ascends.

आरोहन – न॰ – (आरोहण) चढ़ाई। climbing, ascending.

आलकमंदा – स्त्री॰ – (आलकमन्दा) अलकापुरी, कुबेर की नगरी। the capital town of Kuber.

आलका – स्त्री॰ – (आलका) देखें – आलकमंदा। see Ālakmandā.

आलग्गित – कृदन्त – (आलग्न) संलग्न, लगा हुआ, लटकता हुआ। hung on, fastened.

आलग्गेति – क्रि॰ – ($\sqrt{}$ ली - इलेषणे - लीयते) लगा रहता है, सटा रहता है। remains fastened, remains hanging.

आलपति – क्रि॰ – (आलपति) बातचीत करता है। converses, discusses.

आलपन – न॰ – (आलपन) संलाप, बातचीत, सम्बोधन करना। conversation, dialogue.

आलम्ब – पु॰ – (आलम्ब) आश्रय, सहारा, लटके रहने का आधार । support, help, anything to hang on.

आलम्बणदण्ड – पु॰ – (आलम्ब + दण्ड) हाथ के सहारे की छड़ी । stick for support, walking stick.

आलम्बति – क्रि॰ – (आलम्ब्यते) लटकता है, पकड़े रहता है, सहारा लिए रहता है । hangs on to, catches hold of.

आलम्बन (1) – न॰ – (आलम्बन) इन्द्रिय का विषय, जैसे घ्राण का विषय गन्ध । sense object.

आलम्बन (2) – (आलम्बन) लटकना, सहारा । hanging down from, support.

आलम्बर – पु॰ – (आलम्बर) एक प्रकार की भेरी । a kind of drum.

आलय – पु॰ – (आलय) स्थान, इच्छा, आसक्ति, बहाना । abode, desire, attachment, pretence.

आलबालक – न॰ – (आलबालक) आलबाल, पेड़ की जड़ में पानी देने हेतु मिट्टी से बनाया गया थावला या थाला । a circular earthen ridge around the plant for watering.

आळवी – स्त्री॰ – (आलवी) श्रावस्ती तथा राजगृह के बीच में बसा हुआ बुद्धकालीन नगर । an ancient town of Buddhist period, situated between Śrāvastī and Rājagṛha.

आलस – न॰ – (आलस्य) आलस्य । laziness.

आलसिय/आलस्य – देखें आलस । see Ālasa.

आलान – न॰ – (आलान) हाथी बाँधने का स्तम्भ । a stake or post to which an elephant is tied.

आलाप – पु॰ – (आलाप) संलाप, बातचीत । conversation.

आळार-कालाम – गृह-त्याग के अनन्तर सिद्धार्थ कुमार ने सर्वप्रथम जिस आचार्य से शिक्षा ग्रहण की । the teacher whom Siddharth from after his renunciation, first received education.

आलि – स्त्री॰ – (आलि) पंक्ति, एक प्रकार की मछली । row, a kind of fish.

आलि – पु॰/स्त्री॰ – (आलि) कुल्या, नहर तटबन्ध, खाई । dike, embankment.

आलिखति – क्रि॰ – (आलिखति) आलेखन करता है, चित्र बनाता है । delineates, sketches some figure.

आलिङ्गति – क्रि॰ – (आ + लिङ्गति) आलिङ्गन करता है । embraces, clasps.

आलिङ्गन – न॰ – (आलिङ्गन) गले लगना । चिपट जाना । embracing.

आलित्त – कृद॰ – (आ + लिप्त) (1) पोता हुआ, लीपा हुआ (2) लिप्त । (1) besmeared (2) indulged.

आलिन्द – पु॰ – (आलिन्द) घर का बरामदा । a verandah before the door of house.

आलिम्पन – न॰ – (आलिम्पन) लीपना-पोतना । besmearing.

आलिम्पित – कृदन्त – (आ + √ लिम्प + क) लीपा हुआ । besmeared.

आलिम्पेति – क्रि॰ – (आलिम्पति) लीपता है । besmears.

आली – स्त्री॰ – (आलि) सहेली, सखी । woman's female friend.

आलु – न॰ – (आलुकम्) आलू । potato.

आलुम्पति – क्रि॰ – (आ + √ लुम्प =

आलुम्पयति) तहस-नहस कर डालता है, खोद डालता है। destroys.

आलुळति – क्रि॰ – (आ + √लोड् - उन्मादे = आलोडति) झकझोर देता है, हलचल करता है। stirs, agitates, shakes.

आलेप – पु॰ – (आलेप) लेप, लीप-पोत। plaster, ointment.

आलेपन – न॰ – (आलेपन) लेप, लीप-पोत। smearing, plastering.

आलोक – पु॰ – (आलोक) प्रकाश। light.

आलोकन – न॰ – (आलोकन) (1) खिड़की (2) बाहर देखना। (1) window (2) looking out.

आलोक-सन्धि – पु॰ – (आलोक-सन्धि) झरोखा। an opening to let the light in.

आलोकित – कृद॰ – (आलोकित) देखा हुआ। seen.

आलोकेति – क्रि॰ – (आ + √लोक्) बाहर देखता है। beholds, looks at.

आलोप – पु॰ – (आ + √लुप = छेदने) ग्रास भोजन का कौर, आहार-पिण्ड। morsel of food.

आलोळ – पु॰ – (आ + लोड् - उन्मादे) मन्थन, हलचल। stirring, shaking.

आलोळेति – क्रि॰ – (आलोडयति) मन्थन करता था, हलचल करता है, (छाछ) बिलोता है। shakes, jumbles, churns.

आळाहन – न॰ – (आदहन - √दह्) दाह-क्रिया का स्थान, श्मशान। place for burning dead body.

आवज्जति – क्रि॰ – (आ + वज्जयति) ध्यान देता है, प्रभावित करता है। notices, pays attention, reflects, inclines.

आवज्जेति – क्रि॰ – (आवज्जयति) देखें आवज्जति। see Āvajjati.

आवट्ट – कृद॰ – (आवृत्त) आवृत्त ढका हुआ। covered.

आवट्ट – पु॰ – (आवर्त्त) परिधियुक्त, चक्कर, गोल घेरा। circumference, whirl-pool, twisting.

आवट्टति – क्रि॰ – (आवर्त्तति) उलटता है, पलटता है। turns around, twists, revolves.

आवट्टन – न॰ – (आवर्त्तन) (1) आवर्तन (2) किसी भूत-प्रेत का सिर आना। (1) revolving, temptation (2) possession by some evil spirit.

आवट्टनी – स्त्री॰ – (आवर्त्तनी) जादू आवर्तनी-माया। enticing, adverting to māyā.

आवट्टेति – क्रि॰ – (आवर्त्तयति) घुमा देता है, जादू कर देता है। turns round, entices, converts.

आवत्त – कृद॰ – (आवर्त्त) पीछे लौटा हुआ। fallen back on, bent, turned.

आवत्तक – क्रि॰ – (आवर्त्तक) पीछे लौटने वाला। coming back, one who returns.

आवत्तति – क्रि॰ – (आवर्त्तति) वापस लौटता है, लौटता है, पीछे मुड़ता हैं। turns round, goes back.

आवत्तन – न॰ – (आवर्त्तन) वापस लौटना। turning, return.

आवत्तिय – वि॰ – (आवर्त्ती) जो वापस लौट सके या वापस लौटाया जा सके। turnable, returnable.

आवत्तेति – क्रि॰ – (आवर्त्तयति) लौटाता है। turns round, converts.

आवत्थिक – वि॰ – (आवस्तिक) सहज योग्य मौलिक, स्वाभाविक। original, befitting, inherent.

आवपति – क्रि॰ – (आ + √ वप् = वपने) बोता है। sows.

आवपन – न॰ – (आ + √ वप् = वपने + ल्युट्) बुवाई। sowing.

आवर – वि॰ – (आ + √ वृ = आच्छादने) बाधक। causing hindrance, troublesome.

आवरण – न॰ – (आवरण) परदा, ढक्कन। shutting off, a screen.

आवरणीय – वि॰ – (आवरणीय) परदा रखने योग्य। apt to obstruct.

आवरति – क्रि॰ – (आवारयति / आवारयते) बाधा उपस्थित करता है। shuts out, obstructs.

आवरित – कृद॰ – (आवरित) बाधित। obstructed, shut out.

आवरिय – पूर्व क्रि॰ – (आवारयित्वा) बाधा उपस्थित कर, परदा डालकर। having obstructed.

आवलि – स्त्री॰ – (आवलि) अवली, पंक्ति। row.

आवली – स्त्री॰ – (आवलि) पंक्ति, माला। row, garland.

आवसति – क्रि॰ – (आवसति) वास करता है, रहता है। resides, inhabits.

आवसथ – पु॰ – (आवास-स्थल) निवास-स्थान। abode, dwelling, rest-house.

आवहति – क्रि॰ – (आ + √ वह् = आवहति) लाता है। brings.

आवाट – पु॰ – (आवाट) गड्ढा। pit.

आवहन – न॰ – (आ + √ वह् + ल्युट्) लाना। bringing, conveyance.

आवाप – पु॰ – (आपाकः) कुम्हार का आँवा, भट्टी। potter's furnace, an oven.

आवास – पु॰ – (आवास) निवास-स्थान, घर। abode, dwelling, rest-house.

आवासिक – वि॰ – (आवासिक) नैवासिक। a resident.

आवि – अव्यय – (प्रत्यक्षतः) प्रकट रूप से, सबकी आँखो के सामने। openly, before one's eyes.

आविज्झति – क्रि॰ – (आ + √ विध्) बींध देता है, चारों ओर से घेर लेता है। encircles, pierces through.

आविज्झन – न॰ – (आ + √ विध + ल्युट् = आविध्यन) घेरना, बींधना। encircling, piercing.

आविज्जति – क्रि॰ – (आ + √ व्यज = वीजने) बिलोता है, मथता है, उद्विग्न होता है। churns, pulls, agitates.

आविज्जनक – वि॰ – (आ + व्यजनक) झूलता या लटकता हुआ। swinging round, hanging loose.

आविट्ठ – कृद॰ – (आ + √ विश् + क्त = आविष्ट) प्रविष्ट। entered, approached.

आविद्ध – कृद॰ – (आविद्ध) बींधा गया, घेरा गया। pierced, encircled.

आविल – वि॰ – (आविल) गन्दला, मलिन। dirty.

आविलत्त – कृद॰ – (आविलत्त्व) गन्दलापन। dirtyness.

आविसति – क्रि॰ – (प्र + √ विश्) प्रवेश करता है। enters.

आवुणाति – क्रि॰ – (आ + √ ग्रथ् = आग्रथ्नाति) पिरोता है, धागा बाँधता है। strings upon, fixes on.

आवुत्त – वि॰ – (आवृत्त) घिरा हुआ। hidden, covered.

आवुत्थ – कृद॰ – (आवसति) बसा हुआ। inhabitant.

आवुध – न॰ – (आयुध) शस्त्रास्त्र। weapons.

आवुसो – अव्यय – (आयुष्य) भिक्षु वर्ग में व्यवहृत आदरयुक्त सम्बोधन। a form of polite address among monks.

आवेट्ठन – न॰ – (आवेष्ठन) लपेटना। ravelling, wrapping round.

आवेठेति – क्रि॰ – (आवेष्टयति) लपेटता है। wraps over, twists.

आवेणिक – वि॰ – (अद्वितीयक) विशेष, असाधारण। special, exceptional.

आवेला – स्त्री॰ – (आवेला) बेला पुष्प की शिरोमाल। garland for the head.

आवेल्लित – कृद॰ – (आ + √ वल् + क्त = आवलित) कुञ्चितु, घुँघराला, बंकिम। curled, curved.

आवेसन – न॰ – (आवेशन) प्रवेश-द्वार। entrance.

आवेसिक – (त्रिलिङ्गी) – (आवेशिक) आगन्तुक। stranger.

आसंक-जातक – (जा॰ सं॰ 380) – (आशंका जातकम्) इस जातक कथा में आशंका नामक तरुणी द्वारा काशी नरेश को यह उपदेश दिया गया है कि असफलताओं से हार न मानने वाले को सफलता मिल ही जाती है। the Jātaka tale (No. 380) concludes that one who does not leave his objective due to failures, attains success.

आसंकति – क्रि॰ – (आ + शङ्क्यते) आशंका करता है, सन्देह करता है। suspects, distrusts.

आसंका – स्त्री॰ – (आशङ्का) शंका, सन्देह, भय। doubt, suspicion, fear.

आसंकित – कृद॰ – (आ + √ शङ्कु + क्त) सशंकित, आशंकायुक्त। suspicious, apprehensive, doubtful.

आसंगवचन – न॰ – (आ + √ सञ्ज् – सझ्झे – आसङ्ग) आसक्ति, वंचना। attachment, accomplishment.

आसंसत्थ – वि॰ – (आ + √ शंस् = आशंसित) प्रशंसित, प्राप्त आशीष। hoped for, wished.

√ आस – (√ आस् = उपवेशने) बैठना, जमकर बैठना, करते रहना। to sit, to settle down, remain, to do something ceaselessly.

आसज्ज – पूर्व क्रिया – (आ + साद्य) प्राप्त-कर, पहुँचकर, समीप जाकर। having approached.

आसज्जति (1) – क्रि॰ – (आ + सज्जति) आसक्त होता है। gets entangled in attachment.

आसज्जति (2) – क्रि॰ (अवसादयति) पीड़ा देता है, विरोध करता है। harms, torments.

आसज्जन (1) – न॰ – (आ + √ साद् + ल्युट्) निग्रह, निन्दा। knocking against, insult.

आसज्जन (2) – न॰ – (आ + √ सञ्ज + ल्युट्) आसक्ति। attachment.

आसति – क्रि॰ – (आस्ते) बैठता है। sits.

आसत्त – कृद॰ – (आसक्त) लिप्त, आसक्त। attached to, accursed.

आसन – न॰ – (आसन्द) बैठने का आसन।
seat.

आसन-साला – स्त्री॰ – (आसन-शाला)
योगासन के अभ्यास का स्थान। hall
for practising yoga.

आसन्दि – स्त्री॰ – (आसन्दी) कुर्सी, चौकी।
chair.

आसन्न (1) – क्रि॰ वि॰ – (आसन्न) पास में
सन्निकट। near, immediate.

आसन्न (2) – न॰ – (आसन्न) प्रतिवेश,
पड़ोस। neighbourhood.

आसभ – वि॰ – (आ + वृषभ) वृषभ-सदृश
उन्नत, बलिष्ठ। strong like bull, of
powerful.

आसय – पु॰ – (आशय) आशय, निवास-
स्थान, संचय, इरादा। (1) abode (2)
intention (3) deposit (4)
inclination.

आसव – पु॰ – (आसव) स्रवित होने वाला,
मद्य पूय, अकुशल-विचार, दुर्भाव।
distilled material, discharge
from a sore, intoxicating liquor.

आसव-क्खय – पु॰ – (आस्रव-क्षय) दुर्भावों
का   क्षय।   destruction   of
intoxicating ideas.

आससान – वि॰ – (आशंसमान) इच्छा करते
हुए। desiring, wishing.

आसा – स्त्री॰ – (आशा) आशा, इच्छा।
hope, desire.

आसा-भङ्ग – पु॰ – (आशा-भङ्ग) निराश
होना। disappointment.

आसाटिका – स्त्री॰ – (आसाटिका) मक्खी
का अण्डा। fly's egg.

आसादेति – क्रि॰ – (आसादयति) अपमानित
करता है, दुःखी करता है, पीड़ित करता
है। offends, insults, assails.

आसार – पु॰ – (आसार) मूसलाधार वर्षा,
अतिवृष्टि। torrential rain.

आसाळ्ह – पु॰ – (आषाढ) आषाढ़ का
महीना। name of a month Āṣāḍha.

आसि – क्रि॰ – (आसीत्) (वह) था। (he)
was.

आसिञ्चति – क्रि॰ – (आ + सिञ्चति)
छिड़कता है, सींचता है। sprinkles,
pours over.

आसिट्ठ – कृदन्त – (आशिष्ट) आशीर्वाद-
प्राप्त। wished or longed for,
blessed.

आसित्त – कृद॰ – (आसिक्त) सींचा हुआ।
sprinkled, watered.

आसित्तक – न॰ – (आ + सिक्तक) मसाला।
condiment.

आसित्तकुपधान – न॰ – (आशीतकोपधान)
मसाला कूटने का पात्र। condiment
mixer, grinder.

आसिलेसा – स्त्री॰ – (आश्लेषा) आश्लेष
नामक नक्षत्र। name of a nakṣatra
(star).

आसिं – क्रि॰ – (मैं) था। (I) was.

आसिंसक – वि॰ – (आशंसक) इच्छा करने
वाला, आशान्वित। wishing, aspiring
after.

आसिंसति – क्रि॰ – आशा करता है, इच्छा
करता है। hopes for, desires.

आसिंसना – स्त्री॰ – (आशंसा) इच्छा,
आशा। wish, hope, desire.

आसी – स्त्री॰ – (आशीष) आशीर्वाद।
blessing

आसी – स्त्री॰ – (आशी) सांप का फन।
fang of a snake.

आसीतिक – वि॰ – (आशीतिक) अस्सी वर्ष का। of eighty years.

आसीन – कृद॰ – (आसीन) बैठा हुआ। sitting.

आसीविस – पु॰ – (आशीविष) सर्प। snake.

आसु – अव्यय – (आशु) क्षिप्र, शीघ्रता से। quickly.

आसुं – क्रि॰ – (आसन्) (वे) थे। (they) were.

आसुम्भति – क्रि॰ – (आ + घुम्म् = आघुम्मति) किसी तरल पदार्थ को फेंकता है। glides, throws down some liquid.

आसेवति – क्रि॰ – (आसेवते) अभ्यास करता है, संगति करता है। practises, associates.

आसेवना – स्त्री॰ – (आसेवना) अभ्यास, संगति। practice, association.

आह – क्रि॰ – (आह) उवाच (उसने) कहा। (he has) said.

आहच्च – वि॰ – (आंहार्य) जो हटाया जा सके। removable.

आहच्च-पाद – न॰ – (आहार्य-पाद) पलंग जिसका पाया हटाया जा सके। a folding cot with removable legs.

आहट – कृद॰ – (आ + हृत) लाया हुआ, आहरण किया हुआ। brought.

आहत – कृद॰ – (आ + √हन् + क्त) चोट खाया हुआ। struck, affected with, afflicted.

आहनति – क्रि॰ – (आ + √हन् = आहनति) मारता है, चोट पहुँचाता है। beats, knocks down.

आहनन – न॰ – (आ + √हन् + ल्युट् = आहनन), चोट पहुँचाना। beating, knocking.

आहरण – न॰ – (आ + √हृ + ल्युट् = आहरण) लाना। bringing.

आहरति – क्रि॰ – (आहरति) लाता है। brings, fetches.

आहव – न॰ – (आहव) संग्राम, युद्ध। war, battle.

आहवनीय – न॰ – (आहवनीय) यज्ञाग्नि। the sacred fire.

आहार – पु॰ – (आहार) भोजन। food.

आहारट्ठितिक – वि॰ – (आहार स्थितिक) आहार पर निर्भर। subsisting on food.

आहारेति – क्रि॰ – (अश्नाति) भोजन ग्रहण करता है। takes food, eats.

आहाव – न॰ – (वै + आहाव) कुएँ के पास की लकड़ी की बनी कहवत जैसी नाँद जिसमें रहट या ढेकुल का पानी गिरकर नालियों में प्रवाहित होता था। a wooden tub adjacent to a well, leading to a drain.

आहिण्डति – क्रि॰ – (आ + √हिण्ड् = अहिण्डति) घूमता है, इधर-उधर डोलता है। wanders about, roams.

आहुति – स्त्री॰ – (आहुति) यज्ञ-आहुति। oblation, offering.

आहुणेय्य – वि॰ – (आहवनीय / आहुणेय) {प्र + आहरण = पाहुन} भेंट देने योग्य। worthy of adoration offerings.

आहुन्दरिक – वि॰ – (आहुण्डित) ठसाठस। crowded, blocked up.

आळहक – न॰ – (आलान) गजबन्धन, हाथी बांधने का खूँटा। the post or pillar to tie an elephant.

इ

इ – पालि वर्णमाला का तीसरा स्वर। the third vowel of Pāli alphabet.

इक्क – पु॰ – (ऋक्ष) रीछ, भालू। bear.

इक्खण – न॰ – (ईक्षण) देखना। seeing, looking at.

इक्खणिक – पु॰ – (ईक्षणिक) ज्योतिषी। fortune-teller, astrologer.

इक्खति – क्रि॰ – (ईक्षते) देखता है। looks at, sees.

इक्खित – कृद॰ – (ईक्षित) दिखाई दिया। seen, looked at.

इञ्ज – पु॰ – (इञ्ज) इशारा, संकेत। gesture, hint.

इञ्जित – न॰ – (इञ्जित) चेष्टा, इशारा। gesture, sign, motion.

इङ्गिरीलि – स्त्री॰ – (इङ्गिरील) अंग्रेजी भाषा के लिए पालि शब्द। the Pāli name for English language.

इंगुदी – स्त्री॰ – (इङ्गुदी) हिंगोट का पेड़। the wild staff tree.

इङ्घ – अव्यय – (इङ्घ-इध) इधर देखें। look here.

√इच्छ – (√इच्छ) इच्छा करना, चाहना। to desire.

इच्छ – वि॰ – (इच्छ) इच्छुक के अर्थ में सामासिक पदों में प्रयुक्त। (In compounds) wishing, longing, desirous of.

इच्छक – वि॰ –(इच्छक) इच्छा करने वाला। desirous.

इच्छति – क्रि॰ – (इच्छति) इच्छा करता है। wishes, desires.

इच्छा – स्त्री॰ – (इच्छा) चाह, कामना। wish, desire.

इच्छानङ्गल – (इच्छानङ्गल) कोसल जनपद का एक ब्राह्मण गाँव। a brāhmaṇa village of Kośal state.

इच्छानंगल – पु॰ – (इच्छानंगल) श्रावस्ती से अनतिदूर स्थित एक बुद्धकालीन ग्राम। भगवान बुद्ध के द्वारा इच्छानंगल जाकर उपदेश करने का उल्लेख अंगुत्तरनिकाय में हुआ है। Icchānaṅgala, the village of Buddhistic period, not very far from Śrāvastī, where the Buddha delivered sermons as referred to in Aṅguttara Nikāya.

इज्झति – क्रि॰ – (इध्यति) सफल होता है, उन्नति करता है। thrives, succeeds.

इज्झन – न॰ – (इध्यान) सफलता, वृद्धि। success, thriving.

इञ्जति – क्रि॰ – (इञ्जति) हिलना, कम्पित होना। moving, stirring.

इञ्जन – न॰ – (इञ्जन) गति, हलचल, कम्पन। motion, movement.

इट्ठ – वि॰ – (इष्ट) इच्छित इष्ट, अनुकूल। desired, pleasing, favourable.

इट्ठक/इट्ठिका – स्त्री॰ – (इष्टिक/इष्टिका) ईंट, ईंटा। brick.

इट्ठगंध – त्रिलिङ्गी – (इष्टगन्ध) मोहन गन्ध, सुगन्धित। pleasant smell.

इट्ठविपाक – पु॰ – (इष्ट-विपाक) शुभ परिणाम। welfare, pleasant, good result.

इटुट्रस्सासिंसना – स्त्री॰ – (इष्ट आशंसना) शुभाशीष, शुभ आशीर्वाद। blessing, benediction.

इट्ठिय – महेन्द्र के साथ बौद्ध धर्म प्रचारार्थ सिंहल द्वीप जाने वालों में से एक प्रमुख भिक्षु। one of the monks who accompanied Mahendra on his visit to Ceylon (Sri Lanka).

इण – न॰ – (ऋण) ऋण। debt.

इणट्ठ – वि॰ – (ऋणस्थ) ऋणी। one who is in debt.

इण-पण्ण – न॰ – (ऋण-पर्ण) ऋण-पत्र, हुण्डी, तमस्सुक। promissory note.

इण-मोक्ख – पु॰ – (ऋण-मोक्ष) ऋण-मोक्ष। release from debt.

इण-सामिक – पु॰ – (ऋण-स्वामिक) ऋण देने वाला। creditor.

इण-सोधन – न॰ – (ऋण-शोधन) ऋण, उतारना। discharge of debt.

इणयिक – पु॰ – (ऋणिक) ऋणी, कर्जदार। debtor.

इणुक्खेप – न॰ – (ऋणक्षेप) ऋण, उधार। debt.

इतर – क्रि॰ वि॰ – (इतर) दूसरा। the other.

इतरीतर – वि॰ – (इतरेतर) कोई। any, whatsoever.

इति – अव्यय – (इति) ऐसा। वाक्य की समाप्ति का संकेत बहुधा इसका आरम्भिक स्वर 'इ' लुप्त रहता है, जैसे ति किर सुतम् ऐसा मैंने सुना। this word is used to show that the narration has ended, very often its former (i) is elided and only (ti) remains.

इतिवृत्त – न॰ – (इतिवृत्त) वृत्तान्त, घटना, कथन। event, occurrence, statement.

इतिवुत्तक – न॰ – *खुद्दक निकाय* की चौथी पुस्तक इसकी प्रथम पंक्ति एक विध है – कहने के अधिकारी भगवान बुद्ध द्वारा यह कहा गया। the fourth book of *Khuddaka Nikāya* a treatise of *suttā*s beginning with the phrase 'thus it is said'.

इतिह – न॰ – (इति = इत्थ + ह + निश्चयेन) परम्परागत उपदेश। traditional legend, advice.

इतिहा – पु॰ – (ऐतिह्य) पुरावृत्त। traditional beliefs.

इतिहास – पु॰ – (इतिहास) प्राचीन घटनाओं का ब्यौरा, परम्परा का इतिवृत्त। history, tradition, account of former events.

इतो – अव्यय – (इतः) इससे आगे। from here, from now, hence.

इतो-पट्ठाय – अव्यय – (इतः प्रस्थाय) यहाँ से आरम्भ करके। henceforth.

इत्तर – वि॰ – (अल्पतर) संक्षिप्त, थोड़ा। brief, very small or few.

इत्तर-काल – पु॰ – (अल्पतर काल) थोड़ा सा समय। a short period.

इत्थत्त (1) – न॰ – (इत्थं + त्व) वर्तमान अवस्था। the present state.

इत्थत्त (2) – न॰ – (स्त्रीत्व) स्त्रीपना, नारीपना। womanhood, femininity.

इत्थं – क्रि॰ वि॰ – (इत्थं) इस प्रकार। thus, in such a way.

इत्थं-नाम – (इत्थं नाम) इस नाम का। called thus, so-called.

इत्थं-भूत – वि॰ – (इत्थं-भूत) इस प्रकार का। being thus, of this kind.

इत्थागार – पु॰ – (स्त्र्यागार) स्त्रियों के रहने का हिस्सा। harem, seraglio.

इत्थि-इत्थिका – स्त्री॰ – (स्त्री / स्त्रिका) नारी, औरत । woman, female.

इत्थि-धुत्त – (स्त्री-धूर्त्त) स्त्रियों के चक्कर में रहने वाला । one who indulges in woman.

इत्थि-लिङ्ग – स्त्री॰ – (स्त्रीलिङ्ग) स्त्रीत्व का चिह्न । female organ, feminine quality, sign of femininity.

इत्थि-निमित्त – न॰ – (स्त्री निमित्त) स्त्रीत्व का चिह्न, नारीन्द्रिया । female organ.

इदं – न॰ – (इदम्) इम (सर्वनाम) का कर्त्ता, कर्म (एकवचन) । this (pronoun).

इदपच्चयता – स्त्री॰ – (इत + प्रत्ययता) 'इस' का हेतु होना । having its foundation on it.

इदानि – क्रि॰ वि॰ – (इदानीम्) इस समय, अब । now, at this time.

इद्ध – कृद॰ – (ऋद्ध) सम्पन्न जैसे सम + ऋद्ध = समृद्ध । prosperous, opulent.

इद्धि – स्त्री॰ – (ऋद्धि) ऋद्धि, जैसे समृद्धि । prosperity, potency.

इद्धि-बल – न॰ – (ऋद्धि-बल) अलौकिक शक्ति । supernatural power.

इद्धिमन्तु – वि॰ – (ऋद्धिमान्) अलौकिक बल सम्पन्न । possessing psychic power.

इद्धि-विसय – पु॰ – (ऋद्धि-विषय) अलौकिक शक्ति क्षेत्र । extent of psychic power.

इध – क्रि॰ वि॰ – (इध) यहाँ, इस जन्म में इस लोक में । here, in this world, in this life.

इधुम – न॰ – (इन्धन) जलावन । firewood.

इन्द – पु॰ – (इन्द्र) (वैदिक) इन्द्र (देवताओं का अधिपति) । Vedic god Indra, the king of *devatā*s.

इन्द-खील – नगर-द्वार के बाहर गड़ा हुआ मजबूत खम्भा । a strong pole before a city gate.

इन्द-गज्जित – न॰ – (इन्द्र-गर्जितम्) बादलों का गर्जन । the thunder.

इन्द-गोपक – पु॰ – (इन्द्र-गोपक) वर्षा ऋतु में पृथ्वी से बाहर आने वाले लाल रंग के कीड़े, वीर बहूटियाँ । a kind of red insect which comes out from the ground after rainfall.

इन्द-अग्गि – पु॰ – (इन्द्राग्नि) बिजली । lightning.

इन्द-जाल – न॰ – (इन्द्रजाल) इन्द्रजाल, जादू । magic.

इन्द-जालिक – पु॰ – (इन्द्रजालिक) जादूगर । magician, juggler.

इन्द-धनु – न॰ – (इन्द्रधनु) इन्द्रधनुष । rainbow.

इन्द-नील – पु॰ – (इन्द्रनील) नीलम, नीलमणि । sapphire.

इन्दपत्त – पु॰ – (इन्द्रप्रस्थ) कुरु जनपद का एक नगर, इन्द्रप्रस्थ । आधुनिक दिल्ली इन्द्रप्रस्थ की भूमि पर ही बसी हुई है । the capital city of Pāṇḍavas, modern Delhi is situated at the same location.

इन्द-यव – पु॰ – (इन्द्रयव) इन्द्र जौ, एक प्रकार की घास जिसके दाने जौ जैसे होते हैं, जई । a kind of weed, its seeds look like barley.

इन्द-वारुणि – स्त्री॰ – (इन्द्रवारुणी) खीरा, ककड़ी । cucumber.

इन्दसाल – पु॰ – (इन्द्रसाल) इन्द्रसाल (वृक्ष) । a tree *Vetaria Acuminata*.

इन्दावुध – न॰ – (इन्द्रायुध) इन्द्र का वज्र । thunderbolt.

इन्दीवर – न॰ – (इन्दीवर) नीलकमल। blue waterlily.

इन्द्रिय – न॰ – (इन्द्रिय) चक्षु आदि इन्द्रियाँ। sense-organs.

इन्द्रिय-गुत्ति – स्त्री॰ – (इन्द्रिय-गुप्ति) इन्द्रियों का संरक्षण। keeping watch over the senses.

इन्द्रिय-दमन – न॰ – (इन्द्रिय-दमन) इन्द्रियों का दमन। subjugation of senses.

इन्द्रिय-संवर – पु॰ – (इन्द्रिय-संवर) इन्द्रियों का संयम। control of senses.

इन्द्रिय-जातक – (जा॰ सं॰ 423) – नारद तपस्वी का एक अप्सरा के द्वारा लुभाये जाने की यह जातक कथा इन्द्रियों की प्रबलता का बोध कराती है। the Jātaka tale (No. 423) related to the story of ascetic Nārada's temptation by a courtesan which emphasises the stronghold of senses.

इन्दु – पु॰ – (इन्दु) चन्द्रमा। moon.

इन्धन – न॰ – (इन्धन) ईंधन, जलावन। fuel, firewood.

इब्भ – वि॰ – (इभ्भ) धनी, स्वामी। rich, lord.

इभ – पु॰ – (इभ) हाथी। an elephant.

इभ-पिप्फली – स्त्री॰ – (इभ-पिप्फली) काली मिर्च के समान तिक्त लम्बाकार पिप्पली नामक औषधि। a kind of long 'pepper'.

इरिण – न॰ – (अरण्य) महान जंगल, रेगिस्तान, बंजर भूमि। great forest, desert, baren land.

इरियति – क्रि॰ – (√ईर/ईरयति) कँपा देता है, हलचल करता है। moves, stirs, shakes.

इरिया/इरियना – स्त्री॰ – (√ईर + गमन प्रकार) चाल-ढाल। movement of the body, posture.

इरिया-पथ – पु॰ – (ईरिय पथ) अङ्ग-संचालन। अंग चालन की चार स्थितियाँ चलना, खड़ा होना, बैठना, लेटना। deportment, four postures, viz., walking, standing, sitting and lying down.

इरीण – न॰ – (अरण्य) कान्तार। a great forest.

इरु – स्त्री॰ – (ऋक्) ऋचा। the ślokas of Ṛgveda.

इरुब्बेद – पु॰ – (ऋग्वेद) ऋग्वेद। Ṛgveda.

इल्ली – स्त्री॰ – (इल्ली) एक छोटी तलवार। a kind of short sword.

इल्लीस जातक – (जा॰ सं॰ 78) – (इल्लीस जातकम्) इल्लीस नामक कंजूस सेठ की कथा। the Jātaka tale (No. 78) related to a miser banker who becomes generous by effective teachings.

इस्सा – पु॰ – (ईषा मृग) सिंह की भाँति मूछों वाला एक मृग। a species of antelope.

इस्सा-सिंग – पु॰ – (ईषा-शृंग) ईषा मृग की मूँछें। the antlers of 'issa' antelope.

इसि – पु॰ – (ऋषि) ऋषि। a sage.

इसि-पब्बज्या – स्त्री॰ – (ऋषि प्रव्रज्या) ऋषियों के ढंग की प्रव्रज्या। renunciation like that of ṛṣis of Vedic age.

इसिगिलि – न॰ – (इसिगिल) राजगृह के आसपास के पाँचों पर्वतों में से एक। one of the five mountains near ancient Rājagṛha.

इसिपतन – न॰ – (**ऋषिपत्तन**) बनारस के पास के प्रसिद्ध भिगदाय की भूमि (वर्तमान सारनाथ)। यहीं भगवान् बुद्ध का धर्म-चक्र प्रवर्तित हुआ था। famous deer park near Varuṇā river, modern Sārnāth is situated at same location.

इस्स – पु॰ – (**ऋक्ष**) भालू। a bear.

इस्सति – क्रि॰ – (**ईष्यति**) ईर्ष्या करता है। envies.

इस्सत्थ (1) – न॰ – (**इषुशास्त्र**) धनुर्विद्या। archery.

इस्सत्थ (2) – पु॰ – (**इषुज्ञ**) धनुर्धर। skilled in archery.

इस्सर – पु॰ – (**ईश्वर**) स्वामी, मालिक, ईश्वर (सृष्टि रचयिता)। lord, master, the creator (of the world).

इस्सर-जन – पु॰ – (**ऐश्वर्यशाली**) धनी या प्रभावशाली लोग। rich or influential people.

इस्सर-निम्माण – न॰ – (**ईश्वर-निर्माण**) ईश्वर-निर्माण, सृष्टि-संरचना। the creation of God.

इस्सर-निम्माण-वादी – पु॰ – (**ईश्वर निर्माणवादी**) जो ईश्वर के सृष्टि-रचयिता होने में विश्वास करता है। one who believes in a creator, i.e., God.

इस्सरिय – न॰ – (**ऐश्वर्य**) ऐश्वर्य, प्रभुता, वैभव। supremacy, domination, wealth.

इस्सरिय-मद – पु॰ – (**ऐश्वर्य-मद**) ऐश्वर्य-मद। pride of supremacy or wealth.

इस्सरियता – स्त्री॰ – (**ऐश्वर्यता**) ऐश्वर्य-भाव। the sense of supremacy.

इस्सा – स्त्री॰ – (**ईर्ष्या**) ईर्ष्या, द्वेष, वैर। jealousy, ill-will, envy.

इस्सा-मनक – वि॰ – (**ईर्ष्या मानक**) ईर्ष्यालु। jealous.

इस्सास – पु॰ – (**इष्वासः**) धनुर्धर। an archer.

इस्सुकी – वि॰ – (**ईर्ष्यालु**) ईर्ष्यालु। envious, jealous.

इह – अव्यय – (**इह**) यहाँ। here.

इह-लोक – न॰ – (**इह लोक**) यह लोक, यह जन्म। this world, present existence.

इहलौकिक – पु॰ – (**इह लौकिक**) इस लोक से सम्बन्धित, सांसारिक। related to worldly affairs.

ई – पालि वर्णमाला का चौथा स्वर। the fourth vowel of Pāli alphabet.

ईघ – पु॰ – (**दौर्गत्यम्**) आपदा, विपदा। distress, danger.

ईति – स्त्री॰ – (**ईति**) विपदा, आपदा। calamity.

ईतिक – वि॰ – (**ईतिक**) ईतिग्रस्त, आपदा-ग्रस्त।

ईदिस – वि॰ – (**ईदृश/ईदृक्**) ऐसा। in this way such as this.

ईरति – क्रि॰ – (√**ईरयति**) चलाता है, हिलाता-डुलाता है। moves, stirs, shakes.

ईरित – कृदन्त – (**ईरित**) झकझोरा गया, कम्पित। moved, shaken, stirred.

ईरेति – क्रि॰ – (**उदीरयति**) बोलता है। speaks.

ईस – पु॰ – (**ईश**) प्रभु, ईशु, स्वामी। lord, master, ruler.

ईसं – अव्यय – (**ईषत्**) थोड़ा, अल्प। a little, a few.

ईसकं – वि॰ – (**ईषक**) तनिक, थोड़ा सा। little, few.

ईसकं – क्रि॰वि॰ – (**ईषकम्**) तनिक, थोड़ा सा। little, a slightly.

ईसम्पण्डु – वि॰ – (**ईषत्पाण्डु**) भूरा रंग। brown coloured.

ईसत्थ – पु॰ तथा न॰ – (**ईषत्**) देखें ईसक। see 'Isaka'.

ईसदत्थ – पु॰ तथा न॰ – (**ईषद्**) थोड़े का पर्यायवाची। same as 'Iskam'.

ईसा – स्त्री॰ – (**ईषा**) गाड़ी या हल का फड़, लकड़ी का दण्ड जो हल या गाड़ी खींचने में काम आता है। pole of a plough.

ईसा-दन्त – वि॰ – (**ईषा–दन्त**) हल के फाल के समान दान्तों वाला हाथी। the elephant having like a long tusks plough pole.

ईहति – क्रि॰ – (**ईहति**) प्रयत्न करता है। attempts, strives.

ईहा – स्त्री॰ – (**ईहा**) प्रयत्न, प्रयास। exertion, endeavour.

ईहान – न॰ – (**ईहान**) देखें – ईहा। see Iha.

उ

उ – पालि वर्णमाला का पाँचवा स्वर। the fifth vowel of Pāli alphabet.

उक्कंस – पु॰ – (उत्कर्ष) उत्थान, श्रेष्ठता, समृद्धि। excellence, superiority.

उक्कंसक – वि॰ – (उत्कर्षक) उत्थानक, प्रोत्साहक, श्रेयस्कर। exalting, praising.

उक्कंसना – स्त्री॰ – (उत्कर्षणा) प्रोत्साहन, बढ़ावा देना। extolment, eulogization.

उक्कंसेति – क्रि॰ – (उत्कर्षयति) बड़ाई करता है। eulogizes.

उक्कटि्ठ – वि॰ – (उत्कृष्ट) उत्कृष्ट, श्रेष्ठ। superior.

उक्कट्ठता – स्त्री॰ – (उत्कृष्टता) श्रेष्ठता, उत्कृष्टता। superiority, eminence.

उक्कट्ठा-गाम – पु॰ – (उक्कट्ठा-ग्राम) उक्कट्ठा कोसल देश का एक प्रसिद्ध ब्राह्मण ग्राम (वैदिक धर्मानुयाइयों का ग्राम था। कोसल राजा प्रसेनजित की ओर से यह ग्राम ब्राह्मण विद्वान् पोक्खरसादि (पुष्करसाति) को दिया गया था। उक्कट्ठा आजकल 'उकरा' ग्राम के नाम से जाना जाता है। उक्कट्ठा का समीपवर्ती बुद्धकालीन सुभगवन आजकल सुभागपुर के नाम से प्रसिद्ध है। ये दोनों स्थान गोण्डा जनपद के विकास क्षेत्र पंडरीकृपाल के अन्तर्गत विद्यमान हैं। Ukkaṭṭhā was a famous brāhmaṇa village which was donated by Prasenjit, king of Kosal, to a learned brāhmaṇa Pokkharsādi (Puṣkarsāti). This Ukkaṭṭha village is known today by the name of Ukarā (situated in Paṇḍarī Kṛpāla Development Block in district Gonda of U.P.). Subhagvan, a Buddhistic place situated near Ukkaṭṭhā is known today as Subhāgapura.

उक्कण्ठति – क्रि॰ – (उत्कण्ठति) उत्कण्ठित होता है, असन्तुष्ट होता है। becomes dissatisfied, feels anxiety, gets pain due to seperation of his/her beloved.

उक्कण्ठा – स्त्री – (उद् + कण्ठ् + अ + टापू = उत्कण्ठा) (1) चिन्तातुरता, बेचैनी, (2) प्रिय को पाने की लालसा (3) किसी प्रिय वस्तु या व्यक्ति के खो जाने का शोक, खेद। (1) anxiety, uneasiness, eagerness to meet the loving object or person, misery caused by beloved.

उक्कण्ठना – स्त्री॰ – (उत्कण्ठना) उत्कण्ठा, असंतोष। same as Ukkaṇthā.

उक्कण्ठित – कृदन्त – (उत्कण्ठित) उत्कण्ठित, असंतुष्ट। p.p. of Ukkaṇṭhati.

उक्कण्ण – वि॰ – (उत्कर्ष) जिसके कान सीधे खड़े हों। having the ears erect, attentive.

उक्कंतति – क्रि॰ – (उत्कृन्तति) काटता है, फाड़ डालता है। cuts or tears out.

उक्कमति – क्रि॰ – (उत् √क्रम) एक ओर हट जाता है। goes aside.

उक्कल – पु॰ – (उत्कल) प्राचीन उत्कल प्रदेश का आधुनिक नाम उड़ीसा है। ancient 'Utkal' is presently named 'Orissa.'

उक्किलिस्सति – क्रि॰ – (उत्क्लिश्यते) पतित होता है। becomes depraved.

उक्का – स्त्री॰ – (उल्का) मशाल, उल्का (-पात) लोहार की भट्ठी। torch, a fiery phenomenon in the sky, meteor.

उक्काचेति – स्त्री॰ – (उत्काचयति) उलीचता है तुलना करें उत्कलापयति – बुहारता है। empties with a bucket.

उक्कार – पु॰ – (उच्चार) गोबर, मल। dung, excrement.

उक्कार-भूमि – स्त्री॰ – (उच्चार-भूमि) मैला-स्थान, विष्ठा करने की जगह। dung hill, unclean place.

उक्कासति – क्रि॰ – (उत्कासते) खाँसता है, गला साफ करता है। clears one's throat by coughing.

उक्कासित – कृदन्त – उक्कासति का भूतकालिक विशेषण। the p.p. of Ukkāsati.

उक्किरण – कृदन्त – (उत्कीर्ण) खोदा हुआ। excavated dug up.

उक्किलेदेति – क्रि॰ – (उद् + √ क्लिद् = उत्क्लेदयति) मैल बाहर करता है। takes the dirt out.

उक्कुज्ज – वि॰ – (उत्कुब्ज) सीधा करके रखा हुआ। set up, straightened.

उक्कुज्जेति – क्रि॰ – (उत्कुब्जयति) औंधे को सीधा करता है। turns up, straightens.

उक्कुटिक – वि॰ – उकड़ूँ बैठा हुआ। squatting.

उक्कुट्ठि – स्त्री॰ – (आक्रुष्टि) चिल्लाना, घोषणा करना। shouting out, acclamation.

उक्कुस – पु॰ – (उत्क्रोश) उत्क्रोश, समुत्क्रोश। outcry clamour.

उक्कूल – वि॰ – (उत्कूल) ढालू, ढलवान। steep, sloping up.

उक्कोच – पु॰ – (उत्कोच) घूस। bribe.

उक्कोटन – न॰ – (उत्कोटन, उत्कोचन) रिश्वत लेकर न्याय न करना। perverting justice by taking bribe.

उक्कोटेति – क्रि॰ – (उत् √ कुट् = उत्कोट्यति) निर्णीत मुकद्दमे को विधिक त्रुटि दिखाकर नये सिरे से उठाता है। opens a settled case due to some legal flaw.

उक्खलि – स्त्री॰ – (क्षुद्र उखः) छोटा बर्तन। a small pot.

उखा – स्त्री॰ – (उखा) मिट्टी का बर्तन जिसमें साल भर अग्नि रखी जाती है, हँडिया। a ritual fire-pot.

उखलिका – स्त्री॰ – (उखलिका) मिट्टी का छोटा बर्तन (मेलिया, भुरकी)। a small earthen pot.

उक्खित्त – कृद॰ – (उत्क्षिप्त) उठाया गया या हटाया गया। lifted up, thrown out.

उक्खित्त-पलिघ – वि॰ – (उत्क्षिप्त परिघः) जिसे बाधा-रहित कर दिया जाए। having the obstacle removed.

उक्खिपति – क्रि॰ – (उत्क्षिपति) (1) ऊपर उठाता है, धारण करता है, फेंकता है (2) स्थगित करता है। (1) holds, throws away, raises, (2) suspends.

उक्खिपन – न॰ – (उत्क्षेपण) ऊपर फेंकना। lifting up, raising.

उक्खेपन – देखें उक्खिपन। see Ukkhipan.

उक्खेपक – वि॰ – (उत्क्षेपक) ऊपर फेंकने वाला। one who throws or tosses up.

उक्लाप – पु॰ – (उत्क्लाप) कूड़ा-कचरा। dirt, rubbish.

उक्लाप – वि॰ – (उत्क्लाप) गन्दा। dirt, unclean.

उग्ग – वि॰ – (उग्र) घोर, प्रचण्ड। violence, fierce.

उग्गच्छति – क्रि॰ – (उद् + गच्छति) ऊपर जाता है। goes up, rises.

उग्गजति – क्रि॰ – (उद् गर्जति) घोर गर्जन करता है। shouts loudly, thunders.

उग्गण्हन – न॰ – (उद् + ग्रहण) सीखना, पढ़ना। learning, study.

उग्गण्हाति – क्रि॰ – (उद् + गृह्णाति) सीखता है, पढ़ता है। learns, studies.

उग्गण्हापेति – क्रि॰ – (उद् + गृह्णति) सिखाता है, शिक्षा देता है। teaches, instructs.

उग्गनगर – पु॰ – (उग्रनगर) कोसल देश का एक बुद्धकालीन नगर। यहाँ के 'भद्दाराम' नामक विहार में भगवान बुद्ध ठहरे थे स्थविर उग्ग यहीं के निवासी थे। Ugganagar was a famous Buddhistic town of Kosal. Lord Buddha had stayed here in the Vihāra, known as Bhaddārāma. Monk Ugga was a resident of this place.

उग्गह्ल – पूर्व क्रि॰ – (उद् + गृह्य) सीख करके। having learnt or taken up.

उग्गत – कृद॰ – (उद्गत) उन्नत, ऊपर उठा हुआ। risen up, reached to the top.

उग्गथन – न॰ – (उद् + घट्टन) बजाने वाला कंगन, आभरण विशेष। a tinklet, an ornament.

उग्गम – पु॰ – (उद्गम्) ऊपर उठना। rise, going up.

उग्गमन – न॰ – (उद्गमन) चढ़ाई वृद्धि। rise, increase.

उग्गहित – कृद॰ – (उद्गृहीत) सीखा हुआ, ऊपर उठा हुआ, बलात् ले लिया गया। learnt, raised, taken with force.

उग्गहेतु – पु॰ – (उद् + गृहीता) ग्रहण करने वाला, सीखने वाला। one who learns or takes up.

उग्गहेत्वा – पूर्व क्रि॰ – (उद् + गृह्य) सीखकर। having learnt or taken up.

उग्गार – पु॰ – (उद्गार) उल्टी, डकार। vomit, spittle.

उग्गाहक – वि॰ – (उद्ग्राहक) सीखने वाला। learner.

उग्गिरति – क्रि॰ – (उद्गिरति) मुँह से शब्द निकालता है, डकार लेता है। utters, speaks, belches.

उग्गिरण – न॰ – (उद्गिरण) उद्गार। utterance.

उग्गिलति – क्रि॰ – (उद् + गिलति) थूकता है, उल्टी करता है। spits out, vomits.

उग्घटित – वि॰ – (उद्घाटित) अकस्मात घटित। suddenly happened.

उग्घरति – क्रि॰ – (स्यन्दते) बूँद-बूँद टपकता है। oozes.

उग्घंसेति – क्रि॰ – (उद् + घर्षयति) रगड़ता है। rubs.

उग्घाटन – न॰ – (उद्घाटन) उद्घाटन, विवृत करना, खोलना। unfastening, opening.

उग्घाटित – कृद॰ – (उद्घाटित) उद्घाटन किया हुआ। unfastened.

उग्घाटेति – क्रि॰ – (उद्घाटयति) उद्घाटन करता है, खोलता है। unfastens, opens.

उग्घात – पु॰ – (उद्घात) आघात, झटका। a jolt or jerk.

उग्घातित – कृद॰ – (उद्घातित) झटका खाया हुआ। jerked, jolted.

उग्घातेति – क्रि॰ – (उद्घातयति) अचानक झटका देता है। jerks suddenly.

उग्घोसना – स्त्री॰ – (उद्घोषणा) घोषणा। proclamation.

उग्घोसित – कृद॰ – (उद्घोषित) घोषित। shouted out, proclaimed.

उग्घोसेति – क्रि॰ – (उद्घोषयति) घोषणा करता है। shouts, proclaims.

उच्च – वि॰ – (उच्च) ऊँचा, श्रेष्ठ। high, noble.

उच्चत्त – न॰ – (उच्चत्व) ऊँचाई। height.

उच्चतरस्सर – पु॰ – (उच्चतर स्वर) उच्च स्वर, तेज आवाज। louder sound.

उच्चय – पु॰ – (उच्चय) संकलन, संग्रह। accumulation.

उच्चसद्दन – न॰ – (उच्च शब्दनम्) घोषणा। announcement.

उच्चा – क्रि॰वि॰ – (उच्चा) ऊँचा, श्रेष्ठ। high, noble.

उच्चा-सद्द – (उच्च शब्द) ऊँचा शब्द। loud word.

उच्चासयन – न॰ – (उच्च शयन) ऊँचा पलङ्ग। high bed.

उच्चार – पु॰ – (उच्चार) गोबर, गूह। dung, faeces, excrement.

उच्चारण – न॰ – (उच्चारण) (1) ऊपर उठाना, (2) (शब्द का) उच्चारण। (1) lifting up, (2) utterance.

उच्चारित – कृदन्त – (उच्चारित) जिसका उच्चारण हुआ है। uttered, pronounced.

उच्चारेति – क्रि॰ – (उच्चारयति) उच्चारण करता है। utters, pronounces.

उच्चालिङ्ग – पु॰ – (आन्त्र कृमिः) इल्ली पेट या आँत का कीड़ा। maw-worm, worm in the intestine.

उच्चावच – वि॰ – (उच्चावच) ऊँचा-नीचा, विविध। high and low, various.

उच्चिनाति – क्रि॰ – (उच्चिनोति) चुनाव करता है। selects, chooses.

उच्छङ्ग – पु॰ – (उत्सङ्ग) गोद। the lap.

उच्छङ्ग-जातक – (जा॰ सं॰ 675) – (उत्संग जातकम्) इस जातक कथा में एक स्त्री का उदाहरण है जिसने राजा की कैद से अपने पति तथा पुत्र को भी छोड़ देने की याचना न कर, अपने भाई को छोड़ देने की याचना की। the Jātaka tale (No. 675) reveals that the husband and son are replaceable but not the brother.

उच्छादन – न॰ – (उत्सादन + अङ्ग + मर्दनम्) मालिश करना, देह-मर्दन करना। the rubbing of the body, massaging.

उच्छादेति – क्रि॰ – (उत्सादयति) मालिश करता है, बदन को रगड़ता है। rubs the body, massages.

उच्छिट्ठ – वि॰ – (उच्छिष्ट) अपवित्र, जूठन। left, impure leavings, polluted.

उच्छिट्टभत्त-जातक (जा॰ सं॰ 212) – (उच्छिष्ट भक्त जातकम्) इस जातक कथा में ऐसी दुष्ट ब्राह्मणी का उल्लेख है जिसने अपने यार का जूठा भात अपने ब्राह्मण को खिलाया। the story (No. 212) of a wicked woman, given in this Jātaka, who gave her lover's left-over food to her own husband.

उच्छिज्जति – क्रि॰ – (उच्छिद्‍यते) मिट जाता है, नष्ट हो जाता है। ceases, becomes annihilated.

उच्छित – वि॰ – (उच्छ्रित) ऊपर को उभरा, ऊँचा, उन्नत। lifted up, raised.

उच्छिन्दति – क्रि॰ – (उच्छिन्दति) काट डालता है, तोड़ डालता है, नाश कर डालता है। cuts down, breaks, destroys.

उच्छिन्न – कृदन्त – (उच्छिन्न) कटा हुआ, टूटा हुआ, विनष्ट। cut, broken, destroyed.

उच्छु – पु॰ – (इक्षु) गन्ना। sugar cane.

उच्छु-यन्त – न॰ – (इक्षु यन्त्र) गन्ना पेरने की मशीन। cane crusher.

उच्छु-रस – पु॰ – (इक्षु रस) गन्ने का रस। the juice of sugar cane.

उच्छेद – पु॰ – (उच्छेद) नाश, विनाश। cutting off, extirpation.

उच्छेद-दिट्ठि – (उच्छेद दृष्टि) शून्यवाद, पुनर्जन्म में अविश्वास का सिद्धान्त। lack of belief in re-birth, belief in the annihilation of the soul.

उच्छेदवादी – पु॰ – पूर्वजन्म को न मानने वाला। one who does not believe in the re-birth, who professes the doctrine of annihilation.

उजु/उजुक – वि॰ – (ऋजु/ऋजुक) सरल, सीधा। straight, upright, frank, simple.

उजुगत – वि॰ – (ऋजुगत) सरल। straight, frank, upright.

उजुता – स्त्री॰ – (ऋजुता) सरलता, सीधापन। straightness, rectitude.

उजुभूत – देखें – 'उजुगत'। see 'Ujugata'.

उजु – क्रि॰ वि॰ – (ऋजुम्) सीधे। straight.

उजुञ्ञा – स्त्री॰ – (उजुन्या) उजुन्या नामक कोसल देश में एक बुद्धयुगीन जनपद भी था और एक महाग्राम भी। इसी महा ग्राम के समीप 'कण्णकत्थल' नामक रमणीक मृगदाव था। अचेल कस्सप से बुद्ध की यहीं भेंट हुई थी। उसे यहीं पर *दीघ निकाय* के 'कस्सप-सीहनाद सुत्त' का उपदेश दिया गया था। एक अन्य अवसर पर बुद्ध द्वारा कोसलराज प्रसेनजित को यहीं पर 'कण्णत्थलक सुत्तन्त' का उपदेश दिया गया था। Ujuññā was the name of a district and also of a big village of Kosala in the Buddhist period. At a short distance was situated a deer-park called Kaṇṇa-katthala. The Buddha had met Achela-Kassapa at this very place and the sermon of Kassapa-Sīhanādasutta of *Dīgha Nikāya* was also delivered here. On another occasion the sermon of Kaṇṇakatthalakak Suttanta was also delivered here to Prasenjit, king of Kosala.

उज्जगघति – क्रि॰ – (उच्चैः हसति) जोर से खिलखिलाकर हँसता है। laughs aloud.

उज्जग्घिका – स्त्री॰ – (उच्च-हासः) जोर की हँसी। loud laughter.

उज्जङ्गल – वि॰ – (उज्जाङ्गल) ऊसर, बंजर या बालू की जमीन। hard, barren soil.

उज्जल – वि॰ – (उज्जल) उज्ज्वल, चमकदार। bright, blazing.

उज्जलति – क्रि॰ – (उज्ज्वलति) चमकता है। shines, blazes up.

उज्जवति – क्रि॰ – (उज्जवति) नदी के चढ़ाव की ओर जाता है। goes upstream.

उज्जवनिका – स्त्री॰ – (उज्जवनिका) धारा-प्रवाह के विपरीत जाने वाली नाव। vessel going upstream.

उज्जहति – क्रि॰ – (उज्जहाति) त्याग देता है, छोड़ देता है। gives up, sacrifices.

उज्जुञ्आ – स्त्री॰ – (उज्जयिनिया) वर्तमान समय में उत्तर प्रदेश के बलरामपुर जनपद और उतरौला तहसील के अन्तर्गत अवस्थित इस बुद्धकालीन महाग्राम के लिए देखें 'उज्जुञ्आ'। this site is presently known as ujjayiniya (district Balrampur of U.P.). For this ancient town see Ujuñña.

उज्जेनी – स्त्री॰ – (उज्जयिनी) अवन्ति जनपद की राजधानी। the capital of Avanti district.

उज्जोत – पु॰ – (उद्द्योत) प्रकाश। light, lustre.

उज्जोतित – कृदन्त – (उद्द्योतित) प्रकाशित। illuminated.

उज्जोतेति – क्रि॰ – (उद् √द्युत् = उद्द्योतयति) प्रकाशित करता है। illuminates.

उज्झति – क्रि॰ – (उज्झू = उज्झति) छोड़ देता है। leaves, forsakes.

उज्झान – न॰ – (उद् + ध्यान) शिकायत। taking offence, complaining.

उज्झान-सञ्ञी – वि॰ – (उद् + ध्यान + संज्ञी) दोषारोपण की भावना वाला। willing to blame.

उज्झापन – न॰ – (उद् + दहन) उत्तेजित करना, जलाना। provoking, burning.

उज्झापेति – क्रि॰ – (उद् + √ध्या – उद्ध्यापयति) चिढ़ाता है, शिकायत करता है। provokes, complains.

उज्झायति – क्रि॰ – (उद्ध्यायति) असन्तोष प्रकट करता है। grumbles.

उज्झित – कृदन्त – (√उज्झू = त्यागने = उज्झित) त्यक्त फेंका गया। abandoned, discharged.

उछति – क्रि॰ – (√उछ् = कणशः आदाने = उछति) शिला (सीला) – फसल कटने-ढोने के उपरान्त गिरी-बची बालियों को चुनता है, भिक्षा या मधुकरी संचित करता है। seeks alms, gleans, gathers left over grains from field after harvest.

उछा – स्त्री॰ – (उछा) मधुकरी। anything gathered for sustenance, or gathering food.

उछा-चारी – पु॰ – (उछा-चारी) मधुकरी के लिए घर-घर फिरने वाला। wanderer for gleaning.

उज्झातब्ब – कृदन्त – (अवज्ञातव्य) घृणास्पद। contemptible, despicable.

उद्ठहति – क्रि॰ – (उत्तिष्ठति) उठ खड़ा होता है। stands up, rises.

उद्ठातु – पु॰ – (उत्थातृ) स्वयं उठ खड़े होने वाला। one who gets up or rouses himself.

उद्ठापेति – क्रि॰ – (उत्थापयति) उठा देता है, बाहर करता है। raises, makes one risen, turns a person out.

उद्ठायक – वि॰ – (उत्थापक) अप्रमादी, क्रियाशील। active, industrious.

उद्ठित – कृदन्त – (उत्थित) उठा हुआ। got up, arisen.

उड्डाहति – क्रि॰ – (उद् + √दह् = उद्दाहति) जलाता है। burns up.

उड्डेति – क्रि॰ – (उद् + √डी = उड्डीयते) उड़ता है। in the air flies, suspends.

उण्ण – न॰ – (ऊर्ण) ऊन। wool, fibre.

उण्णा – स्त्री॰ – (ऊर्णा) भौंहों के बीच के बाल। hairs between the eyebrow.

उण्णा-नाभि – पु॰ – (ऊर्णा – नाभि) मकड़ी। a spider.

उण्णामय – वि॰ – (ऊर्णामय) ऊन का बुना बिछावन। woollen matting.

उण्ह – वि॰ – (ऊष्ण/उष्ण) उण्ण, गरम। hot.

उण्हत्त – न॰ – (उष्णत्व) गरमी। heat.

उण्हंरसि – पु॰ – (उष्ण-रश्मि) सूर्य। sun.

उण्हीस – न॰ – (उष्णीहश) साफा, पगड़ी। turban.

उतु – स्त्री॰ – (ऋतु) ऋतु। season.

उतु-काल – पु॰ – (ऋतुकाल) मासिक धर्म का समय। the menses period.

उतु-परिस्सय – पु॰ – (ऋतु-परिश्रव) ऋतु परिवर्तन से होने वाले कष्ट। troubles caused by the change of season.

उतु-सप्पाय – पु॰ – (ऋतुसाम्य) ऋतु की अनुकूलता। the favour of the season.

उतुनी – स्त्री॰ – (ऋतुमती) ऋतु स्राव वाली स्त्री। a woman during the menses period.

उत्त – कृदन्त – (उक्त) उक्त कहा गया। said, narrated.

उत्तण्डुल – वि॰ – (उद् + तण्डुल) ठीक से न पका, कच्चा भात। badly cooked rice, having some unboiled grains.

उत्तत्त – कृदन्त – (उत्तप्त) (1) गरम किया हुआ (2) चमकता हुआ। (1) heated, molten, (2) shining.

उत्तम – वि॰ – (उत्तम) श्रेष्ठ। best, noble.

उत्तमङ्ग – न॰ – (उत्तमाङ्ग) शरीर का प्रमुख अव्यय – शिर। the most important part of the body-head.

उत्तमङ्गरुह – न॰ – (उत्तमाङ्गरुह) सिर के बाल। hair of the head.

उत्तमण – पु॰ – (उत्तमर्ण) ऋणदाता। creditor.

उत्तमत्थ – पु॰ – (उत्तमार्थ) परमार्थ। the highest gain.

उत्तमा – स्त्री॰ – (उत्तमा) श्रेष्ठ स्त्री, सुन्दर नारी। a noble woman.

उत्तम-पोरिस – पु॰ – (उत्तम पुरुष) श्रेष्ठतम-पुरुष। noble man.

उत्तर (1) – वि॰ – (उत्तर) (1) उच्चतर (2) उत्तर दिशा। (1) higher (2) the north.

उत्तर (2) – न॰ – (उत्तर) प्रश्न का उत्तर। reply, answer.

उत्तरकुमार – पु० – (उत्तर) बुद्धयुगीन उत्तर कोसल साम्राज्य के अन्तर्गत उज्जयिनी (उजुञ्ञा या उज्जुञ्ञा) एक जनपद था जिसकी राजधानी उजुञ्ञा महाग्राम में थी उसका शासक 'उत्तर' सम्राट प्रसेनजित का सामन्त और अति धनाढ्य व्यक्ति था। वर्तमान उतरौला नगर का नामकरण उसी के नाम पर हुआ। The ruler of Ujjuññā (Ujjayinī). He was a feudal lord, and also a banker of Prasenjit, the ruler of Uttara Kosal. The great village of Ujjai (presently situated in Balrampur distt of U.P.) had been its capital. Modern town of Uttaraula has been named after Uttar Kumar.

उत्तर-कुरु – पु० – (उत्तर कुरु) प्राचीन कुरु जनपद का उत्तरी अंचल। northern part of ancient Kuru Janapada (district).

उत्तर कोसल – बुद्धकालीन शक्तिशाली कोसल राष्ट्र का उत्तरी प्रखण्ड। कोसल की गणना बुद्धयुगीन भारत के सोलह महाजनपदों में हुई है। कोसल राष्ट्र बुद्ध के समय सम्राट प्रसेनजित द्वारा शासित था। काशी प्रान्त भी उनके अधीन था जिसे उन्होंने अपनी बहन कोसला देवी के विवाह के अवसर पर यौतुक-धन के रूप में उपहार स्वरूप दे दिया था। सरयू नदी उत्तर कोसल को दक्षिण कोसल से पृथक करती थी। बौद्ध ग्रन्थों में उत्तर कोसल के बहुत से ग्रामों का उल्लेख मिलता है जिनमें – इच्छानंगल, उक्कट्ठा, एकसाला, ओपसाद, चण्डालकप्प, दण्डकप्प, नगरविन्द, नळकप्पान, पंकधा, वेनागपुर, वेणुद्वार, सेतव्या प्रमुख है। The northern division of ancient Kosala country included in the list of sixteen *mahājanapada*s of Buddhist India. It was ruled by the powerful emperor Prasenjit, the son of Mahā Kosal, Kāśī had been under== his rule which was gifted to his sister Kosalādevī on the occasion of her marriage with Bimbisāra, the ruler of Magadha, Uttara Kosala was divided by river Sarayū from Dakṣiṇa Kosala.

उत्तरत्थरण – न० – (उत्तरास्तरण) ऊपर का बिछावन। the upper bed sheet.

उत्तरच्छद – पु० – (उत्तरच्छद) चँदवा। awning, canopy.

उत्तरसुवे – क्रि० वि० – (उत्तरश्वः) परसों। day after tomorrow.

उत्तर सेट्ठि – उत्तर नामक क्षत्रिय जो उत्तर कोसल नरेश प्रसेनजित के कुल का एक धनाढ्य व्यक्ति तथा उनमें प्रतिष्ठित सामन्त था। प्राचीन श्रावस्ती अंचल के अन्तर्गत उज्जयिनी महाग्राम उसकी राजधानी थी। उत्तर के एक पुत्र था उत्तर कुँअर जिसे आदर से सभी उत्तर-सेट्ठि-पुत्त (उत्तर सेठ का पुत्र) कहकर सम्बोधित करते थे। उत्तर सेट्ठि-पुत्त के सम्बन्ध में तिपिटक में उल्लेख मिलता है। वर्तमान बलरामपुर (उ. प्र.) जनपद के अन्तर्गत स्थित उतरौला नगर का नामकरण उत्तर कुँअर के ही नाम पर हुआ है। Uttar was a banker, and from the same clan, of Prasenjit the ruler of Uttar Kośāla. The big village of Ujjainī within the ancient Śrāvasthi district was its capital. Uttar's one son, prince Uttar, was affectionately called Uttar Sett Pūtra. Information on him is available in the Tripīṭika. The present day town of Uttaraula in Balarampur district of U.P. is named after him.

उत्तर-पञ्चाल – पु० – (उत्तर–पाञ्चाल) राष्ट्र-विशेष. जिसकी राजधानी कम्पिल्ल थी। Ancient Pañcāla district having Kampilla as its capital.

उत्तरण – न० – (उत्तरण) पार होना, (परीक्षा में) उत्तीर्ण होना। crossing (a river), passing (an exami-nation).

उत्तरति – क्रि० – (उत्तरति) जल से बाहर आता है। comes out of water.

उत्तरा – स्त्री० – (उत्तरा) उत्तर दिशा। north direction.

उत्तरा-नन्द-माता – स्त्री० – (उत्तरानन्द माता) बुद्ध का उपस्थान करने वाली गृहस्थ उपासिकाओं में प्रमुख। the main lady among the household-worshippers of Buddhā.

उत्तरापथ – पु० – (उत्तर-पथ) उत्तरी भारत का बुद्धकालीन प्रमुख व्यापारिक मार्ग जो राजगृह से श्रावस्ती होकर तक्षशिला तक जाता था। The famous trade route of north India in Buddhist times from Rājagṛha, to Takṣaśilā via Śrāwastī.

उत्तरायण – न० – (उत्तरायण) सूर्य की उत्तरायण, दक्षिणायन दो गतियों में से पहली। movement of sun towards north, roughly January 14 to July 14.

उत्तरासङ्ग – पु० – (उत्तरासङ्ग) ऊपर का कपड़ा। upper garment.

उत्तरि-उत्तरि – क्रि. वि. – (उत्तर) अधिक, बढ़कर, अधिकतर। over, beyond, further.

उत्तरि-करणीय – (उत्तर + करणीय) अतिरिक्त कार्यभार। moreover.

उत्तरि-भञ्ज – पु० – (उत्तरपेय:) भोजन की समाप्ति पर दिया जाने वाला मधुर खाद्य पदार्थ। sweet dish, dessert.

उत्तरि-मनुस्स-धम्म – पु० – (उत्तर-मनुष्य-धर्म) परामानुषिक स्थिति। transcendental norm.

उत्तरि-साटक – पु० – (उत्तर शाटक) ऊपर का वस्त्र। upper garment.

उत्तरितर – वि० – (उत्तरोत्तर) अधिकाधिक श्रेष्ठ। more superior.

उत्तरीय – न० – (उत्तरीय) प्रावरण, दुपट्टा, गमछा। garment, upper or outer.

उत्तसति – क्रि० – (उद् + त्रसति) त्रस्त होता है, चौकन्ना हो जाता है। terrified, becomes alarmed due to fear.

उत्तसन – न० – (उत् + त्रास) त्रास, भय। terror.

उत्तस्त – कृदन्त – (उद् + त्रस्त) भयभीत, त्रस्त। terrified, frightened.

उत्तान/उत्तानक – वि० – (उत्तान) आकाश की ओर मुँह करके लेटा हुआ। lying on one's back.

उत्तान-सेय्यक – वि० – (उत्तर-शायी) शिशु उत्तान नन्हा, बच्चा। an infant.

उत्तानीकम्म/उत्तानीकरण – न० – स्पष्टी-करण। exposition, manifestation.

उत्तानीकरोति – क्रि० – (उत्तानीकरोति) स्पष्ट करता है। makes clear, clarifies.

उत्तापेति – क्रि० – (उत्तापयति) कष्ट देता है, त्रास देता है। torments, troubles.

उत्तारित – कृदन्त – (उत्तारित) पार उतारा हुआ। taken across.

उत्तारेति – क्रि॰ – (उत्तारयति) पार उतारता है, रक्षा करता है, सहायता करता है। takes across, assists, saves.

उत्तास – पु॰ – (उद् + त्रास) त्रास, भय। terror, fear.

उत्तासन – न॰ – (उद् + त्रासन) त्रास देना, मृत्युदण्ड देना। impalement.

उत्तासित – कृदन्त – (उद् + त्रस्त = उत्त्रास्त) जिसे त्रास दिया गया है, जिसे मृत्युदण्ड दिया जाता है। impaled.

उत्तासेति – क्रि॰ – (उद् + त्रासयति) त्रास देता है, डराता है। frightens, terrifies.

उत्तिट्ठति – क्रि॰ – (उत्तिष्ठति) उठ खड़ा होता है। stands up, rises.

उत्तिण – वि॰ – (उद् + तृण = उतृण) तृण-रहित। grassless.

उत्तिण्ण – कृदन्त – (उत्तीर्ण) उत्तीर्ण हो गया, पार कर गया, उस पार चला गया। passed (exams) crossed over, reached the other shore or bank.

उत्रास – पु॰ – (उद् + त्रास) त्रास, भय। see 'Uttāsa'.

उत्रासी – वि॰ – (उद् + त्रस्त) त्रसित, भयभीत, कायर। see 'Uttāsī'.

उद – अव्यय – (उत) अथवा या। or.

उदक – न॰ – (उदक) पानी। water.

उदक-काक – पु॰ – (उदककाक) जल काक, पनकौआ। a kind of bird, i.e., water crow.

उदक-धारा – स्त्री॰ – (उदक धारा) वारिस धारा, जल-धारा। a torrent of water.

उदक-बिन्दु – न॰ – (उदकबिन्दु) जल-बिन्दु। a drop of water.

उदक-माणिक – पु॰ – (उद् + कुम्भ) जल रखने का बड़ा बर्तन। a big jar to keep water.

उदक-साटिका – स्त्री॰ – (उदक शाटिक) नहाने का वस्त्र। bathing dress, bath robe.

उदकच्छ – न॰ – (उदकच्छ) दलदल। marshy land.

उदकायतिक – (जलनेत्री) पानी का पाइप। water-pipe.

उदकुम्भ – पु॰ – (उद्कुम्भ) देखें उदकमाणिक। see 'Udaka māṇika.'

उदकोघ – पु॰ – (उदकोध) पानी की बाढ। flood of water.

उदग्ग – वि॰ – (उदग्र) प्रसन्नचित्त। exultant, joyful.

उदञ्चन – न॰ – (उदञ्चन) छोटी बाल्टी, जलपात्र। a small vessel with a handle to take out water from a bucket, a mug.

उदञ्चनी-जातक – (जा॰ सं॰ 106) – (उदञ्चनी जातकम्) स्त्री के आकर्षण के वशीभूत हुए पुत्र को पिता ने उसके साथ जाने की आज्ञा दी। the son greatly enamoured of a woman was permitted by father to reside with her but realising her untrue love returned soon (Jātaka tale No. 106).

उदण्ह – न॰ – (उद् + अहीन = दिवसाभ्यः) सूर्योदय। the dawn.

उदधि – पु॰ – (उदधि) समुद। ocean.

उदपादि – क्रि॰ – (उत्पन्न) पैदा हुआ, उत्पन्न हुआ। arose, originated.

उदपान – पु॰ न॰ – (उदपान) कुआँ। a well.

उदपान-दूसक-जातक – (जा॰ सं॰ 271) – (उदपादन-दूषक जातकम्) कुएँ के जल को खराब करने वाले गीदड़ की कथा। the Jātaka tale (No. 291) related to jackal who was in the habit of fouling the well as a family tradition.

उदय – पु॰ – (उदय) उन्नत, वृद्धि, आय, ब्याज। growth, increase, income, interest (from money).

उदय-जातक – न॰ – (जातक सं॰ 458) – उदय भद्द तथा उदय भद्दा की कथा। the Jātaka tale (No. 458) related to Udai Bhadda and Udai Bhaddā.

उदयत्थगम – पु॰ – (उदयास्तगम) उन्नति तथा पतन। rise and fall.

उदय-ब्बय – पु॰ – (उदयव्ययः) उत्थान-पतन, लाभ-हानि, जीवन-मरण। rise and fall, profit and loss, life and death.

उदयन्त – कृदन्त – (उदयन) उठता हुआ, वृद्धि को प्राप्त होता हुआ। rising, increasing.

उदयति – क्रि॰ – (उदयति) उदय होता है। rises.

उदर – न॰ – (उदर) पेट। stomach.

उदरग्गि – पु॰ – (उदराग्नि / जठराग्नि) भूख। hunger.

उदरावदेहकं – क्रि॰ वि॰ – पेट को गले तक भरना। gluttoning.

उदरिय – न॰ – (उदरीय) पेट में स्थित बिना पचा हुआ भोजन। undigested food in the stomach.

उदहारक – पु॰ – (उद + हारक) पानी लाने वाला, कहार। one who fetches water.

उदहारिका – स्त्री॰ – (उदहारिका) पानी भरने वाली, कहारिन। the woman who fetches water.

उदहरिय – वि॰ – (उदक + आहरणम्) पानी भर लाने की क्रिया। the act of carrying water.

उदागच्छति – क्रि॰ – (उदागच्छति) सम्पूर्ण होता है। becomes complete.

उदान – न॰ – (उदान) उल्लासपूर्ण कथन। emotional utterance.

उदान – न॰ – (उदान) *खुद्दक निकाय* का तीसरा ग्रन्थ। the third divison of *Khuddaka Nikāya*.

उदानेति – क्रि॰ – (उदानेति) उल्लासपूर्ण उद्गान करता है। utters with intense emotion.

उदार – वि॰ – (उदार) विशाल हृदय, महान्। excellent, lofty.

उदासीन – वि॰ – (उदासीन) उपेक्षायुक्त, अक्रियाशील। indifferent, inactive.

उदाहट – कृ॰ – (उदाहृत) उदाहरणस्वरूप प्रयुक्त कथन। quoted as an example.

उदाहरण – न॰ – (उदाहरण) मिसाल, उदाहरण। example, instance.

उदाहरति – क्रि॰ – (उदाहरति) सस्वर पाठ करता है, उच्चारण करता है। utters, recites.

उदाहार – पु॰ – (उदाहार) कथन। utterance, speech.

उदाहु – अव्यय – (उताहु) अथवा, या। or.

उदिक्खति – क्रि॰ – (उद + √ईक्ष = उदीक्षति) निहारता है, देखता है, अवलोकन करता है। looks at, surveys.

उदिक्खतु – पु॰ – (उद + ईक्षेता) देखने वाला, नजर डालने वाला। one who looks at.

उदिक्खित- उदिक्खित – कृ॰ – (उद् + ईक्षित) अवलोकित। seen.

उदिच्च – वि॰ – (उदीच्य) श्रेष्ठ उत्तर भारतीय कुल में उत्पन्न। noble person belonging north India.

उदित – कृदन्त – (उदित) उदय हुआ, ऊपर उठा। risen, highly elevated.

उदीचि – स्त्री॰ – (उदीचि) उत्तर दिशा। the north, northern direction.

उदीरण – न॰ – (उद् + ईरण) कथन। utterance, saying.

उदीरित – कृ॰ – (उदीरित) कहा गया, कथित। said, uttered.

उदोरेति – क्रि॰ – (उदीरयति) कहता है, बोलता है। says, utters.

उदुक्खल – पु॰ – (उदूखल/उलूखल) धान कूटने का ऊखल या ओखली। a wooden mortar used for pounding rice.

उदुम्बर – पु॰ – (उदुम्बर) गूलर का वृक्ष। the glomerouse (figus glomerata) fig-tree.

उदुम्बर-जातक – (जा॰ सं॰ 298) – एक बन्दर द्वारा दूसरे बन्दर के ठगे जाने की कथा। the Jātaka tale (No. 298) describes the cheating of a red-faced monkey by a black-faced one.

उदेति – क्रि॰ – (उदयति) उदय होता है, वृद्धि को प्राप्त होता है। rises, increases.

उदेन – पु॰ – (उदयन) इतिहास प्रसिद्ध कोशाम्बी नरेश। the king of Kosāmbī, a historical personality.

उद्द – पु॰ – (उद्र) ऊदबिलाव। an otter, a fish eating mammal.

उदक-रामपुत्त – (उद्दक – रामपुत्त) गृहत्याग के अनन्तर जिन आचार्यों से गौतम बुद्ध ने शिक्षा ग्रहण की उनमें से एक। one of the teachers from whom Gautama, after leaving home and before being enlightened, received instructions.

उद्धलोमी – पु॰ – (ऊर्ध्वलोमिन्) ऊर्ध्व-लोमी कम्बल जिसके दोनों सिरों पर रोएँ (बाल) हों। a kind of a blanket having fringe on both sides.

उद्दस्सेति – क्रि॰ – (उद् + दर्शयति) दिखलाता है। shows.

उद्दान – न॰ – (उद्दान) (1) सूची, तालिका (2) समूह। (1) a list, a table of contents, (2) a cluster.

उद्दाप – पु॰ – (उद्दाप) प्राकार की नींव। a bastion.

उद्दाम – वि॰ – (उद्दाम) उच्छृंखल, चञ्चल, बेलगाम। out of bounds, restless, free.

उद्दालन – न॰ – (उद्दालन) विदीरण, फाड़ डालना। tearing out.

उद्दाल – पु॰ – (उद्दालक) लसोड़ा का वृक्ष। the tree *Cassia Fistula* or *Cardia Mixa*.

उद्दालक-जातक – (जा॰ सं॰ 487) – उद्दालक पुरोहित की कथा। the Jātaka tale (No. 487) related to an ascetic named Uddālaka.

उद्दालेति – क्रि॰ – (उद्दालयति) विदीर्ण कर देता है, फाड़ डालता है। tears out.

उद्दिट्ठ – कृदन्त – (उद्दिष्ट) बताया हुआ, इशारा किया हुआ। pointed out, allotted.

उद्दिसति – क्रि॰ – (उद्दिशति) इंगित करता है, उच्चारण करता है। points out, allots, recites.

उद्दिसापेति – क्रि॰ – (उद् + दिश् + आपयति) पाठ कराता है। makes recite.

उद्दीपना – स्त्री॰ – (उद्दीपना) (1) व्याख्या (2) उदीप्त करना। (1) explanation, (2) sharpening.

उद्देक – पु॰ – (उद्रक) डकार। a belch, spouting out.

उद्देस – पु॰ – (उद्देश्य) संकेत, व्याख्या, पाठ। indication, propounding, recitation.

उद्देसक – पु॰ – (उद्देशक) संकेत करने वाला, व्याख्याता, पाठ करने वाला। one who points out or recites.

उद्देहक – वि॰ – (उद्वेलक) उबलने वाला। bubbling or seething up.

उद्ध – वि॰ – (ऊर्ध्व) ऊपर का। upper, upward.

उद्धग्ग – वि॰ – (ऊर्ध्वाग्र) ऊपर की ओर मुंह वाला, प्रसिद्ध। with face turned upwards, prominent.

उद्धगति – स्त्री॰ – (ऊर्ध्वगति) ऊर्ध्वगति। going upward.

उद्धच्च – न॰ – (औद्धत्य) उद्धतपना। haughtiness.

उद्धट – कृदन्त – (उद्घृत) खींचा हुआ, नष्ट किया हुआ। pulled out, uprooted.

उद्धत – वि॰ – (उद्धत) उद्धत। haughty.

उद्धदेहिक – कृदन्त – मृतक-दान, श्राद्ध। ritual of alms for dead.

उद्धन – न॰ – (उद्दहन) तन्दूर, चूल्हा। fire place, an oven.

उद्धपाद – वि॰ – (ऊर्ध्वपाद) ऊपर की ओर पांव वाला। having heels upwards.

उद्धम्म – पु॰ – (उद्धर्म) कुमत, मिथ्यामत। false.

उद्धरण – न॰ – (उद् + हरण) ऊपर उठाना, जड़ खोदना। lifting, pulling out, uprooting.

उद्धरति – क्रि॰ – (उद् + हरति) उठाता है, जड़ खोदता है। raises, lifts, pulls out, uproots.

उद्ध – क्रि॰वि॰ – (ऊर्ध्वम्) उन्नत, ऊपर, आगे। high up, above, ahead.

उद्धंगम – वि॰ – (ऊर्ध्वगामी) ऊपर जाने वाला। going upward.

उद्धंभागिय – वि॰ – (ऊर्ध्वभागीय) ऊपरी भाग से सम्बन्धित। belonging to the upper part.

उद्धंविरेचन – न॰ – (ऊर्ध्वविरेचन) वमन। vomitting.

उद्धंसोत – वि॰ – (ऊर्ध्वस्रोतस्) जीवन स्रोत पर ऊपर की ओर चढ़ना। going upward in the stream of life.

उद्धंसेति – क्रि॰ – (उद् + ध्वंसयति) विध्वंस करता है, विनाश करता है। destroys, ruins.

उद्धार – पु॰ – (उद्धार) बाहर खींच लाना। withdrawal, pulling out.

उद्धुमात/उद्धुमातक – (आ √ध्या = शब्दाग्नि) सूजा हुआ, फूला हुआ। swollen, bloated.

उद्धुमायति – क्रि॰ – (आधमति) सूज जाता है। swells, bloats.

उद्रय/उद्धय – वि॰ – (उद्रय/उद्धय) कारण होना (केवल समास में प्रयुक्त)। to be the cause (only in compounds).

उद्रीयति – क्रि॰ – (उद् √ रिच - रेचने = उद्रीयति) टूट पड़ता है, टुकड़े-टुकड़े हो जाता है। bursts, fallen in pieces.

उद्रीयन – न॰ – (उद्रीयन) टूट पड़ना, गिर पड़ना। bursting, falling down.

उद्रेक – पु॰ – (उद् √ रिच् = रेचने) वमन। vomitting.

उन्दु – पु॰ – (उन्दूर) चूहा। mouse.

उन्दुर – देखें 'उन्दु।' see 'Undu.'

उन्न – वि॰ – (√ उद - कलेदने + क्त = उन्न) गीला, आर्द्र, दयालु। wet, compassionate.

उन्नत – कृदन्त – (उन्नत) ऊपर उठा हुआ। lifted up, tall, stately.

उन्नति – स्त्री॰ – (उन्नति) प्रगति, वृद्धि, समृद्धि। elevation, increase, prosperity.

उन्नदति – क्रि॰ – (उन्नदीत) महाध्वनि करता है, चिल्लाता है। makes high sound, cries loudly.

उन्नम – पु॰ – (उन्नम) ऊँचाई। elevation.

उन्नमति – क्रि॰ – (उन्नमति) ऊपर उठता है। rises up, prospers.

उन्नल – वि॰ – (उद्धत) अभिमानी, अहंकारी। insolent, arrogant, proud.

उन्नाद – पु॰ – (उद् + नाद) महाध्वनि, घोररव, चिल्लाहट। a loud sound, high sound.

उन्नादेति – क्रि॰ – (उद् √ नद् = उन्नादयति) शोर करता है। makes high sound.

उप/उपसर्ग – (उप) समीप आदि अनेक अर्थों का बोधक। a prefix used in the sense of nearness etc.

उपक – वि॰ – (उपक) समीप जाना। approaching, frequenting.

उपग – देखें 'उपक'। see 'Upak'.

उपकच्छ – न॰ – (उपकच्छ) बगल, काँख। armpit.

उपकट्ठ – वि॰ – (उपकस्थ) समीपस्थ, निकटस्थ। near, approaching.

उपकड्ढति – क्रि॰ – (उप √ कर्ष = उपकर्षति) खींचता है। drags, pulls near.

उपकण्णक – न॰ – (उप + कर्णक) ऐसा स्थान, जहाँ से दूसरों की आपसी बात-चीत सुनाई दे सके। the place where from the whispering of the other can be heard.

उपकप्पति – क्रि॰ – (उप + कल्पति) पास जाता है, योग्य होता है, अनुकूल होता है। approaches, proves, beneficial or suitable.

उपकप्पन – न॰ – (उपकल्पन) समीप जाना, उपयोगी होना, योग्य होना। approaching, being beneficial or suitable.

उपकरण – न॰ – (उपकरण) साधन। instrument.

उपकरोति – क्रि॰ – (उपकरोनि) उपकार करता है। helps, supports, serves.

उपकार – पु॰ – (उपकार) उपकृति, सहायता। help, assistance.

उपकारक – पु॰ – (उपकारक) भलाई करने वाला, उपकार करने वाला। doing favour, productive of good results.

उपकिण्ण – कृदन्त – (उपकीर्ण) विकीर्ण बिखेरा हुआ। scattered.

उपकूजति – वि॰ – (उपकूजति) पक्षी चहचहाता है। sings, chirps.

उपकूजित – भू॰कृ॰ – (उपकूजति) पक्षियों के कलरव से मण्डित। filled with chirping of birds.

उपकूल – वि॰ – (उपकूल) नदी-तट। the river bank.

उपकूलित – कृदन्त – उबाला हुआ, भूना हुआ। boiled, roasted.

उपक्कम (1) – पु॰ – (उपक्रम) साधन, उपाय। means, expedient.

उपक्कम (2) – पु॰ – (उपक्रम) आक्रमण, धावा। approach, attack.

उपक्कमति – क्रि॰ – (उपक्रमति) प्रयास करता है, आक्रमण करता है। strives, attacks.

उपक्कमन – न॰ – (उपक्रमण) आक्रमण, समीप जाना। attack, approach.

उपकिकलिट्ठ – वि॰ – (उपक्लिष्ट) मैला, दागी। soiled, impure, stained.

उपक्किलेस – पु॰ – (उपक्लेश) अशुद्धि, चित्त-मैल। impurity, defilement.

उपक्कीतक – पु॰ – (उपक्रीतकः) क्रीत, मृत्यु, क्रीत दास, खरीदा हुआ गुलाम। a bought slave.

उपक्कुट्ठ – कृदन्त – (उपक्रुष्ट) जिस पर दोषारोपण हुआ हो, जिस पर डाँट पड़ी हो। blamed, scolded, accused.

उपक्कोस – पु॰ – (उपक्रोश) दोषारोपण। censure, complaint.

उपक्कोसति – क्रि॰ – (उप $\sqrt{}$ क्रश) शिकायत या दोषारोपण करता है। complaints, censures.

उपक्खट – वि॰ – (उपक्षित) पास बसाया हुआ। dwelled near.

उपक्खर – पु॰ – (उप + अप) रथ का अङ्ग-विशेष। particular part of a chariot.

उपक्खलन – न॰ – (उपस्खलन) स्खलन, पाँव लड़खड़ाना। stumbling, tripping.

उपग – वि॰ – (उपग) जाता हुआ, समीप जाता हुआ। going to, reaching.

उपगच्छति – क्रि॰ – (उपगच्छति) पास जाता है। approaches, goes near.

उपगत – कृदन्त – (उपगत) पास गया। approached, drawn near.

उपगमन – न॰ – (उपगमन) पास जाना। approaching.

उपगूहति – क्रि॰ – (उपगूहति) भेंटता है, गले मिलता है, आलिंगन करता है। embraces.

उपगूहन – न॰ – (उप $\sqrt{}$ गूह + ल्युट् = उपगूहन) आलिंगन, गले मिलना। embracing.

उपग्घात – पु॰ – (उपाघात) झटका। sudden jerk.

उपघात – पु॰ – (उपघात) आघात, चोट। hurt, injury, knocking against.

उपघातक – वि॰ – (उपघातक) आघात या चोट पहुँचाने वाला। one who hurts or destroys.

उपघाती – वि॰ – (उपघाती) देखें 'उपघातक'। see 'Upaghātaka'.

उपचय – पु॰ – (उपचय) संचय, संग्रह। accumulation, collection.

उपचरति – क्रि॰ – (उपचरति) व्यवहार करता है, उद्यत रहता है। deals with, gets ready.

उपचरित – कृदन्त – (उपचरित) अभ्यस्त, सेवित। practised, served.

उपचार – पु॰ – (**उपचार**) सेवा, उपचार, निदान। service, treatment, remedy, bribe.

उपचिका – स्त्री॰ – (**उपचिका**) दीमक। termite, white ant.

उपचिण्ण – कृदन्त – (**उपचीर्ण**) (1) अभ्यस्त (2) एकत्रित। (1) practised (2) accumulated.

उपचित – कृदन्त – (**उपचित**) संगृहीत। collected, accrued.

उपचिनाति – क्रि॰ – (**उपचिनोति**) (1) एकत्र करता है (2) दीवार चुनता है। (1) collects (2) builds.

उपच्चगा – क्रि॰ – (**उपत्यगात्**) लाँघ गया, आगे बढ़ गया, बढ़ निकला। overcome, passed.

उपच्छिन्दति – क्रि॰ – (उप √छिन्द्= उपछिन्दति) तोड़ डालता है, नष्ट कर डालता है, बाधक होता है। breaks, destroys, interrupted.

उपच्छिन्न – कृदन्त – (**उपच्छिन्न**) तोड़ दिया गया, काट दिया गया, नष्ट कर दिया गया। broken, destroyed, interrupted.

उपच्छेद – पु॰ – (**उपच्छेद**) विरति, रुकावट, विनाश। stoppage, destruction.

उपच्छेदक – वि॰ – (**उपच्छेदक**) रुकावट डालने वाला, नष्ट करने वाला। obstructionist, destroyer.

उपजानाति – क्रि॰ – (**उपजानाति**) सीखता है, प्राप्त करता है। learns, attains.

उपजीवति – क्रि॰ – (**उपजीवति**) किसी के आश्रय से जीता है। lives on, depends on.

उपजीवी – क्रि॰ – (**उपजीवी**) किसी के आश्रय से जीने वाला। parasite.

उपज्झाय – पु॰ – (**उपाध्याय**) अध्यात्म शिक्षा देने वाला आचार्य। spiritual teacher, preceptor.

उपञ्ञात – कृ॰ – (**उपज्ञात**) आत्मसात किया हुआ, सीखा हुआ, ज्ञात। learnt, fully known, found out.

उपट्ठपेति – क्रि॰ – (**उपस्थापयति**) समर्पित करता है, सेवा में उपस्थित रहता है। provides, puts forth, waits on.

उपट्ठहति – क्रि॰ – (**उपस्थित**) प्रतीक्षा करता है, सेवा करता है, सेवा में उपस्थित रहता है, समझता है, उपस्थान करता है। waits or attends on, cares for, serves, understands.

उपट्ठाक – पु॰ – (**उपस्थातृ**) सेवक। servitor, attendant.

उपट्ठान – न॰ – (**उपसेवन**) सेवा। servicing.

उपट्ठान-साला – स्त्री॰ – (**उपस्थान-शाला**) सभा-भवन। conference hall.

उपट्ठित – कृदन्त – (**उपस्थित**) उपस्थित, तैयार। present, ready.

उपट्ठेति – क्रि॰ – (**उपस्थाति**) सेवा में रहता है, गौरव प्रदर्शित करता है। serves, respect, pays honours.

उपडय्हति – क्रि॰ – (उप √दह = उपदहयेत) जलता है। burning.

उपड्ढ – वि॰ – (**उपार्द्ध**) आधा। half.

उपतप्पति – वि॰ – (**उपत्तपति**) अनुतप्त होता है। becomes vexed or tormented.

उपताप – पु॰ – (**अनुताप**) पश्चात्ताप। remorse, repentence.

उपतापक – वि॰ – (**उपतापक**) अनुताप तथा पश्चात्ताप का कारण। the cause of repentence.

उपतापेति – क्रि॰ – (उपतापयति) कष्ट देता है, पीड़ा पहुँचाता है। causes pain, torments.

उपतिट्ठति – क्रि॰ – (उपतिष्ठति) समीप खड़ा होता है, देखभाल करता है। stands by, looks after.

उपतिस्स – (उपतिस्स) धर्म सेनापति सारिपुत्र का गृहस्थ नाम। the clan name of Sāriputta the chieftain of Upatissagām.

उपत्थद्ध – वि॰ – (उपस्तब्ध) कड़ा, कठोर, सहारे खड़ा हुआ। stiff, supported by.

उपत्थम्भ – पु॰ – (उपस्तम्भ) अवलम्ब, टेक, सहारा। support, encouragement.

उपत्थम्भेति – क्रि॰ – (उपस्तम्भयति) सहारा देता है। gives support, props up, sustains.

उपत्थर – पु॰ – (उपस्तरण) बिछावन, दरी, आस्तरण। matting, rug, covering.

उपदस्सेति – क्रि॰ – (उपदर्शयति) प्रदर्शित करता है। shows, manifests, exhibits.

उपदहति – क्रि॰ – (उपदहति) देता है, कारणीभूत होता है। gives, furnishes, causes.

उपदा – न॰ – (उपदा) भेंट, उपहार। gift, present.

उपदिट्ठ – कृदन्त – (उपदिष्ट) निर्दिष्ट, उपदिष्ट। advised, pointed out.

उपदिसति – क्रि॰ – (उपदिशति) उपदेश देता है। preaches, advises.

उपदिसन – न॰ – (उपदिश) उपदेश। advice, counsel, preaching.

उपदिस्सति – क्रि॰ – (उपदृश्यते) प्रकट होता है। appears, being shown or exhibited.

उपदेस – (उपदेश) उपदेश। advice, instruction.

उपद्दव – पु॰ – (उपद्रव) उपद्रव, दुर्भाग्य। distress, misfortune.

उपद्दवेति – क्रि॰ – (उपद्रवेति) कष्ट पहुँचाता है। troubles, annoys.

उपद्दुत – कृदन्त – (उपद्रुत) उपद्रुत, कष्ट का भागी, त्रस्त। oppressed, annoyed.

उपधान – न॰ – (उपधान) तकिया। pillow.

उपधारण – न॰ – (उपधारण) दूध का बर्तन। milk-pot, a receptacle.

उपधारणा – स्त्री॰ – (उपधारणा) अवधारणा, विचार। consideration.

उपधारित – कृदन्त – (उपधारित) अवधारित, विचारित, निश्चयकृत। surmised, considered, looked out for.

उपधारेति – क्रि॰ – (उपधारयति) विचार करता है, परिणाम निकालता है। looks out for, thinks, considers.

उपधावति – क्रि॰ – (उपधावति) दौड़-धूप करता है। runs after.

उपधावन – न॰ – (उपधावन) पीछे दौड़ना। substratum of rebirth, attachment.

उपधि – पु॰ – (उपधि) पुनर्जन्म का कारण, आसक्ति। attachment cause for rebirth.

उपनच्चति – क्रि॰ – (उपनृत्यति) सहनृत्य करता है। assists in dance.

उपनत – कृदन्त – (उपनत) आनत, झुका हुआ। bent down.

उपनदति – क्रि॰ – (उप √नद् = उपनदति) आवाज देता है। sounds, roars.

उपनद्ध – कृदन्त – (उपनद्ध) शत्रु-भाव रखना। keeping enmity.

उपनध्यति – क्रि॰ – (उपनद्धति) शत्रु-भाव रखता है। keeps enmity.

उपनमति – क्रि॰ – (उपनमति) झुकता है, समर्पण व्यक्त करता है। brings near, offers.

उपनमन – न॰ – (उपनमन) झुकना, नम्र होना। bending on, bringing near.

उपनयन – न॰ – (उपनयन) उपनयन संस्कार। the ceremony of imitation of dviyas (twice-born), sacred thread ceremony.

उपनह्यति – क्रि॰ – (उपनह्यति) शत्रु-भाव रखता है। bears enmity towards, wraps with.

उपनह्ना – स्त्री॰ – (उपनह्यना) शत्रु-भाव। enmity, wrapping over.

उपनामित – कृदन्त – (उपनामित) पास लाया गया, भेंट। brought near, offer.

उपनामेति – क्रि॰ – (उपनामयति) पास लाता है, भेंट लाता है। brings near, offers.

उपनायिक – वि॰ – (उपनायिक) समीप आता हुआ, लाता हुआ। approaching, conveying.

उपनाह – पु॰ – (उपनाह) वैर, शत्रु-भाव। ill-will, enmity.

उपनाही – वि॰ – (उपनाही) दुर्भाव रखने वाला, छिद्रान्वेषी। jealous, malicious, peevish.

उपनिक्खमति – क्रि॰ – (उपनिष्क्रमति) अभिनिष्क्रमण करता है। renounces.

उपनिक्खित्त – कृदन्त – (उपनिक्षिप्त) निक्षिप्त रखा गया। deposited, laid down.

उपनिक्खित्तक – पु॰ – (उपनिक्षेपक) जमा करने वाला, चर-पुरुष। depositor.

उपनिक्खिपति – क्रि॰ – (उपनिक्षिपति) निक्षेप करता है, रखता है। deposits, lays down.

उपनिक्खिपन – न॰ – (उपनिक्षेपण) निक्षेप, रखना। putting down, depositing near.

उपनिक्खेप – पु॰ – (उपनिक्षेप) (article) put down, wealth deposited near.

उपनिघंसति – क्रि॰ – (नि √घृष - घर्षणे = निघर्षति) रगड़ता है। rubs up, crushes up.

उपनिज्झान – न॰ – (उप + नि + ध्यान) विचार, मनन। consider, reflection.

उपनिज्झायति – क्रि॰ – (उप + नि + √ध्यौ = उपनिध्यायति) ध्यान करता है, मनन करता है। meditates upon, reflects on.

उपनिधा – स्त्री॰ – (उपनिधा) तुलना। comparison.

उपनिधि – पु॰ – (उपनिधि) वचन, प्रतिभूति, धरोहर। promise, pledge.

उपनिधाय – अव्यय – (उपनिधाय) तुलना करके। having compared.

उपनिपज्जति – क्रि॰ – (उप + नि √पद् = उपनिपद्यति) पास लेट जाता है। lies down close to.

उपनिबद्ध – कृदन्त – (उपनिबद्ध) सटा हुआ। tied close to, sticks together.

उपनिबन्ध – पु॰ – (उपनिबन्ध) निकट सम्बन्धी। of close relation.

उपनिबन्ध – वि॰ – (उपनिबन्ध) आश्रित, निभृत। close connection, dependence.

उपनिबन्धति – क्रि॰ – (उप + निबन्धति) सटाकर बाँधता है, मिन्नत करता है। ties close to, entreats, requests.

उपनिबन्धन – न॰ – (उपनिबन्धन) समीपी, सम्बन्ध, दुराग्रह। close connection, importunity.

उपनिसा – स्त्री॰ – (उपनिसा) कारण, साधन, समान भाव। sits close to.

उपनिसीदति – क्रि॰ – (उप + नि √ सद् = उपनिसीदति) समीप बैठता है। associates closely.

उपनिसेवति – क्रि॰ – (उप + नि √ सेव = उपनिसेवते) संगति करता है। associates closely.

उपनिस्सय – पु॰ – (उप + निश्रय) आधार, आश्रय। basis, support, sufficing condition.

उपनिस्सयति – क्रि॰ – (उप + नि √ श्रि = उपनिश्रयति) संगति करता है। associates closely.

उपनिस्साय – क्रि॰ वि॰ – (उप निःश्रृत्य) निर्भर होकर, आश्रय ग्रहण कर। depending on.

उपनिस्सित – कृदन्त – (उपनिश्रित) निभृत, आश्रित। dependent.

उपनीत – कृदन्त – (उपनीत) लाया गया, पाला गया। brought up.

उपनीय – पूर्व क्रि॰ – (उप √ नी + ल्यप् = उपनीय) पास लाकर। having brought near.

उपनीयति – क्रि॰ – (उप √ नी का कर्मवाच्य उपनीयते) लाया जाता है, ले जाया जाता है। to be brought up, to be carried away.

उपनील – वि॰ – (उपनील) नील वर्ण। of blue colour.

उपनेति – क्रि॰ – (उपनयति) पास लाता है, भेंट करता है। brings up, conduces, presents, contributes.

उपन्त सेल – पु॰ – (उपान्त शैल) उपत्यका। foot of a mountain, foothills.

उपन्तिक – वि॰ – (उपान्तिक) समीप। near.

उपन्तिक – न॰ – (उपान्तिक) पास-पड़ोस। neighbourhood.

उपपज्जति – क्रि॰ – (उपपद्यते) पुनर्जन्म ग्रहण करता है। gets rebirth.

उपपति – न॰ – (उपपति) प्रेमी, यार, जार। paramour, lover.

उपपत्ति – स्त्री॰ – (उपपत्ति) जन्म, पुनर्जन्म। birth, rebirth, approach.

उपपन्न – कृदन्त – (उपपन्न) सम्पूर्ण (पूर्ण) जन्म (पुनर्जन्म) ग्रहण किया। possessed, got rebirth.

उपपरिक्खण – न॰ – (उपपरीक्षण) जाँच, परीक्षा। investigation, examination.

उपपरिक्खति – क्रि॰ – (उप + परीक्षते) जाँच करता है, परीक्षा लेता है। investigates, examines.

उपपरिक्खा – स्त्री॰ – (उप-परीक्षा) जाँच, परीक्षा। investigation, examination.

उपपातिक – वि॰ – बिना माता-पिता के उत्पन्न होने वाले सत्व जैसे देवता। self-born without union of male and female.

उपपादित – कृदन्त – (उत्पादित) समुत्पन्न। born, produced.

उपपादेति – क्रि॰ – (उत्पादयति) उत्पन्न करता है। produces.

उपपारमी – स्त्री॰ – (उप-पारमी) छोटी पारमिताएँ (गुण विशेष की पराकाष्ठाएँ)। minor perfection.

उपपीळक – (उत्पीडक) पीड़ा देने वाला, कष्ट देने वाला। oppressor.

उपपीळा – स्त्री॰ – (उपपीडा) पीड़ा, कष्ट। oppression, suffering, harassment.

उपफ्कुसति – क्रि॰ – (उप स्पृशति) स्पर्श करता है। touches.

उपप्लवति – क्रि॰ – (उप प्लवते) तैरता है। swims.

उपब्बजति – क्रि॰ – (उप्रव्रजति) जाता है, विदा होता है। sets out, leaves house to become an ascetic.

उपब्बूळह – वि॰ – (उपव्यूढ) भीड़ वाली जगह। crowded place, in full swing.

उपबूहन – न॰ – (उपबृंहन) वृद्धि, समृद्धि। increase, augmentation.

उपबूहति – क्रि॰ – (उपबृंहति) बढ़ाता है, फैलाता है। increases, augments.

उपभुञ्जक – वि॰ – (उपभोक्ता) खाने वाला, भोगने वाला। one who eats, enjoys or undergoes.

उपभुञ्जति – क्रि॰ – (भुङ्क्ते) भोगता है। eats, enjoys.

उपभोग – पु॰ – (उपभोग) उपयोग, भोगना। use, enjoyment.

उपभोगी – वि॰ – देखें 'उपभुञ्जक'। see 'Upabhuñjaka.'

उपमा – स्त्री॰ – (उपमा) समानता। simile, parable, comparison.

उपमान – न॰ – (उपमान) देखें 'उपमा'। see - 'Upamā.'

उपमातु – स्त्री॰ – (उपमाता) धाय, दाई। a midwife.

उपमान – न॰ – (उपमान) तुलना, जिससे तुलना की जाये। to be compared with.

उपमेति – क्रि॰ – (उपमेति) तुलना करता है। compares.

उपमेय्य – वि॰ – (उपमेय) उपमा का विषय, जिसकी तुलना की जाये। to be compared.

उपय – पु॰ – (उपय) आसक्ति। attachment.

उपयम – न॰ – (उपयम) विवाह। marriage.

उपयाचति – क्रि॰ – (उपयाचते) याचना करता है, माँगता है। beg, solicits, asks for.

उपयाचितक – न॰ – (उपयाचना) याचना, माँग। begging, entreatment, praying.

उपयाति – क्रि॰ – (उपयाति) समीप जाता है। approaches.

उपयान – न॰ – (उपयान) पहुँच। approachment.

उपयानक – न॰ – (कर्कटः) कुलीर, कर्कटक, केकड़ा, जल बिल्व, पङ्कवास। crab, cancer.

उपयुञ्जति – क्रि॰ – (उपयुज्यते) सम्बन्ध जोड़ता है, अभ्यास करता है, उपयोग करता है। connects with, practises, uses.

उपयुक्त – वि॰ – (उपयुक्त) उचित, ठीक। befitting, appropriate.

उपयोग – पु॰ – (उप + योग) सम्बन्ध, इस्तेमाल। use.

उपरचित – कृदन्त – (उपरचित) निर्मित। constructed.

उपरज्ज – न॰ – (उपराज्य) उप-राजपना। viceroyalty.

उपरत – कृदन्त – (उपरत) विरत, विरत हुआ। desisting or abstaining from, ceased.

उपरति – स्त्री॰ – (उपरति) विरति, संयम। ceasing, restrainment.

उपरमति – क्रि॰ – (उपरमते) विरत रहता है, संयत रहता है। desists, ceases, restrains from.

उपराजा – पु॰ – (उपराजा) वाइसराय, राजा का स्थानापन्न। viceroy, the substitute of a king.

उपरि – अव्यय – (उपरि) पर, ऊपर। on, above, upper, upon.

उपरिट्ठ – वि॰ – (उपरिस्थ) सर्वोपरि। topmost, situated above.

उपरि-पासाद – पु॰ – (उपरिप्रासाद) हवेली का सबसे ऊपर का तल्ला। the upper storey of a palace.

उपरि-भाग – पु॰ – (उपरिभाग) ऊपर का हिस्सा। the upper portion.

उपरि-मुख – वि॰ – (उपरिमुख) ऊपर की ओर मुँह वाला। facing upward.

उपरित्त – अव्यय – (उपरित्र) ऊपर होने का भाव। state of being higher.

उपरिम – वि॰ – (उपरिम) सर्वोपरि। uppermost.

उपरूज्झति – क्रि॰ – (उपरुध्यते) अवरोध को प्राप्त होता है, रुक जाता है। being obstructed, stops, ceases.

उपरूद्ध – वि॰ – (उपरुद्ध) रुद्ध, बाधित, रोका गया। ceased, stopped, obstructed.

उपरूळह – कृदन्त – (उपरुढ) वर्धित, प्ररूढ़ उगा हुआ। grown.

उपरोचति – क्रि॰ – (उपरोचते) प्रसन्न करता है। pleases.

उपरोदति – क्रि॰ – (उपरोदिति) रोता है, विलाप करता है। cries in wail, laments.

उपरोधेति – क्रि॰ – (उपरुणद्धि) बाधा डालता है। obstructs.

उपरोप – न॰ – (उपरोप्य) बेरन, पौधा। seedling, plant.

उपल – पु॰ – (उपल) पत्थर। stone.

उपलक्खण – न॰ – (उपलक्षण) भेदक पहचान का चिह्न। distinctive feature.

उपलक्खणा – स्त्री॰ – (उपलक्षणा) विभेदीकरण, विवेक द्वारा पृथक् करना। discrimination.

उपलक्खित – कृदन्त – (उपलक्षित) उपलक्षित, विवेक द्वारा पृथक्कृत। discriminated.

उपलक्खेति – क्रि॰ – (उपलक्षयति – ते) विवेक द्वारा पृथक् करता है। discriminates.

उपलद्ध – कृ॰ – (उप √लभ् + क्त = उपलब्धु) प्राप्त। obtained.

उपलब्धि – स्त्री॰ – (उपलब्धि) प्राप्ति। achievement.

उपलब्भति – क्रि॰ – (उपलभ्यते) प्राप्त होता है, विद्यमान होता है। is founded, acquired possessed.

उपलभति – क्रि॰ – (उपलभति) हासिल करता है, प्राप्त करता है। gets, acquires.

उपलापन – न॰ – (उपलापन) प्रेरणा, बकवास। persuasion, humbug.

उपलापेति – क्रि॰ – (उपलापयति = प्रेरयति) प्रेरित करता है, खुशामद करता है। persuades, coaxes.

उपलालेति – क्रि॰ – (उपलालयति) दुलारता या दुलारता है, लालन करता है। fondles, caresses.

उपलिक्खति – क्रि॰ – (उपलिखति) उकेरता है, उत्कीर्ण करता है। engraves.

उपलिप्पति – क्रि॰ – (उपलिम्पति) लीपता है, लेप या लेपन करता है। smears, taints, defiles.

उपलिम्पति – क्रि॰ – (उपलिम्पति) देखें 'उपलिप्पति'। see 'Upalippati.'

उपलेप – पु॰ – (उपलेप) लेप। coating, smearing.

उपलोहितक – वि॰ – (उपलोहितक) लाल रंग का। of red colour.

उपवज्ज – वि॰ – (उपवद्य) निन्द्य, वर्ज्य सदोष। blameworthy.

उपवण्णेति – क्रि॰ – (उपवर्णयति) वर्णन करता है। describes.

उपवत्त/उपवत्तन – हिरण्यवती के तट पर कुसीनारा के मल्लों का शाल-वन। यहीं भगवान् बुद्ध का परिनिर्वाण हुआ था। The Śāla garden of Malla kṣatriyas of Kusīnārā, situated on the bank of Hiraṇyavatī, where the lord Buddha attained salvation.

उपवत्तति – क्रि॰ – (उपवत्ततेे) विद्यमान होता है। exists.

उपक्तन – वि॰ – (उपवर्त्तन) समीप, विद्यमानता। existing near.

उपवदति – क्रि॰ – (उपवदति) दोषारोपण करता है, अपमानित करता है। blames, insults.

उपवन – न॰ – (उपवन) उद्यान, नगर के समीप स्थित छोटा वन। small forest situated near the town, grove.

उपवसति – क्रि॰ – (उपवसति) वास करता है, रहता है। dwells in, lives in.

उपवाद – पु॰ – (उपवाद) दोष, अपमान। blame, insult.

उपवादक – वि॰ – (उपवादक) दोष देने वाला, अपमान करने वाला। one who blames or insults.

उपवादी – पु॰ – (उपवादी) देखें 'उपवादक'। see 'Upavādaka'.

उपवायति – क्रि॰ – (उप √ वा = उपवाति) (वायु) बहती है, (हवा) चलती है। blows towards.

उपवास – पु॰ – (उपवास) आहार-त्याग, व्रत। fasting, abstaining from enjoyment.

उपवासन – न॰ – (उपवासन) सुगन्धित करना। perfuming.

उपवासित – वि॰ – (उपवासित) सुवासित, सुगन्धीकृत, सुगन्धित। perfumed.

उपवासेति – क्रि॰ – (उपवासयति) सुगन्धित करता है। perfumes.

उपवाहन – न॰ – (उपवाहन/उपवहन) ढोना, बहाकर ले जाना। carrying by flouring water.

उपविज्ञा – स्त्री॰ – (आसन्न प्रसवा) ऐसी स्त्री जिसको प्रसव शीघ्र होने वाला हो। woman who is shortly giving birth to a baby.

उपविसति – क्रि॰ – (उपविशति) समीप आता है, समीप बैठ जाता है। sits nearby, approaches.

उपवीण – पु॰ – (उपवीण) वीणा का सिरा। the neck of a lute.

उपवीत (1) – कृदन्त – (उपवीत) बुना हुआ। woven.

उपवीत (2) – वि॰ – (उपवती) उपनयन सम्पन्न। having sacred thread.

उपवीयति – क्रि॰ – (उपवयति) बुनता है। weaves.

उपवुत्त – कृदन्त – (उपवादित) दोषारोपित किया गया। blamed, insulted.

उपवुत्थ – कृदन्त – (उपोसभ) व्रत रखा गया। having kept a fast.

उपवेसन – न॰ – (उपवेशन) बैठना। sitting.

उपव्हयति – क्रि॰ – (आ √ ह्वे = आह्वयति) बुलाता है। calls, invokes (god).

उपसंवसति – क्रि॰ – (उपसंवसति) किसी के साथ रहता है। lives with someone.

उपसंहरण – न॰ – (उप संहरण) समापन वृत्त, एकत्र करना, तुलना करना, निष्कर्ष की प्रस्तुति, समापन, संक्षेप। in conclusion, to recollect, in short.

उपसंहरति – क्रि॰ – (उपसहरति) इकट्ठा करता है, निष्कर्ष देता है, उपसंहार करता है। concentrates, concludes in the end.

उपसंहार – पु॰ – (उपसंहार) देखें 'उपसंहरण'। see Upsaṁharaṇa.

उपसङ्कमति – क्रि॰ – (उपसंकामति) पास जाता है। approaches.

उपसङ्कमन – न॰ – (उपसंक्रमण) पहुँच, समीप, गमन। approach.

उपसङ्कमित्वा – पूर्व क्रि॰ – (उपसंक्रम्य) पास जाकर, पहुँचकर। approaching, getting nearby.

उपसग्ग – पु॰ – (उपसर्ग) (1) – बाधा (2) किसी क्रिया के पूर्व में आने वाले वर्ण समूह (उपसर्ग)। (1) a prefix (2) danger.

उपसन्त – कृदन्त – (उपशान्त) शान्त-चित्त। mind being calmed.

उपसम – पु॰ – (उपशम) शान्ति, सन्तोष। calmness, appeasement, peace.

उपसमन – न॰ – (उपशमन) देखें 'उपसम'। see 'Upasama.'

उपसमेति – क्रि॰ – (उपशाम्यति) सन्तुष्ट करता है, शान्त करता है। appears, gets calmed, appeases.

उपसम्पज्ज – कृदन्त – (उपसम्पद्य) पहुँच-कर, प्रविष्ट होकर, उपसम्पन्न, भिक्षु होकर। having attained having enterd, having become fully ordained.

उपसम्पज्जति – क्रि॰ – (उपसम्पद्यते) पहुँचता है, प्रविष्ट होता है, (भिक्षु) उपसम्पन्न होता है। attains, enters, becomes fully ordained.

उपसम्पदा – स्त्री॰ – (उपसम्पदा) बौद्ध भिक्षु की संघ के द्वारा दी जाने वाली दीक्षा। higher ordination of a Buddhist monk.

उपसम्पन्न – कृदन्त – (उपसम्पन्न) उपसम्पदा प्राप्त भिक्षु। a monk who has attained 'Upasampadā'.

उपसम्पादेति – क्रि॰ – (उपसम्पादयति) भिक्षु को उपसम्पदा की दीक्षा देता है। ordinates 'Upasampadā' to a monk.

उपसम्फस्सति – क्रि० – (उपसंस्पृशति) गले मिलता है, आलिंगन करता है।embraces.

उपसम्मति – क्रि० – (उपशाम्यति) शान्त होता है, सन्तुष्ट होता है। becomes calmed, ceases.

उपसाळह-जातक – (जा० सं० 166) – एक ब्राह्मण की कथा जिसने अपने लड़कों को आदेश दिया था कि उसकी दाह-क्रिया ऐसी जगह की जाये, जहाँ पहले किसी की दाह क्रिया न हुई हो। the Jātaka tale (No. 166) which concludes that there is none immortal in the world.

उपसिंघति – क्रि० – (शयनकाले नासिकया कर्कश ध्वनि सहितं श्वसति) नाक बजाता है। snores.

उपसिंघन – (न०) – (शयन-काले नासिकया कर्कश सहितम् श्वसनम्) नाक बजाना। snoring.

उपसुस्सति – क्रि० – (उपशुष्यति) सूख जाता है। becomes dry.

उपसुस्सन – न० – (उपशुष्यन) सूख जाना। to become dry.

उपसेचन – न० – (उपसिञ्चन) भोजन को स्वादिष्ट बनाने के लिए उस पर (नमक-मिर्च) छिड़कना। sprinkling of salt, spice, etc., to make food dainty and tasty.

उपसेनिया – स्त्री० – (उपशयनी) जो लड़की सदैव अपनी माँ के पास रहना चाहे, लाड़ली। the girl who wants to live, always with her mother.

उपसेवति – क्रि० – (उपसेवते) अभ्यास करता है, संगति करता है। practises, associates, frequents.

उपसेवना – स्त्री० – (उपसेवना) अभ्यास, संगति। practice, associated, frequented.

उपसेवित – कृ० – (उपसेवित) जिसने अभ्यास किया हो, जिसने संगति की हो। practised, associated, frequented.

उपसेवी – वि० – (उपसेवी) अभ्यास करने वाला, संगति करने वाला। one who associates, uses or practises.

उपसोभति – क्रि० – (उपशोभते) सुशोभित होता है, सुन्दर लगता है। appears beautiful, looks attractive.

उपसोभित – कृदन्त – (सुशोभित) सुशोभित। embellished, beautified.

उपसोभेति – क्रि० – (उपशोभयति) सुशोभित कराता है। gets beautified, makes embellished.

उपसोसेति – क्रि० – (उपशोषयति) सुखाता है। makes dry.

उपस्सट्ठ – (उपसृष्ट) दमित, जिसका दमन किया गया। oppressed, or afflicted with.

उपस्सय – पु० – (उपाश्रय) निवास-स्थान। home, abode, dwelling.

उपस्सास – पु० – (उपश्वास) साँस लेना। breathing in.

उपस्सुति – स्त्री० – (उपश्रुति) उपश्रुति, दूसरों की गुप्त बात-चीत का श्रवण। listening to private whisperings of others, snooping at others talk.

उपस्सुतिक – वि० – (उपश्रुतिक) दूसरों की बात-चीत सुनने वाला। one who listens to the private whispering of others.

उपहञ्ञति – क्रि० – (उपहन्यते) भ्रष्ट होता

है, चोट खाता है । becomes spoilt or injured.

उपहत – कृदन्त – **(उपहत)** बरबाद कर डाला गया, चोट खाया हुआ । injured, destroyed.

उपहत्त – पु॰ – **(उपहत्ता)** लाने वाला । one who conveys or bears, bearer.

उपहनति – क्रि॰ – **(उपहनति)** हानि पहुँचाता है, चोट पहुँचाता है । injures, destroys.

उपहरण – न॰ – **(उपहरण)** भेंट । gift, present.

उपहरति – क्रि॰ – **(उपहरति)** भेंट लाता है । gifts, offers present.

उपहार – पु॰ – **(उपहार)** भेंट, पुरस्कार । gift, present, prize.

उपहिंसति – क्रि॰ – **(उपहिंसति)** हानि पहुँचाता है, चोट पहुँचाता है । ruins, injures.

उपागच्छति – क्रि॰ – **(उपागच्छति)** समीप आता है । comes near, approaches, attains.

उपागत – कृदन्त – समीप आया हुआ । reached, attained.

उपातिधावति – क्रि॰ – **(उपातिधावति)** दौड़ता रहता है । runs on or runs into.

उपातिपन्न – कृदन्त – **(उपातिपन्न)** गिरा हुआ, शिकार हुआ । fallen, a prey to.

उपातिवत्त – कृ॰ – **(उपातिवृत्त)** सीमातिक्रान्त हुआ । gone beyond, escaped from, free from.

उपातिवत्तति – क्रि॰ – **(उपातिवत्तते)** सीमोल्लंघन करता है । goes beyond, oversteps.

उपादा – क्रि॰ वि॰ – **(उपादाय)** उपादाय का संक्षिप्त रूप, सकारण । a shortened

gerund of *upadiyati*, i.e., of *upadaya*.

उपादान (1) – न॰ – **(उपादान)** आसक्ति, ईंधन । fuel, attachment, grasping.

उपादान (2) – क्रि॰ – **(उपादान)** सांसारिक पदार्थों से इन्द्रियों व मन को विरत करना । to detatch mind and senses from worldly objects.

उपादानक्खन्ध – पु॰ – **(उपादान स्कन्ध)** आसक्ति के रूप, वेदना, आदि, स्कन्ध । the state of clinging, to or grasping at existence.

उपादानक्खय – पु॰ – **(उपादान क्षय)** आसक्ति का क्षय । extinction of attachment.

उपादानिय – वि॰ – **(उप + आ √दा + यत्)** आसक्ति से सम्बन्धित । connected with grasping.

उपादाय – पूर्व क्रि॰ – **(उप + आ √दा + ल्यप्)** कारण होकर । having grasped, compared with.

उपादि – पु॰ – **(उपादि)** जीवन का ईंधन रूप, वेदना, आदि, स्कन्ध । stuff of life, substratum of being (*khandhas*) also see Appendix I.

उपादि-सेस – वि॰ – **(उपादि शेष)** जिसमें रूप, वेदना, आदि, स्कन्ध अवशेष हों । having some fuel of life (*upādi-khandhas*) left.

उपादिन्न – कृदन्त – **(उपादात्त)** गृहीत । grasped at, laid hold of.

उपादियति – क्रि॰ – **(उपादाति)** ग्रहण करता है । takes hold of, graspes, clings to.

उपाधि (1) – पु॰ – **(उपाधि)** अलङ्करण निधान, टाईटल, पद, गद्दी । title, designation.

उपाधि (2) – स्त्री॰ – (उपाधि) चालाकी, दूसरे की एवज में रखी वस्तु दुश्चिन्ता। deceit, put in place of another, substitute.

उपान्तभू – स्त्री॰ – (उप + अन्त + भू) उपान्त अर्थात पास (गोंयड़) की जमीन। the land surrounding a township or village.

उपाय – पु॰ – (उपाय) युक्ति, तरकीब, साधन। way, means, resource.

उपाय-कुसल – (उपाय कुशल) साधन-सम्पन्न। clever in resources.

उपाय-कोसल्ल – न॰ – (उपाय कौशल) उपाय-कुशलता। clever expedient, resourceful plan.

उपायन – न॰ – (उपायन) उपहार, भेंट। gift, a tribute.

उपायास – पु॰ – (उपायास) चिन्ता, दुःख, पश्चाताप। anxiety, tribulation, grief.

उपारम्भ – पु॰ – (उपारम्भ) डाँट-डपट। reproach.

उपालि स्थविर – पु॰ – (उपालि स्थविर) भगवान् बुद्ध के महाश्रावकों में से एक। इनका जन्म कपिलवस्तु के नाई परिवार में हुआ था। बुद्ध के परिनिर्वाण के अनन्तर प्रथम संगीति में उपालि स्थविर ही विनय के विषय में प्रमाण माने गये थे। one of Buddha's eminent and immediate disciples, he belonged to a barber's family in Kapilvastu. In Rājagṛha council Upāli took a leading part in deciding all the questions related to *vinaya* (modesty and humility).

उपविसि – क्रि॰ – (उपाविशत्) स्थान ग्रहण किया। took the seat.

उपासक – पु॰ – (उपाशक) गृहस्थ शिष्य। a lay devotee, devotion

उपासकत्त – न॰ – (उपासकत्व) उपासक-भाव। state of devotee, devotion.

उपासति – क्रि॰ – (उपासते) उपासना करता है, सेवा में रहता है। worships, attends or serves.

उपासन – न – (उपासन) (1) सेवा (2) धनुर्विद्या। (1) service, attendance, (2) archery.

उपासिका – स्त्री॰ – (उपासिका) उपासना करने वाली स्त्री। a lady worshipper, a female devotee.

उपासित – कृदन्त – (उपासित) पूजित, सेवित। worshipped, served.

उपासीन – कृदन्त – (उपासीन) पास बैठा हुआ। sitting by.

उपाहत – कृदन्त – (उपाहत) जिसे आघात लगा हो, जिसने चोट खाई हो। struck, afflicted.

उपाहन – न॰ – (उपाहन) पदत्राण, जूता। footwear, i.e., shoes or sandals.

उपेक्खक – वि॰ – (उपेक्षक) उपेक्षा करने वाला। ignorer, one who disregards.

उपेक्खति – क्रि॰ – (उपेक्षते) उपेक्षा करता है। ignores, disregards.

उपेक्खना – स्त्री॰ – (उपेक्षणा) उपेक्षा। negligence, contempt.

उपेक्खा – स्त्री॰ – (उपेक्षा) उपेक्षा-भाव, मध्यस्थ-भाव। disregard, over-looking, neutral feeling.

उपेत – कृदन्त – (उप √ इ + क्त) पास गया हुआ, प्राप्त हुआ। approached, attained.

उपेति – क्रि॰ – (उपेति) पास जाता है, प्राप्त करता है। having approached or attained.

उपेत्वा – पूर्व क्रि॰ – (उपेत्वा) पास जाकर। introduction.

उपोग्घात – पु॰ – (उपोद्घात) प्राक्कथन। introduction, preface.

उपोचित – कृदन्त – (उपोचित) संचित, ढ़ेर लगाया हुआ, सुखद। heaped up, comfortable.

उपोसथ (1) – (उपोसथ) बुद्धमत के आरम्भिक व्रतकाल में महीने की दोनों अष्टमियाँ, अमावस्या तथा पूर्णिमा ये चार उपोसथ (व्रतोपवास) दिवस माने जाते थे। इन्हें 'सब्बथ' दिवस माना जाता था। Buddhism, Early in four days new moon, full moon, and the eighth days after these two — were meant for fasting and were called 'sabbath' days.

उपोसथ-कम्म – न॰ – (उपोसथ कर्म) उपोसथ (व्रत) का क्रियात्मक रूप। observance of 'Uposatha'.

उपोसथागार – न॰ – (उपोसथागार) उपोसथ भवन। hall for observing 'Uposatha'.

उपोसथिक – वि॰ – (उपोसथिक) उपोसथ (व्रत) के दिन आठ शील ग्रहण करने वाला। one who observes eight precepts during 'upasatha'.

उप्पक्क – वि॰ – (उत्पक्व) सूजा हुआ, फूला हुआ। swollen, scorched.

उप्पच्चति – क्रि॰ – (उत्पच्यते / उत्पच्यमान) पकता है। being boiled.

उप्पज्जति – क्रि॰ – (उत्पद्यते) उत्पन्न होता है। borns, arises.

उप्पज्जन – न॰ – (उत्पद्यन) अस्तित्व प्राप्त करना, उत्पन्न होना, जन्म, पुनर्जन्म। coming into existence, birth, rebirth.

उप्पज्जमान – कृ॰ – (उत्पद्यमान) उत्पन्न होने वाला। one who is coming into existence, being born or reborn.

उप्पज्जितब्ब – कृदन्त – (उत्पद्दितव्य) उत्पन्न होने के योग्य। fit to be born.

उप्पटिपाति – स्त्री॰ – (उत्प्रतिपाति) क्रमाभाव, अनियम। lack of order, irregularity.

उप्पटिपाटिय – वि॰ – (उद् + प्रतिपातीय) क्रम-विरुद्ध। against the order.

उप्पण्डना – स्त्री॰ – (उद् + पण्डनम्) हँसी उड़ाना, मजाक उड़ाना। ridicule, mockery.

उप्पण्डुकजात – वि॰ – (उत्पाण्डुकं जातम्) पीला पड़ गया। having become pale.

उप्पण्डेति – क्रि॰ – (उद् + पण्डयति) (पण्ड – परिहास करता है) मुँह चिढ़ाता है। mocks, derides.

उप्पतति – क्रि॰ – (उत्पतति) उड़ता है, ऊपर उछलता है। flow, jumps up.

उप्पतन – न॰ – (उत्पत्न) उड़ान, उछलन। flight, jump.

उप्पतमान – कृदन्त – (उत्पतमान) उड़ता हुआ, उछलता हुआ। state of flying, jumping.

उप्पतित – कृदन्त – (उत्पतित) उड़ा, उछला। flied, jumped.

उप्पतित्वा – पूर्व क्रि० – (उत्पतित्वा) उड़कर, उछलकर। having flown or jumped.

उप्पत्ति – स्त्री० – (उत्पत्ति) उत्पत्ति, पुनर्जन्म। birth, rebirth, production.

उप्पत्ति-भूमि – स्त्री० – (उत्पत्ति-भूमि) जन्म-भूमि। place of birth.

उप्पथ – पु० – (उत्पथ) कुपथ, कुमार्ग। wrong path, wrong course.

उप्पन्न – कृ० – (उत्पन्न) उत्पन्न। arisen, born or reborn.

उप्पब्बजति – क्रि० – (उत् + प्रब्रजति) भिक्षु-संघ से निकल जाता है। पुनः गृहस्थ हो जाता है। one who leaves the community of *bhikkhu*s and enters the household again.

उप्पब्बजित – कृदन्त – (उत् + प्रब्रजित) भिक्षु संघ से निकला हुआ, पुनः गृहस्थ बना हुआ। one who had left the community of *bhikkhu*s and had rejoined, household.

उप्पबाजेति – क्रि० – (उत्प्रब्रज्जयति) भिक्षु – संघ से निकाल देता है, पुनः गृहस्थ बना देता है। turns out of *bhikku*s from Sangha or the community.

उप्पल – न० – (उत्पल) कमल, कँवल। lotus, water-lily.

उप्पलवण्णा-थेरी – (उत्पलवर्णा थेरी) भगवान् बुद्ध की दो प्रधान भिक्षुणियों में से एक वह श्रावस्ती के एक सेठ की पुत्री थी। उसके शरीर का रंग नीलकमल के वर्ण जैसा होने के कारण उसका नाम 'उत्पलवर्णा स्थविरी' पड़ा था। one of the two chief lady disciples of Buddha, she was the daughter of a banker of Śrāvastī, she got

her name because her skin's colour was like that of blue lotus.

उप्पालिनी – स्त्री० – (उत्पालिनी) कँवलों से भरा हुआ तालाब पद्म, पुष्करिणी। a lily pond or, lake of water-lilies.

उप्पाटन – न० – (उत्पाटन) मूलोच्छेदन, उखाड़ना, फाड़ना। uprooting, pulling out, or torn apart.

उप्पाटित – कृ० – (उत्पाटित) उखाड़ा गया। pulled out, uprooted.

उप्पाटेति – क्रि० – (उत्पाटयति) उखाड़ता है, छीलता है। pulls or tears out, uproots, skins.

उप्पात – पु० – (उत्पात) (1) ऊपर उड़ना (2) उल्कापात, उपद्रव, असाधारण घटना। (1) flying up, (2) portent a meteor, adversity portent.

उप्पाद – पु० – (उत्पाद) उत्पन्न की गयी वस्तु। product.

उप्पादक – वि० – (उत्पादक) उत्पादन कर्त्ता, उत्पन्न करने वाला। grower, one who causes growing, producer.

उप्पादन – न० – (उत्पादन) उत्पत्ति। production.

उप्पादेति – पु० – (उत्पादयति) उत्पन्न करता है। produces.

उप्पादेतु – वि० – (उत्पादयिता) उत्पन्न करने वाला। producer.

उप्पादेतुं – कृ० – (उत्पादयितुम्) उत्पन्न करने के लिए। for production.

उप्पीळन – न० – (उत्पीडन) पीड़ा देना, दबाना, दमन करना। pressing, oppressing, crushing.

उप्पीळित – कृ० – (उत्पीडित) पीड़ित। oppressed, crushed.

उप्पीळेति – क्रि॰ – (उत्पीडयति) पीड़ा देता है, दबाता है, कष्ट देता है। presses down, crushes.

उप्पोठन – न – (उद् √स्फुट + ल्युट्) झाड़ना, पीटना। oppressing.

उप्पोठेति – क्रि॰ – (उद् √स्फुट = उत्स्फोटयति) झाड़ता है, पीटता है। oppresses.

उप्लवन – न॰ – (उत् √प्लु = उत्प्लवन) तिरना, तैरना। floating, rising to the surface.

उप्लवति – क्रि॰ – (उत् √प्लु = उत्प्लवते) तिरता है, तैरता है। flows.

उप्लापेति – क्रि॰ – (√लीलीयते अथवा √लुप = लुप्यति) डुबकी लगाता है। dives.

उप्फालेति – क्रि॰ – (स्फाटयति) फाड़ता है। tears, rips or splits open.

उप्फासुलिक (1) – वि॰ – (उत् + पांसुलिक परिकृशः शुष्क मांसः) पसली मात्र दिखाई देने वाला। cripple, emaciated.

उप्फासुलिक (2) – वि॰ – (उत् + पांसुलिक) धूल-धूसरित। soiled by dust.

उब्बट्टन (1) – (उद्वर्तनम्) उबटन, उबटन सरसों तथा सुगन्धित औषधियों से बनी पिष्टी जिससे अंग-मर्दन किया जाता है, बुकवा। cosmetic paste for cleaning and softening of skin an unguent.

उब्बट्टन – क्रि॰ – (उद् √वर्त + ल्युट् = उद्वर्तन) उबटन अर्थात् सुगन्धित पिष्टी से अंग-मर्दन करना। rubbing the body with cosmetic paste or unguent.

उब्बट्टित – कृ॰ – (उद् + वर्त्तित) मला गया, उबटन लगाया गया। rubled.

उब्बट्टेति – क्रि॰ – (उद् + वत्ति) मालिश करता है, उबटन लगाता है। rubs the body with cosmetic paste.

उब्बत्तेति – क्रि॰ – (उद् + वर्त्तयति) ऊपर उठाता है, फुलाता है, सुपथ से हटाता है। causes to rise or swell, leaves a right course.

उब्बन्धेति – क्रि॰ – (उद् + √बन्ध = उद् बध्नाति) फाँसी लटका देता है, गला घोंट देता है। hangs to death.

उब्बन्धन – (उद् + बन्धन) गला घोंटना, फाँसी लगा लेना, फाँसी लटकाना। strangling, hanging oneself.

उब्बहति – क्रि॰ – (उद् + √वह = उद्वहति) खींचता है, ले जाता है, उठाता है। pulls out, takes out, lifts.

उब्बहन (1) – क्रि॰ (उद् + वहन) खींचना, ले जाना, उठाना। pulling out, taking out, lifting.

उब्बहन (2) – न॰ – (उद्वहन) उबहन, कुएँ से जल-पात्र खींचने की रस्सी। thin rope or string for pulling out a water pitcher from a well.

उब्बाळह – कृदन्त – (उद् + बाधित = उद्बाधित) अपबिद्ध, हैरान किया गया। troubled, annoyed, harassed.

उब्बिग्ग – कृ॰ – (उद्विग्न) उद्विग्न। agitated.

उब्बिज्जति – क्रि॰ – (उद् + विज्यते) उद्वेग को प्राप्त होता है। becomes agitated.

उब्बिज्जना – स्त्री॰ – (उद्वेजना) उद्वेग, अशान्ति। agitation, uneasiness.

उब्बिलावितत्त – न॰ – (आह्लादत्त्व) अतिशय उल्लास, आह्लादत्त्व। rejoicing, exulting, elation of mind.

उब्बी – स्त्री॰ – (ऊर्वी) भूमि। earth.

उब्बेग – पु॰ – (उद्वेग) उद्वेग, उत्तेजना। excitement, agitation, anxiety.

उब्बेजेति – क्रि॰ – (उद् + √वीज् = उदवीजयति) उद्वेग उत्पन्न करता है, भयभीत करता है। stimulates, agitates.

उब्बेध – पु॰ – (उद्बेध) ऊँचाई। height.

उब्भट्ठक – वि॰ – सीधा खड़ा हुआ। stood erect, upright.

उब्भत – कृदन्त – (उद् + भृत) वापस ले लिया गया, खींच लिया। withdrawn, pulled out.

उब्भव – पु॰ – (उद्भव) उद्भव, उत्पत्ति। production, birth.

उब्भार – पु॰ – (उद्भार / अपभार) निलम्बन, निष्कासन, स्थानान्तरण। withdrawal, removal.

उब्भिज्ज – पू॰ क्रि॰ – (उद् + भेद्य) बाहर आकर, अंकुरित होकर। having sprung or burst upwards.

उब्भिज्जति – क्रि॰ – (उद् + भिद्यते) ऊपर उछलता है, अंकुरित होता है। springs up, sprouts.

उब्भिद (1)– पु॰ – (उद्भिद) (1) खाने का नमक (2) पु॰ पानी का पौधे का अंकुर। sprout or shoot of a plant.

उब्भिद (2) – न॰ – (उद्भिद) खाने का नमक। kitchen salt.

उब्भिद – पु॰ – (उद्भिद) जलस्रोत, झरना। water-spring, water-fall.

उब्भुजति – क्रि॰ – (उद् + नमति ऊर्ध्वंगमयति) ऊपर 'छढाता है। lifts up.

उभ, उभय – सर्वनाम – (उभ, उभय) दोनों। both.

उभतो – अव्यय – (उभयतः) दोनों ओर से, दोनों तरह से। in both ways or sides.

उभतो-भट्ठ-जातक – (जा॰ सं॰ 139) – इस जातक में एक ऐसे मछुआरे की कथा है, जो अपनी चालाकी में सब कुछ गँवा बैठा। the Jātaka tale (No. 139) concludes that the enterprise of a cunning fisherman leads him to grief.

उभो – सर्वनाम – (उभौ) दोनों (पुरुष)। both (men).

उम्मग्ग – पु॰ – (उन्मार्ग) सुरंग, चोर-रास्ता। a tunnell, devious or wrong way.

उम्मज्जन – न॰ – (उन्मार्जन) शरीर को धोना। washing the body, bathing.

उम्मत्त – वि॰ – (उन्मत्त) पागल। mad, out of mind.

उम्दन्ती-जातक – (जा॰ सं॰ 527) – (उन्मादयन्ती जातकम्) एक सेठ की लड़की की कथा जो अपने सौन्दर्य के कारण देखनें वालों को उन्मत्त बना देती थी। the Jātaka tale (No. 527) of a maiden who made all who saw her, indulge in passion, and of a king who by a supreme effort overcomes his infatuation.

उम्मा – स्त्री॰ – (उमा) अलसी, अतसी। linseed, flax.

उम्माद – पु॰ – (उन्माद) उन्माद, पागलपन। madness.

उम्मादन – न॰ – (उन्मादन) उन्मत्त कर देना। maddening.

उम्मादवन्तु – पु॰ – (उन्मत्त) पागल। mad.

उम्मार – पु॰ – (देहरी/गृहावग्रहण) देहरी, चौखट। doorsill, doorstep.

उम्मि – स्त्री॰ – (ऊर्मि) ऊर्मि, लहर। wave a ray.

उम्मिसति – क्रि॰ – (उन्मिषति) आँख खोलता है। opens one's eyes, wakes-up.

उम्मिहति – क्रि॰ – (उद् √ मिह् = उन्मेहति) पेशाब करता है। urinates.

उम्मीलन – न॰ – (उन्मीलन) उन्मीलन, आँख खोलना। opening of one's eyes.

उम्मीलेति – क्रि॰ – (उन्मीलयति) उन्मीलन करता है, आँख खोलता है। opens one's eyes.

उम्मुक – न॰ – (उल्मुकम्) लुआठी, मशाल। fire-brand.

उम्मुक्क – कृदन्त – (च्युत, संसृत) च्युत, गिरा हुआ। fallen down.

उम्मुख – वि॰ – (उन्मुख) जिसका मुँह आकाश की ओर हो। having one's face upwards.

उम्मुज्जति – क्रि॰ – (उन्मज्जति) तरता है, पानी से बाहर निकलता है। emerges, comes out of water.

उम्मुज्जन – न॰ – (उन्मज्जन) प्लवन, तरुण, (पानी से) बाहर निकलना। emerging, coming out of (water).

उम्मुज्ज-निमुज्जा – स्त्री॰ – (उन्मग्नता-निमग्नता) उतराना-डूबना। emerging and diving.

उम्मूल – वि॰ – (उन्मूल) निर्मूलीकृत, उन्मूल। uprooted.

उम्मूलित – कृदन्त – (उद् √ मूल + क्त = उन्मूलति) जड़ से खोदा हुआ, विनष्ट। uprooted, destroyed.

उम्मूलन – न॰ – (उद् √ मूल + ल्युट्) जड़ खोदना। uprooting.

उम्मूलेति – क्रि॰ – (उन्मूलयति) बर्बाद कर डालता है, जड़ खोदता है। uproots, destroys.

उय्यान – न॰ – (उद्यान) उपवन, वाटिका। a park, pleasure grove.

उय्यान-कीला – स्त्री॰ – (उद्यान क्रीडा) उद्यान क्रीडा। amusement in a park.

उय्यान-पाल – पु॰ – (उद्यानपाल) उद्यान-पालक, माली। a gardener.

उय्यान-भूमि – स्त्री॰ – (उद्यान-भूमि) उद्यान भूमि। pleasure ground.

उय्यानवन्त – वि॰ – (उद्यानवन्त) अनेक उद्यानों वाला। the owner of gardens.

उय्याम – पु॰ – (उद्यम = उद्याय) उद्यम, प्रयत्न। exertion, enterprise, effort.

उय्युञ्जति – क्रि॰ – (उद् √ युज् = उद्युङ्क्ते) काम में जुटता है, प्रयास करता है। undertakes, sets to work, pursues.

उय्युञ्जन – न॰ – (उद् √ युज् + ल्युट् = उद्योजन) उद्यमिता, क्रियाशीलता। activity.

उय्युञ्जन्त – कृदन्त – (उद्योगमान) उद्योग-रत, क्रियाशील। active, busy.

उय्युत्त – कृदन्त – (उद्युक्त) तत्पर, लगा हुआ। striving.

उय्योग – पु॰ – (उद्योग) उद्योग। exertion, effort.

उय्योजन – न॰ – (उद् √ युज + ल्युट्) प्रेरणा। instigation, sending away.

उय्योजित – कृदन्त – (उद् + योजित) प्रेरित, भेज दिया गया। instigated, sent off.

133 उल्लपना

उय्योजेति – क्रि॰ – (उद् + योजयति) प्रेरित करता है, भेज देता है। instigates, sends off.

उय्योधिक – न॰ – (उद् + योद्धन) छाया, युद्ध, छद्म-युद्ध या झूठ-मूठ की लड़ाई। sham fight of an army.

उर – पु॰ तथा न॰ – (उर) वक्ष, छाती। chest.

उर-चक्क – न॰ – (उर-चक्र) यातना देने के लिए छाती पर रखा हुआ लौह-चक्र। an iron-wheel put on the chest to torture.

उर-च्छद – (उरुच्छद्) उरुत्राण, छाती की ढाल। breast-plate.

उर-ताळि – क्रि॰ वि॰ – (उरु ताडनम्) अपनी छाती पीटना। beating one's own breast.

उरग – पु॰ – (उरग) रेंगने वाला जन्तु, सर्प। snake, a creeping reptile.

उरग-जातक (1) – (जा॰ सं॰ 154) – साँप तथा गरुड़ का संघर्ष अपने उद्बोधन से बोधिसत्व द्वारा दोनों स्थायी बैरियों में मैत्री कराने की कथा। the Jātaka tale (No. 154) tells that by preaching Bodhisattva made bitter enemies friendly towards each other.

उरग-जातक (2) – (जा॰ सं॰ 354) पुत्र की मृत्यु पर घर कोई भी नहीं रोया। the Jātak tale (No. 354) describes an incident when the family members did not mourn the death of their beloved youth due to their practices of the thought of death.

उरण – पु॰ – (उरण) भेड़, मेष, मेढ़ा। a sheep, ewe.

उरणी – स्त्री॰ – (उरणी) मादा भेड़, भेड़ी। a female ram.

उरब्भ – पु॰ – (उर्ण √भृ = उरभ्र) मेष, मेढ़ा। a ram.

उरू – वि॰ – (उरु) बड़ा, चौड़ा, प्रमुख। large, wide, eminent.

उरूवेलकप्प – पु॰ – (उरुवेलकप्प) मल्ल जनपद में मल्लों का एक नगर। a town of Malla kṣatriya's situated in Malla Janapada.

उरुवेला – स्त्री॰ – (उरुवेला) बोधगया में बोधिवृक्ष के समीप नेरञ्जरा के तट पर एक स्थान। a sight at the bank of Nerañjarā river near *bodhi* tree in Bodh Gayā.

उलूक – पु॰ – (उलूक) उल्लू। an owl.

उलूक-जातक – (जा॰ सं॰ 270) पक्षियों ने एक राजा की आवश्यकता अनुभव कर उल्लू को अपना राजा बनाये जाने का प्रस्ताव रखा किन्तु उसकी मूर्खता देख हंस को राजा चुना। feeling the necessity of a king, some resolved to crown an owl but seeing its foolishness they chose a goose.

उल्लंघन – न॰ – (उल्लंघन) सीमोल्लंघन। transgression, violation.

उल्लंघेति – क्रि॰ – (उल्लंघयति) कूद जाता है, सीमा लाँघ जाता है। jumps over, violates transgresses.

उल्लपति – क्रि॰ – (उल्लपति/उल्लपेत) आत्म प्रशंसा करता है। speaks in laudatory terms.

उल्लपना – स्त्री॰ – (उल्लपना) आत्म प्रशंसा। extolling, praising.

उल्लिखति – क्रि॰ – (उल्लिखति) अलग करता है, लकीर खींचता हैं। slits, scratches.

उल्लिखन – न॰ – (उल्लिखन) अलग करना, लकीर खींचना। tearing, slitting, scratching.

उल्लित्त – कृ॰ – (उपलिप्त) लेपित, उपलिप्त, लेप किया हुआ। plastered, covered with mortar.

उल्लुम्पति – क्रि॰ – (उप + लिम्पति) ऊपर उठाता है, सहायक होता है। raises up, helps.

उल्लुम्पन – न॰ – (उपलुम्पन) ऊपर उठाना, संरक्षण। raising up, protection.

उल्लोकक – वि॰ – (उद् √लोक् + ण्वुल) द्रष्टा। looker, one who looks on.

उल्लोकन – न॰ – (उद् √लोक + ल्युद्) (1) दृष्टिपात (2) खिड़की। (1) looking up (2) a window.

उल्लोकेति – क्रि॰ – (उद् + लोकयते) देखता है। looks up or looks for.

उल्लोच – पु॰ – (उद् + √लुच्) वितान-चँदोवा। canopy.

उल्लोल (1) – पु॰ – (उद् + लोल = उल्लोल) महोर्मि, बड़ी लहर। large wave.

उल्लोल (2) – वि॰ – (उल्लोल) चंचल। violently moving.

उल्लोलेति – क्रि॰ – (उद् + लोलयति) हलचल पैदा करता है। agitates, creates a commotion.

उसभ – पु॰ – (वृषभ) (1) सांड, वृषभ (2) श्रेष्ठ पुरुष (3) दूरी का माप विशेष (एक उसभ = 140 हाथ, एक हाथ = लगभग 20 इंच)। (1) a bull, (2) a noble person, (3) the length of 140 cubits (one cubit = about 20 inches).

उसीर – न॰ – (उशीर) खस-खस की सुगन्धित जड़। fragrant root of *Anaropogon nuricatum*.

उसु – पु॰ तथा स्त्री॰ – (इषु) तीर। an arrow.

उसुकार – पु॰ – (इषुकार) तीर बनाने वाला। arrow-maker, fletcher.

उसुवडढकी – पु॰ – (इषु + वर्द्धाकिन) इषु-तक्षक, तीर बनने वाला बढ़ई। carpenter who makes arrow.

उसूयक – वि॰ – (√असू + ण्वुल = असूयकः) ईर्ष्या करने वाला। envious, jealous.

उसूयति – क्रि॰ – (असूयति) ईर्ष्या करता है। gets envious or jealous.

उसूया – स्त्री॰ – (असूया) ईर्ष्या। envy, jealousy.

उसूयोपगम – पु॰ – (असूया + उपागम) ईर्ष्या का आगमन। rise of envy.

उस्मा – स्त्री॰ – (ऊष्मा) ऊष्णता। heat.

उस्सङ्की – वि॰ – (उत्शङ्किन) शंकालु, भयभीत। distrustful, mistrustful.

उस्सद/उस्सन्न – वि॰ – (उद् √सद + क्त) उच्छिन्न, नष्ट किया हुआ। destroyed, abolished.

उस्सनता – स्त्री॰ – (उत्सन्नता) उच्छिन्नता, विनाश। decay, abolishment.

उस्सव – पु॰ – (उत्सव) उत्सव। festival, ceremony.

उस्सहति – क्रि॰ – (उत्सहते) कोशिश करता है। attempts.

उस्सहन – न॰ – (उत्सहन) प्रयास, प्रयत्न। attempt, effort.

उस्सापन – न॰ – (उत्थापन) उठाना। raising, lifting up.

उस्सापित – कृदन्त – (उत्थापित) उठाया गया। lifted up, elevated.

उस्सापेति – क्रि॰ – (उत्थापयति) उठाता है, ऊँचा करता है। elevates, lifts up.

उस्सारणा – स्त्री – (उत्सारणा) भीड़। crowd.

उस्सारित – कृदन्त – (उत्सारित) एक ओर ढकेल दिया गया। driven aside, pushed aside.

उस्सारेति – क्रि॰ – (उत्सारयति) एक ओर ढकेल देता है। pushes aside, shoves.

उस्साव – पु॰ – (उत्स्राव) हिमकण, ओस। dew.

उस्साव-बिन्दु – न॰ – (उत्स्राव-बिन्दु) ओस की बूँद। a dew-drop.

उस्साह – पु॰ – (उत्साह) उत्साह। zeal, endeavour, enthusiasm.

उस्साहवन्तु – वि॰ – (उत्साहवन्तु) उत्साही। enthusiastic, zealous, pushing.

उस्साहेति – क्रि॰ – (उत्साहयति) उत्साहित करता है। endeavours, enthuses.

उसिञ्चति – क्रि॰ – (उत्सिञ्चति) पानी उठाता है, सींचता है। lifts water, draws water, irrigates by drip method.

उसिञ्चन – न॰ – (उपसिञ्चन) पानी उठाना, सींचना। irrigation by drip method, watering.

उसित – कृदन्त – (उत्थित) उठाया गया, ऊँचा किया गया। elevated, raised up.

उस्सीसक – न॰ – (उद् + शीशकम्) सिर रखने की जगह, तकिया। round head cushion for carrying pitcher.

उस्सुक – वि॰ – (उत्सुक) उत्सुक, उत्साही, क्रियाशील। zealous, energetic.

उस्सुक्क – न॰ – (औत्सुक्य) औत्सुक्य, उत्साह, क्रियाशीलता। zeal, energy.

उस्सुक्कति – क्रि॰ – (उत्सुक्यते) कोशिश करता है, प्रयत्न करता है। endeavours, tries.

उस्सुक्कापेति – क्रि॰ – (उत्सूक्यति/प्रेरयति) प्रेरित करता है। entices, arouses.

उस्सुसति – क्रि॰ – (उद् √शुष् = उत्शुष्यति) सूख जाता है। dries up, evaporates.

उस्सूर – वि॰ – (उत्सूर्य) सूर्योदय। sunrise.

उस्सूर-सेय्या – स्त्री॰ – (उत्सूर्य शयनम्) सूर्योदय के बाद सोते रहना। sleep after sunrise.

उस्सोलही – स्त्री॰ – (उत्साह) उत्साह। exertion.

उळार – वि॰ – (उदार) उदार, विशाल, श्रेष्ठ, प्रमुख। generous, liberal, magnificent.

उळारत्त – न॰ – (उदारत्व) उदारता, विशालता, श्रेष्ठत्व प्रमुखत्व। generosity, liberality, magnanimity.

उळु – पु॰ – (उडु = उडुप) तारा। star.

उळु-राज – पु॰ – (उडु-राज) उडुपति, चन्द्रमा। moon.

उळुङ्क – पु॰ – (दर्वी) कडछी, करछुल। a ladle.

उळुम्प – पु॰ – (उडुप) डोंगी। a raft, a float.

उळूक – पु॰ – (उलूक) उल्लू। owl.

उल्लुक-पक्खिक – न॰ – (उलूक पाक्षिकम्) उल्लू के परों से बना हुआ पहनावा। a dress made of owl's feathers.

ऊ

ऊ – पाली वर्णमाला का छठा स्वर। sixth vowel of Pāli alphabet.

ऊका – स्त्री॰ – (ऊका) जूँ चीलर। louse.

ऊन – वि॰ – (ऊन) कम, न्यून। less, minus, wanting, deficient.

ऊनत्त/ऊनता – न॰/स्त्री॰ – (ऊनत्व/ ऊनता) कमी, न्यूनता। deficiency.

ऊमी/ऊमि – स्त्री॰ – (ऊर्मि) लहर। wave.

ऊरट्ठि – न॰ – (ऊरस्थि) उरु अर्थात् जाँघ की हड्डी। the thigh-bone.

ऊरू – पु॰ – (उरु) जाँघ। the thigh.

ऊरू-पब्ब – न॰ – (ऊरु-पर्व) घुटने या जाँघ का जोड़। joint of knee.

ऊस – पु॰ – (ऊष) क्षारीय पदार्थ, खारी मिट्टी। a saline substance.

ऊसवन्तु – पु॰ – (ऊषवान्) खारी मिट्टी वाला। having saline substance.

ऊसा – पु॰ – (ऊषा) क्षारीय पदार्थ, खारा पदार्थ। saline substance.

ऊसर – वि॰ तथा न॰ – (ऊषर) क्षार-युक्त ऊसर। saline soil.

ऊहच्च – कृदन्त – (अवहृत्य) खींचा गया, हटा दिया गया। having pulled out or removed.

ऊहदति – क्रि॰ – साफ करता है, मैल दूर करता है। washes, cleans.

ऊहन – न॰ – (√उह + ल्युट् = ऊहनम्) तर्कना, विचार। reasoning, consideration.

ऊहनति (1) – क्रि॰ – (√उहन/अव √हन = उद्‌हनति/अवहनति) खींचता है, हटाता है। removes, modifies, changes.

ऊहनति (2) – क्रि॰ – (अवहनति) पृथक् करता है, अवसारित करता है। cuts off, discharges, emits.

ऊहसति – क्रि॰ – (उद्‌ + हसति) हँसता है, मुँह चिढ़ाता है। laughs at, mocks.

ऊहा – स्त्री॰ – (ऊहा) चिन्तन-मनन। contemplation.

ए

ए — पालि वर्णमाला का सातवां तथा आठवाँ स्वर। पालि में देवनागरी लिपि का 'ऐ' पालि में नहीं है। पालि में 'ए' के दो रूप हैं – ह्रस्व 'ए' और दीर्घ 'ए' जैसे 'एकाकी' शब्द के उच्चारण में ए का दीर्घ रूप है तथा 'एत्थ' के उच्चारण में ए का ह्रस्व रूप। ह्रस्व ए और 'दीर्घ' 'ए' दोनों के लिए समान लिपि-चिह्न है। अतः कुछ वैयाकरण 'ए' की व्यावहारिक स्वर भिन्नता के आधार पर पालि में स्वरों की संख्या दस मानते हैं तो दूसरा वर्ग लिपि-चिह्न के आधार पर पालि स्वरों की संख्या 8 मानने का पदाधार है। the seventh and eighth (ए & ऐ) vowel of Pāli alphabet there is no Devanāgari ऐ in Pali).

एक — वि॰ — (एक) संख्यावाचक शब्द। बहुवचन में 'एक' का अर्थ हो जाता है कुछ जैसे – एके = कुछ लोग। one (only in singular) in plural, it gives the meaning of some.

एक-चर / एक-चारी — वि॰ — (एकचारिन्) अकेलुआ, अकेला रहने वाला। one who lives alone.

एक-देश — पु॰ — (एक देशः) एक विभाग, एक हिस्सा। a portion, a part.

एक-पट्ट — वि॰ — एक तह वाला कपड़ा। having a single fold.

एक-भत्तिक — वि॰ — (एक भुत्तक) एकाहारी, दिन में एक ही बार खाने वाला। having one meal a day.

एकक — वि॰ — (एकक) अद्वितीय, अकेला। single, solitary.

एककूटयुत — पु॰ — (एक कूट्युक्त भवनम्) एक तल्ला भवन। one storeyed building.

एकक्खरकोस — पु॰ — (एकाक्षर कोशः) सोलहवीं शताब्दी में सद्धम्म-कित्ति द्वारा रचित पालि शब्द-सूची जिसमें प्रत्येक शब्द का संस्कृत-पर्याय भी दिया गया है। a well-known Pāli vocabulary, composed in the sixteenth century by Saddhammakitti, it contains Sanskrit meanings for words.

एकक्खी — वि॰ — (एकाक्षिन्) एक आँख वाला। one-eyed person.

एकग्ग — वि॰ — (एकाग्र) एकाग्र। calm, tranquil.

एकग्गता — स्त्री॰ — (एकाग्रता) एकाग्रता। tranquility of mind.

एकच्च / एकच्चिय — वि॰ — (एकत्य) कुछ, चन्द। some, certain, a few.

एकज्झं — अव्यय — (एकध्यम्) एक ही ठौर। together at the same place.

एकतो — अव्यय — (एकतः) एक ओर। together on one side.

एकत्त — न॰ — (एकत्व) (1) एकता (2) अकेलापन (3) अनुकूलता। (1) unity (2) loneliness (3) agreement.

एकदा — क्रि॰ वि॰ — (एकदा) एक बार। once, at one time.

एकन्त — वि॰ — (प्रत्यन्त) निश्चय से पूर्ण, रूप से एक छोर पर। sure, unfailing, extreme.

एकन्तम् – वि॰ – (**एकन्तम्**) देखें एकन्त। see 'Ekant.'

एकन्तन – क्रि॰ वि॰ – (**एकन्तन**) देखें एकन्त। see - 'Ekant.'

एकन्त ⁄ लोमी – पु॰ – (**प्रत्यन्त लोमिन्**) कम्बल जिसके एक छोर पर झब्बा हो। a woollen coverlet with a fringe at one end.

एकन्तरिक – वि॰ – (**एकान्तरिक**) एक का बीच देकर, एक के बाद एक छोड़कर। with a gap of one in between two words, alternate word.

एकपट्लिक – वि॰ – (**एकपट्टलिक**) एक तल्ला वाला (चप्पल)। having a single sole (footwear).

एकपण्ण-जातक – (जा॰ सं॰ 149) – (**एक पर्ण जातकम्**) निम्ब पत्र की तिक्तता के उदाहरण से बोधिसत्व द्वारा एक दुष्ट राजकुमार के व्यवहार परिवर्तन की जातक कथा। the Jātaka tale (No. 149) of an ill behaved prince who changed his conduct by the preaching of Bodhisattva.

एकपद-जातक – (जा॰ सं॰ 238) 'दक्षता' शब्द के द्वारा उपदेश की कथा मनुष्य के उत्कर्ष का मुख्य आधार 'दक्षता' है। इस तथ्य का आख्यान करने वाली जातक कथा। the Jātaka tale (No. 238) Bodhisattva reveals that *dakṣatā* (skill, cleverness or discretion) is the main basis for man's exaltation.

एक-पदिक-मग्ग – पु॰ – (**एकपदिक–मार्ग**) पगडण्डी। a footpath, a foot way-track.

एकमन्तं – क्रि॰ वि॰ – एक ओर। on one side, aside.

एकमेक ⁄ एकेक – वि॰ – (**एकमेक ⁄ एकैक**) एक-एक करके। one by one, each.

एकराज-जातक – क्रि॰ – (जा॰ सं॰ 303) – जातक कथा एक बन्दी राजा का दृष्टान्त प्रस्तुत करती है जो अपने गुणों और कौशल से न केवल दंड मुक्त किया गया अपितु उसने खोया राज्य भी प्राप्त कर लिया। the jātaka tale (No. 303) tells about a captive king who, by his virtue and skill was set free and got back his kingdom.

एकरूप – वि॰ – (**एकरूप**) अपरिवर्तनशील। unbroken.

एकविध – वि॰ – (**एकविध**) एक ही तरह का समान। of one kind, similar.

एकसो – क्रि॰ वि॰ – (**एकशः ⁄ एकैकशः**) एक-एक करके। one by one.

एकंस ⁄ एकंसिक – वि॰ – (**एकांशं, एकांशिक**) निश्चय ही, निश्चित रूप से। certain.

एकंस ⁄ एकंसिक – वि॰ – (**एकांस ⁄ एकांसिक**) एक अंस कंधे के लिए उचित, मात्र एक कन्धे का। pertaining to one shoulder.

एकाकी – त्रिलिङ्गी – (**एकाकी**) एकचर, अकेला। lonely person.

एकाकिनी – स्त्री॰ – (**एकाकिनी**) अकेली स्त्री। lonely (woman).

एकागारिक – पु॰ – (**एकागारिक**) एक कक्ष में निरुद्ध, बन्दी चोर। prisoner, a thief.

एकादस – संख्यावाची वि॰ – (**एकादश**) ग्यारह। eleven.

एकायन – पु॰ – (**एकायन**) एक + अयन (मार्ग) एक ही मार्ग, इकहरा रास्ता। the only way or means.

एकायन – पु॰ – (एकायन) एकल संचार पथ। one way communication.

एकासनिक – वि॰ – (एकाशनिक) दिन भर में एक ही बार खाने वाला। one who takes his meals only once a day.

एकाह – न॰ – (एक + अह = एकाह) एक दिन। one day.

एकाहिक – वि॰ – (एक + आह्निक = एकाह्निक) एक ही दिन रहने वाला। existing for a day.

एकिका – स्त्री॰ – (एकिका / एकाकिनी) अकेली स्त्री। a solitary woman.

एकीभाव – पु॰ – (एकीभाव) एकता, एकान्त। unity, substitute, loneliness.

एकीभूत – वि॰ – (एकीभूत) एकत्रित, सम्बन्धित। united, connected, gathered together.

एकून – वि॰ – (एक + ऊन = एकोन) एक कम। minus one, less or short by one.

एकूनचत्तालीसति – स्त्री॰ – (एकोनचत्वारिंशति) चालीस में एक कम उन्तालीस। thirty-nine.

एकूनतिंसति – स्त्री॰ – (एकोनत्रिंशति) उन्तीस। twenty-nine.

एकूनपञ्ञास – स्त्री॰ – (एकोन पञ्चाश) उनचास। forty-nine.

एकूनवीसति – स्त्री॰ – (एकोनविंशति) उन्नीस। nineteen.

एकूनसट्ठि – स्त्री॰ – (एकोनषष्टिः) उनसठ। fifty-nine.

एकूनसत्तति – स्त्री॰ – (एकोनसप्तति) उनहत्तर। sixty-nine.

एकूननवुति – स्त्री॰ – (एकोननवति) नवासी। eighty-nine.

एकूनसत – न॰ – (एकोनशतम्) निन्यानवे। ninety-nine.

एकूनासीति – स्त्री॰ – (एकोनाशीति) उन्यासी, उनास्सी। seventy-nine.

एकोदिभाव – पु॰ – (एक + दिक् + भाव) एकाग्रता। one pointedness, concentration.

एजा – स्त्री॰ – (√ एज् + कम्पने = एजा) ललक, विचलन, (हिलना)। craving, motion.

एट्ठि – स्त्री – (इष्टि) तलाश, इच्छा, चाह। search, desire.

एण – पु॰ – (एण) कृष्ण मृग, कस्तूरी मृग। a kind of antelope, black deer.

एणिक – पु॰ – (एणिक) एण-वधिक। deer-hunter.

एणिमिग – पु॰ – (एणिमृग) कृष्णसार मृग / कस्तूरी मृग। a kind of antelope, musk deer.

एणेय्य – पु॰ – (ऐणेय) एण नामक मृग से सम्बन्धित (चमड़ी, सींग, बच्चा, आदि)। relating to 'Ena' antelope (skin, horn, fawn, etc.)

एणेय्यक – न॰ – कृष्णसार मृग की नाभि से कस्तूरी निकालने के लिए नाभि में चीरा लगाकर दी जाने वाली यातना। a kind of torture given to musk deer for obtaining the musk.

एत – सर्वनाम – (एतद) वह, यह, पु॰ एसो, -स्त्री॰-ऐसा। that, this, eso (mas. singular), esā (fem. singular).

एतरहि – क्रि॰ वि॰ – (एतर्हि, इदानी) अब। now, at present.

एतादिस – वि॰ – (एतादृश्) ऐसा, इस तरह का। such of this kind.

एति – क्रि॰ – (एति) आता है । comes.

एतिहा – स्त्री॰ – (ऐतिहासिक) इति-वृत्त । historic, description.

एतिय्यह – न॰ – (एतिह्य) परम्परागत वृतान्त । legendary account.

एत्तक – वि॰ – (एत्तुक) इतना । this much, so much.

एत्तावता – क्रि॰ वि॰ – (एतावत) यहाँ तक, इतनी दूर तक । to this extent, by this much.

एत्तो – अव्यय – (इतः) यहाँ से, यहाँ । from this, out of here.

एत्थ – क्रि॰ वि॰ – (अत्र) यहाँ । here.

एदिस/एदिसक – वि॰ – (ईदृश/ईदृशिक) ऐसा, इस प्रकार का । such, such like.

एध – पु॰ – (√ इन्ध/इध्म) ईधन, जलावन । fuel, firewood.

एधति – क्रि॰ – (एधते) प्राप्त करता है, सफल होता है । gains, succeeds in.

एन – सर्वनाम – (एनम) एतद् का एक पद-रूप । 'Eta' takes this form in some cases.

एरक – न॰ – (एरक) चटाई बनाने के काम आने वाली घास-विशेष । a kind of grass used for making mats.

एरक/दुस्स – न॰ – (एरक-आस्तरणम्) एरक की बनी चादर । a kind of garment made of 'eraka grass'.

एरण्ड – पु॰ – (एरण्ड) रेंड का पौधा । the plant Palma Christi, castor oil is extracted from its seed.

एरावण – पु॰ – (एरावत) इन्द्र के हाथी का नाम । name of Indra's elephant.

एरावत – पु॰ – (एरावत) नारंगी, संतरा । mandarin, orange.

एरित – कृदन्त – (ईरित) विकम्पित । shaken.

एरेति – क्रि॰ – (ईरयति) कंपाता है । shakes, sets into motion.

एला (1) – स्त्री॰ – (एला) लार, थूक । saliva.

एला (2) – स्त्री॰ – (एला) इलायची । the seed or plant of cardamom.

एव – अव्यय – (एव) ही । emphatic particle.

एवरूप – वि॰ – (एवरूपम्) ऐसा, इस प्रकार का । such, of such form.

एवं – क्रि॰वि॰ – (एवम्) इस प्रकार । thus, in this way.

एवं – अव्यय – (एवम्) हाँ । yes.

एवम्पि – अव्यय – (एवम् अपि) इस प्रकार भी । also of this kind.

एवमेव – अव्यय – (एवमेव) इसी प्रकार ।

एवंविध – वि॰ – (एवंविध) इस प्रकार । such like.

एसति – क्रि॰ – (एषते) खोजता है । seeks, searches.

एसना – स्त्री॰ – (एषणा) खोज । seeking, longing.

एसन्त/एसमान – कृदन्त – (इष्यमाण) खोजता हुआ । having searched.

एसिकत्थम्भ – पु॰ – (नगर-द्वार स्तम्भ) नगर द्वार के सामने गड़ा हुआ खम्भा । a strong post before a city gate.

एसित – कृदन्त – (एषित) खोजा गया । searched out.

एसितब्ब – कृदन्त – (एषितव्य) खोजने योग्य । to be sought after.

एसो – पु॰ – (एषकः) खोजने वाला । searcher.

एसिनी – स्त्री॰ – (एषिणी) खोजने वाली। a female searcher.

एहलोकिक – वि॰ – (इहलौकिक) इहलोक सम्बन्धी। belonging to this world.

एहिपस्सिक – वि॰ – (एहि-पश्यकः) जो धर्म सभी को कहे कि आओ और परीक्षा करके देखो। that which invites all to come and see, open to all, open to the public.

एहि-भिक्खु – प्राचीनतम समय में किसी को भिक्षु बनाने की पद्धति 'भिक्षु' आ। way of admission to the order- "come O monk".

एळक – पु॰ – (एडक) मेष, भेड़। sheep.

एळगल – वि॰ – (एडगल) जिसके मुँह से लार टपकती है। with oozing saliva.

एळगला – the plant *Cassia Tora*.

एलमूग – पु॰ – (एडमूकः) बहरा तथा गूँगा। deaf and dumb.

एळा – स्त्री – (लाला) थूक। saliva, spittle.

एलालुक – न॰ – (उर्वारुक) ककड़ी, खरबूजा। musk melon, cucumber.

ओ

ओ – पालि वर्णमाल का नौवां-दसवां स्वर। पालि में 'ए' स्वर की भांति 'ओ' के भी ह्रस्व तथा दीर्घ दो रूप हैं। उदाहरणार्थ 'ओक' शब्द में 'ओ' का दीर्घ रूप है। जबकि 'ओक्काक' में 'ओ' का ह्रस्व रूप। लिपि-चिह्न दोनों के लिए एक ही है। संयुक्त व्यञ्जनों के पूर्व आने वाला 'ओ' ह्रस्व बोला जाता है। the ninth/tenth Vowel in Pali alphabet.

ओक – न॰ – (ओक) जल। (1) जल (2) निवास। (1) water (2) abode, habitaion.

ओकड्ढति – क्रि॰ – (अवकर्षति) खींच लाता है, हटा देता है। attracts, drives away.

ओकन्तति – क्रि॰ – (अव + कृन्तति) काटता है। cuts down.

ओकप्पति – क्रि॰ – (अव + √क्लृप् = अवकल्पते) व्यवस्था करता है, तैयारी करता है, विश्वास करता है। arranges, makes ready, feels confident.

ओकप्पना – स्त्री॰ – (अव + कल्पना) ध्यान केन्द्रित करना, विश्वास करना। fixing one's mind (on) putting trust to.

ओकप्पनिय – वि॰ – (अव + कल्पनीय) विश्वसनीय। trustworthy.

ओकप्पेति – क्रि॰ – (अव + कल्पते) विश्वास करता है। fixes one's mind on, puts one's trust in.

ओकम्पेति – क्रि॰ – (अव + कम्पयति) हिलाता है। shakes.

ओकार – वि॰ – (अवकार) नीचपन, विकृति। lowliness, degradation.

ओकास – पु॰ – (अवकाश) खुला स्थान, अवसर, अनुज्ञा। open space, chance, permission.

ओकास-कम्म – न॰ – (अवकाश-कर्म) अनुज्ञा। strewn over.

ओकिण्ण – कृदन्त – (अवकीर्ण) बिखरा हुआ, ढका हुआ। scattering, casting out.

ओकिरण – (अवकीर्णन) बिखेरा जाना, फेंका जाना। scatters, spreads, disperses.

ओकिरति – क्रि॰ – (अवकिरति) बिखेरता है। poured down.

ओक्कन्त – कृदन्त – (अवक्रान्त) आगत, घटित। arrived.

ओक्कन्ति – स्त्री॰ – (अवक्रान्ति) प्रवेश प्रकट होना, घटित होना। entry, appearance, happening.

ओक्कन्तिक – वि॰ – (अवक्रान्तिक) घटित होने वाला। appearing, entering.

ओक्कमति – क्रि॰ – (अवक्रमते) प्रवेश करता है, आता है। enters, comes in, arrives.

ओक्कमन – न॰ – (अवक्रमण) प्रवेश, आगमन। entry, arrival, advent.

ओक्कमन्त – कृदन्त – (अवक्रमण) प्रवेश होता हुआ। entering or arriving having overcome.

ओक्कम्म – पूर्व क्रि॰ – (अवक्रम्य) हटकर।

ओक्काक – पु॰ – (ओक्काक) शाक्यों तथा कोलियों का पूर्वज ओकाक्क नरेश। a king (ancestor) of the Śākyas and Kollians.

ओक्खित्त-चक्खु – वि॰ – (अवक्षिप्त चक्षु) नीची नजर वाला, अवक्षिप्त दृष्टि। with downcast eyes.

ओक्खिपति – क्रि॰ – (अवक्षिपति) फेंकता है, गिराता है। throws, cuts down, drops.

ओगच्छति – क्रि॰ – (अवगच्छति) नीचे जाता है, अस्त होता है। goes down, sinks down.

ओगण – वि॰ – (अवगण) गण से पृथक् हुआ अकेला। separated from the troop.

ओगध – वि॰ – (अवगाहित) सम्मिलित, डूबा हुआ। included, immersed.

ओगय्ह – पूर्व क्रि॰ – (अवगाह्य) मिल जाने पर, डूब जाने पर। having plunged into or entered, having understood.

ओगाह/ओगाहन – न॰ – (अवगाहन) डुबकी लगाना। diving or plunging into.

ओगाहति – क्रि॰ – (अवगाहते/अवगाहति) डुबकी लगाता हुआ। plunges into, enters into, investigates.

ओगाहमान – कृदन्त – (अवगाहन) डुबकी लगाते हुए। diving or plunging into.

ओगाळह – कृ॰ – (अवगाढ) अवगाहित। plunged into.

ओगिलति – क्रि॰ – (अवगिलति) निगलता है। swallows down.

ओगुण्ठित – कृदन्त – (अवगुण्ठित) घूँघट निकला हुआ, ढका हुआ। covered, veiled over.

ओगुण्ठेति – क्रि॰ – (अवगुण्ठयति) घूँघट निकालती है, ढकती है। veils over, covers her own face.

ओगुम्फेति – क्रि॰ – (अवगुम्फयति) (माला) पिरोता है। strings or needles (the garland).

ओग्गत (1) – कृदन्त – (अवगत) अस्तंगत। अवगत, अस्त होना। to set.

ओग्गत (2) – कृदन्त – (अस्तंगत)। came descended down.

ओघ – पु॰ – (ओघ) बाढ़, जलप्लावन। flood.

ओघ-तिण्ण – वि॰ – (ओघतीर्ण) बाढ़ से सुरक्षित। one who has overcome the flood.

ओघनिय – वि॰ – (ओघनीय) जो बाढ़ में आ सकता है। which can come in the flood, like wood.

ओचरक – पु॰ – (अवचरक) गुप्तचर। Intelligence branch, spy.

ओचिण्ण – कृदन्त – (अवचीर्ण) संगृहीत। gathered, heaped.

ओचिनन – न॰ – (अवचीर्णन) संग्रह करना, एकत्र करना। gathering, picking.

ओचिनन्त – कृदन्त – (अव + चीर्णमान) संग्रह करते हुए, एकत्र करते हुए। gathered, collected.

ओचिनाति – क्रि॰ – (अवचिनोति) संग्रह करता है, एकत्र करता है। collects, gathers, picks.

ओछिन्दति – क्रि॰ – (अवछिन्दति) काट डालता है। cuts down.

ओज – पु॰ – (ओज) शरीर-शक्ति, तेज। vigour, splendour.

ओजवन्त – वि॰ – (ओजवन्त) ओजस्वी, तेजवन्त। vigorous, splendorous.

ओजवन्तता – स्त्री॰ – (ओजवत्ता) शक्ति-
वर्धक भाव। vigorousness.

ओजहाति – क्रि॰ – (अवजहाति) छोड़ देता
है, त्याग देता है। परिव्यजति।
abandons, gives up.

ओजा – स्त्री॰ – (ओजस्) शरीर का आधार
ओज। nutritive essence.

ओजिनाति – क्रि॰ – (जयति) जीतता है,
हराता है। conquers, defeats.

ओट्ठ (1) – पु॰ – (ओष्ठ) ओठ। the lip.

ओट्ठ (2) – पु॰ – (उष्ट्र) ऊँट। camel.

ओट्ठुभति – क्रि॰ – (अव √ष्ठीव् –
अवष्ठीवति) थूकता है। splits.

ओड्डित – कृदन्त – (अवडिडत) (जाल)
फेंका गया। snared.

ओड्डेति – क्रि॰ – (पाशं अस्यतिद् अवड्यति)
(जाल) बिछाता है। lays snares.

ओणमति – क्रि॰ – (अवनमति) झुकता है।
bends down, stoops.

ओणमन – न॰ – (अवनमन) झुकना।
bending down, stooping.

ओणमित – कृदन्त – (अवनमित) अवनत,
झुका हुआ। stooped, bent down.

ओतरण – न॰ – (अवतरण) उतरना, नीचे
आना। descending landing, taking
birth, incarnate.

ओतरति – क्रि॰ – (अवतरति) नीचे उतरता
है। gets down.

ओतरन्त – कृदन्त – (अवतरन) नीचे उतरते
हुए। getting down.

ओतापेति – क्रि॰ – (उत्तापयति) धूप में
तपता है। exposes to the sun.

ओतार – पु॰ – (अवतार) उतराव, पहुँच,

अवसर, दोष। descent, access,
chance, fault.

ओतार-गवेसी – वि॰ – (अवतरण गवेसी)
अवसर खोजने वाला। seeking an
opportunity.

ओतारण – न॰ – (अवतारण) उतराव।
lowering down.

ओतारेति – क्रि॰ – (अवतारयति) उतारता
है। lowers down.

ओतिण्ण – कृदन्त – (अवतीर्ण) अवतरित।
lowered down.

ओत्तप्प – न॰ – (अवत्ताप) पाप-भीरूता।
shrinking back from, doing
wrong.

ओत्तप्पति – क्रि॰ – (अवतप्यति) पाप करने
से भयभीत होता है। feels a sense of
guilt, is afraid of doing evil.

ओत्तप्पी – वि॰ – (अवत्तापी) पाप-भीरू।
afraid of wrong.

ओत्थट – कृदन्त – (अवत्थत) फैला हुआ,
द्वारा ढका हुआ। spread over,
hidden by.

ओत्थरक – न॰ – (अवस्तरक) महीन छन्नी।
a kind of strainer, a filter.

ओत्थरति – क्रि॰ – (अवस्तरति) फैलाता है,
नीचे जाता है, छानता है। spreads
over, spreads out, filters.

ओदक – न॰ – (उदक) जल। water.

ओदकन्तिक – वि॰ – (उदकान्तिक) जिसका
अन्त जल में हो। one who dies in
the water, one who drowns.

ओदकन्तिक (ओदकान्तिक) – न॰ –
(उदकान्तिक) जलाशय का निकटवर्ती
स्थान। a place near the water.

ओदग्य – न॰ – (औदाग्र) उन्नतता, उदग्र भाव, तेजस्वी भाव । exultation, elevation, feeling of greatness.

ओदन – न॰ तथा पु॰ – (ओदन) पकाया हुआ चावल, भात । boiled rice.

ओदनिक – पु॰ – (ओदनिक) रसोइया । a cook.

ओदनिय – वि॰ – (ओदनीय) ओदन सम्बन्धी । made of rice, rice gruel.

ओदरिक – वि॰ – (औदरिक) अतिभदक, उदर पिशाच, पेटू। living for one's belly, voracious, gluttonous.

ओदहति – क्रि॰ – (अवधत्ते/अवदधाति) रखता है, ध्यान देता है। pays attention, listens.

ओदहन – न॰ – (अवधान) ध्यानावस्थित होना । paying attention, devotion.

ओदात – वि॰ – (अवदात) उत्कृष्ट, शुभ्र, स्वच्छ । clean, white, noble.

ओदात-कसिण – न॰ – श्वेत रंग का चित्त को एकाग्र करने हेतु श्वेत पट्ट । meditation on the white colour.

ओदात-वण्ण – वि॰ – (अवदात वर्ण) श्वेत, शुभ्र । white.

ओदात-वसन – वि॰ – (अवदात वसन) शुभ्र-वासक, श्वेत वस्त्रधारी । dressed in white.

ओदिस्स – क्रि॰ – वि॰ – (उद्दिश्य) उद्देश्य से। aiming at, having a particular purpose, definitely, specifically.

ओदिस्सक – वि॰ – (उद्दिश्यक) मुख्य रूप से, विशेष रूप से। with a particular purpose, definitely, specifically.

ओदुम्बर – वि॰ – (औदुम्बर) गूलर-वृक्ष सम्बन्धी । related to an 'Udumbar', the glamorous fig tree or Ficus Religiosa.

ओधि – पु॰ – (अवधि) अवधि, सीमा। period, boundary, limit.

ओधिसो – क्रि॰ वि॰ – सीमित मात्रा में। limited.

ओधुनाति – क्रि॰ – (अवधुनोति) बुरी तरह पिटाई करता है, धुनता है (रूई)। beats hard, to card cotton.

ओनद्ध – कृदन्त – (अव + नद्ध) बँधा हुआ, ढका हुआ, लिपटा हुआ । bound, covered up, wrapped over.

ओनन्धति – क्रि॰ – बाँधता है, ढकता है, लपेटता है। binds, covers up, wraps over.

ओनमक – वि॰ – (अवनमक) झुकता हुआ। bent down.

ओनमति – क्रि॰ – (अवनमति) झुकता है। bends down, stoops.

ओनमन – न॰ – (अवनमन) झुकना। bending, stooping.

ओनह्हति – क्रि॰ – (अव $\sqrt{}$नह = अवनह्हति) ढकता है, बाँध डालता है। ties down, covers over, shrouds, binds.

ओनहन – न॰ – (अवनहन) ढकना। covering.

ओनीत – कृदन्त – (अवनीत) हटाया गया, ले जाया गया। taken away, removed.

ओनेति – क्रि॰ – (अवनयति) दूर हटा है, दूर ले जाता है। takes away, removes.

ओनोजन – न॰ – (अव $\sqrt{}$निज + ल्युट् = अवनेजन) धुलाई, सफाई, अपने हाथ धो

डालना। washing off, cleaning, washing one's hands.

ओनोजेति – क्रि॰ – (अव √ निज् = अवनेनेक्ति) धोता है। washes.

ओनोजित – कृदन्त – (अवनेजित) धोकर साफ किया हुआ, धोया हुआ। cleanend with water, washed.

ओपक्कमिक – वि॰ – (उप + क्रमिक) किसी उपक्रम अथवा उपाय-विशेष से किया गया कष्ट। pain caused by some contrivance.

ओपक्खी – वि॰ – (अव + पक्षी) अशक्त, जिसके पर कटे हों। powerless, wingless, weak.

ओपतति – क्रि॰ – (अव + उत्पतति) (1) गिरता है (2) उड़ जाता है। (1) falls, (2) flies away.

ओपतित – कृदन्त – (अवपतित) गिरा हुआ। fallen.

ओपत्त – वि॰ – (अवपत्र) पत्र-विहीन ऐसा पेड़ जिराके पत्ते गिर गए हों। leaf less, a tree without leaves.

ओपधिक – वि॰ – (औपधिक) पुनर्जन्म के आधार-सम्बन्धी। forming a substratum for rebirth.

ओपनयिक – वि॰ – (उपनयिक) पास ले जाने वाला। leading to.

ओपपातिक – वि॰ – (औत्पातिक) प्रत्यक्ष कारण के बिना उत्पन्न, असहज रूप से उत्पन्न हुआ। arisen or produced born without cause.

ओपम्म – न॰ – (औपम्य) उपमा, तुलना। simile, comparison.

ओपरज्ज – न॰ – (औपराज्य) उपराजपन। viceroyalty.

ओपवव्ह – वि॰ – (आरोहणीय) चढ़ने के योग्य। fit for riding.

ओपसमिक – वि॰ – (औपशमिक) शान्ति-कारक। quieting.

ओपात – पु॰/न॰ – (अवपात) (1) गड्ढा (2) पतन। (1) pit (2) fall.

ओपातेति – क्रि॰ – (अवपातयति) गिराता है। makes fall, interrupts.

ओपान – न॰ – (निपान) कूप, इनार, कुआँ। well (for water).

ओपारम्भ – वि॰ – (उपारम्भ) सहायक। acting as a support, helpful.

ओपायिक – वि॰ – (औपायिक) योग्य। suitable.

ओपिलापित – कृदन्त – (अवप्लावित) तैराया गया। floated.

ओपिलापेति – क्रि॰ – (अवप्लावयति) तैराता है। makes something float.

ओपुणाति – क्रि॰ – (अवप्रनाति) पवित्र करता है। imparts sanctity, sanctifies.

ओपुप्फ – न॰ – (अवपुष्प) कलिका, मुकुल कली। bud, young flower.

ओबंधति – क्रि॰ – (अववध्नाति) बाँधता है। binds, ties with.

ओभग्ग – कृदन्त – (अव √ भञ्ज् + ल्युट्) टूटा हुआ। broken.

ओभज्जति – क्रि॰ – (अवभञ्जति) तोड़ डालता है। breaks.

ओभत – कृदन्त – (अवभृत) ले जाया गया। taken away, carried away.

ओभरति – क्रि॰ – (अवभरति) ले जाता है। takes or carries away.

ओभास – पु॰ – (अवभास) चमक, दीप्ति,

तेज प्रकाश। shine, splendour, light, lustre.

ओभासति (1) – क्रि॰ – (अव √ भास = अवभासते) चमकता हैं। shines.

ओभासति (2) – क्रि॰ – (अव √ भाष = अव भाषते) अपशब्द कहता है, गाली देता है। abuses.

ओभासन – न॰ – (अवभासन) चमक। shining.

ओभासित – कृदन्त – (अवभासित) प्रकाशित। illuminated.

ओभासेति – क्रि॰ – (अवभासयति) चमकाता है। gets illuminated.

ओभासेन्त – कृदन्त – (आभासमान) चमकते हुए। radiating, illuminating.

ओभोग – पु॰ – (संपुटीकरण) (1) झुकना लपेटना (2) चीवर का तह करना। (1) winding, bending (2) the fold of a robe.

ओम/ओमक – वि॰ – (वैदिक अवम् का तमप् बोधक रूप) निम्न कोटि का। lower in rank, inferior.

ओमट्ठ – कृदन्त – (अव √ मृश् + क्त = अवपृष्ट) संस्पृष्ट, छुआ गया, मैला किया गया। touched, made unclean, polluted.

ओमद्दति – क्रि॰ – (अव + मर्दति) मलता है, दबाता है। rubs, oppresses.

ओमसति – क्रि॰ – (अव + मृशति) स्पर्श करता है। touches.

ओमसना – स्त्री॰ – (अवमर्षण) स्पर्श। touching, touch.

ओमान – न॰ – (अवमान) अपमान, तिरस्कार, अगौरव। disregard, disrespect, contempt.

ओमिस्सक – वि॰ – (अवमिश्रक) मिश्रित। mixed.

ओमुक्क – वि॰ – (अव + √ मुच + क्त) फेंका गया। cast off.

ओमुञ्चति – क्रि॰ – (अवमुञ्चति) खोलता है, (वस्त्र) उतारता है। takes off, unfastens (clothes), undresses.

ओमुत्त – कृदन्त – (अवमुक्त) मुक्त हुआ, स्वतन्त्र हुआ। released, freed, independent.

ओमुत्तेति – (अवमूत्रयति) मूत्र करता है। urinates.

ओयाचति – क्रि॰ – (अवयाचते) बुरा चाहता है, शाप देता है। wishes ill, curses.

ओर – न॰ – (ओर) इस ओर, यह संसार। this side, this world.

ओर – वि॰ – (अवर) अवर, हीनता, कनीयान। inferior.

ओर-पार – न॰ – (ओर–पार) इस ओर, उस पार, इहलोक-परलोक। this side-that side, the world here and above.

ओर-मत्तक – वि॰ – (अवर–मात्रक) तुच्छ, मामूली। insignificant, ordinary.

ओरब्भिक – पु॰ – (औरब्भिक) उरम अर्थात् भेड़ों का व्यापार करने वाला, या भेड़ मारने वाला कसाई। dealer or butcher of sheep.

ओरमति – क्रि॰ – (अवरमते) विरभ, इधर ही रुक जाता है। stays put on this side.

ओरमापेति – क्रि॰ – (अव रमापयति) (किसी अन्य को) रोक देता है। makes someone desist.

ओरम्भागिय – वि॰ – (ओरिय भागीय ऐहिक)

इस लोक-सम्बन्धी । related to this world.

ओरस – वि॰ – (औरस) आत्मज, स्वकीय पुत्र । legitimate son, own son.

ओरिम – वि॰ – (ओरिम) इस तरफ का, इस ओर का । of this world, of this side.

ओरिम/तीर – न॰ – (ओरिम-तीर) नजदीक का तट । the nearest shore.

ओरुद्ध – कृदन्त – (अवरुद्ध) बाधित, जिसके मार्ग में बाधा डाली गयी हो । restrained, subdued.

ओरुन्धति – क्रि॰ – (अवरुन्धति) प्राप्त करता है, पत्नी बनाता हैं । obtains, takes for a wife.

ओरूळ्ह – पु॰/कृ॰ – (अवरुद्ध) उतरा हुआ, expelled, removed.

ओरोध – पु॰ – (अवरोध) रनिवास । a harem.

ओरोध – पु॰ – (अवरोध) बाधा । obstruction, check.

ओरोपन – न॰ – (अवरोपण) उतारना, हटाना । taking down, removing.

ओरोपेति – क्रि॰ – (आरोपयति) उतारता है, हटाता है । takes or lowers down.

ओरोहण – न॰ – (अवरोहण) उतरना । descent, coming down.

ओरोहति – क्रि॰ – (अवरोहति) (नीचे) उतरता है । descends, comes down.

ओलग्गेति – क्रि॰ – (अव √लग्ग् = अवलग्नाति) रोकता है । stops, restrains, puts off.

ओलंघना – स्त्री॰ – (अवलंघना) नीचे झुकना । bending down.

ओलंघेति – क्रि॰ – (अवलंघयति) नीचे कूदाता है । makes someone jump down.

ओलम्ब – वि॰ – (अवलम्ब) अवलम्ब, लटकने की स्थिति । hanging down.

ओलम्बति – क्रि॰ – (अवलम्बति) नीचे रोकता है, नीचे से थाम लिया जाता है । hangs on to, is supported by, rests on.

ओलम्बन – न॰ – (अवलम्बन) (1) आश्रय, आधार सहारा, (2) धारण, ग्रहण । (1) base, support (2) hold, assumption.

ओलिखति – क्रि॰ – (अवलिखति) लकीर खींचता है, खरोंचता है । draws a line, scratches.

ओलिगल्ल – पु॰ – (व्युत्पत्ति सन्दिग्ध प्रणालि:, जल परिवाह:) चहबच्चा, नाबदान । a dirty pool near a village, gutter, drain.

ओलीन – कृ॰ – (अवलीन) प्रमादी, सुस्त, ढीला-ढाला । infatuated, adhering, sticking.

ओलीयति – क्रि॰ – (अवलीयते) आलस्य या प्रमाद करता है । sticks, clings to.

ओलुग्ग – कृ॰ – (अवलग्न) टुकड़े-टुकड़े हो चुका । fallen to pieces.

ओलुज्जति – क्रि॰ – (अवरुज्यते) टुकड़े-टुकड़े हो जाता है । falls to pieces.

ओलुम्पेति – क्रि॰ – (अवलुम्पति) छिलका उतारता है, पकड़ता है, चुनता है, चुगता है । strips off, picks up, plucks.

ओलोकन – न॰ – (अवलोकन) अवलोकन, देखना । looking at.

ओलोकनक – न॰ – (अवलोकनक) गवाक्ष, खिड़की, झरोखा । a window.

ओलोकेति – क्रि॰ – (अवलोकयति) देखता है । looks at.

ओळारिक – वि॰ – (आढय, स्थूलः) पीवर, मोटा, ताजा, स्थूल। gross, coarse, material.

ओवज्जमान – कृदन्त – (आवद्य आवद्द्य) उपदिष्ट, अनुशासित। instructed, disciplined.

ओवट्टिक – स्त्री॰ – (आवर्त्तिक) कमरबन्द। girdle, waist-band.

ओवदति – क्रि॰ – (उपदिशति) उपदेश देता है। gives advice, preaches.

ओवदन – न॰ – (आ √वद् + ल्युट्) उपदेश देना। teaching, advising.

ओवदितब्ब – कृदन्त – (आ √वद् + तव्यत्) उपदेश देने के योग्य। fit for preaching, advisable.

ओवमति – क्रि॰ – (आ + वमति) उल्टी करता है, कै करता है। throws up, vomits.

ओवरक – न॰ – (गर्भगृह) अन्दर का कमरा। inner chamber, sanctum sanctorum in a temple.

ओवरति – क्रि॰ – (अव + वारयति) रोकता है। restricts, bans.

ओवस्सति – क्रि॰ – (आ + वर्षति) बरसता है। rains.

ओवस्सापेति – क्रि॰ – (आ + वर्षापयति) बारिश में भिगवाता है। drenches in the rain.

ओवहति – क्रि॰ – (अव + वहति) नीचे ले जाता है। carries down.

ओवाद – पु॰ – (आ + वाद) उपदेश। teaching, preaching.

ओवादक – पु॰ – (आ + वादक) उपदेश देने वाला। preacher.

ओवादक्खम – वि॰ – (आ + वाद + क्षम) उपदेश करने की क्षमता वाला। competent, or eligible to be preached, a disciple.

ओविज्झति – क्रि॰ – (आ + विध्यति) बींधता है। pierces through.

ओसक्कति – क्रि॰ – (अव + शक्नोति = अवसर्पति) पीछे हटता है। draws back, moves back.

ओसज्जति – क्रि॰ – (अव √सज्जू = अवसञ्जति) छोड़ता है। emits, evacuates.

ओसध – न॰ – (औषधि) औषधि, दवाई। any medicine (whether of herbs or other ingredients).

ओसधी – स्त्री॰ – (औषधि) दवाई का पौधा। herb for medicine.

ओसधीस – पु॰ – (ओषधीश) चन्द्रमा। moon.

ओसन्न – वि॰ – (अवसन्न) उत्सन्न, त्यक्त, छोडा हुआ। given out, exhausted.

ओसप्पति – क्रि॰ – (अवसर्पति) पीछे हटता है। draws back, gives way.

ओसरण – न॰ – (अव √सृ + ल्युट् = अवसरण) वापसी। (1) return to, going into (2) withdrawal.

ओसरति – क्रि॰ – (अवसरति) वापस आता है। returns, visits.

ओसान – न॰ – (अवसान) समाप्ति। stopping, ceasing, ending.

ओसापेति – क्रि॰ – (अवसापयति) अवसान करता है, समाप्त करता है। brings to an end, completes, finishes.

ओसारक – न॰ – (अवसारकः) आलिन्द, ओसारा। verandah, out-house.

ओसारणा – स्त्री॰ – (अवसारणा) पुनः स्थापना, पुनर्नियुक्ति, बहाली। restoration, rehabilitation.

ओसारेति – क्रि॰ – (अवसारयति) पुनर्नियुक्त करता है। expounds, puts in, restores.

ओसिञ्चति – क्रि॰ – (अवसिञ्चति) फुहार विधि सींचता है। sprinkles, as a part of ritual.

ओसीदन – न॰ – (अवसीदन) डूबना। sinking.

ओसीदापन – न॰ – (अवसादन) डुबाना। submerging, causing to sink, drawning.

ओसीदापेति – क्रि॰ – (अवसादयति) डुबाता है। submerges, causes sinking, drowns.

ओस्सग्ग – न॰ – (अव $\sqrt{}$ सृज = अवसर्ग) अनवधानता, शिथिलीकरण। inattention, carelessness, absent-mindedness.

ओस्सजति – क्रि॰ – (अवसृजति) ढीला छोड़ता है, मुक्त कर देता है। releases, frees.

ओस्सजन – न॰ – (अवसृजन) मुक्ति, परित्याग। release, dismissal, giving up.

ओहरति – क्रि॰ – (आ + $\sqrt{}$ हृ = आहरति) ले जाता है। takes away.

ओहाय – पूर्व क्रि॰ – (अव $\sqrt{}$ हा + क्त्वा = अवहाय) छोड़कर। having left or given up.

ओहरण – न॰ – (अवहरण) (1) हटाना (2) हजामत करना। (1) removing, (2) shaving.

ओहित – कृदन्त – (अवहित / अपहित) छिपा हुआ। taken down concealed.

ओहीन – कृदन्त – (अवहीन) पीछे छूटा हुआ। left behind.

ओहीयति – क्रि॰ – (अव $\sqrt{}$ हा – = अवजहाति) पीछे रह जाता है। stays behind.

ओहीयन – न॰ – (अवहायन) पीछे रह जाना। staying behind.

ओहीयमान – कृ॰ – (अवहीमयान) पीछे रह जाता है। stood behind or stayed back.

क

क (1) – (क) देवनागरी एवं पालि वर्णमाला का प्रथम व्यञ्जन। the first consonant of Devanāgarī and Pāli alphabet.

क (2) – सर्व॰ – (कः) प्रश्नवाचक किम् सर्वनाम का एक रूप जिसका प्रयोग कौन, क्या, कौन-सा अर्थों में होता है। an interrogative.

कंस – न॰ – (कांस्य) काँसा नामक धातु। bronze, bell metal.

ककच – पु॰ – (क्रकच) आरा। a saw.

ककण्टक – पु॰ – (कुलाहकः)सरटः, प्रतिसूर्यकः गिरगिट। chameleon.

ककण्टक-जातक – (जा॰ सं॰ 546) – महाउम्मग-जातक में आगत ककण्टकपञ्ह कथा। एक गिरगिट की कहानी के माध्यम से नगण्य लाभ पर इतराने वाली ओछी बुद्धि का दृष्टान्त है। The jātaka tale no. 546 showing the story of a Chameleon.

ककु – पु॰ – (ककु) शिखर, चोटी, कूब। summit, a hump.

ककुट्ठा – कुसीनारा के समीप की एक नदी, जिसमें परिनिर्वाण से पूर्व भगवान् बुद्ध ने स्नान किया था और जिसका जल ग्रहण किया था। a river near Kusīnārā, in which Lord Buddha bathed and of whose water he drank.

ककुद – पु॰ – (ककुद्) राजचिह्न, शिखर, साँड का डिल्ला। summit, hump of a bull.

ककुध – पु॰ – (ककुद्) (1) साँड की गर्दन पर कूबड़ जैसा डिल्ला (2) अर्जुन वृक्ष। (1) the hump of a bull (2) the tree *Terminalia Arjuna*.

ककुध-भण्ड – न॰ – (ककुद्-भाण्ड) सत्ता का प्रतीक चिह्न, राजत्व के प्रतीक पाँच अवयव – मुकुट, छत्र, खड्ग, पदत्राण, और चमर। ensign of royalty, the five regalia — diadem, canopy, sword, slippers and chowry of Yak's tail.

कक्क – न॰ – (उद्वर्तनम = अनुविलेपः) उबटन, लेप-विशेष। a paste, ointment.

कक्कट – पु॰ – (कर्कट) गेंगटा, केकड़ा। a crab.

कक्कटक-जातक – (जा॰ सं॰ 267) – हाथी रूप में जन्में बोधिसत्त्व द्वारा हाथियों को खाने वाले भयानक केकड़े के वध की कथा। the story (No. 267) of Bodhisattva (as an elephant) who killed the elephant-eater crab.

कक्कर – पु॰ – (तित्तिरः) तीतर। a partridge.

कक्कर-जातक – (जा॰ सं॰ 209) – उसे पकड़ने के लिए एक बुद्धिमान पक्षी द्वारा प्रयत्नशील किसान को छकाने की कथा। the jātaka tale (No. 209) tells how a wise bird befooled the farmer trying to catch the bird.

कक्करता – स्त्री॰ – (कर्कशता) कर्कश भाव। harshness, the state of rigidity.

कक्कस – वि॰ – (कर्कश) कठोर, कर्कश।
rough, harsh.

कक्कारी – स्त्री॰ – (कर्कटी) तोयफला,
चिर्भटी, ककड़ी। cucumber, female
tortoise.

कक्कारू-जातक – (जा॰ सं॰ 326) – अपात्र
दुर्गुणी, लोभी पुरोहित द्वारा मिथ्या वचनों
से ग्रहण की गयी दिव्य-माला पहनने से
विपदा में पड़ने की कथा। the Jātaka
tale (No. 326) of a fraud paṇḍit.

कक्कारेति – क्रि॰ – खखारता है। coughs
up in order to clear the throat.

कक्खल – वि॰ – (कर्कश) खुरदरा। rough,
harsh, hard.

कक्खळता – स्त्री॰ – (कर्कशता) कठोरपन।
harshness, rigidity.

कङ्क – पु॰ – (कङ्क) श्वेत चील, सारस-
बगुला। heron, white vulture.

कंकट – पु॰ – (कङ्कट) लौह कवच, अंकुश।
armour, goad to drive an
elephant.

कङ्कण न॰ (कङ्कण) कंगन। a bracelet.

कङ्खावितरणी – (कङ्खावितरणी) विनय पिटक
के प्रातिमोक्ष पर बुद्धघोषाचार्य द्वारा रचित
अट्ठकथा। the Aṭṭhakathā of
Pātimokha under Vinaya Pīṭaka
written by Buddhaghoṣa.

√कङ्ख – (भू॰) (इच्छायां – √कांक्ष् =
कांक्षति) चाहना। to desire.

कंखति – क्रि॰ – (आ √शङ्क् = आशङ्कते)
सन्देह करता है। doubts, suspects.

कंखना – स्त्री॰ – (शङ्कना) शङ्का, सन्देह।
doubt, suspicion.

कंखनीय – कृ॰ – (आ + शङ्क् + अनीयर् =
आ + शङ्कनीय) सन्दिग्ध। doubtful.

कंखा – स्त्री॰ – (आशङ्का) सन्देह। doubt.

कंखी – वि॰ – (आशङ्की) आशंका वाला,
सन्देह करने वाला। one who doubts.

कङ्गु – स्त्री॰ – (कङ्गु) कदन्न, बाजरा।
millet seed.

कच – न॰ – (कच) बाल। hair.

कचवर – पु॰ – (अवस्करः) कूड़ा-करकट।
sweepings, rubbish.

कच्चानि-जातक – (जा॰ सं॰ 417) धर्म के
श्राद्ध की कथा जो दर्शाती है कि पत्नी
कैसे मातृभक्त पति को माता से विमुख
बना देती है। the Jātaka tale (No.
417) tells how the wife makes
the husband angry with his old
beloved mother.

कच्चायन-व्याकरण – कच्चायन द्वारा रचित
व्याकरण। a famous book on Pāli
grammar written by Kaccāyana.

कच्चि – अव्यय – (कच्चित्) सन्देहार्थक-
पद। an indefinite interrogative
particle expressing doubts.

कच्छ (1) – पु॰ – (कच्छ) दलदली भूमि।
marshy land.

कच्छ (2) – न॰ – (कक्ष) काँख, बगल,
भुजमूल का निचला भाग। arm-pit.

कच्छक – पु॰ – (अञ्जीरः) अंजीर का
पेड़। a kind of fig tree.

कच्छन्तर – पु॰ – (कक्षान्तर) (1) राजा का
अपना कमरा (2) बगल के नीचे।
(1) interior of a royal palace
(2) below the armpit.

कच्छप – पु॰ – (कच्छप) कछुआ। a
tortoise, a turtle.

कच्छप-जातक – (जा॰ सं॰ 178) – एक
कछुवे की कथा जिसने सूखा पड़ने पर

भी अतिशय मोहवश अपना तालाब नहीं छोड़ा और कुम्हार की कुदाल से कटकर मर गया। the Jātaka tale (No. 178) which shows the folly of a tortoise who did not leave his tank when it became dry in summer and was killed with a potter's pick-axe.

कच्छप-जातक – (जा॰ सं॰ 215) – एक कछुवे की कथा जो अति-मुखरता के दोषों और मौन रखने के गुणों पर प्रकाश डालती है। a tortoise tale (No. 215) that reveals the demerits of talkativeness and highlights the virtues of silence.

कच्छप-जातक – (जा॰ सं॰ 273) – यह कथा बतलाती है कि मजाक में की गयी शरारत किस प्रकार विपदा बनकर गले पड़ती है। This tale (No. 273) tells how a mischief causes danger.

कच्छपुट – वि॰ – (कक्षपुट) बगल काँख में बाँधकर सौदा बेचने वाला। hawker who has a bundle hanging from one shoulder.

कच्छबन्धन – न॰ – (कक्ष्य-बन्धन) कमर-बन्द। girdle.

कच्छा (1) – स्त्री॰ – (कक्षा) करधनी, मेखला, हाथी की रस्सी। girdle, rope for elephant.

कच्छा (2) – स्त्री॰ – (कक्षा) कटी, जघन, काछ। secluded place of a building, private chamber.

कच्छा (3) – (कक्ष्या) करधनी, मेखला, हाथी की रस्सी। girdle, the rope for an elephant, girth.

कच्छा-बन्ध – स्त्री॰ – (कच्छा-बन्धनम्) कौपीन। undergarment.

कच्छु (1) – स्त्री॰ – (कच्छु) खुजलाहट, चर्म रोग-विशेष। a kind of skin desease, itch, seals.

कच्छु (2) – पु॰ – (कौञ्चफलम्) केवाच का फल जिसे त्वचा पर रगड़ने से खुजली पैदा होती है। flower of Dolichos pruriens plant, causes itching when applied on skin.

कजङ्गल – पु॰ – (कजङ्गल) मध्यमण्डल की बुद्ध-कालीन पूर्वी सीमा। the eastern boundary of Majjhima Pades in Buddhist period.

कज्जल – न॰ – (कज्जल) काजल, अञ्जन। black ointment for eyes, collyrium, salve for eyes.

कञ्चन – न॰ – (कञ्चन) स्वर्ण, सुवर्ण, कनक। gold.

कञ्चन-वण्ण – वि॰ – (कञ्चन वर्ण) सोने का सा रंग वाला, सुनहला। golden, of gold colour.

कञ्चुक – पु॰ – (कञ्चुक) जाकेट, कवच, केंचुल। jacket, overcoat, armour, the slough of a snake.

कञ्चुकी – पु॰ – (कञ्चुकी) राजकीय सेवक। a royal attendant.

कञ्जिक – न॰ – (कञ्जिकम्) गृहाम्ल, काँजी। a kind of sour gruel, vinegar.

कञ्जिय – देखें कञ्जिय (कञ्जिक) see Kañjik.

कञ्जा – स्त्री॰ – (कन्या) कुमारी, कन्या। girl, maiden, virgin.

√कट (भू॰) मर्दने – (√कट् = छेदने) काटना, चूर-चूर करना। to cut into small pieces.

कट (1) – कृ॰ – (√ कृ + क्त = कृत)
किया गया । performed, done.

कट (2) – पु॰ – (कट) चटाई । mat-
made of stalk.

कटक (1) – न॰ – (कटक) बाजूबन्द । a
bracelet.

कटक (2) – न॰ – (कटक) पर्वत की घाटी,
गुहा । cave, middle part of a
mountain, ridge.

कटकटायति – क्रि॰ – (कटकटायते) (दाँतों
से) कट-कट करता है । grinds the
teeth.

कटच्छु – पु॰ – (दर्वी) करछुल, कड़छी । a
ladle, a scoop.

कटल्लक – न॰ – (काष्ठ पुत्तलिका)
कठपुतली । a puppet.

कटसार – पु॰ – (कटसार) चटाई । a mat.

कटसी – स्त्री॰ – (कटस्थली, कटसी)
शमशान-भूमि । cemetry.

कटाह – पु॰ – (कटाह) कड़ाह । a big
frying pan, couldron, well.

कटाहक-जातक – (जा॰ सं॰ 125) दासीपुत्र
कटाहक की कथा बतलाती है कि कैसे
झूठी डींग हाँकने वाले का घमंड रहस्य
खुल जाने की आशंका से शान्त हो जाता
है । Jātaka tale (No. 125) tells how
the pretensions of a person who
used to boast of his lineage are
exposed, and how he becomes
sober.

कटि – स्त्री॰ – (कटि) कमर । waist, hip,
buttocks.

कटु – वि॰ – (कटु) तिक्त, कड़आ । bitter,
pungent.

कटुक – वि॰ – (कटुक) तेज, तिक्त, कड़आ ।
sharp, bitter, pungent.

कटुक-भण्ड – न॰ – (उपस्कारः) उपस्कर
सामग्री । मसाले । spices.

कटुक-विपाक – वि॰ – (कटुक-विपाक)
दुष्परिणाम । bitter results, bitter
consequence.

कटुक-रोहिणी – स्त्री॰ – (कटुरोहिणी) कटुका,
कटुभाषिणी । a woman using
seurrilous, abusive words.

कटुवियकत – वि॰ – (कलुषीकृत) कलुषित
किया हुआ । made impure,
polluted.

कटुका – स्त्री॰ – देखें 'कटुरोहिणी' । see
Kaṭurohiṇi.

कट्ठ – न॰ – (काष्ठ) काष्ठ, लकड़ी ।
peice of wood, timber, stick.

कट्ठक – पु॰ – (काष्ठकः / वंश-वृक्ष) बाँस
का पेड़ । bamboo plant.

कट्ठत्थर – न॰ – (काष्ठस्तर) लकड़ी के
तख्तों का आस्तरण । a bed of wooden
planks, a mat made of twigs.

कट्ठमय – वि॰ – (काष्ठमय) लकड़ी का
बना । made of wood.

कट्ठहारि-जातक – (जा॰ सं॰ 7) – दुष्यन्त
के शकुन्तला को अंगूठी देने की तरह
राजा ने मुग्ध होकर लकड़ी चुनने वाली
स्त्री को अपनी अंगूठी दी । उसका
अपरिचित पुत्र बड़ा होकर राज्य का
उत्तराधिकारी बना । This Jātaka tale
(No. 7) tells how the son of a
beautiful poor woman, to whom
the king had gifted his signed
ring, inherited the kingdom.

कटिठस्स – न॰ – कढ़ी हुई रेशमी चादर ।
a silken coverlet embroidered
with gems.

कठल – न॰ – (घटशकलम्) ठीकरे। potsherd, fragment of an earthen vessel.

कठित – न॰ – (उत्क्वथित) उबाला हुआ। boiled.

कठिन (1) – वि॰ – (कठिन) कठोर, कर्कश, मुश्किल। rough, hard, stiff, difficult.

कठिन (2) – न॰ – (चीवर-विशेषः) भिक्षुओं को प्रतिवर्ष दिया जाने वाला चीवर विशेष। the tattered, dress (cloth) annually supplied to the monks.

कठिनत्थार – पु॰ – कठिन चीवरों का भेंट करना। dedication of the rough robes, to a monk.

√ कड्ढ – (भू॰) कड्ढने – (आ √ कृष् = कर्षणे) खींचना, निकालना। to pull, remove.

कड्ढति – क्रि॰ – (कर्षति) खींचता है। draws, pulls outs.

कड्ढन – न॰ – (कर्षण) खींचना, चूसना। to draw, to pull out.

√ कण – (भू॰) सद्दत्थे – (√ क्वण = क्वणति) बजना, शब्द करना। to ring, to sound.

√ कण – (भू॰) – (निमीलने) मूंदना। to be shut-up, to be covered, to be hidden.

कण – पु॰ – (कण) (चावल के टूटे) कण। the broken pieces of rice, grain, granule.

कणय – पु॰ –(कुन्तः) बरछी। a spear.

कणवीर – पु॰ – (कर्णवीर/करवीर) करवीर नामक एक विषैला पौधा। the oleander plant, a poisonous shrub.

कणवेर-जातक – (जा॰ सं॰ 318) – सामा नामक राज्य-गणिका द्वारा मृत्यु-दण्ड प्राप्त दस्यु को कारागार-मुक्त कराने तथा मुक्त दस्यु द्वारा सामा को ही लूट लेने की कथा। the Jātaka tale (No. 318) tells about a robber who was arrested and was condemned to death. The chief courtesan of the city, Sāmā, bribed the authority and got him free but the robber looted her ornaments and escaped.

कणाजक – न॰ – (कणजूषकम्) टूटे चावलों की खिचड़ी। the porridge of broken rice.

कणिका – स्त्री॰ – (कणिका/कर्णिकार) कनेर नामक पुष्प तरु। Cascariao Vata plant having flowers of golden colour.

कणिकार – पु॰ – (कर्णिकार) कनेर नामक फूलदार वृक्ष-विशेष। see Kanika.

कणेरिक – न॰ – (कुटीर) झोंपड़ी। the hut.

कणिट्ठ – वि॰ – (कनिष्ठ) सबसे छोटा। youngest.

कणिट्ठक – पु॰ – (कनिष्ठ) अनुज, छोटा भाई। the younger brother.

कणिट्ठा – स्त्री॰ – (कनिष्ठा) छोटी बहन। the younger sister.

कणेरू (1) – पु॰ – (करेणु) हाथी। elephant.

कणेरू (2) – स्त्री॰ – (करेणू) हथिनी। a she elephant.

कण्टक – न॰ – (कण्टकम्) काँटा, मछली की नन्ही हड्डी, नोकदार यन्त्र। a thorn, a small fish bone, any instrument with a sharp point.

कण्टक-अपस्सय – पु॰ – (कण्टक- अपाश्रयः) कण्टक सेज, काँटों की शय्या। a bed made of an outstretched skin under whih are iron spikes or thorns.

कण्टकाधान – न॰ – (कण्टकाधन) काँटो की झाड़ी। thorny-hedge.

कण्टकीफल – पु॰ – (कण्टकीफलम्) पनस फलम्, कटहल। jackfruit.

√कण्ठ – चु॰ – शोके – (√शुच = शोचति) शोक करना। to mourn.

कण्ठ – पु॰ – (कण्ठ) ग्रीवा, गला। the neck, the throat.

कण्ठज – वि॰ – (कण्ठज) कण्ठ अथवा गले से उच्चारित। guttural sounds.

√कण्ड – (भू॰,चू॰) – भेदने – (√भञ्ज् = भनक्ति) भेदना, तोड़ना। to pierce, to break.

कण्ड (1) – पु॰ – (काण्ड) सर्ग, परिच्छेद। a portion, a chapter.

कण्ड (2) – (काण्ड) बाण, तीर। an arrow or shaft.

कण्डक – वि॰ – सुरक्षित। guarded, protected.

कण्डर – न॰ – (कण्डरा) प्रधान, स्नायु, प्रधान शिरा। tendons, artery of blood.

कण्डरा – स्त्री॰ – (कण्डरा) नितम्ब, कटि-प्रोथ, पुट्ठा। haunch, hip.

कण्डरि-जातक – न॰ – (जा॰ सं॰ 314) – रानी किन्नरा के एक कोढ़ी पर आसक्त हो जाने की कथा। जो नारियों की विश्वासघातिनी प्रकृति का आख्यान करती है। the Jātaka story (No. 314) of a queen which reveals the distrust fulness of women.

कण्डिन-जातक – (जा॰ सं॰ 13) एक मृग के मृगी पर आसक्ति विषयक कथा जो बुद्ध के तीन अप्रशस्त कर्मों का आख्यान करती है (1) दूसरे की मृत्यु का कारण बनना (2) क्षेत्र का स्त्री द्वारा शासित होना (3) पुरुष का स्त्री की अधीनता। the story (No. 13) tells about the three folly acts mentioned by the Buddha, they are (1) To cause another death (2) The land ruled by women. (3) The men who yield to woman's dominance.

कण्डु – स्त्री॰ – (कण्डू) खाज, खुजली। itching, scratching.

कण्डुति – स्त्री॰ – (कण्डू) खाज, खुजली। itching, scratching.

√कण्डुव – (√कण्डू = कण्डूयति - ते) खुजलाना। itches, scratches.

कण्डूवति – क्रि॰ – (√कण्डू = कण्डूयति) खुजलाता है। itches, scratches.

कण्डोलिका – स्त्री॰ – (कण्डोलिका) टोकरी। a basket.

√कण्ण – चु॰ – सवने – (आ √कण् = आकर्णयति) सुनता है। listens, hears.

कण्ण – न॰ – (कर्ण) कान। ear.

कण्ण-कटुक – वि॰ – (कर्ण-कटु) कर्कश, सुनने में अप्रिय। harsh words.

कण्ण-गूथ – न॰ – (कर्ण-गूथ) कान का मैल। ear wax.

कण्ण-मल – न॰ – (कर्णमल) देखें कण्ण-गूथ। see Kaṇṇa-gūtha.

कण्ण-छिद्द – न॰ – (कर्ण-छिद्र) कान का छेद। orifice of the ear.

कण्णच्छिन्न – वि॰ – (कर्णच्छिन्न) कनकटा, कान-कटा। one whose ear/ears are cut-off.

कण्ण-जप्पक – वि॰ – (कर्ण-जल्पक) कानाफूसी करने वाला। one who whispers.

कण्ण-जलूका – स्त्री॰ – (कर्ण-जलूका) कर्णखर्जू, कनखजूरा। a small kind of centipede.

कण्ण-भुसा – स्त्री॰ – (कर्णाभूषण) कर्णाभूषण। ornament for the ear.

कण्ण-मूल – न॰ – (कर्णमूल) कान की जड़। root of the ear.

कण्ण-विज्झन – न॰ – (कर्ण-वेधन) कान को बींधना। perforation of the ear.

कण्ण-वेठन – न॰ – (कर्ण-वेष्टन) कान की बाली, कान का आभरण विशेष। ear-ring.

कण्ण-सक्खलिका – स्त्री॰ – (कर्ण-शाष्कुली) कान का बाह्य भाग। outer part of the ear.

कण्ण-सुख – वि॰ –(कर्ण-सुख) सुनने में सुखद। pleasant to the ear (melodious).

कण्ण-सूल – न॰ – (कर्ण-शूल) कान का दर्द। ear-ache.

कण्णधार – पु॰ – (कर्ण-धार) मल्लाह, नौका की पतवार पकड़ने वाला। helmsman (of a vessel).

कण्णिका – स्त्री॰ – (कर्णिका) (1) भवन का शिखर (2) कान का आभरण। (1) a house top (2) an ornament for the ear.

कण्ह (1) – वि॰ – (कृष्ण) कृष्ण, काला। kṛṣṇa, black.

कण्ह (2) – पु॰ – (कृष्ण) श्याम वर्ण, विष्णु, काला रंग। the black colour the god Viṣṇu.

कण्ह-जातक – (जा॰ सं॰ 440) – कृष्ण तपस्वी की उग्र तपश्चर्या की कथा। The Jātaka tale (No. 440) tells about Kṛṣṇa's rigid asceticism.

कण्ह-तुण्ड – पु॰ – (कृष्ण-तुण्ड) काले मुख वाला बन्दर। black faced monkey.

कण्ह-दीपायन-जातक – (जा॰ सं॰ 444) – कोशाम्बी के दीपायन तथा मण्डव्य नामक दो ब्राह्मणों की कथा। the story (No. 444) of two brāhmaṇas Dīpāyana and Māṇḍavya of Kośāmbī.

कण्ह-पक्ख – पु॰ – (कृष्ण-पक्ष) महीने का कृष्ण-पक्ष। dark half of a month, full moon to new moon.

कण्ह-वत्तनी – पु॰ – (कृष्ण वर्त्त्यन) अग्नि, आग। fire.

कण्ह-विपाक – वि॰ – (कृष्ण-विपाक) दुष्परिणाम। evil results.

कण्ह-सप्प – पु॰ – (कृष्ण सर्प) विषैला काला साँप। a venomous black snake.

√ कत – रु॰ – छेदने – (√ कृत् = कृन्तति) काटना। to cut.

कत – कृ॰ – (कृत) किया हुआ। done.

कत-कल्याण – वि॰ – (कृत-कल्याण) शुभ-कर्मी। one who has done good deeds.

कत-किच्च – वि॰ – (कृत-कृत्य) कृत-कृत्य, जो करणीय कर चुका। having fulfilled one's obligation.

कतञ्जली – वि॰ – (कृताञ्जलि) प्रणामार्थ जिसने दोनों हाथ जोड़ रखे हों। having raised and joined one's hands in salutation.

कतज्ञुता – स्त्री॰ – (कृतज्ञता) कृतज्ञता। gratefulness.

कतज्ञू – वि॰ – (कृतज्ञ) अहसानमन्द, कृतज्ञ। grateful.

कत-पटिसंथार – वि॰ – जिसका स्वागत हुआ हो। having been received cordially.

कत-परिचय – वि॰ – (कृत-परिचयः) अभ्यस्त, परिचित। aquainted.

कत-पातरस – वि॰ – (कृत प्रातराश) जिसने प्रातःकाल का आहार कर लिया हो। who has taken breakfast.

कत-पुञ्ज – वि॰ – (कृत-पुण्य) जिसने पुण्य किये हों। one who has performed sublime deeds.

कत-भत्त-किच्च – वि॰ – (कृतभत्तकृत्य) जिसने भोजन समाप्त कर लिया। one who has taken one's meals.

कत-वेदी – वि॰ – (कृत-वेद्य) कृतज्ञ। grateful.

कत-सक्कार-संग्रह – वि॰ – (कृत- सत्कार संग्रह) जिसे आतिथ्य प्राप्त हुआ। one who has received hospitality.

कत-संड्केत – वि॰ – (कृत सङ्केत) पूर्वकृत-संकेत। sign made beforehand.

कताधिकार – वि॰ – (कृताधिकार) जिसने कोई संकल्प-विशेष किया हो। one who has formed a resolution or aspiration.

कतापराध – वि॰ – (कृतापराध) अपराधी, दोषी। culprit, guilty.

कताभिसेक – वि॰ – (कृताभिषेक) जिसका अभिषेक हुआ हो। anointed, consecrated.

कतत्त – न॰ – (कृतत्व) कर्तव्य। necessary, duty obligation.

कतम – वि॰ – (कतमः) कौन, कौन-सा, बहुतों में से कौन। which, and what of the many.

कतमत्ते – अव्यय – (कृतमात्रे) अधिकरण, ज्यों ही कोई कार्य सम्पन्न हुआ। locative, as soon as something has been done.

कतर – वि॰ – (कतर) (दोनों में से) कौन सा। which of the two.

कति – अव्यय/सर्वनाम (कति) कितने। how many.

कति-वस्स – वि॰ – (कतिवर्ष) कितने वर्ष का। how many years.

कतिविध – वि॰ – (कतिविध) कितने प्रकार का। how many kinds.

कतिका – स्त्री॰ – (कथिका) वार्तालाप। conversation.

कतिकावत्त – न॰ – (कथिकावृत्त) अनुबन्ध, निश्चय करणीय। an agreement, a pact.

कतिपय – वि॰ – (कतिपय) कुछ, कई। some, several.

कतिपाह – न॰ – (कतिपयाह) कुछ दिन। a few days.

कतिपाहं – क्रि॰ वि॰ – (कतिपयाहम्) कुछ दिन के लिए। for a few days.

कतिमि – वि॰ – (कतिमिति) कौन-सी तिथि। which date.

कतूपकार (1) – वि॰ – (कृतोपकारः) उपकृत, उपकार से लाभान्वित। helped or assisted by.

कतूपकार (2) – पु॰ – (कृतोपकारः) जिसके द्वारा उपकार किया गया है, उपकारी। who has helped benefactor someone.

कतुपासन – वि॰ – धनुष-विद्या में चतुर। skilled in archery.

कते – क्रि॰ वि॰ – (कृते) उसके लिए। for someone.

कतोकास – वि॰ – (कृतावकाशः) आज्ञा प्राप्त, अवसर प्राप्त। being permitted, giving leave, take opportunity.

कत्तब्ब (1) – कृ॰ – (√ कृ + तव्यत् = कर्त्तव्य) करणीय। fit to be done.

कत्तब्ब (2) – न॰ – (कर्त्तव्य) कर्त्तव्य। duty, obligation.

कत्तर – वि॰ – (लघुतर) बहुत छोटा। very small.

कत्तर-दण्ड – पु॰ – (लघु-दण्ड) छड़ी। walking stick.

कत्तर-यटिठ – स्त्री॰ – (लघु यष्टि) छड़ी। walking stick.

कत्तर-सुप्प – पु॰ – (क्षुद्र शूर्प) अनाज साफ करने का छोटा सूप, सुपेला। a small winnowing basket.

कत्तरिका – स्त्री॰ – (कर्त्तरिका) कैंची। scissors, shears.

कत्तिक-मास – (कार्त्तिक मास) कार्तिक मास, कातिक का महीना। month of Kārttik (October-November).

कत्तिका – स्त्री॰ – (कृत्तिका) सत्ताइस नक्षत्रों में से एक कृत्तिका नक्षत्र। one Nakṣatra called Kṛttikā out of twenty-seven *nakṣatra*s.

कत्तु – पु॰ – (कर्त्तृ) कर्त्ता, लेखक, वाक्य का कर्त्ता अंश। author, the subject of a sentence.

कत्तु-काम – वि॰ – (कर्त्तु-काम) करने की इच्छा वाला। willing to do.

कत्तुं – कृ॰ – (√ कृ + तुमुन् = कत्तुर्म्) करने के लिए। for doing.

√ कत्थ – (भू॰) – सिलाघायं – (√ इलाघ् = इलाघते) प्रशंसा करना। to appreciate.

कत्थ – क्रि॰ वि॰ – (कुत्र) कहाँ। where.

कत्थचि – अव्यय – (कुत्रचित्) कहीं न कहीं। somewhere.

कत्थति – क्रि॰ – (कत्थयति) शेखी मारता है। boasts.

कत्थन – न॰ – (कत्थन) आत्म-श्लाघा, स्व-प्रशंसा। boasting.

कत्थना – स्त्री॰ – (कत्थना) डींग, शेखी। boasting.

कत्थी – वि॰ – (कत्थी) शेखी मारने वाला। boaster, boastful.

कत्त्वा – कृ॰ – (√ कृ + त्वा = कृत्त्वा) करके। having done.

√ कथ – चु॰ – वाक्यापबन्धे – (√ कथ = कथयति) कहना। to say.

कथुह्दिका – स्त्री॰ – (कस्तूरिका) कस्तूरी। musk.

कथं – क्रि॰ वि॰ – (कथम्) कैसे। how.

कथंकथा – स्त्री॰ – (कथं–कथा) अनिश्चय, सन्देह। doubt, uncertainty.

कथंकथी – वि॰ – (कथं–कथी) अनिश्चयी, सन्देही। one who is doubtful, who is suspicious.

कथंकर – वि॰ – (कथं–कर) वैसी क्रिया। same acting.

कथं-भूत – वि॰ – (कथं–भूत) कैसा, किस प्रकार का। what kind, what like.

कथं-विध – वि॰ – (कथं–विध) किस प्रकार का। of what sort, of what kind.

कथं-पकार – वि॰ – (कर्थं-प्रकार) किस प्रकार का। of what kind.

कथंसील – वि॰ – (कथं-शील) कैसे शील का। of what character.

कथन – न॰ – (कथन) बातचीत कहना। talk, conversation.

कथा – स्त्री॰ – (कथा) वार्ता, बातचीत, कहानी। exchange of words, talk, story.

कथापाभत – न॰ – (कथावस्तु) कथा का विषय। subject or topic of the conversations.

कथामग्ग – पु॰ – (कथामार्ग) कथा का वर्णन। a narrative, a story.

कथावत्थु (1) – न॰ – (कथावस्तु) चर्चा अथवा विवाद का विषय। subject of the discussion.

कथावत्थु (2) – (कथावस्तु) 'अभिधम्म' के सात प्रकरणों में से पाँचवा प्रकरण। the 5th chapter out of the seven chapters of 'Abhidhamma'.

कथा-सल्लाप – पु॰ – (कथा संलाप) मैत्री-पूर्ण बातचीत। a friendly conversation.

कथापेति – क्रि॰ – कहलवाता है, सन्देश भेजता है। sends a message.

कथित – कृ॰ – (√ कथ् + क्त = कथित) कहा गया। said.

कथेति – क्रि॰ – (कथयति) कहता है। says.

कथेत्वा – पुर्व क्रि॰ – (√ कथ + त्वा = कथयित्वा) कहकर। having said, having spoken.

कदन्न – न॰ – (कदन्न) खराब अन्न। spoiled grains, bad food.

कदम्ब – पु॰ – (कदम्ब) समूह। mass, group, assembly.

कदम्बक – न॰ – (कदम्ब / कदम्बक) कदम्ब का वृक्ष। the tree Nauclea Cadamba.

कदर – पु॰ – (कदर) कदम्ब वृक्ष के फूल। the flower of Nauclea Cadamba.

कदरिय – वि॰ – (कदर्य) कंजूस। miser.

कदलि – स्त्री॰ – (कदली) केले का पेड़। the plantain tree, banana plant.

कदलि-फल – न॰ – (कदलीफलम्) केले का फल। banana fruit.

कदलि-मिग – पु॰ – (कदली मृग) मृग-विशेष, जिसकी चमड़ी मूल्यवान मानी जाती है। a kind of deer (antelope) whose skin is much valued.

कदा – क्रि॰ वि॰ – (कदा) कब। when.

कदाचि – अव्यय – (कदाचिद्) कभी-कभी। sometimes.

कद्दम – पु॰ – (कर्दम) कीचड़, कर्दम, काँदो। mud, mire.

कद्दम-बहुल – वि॰ – (कर्दम-बहुल) जहाँ कीचड़ का बाहुल्य हो। full of mud.

कद्दमोदक – न॰ – (कर्दमोदक) मटमैला पानी। muddy water.

√ कन – भू॰ – (दिंतिशतिकन्तिसु = √ काश = काशते) चमकना। to shine, to glitter.

कनक – न॰ – (कनक) स्वर्ण, सोना। gold.

कनकच्छवि – वि॰ – (कनकच्छवि) सुनहरी चमड़ी, सुनहली कान्ति वाला। of golden complexion.

कनकप्पभा – स्त्री॰ – (कनक-प्रभा) स्वर्ण-प्रभा। the colour of gold.

कनक-विमान – न॰ – (कनक-विमान) सुनहरा महल। a golden palace.

कनय – पु॰ – (कनय) आयुध-विशेष। particular weapon.

कनिट्ठ – न॰ – (कनिष्ठ) सबसे छोटा भाई। youngest brother.

कनिट्ठा – स्त्री॰ – (कनिष्ठा) सबसे छोटी लड़की। youngest girl.

कनिय – वि॰ – (कनीयन) छोटा। younger.

कनीनिका – स्त्री॰ – (कनीनिका) आँख का तारा। the pupil of the eye.

कन्त (1) – वि॰ – (कान्त) प्रियकर, अनुकूल। lovely, pleasant.

कन्त (2) – पु॰ – (कान्त) पति, प्रियतम। husband, the beloved one.

कन्तति – क्रि॰ – (कृन्तति √कृन्त्) काटता है। cuts, shears.

कन्तन – न॰ – (कृन्तन) कताई, काट। spinning/incision.

कन्ता – स्त्री॰ – (कान्ता) औरत, पत्नी। the woman, the wife.

कन्तार – पु॰ – (कान्तार) निर्जन प्रदेश, जंगल, बियाबान। wilderness, desert.

कन्तार-नित्थरण – न॰ – (कान्तार-निस्तरण) निर्जन क्षेत्र से गुजरना। passing through a desert.

कन्ति – स्त्री॰ – (कान्ति) द्युति, शोभा। lustre.

कन्तित – कृ॰ – (कृन्तित / कर्त्तित) काटा गया। has/had been cut.

कन्तिमत्त – वि॰ – (क्रान्तिमान्) चलता हुआ। walking.

कन्थक – पु॰ – (कन्थक) वह घोड़ा जिस पर बैठकर सिद्धार्थ गौतम ने महाभिनिष्क्रमण किया था। the horse on which

Gautama left his father's palace with his attendant Chandaka.

√कन्द – भू॰ – (व्हानरोदनेसु = √क्रन्द् - क्रन्दति) रोना। to lament, to cry in grief.

कन्द – पु॰ – (कन्द) कन्द-मूल। a tuber, yam.

कन्दगलक-जातक – (जा॰ सं॰ 210) खदिरवनिय नामक कठफोड़े तथा कन्दगलक नामक उसके मित्र की कथा जो यह शिक्षा देती है कि अहंकार व्यक्ति के विनाश का कारण बन जाता है। the Jātaka tale (No. 210) tells how false pride and egoism ruin a person.

कन्दति – क्रि॰ – (√क्रन्द = क्रन्दति) चिल्लाता है, रोता है, पश्चात्ताप करता है। cries, wails, laments.

कन्दन्त – कृ॰ – (√क्रन्द + शतृ = क्रन्दन) रोता हुआ। weeping.

कन्दर – पु॰ – (कन्दरा) गुहा, गुफा, कन्दरा। grotto on the slope of a mountain, cave, gorge.

कन्दरा – स्त्री॰ – (कन्दरा) गुहा, गुफा। cave, covern, grotto on the slope of mountain.

कन्दुक – पु॰ – (कन्दुक) क्रीडा, कन्दुक, गेंद। a ball used in games.

कपण – वि॰ – (कृपण) कंजूस, दरिद्र। a miser, poor.

कपण – पु॰ – (कृपण) भिखारी, दयनीय। a beggar, insignificant.

कपल्ल – न॰ – (तप्तकम्) चूल्हे का तवा। a frying pan.

कपल्लक – पु॰/न॰ – (तप्तकम्) चूल्हे का तवा। a frying pan.

कपल्लक-पूव – पु॰/न॰ – (तप्तकापूपः) तवे का पुआ, चीला। a pan-cake.

कपाल – न॰ – (कपाल) खप्पर, एक प्रकार का भिक्षा पात्र, कासा, माथा, खोपड़ी। beggar's bowl, skull, forehead.

कपालसीस – पु॰ – (कपाल-शीर्ष) खोपड़ी। the skull, also see 'Kapāla'.

कपाल्लक – देखें 'कपाल'। see 'Kapāla'.

कपि – पु॰ – (कपि) लंगूर, बंदर। ape, monkey.

कपिकच्छ – न॰ – (कपिकच्छू) केवाँच नामक पौधा जिसके छूने से बदन में खुजली उठती है। the plant *Mucano Pruritus* which causes itching.

कपि-जातक – (जा॰ सं॰ 250) – जातक कथा बतलाती है कि चतुर व्यक्ति के आगे धूर्त की चाल किस प्रकार विफल हो जाती है। this tale (No. 250) tells how a wicked man meets failure by his own conspiracy.

कपि-जातक – (जा॰ सं॰ 404) – एक दुष्ट बन्दर की कथा जो शिक्षा देती है कि कैसे एक दुष्ट अपनी करतूत द्वारा पूरे समुदाय को विपत्ति में डाल देता है। this tale (No. 404) tells how the folly of a wicked causes harm to the entire community.

कपिञ्जल – पु॰ – (कपिञ्जल) तीतर प्रजाति का एक पक्षी। a kind of partrige.

कपित्थ – पु॰ – (कपित्थ) कैथ नामक वृक्ष और उसका फल। elephant apple, or the wood-apple tree (fernia elephantum) and its fruit.

कपिल (1) – / पु॰ – (कपिल) (1) भूरा (2) भूरा रंग। (1) tawny (2) tawny colour (reddish brown).

कपिल (2) – पु॰ – (कपिल) सांख्य दर्शन के प्रवर्त्तक महर्षि कपिल। name of a sage who introduced Sāṃkhya philosophy.

कपिलवत्थु – स्त्री॰ – (कपिलवस्तु) शाक्यों की राजधानी कपिलवस्तु। the capital town of Śuddhodana, the father of Siddhārtha.

कपिला – स्त्री॰ – (कपिला) शिंशिपा, शीशम का पेड़। sissu tree, *Dalbergia sissu*, Indian rosewood tree.

कपिसीस – पु॰ – (कपिलशीर्ष) अर्गल-स्तम्भ। lintel of the door.

कपोत – पु॰ – (कपोत) पारावत, कबूतर। pigeon.

कपोत-जातक (1) – (जा॰ सं॰ 42) – लालच से व्यक्ति किस प्रकार विनष्ट होता है इसका आख्यान करने वाली जातक कथा। this tale (No. 42) tells how a greedy man gets himself ruined.

कपोत-जातक (2) – (जा॰ सं॰ 375) – बहुत कुछ उक्त कपोत जातक के समान ही। tale (No. 375), similar to the above Jātaka story.

कपोत-पालिका – स्त्री॰ – (कपोतपालिका) चिड़ियाखाना, पक्षीशाला। aviary, a large cage for keeping birds.

कपोल – पु॰ – (कपोल) गाल। the cheek.

√कप्प – भू॰ – (सामत्थिये - √क्लृप् = कल्पते) समर्थ होना। to be capable.

√कप्प – चु॰ – (वितक्के - √तर्क = तर्कयति) सोचना। to think.

कप्प (1) – पु॰ –(कल्प) ब्रह्मा का दिन। a day of Brahmā, consisting of 4320,000,000 year of mortals.

कप्प (2) – पु॰ – (कल्प) योग्य, अनुरूप। capable, practicable.

कप्पक – पु॰ – (कल्पक) केश-कल्पक, नाई, राजमहल का कर्मचारी। barber, a royal attendant.

कप्पक्खय – पु॰ – (कल्पक्षय) कल्प का क्षय, प्रलय। the great flood, final destruction of the universe.

कप्पट्ठायी – वि॰ – (कल्पस्थायी) कल्प स्थायी, एक कल्प तक विद्यमान रहने वाला। capable to remain for one *kalpa*, lasting a world cycle.

कप्प-रुक्ख – पु॰ – (कल्पवृक्ष) कामना पूरी करने वाला वृक्ष। a celestial tree fulfilling all wishes.

कप्प-विनास – पु॰ – (कल्प-विनाश) कल्प क्षय, कल्प के अन्त में, संसार का विनाश, प्रलय। destruction of the universe.

कप्प-विनासक – वि॰ – (कल्प-विनाशक) सृष्टि का संहारकर्त्ता। the destroyer of the universe.

कप्पट – पु॰ – (कर्पट) पुराना कपड़ा, चीथड़ा। old rag, torn garments.

कप्पति – क्रि॰ – (कल्पते) योग्य होता है। seems proper or befitting.

कप्पना (1) – स्त्री॰ – (कल्पना) (1) कल्पना (2) व्यवस्थित करना। imagination, putting into order.

कप्पना (2) – क्रि॰ – (√ क्लृपू) बनाना, रचना करना। to make.

कप्पबिन्दु – न॰ – (कल्प-बिन्दु) भिक्षु के चीवर पर बना हुआ काला निशान। a small black dot mark made on a monk's rope.

कप्पर – पु॰ – (कूर्पर/कफोणिः) कुहनी, कोहनी। the elbow.

कप्पास – न॰ – (कार्पास) कपास। cotton.

कप्पास-पटल – न॰ – (कार्पास-पटल) कपास की तह। a layer of cotton.

कप्पास-मय – वि॰ – (कार्पासमय) रुई से निर्मित। made of cotton.

कप्पासिक – वि॰ – (कार्पासिक) रुई का बना हुआ। made of cotton.

कप्पासी – पु॰ – (कार्पासी) कपास का पौधा। cotton plant.

कप्पिक – वि॰ – (कल्पिक) कल्प से सम्बन्धित (इसका प्रयोग प्रायः सामासिक पदों मे होता है। belonging to a world cycle (used in compounds).

कप्पित – कृ॰ – (कल्पित) रचित, तैयार किया हुआ। made, invented.

कप्पिय – वि॰ – (कल्पीय) योग्य, उचित। appropriate, lawful, proper.

कप्पिय-कारक – पु॰ – जो व्यक्ति भिक्षुओं की उचित आवश्यकताएँ पूरी करता है। an attendant of a monk, one who provides necessary things.

कप्पिय-भाण्ड – न॰ – (कल्पीय-भाण्ड) वे बर्तन जिनका उपयोग भिक्षुओं के लिए विहित है। things (vessels) allowable to the monk.

कप्पुर – न॰ – (कर्पूर) कपूर। camphor.

कप्पूर – पु॰ – (कर्पूर) कपूर। camphor.

कप्पेति – क्रि॰ – (कल्पयति) तैयार करता है, काटता है, बनाता है। prepares, harnesses, considers.

कप्पेत्वा – पूर्व क्रि॰ – (कल्पयित्वा) तैयारी करके काटकर। having harnessed, trimmed or prepared.

कबर – वि॰ – (कर्बुर) चित्तीदार, कर्बर, चितकबरा। spotted, variegated.

कबरमणि – न॰ / पु॰ – (कर्बरमणि) लहसुनिया रत्न। cat's eye-jewel.

कबल – पु॰ तथा न॰ – (कवल) ग्रास, कौर। a loaf, a lump.

कवलिंकार – पु॰ – (कवलीकार) मुँह भरा कौर। a mouthful loaf.

कवलिंकाराहार – पु॰ – (कवलीकार आहार) भोजन। material food.

कब्ब – न॰ – (काव्य) काव्य, काव्यात्मक रचना। poem, poetical composition.

√कम – भू॰ – (पदविक्षेपे = √क्रम् – क्रामति) चलना। to walk.

√कम – चु॰ – (इच्छायं = √काम् – कामयते) कामना करना। to desire, to wish for.

कम – पु॰ – (क्रम) ढंग, तरीका, क्रम। order, manner, way.

कमति – क्रि॰ – (√क्रम = क्रामति) चलता है, प्रवेश करता है, जाता है। goes, enters into.

कमण्डलु – पु॰ तथा न॰ – (कमण्डलु) कमण्डल। water pot of ascetics.

कमनीय – वि॰ – (कमनीय) वाञ्छनीय, सुन्दर, आकर्षक। desirable, lovely, beautiful.

कमल – न॰ – (कमल) जलज, कँवल। lotus.

कमल-दल – न॰ – (कमल-दल) कमल की पंखुड़ी। petal of a lotus.

कमलासन – पु॰ – (कमलासन) कमल पर आसन लगाने वाले ब्रह्मा। Brahmā, the creator, who is shown sitting on a lotus.

कमलिनी – स्त्री॰ – (कमलिनी) कँवल का तालाब या झील। lotus pond or lotus lake.

कमितु – न॰ – (कामुक) कामुक। lustful.

कमुक – न॰ – (क्रमुकम्) पूगफल, क्रमुक, सुपारी। arecanut.

√कम्प – (भू॰) – चलने – (√कम्प् – कम्पते) काँपना। to tremble.

कम्पक – वि॰ – (कम्पक) कँपा देने वाला। one who shakes.

कम्पति – क्रि॰ – (कम्पते) काँपता है। trembles, wavers.

कम्पमान – कृ॰ – (√कम्प् + √शानच् = कम्पमान) काँपता हुआ। trembling.

कम्पित – कृ॰ – √कम्प + √क्त = कम्पित) काँप उठा, दहला हुआ। shaken, agitated.

कम्पिय – वि॰ – (कम्पनीय) जो कँपाया जा सके, जो हिलाया जा सके। shakeable, moveable.

कम्पेति – क्रि॰ – (कम्पयति) कँपाता है। causes to tremble or shake.

कम्पेत्वा – पूर्व क्रि॰ – (√कम्प् + त्वा – कम्पयित्वा) हिलाकर, कँपाकर। having shaken.

√कम्ब – (भू॰) – संवरणे – (संवरणे) आच्छादित करना। to cover with.

कम्बल – न॰ – (कम्बल) कंबल। blanket.

कम्बली – वि॰ – (कम्बली) कम्बल वाला, ऊनी परिधान धारण करने वाला। one who has a woollen blanket or woollen garment for his dress.

कम्बु – पु॰ तथा न॰ – (कम्बु) सीपी, शंख, हाथी। shell, conch, elephant.

कम्बुगीव – वि॰ – (कम्बुग्रीव) शंख जैसी त्रि-रेखायुक्त गर्दन वाला। having a neck marked with three lines.

कम्बोज – पु॰ – (कम्बुजः) बुद्धयुगीन भारत के सोलह महाजनपदों में से एक जो गान्धार के पास स्थित था। one of the sixteen *mahājanpada*s (states) of Buddhistic India. It was situated near Gāndhāra.

कम्म – न॰ – (कर्म) काम, कार्य। deed, work, action.

कम्म-कर-कम्मकार – पु॰ – (कर्मकार) मजदूर, श्रमिक। workman, labourer.

कम्म-करण – न॰ – (कर्म-करण) परिश्रम, सेवा। labour, service.

कम्म-कारणा – स्त्री॰ – (कर्म-कारणा) शारीरिक दण्ड। physical punishment.

कम्म-क्खय – पु॰ – (कर्म-क्षय) पूर्वजन्म के कर्मों का क्षय। consummation of the actions (deeds) and their results performed in the previous life.

कम्मज – वि॰ – (कर्मज) कर्म से उत्पन्न। produced by *karma*.

कम्मजात – न॰ – (कर्मजात) नाना प्रकार के कर्म। various actions or deeds.

कम्म-दायाद – वि॰ – (कर्म-दायाद) कर्म का उत्तराधिकारी। inheriting the consequences of one's own deeds.

कम्म-नानत्त – न॰ – (कर्म-नानात्व) कर्मों का नानाविध होना। multifoldness of *karma*.

कम्म-निब्बत्त – वि॰ – (कर्म-निर्वृत्त) कर्मों के द्वारा उत्पन्न। produced through *karma*.

कम्म-पथ – पु॰ – (कर्म-पथ) कर्म-मार्ग। the ways of action.

कम्म-प्पच्चय – वि॰ – (कर्म-प्रत्यय) कर्माधारित। having *karma* as a basis.

कम्म-फल – न॰ – (कर्म-फल) कर्म-फल, कर्म का परिणाम। the result or fruit of *karma*.

कम्म-बन्धु – वि॰ – (कर्म-बन्धु) कर्म ही जिसका बन्धु हो। having bound by karma.

कम्म-बल – न॰ – (कर्म-बल) कर्म ही जिसका बल हो। one who depends upon the power of *karma*.

कम्म-योनि – वि॰ – (कर्म-योनि) कर्म से ही जिसकी उत्पत्ति हुई हो। one having *karma* as origin.

कम्म-वाद – पु॰ – (कर्म-वाद) कर्मों और उनके फलों के कारण-कार्य-भाव तथा उसकी महत्ता को मानने वाला सिद्धान्त। view or belief in *karma* its cause and effect.

कम्म-वादी – वि॰ – (कर्म-वादी) कर्मफल के सिद्धान्त को मानने वाला। one who believes in *karma-vāda*.

कम्म-विपाक – पु॰ – (कर्म-विपाक) कर्मों का फल। the result of own actions.

कम्म-वेग – पु॰ – (कर्म-वेग) कर्मों का वेग। the impetus of *karma*.

कम्म-समुट्ठान – वि॰ – (कर्म-समुत्थान) कर्मोत्पन्न। arising from *karma*.

कम्म-सम्भव – वि॰ – (कर्म-सम्भव) कर्मों से उत्पन्न। produced by karma.

कम्म-सरिक्खक – वि॰ – (कर्म-सदृशक) कर्मों से सदृश विपाक। similar in consequence to the deed done.

कम्म-सक – वि॰ – (**कर्म-स्वक**) कर्म ही जिसका निज सर्वस्व है। one who believes *karma* as one's own property.

कम्मयूहन – न॰ – कर्मों की ढेरी। देखें कम्मायूहन। see Kammāyūhana.

कम्म-उपचय – पु॰ – (**कर्म-उपचय**) कर्मों का संग्रह। accumulation of karma.

कम्मज-वात – पु॰ – (**कर्मज-वात**) प्रसव-वेदना। pangs of childbirth.

कम्मञ्ञ – वि॰ – (**कर्मज्ञ**) जो कर्म के स्वरूप और उसकी प्रविधि का ज्ञाता है। one who knows the deed and its best performances.

कम्मञ्ञता – स्त्री॰ – (**कर्मज्ञता**) कर्म के स्वरूप और उसके ढंग का ज्ञाता होने का भाव। the ability of knowing and performing *karma*.

कम्मट्ठान (1) – न॰ – (**कर्म-स्थान**) ध्यान का विषय, जिस पर चित्त एकाग्र किया जाता है। an object for meditation, object of concentration.

कम्मट्ठान (2) – न॰ – (**कर्मस्थान**) कार्यालय, कर्मशाला। public office, place of industry.

कम्मट्ठानिक – पु॰ – (**कर्मस्थानिक**) योगाभ्यास करने वाला। a person practising meditation.

कम्मधारय – पु॰ – (**कर्मधारय**) समास के छह प्रकारों में से एक। कर्मधारय-समास जो विशेषण-विशेष्य पदों पर आधारित होता है। The adjectival compound.

कम्मन्त – न॰ – (**कर्मान्त**) काम, कारोबार। work, industry, business.

कम्मन्तट्ठान – (**कर्मान्तस्थान**) कारोबार की जगह। place of industry.

कम्मन्तिक – वि॰ – (**कर्मान्तिक**) श्रमिक, मजदूर। labourer.

कम्मप्पत्त – वि॰ – (**कर्म-प्राप्त**) जो विनय-कर्म करने के लिए एकत्र हुए हों। those who have assembled to take part in an auspicious ceremony.

कम्मवाचा – स्त्री॰ – (**कर्म-वाचन**) विनय-कर्म का पाठ। the recitation of the text constituted in Vinaya Piṭaka.

कम्मस्सामी – पु॰ – (**कर्म-स्वामी**) कारोबार का स्वामी। owner of the industry.

कम्माधिट्ठायक – पु॰ – (**कर्माधिष्ठाता**) कारोबार का निरीक्षक। superintendent of work.

कम्मानुरूप – वि॰ – (**कर्मानुरूप**) कर्मानुसार। suitable to one's action.

कम्मार – पु॰ – (**कर्मकार**) लोहार या सुनार। goldsmith or blacksmith.

कम्मार-भण्ड – न॰ – (**कर्मकार-भाण्ड**) सुनार या लोहार का उपकरणादि सामान। tools of black and goldsmith.

कम्मार-साला – स्त्री॰ – (**कर्मार-शाला**) लोहार या सुनार की काम करने की जगह। the place of blacksmith or a gold-smith.

कम्मारम्भ – पु॰ – (**कर्मारम्भ**) कार्य-विशेष का आरम्भ करना। commencement of an undertaking.

कम्मारह – वि॰ – (**कर्मार्ह = कर्म + अर्ह**) काम के योग्य। entitled to take part in.

कम्माराम – वि॰ – (**कर्माराम**) कार्य में रस लेना। delighting in activity.

कम्मारामता – स्त्री॰ – (कर्मारामता) सांसारिक कार्यों में मन लगे रहने की भावना। taking pleasure in worldly activities.

कम्मास – वि॰ – (कल्माष) कर्बर, चितकबरा बेमेल। variegated, of various colours or hues.

कम्मास-दम्म – कुरुओं का एक नगर, जहाँ भगवान बुद्ध एक से अधिक बार ठहरे और जहाँ उन्होंने महासतिपट्ठानसुत्त सदृश महत्त्वपूर्ण सूत्रों का उपदेश दिया। a place in Kuru state at the time of Buddha.

कम्मिक – पु॰ – (कर्मिक) कर्मकर, काम करने वाला, मजदूर। a labourer.

कम्पता – स्त्री॰ – (काम्यता) इच्छा। desire.

कय – पु॰ – (क्रय) क्रय, खरीद। purchase.

कय-विक्कय – पु॰ – (क्रय-विक्रय) क्रय-विक्रय, खरीद-फरोख्त। buying and selling.

कय-विक्कयी – पु॰ – (क्रय-विक्रयी) व्यापारी। a trader or broker.

कयिक – पु॰ – (क्रयिक/क्रेता) खरीदार। purchaser.

√ कर – त॰ – करणे – (√ कृ = करोति/ कुरुते) करना। to do.

कर – पु॰ – (कर) (1) हाथ (2) किरण (3) टैक्स (4) हाथी की सूँड। (1) the hand, (2) a ray, (3) tax (4) the trunk of an elephant.

करक (1) – पु॰ – (करकम्) अनार का वृक्ष। pomegranate plant.

करक (2) – न॰ – (करक) करवा, जल-पात्र। a drinking vessesl.

करका – स्त्री॰ – (करका) हिम उपल, ओले। hail-storm, hail-shower.

करग्ग – पु॰ – (कराग्र) हाथ का अगला भाग, हाथ का सिरा। tip of the hand.

करज – पु॰ – (कर + ज) कर-नख:, कररुह, करशूक, हाथ का नाखून। nail (of the hand).

करजकाय – पु॰ – (करजकाय) देह (जो नाना प्रकार के मलों से निर्मित है) the body (which is born of impurity).

करञ्ज – पु॰ – (करञ्जक) करञ्ज, करंजुआ (एक झाड़ीनुमा कंटीला पौधा जो जूड़ी ताप की दवा के काम आता है)। the tree *Pangamia glabra* (used medicinally).

करतल – न॰ – (करतल) हाथ की हथेली। the palm of the hand.

कर-पुट – पु॰ – (कर-पुट) अञ्जलि, जुड़े हुए हाथ। folded hands, to show respect.

कर-भुसा – स्त्री॰ – (कर-भूषण) हाथ का आभरण, पहुँची, बाजूबन्द। an ornament, for the hand, a bracelet.

करण – न॰ – (करणम्) (1) करना, बनाना (2) उत्पत्ति। doing/making/ production.

करणत्थ – पु॰ – (करणार्थ) साधन बनने का भाव। the sense of instrumentality, sense fo usefulness.

करणविभत्ति – स्त्री॰ – (तृतीया विभक्ति) करण कारक। the instrumental case.

करणीय – वि॰ – (√ कृ + अनीयर = करणीय) कर्तव्य। right to be done, duty, obligation.

करण्डक – पु॰ – (करण्डक/करण्ड) डलिया, टोकरी, पिटारी। a casket, a small box, receptacle.

करभ – पु॰ – (करभ) (1) ऊँट (2) कलाई। (1) camel (2) the wrist.

करमद्द – वि॰ – (कर-मर्द) करौंदा का पेड़। gooseberry, the thorny plant *Carissa carandus*.

करमद्दक – वि॰ – (करमर्दक) हाथों से देह की मालिश करने वाला। one who massages the body.

करमर – पु॰ – (कारागुप्तः) बन्दी, प्रग्रहः, कैदी। prisoner.

करमरानीत – वि॰ – (युद्धबन्दी) युद्धबन्दी। one who is captured in a war, a prisoner of war.

करवीक – पु॰ – (काकलीखः) कुहूख, परभृत, कोयल। the Indian cuckoo.

करवीक-भाणी – वि॰ – (कोकील-कण्ठी) स्पष्ट तथा मधुर स्वर वाला। possessing melodious voice.

करवीर – पु॰ – (करवीर) करवीर या कनेर। the *Oleander* plant.

करसाखा – स्त्री॰ – (कर-शाखा) अङ्गुलि, अँगुली। finger.

करहचि – अव्यय – (कर्हिचिद्) कभी-कभी। seldom/at times.

करहाट – न॰ – (करहाट) कमल की जड़। root of a lotus.

करिसापणण – पु॰ – (कार्षापण) कार्षापण। पाँचवी-छठी शताब्दी ईसा पूर्व में उत्तर भारत, मुख्यतया कोसल साम्राज्य, में विनिमय का मुख्य माध्यम कार्षापण नामक सिक्का था। यह सोने, चाँदी तथा ताँबे से निर्मित विभिन्न आकार और भार का तथा विभिन्न मूल्यों के लिये होता था। An ancient coin used in Kosala state in north India for dealing in gold, silver, copper and other items.

करी – पु॰ – (करिन्) गज, कुंजर, वारण, हाथी। an elephant.

करीयति – क्रि॰ – (क्रियते) किया जाता है। is being done.

करीयमान – क्रि॰ – (√क्रि + शानच् = क्रियमाण) किया जाता हुआ। having being done.

करीर – पु॰ – (करीर) कलश, वंशाकुर, करील का पेड़। a jar, the shoot of bamboo, a thorny plant, Capparis Aphylla, grown in deserts and eaten by camels.

करीस – न॰ – (करीष) विष्ठा, सूखा, गोबर। dry dung, dung.

करीस-मग्ग – पु॰ – (करीष मार्ग) गुदा। the anus.

करुणं – क्रि॰ वि॰ – (करुणम्) करुणापूर्वक। pitiably.

करुणा – स्त्री॰ – (करुणा) दया। compassion, pity.

करुणायति – क्रि॰ – (करुणायते) दया, अनुभव करता है। feels pity for.

करेणु – स्त्री॰ – (करेणु) हथिनी। she-elephant.

करेरि – पु॰ – (करेरि) कूजा का पेड़, वृक्ष-विशेष। The *muskrobe* tree.

करोति – क्रि॰ – (करोति) करता है। does, performs, acts.

करोन्त – कृ॰ – (√क्रि + शतृ = कुर्वन्) करते हुए। doing.

√कल – चु॰ – संख्यान – (√गप्पू = गणयति ⁄ ते) गिनना। to count.

कल – पु॰ – (कल) प्रायः समास रूप में प्रयुक्त जैसे – कलख, मधुर आवाज। sweet low sound (often used in compounds).

कलंक – पु॰ – (कलङ्क) चिह्न, दाग, धब्बा। stain, blot, blame.

कलण्डुक-जातक – (जा॰ सं॰ 127) – छल-छद्म के सहारे एक निर्धन सेवक का छन कुबेर की पुत्री से परिणय की कथा। this tale (No. 127) tells how by a fraud a poor got himself married with a banker's daughter.

कलत्त – न॰ – (कलत्रम्) पत्नी। wife.

कलन्दक – पु॰ – (चरमपुच्छः वृक्षशायिका) गिलहरी। squirrel.

कलन्दक-निवाप – पु॰ – (कलन्दक निवाप) वेलुवन का वह स्थान जहाँ गिलहरियों को नियम से खाना मिलता था। locality of Venu-vana where squirrels were fed at the time of the Buddha.

कलभ – पु॰ – (कलभ) हाथी का बच्चा। a young elephant.

कलल – न॰ – (कलल) कीचड़। mud, mire.

कलल-मक्खित – वि॰ – (कलल म्रक्षित) कीचड़ सना हुआ। smeared or spoiled with mud.

कलल-रूप – न॰ – (कलल-रूप) गर्भ की आरम्भावस्था। the first stage in the formation of the foetus.

कलविंक – पु॰ – (कलविङ्क) चटक, गौरैया, चिड़िया। a sparrow.

कलस – न॰ – (कलश) कलश, जल-पात्र। a small waterpot.

कलसिगाम – पु॰ – (कलसिग्राम) अलसन्दा (अलैक्जैण्डरिया) द्वीप का वह स्थान, जहाँ मिलिन्द नरेश पैदा हुआ था। the village of Alexandria where king Milinda was born.

कलह – पु॰ – (कलह) झगड़ा। quarrel, dispute.

कलह-कारक – वि॰ – (कलह-कारक) झगड़ने वाला। a quarreller.

कलह-कारण – न॰ – (कलह-कारण) झगड़े का कारण। the cause of dispute.

कलह-सद् – पु॰ – (कलह-शब्द) झगड़े की आवाज। a brawl, squabble.

कला – स्त्री॰ – (कला) (1) सम्पूर्ण का एक भाग (2) कला शिल्प। fraction of a whole, an art.

कलाप – पु॰ – (कलाप) बण्डल, तरकश, महाभूतों के कणों का समूह। (1) a bundle, heap (2) a quiver (3) a group of elementary particles.

कलापी – पु – (कलापी) (1) मोर (2) तरकश वाला। (1) peacock (2) one who has a quiver.

कलायमुट्ठी-जातक – (जा॰ सं॰ 176) एक बन्दर की कथा, जिसने एक मटर के दाने के लिए मुट्ठी के सभी मटर गँवा दिये। the story (No. 176) of a monkey who lost handful of peas for the sake of one pea.

कलि – पु॰ – (कलि) हार, दुर्भाग्य, पाप, कष्ट। defeat, bad luck, sin, distress.

कलिका – स्त्री॰ – (कलिका) फूल की कली। the bud of flower.

कलिग्गह – पु॰ – (कलिग्रह) हार का पाँसा। dice of a losing throw.

कलियुग – पु॰ – (कलियुग) सतयुग, त्रेता-युग आदि का अंतिम युग। the last of four aeons.

कलिङ्गर – पु॰ तथा न॰ – (कलिङ्गर) लट्ठा, लकड़ी का सड़ा हुआ लट्ठा। a log-rotten piece of wood.

कलिल – न॰ – (कलिल) गहन। dense.

कलीर – न॰ – (कलीर) ताड़ वृक्ष के तने का ऊपरी कोमल भाग। the soft part at the top a palm tree.

कलुस – न॰ – (कलुष) कलुष, पाप-कर्म, अपवित्रता। sin, impurity.

कलेवर/कलेबर – न॰ – (कलेवर) शरीर। the body.

कल्याण – वि॰ – (कल्याण) भलाई, शुभ। welfare, goodness.

कल्याण-काम – वि॰ – (कल्याण-कामी) भला चाहने वाला। well wisher.

कल्याण-कारी – वि॰ – (कल्याणकारी) शुभ-कर्मी। desiring welfare/well-wisher.

कल्याण-दस्सन – वि॰ – (कल्याण-दर्शन) सुन्दर। lovely, handsome.

कल्याण-धम्म – वि॰ – (कल्याण-धर्म) शुभ कार्म। good conduct.

कल्याण-पटिभाण – वि॰ – (कल्याण-प्रतिभान) शीघ्र बोध वाला, प्रतिभावान। having quick understanding, intelligent.

कल्याण-मित्र – पु॰ – (कल्याण-मित्र) शुभ-चिंतक मित्र। a well-wisher friend.

कल्याण-अज्झासय – वि॰ – (कल्याण-अध्याशय) शुभ-चेतना। having intention to do good.

कल्याण-धम्म-जातक – (जा॰ सं॰ 101) – साँस के बहरेपन के कारण बहू ने कुछ कहा और सास ने दूसरा ही समझा। the story (No. 101) of a deaf mother-in-law who created a mischief by her mishearing.

कल्याणी – स्त्री॰ – (कल्याणी) (1) सुन्दर स्त्री (2) लंका की नदी तथा एक नगरी। (1) a beautiful woman (2) name of a river and town in Ceylon.

कल्लता – वि॰ – (कल्य) दक्ष, योग्य, स्वस्थ। clever, able, healthy.

कल्ल – स्त्री॰ – (कल्यता) दक्षता। ability.

कल्ल-सरीर – वि॰ – (कल्य शरीर) स्वस्थ शरीर वाला। of sound physique.

कल्लहार – न॰ – (कल्हार) कुमुद, श्वेत कँवल। night lotus, white lotus.

कल्लोल – पु॰ – (कल्लोल) महातरङ्ग, बड़ी लहर। a billow.

कवच – पु॰ – (कवच) जिरह-बख्तर, सन्नाह। armour, a coat of nail.

कवंध – पु॰ – (कबन्ध) बिना सिर का शरीर, धड़। headless body, trunk of the body.

कवाट – पु॰ तथा न॰ – (कपाट) खिड़की दरवाजे के किवाड़। the shutter of door or window.

कवि – पु॰ – (कवि) काव्य-रचना करने वाला, कवि, शायर। a poet.

कविट्ठ (1) – पु॰ – (कपित्थ) कैथ का वृक्ष। the wood-apple or the elephant-apple tree (fernia elephantum).

कविट्ठ (2) – न॰ – (कपित्थम्) कैथ का फल। the wood-apple or the elephant-apple.

कविता – स्त्री॰ – (कविता) काव्य-रचना, काव्य-कृति। poetry.

कवित्त – न॰ – (कवित्व) कवित्व, कवि की अवस्था या काव्य-सामर्थ्य। poetic sense.

√**कस** – भू॰ – गति हिंसा विलेखनेसु – (कृष्/कर्षति) जोतना। to plough.

कसट (1) – पु॰ – (अवस्करः) कूड़ा-करकट। rubbish, waste.

कसट (2) – पु॰ – (कषायः) कसैला। of acrid taste.

कसति – क्रि॰ – (कर्षति) हल चलाता है। ploughs, tills the land.

कसन – न॰ – (कर्षण) हल चलाना। tilling, ploughing.

कसंत/कस्समान – कृ॰ – (कर्षन्त/कर्षमाण) हल चलाता हुआ। tilling, ploughing.

कसम्ब – पु॰ – (अवस्करः) कूड़ा-करकट। the refuse, a filth, rubbish, waste.

कसम्ब-जात – वि॰ – (अवस्कर-जात) कूड़ा-करकट में से उत्पन्न, दुश्चरित्र। immoral, impure, of bad character.

कसा – स्त्री॰ – (कशा) चाबुक। a whip.

कसाहत – वि॰ – (कशाहत) चाबुक के आघात प्राप्त। being whipped or flogged.

कसाय – न॰ – (कषाय) काढ़ा, जोशान्दा। decoction.

कसाव – पु॰/न॰ – (काषाय) (1) कसैला स्वाद (2) काषाय रंग। (1) the acrid taste (2) of orange colour.

कसि – स्त्री॰ – (कृषि) कृषि, खेती-बाड़ी। cultivation, agriculture.

कसि-कम्म – न॰ – (कृषि-कर्म) खेती। agriculture.

कसि-भण्ड – न॰ – (कृषि-भाण्ड) कृषि के औजार। agricultural implements.

कसिण (1) – वि॰ – (कृत्स्न) सम्पूर्ण, समस्त। the whole, entire.

कसिण (2) – न॰ – (कृत्स्न) चित्त को एकाग्र करने का साधन। an object for meditation.

कसिण-परिकम्म – न॰ – (कृत्स्न-परिकर्म) योगाभ्यास की पूर्व तैयारी। duties to be performed before meditation.

कसिण-मण्डल – न॰ – (कृत्स्न-मण्डल) योगाभ्यास के लिए कागज या दीवार पर खींचा गया चक्र। diagram or picture illustrating yogasanas.

कसितट्ठान – न॰ – (कर्षित स्थान) हल चलाई हुई भूमि। ploughed field.

कसित्वा – पूर्व क्रि॰ – (कर्षयित्वा) हल चलाकर। having ploughed.

कसिर (1) – वि॰ – (कसिर) कष्टसाध्य, कठिन। difficult, miserable.

कसिर (2) – न॰ – (कसिर) कठिनाई, कठिनता। trouble, misery, difficulty.

कसिरेन – क्रि॰ वि॰ – (कसिरेण) कठिनाई से। with difficulty.

कस्मीर – पु॰ – (कश्मीरः) उत्तर भारत का प्रदेश, आधुनिक काश्मीर। a northern State of India, modern Kashmir.

कस्सक – पु॰ – (कर्षक) कृषक, किसान। farmer, cultivator, agriculture.

कस्सति – क्रि॰ – (कर्षति) खींचता है। drags.

कस्सपमन्दिय-जातक – (जा॰ सं॰ 312) – वृद्धों की तरूणों के साथ सहनशीलता का बर्ताव करने की शिक्षा देने वाली जातक कथा। this Jātaka tale (No. 312) teaches that the old should have patience with the young.

कहं – क्रि॰ वि॰ – (कुत्र) कहाँ। where.

कहापण – न॰ – (कार्षापण) स्वर्ण-मुद्रा, कार्षापण, देखें 'करिसापण्ण'। see Karisāpanna.

कहापणक – न॰ – (कहापणक) दण्ड-विधान, जिसमें अपराधी के मांस के कार्षपणों के समान छोटे-छोटे टुकड़े कर दिये जाते हैं। a penalty involving torture which consisted of cutting off small pieces of flesh.

√**का** – दि॰ – सदे = (√ रु = रौति) शब्द करना। make word.

काक – पु॰ – (काक) कौआ। a crow.

काक-जातक – (जा॰ सं॰ 140) – यह कथा बतलाती है कि किस प्रकार एक दुष्ट की करतूत समूची जाति के विनाश का कारण बन जाती है। the story (No. 140) tells how the act of a wicked person causes the ruin of the community.

काक-जातक – (जा॰ सं॰ 146) – कौवा तथा उसकी कौवी शराब पीकर मस्त हो गये। कौवी को समुद्र की लहर बहा ले गई। कौवे का विलाप सुन सभी कौवे समुद्र के शत्रु बन बैठे। (tale No. 146) the crow and his spouse took liquor and were intoxicated. The female crow was washed away by the sea. Hearing the laments of the crow all the crows turned hostile to the sea.

काक-जातक – लोभी कौवे की दोस्ती में कबूतर के प्राण संकट में पड़ गये। A Jātaka tale tells how the friendship of a wicked crow put a life of a pigeon in danger.

काक-पाद – (काक–पाद) कौवे का पाँव, क्रॉस-चिह्न। crow's feet or legs, cross-mark.

काक-पेय्य – वि॰ – (काक–पेय) लबालब भरा हुआ, ताकि कौआ भी पी सके। full to the brim so that a crow can easily drink.

काक-वर्ण – वि॰ – (काकवर्ण) कौवे के रंग का। of the colour of crow.

काकच्छति – क्रि॰ – (नासिकां घर्घरायते) नाक बजाता है। snores.

काकणिका – स्त्री॰ – (काकणी) कौड़ी कर्पर्दिका। a small shell used as a coin of very low value.

काकतालीय – न॰ – (काकातालीय न्याय) काकतालीय-न्याय, अकस्मात घटित इस प्रकार का कोई संयोग जैसे कोई गंजा जेठ की दुपहरी में छाया के लिए ताड़ वृक्ष की जड़ पर खड़ा हुआ तभी कौवा आकर पके ताड़ फल पर बैठा और ताड़-फल टूटकर गंजे की खोपड़ी पर गिरा जिससे उसकी मृत्यु हो गयी। Kāktalīya rule — a crow sat on a palm fruit, the fruit fell on the bald head of a man below and the man died.

काकतिन्दुक – पु॰ – (काकतिन्दुक) काकेन्दु या कुचला का पेड़। a kind of ebony named 'Kuchila' in Sanskrit.

काकपक्ख – पु॰ – (काकपक्ष) बालकों की कनपटी पर स्थित बालों का गुच्छा, अलक। side locks of hair on the temples of the boys.

काकली – स्त्री॰ – (काकलि) कल सूक्ष्म ध्वनि, धीमा स्वर। low sweet toned sound.

काकसूर – वि॰ – (काक-शूर) कौवे की तरह शूर, निर्लज्ज। clever, as a crow, a shameless fellow.

काकाति-जातक – (जा॰ सं॰ 327) – बनारस के राजा की काकाति नामक पटरानी पर गरुड़ मोहित हो गया और उसे उड़ा ले गया। Garuḍa was enamoured of Kākāti the queen of the king of Banaras and eloped with her.

काकी – स्त्री॰ – (काकी) कौवी। a female crow.

काकोल/काकोळ – पु॰ – (काकोळ) काला कौआ, जंगली कौआ। a raven, black crow.

काच – पु॰ – (काच) काँच। glass, crystal.

काच-तुम्ब – पु॰ – (काच-तुम्ब) काँच की बोतल। a glass bottle, a glass jar.

काचमय – वि॰ – (काचमय) काँच से निर्मित। made of glass.

काज – पु॰ – (काज-वेणुशिक्या) स्कन्ध-वाहिनी, बहंगी। a sling, a carrying pole.

काज-हारक – पु॰ – (काजहारक) बहंगी ढोने वाला। a sling carrier.

काट – पु॰ – (शिश्नः) उपस्थ, लिङ्ग, पुरुषेन्द्रिय। the male organ.

काण – वि॰ – (काणः) काना, एक आँख का अंधा। one-eyed man.

कातब्ब – न॰ – (कर्त्तव्य) कर्तव्य। duty that is to be done.

कातर – वि॰ – (कातर) दुःखी, दरिद्र। distress, poor.

कातवे/कातु – कृ॰ – (कर्त्तवै/कर्त्तुम्) करने के लिए। for performing, for doing.

कातुकाम – वि॰ – (कर्तुकामः) करने की इच्छा वाला। willing to do, desirous of doing.

कादम्ब – पु॰ – (कादम्ब) भूरे रंग वाली बत्तख की विशेष जाति, कलहंस। a kind of goose with grey wings.

कानन – न॰ – (कानन) जंगल। forest, grove.

कापिलवत्थव – वि॰ – (कपिल-वास्तव) कपिलवस्तु का। belonging to Kapilavastu.

कापुरिस – पु॰ – (कापुरुष) कायर अथवा घृणित व्यक्ति। a coward, wretch, contemptible.

कापोतक – वि॰ – (कापोतक) कबूतर के समान सफेद। white colour of a pigeon.

कापोतिका – स्त्री॰ – (कापोतिका) एक तरह की लाल रंग की मदिरा। a kind of liquor (which is of red colour).

काम – पु॰ – (काम) कामना, कामुकता। pleasure, lust, enjoyment.

काम-गिद्ध – वि॰ – (काम-गृद्ध) इन्द्रिय सुख का लोभी। greedy of sensual pleasure.

काम-गुण – पु॰ – (काम-गुण) इन्द्रिय सुख। sensual pleasure.

काम-गेध – पु॰ – (कामासक्ति) इन्द्रिय सुख के प्रति आसक्ति। attachment to a sensual pleasure.

कामच्छन्द – (कामच्छन्द) कामुकता। sensual excitement.

काम-तण्हा – स्त्री॰ – (काम–तृष्णा) काम-पिपासा, काम-तृष्णा। thirst for pleasure.

काम-दद – वि॰ – (कामदता) इच्छित वस्तु का देना। giving what is desired.

काम-धातु – स्त्री॰ – (काम–धातु) इच्छा-लोक। the world of desire.

काम-पङ्क – पु॰ – (काम–पङ्क) इच्छाओं का कीचड़। the desire of lust.

काम-परिळाह – पु॰ – (काम परिदाह) काम-ज्वर। the fever caused by passion.

काम-भव – पु॰ – (काम–भव) कामनाओं का संसार। the sphere dominated by pleasure.

काम-भोगी – वि॰ – (काम–भोगी) इन्द्रिय-सुख का भोगने वाला। enjoying the pleasure of senses.

काम-मुच्छा – स्त्री॰ – (काम–मूर्च्छा) काम-मूर्च्छा। sensual stupor.

काम-रति – स्त्री॰ – (काम–रति) कामुकता का आनन्द। amorous enjoyment.

काम-राग – पु॰ – (काम–राग) काम-चेतना। sensual passion.

काम-लोक – पु॰ – (काम–लोक) कामनाओं का लोक। the world of sensual pleasure.

काम-वितक्क – पु॰ – (काम–वितर्क) कामनाओं सम्बन्धी विचार। thought concerning sensual pleasures.

काम-संकप्प – पु॰ – (काम–संकल्प) कामनाओं के सम्बन्ध में संकल्प-विकल्प। aspiration after pleasure.

काम-सञ्ञोजन – न॰ – (काम–संयोजन) कामनाओं के बन्धन। hindrance formed by pleasure (body of pleasure).

काम-सुख – न॰ – (काम–सुख) कामेन्द्रिय-जनित सुख। happiness arising from sensual pleasure.

काम-सेवना – स्त्री॰ – (काम–सेवना) मैथुन धर्म का सेवन। (indulgence in) sexual intercourse.

काम-जातक – (जा॰ सं॰ 467) – एक राजकुमार की कथा जो कामनाओं की अन्तहीन वृद्धि का दृष्टान्त प्रस्तुत करती है। the Jātaka story (No. 467) of a prince showing the futility of wishes.

कामनीत-जातक – (जा॰ सं॰ 228) – कामनाओं की अतृप्ति का दृष्टान्त प्रस्तुत करने वाली कथा। the Jātaka story (No. 228) explaining the insatiability of desires.

कामता – स्त्री॰ – (कामता) आकांक्षा, इच्छा। longing, willingness.

कामी (1) – वि॰ – (कामी) कामेन्द्रिय सुखों से सम्पन्न। one who possesses the objects of sensual pleasure.

कामी (2) – वि॰ – (कामी) समस्त पदों में यह 'इच्छुक' अर्थ में आता है जैसे राज्य-कामी अर्थात् राज्य चाहने वाला। in compounds, desirous of lust, lewd.

कामुक – वि॰ – (कामुक) कामी व्यक्ति, रागी। sexual, lustful, lewd.

कामेति – क्रि॰ – (कामयते) कामना करता है, इच्छा करता है। craves, desires.

कामेतब्ब – कृ॰ – (कामयितव्य) इच्छा किये जाने के योग्य। desirable.

काय – पु॰ – (काय) ढेर, संग्रह, शरीर। a heap, the collection, the body.

काय-कम्म – न॰ – (काय–कर्म) शारीरिक कर्म। bodily action, physical action.

काय-कम्मञ्ञता – स्त्री॰ – (काय–कर्मण्यता) शरीर की कमनीयता। beauty of the body.

काय-गत – वि॰ – (काय–गत) शरीर सम्बन्धी। relating to the body.

काय-गन्थ – पु॰ – (काय–ग्रन्थि) शारीरिक बन्धन। bodily fetter.

काय-गुत्त – वि॰ – (काय–गुप्त) शरीर से संयत। careful in guarding one's own body.

काय-डाह – (काय–दाह) शरीर-ज्वर। inflammation of body.

काय-दरथ – पु॰ – (काय–क्लेश) शारीरिक कष्ट। bodily distress.

काय-दुच्चरित – न॰ – (काय–दुश्चरित) शारीरिक दुश्चारित। misconducted by the body.

काय-द्वार – न॰ – (काय–द्वार) शारीरिक इन्द्रिय। the outlet of bodily senses.

काय-धातु – स्त्री॰ – (काय–धातु) स्पर्शेन्द्रिय। the faculty of touch.

कायप्पकोप – पु॰ – (कायः प्रकोप) शारीरिक दुष्कर्म। misbehaviour.

कायप्पचालकं – क्रि॰ वि॰ – (काय-प्रचालकम्) शरीर का हिलना-डुलना। swaying the body.

काय-पटिबद्ध – वि॰ – (काय–प्रतिबद्ध) शरीर से सम्बन्धित। connected with the body.

काय-प्पयोग – पु॰ – (काय–प्रयोग) शारीरिक साधन। instrumentality of the body.

काय-परिहारिक – वि॰ – (काय–परिहार) शरीर का पालन। tending the body.

काय प्पसाद – पु॰ – (काय–प्रसाद) स्पर्शेन्द्रिय का स्पष्ट बोध। sense of touch.

काय-प्पसद्धि – स्त्री॰ – (काय–प्रशान्ति) इन्द्रियों की प्रशान्ति। serenity of the senses.

काय-पागब्भिय – न॰ – (काय–प्रगल्भता) शारीरिक प्रगल्भता, शारीरिक असंयम। immodesty.

काय-बंधन – न॰ – (काय–बन्धन) कमरबन्द, कमर की पट्टी। waist-band, girdle.

काय-बल – न॰ – (कायबल) शारीरिक बल। physical strength.

काय-मुदुता – स्त्री॰ – (काय–मृदुता) शरीर या इन्द्रियों की कोमलता। pliability of senses.

काय-लहुता – स्त्री॰ – (काय–लघुता) शरीर या इन्द्रियों का हल्कापन। buoyancy of senses.

काय-वङ्क – पु॰ – (काय–वक्र) टेढ़े कार्य। crookedness of action.

काय-विकार – पु॰ – (काय–विकार) अंगों से संकेत। gesture.

काय-विञ्ञत्ति – स्त्री॰ – (काय–विज्ञप्ति) शारीरिक सूचना। intimation through the body, gesture.

काय-विञ्ञाण – न॰ – (काय–विज्ञान) स्पर्श द्वारा चेतना। consciousness by means of touch.

काय-विज्ञेय्य – वि॰ – (काय-विज्ञेय) स्पर्श द्वारा जानने योग्य। to be perceived by the sense of touch.

काय-विवेक – पु॰ – (काय-विवेक) शारीरिक एकान्त। seclusion of the body.

काय-वेय्यावच्च – न॰ – (काय-व्यावृत्त) शारीरिक सेवा कार्य। manual labour.

काय-संसग्ग – पु॰ – (काय-संसर्ग) शारीरिक संसर्ग। bodily contact.

काय-सक्खी – वि॰ – (काय-साक्षी) शरीर का सत्य से साक्षात् कृत। he who has realised the final truth through the body.

काय-संखार – पु॰ – (काय-संस्कार) शरीर का सूक्ष्म स्वरूप। substratum of the body.

काय-समाचार – पु॰ – (काय-समाचार) शारीरिक सदाचरण। good conduct.

काय-सम्फस्स – पु॰ – (काय-संस्पर्श) स्पर्शेन्द्रिय। the sense of touch.

काय-सुचरित – न॰ – (काय-सुचरित) शारीरिक सदाचरण। good conduct in action.

काय-सोचेय्य – न॰ – (काय-शुचिता) शारीरिक पवित्रता। purity of the body.

कायविच्छिन्द-जातक – (जा॰ सं॰ 293) – धार्मिक जीवन बिताने के संकल्प एवं आचरण से रोग नष्ट होने का दृष्टान्त। the tale describes how diseases are removed by good conduct and pious life.

कायिक – वि॰ – (कायिका) शारीरिक। physical.

कायिक-दुक्ख – न॰ – (कायिका-दुःख) शारीरिक वेदना। bodily pain.

कायुजुकता – स्त्री॰ – (काय-ऋजुता) शरीर का सीधापन। straightness of the body.

कायूपग – वि॰ – (कायोपग) शरीर से आसक्त, नया जन्म ग्रहण करने वाला। attached to the body, going to be born.

कायूर – न॰ – (केयूर) भुजबन्ध, बाजूबन्द। a bracelet worn on the upper arm.

कार (1) – पु॰ – (कार/कारक) क्रिया, कर्म, सेवा। deed, service, act of homage.

कार (2) – वि॰ – (कार) समस्त पद में 'बनाने वाला' के अर्थ में जैसे रथकार – रथ बनाने वाला। often used in compounds as *rathkāra* chariot-maker.

कारक (1) – पु॰ – (कारक) कर्ता, करने वाला। the doer.

कारक (2) – न॰ – (कारकम्) क्रिया से सम्बन्ध बताने वाला। syntax.

कारण – न॰ – (कारण) हेतु, कारण। reason, cause.

कारणा – स्त्री॰ – (कारणा) जैसे किं कारणा? कार्य का माध्यम किस हेतु से? क्यों?। means of, as kiṁ kāraṇam? why?

कारण्डिय-जातक – (जा॰ सं॰ 366) – बिना किसी की योग्यता-अयोग्यता परखे हर किसी को उपदेश देने वाले आचार्य का दृष्टान्त। this Jātaka tale (No. 366) shows the result of preaching to all without examining the eligibility of the listeners is fruitless.

कारणा – स्त्री॰ – (**कारणा**) यातना, शारीरिक दण्ड। torture, bodily punishment.

कारणिक – पु॰ – (**कारणिक**) यातना देने वाला। a torturer.

कारवेल्ल – पु॰ – (**कारवेल्ल**) कारवेल्लक, करैला। bitter-gourd.

कारा – स्त्री॰ – (**कारा**) कारागार, जेल। a prison, jail.

काराघर – न॰ – (**कारागृह**) कारागार, जेलखाना। a prison, jail.

कारापक – पु॰ – (**कार्यापक**) कार्य कराने वाला। one who orders to do something.

कारापिका – स्त्री॰ – (**कार्यापिका**) कार्य कराने वाली। the women who gets things done.

कारापन – न॰ – (**कार्य-निष्पादन**) कार्य करना, दूसरे से करवाना। to get done, causing to do, ordering to do.

कारापित – कृ॰ – (**कारित**) करवाया गया। having got done.

कारापेति – क्रि॰ – (**कारयति**) करवाता है। gets done.

कारा-भेदक – वि॰ – (**कराभेदक**) जेल से भाग आने वाला। one who has broken out of a jail.

कारिका – स्त्री॰ – (**कारिका**) व्याख्या। commentary.

कारिय – न॰ – (**कार्य**) कार्य, कर्तव्य। duty, action.

कारी – पु॰ – (**कारी**) करने वाला (समस्त पदो में प्रयुक्त)। doer (used in compounds).

कारुञ्ञ – न॰ – (**कारुण्य**) करुणा। compassion.

कारुणिक – वि॰ – (**कारुणिक**) दयालु। compassionate.

कारेति – क्रि॰ – (**कारयति**) करवाता है। gets done.

काल – पु॰ – (**काल**) समय। time.

कालस्सेव – क्रि॰ – (**कालस्य + एव**) समय रहते। early.

कालेन – क्रि॰ वि॰ – (**कालेन**) ठीक समय पर। at proper time.

कालेन-कालं – क्रि॰ वि॰ – (**कालेन = कालम्**) समय-समय पर। from time to time.

कालं-करोति – क्रि॰ – (**कालम् करोति**) मर जाता है। dies.

कालंकत – कृ॰ – (**कालम् + कृत**) मर गया। died.

काल-किरिया – स्त्री॰ – (**काल-क्रिया**) मृत्यु। death.

काल-कण्णी – पु॰ – (**काल-कर्णी**) मनहूस। an unfortunate person, a wretch.

काल-पवेदन – न॰ – (**काल-प्रबोधन**) समय की सूचना। announcement of time.

काल-वादी – वि॰ – (**काल-वादी**) समयोचित बोलने वाला। speaking at the proper time.

कालञ्ञु – वि॰ – (**कालज्ञ**) (उचित) समय का जानकार। one who knows the proper time.

कालंतर – न॰ – (**कालान्तर**) व्यवधान, समय-विभाग। interval, period.

कालिक – वि॰ – (**कालिक**) समय-सम्बन्धी। temporal.

कालिङ्ग – (**कालिङ्ग**) पूर्व भारत का कालिंग नामक प्रदेश। name of a state of eastern India.

कालुसिय – न॰ – (कालुष्य) कलुषता, मैल, पाप । dirt, obscurity.

कावेय्य – न॰ – (काव्यम्) काव्य । poetry.

√कास – भू॰ – (दित्तियं = √काश्/ काशते) चमकना to shine.

कास (1) – पु॰ – (काश) कास नामक तृण गुल्म और उसका फूल । a kind of reed and its flower.

कास (2) – पु॰ – (कास) खांसी, दमा । cough, asthma.

कासाय/कासाव – न॰ – (काषाय) काषाय वस्त्र । yellow robe.

कासाय/कासाव – वि॰ – (काषाय) गैरिक वर्ण युक्त । of orange colour.

कासि – स्त्री॰ – (काशी) सोलह महाजनपदों में से एक । इसकी राजधानी वाराणसी थी । a state of India in ancient days Vārāṇasī was its capital.

कासिक – वि॰ – (काशिक) काशी का, काशी में निर्मित । belonging to or made in Kāsī.

कासु – स्त्री॰ – (गर्त्तः खातम्) गड्ढा । a pit.

काल – वि॰ – (कृष्ण) काला । black.

काल – पु॰ – (कृष्ण-वर्ण) काला रंग । black colour.

काल-कूट – (कालकूट) हिमालय पर्वत का एक शिखर । name of a summit of Himālaya.

काल-केस – वि॰ – (कृष्ण-केशः) काले बाल वाला । a black-haired.

काल-तिपु – न॰ – (काल-त्रपु) काला सीसा, कृष्ण सीसकम् । the black lead.

काल-पक्ख – पु॰ – (कृष्ण पक्ष) अँधेरा पाख, कृष्ण पक्ष । the moonless fortnight.

काल-लोण – न॰ – (कृष्ण लवणम्) काला नमक । black salt.

काल-सीह – न॰ – (काल-सिंह) काला सिंह । a kind of lion.

काल-सुत्त – न॰ – (कृष्णसूत्र) काला-सूत्र । carpenter's measuring thread.

काल-हंस – पु॰ – (कलहंस/कृष्णहंस) काला हंस । a black swan.

कालहक – वि॰ – (कलङ्क) लाञ्छनम्, काला चिह्न । a black spot.

कालक – न॰ – (कालकम्) काला धब्बा, धान में का काला दाना । a black spot, black grain in the rice.

कालकण्णी-जातक – (जा॰ सं॰ 83) – अनाथ-पिण्डिक के कालकण्णी मित्र की कथा के समान । the story (No. 83) is similar to the tale of Kāḷakaṇṇī.

कालकण्णी – अनाथ पिण्डिक के निर्धन मित्र कालकर्णी की कथा कृष्ण सुदामा की याद दिलाती है । tale of Kālakaṇṇī related to his friendship with Anāthapiṇḍika reminds the true friendship of Kṛṣṇa and Sudāmā.

कालबाहु-जातक – (जा॰ सं॰ 329) – यह कथा बताती है कि चालबाजियों के सहारे प्राप्त सस्ती लोकप्रियता शीघ्र नष्ट हो जाती है । the story (No. 329) tells that the cheap popularity earned by mere tricks vanishes very soon.

कालाम – पु॰ – (कालाम) गोत्र-विशेष । कालामों को ही भगवान् बुद्ध ने प्रसिद्ध कालाम-सुत्त का उपदेश दिया था ।

Kṣatriya clan at the time of the Buddha. Ālāra-kālāma of this clan was the teacher of Gautama before he was enlightened. The Buddha has preached the famous Kālāma- Sutta amongst the Kālāma.

कालायस – न॰ – (कृष्णायस्) कच्चा लोहा, काला लोहा। (black) iron, ore of iron.

कालावक – पु॰ – (कालकुम्भिन्) एक प्रकार का हाथी। a kind of elephant.

कालिंग-बोधि-जातक – (जा॰ सं॰ 479) – कालिंग नरेश के दो पुत्रों की कथा। it is the tale of the two sons of the king of Kaliṅga.

कासाव-जातक – (जा॰ सं॰ 221) – काषाय वस्त्र के कारण हाथी द्वारा दुष्ट आदमी को क्षमा कर देने की कथा। the story (No. 221) concludes that even animals pay respect to those who appear to be leading a pious life.

किकी – पु॰ – (किकीवि ∕ चाषः) मादा नीलकण्ठ पक्षी। the blue female jay bird.

किंकर – पु॰ – (किङ्कर) नौकर, सेवक। servant, attendant.

किंकिणी – स्त्री॰ – (किङ्किणी) छोटी घंटी, घुँघरु। a jingling bell.

किंकिणिक-जाल – न॰ – (किङ्किणिक जाल) घुँघरुओं की जाली। a net of tinkling bells.

किच्च – न॰ – (कृत्य) कर्त्तव्य, कार्य, कृत्य। duty, job.

किच्चकारी – वि॰ – (कृत्यकारी) कर्तव्य-पालक। devoted to one's own duty, dutiful.

किच्चाकिच्च – न॰ – (कृत्याकृत्य) कृत्य तथा अकृत्य, करणीय तथा अकरणीय। what should be done and what not to be done.

किच्छ (1) – वि॰ – (कृच्छ्) कठिन, दुःखद। difficult, painful.

किच्छ (2) – न॰ – (कृच्छ्) कठिनाई, दुःख। difficulty, distress.

किच्छति – क्रि॰ – (कृच्छ्रति) दुःख झेलता है, कष्ट पाता है। becomes troubled, gets worried.

√ **किञ्च** – भू॰ – यद्ने – (√ चूर्ण∕ चूर्णयति) चूर-चूर कर देना। reduce pulverise, to powder.

किंचन – न॰ – (किञ्चन) कुछ, सांसारिक आसक्ति। something, worldly attachment.

किंचापि – अव्यय – (किञ्चिदपि) कुछ भी, कैसे भी, कितना भी, लेकिन। whatever, however much, but.

किंचि – अव्यय – (किञ्चिद्) कुछ। something.

किंचिक्ख – न॰ – तुच्छ। trifle.

किंजक्ख – पु॰ तथा न॰ – (किंजल्क) पुष्प रेणु, पराग केसर। filament, pollen.

किट्ठ – न॰ – उगता हुआ धान। growing corn.

किट्ठाद – वि॰ – धान खाने वाला। corn-eater.

किट्ठा-सम्बाध-समय – (पु॰) – खेती पक जाने का समय। harvest time.

किणन्त – कृ॰ – (क्रीणन्) खरीदते हुए। buying.

किणित्वा – पूर्व क्रि॰ – (क्रीत्वा) खरीदकर। having bought.

किण्ण (1) – कृ० – (कीर्ण) बिखरा हुआ। scattered.

किण्ण (2) – न० – (कीर्ण) खमीर। yeast.

कितव – पु० – (कितव) ठग। a cheat, an imposter.

√ कित्त – चु० – संसदे – (√ कृत-कीर्त्तयति) स्तुति भाव से बार-बार नाम लेना। to repeat the name.

कित्तक-सर्वनाम – (कित्तक) कितना, किस सीमा तक, कितने। how much? to what extent? how many?

कित्तन – न० – (कीर्त्तनम्) कीर्तन, प्रशंसा, स्तुति। praising, expounding.

कित्तावता – क्रि० वि० – (कियत् तावत्) कहाँ किस सम्बन्ध में। how for? in what respect?

कित्ति – स्त्री० – (कीर्त्ति) कीर्ति, प्रसिद्धि। fame, renown.

कित्ति-घोस – पु० – (कीर्ति-घोष) यश। reputation, glory.

कित्ति-मन्तु – वि० – (कीर्तिमान) यशस्वी। famous.

कित्तिम – वि० – (कृत्रिम) कृत्रिम। artificial.

कित्ति-सदद – पु० – (कीर्ति-शब्द) यशोगान, ख्याति। reputation.

कित्तेति – क्रि० – (कीर्त्तियति) प्रशंसा करता है। praises, extols.

किन्नर – पु० – (किन्नर) (1) पक्षी-विशेष (2) जंगल में रहने वाली जाति-विशेष। (1) a kind of bird (2) a forest-dwelling a demi-god tribe.

किन्नरी – स्त्री० – (किन्नरी) किन्नर स्त्री। a kinnara, a demi-god, a kind of violin woman, wife of.

किपिल्लिका – स्त्री० – (पिपीलिका) चींटी।an ant.

किब्बिस – न० – (किल्विष) अपराध।wrong doing, crime.

किब्बिसकारी – पु० – (किल्विषकारी) अपराधी। a criminal.

किमि – पु० – (कृमि) कीड़ा, कृमि। a worm, vermin.

किमि-कुल – न० – (कृमि-कुल) कीड़ों का समूह। a crowd of worms.

किमक्खायी – वि० – (किम् आख्यायी?) किस उपदेश की चेष्टा। preaching what.

किमत्थं – क्रि० वि० – (किमर्थम्) किसलिए। for what purpose?

किमत्थिय – वि० – (किमर्थम्) किस उद्देश्य से। for what purpose?

किमपक्क-फल – न० – (किम्पक्व फल) आम की शक्ल का जहरीला फल। a poisonous fruit of a cucurbitaceous plant, fruit of Trichosanthes palmata, in the shape of a mango.

किमपक्क-जातक – (जा० सं० 85) – यह जातक कथा बतलाती है कि इन्द्रिय सुख 'किम्पक्व फल' की भांति उपभोग के समय मधुर और आकर्षक लगता है उसका विष मृत्यु का कारण बन जाता है। the story (No. 85) tells that lusts of the sense-organs are like the fruit of *kiṁpakka* tree, sweet and attractive in the hour of enjoyment but leading later to death.

किमपुरिस – (किम्पुरुष) देखें किन्नर। see Kinnara.

किंसुकोपम-जातक – (जा॰ सं॰ 248) – बुद्ध द्वारा चार भिक्षुओं को चार भिन्न-भिन्न कर्म स्थान दिये गये चारों ने अर्हत्व लाभ किया। The story (No. 248) tells that one should not bother about the variety of the means. There are various paths reaching to the same goal.

किंच्छन्द-जातक – (जा॰ सं॰ 511) – रिश्वत लेने वाले न्यायाधीश पुरोहित की दुःख-सुख से परिपूर्ण कथा। the story (No. 511) tells about the alternates of bliss and misery in life.

√ किर – तु॰ – (विकिरणे = √ कृ + किरति) बिखेरना। to scatter, to strew.

किर – अव्यय – (किल) वास्तव में (एक अनुश्रुतिसूचक प्रयोग)। really, truely, (refers to a hearsay).

किरण – पु॰ तथा न॰ – (किरण) (सूर्य या चन्द्र की) किरण। ray, effulgence.

किरति – क्रि॰ – (किरति) बिखेरता है। scatters.

किरात – पु॰ – (किरात) एक जँगली जाति-विशेष। a forest tribe-dwelling.

किरिय – न॰ – (क्रिया) क्रिया। action, performance.

किरियवाद – पु॰ – (क्रियावाद) कर्म-फल में विश्वास। belief in the consequence of action, fruits of action.

किरिय-वादी – पु॰ – (क्रिया-वादी) कर्म-फल में विश्वासी। one who believes in the theory of fruits of action.

किरीट – न॰ – (किरीट) राज-मुकुट। a crown, diadem.

किलञ्ज – स्त्री॰ – चटाई। mat of rushes.

किमन्त – कृ॰ – (क्लान्त) थका हुआ। tired, exhausted.

किलम – भू॰ – (ग्लानौ) ग्लानि कम होना। reduce exhaustion, reduce sickness or depression.

किलमति – क्रि॰ – (क्लामति / क्लाम्यति) थकता है। becomes fatigued, tired.

किलमथ – पु॰ – (क्लमथ) थकावट। fatigue, weariness.

किलमन्त – कृ॰ – (क्लाम्यन्) थकता हुआ। becoming weary.

किलमित – कृ॰ – (क्लमित / क्लान्त) थका हुआ। tired, fatigued.

किलमेति – क्रि॰ – (क्लमयति) थकाता है। makes weary.

किलास – पु॰ – (किलास) त्वचागत कुष्ठ, कोढ़। skin-leprosy.

किलिट्ठ – कृ॰ – मैला। dirty.

किलिन्न – कृ॰ – (√ क्लिद् + क्त = क्लिन्न) भीगा हुआ। wet, soiled, moist.

√ किलिस – वि॰ – (उपतापे) क्लेश पाना। becomes anguished, distressed.

किलिस्सति – क्रि॰ – दाग लगाता है, अशुद्ध होता है। blemished, impure.

किलिस्सन – न॰ – मैला होना, दाग लगना। to spoil, to pollute.

किलेस – पु॰ – (काम-क्लेश) कामुकता। passion, lust.

किलेसक्खय – (कामक्लेश-क्षय) कामुकता का क्षय। reduction of passion.

किलेसप्पहाण – (कामक्लेश-प्रहाण) कामुकता का नाश। destruction of passion or desires.

किलेस-वत्थु – (कामक्लेश-वस्तु) आसक्ति के पात्र। objects of passion or lust.

किलेसेति – क्रि॰ – (कुलुषयति) धब्बा या दाग लगाता है। makes someone impure or blemished.

किलोमक – न॰ – (क्लोमक) फुप्फुस का आवरण। the pleura.

किस – वि॰ – (कृश) कृश, दुबला-पतला। lean, emaciated.

किं – सर्वनाम – (किम्) क्या। what?

को – पु॰ – (कः) कौन, (पुरुष)। who? (male).

का – स्त्री॰ – (का) कौन (स्त्री)। who? (female).

कं – न॰ – (कम्) किस वस्तु की? what? (thing).

किं – कारण – क्रि॰वि॰ – (किं कारणात्) किस कारण से? by reason of what?

किंवादी – वि॰ – (किंवादी) किस मत का। what view are you holding?

√ **की** – (कि॰) – (द्रव्यविनिमय) खरीदना। to buy.

कीट – पु॰ – (कीट) कीड़ा। an insect, a moth.

कीत – कृ॰ – (क्रीत) खरीदा हुआ। purchased.

कीदिस – वि॰ – (कीदृश) कैसा? of what kind? what like?

कीर – पु॰ – (कीर) तोता। a parrot.

√ **कीळ** – (भू॰) – (बन्धे) बाँधना। to fasten, to tie.

√ **कीळ** – (भू॰) – (क्रीडायाम्) खेल करना। to play.

कील – पु॰ – (कीलक) खूँटा। a stake.

कीव – अव्यय – (कियत्) कितना? कब तक? how much? how long?

कीवतिक – वि॰ – (कियत्तिक) कितन? कितना? how many? how much?

कीळति – क्रि॰ – (क्रीडति) खेलता है। plays.

कीळनक – न॰ – (क्रीडनक) खिलौना। a toy.

कीळना-केळी – स्त्री॰ – (क्रीडा-केलि) क्रीडा-विनोद। sport, enjoyment.

कीळा-गोलक – न॰ – (क्रीडा-गोलक/कन्दुक) खेलने का गेंद। a ball to play with.

कीळा-पसुत – वि॰ – (क्रीडा-पसृत) खेल में लगा हुआ। engaged in playing.

कीळा-भण्डक – न॰ – (क्रीडा-भाण्डक) खिलौना। a plaything, a toy.

कीळा-व्यमण्डल – न॰ – (क्रीडा-मण्डल) क्रीडा-भूमि। play ground.

कीळा-पनक – वि॰ – (क्रीडनक) खिलाड़ी, न खिलौना। one who a toy plays.

कीळापेति – क्रि॰ – (क्रीडापयति) खिलाता है। causes to play, makes one play.

कीळित – कृ॰ – (क्रीडित) खेला हुआ। played.

कुकुत्थक – पु॰ – एक प्रकार का पक्षी। a wild cock (Phasianus gallus).

कुक्कु – पु॰ – (अन्तःप्रकोष्ठिक) लगभग 20 इंच या हाथ भर का माप। a cubit.

कुक्कु-जातक – (जा॰ सं॰ 396) – राजा ब्रह्मदत्त को समझाने के लिए दी गयी अनेक उपमाओं से युक्त कथा। it (tale No. 396) contains several parables which the Bodhisattva as counsellor to Brahmadatta narrated to him.

कक्कुच्च – न॰ – (कौकृत्य) कौकृत्य, पश्चात्ताप। remorse, grief.

कुक्कुचायति – क्रि॰ – पश्चात्ताप करता है। to grieve, to feel remorseful.

कुक्कुट – पु॰ – (कुक्कुट) मुर्गा। a cock.

कुक्कुट-जातक – (जा॰ सं॰ 383) – एक बिल्ली ने एक मुर्गे की पत्नी बनने की बात बना उसे ठगना चाहा किन्तु सफल न हुई। the story (No. 383) tells that one should not be tempted by the sight of a woman.

कुक्कुट-जातक – (जा॰ सं॰ 448) – एक बाज ने एक मुर्गी को ठगना चाहा। the story (No. 448) tells that there could be no friendship between birds with opposite natures like fowl and falcon.

कुक्कुटी – स्त्री॰ – (कुक्कुटी) मुर्गी। a hen.

कुक्कुर – पु॰ – (कुक्कुर) कुत्ता। a dog.

कुक्कुर-वतिक – वि॰ – (कुक्कुर-व्रतिक) कुकुर व्रती। imitating a dog (in austerity).

कुक्कुर-जातक – (जा॰ सं॰ 22) – राजा द्वारा अपने कुत्तों के अपराध के कारण दूसरे निरपराध कुत्तों को भी मरवाने की आज्ञा देने का दृष्टान्त। the tale (No. 22) shows how the offence committed by one affects the entire community.

कुक्कुळ – पु॰ – गरम राख। एक नरक का नाम। hot ashes, name of a hell.

कुंकुम – न॰ – (कुङ्कुमं) केसर। saffron.

कुच्छि – पु॰ – (कुक्षि) कोख, पेट। the belly or womb.

कुच्छिट्ठ – वि॰ – (कुक्षिस्थ) कुच्छि-स्थित, कोख में स्थित। deposited in the womb.

कुच्छि-दाह – पु॰ – (कुक्षि-दाह) पेट की जलन। inflammation in the stomach.

कुच्छित – कृ॰ – (कुत्सित) कुत्सित, घृणित। contemptible, vile.

√कुज – भू॰ – (कूजने) चहकना। to chirp.

कुज – पु॰ – (कुज) वृक्ष-विशेष, मङ्गल ग्रह। a tree, the planet mars.

कुज्झति – क्रि॰ – (कुध्यति) क्रोधित होता है। becomes angry.

कुज्झन – न॰ – (क्रोधनम्) क्रोध। anger, irritation.

कुज्झित्वा – पूर्व क्रि॰ – (√कुध् + त्वा = कुद्ध्वा) क्रुद्ध होकर। being angry.

कुञ्चनाद – पु॰ – (कौञ्चनाद) कौञ्च-नाद, हाथी की चिंघाड़। trumpeting (of an elephant).

कुञ्चिका – स्त्री॰ – (कुञ्चिका) चाबी। a key.

कुञ्चिका-विवर – न॰ – (कुञ्चिका-विवर) चाबी का छेद। keyhole.

कुञ्चित – कृ॰ – (कुञ्चित) मुड़ा हुआ। bent, curled.

कुञ्ज – न॰ – (कुञ्ज) घाटी-लताओं, आदि से ढँका स्थान। a place over-run with plants, a place half covered, a dell.

कुञ्जर – पु॰ – (कुञ्जर) हाथी। elephant.

√कुट – (तु॰) – (कौटिल्ये) टेढ़ा होना। bend, crooked.

√कुट – (भू॰) – (छेदने) काटना। to cut.

√ कुट – (चु॰) – (आकोटने) मारना पीटना। to beat.

कुट – पु॰ तथा न॰ – (कुट) जल-पात्र। water vessel.

कुटज – पु॰ – (कुटज) कुरैया नामक औषध-विशेष, बूटी-विशेष। a kind of medicinal herb.

कुटि – स्त्री॰ – (कुटी) झोंपड़ी। a hut.

कुटि-दूसक-जातक – (जा॰ सं॰ 321) – बये ने बरसात में भीगे बन्दर को उपदेश दिया। बन्दर ने बये का घोंसला ही उजाड़ दिया। the famous story (No. 321) of the monkey who on being given good advice got enraged and destroyed the bird's nest.

कुटिल – वि॰ – (कुटिल) टेढ़ा, वक्रा। bent, crooked.

कुटिलता – स्त्री॰ – (कुटिलता) दुष्टता, टेढ़ापन। crookedness, dishonesty.

कुटुम्ब – न॰ – (कुटुम्ब) परिवार। family.

कुटुम्बिक – पु॰ – (कुटुम्बिक) परिवार का मुखिया। the head of a family, a householder.

कुट्ठ – न॰ – (कुष्ठ) (1) कुष्ठ (2) एक पौधा-विशेष। (1) leprosy (2) a kind of fragrant plant.

कुट्ठी – पु॰ – (कुष्ठी) कोढ़ी। a leper.

कुठारी – स्त्री॰ – (कुठारी) कुल्हाड़ी। an axe, hatchet.

कुडुव – पु॰ – (कुडव) कुडव। an opening bud.

कुडुमल – पु॰ – (कुड्मल) किसलय, कोपल, मुकुल। an opening bud.

कुड्ड – न॰ – (कुड्य) दीवार। wall.

√ कुण – (भू॰) – (शब्दार्थे) आवाज करना। to sound.

कुणप – पु॰ – (कुणप) शव, लाश। corpse, carcase.

कुणप-गन्ध – पु॰ – (कुणप-गन्ध) लाश की सड़ाँध। smell of rotting corpse.

कुणाल – पु॰ – (कुणाल) कोकिल, कोयल। the Indian cuckoo.

कुणाल-जातक – (जा॰ सं॰ 536) – नारियों की चपलता, कामुकता और अविश्वसनीयता की कथा। the story (No. 536) that illustrates the wickedness of woman.

कुणी – पु॰ – (कुणी) खंज, लंगड़ा। a cripple.

कुण्ठ – वि॰ – (कुण्ठ) भोथरा, थोथरा। blunt.

कुण्ठेति – क्रि॰ – (कुण्ठयति) कुण्ठित कर देता है। makes blunt.

कुण्डक – (कुण्डक) चावलों से प्राप्त भूसी के नीचे का चूर्ण। the powder obtained from the inner rind of rice.

√ कुण्ड – (भू॰) – (दहे) जलाना। to burn.

कुण्डक-पूव – (कुण्डक-पूपय) कुण्डक से बने पूए। cake made of rice powder.

कुण्डल – न॰ – (कुण्डल) कान की बाली। an earring, a curl.

कुण्डल-केस – वि॰ – (कुण्डल-केश) घुँघराले बाल। curled hair.

कुण्डलावत्त – वि॰ – (कुण्डलावर्त्त) स्प्रिंग्-दार घुमाव। twisted round.

कुण्डली – वि॰ – (कुण्डली) जिनके कान में कुण्डल हो या जिसके बाल घुँघराले हों। having earrings or curls.

कुणिडका – स्त्री॰ – (कुण्डिका) कुण्डी, मिट्टी का जल-पात्र। a pitcher, water jug.

कुच – (तु॰) – (संकोचे) सिकुड़ना। to feel shy.

कुतूहल – न॰ – (कुतूहल) उत्तेजना, कौतूहल। excitement, curiosity.

कुतो – क्रि॰ वि॰ – (कुतः) कहाँ से? where from?

कुत्त – न॰ – आचरण, नखरा। behaviour, demeanour.

कुत्तक – न॰ – बड़ा गलीचा। a big carpet.

कुत्ति – स्त्री॰ – सजावट। decoration.

कुत्थ/कुत्र – क्रि॰ वि॰ – (कुत्र) कहाँ?. where?

कुथित – कृ॰ – (क्वथित) उबाला गया। boiled.

कुदस्सु – अव्यय – कब? when?

कुदाचन/कुदाचनं – अव्यय – (कदाचन) कभी, किसी समय। sometimes, at any time.

कुद्दाल – पु॰ – (कुद्दाल) कुदाली। a spade or hoe.

कुद्दाल-जातक – (जा॰ सं॰ 76) – कुद्दाल पण्डित अपनी कुदाली के प्रति असीम आसक्ति के कारण छह बार गृहस्थ बना और गृहस्थी के झंझटों के कारण छह बार साधु। यह है आसक्ति का कुफल। the tale (No. 76) tells about the evils of deep attachment.

कुद्ध – कृ॰ – (कुध) क्रुद्ध। angry, irritated.

कुदरूसक – पु॰ – धान्य-विशेष। a kind of grain.

√ कुद्द – (दि॰) – (क्रोधे) क्रोध करना। to be angry.

कुन्त (1) – पु॰ – (कुन्त) भाला, बर्छी। scepter, lance, spear.

कुन्त (2) – पु॰ – (कुन्त) सारस पक्षी, कौडिल्ला पक्षी। a kind of bird-kaudilla.

कुन्तनी – स्त्री॰ – (कुन्तनी) मादा सारस, बगुली। female crane or female heron.

कुन्तनी-जातक – (जा॰ सं॰ 343) – यह जातक कथा बताती है कि दुर्बल को सताने वाला अपने से बलवतर किसी अन्य का कोपभाजन बन जाता है। the story (No.343) tells how the torturer of the poor gets himself tortured by some stronger one.

कुन्तल – पु॰ – (कुन्तल) केश-राशि। bunch of hair.

कुन्थ – पु॰ – (कुन्थ) चींटी विशेष। a sort of ant.

कुन्द – न॰ – (कुन्द) जूही के समान श्वेत-पुष्प वाला एक पौधा। a kind of jasmine.

कुन्नदी – स्त्री॰ – (कुनदी) नाला, छोटी नदी। rivulet.

कुपथ – पु॰ – (कुपथ) कुमार्ग। wrong path.

√ कुप – (दि॰) – (कोपे) क्रोध करना। to show anger.

कुपित – पु॰ – (कुपित) क्रुद्ध। angry offended.

कुपुरिस – पु॰ – (कुपुरुष) दुष्ट आदमी। bad person.

कुप्प – (कुप्य) अस्थिर, चञ्चल। excited, agitated.

कुप्पति – क्रि॰ – (कुप्यति) क्रोधित होता है,

उत्तेजित होता है। becomes angry or agitated.

कुप्पन – न॰ – (कोपनम्) उत्तेजना, क्रोध। agitation, anger.

कुब्बति – क्रि॰ – (करोति/कुरुते) करता है। does, acts, performs.

कुब्बनक – न॰ – (कुवनक) छोटा जंगल, झाली। a small forest, brushwood.

कुब्बन्त – कृ॰ – (कुर्वन्/कुर्वाणः) करता हुआ। doing, acting, performing.

कुब्बर – पु॰ – (अक्षः, ध्रुवः) गाड़ी के पहियों की धुरी। pole of a carriage.

कुमति – स्त्री॰ – (कुमति) दुर्बुद्धि, मिथ्या दृष्टि। a wrong view.

कुमार – पु॰ – (कुमार) किशोर, लड़का। a boy, a youngster, a lad.

कुमार-कीळा – स्त्री॰ – (कुमार-क्रीडा) कुमार-क्रीडा। amusement of a boy.

कुमार-पञ्ह – खुद्दक पाठ (सुत्त पिटक) का चौथा परिच्छेद। सात वर्ष के सोपाक अर्हत् से पूछे गए प्रश्न। the fourth chapter of the Khuddaka-pāṭha.

कुमारिका – स्त्री॰ – (कुमारिका) कुमारी, कुँवारी। a girl, a virgin.

कुमुद – न॰ – (कुमुद) श्वेत कँवल। white water-lily.

कुमुदं – न॰ – (कुमुदं) एक पर 105 शून्य लगाकर व्यक्त की जाने वाली संख्या। the number denoted by one with 105 zeros.

कुमुद-नाल – न॰ – (कुमुद-नाल) कुमुद-नाल, श्वेत कमल की नलिका। the stalk of white water-lily.

कुमुद-वण्ण – वि॰ – (कुमुद-वर्ण) श्वेत-कमल के वर्ण का। of the colour of white lily.

कुम्भ – पु॰ – (कुम्भ) घड़ा। a water pot, pitcher.

कुम्भक – न॰ – (कुम्भक) जहाज का मस्तूल। the mast (of a ship).

कुम्भकार – पु॰ – (कुम्भकार) कुम्हार। a potter.

कुम्भकार-जातक – (जा॰ सं॰ 408) – वासना-सिक्त विचारों की दुर्दमनीयता का आख्यान करने वाली कथा। the story (No. 408) tells how difficult it is to win over lustful thoughts.

कुम्भकार-साला – स्त्री॰ – (कुम्भकार-शाला) बर्तन बनाने का स्थान। pottery (a place where earthenware is prepared).

कुम्भ-दासी – स्त्री॰ – (कुम्भ-दासी) पनिहारिन, कुएं या नदी से पानी लाने वाली दासी। a female servant who brings water from a well or river.

कुम्भ-जातक – (जा॰ सं॰ 512) – शराब का कैसे अकस्मात् प्रचलन हुआ तथा उसके प्रसार की कथा। the story (No. 512) tells how surā was accidently discovered.

कुम्भण्ड – न॰ – (कूष्माण्ड) कद्दू। a pumpkin.

कुम्भी – स्त्री॰ – (कुम्भी) मिट्टी का बर्तन। a small earthen pot.

कुम्भील – पु॰ – (कुम्भील) मगरमच्छ। crocodile.

कुम्भील-जातक – (जा॰ सं॰ 206) – देखें वानरिन्द-जातक। see Vānarinda Jātaka.

कुम्म – पु॰ – (कूर्म) कछुआ। a tortoise.

कुम्मग्ग – पु॰ – (कुमार्ग) कुमार्ग। wrong path.

कुम्मास – (कुल्माष) चावल या कोई अन्न उबालकर, गुड़ या खांड शक्कर मिलाकर मथकर बनाया गया लस्सी। a sweet dish.

कुम्मासपिण्ड-जातक – (जा॰ सं॰ 415) – कुल्माष-पिंड के दान की कथा।

√ कुर – (तु॰) – (छेदने) काटना। to cut.

√ कुर – (तु॰) – (शब्दे) शब्द करना। to utter, to chirp.

कुर – न॰ – भात। boiled rice.

कुरण्डक – पु॰ – (कुरण्टक) कुरबक नामक पौधा जिसमें पीले फूल लगते हैं। yellow amaranth, a kind of flower plant.

कुरर – पु॰ – (कुरर) टिट्टिभ, टिटहरी। मछली खाने वाला पक्षी-विशेष। an osprey, fishing eagle.

कुररी – स्त्री॰ – (कुररी) मादा टिट्टिभ, टिटहरी। female osprey.

कुरु – (कुरु) प्राचीन भारत के सोलह महाजनपदों में से एक। one of the sixteen states of ancient India.

कुरुंग – पु॰ – (कुरुंग) हरिण की एक जाति। a kind of deer.

कुरंग-मिग-जातक – (जा॰ सं॰ 21) – इस जातक में बताया गया है कि कैसे सच्चे मित्र परस्पर सहायक बनकर आपदाओं को पार करते हैं। the story (No. 21) illustrates how fast friends overcome danger with mutual help.

कुरु-धम्म-जातक – (जा॰ सं॰ 276) – पंचशील अथवा धम्म के पालन से कुरु जनपद की समृद्धि की कथा। this tale (No. 276) tells how the Kuru became prosperous by observing Pañcaśīla following the *dhamma*.

कुरुमान – कृ॰ – (कुर्वाणः) करते हुए। doing, performing.

कुरु-रट्ठ – (कुरु राष्ट्र) उत्तर भारत का कुरु राष्ट्र। a nation (state) of ancient northern India.

कुरूर – वि॰ – (क्रूर) नृशंस, क्रूर, अत्याचारी। cruel, fierce.

कुल – न॰ – (कुल) परिवार, वंश, जाति। family, clan, caste.

कुल-गेह – न॰ – (कुल-गृह) ज्ञाति-गृह, माता-पिता का घर। ancestral home, parent's house.

कुलङ्गर – पु॰ – (कुलङ्गर) कुल-विनाशक। one who brings his family to ruin.

कुल-तन्ति – स्त्री॰ – (कुल-तन्तु) कुल-परम्परा। the line and traditions of a family.

कुल-दूसक – पु॰ – (कुल-दूषक) कुल की बदनामी करने वाला। one who earns a bad repute for his family.

कुल-धीता – स्त्री॰ – (कुल-धी) कुल-ललना, कुलीन बेटी। daughter of a respectable family.

कुल-पुत्त – पु॰ – (कुल-पुत्र) कुल-पुत्र। son of a good family.

कुल-वंस – न॰ – (कुल-वंश) वंश-वृक्ष, वंश-परम्परा। lineage, progeny.

कुलटा – स्त्री॰ – (कुलटा) चरित्रहीन स्त्री, कुलटा, दुष्टा नारी। characterless woman.

कुलत्थ – पु॰ – (कुलत्थ) कुलथी या मोठ नामक दलहन पौधा। vetch, a kind of plant.

कुल-पालिका – स्त्री॰ – (कुल–पालिका) कुल-स्त्री, कुल का पालन करने वाली। the lady maintaining the family well.

कुलल – पु॰ – (कुलाल) (1) जंगली मुर्गा, (2) उल्लू। (1) a wild cock, a wild fowl (2) an owl.

कुलाल – पु॰ – (कुलाल) कुम्हार। a potter.

कुलाला-चक्क – न॰ – (कुलाल–चक्र) कुम्हार का चाक। the wheel of a potter.

कुलावक-जातक – (जा॰ सं॰ 31) – गाँव के उन्तीस परिवारों के मुखिया मघ की समाज-सेवा की कथा। this tale (No. 31) describes about the social service of Magha the headman of 29 families.

कुलिस – न॰ – (कुलिश) वज्र, (इन्द्रायुध) गदा। steel, thunderbolt, a mace.

कुलीन – वि॰ – (कुलीन) श्रेष्ठ कुल का। belonging to a recognised clan.

कुलीर – पु॰ – (कुलीर) केकड़ा। a crab.

कुलीर-पाद – वि॰ – (कुलीर–पाद) केकड़े जैसे पाँवों वाला। having the legs in the shape of a crab.

कुलूपग – वि॰ – (कुलोपग) परिवार विशेष से सुपरिचित। one who frequents a family.

कुल्ल – पु॰ – (तरण्डकः) बेड़ा। a raft.

कुवलय – न॰ – (कुवलय) नीलकमल। a blue water-lily.

कुवेर – पु॰ – (कुबेर) धन के स्वामी, यक्षा-धिपति। the king of *yakṣas*, the master of wealth.

√**कुस** – (भू॰ चु॰) – (आक्रोशे) आक्रोश, बुरा भला कहना। curse, abuse.

कुस – पु॰ – (कुश) कुश (दर्भ) नामक नुकीला तृण। a kind of grass having sharp leaves, (used in Hindu religions ceremonies).

कुसग्ग – न॰ – (कुशाग्र) कुश का नुकीला सिरा। the sharp point of the *kuśa*.

कुसचीर – न॰ – (कुशचीर) कुश-निर्मित पहनावा। garment made of *kuśa*-grass.

कुस-जातक – (जा॰ सं॰ 531) – यह जातक कथा दृष्टान्त प्रस्तुत करती है कि नारी की आसक्ति में फंसकर शक्तिमान व्यक्ति भी दीन-हीन होकर कष्ट भोगते हैं। the story (No. 531) shows how even mighty men may lose their power and come to misery through love of a woman.

कुसल (1) – न॰ – (कुशल) शुभ कर्म। good deeds, auspicious deeds.

कुसल (2) – वि॰ – (कुशल) निपुण, दक्ष। competent, skilled.

कुसल-कम्म – न॰ – (कुशल–कर्म) शुभ-कर्म, सदाचरण। meritorious action, right conduct.

कुसल-चेतना – स्त्री॰ – (कुशल–चेतना) शुभ-चिंतन। right volition.

कुसल-धम्म – पु॰ – (कुशल धर्म) सदाचार अथवा नैतिकतापूर्ण आचरण के विषय। points of righteousness.

कुसल-विपाक – पु॰ – (कुशल–विपाकः) शुभ कर्मों का फल। result of good deeds.

कुसलता – स्त्री॰ – (कुशलता) दक्षता, कुशलता। accomplishment.

कुसा – स्त्री॰ – (नासा–बन्धन) नाक की नकेल। a nose string used as rein, a nose halter of camel which serves as rein.

कुसि – पु॰ – चीवर के अंश। part of a mendicants dress.

कुसीनारा – स्त्री॰ – (कुशीनारा) मल्ल क्षत्रियों की राजधानी। the capital city of the Malla *janapada*.

कुसीत – वि॰ – आलसी। indolent, lazy.

कुसीतता – स्त्री॰ – आलस्य। laziness, indolence.

कुसुम – न॰ – (कुसुम) फूल। flower.

कुसुमित – वि॰ – (कुसुमित) पुष्पित। flowering, blooming.

कुसुब्भ – न॰ – गड़ही, छोटा गड्ढा, छीलर। a small pit.

कुसुम्भ – न॰ – (कुसुम्भ) एक प्रकार का कंटीला कुसुम नामक पौधा जिसके फूल वस्त्र रंगने के काम आते हैं। the saf-flower (for dying red).

कुसूल – पु॰ – (कुशूल) धान्यक, धान्यागार। a granary.

कुसेसय – न॰ – (कुशेशय) कमल, पद्म। lotus.

कुह/कुहक – वि॰ – (कुहुक) जादू करने वाला, ठग, ढोंगी। deceitful, a cheat.

कुहक-जातक – (जा॰ सं॰ 89) – तपस्वी द्वारा धनी गृहस्थ की सोना हड़पने के षड्यन्त्र की कहानी। it is the story (No. 89) of a juggler ascetic who tried to usurp the wealth of a rich householder.

कुहण – न॰ – (कुहुक) ढोंग। deceit, jugglery.

कुहणा – स्त्री॰ – (कुह) ठगी, ढोंग। deceit, fraud.

कुहर – न॰ – (कुहर) विवर, बिल, छिद्र। a hole, cavity.

कुहिं – अव्यय – (कुत्र) कहाँ। where?

कुहेति – क्रि॰ – (√कुह = कुहते) ठगता है। deceives.

कूजति – क्रि॰ – (कूजति) चहकता है, कूजता है। chirps.

कूजन – न॰ – (कूजन) पक्षियों की चहचहाहट। chirping of birds.

कूजंत – कृ॰ – (कूजन) कूजता हुआ। chirping.

कूट – वि॰ – (कूट) मिथ्या, छलयुक्त। false, deceitful.

कूट-गोण – पु॰ – (कूट-बलीवर्द) दुष्ट बैल। untamed bull.

कूट-अट्ट – न॰ – (कूटवाद) झूठा मुकदमा। a false suit.

कूट-अट्टकारक – पु॰ – (कूटवाद–कारक) झूठा मुकदमा दायर करने वाला। a false complainant.

कूट-जटिल – पु॰ – (कूट-जटिल) ढोंगी तपस्वी। fradulent ascetic.

कूट-वाणिज – पु॰ – (कूट-वणिक्) ठग व्यापारी। a dishonest trader.

कूट-वाणिज-जातक – (जा॰ सं॰ 98) – पण्डित तथा अपण्डित नाम के दो व्यापारियों के बीच घटित ठगी के कारनामे। the story (No. 98) of a dishonest merchant who tries to cheat his honest co-merchant.

कूट-वाणिज-जातक – (जा॰ सं॰ 218) – एक सद्गृहस्थ ने एक व्यापारी को अपने लोहे के हल सुरक्षित रखने के लिए

दिये। वापिस माँगने पर उसका वह मित्र बोला चूहे खा गये। चतुर गृहस्थ ने भी उसे उसके कृत्य का मजा चखाया। it is the story (No. 218) of a cheating merchant, who said that rat ate the iron plough.

कूटागार – न॰ – (कूटागार) शिखरिका, शिखर वाला भवन। a pinnacled building.

कूप – पु॰ – (कूप) कुआँ। well.

कूपक – पु॰ – (कूपक) मस्तूल। the mast.

कूल – न॰ – (कूल) नदी-तट, नदी का किनारा। river-bank, embankment.

√ कूल – (भू॰) – (आवरणे) ढकना। to cover.

केका – स्त्री॰ – (केका) मोर की आवाज। the cry of a peacock.

केणि – पु॰ – (क्षेपणी) नौका का चप्पू। an oar.

केतकी – स्त्री॰ – (केतकी) क्रकचा, केतकः गन्धः पुष्पा केवड़ा नामक पौधा जिसके पत्ते काँटेदार और फूल मोहक गन्ध लिये होते हैं। the screw pine plant.

केतन – न॰ – (केतन) पताका। a flag.

केतव – न॰ – (कैतवम्) धूर्तता, शठता। crookedness, knavery.

केतुं – पु॰ – (केतु) झण्डा, पताका। flag.

केतु-कम्यता – स्त्री॰ – (केतु–काम्यता) प्रमुखता की कामना। vainglory, desire for prominence.

केतु-मन्तु – वि॰ – (केतु–मान) पताकाओं से सुसज्जित। adorned with flags.

केतुं – कृ॰ – (√ की + तुमुन = केतुम्) खरीदने के लिए। to buy, for purchase.

केदार – पु॰ तथा न॰ – (केदार) धान का खेत अथवा क्यारी। field of rice.

केदार-पालि – स्त्री॰ – (केदार–पालि) धान के खेतों के बीच की मेंड। a narrow embankment in paddy fields.

केयूर – न॰ – (केयूर) बाजूबंद। a bracelet (an ornament) for the upper arm.

केय्य – वि॰ – (क्रयणीय) खरीदने योग्य। fit to be bought, purchasable.

केराटिक – वि॰ – (प्रतारक / पाखण्डी) ठग, ढोंगी। a deceitful, hypocritic.

केराटिय – न॰ – (प्रतारणा, आडम्बरः) ठग, ढोंगी। deceit, fraud.

√ केल – (भू॰) – (चलने) हिलना। to move.

केलास – पु॰ – (कैलाश) कैलास पर्वत। name of a sacred mountain in the Himālayas.

केलि – स्त्री॰ – (केलि) विनोद, क्रीड़ा। amorous sport, a pastime.

केलिसील-जातक – (जा॰ सं॰ – 202) – हँसोड़ राजा को इन्द्र ने लोगों के परिहास का भाजन बनाया। the story (No. 202) of a king who could not look at anyone old or decrepit without passing jokes on them.

केवट्ट – पु॰ – (केवर्त्त) मछुवा। a fisherman.

केवल – वि॰ – (केवल) अमिश्रित, एकान्त, समस्त। lonely, unmixed, whole.

केवल-कप्पं – वि॰ – (केवल कल्पम्) लगभग सारा। almost the whole.

केवल-परिपुण्णं – वि॰ – (केवल परिपूर्ण) सम्पूर्ण। the whole.

केवलि – वि॰ – (केवली) सम्पूर्णता प्राप्त अर्हत्। who has attained the whole perfectness; an *arhant*.

केस – पु० – (केश) सिर के बाल। hair of the head.

केसोहारक – पु० – (केश-हारक) नाई। a barber.

केस-कम्बल – न० – (केस-कम्बल) बालों का बना कम्बल। blanket made of hair.

केस-कलाप – पु० – (केश–कलाप) केश-गुच्छ। a tress of hair.

केस-कल्याण – न० – (केश-कल्याण) केशों का सौन्दर्य। beauty of hair.

केस-धातु – स्त्री० – (केश–धातु) भगवान् बुद्ध की पवित्र केश-धातु। hair relic.

केसर – न० – (केसर) पुष्प-रेणु, पराग, अयाल (पशुओं के कन्धे के बाल)। hair mane (of animals).

केसर-सीह – पु० – (केसरी सिंह) केसरी, बबर शेर, शेर की एक प्रजाति जिसकी गरदन पर लम्बे बाल होते हैं। a maned lion.

केसव – वि० – (केशवान) लम्बे घने केशों वाला। of rich hair.

केसव – पु० – (केशव) केशव (वासुदेव कृष्ण)। God Viṣṇu, lord Kṛṣṇa.

केसव-जातक – (जा० सं० 346) – इस कथा का वही निष्कर्ष है जो रहीम ने कहा है : अमिय पियावत मान बिनु,रहिमन मोहि न सुहाय। this story (No. 346) points out that the best food is that which is given in love, love is the best flavouring for food.

केसोरोपन – न० – (केश-कर्त्तन) बालों को मूंड़ना, बालों को काटना। shaving of hair.

केसोहारण – न० – (केश-कर्त्तनम्) बालों को मूंड़ना, बालों को काटना। shaving of hair.

केसोहारक – पु० – (केश सुधारक) केश प्रसाधक, नाई। barber.

को – पु० – (कः) कौन? who?

कोक – पु० – (कोकः) वृक:, भेड़िया। a wolf.

कोकनद – न० – (कोकनद) पद्म, लाल कमल। a red lotus.

कोकिल – पु० – (कोकिल) कोयल। Indian cuckoo.

कोचि – अव्यय – (कोचिद्) कोई। someone, whoever.

कोच्छ (1) – न० – (कटम्) पेड़ की छाल, उशीर (गँडरा) नामक घास, मूँज, भादा, जलनेत आदि से बनायी गयी बैठने हेतु चटाई। a kind of seat or settee made of bark, grass or rushes.

कोच्छ (2) – न० – (कंकती／कंकतिका) कंघी (केश सुलझाने हेतु)। a comb for hair dressing.

कोच्छ-कार – पु० – (कंकति कारः) कंघी बनाने वाला। a comb-maker.

कोज – पु० – (कवच) कवच, वर्म। armour.

कोजव – पु० – (गोणका) गलीचानुमा बालों का बना आवरण, आच्छादन। a rug or cover with long hair.

कोकालिक-जातक – (जा० सं० 331) – एक वाचाल राजा को वाचालता के विरुद्ध दिया गया परामर्श this story (No.331) points out that the garrulous meets ill fate more.

कोञ्च – पु० – (क्रौञ्च) सारस। a heron.

कोञ्चनाद – पु० – (क्रौञ्चनाद) हाथी की चिंघाड़। trumpeting of an elephant.

कोट – न० – (कोट) शिखर। summit.

कोटचिका – स्त्री॰ – (च्युतिः /योनिः) चूत्। the female organ.

कोटि – स्त्री॰ – (कोटि) (1) शिखर (2) करोड़। (1) summit, point (2) ten-million.

कोटिप्पकोटि – स्त्री॰ – (कोटि-प्रकोटि) एक के दाहिनी ओर इक्कीस ओर शून्य लगाकर बनायी गई संख्या। number or figure one followed by 21 zeroes.

कोटिप्पत्त – वि॰ – (कोटि-प्राप्त) सिरे तक पहुँच गया, भली प्रकार समझ गया। having reached the end, fully grasped.

कोटिल्ल – न॰ – (कौटिल्य) दुष्टता, कुटिलता, टेढ़ापन। crookedness.

कोटिसिम्बलि-जातक – (जा॰ सं॰ 412) – इस कथा का निष्कर्ष यह है कि जब विश्वास न करने का समुचित कारण हो तो विश्वास न करना ही उचित है। story (No. 412) says it is right to distrust where the reason for distrust is proper .

कोटुम्बर – न॰ – (पाटम्बर) वस्त्र-विशेष। a kind of cloth.

कोट्टन – न॰ – (कुद्दटन) कूटना। pounding.

कोट्ठ – पु॰ – (कोष्ठ) कोठा। a store room.

कोट्ठक – पु॰ तथा वि॰ – (कोष्ठक) (1) दुर्ग (2) द्वार (3) छिपने का स्थान। (1) a gateway (2) stronghold (3) place for concealment.

कोट्ठागार – न॰ – (कोष्ठागार) धान्यागार। a granary.

कोट्ठागारिक – पु॰ – (कोष्ठागारिक) भाण्डागारिक। a storekeeper.

कोट्ठासय – वि॰ – (कोष्ठाशय) पेट में रहने वाला। existing in the abdomen.

कोट्ठास – पु॰ – (कोष्ठांश) हिस्सा, भाग। share, portion.

कोण – पु॰ – (कोण) कोना, सिरा, धनुष। corner, end, bow.

कोण्डञ्ञ कोण्डञ्ञ – प्रसिद्ध ब्राह्मण-क्षत्रिय गोत्र। a famous lineage of brāhmanas, kṣatriyas.

कोतूहल – न॰ – (कुतूहल) उत्तेजना, जिज्ञासा। excitement, curiosity.

कोत्थु/कोत्थुक – पु॰ – (क्रोष्टः) शृगाल, गीदड़। a jackal.

कोदण्ड – न॰ – (कोदण्ड) धनुष। a bow.

कोध – पु॰ – (क्रोध) क्रोध, गुस्सा। anger.

कोधन – वि॰ – (क्रोधन) विक्षुब्ध, असंयत चित्त। peevish, uncontrolled (of mind).

कोप – पु॰ – (कोप) क्रोध, गुस्सा। anger.

कोपनेय्य – वि॰ – (कोपनेय) क्रोध उत्पन्न करने वाला। to arouse anger.

कोपी – वि॰ – (कोपी) क्रोधी। ill-tempered.

कोपीन – न॰ – (कोपीनम्) लँगोटी। an undergarment for men.

कोपेति – क्रि॰ – (कोपयति) क्रोध उत्पन्न कराता है। makes angry, irritates.

कोमल – वि॰ – (कोमल) नर्म। soft.

कोमार – वि॰ – (कौमार) कुमार-सम्बन्धी। juvenile.

कोमार-भच्च (1) – न॰ – (कौमार-भृत्य) बच्चों की चिकित्सा। the medical treatment of infants.

कोमार-भच्च (2) – (कौमार-भृत्य) किसी राजकुमार द्वारा पोषित। brought up by a prince.

कोमाय-पुत्त-जातक – (जा॰ सं॰ – 299) – कथा बतलाती है कि चतुर कोमायपुत्त ने किस प्रकार ढोंगी तपस्वियों का आश्रम हथिया लिया। the story (No. 299) tells how the wise ascetic occupied the huts of juggler ascetics.

कोमुदी – स्त्री॰ – (कौमुदी) शरद पूर्णिमा चाँदनी। Kārtika, the full moon night in the month of Kārtika.

कोरक – पु॰ तथा न॰ – (कोरक) कोपल। a bud.

कोरब्य/कोरव्य – वि॰ – (कोरव्य) कुरु वंश का, कुरु राष्ट्र का निवासी। a descendant of Kuru.

कोल – पु॰ तथा न॰ – (कोलम्) रस-भरी का फल। a jujube fruit.

कोलक – न॰ – (कोलकम् /कालकम्) काली मिर्च। black pepper.

कोलम्ब – पु॰ – (कोलम्ब) बड़ा घड़ा या मर्त्तबान। a big jar or pitcher.

कोलाप – पु॰ – (तरु-कोदर) खोखला पेड़। a dead or hollow tree.

कोलाहल – न॰ – (कोलाहल) शोर-गुल। tumult, hue and cry.

कोलित – (कोलित) मोद्गल्यायन स्थविर का गृहस्थ नाम। the former name of monk Mahāmoggallāna.

कोलिय – पु॰ – (कोलिय) शाक्यों के समान ही एक दूसरी जाति। name of a clan akin to Śākyas.

कोलेय्यक – वि॰ – (कोलेय्यक) अच्छी नस्ल का (विशेष रूप से कुत्तों की नस्ल)। of good breed (said of dogs).

कोविदं – वि॰ – (कोविद) दक्ष, निपुण, पण्डित। clever, well-versed.

कोस – पु॰ – (कोश) भण्डार, खजाना, म्यान। storeroom, treasury, sheath.

कोसक – पु॰ तथा न॰ – (कोसक) पानी पीने का पात्र। a cup, drinking vessel.

कोसज्ज – न॰ – (कौसीद्य) आलस्य, कुसीदत्व। idleness, sloth, indolence.

कोसम्बी – स्त्री॰ – (कोशाम्बी) वत्स्य-देश की राजधानी। name of the capital of Vatsa State.

कोसल – पु॰ – (कोसल) कोशल जनपद। one among the sixteen *mahājanapada*s (States) of India at the time of the Buddha.

कोसल्ल – न॰ – (कौशल) कौशल, निपुणता, दक्षता। proficiency.

कोसारक्ख – पु॰ – (कोषाध्यक्ष) कोषपालक, खजांची। treasurer.

कोसिक – पु॰ – (कौशिक) (विश्वामित्र का शोकपरक नाम (1) अकौशिक (2) उल्लू। (1) the title of Viśvāmitra (2) owl.

कोसिनारक – वि॰ – (कौशिनारक) कुसीनारा सम्बन्धी। belonging to Kusīnārā.

कोसिय-जातक (1) – (जा॰ सं॰ 130) – रोग का बहाना बना दिन भर लेटी रहने और रात को मौज मस्ती मनाने वाली दुष्टा का अचूक इलाज। the story (No. 130) tells how to cure a bad wife who remains in bed by day feigning sickness and spends her night in enjoyment.

कोसिय-जातक (2) – (जा॰ सं॰ 226) – अनुपयुक्त काल पर किया गया आचरण घातक बन जाता है इसका एक दृष्टान्त। the story (No. 226) tells that the act done at inappropriate time may cause miseries.

कोसी – स्त्री॰ – (कोशी) खड्ग-कोश, म्यान। a sheath.

कोसेय्य (1) – न॰ – (कौशेय) रेशम, रेशम से बना वस्त्र। silk, silk cloth.

कोसेय्य (2) – वि॰ – (कौशेय) रेशमी। silken.

कोसोहित – वि॰ – (कोशावृत्त) कोश से ढका हुआ, कोशावृत्त। ensheathed.

√ **कोह** – (चु॰) – (छेदने) काटना। to cut.

कोहञ्ञ – न॰ – (पाखण्ड) ढोंग। hypocrisy, deceit.

√ **क्लम** – (भू॰) – (ग्लानौ) परेशान होना। to be tired.

√ **क्लिस** – (दि॰) – (उपतापि) क्लेश उठाना। to suffer.

क्व – अव्यय – (क्व) कहाँ? where?

क्वचि – अव्यय – (क्वचिद्) कहीं? some - where?

ख

ख (1) – पालि वर्णमाला का दूसरा व्यञ्जन। the second consonant of Pāli alphabet.

ख (2) – न॰ – (ख) आकाश, शून्य। the sky.

खग – पु॰ – (खग) पक्षी। bird.

खगन्तर – पु॰ – (काष्ठकूटः) दार्वाघाटः शतच्छद, कठफोड़ा पक्षी। a wood-pecker.

खगादि – पु॰ – (खग) पक्षी। fowl.

खगादिबन्धन – पु॰ – (खगबन्धन) पक्षियों को फँसाने का जाल। net for catching fowl.

खग्ग – पु॰ – (खड्ग) तलवार। sword.

खग्ग-कोस – पु॰ – (खड्ग-कोश) तलवार की म्यान। sheath for a sword.

खग्ग-गाहक – पु॰ – (खङ्गधारी) असि-धारक, कृपाण-धारी। a sword bearer.

खग्ग-तल – न॰ – (खड्ग-तल) तलवार का फलक। blade of a sword.

खग्ग-धर – वि॰ – (खड्ग-धर) देखें खग्ग-गाहक। see Khagga-gāhaka.

खग्ग-विसाण – पु॰ – (खड्ग-विषाण) गैंडा। rhinoceros.

खचति – क्रि॰ – (खचति) जड़ता है, (अँगूठी में नगीना जड़ता है)। inlays, adorns with.

खज्ज – (भू॰) (गतिवैकल्पे) लंगड़ाना। to cripple.

खज्ज (1) – वि॰ – (खाद्य) खाद्य। to be eaten or eatable.

खज्ज (2) – न॰ – (खज्जकम्) खाजा नामक मिष्ठान्न। a kind of sweet-meat.

खज्जकन्तर – न॰ – (खाद्यकान्तरम्) नाना-विध मिठाईयाँ। various kinds of sweets.

खज्जु – स्त्री॰ – (खज्जु/कण्डू) खाज। itch.

खज्जूरी – स्त्री॰ – (खर्जूर) खजूर का वृक्ष व फल। date-palm.

खज्जोपनक – पु॰ – (खद्योत) जुगनू। the fire-fly, a glow-worm.

खञ्ज – वि॰ – (√ खजि = गति वैकल्ये - खञ्जः) लँगड़ा। lame, crippled.

खञ्जति – क्रि॰ – (√ खजि - खञ्जति) लँगड़ाता है। cripples, walks limping.

खञ्जन – पु॰ – (खञ्जन) खञ्जन पक्षी। a wag tail, bird.

खञ्जन – न॰ – (खञ्जन) लँगड़ाना। limping.

खटक – पु॰ (खटक) मुट्ठी। fist.

खण – पु॰ – (क्षण) क्षण, अवसर। a moment, an opportunity.

खणेन – क्रि॰ वि॰ – (क्षणेन) क्षण में। in a moment.

खणातीत – वि॰ – (क्षणातीत) अवसरातीत, जो अवसर से चूक गया। having missed the opportunity.

खणति – क्रि॰ – (खनति) खोदता है। digs, uproots.

खणन – न॰ – (खनन) खोदना । digging.

खणिक – वि॰ – (क्षणिक) क्षणिक । momentary.

खणित्ती – स्त्री॰ – (खनित्री) खन्ति, कुदाल । a pick-axe, a crow-bar.

खण्ड – पु॰ – (खण्ड) हिस्सा, टुकड़ा । a bit, broken piece.

खण्ड-दन्त – वि॰ – (खण्ड दन्त) टूटे दाँत वाला । having broken teeth.

खण्ड-फुल्ल – न॰ – (खण्डावशेषः) धवसांवशेष, खँडहर । broken and shattered portions (of a building).

खण्डन – न॰ – (खण्डन) नष्ट करना, टूटना, बात काट देना । breaking, destroying, refuting.

खण्डहाल-जातक – (जा॰ सं॰ 542) – रिश्वतखोर पुरोहित की कथा जो राजा के पुत्र की हत्या कराने के षड्यन्त्र में स्वयं मृत्यु का ग्रास बन गया । the story (No. 542) of a wicked chaplain who not only failed in his conspiracy of killing the prince but was murdered for his guilt.

खण्डाखण्ड – वि॰ – (खण्डाखण्ड) टुकड़े-टुकड़े टूटा हुआ । broken into pieces.

खण्डिका – स्त्री॰ – (खण्डिका) खण्डित टुकड़ा । a piece, a broken bit.

खण्डिच्च – न॰ – (खण्डित्व) खण्डित होना । the state of being broken.

खण्डेति – क्रि॰ – (खण्डयति) टुकड़े-टुकड़े करता है । breaks into pieces.

खत (1) – कृ॰ – (क्षत) घायल, चोट लगा हुआ । wounded, injured.

खत (2) – न॰ – (क्षतम्) घाव, चोट । wound, injury.

खत्त (1) – न॰ – (क्षत्र) सम्प्रभुता । sovereign.

खत्त (2) – धम्म – (क्षात्र-धर्म) क्षात्र-धर्म, राजनीति । political science, belonging to kṣatriyas.

खत्तिय – पु॰ – (क्षत्रिय) क्षत्रिय, वि॰ – क्षत्रिय वर्ण का । of warrior, of kṣatriyas.

खत्तिय-कञ्आ – स्त्री॰ – (क्षत्रिय कन्या) क्षत्रिय कन्या । a maiden of the kṣatriya race.

खत्तिय-कुल – न॰ – (क्षत्रिय कुल) क्षत्रिय वंश । the warrior caste.

खत्तिय-परिसा – स्त्री॰ – (क्षत्रिय परिषद्) क्षत्रिय-सभा । the council of kṣatriyas.

खत्तिय-महासाल – पु॰ – (क्षत्रिय-महाशाल) क्षत्रिय धन, कुबेर । a millionaire of Kṣatriya clan.

खत्तिय-सुखुमाल – वि॰ – (क्षत्रिय सुकुमार) राजकुमार के समान कोमल शरीर वाला । tender and delicate like a prince.

खत्तिया – स्त्री॰ – (क्षत्रिया) क्षत्राणी । a women of kṣatriya race.

खत्तियानी – स्त्री॰ – (क्षत्राणी) देखें खत्तिया । see Khattiyā.

खत्तु – पु॰ – (क्षतृ) सूत, सारथी, राजा का सलाहकार । a charioteer, a king's adviser.

खदिर – पु॰ – (खदिर) खैर का पेड़ । the tree Acacia catechu having very hard wood.

खदिरङ्गार – पु॰ – (खदिराङ्गार) खैर या बबूल के लकड़ी का कोयला । embers of Acacia wood.

खदिराङ्गार-जातक – (जा० सं० 40) – जलते कोयलों के गड्ढे में गिर पड़ने का खतरा मोल लेकर भी दान से विरत न होने वाले दानशील की कथा बताती है कि सद्धर्म पर अडिग व्यक्ति के पथ के शूल भी फूल बन जाते हैं। the story (No. 40) tells that the obstacles melt away from the path of the person who is devoted to the noble deeds.

खन्ति – स्त्री० – (क्षान्ति) सहनशीलता। patience, forbearance.

खन्ति-बल – न० – (क्षान्ति-बल) सहन-शक्ति। power of patience.

खन्तिमन्तु – वि० – (क्षान्तिमान्) सहनशील। forbearing, one having patience.

खन्तिक – वि० – (क्षान्तिक) अ.मुक मत का। (इसका प्रायः प्रयोग सामासिक पद के रूप में होता है जैसे – अञ्ञ-खन्तिक = अन्य मत का)। it is often used in compounds, as Añña-Khantika = of another belief.

खन्तिक-वण्ण-जातक – (जा० सं० 225) – एक राजदरबारी ने राजा के रनिवास में गड़बड़ी की और उसी राजदरबारी के नौकर ने अपने मालिक के घर में। राजा के सामने मामला पेश हुआ, तो राजा ने राजदरबारी को सहनशील बने रहने की सलाह दी। the story (No. 225) presents an example of 'as you sow so shall you reap'.

खन्तिवादी-जातक – (जा० सं० 313) – क्षमाशीलता का उपदेश करने वाले तपस्वी की क्षान्ति की परीक्षा में राजा ने उसके हाथ कटवा दिये तपस्वी ने फिर भी राजा की नासमझी कहकर प्रभु से उसकी भलाई की ही प्रार्थना की। the Jātaka tale (No. 313) mentions an example of supreme forgiveness. It tells how an angry man loses all his prosperity.

खन्तु – पु० – (क्षन्तृ) क्षमाशील। one who forbears, gentle.

खन्ध – पु० – (स्कन्ध) स्कन्ध, पेड़ का तना, ढेर, परिच्छेद, रूप-वेदनादि पाँच स्कन्ध। bulk, the trunk of the bady or tree, mass, heap, a chapter, a sensorial aggragate.

खन्ध-पञ्चक – (स्कन्ध-पञ्चक) रूप, वेदना, संज्ञा, संस्कार और विज्ञान। the five sensorial aggregates, viz. rūpa (bodily form), vedanā (sensation), saṁjnā (perception), saṁskāra (aggregate of formations), and vijñāna (consciousness or thought faculty).

खन्धक – पु० – (स्कन्धक) विभाग, परिच्छेद। division or chapter.

खन्ध-कोट्ठास – पु० – (स्कन्ध कोष्ठकाः) शरीर का भाग। the organs of the body.

खन्धदेस – न० – (स्कन्ध देश) आसन, पाँच स्कन्धों का आधार। the seat of five sensorial aggregates.

खन्धवत्त-जातक – (जा० सं० 203) – यह कथा शिक्षा देती है कि नियमित मैत्री-भावना करने से शत्रुकोप से बचा जा सकता है। the story (No. 203) reveals that the constant effort of loving behaviour turns enmity into friendship.

खन्धावार – पु० – (स्कन्धावार) छावनी। a military camp.

खम – वि० – (क्षमः) क्षमाशील। forgiving, enduring.

खमति – क्रि॰ – ($\sqrt{}$ क्षम् = क्षाम्यति / क्षमते) क्षमा करता है । endures, forbears.

खमन – न॰ – (क्षान्ति) क्षमा । tolerance, endurance.

खमापन – न॰ – (क्षमापन) क्षमा-याचना करना । asking for pardon.

खमापेति – क्रि॰ – (क्षमयति) क्षमा-याचना करता है । asks one's pardon.

खमितब्ब – कृ॰ – (क्षन्तव्य) क्षमा देने योग्य । fit to be forgiven.

खमित्वा – पूर्व क्रि॰ – (क्षमित्वा) क्षमा देकर । having forgiven.

खम्भकत – (स्कम्भकृत) हाथों को कमर पर रखकर खंभे की तरह खड़ा हुआ । with one's arms standing on the hips, kimbo.

खय – पु॰ – (क्षय) क्षय, नाश । decay, consummation of.

खयानुपस्सना – स्त्री॰ – (क्षय + अनुपश्यना) संसार के क्षयशील स्वभाव का ज्ञान । knowledge of the fact about the world's ultimate decay.

खर (1) – वि॰ – (खर) कष्टप्रद, कठोर, तीव्र प्रचण्ड । rough, hard, sharp, painful.

खर (2) – पु॰ – (खर) गर्दभ, गदहा । a donkey.

खरपुत्त-जातक – (जा॰ सं॰ 286) – नागराज की कृपा से एक राजा के विलक्षण शक्तियों का स्वामी बन जाने किन्तु पत्नी मोह मे सर्वस्व गँवा देने की कथा । the story (No. 286) of a king who by the grace of Nāgrāja achieved magical power and prosperity but due to his attachment for his wife lost all.

खरत्त – न॰ – (खरत्व) कर्कशता, चण्डता, कठोरता । roughness, hardness.

खरादिय-जातक – (जा॰ सं॰ 15) – भानजे मृग ने मामा से मृगों की प्राण रक्षा की विधि सीखने में प्रमाद किया फलतः मृत्यु का ग्रास बना । (tale No. 15), the disobedient young deer did not learn the skill of a parent deer and was killed by a hunter.

खल – न॰ – (खल) खलिहान । threshing floor (for corn).

खलगग – न॰ – (खलाग्र) धान का भूसा निकालने का आरम्भ । the start of threshing.

खलति – क्रि॰ – (स्खलति) स्खलित होता है, लड़खड़ाता है । stumbles.

खलित – न॰ – ($\sqrt{}$ स्खल + क्त = स्खलित) स्खलित, अपराधकृत । stumbled.

खलीन – पु॰ – (खलीन) घोड़े की लगाम । rein, bit (of a horse).

खलु – अव्यय – (खलु) वास्तव मे । indeed, surely.

खलुङ्क – पु॰ – (हीनाश्व) घटिया किस्म का घोड़ा । inferior type of horse, vile horse.

खल्लाट – वि॰ – (खल्वाट) खल्वाट, गंजा । bald headed.

खल्लाट-सीस – वि॰ – (खल्वाट शीर्ष) गंजे सिर वाला । having a bald head.

खल्लाटीय – न॰ – (खल्लाटता) गंजापन । baldness.

खलोपि – स्त्री॰ – (कुम्भी) एक प्रकार का बर्तन, मटकी । a kind of pot.

खळ (1) – वि॰ – (खड) कठोर । harsh.

खळ (2) – पु॰ – (खल) दुष्ट पुरुष। rascal, a vile person.

खाणु – पु॰ – (स्थाणु) खम्भा (लकड़ी का) पेड़ का ठूँठ। stump of a tree, a post.

खात – कृ॰ – (खनित) खोदा गया। dug out.

खादक – वि॰ – (खादक/भक्षक) खाने वाला। one who eats, living on.

खादति – क्रि॰ – (√खाद् = खादति) खाता है। eats, chews.

खादन – न॰ – (खादन) खाना। eating.

खादनीय – वि॰ – (√खाद + अनीयर = खादनीय) खाने योग्य, सुस्वादु। fit for eating, tasty.

खादापन – न॰ – खिलाना। feeding.

खादापित – कृ॰ – खिलाया गया। having been fed.

खादापेति – क्रि॰ – (खादयति) खिलाता है। feeds, gets another to take meals.

खादित – कृ॰ – (√खाद् + क्त = खादित) खाया गया। eaten up.

खादितब्ब – कृ॰ – (खादितव्य) खाने योग्य। fit for eating.

खादितुं – कृ॰ – (√खाद् + तुमुन् = खादितुम्) खाने के लिए। for eating.

खायति – क्रि॰ – (ख्यायते) प्रतीत होता है। seems to be, appears like.

खायित – वि॰ – (खादित) खाया गया। eaten up.

खार – पु॰ – (क्षार) क्षार, खार। alkaline substance.

खारक – वि॰ – (क्षारक) क्षार। alkaline.

खारी – स्त्री॰ – (खारी) बहंगी से लटकी हुई टोकरी, खारिया। basket suspended from a pingo.

खारी-काज – पु॰ तथा न॰ – (वेषु-शिम्या/स्कन्धवाहिनी) बहँगी की टोकरी तथा बहँगी। shoulder yoke with basket, pingo basket and the pingo.

खालेति – क्रि॰ – (क्षालयति) धोता है, कुल्ला करता है। washes, rinses.

खिड्डा – स्त्री॰ – (क्रीडा) खेल, क्रीडा। play, amusement.

खिड्डा-दासक – न॰ – (क्रीडादास) जो खेल का दास बना हुआ हो। addicted to games.

खिड्डा-पदोसिक – वि॰ – (क्रीडा प्रदोषिक) खेल-कूद के कारण खराब हुआ। spoiled due to excess of playing.

खिड्डा-रति – स्त्री॰ – (क्रीडा रति) क्रीडा में अतिशय रूचि। enjoyment of playing.

खित्त – कृ॰ – (√क्षिप + क्त = क्षिप्त) फेंका हुआ। thrown, cast away.

खित्त-चित्त – (क्षिप्त-चित्त) विक्षिप्त-चित्त। one whose mind is deranged.

खिप – पु॰ – (क्षिप) फाँसने के लिए फेंका गया जाल, मछली पकड़ने का जाल। anything thrown over, a fish trap.

खिपति – क्रि॰ – (क्षिपति) फैलाता है। castes, throws over, sneezes.

खिपि – क्रि॰ – (अक्षिपत्) फेंका, फैलाया। threw, spread.

खिपन्त – कृ॰ – (√क्षिप् + शतृ = क्षिपन क्षिपन्तः) फेंकते हुए। which has been spread or thrown away.

खिपमान – कृ॰ – (√ क्षिप् + शानच् = क्षिप्यमाण) फेंके जाते हुए । which had already been spread of thrown.

खिपित्वा – कृ॰ – (√ क्षिप् + त्वा = क्षिप्त्वा) फेंक करके । having thrown away or spread.

खिपन – न॰ – (क्षिप् + ल्युट्) फेंकना, फैलाना । throw, cast.

खिपित – कृ॰ – (क्षेपित / क्षिप्त) फेंका गया । thrown.

खिप्प – वि॰ – (क्षिप्र) द्रुत, शीघ्र, क्षिप्र । quick.

खिप्पतरं – क्रि॰ वि॰ – (क्षिप्रतर) अति द्रुत, अति शीघ्र । very soon.

खिप्पं – क्रि॰ वि॰ – (क्षिप्रम्) शीघ्र । quickly.

खिल – न॰ – (ऊषरः) कठोरता । callousness, hardness.

खीण – कृ॰ – (√ क्षि + त = क्षीण) कृश, क्षीण, क्षय प्राप्त । exhausted, wasted.

खीण-मच्छ – वि॰ – (क्षीण–मत्स्य) मछलियों से रहित । without fish.

खीण-बीज – वि॰ – (क्षीण–बीज) पुनर्जन्म के बीज से रहित । one who is without the seed of existence.

खीणासव – वि॰ – (क्षीणासव) जिसके आस्रव अर्थात् चित्त-मैल क्षीण हो गये । whose mind is free from mental obsessions.

खीयति – क्रि॰ – (क्षयति) क्षय होता है, नष्ट होता है । becomes exhausted, becomes dejected.

खीयमान – कृ॰ – (√ क्षि + शानच् = क्षीयमाण) being exhausted, being dejected.

खीयितब्ब – कृ॰ – (√ क्षि / √ क्षे + तव्यत् = क्षयितव्य) क्षीण होने योग्य । fit to be exhausted.

खीर – न॰ – (क्षीर) क्षीर, दूध । milk.

खीरण्णव – पु॰ – (क्षीराण्णव) श्वेत समुद्र, क्षीरार्णव । the white sea, ocean of milk.

खीरपक – वि॰ – (क्षीरप / क्षीरपक) दुध-मुहाँ, दूध चूसता हुआ । sucking the milk.

खीरिका – स्त्री॰ – (क्षीरिका) एक वृक्ष विशेष । the tree *Buchanania latifolia*.

खीरोदन – न॰ – (क्षीरोदन) दूध-भात । milk-rice.

खील – पु॰ – (कीलकम्) स्थाणु, कील, खूँटा । a peg, a stake, a post.

खुंसेति – क्रि॰ – (आक्रोशति) गाली देता है । abuses.

खुज्ज – वि॰ – (कुब्ज) कुबड़ा । a humpbacked person.

खुदा – स्त्री॰ – (क्षुधा) क्षुधा, भूख । hunger.

खुद्दक – वि॰ – (क्षुद्रक) छोटा, तुच्छ । small, inferior, insignificant.

खुद्दक-निकाय – पु॰ – (क्षुद्रक निकाय) पाँचों निकायों में से एक । name of a collection of canonical books.

खुद्दक-पाठ – पु॰ – (खुद्दक–पाठ) खुद्दक-निकाय की पहली पोथी खुद्दक पाठ । the first book of Khuddaka Nikāya.

खुद्दा – स्त्री॰ – (क्षुद्रा) भुनगा, मधुमक्खी, शहद की छोटी मक्खी क्षुद्रा । kind of small honey-bees.

खुद्दानुखुद्दक – वि॰ – (क्षुद्रानुक्षुद्रक) छोट-मोटे (नियम) । the lesser and minor (precepts).

खुप्पिपासा – स्त्री० – (क्षुत्-पिपासा) भूख और प्यास। hunger and thirst.

खुभति – क्रि० – (√ क्षुभ् = क्षोभते) क्षुब्ध होता है। becomes agitated or disturbed.

खुर – न० – (क्षुर) (1) उस्तरा (2) पशु का खुर। (1) razor (2) hoof (of an animal).

खुरग्ग – न० – (क्षुराग्र) मुण्डन संस्कार का स्थान। the hall of tonsure.

खुर-कोस – पु० – (क्षुरकोश) उस्तरे का खोल। sheath for a razor.

खुर-चक्क – न० – (क्षुर-चक्र) उस्तरे जैसा तेज चक्र। a razor sharp-disc.

खुर-धारा – स्त्री० – (क्षुरधारा) उस्तरे की धार। the blade of a razor.

खुर-भण्ड – न० – (क्षुरभाण्ड) नाई का सामान। the outfit of a barber.

खुर-मुण्ड – (क्षुर-मुण्ड) मुँडा हुआ सिर। a close-shaven.

खुरप्प – पु० – (क्षुरप्र) एक प्रकार का तीर। a kind of arrow.

खुरप्प-जातक – (जा० सं० 265) – यह कथा उदाहरण प्रस्तुत करती है कि शूरता भरे कार्य करने वाले प्राणों की चिन्ता नहीं करते। the story (No. 265) reveals that he who does heroic deeds does not worry about life.

खेट – न० – (खेट) ढाल। a sheild.

खेटक – न० – (खेटक) ढाल। a sheild.

खेत्त – न० – (क्षेत्र) खेत, क्षेत्र। field, plot of land, suitable place.

खेत्तोपम – न० – (क्षेत्रोपम) क्षेत्र के समान। alike a field.

खेत्त-कम्म – न० – (क्षेत्र-कर्म) खेत सम्बन्धी कार्य। work in the field.

खेत्त-गोपक – पु० – (क्षेत्र-गोपक) खेत का रखवाला। field-watcher, cultivator.

खेत्त-सामिक – पु० – (क्षेत्र-स्वामिक) खेत का स्वामी। owner of a field.

खेत्ताजीव – पु० – (क्षेत्राजीव) कृषक, किसान। cultivator.

खेद – पु० – (खेद) अफसोस। regret.

खेप – पु० – (क्षेप) फेंक। a throw.

खेपक – पु० – (क्षेपक) धनुर्धर, धनुर्धारी। an archer.

खेपन – न० – (क्षेपण) प्रायः समस्त पद के रूप में प्रयुक्त जैसे: काल-क्षेपण = काल क्षेप। often used in compounds as kāla-kṣepaṇa.

खेपेति – क्रि० – (√ क्षिप् + णिच् = क्षेपयति) काल-क्षेप करता है। spends (time), causes to be wasted.

खेम – वि० – (क्षेम) क्षेम, शान्ति। the serenity, safety.

खेमट्ठान – न० – (क्षेम-स्थान) शान्ति-स्थान। the place of safety and happiness.

खेमप्पत्त – वि० – (क्षेम-प्राप्त) क्षेम-प्राप्त। having attained tranquility.

खेम-भूमि – स्त्री० – (क्षेम-भूमिः) कल्याण-भूमि। a peaceful place.

खेमी – पु० – (क्षेमी) सूखपूर्वक रहने वाला। one who enjoys security.

खेळ – पु० – (ष्वेडे = ष्ठीवनम्) थूक। saliva.

खेळ-मल्लक – पु० – (ष्वेड-मल्लक) थूकदान, पीकदान। a spittoon.

खेळ-सिंघानिका – स्त्री॰ – (क्ष्वेड-शिंघाण) थूक-सींढ, नाक की मैल। nose-phlegm.

खेळासिक – वि॰ – (क्ष्वेडाशनः) थूक चाटने वाला (अपशब्द)। phlegm-eater (an abusive term).

खो – अव्यय – (खलु) वास्तव में। indeed, really.

खोभ – पु॰ – (क्षोभ) क्षोभ। shock, agitation.

खोम – न॰ – (क्षौम) सन का कपड़ा। linen cloth.

खोम-दुस्स – न॰ – (क्षौम-दुष्य) तीसी का बना। flaxen.

ख्यात – वि॰ – (ख्यात) प्रसिद्ध। renowned.

ख्यापन – न॰ – (ख्यापन) प्रसिद्धि। fame.

ग

ग – पालि वर्णमाला का तीसरा व्यञ्जन. the third consonant of Pāli alphabet.

गगन – न॰ – (**गगन**) आकाश। sky.

गगन-गामी – वि॰ – (**गगन-गामी**) नभ चर, आकाश में विचरने वाला। flying through the sky.

गग्ग-जातक – (जा॰ सं॰ 155) – यह कथा बताती है कि छींकने पर चिरञ्जीव: 'दीर्घायु हों, ऐसा कहना अनिवार्य क्यों माना गया। when someone sneezes others around him shout 'long life' the story (No. 155) gives the origin of this custom.

गग्गरा – स्त्री – (**गर्गरा**) चम्पा नगरी की एक पुष्करिणी का नाम। a lotus pond at Campā.

गग्गरायति – क्रि॰ – (**गर्गरायते**) गर्जता है। roars.

गग्गरी – स्त्री॰ – (**गर्गरी**) लोहार की धौंकनी। blacksmith's bellows.

गङ्गा – स्त्री॰ – (**गङ्गा**) नदी, गङ्गा-नदी। river, the Gaṅgā river.

गङ्गातीर – न॰ – (**गङ्गा-तीर**) गङ्गा तट। the bank of Ganga.

गङ्गा-द्वार – न॰ – (**गङ्गा-द्वार**) नदी के समुद्र में गिरने की जगह। mouth of a river.

गङ्गा-धार – पु॰ – (**गङ्गा-धार**) गङ्गा की धारा। a river - basin.

गङ्गा-पार – न॰ – (**गङ्गापार**) गङ्गा का दूसरा तट। the other bank of river Gaṅgā.

गङ्गा-सोत – पु॰ – (**गङ्गा-स्रोत**) गङ्गा का स्रोत। river stream, torrent.

गङ्गा-माल-जातक – (जा॰ सं॰ 421) – एक ऐसे ओसथ-व्रती नौकर की कथा जो निराहार रहकर मर गया। the story (No. 421) of a lay follower who died in his observance of *uposatha*.

गङ्गेय्य – वि॰ – (**गाङ्गेय**) गङ्गा-सम्बन्धी। belonging to the river Gaṅgā.

गच्छ – पु॰ – (**गाछ**) पौधा, (गाछ)। a plant, a shrub.

गच्छति – क्रि॰ – (**गच्छति**) जाता है। goes.

गज – पु॰ – (**गज**) हाथी। elephant.

गज-कुम्भ – पु॰ – (**गज-कुम्भ**) हाथी का सिर। the forehead of an elephant.

गज-पोतक – पु॰ – (**गज-पोतक**) हाथी का बच्चा। a young elephant.

गज्जति – क्रि॰ – (**गर्जति**) गर्जना करता है। roars, thunders.

गज्जना – स्त्री॰ – (**गर्जना**) गर्जना। roaring.

गज्जित – कृ॰ – (**गर्जित**) गर्जित। roar, thunder.

गज्जितु – पु॰ – (**गर्जतृ**) गरजने वाला। one who roars or thunders.

गण – पु॰ – (**गण**) समूह, दल (भिक्षु) संघ। a gang, crowd, chapter of (monks).

गण-पूरक – वि॰ – (गण-पूरक) जिसमें गण-पूर्ति हो। one who completes the quorum.

गण-पूरण – न॰ – (गण-पूरण) गण-पूर्ति। the quorum.

गण-बंधन – न॰ – (गण-बन्धन) सहयोग। co-operation.

गण-सङ्गणिका – स्त्री॰ – (गण-सङ्गणिका) मण्डली में रहने की इच्छा। desire to be in a crowd.

गणक – पु॰ – (गणक) हिसाब-किताब रखने वाला मुंशी। an accountant.

गणनपथातीत – वि॰ – (गणनपथातीत) गिनती से बाहर। gone beyond the calculation.

गणना – स्त्री॰ – (गणना) संख्या। number, counting.

गणाचरिय – पु॰ – (गणाचारी) अनेकों का शिक्षक। the teacher who has many followers.

गणारामता – स्त्री॰ – (गणारामता) मण्डली-प्रेम। desire to be in a crowd.

गणिका – स्त्री॰ – (गणिका) वेश्या। courtesan.

गणिकण्टक – पु॰ – (कण्टकश्रृङ्ग) बारहसिंगा। a stag.

गणित (1) – कृ॰ – (गणित) गिना हुआ। counted.

गणित (2) – न॰ – (गणितम्) गणित-शास्त्र। arithmatic.

गणी – पु॰ – (गणी) गणधर, जिसके अनुयायी हों। one who has a following.

गणेति – क्रि॰ – (गणयति) गिनता है। counts, reckons.

गणिठ – स्त्री॰ – (ग्रन्थि) गाँठ, ग्रन्थि। a knot, a tie.

गणिठका – स्त्री॰ – (ग्रन्थिका) ग्रन्थि। a knot, a tie.

गणिठ-कासाव – न॰ – (काषाय-ग्रन्थि) (1) ग्रन्थियुक्त (2) काषाय वस्त्र। (1) having knots (2) the saffron dress (*cīvara*) of *bhikkus*.

गणिठट्ठान – न॰ – (ग्रन्थि-स्थल) कठिन-स्थल। a difficult and obscure passage.

गणिठपद – न॰ – (ग्रन्थिपद／कूटपद) ग्रन्थि-पद, कठिनाई से समझ में आने वाला पद। an obscure passage.

गणिठपास – पु॰ – (ग्रन्थि-पाश) बेड़ी। shackles.

गण्ड – पु॰ – (गण्ड) फोड़ा। a boil, a protuberance.

गण्डक – पु॰ – (गण्डक) गैंडा। a rhinoceros.

गण्डम्ब – पु॰ – (गण्डम्ब) श्रावस्ती के द्वार पर स्थित आम्र-वृक्ष, जिसके नीचे भगवान् बुद्ध ने यमक-पाटिहारिय नाम का चमत्कार दिखाया था। the historical mango-tree in Sāvatthi under which the Buddha performed some miracles.

गणिडका – स्त्री॰ – (गणिडका) भीतर से खोखला लकड़ी का लट्ठा, जिससे घण्टे बजाने का काम लिया जाता है। a hollowed block of wood used for ringing a bell.

गण्डी – स्त्री॰ – (गण्डी) (1) घंटा (2) जल्लाद का ब्लाक (1) a gong (2) executioner's block.

गण्डी – वि॰ – (गण्डी) फोड़े वाला। having boils.

गण्डुप्पाद – पु॰ – (गण्डूपदः) केंचुआ। an earthworm.

गण्डूस – पु॰ – (गण्डूष) मुँह भर। a mouthful.

गण्हाति – क्रि॰ – (गृह्णाति) ग्रहण करता है। holds of, seizes.

गण्हितब्ब – कृ॰ – (√ग्रह + तव्यत् = गृहीत्वा) ग्रहण करने योग्य। fit for holding.

गण्हित्वा – कृ॰ – (√ग्रह + त्वा = गृहीत्वा) ग्रहण करके। having seized.

गण्ही – क्रि॰ – (अगृह्णात्) ग्रहण किया। held, seized.

गहित – कृ॰ – (√ग्रह + क्त = गृहीत) ग्रहण किया हुआ। seized.

गहितब्ब – कृ॰ – (√ग्रह + तव्यत् = गृहीतव्य) ग्रहण करने योग्य। fit to be seized.

गहेत्वा – कृ॰ – (√ग्रह + त्वा = गृहीत्वा) ग्रहण करके। having seized.

गण्हापेति – क्रि॰ – (ग्राहयति) ग्रहण कराता है। causes to be seized.

गण्हितुं – कृ॰ – (√ग्रह् + तुमुन् = गृहीतुम्) लेने के लिए। for taking, to take.

गत – (√गम + क्त = गत) गया हुआ। gone.

गतक – पु॰ – (गतक) संदेशवाहक। messenger.

गतट्ठान – न॰ – (गत + स्थान) जिस स्थान को जाया गया। the place where one has gone.

गतद्ध – वि॰ – (गत + अध्वन् = गताध्वन्) जिसने अपना रास्ता पूरा कर लिया है।

one who has completed his journey.

गतद्धी – वि॰ – (गताध्वी) जिसने अपना रास्ता पूरा कर लिया। one who has completed his journey.

गतयोब्बन – वि॰ – (गतयौवन) जिसका यौवन चला गया। one who has passed his youth.

गति – स्त्री॰ – (गति) जाना। going.

गतिमन्तु – वि॰ – (गतिमान) निपुण, चतुर, दक्ष। of perfect behaviour.

गत्त – न॰ – (गात्र) शरीर, गात्र। the body.

गथित – कृ॰ – (ग्रथित) बँधा हुआ। bound.

गद – पु॰ – (गद) (1) रोग (2) वाणी। (1) sickness (2) speech.

गदति – क्रि॰ – (गदति) बोलता है। speaks.

गदा – स्त्री॰ – (गदा) एक प्रकार का आयुध, लौह मुद्गर। a kind of weapon, mace, club.

गद्दुल – पु॰ – (गर्दुल) चमड़े का पट्टा। a leash, a leather strap.

गद्दूहन – न॰ – (गोदोहन) गाय दुहना। milking of cow.

गद्रभ – पु॰ – (गर्दभ) गधा। an ass.

गधित – (ग्रथित) बँधा हुआ। bound.

गन्तब्ब – कृ॰ – (√गम् + तव्यत् = गन्तव्य) जाने योग्य। fit to be gone.

गन्तु – पु॰ – (गन्तृ/गन्ता) जाने वाला। one who goes.

गन्तुं – कृ॰ – (√गम् + तुमुन् = गन्तुम्) जाने के लिए। to go.

गन्त्वा – पूर्व क्रि॰ – (√गम् + त्वा = गत्वा) जाकर। having gone.

गन्थ – पु० – (ग्रन्थ) ग्रन्थ। a composition, a text.

गन्थकार – पु० – (ग्रन्थकार) कृतिकार, ग्रन्थकार। an author, compiler of a book.

गन्थधुर – न० – (ग्रन्थ-धुर्य) पठन-पाठन का कार्य। the burden of studying scriptures.

गन्थप्पमोचन – न० – (ग्रन्थ-प्रमोचन) ग्रन्थ विमोचन, पुस्तक का लोकार्पण। releasing of the book.

गन्थति – क्रि० – (ग्रथ्नाति) गांठ बाँधता है। binds or fastens together.

गन्थन – न० – (ग्रन्थन) ग्रन्थन, गाँठ बाँधना। knitting.

गन्थेति – क्रि० – (ग्रन्थयति) गाँठ बँधवाता है। gets fastened together.

गन्ध – पु० – (गन्ध) महक, सुगन्ध। smell, odour.

गन्ध-कुटि – स्त्री० – (गन्ध-कुटी) भगवान बुद्ध के रहने की कोठरी। the dwelling chamber of the Buddha

गन्ध-चुण्ण – न० – (गन्ध-चूर्ण) सुगन्धित चूर्ण। scented powder.

गन्ध-जात – न० – (गन्ध जात) सुगन्धियों के प्रकार। kinds of perfumes.

गन्ध-तेल – न० – (गन्ध-तैल) सुगन्धित तेल। scented oil.

गन्ध-पञ्चङ्गुलिक – न० – (गन्ध पञ्चाङ्गुलिक) सुगन्धित तेल से सिक्त पाँच अँगुलियों की छाप। the five fingure mark with scented oil.

गन्धब्ब – पु० – (गन्धर्व) (1) संगीतकार (2) जन्म ग्रहण करने वाला जीव (3) गन्धर्व। (1) a musician (2) a being ready to take new existence (3) a mythical race of celestial musicians.

गन्धब्बाधिप – पु० – (गन्धर्वाधिप) गन्धर्वों का प्रधान। the headman of the gandharvas.

गन्धमादन – पु० – (गन्धमादन) हिमालय का एक पर्वत। name of a mountain in Himālayas.

गन्धवंस – न० – (गन्धवंस) बर्मा में लिखा गया एक पालि ग्रन्थ। यह नन्दपञ्ञ आरण्यक की रचना माना जाता है। a late Pāli work written in Burma. It relates the history of Pāli canon.

गन्ध-सार – पु० – (गन्ध-सार) चन्दन, चन्दन वृक्ष। sandal, sandalwood.

गन्धापण – पु० – (गन्धापण) सुगन्धित तेल बेचने वाले अर्थात् गन्धी की दुकान। the shop selling fragrant items .

गन्धार – पु० – (गान्धार) प्राचीन सोलह जनपदों में से एक वर्तमान कन्धार। इसकी राजधानी तक्षशिला थी। one of the sixteen *janapadas* of Buddhist India with its capital at Takṣaśilā presently it is known as Kandhar.

गन्धारी – स्त्री० – (गान्धारी) गन्धार से सम्बन्धित (जादू-टोना)। a magical charm related to Kandhar.

गन्धिक – वि० – (गन्धिक) देखें गन्धी। same as gandhi.

गन्धी – वि० – (गन्धी) सुगन्धित द्रव्यों को बेचने वाला। a shopkeeper selling fragrant items.

गन्धोदक – न० – (गन्धोदक) सुगन्धित जल। scented water.

गब्बित – वि॰ – **(गर्वित)** गर्वित, अहंकारी। proud, arrogant.

गब्भ – पु॰ – **(गर्भ)** अन्दरूनी भाग, गर्भ। interior, the womb.

गब्भ-गत – वि॰ – **(गर्भगत)** गर्भस्थ। gone to the womb.

गब्भ-परिहरण – न॰ – **(गर्भ परिरक्षण)** गर्भ-संरक्षण। protection of the embryo.

गब्भ-पातन – न॰ – **(गर्भपातन)** गर्भपात। destruction of the embryo.

गब्भ-मल – न॰ – **(गन्ध-मूल)** बच्चे के जन्म के समय उसके शरीर के साथ लगा हुआ घृणित अंश। accompanying dirty matter of child-birth.

गब्भ-वुट्ठान – न॰ – **(गर्भोत्थान-प्रसवः)** प्रसव। child-birth.

गब्भर – न॰ – **(गह्वर)** गुफा। a cave.

गब्भासय – पु॰ – **(गर्भाशय)** बच्चादानी। the uterus.

गब्भिनी – स्त्री॰ – **(गर्भिणी)** गर्भिणी स्त्री। a pregnant woman.

गभीर – वि॰ – **(गभीर)** गहरा। deep.

गम – पु॰ – **(गम)** गमन, यात्रा। journey.

गमन – न॰ – **(गमन)** जाना। going.

गमनन्तराय – पु॰ – **(गमनान्तराय)** गमन में बाधा। obstacles to one's departure.

गमन-कारण – न॰ – **(गमन–कारण)** जाने का कारण। reason for going.

गमनागमन – न॰ – **(गमनागमन)** जाना-आना। going and coming.

गमनीय – कृ॰ – **(√ गम् + अनीयर् = गमनीय)** जाने योग्य। ought to go, fit to be gone.

गमिक – वि॰ – **(गमिक, गन्ता)** जाने वाला, यात्रा पर निकलने वाला। setting out for a journey.

गमिक-क्त – न॰ – **(गमिक–वृत्ति)** यात्रा की तैयारी। preparations for journey.

गमेति – क्रि॰ – **(√ गम् + णिच् = गमयति)** भेजता है, समझता है। sends, understands.

गम्भीर – वि॰ – **(गम्भीर)** गहरा। deep.

गम्भीरावभास – वि॰ – **(गाम्भीर्यावभास)** गम्भीरता की प्रतीति। having the appearance of depth.

गम्म – वि॰ – **(ग्राम्य)** देहाती, गँवार, ग्राम्य। vulgar.

गम्म – वि॰ – **(गम्य)** जानने लायक। what should be understood or attained.

गया – न॰ – **(गया)** बोधि-वृक्ष तथा बनारस के बीच की सड़क पर स्थित प्रसिद्ध नगर। a famous town situated on the road between *bodhi*-tree and Varanasi.

गया-सीस – पु॰ – **(गयाशीर्ष)** गया के पास का एक पर्वत। a hill situated near Gayā.

गय्ह – वि॰ – **(ग्राह्य)** ग्रहण करने योग्य। fit to be taken, acceptable.

गय्हति – क्रि॰ – **(गृह्यते)** ग्रहण किया जाता है। is taken or accepted.

गरहति – क्रि॰ – **(गर्हते/गर्हयति)** दोष देता है, निन्दा करता है। reproaches, blames.

गर्ही – सा॰ भू॰ – **(अगर्हत्)** निन्दा की। blamed.

गर्हित – कृ॰ – (√ **गर्ह्** + **क्त**) निन्दित।
blamed

गर्हन्त – कृ॰ – (√ **गर्ह्** + **शतृ**) निन्दित
होता हुआ। being blamed.

गर्हमान – कृ॰ – (**गर्ह्** + **शानच्**) निन्दित
होता हुआ। being blamed.

गरहन – न॰ – (**गर्हन**) दोषारोपण।
reproach.

गरहित-जातक – (जा॰ सं॰ 219) – कथा
बताती है कि सज्जन के बढ़ते यश से
व्यथित दुर्जन सज्जन के प्रति मिथ्यापवाद
का दुष्प्रचार कर सन्ताप को शान्त करना
चाहता है। the story (No. 219) tells
that pained by the increasing
fame of the noble one, a wicked
person wants to soothen his
pain by levelling false
allegations against him.

गरही – पु॰ – (**गर्ही**) दोषारोपण करने वाला।
one who blames.

गरु – वि॰ – (**गुरु**) भारी, गम्भीर, सम्मान्य।
heavy, serious, grave.

गरु-कातब्ब – वि॰ – (**गुरु कर्तव्य**) सम्मान
के योग्य। worthy of esteem.

गरु-कार – पु॰ – (**गुरुकार**) पूज्य भाव,
सम्मान। esteem, honour, respect.

गरु-गब्भा – स्त्री॰ – (**गुरु–गर्भा**) गर्भवती,
गर्भिणी। a pregnant woman.

गरुट्ठानीय – वि॰ – (**गुरुस्थानीय**) आचार्य।
one who takes the place of a
teacher.

गरुक – वि॰ – (**गुरुक**) भारी, गम्भीर।
heavy, serious.

गरु-करोति – क्रि॰ – (**गुरु करोति**) आदर
करता है। respects.

गरुत्त – न॰ – (**गुरुत्व**) गरिमा, गुरुत्व।
heaviness, respect.

गरुळ – पु॰ – (**गरुड**) गरुड़ नामक एक
काल्पनिक पक्षी। a mythical bird
(vehicle of Viṣṇu), a harpy.

गल – पु॰ – (**गल**) गला। neck, throat.

गलग्गाह – पु॰ – (**गालग्राह**) गले से
पकड़ना। taking by the neck.

गल-नाळी – स्त्री॰ – (**गल–नालिका**) गले
की नाली। the larynx.

गलप्पमाण – वि॰ – (**गलप्रमाण**) गले तक।
going up to the neck.

गल-वाटक – पु॰ – (**गल–वर्त्तक**) गले का
घेरा। the bottom of the throat.

गलति – क्रि॰ – (**गलयते**) बहता है। flows,
trickles, flowed.

गलि – सा॰ भू॰ – (**अगलत**) टपका।
trickled, flowed.

गलन्त – कृ॰ – (√ **गल्** + **शतृ** = **गलम्**)
बहता हुआ, टपकता हुआ। trickling.

गलमान – कृ॰ – (√ **गल्** + **शतृ** = **गलन्**)
टपकता हुआ। trickling.

गलित – कृदन्त – (**गलित**) बहा हुआ।
trickled, flowed.

गव – पु॰ – (**गव**) वृषभ। a bull.

गवक्ख – पु॰ – (**गवाक्ष**) गवाक्ष, झरोखा।
ventilator.

गव-घातन – न॰ – (**गव–घातन**) गो-हत्या।
cow-slaughter.

गव-पान – न॰ – (**गव्य–पान**) पायस, खीर
(दूध-भात)। milk-rice.

गवज – पु॰ – (**गवय**) देखें गवय। see
Gavaya.

गवय – पु॰ – (गवय) नील गाय। the gayal, white footed antelope or deer.

गवि – पु॰ – (गवि) हवि, हव्य-सामग्री, घी। anything offered as an oblation in fire (ghee).

गवेसक – वि॰ – (गवेषक) खोजने वाला। one who seeks or looks for.

गवेसति – क्रि॰ – (गवेषते) खोजता है। seeks, looks for.

गवेसन – न॰ – (गवेषणा) खोज, अनु-सन्धान, गवेषणा। search, seeking.

गवेसी – पु॰ – (गवेषी) खोजने वाला। one who seeks.

गह (1) – पु॰ – (ग्रह) जो आधिपत्य संभालता है, जो ग्रहण करता है। one who takes possession of.

गह (2) – (गृह) घर। house.

गह (3) – पु॰ – (ग्रह) ग्रह (मंगल आदि)। a planet.

गह-कारक – पु॰ – (गृह-कारक) घर का निर्माता। house builder, architect.

गह-कूट – न॰ – (गृहकूट) घर का शिखर। the peak of a house.

गहट्ठ – पु॰ – (गृहस्थ) गृहस्थ। a house-holder.

गहण – न॰ – (ग्रहण) अधिग्रहण, ग्रहण करना। taking, seizing, acquiring.

गहणिक – वि॰ – (ग्रहणिक) अच्छी पाचन-शक्ति वाला। having a good digestion.

गहणी – स्त्री॰ – (ग्रहणी) पाचन-शक्ति। digestion.

गहन – न॰ – (गहन) घना। thicket, dense.

गहनट्ठान – न॰ – (गहन-स्थान) जंगल में ऐसा स्थान जहाँ घुसना दुष्कर हो। impenetrable place in a jungle.

गहपतानी – स्त्री॰ – (गृह-पत्नी) गृह-पत्नी। wife, house-mistress.

गहपति – पु॰ – (गृह-पति) गृहस्वामी, गृहपति। the householder, husband.

गहपति-जातक – (जा॰ सं॰ 199) – यह कथा स्त्रियों के सहज दुश्शील स्वभाव का आख्यान करती है। the story (No. 199) reveals that women were always sinful.

गहपति-महासाल – पु॰ – (महाशाल गृहपति) धनी गृहपति। a wealthy house holder.

गहित – कृ॰ – ($\sqrt{}$ ग्रह + क्त = गृहीत) गृहीत। taken, seized.

गलगलायति – क्रि॰ – (गलगलायते) गल-गल शब्द करते हुए बरसता है। rains heavily making the sound *galgal*.

गलोचि – स्त्री॰ – (गडुचि) गडुच। a medicinal creeper *Tinospara cordifolia*.

गाथा – स्त्री॰ – (गाथा) दो पंक्तियों का छन्द-विशेष, त्रिपिटक के नौ अंगों में से एक। a verse, stanza, a couplet of a particular metre.

गाध (1) – वि॰ – (अगाध) गहरा। deep.

गाध (2) – पु॰ – (अगाधता) गहराई। depth.

गाधति – क्रि॰ – (गाधते) दृढ़ (खड़ा) रहता है। has a firm footing.

गान – न॰ – (गानम्) गाना। song.

गाम – पु॰ – (ग्राम) गाँव, ग्राम। village.

गामक – पु॰ – (ग्रामक) एक छोटा गाँव। a small village.

गाम-घात – पु॰ – (ग्राम-घात) गाँव की लूट। plundering of a village.

गाम-जेट्ठ – पु॰ – (ग्राम-ज्येष्ठ) गाँव का मुखिया। the village-headman.

गाम-दारक – पु॰ – (ग्राम-दारका) गाँव का लड़का। youngster of a village.

गाम-दारिका – स्त्री॰ – (ग्राम-दारिका) गाँव की लड़की। a village-damsel.

गाम-द्वार – न॰ – (ग्राम-द्वार) गाँव का प्रवेश-द्वार, गाँव का निकास। the entrance to a village.

गाम-धम्म – पु॰ – (ग्राम्य-धर्म) ग्राम्य-धर्म, मैथुन कर्म। sexual intercourse.

गाम-भोजक – पु॰ – (ग्राम-भोजक) गाँव का मुखिया। the village headman.

गाम-वासी – पु॰ – (ग्राम-वासी) ग्राम-वासी। a villager.

गाम-सीमा – स्त्री॰ – (ग्राम-सीमा) गाँव की सीमा। the boundary of a village.

गामणी – पु॰ – (ग्रामणी) गाँव का मुखिया (ग्रामणी)। headman of the village.

गामणी-जातक – (जा॰ सं॰ 8) – देखें संवर-जातक। see Saṁvar Jātaka.

गामिक – पु॰ –(ग्रामिक) ग्रामीण। a villager.

गामी – वि॰ – (गामी) गमनोत्सुक, जाने वाला, समास में प्रयुक्त जैसे – अग्रगामी। it is used in compounds as : *agga-gāmī*, (going ahead).

गायक – पु॰ – (गायक) गाने वाला। singer.

गायति – क्रि॰ – (गायति) गाता है। sings.

गायन – न॰ – (गायन) गाना। singing, chant, song.

गायिका – स्त्री॰ – (गायिका) गाने वाली। a female singer.

गारय्ह – वि॰ – (गर्ह्य) निन्दनीय। contemptible.

गारव – पु॰ – (गौरव) गौरव। reverence.

गालह – वि॰ – (गाढ) मजबूत, कसा हुआ। string, tight.

गावी – स्त्री॰ – (गो) गौ। cow.

गावुत – न॰ – (गव्यूति) गव्यूति, दूरी का माप (लगभग दो मील)। a measure of about two miles.

गावो – पु॰ – (गावः) पशु (बहुवचन)। cattle.

गाह – पु॰ – (ग्राह) (1) पकड़ (2) दृष्टि (3) मत। (1) grip (2) obsession (3) a view.

गाहक – वि॰ – (ग्राहक) लेने वाला, ग्रहण करने वाला, ग्राहक। holder, bearer, customer.

गाहति – क्रि॰ – (गाहते) भीतर जाता है, डुबकी लगाता है। immerses, plunges into.

गाहन – न॰ – (गाहन) भीतर जाना, डुबकी लगाना। submersion, plunging.

गाहपच्च – पु॰ – (गार्हपत्य) गार्हपत्य, गृहस्थ के घर में नित्य विराजमान अग्नि। the ritual fire worshipped by householder.

गाहापक – वि॰ – (ग्राहपक) ग्रहण कराने वाला। one who causes to take or hold.

गाहापेति – क्रि॰ – (ग्राहयति) ग्रहण करवाता है। causes to take or hold.

गाहित – कृ॰ – (√ग्रह + क्त = गृहीत) ग्रहण किया हुआ। taken.

गाहितव्य – कृ॰ – (√ग्रह् + तव्यत् = ग्राहितव्य) ग्रहण करने योग्य। fit to behold.

गाहीय – कृ॰ – (√ग्रह + अनीयर् = ग्रहणीय) ग्रहण करने योग्य। fit to behold.

गाही – वि॰ – (ग्राहक) गाहक (ग्राहक)। purchaser, holder, bearer, buyer.

गाहेति – क्रि॰ – (ग्राहयति) ग्रहण कराता है। causes to take or hold.

गिंगमक – न॰ – (गिंगमक) आभरण विशेष। a kind of ornament.

गिज्झ – पु॰ – (गृद्ध) गीध। vulture.

गिज्झ-कूट – (गृद्ध-कूट) राजगृह के पास गृध-कूट पर्वत। a hill called the vulture's peak near Rājagṛha.

गिज्झ-जातक (1) – (जा॰ सं॰ 164) – कृतज्ञ गीधों द्वारा जहाँ-तहाँ से लोगों के आभूषण आदि उठा-उठा लाकर सेठ के मकान में गिराने की कथा। the story (No. 164) highly praises the quality of gratefulness.

गिज्झ-जातक (2) – (जा॰ सं॰ 427) कथा बतलाती है कि किस प्रकार अभिमानी सुपत्त गीध के पिता की आज्ञा का तिरस्कार करते हुए अहंकारवश प्राणों से हाथ धोना पड़ा। the story (No. 427) tells about a vulture who discarding the advice of his father flew in the high sky and was dashed to death.

गिज्झ-जातक (3) – (जा॰ सं॰ 399) – यह कथा बतलाती है कि असहाय माता-पिता की सेवा में समर्पित रहने वाले की प्रशस्त

भावना से क्रूर जन भी द्रवित हो जाते हैं। the story (No. 399) reveals that the cruel persons too have a soft corner for those who perform noble deeds.

गिज्झति – क्रि॰ – (गृद्धयति) लोभ करता है। longs for, desires.

गिज्झका – स्त्री॰ – (इष्टका/इष्टिका) ईंट। brick

गिज्झकावसथ – पु॰ – (इष्टकावास) ईंटों का बना घर। a house made of bricks.

गिद्ध – कृ॰ – (√गृध् + क्त = गृद्धः) लुब्ध। greedy.

गिद्धि – स्त्री॰ – (गृद्धिः) लोलुपता, लोभ, आसक्ति। greed, attachment.

गिद्धी – वि॰ – (गृद्धः/गीधः) लोभी। greedy for, desirous of.

गिनि – पु॰ – (अग्नि) आग। fire.

गिम्ह – पु॰ – (ग्रीष्म) गरमी, ग्रीष्म ऋतु। heat, hot season, summer.

गिम्हान – पु॰ – (ग्रीष्म) ग्रीष्म ऋतु। summer.

गिम्हिक – वि॰ – (ग्रीष्मिक) ग्रीष्म ऋतु सम्बन्धी। belonging to summer.

गिरग्ग-समज्जा – स्त्री॰ – (गिरि + अग्र + समारोह) समय-समय पर मनाया जाने वाला पहाड़ वाला उत्सव। a kind of celebration performed by hill tribes.

गिरा – स्त्री॰ – (गिरा) वाणी। word, utterance.

गिरि – पु॰ – (गिरि) पर्वत। mountain.

गिरि-गब्भर – न॰ – (गिरि-गह्वर) पर्वत-गुफा। a mountain cleft, a cave, ridge.

गिरि-गुहा – (गिरि-गुहा) पर्वत-कन्दरा। a mountain cleft, a cave.

गिरि-दन्त-जातक – (जा॰ सं॰ 184) – अपने लंगड़े प्रशिक्षक की नकल में लँगड़ाने वाले घोड़े की कथा कुसंगति के दुष्प्रभाव का उदाहरण है। the story (No. 184) tells about the bad effect of evil association.

गिरिब्बज – पु॰ – (गिरिव्रज) मगधों की राजधानी। name of a former capital of Magadha.

गिरि-राज – पु॰ – (गिरिराज) मेरु पर्वत। the mount Meru.

गिरि-सिखर – न॰ – (गिरि-शिखर) गिरि-शिखर। peak, top of a mountain.

गिलति – क्रि॰ – (√गृ = गिरति) निगल जाता है। swallows, devours.

गिलन – न॰ – (नि + √गृ + क्वतु = निगरणम्) निगलना। swallowing.

गिलान – वि॰ – (ग्लान) अस्वस्थ, रुग्ण, रोगी। sick, unwell.

गिलान-पच्चय – पु॰ – (रुग्ण + पथ्य) रोगी का पथ्य। support for the sick.

गिलान-भत्त – न॰ – (रुग्णाहरम्) रोगी का भोजन। food for the sick.

गिलान-साला – स्त्री॰ – (रुग्ण-शाला) रोगी-शाला। a hall for the sick.

गिलानालय – पु॰ – (व्याधि+उपाश्रयः) रोग का बहाना। pretence of illness.

गिलानुपट्ठाक – पु॰ – (रुग्णोपसेवकः) रोगी का सेवक, परिचारक, तीमारदार। one who attends the sick.

गिलानुपट्ठान – न॰ – (रुग्ण परिचर्या) रोगी-सेवा, तीमारदारी, रुग्ण परिचर्या। nursing of the sick.

गिलायति – क्रि॰ – (√ग्लै = ग्लायति) बीमार पड़ता है। falls ill, becomes sick.

गिलित – कृ॰ – (निगलित) खाया हुआ। eaten.

गिही – वि॰ – (गृही) गृहस्थी में तत्पर, गृहस्थ। one who leads a domestic life.

गिही-भोग – पु॰ – (गृही-भोगः) गृहस्थ के भोग। enjoyment of a layman.

गिही-व्यञ्जन – न॰ – (गृही-लक्षणम्) गृहस्थ की विशेषताएँ। characteristics of a layman.

गिही-संसग्ग – पु॰ – (गृही-संसर्ग) गृहस्थों के साथ संसर्ग। association with layman.

गीत (1) – न॰ – (गीतम्) गीत। song.

गीत (2) – कृ॰ – (√गै + क्त = गीत) गाया हुआ। sung.

गीत-ख – पु॰ – (गीत-खः) गीत की ध्वनि। sound of song.

गीत-सद्द – पु॰ – (गीत-शब्दः) गीत के शब्द, गीत की ध्वनि। sound of a song.

गीतका – स्त्री॰ – (गीतिका) (1) छोटा गीत (2) गीतिका नामक छन्द। song, a particular poetic metre.

गीवा – स्त्री॰ – (ग्रीवा) गर्दन, ग्रीवा। the neck.

गीवेय्यक – न॰ – (ग्रैवेयक) कण्ठहार, गर्दन का गहना। an ornament for the neck.

गुग्गुल – पु॰ – (गुग्गुलु) गुग्गल, गूगुल का पेड़। bdellium (a fragrant gum resin) of *Amyris Agallochum* tree.

गुञ्जा – स्त्री॰ – **(गुञ्जा)** (1) घुँघची, चिरमठी (2) रत्ती-भर (तौल) । (1) berry or seed of shrub *Abru precatrius*, (2) in weighing gold.

गुण (1) – पु॰ – **(गुण)** स्वभावगत विशेषता जैसे सद्गुण या दुर्गुण, धागा । characte-ristics, thread.

गुण (2) – **(गुण)** प्रकृति के तीन गुण : सत, रज, तम । three characteristics of matter *sattva* (light), *raja* (action) and *tama* (darkness).

गुण-कथा – स्त्री॰ – **(गुण-कथा)** प्रशंसा । praise.

गुण-कित्तन – न॰ – **(गुण-कीर्त्तनम्)** गुणों की अनवरत चर्चा । telling about one's virtues.

गुण-गण – पु॰ – **(गुण-गण)** गुणों का समूह । accumulation of virtues.

गुणवन्तु – वि॰ – **(गुणवान)** गुणी, गुनवन्तु, गुणवान । virtuous.

गुणानुपेत – वि॰ – **(गुणानुपेत)** गुणी । endowed with good qualities.

गुणहीन – वि॰ – **(गुण-हीन)** गुण-रहित । devoid of virtues.

गुण-जातक – (जा॰ सं॰ 157) – संकट में प्राण रक्षा करने वाले शृगाल के प्रति एक शेर की कृतज्ञता की यह कथा सुपात्र को दिये गये सात्त्विक दान की महिमा दर्शाती है । the story (No. 157) of a lion grateful to the jackal who saved his life in danger reveals the virtue of gratefulness.

गुणक – वि॰ – **(गुणक)** जिसके सिरे पर गाँठ हो । having knots at the ends.

गुण्ठक – वि॰ – **(गुण्ठक)** ढका हुआ । covered.

गुण्ठिका – स्त्री॰ – **(गुण्ठिका)** धागे का गोला । a ball of thread.

गुण्ठेति – क्रि॰ – **(√ गुण्ठ् = गुण्ठयति)** ढकता है, लपेटता है । wraps, covers.

गुण्डिक – पु॰ – **(गुण्डिक)** धागे की घुण्डी, देखें गुण्ठिक । see Gunthika.

गुणेतर – वि॰ – **(गुण + इतर)** दोष । bad qualities, blemish.

गुत्त – कृ॰ – **(√ गुप् + त = गुप्त)** संरक्षित । guarded, protected.

गुत्त-द्वार – वि॰ – **(गुप्त-द्वार)** संयतेन्द्रिय । with well guarded senses.

गुत्ति – स्त्री॰ – **(गुप्ति)** संरक्षा । protection.

गुत्तिक – पु॰ – **(गुप्तिक/गोप्ता)** आरक्षक, चौकीदार । watchman.

गुत्तिल-जातक – (जा॰ सं॰ 243) – यह कथा बतलाती है कि विद्या-प्राप्ति के अनन्तर अपने ज्ञान के अहंकार में गुरु की अवहेलना करने वाला दुर्गति को प्राप्त होता है । the story (No. 243) reveals that the pupil who being proud of his learning, disregards his teacher and creates misfortune for himself.

गुद – न॰ – **(गुद)** गुदा । anus.

गुम्ब – पु॰ – **(गुल्म)** झाड़ी । a bush, a thicket.

गुम्बिय-जातक – (जा॰ सं॰ 366) – यह कथा बतलाती है कि कामेन्द्रिय-जनित-सुख, विषमिश्रित मधु की भाँति दुःख परिणामी है । the story (No. 366) reveals that sensuous pleasures are like honey sprinkled with deadly poison.

गुह्ह (1) – वि॰ – (गुह्ह्य) गोपनीय, छिपाने योग्य। fit to be hidden.

गुह्ह (2) – न॰ – (गुह्ह्यम्) रहस्य। secret.

गुह्ह-भण्डक – न॰ – (गुह्ह्येन्द्रिय) शिश्न अथवा जननेन्द्रिय। the male or female genital.

गुरु – पु॰ – (गुरु) शिक्षक। a teacher.

गुरु-दक्खिणा – स्त्री॰ – (गुरु–दक्षिणा) गुरु को दी जाने वाली दक्षिणा। the presents to the teacher given by pupils at the completion of their study.

गुहा – स्त्री॰ – (गुहा) गुफा। cave, a cavern.

गुल – न॰ – (गुड) (1) भेली, गुड (2) गोली (3) गेंद। (1) ball like form of boiled sugarcane, malasses, (2) pill (3) ball.

गुल-कीळा – स्त्री॰ – (गुलि-क्रीडा) गोलियों की क्रीडा। a play with small balls.

गुलिका – स्त्री॰ – (गुलिका) गोली। pills.

गूथ – न॰ – (गूथ) पुरीष, विष्ठा, गोबर। excrement, cowdung.

गूथ-गत – न॰ – (गूथ–गत) विष्ठा का ढेर। heap of dung.

गूथ-पाणक – (गूथ–कीटः) गूँह में रहने वाला कीड़ा। an insect living on excrement.

गूथ-भक्ख – वि॰ – (गूथ–भक्ष/भक्षक) मल-भक्षी, विष्ठा-भक्षी। an excrement eating worm, living on dung.

गूथ-भाणी – पु॰ – (गूथ–भाषिक) दुर्वच, बुरा बोलने वाला। of foul speech.

गूथ-पाण-जातक – (जा॰ सं॰ 227) – एक गुबरैले ने भूमि पर गिरी पड़ी शराब चख ली। वह मदमस्त हो गया। उधर आ रहा हाथी पड़ी हुई शराब की गंध सूंघ घृणावश लौट चला। गुबरैले ने सोचा हाथी मुझसे डरकर लौट पड़ा है तो उसने हाथी को लड़ने की चुनौती दी। हाथी लौट पड़ा उसने गुबरैले के ऊपर ही पेशाब कर दिया। जिससे दबकर गुबरैला तत्काल मर गया। (Story No. 227), a dung beetle drank some liquor dropped by some merchants. An elephant who was passing by smelt the liquor and returned in disgust. The beetle thinking that the elephant was frightened of him challenged him to fight. The elephant returned and dropped some dung on the beetle killing him on the spot.

गूहति – क्रि॰ – (√गूह्=गूहति) छिपाता है। hides, conceals.

गूहन – न॰ – (गूहन) छिपाव। concealment.

गूहित – कृ॰ – (√गूह + क्त = गूहित) छिपा हुआ। hidden, concealed.

गूळ्ह – कृ॰ – (गूढ) गुप्त, छिपा हुआ। hidden, covered, secret.

गेण्डुक – पु॰ – (गेन्दुक) गेंद। ball for playing.

गेध – पु॰ – (गर्द्धः) लोभ। greed.

गेधित – कृ॰ – (गर्द्धित) लुब्ध। greedy.

गेय्य – वि॰ – (गेय) (1) गाने योग्य (2) त्रिपिटक के नौ अंगों में से एक, गेय्य अंश। (1) which is to be sung (2) one of the nine forms of Tripīṭak.

गेरुक – न॰ – (गैरिक) गेरु का रंग। a saffron colour.

गेलञ्ज – न॰ – (ग्लानता/ग्लानत्व) अस्वस्थता, व्याधि। sickness, illness.

गेह – पु॰ तथा न॰ – (गेह) निवास-भवन, घर। house, dwelling place.

गेहङ्गन – न॰ – (गेह-अङ्गणम्) घर का आँगन। the court-yard of a house.

गेहजन – पु॰ – (गेहजन) गृह-जन, कुटुम्बी परिवार के सदस्य। members of a household.

गेहट्ठान – न॰ – (गेहस्थान) घर के लिए जगह। site for a house.

गेह-द्वार – न॰ – (गेहद्वार) घर का दरवाजा। the gate or the front of a house.

गेह-निस्सित – वि॰ – (गेह-निःश्रृत) घर पर आश्रित। connected with the family life.

गेहप्पवेसन – न॰ – (गृह-प्रवेशनम्) गृह-प्रवेश का संस्कार। the ceremony of entering a new building.

गो – पु॰ तथा स्त्री॰ – (गो) गाय, बैल, साँड पशु। an ox, cattle in general.

गो-कण्टक (1) – न॰ – (गो-कण्टक) पशुओं के खुर। the hoof of cattle.

गो-कण्टक (2) – न॰ – (गो-कण्टक) गोखरू। thistle, a thorny medicinal plant *Astera-cantha, Ruellia-longifolia*.

गो-कुल – न॰ – (गोकुल) गो-घर, गौ-शाला। cow-shed.

गो-गण – पु॰ – (गो-गण) पशु-समूह। herd of cattle.

गो-घातक – पु॰ – (गो-घातक) कसाई। a butcher.

गोकुलिक – पु॰ – (गो-कुलिक) वज्जिपुत्तकों का एक उपभेद। a class of Vajji-kṣatriyas.

गोचर – पु॰ – (गोचर) चारागाह। pasture.

गोचर-गाम – पु॰ – (गोचर-ग्राम) भिक्षाटन-क्षेत्र। a village from where a monk obtains his foods.

गोच्छक – पु॰ – (गुच्छक) गुच्छा। a cluster or bunch.

गोट्ठ – न॰ – (गोष्ठ) गौओं का बाड़ा। cow-shed.

गोण – पु॰ – (गोण) बैल, वृषभ। an ox, a bull.

गोणक – पु॰ – (गोणक) (1) एक प्रकार का बैल (2) बकरों के बाल से बना थैला। (1) a kind of ox (2) a sack made of goat-hair.

गोतम – वि॰ – (गौतम) (1) गौतम-गोत्र सम्बन्धी (2) शाक्यों का गोत्र। (1) belonging to the Gautama clan (2) Śākya clan.

गोतमी – स्त्री॰ – (गौतमी) गौतम-गोत्र की। a woman of Gautama clan.

गोत्त – न॰ – (गोत्र) गोत्र। clan, ancestry, lineage.

गोत्रभू – (गोत्रभू) एक पारिभाषिक शब्द। वह जो सांसारिक न रहा, बल्कि निर्वाण जिसका उद्देश्य हो गया हो। one who destroys the linage.

गोध-जातक – (जा॰ सं॰ 138) – कथा बतलाती है कि सतर्क व्यक्ति नीयत भाँपकर विपदा से बचाव कर लेते हैं। the story (No. 138) tells that alertness is essential for one's protection.

गोध-जातक – (जा॰ सं॰ 141) – एक गोह-बच्चे के गिरगिट से यारी की यह कथा बतलाती है कि विषय प्रकृति वालों की मैत्री कष्ट का कारण बनती है। this story (No. 141) of an iguana and chameleon tells that unnatural intimacy causes loss.

गोध-जातक – (जा॰ सं॰ 333) – अर्द्धांगिनी कही जाने वाली पत्नी को भी प्रदेय भोग न देने वाले राजकुमार की कथा। the story (No. 333) of a prince who ate the whole food himself and did not give any to his hungry wife.

गोध-जातक – (जा॰ सं॰ 325) – यह कथा बतलाती है कि किस प्रकार एक गोध ने ढोंगी तपस्वी को उसकी करतूत का फल चखाया। the story (No. 325) tells how a clever iguana got rid of a treacherous monk.

गोधा – स्त्री॰ – (**गोधा**) गोह। an iguana.

गोधावरी – स्त्री॰ – (**गोदावरी**) दक्षिणापथ की एक नदी गोदावरी। Godāvarī the longest river in south India.

गोधूम – पु॰ – (**गोधूम**) गेहूँ। wheat.

गोनस – पु॰ – (**गोनस**) एक प्रकार का विषैला सर्प। a viper.

गोपक – पु॰ – (**गोपक**) पहरेदार, चौकीदार। watchman.

गोपानसी – स्त्री॰ – (**गोपानसी**) छान-छप्पर को थामने वाली लकड़ी या बाँस की कैंची, टेउकी (अवधी)। a bent beam supporting the framework of a roof.

गोपी – स्त्री॰ – (**गोपी**) ग्वाले या चरवाहे की स्त्री। a wife of cow herd, cow-herdess.

गोपुर – न॰ – (**गोपुर**) द्वार। gateway.

गोपेति – क्रि॰ – (√ **गुप** = **गोपयति**) रक्षा करता है। guards, watches.

गोपेतु – पु॰ – (**गोप्ता**) रक्षक। a guard, watchman.

गोप्फक – न॰ – (**गोफण**) ढोल बाँस, गुलेल। sling.

गोमय – न॰ – (**गोमय**) गोबर। cowdung.

गोमिक – वि॰ – (**गोमिन्**) गायों अथवा पशुओं का मालिक। owner of cows.

गोमी – वि॰ – (**गोमिन्**) पशुओं का मालिक। owner of cows.

गोमुत्त – न॰ – (**गोमूत्र**) गोमूत्र। urine of the cows.

गो-यूथ – पु॰ – (**गो–यूथ**) गायों का झुण्ड। a herd of cattle.

गोरक्खा – स्त्री॰ – (**गो–रक्षा**) गौ-रक्षा, गौ-पालन। protection of cows, cow-keeping.

गोळक – पु॰ तथा न॰ – (**गोलक**) गेंद। a ball.

गोसीस – पु॰ – (**गोशीर्ष**) पीला चन्दन। the yellow sandalwood.

घ

घ – पालि वर्णमाला का चतुर्थ व्यञ्जन the fourth consonant of Pali alphabet.

घंसति – क्रि॰ – (√ घृष् = घर्षति) रगड़ता है। rubs.

घच्चा – स्त्री॰ – (√ हन् = घात > घात्य) विनाश। destruction.

घट – पु॰ – (घट) घड़ा। pitcher.

घटक (1) – पु॰ तथा न॰ – (घटक) छोटा बर्तन। a small jar.

घटक (2) – न॰ – (घटक) अवयव। a constituent part.

घट-जातक – (जा॰ सं॰ 355) – कोसल नरेश वंक के मन्त्री घटकुमार के अपकर्ष और उत्कर्ष की कथा। the story (No. 355) related to the life of Ghaṭa Kumār, minister of Vaṅka, the king of Kosala.

घट-जातक – (जा॰ सं॰ 454) – किस प्रकार घट पण्डित ने अपने भाई वासुदेव का कष्ट दूर किया। the story (No. 454) tells how Ghaṭa paṇḍit assuaged the grief of his brother Vasudev by his intelligence.

घटति – क्रि॰ – (घटते) कोशिश करता है, प्रयास करता है। tries, strives.

घटित – कृ॰ – (√ घट + क्त = घटित) happened.

घटमान – कृ॰ – (√ घट् + शानच = घटमान) being happened.

घटना – स्त्री॰ – (घटना) घटना, संयोग, मेल। fixing, combination, incident.

घटा – स्त्री॰ – (घटा) समुदाय, भीड़। collection, mass.

घटासन-जातक – (जा॰ सं॰ 133) – बुद्धिमान वही है जो परिस्थिति और नीयत का अनुमान कर आने वाली आपदा से समय रहते सचेत हो जाता है। (story No. 133) he is called wise who by assessing the situation and observing the intention realizes the forthcoming trouble and becomes alert.

घटिका – स्त्री॰ – (घटिका) सुराही। an earthen jar for keeping water.

घटी – स्त्री॰ – (घटी) जल-पात्र। water-pot.

घटीकार – पु॰ – (घटीकार) कुम्भकार, कुम्हार। a potter.

घटी-यन्त – न॰ – (घटी–यन्त्र) घटी-यन्त्र, रहट। Persian wheel for drawing water out from a well.

घटीयति – क्रि॰ – (घट्यते) सम्बन्धित होता है। becomes combined or connected.

घटेति – क्रि॰ – (घटते) प्रयत्न करता है। connects, strives.

घट्टन – न॰ – (घट्टन) संघर्ष। striking, knocking, against.

घट्टेति – क्रि॰ – (घातयति) चोट पहुँचाता है, रुष्ट करता है। offends, knocks against.

घण्टा – स्त्री॰ – (घण्टा) (बजाने का) घण्टा। a bell.

घत – न॰ – (घृत) घृत, घी। clarified butter, ghee.

घत-सित्त – वि॰ – (घृत-सिक्त) घृत से सिंचित जिस पर घी डाला गया हो। sprinkled with ghee.

घन – वि॰ – (घन) मोटा, स्थूल। thick, dense, solid.

घनतम – वि॰ – (घनतम्) अतिशय सघन, अत्यन्त स्थूल। very thick, much dense.

घन-पुफ्फ – न॰ – (घन-पुष्प) फूलों वाला गलीचा। a woollen coverlet embroidered with flowers.

घनसार – न॰ – (घनसार) कपूर। camphor.

घनोपल – न॰ – (घनोपल) ओले। hail, storm.

घम्म – पु॰ – (धर्म) ऊष्णता। heat.

घम्म-जल – न॰ – (घर्म-जल) पसीना। sweat.

घम्माभितत्त – वि॰ – (घर्माभितप्त) गरमी से हैरान। overpowered by heat.

घर – न॰ – (गृह) गृह। house.

घर-गोलिका – स्त्री॰ – (गृहगोधिका) छिपकली। lizard.

घर-बन्धन – न॰ – (गृह-वन्धन) परिणय, विवाह। performance of marriage.

घर-मानुष – पु॰ – (गृह-जन) घर के लोग। members of house.

घर-सप्प – वि॰ – (गृह-सर्प) मूषक-सर्प, धामिन सांप। a rat-snake.

घराजिर – न॰ – (गृहाजिर) घर का आंगन। house-yard.

घरावास – पु॰ – (गृहावास) गृहस्थ जीवन। the household life.

घरणी – स्त्री॰ – (गृहिणी) गृहिणी। house-wife, mistress of a house.

घस – वि॰ – (√घस् + घसः) खाने वाला। one who eats, grazes.

घसति – क्रि॰ – (√घस् = घसति) खाता है। eats.

घंसेति – क्रि॰ – (√घृष् = घर्षति) रगड़ता है, संघर्ष करता है। rubs, knocks against.

घात – पु॰ – (√हन् = घात) चोट हत्या. blow, killing.

घातन – न॰ – (घातन) हत्या। murder, slaying.

घातक – पु॰ – (घातक) हत्यारा, लुटेरा। killer, robber.

घाती – पु॰ – (घाती) घात करने वाला, हत्यारा, लुटेरा। murderer, robber.

घातपेति – क्रि॰ – (घातयति) हत्या करवाता है, लुटवाता है। causes murder, gets plundered.

घातेति – क्रि॰ – (घातयति) हत्या करता है, लूटता है। kills, robs.

घाण – न॰ – (घ्राण) नासिक, नाक। nose.

घाण-विञ्ञाण – न॰ – (घाण-विज्ञान) घ्राणेन्द्रिय के माध्यम से उत्पन्न होने वाला ज्ञान। perception of smell.

घायति – क्रि॰ – (जिघ्रति) सूँघता है। smells.

घायित – कृ॰ – (√घस् + क्त = घसित) खाया हुआ। eaten.

घास – पु० – (घास) घास, जानवरों का आहार, चारा। fodder, a kind of grass.

घासच्छादन – न० – (घास + आच्छादनम्) भोजन-वस्त्र। food and clothing.

घास-हारक – वि० – (घास+हारक) घास लाने वाला। one who fetches the fodder or grass.

घुट्ठ – कृ० – ($\sqrt{}$ घुष + क्त = घोषित) घोषित। proclaimed, announced.

घोटक – पु० – (घोटक) बिना सधा हुआ घोड़ा। an untamed horse, a wild horse.

घोर – वि० – (घोर) भयानक। terrible, awful.

घोरतर – वि० – (घोरतर) अधिक भयानक। more terrible.

घोस – पु० – (घोष) उदघोष, घोषणा, शब्द। sound, shout, utterance.

घोसक – पु० – (घोषक) घोषणा करने वाला। one who shouts or proclaims.

घोसापेति – क्रि० – (घोषयति) घोषणा कराता है। gets announced, proclaimed.

घोसिताराम – कोशाम्बी का प्रसिद्ध विहार। a famous monastery of Kośāmbī.

घोसेति – क्रि० – (घोषयति) घोषणा कराता है। announces, proclaims.

च

च (1)– पालि वर्णमाला का छठा व्यञ्जन। the sixth consonant in the Pāli alphabet.

च (2) – अव्यय – (च) और तब, अब। and then, now.

चकित – वि॰ – (चकित) हैरान, भयभीत। disturbed, afraid.

चकोर – पु॰ – (चकोर) चकोर। the Indian red legged partridge, found in Punjab, eats white ants.

चक्क – न॰ – (चक्र) चक्र, चक्का, पहिया। circle, disc, wheel.

चक्क-अङ्कित – वि॰ – (चक्राङ्कित) चक्र के निशान वाला। having a wheel-mark.

चक्क-गब्भ – पु॰ – (चक्र–गर्भ) ब्रह्माण्ड चक्र का अन्तर्वर्ती भाग। the interior of a world circle.

चक्क-पब्बत – पु॰ – (चक्र-पर्वत) चक्राकार पर्वत श्रेणी जो पृथ्वी को वलय की भाँति घेरे हुए है। the wheeling encircling the earth.

चक्क-पाणी – पु॰ – (चक्र-पाणि) चक्रपाणि, विष्णु। the god Viṣṇu (with discus weapon in his hand).

चक्क-युग – न॰ – (चक्र-युग) पहियों का जोड़ा। a pair of wheels.

चक्क-रतन – न॰ – (चक्र-रत्न) चक्रवर्ती राजा का रत्न-चक्र। jewelled wheel of an emperor.

चक्क-वत्ती – पु॰ – (चक्रवर्ती) चक्रवर्ती राजा। emperor.

चक्क-समारूळ्ह – वि॰ – (चक्र-समारूढ) चक्रों (रथों) पर चढ़े हुए। mounted on their vehicles.

चक्कवाक – पु॰ – (चक्रवाक) चकवा। the ruddy goose.

चक्कवाक-जातक – (जा॰ सं॰ 434) – कथा का निष्कर्ष है कि संतोष सौन्दर्य प्रदान करता है जैसे चकवा-चकवी का, और लोभ सौन्दर्य नष्ट करता है जैसे–कौवे का। the story (No. 434) concludes that happiness gives beauty to a person.

चक्कवाक-जातक – (जा॰ सं॰ 451) – उपरोक्त जातक सं॰ 434 के समान। as the above tale.

चक्क-वाल – पु॰ – (चक्र-वर्त्तः) घेरा, क्षेत्र, चक्रवार। limit, boundary.

चक्कव्ह – पु॰ – (चक्रव्य) चक्रवाक, चकवा। the ruddy goose.

चक्किक – वि॰ – (चाक्रिक) सामूहिक स्तुति पाठ करने वाले। proclaimer, announcer.

चक्ख – (भू॰) – दस्सने – ($\sqrt{}$ दृश् = पश्यति) देखना। to see.

चक्खु – न॰ – (चक्षु) आँख। the eye.

चक्खुक – वि॰ – (चक्षुक) आँख वाला, दृष्टि वाला। having eyes.

चक्खुदद – वि॰ – (चक्षुदद) आँख देने वाला, अर्थात् दृष्टि प्रदान करने वाला। one who gives the eye of understanding.

चक्खु-धातु – स्त्री० – (चक्षु-धातु) दृष्टि। vision.

चक्खु-पथ – पु० – (चक्षु-पथ) दृष्टिपथ। the range of vision.

चक्खु-भूत – वि० – (चक्षुभूत) सम्यक् दृष्टि वाला। who possesses right understanding.

चक्खुमन्तु – वि० – (चक्षुमान) आँख वाला। endowed with eyes (understanding).

चक्खु-लोल – वि० – (चक्षु-लोल) आँख का लोभी, चञ्चल दृष्टि। greedy to see many things, roving vision.

चक्खु-विञ्ञाण – न० – (चक्षु-विज्ञान) दृष्टि के द्वारा प्राप्त ज्ञान। visual cognition.

चक्खु-विञ्ञेय – वि० – (चक्षु-विज्ञेय) दृष्टि द्वारा जाना जा सकने योग्य। which can be percieved by sense of sight.

चक्खु-सम्फस्स – पु० – (चक्षु-संस्पर्श) चक्षु-स्पर्श। contact with the vision.

चक्खुस्स – वि० – आँख को अच्छा लगने वाला या आँख के लिए अच्छा। good for eyes.

चङ्कम – पु० – (चङ्कम) चक्रमण-स्थल। a terraced foot path.

चङ्कमन – न० – (चङ्क्रमणम्) चंक्रमण की क्रिया। to walk up and down as an exercise.

चङ्कमति – क्रि० – (चङ्क्रमते) चंक्रमण करता है। walks up and down.

चङ्ववार – पु० – (द्रोणी) खोखले काष्ठ से बनायी गयी अदिया या डोकनी, नन्हीं कठवत जैसी कटोरी के आकार का लकड़ी का पात्र जिससे दही-दूध नापते निकालते हैं। a small wooden bowl for measuring milk.

चङ्घोटक – पु० – (चङ्घोटक/द्रोणी) छोटी टोकरी, खोखले काष्ठ से निर्मित द्रोणी। a hollow vessel, a bowl.

चच्चर – न० – (चत्वर) आँगन, चौरस्ता। a courtyard, a cross-road, junction.

√चज – (भू०) – हानियं – (√त्यज् = त्यजति) छोड़ना। to leave.

चजति – क्रि० – (√त्यज् = त्यजति) त्याग देता है। gives up, abandons.

चजन – न० – (व्यजनम्) त्याग। giving up.

चञ्चल – वि० – (चञ्चल) अस्थिर। unsteady.

√चट – (चु०) – भेदने – (कुट्टनम्) कूटना। to pound.

चटक – पु० – (चटक) गौरैया नामक चिड़िया। a sparrow.

चणक – पु० – (चणक) चना। gram, chickpea.

चण्ड – वि० – (चण्ड) भयानक, प्रचण्ड। fierce, violent.

चण्डपज्जोत – पु० – (चण्ड-प्रद्योत) बुद्ध का समकालीन अवन्ति नरेश चण्ड-प्रद्योत। the ruler of Avantī at the time of Buddha.

चण्डासोक – पु० – (चण्डाशोक) भाइयों की निर्दयतापूर्वक हत्या करने के कारण अशोक को दिया गया नाम कालान्तर में यह नाम बदलकर धम्मासोक पड़ा। the name given to Aśoka because he very cruelly killed his brothers the name was later changed into Dhammāsoka.

चण्डाल – पु॰ – (चाण्डाल) जाति बहिष्कृत अथवा अस्पृश्य। an outcaste or untouchable.

चण्डाल-कुल – न॰ – (चाण्डाल–कुल) नीचतम कुल। the lowest caste.

चण्डाली – स्त्री॰ – (चाण्डाली) चण्डाल स्त्री। a caṇḍāla woman, impure woman, untouchable women.

चण्डिक्क – न॰ – (चण्डता / चाण्डिक्य) भयानकता, प्रचण्ड-भाव। ferocity.

चतु – वि॰ – (चतुः) चार। four.

चतुक्कण्ण – वि॰ – (चतुष्कोण) चौकोन, चतुष्कोण। rectangular, having four corners.

चतुक्खत्तुं – क्रि॰ वि॰ – (चतुष्कर्तुम्) चार-बार। four times.

चतुग्गुण – वि॰ – (चतुर्गुणः) चौगुना। four times.

चत्तालीसति – स्त्री॰ – (चतुश्चत्वारिंशत्) चवालीस। forty-four.

चतुज्जाति-गन्ध – पु॰ – (चतुर्जाति गन्धः) चार प्रकार की सुगन्धि जिसमें केशर, चमेली, तुरुष्क, और एक यूनानी पुष्प सम्मिलित है। four kinds of perfumes, viz. saffron, jasmine, turuṣka and a greek plant.

चतुत्तिंसति – स्त्री॰ – (चतुस्त्रिंशत्) चौंतीस। thirty-four.

चतुद्दस – वि॰ – (चतुर्दश) चौदह। fourteen.

चतुद्दिसा – स्त्री॰ – (चतुःदिक्) चारों दिशाएँ। the four directions.

चतुद्द्वार – वि॰ – (चतुर्द्वार) चार द्वारों वाला। having four gates.

चतुनवुति – स्त्री॰ – (चतुर्नवतिः) चौरानबे। ninety-four.

चतुपच्चय – पु॰ – (चतुः प्रत्यय) भिक्षु की भोजन, चीवर, औषधि और आवास ये चार आश्यकताएँ। the four requisites, viz. food, clothing, medicine and lodgings of a disciple.

चतुपण्णास – स्त्री॰ – (चतुः पञ्चाशत) चौवन। fifty-four.

चतु-परिसा – स्त्री॰ – (चतुः परिषत्) चार प्रकार की परिषद अर्थात् भिक्षु, भिक्षुणियों, उपासक तथा उपासिकाएँ। the four-fold assembly, viz. monks, nuns, laymen and lay women.

चतु-भूमक – वि॰ -- (चतुः + भौमिक) चार तल्लों का। having four storeys or stages.

चतु-मधुर – न॰ – (चतुः + मधुर) चार प्रकार के मधुर-पदार्थ-घृत, मधु, शर्करा तथा तिल। the four sweets, ghee, honey, sugar and sesame.

चतुरङ्गिक – वि॰ – (चतुरङ्गिक) चार हिस्सों वाला। consisting of four divisions.

चतुरङ्गिनी – स्त्री॰ – (चतुरङ्गिणी) चार अंगों वाली सेना गज, रथ, घुड़सवार और पैदल। an army consisting of elephants, chariots, cavalry and infantry.

चतुरङ्गुल – वि॰ – (चतुरङ्गुलः) चार अंगुल भर की माप। measuring four inches.

चतुरस्स – वि॰ – (चतुरस्र) चौकोन, चौकोर। quadrangular.

चतुरस्सक – पु॰ – (चतुरस्रक) चार तल्ले का महल। a four-storey building.

चतुरंस – वि॰ – (चतुरंशक) चतुष्कोण। having four corners.

चतुरासीति – स्त्री॰ – (चतुरशीतिः) चौरासी। eighty-four.

चतुवीसति – स्त्री॰ – (**चतुर्विंशति**) चौबीस। twenty-four.

चतुसट्ठि – स्त्री॰ – (**चतुः षष्ठिः**) चौंसठ। sixty-four.

चतु-सत्तति – स्त्री॰ – (**चतुः-सप्ततिः**) चौहत्तर। seventy-four.

चतुक्क – न॰ – (**चतुष्क**) चौका, चौरस्ता। crossing of four roads, square plot of ground.

चतुद्वार-जातक – (जा॰ सं॰ 439) महामित्त देखें महामित्त-विन्दक जातक। see Mahamitta-Vindak Jātaka.

चतुत्थ – वि॰ – (**चतुर्थ**) चौथा। fourth.

चतुत्थी – स्त्री॰ – (**चतुर्थी**) चतुर्थी तिथि, पक्ष का चौथा दिन। the fourth day of fortnight.

चतुत्थी – स्त्री॰ – (**चतुर्थी**) सम्प्रदान कारक के लिए प्रयुक्त होने वाली 'चतुर्थी विभक्ति'। the fourth (dative) case, ceremony on fourth day after marriage.

चतुधा – क्रि॰ वि॰ – (**चतुर्धा**) चार तरफ से। in four ways.

चतुपोसथिक-जातक – (जा॰ सं॰ 441) वस्तुतः यह पुण्णक जातक के अन्तर्गत हैं। अतः वहीं से विवरण प्राप्त करें। see Puṇṇaka Jātaka.

चतुप्पद – वि॰ – (**चतुष्पाद**) चतुष्पाद, चार पैरों वाला जानवर। a quadruped.

चतुब्बिध – वि॰ – (**चतुविध**) चार प्रकार से। four-footed.

चतुभाणवार – पाँच निकायों में से और विशेष रूप से खुद्दक पाठ में से सत्ताईस उद्धरणों का एक संग्रह। a compilation of twenty-seven extracts from the five Nikāyas, chiefly from the Khuddaka Pāṭh.

चतुमट्ठ-जातक चतुमट्ठ-जातक – (जा॰ सं॰ 187) – चित्रकूट पर्वत से आये दो हंसों की एक दुष्ट श्रृगाल द्वारा बाधित कथा। the story (No. 187) of two geese from Citrakūṭa which were separated by a wicked jackal.

चतुर – वि॰ – (**चतुर**) होशियार, बुद्धिमान। clever, skilled, shrewd.

चतुरोपधि – पु॰ – (**चतुरूपाधि**) चार प्रकार के बन्धन जाति, व्याधि, जरा और मरण। fourfold bonds — caste, disease, old age and death.

चत्त – कृ॰ – (**त्यक्त**) त्यक्त, त्यागा हुआ। given up, secrificed.

चन – अव्यय – (**चन**) 'कभी-कभी' के अर्थ-वाचक 'कुदाचन' शब्द का एक अंश। a particle used to express a portion of a whole : *Kudācan* - sometimes.

चनं – अव्यय – (**चनम्**) देखिये चन। see Cana.

√चन्द – भू॰ – (**दित्तिहिलादनेसु**) चमकना। to shine.

चन्द – पु॰ – (**चन्द्र**) चाँद। the moon.

चन्दग्गाह – पु॰ – (**चन्द्रग्रहण**) चन्द्र-ग्रहण। eclipse of the moon.

चन्द-मण्डल – न॰ – (**चन्द्र-मण्डल**) चन्द्रमा की गोलाकृति। the disc of the moon.

चन्द-किन्नर-जातक – (जा॰ सं॰ 485) – इस जातक में एक ऐसी किन्नरी का वर्णन है जो समस्त ऐश्वर्य सुखों का प्रलोभन ठुकराकर केवल पति-प्रेम का वरण करती है। the story (No. 485) reveals the undying affection of a noble woman for her husband.

चन्दन – पु॰ – (चन्दन) चन्दन का एक वृक्ष। न॰ चन्दन की लकड़ी। sandal tree (n) sandalwood.

चन्दन-सार – पु॰ – (चन्दन–सार) चन्दन का सार। the essence of sandalwood.

चन्दाभ-जातक – (जा॰ सं॰ 135) – इस कथा के अनुसार चन्द्र तथा सूर्य पर चित्त एकाग्र करने वाले आभास्वर लोक में उत्पन्न होते हैं। according to the Jātaka (No. 135) who-ever concentrate their sight on the sun and the moon would be born in the Ābhāssar world.

चन्दनिका – स्त्री॰ – (चन्दनिका) मलमुण्ड, नाबदान। a cesspool, a cesspit.

चन्दप्पभा – स्त्री॰ – (चन्द्र-प्रभा) चन्द्रिका, चाँदनी। moonlight.

चन्दभागा – पु॰ – (चन्द्रभागा) चन्द्रभागा नामक नदी जिसे आजकल चेनाब कहा जाता है। ग्रीक वासियों ने इसे आक्सिन कहा है। a famous river flowing from the Himālayas. Candabhāgā is identified with the Cenāb river of Punjab.

चन्दिका – स्त्री॰ – (चन्द्रिका) चन्द्रप्रभा, चाँदनी। moonlight.

चन्दिमा – पु॰ – (चन्द्रमा) चाँद। the moon.

चपल – वि॰ – (चपल) चंचल, अस्थिर। fickle, unsteady.

चपु-चपु – कारकं – क्रि॰ वि॰ – (चपचप कारकम्) चप-चप आवाज करते हुए (भोजन) करना। making capa - capa sound while eating or drinking.

चमर – पु॰ – (चमर) हिमालय प्रदेश की सुरा गाय। the Tibetan yak ox (found in Himalayan regions), covered with long silky hair.

चमू – स्त्री॰ – (चमू) सेना। an army.

चमूपति – पु॰ – (चमू-पतिः) सेनापति। general of an army.

चम्पक – पु॰ – (चम्पा) चम्पा नामक पुष्प-वृक्ष। the tree Michelia Champaka.

चम्पा – स्त्री॰ – (चम्पा) इसी नाम की नदी के किनारे का एक नगर। यह अंग देश की राजधानी था। वर्तमान भागलपुर। name of a town which was the capital of Aṅga. Today Campā is known as Bhāgalpur.

चम्पेयक-जातक – (जा॰ सं॰ 506) – यह जातक कथा शिक्षा देती है कि दृढ़ निश्चयी के मनोरथ अन्ततः पूर्ण हो ही जाते हैं। the teaching of this Jātaka tale (No. 506) is that where there's a will there is a way.

चम्म – न॰ – (चर्म) चर्म। leather.

चम्मकार – पु॰ – (चर्मकार) चमार। a tanner.

चम्म-खण्ड – पु॰ – (चर्म-खण्ड) आसन की तरह उपयोग में आने वाला चर्म-खण्ड। a piece of leather used as a rug.

चम्म-पसिब्बक – पु॰ – (चर्म–प्रसेवकः) चमड़े का थैला। a leather-bag.

चय – पु॰ – (चय) संग्रह, ढेर। collection, heap.

√चर – (भू॰) – गतिभक्खणेसु – (√चर् = चरति) चलना। to walk.

चर – पु॰ – (चर) घूमने वाला, चर-पुरुष (गुप्तचर)। one who walks or frequents, a spy.

चरक – (चरक) देखें – चर। see Cara.

चरण – न॰ – (चरणम्) (1) चलना-फिरना, (2) पाँव (3) आचरण। (1) walking about (2) foot (3) behaviour.

चरति – क्रि॰ – (√ चर् = चरति) (1) चलता फिरता है (2) आचरण करता है। (1) walks or roams about (2) behaves, performs.

चरन्त – कृ॰ – (√ चर + शतृ = चरन्) चलते हुए, आचरण करते हुए। walking, behaving.

चरमान – कृ॰ – (√ चर् + शानच् = चरमाण) देखें चरन्त। see Caranta.

चराचर – न॰ – (चराचर) समस्त चलाचल वस्तु। moving and static, the whole.

चरापेति – क्रि॰ – (चारयति) चलाता है। makes to move.

चरित – न॰ – (चरित) (1) चरित्र, (जीवन) चरित। (1) character, behaviour (2) life.

चरित – कृ॰ – (√ चर + क्त = चरित) कृत। acted.

चरितब्ब – कृ॰ – (√ चर + तव्यत् = चरितव्य) आचरण के योग्य, चलने योग्य। fit for walking, fit for behaviour.

चरिम – वि॰ – (चरिम) अन्तिम। the last, subsequent.

चरिया – स्त्री॰ – (चर्या) आचरण, चरित। conduct, behaviour.

चरिया-पिटक – खुद्दक निकाय के पन्द्रह ग्रंथों में से एक। यह खुद्दक निकाय का अन्तिम ग्रन्थ माना जाता है। one among the fifteen books compiled in Khuddaka Nikāya.

चरु – पु॰ – (चरु) यज्ञीय द्रव्य, यज्ञार्थ तण्डुल पाक। an oblation of.

√ चल – (भू॰) – कम्पने – (√ कम्प् = कम्पते) काँपना। to tremble.

चल – वि॰ – (चल) अस्थिर। moving, unsteady.

चल-चित्त – वि॰ – (चल-चित्त) अस्थिर चित्त। having a fickle mind.

चलति – क्रि॰ – (√ चल् = चलति) चंचल होता है, काँपता है। moves, trembles.

चलन – न॰ – (चलनम्) हिलना-डुलना, काँपना। movement, trembling, agitation.

चलनी – पु॰ – (चल्नी) वात-मृग। a kind of deer.

चवति – क्रि॰ – (√ च्यु = च्यवते) गिरता है, च्युत होता है, फिसलता है। falls down, slips.

चवन – न॰ – (√ च्यु + ल्युट् = च्यवनम्) गिरना, पतन, मृत्यु। falling, loss.

चसक – न॰ तथा पु॰ – (चषक) पान-पात्र। a bowl for drink.

चाग – पु॰ – (त्याग) (1) त्याग (2) उपहार। (1) giving up, abandoning (2) gift.

चागानुस्सति – स्त्री॰ – (त्यागानुस्मृति) अपनी उदारता का अनुस्मरण। rememberance of one's generosity.

चागी – पु॰ – (त्यागी) त्यागी। one who donates or abandons.

चाटि – स्त्री॰ – (चाटि) एक बर्तन। a jar, a pot.

चाटुकम्यता – स्त्री॰ – (चाटुकर्मता / चाटुकारिता) चाटुकारिता, खुशामद। flattery, favourable conversation.

चातक – पु॰ – (चातक) पपीहा या चातक पक्षी। a hornbill.

चातुद्दसी – स्त्री॰ – (**चतुर्दशी**) पक्ष की चतुर्दशी तिथि। the fourteenth day of a fortnight.

चातुद्दिस – वि॰ – (**चतुर्दिक्**) चारों दिशाओं से सम्बन्धित। belonging to the four directions.

चातुद्दीपक – वि॰ – (**चातुर्द्दीपक**) चारों द्वीपों पर छाया हुआ। covering the four continents or sweeping the whole earth.

चातुम्महापथ – पु॰ – (**चातुर्महापथ**) चार सड़को के मिलने की जगह, चौरस्ता। the place where four roads meet, a cross-way.

चातुम्महाभूतिक – वि॰ – (**चातुर्महाभूत**) पृथ्वी, जल, तेज और वायु नाम के चार महाभूतों से सम्बन्धित। consisting the four great elements earth, water, heat and air.

चातुम्महाराजिक – वि॰ – (**चातुर्महाराजिक**) निम्नतम देवलोक में रहने वाले चातुर्महाराजिक देवताओं से सम्बन्धित। belonging to four Deva kings inhabiting the lowest Devaloka.

चातुरिय – न॰ – (**चातुर्य**) चतुराई। skill, shrewdness.

चाप – पु॰ – (**चाप**) धनुष। a bow.

चापल्ल – न॰ – (**चापल्य**) चपलता। fickleness.

चामर – न॰ – (**चामर**) चँवर, चवरी गाय की पूँछ से बनी चँवरी। the tail of the yak used as a whisk.

चामिकर – न॰ – (**चामीकर**) स्वर्ण। gold.

चार – पु॰ – (**चारः**) आचार, चलन। motion, action, going.

चारक – वि॰ – (**चारक**) चलाने वाला। one who causes to move.

चारक – पु॰ – (**चारकः**) कारागार। a prison.

चारण – न॰ – (**चारण**) चलाया जाना, व्यवस्था। causing to move, management.

चारिका – स्त्री॰ – (**चारिका**) भ्रमण, यात्रा। wandering, journey.

चारित्त – न॰ – (**चारित्र्यम्**) आदत, आचरण, अभ्यास। custom, conduct, practice.

चारु – वि॰ – (**चारु**) सुन्दर, आकर्षक। charming, pleasant.

चारु-दस्सन – वि॰ – (**चारु-दर्शन**) रूपवान, सुन्दर। lovely to behold.

चारेति – क्रि॰ – (**चारयति**) चलाता है, (इन्द्रियों को) दौड़ता है। pastures, feasts one's senses.

चाल – पु॰ – (**चाल**) आघात। a shock, a sudden agitation.

चालेति – क्रि॰ – (**चालयति**) चलाता है। shakes, agitates.

चावना – स्त्री॰ – ($\sqrt{}$ च्यु + णिच् = च्यावन) गिरावट, हटाना। causing to fall.

चावेति – क्रि॰ – (**च्यावयति**) गिराता है। causes to fall.

$\sqrt{}$ च – (जि॰) – चये – ($\sqrt{}$ चि = चिनोति / चिनुते) चुनना, चयन करना। to select, to collect.

चि – (कोचि) अव्यय – (**किञ्चिद्**) कोई। someone (an indefinite interrogative particle).

$\sqrt{}$ चिक्ख – (भू॰) – वचने ($\sqrt{}$ चक्ष् = आचक्षते) कहना। to say, to tell.

चिक्खल्ल – न॰ – (चिकिल) कीचड़, दलदल । mine, mud.

चिङ्गुलक – (चिङ्गुलक) ताड़ की पत्ती (या कागज आदि) को गोलाकार काटकर केन्द्र में कोई कीली छुरे की भांति लगाकर हवा के रुख को सामने दौड़कर पंखे की भांति नचायी जाने वाली फिरकी । a toy wind mill made of palm-leaves (or paper, etc.).

चिङ्गुलायति – क्रि॰ – (चिङ्गुलायते) अपनी धुरी पर फिरकी की तरह घूमता है । revolves like windmill blades.

चिटिचिटायति – क्रि॰ – (चिटिचिटायते) चिट-चिट करता है । makes cit-cit sound.

चिञ्वा – स्त्री॰ – (चिञ्चा) इमली का वृक्ष । tamarind tree.

चिण्ण – कृ॰ – (चीर्ण) अभ्यस्त । made a habit of.

चिण्ह – न॰ – (चिह्न) चिह्न, निशान । made a mark.

√चित – (चु॰) – संचेतने – (√चित = चेतति/चेतयते) होश में आना, चेत करना । to come to senses, to think.

चित – कृ॰ – (√चि + क्त = चित) एकत्रित, चयनीकृत । heaped.

चितक – पु॰ – (चिता) चिता । funeral pyre.

चिति – स्त्री॰ – (चिति) ढेर । a heap, a cairn.

चित्त-सम्भूत-जातक – (जा॰ सं॰ 498) – चित्त तथा सम्भूत दोनों चण्डाल-भाइयों के जाति-अभिमानियों द्वारा पीटे जाने की कथा । the Jātaka story (No. 498) of two cāṇḍāla brothers who were beaten by caste-boasters.

चित्त (1) – न॰ – (चित्त) चित्त, मन, विचार । mind, thought.

चित्त (2) – न॰ – (चित्रम्) चित्र, तस्वीर । a picture, a portrait, a painting.

चित्त (3) – वि॰ – (चित्र) विचित्र । चित्र, विचित्र, सुन्दर । peculiar, wonderful.

चित्तक्खेप – पु॰ – (चित्तक्षेप) चित्त का विक्षेप । derangement of the mind.

चित्तपसादद्धि – स्त्री॰ – (चित्त प्रसादिता) चित्त की शान्ति । serenity of mind.

चित्त-मुदुता – स्त्री॰ – (चित्त-मृदुता) चित्त की कोमलता । plasticity of mind.

चित्तविक्खेप – पु॰ – (चित्त-विक्षेप:) विक्षिप्त । madness.

चित्त-समथ – पु॰ – (चित्त सामर्थ्य) विचारों का एकीकरण, चित्त की एकाग्रता । collectedness of thoughts.

चित्तानुपस्सना – स्त्री॰ – (चित्तानुपश्यना) विचारों का अनुचिन्तन-मनन । a critique of heart.

चित्ताभोग – पु॰ – (चित्ताभोग) विचार । a consideration.

चित्तुजुकता – स्त्री॰ – (चित्त-ऋजुता) चित्त का सीधापन । rectitude of mind.

चित्तुत्रास – पु॰ – (चित्त-त्रास) चित्त का त्रास, भय । terror, fear.

चित्तुप्पाद – पु॰ – (चित्तोदपाद) विचार का उदय । rise of a thought.

चित्तकत (1) – वि॰ – (चित्रकृत) सज्जित, चित्रित । adorned.

चित्तकत (2) – (चित्तकृत) चित्त द्वारा कल्पित । made by mind.

चित्तकथिक – वि॰ – (चित्रकथिक:) श्रेष्ठ-वक्ता । a brilliant speaker.

चित्त-कम्म – न॰ – (चित्र-कर्म) चित्रकला। drawing and painting, an art of painting.

चित्त-कार – पु॰ – (चित्रकार) चित्रकार। a painter.

चित्ततर – वि॰ – ($\sqrt{}$ चित्र – तर) अति विचित्र, विचित्रतर। more varied or diversified.

चित्तागार – न॰ – (चित्रागार) चित्रशाला, चित्रवीथी, चित्रागार। a picture gallery.

चित्तक – न॰ – (चित्रक) सम्प्रदाय बोधक तिलक जो मस्तक पर अंकित किया जाता हैं। a sectarian mark on the forehead.

चित्तक – पु॰ – (चित्रक) चित्तीदार मृग। spotted deer.

चित्तीकार – पु॰ – (चित्तार्पण) आदर, सत्कार। respectful consideration.

चिनाति – क्रि॰ – (चिनाति) ढेर लगाता है, संग्रह करता है। heaps, collects.

$\sqrt{}$ चिन्त – (भू॰) – चिन्तापं – ($\sqrt{}$ चिन्त् = चिन्तयति) चिन्तन करना। to think.

चिन्तक – पु॰ – (चिन्तक) सोचने वाला, विचारक। a thinker.

चिन्ता – स्त्री॰ – (चिन्ता) चिन्ता, विचार। thinking, thought.

चिन्तामणि – पु॰ – (चिन्तामणि) इच्छापूर्ति करने वाली मणि। a wish-fulfilling gem.

चिन्तामय – वि॰ – (चिन्तामय) चिन्तनयुक्त, विचार-युक्त। consisting of thoughts.

चिन्तित – कृ॰ – ($\sqrt{}$ चिन्त + क्त = चिन्तित) विचार किया हुआ, आविष्कृत। thought out, invented.

चिन्ती – (चिन्ती) (समास में) सोचता हुआ। (in compounds) thinking of.

चिन्तेतब्ब – कृ॰ – ($\sqrt{}$ चिन्त् + तव्यत् = चिन्तयितव्य) विचारणीय। fit to be considered.

चिन्तेति – क्रि॰ – ($\sqrt{}$ चिन्त् = चिन्तयति) सोचता है। thinks, consider.

चिन्तमान – कृ॰ – ($\sqrt{}$ चिन्त् + शानच् = विचिन्तमान) सोचता हुआ। remaining in thought.

चिन्तेय्य – वि॰ – (चिन्त्य) विचारणीय। fits be considered.

चिमिलिका – स्त्री॰ – (चिलिमिका) आच्छादान, आवरण (फारसी चिलमन)। a kind of cloth, a coverlet made from palm leaves, bark, etc.

चिर – वि॰ – (चिरम्) बहुत देर तक रहने वाला। lasting long.

चिरकालं – वि॰ – (चिरकालम्) दीर्घकाल। a long time.

चिरटिठृतिक – वि॰ – (चिरस्थितिक) चिर-स्थायी। lasting long, perpetual.

चिरतर – वि॰ – (चिरतरम्) और भी अधिक देर। a further long time.

चिरनिवासी – वि॰ – (चिर-निवासी) बहुत समय से रहने वाला। dwelling for a long time.

चिरपब्बजित – वि॰ – (चिर-प्रव्रजित) देर से प्रव्रजित। having long since become a monk.

चिरप्पवासी – वि॰ – (चिर-प्रवासी) चिर काल से प्रवास पर गया हुआ। a person long absent from his home.

चिरत्तं – वि॰ – (चिरत्वम) चिरकाल का भाव। a long time.

चिरत्ताय – वि॰ – (चिरत्वाय) चिरकाल के लिए । for a long time.

चिरं – क्रि॰ वि॰ – (चिरम्) चिरकाल तक । for a long time.

चिरस्सं – क्रि॰ वि॰ – (चिरस्यम्) अति बिलम्ब, अन्त में । a very long time, at last.

चिरातीत – वि॰ – (चिरातीत) चिरभूत (काल) । having passed a long time.

चिराय – क्रि॰ वि॰ – (चिराय) चिरकाल के लिए । for a long time.

चिरायति – क्रि॰ – (चिरायते) देर करता है । delays.

चिरायित – भूतकाल, past time.

चिरायन्त – (चिरायन्त) चिरभूत, delay.

चिरायित्वा – पूर्व क्रि॰ – (चिरायित्वा) भूत, past.

चिरेन – क्रि॰ वि॰ – (चिरेण) बहुत समय बाद । after a long time.

चिनं-पिट्ठ – न॰ – (चीन-पृष्ठ) लाल-सीसा । red lead.

चीन-रट्ठ – न॰ – (चीन राष्ट्र) चीन राष्ट्र । China.

चीर – न॰ – (चीरम्) छाल, छाल का कपड़ा । fibre, a bark dress.

चीरक – न॰ – (चीरकम्) देखिए - चीर । see Cīra.

चीरी – स्त्री॰ – (चीरी) झींगुर । a cricket.

चीवर – न॰ – (चीवर) बौद्ध भिक्षु का काषाय-वस्त्र । the saffron robe of a Buddhist monk.

चीवर-कण्ण – न॰ – (चीवर-कर्ण) चीवर का कोना । the lappet of a robe.

चीवर-कम्म – न॰ – (चीवर-कर्म) चीवर का बनाना । robe making.

चीवर-कार – पु॰ – (चीवर-कार) चीवर बनाने वाला । robe maker.

चीवर-दान – न॰ – (चीवर-दान) चीवर अथवा चीवरों का देना । donation of robes.

चीवर-दुस्स – न॰ – (चीवर-दुष्य) चीवर बनाने के लिए वस्त्र । cloth for making robes.

चीवर-रज्जु – स्त्री॰ – (चीवर-रज्जु) चीवर टाँगने की रस्सी । a rope for hanging the robes.

चीवर-वंस – पु॰ – (चीवर-वंश) चीवर टाँगने के लिए बाँस । bamboo for hanging up robes.

चुण्ण (1) – न॰ – (चूर्णम्) चूर्ण । powder.

चुण्ण (2) – न॰ – (चूर्णम्) पाउडर रूप में साबुन । soap-powder.

चुण्ण-विचुण्ण – वि॰ – (चूर्ण-विचूर्ण) चूर्ण-विचूर्ण, छोटे-छोटे कणों में खण्डित । crushed to bits, smashed.

चुण्णक – न॰ – (चूर्णक) सुगन्धित चूर्ण । a scented powder.

चुण्णक-जात – वि॰ – (चूर्णक-जातम्) चूर्ण किया हुआ । reduced to powder.

चुण्णक-चालनी – स्त्री॰ – (चूर्णक-चालनी) चूर्ण छानने की छलनी । a sieve.

चुण्णित – कृ॰ – (चूर्णित) चूर्ण किया हुआ, पीसा हुआ । powdered.

चुण्णेति – क्रि॰ – (चूर्णयति) चूर्ण कर डालता है । grinds to powder.

चुत – कृ॰ – (च्युत) स्खलित, गिरा हुआ । fallen.

चुति – स्त्री॰ – (च्युति) स्खलना, च्युत होना, अदृश्य हो जाना । shifting, vanishing.

चुदित – कृ॰ – (गर्हित) दोषारोपित । indited, accused.

चुदितक – पु॰ – (गर्हित / अभियुक्त) दोषारोपित । an accused, reproved.

चुद्दस – वि॰ – (चतुर्दश) चौदह । fourteen.

चुन्द – चुन्द नामक एक शिल्पी जो पावा का निवासी था। कुसीनारा के रास्ते में पावा पहुँचने पर भगवान् बुद्ध चुन्द 'कम्मार-पुत्त' के ही आम्रवन में ठहरे थे। उसी के यहाँ का भोजन भगवान् का अन्तिम भोजन सिद्ध हुआ । a smith living in Pāvā. When the Buddha reached Pāvā on his way to Kuśīnārā he stayed in Cunda's mango-grove. The meals taken at his home was the last meal of the Buddha.

चुन्दकार – पु॰ – (कुन्दिम्) कुँदेर, खरीदने वाला । a turner.

चुन्दभण्ड – न॰ – (कुन्द-भाण्डम्) कुँदेरी के उपकरण । the implements of a turner.

चुबुक – न॰ – (चिबुक) ठोड़ी । chin.

√चुम्ब – (भू॰) – वदन संयोगे – (√चुम्ब = चुम्बति) चूमना । to kiss.

चुम्बटक – न॰ – (चुम्बटक) गेण्डुरी । a coiled pad for putting vessels.

चुम्बति – क्रि॰ – (√चुम्ब = चुम्बति) चूमता है । kisses.

√चुर – (तु॰) – चोर्ये – (√चुर = चोरयति) चुराना । to steal.

चुल्ल – वि॰ – (चुल्ल) नन्हा, छोटा । small, minor.

चुल्लन्तेवासिक – पु॰ – (चुल्ल + अन्तेवासिकः) नन्हा शिष्य । little disciple, young disciple.

चुल्ल – पितु – पु॰ – (कनीयान्-पिता / पितृत्य) चाचा । uncle.

चुल्ल-उपट्ठाक – पु॰ – (लघु –सेवक) लघु-सेवक, निजी सेवक । a personal attendant.

चुल्लक-सेटिठ-जातक – (जा॰ सं॰ 4) – मरी चुहिया की पूँजी से आरम्भ करके, धन्ना सेठ व्यापारी बन जाने की रोचक कथा । the story (No. 4) of a merchant who started business with a dead mouse as capital and became rich later.

चुल्लकालिङ्ग-जातक – (जा॰ सं॰ 301) – कथा में वर्णित दन्तपुर नरेश कालिङ्ग की युद्ध-लिप्सा मनुष्य की बर्बरता का द्योतक है । the story (No. 301) gives an example how a proud man invites destruction for himself.

चुल्लकुणाल-जातक – देखें कुणाल जातक। see Kuṇāla Jātaka.

चुल्लधनुग्गह-जातक – (जा॰ सं॰ 374) – कथा बताती है कि लोलुप व्यक्ति अप्राप्त को पाने की लालसा में प्राप्त को भी गवाँ बैठता है । (story No. 374) The greedy man loses also that which is in his possession hankering for what is not with him.

चुल्लधम्मपाल-जातक – (जा॰ सं॰ 350) – पुत्र के प्यार में निमग्न रानी द्वारा पति के सत्कार में खड़ी न हो पाने की धृष्टता से क्रोधोन्मत्त नरेश पति ने ईर्ष्यावश पुत्र की बोटी-बोटी कटवा दी, पत्नी पुत्र-शोक में चल बसी तथा नराधम नृपति महल में लगी आग में भस्म हो गया। सच है कि क्रोध सर्वनाश का मूल है । (story No. 350) being lost in love for her young son the queen could not come forward to honour her husband. Seeing her insolence the king was so enraged that he cut the son to pieces and killed the queen too. Immediately the palace was ablaze and the king was burnt to ashes. It is true that the rage is the root cause of complete destruction.

चुल्लनन्दिय-जातक – (जा॰ सं॰ 222) – इस कथा का निष्कर्ष है कि नृशंस दूसरों को तो यातना देता ही है। अपना भी सर्वनाश कर डालता है। (story No. 222) the moral of this story is that a cruel man causes suffering for others as well as ruins himself too.

चुल्लनारद-जातक – (जा॰ सं॰ 477) – यह कथा तरुणी पर आसक्त तपस्वी-पुत्र के पुनः सुपथगामी होने का एक दृष्टान्त है। The story (No. 477) is of a hermit-son who was earlier indulged in a young woman later on returned to the sacred path.

चुल्लपदुम-जातक – (जा॰ सं॰ 193) – त्रिया-चरित्र की विलक्षणता दर्शाने वाली एक रोचक कथा। a very interesting tale (No. 193) of a beguiling woman.

चुल्लपलोभन-जातक – (जा॰ सं॰ 263) – यह कथा रमणियों के प्रलोभन तथा उसमें फँसने वाले पुरुषों की दुर्दशा का वर्णन करती है। the story (No. 263) tells about the wiles of woman and plights of the man who falls victim to her charms.

चुल्लबोधि-जातक – (जा॰ सं॰ 443) – कथा शिक्षा देती है कि व्यक्ति को क्रोध

नहीं करना चाहिए क्योंकि क्रोध जब जगता है तो उसे दबा पाना बहुत कठिन होता है। the story (No. 433) tells that one should not give way to anger because anger once awakened is difficult to be curbed.

चुल्लसुतसोम-जातक – (जा॰ सं॰ 525) – कथा बतलाती है कि भोग की सीमा और मर्यादा का समुचित ध्यान और तदनुरूप आचरण करने वाला सर्वत्र सम्मान पाता है। the story (No. 525) tells that one who realizes the limitation of enjoyment and the value of renunciation and acts accordingly is praised by all.

चुल्लहंस-जातक – (जा॰ सं॰ 533) – कथा बताती है कि उदारता स्वयं में एक वरदान है। उदार व्यक्ति के आगे क्रूर भी नतमस्तक हो जाते हैं। the story (No. 533) concludes that generosity is itself a reward.

चुल्ली – स्त्री॰ – (**चुल्ली/चुल्लिः**) चूल्हा। fireplace.

चूचुक – न॰ – (**चूचुक**) चूँची, स्तन का अगला भाग। nipple of breast.

चूलजनक-जातक – (जा॰ सं॰ 52) देखें महाजनक जातक। see Mahājanak Jātaka.

चूल-वग्ग – (**चूल-वर्ग**) विनय पिटक के दोनों खन्धकों में से दूसरा। the second of the two volumes known as the two Khandakas of the Vinaya Piṭaka.

चूळा – स्त्री॰ – (**चूडा**) सिर के बाल, जूड़ा। hair on the top of the head.

चूळामणि – पु॰ – (चूडामणि/चूडारत्नम्) चूड़े या जूड़े में पहनी जाने वाली मणि। jewel worn on top of the head.

चूलिका – स्त्री॰ – (चूडिका) बालों का गुच्छ। mass of hair.

चे – अव्यय – (च + इद् = चेद) यदि। if.

चेट – पु॰ – (चेट) सेवक, बालक। servant, a page boy.

चेटक – पु॰ – (चेटक) नौकर, गुलाम। servant, a slave.

चेटिका – स्त्री॰ – (चेटिका) सेविका, बालिका। a maid servant, aslove.

चेटी – स्त्री॰ – (चेटी) सेविका, बालिका। a maid servant.

चेत – पु॰ तथा न॰ – (चेतः) चेत, विचार, सोच, इरादा। thought, intention.

चेतक – पु॰ – (चेतक) वन्य जन्तु। a wild beast.

चेतना – स्त्री॰ – (चेतना) बुद्धि, मीत, ज्ञान। mind, intelligence or intellect knowledge.

चेतयति – क्रि॰ – (√चित् = चेतति) समझता है। understands.

चेतयति – क्रि॰ – (√चित् = चेतयते) सोचता है। thinks.

चेतस – वि॰ – (चेतस्) चित्त, अन्तःकरण, मन, सामासिक पदों में जैसे पाप-चेतस् = पापी मन। mind, intelligence, consiousness used in compounds as; pāpa-cetas.

चेतसिक – वि॰ – (चेतसिक) चैतसिक, चित्त-सम्बन्धी। mental, a mental property.

चेतापेति – क्रि॰ – अदला-बदली करता है। gets in exchange, barters.

चेतिय – न॰ – (चैत्य) चैत्य, धातु-गर्भ। a sepulchral monument, a *pagoḍā*.

चेतियङ्गण – न॰ – (चैत्याङ्गणम्) चैत्य का आंगन। the open space around a *pagoḍā*.

चेतिय-गब्भ – पु॰ – (चैत्य गर्भ) चैत्य का केन्द्रीय प्रकोष्ठ। the dome of a *pagoḍā*.

चेतिय-पब्बत – (चैत्य पर्वत) श्रीलंका स्थित चैत्य-पर्वत, आधुनिक मिहिम तल। name of a mountain in Ceylon.

चेतिय-जातक – (जा॰ सं॰ 422) – चेति-नरेश, अपचर तथा विश्व के प्रथम मिथ्यावादी की कथा। contains the story (No. 422)of Apacara, the king of Ceti and the world's first liar.

चेतिति – क्रि॰ – (चेतयति) देखें चेतयति। see Cetayati.

चेतोखिल – न॰ – (चित्त-हानि) चित्त-हानि। hollowness, waste of mind.

चेतोपणिधि – स्त्री॰ – (चेतसोपनिधि) संकल्प, निश्चय। resolution, aspiration.

चेतोपरिञ्ञाण – न॰ – (चेतस + परिज्ञानम्) दूसरों के मनोगत भावों का ज्ञान। understanding others thoughts.

चेतोपदास – पु॰ – (चित्त-प्रसादः) चित्त की प्रसन्नता। gladdening of heart.

चेतोविमुत्ति – स्त्री॰ – (चित्त-विमुक्ति) चित्त की विमुक्ति। emancipation of heart.

चेतोसमथ – पु॰ – (चित्तोपशमः) चित्त की शान्ति। calmness of mind.

√चेल – (भू॰) – चलने – (√चल् = चलति) चलना। to move, to walk.

चेल – न॰ – (चेलम्) परिधान, वस्त्र । cloth, garment.

चेल-वितान – न॰ – (चेल-वितानम्) चँदवा । an awning.

चेलुक्खेप – न॰ – (चेलोत्क्षेप) शाबासी में वस्त्रों का उछालना । waving of garments (as a sign of applause).

चोच – न॰ – (मोचम्/कदली फलम्) केले की फली । banana fruit.

चोच-पान – न॰ – (मोच-पानम्) केले से बनाया गया मधुर पेय । a sweet drink made of bananas.

चोदक – पु॰ – (चोदक) प्रेरक, दोषारोपक । impeller, one who censures or complains.

चोदना – स्त्री॰ – (चोदना) प्रेरणा, दोषारोपण । stimulation, reproof, accusation.

चोदित – कृ॰ – (√चुद् + क्त = चोदित) प्रेरित, दोषारोपित । stimulated, accused.

चोदेति – क्रि॰ – (√चुद् = चोदयति) उकसाता है, प्रेरित करता है, दोषारोपण की प्रेरणा करता है । incites, reproves, accuses.

चोपन (1) – न॰ – (चोपन) स्पन्दन, चलन । action, activity.

चोपन (2) – वि॰ – (चोपन) मन्द चाल पैदा करने वाला । causing slow motion.

चोर – पु॰ – (चौर) चोर, डाकू । thief, dacoit.

चोर-घातक – पु॰ – (चौर-घातक) जल्लाद । executioner of robbers.

चोर-उपद्दव – (चौर–उपद्रवः) डाकुओं के द्वारा किया जाने वाला आक्रमण । an attack from robbers.

चोरिका – स्त्री॰ – (चौर-कर्म) चोरी । theft.

चोरी – स्त्री॰ – (चौरिणी) चोरिणी, चोट्टी । a female thief.

चोळ – पु॰ – (चोल) बण्डी (जैकेट) नामक वस्त्र । a jacket.

चोळ-रट्ठ – न॰ – (चोल राष्ट्र) चोळ राष्ट्र बुद्धकालीन दक्षिण भारत का एक प्रदेश जिसमें आजकल तंजौर व त्रिचनापल्ली शामिल हैं । a nation of south India at the time of the Buddha. Presently it contains the districts of Tanjore and Trichinapalli (Tiruchirapalli).

चोळक – न॰ – (चोलकम्) (1) बण्डी, कवच (2) चीथड़ा । (1) jacket, armour (2) a piece of cloth, a rag.

चोळिय – वि॰ – (चोलिय) चोळ देश का । belonging to the Coḷa country.

छ

छ – पालि वर्णमाला का छठा व्यञ्जन। the sixth consonant of Pali alphabet.

छ – वि॰ – (षड्) छह। six.

छक्खत्तुं – क्रि॰ वि॰ – (षड्-कृत्वा) छ गुना, छह बार। six times.

छचत्तालीसति – स्त्री॰ – (षट्चत्वारिंशत्) छियालिस। forty-six.

छद्वारिक – वि॰ – (षड्द्वारिक) छह इन्द्रिय (पाँच ज्ञानेन्द्रिय छठा मन) से सम्बन्धित। belonging to the six outlets of the senses.

छनवुति – स्त्री॰ – (षण्णवतिः) छियानबे। ninety-six.

छपञ्ञास – स्त्री॰ – (षट्-पञ्चाशत्) छप्पन। fifty six.

छब्बाग्गिय – वि॰ – (षड्-वर्गीय) षडवर्गीय भिक्खु, बुद्ध के समकालिक छह भिक्षु जिनका बौद्ध ग्रन्थों में प्रायः उल्लेख हुआ है – अस्सजि, पुनब्बसु, पाण्डुक, लोहितक, मेत्तेय और भुम्मज। belonging to the groups of six *bhikkus* Assaji, Punabbasu, Pānduk, Lohitak, Metheya and Bhubbaj.

छब्बण्ण – वि॰ – (षड्-वर्ण) छह वर्णों का। consisting of six colours.

छब्बसिक – वि॰ – (षड्-वार्षिक) छह वार्षिक। existing throughout six years.

छब्बिध – वि॰ – (षड्-विध) छह प्रकार का। sixfold.

छब्बीसति – स्त्री॰ – (षड्-विंशति) छब्बीस। twenty-six.

छसट्ठि – स्त्री॰ – (षट्षष्टिः) छियासठ। sixty-six.

छसत्तति – स्त्री॰ – (षट्-सप्ततिः) छिहत्तर। seventy-six.

छक – न॰ – (छग) विष्ठा। dung.

छकन – न॰ – (छगण) सूखा गोबर, करसी। lumps of dry cow-dung.

छकल – पु॰ – (छगल) बकरा। goat.

छक्क – न॰ – (षडकम्) छह-छह का समूह। a set of six.

छट्ठ – वि॰ – (षष्ठ) छठा। sixth.

छट्ठी – स्त्री॰ – (षष्ठी) छठी, सम्बन्ध कारक सूचक षष्ठी विभक्ति। the sixth care, i.e., genitive case.

√छड्ड – (चु॰) – छड्डने (√क्षिप् = क्षिपति) फेंकना। throws.

छण – पु॰ – (क्षण) उत्सव-क्षण, त्योहार, उत्सव। a festival.

छत्त – न॰ – (छत्रम्) छाता, छतरी। umbrella.

छत्त – पु॰ – (छात्रः) छात्र, विद्यार्थी। student.

छत्तकार – पु॰ – (छत्रकार) छाता बनाने वाला। one who makes umbrella, a sunshade maker.

छत्त-गाहक – पु॰ – (छत्र-ग्राहक) अपने स्वामी का छत्र वहन करने वाला, छत्र-वाहक। one who carries his master's umbrella.

छत्त-नालि – स्त्री॰ – (छत्र-नालकम्) छाते की बेंत। the handle of an umbrella.

छत्त-दण्ड – न॰ – (छत्र-दण्डम्) देखें छत्त-नालि। see Chatta-nāli.

छत्त-पाणि – पु॰ – (छत्र-पाणि) देखें छत्त-गाहक। see Chatta-gāhaka.

छत्त-मङ्गल – न॰ –(छत्र-मङ्गलम्) मठ या चैत्य पर छत्र रोहण का उत्सव। coronation festival, pinnacle rising of a *pagoḍā*.

छत्त-उस्सापन – न॰ – (छत्र / क्षत्रोत्थापन) राजकीय छत्र का उठाना। raising of royal umbrella, coronation.

छत्तिंसति – स्त्री॰ – (षट्त्रिंशत्) छत्तीस। thirty-six.

√ छद – (चु॰) – संवरणे – (√ छद् = छादयति) ढकना, छिपाना। to cover.

छद – पु॰ – (छद्) आवरण, छदन, ढाकने का वस्त्र। anything that covers.

छदन – न॰ – (छद्मन्) मकान की छत। roof of a house.

√ छद्द – (चु॰) – वमने – (√ छर्द = छर्दयति छर्दति) वमन करना। to vomit.

छद्दन्त – वि॰ – (षड्दन्तः) छह दाँतों वाला। having six teeth.

छद्दन्त-जातक – (जा॰ सं॰ 514) – हस्ति-राज छद्दन्त की कथा बताती है कि जीवन दुःख और सुख दोनों के ताने-बाने से बुना जाता है। the story (No. 514) tells the life is entwined with joy and grief.

छद्दिका – स्त्री॰ – (√ छर्द /छर्दिका) वमन। vomitting.

छद्धा – क्रि॰ वि॰ – (षड्धा) छह प्रकार से। in six ways.

छधा – क्रि॰ वि॰ – (षड्धा) छह प्रकार से। sixfold.

छन्द – पु॰ – (छन्द) इच्छा, कामना। impulse, will, wish.

√ छन्द – (भू॰) – इच्छाएँ – (√ छन् = छन्दति) मौज करना। enjoy.

छन्द-राग – पु॰ – (छन्द-राग) उत्तेजक कामना। exciting desire.

छन्दक – न॰ – (छन्दक) अभिमत, चन्दा। vote a voluntary collection.

छन्दता – स्त्री॰ – (छन्दता) इच्छा, कामना। impulse, desire.

छन्दागति – स्त्री॰ – (छन्द + अगति) पक्षपात- पूर्ण व्यवहार। a wrong way of behaviour under impulse.

छन्न (1) – कृ॰ – (√ छद् + त = छन्न) ढका गया। covered.

छन्न (2) – वि॰ – (छन्द) ठीक, योग्य। proper, suitable.

छन्न – पु॰ – (छन्दक) गौतम के जन्म के दिन ही पैदा हुआ उनका सारथी तथा (बाद में) साथी। Gautama's charioteer and companion (later) born on the same day as Gautama.

छप्पञ्च – वि॰ – (षड्-पञ्च) छह या पाँच। six or five.

छप्पद – पु॰ – (षड्पद) मधु मक्षिका, शहद की मक्खी। a bee, honey-bee.

छमा – स्त्री॰ – (क्षमा) पृथ्वी, क्षमा। earth, indulgence, forgiveness.

छम्भति – क्रि॰ – (√ स्तम्भ् = स्तम्भते) भय से जड़ीभूत हो जाता है। becomes paralysed with fear.

छंरस – पु॰ – (षडरस्) भोजन के छह प्रकार के स्वाद–तिक्त, मधुर, खट्टा, कड़ुवा कसैला और नमकीन। the six main tastes and flavours of food.

छव – पु॰ – (शव) शव, लाश। a corpse.

छव-कुटिका – स्त्री॰ – (शव–कुटिका) श्मशान। cremation ground.

छवट्ठिक – न॰ – (शवस्थिकम्) कंकाल से पृथक् की गयी हड्डी। a bone separated from a corpre.

छव-दाहक – पु॰ – (शव–दाहक) शव जलाने वाला। one who officially burns the dead.

छवालात – न॰ – (शव + आलातम्) चिता की आग। fire from a pyre.

छवक-जातक – (जा॰ सं॰ 309) – the story (No. 309) tells about the origin of a custom that the learners, should sit on a higher seat and the preacher on the lower.

छवि – स्त्री॰ – (छवि) चमड़ी। the outer skin, tegument.

छवि-कल्याण – न॰ – (छवि–कल्याण) चमड़ी का सौन्दर्य। beauty of the skin.

छवि-वण्ण – पु॰ – (छवि–वर्ण) चमड़ी का रंग। beauty of complexion.

छळङ्ग – वि॰ – (षडङ्ग) छह अंगों से युक्त। consisting of six parts.

छळभिञ्ञा – स्त्री॰ – (षड् + अभिज्ञा) छह प्रकार के दिव्य ज्ञान। six branches of higher knowledge.

छळंस – वि॰ – (षडसं) छकोन, षटकोण। having six sides or corners.

छा – स्त्री॰ – (बुभुक्षा) भूख-प्यास। hunger and thirst.

छात – वि॰ – (बुभुक्षित) भूखा। hungry.

छातक – न॰ – (बुभुक्षा) भूख, अकाल। hunger, famine.

छादन – न॰ – ($\sqrt{छद्}$ + ल्यूट् = छादन) आवरण, आच्छादन, शरीर ढकने के वस्त्र। covering, clothing, concealment.

छादना – स्त्री॰ – ($\sqrt{छद्}$ = ल्यूट + टापू) आवरण, आच्छादन, शरीर ढकने के वस्त्र। covering, clothing, concealment.

छादनीय – कृ॰ – ($\sqrt{छद्}$ + अनीयर = छादनीय) ढकने योग्य। fit to be covered.

छादेतब्ब – कृ॰ – ($\sqrt{छद्}$ + तव्यत् = छादितव्य) अस्वीकार करना, ढका हुआ। to reject, covered.

छादेति – क्रि॰ – ($\sqrt{छद्}$ = छादयति) ढकता है। covers.

छाप – पु॰ – (शाव) पशु-शावक, पशुओं का छौना। the young one of an animal.

छापक – पु॰ – (शावक) पशु-शावक, पशुओं का छौना। the young one of an animal.

छाया – स्त्री॰ – (छाया) छाया, साया। shade, shadow.

छायामान – न॰ – (छायामान) छाया की माप। the measuring of shadow.

छायारूप – न॰ – (छायारूप) छाया-चित्र, फोटो। a photograph, portrait.

छारिका – स्त्री॰ – (क्षारिका) राख। ashes.

छाह – न॰ – (षड् + अहन् = षडाह) छह दिन। six days.

छि – अव्यय – (हि) निपात, निश्चयार्थ। surely.

छिग्गल – न॰ – (छिद्रल) छिद्रयुक्त। containing holes, pierced.

छिज्जति – क्रि॰ – (√ छिद् - णिच् = छिद्यते) कटता है। becomes cut or broken.

√ छिद – (रु॰) – द्वेधाकरणे – (√ छिद् = छिनाति) काटना। to cut.

छिद – वि॰ – (छिद्) सामासिक पदों में प्रयुक्त जैसे – बन्धन छिद = बन्धनों को छिन्न-भिन्न करने वाला। used in compounds as *bandhan + chid* = one who breaks the bond.

छिद्द – न॰ – (छिद्र) छिद्र, सूराख, दोष। a hole, a fault.

छिद्दक – वि॰ – (छिद्रक) दोषों अथवा छिद्रों वाला। having holes or pores.

छिद्दगवेसी – वि॰ – (छिद्रान्वेषी) दूसरों के दोष खोजने वाला। looking for other's faults or weak points.

छिद्दावच्छिद्दक – वि॰ – (छिद्रावछिद्रक) तमाम छिद्रों-दोषों से भरपूर। full of faults.

छिद्दित – कृ॰ – (छिद्रित) छेदा हुआ। perforated.

छिन्दति – क्रि॰ – (√ छिन्द् = छिन्दति) काटता है। cuts, destroy.

छिन्दिय – वि॰ – (छेद्य) जो काटा जा सके, जो टूट सके। can be cut, breakable.

छिन्न – कृ॰ – (√ छिद् + क्त = छिन्न) टूटा हुआ, नष्ट हुआ। cut, destroyed.

छिन्नास – वि॰ – (छिन्नाश) भग्नाश, निराश। hopeless.

छिन्ननास – वि॰ –(छिन्न + नासः) जिसकी नाक कटी हो। one whose nose is cut-off.

छिन्न-भत्त – वि॰ – (छिन्न-भत्त) छिन्नाहार, जिसे आहार न मिलता हो। starved, famished.

छिन्न-वत्थ – वि॰ – (छिन्न-वस्त्र) जिसके वस्त्र लुट गये हों। whose garments are taken by force.

छिन्न-हत्थ – वि॰ – (छिन्न-हस्त) जिसके हाथ काट लिये गये हों। whose hands are cut off.

छिन्न-इरियापथ – वि॰ – (छिन्न + ईर्यः) जो चल-फिर न सकता हो। unable to walk, a cripple.

√ छु – (तु॰) – सम्फस्से – (√ स्पश् = स्पृशति) छूना। to touch.

छुद्ध – कृ॰ – (√ क्षुभ + क्त = क्षुब्ध) क्षुब्ध, उत्तेजित। thrown away, rejected.

छुपति – क्रि॰ – (√ स्पश् = स्पृशति) स्पर्श करता है। touches.

छुपन – न॰ – (स्पर्शनम्) स्पर्श। touching.

छुरिका – स्त्री॰ – (क्षुरिका) छुरी, चाकू। a dagger, a knife.

छूरिका – स्त्री॰ – (क्षुरिका) छुरी, चाकू। a dagger, a knife.

छेक – वि॰ – (छेक) दक्ष, होशियार। clever, skillful.

छेकता – स्त्री॰ – (छेकता) दक्षता, होशियारी। cleverness, skill.

छेज्ज – वि॰ – (√ छिद् + यत् = छेद्य) काट डालने योग्य। fit to be cut-off, liable to break.

छेज्ज – न॰ – (छेदनम्) दण्डस्वरूप अंग-छेदन। punishment by cutting off one's limbs.

छेतब्ब – ($\sqrt{}$ छिद् + तव्यत् = छेद्रितव्य / छेतव्य) काट डालने योग्य। ought to be cut-off.

छेत्तु – पु० – (छेत्ता) काटने वाला। one who cuts.

छेत्वा – पूर्व क्रि० – (छित्वा) काटकर। having cut off.

छेत्वान – पूर्व क्रि० – (छित्वा) काटकर। having cut off.

छेद – पु० – (छेद) छेदन, काट। cutting, severing.

छेदक – पु० – (छेदक) काटने वाला। cutter, breaker.

छेदन – न० – (छेदन) काट। cutting, severing.

छेदापन – न० – (छेदायनम्) कटवाना। to get cut-off.

छेदापेति – क्रि० – (छेदयति) कटवाता है। gets cut-off.

छेदापेतब्ब – कृ० – (छेदयितव्य) कटवाने योग्य। to get cut-off.

छेप्पा – स्त्री० – (पुच्छः) पूँछ, दुम। a tail.

ज

ज – पालि वर्णमाला का आठवाँ व्यञ्जन। the eighth consonant of Pāli alphabet.

जगती – स्त्री॰ – (जगती) (जगति, समास पदों में ही) पृथ्वी, दुनिया। the earth, the world.

जगतिप्पदेस – पु॰ – (जगतिप्रदेशः) पृथ्वी का एक प्रदेश। a spot on the earth.

जगति-रुह – पु॰ – (जगतीरुह / भूरुह) वृक्ष। tree.

√जग्ग – (भू) – निद्दाखये – (√जागृ = जागत्ति) जागना। to wake up.

जग्गति – क्रि॰ – (जागर्त्ति) देख-भाल करता है, पोषण करता है, जागता है। watches over, nourishes, lies awake.

जग्गित्वा – पूर्व क्रि॰ – (जागरित्वा) जागकर। being woken up.

जग्गन – न॰ – (जागरण) जागरण। watchfulness.

जग्घति – क्रि॰ – (जग्घति / परिहसति) मजाक बनाता है। makes fun of, jokes.

जग्घना – स्त्री॰ – (जग्घन / परिहास) मजाक। joke, fun.

जग्घित – न॰ – (जग्घित / परिहसित) मजाक। joke, fun.

जङ्गम – वि॰ – (जङ्गम) चल (सम्पत्ति)। movable (property).

जङ्गल – न॰ – (जङ्गल) अरण्य, मरुस्थल। jungle, wilderness.

जङ्घ-मग्ग – पु॰ – (जङ्घामार्ग / चरणवीथिः) पगडण्डी। foot-path.

जङ्घापेसन – न॰ – (जङ्घाप्रेषण) पैदल द्वारा संदेश पहुँचाना। carrying messages on foot.

जङ्घपेसनिक – न॰ – (जङ्घप्रेषणिक) संदेश वाहक, हरकारा। one who carries messages on foot, mail runner.

जङ्घा – स्त्री॰ – (जङ्घा) जाँघ। the thigh, leg, hip.

जङ्घा-बल – न॰ – (जङ्घा-बलम्) जाँघ की शक्ति। strength of the leg.

जङ्घा-विहार – पु॰ – (जङ्घा-विहार) सैर, चहल-कदमी। a walk.

जङ्घेय्य – न॰ – (जङ्घेय्य) जाँघ-भर ढकने का वस्त्र। a knee-piece.

जच्च – वि॰ – (जात्य) जन्म-सम्बन्धी। having such a birth.

जच्चन्ध – वि॰ – (जन्मान्ध) जन्म से अन्धा। a blind from birth.

जच्चा – (जात्या) जन्म से। from birth.

जज्जर – वि॰ – (जर्जर) जरा से जर्जर। feeble with age, withered.

जञ्ञ – वि॰ – (जन्य) पवित्र, श्रेष्ठ, आकर्षक, कुलीन। pure, noble, charming, of good birth.

जट – न॰ – (जट) मूठ, मुठिया। the handle (of a knife, etc.).

जटा – स्त्री॰ – (जटा) जटा (केश) पेड़ों की उलझी डालियाँ (आलंकारिक अर्थ में) कामनाओं का उलझाव। tangle, plaiting, matted hair.

जटाधर – पु॰ – (जटाधरः) जटाधारी। an ascetic wearing matted hair.

जटित – कृ॰ – (√जट + क्त = जटित) उलझा हुआ। entangled, plaited.

जटी – पु॰ – (जटी) जटाधारी, तपस्वी। an ascetic wearing matted hair.

जटिल – पु॰ – (जटिल) जटाधारी, तपस्वी। see Jaṭī.

जठर – पु॰ तथा न॰ – (जठर) पेट। the belly, the stomach.

जठरग्गि – पु॰ – (जठराग्नि) जठराग्नि, भूख। fire in the stomach which aids digestion, hunger.

जण्णु – पु॰ – (जानु) घुटना। the knee.

जण्णुमत्त – वि॰ – (जानु-मात्र) घुटने तक आजानु। up to the knee.

जण्हु – न॰ – (जानु) घुटना। the knee.

जण्हुमत्त – वि॰ – (जानु-मात्र) घुटने तक। up to the knee.

जतु – न॰ – (जतु) लाख। lac.

जतुमट्ठक – न॰ – (जतु-मस्तकम्) सील-बन्द, लाखा-बन्द। (something) encased with lac.

जतुका – स्त्री॰ – (जतू) चमगादड़। a bat, vampire.

जत्तु – न॰ – (जत्रु) कंधा, कन्धे की हड्डी, हँसली। shoulder, a collar-bone.

जन – पु॰ – (जनः) व्यक्ति, लोग। a person, a man.

जन-काय – पु॰ – (जन-काय) जन समुदाय, जनता। a crowd of people.

जनपद – पु॰ – (जनपद) प्रान्त, जिला, देहात। a province, a district, country-side.

जनपद-कल्याणी – स्त्री॰ – (जनपद-कल्याणी) देश की सुन्दरतम तरुणी। the most beautiful girl in a country.

जनपद-चारिका – स्त्री॰ – (जनपद-चारिका) देश-भ्रमण। travelling in a country.

जनसम्मद्द – पु॰ – (जन-संमर्द) लोगों की भीड़। crowding of people.

जनक (1) – पु॰ – (जनक) उत्पन्न करने वाला, पिता। a producer, father.

जनक (2) – वि॰ – (जनक) उत्पन्न करता हुआ। producing.

जनन – न॰ – (जनन) उत्पत्ति। production.

जननी – स्त्री॰ – (जननी) माता, माँ। the mother.

जनसंध-जातक (जातक सं॰ 468) जनसंध की दानशीलता की कथा। the story of a king's righteousness.

जनाधिप – पु॰ – (जनाधिप) राजा। king.

जनालय – पु॰ – (जनालय) मण्डप। a pavilion.

जनिका – स्त्री॰ – (जनिका) माता, माँ। the mother.

जनित – कृ॰ – (√जन + क्त = जनित) उत्पन्न हुआ। born, generated.

जनिन्द – पु॰ – (जनेन्द्र) राजा। the king.

जनेति – क्रि॰ – (√जन् = जनयति) उत्पन्न करता है। generates, produces, gives birth.

जनेन्त – कृ॰ – (√जन् + शतृ = जनयन) उत्पन्न करता हुआ। producing, giving birth.

जनेत्वा – पूर्व क्रि. – (√ जन् + त्वा = जनयित्वा) उत्पन्न कर। having produced, having given birth.

जनेतु – पु. – (जनयिता) उत्पन्न करने वाला। producer, father.

जनेत्ती – स्त्री. – (जनयित्री) माँ। the mother.

जन्ताघर – (वाष्पस्नान गृह) वाष्प स्नान का घर। a room for steam-bath.

जन्तु – पु. – (जन्तु) जीव। a creature.

जप – पु. – (जप) जपना। muttering of prayer.

जपति – क्रि. – (जपति) जाप करता है। utters the prayer repeatedly, repeats the name of a deity.

जपित – क्रि. – (√ जप् + त = जपित) जप किया हुआ। muttered, mumbled (prayer).

जपित्वा – कृ. – (√ जप् + त्वा = जप्त्वा) जप करके। having muttered.

जपा – स्त्री. – (जपा) जवाकुसुम, जपा, अड़हुल की एक किस्म जिसकी पंखुड़ियां लिपटी रहती हैं। china-rose, hibiscus flower.

जप्पना – स्त्री. – (जल्पना) लोभ, जल्पना। whispering.

जप्पा – स्त्री. – (जल्पना) देखें जप्पना। see Jappanā.

जम्बाली – स्त्री. – (जम्बालिनी) गंदा नाला। a dirty pool.

जम्बीर (1) – पु. – (जम्बीर) जँभीरी नींबू का पेड़। a kind of lemon plant.

जम्बीर (2) – न. – (जम्बीरम्) जँभीरी नींबू (फल)। a kind of lemon fruit which resembles an orange.

जम्बु – स्त्री. – (जम्बु) जामुन। the rose-apple, a kind of black plum, Eugenia Jambolana.

जम्बुक-जातक – (जा. सं. 535) – शेर की मित्रता प्राप्त कर शृगाल का अहंकार इतना बढ़ा कि शेर द्वारा मना किये जाने पर भी हाथी को युद्ध की चुनौती देकर प्राणों से हाथ धो बैठा। (story No. 535), getting the friendship of a lion the jackal was so proud that he challenged an elephant for fighting and was ultimately killed.

जम्बुखादक-जातक – (जा. सं. 294) – लोमड़ी की खुशामद के चक्कर में कौवे ने लोमड़ी के लिए फल गिराये। (story No. 294), the singers of each other's praises are discarded everywhere.

जम्बुदीप – पु. – (जम्बुदीप) एशिया महाद्वीप का प्राचीन भारतीय नाम। the ancient name of Asia.

जम्बु-सण्ड – (जम्बुषण्ड) जामुन का बगीचा। the *jāmun*-grove.

जम्बुक – पु. – (जम्बुक) गीदड़। jackal.

जम्बोनद – न. – (जाम्बुनद) स्वर्ण का प्रकार (जो जम्बू नदी से प्राप्त होता है)। gold (obtained from Jambu river).

जम्भ – वि. – (जम्भ) गँवार, निकृष्ट। vulgar, contemptible.

जम्भति – क्रि. – (√ जम्भू = जम्भति) जँभाई लेता है। yawns.

जम्भना – स्त्री. – (जम्भा) जँभाई। yawn.

जय – पु. – (जय) विजय। victory.

जयग्गाह – पु. – (जयग्रह) विजय-पाँसे का अनुकूल पड़ना। the lucky dice.

जय-पान – न॰ – (**जय-पानम्**) विजयोत्सव में सामूहिक मदिरापान। the drink of victory.

जय-सुमन – न॰ – (**जपा सुमन**) जवा-कुसुम, विजय सुमन। अड़हुल की एक प्रजाति। the red china rose, hibiscus flower.

जयति – क्रि॰ – (√ **जि = जयति**) जीतता है। wins, attains victory.

जयद्दिस-जातक – (जा॰ सं॰ 513) – कम्पिल्ल नरेश जयद्दिस के दो पुत्रों को एक चुड़ैल द्वारा खा डालने तथा तीसरे शिशु को ले जाकर पुत्र रूप में पालने तथा उक्त राजा के चौथे पुत्र द्वारा चुड़ैल की मृत्यु उपरान्त अपने तीसरे भाई के उद्धार की रोमांचक कथा। the sad story (No. 513) of the king of Kampilla whose two sons were eaten by an ogress, one newly born son was snatched and looked after by her as own son. The fourth son of the king sought his third brother when the ogress had died.

जया – स्त्री॰ – (**जया**) पत्नी। wife.

जया – स्त्री॰ – (**ज्या**) धनुष की डोरी। the string of a bow.

जयम्पति – पु॰ – (**जाया-पति-दम्पति**) पत्नी तथा पति। couple of husband and wife.

जर – पु॰ – (**ज्वर**) ज्वर। fever.

जरग्गव – पु॰ – (**जरद्गव**) बूढ़ा बैल। an old ox.

जरता – स्त्री॰ – (**जरता**) बुढ़ापा। old age, decay.

जरा – स्त्री॰ – (**जरा**) बुढ़ापा। old age.

जरा-दुक्ख – न॰ – (**जरा-दुःख**) बुढ़ापे का दुःख। suffering through the old age.

जरा-धम्म – वि॰ – (**जरा-धर्म**) ह्रास धर्म। subject to growing old or decaying.

जरा-भय – न॰ – (**जरा-भय**) बुढ़ापे का भय। fear of old age or decay.

जरूदपान-जातक – (जा॰ सं॰ 256) – धन के मोह में अधिक और अधिक खोदने वाले साथ्थों ने प्राण गँवाये। (story No. 256) the endless hunger for wealth leads the greedy to his ruins.

जल – न॰ – (**जलम्**) पानी। water.

जल-गोचर – वि॰ – (**जल-गोचर**) जल-चर, पानी में रहने वाला। aquatic animal.

जलचर – पु॰ – (**जलचर/मीनः**) मछली। fish.

जलज – न॰ – (**जलजम्**) पद्म, कमल। lotus.

जलद – पु॰ – (**जलद**) मेघ, बादल। cloud.

जलधि – पु॰ – (**जलधि**) वारिधि, समुद्र। ocean.

जल-निग्गम – पु॰ – (**जल-निर्गमः**) जल का बहाव, नाली। an outlet for water.

जलनिधि – पु॰ – (**जलनिधि**) समुद्र। ocean.

जलति – क्रि॰ – (**ज्वलित**) चमकता है, जलता है। shines, burns.

जलन – न॰ – (**ज्वलन**) चमक, जलन। shine, burning.

जलाधार – पु॰ – (जलाधार) जल-संग्रह-स्थल। reservoir, lake.

जलाबु – पु॰ – (जरायु) गर्भाशय। the placenta with the membrane enveloping the foetus.

जलाबुज – वि॰ – (जरायुज) मनुष्य की तरह के वे प्राणी जो जरायु से लिपटे हुए हैं। animal whose foetus is covered by a membrane, like in human beings.

जलासय – पु॰ – (जलाशय) पोखर, झील, पुष्करिणी। a lake, an artificial tank.

जलूका – स्त्री॰ – (जलूका) जोंक। a leech.

जल्ल – न॰ – (जल्ल) गन्दगी, कीचड़। wet-dirt, filth, slime.

जळ – वि॰ – (जड) जड़, अचेतन। stiff, inanimate.

जव – पु॰ – (जव) गति, शक्ति, तेजी। speed, energy, quickness.

जवति – क्रि॰ – (√जू = जवति) दौड़ता है। runs.

जवन – न॰ – (जवनम्) दौड़. race.

जवन-हंस-जातक – (जा॰ सं॰ 476) – यह कथा तथ्य का निरूपण करती है कि शरीर रचना के संघटकों के क्षय की गति संसार के किसी भी वेगवान पदार्थ की गति से तीव्रता है। the story (No. 476) concludes that the decay of elements of life is fleeter than any other thing of the world.

जव-सकुण-जातक – (जा॰ सं॰ 308) – कठफोड़े ने शेर के मुँह में फँसी हुई हड्डी निकालकर शेर की जान बचाई किन्तु कृतघ्न शेर ने इसे अपनी महान् उदारता बताई कि जबड़े के भीतर आकर भी उसे जीवित छोड़ दिया। the story (No. 308) is related to the ingratitude of a lion who was saved by a wood-pecker by removing the bone struck in the throat of the lion. Later the wood-pecker saw the lion eating the carcase of a buffalo and asked for a bone. The lion refused saying it was enough for him to have escaped death after putting his head into a lion's mouth.

जवनिका – स्त्री॰ – (जवनिका) परदा। curtain.

जवाधिक – पु॰ – (जवाधिक) शीघ्रगामी (घोड़ा)। extremely swift.

जहति – क्रि॰ – (√हा = जहाति) छोड़ता है। lives, gives up.

जागर – वि॰ – (जागरितृ) जागने वाला। wakeful, awake.

जागर-जातक – (जा॰ सं॰ 404) – इस कहानी का सारांश है कि कभी-कभी देखने में गंवार और बुद्धू प्रतीत होने वाले लोग भी विलक्षण ज्ञानी और प्रतिभावान प्रमाणित होते हैं। the story (No. 404) tells that sometimes such persons who seem to be laymen by appearance prove to be extra-ordinary geniuses.

जागरति – क्रि॰ – (√जाग्र = जागर्ति) जागता रहता है, पहरा देता है। wakes up, remains watchful.

जागरण – न॰ – (जागरण) जागते रहना। waking.

जागरिय – न॰ – (जाग्रत्) जागरणशील, जागरूक। conscious.

जागरियानुयोग – पु॰ – (जाग्रत् + अनुपयोग) जागते रहना। waking continuously.

जाणु – पु॰ – (जानु/जानुकम्) घुटना। the knee.

जाणु-मण्डल – न॰ – (जानु-मण्डल) टखना। knee-cap.

जाणु-मत्त – वि॰ – (जानु-मात्र/आजानु) घुटने तक। up to the knee.

जात – कृ॰ – (√जन् + क्त = जात) उत्पन्न, घटित। born, arisen.

जात – न॰ – (जात्) संग्रह, प्रकार। a collection, variety.

जात-दिवस – पु॰ – (जात-दिवस) जन्म-दिन। birth-day.

जात-रूप – न॰ – (जातरूप) सोना। gold.

जात-वेद – पु॰ – (जातवेद/जातवेदस्) अग्नि। fire.

जातस्सर – पु॰ तथा न॰ – (जातस्सर) एक प्राकृतिक झील। name of a natural lake.

जातक – न॰ – (1) जन्म-कथा (2) सुत्तपिटक के खुद्दक निकाय का दसवाँ ग्रन्थ, जिसमें बुद्ध के पूर्व-जन्मों की कथाओं का वर्णन है। (1) birth tales, (2) the tenth book of Khuddaka Nikāya of the Sutta Piṭaka containing tales of the former births of the Buddha.

जातकट्ठकथा – जातक की अट्ठकथा। इसमें जातक के पद्य भाग का सम्बन्धित गद्य विस्तार है। a commentary on the Jātaka. It comprises all the verses of the Jātaka and gives also in prose the stories connected with the verses.

जातक-भाणक – पु॰ – (जातक-भाणक) जातक कथा सुनाने वाले। a preacher of the Jātakas.

जातत्त – न॰ – (जातत्व) उत्पत्ति भाव। the fact of being born.

जाति – स्त्री॰ – (जाति) जन्म, पुनर्जन्म, जाति, वंश-परम्परा। birth, rebirth, race, nation, genealogy.

जाति-कोस – पु॰ – (जाति-कोश) जावित्री का छिलका। mace (of nutmeg).

जातिक्खय – पु॰ – (जाति-क्षय) पुनर्जन्म की संभावना का न रहना। destruction of the chance of being reborn.

जातिक्खेत्त – न॰ – (जाति-क्षेत्र) जन्म-स्थान। birthplace, the realm of rebirth.

जातित्थद्ध – वि॰ – (जात्याभिमानी) जन्माभिमानी। proud of (one's own) birth.

जाति-निरोध – पु॰ – (जाति-निरोध) पुनर्जन्म का निरोध। extermination of rebirth.

जाति-फल – न॰ – (जाति-फल) जावित्री। nutmeg.

जाति-मन्तु – वि॰ – (जातिमान) अच्छी जाति का, गुणवान। of good birth, having genuine qualities.

जाति-वाद – पु॰ – (जातिवाद) जाति (वंश-परम्परा) के सम्बन्ध में विवाद। discussion.

जाति-सम्पन्न – वि॰ – (जाति-सम्पन्न) अच्छी जाति का। of good birth, belonging to noble family.

जाति-सुमना – स्त्री॰ – (जाति-पुष्प) चमेली। jasmine.

जातिस्सर – वि॰ – (जातिस्मर) पूर्व जन्मों की स्मृति। remembering former births.

जाति-हिंगुलुक – न॰ – (जाति-हिङ्गुलुक) सेंदुर, ईंगुर। vermillion.

जातिक – वि॰ – (जातिक) जातिगत, जाति-सम्बन्ध। belonging to class, clan or nation of.

जातु – अव्यय – (जातु) निश्चय से। surely, undoubtedly.

जानन – न॰ – (जानन) ज्ञान, पहचान। knowledge, recognition.

जाननक – वि॰ – (जाननक) जानने वाला। knowing.

जाननीय – वि॰ – (जाननीय) जानने योग्य। what should be known.

जानपद (1) – वि॰ – (जानपद) जनपद सम्बन्धी। belonging to the country.

जानपद (2) – पु॰ – (जानपदः) ग्रामीण, देहाती। a rustic country folk.

जानपदिक – देखें – जानपद। see Jānapada.

जानाति – क्रि॰ – (√ ज्ञा = जानाति) जानता है। knows, finds out.

जानापेति – क्रि॰ – (√ ज्ञा + णिच् = ज्ञापयति) जनवाता है। makes known, informs.

जानि – स्त्री॰ – (जानि) समास के अन्त में प्रायः प्रयुक्त पत्नी (जाया)। sweet-heart, wife.

जानि-पति – पु॰ – (जानि-पति/जाया पति) पत्नी तथा पति। wife and husband.

जामातु – पु॰ – (जामाता) जँवाई। son-in-law.

जायति – क्रि॰ – (√ जन् = जायते) उत्पन्न होता है। becomes born.

जायत्तन – न॰ – (जायात्व) पत्नीभाव। the state of a wife.

जायन – न॰ – (जायन) जन्म। birth, arising.

जाया – स्त्री॰ – (जाया) पत्नी। wife.

जाया-पति – पु॰ – (जाया-पति/दम्पती) पत्नी तथा पति। wife and husband, couple.

जार – पु॰ – (जार) यार, उपपति। a paramour, a lover, an adulterer.

जारत्तन – न॰ – (जारत्वम्) यारी, उपपतित्व। the state of paramour.

जारी – स्त्री॰ – (जारिणी) छिनाल, उपपत्नी। an adulteress, woman of loose character.

जाल – न॰ – (जाल) (मछली पकड़ने का) जाल, उलझन। a net (for catching fish) entanglement.

जाल-पूपं – पु॰ – (अपूपः/पिष्टकः) पुआ। pancake.

जालक – पु॰ – (जालक) छोटा जाल, कोंपल। a small net, a bud.

जालक्खिक – न॰ – (जालाक्षि/जालरन्ध्र) जालरन्ध्र। mesh of a net.

जाला – स्त्री॰ – (ज्वाला) ज्वाला। flame.

जालाकुल – वि॰ – (ज्वालाकुल) ज्वालाओं से घिरा। surrounded by flames.

जालिक – पु॰ – (जालिक) जाल का उपयोग करने वाला मछुआ। a fisherman who uses a net.

जालिका – स्त्री॰ – (जालिका) लोहे की जाली का बना कवच। an armour made of iron-chains.

जालिनी (1) – स्त्री॰ – (ज्वालिनी/तृष्णा) तृष्णा। lust, desire.

जालिनी (2) – स्त्री॰ – (**जालिनी**) जालीदार खिड़की । a lattice-window.

जालेति – क्रि॰ – (**ज्वालयति**) जलाता है। kindles, causes to burn.

जिगिंसक – वि॰ – (**जिघत्सु**) खाने का इच्छुक । desirous of (consuming).

जिगिंसति – क्रि॰ – ($\sqrt{}$ **जि** + **घस्** = **जिघित्सति**) खाने की इच्छा करता है। desires to eat or consume.

जिगुच्छक – वि॰ – (**जुगुप्सक**) जुगुप्सा करने वाला, घृणा करने वाला । one who hates.

जिगुच्छति – क्रि॰ – (**जु** + $\sqrt{}$ **गुप्** = **जुगुप्सति**) घृणा करता है। hates, dislikes.

जिगुच्छन – न॰ – (**जुगुप्सा**) घृणा । disgust, abhorrence.

जिगुच्छना – स्त्री॰ – (**जुगुप्सना**) घृणा, अरुचि । hatred, disgust.

जिघच्छति – क्रि॰ – ($\sqrt{}$ **घस्** = **जिघत्सति**) भूखा होता है, खाना चाहता है। desire to eat.

जिघच्छा – स्त्री॰ – (**जिघत्सा**) भूख । hunger.

जिञ्जुक – पु॰ – (**जिञ्जुक**) गुञ्जा, जंगली घुँघची मुलेठी । wild liquorice.

जिण्ण – कृ॰ – (**जीर्ण**) बूढ़ा, क्षीण । old, decayed.

जिण्णवसन – न॰ – (**जीर्णवसन**) पुराना वस्त्र । old cloth.

जित – कृ॰ – ($\sqrt{}$ **जि** + **क्त** = **जित**) जीता हुआ, जीत लिया गया। conquered, subdued.

जितत्त – न॰ – (**जितत्व**) जीत, वि, आत्म-विजयी । one who has subdued one's senses.

जिति – स्त्री॰ – (**जिति / जयः**) जय, विजय । victory.

जिन – पु॰ – (**जिन**) विजेता, जीतने वाला, बुद्ध । the conquerer, the victor, the Buddha.

जिन-चक्क – न॰ – (**जिन-चक्र**) बुद्ध मत । the doctrine of the Buddha.

जिन-पुत्त – पु॰ – (**जिन-पुत्र**) बुद्ध-पुत्र, बुद्ध का शिष्य । a disciple of the Buddha.

जिन-सासन – न॰ – (**जिन-शासन**) बुद्ध की शिक्षा । the Buddha's teaching.

जिनाति – क्रि॰ – ($\sqrt{}$ **जि** = **जयति**) जीतता है । conquers, subdues

जिम्ह – वि॰ – (**जिह्म**) कुटिल, टेढ़ा, बेईमान । crooked, slant, dishonest.

जिम्हता – स्त्री॰ – (**जिह्मता**) कुटिलता । crookedness.

जिया – स्त्री॰ – (**ज्या**) धनुष की डोरी । a bow-string.

जिव्हा – स्त्री॰ – (**जिह्वा**) जीभ । the tongue.

जिव्हग्ग – न॰ – (**जिह्वाग्र**) जीभ का सिरा । the tip of the tongue.

जिव्हायतन – न॰ – (**जिह्वायतन**) रसेन्द्रिय, रसना । the organ of taste.

जिव्हाविञ्ञाण – न॰ – (**जिह्वा-विज्ञान**) जिह्वा के द्वारा प्राप्त ज्ञान । the cognition of taste.

जिव्हिन्द्रिय – न॰ – (**जिह्वेन्द्रिय**) जिह्वा । the sense of taste.

जीन – वि॰ – (**जीन**) हीन । diminished, wasted, deprived of.

जीमूत – पु० – (जीमूत) बादल। rain-cloud.

जीयति – क्रि० – (√जॄ = जीय्यते) जरा को प्राप्त होता है, बूढ़ा होता है, पुराना पड़ता है। becomes diminished, becomes old, decays.

जीरक – न० – (जीरकम्) जीरा। cummin seed.

जीरति – क्रि० – (√जॄ = जीय्यते) देखें जीयति। see Jīyati.

जीरण – न० – (जीरणम्/जीर्णता) जीर्णता। decaying, digestion.

जीरापेति – क्रि० – (√जॄ = णिच्) जरा प्राप्ति का कारण बनता है, हजम कराता है। causes to decay or digest.

जीव – पु० – (जीव) जीवन, आत्मा, जीव। the life, soul.

जीव-दन्त – पु० – (जीव-दन्त) जीवित हाथी के दाँत। the tusks of a living elephant.

जीवक – पु० – (जीवक) (1) जीने वाला (2) बुद्ध का समकालीन प्रसिद्ध वैद्य। (1) one who lives (2) a renowned physician at the time of Buddha.

जीवकम्बवन – न० – (जीवकाम्रवनम्) राजगृह का वह आम्रवन, जो जीवक ने बुद्ध प्रमुख भिक्षु संघ को दान कर दिया था। the famous mango-grove of Rājagṛha which was donated to Bhikku-saṅgha by Jīvaka.

जीवति – क्रि० – (√जीव = जीवति) जीता है। lives, subsists on.

जीवन – न० – (जीवन) जीना। living.

जीविका – स्त्री० – (जीविका) जीवन-यात्रा का साधन। livelihood.

जीवकं-कप्पेति – क्रि० – (जीविकां कल्पयति) जीविका चलाता हैं। gets one's living.

जीवित – न० – (जीवितम्) जीवन। life, span of life.

जीवितक्खय – पु० – (जीवित-क्षयः) जीवन की हानि। the dissolution of life, death.

जीवित-दान – न० – (जीवित-दान) जीवन का दान। saving of life.

जीवित-परियोसान – न० – (जीवित-पर्यवसान) जीवन का अन्त। the end of life.

जीवित-मद – पु० – (जीवित-मद) जीवन-मद। the pride of life.

जीवित-वृत्ति – स्त्री० – (जीवित-वृत्ति) जीविका, जीवन-वृत्ति। livelihood.

जीवित-संखय – पु० – (जीवित-क्षयः) जीवन का अन्त। the solution of life.

जीविताशा – स्त्री० – (जीविताशा) जीवन की आशा। desire for life.

जीवितिन्द्रिय – न० – (जीवितेन्द्रिय) जान, जीवन। the faculty of life, vitality.

जीवित-संसय – पु० – (जीवित-संशयः) जीवन के लिए खतरा। danger of life.

जीवी – पु० – (जीवि) जीने वाला (प्रायः समास में प्रयुक्त जैसे - दीर्घ-जीवी)। one who lives (in compounds) leading a life of.

जुण्ह – वि० – (जूर्णि) चमकदार। glowing fire, blaze, shining.

जुण्ह-पक्ख – पु० – (जूर्णि-पक्ष) शुक्ल पक्ष। moonlit fortnight, bright half of the month.

जुण्ह-जातक – (जा॰ सं॰ 456) – जातक कथा की शिक्षा है कि शासक को अधीनस्थ विद्वद् वर्ग के कथन की अनसुनी नहीं करनी चाहिए। the story (No. 456) reveals that the ruler should not neglect the intellectuals.

जुण्हा – स्त्री॰ – (जूर्णा) चाँदनी, चाँदनी रात का। moonlight, a moonlit night.

जुति – स्त्री॰ – (द्युति) द्युति, चमक। effulgence, brightness.

जुतिक – वि॰ – (द्युतिक) चमकदार। having brightness.

जुतिधर – वि॰ – (द्युतिधर) प्रकाशमान। resplendent, brilliant.

जुतिमन्तु – वि॰ – (द्युतिमान) दीप्तिमान, प्रकाशमान। brilliant.

जुहति – क्रि॰ – (√हु = जुहोति) आहुति डालता है। pours offering (libation) into fire.

जुहन – न॰ – (हवन) यज्ञ में आहुति डालना। pouring libation into fire.

जूत – न॰ – (द्यूत) द्यूत, जुआ। gambling.

जूत-कार – पु॰ – (द्यूतकार) जुआरी। gambler.

जे – निपात – (रे) नीच कुल की स्त्री को सम्बोधन करने के लिए अव्यय-पद। a particle, used to address a slave woman or a woman of low grade.

जेगुच्छ – वि॰ – (जुगुप्सित) घृणित। contemptible, loathsome.

जेगुच्छी – पु॰ – (जुगुप्सिक) घृणा करने वाला। hater, one who detests or avoids.

जेट्ठ – वि॰ – (ज्येष्ठ) ज्येष्ठ। elder, supreme, foremost.

जेट्ठतर – वि॰ – (ज्येष्ठतर) ज्येष्ठतर। older or senior.

जेट्ठ-भगिनी – स्त्री॰ – (ज्येष्ठभगिनी) बड़ी बहिन। elder sister.

जेट्ठ-भातु – पु॰ – (ज्येष्ठ भ्राता) बड़ा भाई। elder brother.

जेट्ठ-मास – (ज्येष्ठ-मास) ज्येष्ठ महीना। the month of Jeṭha, i.e., May June.

जेट्ठापचायन – न॰ – (ज्येष्ठापचायन) बड़ों का सम्मान। respect to the elders.

जेतब्ब – कृ॰ – (√जि + तव्यत् = जेतव्य) जीतने योग्य। fit to be conquered.

जेतवन – न॰ – (जेतवन) श्रावस्ती का वह प्रसिद्ध उद्यान जिसमें अनाथपिण्डिक का जेतवनाराम बना था। the famous garden of Śrāvastī, where the Jetavanārām of Anāthapiṇḍika was built.

जेति – क्रि॰ – (√जि = जयति) जीतता हैं। conquers, wins over.

जेतुमिच्छा – स्त्री॰ – (विजिगीषा) जीतने की इच्छा। the desire to win.

जेय्य – कृ॰ – (√जि + ण्यत् = जेय) जीतने योग्य। fit to be conquered.

जोतक – वि॰ – (द्योतक) द्योतक illuminating, one who makes clear.

जोतति – क्रि॰ – (√द्युत् = द्योतते) चमकता है। shines.

जोतन – न॰ – (द्योतन) चमक। shining

जोति (1) – स्त्री॰ – (द्युति, ज्योति) ज्योति, प्रकाश। light, radiance.

जोति (2) – न॰ – (ज्योतिष्) ज्योति-पिण्ड, तारा। a star.

जोति (3) – पु॰ – (ज्योति/स्फुलिङ्ग) ज्योति, स्फुलिंग, चिनगारी। a crystal generating heat.

जोति-पाषाण – पु॰ – (ज्योति-पाषाण) चकमक पत्थर। a crystal generating heat.

जोतिसत्थ – न॰ – (ज्योतिष-शास्त्र) नक्षत्र-शास्त्र, खगोल-विद्या। astronomy.

जोतेति – क्रि॰ – (द्योतयति) प्रकाशित करता है। illuminates, explains, makes clear.

झ

झ – पालि वर्णमाला का नवम् व्यञ्जन। the ninth consonant of Pāli alphabet.

झज्झरी – स्त्री. – झंझट। botheration, difficulty.

झत्वा – पूर्व क्रि. – (दग्ध्वा) जलाकर। having burnt.

झल्लिका – स्त्री. – (झिल्लिका) झींगुर, भृङ्गारी, झिल्ली। a cricket (insect).

झस – पु. – (झष) मछली। fish.

झसा – स्त्री. – (पुलागवल्ली) नागबाला, पान की लता। a betal creeper.

झाटल – पु. – (झाटुः) कण्ट गुल, काँटेदार झाड़ी। a thorny shrub.

झान – न. – (ध्यान) ध्यान। meditation.

झान-अङ्ग – न. – (ध्यान-अङ्ग) ध्यान का अङ्ग। a constituent of meditation.

झान-रत – वि. – (ध्यान-रत) ध्यान-रत। fond of meditation.

झान-विमोक्ख – पु. – (ध्यान-विमोक्ष) ध्यान द्वारा विमुक्ति। emancipation through meditation or contemplation.

झानसोधन-जातक – (जा. सं. 134) – इस कथा में "न संज्ञा, न-असंज्ञा" का विवेचन किया गया है। the story (No. 134) presents an explanation of consciousness unconsciousness.

झानिक (1) वि. – (ध्यानिक) (1) जिसने ज्ञान प्राप्त किया हो। (2) ध्यान-सम्बन्धी। (1) one who has obtained knowledge wisdom, (2) related to meditation.

झापक – पु. – (दाहक / धुक्षक) आग लगाने वाला। one who sets fire to.

झापन – न. – (दाहन / धावन) आग लगाना। setting fire to.

झापित – कृ. – (√दह् + क्त = दग्ध) जलाया गया। burnt.

झापियति – क्रि. – (√दह् + णिच् = दह्यते) जलाया जाता है। becomes burnt.

झापेति – क्रि. – (√दह् = दाहयति / √धुक्ष् = धुक्षते) जलाता है। burns.

झापेत्वा – पूर्व क्रि. – (√दह् + त्वा = दग्ध्वा) जलाकर। having burnt.

झाबुक – पु. – (झाबुक) पिचुल, झाऊ। *Tamarix Indica.*

झाम – वि. – (दग्ध) जला हुआ। burnt.

झामक – वि. – (दग्ध) जला हुआ। burnt.

झायक – पु. – (ध्यायी / ध्यानी) ध्यानी। one who meditates, meditator.

झायति (1) – क्रि. – (ध्यायते) ध्यान लगाता है। meditates.

झायति (2) – क्रि. – (धावयति) जलाता है। burns.

झायन (1) – न. – (ध्यान) ध्यान लगाना। being in meditation.

झायन (2) – न. – (धुक्षनम्) ज्वलन, दाहन। burning.

झायी – पु. – (ध्यायी) ध्यान लगाने वाला। burning.

ञ

ञ – पालि वर्णमाला का दसवां व्यञ्जन। the tenth consonant of Pāli alphabet.

ञत्त – न॰ – (ज्ञात) ज्ञात। known.

ञत्ति – स्त्री॰ – (ज्ञप्ति/विज्ञप्ति) विज्ञप्ति, घोषणा। announcement, declaration.

ञत्वा – पूर्व क्रि॰ – (√ ज्ञा + त्वा = जानकर) विज्ञप्ति, घोषणा। having known, having learnt.

ञाण – न॰ – (ज्ञान) ज्ञान, बुद्धि। wisdom, insight.

ञाण-करण – वि॰ – (ज्ञान-करण) ज्ञान देने वाला। enlightening.

ञाण-चक्खु – न॰ – (ज्ञान-चक्षु) ज्ञान की आँख। the eye of knowledge.

ञाण-जाल – न॰ – (ज्ञान्-जालम्) ज्ञान का जाल। the net of knowledge.

ञाण-दस्सण – न॰ – (ज्ञान-दर्शनम्) ज्ञान-दर्शन, सम्पूर्ण ज्ञान। perfect knowledge.

ञाण-विप्पयुत्त – वि॰ – (ज्ञान-विप्रयुक्त) ज्ञान-शून्य। void of knowledge.

ञाण-सम्पयुत्त – वि॰ – (ज्ञान-सम्प्रयुक्त) ज्ञान-युक्त। associated with knowledge.

ञाणी – वि॰ – (ज्ञानी) ज्ञानी। possesser of knowledge.

ञात – कृ॰ – (ज्ञात) ज्ञात, प्रसिद्ध, साक्षात्कृत। well known, realized.

ञातक – पु॰ – (ज्ञातृक) रिश्तेदार। kinsman, relative.

ञाति-कथा – स्त्री॰ – (ज्ञाति-कथा) रिश्तेदारों की चर्चा। talk about relatives.

ञाति-धम्म – पु॰ – (ज्ञाति-कर्त्तव्य) रिश्तेदारों का कर्तव्य। the duties of relatives.

ञाति-परिवट्ट – न॰ – (ज्ञाति-परीवर्त्त) रिश्तेदारों की मण्डली। the circle of relation, circle of relatives.

ञाति-पेत – पु॰ – (ज्ञाति-प्रेत) मृत रिश्तेदार। deceased relatives.

ञाति-व्यसन – न॰ – (ज्ञाति-व्यसन) रिश्तेदारों का दुःख। misfortune of relatives.

ञाति-सङ्ग्रह – पु॰ – (ज्ञाति-संग्रह) रिश्तेदारों के साथ सद्व्यवहार। good treatment towards kinsmen.

ञाति-सालोहित – पु॰ – (ज्ञाति-सलोहित) रक्त-सम्बन्धी। blood relation.

ञापन – न॰ – (ज्ञापन) घोषणा। announcement.

ञापेति – क्रि॰ – (ज्ञापयति) प्रकट करता है, घोषित करता है। announces, declares to the public.

ञाय – पु॰ – (ज्ञाय) विधि, पद्धति, उचित ढंग। method, system, right manner.

ञाय-पटिपन्न – वि॰ – (ज्ञाय-प्रतिपन्न) सुपथगामी। walking in the right-path.

ञेय्य – वि॰ – (ज्ञेय) ज्ञान का विषय। what should be understood or realized.

ञेय्य-धम्म – पु॰ – (ज्ञेय-धर्म) जिसे सीखना या जानना जरूरी हो। which must be understood.

ट

टण्क – पु॰ – (टङ्क) पत्थर काटने की छैनी।
an instrument to cut-stones.

टीका – स्त्री॰ – (टीका) व्याख्या। sub-
commentary.

टीकाचरिय – पु॰ – (टीकाकार)
अनुटीकाकार। sub-commentator.

ठ

ठत्वा – पूर्व क्रि॰ – ($\sqrt{}$ स्था + त्वा = स्थित्वा) खड़े होकर। having stood.

ठपन – न॰ – (स्थपनम्) स्थापित करना। setting up, placing, keeping.

ठपापेति – क्रि॰ – ($\sqrt{}$ स्था + णिच् = स्थापयति) स्थापित कराता है। causes to settle, fixes.

ठपित – कृ॰ – (स्थापित) स्थापित। placed, set-up, fixed.

ठपेति – क्रि॰ – (स्थापयति) रखता है, निश्चित करता है। placed, sets up, fixes.

ठपेत्वा – पूर्व क्रि॰ – ($\sqrt{}$ स्था + त्वा – स्थापयित्वा) रखकर, एक ओर करके। having placed, set aside.

ठान – न॰ – (स्थान) स्थान, कारण। place, locality, cause.

ठानसो – क्रि॰ वि॰ – (स्थानशः) सकारण। with reason.

ठानीय – न॰ – (स्थानीय) स्थानीय, स्थान देने योग्य। local, fit to be placed.

ठापक – वि॰ – (स्थापक) खड़ा रहने वाला, स्थापित करने वाला या रखने वाला। one who places or keeps.

ठायी – वि॰ – (स्थायी) स्थित हुआ, स्थायी। permanent, standing.

ठित – कृ॰ – (स्थित) स्थित। stood.

ठितक – वि॰ – (स्थितक) खड़ा होने वाला। one who stands.

ठितट्ठान – न॰ – (स्थित स्थान) जहाँ आदमी खड़ा था। the place where one was standing.

ठितत्त – न॰ – (स्थितत्व) स्थितत्व, वि॰ संयत। the fact of standing, self-controlled.

ठिति – स्त्री॰ – (स्थिति) स्थिति। stability, duration.

ठिति-भागीय – वि॰ – (स्थिति-भागीय) स्थायित्व से सम्बन्धित। lasting, connected with duration.

ठितिक – वि॰ – (स्थितिक) समास में प्रयुक्त निर्भय, स्थायी। used in compounds lasting, enduring.

ड

डसति – क्रि॰ – ($\sqrt{}$ **दंश = दंशति**) डंक मारता है। bites.

डसन – न॰ – (**दंशन**) डंक मारना। biting.

डह्यति – क्रि॰ – ($\sqrt{}$ **दह्** कर्म वा॰ = **दह्यते**) जलाया जाता है। becomes burnt.

डहति – क्रि॰ – ($\sqrt{}$ **दह्** = **दहति**) जलाता है। burns, sets fire to.

डंस – पु॰ – (**दंश**) डाँसा, डाँस। a gad-fly.

डाक – पु॰ तथा न॰ – (**शाक**) खाने योग्य पौधे। edible herbs.

डाह – पु॰ – (**दाह**) चमक, गरमी, जलन। glow, heat, inflammation.

डीयन – न॰ – (**डयनम्**) उड़ना। flying.

डेति – क्रि॰ – ($\sqrt{}$ **डी** = **डयते / डीयते**) उड़ता है। flys.

त

त (1) – पालि वर्णमाला का सोलहवाँ व्यञ्जन the sixteenth consonant of Pāli alphabet.

त (2) – सर्वनाम – *(तद् - सो - पुल्लिंग)* वह। he.

त (3) – सर्वनाम – *(तद् - स्त्रीलिंग - सा)* वह। she.

त (4) – सर्वनाम – *(तद् - नपु॰ - तद्)* वह (वस्तु)। that (article).

तक्क – पु॰ – *(तर्क)* विचार, तर्क। thought, reasoning, logic.

तक्क – न॰ – *(तक्र)* मट्ठा, पञ्च गोरसों में से एक। butter-milk.

तक्क-जातक – *(जा॰ सं 63)* – गंगा में डूबती हुई कामासक्त दुराचारिणी सेठ-कन्या ने उबारने वाले को ही मरवा देने का षड्यन्त्र रचा। the wicked woman planned to get her husband murdered for a new lover (story No. 63).

तक्कन – न॰ – *(तर्कणा)* तर्क करना, विचार करना। thinking, reasoning.

तक्कर (1) – पु॰ – *(तस्कर)* तस्कर, चोर। a thief.

तक्कर (2) – वि॰ – *(तत्करः)* कर्त्ता पुरुष। a doer.

तक्करू-जातक – देखें कक्करु जातक। see Kakkaru Jātaka.

तक्कल-जातक – *(जा॰ सं॰ 446)* – वसिट्ठक ने अपनी भार्या के कहने से अपने बूढ़े पिता को मारकर गाड़ देने की तैयारी की, किन्तु उसके सात वर्षीय पुत्र ने यहां एक और गड्ढा खोदा, पूछने पर बताया कि जब आप बूढ़े हो जायेंगे तो यह काम आएगा। इस प्रकार उसने अपने बाप की आँख खोल दी। the story (No. 446) tells that a villager Vāsiṭṭhaka who on the insistence of his wife got ready to kill his useless old father and bury in a pit but his seven years old son overheard the planning. The boy began digging another pit. On being asked the reason he said it was for his father when he should be too old to be supported. This remark opens Vāsiṭṭhaka's eyes.

तक्कसिला – स्त्री॰ – *(तक्षशिला)* गन्धार की राजधानी, यहीं प्रसिद्ध तक्षशिला विश्वविद्यालय था। the capital of Gandhār, it was famous for its reputed university.

तक्कसिला-जातक – देखें तेलपत्त जातक। see Telapatta Jātaka.

तक्कारी – स्त्री॰ – *(तक्कारी / अरणि)* वैजयन्ती, अरणि नामक अग्निमन्थ वृक्ष। the tree (a kind of *Acacia*).

तक्काल – न॰ – *(तत्काल)* उस समय। at the same time, immediate.

तक्कारिय-जातक – *(जा॰ सं॰ 481)* – ब्राह्मण ने अपनी चुप न रह सकने की सामर्थ्य के कारण जान को खतरे में डाला। the story (No. 481) tells how the talkative brāhmaṇa created a danger to his life by his bad habit of, talking too much.

तक्किकं – पु॰ – (तार्किक) तार्किक। a sophist, a logician.

तक्की – पु॰ – (तार्किक) देखें तक्किक। see Takkika.

तक्केति – क्रि॰ – (√तर्क् = तर्कयति) सोचता है, तर्क करता है। thinks, reasons, argues.

तक्कोल – न॰ – (तक्कोल) एक प्रकार की सुगन्धि। a kind of perfume.

तगर – न॰ – (तगर) सुगन्धित द्रव्य। a fragrant substance.

तगगरुक – वि॰ – (तद् + गरुक) उधर झुका हुआ। bent thereon.

तग्ध – अव्यय – (तग्घ) यथार्थ रूप से। an affirmative particle giving the sense of truly, surely.

तच – पु॰ – (त्वक्/त्वचा) चमड़ी। skin.

तच-गन्ध – पु॰ – (त्वक्-गन्ध) छाल की सुगन्ध। the smell of a bark.

तच-पञ्चक – न॰ – (त्वक्-पञ्चक) शरीर के केश, लोम, नख, दन्त तथा त्वचा, पाँच अव्यय। the five constituents of body, viz., *kesa, loma, nakha, danta* and *tvacā* (hair on the head, hair on body, nail, tooth and skin).

तच-परियोसान – वि॰ – (त्वक्-पर्यवसान) 'त्वचा' तक सीमित। limited by the skin.

तचसार-जातक – (जा॰ सं॰ 368) – कथा बतलाती है कि दूसरों के लिए गड्ढा तैयार करने वाला कैसे स्वयं ही उसमें जा फँसता है। the story (No. 368)

gives an instance how a wicked falls into the well which was dug by him for others.

तचुब्भव – वि॰ – (त्वगुद्भवः) त्वक्-निर्मित, छाल-निर्मित। rising from the skin, skin eruption.

तच्छ (1) – वि॰ – (तथ्य) सत्य, यथार्थ। true, real.

तच्छ (2) – न॰ – (तथ्यम्) सत्य। truth.

तच्छक – पु॰ – (तक्षक) बढ़ई, लकड़ी छीलने वाला। carpenter, chipper of wood.

तच्छति – क्रि॰ – (√तक्ष् = तक्षति) छीलता है। chips, chops, makes thin.

तच्छन – न॰ – (तक्षणम्) छीलना। chipping off.

तच्छनी – स्त्री॰ – (तक्षणी) बसूला। chip-axe.

तच्छसूकर-जातक – (जा॰ सं॰ 286) – कथा बताती है कि कैसे सूअर ने अपने साथियों को संगठित कर शेर को मार गिराया। the story (No. 286) tells how a boar united his companions and succeeded in killing the tiger.

तच्छेति – क्रि॰ – (√तक्ष् = तक्षति) तराशता है, छीलता है। hews, chops.

तज्ज – वि॰ – (√तद् + ज = तज्ज) उससे उत्पन्न। arising from that.

तज्जना – स्त्री॰ – (तर्जना) तर्जना, भय का कारण। threat, menace.

तज्जनीय – कृ॰ – (√तर्ज् + अनीयर = तर्जनीय) तर्जना करने के योग्य। to be blamed or censured.

तज्जनी – स्त्री॰ – (तर्जनी) तर्जनी उँगली। pointing finger.

तज्जेति – क्रि॰ – (√ तर्ज् = तर्जति) तर्जना करता है, डराता है, धमकाता है। threatens, frightens.

तट (1) न॰ – (तट) (नदी का) तट। a river bank.

तट (2) – पु॰ – (तट) पर्वत या चट्टान की ढलान। slope of a mountain or rock.

तटतटायति – क्रि॰ – (तटतटायते) तट-तट शब्द करता है। makes the sound *taṭa-taṭa.*

तट्टक – न॰ – (तट्टक) थाली, तश्तरी, ताट (मराठी)। a tray, a porringer.

तट्टिका – स्त्री॰ – (तट्टिका) एक छोटी चटाई, बैठने के लिए छोटा चर्मासन। a small mat, a piece of hide to sit on.

तण्डुल – न॰ – (तण्डुल) चावल के दाने। rice grains.

तण्डुलनालि-जातक – (जा॰ सं॰ 5) – यह कथा बतलाती है कि अयोग्य के मूर्खतापूर्ण निर्णय किस प्रकार दूसरों की हानि करते हैं। the story (No. 5) tells how the stupidity of an incompetent man deprives others of their profit.

तण्डुल-मुट्ठि – पु॰ – (तण्डुल-मुष्टि) चावल की मुट्ठी। a handful of rice.

तण्हा – स्त्री॰ – (तृष्णा) कामना, स्पृहा, तृष्णा। craving, lust, attachment.

तण्हाक्खय – पु॰ – (तृष्णा-क्षयः) तृष्णा का क्षय। the destruction of craving.

तण्हा-जाल – न॰ – (तृष्णा-जाल) तृष्णा जाल। the snare of craving.

तण्हा-दुतिय – वि॰ – (तृष्णा-द्वितीय) तृष्णा सहित। for whom craving is like a companion.

तण्हा-पच्चय – वि॰ – (तृष्णा-प्रत्यय) तृष्णा द्वारा उद्भूत। caused by craving.

तण्हा-मूलक – वि॰ – (तृष्णा-मूलक) तृष्णा जिनके मूल में हो। craving-based.

तण्हा-विचारित – कृ॰ – (तृष्णा-विचारित) तृष्णा का विचार। thought of craving.

तण्हा-संखय – पु॰ – (तृष्णा-संक्षय) तृष्णा का मूलोच्छेद। complete destruction.

तण्हा-संयोजन – न॰ – (तृष्णा-संयोजन) तृष्णा का बन्धन। the fetter of craving.

तण्हा-सल्ल – न॰ – (तृष्णा-शल्य) तृष्णा-शल्य। the dart of craving.

तण्हीयति – क्रि॰ – (तृष्णायते) तृष्णा करता है। remains in thirst for.

तत – कृ॰ – (√ तन् + क्त = ततः) फैला हुआ, ताना हुआ। extended, spread out.

ततिय – वि॰ – (तृतीय) तृतीया। the third.

ततिया – स्त्री॰ – (तृतीया) तृतीया, तीसरी। the third.

ततियं – क्रि॰ वि॰ – (तृतीयम्) तीसरी बार। third time.

ततो – अव्यय – (ततः) वहाँ से, उससे, उस लिए। from there, from that, thereupon.

ततो-निदानं – क्रि॰ वि॰ – (ततः निदानम्) उस कारण से। on account of that.

ततो-पट्ठाय – अव्यय – (ततो-प्रस्थाय) उस समय से आरम्भ करके। thenceforth, since.

ततो-परं – अव्यय – (ततः परम्) उसके बाद । beyond that.

तत्त (1) – न॰ – (तत्त्व) तत्त्व, वास्तविकता । the real nature, reality.

तत्त (2) – कृ॰ – ($\sqrt{}$ तप् + क = तप्त) तप्त, तपा हुआ, संतृप्त । hot, heated, glowing.

तत्त-तो – अव्यय – (तत्त्वतः) वास्वविक रूप से । in fact.

तत्तक – वि॰ – (तत्त्वक/त्त्रक) उतने तक, उतने माप तक । that much, of such size.

तत्थ – क्रि॰ वि॰ – (तत्र) वहाँ, उस स्थान पर । there, at that place.

तत्र – क्रि॰ वि॰ – (तत्र) देखें तत्थ । see Tattha.

तथ (1) – वि॰ – (तथ्य) तथ्य । true, real.

तथ (2) – न॰ – (तथ्य) सत्य । truth, reality.

तथता – स्त्री॰ – (तथ्यता) वास्तविकता, सत्यता । reality, such likeness.

तथत्त – न॰ – (तथ्यत्व) सत्यता । reality.

तथवचन – वि॰ – (तथ्य-वचन) सत्य वचन । true word, spoken truth.

तथा – क्रि॰ वि॰ – (तथा) उसी प्रकार, वैसे । thus, so, in that way.

तथाकारी – वि॰ – (तथाकारी) वैसा करने वाला । acting in the same manner.

तथागत – वि॰ (तथागत) (1) भगवान् बुद्ध का स्वयं अपने लिए व्यवहृत वचन (2) जैसे आया अथवा गया । (1) an adjective used by lord Buddha for himself (2) the enlightened one.

तथागत-बल – न॰ – (तथागत–बलम्) तथागत की दस विशिष्ट शक्तियाँ । the supreme intellectual powers of a Tathāgata.

तथा-भाव – पु॰ – (तथा-भावः) वैसा-पन । suchness, such a condition.

तथा-रूप – वि॰ – (तथा-रूप) इस प्रकार का, इस रूप का । such like that.

तथेव – क्रि॰ वि॰ – (तथैव) वैसे ही । in the same way.

तदग्गे – क्रि॰ वि॰ – (तदग्रे) इससे आगे । henceforth.

तदङ्ग – वि॰ – (तदङ्ग) वह अंग, वह प्रकरण । that portion.

तदत्थं – अव्यय – (तदर्थः) उस उद्देश्य के लिए । for that purpose.

तदनुरूप – वि॰ – (तदनुरूप) उसके अनुरूप । conforming with that.

तदह-तदहु – न॰ – (तदह-तदहु) उसी दिन । the same day.

तदहुपोसथे – (तदहुपोसथव्रते) उसी उपोसथ व्रत के दिन । on the same fast-day.

तदा – अव्यय – (तदा) उस समय, तब । at that time, then.

तदुपिय – वि॰ – (तद् + उपेय) उसके अनुरूप, योग्य । agreeing with that, befitting.

तदुपेत – वि॰ – (तदुपेत) उसके साथ । endowed with that.

तनय – पु॰ – (तनय) पुत्र, सन्तान । a son, offspring.

तनया – स्त्री॰ – (तनया) पुत्री । daughter.

तनु (1) – वि॰ – (तनु) कृश, पतला, दुबला । thin, slender, diluted.

तनु (2) – स्त्री॰न॰ – (तनु) शरीर। body.

तनुकत – वि॰ – (तनु + कृत) कृश-कृत, दुबलाया हुआ। made thin.

तनुकरण – न॰ – (तनु + करण) कृश करना, दुबलाना। making thin.

तनुतर – वि॰ – (तनुतर) कृशतर, दुर्बलतर। a thinner.

तनुत्त – न॰ – (तनुत्व) तनुता, कृशता, पतले होने का भाव। a thinness, diminution, reduction.

तनुता – स्त्री॰ – देखें तनुत्त। see Tanutta.

तनु-भाव – पु॰ – (तनुभाव) देखें तनुत्त। see Tanutta.

तनु-रूह – न॰ – (तनोरुह) शरीर पर उगे बाल। hair on the body.

तनोति – क्रि॰ – ($\sqrt{}$ तनू = तनोति) तानता है, फैलाता है। spreads, stretches, extends.

तन्त – न॰ – (तन्तु) तागा, डोरा, धागा। thread, string a loom.

तन्तवाय – पु॰ – (तन्तुवाय) जुलाहा। a weaver.

तन्ताकुलकजात – वि॰ – (तन्त्वाकुलित) धागे की गेंद की तरह उलझा हुआ। entangled like a ball of string.

तन्ति (1) – स्त्री॰ – (तन्त्र) पंक्ति, परम्परा, पवित्र ग्रन्थ। line, a lineage, a sacred text.

तन्ति (2) – स्त्री॰ – (तन्त्री) वीणा, वीणा के तार। cord of a lute.

तन्ति (3) – (तन्ति) रस्सी। string.

तन्ति-धर – वि॰ – (तन्त्र-धर) परम्परा-संरक्षक। bearer of a tradition, traditionalist.

तन्तिस्सर – पु॰ – (तन्त्री-स्वर) तन्त्री का स्वर, सितार की संगीत। string music, sound of a lute.

तन्तु – पु॰ – (तन्तु) धागा। thread.

तन्दा – वि॰ – (तन्द्रा) आलस्य, प्रमाद, प्रमादी। weariness, sloth.

तन्दित – कृ॰ – (तन्द्रित) थका हुआ, सुस्त, अक्रियाशील। weary, lazy, inactive.

तप – पु॰ तथा न॰ – (तप) तपस्या। penance, religious austerity.

तपो-कम्म – न॰ – (तपः कर्म) तपस्या की क्रिया। ascetic practice.

तपो-धन – वि॰ – (तपोधन) तपस्या ही जिसका धन है, तपस्वी। one whose wealth is self-control, an ascetic.

तपोवन – न॰ – (तपोवन) तपस्या का स्थान। a place suitable for religious practices.

तपति – क्रि॰ – ($\sqrt{}$ तप् = तपति) चमकता है। shines.

तपन – न॰ – (तपन) चमक। shining, brightness.

तपनीय (1) – वि॰ – (तपनीय) अनुताप का कारण। cause of remorse.

तपनीय (2) – न॰ – (तपनीय) स्वर्ण, सोना। gold.

तपस्सी – पु॰ – (तपस्वी) तपस्वी, साधु। a hermit.

तपस्सिनी – स्त्री॰ – (तपस्विनी) तपस्विनी। a female hermit.

तपोदा – स्त्री॰ – (तपोदा) राजगृह के बाहर वैभार पर्वत के नीचे एक बड़ा जलाशय। name of a great lake near Vaibhāra mountain.

तप्पण – न॰ – (तर्पण) संतोष। satisfaction.

तप्पति – क्रि॰ – **(तप्यते)** जलता है, चमकता है, अनुतप्त होता है। burns, shines, becomes tormented by remorse.

तप्पर – वि॰ – **(तत्पर)** तत्पर, समर्पित। devoted to, quite given to.

तप्पित – कृ॰ – **(तृप्त)** संतर्पित, संतुष्ट। satiated, satisfied.

तप्पिय – वि॰ – **(तृप्य)** संतुष्ट करने योग्य। fit to be satisfied.

तप्पेति – क्रि॰ – **(तर्पयति)** तृप्त करता है, संतुष्ट करता है। satiates, satisfies.

तप्पेतु – कृ॰ – **(तर्पयितुम्)** संतुष्ट करने के लिए। for satisfying.

तब्बहुल – वि॰ – **(तद् बहुलम्)** प्रायः, अधिकतया वही। often.

तब्बिपक्ख – वि॰ – **(तद्-विपक्ष)** उसके विपक्ष में। antagonistic to that.

तब्बिपरीत – वि॰ – **(तद्-विपरीत)** उसके विपरीत। different from that.

तब्बिसय – वि॰ – **(तद्-विषय)** वही विषय। having that as an object.

तब्भाव – पु॰ – **(तद्-भाव)** वही भाव। that state, the real nature.

तम – पु॰ तथा न॰ – **(तम)** अन्धकार, अज्ञान। darkness, ignorance.

तमो-खन्ध – पु॰ – **(तमः + स्कन्ध)** निबिडतम, अन्धकार-समूह। great darkness.

तमो-नद्ध – वि॰ – **(तमः + नद्ध)** तमसाच्छन्न, अन्धकारच्छन्न। enveloped in darkness.

तमोनुद – वि॰ – **(तमोनुद)** अन्धकार को दूर करने वाला। dispeller of darkness.

तमो-परायण – वि॰ – **(तमो-पारायण)** अन्धकार में जाने की नियति वाला। having a state of darkness for his destiny.

तमाल – पु॰ – **(तमाल)** तमाल अथवा आबनूस नामक वृक्ष। the evergreen tree (catachu) xanthocymus epictorius.

तम्ब (1) – न॰ – **(ताम्र)** ताँबा। copper.

तम्ब (2) – वि॰ – **(ताम्र)** ताँबे के रंग का। copper-coloured.

तम्ब-केस – वि॰ – **(ताम्र-केशः)** ताम्र वर्णी केश वाला। having tawny hair.

तम्ब-चूल – पु॰ – **(ताम्र-चूड)** मुर्गा। cock.

तम्ब-नख – वि॰ – **(ताम्र-नख)** ताम्र-वर्ण नाखून वाला। having brown finger-nails.

तम्ब-नेत्त – वि॰ – **(ताम्र-नेत्र)** ताम्र वर्ण आँखों वाला। having brown eyes.

तम्ब-भाजन – न॰ – **(ताम्र-भाजन)** ताम्र बर्तन। a copper-vessel.

तम्बपण्णि – **(ताम्रपर्णी)** श्रीलंका का वह स्थान जहां गुजरात (भारत) के राजकुमार विजय सिंह का प्रथम पदार्पण हुआ और उनके द्वारा जिसे 'ताम्रपर्णी' नाम दिया गया। the name given to the district in Ceylon (Sri Lanka) where prince of Gujarat Vijai Singh landed for the first, time.

तम्बूल – न॰ – **(ताम्बूल)** पान का पत्ता। betel-leaf.

तम्बूल-पसिब्बक – पु॰ – **(ताम्बूल-प्रसेवक)** पान रखने की थैली। a purse to keep betel.

तम्बू-पेळा – स्त्री॰ – **(ताम्बूल-पेटिका)** पान की पेटी। a betel-box.

तय – न॰ – **(त्रय)** तीन। three.

तयी – स्त्री॰ – (त्रयी) वेद। the Vedas.

तय्यो – वि॰ – (त्रयः) तीन पुरुष। three men.

तयोधम्म-जातक – (जा॰ सं॰ 58) – यह कथा शिक्षा देती है कि जिसमें तीन विशेषताएं –॰ दक्षता, कौशल, पराक्रम और संसाधन है वह पराजित नहीं होता। the story (No. 58) tells that who ever combines the three qualities of dexterity, valour and resource can never be vanquished.

तर – पु॰ – (√ तृ = तरः) तरणी, नौका। boat.

तरङ्ग – पु॰ – (तरङ्ग) लहर। a wave.

तरच्छ – पु॰ – (तरक्षु) लकड़बग्घा। a hyena.

तरण – न॰ – (तरणम्) (तैरकर) पार जाना, उस ओर पहुँचना। going across, passing over.

तरणी – स्त्री॰ – (तरणी) तरी, नौका। ship, boat.

तरति – क्रि॰ – (√ तृ = तरति) तैरता है। crosses or passes over.

तरमान-रूप – वि॰ – (त्वरमाण-रूप) जल्दी में होना। being in a hurry.

तरल – न॰ – (तरला) काँजी, यवागु। watery, rice-gruel.

तरितु – पु॰ – (तरितृ/तरिता) पार जाने वाला। one who crosses or passes over.

तरी – स्त्री॰ – (तरी) नाव। boat.

तरु – पु॰ – (तरु) वृक्ष, पेड़। tree.

तरु-सण्ड – पु॰ – (तरुषण्ड) वृक्षों का समूह। grove of trees.

तरुण – वि॰ – (तरुण) नौजवान। young of tender age.

तल – न॰ – (तल) नीचे का, स्तर, चौपट स्थान, चपटी छत, किसी हथियार का फल। a flat surface, level ground, a flat roof, the blade of a weapon.

तल-घातक – न॰ –(तल-घात) हाथ की चपत। a slap with the palm of a hand.

तल-सत्तिक – न॰ – (ऊर्ध्वकरतलेन तर्जनम्) धमकी की मुद्रा में हथेली तानना। lifting the hand in a threatening form.

तलाक – पु॰ – (तडाग) तालाब। a tank, pond.

तलुण – पु॰ – (तलुण) देखें तरुण। see Taruṇa.

तस – वि॰ – (√ तस् + घञ् = तसः) चञ्चल, अस्थिर। movable, trembling.

तसर – पु॰ – (त्रसरः/सूत्र वेष्टनम्) फिरकी, जुलाहे की नाल। shuttle, for weaving.

तसति – क्रि॰ – (√ त्रस् = त्रसति) काँपता है, भयभीत होता है। trembles, becomes frightened.

तसिना – स्त्री॰ – (तृष्णा) तृष्णा। craving, thirst.

तस्सन – न॰ – (तर्षण) तृषा, पिपासा। thirst.

तहं – क्रि॰ वि॰ – (तत्र) वहाँ, उस स्थान पर। there, at that place.

तहिं – क्रि॰ वि॰ – (तत्र) वहाँ, उस स्थान पर। there, at that place.

ताण – न॰ – (त्राण) त्राण, शरण। protection, refuge, shelter.

तात – पु॰ – (तात) (1) पिता (2) पुत्र (स्नेहपूर्ण आमन्त्रण, बड़ों तथा छोटों, दोनों के लिए)। (1) father (2) son (used as a term of affection for both younger and older.

तादिस – वि० – (तादृक्/तादृश) तादृश, वैसा। such, of such quality.

तादिसक – वि० – (तादृश) देखें तादिस्। see Tādisa.

तापन – न० – (तापनम्) आत्म-क्लेश। scorching, self-mortification.

तापस – पु० – (तापस) तपस्वी। a hermit

तापसी – स्त्री० – (तापसी) तपस्विनी। a female ascetic.

तापित – कृ० – (तप्त) तपाया हुआ, संतृप्त। tormented, scorched.

तापेति – क्रि० – (तापयति) तपाता है, गरमी पहुँचाता है। torments, heats up.

तामबूली – (ताम्बूलिक/ताम्बूलिन) पनवाड़ी, तमोली। betel-leaf seller.

तामलित्ति – स्त्री० – (ताम्रलिप्ति) मिदनापुर जिले का तमलुक पत्तन जहाँ से अशोक ने बोधि वृक्ष की शाखा सिंहल भेजी थी। Tamluk port in Midnāpur district from where Aśoka had transported the branch of *bodhi* tree to Sri Lanka.

तायति – क्रि० – ($\sqrt{}$ त्रै = त्रायते) रक्षा करता है। protects.

तायन – न० – (त्राण) संरक्षण। protection.

तार – पु० – ($\sqrt{}$ तृ = तार) उच्च तीखा, ऊँची (आवाज)। very loud.

तारका – स्त्री० – (तारका) आकाश का तारा। a star.

तारा – स्त्री० – (तारा) आकाश का तारा। a star.

तारा-गण – पु० – (तारा-गण) तारा-समूह। the host of stars.

तारा-पति – पु० – (तारा-पति) चन्द्रमा। the moon.

तारा-पथ – पु० – (तारा-पथ) आकाश। the sky.

तारेतु – पु० – (तारयिता) संतरण में सहायक, संरक्षक। one who helps to cross, saviour.

ताल – पु० – (ताल) ताड़ का वृक्ष। fan-palm tree.

तालट्ठिक – न० – (तालास्थिक) ताड़ के भीतर की गुठली। the inner shell of a palm-nut.

ताल-कन्द – पु० – (ताल-कन्द) ताड़ की कोंपल। the sprout coming out of a palm-tree.

ताल-कन्द – पु० – (ताल-कन्द) कोलम्ब, प्याज जैसी कन्द वाला एक पौधा। a bulbous plant.

तालक्खन्ध – न० – (तालस्कन्ध) ताड़-वृक्ष का तना। the trunk of a palm tree.

ताल-पक्क – न० – (ताल-पक्व) ताड़ का फल। palm-nut.

ताल-पण्ण – न० – (ताल-पर्ण) ताड़ का पत्ता (लेखन हेतु)। palm-leaf (used for writing).

ताल-वन्त – न० – (ताल-वृन्त) ताड़ के पत्ते से बना पंखा। a fan (made of palm-leaf).

तालावत्थुकत – वि० – (उन्मूलित) जड़ से उखाड़ दिया गया। uprooted.

तालु – पु० – (तालु) तालु। the palate.

तालुज – वि० – (तालुज) तालव्य। palatal.

ताव – अव्यय – (तावत्) अब तक। so much, so far.

तावकालिक – वि॰ – (तावत्-कालिक) अस्थायी। for the time being.

तावतक – वि॰ – (तावतक) इतना ही, इतनी देर तक ही। just so much, just so long.

तावता – क्रि॰ वि॰ – (तावता) अब तक। so long, by that much.

तावतिंस – वि॰ – (त्रयस्त्रिंश) तैंतीस संख्या (केवल समास पदों में जहाँ 33 देवताओं का जिक्र हो)। thirty-three (used only in compounds to mention thirty-three gods).

तावतिंस-देवलोक – (त्रयस्त्रिंश-देवलोक) तैंतीस देवताओं का काल्पनिक देवलोक। mythical heavenly abode of thirty three gods.

तावतिंस-भवन – न॰ – (त्रयस्त्रिंश-भवन) तैंतीस देवताओं का भवन। the realm of 33 gods.

तावदेव – अव्यय – (तावदेव) उस समय, तुरन्त। at the moment, instantly.

ताल – पु॰ – (ताल) (1) चाबी (2) गीत की ताल। (1) a key (2) cymbal music.

तालच्छिद् – न॰ – (तालच्छिद्र) चाबी का छेद। key-hole.

तालावचर (1) – न॰ – (ताल+अवचरम्) संगीत। music.

तालावचर (2) – पु॰ – (ताल+अवचरः) संगीतज्ञ। musician.

तालन – न॰ – (ताडनम्) ताड़न, चोट पहुँचाना। beating, striking.

ताली – स्त्री॰ – (ताडने-पातः / आहतिः) चोट। a strike, a blow.

ताळेति – क्रि॰ – (√ताड़ = ताडयति) ताड़ना देता है। beats, flogs.

तास – पु॰ – (त्रास) त्रास, भय, कंपन। terror, fear, trembling.

तासेति – क्रि॰ – (√त्रस् + णिच् = त्रासयति) त्रास देता है। impales, frightens.

ति – वि॰ – (त्रि) तीन। three.

तिक – वि॰ – (त्रिक) तीन का समूह। consisting of three.

तिकटुक – न॰ – (त्रिकटुक) तीन कटु औषधियों, सोंठ, पिप्पली और काली मिर्च का मिश्रण। combination of three medicinal spices, i.e. black pepper, long pepper and dry ginger.

तिकिच्छक – पु॰ – (चिकित्सक) चिकित्सक। a physician.

तिकिच्छति – पु॰ – (चिकित्सति) चिकित्सा करता है। treats medically.

तिकिच्छा – स्त्री॰ – (चिकित्सा) चिकित्सा। the art of healing, medical practice.

तिक्ख – वि॰ – (तीक्ष्ण) तीक्ष्ण, तेज। sharp, acute.

तिक्खत्तुं – क्रि॰ वि॰ – (त्रिकृत्वा) तीन बार। three times.

तिक्खपञ्ञा – वि॰ – (तीक्ष्ण-प्रज्ञा) तीव्र प्रज्ञा वाला, कुशाग्र मति। having sharp intellect.

तिखिण – वि॰ – (तीक्ष्ण) तीक्ष्ण, तेज। sharp.

तिगावुत – वि॰ – (त्रि-गत्यूतिः) तीन गत्यूति की दूरी। measuring three *gavuta*s or about six mile.

तिगोचर – पु॰ – (त्रि-गोचर) तीन जनों द्वारा सुना गया शब्द। the word heard by three persons, hearsay.

तिचीवर – न० – (त्रिचीवरम्) भिक्षु के तीनों चीवर – अन्तःशाटक, मध्यम, उत्तरीय। the three robes of a *bhikku*, i.e., the inner, the under and upper.

तिदिव – पु० – (त्रिदिव) दिव्य लोक। heavenly abode.

तिदिवाधार – पु० – (त्रिदिवाधार) मेरु पर्वत। the Meru mountain.

तिदिवादिभू – पु० – (त्रिदिवादिभू) शक्र, देवेन्द्र। the Śakra or Indra, the king of gods.

तिपिटक – न० – (त्रिपिटक) तीन मञ्जूषाएं, पालि त्रिपिटिक (1) सुत्त-पिटक, (2) विनय-पिटक (3) अभिधम्म-पिटक। the three divisions of Buddhist canon Tripiṭakas, viz. (1) Sutta-piṭaka (2) Vinaya-piṭaka (3) Abhidhamma-piṭaka.

तिपुटा – पु० – (त्रिपुटा/त्रिकूटः) तेवरी, त्यौरी, कोपदृष्टि। frown, angry look.

तिपेटक-तिपेटकी – वि० – (त्रिपिटकज्ञ) त्रिपिटक का ज्ञाता। master of the three Piṭakas.

तियामा – स्त्री० – (त्रियामा) रात्रि। the night.

तियोजन – न० – (त्रियोजनम्) तीन योजन की दूरी। a distance of 3 leagues or six miles or ten kilometres.

तिरक्कार – पु० – (तिरस्कार) तिरस्कार, अपमान, अनादर। contempt, disrespect.

तिलिङ्गिक – वि० – (त्रिलिङ्गिक) जिस शब्द की गिनती तीनों लिङ्गों के अन्तर्गत हो। the word belonging to the three genders.

तिलिच्छ – पु० – (तिलिन्छ) सर्प-विशेष। a kind of snake.

तिलोक – पु० – (त्रिलोकम्) भू भुवः और स्वः (तीनों) लोक। the three worlds, earth, mid-air region, sky.

तिवग्ग – वि० – (त्रिवर्ग) त्रिवर्ग, जीवन के तीन परमार्थ-धर्म, अर्थ और काम। consisting of three divisions, i.e., *dharma*, *artha* and *kāma*.

तिवङ्गिक – वि० – (त्रयङ्गिक) जिसके तीनों अङ्ग हों। having three constituents (*aṅgas*) of *jñāna*.

तिवस्सिक – वि० – (त्रि-वार्षिक) तीन वर्ष का। three years old.

तिविज्जा – स्त्री० – (त्रिविद्या) त्रिविद्या, त्रयी अर्थात् वेद। the three sciences, i.e., the Vedas.

तिविध – वि० – (त्रिविध) त्रिविध, तीन प्रकार का। threefold, of three sorts.

तिट्ठति – क्रि० – (√ स्था = तिष्ठति) ठहरता है, स्थिर होता है। stays, remains.

तिण – न० – (तृण) तृण। grass.

तिणअण्डूपक – न० – घास का गद्दा। a roll of grass.

तिण-उक्का – स्त्री० – (तृणोल्का) तिनकों की मशाल। the torch made of grass.

तिण-गहण – न० – (तृण-ग्रहण) तृण-ग्रहण। a thicket of grass.

तिण-जाति – स्त्री० – (तृण-जाति) तिनकों की जाति। grass-creeper.

तिण-भक्ख – वि० – (तृण-भक्ष) तिनके खाकर रहने वाला। grass eater.

तिण-भिसि – स्त्री० – (तृण-बृशि) पुआल का बना गद्दा। a mat of grass, a pad of grass.

तिण-भुस – न॰ – (तृण-बुसभ) भूसा, करनी। chaff, litter, dry grass.

तिण-संथार – पु॰ – (तृण-संस्तार) तिनकों का बिछौना। the mat of grass.

तिण-हारक – पु॰ – (तृण-हारक) घास बेचने वाला, घसियारा। grass seller, one who carries grass for sale.

तिणागार – न॰ – (तृणागार) तिनकों की कुटिया। a cottage thatched with grass.

तिन्दुक-जातक – (जा॰ सं॰ 117) – देखें तिन्दुक जातक। see Tinduka Jātaka.

तिण्ण – क्रि॰ – (तीर्ण) तीर्ण, पार उतर गया। crossed over, gone through.

तिण्ह – वि॰ – (तीक्ष्ण) प्रखर, तेज। sharp.

तितिक्खति – क्रि॰ – (√ तिज् = तितिक्षते) सहन करता है, क्षमा करता है। endures, forbears.

तितिक्खाति – क्रि॰ – (तितिक्षा) क्षान्ति, सहनशीलता। endurance, patience.

तित्त (1) – वि॰ – (तिक्त) तिक्त, तीता, कड़ुवा। pungent, bitter.

तित्त (2) – कृ॰ – (√ तृप् + क्त = तृप्त) सन्तुष्ट। satisfied.

तित्तक – वि॰ – (तिक्तक) तिक्त, तीता, कड़ुवा। pungent, bitter.

तित्ति – स्त्री॰ – (तृप्ति) तृप्ति। satisfaction.

तित्तिर – पु॰ – (तित्तिर) तीतर। partridge.

तित्तिर-जातक – (जा॰ सं॰ 37) – तीतर, बन्दर और हाथी की कथा के माध्यम से परस्पर स्नेह-सम्मान पूर्ण व्यवहार की शिक्षा। the story (No. 37) tells the value of respect given to companions and elders.

तित्तिर-जातक – (जा॰ सं॰ 117) – बिना मतलब किसी को उपदेश देने का दण्ड। the story (No. 117) tells that how the habit of giving unsolicited advice causes miseries.

तित्तिर-जातक – (जा॰ सं॰ 319) – बहेलिए के पालतू तीतर का पश्चात्ताप जो आवाज करके अन्य तीतरों को बटोर कर बहेलिए का शिकार बनाता था। the story (No. 319) tells that an action becomes a crime only when performed with bad intention.

तित्तिर-जातक – (जा॰ सं॰ 438) – तीतर, गिरगिट और गाय की यह कथा "जैसी करनी वैसी भरनी" का दृष्टान्त है। this story related with a partridge, lizard, a cow and a crooked hermit repeats the saying, "as you sow so shall you reap."

तित्थ – न॰ – (तीर्थ) तीर्थ, पत्तन। a ford, harbour.

तित्थकर – पु॰ – (तीर्थं कर) सम्प्रदाय-विशेष का संस्थापक। founder of a religious order.

तित्थायतन – न॰ – (तीर्थायतन) सम्प्रदाय विशेष के सिद्धान्त। the fundamentals of doctrine.

तित्थ-जातक – (जा॰ सं॰ 25) – कथा बताती है कि बदलाव इस परिवर्तनशील जगत का आधारित तथ्य है। नित्य का अतिमधुर व्यञ्जन भी बिना बदलाव के अरुचिकर बन जाता है। the story (No. 25) reveals the natural law that a man will tire even the daintiest food if it is not changed.

तित्थिय – पु॰ – (तीर्थिक) बौद्धेतर मत का

संस्थापक। founder of non-Buddhistic doctrine.

तित्थय-सावक – पु० – (तिर्थिक श्रावक) बौद्धेतर मतानुयायी शिष्य। the pupil, follower of non-Buddhist doctrine.

तित्थियाराम – पु० – (तीर्थिकारामः) तपस्वियों का आश्रम। the monastery of hermits.

तिथि – स्त्री० – (तिथि) चन्द्र मास की तिथि। a lunar-day.

तिदस – पु० – (त्रिदश) देवता। gods.

तिदसपुर – न० – (त्रिदशपुर) देवनगर। the city of *deva*s.

तिदसिन्द – पु० – (त्रिदशेन्द्र) देवताओं का राजा। the king of gods.

तिदण्ड – न० – (त्रिदण्डम्) तिपाई। a three-legged table.

तिधा – क्रि० वि० – (त्रिधा) तीन तरह से। in three ways.

तिन्त – (आर्द्र / म्लिन्न) गीला, भीगा। wet, moist.

तिन्दुक – पु० – (तिन्दुक) तेंदूँ का पेड़। the tree *Diospyros embryopteris* (its fruit yielding a kind of resin).

तिन्दुक-जातक – (जा० सं० 177) – यह कथा बोधिसत्व की दूरदर्शिता और कार्य-निपुणता का दृष्टान्त है। the story (No. 177) is an illustration of the sagacity of a Buddhist.

तिपञ्ञास – स्त्री० – (त्रिपञ्चाशत्) तिरपन। fiftythree.

तिपल्लत्थ-मिग-जातक – (जा० सं० 16) – कथा का यही सारांश है कि अनुशासन न अति कठोर होना चाहिए और न अति शिथिल। the story (No. 16)

concludes that the rules for discipline should neither be very tight nor very loose.

तिपु – न० – (त्रपु) सीसा। lead.

तिपुस – न० – (कूष्माण्डः / कूष्माण्डकः) कद्दू। a pumpkin.

तिण्ह – वि० – (तीव्र) तीव्र। sharp, acute, piercing.

तिब्ब – वि० – (तीव्र) तीव्र। sharp, fast piercing.

तिमि – पु० – (तिमि) महामत्स्य। name of an enormous fish, whale.

तिमिंगुल – पु० – (तिमिंगल) विशालकाय मछली, जो छोटी मछलियों को निगल जाती है। kind of enormous fish, whale.

तिमिर – न० – (तिमिर) अँधेरा। darkness.

तिमिरायितत्त – न० – (तिमिरत्व) अँधेरापन। gloom, darkness.

तिमिस – न० – (तमिस्र) अँधेरा। darkness.

तिमिसिका – स्त्री० – (तमिस्रिका) घोर अँधेरी रात। a very dark night.

तिम्बरू – पु० – (तिन्दुक) देखें तिंदुक। see Tinduka.

तिरच्छान – न० – (तिरश्चीन) तिर्यग योनि वाले, पशु-कीट। animal, beast.

तिरच्छान-कथा – स्त्री० – (तिरश्चीन कथा) तिर्यग् कथा, कीट पशुओं से सम्बन्धित बतकही। the talk about insects and beasts.

तिरच्छानगत – पु० – (तिरश्चानुगत) तिर्यग योनि वाले, पशु। the beasts and animals in general.

तिरच्छान-योनि – स्त्री० – (तिरश्चीन-योनि) पशु-योनि। the beasts and animals collectively.

तिरियं – क्रि॰ वि॰ – (तिर्यञ्च) आड़े-तिरछे। lying crosswise.

तिरियं-तरण – न॰ – (तिर्यञ्च तरणम्) पार उतारना। ferrying across.

तिरीट – पु॰ – (तिरीट) तिलक नामक वृक्ष। the tree *Symplocos racemosa*.

तिरीटक – न॰ – (तिरीटक) तिरीट की छाल का बना आच्छादन। a garment made of the bark of the Tirīta.

तिरीटवच्छ-जातक – (जा॰ सं॰ 259) – कृतज्ञतासम्पन्न गुणी को सम्मानित होता देख खुशामदी उससे ईर्ष्या ही करते हैं। flatterers became jealous seeing the person who has saved the king's life being honoured by him as an obligation, (story No. 259).

तिरो – अव्यय – (तिरो) प्रायः समस्त पद के रूप में प्रयुक्त पार, बाह्य। across, beyond, outside.

तिरोकरणी – स्त्री॰ – (तिरोकरणी/जवनिका) परदा। curtain.

तिरोकुड्ड – न॰ – (तिरो कुड्यम्) दीवार के बाहर की ओर। outside the wall.

तिरोक्कार – पु॰ – (तिरस्कार) अपमान, तिरस्कार। insult.

तिरोधान – न॰ – (तिरोधान) पिधान, ढक्कन। a lid, a screen.

तिरोभाव – पु॰ – (तिरोभाव) अदृश्य होना। disappearance.

तिल – न॰ – (तिल) तिल। the sesame seed.

तिल-कक्क – न॰ – (तिल-कल्क) तिल का लेप। sesame-paste.

तिल-पिञ्ञाक – न॰ – (तिल-पिण्याक) तिल की खली। the cake obtained by grinding sesame.

तिल-पिट्ठ – न॰ – (तिल-पिष्टि) तिल की खली। sesame grinding.

तिल-मुट्ठि – पु॰ – (तिल-मुष्टि) तिलों की मुट्ठी। a handful of sesame.

तिल-मुट्ठि-जातक – (जा॰ सं॰ 252) – बच्चे को अपराधी प्रवृत्तियों में संलग्न होने से बचाने के लिए दण्ड की भूमिका कितनी महत्त्वपूर्ण होती है, इस पर यह कथा प्रकाश डालती है। this Jātaka tale (No. 252) elaborates the fruitful warning hidden in the saying "spare the rod and spoil the child."

तिल-वाह – पु॰ – (तिल-वाह) गाड़ी भर तिल। a cart-load of sesame.

तिल-सङ्गुलिका – स्त्री॰ – (तिल-सङ्गुलिका) तिल का लड्डू। sesame cake.

तिंसति – स्त्री॰ – (त्रिंशति) तीस। thirty.

तिंसा – स्त्री॰ – (त्रिंश) तीस। thirty.

तीर (1) – न॰ – (तीर) किनारा, तट। shore, riverbank.

तीर (2) – (तीर) बाण। an arrow.

तीर-दस्सी – (तीर-दर्शी) पार-द्रष्टा, तीर-द्रष्टा, अपने पथ को भली-भाँति जानने वाला। seeing the shore; well known of one's way.

√ तीर – (चु॰) – कम्मसमत्तियं – (√ तॄ) पार जाना, लक्ष्य पा लेना। to cross over, to attain an end.

तीरण – न॰ – (तीरण) निर्णय, निश्चय। certainty, estimation, conclusion.

तीरेति – क्रि॰ – (तरति) निश्चय करता है। concludes, makes certain.

तीरित – कृ॰ – (तीर्ण) निश्चय किया गया। decided, concluded, settled.

तीरेत्वा – पूर्व क्रि॰ – (तीर्त्वा) निश्चय करके। having made certain.

तीह – न॰ – (त्र्यहीन) तीन दिन का समय। three days time.

तु – अव्यय – (तु) जैसे-तैसे, लेकिन, अभी, अब, तब। however, but, yet, now, then.

तुङ्ग – वि॰ – (तुङ्ग) ऊँचा, प्रसिद्ध। high, prominent.

तुंग-नासिक – वि॰ – (तुङ्ग-नासिक) ऊँची नाक वाला। having a prominent nose.

तुच्छ – वि॰ – (तुच्छ) खाली, व्यर्थ, त्यक्त। empty, vain, deserted.

तुट्ठ – कृ॰ – (तुष्ट) संतुष्ट। satisfied.

तुट्ठि – स्त्री॰ – (तुष्टि) प्रसन्नता, प्रीति। pleasure, joy.

तुण्डक – न॰ – (तुण्डक) चञ्चु, चोंच। the beak, snout.

तुण्डिल-जातक – (जा॰ सं 388) – महातुण्डिल तथा चुल्ल-तुण्डिल, सूअर-पोतकों की कथा जो अवश्यम्भावी मृत्यु से भयभीत न होने का उपदेश करती है। the story (No. 388) tells that one should not always remain afraid of death which is unavoidable.

तुण्ण-कम्म – न॰ – (तुन्न-कर्म) जुलाहे का काम। weaving or tailoring.

तुण्ण-वाय – पु॰ – (तुन्नवाय) जुलाहा या दर्जी। a weaver or a tailor.

तुण्ही – अव्यय – (तूष्णी) चुप। silent.

तुण्ही-भाव – पु॰ – (तूष्णी-भाव) मौन। silence.

तुण्ही-भूत – वि॰ – (तूष्णीभूत) चुप। silent.

तुण्हीयति – क्रि॰ – (तूष्णीयति) चुप रहता है। remains silent.

तुत्त – न॰ – ($\sqrt{}$ तुद = तोत्र) हाथी को नियंत्रित करने का अंकुश। a pike for guiding elephants.

तुदति – क्रि॰ – ($\sqrt{}$ तुद् = तुदति/तुदते) चुभोता है। pricks, pierces.

तुदित – कृ॰ – ($\sqrt{}$ तुद + क्त = तुदित) चुभोया गया। pierced, pricked.

तुदन – न॰ – (तुदन) चुभोना। pricking.

तुदम्पति – वि॰ – (दम्पति) दम्पति, पत्नी-पति दोनों। couple (husband and wife).

तुमुल – वि॰ – (तुमुल) बड़ा, विशाल। grand, great.

तुम्ब – पु॰ तथा न॰ – (तुम्ब) तुम्बा। पके लौकी-फल से बना जल-पात्र। water-vessel made of bottle-gourd.

तुम्ब-कटाह – पु॰ – (तुम्ब-कटाह) लौकी का बर्तन। calabash or a vessel made of bottle-gourd.

तुम्बी – पु॰ तथा न॰ – (तुम्बी) लौकी, तुम्बी। long gourd, bottle-gourd.

तुम्ह – सर्वनाम (मध्यम पुरुष बहुवचन) – (यूयम्) तुम। you (the second personal pronoun).

तुम्हादिस – (युष्मादृश) तुम्हारे समान। of your kind.

तुरग – पु॰ – (तुरग) घोड़ा। horse.

तुरंग – पु॰ – (तुरङ्ग) अश्व, घोड़ा। a horse.

तुरंगम – पु॰ – (तुरङ्गम्) अश्व, घोड़ा। a horse.

तुरति – क्रि॰ – (√ **तुरण्** = **तुरण्यति**) जल्दी करता है। hastens.

तुरित – वि॰ – (**त्वरित**) शीघ्र। speedy, quick.

तुरितं – क्रि॰ वि॰ – (**त्वरितम्**) शीघ्रता से। quickly, in a hurry.

तुरिय – न॰ – (**तूर्य**) तुरही, तूर्य-बाजा। a musical instrument, bugle, trumpet.

तुरियंतर – न॰ – (**तूर्यन्तर**) वाद्य-विशेष। a musical instrument.

तुरुक्ख – वि॰ – (**तुरुष्क**) तुर्की से सम्बन्धित। belonging to Turkey.

तुलना – स्त्री॰ – (**तुलनम्**) तोलना, विचार करना। weighing, assessing, considering.

तुलसी – स्त्री॰ – (**तुलसी**) तुलसी का पौधा। the basil plant.

तुला – स्त्री॰ – (**तुला**) तराजू। balance, scales, a rafter.

तुलाकूट – न॰ – (**तुलाकूट**) खोटा तराजू। false weighing.

तुला-दण्ड – पु॰ – (**तुला-दण्ड**) तराजू की डण्डी। the beam of a balance.

तुलिय – पु॰ – (**तुलिय**) चमगदुरी, एक विशेष प्रकार का छोटा चमगादड़। flying, fox, mouse-tailed bat.

तुलिय – वि॰ – (**तुलीय / तुलनीय**) जो तोला जा सके। fit for weighing.

तुलेति – क्रि॰ – (**तोलयति**) तोलता है। weighs.

तुल्य – वि॰ – (**तुल्य**) (1) समान (2) जो तोला जा सके। (1) equal, (2) measurable.

तुल्यता – स्त्री॰ – (**तुल्यता**) समानता। equality.

तुल्ल – वि॰ – (**तुल्य**) देखें तुल्य। see Tulya.

तुवं – सर्वनाम – (**त्वं**) तू। you.

तुवटं – क्रि॰ वि॰ – (**त्वरितम्**) शीघ्रता से। quickly.

तुवटदेति – क्रि॰ – (**द्वन्द्वायति**) हिस्सा बाँटता है, भागीदार बनता है। shares with.

तुस्सति – क्रि॰ – (√ **तुष्** = **तुष्यति**) तुष्ट या संतुष्ट होता है। becomes glad or satisfied.

तुस्सना – स्त्री॰ – (**तुष्यणा / तोषण**) संतोष, प्रीति। satisfaction.

तुसित – न॰ – (**तुषित**) छह देवलोकों में से चौथा देवलोक। the fourth of the six deva-lokas.

तुहिन – न॰ – (**तुहिन**) ओस। dew.

तूण – पु॰ – (**तूर्ण / तूणीर**) तरकस। quicker.

तूणीर – पु॰ – (**तूणीर / तूण**) देखें तूण। see Tūna.

तूरिय – न॰ – (**तूर्य**) देखें तुरिय। see Turiya.

तूल – न॰ – (**तूल**) कार्पास, कपास, रूई। cotton.

तूल-पिचु – पु॰ – (**तूल-पिच्चु**) रूई, ऊन। cotton-wool.

तूलिका – स्त्री॰ – (**तूलिका**) (1) चित्रकार की तूलिका (2) रूई का गद्दा। (1) a painter's brush, (2) a cotton-mattress.

ते-असीति – स्त्री॰ – (**त्र्यशीतिः**) तिरासी। eighty-three.

ते-किच्छ – वि॰ – (**चिकित्स्य**) चिकित्सा किय जाने योग्य। curable.

ते-चत्तालीसति – स्त्री॰ – (त्रयश्चत्वारिंशत्) त्रिचत्वारिंश, तैंतालीस । forty-three.

ते-चीवरिक – वि॰ – (त्रि-चीवरक) त्रिचीवर वाला । using three robes.

तेज – पु॰ तथा न॰ – (तेज) ऊष्णता, प्रकाश । heat, radiance.

तेजो-धातु – स्त्री॰ – (तेजस्-धातु) ऊष्णता । the element of heat.

तेजो-कसिण – न॰ – (ध्यानार्थ आभामण्डल) ध्यान लगाने के लिए अग्नि प्रकाश या आभा-मण्डल । contemplation on fire for meditation.

तेजन – न॰ – (तेजनम्) तीर । an arrow.

तेजवन्तु – वि॰ – (तेजवन्त) तेजस्वी, तेजयुक्त । brilliant, glorious, majestic.

तेजित – कृ॰ – (शीशांसित) तेज किया हुआ । sharpened.

तेजेति – क्रि॰ – (√ शान = शीशांसित्र) प्रखर करता है । sharpens.

तेत्तिंसा – स्त्री॰ – (त्रयस्त्रिंशत्) तैंतीस । thirty-three.

तेन – अव्यय – (तेन) इस कारण से । on account of this, because of it.

तेन – हि॰ – अव्यय – (तेन हि) यदि ऐसा हो, ऐसा होने पर । if it is so.

ते-नवुति – स्त्री॰ – (त्रि-नवतिः) तिरानबे । ninety-three.

तेन-पञ्ञासति – स्त्री॰ – (त्रि-पञ्चाशत्/त्रयः पञ्चाशत्) तिरपन । fifty-three.

तेमन – न॰ – (क्लेदनम्) गीला होना, भीग जाना । wetting, moistening.

तेमियति – क्रि॰ – (√ क्लिद् = क्लिद्यति) भीगता है, गीला हो जाता है । gets wet.

तेरस-तेळस – वि॰ – (त्रयोदश) तेरह । thirteen.

तेरो-वस्सिक – वि॰ – (त्रय्-वार्षिकः) तीन वर्ष का । of three years.

तेल – न॰ – (तैलम्) तेल, स्निग्ध पदार्थ । oil.

तेल-घट – पु॰ – (तैल-घट) तेल का घड़ा । oil-jar.

तेल-चाटी – स्त्री॰ – (तैल-कुप्पम्) तेल का बर्तन । a pot for oil.

तेल-धूपित – वि॰ – (तैल-धूपित) तेल में छौंका गया । fried in oil.

तेल-पदीप – पु॰ – (तैल-प्रदीपः) तैल दीप । oil lamp.

तेल-मक्खन – न॰ – (तैल-म्रक्षणम्) तेल से बघारना । anointing with oil.

तेलक – न॰ – (तैलक) थोड़ा सा तिल । a little quantity of oil.

तेल पत्त-जातक – (जा॰सं 96) – कथा। का निष्कर्ष है कि इन्द्रिय-सुखों के फेर में लक्ष्य से विचलित न होने वाला ही सफलता के शिखर पर पहुँचता है । the story (No. 96) tells that one who does not succumb to the wiles of woman and constantly strives for one's object attains glorious victory.

तेलिक – पु॰ – (तैलिकः) तेली । a dealer in oil.

तेलोवाद-जातक – (जा॰ सं॰ 246) – कथा बतलाती है कि निन्दा-परिहास से उत्तेजित न होने वाला ही विजयी होता है । the story (No. 246) tells that who does not become agitated by sneering attains success.

तेसकुण-जातक – (जा० सं० 521) – कथा बुद्ध द्वारा कोसल नरेश प्रसेनजित को दी गयी चेतावनी से सम्बन्धित है। the story (No. 521) is related to the admonitions delivered by the Buddha to the king of Kosala.

तेसट्ठि – स्त्री० – (त्रिषष्टिः) तिरसठ। sixty-three.

तेसत्तति – स्त्री० – (त्रि-सप्ततिः) तिहत्तर। seventy-three.

तोमर – पु० तथा न० – (तोमर) एक आयुध, बर्छी। a spear, a lance.

तोय – न० – (तोयम्) जल। water.

तोरण – न० – (तोरण) तोरण-द्वार, अलंकृत बहिर्द्वार। an arched gateway, a decorative canopy.

तोस – पु० – (तोष) तुष्टि, प्रसन्नता, प्रीति। joy, satisfaction.

तोसना – स्त्री० – (तोषणा) संतोष। satisfaction.

तोसापेति – क्रि० – (√ तुष् + णिच् = तोषयति) तुष्ट करता है, प्रसन्न करता है। makes happy, pleases.

तोसित – कृ० – (तोषित) तुष्ट किया हुआ। having been satisfied.

तोसायमान – कृ० – (तोषायमाण) संतुष्ट किया जाता हुआ। being satisfied.

तोसयित्वा – कृ० – (तोषयित्वा) सन्तुष्ट करके। having satisfied.

त्वं – सर्वनाम – (त्वं) देखें – तुवं। see Tuvaṁ.

तोसेति – क्रि० – (तोषयति) संतोष देता है। gives satisfaction, satisfies.

त्यादो – वि० – (इत्यादयः) बहु, अनेक। many.

थ

थ – पालि वर्णमाला का सत्रहवाँ व्यञ्जन। the seventeenth consonant of Pāli alphabet.

थकन – न॰ – (स्तरणम्) ढक्कन, आच्छादन। covering.

√ थक – (चु॰) – (प्रतिघाते) रोकना। to obstruct.

थकेति – क्रि॰ – (√ स्तृ = स्तृणाति) बन्द करता है, ढकता है। closes, covers.

थकेसि – अतीत क्रि॰ – (अस्तृणात्) बन्द किया। closed, covered.

थकित – कृ॰ – (स्तरित) बन्द किया हुआ। closed, covered.

थकेन्त – कृ॰ – (स्तरन्) बन्द करता हुआ। closing, covering.

थकेत्वा – पूर्व क्रि॰ – (स्तृत्वा) बन्द करके। having closed or covered.

थञ्ञ – न॰ – (स्तन्य) स्तन्य, माँ का दूध। mother's milk.

थण्डिल – न॰ – (स्थण्डिल) कड़ी जमीन। hard or stony ground.

थण्डिल-सायिका – (स्थण्डिल-शायिका) नंगी जमीन पर लेटना (एक प्रकार की तपस्या)। lying on the bare ground (a kind of penance).

थण्डिल-सेय्या – स्त्री॰ – (स्थण्डिल-शय्या) नंगी जमीन पर बिस्तर। a bed on bare ground.

थद्ध – वि॰ – (स्तब्ध) कठोर, कड़ा, जड़ीभूत। hard, stiff, callous.

थद्ध-मच्छरी – पु॰ – (स्तब्ध-मत्सरः) अत्यन्त कंजूस। very miser.

√ थन – (चु) – देवसद्दे – (√ स्तन्) गरजना। the thunder.

थन – न॰ – (स्तन) स्त्री का स्तन, गौ-बकरी का स्तन। the breast of a woman, the udder of a cow, etc.

थनग्ग – न॰ – (स्तनाग्र) चूचुक, चूँची। the nipple of breast.

थनप – पु॰ – (स्तनपायी) स्तनपायी, शिशु। a sucking baby, an infant.

थनयति – क्रि॰ – (√ स्तन = स्तनयति) गरजता है। thunder, roars.

थनित – न॰ – (स्तनित) गर्जन। thunder, roar.

थनेति – क्रि॰ – (स्तनयति) गर्जता है। roars, thunders.

थनेसि – अतीत क्रि॰ – (अस्तानीत्) गरजा, गर्जना की। roaring, roared.

थनित – कृ॰ – (√ स्तन् + क्त = स्तनित) गर्जा हुआ। roared, thundered.

थनेन्त – कृ॰ – (स्तनन्) गर्जता हुआ। roaring thundering.

थनेत्वा – पूर्व क्रि॰ – (√ स्तन् + त्वा = स्तमित्वा) गरजकर। having thundered.

थपति – पु॰ – (स्थपति) (1) राज या थवई (2) बढ़ई। (1) mason (2) carpenter.

थबक – पु॰ – (स्तबक) गुच्छा। a bunch.

√ थम्भ – (भू॰) – पतिबन्धे – (स्तम्भ्) रोकना। to obstruct.

थम्भ – पु॰ – (√स्तम्भ) खम्भा, स्तम्भ। pillar post.

थम्भक – पु॰ – (स्तम्बक) घास की मुट्ठी। a clump of grass.

√थर – भू॰ – सत्थरणे – (√संस्तृ) फैलाना। to spread.

थरु – पु॰ – (त्सरु) तलवार (या अन्य किसी शस्त्र) की मूठ। the hilt or handle of a weapon.

थल – न॰ – (थल/स्थल) भूमि, जमीन। land, dry land.

थल-गोचर – वि॰ – (स्थल-गोचर) स्थल-निवास करने वाला। living on land.

थलज – वि॰ – (स्थलज/भूमिज) भूमि से उत्पन्न। sprung from land.

थलट्ठ – वि॰ – (स्थलस्थ) भूमि पर स्थित। situated on land.

थलपथ – पु॰ – (स्थल-पथ) स्थल-मार्ग। land route.

थव – पु॰ – (स्तवन्) प्रशंसा, स्तुति। praise, eulogy.

थवति – क्रि॰ – (√स्तु + स्तौति) प्रशंसा करता है। praises, extols.

थविका – स्त्री॰ – (स्तबिका) थैली। purse, knapsack.

थाम – पु॰ – (सत्त्वम्) सामर्थ्य, शक्ति। strength, power, vigour.

थामवन्तु – वि॰ – (सत्त्वशाली/सत्त्ववान्) सामर्थ्यवान् शक्तिशाली। strong, powerful, vigorous.

थाल – पु॰ तथा न॰ – (स्थालम्) थाल। a big plate, a big disc.

थाली – स्त्री॰ – (स्थाली) थाली। a plate, a dish.

थालक – न॰ – (स्थालीक) तश्तरी। a saucer.

थालिका – स्त्री॰ – (स्थालिका) प्यालानुमा कटोरा। a bowl.

थाली-पाक – पु॰ – (स्थाली-पाक) (दूध में) पका भात या जौ। boiled rice or barley (in milk).

थावर – वि॰ – (स्थावर) स्थावर, अचर, अचल। immovable (beings), firm.

थावरिय – न॰ – (स्थावरत्व) स्थिरपन, अचलपन। immovability, firmness.

थिर – वि॰ – (स्थिर) दृढ़। firm, lasting.

थिरता – स्त्री॰ – (स्थिरता) स्थिरता। firmness.

थिरतर – स्त्री॰ – (स्थिरतर) दृढ़तर। more firm, more lasting.

थी – स्त्री॰ – (स्त्री) स्त्री। a woman.

थी-रज – पु॰ तथा न॰ – (स्त्री-रज) स्त्रियों का मासिक धर्म। menstrual flux.

थीन – न॰ – (√स्त्यै + क्त = स्त्यान) जड़ता, आलस्य। impliability, unwieldiness.

√थु – (भू॰) – (अभित्थवे - √स्तु) स्तुति करना। to praise.

थु – (जु॰) – (अभित्थवे-√स्तु) स्तुति करना। to praise.

थुति – स्त्री॰ – (स्तुति) स्तुति। praise.

थुति-पाठक – पु॰ – (स्तुति-गायक) चारण भाट। a panegyrist.

थुनाति – क्रि॰ – (स्तनति) कराहता है। moans, groans.

थुनि (अतीत) – क्रि॰ – (अस्तानीत्) कराहा। moaned, groaned.

थुनंत थुनमान – कृ॰ – (स्तनयन) कराहता हुआ। moaning, groaning.

थुनित्वा – पूर्व क्रि॰ – (स्तनित्वा) कराहकर। having moaned or groaned.

थुल्ल – वि॰ – (स्थूल) स्थूल, मोटा विशाल। massive, fat, grave.

थुल्लच्चय – पु॰ – (स्थूल-वाच्यम्) बड़ा अपराध। a grave offence.

थुल्ल-कुमारी – स्त्री॰ – (स्थूल-कुमारी) स्थूल किशोरी, मोटी कुमारी। a fat girl.

थुल्ल-फुसितक – वि॰ – (स्थूल-वृष्टि) बड़ी-बड़ी बूँदों वाली वर्षा। raining with big drops.

थुल्ल-सरीर – वि॰ – (स्थूल शरीर) मांसल मोटे शरीर वाला। a corpulent.

थुस – पु॰ – (तुष) भूसी। chaff, husk of grain.

थुसग्गि – पु॰ – (तुषाग्नि) भूसी का आग। fire of husks.

थुस-पच्छि – स्त्री॰ – (तुष-करण्डकः) भूसी भरी डलिया। a basket to keep chaff.

थुस-सोडक – न॰ – (तुष-शुक्तम्) सिरके का एक प्रकार। a kind of vinegar.

थुस-जातक – (जा॰ सं॰ 338) – आचार्य ने बनारस राज्य के उत्तराधिकारी, अपने शिष्य, राजकुमार को चार गाथाएँ सिखा दी थी। उन्होंने ही उनकी जान बचाई। the story (No. 338) of a king who following the instructions of his teacher could save his life from his enemy-son.

थूण – पु॰ – (स्थूण) खम्भा, थूनी, लौह प्रतिमा पशुओं की। post, pillar, iron image.

थूण – (थानेश्वर) – (थानेश्वर) मज्झिम-देस की पश्चिम सीमा पर एक गाँव। वर्तमान थानेश्वर। modern Thaneshwar city near Delhi.

थूप – पु॰ – (स्तूप) स्तूप। श्रेष्ठ पुरुषों की भस्मी पर बनाया गया गुम्मदाकार समाधि भवन। a tope, *pagodā*, a monument erected over the remains of a holy person.

थूपारह – वि॰ – (स्तूपार्ह) स्तूप-निर्माण द्वारा पूजे जाने योग्य। one who should be honoured by erecting a tope.

थूप-वंस – वाचिस्सर रचित पालि रचना। इस काव्य के एक अंश में अनु-राधपुर के महास्तूप की रचना का वर्णन है। a Pāli poem written by Vācissara (which includes a description of the pagoda at Anuradhapura).

थूपिका – स्त्री॰ – (स्तूपिका) शिखर। a pinnacle, spire.

थूपीकत – वि॰ – (स्तूपीकृतः) स्तूप के आकार की भाँति निर्मित। method of construction of a pagoda.

थूल – वि॰ – (स्थूल) स्थूल। fat, massive.

थूलता – स्त्री॰ – (स्थूलता) स्थूलता। fatness, massiveness.

थूल-साटक – पु॰ – (स्थूल-शाटक) मोटा-वस्त्र। coarse cloth.

थेत – वि॰ – (विश्वस्त) विश्वसनीय। trustworthy.

√थेन – (चु॰) – (चोरिये – √स्तेन) चोरी करना। to steal.

थेन – पु॰ – (स्तेनः) चोर। thief.

थेनक – पु॰ – (स्तेनकः) चोर। thief.

थेनन – न॰ – (स्तेनम्) चोरी। theft.

थेनित – कृ॰ – (स्तेनित) चोरीकृत। stolen.

थेनेति – क्रि॰ – (स्तेनयति／स्तेनयते) चोरी करता है। steals.

थेनेसि, अतीत – क्रि॰ – (अतिस्तेनत्) चोरी की। committed theft.

थेनेन्त – कृ॰ – (स्तेनयन्) चोरी करते हुए। committing theft.

थेनेत्वा – पूर्व क्रि॰ – (स्तेनयित्वा) चोरी करके। having stolen.

थेय्य – न॰ – (स्तेय) चोरी। stealing.

थेय्य-चित्त – न॰ – (स्तेय-चित्त) चोरी का इरादा। intention to steal.

थेय्य-संवासक – वि॰ – झूठ-मूठ भिक्षुओं का वस्त्र धारण कर भिक्षुओं के साथ रहने वाला। one who lives clandestinely (with bhikkus).

थेर – पु॰ – (थेर) ज्येष्ठ भिक्षु, जो कम-से-कम दस वर्ष का उपसम्पन्न भिक्षु हो। a senior monk who has spent at least ten years in his order.

थेर-गाथा – स्त्री॰ – (थेर-गाथा) खुद्दक निकाय का आठवाँ ग्रन्थ। इनकी गाथाएँ बुद्ध के समकालीन भिक्षुओं की रचनाएँ मानी जाती है। the eighth book of the Khuddaka Nikāya. It is believed that the gāthās of this collection were compiled by Theras during the lifetime of Buddha.

थेर-वाद – पु॰ – (स्थविरवाद) स्थविरवाद, स्थविरों का सिद्धान्त। the doctrine of theras, the southern Buddhism.

थेरी – स्त्री॰ – (थेरी) ज्येष्ठ भिक्षुणी, बुढ़िया। a senior nun, an old woman.

थेरी-गाथा – स्त्री॰ – (थेरी-गाथा) खुद्दक निकाय की नौवीं रचना यह स्थविरियों की काव्य-कृतियों का संग्रह माना जाता है। the ninth book of Khuddaka Nikāya. It is a poetic collection of nuns.

थेव – पु॰ – (जल-बिन्दुः) वर्षा जल की बूँद। a drop of rain water.

थोक – वि॰ – (स्तोकम्) थोड़ा। a little, a few.

थोकं-थोकं – क्रि॰ वि॰ – (स्तोकं-स्तोकम्) थोड़ा-थोड़ा, तनिक-तनिक। little by little.

थोम – (चु॰) – सिलाघायं – (√इलाघ्) सराहना करना। to admire.

थोमन – न॰ – (स्तवन) श्लाघा स्तुति। praise.

थोमेति – क्रि॰ – (स्तौति／इलाघते) स्तुति करता है। praises.

द

द – पालि वर्णमाला का अठारहवाँ व्यंजन। the eighteenth consonant of Pāli alphabet.

दक – न० – (उदक) जल। water.

दक-रक्खस – पु० – (उदक-राक्षसः) जल-राक्षस। a water-spirit.

दक-रक्खस-जातक – (जा० सं० 546) – देखें महाउम्मग्ग जातक सं० 546। see Mahāumagga Jātaka no 546.

दकसीतलिक – न० – (उदकजं) श्वेत कुमुद, पुष्प। a white waterlily.

दक्ख – वि० – (दक्ष) निपुण, दक्ष, योग्य। clever, able, skilled.

दक्खक – वि० – (दर्शक) देखने वाला। on looker, viewer.

दक्खता – स्त्री० – (दक्षता) निपुणता, दक्षता। skill, ability.

दक्खति – क्रि० – ($\sqrt{}$ दृश् = पश्यति) देखता है। sees.

अदक्खि अतीत – क्रि० – (अपश्यत्) देखा। saw.

दक्खिण – वि० – (दक्षिण) दक्षिण, दाहिना, दायाँ। south, southern, right (side).

दक्खिणक्खक – वि० – (दक्षिणाक्षक) दाहिनी हँसली। the right collar-bone.

दक्खिण-दिसा – स्त्री० – (दक्षिण-दिक्) दक्षिण दिशा। the south.

दक्खिण-देस – पु० – (दक्षिण-देश) दक्षिण-देश। the southern country.

दक्खिणापथ – पु० – (दक्षिणापथ) (1) भारत का दक्षिणी महापथ (2) दक्षिण भारत। (1) the southern route (2) the Deccan or south India.

दक्खिणायन – न० – (दक्षिणायन) (सूर्य का) दक्षिणायन (पथ)। the southern course of the sun.

दक्खिणारह – वि० – (दक्षिणार्ह) दक्षिणा के योग्य। worthy of a dedicatory gift.

दक्खिणावत्त – वि० – (दक्षिणावर्त्त) दाहिनी ओर मुड़ना। winding to the right.

दक्खिणा – स्त्री० – (दक्षिणा) (1) दक्षिण (दिशा) (2) दक्षिणा। (1) south (2) fee paid to a holy person or priest.

दक्खिणा-विसुद्धि – स्त्री० – (दक्षिणा-विशुद्धि) दक्षिण की पवित्रता। purity of a gift.

दक्खिणोदक – न० – (दक्षिणोदक) दक्षिणा का जल। water of dedication.

दक्खिणेय्य – वि० – (दक्षिणेय) दक्षिणा देने के योग्य। worthy of an offering.

दक्खिणेय्य-पुग्गल – पु० – (दक्षिणेय-पुरुष) दक्षिणा का अधिकारी व्यक्ति। an individual deserving a donation.

दक्खी – पु० – (साक्षी) देखने वाला, अनुभव करने वाला। one who sees or perceives.

दट्ठ – कृ० – (दंशित) डसा गया। bitten.

दट्ठट्ठान – न० – (दंश-स्थान) वह स्थान जहाँ डसा गया। the place where one is bitten.

दट्ठ-भाव – पु॰ – (दंश-भाव) डसे जाने की बात। the fact of being bitten.

दड्ढ – कृ॰ – (√दह् + क्त = दग्ध) जला हुआ। burnt.

दड्ढट्ठान – न॰ – (दग्ध-स्थान) वह स्थान जो जल गया। the place which is burnt.

दड्ढ-गेह – वि॰ – (दग्ध-गेह) ऐसा आदमी जिसका घर जल गया हो। one whose house is burnt.

√दण्ड – (चु॰) – दण्डने – (दण्ड्) सजा देना। to punish.

दण्ड – न॰ – (दण्ड) (1) लकड़ी (2) सजा। (1) stick (2) punishment.

दण्डक-मधु – न॰ – (दण्डक-मधु) डाल पर लटका हुआ मधु का छत्ता। a beehive hanging on a branch.

दण्ड-कम्म – न॰ – (दण्ड-कर्म) सजा। punishment, penalty, atonement.

दण्ड-कोटि – स्त्री॰ – (दण्ड-कोटि) छड़ी की मूठ। the tip of a stick.

दण्ड-दीपिका – स्त्री॰ – (दण्ड-दीपिका) मशाल। a torch.

दण्डनीय – वि॰ – (दण्डनीय) जिसे दण्डित करना उचित हो। liable to be punished.

दण्डप्पत्त – वि॰ – (दण्ड-प्राप्त) जिसे दण्ड दिया गया हो। one who is prosecuted.

दण्ड-परायण – वि॰ – (दण्ड-पारायण) जिसे छड़ी का सहारा हो। supported by a staff, leaning on a stick.

दण्ड-पाणि – वि॰ – (दण्ड-पाणि) जिसके हाथ में घड़ी हो। carrying a stick in one's hand.

दण्ड-पाणि – (दण्डपाणि) शुद्धोदन की दोनों रानियों माया तथा प्रजापति का भाई। इसके पिता का नाम अंजन तथा माता का नाम यशोधरा था। he was the brother of Māyā and Prajāpati the queens of Śākya Śuddhodana. His father was Anjan and mother Yaśodharā.

दण्ड-भय – न॰ – (दण्ड-भय) दण्ड का भय। fear of punishment.

दण्ड-हत्थ – वि॰ – (दण्ड-हस्त) देखें दण्ड-पाणि। see Danda-Pāni.

दत्त – कृ॰ – (√दा + क्त = दत्त) दिया गया। given.

दत्ति (1) – स्त्री॰ – भोजन रखने के लिए छोटा सा बर्तन। a small vessel to keep food in.

दत्ति (2) – स्त्री॰ – (उपदा/उपायनम्) उपहार, भेंट। a gift, offering.

दत्तु – पु॰ – (दन्ध) मूर्ख आदमी। a stupid person.

दत्वा – पूर्व क्रि॰ – (√दा + त्वा = दत्त्वा) देकर। having given.

दद – वि॰ – (दद) समास में प्रयुक्त देता हुआ। giving, bestowing (used in compounds only).

ददित्वा – (√दा + त्वा = दत्त्वा) देखें दत्वा। see Dattvā.

ददाति – क्रि॰ – (√दा = ददाति) देता है। gives, bestows.

दद्दभ-जातक – (जा॰ सं॰ 322) – यह कथा बतलाती है कि बिना बिचारे, देखा देखी काम करने वाले (गतानुगतिक) लोगों का दृष्टान्त प्रस्तुत करती है। the story (No. 322) tells how people without applying their mind adopt a sheep-like habit.

दद्दर-जातक – (जा॰ सं॰ 172) – इस जातक का वही भाव है जैसा कवि तुलसी ने कहा था–"तुलसी पावस के समय, धरी कोकिला मौन। अब तो दादुर बोलिहैं हमें पूछिहैं कौन"। This Jātaka (No. 172) tale reveals that when the fool starts to preach the wise keeps mum.

दद्दर-जातक – (जा॰ सं॰ 304) – यह कथा धैर्य के गुणों पर प्रकाश डालती है। the tale (No. 304) points out the importance of patience.

दद्दरी – पु॰ – (दर्दरी) वाद्य विशेष। a musical instrument.

दद्दु – स्त्री॰ – (दद्रु) दाद। a disease of ring-worm, cutaneous eruption.

दद्दुर – पु॰ – (दर्दुर) मेंढक। frog.

दद्दुल – न॰ – (दद्दुल/दार्दुर) (1) स्पंज की तरह नरम ढाँचा (2) एक प्रकार का चावल। (1) soft skeleton similar to a sponge (2) a variety of rice.

दधि – न॰ – (दधि) दही। curds.

दधि-घट – पु॰ – (दधि-घट) दही का घड़ा। a pot of curds.

दधि-मण्ड – (क॰) – (दधि-भण्ड) मट्ठा, छाछ। whey, butter milk.

दधिवाहन-जातक – (जा॰ सं॰ 186) – कुसंग के दुष्परिणामों का चित्रण करने वाली एक प्रेरक कथा। this story (No. 186) illustrates the effects of evil association.

दन्त (1) – न॰ – (दन्त) दाँत। tooth, tusk, fang.

दन्त (2) – कृ॰ – (√दम् + क्त = दान्त) दमित, संयत। controlled, restrained.

दन्त-कट्ठ – न॰ – (दन्त-काष्ठ) दातुन। tooth cleaner made of the tender branch of neem or some other herbal plant.

दन्त-कार – पु॰ – (दन्तकार) हाथी दाँत का काम करने वाला। an artisan in ivory.

दन्त-पालि – स्त्री॰ – (दन्त-पालि) दाँतों की पंक्ति। row of teeth.

दन्तपोण – पु॰ – (दन्त) दाँत की सफाई करने वाली वस्तु। teeth cleaner.

दन्त-वलय – न॰ – (दन्त-वलय) हाथी दाँत की चूड़ी। an ivory bangle.

दन्त-विदंसक – वि॰ – (दन्त-विदर्शक) दाँत दिखाने वाला। showing one's teeth.

दन्तावरण – न॰ – (दन्तावरण) दन्तच्छद, दाँत का आवरण, होंठ। the lip.

दन्तपुर – न॰ – (दन्तपुर) कलिंग राज्य की राजधानी। the capital of Kaliṅga at the time of Buddha.

दन्तता – स्त्री॰ – (दान्तता) संयत-भाव। state of being restrained.

दन्त-भाव – पु॰ – (दान्त-भावः) संयत भाव। state of being restrained.

दन्तसठ (1) – पु॰ – (दन्ताघातम्) नींबू का फल। lemon fruit.

दन्तसठ (2) – न॰ – (दन्ताघातः) नींबू का पेड़। lemon tree.

दन्ध – वि॰ – (दन्ध) ढीला, मूर्ख। slow, silly, stupid.

दन्धता – स्त्री॰ – (दन्धता) ढिलाई, आलस्य, मूर्खता। stupidity, sluggishness.

दनु – पु॰ – (दनु) दानव माता। mother of *dānava*s, name of a daughter of Daksha.

√दप – (भू॰) – (√दा) दानगति हिंसादानेसु। to give, to donate, to hurt.

दप्प – पु॰ – (दर्प) दर्प। arrogance, wantonness.

दप्पण – न॰ – (दर्पण) दर्पण। a mirror, looking glass.

दप्पित – वि॰ – (दर्पित) अहंकारी, अभिमानी। arrogant, haughty.

दब्ब (1) – वि॰ – (द्रव्य) बुद्धिमान, योग्य। wise, able.

दब्ब (2) – न॰ – (द्रव्य) पदार्थ, धन, लकड़ी। substance, wealth, timber.

दब्ब-जातिक – वि॰ – (द्रव्य-जातिक) समझदार। intelligent.

दब्बतिण – न॰ – (दूर्वा-तृण) दूब नामक घास। a kind of grass, bent grass, panic grass, panicum dactylon.

दब्ब-पुप्फ-जातक – (जा॰ सं॰ 400) – रोहित मछली को लेकर दो ऊदबिलाव आपस में झगड़ रहे थे। मायावी गीदड़ फैसला करने गया उसने मछली का सिर एक को दिया, पूँछ दूसरे को दी, शेष बीच का मोटा हिस्सा स्वयं खा लिया। when two companions quarrel and request an outsider to arbitrate the case both find themselves losers by the cunningness of the arbitrator (story No. 400).

दब्ब-सम्भार – पु॰ – (गृह निर्माण द्रव्यजात) मकान बनाने की सामग्री। collection of building material.

दब्बी – स्त्री॰ – (दर्वी) करछुल, कड़छी। a ladle.

दब्भ – पु॰ – (दर्भ) कुश-ग्रास, कुश नामक घास। kuśa grass, used for sacrificial purposes.

दम/दमन – न॰ – (दमन) संयम। restrainment, control over the senses.

दमक – वि॰ – (दमक/दमनशीलः) संयत, संयत करने वाला। controller, trainer.

दमित – कृ॰ – (√दम् + क्त = दमित) दमन किया हुआ। restrained.

दमिळ – (दमिल/तमिल) दक्षिण भारत की तमिल जाति। of Tamilian race.

दमेति – क्रि॰ – (दमयति) संयत बनाता है। tames, trains, converts.

दमेतु – पु॰ – (दमयिता) दमन करने वाला। one who trains or controls.

दम्पति – पु॰ – (दम्पति) पत्नी और पति। a couple (wife and husband).

दम्म – वि॰ – (दम्य) जिसे दमित अथवा शिक्षित करना हो। to be tamed or trained.

दया – स्त्री॰ – (दया) करुणा। kindness.

दयालु – वि॰ – (दयालु) दया करने वाला। kind, compassionate.

दयित – कृ॰ – (दयित) दयापात्र। sympathized.

दयितब्ब – कृ॰ – (दयितव्य) जिस पर दया करना या जिसके प्रति दया दिखाना उचित हो। fit to be sympathized or helped.

दयिता – स्त्री॰ – (दयिता) औरत। a woman.

दर – पु॰ – (दर) दुःख, कष्ट, चिन्ता। sorrow, anxiety, distress.

दरिमुख-जातक – (जा॰ सं॰ 378) – मगध नरेश के पुत्र ब्रह्मदत्त तथा उसके सहपाठी दरीमुख की कथा। the story (No. 378) of a prince Brahmadutt of Magadha and his class fellows.

√दल – (भू॰) – विदारणे – (√वि + √दृ) फाड़ना। to tear.

√दल – (भू॰) – दित्तियं – (द्युत) चमकना। to shine.

दलिद्द/दलिद्द – वि॰ – (दरिद्र) निर्धन, दरिद्र। poor, wretched.

√दलिद्द – (भू॰) – दुग्गलियं – (√क्षै = क्षायति) क्षीण होना। to decay.

दळ्ह – वि॰ – (दृढ) दृढ़ I, hard, firm, strong.

दळ्हपरक्कम – वि॰ – (दृढ-पराक्रमः) दृढ़ पराक्रमी, उत्साही। energetic, having an unfailing valour.

दळ्हं – क्रि॰ वि॰ – (दृढता-पूर्वकम्) दृढ़ता-पूर्वक। strongly, with firm decision.

दळ्हीकम्म – न॰ – (दृढीकरण) दृढ़ बनाना। giving firmness.

दळ्ह-धम्म-जातक – (जा॰ सं॰ 409) – दळ्ह धम्म नामक बनारस नरेश के मंत्री की कथा। the story of Drḍha-dharma a minister to the king of Varanasi (story No. 409).

दव – पु॰ – (दव) क्रीडा, आग, गरमी। play, sport, fire, heat.

दवकम्यता – स्त्री॰ – (दिव-काम्यता) हँसी-मजाक करने की रुचि। fondness for joking.

दवधु – न॰ – (दाहः) जलन। inflammation.

दव-डाह – पु॰ – (दवदाह/दावाग्नि) जंगली आग। forest fire.

दस – वि॰ – (दश) दस। ten.

दसक – न॰ – (दशक) दशाब्द, दस का समूह। a group of ten.

दसक्खत्तुं – क्रि॰ वि॰ – (दशकृत्वा) दस गुना, दस बार। ten times.

दसधा – क्रि॰ वि॰ – (दशधा) दस प्रकार से। in ten ways.

दस-बल – वि॰ – (दशबल) दस शक्तियों वाला, भगवान् बुद्ध के लिए प्रयुक्त एक विशेषण पद। endowed with ten super normal powers, this adjective is used for the Buddha in Pāli.

दस-विध – वि॰ – (दशविध) दस प्रकार से। tenfold.

दस-सत – न॰ – (दश-शत/सहस्र) सहस्र, हजार। ten hundred, one thousand.

दस-सत-नयन – वि॰ – (सहस्र नेत्र) सहस्र आँखों वाला। having one hundred eyes.

दस-सहस्स – न॰ – (दश-सहस्र) दस हजार। ten thousand.

दस – वि॰ – (दर्शः) प्रायः समास में प्रयुक्त जैसे 'दुद्दस'। used in compounds as duddasa difficult to be seen.

दुद्दस – वि॰ – (दुर्दर्श) जो कठिनाई से दिखाई दे। difficult to be seen.

दसण्ण – पु॰ – (दशार्ण) मध्य भारत का भूमि भाग, दशार्णव। the ancient name of Deccan plateu of middle India.

दसण्णक-जातक – (जा॰ सं॰ 401) – एक राजा ने पुरोहित पुत्र को अपनी रानी सप्ताह भर के लिए दी जिसे लेकर वह भाग ही गया इस पर पश्चात्ताप न करने की बोध कथा। the story (No. 401) tells that to promise a gift, to make it, having made it and not to regret it, these acts are in increasing degrees far harder than swallowing a sword.

दस-ब्राह्मण-जातक – (जा॰ सं॰ 495) – एक ऐसे राजा की कथा जिसके दान की सीमा न थी किन्तु उसका सारा दान दुष्ट आदमियों के पल्ले पड़ता था। the story (No. 495) of such a king who was unparlleled in generosity but all the recipients of his gift were wicked man.

दसरथ-जातक – (जा॰ सं॰ 461) – वनवासी राम, लक्ष्मण तथा सीता को राजा दशरथ की मृत्यु की सूचना पर राम पण्डित द्वारा असाधारण सहनशीलता का परिचय देने वाली कथा। the story (No. 461) reavealing the unparallel virtues of Rāma.

दसन – न॰ – (दशन) दाँत। tooth.

दसनच्छद – पु॰ – (दशनच्छद) ओष्ठ होंठ, अधरोष्ठ। the lips.

दसा – स्त्री॰ – (दशा) (1) वस्त्र की किनारी (2) दशा। (1) the border of a garment, (2) condition.

दसिक-सुत्त – न॰ – (दशिक-सूत्र) किनारी का धागा। a loose thread of a fringe.

दस्सक – वि॰ – (दर्शक) दिखाने वाला। one who shows.

दस्सति (1) – क्रि॰ – (दृश्यते) दिखाई पड़ता है। is being seen.

दस्सति (2) – क्रि॰ – (दास्यति) देगा। will give.

दस्सन – न॰ – (दर्शन) दर्शन, दृष्टि, अन्तः-प्रेरणा। sight, intuition, insight.

दस्सनीय – वि॰ – (दर्शनीय) दर्शनीय, देखने योग्य। beautiful, handsome, fair to behold.

दस्सावी – पु॰ – (दर्शी) समास में प्रयुक्त देखने वाला (भय दस्सावी, भयभीत)। one who sees, only compounds such as *bhaya-dassāvī*.

दस्सु – पु॰ – (दस्यु) दस्यु, डाकू। robber.

दस्सेति – क्रि॰ – (दर्शयति) दिखाता है। shows, exhibits.

दस्सेतु – पु॰ – (दर्शयिता) दिखाने वाला। one who shows.

√दह – (भू॰) – भस्मीकरण – (√दह्) जलाना। to burn.

दह – पु॰ – (दह, ह्रद) झील, जलाशय। a lake.

दहति – क्रि॰ – (√दह् = दहति) जलाता है। burns.

दहन (1) – न॰ – (दहन) ज्वलन, तपन, जलन। inflammation.

दहन (2) – पु॰ – (दहन) अग्नि। fire.

दहर – वि॰ – (दारकः) तरुण, लड़का। young in years, a boy.

दहरा – स्त्री॰ – (दारिका) तरुणी, लड़की। a girl.

√दा – (भू॰) – दारणे – (√दृ) फाड़ना। to tear.

दाडिम – न॰ – (दाडिम) अनार का पेड़ और फल। pomegranate tree and fruit.

√ **दा** – (भू॰) – दाने – (√ दा = ददाति)
देना । to give.

दाढा – स्त्री॰ – (दंष्ट्रा) दाढ़ । jaw, large-
tooth.

दाढा-धातु – स्त्री॰ – (दंष्ट्रा-धातु) (बुद्ध के)
दन्त अवशेष । the tooth relic (of the
Buddha).

ढाढावुध – वि॰ – (दंष्ट्रायुध) दाँतों को शस्त्र
की तरह उपयोग करने वाला । using
tusks as his weapon.

दाढाबली – वि॰ – (दंष्ट्राबली) दाँतों का
बलवान । one whose strength lies
in his tusks.

दात – कृ॰ – (√ दा + क्त = दात) काटा
गया । having been cut.

दातब्ब – कृ॰ – (√ दा + तव्यत् = दातव्य)
देने योग्य । fit to be given.

दातु – पु॰ – (दाता) देने वाला । bestower,
given.

दातुं – कृ॰ – (√ दा + तुमुन् = दातुम्) देने
के लिए । for giving.

दात्त (1) – न॰ – (दात्र) दाँति, दराँति ।
sickle.

दात्त (2) – कृ॰ – (दात्त) काटा गया ।
having been cut.

दान – न॰ – (दानम्) दान । donation,
charity.

दान-कथा – स्त्री॰ – (दान-कथा) दान सम्बन्धी
चर्चा, दान-विषयक उपदेश । talk about
charity.

दानग्ग – न॰ – (दानाग्र) दान देने का
स्थान । a place where alms are
given.

दान-पति – पु॰ – (दानवीर) दान करने में
हिम्मती । master in liberality.

दान-फल – न॰ – (दान-फल) दान-फल ।
the fruit of munificence.

दान-मय – वि॰ – (दान-मय) दान-मय ।
consisting of giving alms.

दान-वट्ट – न॰ – (दानवर्त्त / सदावर्त्त)
अनवरत दान, सतत् दान । constant
giving of alms.

दान-वत्थु – न॰ – (दान-वस्तु) दान देने
की वस्तु । things to be given in
charity.

दान-वेय्यावटिक – वि॰ – (दान-वितरक)
दान बाँटने वाला । a distributor of
alms.

दान-साला – स्त्री॰ – (दान-शाला)
दानशाला । alms-hall.

दान-सील – वि॰ – (दान-शील) दानशील ।
of liberal disposition.

दान-सोण्ड – वि॰ – (दान-शौण्ड) दान-
प्रिय । fond of giving alms.

दानारह – वि॰ – (दानार्ह) दान देने योग्य ।
worthy of receiving alms/gift.

दानव – पु॰ – (दानव) राक्षस । a titan,
demon.

दानि – (इदानीम्) देखें इदानि । see Idāni.

दापन – न॰ – (दापनम्) दिलाना ।
inducement to give.

दापेति – क्रि॰ – (दापयति) दिलाता है ।
induces to give.

दापेतु – पु॰ – (दापयिता) दिलाने वाला ।
one who induces to give.

दाब्बि – स्त्री॰ – (हरिद्रा / हल्दी) सूखी हल्दी ।
turmeric.

दाम – पु॰ – (दाम) माला, रस्सी, जंजीर। a wreath, rope, chain, garland.

दाय – पु॰ – (दाय) (1) जंगल, उद्यान, (2) उपहार। (1) forest, grove (2) gift.

दायपाल – पु॰ – (उद्यान पाल) माली। a gardener.

दायक – पु॰ – (दायक) दाता, सहायक। giver, supporter.

दायज्ज – न॰ – (दायाद्य) उत्तराधिकार। inheritance.

दायज्ज – न॰ – (दायाद) उत्तराधिकारी। one who inherits.

दायति – क्रि॰ – (√दा = दाति) काटता है। reaps, mows.

दायन – न॰ – (दायनम्) काटना। cutting, reaping, mowing.

दायाद – पु॰ – (दायाद्य) उत्तराधिकार। inheritence.

दायादक – वि॰ – (दायाद) उत्तराधिकारी। one who inherits.

दायिका – स्त्री॰ – (दायिका) देने वाली। a female donor.

दायी – वि॰ – (दायी) प्रायः समास में प्रयुक्त देने वाला। donor, giver, generally used in compounds.

दार – पु॰ – (दारा) स्त्री। wife.

दार-भरण – न॰ – (दारा-भरणम्) स्त्री का पालन-पोषण। maintenance of a wife.

दारक – पु॰ – (दारकः) लड़का, बच्चा। a boy, youngster, son.

दारा – स्त्री॰ – (दारा) स्त्री। wife.

दारिका – स्त्री॰ – (दारिका) लड़की, बच्ची। a girl, daughter.

दारित – कृ॰ – (√दृ + क्त = दारित) चीरा गया, फाड़ा गया। split, burst open.

दारेति – (दारयति) फाड़ता है। splits.

दारेत्वा – पु॰ क्रि॰ – (दारयित्वा) फाड़कर, चीरकर। having split.

दारेन्त – कृ॰ – (√दृ + शतृ = दारयन) फाड़ता हुआ, चीरता हुआ। splitting, bursting open.

दारेसि – अतीत क्रि॰ – (अदारयत्) फाड़ा, चीरा। had split or burst open.

दारु – न॰ – (दारु) काष्ठ, लकड़ी। wood, timber, firewood.

दारु-खण्ड – न॰ – (दारु-खण्ड) लकड़ी का टुकड़ा, काष्ठ-खण्ड। a piece of wood.

दारुक्खन्ध – पु॰ – (दारुस्कन्ध) लकड़ी का लट्ठा। a log of wood.

दारु-भण्ड – न॰ – (दारु-भण्डम्) लकड़ी का सामान। furniture, wooden articles.

दारु-मय – वि॰ – (दारुमय) काष्ठमय, लकड़ी का बना। made of wood.

दारु-सङ्घात – वि॰ – (दारु-सङ्घात) लकड़ी से बनाया गया बेड़ा। a raft made of wood.

दारुण – वि॰ – (दारुण) कठोर। severe, harsh.

दालन – न॰ – (दालन) चीरना-फाड़ना। splitting.

दालेति – (दारयति) देखें दारेति। see Dāreti.

दावग्गि – पु॰ – (दावाग्नि) जंगल की आग। forest fire.

दास – पु॰ – (दास) भृत्य, गुलाम। a slave.

दास-गण – पु॰ – (दास–गण) भृत्यों या गुलामों का समूह। a group of slaves.

दासत्त – न॰ – (दासत्व) दास-भाव। slavery, condition of a slave.

दासित्त – न॰ – (दासीत्व) दासी-भाव। condition of a female-slave.

दासी – स्त्री॰ – (दासी) दासी। a female slave.

दाह – पु॰ – (दाह) जलन, गर्मी। burning, inflammation, heat.

दालिद्दिय – न॰ – (दारिद्र्य) दरिद्रता। poverty.

दालिम – (दाडिम) देखें दाड़िम। see Dādim.

√दिक्ख – (भू॰) – दिक्खति – (√दीक्ष्) दीक्षा देना। to baptise, to initiate into monkhood.

दिक्खति (1) – क्रि॰ – (पश्यति) देखता है। sees.

दिक्खति (2) – क्रि॰ – (दीक्षा-गृह्णाति) दीक्षाय् आप्नोति, दीक्षा लेता है। becomes a monk.

दिक्खित्त – कृ॰ – (दीक्षित) दीक्षा-प्राप्त, दीक्षित। consecrated, initiated.

दिगम्बर – न॰ – (दिगम्बर) नग्न साधु। a naked ascetic.

दिगुण – वि॰ – (द्विगुण) द्विगुण, दूना, दो गुना। twofold, double.

दिग्घिका – स्त्री॰ – (दीर्घिका) खाई। a ditch.

दिज – पु॰ – (द्विज) (1) ब्राह्मण (2) पक्षी। (1) a brāhmaṇa (2) a bird.

दिजगण – पु॰ – (द्विजगण) ब्राह्मण या पक्षियों का समूह। a group of brāhmaṇas or birds.

दिट्ठ (1) – कृ॰ – (√दृश् + क्त = दृष्ट) देखा गया। seen.

दिट्ठ (2) – न॰ – (दृश्यम्) दृश्य। vision.

दिट्ठ-धम्म (1) – पु॰ – (दृष्ट-धर्म) यही संसार। this world, this life.

दिट्ठ-धम्म (2) – वि॰ – (दृष्ट-धर्म) सत्य का साक्षात्कृत। one who has realized the final truth.

दिट्ठधम्मिक – वि॰ – (दृष्ट-धार्मिकः) इसी लोक से सम्बन्धित। belonging to this world.

दिट्ठमङ्गलिक – वि॰ – (दृष्ट-माङ्गलिक) शकुन-अपशकुन का विचार करने वाला। one who believes in good and bad omens.

दिट्ठसंसन्दन – न॰ – (दृष्ट-संस्यन्दनम्) दृष्ट अथवा ज्ञात बातों के बारे में तुलनात्मक विवेचन। to compare one's views on things seen or known.

दिट्ठानुगति – स्त्री॰ – (दृष्टानुगतिः) दृष्ट का अनुकरण। imitation of what one sees.

दिट्ठि – स्त्री॰ – (दृष्टि) सिद्धान्त, मत, विश्वास। dogma, theory, belief.

दिट्ठिक – वि॰ – (दृष्टिकः) मत-विशेष को मानने वाला (इस शब्द का प्रयोग प्रायः समास में किया जाता है)। used in compounds-belonging in, having the theory of.

दिट्ठि-कन्तार – पु॰ – (दृष्टि-कान्तार) मतों का जंगल। the wilderness of dogmas.

दिट्ठिगत – न॰ – (दृष्टिगत) मिथ्यामत। a belief, wrong view.

दिट्ठि-गहन – न॰ – (दृष्टि-ग्रहण) मतों का जमघट। the thicket of speculation.

दिट्ठि-जाल – न॰ – (दृष्टि-जालम्) मतों का जाल। the net of sophistry.

दिट्ठि-विपत्ति – स्त्री॰ – (दृष्टि-विपत्तिः) मत की असफलता। failure in theory.

दिट्ठि-विपल्लास – पु॰ – (दृष्ट-विपर्यासः) मतों की विकृति, स्पष्ट मत। contortion of views.

दिट्ठि-विसुद्धि – स्त्री॰ – (दृष्टि-विशुद्धि) स्पष्ट, दृष्टि, स्पष्ट मत। clear vision, right understanding.

दिट्ठि-सम्पन्न – वि॰ – (दृष्टि-सम्पन्न) सम्यक् दृष्टि से युक्त। endowed with right views.

दिट्ठि-संयोजन – न॰ – (दृष्टि-संयोजन) व्यर्थ के मतों का बंधन। the fetter of empty speculation.

दित्त – कृ॰ – (दीप्त) दीप्त। blazing.

दित्ति – स्त्री॰ – (दीप्ति) प्रकाश, दीप्ति। light, brightness.

दिद्ध – वि॰ – ($\sqrt{}$ दिह् + त = दग्ध) सना, लिपटा, पुता, विष में बुझा। smeared with, poisoned.

दिन – न॰ – (दिन) दिन। day.

दिनकर – पु॰ – (दिनकर) सूर्य। the sun.

दिनच्चय – पु॰ – (दिनात्ययः / दिवसावसन) दिन का अवसान, सन्ध्या। exhaustion of the day, evening.

दिन-पति – पु॰ – (दिनपति) सूर्य। the sun.

दिन्दिभ – पु॰ – (टिट्टिभ) टिटिहरी। a lapwing, bird of plover family, peewit, sand-piper.

दिन – कृ॰ – (दिन्न/दत्त) दिया गया। given.

दिन्नादायी – वि॰ – (दिन्नादायी) जो दिया गया हो उसी को ग्रहण करने वाला। one who is taking what is given.

दिन्नक – पु॰ – (दत्तक) (1) दत्तक (पुत्र) (2) दी गयी (वस्तु)। (1) an adopted son 2. given thing.

दिपद – पु॰ – (द्विपद) द्विपद, दो पैरों वाला, मनुष्य। biped, human being.

$\sqrt{}$ दिप – (दि.) दित्तियं – ($\sqrt{}$ दीप्) चमकना। to shine.

दिपदिन्द – पु॰ – (द्विपदेन्द्र) मनुष्येन्द्र, तथागत बुद्ध। the most noble of the biped, i.e., the enlightened one.

दिपदुत्तम – पु॰ – (द्विपदोत्तम) मनुष्यों में श्रेष्ठ, तथागत बुद्ध। the most noble of biped, i.e., the enlightened one.

दिप्पति – क्रि॰ – ($\sqrt{}$ दीप् = दीप्यते) चमकता है। shines.

दिप्पन – न॰ – (दीपनम्) चमकना। shining.

दिब्ब – वि॰ – (दिव्य) दिव्य। divine, celestial.

दिब्ब-चक्खु – न॰ – (दिव्य-चक्षु) दिव्य-चक्षु। the divine eye.

दिब्ब-चक्खुक – वि॰ – (दिव्य-चक्षुकः) दिव्य-चक्षु से युक्त। endowed with the super human eye.

दिब्ब-विहार – पु॰ – (दिव्य-विहार) दिव्य-विहार, करुणा मुदिता आदि भावनाओं में चित्त का लगाना। the supreme condition of heart.

दिब्ब-सम्पत्ति – स्त्री॰ – (दिव्य-सम्पत्ति) दिव्य-सम्पत्ति। heavenly bliss.

दिब्बत – क्रि॰ – (√ दिव् = दीव्यति) क्रीड़ा करता है, मनोविनोद करता है। sports, amuses oneself.

दियड्ढ – पु॰ – (अध्यर्द्ध) डेढ़। one and a half.

√ दिव – (दि॰) – कीलाविजगिंसा-क्षितिगतिसु। (√ दिव् = दीव्यति) चमकना। to shine.

दिव – पु॰ – (दिव) दिव्यलोक। heaven.

दिवस – पु॰ – (दिवस) दिन। day.

दिवसकर – पु॰ – (दिनकर) सूर्य। the sun.

दिवस-भाग – पु॰ – (दिवस-भाग) दिन का समय। the day-time.

दिवा – अव्यय – (दिवा) दिन, दिन में। day, day by day.

दिवाकार – पु॰ – (दिवाकर) सूर्य। the sun.

दिवा-ठान – (दिवा-स्थान) दिन का समय गुजारने की जगह। place where the day-time is spent.

दिवा-विहार – पु॰ – (दिवा-विहार) दिन में विश्राम करना। rest during the heat.

दिवा-सेय्या – स्त्री॰ – (दिवा-शयन) दिन में लेटना। lying down at midday.

√ दिस – (तु) – अतिसज्जने – (√ दिश्) अनुशंसा करना। to admire.

दिस – पु॰ – (द्विषः) शत्रु। enemy.

√ दिस – (भू॰) – पेक्खने – (√ दृश = पश्यति) देखना। to see.

दिसम्पति – पु॰ – (दिशाम्पति / विशाम्पतिः) नरेश। the king.

√ दिस – (चु॰) – (उच्चारण - √ दिश्) अनुशंसा करना। to admire.

दिसा – स्त्री॰ – (दिशा) दिशा। a direction, a point of the compass.

दिसा-काक – पु॰ – (दिशा-काक) स्थल-भूमि की खोज करने के लिए नौका पर रखा हुआ कौआ। a crow kept on board a ship in order to locate a land.

दिसा-कुसल – वि॰ – (दिशा-कुशल) दिशा-ज्ञान में कुशल। one who is able in ascertaining the directions.

दिसा-पामोक्ख – वि॰ – (दिशा-प्रमुख / लोक प्रसिद्ध) लोक प्रसिद्ध। a world-famous.

दिसा-भाग – पु॰ – (दिशा-भाग) विदिशा, दिशा, कोण, चारों दिशाओं की अन्तरवर्त्ती चार उपदिशाएँ। four intermediary directions.

दिसा-मूळ्ह – वि॰ – (दिशा-मूढ) जिसे दिशाओं का ज्ञान नहीं। one who has lost his bearings.

दिसा-वासिक – वि॰ – (दिशा-वासी) देश के विभिन्न प्रान्तरों में अथवा विदेश में रहने वाला। living in another country or in different parts of a country.

दिस्सति – क्रि॰ – (दृश्यते) ऐसा दिखाई देता है, ऐसा प्रतीत होता है। it seems, appears so.

दीघ – वि॰ – (दीर्घ) लम्बा। long.

दीघङ्गुली – वि॰ – (दीर्घाङ्गुलिः) लम्बी अँगुलियों वाली। having long fingers.

दीघजातिक – पु॰ – (दीर्घ-जातिकः) सर्प की जाति का जीव। a being (member) of the snake species.

दीघता – स्त्री॰ – (दीर्घता) लम्बाई। length.

दीघत्त – न॰ – (दीर्घत्व) लम्बाई। length.

दीघ-दस्सी – वि॰ – (दीर्घ-दर्शी) दीर्घ-दर्शी। far-sighted.

दीघ-निकाय – पु॰ – (दीर्घ-निकाय) सुत्त पिटक का पहला ग्रन्थ जिसमें लम्बे आकार के 34 सुत्त हैं। the first book of Sutta-piṭaka which contains 34 Suttas.

दीघ-भाणक – पु॰ – (दीर्घ-भाणक) दीर्घ निकाय का पाठ करने वाला। a reciter or expounder of Dīgha Nikāya.

दीघ-रत्तं – क्रि॰ वि॰ – (दीर्घ-शत्रम्) दीर्घ काल तक। for a long time.

दीघलोमक – वि॰ – (दीर्घ-लोमकः) लम्बे बाल वाला। having long fleece.

दीघ-सोत्थिय – न॰ – (दीर्घ-सूत्रता) लम्बी नींद, प्रमाद, आलस्य। long sleep, slumber, sluggishness.

दीघ-हत्थ – पु॰ – (दीर्घ-हस्तः) लम्बे हाथ वाला। having long arms.

दीधिति – स्त्री॰ – (दीधिति) किरण, प्रकाश, दीप्ति। light, rays, radiance.

√दी – (दि.) – खये – (√क्षै) क्षीण होना। to decay.

दीन – वि॰ – (दीन) गरीब, दीनावस्था को प्राप्त। a poor, miserable.

दीनता – स्त्री॰ – (दीनता) दैन्य, दीन-भाव। wretchedness.

दीनत्व – देखें दीनता। see Dīnata.

दीप (1) – पु॰ – (दीप) दीपक। a lamp.

दीप (2) – न॰ – (दीप) द्वीपी (चीते) की खाल से मढ़ा हुआ रथ। a kind of chariot covered with a cheetah or leopard skin.

दीप (3) – पु॰ – (द्वीप) टापू आश्रय। an island.

दीपक (1) – पु॰ – (दीपक) छोटा दीपक। small lamp.

दीपक (2) – पु॰ – (द्वीपक) छोटा टापू द्वीप। a small island.

दीपक (3) – वि॰ – (दीपक) व्यक्त करने वाला, व्याख्या करने वाला। showing, explaining.

दीपङ्कर – पु॰ – (दीपङ्कर) दीपक जलाने वाला, पु॰, 24 बुद्धों में से सर्वप्रथम। (1) one who lights a lamp (2) the first among 24 Buddhas.

दीपच्चि – स्त्री॰ – (दीपार्चि) दीपक की लौ। flame of a lamp.

दीप-रुक्ख – पु॰ – (दीप-वृक्ष) दीपाधार, दीप-स्तम्भ। a lamp-post.

दीप-सिखा – स्त्री॰ – (दीप-शिखा) दीपक की लौ। flame of a lamp.

दीपालोक – पु॰ – (दीपालोक) दीपक का प्रकाश। light of a lamp.

दीपना – स्त्री॰ – (दीपना) व्याख्या। illustration, explanation.

दीपनी – स्त्री॰ – (दीपनी) व्याख्यात्मक टिप्पणी। an explanatory note.

दीप-वंस – (दीप-वंस) सिंहल का प्राचीनतम ऐतिहासिक काव्य। the oldest historic poetry of Siṁhala.

दीपि – पु॰ – (द्वीपिन्) चीता। a panther, a cheetah.

दीपिक – पु॰ – (द्वीपिकः) चीता। a panther.

दीपि-जातक – (जा॰ सं॰ 426) – बकरी ने मीठे शब्दों से चीते को बहलाना चाहा, किन्तु वह उसे खा ही गया। (story No. 426) the lamb wanted to entice the cheetah with soft words, lent the cheetah ate up the lamb.

दीपिका – स्त्री॰ – (दीपिका) मशाल, व्याख्या। lamp, explanation.

दीपित – कृ॰ – (दीप्त) व्याख्याता, जिसकी व्याख्या की गयी हो। illustrated, explained.

दीपिनी – स्त्री॰ – (द्वीपिनी) चीती। a female panther.

दीपेति – क्रि॰ – (दीपयति) प्रकाशित करता है, स्पष्ट करता है। lights, makes clear.

दु – उपसर्ग – (दुः/दुर्) कठिनता, अभाव दुःख-सूचक उपसर्ग। a prefix implying badness.

दुक – न॰ – (द्विक्) युग्म, जोड़ा, जोड़ी। a pair.

दुकूल – न॰ – (दुकूल) उत्तम कोटि का वस्त्र। a kind of very fine cloth.

दुक्कट – वि॰ न॰ – (दुष्कृत) दुष्कृत, अकुशल कर्म। badly done, wrong action.

दुक्कर – वि॰ – (दुष्कर) दुष्कर, कठिन। difficulty to do or perform.

दुक्कर-भाव – पु॰ – (दुष्कर-भाव) दुष्करता, कठिनता। difficulty.

दुक्ख – न॰ – (दुःख) कष्ट, वि॰ अप्रिय, कष्टदायी। suffering, pain, misery.

दुक्खं – क्रि॰ वि॰ – (दुःखम्) कठिनाई से। with difficulty.

दुक्खक्खय – पु॰ – (दुःख-क्षय) दुःख का क्षय। extinction of misery.

दुक्खक्खन्ध – पु॰ – (दुःखस्कन्ध) दुःख का समूह। aggregate of sufferings.

दुक्ख-निदान – न॰ – (दुःख-निदान) दुःख का मूल। source of misery causing pain.

दुक्ख-निरोध – पु॰ – (दुःख-निरोध) दुःख का नाश। extinction of suffering.

दुक्ख-निरोध-गामिनीपटिपदा – स्त्री॰ – (दुःख-निरोध-गामिनी-प्रतिपदा) दुःख-निरोध की ओर ले जाने वाला मार्ग। the way leading to the extinction of suffering.

दुक्खन्तगू – वि॰ – (दुःखान्तगः) जो दुःख का अन्त कर चुका। one who has conquered suffering.

दुक्ख-पटिकूल – वि॰ – (दुःख-प्रतिकूल) दुःख के प्रतिकूल। averse to pain.

दुक्ख-परेत – वि॰ – (दुःखोपेत) दुःख से दुःखित। afflicted by misery.

दुक्खप्पत्त – वि॰ – (दुःख-प्राप्त) दुःख प्राप्त। being in pain.

दुक्खप्पहाण – न॰ – (दुःख-प्रहानिः) दुःख का दूर करना। removal of misery.

दुक्ख-विपाक – वि॰ – (दुःख-विपाकः) जिसका फल दुःख हो। having pain as its fruit.

दुक्ख-सच्च – न॰ – (दुःख-सत्य) दुःख के सम्बन्ध में सत्य। the truth of misery.

दुक्ख समुदय – पु॰ – (दुःख-समुदय) दुःख की उत्पत्ति के सम्बन्ध में सत्य। the origin of suffering.

दुक्ख-सम्फस्स – वि॰ – (दुःख-संस्पर्श) दुःख का स्पर्श। having an unpleasant touch.

दुक्खसेय्या – स्त्री॰ – (दुःख-शय्या) बे-आराम की नींद। an uncomfortable sleep.

दुक्खानुभवन – न॰ – (दुःखानुभवन) दण्ड भोगना। undergoing sentence or punishment.

दुक्खापगम – पु॰ – (दुःखापगम) दुःख का हटाना। removal of pain.

दुक्खापन – न॰ – (दुःखापन) कष्ट-प्रद। hurting.

दुक्खापेति – क्रि॰ – (दुःखापयति) कष्ट देता है, दुखाता है। afflicts, causes pain.

दुक्खित – वि॰ – (दुःखित) अप्रसन्न। afflicted, grieved.

दुक्खी – वि॰ – (दुःखी) अप्रसन्न। unhappy, ailing.

दुक्खीयति – क्रि॰ – (दूयते) दुःखी होता है। feels pain, feels miserable, feels unhappy.

दुक्खद्रय – वि॰ – (दुःखप्रद) दुःखद। resulting in pain.

दुक्खूपसम – पु॰ – (दुःखोपशम) दुःख का उपशमन। alleviation of suffering.

दुक्खोत्तिन्न – वि॰ – (दुःखोत्तीर्ण) दुःखों को पार कर चुके वाला। one who has overcome the sufferings.

दुग – न॰ – (दुर्ग) दुर्ग, किला। fortress.

दुगत – वि॰ – (दुर्गत) दरिद्र, दुर्गति प्राप्त। poor, miserable.

दुगति – स्त्री॰ – (दुर्गति) दुर्गति। a realm of miserable existence.

दुगन्ध – पु॰ – (दुर्गन्ध) बदबू वि॰ बदबूदार। having a bad smell.

दुगम – वि॰ – (दुर्गम) ऐसी जगह जहाँ जाना कठिन हो। place difficult to go.

दुग्गहीत (1) – वि॰ – (दुर्गृहीत) जिसे ठीक से नहीं समझा। hold or taken wrongly.

दुग्गहीत (2) – न॰ – (दुर्गृहीतम्) मिथ्या-मत। a wrong view.

दुग्ग-संचार – पु॰ – (दुर्ग-संचार) दुर्ग तक पहुँचने का रास्ता, दुर्गम रास्ता। the way to a fort, the way full of obstacles.

दुच्चज – वि॰ – (दुस्त्यज) जिसे त्यागना कठिन हो। difficult to leave or give up.

दुच्चरित – न॰ – (दुश्चरित) दुराचरण। bad conduct, wrong action.

दुजिव्ह – पु॰ – (द्विजिह्व) साँप। snake, a serpent.

दुज्जह – वि॰ – (दुर्जह) जिसे छोड़ना कठिन हो। difficult to give up or remove, or stop.

दुज्जान – वि॰ – (दुर्ज्ञेय) जिसे जानना कठिन हो। difficult to know.

दुज्जीवित – न॰ – (दुर्जीवित) मिथ्या जीविका। improper livelihood.

दुट्ठ – वि॰/कृ॰ – (दुष्ट) दुष्ट, द्वेष-युक्त। spoiled, corrupt, wicked.

दुट्ठ-चित्त – न॰ – (दुष्ट-चित्त) दुष्ट चित्त वाला। evil-minded, malignant.

दुट्ठु – क्रि॰ वि॰ – (दुष्टु) बुरी तरह से। badly.

दुट्ठुल्ल – न॰ – (दुष्टुल्य) फूहड़ बातचीत, वि॰ घटिया। lewd talk, inferior.

दुत्प्पय – वि॰ – (दुष्तृप्य) जिसे आसानी से सन्तुष्ट न किया जा सके। not easily satiable.

दुतिय – वि॰ – (द्वितीय) द्वितीय, दूसरा। second, having as the second.

दुतियक – वि॰ – (द्वितीयक) साथी। a companion.

दुतियं – क्रि॰ वि॰ – (द्वितीयम्) दूसरी बार।
for the second time.

दुतियपलायी-जातक – (जा॰ सं॰ 230) –
गान्धार नरेश की पलायन कथा। (story
No. 230) relating to the
cowardness of the king of
Gandhāra.

दुतिया – स्त्री॰ – (द्वितीया) (1) पत्नी
(2) द्वितीया विभक्ति कर्म-कारक। (1)
the wife (2) the second case, i.e.,
accusative.

दुतियिका – स्त्री॰ – (द्वितीयिका) पत्नी।
the wife.

दुत्तर – वि॰ – (दुस्तर) जो कठिनाई से पार
किया जा सके। difficult to cross
over.

दुहद-जातक – (जा॰ सं॰ 180) – तक्षशिला
शिक्षित तपस्वी और उनके साथियों के
बनारस आगमन पर वाराणसी के लोगों
द्वारा आवभगत की कथा। the story
(No. 180) relating the honour
paid to the Buddha by the
people of Varanasi.

दुहम – वि॰ – (दुर्दमः) जिसका कठिनाई से
दमन किया जा सके। difficult to
control or tame.

दुहस – वि॰ – (दुर्दर्श) जो कठिनाई से
दिखाई दे, या समझ में आये। difficult
to see or understand.

दुहदसतर – वि॰ – (दुर्दशतर) जो और भी
अधिक कठिनाई से दिखाई दे, या समझ
में आये। more difficult to see or
understand.

दुहसा – स्त्री॰ – (दुर्दशा) दुर्दशा, बुरी हालत।
misfortune, unfavourable time.

दुहसापन्न – वि॰ – (दुर्दशापन्न) दुर्दशा-
ग्रस्त। put in miseries.

दुहसिक – वि॰ – (कुदर्शनः) बदशक्ल।
having ugly features.

दुहिन – न॰ – (दुर्दिन) दुर्दिन, बारिश का
दिन या खराब दिन। cloudly or
unlucky day.

दुद्ध – न॰ – (दुग्ध) दुग्ध, दूध। milk.

दुद्ध – कृ॰ – (दुग्ध) दुहा हुआ। milked.

दुंदुभि – स्त्री॰ – (दुन्दुभि) ढोल। a drum.

दुनामक – न॰ – (दुर्नामक ⁄ अर्श) बवासीर।
piles, haemorrhoids.

दुनिक्खित्त – वि॰ – (दुर्निक्षिप्त) अनुपयुक्त
ढंग से रखा गया। improperly
placed.

दुनिग्गह – वि॰ – (दुर्निग्रह) जिसे काबू में
रखना कठिन हो। difficult to subdue
or control.

दुनिमित्त – न॰ – (दुर्निमित्त) अपशकुन।
bad omen.

दुनीत – वि॰ – (दुर्नीत) अनुचित ढंग से ले
जाया गया। wrongly carried.

दुपट्ट – वि॰ – (द्विपट्ट) दो तहों वाला।
having two folds.

दुपञ्ञ – वि॰ – (दुष्प्रज्ञ) मूर्ख। foolish.

दुप्पटिनिस्सग्गिय – वि॰ – (दुष्प्रतिनिःसर्ग्य)
जिसे छोड़ना कठिन हो। difficult to
abstain from, difficult of leave.

दुप्पटिविज्झ – वि॰ – (दुष्प्रतिविध्य) जिसे
समझना कठिन हो। difficult to
understand.

दुप्पमुञ्च – वि॰ – (दुष्प्रमुञ्च्य) जिसे छोड़ना
दूभर हो। difficult to be freed.

दुप्परिहारिय – वि॰ – (दुष्परिहारीय) जिसकी
व्यवस्था करना कठिन हो। difficult to
use or manage.

दुफस्स – पु॰ – (दुःस्पृश्य) दुःखद स्पर्श, अप्रिय स्पर्श। disagreeable touch.

दुफस्स – सं॰ – (दुस्पृश्य) बिच्छू बूटी, बिच्छू पौधा। nettle plant, a stinging plant.

दुब्बच – वि॰ – (दुर्वचः) जो बात न मानता हो, अनाज्ञाकारी। obstinate, disobedient.

दुब्बच-जातक – (जा॰ सं॰ 116) – आचार्य ने बोधिसत्व का कहना नहीं माना। the story (No. 116) tells about the ill fate of the boaster, who didn't listen to Boddisatva.

दुब्बण्ण – वि॰ – (दुर्वर्ण) दुर्वर्ण, भद्दा। of bad colour, ugly.

दुब्बल – वि॰ – (दुर्बल) दुर्बल। feeble, weak.

दुब्बलत्त – न॰ – (दुर्बलत्वम्) दुर्बलता। feebleness.

दुब्बलता – स्त्री॰ – (दुर्बलता) देखें दुब्बलत्त। see Dubbalatta.

दुब्बल-भाव – पु॰ – (दुर्बल-भाव) देखें दुब्बलत्त। see Dubbalatta.

दुब्बल-कट्ठ-जातक – (जा॰ सं॰ 105) – निरन्तर मृत्यु-भय से त्रस्त रहने वाले एक हाथी की कथा। the story of an elephant who lived in constant state of fear of death.

दुब्बा – स्त्री॰ – (दूर्वा) दूर्वा-तृण, दूब। panic grass, bending grass.

दुब्बिजान – वि॰ – (दुर्बोध्य) कठिनाई से समझ में आने योग्य। difficult to understand.

दुब्बिनीत – वि॰ – (दुर्विनीत) दुर्विनीत। obstinate, badly trained.

दुब्बुट्ठिक – वि॰/न॰ – (दुर्वृष्टिक) दुर्वृष्टिक, जहाँ बारिश कम हो, अकाल। rainless, scarcity of rains.

दुब्भक – वि॰ – (दम्भक) कपटी, छली, विश्वासघाती। treacherous, insidious person.

दुब्भति – क्रि॰ – (√दम्म = दम्नोति) विश्वासघात करता है, छल-कपट करता है। deceives, deludes.

दुब्भन – न॰ – (√दम्म् + ल्युट् = दम्यन) धोखा, छल-कपट, विश्वासघात। deceit, fraud.

दुब्भर – वि॰ – (दुर्भर) दूभर, जिसका पालन-पोषण कठिन हो। difficult to bring up or nourish.

दुब्भासित – न॰ – (दुर्भाषित) अपमानसूचक शब्द, अपशब्द। an insulting word, bad speech.

दुब्भिक्ख – न॰ – (दुर्भिक्ष) अकाल, आहार की कमी। famine, scarcity of food.

दुब्भी – वि॰ – (दम्भी) विश्वासघात करने वाला, षड्यन्त्र रचने वाला। plotting against, seeking to injure, who deceives.

दुभ – (चु॰) – जिघंसायं-हिंसा की इच्छा करना। desirous of action, taking trecherous.

दुम – पु॰ – (द्रुम) द्रुम, पेड़। tree.

दुमग्ग – न॰ – (द्रुमाग्र) पेड़ का शिखर, फुनगी। the top of the tree.

दुमन्तर – न॰ – (द्रुमान्तर) नाना प्रकार के पेड़। variety of trees.

दुमिन्द – पु॰ – (द्रुमेन्द्र) वृक्षराज, बोधि-वृक्ष। the king of trees, i.e., the *bodhi*-tree.

दुमुत्तम – पु० – **(द्रुमोत्तम)** देखें दुमिन्द। see Duminda.

दुमुप्पल – पु० – **(द्रुमोत्पल)** कर्णिकार, पीले फूलों वाला कनेर वृक्ष। the tree *Oleander odorum* having yellow flowers.

दुम्मङ्कु – वि० – **(धूम + मङ्कु)** जिसे कठिनाई से चुप कराया जा सके, धूम लपट की भाँति अति नितान्त अस्थिर व्यक्ति, हठी। an obstinate person who can be made to keep quiet only with difficulty.

दुम्मती – पु० – **(दुर्गतिः)** बुद्धि-भ्रष्ट आदमी। a fool, an devil, animated person.

दुम्मन – वि० – **(दुर्मनः)** अप्रसन्न, दुःखी। unhappy, sorrowful.

दुम्मुख – वि० – **(दुर्मुख)** अप्रसन्न मुख वाला। having a sad face.

दुम्मेध – वि० – **(दुर्मेध)** कुबुद्धि। foolish.

दुम्मेध-जातक – (जा० सं० 50) – कथा बताती है कि एक राजा ने दुष्कर्म करने वालों की बलि देने की घोषणा करके प्रजावर्ग को किस प्रकार गर्हित कर्मों से विरत किया। the story (No. 50) tells how a king made his subjects keep away from unrighteousness, by threatening them.

दुम्मेध-जातक – (जा० सं० 122) – यह रोचक कथा बताती है कि ईर्ष्यावश व्यक्ति किस प्रकार अपना ही अहित करने पर उतारु हो जाता है। this interesting story (No. 122) tells how a person being victim of envy puts oneself in troubles.

दुय्योधन – **(दुर्योधन)** दुर्योधन। Duryodhana.

दुह्हति – क्रि० – ($\sqrt{}$ **दुह् से** कर्मवाच्य **दुह्यते)** दुहा जाता है। being milked.

दुरक्ख – वि० – **(दुःरक्ष्य)** जिसका संरक्षण कठिन हो। difficult to protect.

दुरच्चय – वि० – **(दुरत्यय)** जिसे लाँघना कठिन हो। difficult to pass over.

दुरनुबोध – वि० – **(दुरनुबोध)** जिसका बोध कठिन हो। difficult to understand.

दुरतिक्कम – वि० – **(दुरतिक्रमः)** जिसे लाँघना कठिन हो। difficult to pass over.

दुराजान – वि० – **(दुर्बोध्य)** जिसे जानना या समझना कठिन हो। difficult to know or understand.

दुराजान-जातक – (जा० सं० 64) – कथा बताती है कि स्वेच्छाचारिणी पत्नी की उपेक्षा कर देना ही हितकर है। the story (No. 64) tells that it is essential to neglect the capricious wife.

दुससाद – वि० – **(दुरासाद)** जिसके पास पहुँचना कठिन हो। difficult to be approached.

दुरित – न० – **(दुरितम्)** पाप, अकुशल कर्म। sin, bad action.

दुरुत्त (1)– वि० – **(दुरुक्त)** बुरी तरह से कहा गया। badly spoken.

दुरुत्त (2) – न० – **(दुरुक्तम्)** दुर्वचन, अपशब्द। bad speech.

दुल्लब्भ – वि० – **(दुर्लभ्य)** कठिनाई से प्राप्त। obtained with difficulty.

दुल्लब्धि – स्त्री० – **(दुर्लब्धिः)** मिथ्या दृष्टि। a wrong view.

दुल्लभ – वि० – (दुर्लभ) जिसे कठिनाई से प्राप्त किया जा सके। difficult to obtain.

दुवञ्झिक – वि० – (द्वयाञ्झिक) दो अंझों से युक्त। consisting of two portions.

दुविध – वि० – (द्विविध) दो प्रकार का। twofold.

दुवे – वि० – (द्वे) संख्यावाची दो (आदमी या वस्तुएँ)। two (two persons or things).

दुस्स – न० – (दूर्ष/दूश्य) कपड़ा, वस्त्र (उपरिभाग में पहने जाने वाला चादर, पगड़ी, आदि)। woven material, cloth, clothes, garments.

दुस्स-करण्डक – पु० – (दूर्ष/दूश्य-करण्डक) कपड़ों की पेटी। clothes, chest.

दुस्स-कोट्ठागार – न० – (दूर्ष/दूश्य-कोष्ठागार) कपड़ों का भण्डार। a store-room for clothes.

दुस्स-युग – (दूर्ष/दूश्य-युग) कपड़ों का जोड़ा। a pair of garments.

दुस्स-वट्टि – स्त्री० – (दूर्ष/दूश्य-वर्त्ति) कपड़ों का किनारी युक्त थान। a roll of fringed cotton cloth.

दुस्सति – क्रि० – (√द्विष/द्वेष्टि) द्वेष करता है, क्रोधित होता है। becomes angry, offends against.

दुस्सित्वा – पु० क्रि० – द्वेष करके। having offended.

दुस्सन – न० – द्वेष, विकृति, क्रोध। offending, corruption, anger.

दुस्सह – वि० – (दुस्सह) जिसका सहन करना कठिन हो। difficult to bear.

दुस्सील – वि० – (दुश्शील) दुराचारी। of bad character, devoid of morality.

दुहति – क्रि० – (√दुह् - दोग्धि = दुग्धे) (दूध) दुहता है। milks.

दुहन – न० – (दोहन) दुहा जाना। milking.

दुहितु – स्त्री० – (दुहितृ/दुहिता) बेटी, दुहिता। daughter.

दूत – पु० – (दूत) संदेश-वाहक। a messenger, envoy.

दूती – स्त्री० – (दूती) दूतिका, स्त्री-दूत। a woman messenger.

दूतेय्य – न० – (दूतेय्य) संदेश, संदेश-वाहन। errand, commission, carrying of messages.

दूत-जातक – (जा० सं० 260) – एक लोभी आदमी अपने को 'दूत-दूत' कहता हुआ राजा के खाने की मेज तक पहुँच गया। राजा ने पूछा 'तू किसका दूत है?' आदमी का उत्तर था "मैं पेट का दूत हूँ। the story (No. 260) sreveals that all are the messengers of lust and of the belly, the most important for a living being.

दूभक – वि० – (दम्भक) देखें दुब्भक। see Dubbhaka.

दूर – न० – (दूर) दूरी, वि० दूर। distance, adj. distant.

दूरङ्गम – वि० – (दूरङ्गम) दूर तक जाने वाला। going afar.

दूरतो – अव्यय – (दूरतः) दूर से। from a distance.

दूरत्त – न० – (दूरत्व) दूरत्व, दूर होने का भाव। the fact of being distant.

दूसक – वि० – (दूषक) दूषित करने वाला, विकृत करने वाला, गन्दा करने वाला। one who defiles or defames, corrupting, spoiling.

दूसन – न॰ – (दूषण) दूषण, विकृति, गन्दगी।
corruption, defilement.

दूसित – कृ॰ – (दूषित) दूषित। spoiled,
polluted.

दूसेति – क्रि॰ – (दूषयति) दूषित करता है,
खराब करता है, बदनाम करता है, बुरा
व्यवहार करता है। spoils, pollutes,
defames, ill-treats, abuses.

दूहन – न॰ – (दोहन) (1) डाका डालना
(2) दूध दुहना। (1) robbery,
(2) milking.

देड्डभ – पु॰ – (जल-डुण्डुभः) एक विषहीन
जल-सर्प, मज-गिधवा। a poisonless
water snake.

देण्डिम – पु॰ – (दौण्डिम) दौण्डी, डौडी। a
kettledrum.

देति – क्रि॰ – ($\sqrt{दा}$ = ददाति) देता है।
gives.

देय – पु॰ – (देय) देने योग्य। fit to be
given.

देव – पु॰ – (देव) देवता, आकाश, बादल,
राजा। a deity, the sky, a rain
cloud, a king.

देव-कञ्ञा – स्त्री॰ – (देव-कन्या) देव-
कन्या। a heavenly maiden.

देव-काय – पु॰ – (देव-काय) देव-गण। a
group of gods.

देव-कुमार – वि॰ – (देव-कुमार) दिव्य
राजकुमार। a divine prince.

देव-कुसुम – न॰ – (देव-कुसुम) देव-लोक
के फूल। cloves.

देव-गण – पु॰ – (देव-गण) देव-समूह। a
group of gods.

देव-चारिका – स्त्री॰ – (देव-चारिका) देवलोक
में भ्रमण। a journey in heaven.

देवच्छरा – स्त्री॰ – (देव-अप्सरा) देवप्सरा।
a nymph.

देवञ्ञतर – वि॰ – (देवान्यतर) लघु देवता।
an inferior deity.

देवट्ठान – न॰ – (देवस्थान) देवस्थान। a
temple dedicated to a deity.

देवत्तभाव – पु॰ – (देवत-भाव) दैवी-शरीर।
divine condition of body.

देवदत्तिक – वि॰ – (दैवदत्तिकः) देवता द्वारा
दिया गया। given by a deity.

देव-दुन्दुभि – स्त्री॰ – (देव-दुन्दिभि) मेघ
गर्जना। thunder.

देव-दूत – पु॰ – (देवदूत) देवता का दूत।
god's messenger.

देव-देव – पु॰ – (देव-देव) देवताओं का
देवता। the god of gods.

देव-धम्म – पु॰ – (देव-धर्म) दिव्य गुण,
पाप-भीरुता। divine virtue, fear to
sin.

देव-धीतु – स्त्री॰ – (देव-पुत्री) अप्सरा। a
young nymph.

देव-नगर – न॰ – (देव-नगर) देवताओं का
नगर। the city of *deva*s.

देव-निकाय – वि॰ – (देव-निकाय) देवताओं
का समूह। a community of devas.

देव-परिसा – स्त्री॰ – (देव-परिषद्) देव-
परिषद्। an assembly of *deva*s.

देव-पुत्त – पु॰ – (देव-पुत्र) देवता का पुत्र।
son of god.

देव-पुर – न॰ – (देव-पुर) देव-नगर। the
celestial city.

देव-भवन – न॰ – (देव-भवन) देवताओं
का निवास गृह। abode of a deity.

देव-यान – न॰ – (देव-यान) स्वर्ग मार्ग,
आकाश यान। the path to heaven.

देवराजा – पु॰ – (देवराजा) देवताओं का राजा शक्र। the king of *deva*s, i.e., Indra.

देव-रुक्ख – पु॰ – (देव-वृक्ष) देवताओं का वृक्ष पारिजात। a celestial tree.

देव-रूप – न॰ – (देव-रूप) देवता की मूर्ति। an image of a deity.

देव-लोक – पु॰ – (देव-लोक) स्वर्ग-लोक। heaven.

देव-विमान – वि॰ – (देव-विमान) देव-लोक का भवन। heavenly mansion.

देवता – स्त्री॰ – (देवता) देव। a deity.

देवत्त – न॰ – (देवत्व) देवत्व। divinity.

देवदत्त – (देवदत्त) शाक्य मुनि गौतम बुद्ध के मामा सुप्रबुद्ध शाक्य का पुत्र, जो जन्म भर बुद्ध-द्वेषी बना रहा। son of the Śākya Suprabuddha (the maternal uncle of the Buddha) and his wife Amita Devadaka remained life long haters of the Buddha.

देवदह – (देवदह) शाक्यों का एक निगम (कस्बा) बुद्ध ने अनेक बार वहाँ पदार्पण किया था। a township (*nigama*) of Śākyas where the Buddha stayed and preached on various topics.

देवदारु – पु॰ – (देवदारु) देवदार वृक्ष। a kind of pine, i.e., *Avaria longifolia*.

देवधम्म-जातक – (जा॰ सं॰ 6) – देव धम्म अर्थात् पाप से विरति का उपदेश। (story No. 16) it is a preaching about the fear of sin.

देवर – पु॰ – (देवर) देवर, पति का छोटा भाई। husband's younger brother.

देवसिक – वि॰ – (दैवसिक) दैनिक। occurring daily.

देवा – पु॰ – (देव) मानवों से कुछ ऊपर के स्तर के प्राणी। तीन प्रकार के देव माने गये हैं (1) सम्मुति-देवा, जिन्हें देवता मान लिया गया, जैसे राजा तथा राजकुमार, (2) विसुद्धि-देवा, पवित्र देवता-गण जैसे-अर्हत् तथा बुद्ध (3) उप्पत्ति-देवा, उत्पन्न हुए देवता-गण, सात प्रकार के देवता समूहों का वर्णन है, जैसे चातुम्महाराजिक तावतिंस, आदि। a class of beings above the human level. There are three kinds of Devā (1). Sammuti-devā or conventional gods like kings and princes, (2). Viśuddhi-devā who are divine by the purity of their merits as Arahants and Buddha (3). Uppatti-devā, who are born divine, under the third category, the chief seven groups are Catummahārājika, Tāvatimsa, Yāmā, Tusitā, Nammārati, Paranimmitavasatta and Brahma-kāyikā.

देवातिदेव – पु॰ – (देवाधिदेव) देवताओं का देवता। the god of gods.

देवानुभाव – पु॰ – (देवानुभाव) देव-प्रताप। divine power.

देवानम्पिय-तिस्स – (देवानांप्रिय-तिष्य) ६ र्मा- शोक का समकालीन तथा मित्र सिंहल नरेश। king of Ceylon (247-207 BC), who was a contemporary of Dhammāśoka of Bhārat.

देविसि – पु॰ – (देवर्षि) दिव्य-ऋषि। divine seer.

देवी – स्त्री॰ – (देवी) (1) देवी (2) रानी (3) महेन्द्र स्थविर तथा संघमित्रा की माता अर्थात् अशोक-पत्नी का नाम। (1) goddess (2) queen (3) the mother of Mahendra and Sanghamitra, and the wife of Aśoka.

देवुपपत्ति – स्त्री॰ – (देवोत्पत्ति) देवताओं में उत्पत्ति। rebirth among gods.

देस – पु॰ – (देश) देश, प्रदेश। region, country, a district.

देसक – पु॰ – (देशक) देशना करने वाला, उपदेशक। a preacher, one who expounds.

देसना – स्त्री॰ – (देशना) उपदेश। discourse, sermon, preaching.

देसना-विलास – पु॰ – (देशना-विलास) देशना का सौन्दर्य। charm of instruction.

देसिक – वि॰ – (दैशिक) प्रदेश-विशेष से सम्बन्धित। belonging to a country or province.

देसित – कृ॰ – (दिष्ट) उपदिष्ट। preached, pointed out.

देसेति – क्रि॰ – (दिशति) उपदेश देता है। points out, preaches, expounds.

देसेतु – देखें देसक। see Desaka.

देस्स – वि॰ – (द्वेष्य) प्रतिकूल। disagreeable, odious.

देसिय – (द्वेषिय/द्वेषीय) देखें – देस्स। see Dessa.

देह – पु॰ तथा न॰ – (देह) शरीर। the body.

देह-निक्खेपन – न॰ – (देह-निक्षेप) शरीर-त्याग, मृत्यु। laying down the body, death.

देह-निस्सित – वि॰ – (देह-निःश्रित) शरीर सम्बन्धी। connected with or belonging to the body.

देहनी – स्त्री॰ – (देहली) दहलीज। threshold.

देहावयव – पु॰ – (देहावयव) शरीर का कोई अंग। part of a body, an organ.

देही – पु॰ – (देहधारी) देहधारी। that which has a body, a creature.

दोण – न॰ – (द्रोण) बुद्धकालीन एक माप विशेष। चार सेर का एक आढक और चार आढक का एक द्रोण होता था। एक सेर में 8 कुञ्ची और एक कुञ्ची में 8 मुट्ठी होती थी। एक सेर लगभग 6 छटांक के। a measure of capacity at the time of the Buddha. One *droṇa* consisted of four *āḍhaka*'s one *āḍhaka* consisted of four *seers* one *seer* was of eight *kunchi*, and one *kunchi* consisted of eight handfuls. One seer was of about size *chaṇṭāks*.

दोण – पु॰ – (द्रोण) भगवान् बुद्ध का शरीरान्त होने पर भस्मी पर स्तूप बनाने को उत्सुक प्रान्तपतियों के बीच उनकी अस्थियों का बँटवारा करने वाला द्रोण ब्राह्मण ज॰ द्रोण प्रदेश का वासी होने के कारण द्रोण ब्राह्मण कहलाता है। द्रोण प्रदेश आजकल दांग, राप्ती अंचल, नेपाल में है। brāhmaṇa who was at Kuśinār. at the time of Buddha's death and whom the claimant requested to undertake th distribution of the relics of th Buddha.

दोणि – स्त्री॰ – (द्रोणि) द्रोणि, नौका, कठवत। a boat, a canoe, a trough.

दोणिका – स्त्री॰ – (द्रोणिका) देखें दोणि। see Doni.

दोमनस्स – न॰ – (दोर्मनस्व, दुर्मनस्व) असंतोष, चैतसिक दुःख। displeasure, melancholy, grief.

दोला – स्त्री॰ – (दोला, दोलनम्) झूला, पालकी। a swing palanquin.

दोलायति – क्रि॰ – (दोलायते) झुलाता है। to swing, to move to and fro.

दोबारिक – पु॰ – (दौवारिक) द्वारपाल। gate-keeper.

दोस – पु॰ – (दोष) द्वेष, क्रोध, दोष। anger, corruption, defect.

दोसक्खान – न॰ – (दोषाख्यान) दोषारोपण। blaming.

दोसग्गि – पु॰ – (द्वेषाग्नि) द्वेषाग्नि। the fire of anger.

दोसञ्ञू – पु॰ – (दोषज्ञ) धर्माधिकारी। a judge.

दोसापगत – वि॰ – (दोषापगत) दोषरहित। free from fault or defect.

दोसिना – स्त्री॰ – (दोषा) चाँदनी रात। bright, moonlit night.

दोसो – पु॰ – (दोषा) रात्रि। night.

दोह – पु॰ तथा न॰ – (दोह) दूध दुहना, दोहन। milking the cow, a milking vessel.

दोहक (1) – पु॰ – (दोग्धा) दूध दुहने वाला। one who milks.

दोहक (2) – न॰ – (दोहन-पात्रम्) दोहनी। milking pot.

दोहळ – पु॰ – (दौर्हृद/दौहृद/दोहद) गर्भिणी की बलवती इच्छा, दोहद। longing of a pregnant woman.

दोहळिनी – स्त्री॰ – (दौहृदिनी) दोहद की इच्छा वाली। the pregnant woman who has some longing.

दोही (1) – वि॰ – (द्रोही) द्रोह करने वाला, द्रोही, अकृतज्ञ। an ungrateful person.

दोही (2) – पु॰ – (दोहकः) दूध दुहने वाला। milking man.

द्रव – पु॰ – (द्रव) रस, तरल पदार्थ। liquid, juice.

द्वङ्गुल – वि॰ – (द्व्यङ्गुल) दो अङ्गुल भर। measuring two inches.

द्वत्तिक्खत्तुं – क्रि॰ वि॰ – (द्वित्रित्वा) दो-तीन बार। twice-thrice.

द्वत्तिपत्त – न॰ – (द्वित्रिपात्रम्) दो-तीन पात्र। two or three bowls.

द्वत्तिंसति – स्त्री॰ – (द्वात्रिंशति) बत्तीस। thirty-two.

द्वन्द – न॰ – (द्वन्द्व) जोड़ा, द्वन्द्व (समास)। a pair, couple, dyad, the collective compound.

द्वय – न॰ – (द्वय) दो। two.

द्वाचत्तालीसति – स्त्री॰ – (द्वाचत्वारिंशत्) बयालीस। forty-two.

द्वादस – वि॰ – (द्वादश) बारह। twelve.

द्वानवुति – स्त्री॰ – (द्वानवतिः) बानबे। ninety-two.

द्वार – न॰ – (द्वार) दरवाजा। door.

द्वार-कवाट – न॰ – (द्वार-कपाटम्) दरवाजे के किवाड़। panel of door.

द्वार-कोट्ठक – न॰ – (द्वार-कोष्ठक) दरवाजे के ऊपर का कमरा, फाटक के पास का कमरा। room over a gate, room near the gateway.

द्वार-गाम – पु॰ – (द्वार-ग्राम) नगर-द्वार के बाहर का गाँव। village outside the city-gate.

द्वारपाल – पु॰ – (द्वारपाल) चौकीदार, पहरेदार। gateman, gate-keeper.

द्वार-बाहा – स्त्री॰ – (द्वार-स्तम्भ) दरवाजे का खम्भा। door-post.

द्वार-साला – स्त्री॰ – (द्वार-शाला) दरवाजे के समीप की शाला। a hall near the gate.

द्वारिक – वि॰ – (द्वारिक) द्वार से सम्बन्धित, पु॰ द्वारपाल। belonging to a gate, (m.) a door-keeper.

द्वाबीसति – स्त्री॰ – (द्वाविंशति) बाईस। twenty-two.

द्वासट्ठि – स्त्री॰ – (द्वाषष्टिः) बासठ। sixty-two.

द्वासट्ठि-दिट्ठि – स्त्री॰ – (द्वाषष्टिः/दृष्टिः) बासठ, मिथ्या मत। the sixty-two.

द्वासत्तति – स्त्री॰ – (द्वासप्ततिः) बहत्तर। seventy-two.

द्वासीति – स्त्री॰ – (द्वयशीतिः) बयासी। eighty-two.

द्वि – वि॰ – (द्वि) दो। two.

द्विक – न॰ – (द्विक) युग्म, दो की जोड़ी। pair, couple.

द्विक्खुत्तुं – क्रि॰ वि॰ – (द्विकृत्वा) दो बार। twice.

द्विगुण – वि॰ – (द्विगुण) दुगुना। twofold, double.

द्विचत्तालीसति – स्त्री॰ – (द्विचत्वारिंशत्) बयालीस। forty-two.

द्विज – पु॰ – (द्विज) देखें दिज। see Dija.

द्वि-जिव्ह – वि॰ – (द्वि-जिह्व) दो जीभों वाला (सर्प)। a serpent (having two tongues).

द्वि-नवुति – वि॰ – (द्विनवतिः) बानबे। ninety-two.

द्वि-पञ्ञासति – स्त्री॰ – (द्वि-पञ्चाशत्) बावन। fifty-two.

द्वि-मासिक – वि॰ – (द्वि/द्वै मासिक) दो ही महीने का। two months old, existing for two months.

द्वि-सट्ठि – स्त्री॰ – (द्वि-षष्टिः) बासठ। sixty-two.

द्वि-सत – न॰ – (द्वि-शतम्) दो सौ। two hundred.

द्वि-सत्तति – स्त्री॰ – (द्वि-सप्ततिः) बहत्तर। seventy-two.

द्वि-सहस्स – न॰ – (द्वि-सहस्र) दो हजार। two thousand.

द्वि-गोचर – पु॰ – (द्वि-गोचरः) दो जनों के बीच की बातचीत। the talk between two persons..

द्विधा – क्रि॰ वि॰ – (द्विधा) दो तरह। in two ways.

द्विधा-पथ – पु॰ – (द्विधा-पथ) सड़क का दो ओर बँट जाना। two sides of a road.

द्विप – पु॰ – (द्विप) हाथी। an elephant.

द्विरद – पु॰ – (द्विरद) हाथी। an elephant.

द्वीह – न॰ – (द्वयहः) दो दिन। two days.

द्वीह – क्रि॰ वि॰ – (द्वयाह्निक) दो दिन में। in two days.

द्वीह-तीहं – क्रि॰ विशेषण – (द्व्यहं-त्र्यहम्) दो या तीन दिन में। in two or three days.

द्वे – वि॰ – (द्वे) संख्यावाची विशेषण दो। the two.

द्वे-भाव – पु॰ – (द्वे-भाव) दोहरापन। two-foldness.

द्वे-वाचिक – वि॰ – (द्व्य-वाचिकः) दो शब्द ही दोहराने वाला। having only two words.

द्वैज्ञ – वि॰ – (द्वैध) सन्देह, विरोध। two-fold knowledge, doubt.

द्वैधा – क्रि॰ विशेषण – (द्वैधा) दो तरह से। in two ways.

द्वैधा-पथ – पु॰ – (द्वैधा-पथ) अवान्तर पथ। a cross-road.

द्वैल्हक – न॰ – (द्वैधक) शक, सन्देह। doubt.

ध

ध – पालि वर्णमाला का उन्नीसवाँ व्यञ्जन। the nineteenth consonant of Pali alphabet.

धंक – पु॰ – (काक) कौआ। a crow.

धंसित – कृ॰ – (ध्वंसित) ध्वस्त। devastated.

धज – पु॰ – (ध्वज) ध्वजा। flag, emblem.

धजगग – (ध्वजाग्र) ध्वजा का सिरा। the top of a standard.

धजालु – वि॰ – (ध्वजालि) ध्वजाओं से सुसज्जित। adorned with flags.

धजाहट – वि॰ – (ध्वजाहृत) युद्ध में जीतकर लाया हुआ। captured in war, taken as a booty.

धजविहेळ-जातक – (जा॰ सं॰ 391) – दिन में तपस्वी, रात में बनारस के राजा की रानी के पास जाने वाले जादूगर की कथा। the story (No. 391) of a wizard who used to be an ascetic during tea day but went at mid-night to corrupt the queen of Banaras.

धजिनी – स्त्री॰ – (ध्वजिनी) सेना। an army.

धञ्ञ – न॰ – (धान्य) धान्य। grain, corn.

धञ्ञ – वि॰ – (धन्य) सौभाग्य-सम्पन्न। fortunate, lucky.

धञ्ञ-पिटक – न॰ – (धान्य-पिटक) धान्य की टोकरी। a basket of grains.

धञ्ञ-रासि – पु॰ – (धान्य-राशि) धान्य का ढेर। a heap of grain.

धञ्ञवन्तु – वि॰ – (धन्यवन्त) सौभाग्य-सम्पन्न। fortunate, lucky.

धञ्ञगार – वि॰ – (धान्यागार) अनाज का गोदाम। granary.

धत – कृ॰ – ($\sqrt{}$ धृ + त = धृत) धृत, धारण किया हुआ, स्मरण रखा हुआ। kept in mind, known by heart.

धन – न॰ – (धन) धन, दौलत। wealth, riches.

धनगग – पु॰ – (धनाग्र) श्रेष्ठ, धन। super, wealth.

धनत्थिक – पु॰ – (धनार्थिक) धनार्थी, धन की इच्छा रखने वाला। desiring wealth.

धनक्खय – पु॰ – (धनक्षयः) धन का क्षय। reduction of wealth.

धनक्कीत – वि॰ – (धनक्रीत) धन से खरीदा गया। bought for money.

धनत्थद्ध – वि॰ – (धनोद्धत) धन का अभिमानी। proud of wealth.

धन-लोल – वि॰ – (धन-लोलुप) धन का लोभी। greedy of wealth.

धनवन्तु – वि॰ – (धनवान) धनवान। rich, wealthy.

धन-हेतु – (धन-हेतु) धन के लिए। for the sake of wealth.

धनासा – स्त्री॰ – (धनाशा) धन की आशा। craving for wealth.

धनञ्जय-जातक – (जा॰ सं॰ 413) – पुराने योद्धाओं की ओर ध्यान न दे नये योद्धाओं की ही आवभगत करने वाले राजा के

301

पश्चाताप की कथा। the sorrowful tale (No. 413) of a king who used to neglect his old warriors and respect only new-comers.

धनायति – क्रि॰ – (धनायते) धन समझता है। considers something as one's wealth.

धनिक – पु॰ – (धनिक) ऋणदाता। creditor.

धनित – न॰ – (ध्वनित) आवाज, वि॰ ध्वनित, आवाज किया गया। n. sound, adj. sounded, sonant.

धनी – वि॰ – (धनी) धनवान। wealthy.

धनु – न॰ – (धनुः) धनुष, कमान। a bow.

धनुक – न॰ – (धनुष्क) छोटा धनुष। a small bow.

धनुकार – पु॰ – (धनुकार) धनुष बनाने वाला। bow-maker.

धनुकेतकी – पु॰ – (धनु-केतकी) केतकी। the screw-pine.

धनुग्गह – पु॰ – (धनुग्रहः) धनुर्धारी। an archer.

धनुसिप्प – न॰ –(धनुशिशिल्प) धनुर्विद्या, तीरन्दाजी। the art of shooting.

धनुपञ्चसत – न॰ – (धनुः पञ्चशतम्) पाँच सौ धनुष या कोस-भर का फासला। a distance of two miles.

धन्त – कृ॰ – (√ध्मा + क्त = ध्यातः) फूँका हुआ। sounded, blown.

धम – वि॰ – (धमक) (तुरही) बजाने वाला। one who blows, player of a trumpet.

धमक – वि॰ – (धमक) (तुरही) बजाने वाला। player of trumpet.

धमकरक – पु॰ – पानी छानने का साधन। filter or water strainer.

धमति – क्रि॰ – (ध्माति) बजाता है। blows.

धमनि – स्त्री॰ – (धमनी) नस, रग। a vein.

धमनि-संथत-गत्त – वि॰ – (धमति संस्थित-गात्र) – जिसके सारे शरीर पर नसें ही नसें दिखाई दें। having veins showing all over the body (for lack of flesh).

धमेति – क्रि॰ – (ध्माति) बजाता है। blows.

धमापेति – क्रि॰ – (√ध्मा = धमापयति) बजवाता है। causes to blow.

धम्म – पु॰ – (धर्म) धर्म, सिद्धान्त, स्वभाव, सत्य सदाचार। doctrine, nature, truth, the norm, morality, good conduct.

धम्मक्खान – न॰ – (धर्माख्यान) धर्म की व्याख्या। preaching of the doctrine.

धम्म-कथा – स्त्री॰ – (धर्म-कथा) धार्मिक कथा। religious talk.

धम्म-कथिक – पु॰ – (धर्म-कथाकार) उपदेष्टा। one who preaches the norm (*dharma*).

धम्म-कम्म – न॰ – (धर्म-कर्म) विधि सम्मत कार्य, विनय के अनुकूल क्रिया-कलाप। a legally valid act, procedure in accordance with rules.

धम्म-काम – वि॰ – (धर्मकामी) धर्म-प्रिय धर्म चाहने वाला। lover of the truth.

धम्म-काय – वि॰ – (धर्म-काय) धर्म-काय। the normal body.

धम्मक्खन्ध – पु॰ – (धर्म-स्कन्ध) धर्म-स्कन्ध। a portion of the norm (*dhrama*).

धम्म-गण्ठिका – स्त्री॰ – (धर्माधिष्ठान) धर्म न्याय का स्थान। the place of justice.

धम्म-गण्डिका – स्त्री॰ – (धर्माधिष्ठान) देखें

धम्म गणिठका। see Dhamma-
gaṇṭhikā.

धम्म-गरु – वि॰ – (धर्म-गौरव) धर्म का
गौरव। respect for the norm
(*dharma*).

धम्म-गुत्त – वि॰ – (धर्म्य-गुप्तिः) धर्म द्वारा
सुरक्षित। protected by the norm
(*dharma*).

धम्म-घोसक – पु॰ – (धर्म-घोषक) धर्म की
घोषणा करने वाला। one who
announces about the preaching
of the norm (*dharma*).

धम्म-चक्क – न॰ – (धर्म-चक्र) धर्म-चक्र।
the wheel of norm (*dharma*).

धम्म-चक्क-पवत्तन – न॰ – (धर्म-चक्र-
प्रवर्त्तन) धर्म-चक्र प्रवर्तन, धर्म-देशना।
preaching of the universal
righteousness.

धम्मचक्कपवत्तन-सुत्त – (धर्म-चक्र-प्रवर्त्तन
सूक्त) आषाढ़-पूर्णिमा के इसिपतन के
मिगदाय में पञ्च-वर्गीय भिक्षुओं को भगवान
बुद्ध द्वारा दिया गया सर्वप्रथम उपदेश।
name of the first sermon,
preached by the Buddha, to the
Pañcavaggiyas at the Migdāya
in Isipattan, on the full moon
day of Āsādha.

धम्म-चक्खु – न॰ – (धर्म-चक्षु) धर्म-चक्षु।
the eye of wisdom.

धम्म-चरिया – स्त्री॰ – (धर्म-चर्या) धर्माचरण।
observance of righteousness.

धम्मचारी – पु॰ – (धर्माचारी) धर्मानुसार
आचरण करने वाला। one who walks
on the right path.

धम्म-चेतिय – न॰ – (धर्म-चैत्य) पवित्र-
धर्म-ग्रन्थालय। a shrine in which
sacred texts are enshrined.

धम्म-जातक – (जा॰ सं॰ 457) – धर्म तथा
अधर्म का शास्त्रार्थ। (story No. 457)
a debate based on arguments for
dharma and *adharma* (right and
wrong).

धम्मजीवी – वि॰ ← (धर्मजीवी) धर्मानुसार
जीवन जीने वाला। one living
righteously.

धम्मञ्जु – वि॰ – (धर्मज्ञ) धर्मज्ञ, धर्म के
तत्त्वों को जानने वाला। one who
knows the doctrine (of *dhrama*)

धम्मट्ठ – वि॰ – (धर्मिष्ठ) धर्म-स्थित। just,
righteous.

धम्मट्ठिति – स्त्री॰ – (धर्म-स्थिति) धर्म-
स्थिति, धर्म का वास्तविक स्वरूप। the
real nature of the norm (*dharma*).

धम्म-तक्क – पु॰ – (धर्म-तर्क) धर्म तक,
सही तर्क करना। right reasoning.

धम्मता – स्त्री॰ – (धर्मता / धर्मत्व)
स्वाभाविक नियम। general rule,
natural law.

धम्म-दान – न॰ – (धर्म-दानम्) धर्म-दान।
the gift of the norm (*dharma*)

धम्म-दायाद – वि॰ – (धर्म-दायाद) धर्म का
उत्तराधिकारी। spiritual heir.

धम्म-दीप – वि॰ – (धर्म-द्वीप) धर्म-द्वीप।
having the *dharma* (norm) as a
sound footing.

धम्म-देसना – स्त्री॰ – (धर्म-देशना
धर्मोपदेशः) धर्म का उपदेश। exposition
of the norm.

धम्म-देस्सी – पु॰ – (धर्म-द्वेषी) धर्म-द्वेषी।
hater of the norm.

धम्म-धज – वि॰ – (धर्म-ध्वजः) जो धर्म
को ही ध्वजा समझे। having *dhamma*
as one's banner.

धम्मद्धज-जातक – (जा० सं० 220) – एक घूसखोर तथा एक धार्मिक पुरोहित की संघर्ष गाथा। it is a story (No. 220) of a conflict between two priests, one cunning and the other virtuous.

धम्मद्धज-जातक – (जा० सं० 384) – धर्मध्वजी कौवे ने दूसरे पक्षियों को धोखा देकर उन सबके बच्चे खा डाले। the story (No. 384) of a deceitful crow who ate the young ones of other birds but was killed as the result of his cunningness.

धम्मधर – वि० – (धर्म-धरः) धर्मरत, धर्मानुयायी, धर्म-धर। one who knows and follows the norm (*dharma*) by heart.

धम्म-नियाम – पु० – (धर्म-नियम) प्राकृतिक नियम, स्वाभाविक नियम। the natural law, the moral law.

धम्मनी – पु० – (धामिन) मूषक प्रियः, गृह-सर्प, धामिन साँप। the rat snake.

धम्म-पण्णाकार – पु० – (धर्मपहारः) धर्म-भेंट। the present consisting of *dharma*.

धम्म-पद – न० – (धर्मपद) धर्म के पघ, खुद्दक निकाय का दूसरा ग्रन्थ। सम्भवतः यह थेरगाथा व थेरीगाथा के बाद का गाथा-संकलन है। the second book of Khuddaka Nikāya of the Sutta Piṭaka, it is believed that it is a later collection than the Thera-Therī-gāthā.

धम्म-पद-अट्ठकथा – जातक अर्थ-कथाओं की भाँति धम्म-पद की व्याख्यापरक कथाओं से समन्वित टीका। the commentary on the Dhammapada containing stories similar to those of the Jātakas.

धम्मप्पमाण – वि० – (धर्म-प्रमाण) धर्म-माप। measuring by the teaching.

धम्म-भण्डागारिक – पु० – (धर्मभाण्डागारिक) धर्म का खजान्ची, भगवान् बुद्ध के निकटतम शिष्य आनन्द के लिए प्रयुक्त। the treasures of the norm (*dharma*), it is used for Ānanda the chief disciple of the Buddha.

धम्म-भेरि – स्त्री० – (धर्म-भेरी/धर्म-घोष) धर्म का ढोल। the drum of the norm (*dharma*), the announcement of the norm.

धम्म-रक्खित – वि० – (धर्म-रक्षित) धर्म-रक्षित। protected by the norm (*dharma*).

धम्म-रत – वि० – (धर्म-रत) धर्म-रत, धर्म-प्रिय। fond of religious view, religious attitude.

धम्म-रति – स्त्री० – (धर्म-रति) धर्म-प्रीति। delight in moral act.

धम्म-रस – पु० – (धर्म-रस) धर्म-रस। taste of the norm (*dharma*).

धम्म-राजा – पु० – (धर्म-राजा) धर्म राजा, भगवान् बुद्ध के लिए प्रयुक्त। the king of righteousness.

धम्म-लब्ध – वि० – (धर्म-लब्ध) धर्म से प्राप्त। righteously acquired.

धम्मवर – पु० – (धर्मवर) धर्म-श्रेष्ठ। the excellent doctrine.

धम्मवादी – वि० – (धर्मवादी) धर्मानुसार बोलने वाला। speaking according to law.

धम्म-विचय – पु० – (धर्म + वि + चय) धर्म का चयन, धर्म मीमांसा। investigation of doctrine.

धम्म-विदू – पु० – (धर्म-विद्) धर्म का जानकार। one who understands the moral laws.

धम्म-विनिच्छय – पु० – (धर्म-विनिश्चय) धार्मिक निश्चय। righteous decision.

धम्म-विहारी – वि० – (धर्म-विहारी) धर्म के अनुसार आचरण वाला। living according to the moral laws.

धम्म-सङ्गणि – पु० – (धर्म-सङ्गणि) अभिधम्म पिटक के सात प्रकरणों में से पहला ग्रन्थ। the first book among the seven compiled in Abhidhamma Piṭaka.

धम्म-संगीति – स्त्री० – (धर्म-संगीति) धर्म-संगायन। recital of sacred scriptures.

धम्म-संविभाग – पु० – (धर्म-संविभाग) धर्मानुसार बँटवारा। the division according to law.

धम्म-संगाहक – पु० – (धर्म-संग्राहक) धर्म ग्रन्थ का सम्पादन करने वाला। compiler of the religious scriptures.

धम्म-समादान – न० – (धर्म-समादान) धर्म का ग्रहण। acquisition of the norm (dharma).

धम्म-सवण – न० – (धर्म-श्रवण) धर्म का श्रवण। the hearing of the norm (dharma).

धम्म-साकच्छा – स्त्री० – (धर्म-परिचर्चा) धार्मिक चर्चा। discussion about morality.

धम्म-सेनापति – पु० – (धर्म-सेनापति) धर्म-सेनापति प्रायः भगवान् बुद्ध के अग्रश्रावक सारिपुत्र के लिए प्रयुक्त हुआ हैं। generalissimo of the law in Pāli-books, it has been used for Sāriputta the chief pupil of the Buddha.

धम्म-सोण्ड – वि० – (धर्म-शौण्ड / धर्म रतः) धर्म-प्रेमी। fond of the norm.

धम्म-स्सामी – पु० – (धर्म-स्वामी) धर्म का अधिकारिक ज्ञाता-व्याख्याता। the lord of the norm.

धम्माधिपति – वि० – (धर्माधिपतिः) धर्म को स्वामी मानने वाला। respecting the law as one's guide.

धम्मानुधम्म – पु० – (धर्मानुधर्म) धर्माचरण, धर्मानुसार आचरण। conformity with the law.

धम्मानुवत्ती – वि० – (धर्मानुवर्त्ती) धर्मानुयायी। acting in conformity with the norm (dharma).

धम्माभिसमय – पु० – (धर्मा-भिसमय) धर्म-विचक्षणा, धर्म की समझ। understanding of the truth.

धम्मामतं – न० – (धर्मामृतम्) धर्म-रूपी अमृत। the nectar of the norm (dharma).

धम्मादास – पु० – (धर्मादर्श / धर्म-दर्पण) धर्म-दर्पण। the mirror of the norm (dharmu).

धम्माधार – वि० – (धर्माधार) धर्म ही सहारा। being a support to the norm (dharma).

धम्मासन – न० – (धर्मासन) धर्मासन। a pulpit.

धम्मिक – वि० – (धार्मिक) धार्मिक, धर्मानुकूल। righteous.

धम्मिल्ल – पु० – (जटाग्रन्थिः / केशबन्धः) जूड़ा, बालों की गाँठ। a knot of hair, braided hair.

धम्मीकथा – स्त्री॰ – (धर्मी-कथा/धर्म-कथा) धार्मिक कथा। religious talk.

√धार – (भू॰) – (धारणे) धारण करना। to hold, to wear.

√धार – चु॰ – (धारणे) धारण करना। to hold, to wear.

धर – वि॰ – (धरः) समास पद के रूप में प्रयुक्त जैसे – सत्य को धारण करने वाला। (used in compounds) bearing, holding, keeping in mind.

धरणी – स्त्री॰ – (धरणी) पृथ्वी। the earth.

धरणीरुह – पु॰ – (धरणी रुह/भूरुह) वृक्ष। a tree.

धरति – क्रि॰ – (√धृ = धारयति) धारण करता है, जारी रहता है। lasts, continues, lives.

धरा – स्त्री॰ – (धरा) भूमि। the earth.

धव – पु॰ – (धवः) पति, धव नामक वृक्ष। the husband, the *acacia* tree.

धवल – वि॰ – (धवल) श्वेत, स्वच्छ, पु॰ श्वेत रंग। white, clean, white colour.

धा – (भू॰) – (धारणे) धारण करना। to hold, to wear.

धात – कृ॰ – (√धा + क्त = घात) भरा-पेट, संतुष्ट। fed, satiated.

धातकी – स्त्री॰ – (धातकी) अग्नि ज्वाला। flame of fire.

धाती – स्त्री॰ – (धात्री) दाई। a nurse, foster mother.

धातु – स्त्री॰ – (धातु) स्वाभाविक अवस्था, पवित्र (अस्थि) धातु, शब्द का मूल स्वरूप, शारीरिक धातु, इन्द्रिय। an element, natural condition, a relic, root of a world, semen, faculty of senses.

धातु-कथा – स्त्री॰ – (धातु-कथा) (1) धातुओं की व्याख्या (2) अभिधम्म पिटक का तीसरा ग्रन्थ। (1) an explanation about elements, (2) the third book of the Abhidhamma Piṭaka.

धातु-घर – न॰ – (धातु-गृह) पवित्र धातु-गृह। a relic chamber.

धातु-नानत्त – न॰ – (धातु-नानात्व) धातुओं के विविध प्रकार। diversity of nature or elements.

धातु-विभाग – पु॰ – (धातु-विभाग) धातुओं का पृथक्-पृथक् विश्लेषण। separation of elements, distribution of relics.

धातुक – वि॰ – (धातुक) धातु की प्रकृति लिये (समास रूप में प्रयुक्त)। having the nature of (used in compounds).

धाना – स्त्री॰ – (धाना) भुना हुआ जौ या चावल। fried barley or rice.

धार – वि॰ – (धार) समास के रूप में प्रयुक्त जैसे–सूत्र-धार अर्थात् सूत्र को धारण करने वाला। (used in compounds) bearing, holding, wearing.

धारक – वि॰ – (धारक) समस्त पद के रूप में प्रयुक्त धारण करने वाला, पालन-पोषण करने वाला, याद रखने वाला। used in compounds : bearing, holding, wearing.

धारण – न॰ – (धारण) धारण करना। act of holding or protecting.

धारा – स्त्री॰ – (धारा) जल-धारा। a torrent, stream, shower.

धाराधर – पु॰ – (धाराधर) बादल। cloud.

धारित – कृ॰ – (धृत/धारित) धारण किया हुआ। held, worn.

धारी – वि॰ – (धारी) समास रूप में प्रयुक्त – धारण करने वाला। (used in compounds) bearing, holding, wearing.

धारेति – क्रि॰ – (धारयति) धारण करता है। bears, holds, wears.

धारेतु – वि॰ – (धारयिता) धारण करने वाला। bearer, holder, wearer.

धारेन्त – कृ॰ – (धारयन) धारण करता हुआ। remains holding or bearing.

धारेसि – अतीत – क्रि॰ – (अधारयत) धारण किया। held, worn.

धारेत्वा – पूर्व क्रि॰ – (धारयित्वा) धारण करके। having held or worn.

धाव – (भू॰) – (धावने) दौड़ना। to run.

धावति – क्रि॰ – (√धाव् = धावति) दौड़ता है। runs.

धावन्त – कृ॰ – (धावन) दौड़ता हुआ। running.

धावि – अतीत क्रि॰ – (अधावत) दौड़ा। ran, had run.

धावित – कृ॰ – (धावित) दौड़ा हुआ। run.

धाविय – पु॰ क्रि॰ – देखें धावित्वा। see Dhāvitvā.

धावित्वा – पु॰ क्रि॰ – (धावित्वा) दौड़कर। having run.

धावन – न॰ – (धावन) दौड़। running.

धावी – वि॰ – (धावी) दौड़ने वाला। one who runs.

धि – अव्यय – (धि) धिक्कार। fie, shame, woe.

धिक्कत – वि॰ – (धिक्कृत) घृणित। despised, detested, reviled.

धिति – स्त्री॰ – (धृति) धैर्य, सहन-शक्ति। energy, courage.

धितिमन्तो – वि॰ – (धृतिमान) धृतिमान। energetic, resolute.

धी – स्त्री॰ – (धी) बुद्धि। wisdom.

धीमन्तो – वि॰ – (धीमान) बुद्धिमान। energetic, resolute.

धीतलिका – स्त्री॰ – (पुत्तलिका) गुड़िया। a doll.

धीतु – स्त्री॰ – (दुहिता) धी, बेटी। daughter.

धीतु-पति – पु॰ – (दुहितृ-पति) जामाता, जँवाई। son-in-law.

धीयति – क्रि॰ – (√धि = धियति) धारणा करता है, पकड़ता है, उत्पन्न होता है। is contained, appears.

धीयमान – कृ॰ – उत्पन्न होने वाला। one who appears, one who shows up.

धीर – वि॰ – (धीर) ध्यानशील, बुद्धिमान। intent, wise.

धीरत्त – न॰ – (धीरत्व) धीरज, धीरता, धैर्य-भाव। firmness, calmness.

धीवर – पु॰ – (धीवर) मछुआ। fisherman.

धुत – कृ॰ – (√धू + क्त = धुत) धुना गया, हटाया गया। shaken off, removed.

धुतङ्ग – न॰ – (धूताङ्ग) तपस्वियों के व्रत-विशेष। a special fast of an ascetic.

धुत-धर – वि॰ – (धुत-धर) धुतङ्गधारी। one who practises *dhutaṅga*.

धुतवादी – पु॰ – (धूतवादी) देखें धुतधर। see Dhutadhara.

धुत्त – पु॰ – (धूर्त्त) धूर्त। scoundrel, a cheat.

धुत्तक – पु॰ – (धूर्त्तक) धूर्त। scoundrel, a cheat.

धुत्तिका – स्त्री॰ – (धूर्त्तिका) धूर्तक का स्त्रीलिङ्ग। feminine of Dhurttaka.

धुत्ती – (धूर्त्ती) देखें धुत्तिका। see Dhurttikā.

धुनन – न॰ – (धूनन) हटाना, दूर करना, झाड़ फेंकना। shaking off, doing away with.

धुनाति – क्रि॰ – (√धू = धुनाति/धुनोति) हिलाता है, दूर करता है। moves, shakes.

धुनन्त – कृ॰ – (धुनन) धुनता हुआ। shaken off.

धुनितब्ब – कृ॰ – (धुनितव्य) धुनने योग्य। fit for shaking off.

धुनित्वा – पु॰ क्रि॰ – (धुनित्वा) धुनकर। having shaken off.

धुपित – कृ॰ – (√धूप् + क्त = धूपित) गर्म किया गया। fumigated, heated.

धुर – न॰ – (धुर) उत्तरदायित्व। responsibility, a charge.

धुर-गाम – पु॰ – (धुर-ग्राम) पड़ोसी ग्राम। neighbouring village.

धुरंधर – वि॰ – (धुरन्धर) पदाधिकारी। taking the responsibility.

धुर-निक्खेप – पु॰ – (धुर-निक्षेप) पद-परित्याग। giving up responsibility.

धुर-भत्त – न॰ – (धुर-भत्त) नियमित भोजन। regularly given meal.

धुर-वहन – न॰ – (धुर-वहन) पद-धारण। bearing of the official responsibility.

धुरवाही – पु॰ – (धुरवाही) भारवाहक पशु। animal bearing a burden.

धुर-विहार – पु॰ – (धुर-विहार) पड़ोसी विहार। neighbouring monastery.

धुव – वि॰ – (ध्रुव) स्थायी। stable, permanent.

धुवं – क्रि॰ वि॰ – (ध्रुवं) ध्रुव, लगातार, सिलसिलेवार। regularly, constantly.

धूत – देखें धुत। see Dhuta.

धूप – पु॰ – (धूप) धूप (बत्ती)। incense.

धूपन – न॰ – (धूपनम्) (1) धूप जलाना, (2) छौंकना। (1) fumigation by incense (2) flavouring, seasoning.

धूपायति – क्रि॰ – (धूपायति) धुआँ देता है। fumigates.

धूपायी – कृ॰ – (धूपायित) धुआँ दिया। fumigated.

धूपायन्ति – कृ॰ – (धूपायन) धुआँ देता हुआ। having been fumigated.

धूपायित – कृ॰ – (धूपायित) धुआँ दिया हुआ। fumigated.

धूपेति – क्रि॰ – (धूपायति) छौंकता है। fumigates.

धूपित – कृ॰ – (धूपित) छौंका हुआ। flavoured, fumigated.

धूपेत्वा – पु॰ क्रि॰ – (धूपेत्वा) छौंककर। having fumigated.

धूम – पु॰ – (धूम) धुआँ। smoke, fumes.

धूम-केतु – पु॰ – (धूमकेतु) धूमकेतु तारा। a comet, fire.

धूम-जाल – न॰ – (धूम-जाल) धुएँ का जाल। a mass of smoke.

धूम-नेत्त – न॰ – (धूम-नेत्र) धुआँ निकलने का रास्ता। an outlet for smoke.

धूम-सिख – पु० – (धूम-शिखा) धूम्र-शिखा, आग। fire.

धूमयति – क्रि० – (धूमायति) धूमापात करता है, धुआँ करता है। smokes, smoulders.

धूमायति – क्रि० – (धूमायति) देखें धूमयति। see Dhūmayati.

धूमायितत्त – न॰ – (धूमायितत्वम्) धुँधला करना, अस्पष्ट करना। smoke abscuration clouding over, becoming like.

धूलि – स्त्री० – (धूलि) धूल। dust.

धूसर – वि० – (धूसर) मटमैला। dust-coloured.

धेनु – स्त्री॰ – (धेनु) गौ। a cow.

धेनुप – पु॰ – (धेनुप) दूध पीता बछड़ा। sucking calf.

धोत – कृ॰ – (धौत) धोया हुआ। washed.

धोन – वि॰ – (धीमान) बुद्धिमान। wise.

धोरह्न – वि॰ – (धौरेय) भार वहन करने में समर्थ। able to bear a burden, to carry the yoke.

धोवति – क्रि॰ – (प्रक्षालयति) धोता है। washes, rinses, cleans.

धोवन – न॰ – (प्रक्षालनम्) धोना। washing, cleaning.

न

न – पालि वर्णमाला का बीसवाँ व्यञ्जन। the twentieth consonant of Pāli alphabet.

न – अव्यय – (न) नहीं। (negative particle) no, not

नकुल – पु॰ – (नकुल) नेवला। mongoose.

नकुल-जातक – (जा॰ सं॰ 165) – साँप तथा नेवले में भी मैत्री-सम्बन्ध स्थापित होने की कथा। the story (No. 165) tells how two bitter enemies became friends when their distrust caused by misunderstanding was removed.

नक्क – पु॰ – (नक्र) घड़ियाल। crocodile.

नक्खत्त – न॰ – (नक्षत्र) नक्षत्र। star, constellation.

नक्खत्त-कीळा – स्त्री॰ – (नक्षत्र-क्रीडा) नक्षत्र-क्रीडा। a festival celebrated at the appearance of some constellations.

नक्खत्त-पाठक – पु॰ – (नक्षत्र-पाठक) ज्योतिषी। an astrologer.

नक्खत्त-योग – पु॰ – (नक्षत्र-योग) नक्षत्रों का योग, जन्म-पत्री। conjunction of the planets, horoscope.

नक्खत्त-राज – पु॰ – (नक्षत्र-राज) चन्द्रमा। the moon.

नक्खत्त-जातक – (जा॰ सं॰ 49) – कथा बतलाती है कि नक्षत्र के अनुसार शादी करने पर तुले वर-पक्ष ने किस प्रकार अपना काम बिगाड़ डाला। the story (No. 49) tells how a family created trouble due to the foolish habit of consulting stars.

नख – पु॰ तथा न॰ – (नख) नाखून। nail (of finger or toe).

नख-पञ्जर – पु॰ – (नख-पञ्जर) पंजा। claw.

नखी – वि॰ – (नखी) पंजों वाला। having claws.

नग – पु॰ – (नग) वृक्ष अथवा पर्वत। tree or mountain.

नगर – न॰ – (नगर) छोटा शहर। town, a citadel.

नगर-गुत्तिक – पु॰ – (नगर-गोप्ता) नगरा-धिपति। mayor.

नगर-वर – न॰ – (नगर-वर) श्रेष्ठ नगर। a noble city.

नगर-वासी – पु॰ – (नगर-वासिन) नागरिक। a citizen.

नगर-सोधक – पु॰ – (नगर-शोधक) नगर-शोधक, शहर की सफाई करने वाला। a town-cleaner.

नगर-सोभिनी – स्त्री॰ – (नगर-शोभिनी)। नगर-वधू। the city belle, town courtesan.

नग्ग – वि॰ – (नग्न) नग्न, नंगा। naked, nude.

नग्ग-चरिया – वि॰ – (नग्न-चर्या) नग्न रहना। nudity.

नग्ग-समण – वि॰ – (नग्न-श्रमण) नग्न-श्रमण। naked ascetic.

नग्गिय – न॰ – (नग्नता) नग्नता, नंगापन। nudity.

नङ्गल – न॰ – (लाङ्गलम्) हल। a plough.

नङ्गल-फाल – पु॰ – (लाङ्गल-फालः) हल का फाल। plough-share.

नङ्गलीस-जातक – (जा॰ सं॰ 123) – एक मूर्ख विद्यार्थी की कथा जो हर वस्तु की उपमा हल की फाल से ही देता था। the story (No. 123) of a stupid student who used the simile of plough shaft for everything.

नङ्-गुट्ठ-जातक – (जा॰ सं॰ 144) – यज्ञाग्नि के निकट बँधी गौ को तापस की अनुपस्थिति में चोरों ने खा डाला। यह देख यज्ञदेव की श्रद्धा से विरत होकर तापस ने अग्नि बुझा दी। (story No. 144) the hermit seeing that thieves have eaten his cow which was tied near the sacrificial fire lost his belief, put out the fire and became a recluse.

नङ्गुल – (लाङ्गुल) पूँछ, दुम। tail.

न चिरस्सं – क्रि॰ विशेषण – (न चिरात्) अचिर काल में, थोड़े समय में। shortly, before long.

नच्च – न॰ – (नृत्य) नृत्य, नाटक। dance, play.

नच्च-जातक – (जा॰ सं॰ 32) – शील और गरिमा के महत्त्व पर प्रकाश डालने वाली जातक कथा। a story (No. 32) emphasizing the value of modesty.

नच्चट्ठान – न॰ – (नृत्य-स्थान) नृत्य-स्थान, नाटक-गृह। dancing place, a theatre.

नच्चक – पु॰ – (नर्त्तक) नाचने वाला, नाटक का पात्र। dancer, actor.

नच्चति – क्रि॰ – (√नृत् = नृत्यति) नाचता है। dances.

नच्चि – अतीत क्रि॰ – (अनृत्यत्) नाचा। danced.

नच्चन्त – कृ॰ – (नृत्यन्) नाचता हुआ। dancing.

नच्चित्वा – पु॰ क्रि॰ – (नर्तित्वा) नाचकर। having danced.

नच्चन – न॰ – (नृत्य) नाचना, नाच। dance, dancing.

नट – पु॰ – (नट) नृत्यकार। dancer, actor.

√नट – (चु॰) – नाट्ये – (√नट्) नाट्य या अभिनय करना। to act in drama.

√नट – (भू॰) – नच्चे – (√नृत्) नाचना। to dance.

नटक – पु॰ – (नर्त्तक) नृत्यकार। dancer, actor.

नट्टु – न॰ – (नृत्य) नृत्य, नाटक। dance, play.

नट्टक – पु॰ – (नर्त्तक) नृत्यकार। dancer, actor.

नट्ठ – कृ॰ – (नष्ट) नष्ट हुआ। lost, perished.

नत – कृ॰ – (√नम् + क्त = नत) झुका हुआ। bent, stooping, inclined.

नति – स्त्री॰ – (नति) नम्रता, झुकाव। bending, inclination, bowing down.

नत्त – न॰ – (नृत्य) नृत्य, नाटक। dance, play.

नत्तक – पु॰ – (नर्त्तक) नृत्यकार। dancer, actor.

नत्तकी – स्त्री॰ – (नर्त्तकी) नर्तकी। female dancer, actress.

नत्तन – न॰ – (नर्त्तन) नृत्य, नाटक। dance, play.

नत्तमाल – पु॰ – (तमाल) वृक्ष-विशेष। the tree Xanthochymus Pictorius, black catechu tree.

नत्तु – पु॰ – (नप्तृ) नाती। grandson.

नत्थि – क्रि॰ – (न + अस्ति = नास्ति) नहीं है। no, not present.

नत्थिक-दिट्ठ – न॰ – (नास्तिक-दृष्टिः) नास्तिक मत। nihilistic view.

नत्थिक-वादी – पु॰ – (नास्तिक-वादी) नास्तिक। one who professes a nihilistic view.

नत्थिता – स्त्री॰ – (नास्तिता) नास्तिता। absence.

नत्थि-भाव – पु॰ – (नास्ति-भाव) न होने का भाव। absence.

नत्थु – स्त्री॰ – (नासा / नासिका) नाक। nose.

नत्थु-कम्म – न॰ – (नस्य-कर्म) नाक की चिकित्सा, नाक के माध्यम से चिकित्सा। nose treatment, treatment through nose.

√नद – (भू) – अत्यत्त सद्दे – (√नद्) नाद करना। to sound.

नदति – (√नद् = नदति) गर्जता है। roars, makes a noise.

नदि – अतीत क्रि॰ – (अनदत्) गरजा, गर्जन किया। roared, made a loud noise.

नदन्त – कृ॰ – (नदन्) गर्जन करता हुआ। roaring, made a loud noise.

नदित – कृ॰ – (√नद् + क्त = नदित) गर्जना से गुंजायमान। roared, made a loud noise.

नदित्वा – पु॰ क्रि॰ – (नदित्वा) गर्जन करके। having roared.

नदन – न॰ – (नदन) गर्जन। roar.

नदी – स्त्री॰ – (नदी) नदी, दरिया। river.

नदी-कूल – न॰ – (नदी-कूल) नदी-तट। river bank.

नदी-दुग्ग – न॰ – (नदी-दुर्ग) जहाँ पहुँचने में नदी बाधक हो। a place in accessible because of rivers.

नदी-मुख – न॰ – (नदी-मुख) नदी का मुहाना। mouth of a river.

नद्ध – कृ॰ – (√नह् + क्त = नद्ध) बँधा हुआ। tied, wrapped, twisted with.

नद्धि – स्त्री॰ – (नद्धि) चमड़े की रस्सी। a thong, a narrow strip of leather.

नन्द-थेर – शुद्धोदन तथा महाप्रजापति गौतमी की सन्तान। सिद्धार्थ गौतम का सौतेला भाई। son of Śuddhodana and Mahāprajāpatī Gautamī and half brother of the Buddha.

√नन्द – (भू) समिद्धिय – (√नन्द्) समृद्ध होना, नव-नन्द नाम से प्रसिद्ध नौ राजागण। the famous nine kings of Nanda dynasty known as Nava-Nanda.

नन्द-जातक – (जा॰ सं॰ 39) – यह कथा शिक्षा देती है कि धन एक ऐसी वस्तु है जिसकी लालच में जाने-परखे लोगों की भी नीयत डोल जाती है। the story (No. 39) reveals that the wealth makes the honest and modest persons too proud and insolent.

ननन्दा – स्त्री॰ – (ननान्दृ) ननद। husband's sister.

ननु – अव्यय – (ननु) निश्चय से। certainly, surely.

नन्दक – वि॰ – (नन्दक) खुशी देने वाला, आनन्ददायक। rejoicing.

नन्दति – क्रि॰ – (√नन्द् = नन्दति) प्रसन्न होता है। becomes glad, rejoice.

नन्दि – अतीत क्रि॰ – प्रसन्न हुआ। become rejoiced.

नन्दित – कृ॰ – (नन्दित) प्रसन्नचित्त। rejoiced.

नन्दमान – कृ॰ – (नन्दमान) प्रसन्न होता हुआ। being rejoiced.

नन्दितब्ब – कृ॰ – (नन्दितव्य) प्रसन्न करने योग्य। rejoiceable.

नन्दित्वा – पु॰ क्रि॰ – (नन्दित्वा) प्रसन्न करके। having rejoiced.

नन्दन – न॰ – (नन्दन) प्रसन्नता, इन्द्र-नगर का उद्यान। rejoicing a garden in Indra's city.

नन्दि – स्त्री॰ – (नन्दि) मनोविनोद। pleasure, joy, delight.

नन्दिक्खय – पु॰ – (नन्दिक्षय) तृष्णा का क्षय। diminution of craving.

नन्दि-राग – पु॰ – (नन्दि-राग) अनुराग। passioned delight.

नन्दि-संयोजन – न॰ – (नन्दि-संयोजन) तृष्णा का बंधन। the fetter of craving.

नन्दियमिग-जातक – (जा॰ सं॰ 385) – कथा बताती है कि किस प्रकार एक मृग की सच्चरित्रता ने उसकी तथा उसके माता-पिता की रक्षा की। the story (No. 385) tells how the virtues of a deer protected the lives of his parents and the community.

नन्दि-विसाल-जातक – (जा॰ सं॰ 28) – कथा बतलाती है कि किस प्रकार एक स्वामिभक्त वृषभ ने शर्त जीतकर अपने मालिक को धनी बनाया। the story (No. 28) tells how a devoted bullock by winning a wager made his master, wealthy.

नय्हति – क्रि॰ – (√नह् - नह्यति = नह्यते) बाँधता है। ties, wraps, twists with.

नय्हि – अतीत क्रि॰ – (अनह्यत्) बाँधा। tied, wrapped, twisted with.

नय्हित्वा – पु॰ क्रि॰ – (√नह् + क्त = नध्वा) बाँधकर। having tied on wrapped or twisted with.

नपुंसक – पु॰ – (नपुंसक) नंपुसक, पुरुषत्व-हीन। eunuch.

नभ – पु॰ तथा न॰ – (नभ) आकाश। the sky.

√नम – (भू) – नमने – (√नम्) नमस्कार करना। to salute.

नमक्कार – पु॰ – (नमस्कार) प्रणति, नमस्कार। homage, veneration, bowed down.

नमति – क्रि॰ – (√नम् = नमति) झुकता है। bends, bows down.

नमि – अतीत क्रि॰ – (अनमत्) झुका। bend, bowed down.

नमन्त – कृ॰ – (नमन्) झुकता है। bowing down.

नमित्वा – पु॰ क्रि॰ – (नत्वा) झुककर। bowing down.

नमितब्ब – कृ॰ – (नमितव्य) झुकना चाहिए। fit for bowing down.

नमस्सति – क्रि॰ – (नमस्करोति) नमस्कार करता है। bows, down.

नमस्सि – अतीत क्रि॰ – (**प्रणमत्**) नमस्कार किया। bowed down.

नमस्सित्वा – पु॰ क्रि॰ – (**नमस्कृत्य**) नमस्कार करके। having bowed down.

नमस्सितुं – पु॰ क्रि॰ – (**नमस्कर्तुम**) नमस्कार करने के लिए। to bow down.

नमस्सन – न॰ – (**नमस्करण**) नमस्कार। veneration, worship.

नमस्सना – स्त्री॰ – (**नमस्कृति**) नमस्कार। veneration, worship.

नमुचि – पु॰ – (**नमुचि**) नष्ट करने वाला, मृत्यु 'मार' का नाम। destroyer, the death.

नमो – अव्यय – (**नमः**) नमस्कार है। my adoration to.

नम्मदा – स्त्री॰ – (**नर्मदा**) नर्मदा नदी। the Narmadā river.

√ नय – (**भू॰**) – गमनत्थे – (**√ नी**) ले जाता है। takes with him.

नय – पु॰ – (**नय**) क्रम, पद्धति, ढंग, ठीक परिणाम। method, plan, manner, inference, right conclusion.

नयति – क्रि॰ – (**√ नी = नयति**) ले जाता है, मार्गदर्शन करता है। leads, guides, conducts.

नयन – न॰ – (**नयन**) (1) आँख (2) ले जाना। (1) the eye (2) carrying.

नयनावुध – पु॰ – (**नयनायुध**) जिसके नयन ही उसके शस्त्र हों–यमराज। one whose eyes are one's weapons, i.e., the king Yama.

नय्हति – क्रि॰ – (**√ नह् = नह्यति**) बाँधता है। ties, wraps, twists with.

नय्हित्वा – पु॰ क्रि॰ – (**√ नह् + त्वा**) बाँधकर। having tied, wrapped or twisted with.

नर – पु॰ – (**नर**) आदमी। man.

नरक – न॰ – (**नरक**) नरक, जहन्नुम। purgatory, the hell.

नर-देव – पु॰ – (**नरदेव**) राजा। a king.

नर-वीर – पु॰ – (**नर-वीर**) नरों में वीर, प्रायः भगवान् बुद्ध के लिए प्रयुक्त। a hero, often used for the Buddha.

नर-सीह – पु॰ – (**नर-सिंह**) नरों में सिंह, प्रायः भगवान् बुद्ध के लिए प्रयुक्त। a lion amongst men, often used for the Buddha.

नराधम – पु॰ – (**नराधम**) अधम आदमी, नीच पुरुष। a wicked or wile man.

नरासभ – पु॰ – (**नरर्षभ**) मनुष्यों का स्वामी, प्रायः भगवान बुद्ध के लिए प्रयुक्त। the lord of men, often used for the Buddha.

नरुत्तम – पु॰ – (**नरोत्तम**) आदमियों में श्रेष्ठ, प्रायः भगवान् बुद्ध के लिए प्रयुक्त। the best of men, often used for the Buddha.

नळपान-जातक – (जा॰ सं॰ 20) – यह जातक कथा बतलाती है कि जलाशय के चारों ओर लगी नरकुल का तना खोखला क्यों होता है। this story (No. 20) explains the hollowness of the canes which grew round the lake.

नलाट – न॰ – (**ललाट**) ललाट, मस्तक। the forehead.

नलिनी – स्त्री॰ – (**नलिनी**) (1) कमलों वाला जलाशय, कमलों से युक्त पुष्पकरणी (2) कमलिनी। (1) a lotus pond (2) lotus.

नव – वि॰ – (**नव**) (1) नया (2) नौ की संख्या। (1) new (2) nine.

नव-कम्म – न॰ – (नवकर्म्म) (1) नया काम (2) नया रूप देना। (1) new work (2) repair.

नव-कम्मिक – वि॰ – (नव-कार्मिक) नया काम (भवन निर्माण) कराने वाला। an expert in architecture.

नवङ्ग – वि॰ – (नवाङ्ग) जिसके नौ हिस्से हों। having nine portions.

नव-नवुति – स्त्री॰ – (नव-नवतिः) निन्नानबे। ninety-nine.

नवक (1) – पु॰ – (नवक) नवागन्तुक, तरुण जो नया-नया संघ में प्रविष्ट हुआ हो। a newcomer, a young person.

नवक (2) – न॰ – (नवकम्) नौ व्यक्तियों/वस्तुओं का समूह। a group of nine.

नवकतर – वि॰ – (नवकतर) तरुण से भी तरुण। youngest.

नवनीत – न॰ – (नवनीतम्) मक्खन। fresh butter.

नवम – वि॰ – (नवम) नौवाँ। ninth.

नवमी – स्त्री॰ – (नवमी) चान्द्र मास की नवमी तिथि। the ninth day of a lunar month.

नवुति – स्त्री॰ – (नवतिः) नब्बे। ninety.

√नस – (दि॰) – अदस्सनं – (√नश्) नष्ट होना। to decay.

नस्सति – क्रि॰ – (√नश् = नश्यति) नष्ट होता है, लुप्त होता है। perishes, disappears.

नस्सि – अतीत क्रि॰ – (अनश्यत्) नष्ट हुआ। perished, disappeared.

नस्सन्त – कृ॰ – (नश्यन) नष्ट होता हुआ। perished, disappeared.

नस्सित्वा – पु॰ क्रि॰ – (√नश् + त्वा = नष्ट्वा) नष्ट होकर। perishing, disappearing.

नस्सन – न॰ – (नश्यन) नाश। disappearance, loss.

√नह – (दि॰) – (बन्धने) बांधना। to tie.

नहति – कृ॰ – (√स्ना + त = स्नात) स्नान किया हुआ, नहाया हुआ। one who has bathed.

नहान – न॰ – (स्नान) स्नान। bathing.

नहानिय – न॰ – (स्नानीय) स्नान-सामग्री। the things used during bath.

नहापक – पु॰ – (स्नपक) नहलाने वाला। a bath attendant.

नहापन – न॰ – (स्नापन) स्नान, धोना। bathing or washing (something else).

नहापित – पु॰ – (नापित) नाई। a barber, hair dresser.

नहापेति – क्रि॰ – (स्नपयति) नहलाता है। gives a bath.

नहापेसि – अतीत क्रि॰ – (अस्नपयत्) नहलाया। gave a bath.

नहापेत्वा – पु॰ क्रि॰ – (स्नपयित्वा) स्नान करके। having given a bath.

नहायति – क्रि॰ – (स्नाति) नहाता है। takes bath.

नहायि – अतीत क्रि॰ – (अस्नात्) नहाया। took bath.

नहायित्वा – पु॰ क्रि॰ – (स्नात्वा) नहाकर। having taken bath.

नहायितुं – (स्नातुम्) नहाने के लिए। for taking bath.

नहायन – न॰ – (स्नान) स्नान। bath.

नहारु – पु॰ – (नहारु) रग, नस। a sinew, a tendon.

नहि – अव्यय – (नहि) नहीं । no, not.

नहुत – न॰ – (नहुत) दस हजार। ten thousand, a myriad.

नळ – पु॰ – (नल) सरकण्डा, नली। a reed, a tube.

नलकार – पु॰ – (नलकार) टोकरी बनाने वाला । basket-maker.

नल-कलाप – पु॰ – (नल-कलाप) सरकण्डों का ढेर । a bundle of reeds.

नळ-मीन – पु॰ – (नल-मीन) समुद्री केकड़ा। a shrimp.

नळागार – न॰ – (नलागार) सरकण्डों से बनी झोपड़ी । a hut made of reeds.

नळिनिका-जातक – (जा॰ सं॰ 526) – राजकुमारी नलिनिका की कथा जिसे ऋषि शृंगि को तप-भ्रष्ट करने के लिए भेजा गया था। the story (No. 526) of princess Nalinikā who was sent to destroy the virtue of *ṛṣi* Śṛṅga.

नाक – पु॰ – (नाक) स्वर्ग। heaven.

नाग – पु॰ – (नाग) (1) सर्प (2) हाथी (3) वृक्ष-विशेष (4) श्रेष्ठ पुरुष। (1) a cobra (2) an elephant (3) betel plant (4) noble person.

नाग-दन्त – न॰ – (नागदन्त) हाथी दाँत की कील, खूँटी। an ivory peg, a peg on a wall.

नाग-दीप – (नाग-द्वीप) सिंहल द्वीप का उत्तरी भाग, वर्तमान जाफना। the northern part of Ceylon, the modern Jaffna.

नाग-बल – वि॰ – (नाग-बल) हाथी के बल सदृश बलवाला। having the strength of an elephant.

नाग-बला – स्त्री॰ – (नागबला) गंगेरन (लता विशेष) । a kind of creeper used in medicine.

नाग-भवन – न॰ – (नाग-भवन) नागों का निवास स्थल । the reign of the Nāgas.

नाग-माणवक – पु॰ – (नाग-माणवक) नाग तरुण । a young man of the Nāga race.

नाग-माणविका – स्त्री॰ – (नाग-माणविका) नाग-तरुणी, नाग-कुमारी। a Nāga maiden.

नाग-राज – पु॰ – (नागराज) नागों का राजा। king of the Nāgas.

नाग-रुक्ख – पु॰ – (नाग-वृक्ष) नाग-वृक्ष। the orange tree.

नाग-लता – स्त्री॰ – (नाग-लता) पान की बेल । the betel-creeper.

नाग-लोक – पु॰ – (नाग-लोक) नाग-संसार । the Nāga-world.

नाग-वन – न॰ – (नाग-वन) नागों का वन। grove or a forest where there are elephants.

नागसेन-थेर – मिलिन्द राजा से शास्त्रार्थ करने वाले प्रसिद्ध नागसेन स्थविर। an *arhant* celebrated for his discussions with king Milinda.

नागर – वि॰ – (नागर) नगर वाला, शहरी, सभ्य, नागरिक। belonging to city, urbane, a citizen.

नागरिक – वि॰ – (नागरिक) देखें नागर। see Nāgara.

नाटक – न॰ – (नाटक) ड्रामा। a drama.

नाटकित्थि – स्त्री॰ – (नटी) नृत्य-कुमारी। a dancing girl.

नानच्छन्द-जातक – (जा॰ सं॰ 289) – पुरोहित ने घर के लोगों से परामर्श किया कि वह

राजा से क्या चीज माँगे। किसी ने किसी चीज का नाम लिया, किसी ने दूसरी चीज का। इस प्रकार अनेक माँगें सामने आईं। the story (No. 289) tells about the manifoldness of desire.

नाथ – पु॰ – **(नाथ)** संरक्षण, संरक्षक, लोकनाथ, लोकों के संरक्षक, भगवान् बुद्ध के लिए प्रयुक्त नाम। protection, protector, it is often used for the Buddha in Pāli.

नाद – पु॰ – **(नाद)** आवाज। sound, roar.

नानता – स्त्री॰ – **(नानात्व)** नानत्व, विवि-धता। diversity, variety, manifoldness.

नानत्त – न॰ – **(नानात्व)** नानत्व, विविधता। diversity, variety, manifoldness.

नानत्त-काय – वि॰ – **(नानात्व-काय)** नाना प्रकार के शरीरों वाला। having variety of bodily states.

नाना – अव्यय – **(नाना)** अनेक, भिन्न-भिन्न। various, differently.

नाना-करण – न॰ – **(नाना-करण)** अनेक कारण। diversity, difference.

नाना-गोत्त – वि॰ – **(नाना-गोत्र)** अनेक गोत्र। of many kinds of descent.

नाना-जच्च – वि॰ – **(नाना-जात्य)** अनेक जातियों का। of many nations.

नाना-जन – पु॰ – **(नाना-जन)** अनेक प्रकार की जनता। many kinds of folk.

नाना-तित्थिय – वि॰ – **(नाना तैर्थिक)** नाना सम्प्रदाय के लोग। of various sects.

नाना-प्रकार – वि॰ – **(नाना-प्रकार)** अनेक प्रकार। various, manifold.

नाना-रत्त – वि॰ – **(नाना-रक्त)** नाना वर्ण। of various colours.

नानावाद – पु॰ – **(नानावाद)** नानावाद। different views.

नाना-विध – वि॰ – **(नानाविध)** नाना प्रकार का। various.

नाना-संवास – वि॰ – **(नाना-संवास)** जो अलग-अलग रहते हों। living in different places.

नाभि – स्त्री॰ – **(नाभि)** नाभी, पेट का मध्य बिन्दु, चक्र का मध्य भाग। the navel, the navel or central block of a wheel.

नाम – न॰ – **(नाम)** नाम, व्यक्तित्व का चैतसिक भाग। name, the immaterial factors such as consciousness preception.

नाम-करण – न॰ – **(नामकरण)** नाम रखना। naming.

नाम-गहण – न॰ – **(नाम-ग्रहण)** नाम ग्रहण करना। receiving a name.

नाम-धेय (1) – **(नामधेय)** नाम। name.

नामधेय (2) – वि॰ – **(नामधेय)** नाम वाला। having the name.

नामधेय्य – देखें नामधेय। see Nāmadheya.

नाम-पद – न॰ – **(नाम-पद)** नाम, संज्ञा। a noun.

नामक – वि॰ – **(नामक)** नाम से, नाम मात्र का (केवल समास में प्रयुक्त)। by name (in compounds).

नामसिद्धि-जातक – (जा॰ सं॰ 97) – शिष्य अच्छा सा नाम खोजने जाकर अपने पहले वाले 'नाम' 'पापक' से ही संतुष्ट होकर लौट आया। the story (No. 97) tells that one should not worry about his name's meaning as the name signifies nothing.

नामेति – क्रि॰ – (नमयति) झुकाता है। bends, yields.

नामेसि – अतीत क्रि॰ – (अनमयत्) झुकाया। bent.

नामित – कृ॰ – (नामित) झुकाया गया। has been yielded or bent.

नामेत्वा – पु॰ क्रि॰ – (नमयित्वा) झुकाकर। getting bent.

नायक – पु॰ – (नायक) नेता, मार्गदर्शक। leader.

नायिका – स्त्री॰ – (नायिका) मार्गदर्शिका। a female leader.

नारङ्ग – पु॰ – (नारङ्ग) नारंगी का पेड़। the mandarin orange tree.

नाराच – पु॰ – (नाराच) लोहे की छड़, एक प्रकार का तीर। an iron bar, a kind of arrow.

नारी – स्त्री॰ – (नारी) औरत। woman.

नालं – अव्यय – (न + अलम्) अपर्याप्त, प्रतिकूल। not enough, unsuitable.

नालंदा – राजगृह के पास का प्रसिद्ध स्थान, जहाँ भगवान् बुद्ध कई बार ठहरे थे और जहाँ बाद में जगत् प्रसिद्ध बौद्ध विश्वविद्यालय बना। a town near Rājagṛha, the Buddha stayed here several times, the world renowned ancient Bauddha university was situated there.

नाल – पु॰ – (नाल) नालिका, नाली। a stalk, tube.

नालगिरि – राजगृह की राजकीय हस्तिशाला का हाथी, जिसे देवदत्त की प्रेरणा से गौतम बुद्ध को शारीरिक हानि पहुँचाने के लिए उन पर छोड़ा गया था। an elephant of the royal stalls at Rājagṛha, once it was used by Devadatta to kill the Buddha but he could not succeed.

नालि – स्त्री॰ – (नालि) माप-विशेष। a measure of capacity, a tube.

नालि-मत्त – वि॰ – (नालि-मात्र) केवल एक नालि की माप का। about a measure.

नालिका – स्त्री॰ – (नालिका) नालि। a tube, a bottle.

नालिका-यन्त – (नालिका-यन्त्र) घड़ी। an instrument to measure time.

नालिकेर – पु॰ – (नालिकेर) नारियल। the coconut tree or its fruit.

नालि-पट्ट – पु॰ – (नालि-पत्र) टोपी। a cap, hat.

नावा – स्त्री॰ – (नावा, नौका) जहाज। a ship.

नावा-तित्थ – न॰ – (नावा-तीर्थ) नौका का पत्तन। harbour.

नावा-संचार – पु॰ – (नावा-संचार) नौकाओं का आना-जाना। the transit of ships.

नाविक – पु॰ – (नाविक) मल्लाह, माँझी। boatman.

नाविकी – स्त्री॰ – (नाविकी) मल्लाहिन, माँझी की स्त्री। a boatsman's wife.

नावुतिक – वि॰ – (नावुतिकः) नब्बे वर्ष का। of ninety years.

नास – पु॰ – (नाश) नाश, मृत्यु। ruin, destruction, death.

नासन – न॰ – (नाशन) नाश करना, त्याग देना, निकाल बाहर कर देना। killing, destruction, expulsion.

नासा – स्त्री॰ – (नासा) नाक, नासिका। the nose.

नासा-रज्जु – स्त्री॰ – (नासा-रज्जु) नकेल। a nose-rope (to curb an ox., etc.).

नासिका – स्त्री॰ – (**नासिका**) नाक। the nose.

नासेति – क्रि॰ – (**नाशयति**) नष्ट करता है, खराब कर देता है, मार डालता है। kills, ruins, destroys.

नासेसि – अतीत क्रि॰ – (**अनाशयत्**) नष्ट किया। killed, ruined, destroyed.

नासित – कृ॰ – (**नष्टीकृत**) नष्ट किया हुआ। ruined, destroyed.

नासेत्वा – पु॰ क्रि॰ – (**नाशयित्वा**) नष्ट करके। having ruined, having destroyed.

नासितब्ब – कृ॰ – (**नाशितव्य**) नष्ट करने योग्य। fit to be ruined or destroyed.

निकट – न॰ – (**निकट**) पड़ोस, वि॰, पास। neighbourhood, adj. near.

निकट्ठु – वि॰ – (**निकृष्ट**) पतित, नीच, निकृष्ट। low, mean.

निकटि – स्त्री॰ – (**निकृति**) नीच कर्म, कपट, छल। baseness, fraud, deceit.

निकत – वि॰ – (**निकृत**) छली, कपटी। deceitful.

निकति – स्त्री॰ – (**निकृत्त**) देखें निकटि। see Nikaṭi.

निकन्त – कृ॰ – (**निकृत्त**) कटा हुआ। cut.

निकन्तति – क्रि॰ – (नि √ कृत् = निकृन्तति) काटता है। cuts, twists.

निकन्ति – अतीत क्रि॰ – (**अकृन्तत्**) काटा। cut.

निकन्तित – कृ॰ – (**निकृन्तित**) कटा हुआ। has been cut.

निकन्तित्वा – पु॰ क्रि॰ – (**निकृन्तित्य**) काटकर। having cut.

निकर – पु॰ – (**निकर**) समूह। multitude.

निकस – पु॰ – (**निकष**) कसौटी। touchstone, emery stone.

निकामना – स्त्री॰ – (**कामना**) इच्छा। desire.

निकामलाभी – वि॰ – (**निष्कामलाभी**) बिना कठिनाई से प्राप्त करने वाला। one who has obtained something without difficulty.

निकामेति – क्रि॰ – (**कामयते**) इच्छा करता है, चाहता है। craves, desires.

निकामेसि – अतीत क्रि॰ – (**अकामयत्**) इच्छा की। desired.

निकामित – कृ॰ – (**कान्तः**) इच्छा किया हुआ। desired, craved.

निकामेन्त – (**कामयन्**) इच्छा करता हुआ। craving, desiring.

निकाय – पु॰ – (**निकाय**) समूह, सम्प्रदाय, संग्रह। group, sect, a collection.

निकास – पु॰ – (**निकाश**) दृष्टि-सीमा के भीतर की वस्तु, पड़ोस। within sight neighbourhood.

निकिट्ठ – वि॰ – (**निकृष्ट**) नीच, निकृष्ट। low, vile.

निकुञ्ज – पु॰ तथा न॰ – (**निकुञ्ज**) वृक्षों तथा झाड़ियों से ढका घना स्थान। a glen, a thicket.

निकूजति – क्रि॰ – (**निकूजति**) कूजता है। chirps, warbles.

निकूजि – अतीत क्रि॰ – (**न्यूकूजत्**) शब्द किया। chirped, warbled.

निकूजित – कृ॰ – (**निकूजित**) शब्द किया हुआ। warbled.

निकूजमान – कृ॰ – (**निकूजन्**) शब्द करता हुआ। chirping, warbling.

निकेतन – न॰ – (निकेतन) निवास-स्थान, घर। abode, home.

निक्कङ्ख – वि॰ – (निःशङ्क) निशंक, सन्देह-रहित, असंदिग्ध, विश्वस्त। not afraid, fearless, not doubting, confident.

निक्कड्ढन – न॰ – (निष्कर्षण) बाहर खींच लाना। dragging out, expulsion.

निक्कण्टक – वि॰ – (निष्कण्टक) निष्कण्टक, कांटों या शत्रुओं से रहित। free from thorns or enemies.

निक्कद्दम – वि॰ – (निष्कर्दम) कर्दम-रहित, कीचड़-रहित। free from mud, clean, without blemish.

निक्कम – पु॰ – (निष्क्रम) प्रयत्न। exertion, try.

निक्करुण – वि॰ – (निष्करुण) करुणा-विहीन। merciless.

निक्कसाव – वि॰ – (निष्कषाय) अपवित्रता से मुक्त। free from impurity.

निक्काम – वि॰ – (निष्काम) कामना-रहित। without craving or lust.

निक्कारण – वि॰ – (निष्कारण) बिना कारण के। causeless, groundless.

निक्कारणा – क्रि॰ वि॰ – (निष्कारणा) कारण-रहित। without reason, cause or purpose.

निक्किलेस – वि॰ – (निष्क्लेश) विकार-रहित। free from depravity, unstained.

निक्कुज्ज – वि॰ – (निःकुब्ज) फेंका गया। upset, thrown over.

निक्कुज्जेति – क्रि॰ – (निष्कुब्जयति) उलट देता है। turns upside down.

निक्कुजित – कृ॰ – (निष्कुब्जित) उलट दिया गया। turned upside down.

निक्कुज्जेत्वा – पु॰ क्रि॰ – (निष्कुब्जित्वा) उलटकर। turning upside down.

निक्कुज्जिय – (निष्कुब्जीय) उलट देने योग्य। fit to be turned upside down.

निक्कुह – वि॰ – (निष्कुह) बिना ढोंग का। not deceitful.

निक्कोध – वि॰ – (निष्क्रोध) क्रोध-रहित। free from anger.

निक्केस-सीस – पु॰ – (निष्केश-शीश) गंजा सिर। bald head.

निक्ख – पु॰ – (निष्क) निष्क नामक स्वर्ण-मुद्रा, पच्चीस धरण के बराबर तौल। a big gold coin, a weight equal to 25 dharaịns.

निक्खन्त – कृ॰ – (निष्क्रान्त) (घर से) बाहर निकला हुआ। gone out, departed from.

निक्खम – पु॰ – (निष्क्रम) निष्क्रमण। going out, departure.

निक्खमण – न॰ – (निष्क्रमण) निष्क्रमण, विदाई। going out, departure.

निक्खमति – क्रि॰ – (निष्क्रमति) (घर से) बाहर जाता है, गृहस्थ जीवन का त्याग कर देता है। goes forth from, leaves the household life.

निक्खमि – अतीत क्रि॰ – (निष्क्रमत्) निकला, संन्यस्त हुआ। went forth from, left the household.

निक्खमन्त – कृ॰ – (निष्क्रमन) निकलता हुआ। going forth from.

निक्खमित्वा – पु॰ क्रि॰ – (निष्क्रम्य) निकलकर, संन्यस्त होकर। having gone forth from, having left the household.

निक्खम्म – पु॰ क्रि॰ – (निष्क्रम्य) देखें निक्खमित्वा। see Nikkhamittvā.

निक्खमितब्ब – कृ॰ – (निष्कमितव्य) निष्क्रमण करने योग्य। fit for going forth from, fit for leaving the household.

निक्खमितुं – कृ॰ – (निष्कमितुम्) निष्क्रमण करने के लिए। for Nikkhamana.

निक्खमनीय – पु॰ – (निष्क्रमणीय) सावन का महीना। इस महीने में बच्चे को बाहर निकालकर सूर्य का दर्शन कराया जाता है। the month of Śrāvaṇa.

निक्खामेति – क्रि॰ – (निष्कामयति) निकाल बाहर करता है। makes to go out.

निक्खामेसि – अतीत क्रि॰ – (निष्कामयत्) निकाला। made to go out.

निक्खामित – कृ॰ – (निष्क्रान्त) निकाला हुआ। being made to go out, taken out.

निक्खामेन्त – कृ॰ – (निष्कामयन्) निकालता हुआ। making to go out.

निक्खामेत्वा – पु॰ क्रि॰ – (निष्काम्य) निकालकर। having made to go out.

निक्खिक – पु॰ – (निष्काध्यक्ष) कोषाध्यक्ष, खजांची। treasurer.

निक्खित्त – कृ॰ – (निक्षिप्त) रखा गया। laid or put down.

निक्खिपति – क्रि॰ – (निक्षिपति) एक ओर रख देता है। lays down or aside, puts down.

निक्खिपि – अतीत क्रि॰ – (न्यक्षिपत्) रखा। laid down or aside, put down.

निक्खिपन्त – कृ॰ – (निक्षिपन्) रखता हुआ। laying down or aside.

निक्खिपित्वा – पु॰ क्रि॰ – (निक्षिप्य) रखकर। having laid down aside.

निक्खिपितब्ब – कृ॰ – (निक्षिप्तव्य) रखने के योग्य। fit to be laid down or aside.

निक्खेप – पु॰ – (निक्षेप) निक्षेप, रख देना। putting down, casting off, discarding.

निक्खेपन – न॰ – (निक्षेपण) देखें निक्खेप। see Nikkhepa.

निखणति – क्रि॰ – (निखनति भी) खनता है, खोदता है। digs into.

निखनि – अतीत क्रि॰ – (न्यखनत्) खोदा। dug.

निखात – कृ॰ – (निखात) खोदा हुआ। dug up.

निखनन्त – कृ॰ – (निखनन्) खोदते हुए। digging.

निखनित्वा – पु॰ क्रि॰ – (निखनित्वा) खोदकर। having dug.

निखादन – न॰ – (निखादन) छेनी। a chisel.

निखिल – वि॰ – (निखिल) समस्त। all, entire, whole.

निगच्छति – क्रि॰ – (निगच्छति) अनुभव करता है, सहन करता है। undergoes, experiences, endures.

निगण्ठ – पु॰ – (निर्ग्रन्थ) जैन सम्प्रदाय का संन्यासी। a member of the Jain order.

निगण्ठनाथ-पुत्त – पु॰ – (निर्ग्रन्थनाथपुत्र) बुद्ध के समकालीन छह प्रसिद्ध आचार्यों में से एक। जैनों के अन्तिम तीर्थंकर वर्धमान महावीर। one among six renowned philosophers contemporary to the Buddha, it is often used for Vardhmāna Mahāvīra.

निगति – स्त्री॰ – (नियति) भाग्य, अवस्था, आचरण। fate, condition, conduct.

निगम – पु॰ – (निगम) करबा। town.

निगमन – न॰ – (निगमन) व्याख्या, उद्धरण, दृष्टान्त। conclusion, explanation.

निगल – पु॰ – (निगड) हाथी के पैर की जंजीर। a chain for the elephant's feet.

निगूहति – क्रि॰ – (निगूहति) ढकता है, छिपाता है। covers up, conceals, hides.

निगूहि – अतीत क्रि॰ – (न्यगूहत्) छिपाया। covered, concealed.

निगूहित – कृ॰ – (निगूहित) छिपाया हुआ। hidden, concealed, covered.

निगूळ्ह – कृ॰ – (नि + √गुह् + त = निगूढ) छिपाया हुआ। which has been covered, concealed or hidden.

निगूहित्वा – पू॰ क्रि॰ – (निगूह्य) छिपाकर। having concealed, covered or hidden.

निगूहन – न॰ – (निगूहन) छिपाना। concealment.

निगगच्छति – क्रि॰ – (निर्गच्छति) बाहर जाता है। goes out, proceeds from.

निगगण्ठ – वि॰ – (निर्ग्रन्थि) ग्रन्थि-रहित। free from all ties, indigent.

निगगण्हन – न॰ – (निग्रहण) निग्रह करना, डाँटनाडपटना। suppression, punishment.

निगगण्हाति – क्रि॰ – (निगृह्णाति) दोषारोपण करता है, डाँटता-डपटता है। restrains, subdues, apprehends, accuses.

निगगण्हि – अतीत क्रि॰ – (न्यगगृहीत) निग्रह किया। restrained, subdued

निगगहीत (1) – कृ॰ – (निगृहीत) निग्रह किया गया। restrained, seized, arrested.

निगगहीत (2) – न॰ – (निगृहीत) अनुस्वार। the nasal sound which is marked by a dot above the line.

निगगण्हन्त – कृ॰ – (निग्रहणन) निग्रह करता हुआ। restrained or seized or arrested.

निगगय्ह – पु॰ क्रि॰ – (निगृह्य) निग्रह करके। having restrained or seized or arrested.

निगगहित्वा – पु॰ क्रि॰ – (निगृह्य) देखें निगगय्ह। see Niggayha.

निगगम – पु॰ – (निर्गम) बाहर जाना, बाहर निकलना। going out, departure.

निगगमन – न॰ – (निर्गमन) बाहर जाना, विदा होना। going out, departure.

निगगय्ह-वादी – पु॰ – (निगृह्यवादी) निग्रह करने वाला, दोष दिखाने वाला। one who speaks reprovingly, critic.

निगगोध मिग-जातक – (जा॰ सं॰ – 12) – निगगोध मृग ने अपनी जान देकर भी अपने पक्ष की मृगी और उसके बच्चे की प्राण-रक्षा करनी चाही अन्ततः वह सभी के प्राण बचाने में सफल हुआ। the story (No. 12) of a deer who by his act of magnanimity could save not only the life of a pregnant-doe but of the entire community.

निगगह – पु॰ – (निग्रह) निग्रह, दोषारोपण करना। restraint, suppression, punishment.

निगगहेतब्ब – कृ॰ – (निगृहीतव्य) निग्रह करने योग्य। fit for restraint suppression, punishment.

निग्गाहक – पु॰ – (निग्राहक) निग्रह करने वाला। one who causes censue or punishment.

निग्गुण्डि – स्त्री॰ – (निर्गुण्डि) निर्गुण्डी नामक ओषधीय बूटी-विशेष। a medicinal shrub.

निग्गुण्डी – स्त्री॰ – (निर्गुण्डी) देखें निग्गुण्डि। see Niggundi.

निग्गुम्ब – वि॰ – (निर्गुल्म) जहाँ झाड़-झंखाड़ न हो। having no cluster or clump of roots.

निग्घातक – पु॰ – (निर्घातक) हत्यारा, विनाशक। killer, devastator.

निग्घातन – न॰ – (निर्घातन) हत्या, विनाश। killing, destruction, devastation.

निग्घोस – पु॰ – (निर्घोष) निर्घोष, चिल्लाना। shouting.

निग्रोध – पु॰ – (निग्रोध) वट-वृक्ष, बरगद का पेड़। the banyan tree.

निग्रोध-पक्क – न॰ (निग्रोध पक्वफलम्) वट का पका फल। the ripe fruit of banyan.

निग्रोध-परिमण्डल – वि॰ – वट का घेरा। circumference of a banyan tree.

निघंस – पु॰ – (निघर्ष) रगड़ना। rubbing against, chafing.

निघंसन – न॰ – (निघर्षण) रगड़ना। rubbing against, chafing.

निघंसति – क्रि॰ – (निघर्षति) रगड़ता है। rubs, chafer, erases.

निघंसि – अतीत – क्रि॰ – (न्यघर्षत्) रगड़ा। rubbed, chafed.

निघंसित – कृ॰ – (निघर्षित) रगड़ा हुआ। rubbed, chafed.

निघंसित्वा – पु॰ वि॰ – (निघर्षित्वा) रगड़कर। having rubbed, having chafed.

निघण्डु – पु॰ – (निघण्टु) निघुंटु, पर्याय वचनों का कोश। a dictionary of synonyms.

निघात – पु॰ – (निघात) मारना। striking down, destroying.

निचय – पु॰ – (निचय) संग्रह, धन-संचय। accumulation, money collection.

निचित – कृ॰ – (नि + √चि + क्त = निचित) संगृहीत। accumulated.

निचुल – न॰ – (निचुल) (1) बेंत या वेतस् का पौधा (2) ऊपर का वस्त्र। cane-plant, upper garment.

निच्च – वि॰ – (नित्य) नित्य, लगातार। constant, continuous.

निच्च – क्रि॰ वि॰ – (नित्यम्) नित्य, सदैव, लगातार। constantly, always perpetually.

निच्च-कालं – क्रि॰वि॰ – (नित्यकालम्) सदैव, निरन्तर, अनवरत। always, constantly.

निच्च-दानं – न॰ – (नित्यदान) स्थायी दान। perpetual gift.

निच्च-भत्त – न॰ – (नित्य भोज्य दानम्) सतत् भोजन-दान। a continuous food supply.

निच्च-सील – न॰ – (नित्यशील) सतत्शील-पालन, पंचशील। uninterrupted, observance of virtue, daily deservance.

निच्चता – स्त्री॰ – (नित्यता) नित्यता। continuity, permanence.

निच्चम्म – वि॰ – (निश्चर्म) चर्म-रहित। skin-less, flogged off.

निच्चल – वि॰ – (निश्चल) निश्चल, स्थिर। motionless, steady.

निच्चोल – वि॰ – (**निश्चोल**) निर्वस्त्र, नंगा। clothless, naked, nude.

निच्चय – पु॰ – (**निश्चय**) निश्चय। resolution, determination.

निच्छरण – न॰ – (**निस्सरण**) बाहर भेजना, बाहर निकालना। sending out, emanation.

निच्छरति – कृ॰ – (**निस्सरति**) बाहर जाता है। emanates, goes forth, goes out from.

निच्छरि – अतीत क्रि॰ – (**निरसरत्**) बाहर निकला। went forth, out from, went out.

निच्छरित – कृ॰ – (**निस्सृत**) बाहर निकला हुआ। gone forth or out from.

निच्छरित्वा – पूर्व क्रि॰ – (**निस्सृत्य**) बाहर निकलकर। having gone forth or out from.

निच्छन्द – वि॰ – (**निश्छन्द**) बिना। without desire, excitement.

निच्छारित – कृ॰ – (**निस्सारित**) प्रकट किया हुआ। emitted, sent out.

निच्छारेति – क्रि॰ – (**निस्सारयति**) प्रकट करता है, बोलता है। emits, sends out, speaks, reveals.

निच्छारेत्वा – पु॰ क्रि॰ – (**निस्सारयित्वा**) प्रकट करके। having sent out, having spoken, having revealed.

निच्छारेसि – अतीत क्रि॰ – (**निरसारयत्**) प्रकट किया, बोला। sent out, spoke, emitted, revealed.

निच्छित – कृ॰ – (**निश्चित्**) निश्चित्; विचारित, मीमांसित। considered, investigated.

निच्छनाति – क्रि॰ – (**निश्चिनोति**) विचार करता है, विमर्षण करता है। descriminates, considers, investigates.

निज – वि॰ – (**निज**) स्वकीय, अपना। one's own.

निज-देस – पु॰ – (**निजदेश**) अपना देश, स्वदेश। one's own country.

निज्जट – वि॰ – (**निर्जट / निर्जटिल**) सुलझा हुआ। disentangled.

निज्जर – वि॰ – (**निर्जर**) जरा-रहित, ह्रास-रहित, जिसे बुढ़ापा न व्यापे। free from old age or ageing.

निज्जरेति – क्रि॰ – (**निर्जरयति**) नष्ट करता है, विनाश करता है। destroys, annihilates.

निज्जिण्ण – कृ॰ – (**निजीर्ण**) जरा-प्राप्त, ह्रास प्राप्त। exhausted.

निज्जिव्ह – वि॰ – (**निर्जिह्व**) जिह्वा-विहीन, बिना जीभ के। tongueless, dumb.

निज्जिव्ह – सं॰ – (**निर्जिह्व**) जंगली मुर्गा। a jungle cock.

निज्जीव – वि॰ – (**निर्जीव**) निर्जीव। lifeless.

निज्झान – न॰ – (**निध्यान**) अन्तर्दृष्टि। insight.

निज्झायति – क्रि॰ – (**निध्यायते**) ध्यान लगाता है। meditates.

निट्ठा – स्त्री॰ – (**निष्ठा**) अन्त, सारांश, निष्ठा। the end, conclusion, perfection.

निट्ठाति – क्रि॰ – (**निष्ठाति**) समाप्त होता है, समाप्त करता है। is at an end, becomes finished.

निट्ठान – न॰ – (**निष्ठान**) समाप्ति। completion, ending.

निट्ठासि – अतीत क्रि॰ – (न्यष्ठात्) समाप्त किया । completed, finished.

निट्ठापित – कृ॰ – (निष्ठापित) पूरा कराया हुआ । got completed or finished.

निट्ठापेति – क्रि॰ – (निष्ठापयति) पूरा कराता है, समाप्त कराता है । accomplishes, finishes, carries out.

निट्ठापेत्वा – पु॰ क्रि॰ – (निष्ठापयित्वा) पूरा करके । having accomplished or finished.

निट्ठापेन्त – कृ॰ – (निष्ठापयन्) पूरा करता हुआ । getting accomplished or finished.

निट्ठित – कृ॰ – (निष्ठित) समाप्त, सम्पूर्ण । finished, completed.

निट्ठुभति – क्रि॰ – (नि + √ष्ठिव् = निष्ठीवति) थूकता है । spits out, expectorates.

निट्ठुभन – न॰ – (निष्ठीवनम्) थूकना, थूक । spittle, spitting.

निट्ठुभि – अतीत क्रि॰ – (न्यष्ठीवत्) थूका । spitted.

निट्ठुभित – कृ॰ – (निष्ठ्यूत) थूका हुआ । spit out.

निट्ठुभित्वा – कृ॰ – (निष्ठीव्य) थूक करके । having spitted.

निट्ठुर – वि॰ – (निष्ठुर) निष्ठुर, कठोर, निर्दयी । rough, hard, cruel.

निट्ठुरिय – न॰ – (निष्ठुरता) निष्ठुरता, निर्दयता । harshness, cruelty.

निड्ड – न॰ – (नीड) नीड़, घोंसला, विश्राम-स्थल । nest, resting place.

निड्डेति – क्रि॰ – (निः √डी = निर्डयते) घास-पात हटाता है । removes weeds.

निण्णय – पु॰ – (निर्णय) निर्णय । decision, discrimination.

नितम्ब – पु॰ – (नितम्ब) (1) चूतड़ (2) पर्वत का किनारा । (1) the hip (2) the ridge of a mountain.

नित्तण्ह – वि॰ – (निस्तृष्ण) तृष्णा-रहित । free from desire.

नित्तल – वि॰ – (नितल) गोल । round shape, a ball.

नित्तिण्ण – कृ॰ – (निस्तीर्ण) पार हुआ, तीर्ण हुआ । got out of, having crossed over.

नित्तुदन – न॰ – (निस्तुदन) घोंपना, चुभाना । pricking, piercing.

नित्तेज – वि॰ – (निस्तेज) क्षीण-प्रताप, तेज-रहित । powerless, abashed.

नित्थरण – न॰ – (निस्तरण) पार हो जाना, तर जाना, समाप्ति । getting across, traversing, over-coming end.

नित्थरति – क्रि॰ – (निस्तरति) पार होता है । crosses over, gets over.

नित्थरि – अतीत क्रि॰ (न्यस्तरत्) पार हुआ । had crossed over, got over.

नित्थरित – कृ॰ – (निस्तृत) पार हुआ । crossed over, got over.

नित्थरित्वा – पु॰ क्रि॰ – (निस्तृत्य) पार होकर । having crossed over, got over.

नित्थुनन – न॰ – (निस्तनन) कराहना । a moan, a groan.

नित्थुनाति – क्रि॰ – (निः √स्तन् = निस्तनयति) कराहता है । moans, groans.

नित्थुनन्त – कृ॰ – (निस्तनयन्) कराहता हुआ । moaning, groaning.

नित्थुनि – अतीत क्रि॰ – (न्यस्तनयत्) कराहा। moaned, groaned.

नित्थुनित्वा – पु॰ क्रि॰ – (निस्तनयित्वा) कराह करके। having moaned, groaned.

निदस्सन – न॰ – (निदर्शन) उदाहरण, साक्षी, तुलना। an example, comparison, evidence, witness.

निदस्सित – कृ॰ – (निदर्शित) दर्शाया हुआ, व्याख्यात, परिभाषित। explained.

निदस्सिय – पु॰ क्रि॰ – (निदर्श्य) व्याख्या करके, परिभाषा करके। getting explained or defined.

निदस्सितब्ब – कृ॰ – (निदर्शितव्य) दर्शाने योग्य। fit to be explained or defined.

निदस्सेति – क्रि॰ – (निदर्शयति) परिभाषित करता है, दर्शाता है, व्याख्या करता है। points out, explains, defines.

निदस्सेसि – अतीत क्रि॰ – (न्यदर्शयत्) दरसाया। explained, defined.

निदस्सेत्वा – पु॰ क्रि॰ – (निदर्श्य) देखें निदस्सिय। see Nidassiya.

निदहति – क्रि॰ – (निधन्ते/निदधाति) खजाना गाड़ता है। deposits, buries some treasure.

निदहि – अतीत क्रि॰ – (न्यदधात्) खजाना गाड़ा। buried, the treasure.

निदहित – कृ॰ – (निहित) निहित, खजाना गाड़े हुए। getting the treasure buried.

निदहित्वा – पु॰ क्रि॰ – (निधाय) खजाना गाड़कर। having buried the treasure.

निदाघ – पु॰ – (निदाघ) सूखा, ग्रीष्म-काल, गरमी। drought, heat, summer.

निदान – न॰ – (निदान) मूल, कारण, उत्पत्ति। source, cause, origin.

निदान-कथा – स्त्री॰ – (निदान-कथा) जातकट्ठकथा का आरम्भिक अंश, भूमिका भाग। introduction to the Jātaka-Kaṭṭha-kathā.

निद्दय – वि॰ – (निर्दय) निर्दय। merciless, cruel, pitiless.

निद्दर – वि॰ – (निर्भय/निर्दर) दुःख-रहित, भय-रहित। free from anguish, pain or fear.

निद्दा – स्त्री॰ – (निद्रा) निद्रा, नींद। sleep.

निद्दायान – न॰ – (निद्रागमनम्) शयन। sleeping.

निद्दारामता – स्त्री॰ – (निद्राप्रियता) निद्रा-प्रियता। fondness of sleep.

निद्दालु – वि॰ – (निद्रालु) निद्रालु। fond of sleep.

निद्दासीली – वि॰ – (निद्राशील) निद्रालु। of dews of habits.

निद्दायति – क्रि॰ – (निद्रायते) सोता है। sleeps.

निद्दायन – न॰ – (निद्रागमन) शयन। sleeping.

निद्दायन्त – कृ॰ – (निद्रामाण) सोता हुआ। being slept.

निद्दायि/निद्दायित्वा – पु॰ क्रि॰ – (शयित्वा) सोकर। having slept.

निद्दिट्ठ – कृ॰ – (निर्दिष्ट) निर्दिष्ट, निर्देश किया हुआ। pointed out, explained, defined.

निद्दिसति – क्रि॰ – (निः √दिश् = निर्दिशति) निर्देश करता है। points out, explains.

निद्दिसि – अतीत क्रि॰ – (न्यदर्शत्) निर्देश किया। pointed out, explained.

निद्दिसितब्ब – कृ॰ – **(निर्दिशितव्य)** निर्देश करने योग्य। fit to be pointed out, fit to be explained.

निद्दिसित्वा – पु॰ क्रि॰ – **(निर्दिश्य)** निर्देश करके। having pointed out or explained.

निद्दुक्ख – वि॰ – **(निर्दुःख)** दुःख-रहित। free from pains or misery.

निद्देस – पु॰ – **(निर्देश)** विश्लेषणात्मक व्याख्या, खुद्दक निकाय के अन्तर्गत गिना जाने वाला टीका-ग्रन्थ। analytic explanation, one of the fifteen books of Khuddaka Nikāya.

निद्दोस – वि॰ – **(निर्दोष)** निर्दोष, निर्मल। faultless, undefiled, pure.

निद्धन – वि॰ – **(निर्धन)** निर्धन। poor, without property.

निद्धन्त – कृ॰ – **(निर्धमन्)** फूँक मारते हुए। blowing off, having ejected.

निद्धमति – क्रि॰ – **(नि √ध्मा = निद्धमति)** फूँक मारता है, बाहर निकालता है। blows off, to eject.

निद्धमि – अतीत – क्रि॰ – **(न्यद्धमत्)** फूँक मारी। blown off, ejected.

निद्धमित्वा – पु॰ क्रि॰ – **(निध्माय)** फूँक मारकर। having blown off, having ejected.

निद्धमन – न॰ – **(निर्धमन)** नाली, नहर। a drain, canal, ejection.

निद्धमन-द्वार – न॰ – **(निर्धमन-द्वार)** तालाब के पानी का निकास। sluice of a tank.

निद्धारण – न॰ – **(निर्धारण)** निश्चित करना। specification.

निद्धारित – कृ॰ – **(निर्धारित)** निश्चित किया हुआ। specified.

निद्धारेति – क्रि॰ – **(निर्धारयति)** निश्चय करता है। specifies.

निद्धारेसि – अतीत क्रि॰ – **(निरधारयत्)** निश्चित किया। specified.

निद्धारेत्वा – पु॰ वि॰ – **(निर्धारयित्वा)** निश्चित करके। having specified.

निद्धुनन – न॰ – **(निधूनन)** धुनना। shaking.

निद्धु-नाति – क्रि॰ – **(निर्धुनोति / निर्धुनाति)** धुनता है। moves, shakes.

निद्धुनि – अतीत क्रि॰ – **(न्यधुनोत्)** धुना। moved, shaken.

निद्धुनित्वा – पु॰ वि॰ – **(निधूय)** धुनकर। having moved, having shaken.

निद्धोत – कृ॰ – **(निर्धौत)** धोया हुआ, साफ किया हुआ, तेज किया हुआ। washed, cleaned, sharpened.

निधन – पु॰ तथा न॰ – **(निधन)** मृत्यु। death.

निधान – न॰ – **(निधान)** जमा किया हुआ, छिपा खजाना। deposit, a hidden treasure.

निधापित – कृ॰ – **(निधापित)** रखवाया हुआ। got deposited.

निधापेति – क्रि॰ – **(निधापयति)** रखवाता है, गड़वाता है। causes to deposit.

निधापेसि – अतीत क्रि॰ – **(न्यधापयत्)** रखवाया, गड़वाया। made deposited.

निधाय – पु॰ क्रि॰ – **(नि + √धा + ल्यप् = निधाय)** रखवाकर, गाड़कर। having deposited or kept aside.

निधि – पु॰ – **(निधि)** छिपा खजाना। hidden treasure.

निधि-कुम्भि – स्त्री॰ – **(निधि-कुम्भ)** खजाने का घड़ा। a treasure pot.

निधीपति – क्रि॰ – (निधीयते) रखवाया जाता है, गड़वाया जाता है। got to be deposited.

निधेति – क्रि॰ – (निधत्ते) रखता है, गाड़ता है। deposits, hides or puts aside.

निधेसि – अतीत क्रि॰ – (न्यदधात्) गाड़ा। deposited.

√ निन्द – (भू॰) – (गहरायं – √ निन्द्) निन्दा करना। to blame, insult.

निन्दति – क्रि॰ – (निन्दति) निन्दा करता है। blames, insults.

निन्दित – कृ॰ – (√ निन्द् + क्त = निन्दित) अपमानित, गर्हित। blamed, insulted.

निन्दित्वा – कृ॰ – (√ निन्द् = निन्द्य) निन्दा करके। having blamed, having insulted.

निन्दितब्ब – कृ॰ – (निन्दितव्य) निन्दा करने योग्य। fit to be blamed.

निन्दन – न॰ – (निन्दन) अपमान, अगौरव। insult, disparagement.

निन्दना – स्त्री॰ – अपमान, अगौरव। देखें निन्दन। see Nindana.

निन्दिय – वि॰ – (√ निन्द् + अनीयर = निन्दनीय) निन्दनीय, निन्दा के योग्य। blameworthy, faulty.

निन्न (1) – वि॰ – (निम्न) नीचा, निम्न। low lying, bent down, sunken.

निन्न (2) – न॰ – (निम्न) निम्न भूमि। low land, depression.

निन्नता – स्त्री॰ – (निम्नता) निम्नता। lowliness, inclination.

निन्नगा – स्त्री॰ – (निम्नगा) नदी। river.

निन्नहुत – न॰ – (नियुत) प्रयुत, नियुत दस लाख का बोध कराने वाली संख्या। number denoting one million or ten lacs.

निनाद – पु॰ – (निनाद) स्वर-माधुर्य, लय, राग। melody, tune.

निनादी – वि॰ – (निन्नादी) ऊँची आवाज वाला, मधुर स्वर वाला। a sounding loud, having a melodious voice.

निनामेति – क्रि॰ – (नमति) झुकता है। bends down.

निनामित – कृ॰ – (√ नम् + क्त = नत) झुका हुआ। bent.

निनामेत्वा – कृ॰ – (√ नम् + त्वा = नत्वा) झुककर। bent down.

निनामेसि – अतीत क्रि॰ – (अनमत्) झुक गया। bent.

निनिमित्त – न॰ – (निर्निमित्त) इच्छानुसार। according to wish.

निनेजक – पु॰ – (निः + √ एज् + ण्वुल = निर्नेजक) धोबी। washerman.

निनेतु – पु॰ – (निर्णेतृ / निर्णेता) निर्णायक, निर्णय करने वाला। one who decides, one who leads down to.

निपक – वि॰ – (नि + √ ण + ण्वुल् = निपाक / निपुण) निपुण, दक्ष, बुद्धिमान। clever, wise.

निपच्च – क्रि॰ – (नि + √ पत् + ल्यप् = निपत्य) गिरकर। having fallen down, or bowed down.

निपच्चाकार – पु॰ – (निपत्याकार) नम्रता। humbleness, obedience, repect.

निपज्ज – पु॰ क्रि॰ – (नि + √ पद् + ल्यप् = निपद्य) लेटकर। having slept or lying down.

निपज्जति – क्रि॰ – (नि + √पद् = निपद्यते) लेटता है। lies down, sleeps.

निपज्जन्त – कृ॰ – (नि + √पद् + शतृ = निपद्यन) लेटता हुआ। having slept, laid down.

निपज्जि – अतीत क्रि॰ – (नि √पद् = न्यपदत्) लेट करके। laid down.

निपज्जित्वा – कृ॰ – (नि √पद + ल्यप् = निपद्य) देखें निपज्ज। see Nipajja.

निपन्न – कृ॰ – (नि √पद् + क्त = निपन्न) लेट चुका था। had slept, had laid down.

निपज्जन – न॰ – (नि √पद + ल्युट् = निपद्यन) लेटना। lying down, sleeping.

निपठ – पु॰ – (पाठः) पाठ। lesson.

निपाठ – पु॰ – (पाठः) पढ़ना। reading.

निपतति – क्रि॰ – (नि √पत् = निपतति) गिरता है। falls down.

निपातित – कृ॰ – (नि √पत् - णिच् + क्त = निपातित) पिछाड़ा अथवा गिराया गया। fallen down or thrown.

निपन्न – कृ॰ – (नि √पत् + क्त = निपन्न) लेटा। laid down, slept.

निपात – पु॰ – (निपात) (1) गिरना, उतरना (2) अव्यय-प्रत्यय। (1) falling down, descent (2) an indeclinable particle.

निपातन – न॰ – (निपातन) पिछाड़ना, गिराना। falling upon, throwing down.

निपाती – वि॰ – (निपाती) गिराने वाला, फेंकने वाला, मारने वाला। one who causes to fall down, one who throws or kills.

निपातेति – क्रि॰ – (निपातयति) गिरने देता है, गिराता है। causes to fall down.

निपातेत्वा – कृ॰ – (नि √पत + णिच + त्वा = निपातयित्वा) पिछाड़ करके या गिरा करके। having fallen down or thrown.

निपातेन्त – कृ॰ – (नि + √पात् + शतृ - निपातयन्) गिराते या पिछाड़ते हुए। fallen down or thrown out.

निपातेसि – अतीत क्रि॰ – (न्यपातयत्) गिराया या पिछाड़ा। made to fall or throw out.

निपान – न॰ – (निपान) पशुओं की जल पीने की जगह, नाँद। a watering place for cattle, a trough for cattle.

निपुण – वि॰ – (निपुण) दक्ष, होशियार। skilled, ccmpetent, clever.

निपक्क – वि॰ – (निपक्व) उबला हुआ। boiled, infused.

निप्पदेस – वि॰ – (निःप्रदेश) जो एक देशी न हो, सर्वव्यापक। all embracing, cosmopolitan.

निप्पपञ्च – वि॰ – (निष्प्रपञ्च) प्रपञ्चरहित। free from defilement or diffusiveness..

निप्पभ – वि॰ – (निष्प्रभ) निष्प्रभ, निस्तेज। lustreless, without splendour.

निप्परियाय – वि॰ – (निष्पर्याय) बिना किसी भेद के। without distinction, or difference.

निष्प्लाप – वि॰ – (निष्प्रलाप) प्रलाप-रहित। free from chaf of prattle.

निष्पाप – वि॰ – (निष्पाप) निष्पाप। sinless.

निष्पितिक – वि॰ – (पितृहीन) पिता-विहीन। fatherless.

निष्पीळन – न॰ – (निष्पीडन) पीड़ना, दबाना, निचोड़ना। squeezing, pressing.

निष्पीडित – कृ॰ – (निः √पीड् + क्त = निष्पीडित) squeezed, pressed.

निष्पीडेत्वा – कृ॰ – (निः √पीड् + ल्यप् = निष्पीड्य) having squeezed or pressed.

निष्पीडेसि – अतीत क्रि॰ – (न्यपीडयत्) had squeezed or pressed.

निष्पुरिस – वि॰ – (निष्पुरुष) पुरुष-विहीन, स्त्रियाँ ही स्त्रियाँ। composed entirely of women.

निष्पोथन – न॰ – (निः √तड् = निस्ताडनम्) पीटना। beating. (नोट - पालि में √पुथ धातु का अर्थ है पीटना)

निष्फज्जति – क्रि॰ – (निष्पादयति) निष्पादन करता है। produces, makes happen.

निष्फज्जमान – कृ॰ – (निष्पद्यमान) निष्पन्न होता हुआ। being produced.

निष्फज्जि – अतीत क्रि॰ – (निरपद्यत्) had produced.

निष्फज्जित्वा – कृ॰ – (निष्पद्य) having produced.

निष्फन्न – कृ॰ – (निष्पन्न) produced.

निष्फज्जन – न॰ – (निष्पादन) परिणाम, प्रभाव, प्राप्ति। result, accomplishment, achievement.

निष्फत्ति – स्त्री॰ – (निष्पत्ति) निष्पत्ति, प्राप्ति। result, accomplishment, achievement.

निष्फल – वि॰ – (निष्फल) निष्फल। fruitless, vain.

निष्फादक – वि॰ – (निष्पादक) निष्पादक, उत्पन्न करने वाला। one who produces, producer.

निष्फादन – न॰ – (निष्पादन) उत्पत्ति। production, accomplishment.

निष्फादित – कृ॰ – (निष्पादित) उत्पन्न किया हुआ। produced.

निष्फादेति – क्रि॰ – (निष्पादयति) उत्पन्न करता है। produces, bring forth.

निष्फादेत्वा – कृ॰ – (निष्पाद्य) उत्पन्न करके। having produced.

निष्फादेन्त – कृ॰ – (निष्पादयन्) उत्पन्न करता हुआ। getting produced.

निष्फादेसि – अतीत क्रि॰ – (निरपादयत्) उत्पन्न किया। produced.

निष्फादेतु – पु॰ – (निष्पादक/निष्पादयिता) उत्पन्न करने वाला, उत्पादक। producer.

निष्फोटन – न॰ – (ताडनम्) पीटना। beating.

निष्फोटित – कृ॰ – (ताडित) पीटा हुआ, ताडित। beaten.

निष्फोटेति – क्रि॰ – (ताडयति) पीटता है। beats.

निष्फोटेत्वा – कृ॰ – (ताडयित्वा) पीटकर। having beaten.

निष्फोटेन्त – कृ॰ – (ताडयन्) पीटता हुआ। having beaten.

निष्फोटेसि – अतीत क्रि॰ – (अताडयत्) पीटा। had beaten.

निबद्ध – वि॰ – (निबद्ध) बँधा हुआ, नियमित, लगातार। constant, regular, continuous.

निबन्ध – पु॰ – (निबन्ध) बंधन। bonding, fastening, binding.

निबन्धन – न॰ – (निबन्धन) बंधन। bonding, binding, fastening.

निबन्धति – क्रि॰ – (नि √बन्ध् = निबध्नाति) बाँधता है, प्रेरित करता है। binds, urges, importunes.

निब्बट्ट – वि॰ – (निर्वृत्त) निष्पन्न, जो पूरा किया जा चुका हो, चिरत। satisfied, completed, produced, freed from attachment.

निब्बट्टेति – क्रि॰ – (निवर्त्तयति) हटाता है। removes.

निब्बटेत्वा – कृ॰ – (नि √वृत् + ल्यप् = निवृत्य) लौटकर, पलटकर। returning, turning back.

निब्बत्त – कृ॰ – (निवर्तित) पुनः अस्तित्व प्राप्त, जिसका पुनर्जन्म हुआ है। taken rebirth, who has come in to existence.

निब्बत्तनक – वि॰ – (निवर्त्तनक) उत्पादक। producer.

निब्बत्त – कृ॰ – (निवृत्त) आस्तिव गृहीत, पुनर्जन्म प्राप्त। having existed, being reborn.

निब्बत्तति – क्रि॰ – (निवर्तते) उत्पन्न होता है, जन्म ग्रहण करता है। comes in to existence.

निब्बत्तन – न॰ – (निवर्त्तन) उत्पत्ति। coming forth, birth or rebirth, origin.

निब्बत्तन्त – कृ॰ – (निवर्त्तमान) पुनर्जन्म ग्रहण करने वाला। one being born again.

निब्बत्तित्वा – (निवृत्य) पुनर्जन्म पाकर। getting rebirth.

निब्बत्ति – स्त्री॰ – (निवृत्ति) जन्म ग्रहण, प्रकट होना। to be born, to appear, to manifest.

निब्बत्तापन – न॰ – (निवर्त्तन) पुनर्जन्म। reproduction, rebirth.

निब्बत्तेन्त – कृ॰ – (निवर्त्तयन्) उत्पन्न करता हुआ। getting produced.

निब्बत्तेत्वा – कृ॰ – (निवृत्य) उत्पन्न करके। having produced.

निब्बत्तित – कृ॰ – (निवर्त्तित) उत्पन्न किया हुआ। produced.

निवत्तेतब्ब – कृ॰ – (निवर्त्तितव्य) उत्पन्न किया जाने योग्य। fit to be produced.

निब्बत्तेति – क्रि॰ – (निवर्त्तयति) उत्पन्न करता है। produces.

निब्बन – वि॰ – (तृष्णा निवृत्त) तृष्णा-रहित। free from craving.

निब्बनथ – वि॰ – (तृष्णा मुक्त) तृष्णा-मुक्त। free from craving.

निब्बसन – वि॰ – (निर्वसन) निर्वसन, बिना वस्त्र के। cast of cloth.

निब्बाति – क्रि॰ – (निर्वाति) बुझ जाता है, ठण्डा पड़ जाता है, उत्तेजना-रहित हो जाता है। gets cold, becomes passionless, becomes extinguished.

निब्बातुं – कृ॰ – (निर्वाणं प्राप्तुम) देखें निब्बायितुं। see Nibbāyitum.

निब्बान – न॰ – (निर्वाण) निर्वाण, (अग्नि का) बुझ जाना, मोक्ष। extinction (of a fire), emancipation.

निब्बान-गमन – वि॰ – (निर्वाण-गमन) निर्वाण-गमन। leading to *nibbāna*.

निब्बान-धातु – स्त्री॰ – (निर्वाण-धातु) निर्वाण-क्षेत्र। the sphere of *nibbāna*.

निब्बान-पत्ति – स्त्री॰ – (निर्वाण-प्राप्ति) निर्वाण-प्राप्ति। attainment of *nibbāna*.

निब्बान-सच्छिकिरिया – स्त्री॰ – (निर्वाण-साक्षात्कार) निर्वाण का साक्षात् करना। realisation of *nibbāna*.

निब्बान-सम्पत्ति – स्त्री॰ – (निर्वाण-सम्प्राप्ति) निर्वाण की प्राप्ति। the bliss of *nibbāna*.

निब्बानाभिरत – वि॰ – (निब्बान-अभिरत) निर्वाण-प्राप्ति में अनुरक्त। finding delight in *nibbāna*, fond of *nibbāna*.

निब्बापन – न॰ – (निर्वापन) शान्त होना, बुझना। cooling, quenching, extinction.

निब्बापेति – क्रि॰ – (निर्वापयति) बुझा देता है। extinguish.

निब्बायति – क्रि॰ – (निर्वाणं लभते) निर्वाण-प्राप्त होता है। ceases to exist, becomes cool.

निब्बायितुं – कृ॰ – (निर्वाणं प्राप्तुम्) निर्वाण प्राप्त करने के लिए। to cease to exit.

निब्बाहन – न॰ – (बहिस्करण) हटाना। removal, clearance.

निब्बिकार – पु॰ – (निर्विकार) निर्विकार, अपरिवर्तनशील। unchanging, steadfast.

निब्बिचिकिच्छ – वि॰ – (निर्विचिकित्स) सन्देह-रहित। doubtless.

निब्बिज्ज – कृ॰ – (निर्वेदित) निर्वेद-प्राप्त। disgusted, disheartened.

निब्बिज्जति – क्रि॰ – (निर्वेत्ति/निर्वेदन् अनुभवति) निर्वेद प्राप्त करता है। becomes disgusted.

निब्बिज्झति – क्रि॰ – (निर्बिध्यति) बींधता है। pierces.

निब्बिदा – स्त्री॰ – (निर्विदा) निर्वेद। disgust, weariness.

निब्बिन्दति – क्रि॰ – (निर्विद्यते) निर्वेद-प्राप्त होता है। gets wearied of, becomes disgusted with.

निब्बिस – वि॰ – (निर्विष) विषहीन, निर्विष। poison-less.

निब्बिस – न॰ – (निवेश) मजदूरी। wages.

निब्बिसेस – वि॰ – (निर्विशेष) समान, एक जैसा। similar, showing no difference.

निब्बुति – स्त्री॰ – (निर्वृत्ति) शान्ति, परम सुख। peace, the final bliss.

निब्बुय्हति – क्रि॰ – (निर्व्यूह्यति/संतरति) तैरता है। floats, swims, buoyed up.

निब्बेठन – न॰ – (निर्वेष्टन) उधेड़ना, व्याख्या। unwinding, explanation.

निब्बेठेति – क्रि॰ – (निर्वेष्टयति) उधेड़ता है। unwinds, explains.

निब्बेध – पु॰ – (निर्वेध) घुसाना, घुसेड़ना। penetration, piercing.

निब्बेमतिक – वि॰ – (निर्वैमतिक) एकमत। of one accord, unanimous.

निब्भय – वि॰ – (निर्भय) निर्भय। fearless, brave.

निब्भोग – वि॰ – (निर्भोग) व्यर्थ, बेकार। useless, deserted.

निभ – वि॰ – (निभ) समान। equal to, resembling.

निभा – स्त्री॰ – (निभा/विभा) प्रकाश, चमक-दमक। lustre, light.

निभाति – क्रि॰ – (निभाति/विभाति) चमकता है। shines.

निभासि – अतीत क्रि॰ – (अभासत्) चमका
है । shone.

निमन्तक – वि॰ – (निमन्त्रक) निमंत्रण देने
वाला । one who invites.

निमन्तन – न॰ – (निमन्त्रण) निमंत्रण ।
invitation.

निमन्तेति – क्रि॰ – (निमन्त्रयति) निमंत्रण
देता है । invites.

निमन्तित – कृ॰ – (निमन्त्रित) आमन्त्रित ।
invited.

निमन्तिय – कृ॰ – (निमन्त्रणीय) निमन्त्रित
किये जाने योग्य । fit to be invited.

निमन्तेत्वा – कृ॰ – (निमन्त्रयित्वा) आमन्त्रित
करके । having invited.

निमन्तेन्त – कृ॰ – (निमन्त्रयन्) नियन्त्रित
करते हुए । getting invited.

निमन्तेसि – अतीत क्रि॰ – (न्यमन्त्रयत्)
निमन्त्रित किया । invited.

निमि-जातक –(जा॰ सं॰ 541) – सिर का
सफेद बाल दिखाई देने पर अपने अनेक
पूर्वजों की तरह निमि राजा ने भी सिंहासन
का त्याग कर दिया । the story (No.
541) gives a clarification of the
doubt whether a holy life is more
fruitful or, giving alms.

निमित्त – न॰ – (निमित्त) चिह्न, शकुन,
कारण । sign, omen, cause, portent.

निमित्तगाही – वि॰ – (निमित्त-ग्राही) ऊपरी
चिह्नों से आकर्षित । sensuously
attracted, led away by outward-
signs.

निमित्त-पाठक – पु॰ – (निमित्त-पाठक)
शकुनों की व्याख्या करने वाला, भविष्य
वक्ता । one who prognosticates.

निमिनाति – क्रि॰ – आदान-प्रदान करता
है । exchange for, barters.

निमिस – पु॰ – (निमिष) आँख का झपकना ।
winking, blink.

निमिसति – क्रि॰ – (निमिषति) आँख झपकता
है, आँख मारता है । winks, shuts, or
closes the eyes.

निमीलन – न॰ – (नि · √मील + क्त =
निमीलन) आँख का झपकना, बन्द करना ।
winking, shutting the eyes.

निमीलित – कृ॰ – (नि √मील + क्त =
निमीलित) मुद्रित । closed.

निमीलित्वा – कृ॰ – (नि √मील + ल्यप् =
निमील्य) आँख झपका करके । winked,
having shut the eyes.

निमीलेति – क्रि॰ – (निमीलति) आँख
झपकता है, आँख बंद करता है । winks,
shuts, closes the eyes.

निमुज्ज – कृ॰ – (नि √मज्ज् + क्त =
निमग्न) डुबकी लगाया हुआ । sunk,
plunged into.

निमुज्जति – क्रि॰ – (नि √मज्ज् =
निमज्जति) डुबकी लगाता है । sinks
down, plunges into.

निमुज्जा – स्त्री॰ – (निमज्जन) डुबकी मारना,
डुबकी । diving, sinking, ducking.

निमुज्जन – न॰ – (नि √मज्ज् + ल्युट् =
निमज्जन) डुबकी लगाना । sinking,
diving.

निमेस – पु॰ – (निमेष) देखें निमिस । see
Nimisa.

निम्ब – पु॰ – (निम्ब) नीम का वृक्ष । the
margosa tree.

निम्मकिखक – वि॰ – (निर्मक्षिक) मक्खी-रहित । free from flies or larvae.

निम्मज्जन – न॰ – (निर्मार्जन) निचोड़ना । squeezing.

निम्मथन – न॰ – (निर्मन्थन) पीसना । crushing, pressing.

निम्मथति – क्रि॰ – (निर्मथ्नाति) पीस डालता है, दबा देता है । crushes, presses.

निम्मथेति – क्रि॰ – (निर्मथ्नाति) पीस डालता है, दबा देता है । crushes, presses, grinds.

निम्मद्दन – न॰ – (निर्मर्दन) मर्दित करना, दबा देना । to crush, subdue.

निम्मल – वि॰ – (निर्मल) स्वच्छ, शुद्ध, निर्मल । clean, pure.

निम्मंस – वि॰ – (निर्मांस) मांस-रहित । free from flesh.

निम्मात-पितिक – वि॰ – (निः मातृपितृक) अनाथ, माता-पिता-रहित । orphan, parentless.

निम्मातु – पु॰ – (निर्माता) निर्माण करने वाला, रचयिता । the creator, maker, builder.

निम्माण – न॰ – (निर्माण) रचना, कृति । creation, production.

निम्मान (1) – न॰ – (निर्माण) रचना, कृति । creation, production.

निम्मान (2) – वि॰ – (निर्मान) मान-रहित । free from pride.

निम्मित – कृ॰ – (निर्मित) निर्मित । created, built.

निम्मिनाति – क्रि॰ – (निर् √मी = निर्मिनाति) निर्माण करता है । creates, builds.

निम्मिणाति – क्रि॰ – (निर्मिनाति) देखें निम्मिनाति । see Nimmināti.

निम्मूल – वि॰ – (निर्मूल) निर्मूल । rootless.

निम्मोक – वि॰ – (निर्मोक) साँप की केंचुल । the slough of a serpent.

निय-नियक – वि॰ – (नीय, नियक) स्वकीय, अपना । समस्त पदों में प्रयुक्त जैसे मान + नीय । one's own (used in compounds).

नियत – वि॰ – (नियत) निश्चित, स्थिर । fixed, certain.

नियति – स्त्री॰ – (नियति) भाग्य, किस्मत, आवश्यकता । luck, fate, destiny, necessity.

नियम – पु॰ – (नियम) मर्यादा, निश्चित होना, स्थिर होना । limitation, certainty, stability.

नियमन – न॰ – (नियमन) स्थिरता, नियमा-धीन । fixing, settling.

नियमेति – क्रि॰ – नियमित करता है, नियन्त्रित करता है । fixes, controls.

नियाम – पु॰ – (नियमत्व) नियम होना, तरीका । certainty, limitation, definiteness.

नियामता – स्त्री॰ – (नियमत्त्वा) देखें नियाम । see Niyāma.

नियामक – पु॰ – (नियामक) (1) जहाज का कप्तान (2) सेनापति (3) नियम में चलाने वाला । (1) captain of the ship (2) commander (3) regulator.

नियुज्जति – क्रि॰ – (नियुनक्ति / नियुङ्क्ते) कार्यरत होता है । engages in.

नियुज्जि – अतीत क्रि॰ – (न्यमुनक) कार्य-रत हुआ । engaged in.

नियुत्त – कृ॰ – (नि √युज् + क्त = नियुक्त) नियुक्त । appointed to, engaged in.

नियोग – पु० – (नियोग) आज्ञा, हुक्म, आवश्यकता। command, order.

नियोजन – न० – (नियोजन) नियुक्त करना, आज्ञा देना। urging, ordering, committing.

नियोजित – कृ० – (नि √युज् + क्त = नियोजित) नियोजित। a representative.

नियोजेति – क्रि० – (नि √युज् = नियोजयति) नियुक्त करता है, प्रेरित करता है। urges, incites, commits.

निय्यति – क्रि० – (नीयते) ले जाया जाता है। guided, conducted, or carried.

निय्यातन – न० – (नियार्तन) समर्पण, सौंपना, वस्तु लौटाना। surrender, offering dedication, returning (of something).

निय्यात – कृ० – (निर √या + क्त = नियांत) बाहर गया हुआ। gone out.

निय्याति – क्रि० – (नियांति) बाहर जाता है। goes out.

निय्यातु – पु० – (नियीतृ) (1) नेता, मार्ग-दर्शक (2) बाहर जाने वाला (3) निराने वाला। (1) guide, (2) one who goes out (3) one who weeds out the crop.

निय्यातेति – क्रि० – (निय्यादेति, नीमादेति भी) सौंपता है, समर्पित करता है। to hand over, to pay off.

निय्यान – न० – (नियांन) बहिर्गमन, विदाई। going out, departure, release.

निय्यानिक – वि० – (नियांनिक) मुक्ति की ओर अग्रसर करने वाले। leading to salvation.

निय्यास – पु० – (नियांस) पेड़ों से निकलने वाला रस, गोंद, आदि। gum, exudation of trees.

निय्यूह – पु० – (नियूंह) शिखर, द्वार। summit, peak.

निरंकरोति – क्रि० – (निराकरोति) तिरस्कार करता है, उपेक्षा करता है। disregard, repudiates.

निरग्गल – वि० – (निर्गल) बाधा-रहित, मुक्त। unobstructed, free.

निरत – वि० – (निरत) लगा हुआ। attached to.

निरत्थ – वि० – (निरर्थक) देखें निरत्थक। see Niratthaka.

निरत्थक – वि० – (निरर्थक) निरर्थक। useless, incompetent, vain.

निरन्तर – वि० – (निरन्तर) लगातार। continuous.

निरन्तरं – क्रि० वि० – (निरन्तरम्) लगातार। continuously.

निरपराध – वि० – (निरपराध) निर्दोष। innocent, guiltless.

निरपेक्ख – वि० – (निरपेक्ष) अपेक्षा-रहित, जिसकी परवाह न हो। indifferent, disregarding.

निरपेख – वि० – (निरपेक्ष) देखें निरपेक्ख। see Nirapekkha.

निरब्बुद (1) – वि० – (निरर्बुद) बाधा-रहित, दुःख रहित। free from troubles or tumors.

निरब्बुद (2) – न० – (निरर्बुद) एक विशाल संख्या। a large number.

निरब्बुद (3) – पु० – (निरर्बुद) नरक। hell.

निरय – पु० – (निरय) नरक। hell.

निरय-गामी – वि॰ – (निरयगामी) नरक-गामी । leading to hell.

निरय-दुक्ख – न॰ – (निरय-दुःख) नरक का दुःख । the pain of hell.

निरय-पाल – पु॰ – (निरयपाल) नरक का अधिपति । a guardian in hell.

निरय-भय – न॰ – (निरय-भय) नरक का भय । the fear of hell.

निरय-संवत्तनिक – वि॰ – (निरय संवर्त्तनिक) नरक की ओर ले जाने वाला । leading one to hell.

निरवसेस – वि॰ – (निरवशेष) सम्पूर्ण । inclusive, without remainder.

निरसन – वि॰ – (निरशन) निराहार । fasting.

निरस्साद – वि॰ – (निरास्वाद) बे-स्वाद । tasteless, dull.

निराकति – स्त्री॰ – (निराकृति) दूर करना । expelling.

निराकुल – वि॰ – (निराकुल) उलझन-रहित, बाधा-रहित । unagitated, not confused.

निरातङ्क – वि॰ – (निरातङ्क) आतङ्क-रहित, रोग-रहित । free from fear, free from disease.

निरामय – वि॰ – (निरामय) निरोग । free from disease.

निरामिस – वि॰ – (निरामिष) मांस-रहित, अभौतिक । having no meat, non-material.

निरारम्भ – वि॰ – (निरालम्भ) बिना पशुओं की हत्या किये । without killing of animals.

निरालम्ब – वि॰ – (निरालम्ब) निराधार । unsupported, groundless.

निरालय – वि॰ – (निरालय) आसक्ति-रहित, गृह-रहित । free from desire, homeless.

निरास – वि॰ – (निराशा) आशा-रहित, इच्छा-रहित । desireless.

निरासङ्क – वि॰ – (निरशङ्क) शंका-रहित । unsuspicious, not doubting.

निरासंस – वि॰ – (निराशंस) इच्छा-रहित, आशा-रहित । without expectations, without desires.

निरासव – वि॰ – (निरासव) आसव-रहित । non-alchoholic.

निराहार – वि॰ – (निराहार) आहार-रहित, व्रती । want of food, fasting.

निरिन्धन – वि॰ – (निरिन्धन) ईंधन-रहित । without fuel.

निरुज्झि – अतीत क्रि॰ – (नि + रुरोध) अवरुद्ध किया । ceased.

निरुद्ध – कृ॰ – (नि √रुध + क्त = निरुद्ध) अवरुद्ध कर दिया । ceased.

निरुद्ध्य – कृ॰ – (नि √रुध + ल्यप् = संनिरुद्ध्य) अवरुद्ध किया । having ceased.

निरुज्झन – न॰ – (निरोधन) निरोध । ceasing, dissolving.

निरुत्तर – वि॰ – (निरुत्तर) उत्तर-विहीन, सर्वोत्तम । not answerable, one who has no superior.

निरुत्ति – स्त्री॰ – (निरुक्ति) निरुक्त शास्त्र, बोली, व्याकरण-संबंधी विश्लेषण । philology.

निरुत्ति-पटिसम्भिदा – स्त्री॰ – (निरुक्ति-प्रतिसंविद्) निरुक्त का ज्ञान । knowledge of philological analysis.

निरुदक – वि॰ – (**निरुदक**) जल-रहित। waterless.

निरुद्ध – कृ॰ – (**निरुद्ध**) निरोध को प्राप्त हुआ। ceased to exist.

निरुपद्दव – वि॰ – (**निरुपद्रव**) उपद्रव-रहित। harmless, without mishap, secure.

निरुपधि – वि॰ – (**निरुपधि**) राग-रहित, आसक्ति-रहित। free from passions or attachment.

निरुपम – वि॰ – (**निरुपम**) उपमा-रहित। incomparable.

निरुस्सास – वि॰ – (**निःश्वास**) आश्वास, प्रश्वास-रहित। without breathing.

निरुस्सुक – वि॰ – (**निरुत्सुक**) औत्सुक्य-रहित, उपेक्षायुक्त। spiritless, half-hearted, without esthusiasm.

निरोग – वि॰ – (**निरोग / नीरोग**) नीरोग, स्वस्थ। healthy.

निरोज – वि॰ – (**निस्स्वाद**) स्वाद-रहित, बे-मजा। tasteless.

निरोध – पु॰ – (**निरोध**) (1) रोक (2) – पुनरुत्पत्ति का रुक जाना। (1) obstruction, check (2) cessation or birth.

निरोध-धम्म – वि॰ – (**निरोध-धर्म**) निरोध-स्वभाव। subject to destruction.

निरोध-समापत्ति – (**निरोध-समापत्ति**) attainment of cessation of consciousness.

निरोधेति – क्रि॰ – (**निरोधयति**) निरोध को प्राप्त करता है। annihilates, dissolves, destroys.

निलय – पु॰ – (**निलय**) घर, निवास-स्थान। home, habitation.

निलीयति – क्रि॰ – (**निलीयते**) छिपता है। hides, keeps oneself hidden.

निल्लज्ज – वि॰ – (**निर्लज्ज**) निर्लज्ज, बेशरम। shameless.

निल्लेहक – वि॰ – (**लेहक**) चाटने वाला। one who licks.

निल्लोप – पु॰ – (**निस् √लुप = निर्लोपः**) लूट, डाका। plundering.

निवत्त – कृ॰ – (**निवृत्त**) रुका, निरुद्ध, वीतराग। held back, freed from attachment.

निवत्तति – क्रि॰ – (**निवर्त्तते**) रुक जाता है, लौट पड़ता है। returns, abstains.

निवत्तन – न॰ – (**निवर्त्तन**) रुकना, वापिस आना, हटना या हटाना। stoppage, return, turning back, remaining behind.

निवत्ति – स्त्री॰ – (**निवृत्ति**) देखें निवत्तन। see Nivattana.

निवत्तेति – क्रि॰ – (**निवर्त्तयति**) रोकता है, लौटता है। stops, makes go back.

निवत्थ – कृ॰ – वस्त्र पहने हुए। clothed in, fully with dressed.

निवसति – क्रि॰ – (**निवसति**) रहता है, वास करता है। lives, dwells, inhabits.

निवह – पु॰ – (**निवह**) ढेर, संग्रह। heap, multitude.

निवातक – न॰ – (**निर्वातक**) शान्त, सुरक्षित स्थान। calm or sheltered place, opportunity for hiding.

निवातवुत्ति – वि॰ – (**निर्वात-उक्ति / विनम्र**) विनम्र। hiding, humble, polite.

निवाप – पु॰ – (**निवाप**) पशुओं का आहार, श्राद्ध। fodder, bait, food for feeding cattle.

निवारण – न॰ – (निवारण) रोकना। prevention, warding off.

निवारिय – वि॰ – (निवारणीय) रोकने योग्य। what should be prevented or checked.

निवारेति – क्रि॰ – (निवारेति) रोकता है। prevents, forbids, keeps back.

निवारेतु – पु॰ – (निवारयिता) रोकने वाला। one who prevents, forbids or obstructs.

निवास – पु॰ – (निवास) रहना, रहने की जगह। abode, resting place.

निवास-भूमि – स्त्री॰ – (निवास-भूमि) रहने की जगह। dwelling place.

निवासन (1) – न॰ – (निवासन) अन्तर्वसन, अन्दर पहनने का कपड़ा। under-garment, clothing.

निवासन (2) – न॰ – (निवासन) रहने की जगह। dwelling place.

निवासिक – पु॰ – (निवासी) रहने वाला। who dwells, lives or stays.

निवासी – पु॰ – (निवासी) देखें निवासिक। see Nivāsikā.

निवासेति – क्रि॰ – (वस्त्र-धारयति) वस्त्र पहनता है। dresses oneself, gets clothed.

निविट्ठ – कृ॰ – (निविष्ट) स्थित, समाहित, स्थिर हुआ। settled, established in, devoted to.

निविसति – क्रि॰ – (निविशति) घुसता है, रुकता है। penetrates into, encamps.

निवुत – कृ॰ – (निवृत्त) घिरा हुआ। encircled, surrounded.

निवुत्थ – कृ॰ – (निवसित) रहा हुआ। lived, dwelled.

निवेदक – वि॰ – (निवेदक) निवेदन करने वाला। one who informs or announces.

निवेदत्वा – कृ॰ – (निवेद्य) निवेदन करके। having announced.

निवेदित – कृ॰ – (निवेदित) निवेदन किया हुआ। announced.

निवेदिय – कृ॰ – (निवेदनीय) निवेदन करने योग्य। fit to be announced.

निवेदेति – क्रि॰ – (निवेदयति) निवेदन करता है। announces, makes known, communicates.

निवेदेसि – अतीत क्रि॰ – (न्यवेदत्) निवेदन किया। announced.

निवेस (1) – पु॰ – (निवेश) निवास-स्थान। settlement, abode, house.

निवेस (2) – पु॰ – (निवेश) ठहराव, घुसाव। penetration, encamping.

निवेसन – न॰ – (निवेशन) देखें निवेश। see Niveśa.

निवेसेति – क्रि॰ – (निवेशयति) स्थापित करता है, घुसाता है, निर्धारित करता है। establishes in, settles, arranges.

निवेसेसि – अतीत क्रि॰ – (न्यवेशयत्) established, settled, arranged.

निवेसित – कृ॰ – (निवेशित) स्थापित, निर्धारित। established, settled, arranged.

निवेसित्वा – कृ॰ – (निवेश्य) स्थापित अथवा निर्धारित करके। having established or settled.

निसग – पु॰ – (निसर्ग) देना, प्रकृति, निसर्ग। innate, nature, disposition.

निसज्ज – पू॰ क्रि॰ – (नि √सद् + ल्यप् = निषद्य) बैठकर। having sat down.

निसज्जा (1) – स्त्री॰ – **(निषीदन)** बैठना। sitting down.

निसज्जा (2) – स्त्री॰ – **(निषद्या)** चारपाई, पथिकों के लिए विश्रामगृह। bed, rest-house, for wayfarers.

निसद – पु॰ – **(निसद्)** चक्की का निचला पाट। the lower stone for grinding.

निसद-पोत – पु॰ – **(निसद्-पोत)** चक्की का ऊपरी पाट। the upper stone for grinding.

निसभ – पु॰ – **(वृषभ)** अग्रगामी वृषभ, नर-श्रेष्ठ। the leading ox, the best of men.

निसम्म – पू॰ क्रि॰/क्रि॰ वि॰ – **(निशम्य)** विचार करके, सुख करके। having considered, having heard.

निसम्मकारी – वि॰ – **(निशम्यकारी)** सोच-विचारकर करने वाला। acting considerately.

निसा – स्त्री॰ – **(निशा)** रजनी, रात्रि। night.

निसाकर – पु॰ – **(निशाकर)** चन्द्रमा। the moon।

निसाण – पु॰ – **(निशाण)** सान चढ़ाने का पत्थर, सिल्ली। whetstone, a hone.

निसाद – पु॰ – **(निषाद)** सात स्वरों में से एक, निषाद नामक नस्ल विशेष। one of the seven sounds, name of a race.

निसानाथ – पु॰ – **(निशानाथ)** चन्द्रमा। the moon.

निसामक – वि॰ – **(निशामक)** द्रष्टा, दर्शक, ध्यान लगाकर सुनने वाला। one who sees, knows or hears attentively.

निसामन – न॰ – **(निशमन)** देखना-सुनना। beholding.

निसामेति – क्रि॰ – **(निशामयति)** जानता-सुनता है। sees, knows.

निसित – वि॰ – **(निशित)** तीक्ष्ण, तेज। sharp.

निसिन्न – कृ॰ – (नि √सद् + क्त = निषण्ण) बैठा हुआ। sat down.

निसिनक – वि॰ – **(निषण्णक)** बैठा हुआ। sitting down.

निसीथ – पु॰ – **(निशीथ)** मध्य रात्रि। the mid-night.

निसीदति – क्रि॰ – (नि √सद् = निषीदति) बैठता है। sits.

निसीदन – न॰ – **(निषीदन)** बैठना, बैठने की जगह। sitting, seat.

निसीदापन – न॰ – बैठाना। causing to sitdown.

निसीदापेति – क्रि॰ – **(निषीदयति)** बैठाता है। causes to sit down.

निसूदन – न॰ – **(नि+सूदन)** हत्या करना। killing.

निसेध – पु॰ – **(निषेध)** रोकथाम। prohibition, prevention.

निसेधक – वि॰ – **(निषेधक)** निषेध करने वाला। one who prevents or obstructs.

निसेधेति – क्रि॰ – **(निषेधयति)** निषेध करता है। prevents, prohibits.

निसेधित – कृ॰ – **(निषिद्ध)** निषिद्ध, वर्जित, मना। prohibited, prevented.

निसेधेत्वा – कृ॰ – **(निषिद्धय)** मना करके, निषेध करके। having prohibited or prevented.

निसेधेन्त – कृ॰ – **(निषेधयन्)** निषेध करते हुए। getting prohibited.

निसेधेसि – अतीत क्रि॰ – (न्यवेधयत्) निषिद्ध कर दिया। prohibited.

निसेवति – क्रि॰ – (निषेवतेः) संगति करता है। associates, pursues, indulges in.

निसेवि – अतीत क्रि॰ – (सिषेवे) सेवा की, संगति की। associated, pursued.

निसेवित – कृ॰ – (निषेवित/सेवित) संगति करता है। associated, pursued.

निसेवित्वा – कृ॰ – (निषेव्य, सेवित्या) सेवा करके। having associated, having pursued.

निसेवन – न॰ – (निसेवन) संगति करना, उपयोग करना, अभ्यास करना। associating, using, practising.

निस्सग्ग – पु॰ – (निसर्ग) परित्याग। giving up.

निस्सग्गिय – वि॰ – (निसर्गीय/निसर्ग्य) परित्याग करने योग्य। what ought to be rejected or abandoned.

निसस्ग – वि॰ – (निस्सङ्ग) संग-रहित। unattached, unselfish.

निस्सजति – क्रि॰ – (निस्सृजति) ढीला छोड़ता है, त्याग देता है। gives up, lets loose.

निस्सज्ज – कृदन्त – (निः √सृज् + ल्यप् = निस्सृज्य) त्यागकर। having given up.

निस्सज्जि – अतीत क्रि॰ – (निः ससर्ज) छोड़ दिया। had given up.

निस्सज्जित्वा – कृ॰ – (निः √सृज् + ल्यप् = निसृज्य) देखें – निस्सज्ज। see Nissajja.

निस्सट्ठ (1) – कृ॰ – (निः √सृज् + क्त = निः सृष्ट) त्यागा हुआ। given up.

निस्सट्ठ (2) – कृ॰ – (निः सृत) छोड़ा हुआ, त्यागा हुआ, बाहर निकला हुआ। came out from, given up, let loose.

निस्सत्त – वि॰ – (निःसत्त्व) सत्त्व (प्राणी) - विहीन। soulless.

निस्सद्द – वि॰ – (निःशब्द) निःशब्द, शान्त। silent, noiseless.

निस्सन्द – पु॰ – (निःस्यन्द) (1) परिणाम (2) रिसना। (1) result (2) trickling down.

निस्सय – पु॰ – (निःश्रय) (1) आश्रय (2) संरक्षण। (1) support (2) protection.

निस्सयति – क्रि॰ – (निः √श्र = निःश्रयति) आश्रय ग्रहण करता है, सहारा लेता है। leans on, relies on, depends on.

निस्सरण – न॰ – (निस्सरण) बाहर जाना, विदाई, पलायन। going out, departure, escape.

निस्सरति – क्रि॰ – (निस्सरति) निकल जाता है, विदा होता है। departs, escapes from.

निस्सरि – अतीत क्रि॰ – (निस्सार) विदा हो चुका था। had departed.

निस्सट – कृ॰ – (निःसृत) विदा हुआ। departed.

निस्सठ – कृ॰ – (निःसृष्ट) त्यागना। dismissed, given up, handed over.

निस्सत्त – वि॰ – (निःसत्त्व) प्राणहीन। soulless.

निस्सद्द – वि॰ – (निःशब्द) शब्द हीन, मौन। silent, noiseless.

निस्सरित्वा – कृ॰ – (निःसृत्य) विदा होकर के। having departed.

निस्साय – अव्यय – उसके द्वारा, उससे। through him, from him.

निस्सार – वि॰ – **(निस्सार)** सार-रहित। worthless, unsubstantial.

निस्सारज्ज – वि॰ – विश्वस्त, दावे के साथ। with confidence, truthful.

निस्सारण – न॰ – **(निस्सारण)** बाहर निकालना, विदाई। going out, departure, escape.

निस्साव – पु॰ – **(निःस्राव)** चावल का मांड़। scum of boiled rice.

निस्सित – कृ॰ – **(निश्रित)** आश्रित। dependent on, living by means of.

निस्सितक – वि॰ – **(निःश्रितक)** आश्रय ग्रहण करने वाला, अनुयायी शिष्य। an adherent, one who is supported by.

निस्सिरीक – वि॰ – **(निःश्रीक)** दुर्भाग्यपूर्ण, दुःखी, वैभवहीन। unfortunate, miserable, woeful.

निस्सेणि – स्त्री॰ – **(निःश्रेणि)** सीढ़ी। ladder or staircase.

निस्सेस – वि॰ – **(निःशेष)** सम्पूर्ण। entire, the whole.

निस्सेसं – वि॰ – **(निःशेषम्)** सम्पूर्ण रूप से। entirely.

निस्सोक – वि॰ – **(निःशोक)** शोक-रहित। free from sorrow.

निहत – कृ॰ – **(नि √हन् + क्त = निहत)** उन्मूलित, पराजित। struck down, hit, defeated.

निहतमान – वि॰ – **(निहतमान)** निरंहकारी, विनम्र, विनीत। prideless, polite.

निहनति – क्रि॰ – **(नि √हन् = निहन्ति)** जान से मारता है, मिटा देता है। slays, puts down, destroys.

निहनि – अतीत क्रि॰ – **(निजधान)** मार डाला, नष्ट कर डाला। had killed, had destroyed.

निहंत्वा – कृ॰ – **(नि √हन् + ल्यप् = निहत्वा)** मार करके। having slain, having destroyed.

निहीन – वि॰ – **(हीन)** नीच, तुच्छ, थोड़ा, महत्त्वहीन। low, vile, of little importance.

निहीन-कम्म – न॰ – **(हीन कर्म)** नीच कर्म, पाप कर्म। sinful action.

निहीन-पञ्ञ – वि॰ – **(हीनप्रज्ञ)** दुर्बुद्धि। of inferior wisdom.

निहीन-सेवी – वि॰ – **(नीचसेवी/हीनसेवी)** कुसंगति में रहने वाला। having bad association, of vile pursuit.

निहीयति – कृ॰ – **(नि √ही + क्त = निहीन)** नष्ट। destroyed.

निहीयति – क्रि॰ – **(नि √ही = निहीयते)** नाश को प्राप्त होता है। comes to ruin, becomes destroyed.

निहीयमान – कृ॰ – **(निहीयमान)** नाश को प्राप्त होता हुआ। being destroyed or coming to ruin.

√नी॰ – **(भू)** – पापुणने **(√नी)** पहुंचना, प्राप्त करना। to lead, to carry, to obtain.

नीघ – पु॰ – **(नीघ)** दुःख, अव्यवस्था। misery, confusion.

नीच – वि॰ – **(नीच)** निकृष्ट। low, inferior.

नीच कुल – न॰ – **(नीच-कुल)** नीच जाति। low caste.

नीच कुलीनता – स्त्री॰ – (नीच कुलत्व) नीच कुल में जन्म ग्रहण करने का भाव। state of having a low birth.

नीचासन – न॰ – (नीचासन) नीवा आसन। a low seat.

नीत – कृदन्त – ($\sqrt{}$नी + क्त = नीत) ले जाया गया। carried, guided, led away.

नीतत्थ – पु॰ – (नीतार्थ) अनुमानित अर्थ। inferred meaning.

नीति – स्त्री॰ – (नीति) कानून, मार्गदर्शन। law, guidance.

नीति-सत्थ – न॰ – (नीति-शास्त्र) नीति-शास्त्र। the book of moral laws.

नीप – पु॰ – (नीप) कदम्ब वृक्ष। the tree *Nauclea cadamba*, a species of Asoka.

नीयति – क्रि॰ – (नीयते) ले जाया जाता है। being carried or led away.

नीयाति – क्रि॰ – (निर्याति) देखें निय्याति। see Niyyāti.

नीर – न॰ – (नीर) जल। water.

$\sqrt{}$नील – (भू॰) – वण्णे – (नील रञ्ज्) नीला रंगता है। to colour in blue.

नील – वि॰ – (नील) नीला। blue.

नील – पु॰ – (नील) नीला रंग। blue colour.

नील-कसिण – न॰ – ध्यान लगाने के लिए नील वर्ण गोलाकार। a blue disc used for meditation.

नील-गीव – पु॰ – (नील-ग्रीव) नील ग्रीवा, मोर। peacock.

नीलमणी – पु॰ – (नील-मणि) नीलम। a sapphire.

नील-वण्ण – वि॰ – (नील-वर्ण) नील वर्ण, नीले रंग का। having the blue colour.

नील-वल्ली – स्त्री॰ – (नील-वल्ली) नील वर्ण लता। a kind of medicinal creeper which is of blue colour.

नील-सप्प – पु॰ – (नील-सर्प) नीला सांप। the whip snake.

नीलिनी – स्त्री॰ – (नीलिनी) नील का पौधा। the indigo plant.

नीली – स्त्री॰ – (नीली) नील का पौधा। the indigo plant.

नीलुप्पल – न॰ – (नीलोत्पल) नीलकमल। blue waterlily.

नीवरण – न॰ – (नीवरण) बाधा। obstacle or hindrance.

नीवार – पु॰ – (नीवार) जलाशय में बिना बोये उगने वाला तिन्नी नामक धान। a kind of wild rice plant.

नीहत – कृ॰ – (नीहृत) बाहर निकाला हुआ। taken out, driven away.

नीहरण – न॰ – (नीहरण) बाहर निकालना। taking out, carrying away.

नीहरति – क्रि॰ – (नी $\sqrt{}$ह = नीहरति) बाहर ले जाता है। takes out, drives away.

नीहरन् – कृ॰ – (नी $\sqrt{}$ह + शतृ = नीहरन्) बाहर ले जाया जाता हुआ। being taken away or driven out.

नीहरि – अतीत क्रि॰ – (नीजहार) हर लिया गया। had been taken out or driven out.

नीहरित्वा – कृ॰ – (नी $\sqrt{}$ह + ल्यप् = नीहृत्व) having driven out or taken out.

नीहार – पु॰ – (**नीहार**) (1) बाहर निकालना (2) पथ, ढंग। (1) ejection, carrying out, (2) the way, manner.

नीहित – कृ॰ – (**निहित**) रखा हुआ, व्यवस्थित। deposited, arranged.

नील – न॰ – (**नीड**) नीड़, घोंसला। nest.

नीलज – पु॰ – (**नीडज**) पक्षी। a bird.

नुद – (तु॰) – ($\sqrt{}$ **नुद** = क्षेपणे) फेंकना। to throw.

$\sqrt{}$ **नुंद** – वि॰ – (**नुद:**) निकाल बाहर करने वाला, दूर करने वाला। expelling, dispelling.

नुदक – वि॰ – (**नुदक**) देखें नुद। see Nuda.

नुदति – क्रि॰ – (**नुदति**) दूर हांक देता है, भगा देता है। drives away, expels, rejects.

नुत्वा – कृ॰ – ($\sqrt{}$ **नुद्** + क्त्वा = नुत्वा) दूर हांककर, भगाकर। having expelled or driven away.

नुदि – क्रि॰ – (**नुनोद**) दूर हांका जा चुका, भगा दिया गया। had been driven away or expelled.

नुण्ण/नुन्न – कृ॰ – ($\sqrt{}$ **नुद्** + क्त = नुन्न) हांका गया, भगाया गया। driven away, removed.

नूतन – वि॰ – (**नूतन**) नया। new, fresh.

नूनं – अव्यय – (**नूनम्**) निश्चय से। indeed, surely, certainly.

नूपुर – न॰ – (**नुपुर**) पैंजनी, पैर में पहनने का गहना। anklet.

नूही – स्त्री॰ – (**स्नुही / नुहि**) समन्तदुग्धा, सेहुड, थूहड़। a particular thorny plant Euphorhia Antiquorum,

its milky juice is used as an emetic.

नेक – वि॰ – (**अनेक**) अनेक। several, many.

नेकाकार – वि॰ – (**अनेकाकार**) अनेक प्रकार का। various, diverse.

नेकतिक – पु॰ – (**अनेकतिक**) ठग, ठोंगी। a cheat, an imposter.

नेकतिक – वि॰ – धोखाधड़ी करने वाला, जालसाज। deceitful, fraudulent.

नेकायिक – वि॰ – (**नैकायिक**) सुत्तपिटक के पांचो निकायों का जानकार, स्मृतिकार। versed in the five collections of the scriptures, belonging to a sect.

नेक्ख – न॰ – (**निकषा**) स्वर्णमुद्रा, निकष। a heavy gold coin of ancient India.

नेक्खम्म – न॰ – (**निष्कम**) संसार-त्याग। renunciation.

नेक्खम्म-वितक्क – न॰ – (**निष्कम-वितर्क**) अभिनिष्क्रमण संबंधी विचार। thought of self abnegation.

नेक्खम्म-सङ्कप्प – पु॰ – (**निष्कम-संकल्प**) अभिनिष्क्रमण संबंधी संकल्प। see Nekkhamma-Vittaka.

नेक्खम्म-सुख – न॰ – (**निष्कम-सुख**) अभिनिष्क्रमण का सुख। the happiness of renunciation.

नेक्खम्म-अभिरत – वि॰ – (**निष्कम-अभिरत**) निष्क्रमण के प्रति अभिरुचि। fond of renunciation.

नेगम – वि॰ – (**नेगम**) निगम सम्बन्धी, नगर सम्बन्धी। belonging to a market town.

नेति – क्रि॰ – ($\sqrt{}$ **नी** = नयति) ले जाता है। leads, guides.

नेतु – पु० – (नेतृ/नेता) नेता। leader.

नेत्त – पु० – (नेत्र) आंख। the eye.

नेत्त-तारा – स्त्री० – (नेत्र-तारकम्) आंख की पुतली। pupil of the eye.

नेत्ति – स्त्री० – (नेत्रि) (1) तृष्णा (2) नाली। (1) craving (2) conduct.

नेत्तिक – पु० – (नेत्रिक) खेत सींचने के लिए नाली बनाने वाला। one who makes conduits for irrigation.

नेत्तिस – पु० – (निस्त्रिंश) खड्ग, तलवार। a sword.

नेपक्क – न० – (नैपुण्य) बुद्धिमानी, सूझ-बूझ। a prudence.

नेपच्छ – न० – (नेपथ्य) नट की वेशभूषा। costume of an actor.

नेपुञ्ज – न० – (नैपुण्य) निपुणता, दक्षता। skill.

नेमि – स्त्री० – (नेमि) पहिए का हाल। the rim of a wheel.

नेमित्तिक – पु० – (नैमित्त) ज्योतिषी। astrologer.

नेमिंधर – पु० – (नेमिन्धर) पर्वत-विशेष का नाम। name of a mountain.

नेय्य – वि० – (नेय्य/नेय) ले जाने योग्य। fit to be led or carried.

नेरञ्जरा – स्त्री० – (नेरञ्जरा) बुद्धत्व प्राप्ति के बाद भगवान् बुद्ध इसी नदी के तट पर थे। name of the river whose bank the Buddha reached after enlightenment.

नेरयिक – वि० – (नैरयिक/नारकीय) नरक या निरथ में उत्पन्न, नरकवासी। born in hell, one doomed to suffer in the hell.

नेरु – पु० – (मेरु) उच्चतम अर्थात् सबसे ऊंची चोटी वाले पर्वत का नाम। देखें मेरु। name of the highest mountain. See Meru.

नेरु-जातक – (जा० सं० 379) – स्वर्ण वर्ण मेरु (नेरु) पर्वत की चमक-दमक के कारण किसी ने भी स्वर्ण वर्ण राजहंस की ओर ध्यान नहीं दिया। the story (No. 379) tells that common people are attracted by lustre and not by virtue.

नेवासिक – पु० – (निवासी) रहने वाला। a resident, an inmate.

नेसज्जिक – वि० – (निषदिक) बैठा रहने वाला। remaining in a sitting position.

नेसाद – पु० – (निषाद) देखें निसाद। see Nisāda.

नो – अव्यय – (नो) नहीं। no, not.

नोनीत – न० – (नवनीत) मक्खन। fresh butter.

न्यास – पु० – (न्यास) धरोहर। mortgage, pawn.

न्हात – कृ० – (√ स्ना + क्त = स्नात) देखें – न्हात। see Nahāta.

न्हान – न० – (स्नान) देखें नहान। see Nahāna.

न्हारु – न० – (न्हारु) देखें नहारु। see Nahāru.

प

पकट्ठ – वि॰ – (प्रकर्षः), अति श्रेष्ठ। most valuable.

पकट – वि॰ – (प्रकल्पित), कृत, निर्मित। in the name, done, made.

पकति – स्त्री॰ (प्रकृति), प्राकृतिक या मूल रूप, स्वाभाविक या मूल स्थिति। original or natural form.

पकति-गमन चित्त – नपु॰ – (प्रकृतिः गमनम्), स्वाभाविक चाल। usual walk.

पकति-चित्त – नपु॰ – (प्राकृतिसिद्धः), स्वाभाविक चित्त। natural consciousness.

पकति-सील – नपु॰ – (प्रकृति शीलः), स्वाभाविक शील। natural virtue.

पकतिक – वि॰ – (प्राकृतिक), प्राकृतिक। having the nature of.

पकतिज – वि॰ तथा नपु॰ – (प्रकृतो लयः), प्रकृति से उत्पन्न। by nature.

पकप्पना – स्त्री॰ – (परिकल्पनाम्), तर्क, योजना, व्यवस्था। reasoning, planning, arrangement.

पकप्पेति – क्रिया – (परिकल्पति), विचार करना। to consider; to think over.

पकम्पति – क्रिया – (प्रकम्पति), काँपना। to tremble.

पकरण – नपु॰ – (प्रकरणम्), अवसर साहित्यिक कृति या व्याख्या। an occasion, a literary work or exposition.

पकार – पु॰ – (प्रकारः), ढंग, पद्धति। mode; method.

पकास – पु॰ – (प्रकाशः), चमक, कथन। brightness, annunciation.

पकासक – पु॰ – (प्रकाशकः), प्रकाशक, घोषणा करने वाला। publisher, one who announces.

पकासेति – क्रिया – (प्रकाशेति), प्रकट करना, प्रकाशित करना। to make known; to illustrate; to publish.

पकासन – नपु॰ – (प्रकाशन), घोषणा, पुस्तक। announcement, publication.

पकिण्णक – वि॰ – (प्रकीर्णक), प्रकीर्ण, बिखरा हुआ। scattered about.

पकित्तेति – क्रिया – (प्रकीर्तनमति), प्रशंसा करना, व्याख्या करना। to speak highly; to praise.

पकुप्पति – क्रिया – (प्रकुपित), क्रोधित होना। to be angry.

पकोप – पु॰ – (प्रकोप), क्रोध, विद्वेष। anger; fury; agitation.

पकोपन – नपु॰ – (प्रकोपन), क्रोधित करना। making turbulent; agitating.

पक्क – कृदन्त – (पक्व), पका हुआ, उबला हुआ। ripe; boiled.

पक्कट्ठित – कृदन्त – (पक्तूम्), बहुत उबाला हुआ। much heated; boiled up.

पक्ख – पु॰ – (पक्ष), पहलू, पखवारा। side; party; faction.

पक्खालन – नपु॰ – (प्रक्षालनम्), लड़खड़ाहट, धोना, साफ करना। stumbling; washing; cleaning.

पक्खालेति – क्रि॰ – (प्रक्षालेति), धोना, साफ करना। to wash; to clean.

पक्खिक – वि॰ – (पाक्षिक), एक पखवाड़े से सम्बन्धित। concerning fortnight.

पक्खित्त – कृदन्त – (प्रक्षिप्त), फेंका गया। fallen; thrown; put in.

पक्खिपति – क्रिया – (प्रक्षेपति), फेंकना। to put in, to throw into.

पक्खिपन – नपु॰ – (प्रक्षेपण), फेंकना। putting in; throwing into.

पक्खी – पु॰ – (पक्षकः), पक्षी, पक्षवाला। a bird; the winged one.

पक्खेप – पु॰ – (प्रक्षेपः), आगे फेंकना, उभार। throwing in front; protuberance; bulge; prominence.

पगब्भ – वि॰ – (प्रगल्भः), साहसी, दुस्साहसी। bold, daring.

पगाल्ह – कृदन्त – (प्रगाढ), डूबा हुआ। sunk.

पगह्ति – (प्रगाढति), डुबकी। to dive into; to sink.

पगुण – वि॰ – (प्रगुण), अभ्यस्त, ज्ञान से परिपूर्ण। well-versed; familiar.

पगुणता – स्त्री॰ – (प्रगुणता), दक्षता। competence.

पगेव – अव्यय – (प्रगे), समय से अतिपूर्व। too early.

पगण्हति – क्रिया – (प्रगृह्णाति), ग्रहण करना, धारण करना। to hold up; to take up.

पग्गह – पु॰ – (प्रग्रह), प्रयत्न, सामर्थ्य, उठाना। effort; capability.

पग्गहण – नपु॰ – (प्रग्रहणम्), ग्रहण करना। lifting; holding up.

पग्गहित – कृदन्त – (प्रगृहीत), धरा हुआ, पकड़ा हुआ। held up; stretched out.

पग्गाह – पु॰ – (प्रग्राहः), पराक्रम, उत्साह। energy, support.

पग्घरण – नपु॰ – (प्राघारः), टपकना, चूना, रिसना। trickling; dripping.

पग्घरणक – वि॰ – (प्राघुणकः), चूता हुआ, रिसता हुआ। flowing; trickling.

पघग – पु॰ – (प्रघगः), घर के सामने का छज्जा। covered terrace before a house.

पङ्क – पु॰ – (पङ्कः), कीचड़, गारा। mud; mire.

पङ्कज – नपु॰ – (पङ्कजम्), कमल। a lotus; that which is risen from the mud.

पङ्गु – वि॰ – (पङ्गु), लंगड़ा। lame.

पङ्गुल – वि॰ – (पङ्गुल), लंगड़ा। a cripple.

पचति – क्रिया – (पक्वति), पचति, पकाता है। to cook.

पचन – नपु॰ – (पचनम्), पकाना, to cook.

पचरति – क्रिया – (प्रचारति), अभ्यास करता है, चलता है। to practise; to walk.

पचारक – पु॰ – (प्रचारकः), प्रचारक, विज्ञापक। publisher.

पचारेति – क्रिया – (प्रचारति), प्रचार करता है। publisher.

पचालक – वि॰ – (प्रचालनम्), भूलता, हिलता। swinging; shaking.

पचिनति – क्रि॰ – (प्रचेति), चुगना, चुनना, तोड़ना। to pick; to pluck.

पचुर – वि॰ – (प्रचुर), बहुत, नाना प्रकार का। various; many.

पच्चक्ख – वि॰ – (प्रत्यक्ष), प्रत्यक्ष, दृष्टिगोचर। evident; realised.

पच्चक्खाति – क्रिया – (प्रत्याख्याति), निषेध करना, मना करना। to reject; to refuse.

पच्चक्खान – नपु॰ – (प्रत्याख्यानम्), अस्वीकार करना, निषेध। refusal; rejection.

पच्चग्ग – वि॰ – (प्रत्यग्र), नया, सुन्दर, ताजा। new; beautiful; fresh.

पच्चङ्ग – नपु॰ – (प्रत्यङ्ग), प्रत्यंग। sub-limb.

पच्चत्थिक – पु॰ – (प्रत्यर्थकः), प्रतिपक्षी, विरोधी, शत्रु। enemy; an opponent.

पच्चन्त – पु॰ – (प्रत्यन्त देश), सीमा, प्रदेश। border of a country, countryside.

पच्चय – पु॰ – (प्रत्ययः), हेतु, कारण, उद्देश्य। cause; motive; requisite.

पच्चुपन्न – वि॰ – (प्रत्युत्पन्न), कारण से उत्पन्न, पुनरूत्पादि। reproduction.

पच्चयिक – वि॰ – (प्रत्यायक), विश्वसनीय। trustworthy.

पच्चवेक्खना – स्त्री॰ – (प्रत्यवेक्षणम्), विचार, विवेचन, ध्यान देना। consideration; reviewing.

पच्चस्सोसि – अतीत॰ क्रिया – (प्रतिश्रुति), वचन दिया, प्रतिज्ञा। agreed to; promised.

पच्चाकत – कृदन्त – (परित्यक्त), पराजित, सर्वथा त्यागा हुआ। rejected; defeated.

पच्चागच्छति – क्रिया – (प्रत्यागतिः), वापिस आना, लौटना। to return; to come back.

पच्चागमन – नपु॰ – (प्रत्यागमनम्), वापसी, लौटना। returning; coming back.

पच्चादेस – पु॰ – (प्रत्यादेशः), अस्वीकृति, मना करना। refusal.

पच्चामित्त – पु॰ – (प्रत्यामित्रः), शत्रु, विरोधी। enemy.

पच्चाहरति – क्रिया – (प्रत्याहरति), वापिस लाना। to bring back.

पच्चाहार – पु॰ – (प्रत्याहारः), बहाना, क्षमा-याचना। excuse; apology.

पच्चुट्ठान – नपु॰ – (प्रत्युत्थानम्), सम्मान प्रदर्शित करने के लिए खड़ा होना। rising from one's seat.

पच्चुपकार – पु॰ – (प्रत्युपकारः), उपकार का बदला। help in return.

पच्चुपट्ठान – नपु॰ – (प्रत्युपस्थानम्), सेवा में उपस्थित रहना। appearance; attendance.

पच्चुप्पन्न – वि॰ – (प्रत्युत्पन्नः), वर्तमान। existing, present.

पच्चूस – पु॰ – (प्रत्यूषः), भोर, प्रभात, तड़का। early morning.

पच्चूह – पु॰ – (प्रत्यूहः), बाधा, रूकावट। interruption; hindrance; obstruction.

पच्चेक – वि॰ – (प्रत्येकः), अलग, प्रत्येक। separate; each.

पच्चेक-बुद्ध – पु॰ – (प्रत्येक बुद्धः), जिसने बोधि तो प्राप्त की हो लेकिन दूसरों को उस बोधि का उपदेश न दे, one who is enlightened but does not preach the truth to the world.

पच्चोसक्कति – क्रिया – (प्रत्युद्धरति), वापिस लौटना। to return; to withdraw.

पच्छन्ना – कृदन्त – (प्रछन्न), ढँका हुआ। covered with; hidden.

पच्छा – अव्यय – (पृष्ठतस्), बाद में, पीछे। afterwards; behind.

पच्छाताप – पु० – (पश्चातापः), पछतावा। remorse; repentance.

पच्छा-भाग – पु० – (पृष्ठभागः), पिछला भाग। the hind part.

पच्छाया – स्त्री० – (प्रच्छायम्), सायादार हिस्सा, सघन छाया। shaded part.

पच्छिम – वि० – (पश्चिम), अंतिम। hindmost; western.

पच्छेदन – नपु० – (प्रच्छेदन), काटना, तोड़ना। cutting off; breaking.

पजा – स्त्री० – (प्रजा), जनता, प्राणी, मनुष्य। public; mankind; human being.

पजापति – पु० – (प्रजापति), सृष्टि का मालिक। the lord of creation.

पजापति – नपु० – (प्रजापति), उत्पन्न, होता है। to be born or produced.

पज्ज – नपु० – (पद्यम्), पद्य। a verse; a poem.

पज्जलन – नपु० – (प्रज्वलन), जलना। blazing.

पज्जोत – पु० – (प्रजोत), प्रदीप, प्रकाश। a light; a lamp.

पज्जुन्न – पु० – (प्रद्युम्न), वर्षा के बादल, इन्द्र। rain and cloud; Rain God.

पज्जोत – पु० – (प्रजोत), प्रकाश, प्रदीप। a lamp; a light.

पञ्च – वि० – (पञ्चम्), पाँच। five.

पञ्चक – नपु० – (पञ्चक), पाँच का समूह। a collection of five.

पञ्च-कल्याण – नपु० – (पञ्चकल्याणम्), सौन्दर्य के पाँच चिन्ह। the five beauty marks (of hair, flesh, teeth, skin and age).

पञ्चकामगुण – पु० – (पञ्चकामगुण), पाँच इन्द्रियों के भोग। pleasures of five senses.

पञ्चक्खन्ध – पु० – (पञ्चस्कन्ध), पाँच स्कन्ध। the five aggregates.

पञ्च-गोरस – पु० – (रपञ्चगोरस), दूध, दही, घी, मक्खन एवं छाछ – पाँच गोरस पदार्थ। five products of the cow, viz. milk, curd, ghee, fresh butter and sour milk.

पञ्चङ्गुलिक – वि० – (पञ्चाङ्गुली), पाँच अंगुलियों का निशान, the five-finger mark.

पञ्च-चक्खु – वि० – (पञ्चचक्षुक), पाँच चक्षुओं वाला, having five sorts of visions.

पञ्चचत्तालीसति – स्त्री० – (पञ्चचत्वारिंश), पैंतालीस, forty-five.

पञ्चतिसंति – स्त्री० – (पञ्चत्रिंशतिः), पैंतीस, thirty-five.

पञ्चदास – वि० – (पञ्चदश), पन्द्रह, fifteen.

पञ्चदसी – स्त्री० – (पञ्चदशीख), पूर्णिमा, a full moon.

पञ्चनवुति – स्त्री० – (पञ्चनवतिः), पंचनाव, ninety-five.

पञ्च-नीवरण – (पञ्चनिवरण), पाँच बन्धन, fivefold obstacles for the progress of mind.

पञ्चपञ्आसति – स्त्री० – (पञ्चपचाशत), पचपन, fifty-five.

पञ्च बल – नपु० – (पञ्चबल), पाँच बल, five mental forces.

पञ्च-महानदी – स्त्री० – (पञ्चमहानदी), गंगा, अचिरखती, यमुना आदि पाँच महानदियाँ, the five great rivers.

पञ्च-वर्गिय – (पञ्चवर्गीय), बुद्ध के प्रथम पाँच शिष्यों का सामूहिक नाम। वे पाँच शिष्य थे – कोण्उञ्ज, भद्दिय, वप्प, महानाम,

अस्सजि। belonging to a group of five (the five monks who accompained Gotama when he became an ascetic).

पञ्च-वण्ण – वि॰ – (पञ्चवर्णम्), पाँच वर्ण। of five colours.

पञ्च-सील – नपु॰ – (पञ्चशील), पाँच शील। the five moral precepts.

पञ्चाल – (पाञ्चाल), सोलह जनपदों में से एक। one of the sixteen *janapada*s.

पञ्चालिका – स्त्री॰ – (पञ्चालिका), गुड़िया, पुतली। a doll.

पञ्जर – पु॰ तथा न॰ – (पञ्जरम्), पिंजड़ा। a cage.

पञ्ञ – वि॰ (समास में) – (प्रज्ञ), प्रज्ञावान्। wise; endowed with knowledge.

पञ्ञति – स्त्री॰ – (प्रज्ञप्तिः), नियम, घोषणा, सहमति। designation; name; concept; idea.

पञ्ञवन्तु – वि॰ – (प्रज्ञावत्), समझदार, बुद्धिमान। wise, intelligent.

पञ्ञा-चक्खु – नपु॰ – (प्रज्ञा-चक्षु), the eyes of wisdom.

पञ्ञ-घन – नपु॰ – (प्रज्ञा), घन। the treasure of wisdom.

पञ्ञ-भेद – पु॰ – (प्रज्ञा-भेद), प्रज्ञा के प्रकार। types of wisdom.

पञ्ञ-विमुत्ति – स्त्री॰ – (प्रज्ञा-विमुक्ति), emancipation through insight.

पञ्ञ-सम्पदा – स्त्री॰ – (प्रज्ञा), पूर्ण ज्ञान, प्रज्ञा-सम्पत्ति। the blessing of higher knowledge.

पञ्ञाणा – नपु॰ – (प्राज्ञनम्), चिन्ह, निशान। mark, sign.

पञ्ञापन – नपु॰ – (प्रज्ञापन), घोषणा। declaration.

पञ्ह – त्रिलिङ्गी – (प्रश्न), जिज्ञासा। a question; curiosity.

पट – पु॰ तथा नपु॰ – (पटः), वस्त्र, पहनावा। a cloth.

पटल – नपु॰ – (पटलम्), आवरण। a covering.

पटह – पु॰ – (पटहः), नगाड़ा। a kettle-drum.

पटाका – स्त्री॰ – (पताका), झंडा। a flag.

पटिकत – कृदन्त – (प्रतिकृत्), प्रायश्चित किया गया। redressed.

पटिकार – पु॰ – (प्रतिकारः), प्रतिकार, इलाज। counteraction; remedy.

पटिक्कमन – नपु॰ – (प्रतिकर्मन्), प्रतिक्रमण, पीछे हटना। regression; going back.

पटिक्कूल – वि॰ – (प्रतिकूल), प्रतिकूल। loathsome; disagreeable.

पटिक्खेप – पु॰ – (प्रतिक्षेपः), प्रतिक्षेप, निषेध। refusal; denial.

पटिग्गण्हन – नपु॰ – (प्रतिग्रहणम्), स्वागत। to receive.

पटिघ – पु॰ – (प्रतिघः), क्रोध, विरोध। anger; repulsion.

पटिघात – पु॰ – (प्रतिघात), टक्कर। collision; repulsion.

पटिघोस – पु॰ – (प्रतिघोषः), गूँज। an echo.

पटिच्च – अव्यय, पूर्व॰ क्रिया – (प्रतित्य), हेतु से। on account of.

पटिच्च-समुप्पन्न – वि॰ – (प्रतीत्यसमुत्पन्न), हेतु से उत्पन्न। evolved by reason of the law of causation.

पटिच्च-समुप्पाद – पु॰ – (प्रतीत्य-समुप्पाद), हेतु से उत्पत्ति का नियम। causal genesis.

पटिच्छन्न – कृदन्त – (प्रतिच्छन्न), ढँका हुआ। covered.

पटिजग्गक – पु॰ – (प्रतिजागरक:), पालन-पोषण करने वाला। one who rears; preserver.

पटिजग्गन – नपु॰ – (प्रतिजागर:), पालन-पोषण करना। rearing; caring.

पटिञ्जा – वि॰ – (प्रतिज्ञा), वचन, प्रतिज्ञा, सहमति। promise; vow; consent.

पटिञ्जात – कृदन्त – (प्रतिज्ञात), सहमत हुआ। promised; consented.

पटि-दान – नपु॰ – (प्रतिदानम्), पुरस्कार। reward.

पटिदिस्सि – कृदन्त – (प्रतिदृष्ट), देखा हुआ, दृश्यमान। seen; visible.

पटिघावति – क्रिया – (प्रतिघावति), पीछे की ओर दौड़ना। to run back to.

पटिनन्दना – स्त्री॰ – (प्रतिनन्दनम्), आनन्दित होना। rejoicing.

पटिनिधि – पु॰ – (प्रतिनिधि), प्रति-पुरुष। representative.

पटिनिधि – पु॰ – (प्रतिनिधि) प्रतिमूर्ति, प्रति-निधि। symmetry, representative.

पटिनिवत्त – कृ॰ – (प्रतिनिवृत्त) लौटा हुआ वापस आया हुआ। has come back.

पटिनिवत्तति – क्रि॰ – (प्रतिनिवत्तंते) वापस लौटता है। returned back, comes back.

पटिनिस्सग्ग – पु॰ – (प्रतिनि:सर्ग) परित्याग। rejection, refused, renunciation.

पटिनिस्सज्जति – क्रि॰ – (प्रतिनि:सृजति) त्याग देता है, छोड़ देता है। refuses, dismisses, renounces, forsakes.

पटिनेति – क्रि॰ – (प्रति √ नी = प्रतिनयति) वापस ले जाता है। takes back.

पटिपक्ख – वि॰ – (प्रतिपक्ष) विरोधी, शत्रु। opponent, enemy.

पटिपक्खिक – वि॰ – (प्रतिपक्षी) विरोधी पक्ष का। of opposition, enemy.

पटिपज्जति – क्रि॰ – (प्रतिपद्यते) मार्गारूढ़ होता है, यात्रा पर निकल पड़ता है (पटिपज्जि, पटिपन्न, पटिपज्जमान, पटिपज्जित्वा)। enters upon a path or course, follows a method.

पटिपज्जन – न॰ – (प्रतिपादन) पद्धति, अभ्यास, आचरण। process, practice, behaviour.

पटिपण्ण – न॰ – (प्रतिपर्ण) पत्र का उत्तर। answer of a letter, counterfoil.

पटिपत्ति – स्त्री॰ – (प्रतिपत्ति) आचरण, धार्मिक क्रिया-कलाप। conduct, religious practice.

पटिपथ – पु॰ – (प्रतिपथ) प्रतिकूल मार्ग, उल्टा रास्ता। the opposite way.

पटिपदा – स्त्री॰ – (प्रतिपदा) आचरण, जीवन-मार्ग। line of conduct, lifestyle.

पटिपन्न – कृ॰ – (प्रतिपन्न) मार्गारूढ़। following up teaching.

पटिपहरति – क्रि॰ – (प्रतिपहरति) जवाबी हमला करता है, प्रहार करता है। strikes in return.

पटिपहिणाति – क्रि॰ – (प्रतिप्रहिणोति) वापिस भेजता है। sends back.

पटिपाटि – स्त्री॰ – (प्रतिपाति) क्रम। sequence, order.

पटिपाटिय – क्रि॰ वि॰ – (पात्या) क्रमशः। continuously, successively.

पटिपाद – पु॰ – (प्रतिपाद) पलंग या चारपाई का सहारा। the support of a bed.

पटिपादक – पु॰ – (प्रतिपादक) व्यवस्थापक। organiser.

पटिपादन – पु॰ – (प्रतिपादन) प्रतिपादन, शिक्षण देना। exposition, to impart education.

पटिपादेति – क्रि॰ – (प्रतिपादयति) व्यवस्था करता है, सामग्री पहुँचाता है। organises, manages.

पटिपीळन – न॰ – (प्रतिपीडन) त्रास देना, पीड़ा देना। to hurt, to cause pain.

पटिपीळेति – क्रि॰ – (प्रतिपीडयति) त्रास देता है, पीड़ा देता है, दमन करता है। oppresses, causes pain.

पटिपुग्गल – पु॰ – (प्रतिपुग्गल) प्रतिस्पर्धी। rival, competition.

पटिपुच्छति – क्रि॰ – (प्रतिपृच्छति) बदले में प्रश्न पूछता है। पटिपुच्छि, पटिपुच्छित। asks in return, puts a cross-question in response to a question.

पटिपुच्छा – स्त्री॰ – (प्रतिपृच्छा) बदले में पूछा गया प्रश्न, प्रश्न के उत्तर में पूछा गया प्रश्न। question asked in response, or in response to an answer, a question in return.

पटिपूजना – स्त्री॰ – (प्रतिपूजन) आदर प्रदर्शित करना, गौरव करना। honouring, worshipping.

पटिपूजेति – क्रि॰ – (प्रतिपूजयति) आदर करता है, गौरव करता है। honours, pays reverence.

पटिपेसेति – क्रि॰ – (प्रतिप्रेषयति) वापस भेजता है। sends back.

पटिपस्सद्ध – कृ॰ – (प्रतिप्रसरब्ध) शान्त हुआ। having been calmed, satisfied.

पटिपस्सद्धि – स्त्री॰ – (प्रतिप्रसरब्धि) शान्ति। peace, calmness.

पटिपस्सम्भति – क्रि॰ – (प्रतिप्रसंरभते) शान्त होता है। keeps silence, becomes quiet and peaceful.

पटिपस्सम्भना – स्त्री॰ – (प्रतिप्रसंरम्भणा) देखें पटिपस्सद्धि। see Paṭipassaddhi.

पटिबद्ध – कृ॰ – (प्रतिबद्ध) बंधा हुआ, आकर्षित। attracted, tied, fastened.

पटिबद्ध-चित्त – वि॰ – (प्रतिबद्ध-चित्त) अनुरक्त। bound to, attracted to or by, fond of.

पटिबल – वि॰ – (प्रतिबल) योग्य, सामर्थ्यवान। suitable, eligible, capable.

पटिबाहक – वि॰ – (प्रतिवाहक) विरोध करने वाला, रुकावट डालने वाला, हटाने वाला। one who opposes or interrupts, repelling, preventing.

पटिबाहति – क्रि॰ – (प्रतिवाहति) दूर करता है, हटाता है, बचाता है। removes, saves, sets aside.

पटिबिम्ब – न॰ – (प्रतिबिम्ब) प्रतिबिम्ब, छाया। an image, shadow, reflection.

पटिबिम्बित – वि॰ – (प्रतिबिम्बित) जिसकी छाया पड़ी हो। reflected.

पटिबुज्झति – क्रि॰ – (प्रतिबुध्यति) समझता है, जागता है। understands, comprehensive, wakes up.

पटिबुद्ध – कृदन्त – (प्रतिबुद्ध) ज्ञानी, जागा हुआ। genious, awakened.

पटिभय – न॰ – (प्रतिभय) डर, भय। fear, danger.

पटिभाग – वि॰ – (प्रतिभाग) समान, एक जैसा। similar, resembling, equal partnership.

पटिभाग – पु॰ – (प्रतिभाग) समानता, एक-रूपता, मुकाबला हेतु भागीदारी। similarity, uniformity, equal partnership.

पटिभाति – क्रि॰ – (प्रतिभाति) सूझता है, स्पष्ट होता है। appears, becomes evident.

पटिभाण – न॰ – (प्रतिभाण) प्रत्युत्पन्न मति, हाजिरजवाबी। presence of mind, readiness of speech.

पटिभाणवन्तु – वि॰ – (प्रतिभावन्त) प्रत्युत्पन्न मति वाला, क्षिप्र-प्रज्ञ। possessed of ready wit.

पटिभासति – क्रि॰ – (प्रतिभाषते) उत्तर देता है। answers, gives a reply, replies.

पटिभासि – अतीत क्रि॰ – (प्रतिभासित) उत्तर दिया। answered.

पटिभू – पु॰ – (प्रतिभू) जामिन, जमानत लेने वाला। surety, guarantee.

पटिमग्ग – पु॰ – (प्रतिमार्ग) विरुद्ध मार्ग। confronting road, opposite path.

पटिमण्डित – कृ॰ – (प्रतिमण्डित) सजा हुआ। adorned with.

पटिमल्ल – पु॰ – (प्रतिमल्ल) मुकाबले का पहलवान। opponent in wrestling.

पटिमा – स्त्री॰ – (प्रतिमा) प्रतिमा, मूर्ति। idol, statue, an image.

पटिमानेति – क्रि॰ – (प्रतिमानयति) गौरव करता है, प्रतीक्षा करता है। honours, waits for.

पटिमुक्क – कृ॰ – (प्रतिमुक्त) वस्त्र पहने, बंधा हुआ। clothed, tied.

पटिमुञ्चति – क्रि॰ – (प्रतिमुञ्चति) वस्त्र धारण करता है, बांधता है। wears clothes, puts on a dress, fastens.

पटियादेति – क्रि॰ – (प्रतिपादयति) तैयार करता है, व्यवस्था करता है, सामग्री पहुंचाता है। prepares, arranges, supplies goods.

पटियोध – पु॰ – (प्रतियोध) प्रतिभट, मुकाबले का योद्धा। antagonist.

पटिरव – पु॰ – (प्रतिरव) प्रतिध्वनि, गूंज। echo.

पटिराज – पु॰ – (प्रतिराज) विरोधी राजा। hostile king.

पटिरूप/पतिरूप – वि॰ – (प्रतिरूप) योग्य, ठीक, अनुकूल। fit, proper, suitable.

पटिरूपक/पतिरूपक – वि॰ – (प्रतिरूपक) मिलती-जुलती शक्ल का। resembling someone, disguised as.

पटिरूपता/पतिरूपता – वि॰ – (प्रतिरूपता) स्वरूप की साम्यता। likeness, resemblance.

पटिलब्ध – कृ॰ – (प्रतिलब्ध) प्राप्त। received, obtained.

पटिलभति – क्रि॰ – प्राप्त करता है। obtains, receives, gets.

पटिलाभ – पु॰ – (प्रतिलाभ) उपलब्धि, प्राप्ति। achievement, attainment, obtaining.

पटिलीयति – क्रि॰ – (प्रति √ली = प्रतिलीयते) पीछे हटता है, दूर रहता है। draws back, keeps away from.

पटिलीयन – न॰ – (प्रतिलीयन) दूर रहना, पीछे हटना। keeping away, drawing back.

पटिलोम – वि॰ – (प्रतिलोम) प्रतिकूल, विरुद्ध, विपरीत। opposite, contrary, reverse.

पटिलोम-पक्ख – पु॰ – (प्रतिलोम-पक्ष) विरोध पक्ष, प्रतिपक्ष। opposing party, opposition.

पटिवचन – न॰ – (प्रतिवचन) उत्तर, जवाब। answer, reply.

पटिवत्तन – न॰ – (प्रतिवर्त्तन) पीछे की ओर मुड़ना। moving backward, turning back.

पटिवत्तिय – वि॰ – (प्रतिवर्त्तीय) पीछे लौटने योग्य, लपेटने योग्य। fit to be turned or rolled back.

पटिवत्तु – पु॰ – (प्रतिवक्ता) विरुद्ध भाषण करने वाला, खण्डन करने वाला। one who speaks against or contradicts.

पटिवत्तेति – क्रि॰ – (प्रतिवर्त्तयति) लपेटता है, पीछे हटता है। rolls, turns back.

पटिवदति – क्रि॰ – (प्रतिवदति) उत्तर देता है, खण्डन करता है, विरुद्ध बोलता है। replies, contradicts, speaks against.

पटिवसति – क्रि॰ – (प्रतिवसति) रहता है, निवास करता है। dwells, lives.

पटिवाक्य – न॰ – (प्रतिवाक्य) उत्तर। answer.

पटिवातं – क्रि॰ वि॰ – (प्रतिवातम्) हवा के विरुद्ध। against the wind.

पटिवाद – पु॰ – (प्रतिवाद) प्रतिवाद, आरोपित दोष का खण्डन। retort, recrimination, contradiction of allegations.

पटिविंस – पु॰ – (प्रति + अंशे = प्रत्यंश) हिस्सा। a share, a portion.

पटिविजानाति – क्रि॰ – (प्रतिविजानाति) पहचानता है, जानता है। recognizes, knows.

पटिविज्झति – क्रि॰ – (प्रतिविध्यति) प्रवेश करता है, समझता है। penetrates, comprehends.

पटिविदित – कृ॰ – (प्रतिविदित) ज्ञात, सुनिश्चित। fully known, ascertained.

पटिविद्ध – कृ॰ – (प्रतिविद्ध) प्रविष्ट हुआ, समझ लिया गया। penetrated, comprehended.

पटिविनोदन – न॰ – (प्रतिविनोदन) हटाना, निकाल बाहर करना। dispels, removes, gets rid of.

पटिविभजति – क्रि॰ – (प्रतिविभजति) बांटता है। divides, distributer.

पटिविरत – कृ॰ – (प्रतिविरत) रुका हुआ। abstained from.

पटिविरमति – क्रि॰ – (प्रतिविरमति) रुकता है, विरत रहता है। abstains from.

पटिविरुज्झति – क्रि॰ – (प्रतिविरोधयति) विरुद्ध होता है, झगड़ा करता है। becomes hostile, contradicts.

पटिविरुद्ध – कृ॰ – (प्रतिविरुद्ध) विरुद्ध। opposing, contrary.

पटिविरुहति – क्रि॰ – (प्रतिविरोहति) फिर से उगता है। to grow again.

पटिविरोध – पु॰ – (प्रतिरोध) विरोध-भाव, दुश्मनी, शत्रुता। opposition, hostility, enmity.

पटिविस्सक – पु॰ – (प्रतिवेशिक) पड़ोसी। neighbour.

पटिवेदेति – क्रि॰ – (प्रतिवेदयति) जानता है, ज्ञात कराता है। makes known, informs.

पटिवेध – पु॰ – (प्रतिवेध) अन्तवेध, अन्तः प्रविष्टि। penetration, attainment.

पटिसङ्खत – कृ॰ – (प्रतिसंस्कृत) प्रतिसंस्कार कर दिया गया, मरम्मत कर दी गयी। repaired, prepared.

पटिसंयुत्त – कृ॰ – (प्रतिसंयुक्त) सम्बद्ध। attached, connected with, belonging to.

पटिसंवेदेति – क्रि॰ – (प्रतिसंवेदयति) सहन करता है, अनुभव करता है। one who feels, experiences, suffers.

पटिसंहरण – न॰ – (प्रतिसंहरण) सिकोड़ना, त्याग देना, हटा लेना। folding, removal.

पटिसंहार – पु॰ – (प्रतिसंहार) सिकोड़ना, त्याग देना, हटा लेना। to compress, to renounce, to remove shrivel.

पटिसंहरति – क्रि॰ – (प्रतिसंहरते / ति) सिकोड़ता है, त्याग देता है, हटा लेता है। withdraws, takes back, removes, folds.

पटिसंकरण – न॰ – (प्रतिसंस्करण) प्रतिसंस्करण, मरम्मत। restoration, mending, repairing.

पटिसंकरोति – क्रि॰ – (प्रतिसंस्करोति) प्रतिसंस्कार करता है, मरम्मत करता है। restores, repairs, mends.

पटिसंखरण – न॰ – (प्रतिसंस्करण) देखें पटिसंकरण। see Paṭisaṅkaraṇa.

पटिसंखरोति – क्रि॰ – (प्रतिसंस्करोति) देखें पटिसंकरोति। see Paṭisaṅkaroti.

पटिसंखा – स्त्री॰ – (प्रतिसंख्या) ज्ञान, चेतना, विचार, फैसला। knowledge, consciousness, idea, decision.

पटिसंखान – न॰ – (प्रतिसंख्यान) विचार-विमर्श, मीमांसा। consideration, mindfulness.

पटिसंखाय – पू॰ क्रि॰ – (प्रतिसंख्याय) विचार करके। having considered.

पटिसंखार – पु॰ – (प्रतिसंस्कार) देखें पटिसंखरण। see Paṭisaṅkharaṇa.

पटिसंचिक्खति – क्रि॰ – (प्रतिसञ्चिक्षति) विचार करता है, मीगांरा करता है। discriminates, considers.

पटिसंथार – पु॰ – (प्रतिसंस्तार) मैत्रीपूर्ण स्वागत। friendly welcome, cordial reception.

पटिसंदहति – क्रि॰ – (प्रतिसन्दधाति) जोड़ता है, पुनर्मिलन करता है। reunites.

पटिसंधातु – पु॰ – (प्रतिसन्धाता) मेल कराने वाला, शान्ति संस्थापक। one who reunites, a peace-maker.

पटिसंधान – न॰ – (प्रतिसंधान) पुनर्मिलन। reunion.

पटिसंधि – स्त्री॰ – (प्रतिसन्धि) पुनर्जन्म ग्रहण। reincarnation, conception.

पटिसम्भिदा – स्त्री॰ – (प्रतिसम्भिदा) मीमांसा-पूर्ण ज्ञान। analytic insight, discriminating knowledge.

पटिसम्भिदामग्ग – पु॰ – (प्रतिसम्भिदा मार्ग) खुद्दक निकाय का बारहवां ग्रन्थ। वास्तव में इसकी गणना अभिधम्म ग्रंथों में की जानी चाहिए। the twelfth book of the Khuddaka Nikāya, it really belongs to the literature of the Abhidhamma type and describes how analytical knowledge can be acquired by an *arhanta*.

पटिसम्मोदति – क्रि॰ – (प्रतिसम्मोदयति) मैत्रीपूर्ण बात-चीत करता है। talks or greets in a friendly way.

पटिसर – पु॰ – (प्रतिसर) ताबीज, कौतुक सूत्र। amulet, worn, around arm wrist or neck.

पटिसरण – न॰ – (प्रतिसरण) प्रतिसार, शरण-स्थल, सहायता, संरक्षण। shelter, help, protection.

पटिसल्लान – न॰ – (प्रतिसंलयन) ध्यान-भावना हेतु एकान्त जीवन। retirement for the purpose of meditation, seclusion.

पटिसल्लान-सारुप्प – वि॰ – (प्रतिसंलयन-सारुप्प्य) योगाभ्यास हेतु, एकान्त जीवन के अनुकूल। suitable for seclusion.

पटिसल्लीयति – क्रि॰ – (प्रतिसंल्लीयते) एकान्त जीवन व्यतीत करता है, योगाभ्यास करता है। retires in seclusion, practises yoga.

पटिसामेति – क्रि॰ – (प्रतिसामयति) व्यवस्थित करता है, दूर रहता है। (पटिसमेसि, पटिसमित, पटिसमित्वा)। sets in order, keeps oneself away.

पटिसासन – न॰ – (प्रतिशासन) प्रत्युत्तर। reply, counter message.

पटिसेध – पु॰ – (प्रतिषेध) प्रतिषेध, इन्कार। prohibition, warding off, refusal.

पटिसेधन – न॰ – (प्रतिषेधन) प्रतिषेध, इन्कार। prohibition, refusal.

पटिसेधक – वि॰ – (प्रतिषेधक) प्रतिषेध करने वाला। prohibiting, preventing.

पटिसेधेति – क्रि॰ – (प्रति √ विध् = प्रतिषेधयति) दूर रखता है, दूर हटाता है, मना करता है। wards off, prevents, refuses, prohibits, keeps away.

पटिसेवति – क्रि॰ – (प्रतिसेवते) अनुकरण करता है, सेवन करता है, उपयोग में लाता है। follows, pursues practises, uses.

पटिसेवन – न॰ – (प्रतिसेवन) अभ्यास करना, अनुकरण करना, उपयोग में लाना। practising, using, following.

पटिसोत – वि॰ – (प्रतिस्रोत) स्रोत (बहाव के विपरीत)। against the stream.

पटिस्सत – वि॰ – (प्रतिश्रुत) विचारवान्। mindful, having idea, thoughtful.

पटिस्सव – पु॰ – वचन, स्वीकृति। promise, assent, approval.

पटिसुणाति – क्रि॰ – (प्रतिशृणोति) वचन देता है, सहमत होता है। assents, promises, agrees.

पटिहञ्ञति – क्रि॰ – (प्रतिहन्यते) चोट खाता है। gets struck against, becomes afflicted.

पटिहत – कृ॰ – (प्रतिहत) चोट खाया हुआ। smitten, striken, wounded.

पटिहनन – न॰ – (प्रतिहनन) प्रतिरोध, प्रतिसंघर्ष। resistance, obstruction, repulsion.

पटिहनति – क्रि॰ – (प्रतिहनति) रगड़ खाता है। strikes against, wards off, collides.

पटिहार – पु॰ – (प्रतिहार) द्वार। door.

पटु – वि॰ – (पटु) होशियार, कुशल (आदमी)। clever, skillful.

पटुता – स्त्री॰ – (पटुता) दक्षता। cleverness, skill.

पटोल – पु॰ – (पटोल) परवल, चिचिण्ड़ा। a kind of vegetable 'parwal' (Trichosanthes Dioeca).

पट्ट – न॰ – (पट्ट) तख्ता, वस्त्र, रेशमी वस्त्र, पट्टी। slab, a plate, a strip, a sheet, silk cloth.

पट्टक – न॰ – (पट्टक) देखें पट्ट। see Patta.

पट्टन – न॰ – (पत्तन) नदी तट के पास का नगर। a part, a town on the river bank or on the sea-shore.

पट्टिका – स्त्री॰ – (पट्टिका) पट्टी। a strip (of cloth).

पट्ठपेति – क्रि॰ – (प्रस्थापयति) स्थापित करता है। establishes, begins.

पट्ठान – न॰ – (पट्ठान) प्रस्थान। setting forth, putting forward.

पट्ठानप्पकरण – न॰ – (प्रस्थान प्रकरण) अभिधम्म पिटक का अन्तिम ग्रन्थ इसमें भौतिक तथा अभौतिक चीजों के 24 प्रकार के पच्चयों अथवा हेतुओं का विस्तृत विवेचन है। the last book of the Abhidhamma Piṭaka. It deals with the 24 *paccaya*s or modes of relations between things mental and material.

पट्ठाय – अव्यय – (प्रस्थाय) आरम्भ करके, तब से, उस समय से। beginning with, from then.

√पठ – (भू॰) – (उच्चारणे) उच्चारण करना, पढ़ाना। to recite, to read.

पठति – क्रि॰ – (पठति) पढ़ता है। reads, recites.

पठन – न॰ – (पठन) पढ़ना। reading.

पठम – वि॰ – (प्रथम) पहला। the first.

पठमं – क्रि॰ वि॰ – (प्रथमम्) पहली बार। for the first time.

पठमज्झान – न॰ – (प्रथम ध्यान्) प्रथम ध्यान। at first, meditation for the first time.

पठमतरं – क्रि॰ वि॰ – (प्रथमतरम्) सबसे पहले, यथाशीघ्र। first of all, as early as possible.

पठवी – स्त्री॰ – (पृथ्वी) भूमि, पृथ्वी। land, the earth.

पठवी-ओज – पु॰ – (पृथ्वी-ओज) पृथ्वी का तेज। the sap or essence of the earth.

पठवी-कम्पन – न॰ – (भूकम्प) भूचाल। an earthquake.

पठवी-कसिण – न॰ – (मृत्तिका-कषिण) योगाभ्यास करने के लिए मिट्टी का बना केंद्र-बिन्दु। the seat made of clay used for meditation.

पठवी-चलन – न॰ – (भू-चलन) भूकम्प। an earthquake.

पठवी-चाल – पु॰ – (भूचाल) भूकम्प। an earthquake.

पठवी-धातु – स्त्री॰ – (पृथ्वी-धातु) पृथ्वी-धातु। the earth element.

पठवोज – पु॰ – (पृथ्वी-ओज) पृथ्वी का तेज। the sap or essence of the earth.

पठवी-सम – वि॰ – (पृथ्वी-सम) पृथ्वी-समान। like the earth.

पण – पु॰ – (पण) शर्त, दुकान (आपण)। bet, shop.

√पण – (भू॰) – (व्यवहारस्तुतिसु) व्यापार करना, बड़ाई करना। to trade, to praise.

पणक – पु॰ – (पणक) शैवाल विशेष, सिवार। special algae, duck weed.

पणमति – क्रि॰ – **(प्रणमति)** प्रणाम करता है, झुकता है, पूजा करता है। bows down, worships, adores, greets.

पणय – पु॰ – **(प्रणय)** प्रेमाभिव्यक्ति, विनय, विश्वास। loveful submission, affection, faith.

पणव – पु॰ – **(पणव)** ढोल। tomtom.

पणाम – पु॰ – **(प्रणाम)** प्रणाम, नमस्कार। salutation, adoration, bowing down.

पणामेति – क्रि॰ – **(प्रणामयति)** नमस्कार की मुद्रा में झुकाता है, अञ्जलिबद्ध कराता है। raises the hands in respectful salutation.

पणालि – स्त्री॰ – **(प्रणालि)** नाली। drain.

पणिदहति – क्रि॰ – **(प्रतिदधति)** इच्छा करता है, आकांक्षा करता है। aspires to, longs for.

पणिधान – न॰ – **(प्रणिधान)** आकांक्षा, दृढ़ संकल्प। aspiration, firm determination.

पणिधि – स्त्री॰ – **(प्रणिधी)** आकांक्षा, निश्चय। aspiration, determination.

पणिधाय – पू॰ क्रि॰ – **(पणिधाय)** संकल्प करके। having aspired to.

पणिपात – पु॰ – **(प्रणिपात)** दण्डवत् लेट जाना, पूजा। adoration, prostration, worship.

पणिय – न॰ – **(पण्य)** पणि अर्थात् बाजार की वस्तु, बेचने की चीज। article of trade, article for sale.

पणिहित – कृ॰ – **(पणिहित)** संकल्प-युक्त। directed, bent on, intent.

पणीत – वि॰ – **(प्रणीत)** श्रेष्ठ, बढ़िया। excellent, superior.

पणीततर – वि॰ – **(प्रणीततर)** श्रेष्ठतर, और भी बढ़िया। more exalted, much delicious.

पणेति – क्रि॰ – **(प्रणेति)** दण्डित करता है, निकालता है, रास्ते पर ले जाता है। expels, leads, imposes a fine or punishment.

√ **पण्ड** – (चु॰) – **(परिहारे)** खण्डन करना, नष्ट करना। to cut, to destroy.

√ **पण्ड** – (भू॰) – **(लिङ्ग वैकल्ये)** पुरुषत्व-हीन होना। to become impotent.

पण्डक – पु॰ – **(षण्ड)** हिजड़ा, पुंस्त्वहीन। a eunuch, a weakling.

पण्डर – वि॰ – **(पाण्डुर)** श्वेत, हल्का पीला। white, light yellow, yellowish.

पण्डर-जातक – (जा॰ सं॰ 518) – इस कथा में सांपों की, गरुड़ों से अपने आपको बचाये रखने की युक्ति वर्णित है। the story (No. 518) tells about the tactics of the serpents to save themselves from the Garuḍa(the eagle).

पण्डव – पु॰ – **(पण्डव)** पर्वत-विशेष। name of a mountain.

पण्डिच्च – न॰ – **(पाण्डित्य)** पाण्डित्य। supreme stage of knowledge.

पण्डित – वि॰ – **(पण्डित)** विद्वान। a scholar, a learned man, a wise person.

पण्डितक – पु॰ – **(पण्डितक)** बनावटी पण्डित, पाण्डित्य-दम्भवाला। one who pretends to be a scholar.

पण्डु – वि॰ – **(पाण्डु)** पीला, पीलापन लिये हुए। yellowish, of orange colour.

पण्डुकम्बल – न॰ – **(पाण्डु कम्बल)** पाण्डु रंग का कम्बल। an orange coloured blanket.

पण्डुकम्बल-सिलासन – न॰ – (पाण्डु॒कम्बल शिलासन) देवेन्द्र, शक्र के बैठने का आसन। the seat of Sakra, the king of *deva*s.

पण्डु-पलास – पु॰ – (पाण्डु – पलाश) सूखा पत्ता। a withered leaf.

पण्डु-रोग – पु॰ – (पाण्डु रोग) पीलिया, कमला रोग। jaundice.

पण्डु-रोगी – पु॰ – (पाण्डुरोगी) पाण्डु रोग वाला। one who suffers from jaundice.

पण्डू – पु॰ – (पाण्ड्य) दक्षिण भारत की एक जाति पाण्ड्य। a south Indian caste Pāṇḍya.

पण्ण – न॰ – (पर्ण) पत्ता, पत्र, चिट्ठी। leaf, letter.

पण्णक – पु॰ – (पर्णक) देखें पण्ण। see Paṇṇa.

पण्ण-कुटि – स्त्री॰ – (पर्णकुटी) पर्ण-कुटी, पत्तों की बनी झोंपड़ी। a hut made of leaves.

पण्ण-छत्त – न॰ – (पर्ण-छत्र) पत्तों का छाता, पत्तों का पंखा या पत्तों की छत। a sunshade an umbrella or a fan made of leaves.

पण्ण-सन्थर – पु॰ – (पर्ण-संस्तर) पत्तों का बिछौना। mattress made of leaves.

पण्ण-साला – स्त्री॰ – (पर्णशाला) उटज, कुटीर, कुटिया। a hermitage.

पण्णत्ति – स्त्री॰ – (प्रज्ञाप्ति) देखें पञ्ञति। see Paññatti.

पण्णरस – वि॰ – (पञ्चदश) पन्द्रह। fifteen.

पण्णाकार – पु॰ – (पण्याकार) उपहार, भेंट। a present, a gift.

पण्णास – स्त्री॰ – (पञ्चाश) पचास। fifty.

पणिणक – पु॰ – (पर्णिक) पत्ते बेचने वाला। a green grocer, vendor of green leaves.

पणिणक-जातक – (जा॰ सं॰ 102) – पिता द्वारा पुत्री के सतीत्व की परीक्षा लेने की कथा। the story (No. 102) of a father testing the virginity of his daughter.

पण्य – न॰ – (पण्य) देखें पणिय। see Paṇiya.

पणिह – पु॰/स्त्री॰ – (पार्ष्णि) एड़ी। the heel.

√पत – (भू॰) – (पतने) गिरना। to fall.

√पत – (भू॰) – (गमने) जाना। to go.

पतङ्ग –पु॰ – (पतङ्ग) पक्षी। bird.

पतति – क्रि॰ – (पतति) गिरता है, फिसलता है। falls down, alights on, slides on, slips.

पतन – न॰ – (पतन) गिरावट। falling.

पतनु – वि॰ – (प्रतनु) अत्यंत दुबला-पतला। very thin.

पताका – स्त्री॰ – (पताका) झण्डा। a flag, banner.

पताप – पु॰ – (प्रताप) प्रताप, तेजस्विता। splendour, majesty.

पतापवन्तु – वि॰ – (प्रतापवान) प्रतापी, तेजस्वी। majestic, splendid.

पतापेति – क्रि॰ – (प्र √तप् + णिच् - प्रतापयति) तपाता है। scorches, heats.

पतिरूपं – अव्यय – (प्रतिरूपम्) ठीक। similar, exact.

पति – पु॰ – (पति) स्वामी, भर्ता। lord, husband, master.

पतिकिट्ठ – वि॰ – (प्रतिकृष्ट) निकृष्ट।
vile

पति-कुल – न॰ – (पतिकुल) पति का
खानदान। husband's clan.

पतिट्ठहति – क्रि॰ – प्रतिष्ठित होता है,
स्थापित होता है (पतिट्ठहि, पतिट्ठहन्त,
पतिट्ठहित्वा)। is established,
stands firmly.

पतिट्ठा – स्त्री॰ – (प्रतिष्ठा) प्रतिष्ठा,
सहायता, आश्रय-स्थान। help,
support, shelter.

पतिट्ठातब्ब/पतिटि्ठतब्ब – कृ॰ –
(प्रतिष्ठातव्य) प्रतिष्ठा के योग्य, स्थापित
करने योग्य। fit to be established.

पतिट्ठाति – क्रि॰ – (प्रतिष्ठति) देखें
पतिट्ठहति (पतिट्ठासि, पतिटि्ठत,
पतिट्ठाय, पतिट्ठांतु)। see
Patiṭṭhahati.

पतिट्ठान – न॰ – (प्रतिष्ठान) प्रतिष्ठान,
स्थापना। setting up, support.

पतिट्ठापित – कृ॰ – (प्रतिस्थापयति)
प्रतिष्ठित कराता है। gets established.

पतिट्ठापेतु – पु॰ – (प्रतिष्ठापक) स्थापित
करने वाला। founder, one who
establishes.

पतित – कृ॰ – (पतित) गिरा हुआ। fallen.

पतितिट्ठति – क्रि॰ – (प्रतितिष्ठति) खड़ा
होता है, दुबारा खड़ा होता है। stands
up again.

पतिदान – न॰ – (प्रतिदिन) प्रतिदान, दान
के बदले दान। recompense, return.

पतिबोध – पु॰ – (प्रतिबोध) जागरण, ज्ञान।
waking up, knowledge.

पतिब्बता – स्त्री॰ – (पतिव्रता) पतिव्रता।
faithful wife, chaste woman.

पतिरूप – वि॰ – (प्रतिरुप) देखें पटिरूप।
see Paṭirūpa.

पतिस्सत – वि॰ – (प्रतिश्रृत) देखें पतिस्सत।
see Patissata.

पतीचि – स्त्री॰ – (प्रतीची) पश्चिम दिशा।
the west.

पत्तीत – वि॰ – (प्रतीत) प्रसन्नचित्त। happy,
delighted, cheerful.

पतीर – न॰ – (प्रतीर) किनारा। side, bank,
shore.

पतोद – पु॰ – (प्रतोद) बैलों को हांकने की
लकड़ी, पैना या पैनी। a goad, a
driving stick

पतोदक – न॰ – (प्रतोदक) प्रेरणा, (वि॰)
प्रेरक। impelling, (adj.), impeller.

पतोदक-लट्ठि – स्त्री॰ – (प्रतोदक-यष्टि)
बैलों को हांकने की लाठी। stick for
driving bullocks of a cart.

पत्त (1) – कृ॰ – (प्राप्त) प्राप्त, प्राप्त हुआ।
attained, obtained.

पत्त (2) – पु॰ – (पात्र) भिक्षा-पात्र। an
alms bowl.

पत्त (3) – न॰ – (पत्र) पत्ता, पंख। a leaf,
a feather.

पत्तक्खन्ध – वि॰ – (पन्नस्कन्ध) गिरे हुए
कन्धों वाला, निराश, बुझा-बुझा सा। with
dropping shoulders, dejected,
downcast.

पत्तगत – वि॰ – (पात्रगत) पात्रगत, पात्र में
पड़ा हुआ। that which is in the
bowl.

पत्तगन्ध – पु॰ – (पत्र-गन्ध) पत्तों की गन्ध
। the odour of leaves.

पत्त-गाहक – पु॰ – (पात्र-ग्राहक) दूसरे का
भिक्षा-पात्र लेकर चलने वाला। one who
carries another's bowl.

पत्त-थविका – स्त्री॰ – (पात्र-स्तबिका) भिक्षा-पात्र लटकाने की झोली। case or bag keepings for bowl.

पत्त-पाणि – वि॰ – (पात्र-पाणि) जिसके हाथ मे भिक्षा-पात्र हो। one who holds the bowl.

पत्त-पिण्डिक – वि॰ – (पात्र-पिण्डिक) एक ही पात्र में से खाने वाला। eating from only one vessel.

पत्त-दान – पु॰ – (पत्र-दान) पक्षी विशेष। a particular bird.

पत्तन – न॰ – (पत्तन) देखें पट्टन। see Paṭṭana.

पत्तब्ब – कृ॰ – (प्राप्तत्य) प्राप्तकरणीय। the thing which is obtainable.

पत्ताधारक – पु॰ – (पात्राधार) पात्र का आधार। stand for a bowl.

पत्तानीक – न॰ – (पत्त्यानीक) चार-चार जनों की पैदल सेना। a group of four soldiers.

पत्तानुमोदन – स्त्री॰ – (प्राप्तानुमोदना) प्राप्त पुण्य का अनुमोदन (देवताओं तथा स्वर्गस्थ सम्बन्धियों का दान)। transference of merit.

पत्ति (1) – पु॰ – (पद् + ति = पत्ति) पदाति, पैदल सेना का जवान। foot soldier.

पत्ति (2) – स्त्री॰ – (पत्रक) पत्ती, पेड़ का पत्तों वाला भाग। leaf, leafy portion of a plant.

पत्तिक – पु॰ – (पत्तिक) सेना का छोटा दस्ता, पदाति-गुल्म। an infantry, part of an army.

पत्तिदान – न॰ – (आप्ति-दान) पुण्य या हिस्से का प्रदान। transference of merit or a share.

पत्ती – पु॰ – (पतत्रि) तीर, धनुष का तीर। arrow.

पत्तुन्न – न॰ – (प्रतुन्न) वस्त्र-विशेष। a particular cloth, a kind of cloth.

पत्तुं – कृ॰ – (प्राप्तुम्) प्राप्त करने के लिए। to reach, to attain.

पत्थ – पु॰ – (प्रस्थ) (1) प्रस्थ, धान्य अथवा किसी तरल पदार्थ की चार सेर की माप। (2) एकान्त स्थान। (1) a measure of grain or liquid, four of which makes a *seer*, (2) solitary place.

पत्थट – कृदन्त – (प्रथित) (1) विश्रुत, विनीत, विख्यात। (2) फैलाया हुआ। (1) famous, modest, widely known (2) spread out.

पत्थद्ध – वि॰ – (प्रस्तब्ध) कठोर चट्टान की तरह सीधा। very stiff, straight like a rock.

पत्थना – स्त्री॰ – (प्रार्थना) प्रार्थना, कामना, इच्छा। prayer, desire, aim, aspiration.

पत्थयति – क्रि॰ – (प्रार्थयति) इच्छा करता है, कामना करता है, प्रार्थना करता है। prays, wishes for, requests, aspires.

पत्थयान – कृ॰ – (प्रार्थमान) इच्छा करते हुए, कामना करते हुए। desiring, praying, wishes for.

पत्थर – पु॰ – (प्रस्तर) पत्थर, शिला। a slab, a flat stone.

√पत्थर – (भू॰) – (संथरणे / संस्तरणे) बिछाना। to spread out.

पत्थरति – क्रि॰ – (प्रस्तरति) फैलाता है। spreads out, extends.

पत्थिव – पु॰ – (पार्थिव) पार्थिव, राजा। a king.

पत्थेति – क्रि॰ – (प्रार्थयति) देखें पत्थयति। see Patthayati.

पत्वा – पू॰ क्रि॰ – (प्र √आप - ल्यप् = प्राप्य) प्राप्त करके। having reached, attained or obtained.

√पथ – (तु॰) – (वित्थारे / विस्तारे) फैलाना। to spread out.

पथ – (भू॰) – (गमने) जाना। to go.

पथ – पु॰ – (पथ) मार्ग, रास्ता (गणन-पथ = गिनने की विधि। path, way, road, range of calculation.

पथबी – स्त्री॰ – (पृथिवी) देखें पठवी। see Paṭhavī.

पथावी – पु॰ – (पथिक) राही, यात्री। traveller, passenger.

पथित – वि॰ – (प्रथित) प्रसिद्ध। famous, renowned.

√पद् – (दि॰) – (गमने) जाना। to go.

पद – न॰ – (पद) कदम, वचन, पदवी, स्थान, हेतु, कविता का अनुच्छेद। foot, footstep, a word, position, place, reason, cause, line of stanza.

पद-चेतिय – न॰ – (पदचिह्न) पवित्र, पद-चिह्न। a holy foot-print.

पद-जात – न॰ – (पद जात) नाना प्रकार के पद-चिह्न। various kinds of foot-print.

पदट्ठान – न॰ – (पदस्थान) निकट कारण, नजदीकी वजह। a proximate cause.

पद-पूरण – न॰ – (पाद-पूरण) जिससे पद-पूर्ति हो। an expletive particle.

पद-भाजन – न॰ – (पद - विच्छेद / पदच्छेद) शब्दों का विभाग,

पदान्वय। separation of words, treating each word separately.

पद-भाणक – वि॰ – (पद-भाणक) धर्म-ग्रन्थ के पदों का पाठ करने वाला। one who recites the words of scriptures.

पद-वण्णना – स्त्री॰ – (पदव्याख्या) पदों की व्याख्या। explanation of words.

पद-वलञ्ज – न॰ – (पदलाञ्छन) पद-चिह्न, पद-चिह्नों वाला रास्ता। a track of foot-prints.

पद-विभाग – पु॰ – (पद-विभाग) पदच्छेद, शब्दों का विभाग। separation of words, parsing.

पद-वीतिहार – पु॰ – (पद व्यतिक्रम) कदमों का परिवर्तन। change of steps.

पद-सद्द – पु॰ – (पद-शब्द / पद-चाप) पैरों की आहट। sound of foot-steps.

पदकुसल-मानव-जातक – (जा॰ सं॰ 432) – बारह साल के उपरांत भी पग-चिह्नों का पता लगा सकने के विलक्षण कौशल की कथा। the story (No. 432) of getting the trace of foot-prints though the duration of twelve years had passed.

पदक्खिणा – स्त्री॰ – (प्रदक्षिणा) परिक्रमा। to go round, circumambulation.

पदग – पु॰ – (पदग / पदाति) पैदल सैनिक। an infantry, foot-soldiers.

पदत्त – कृ॰ – (प्रदत्त) दिया गया, बांटा गया। given over, distributed.

पदर – न॰ – (प्रदर) दरार, फटाव, छेद। a board, hole, crack.

पदवि – स्त्री॰ – (पदवी) मार्ग। way, road.

पदहति – क्रि॰ – (प्र √धा = प्रदहति) प्रयत्न करता है, किसी के विरुद्ध संघर्ष

करता है। strives, takes up, confronts.

पदहन – (प्रदहन) देखें पधान। see Padhāna.

पदातवे – कृ॰ – (प्रदातुम्) देने के लिए। for giving.

पदाति – पु॰ – (पदाति) पैदल सैनिक (क्रि॰) देना, लेना, पाना। a foot-soldier, taking, giving, getting.

पदातु – पु॰ – (प्रदाता) दाता, देने वाला। giver, distributor.

पदान – न॰ – (प्रदान) प्रदान, देना। giving, bestowing.

पदालन – न॰ – (प्रदारण) चीरना, फाड़ना। splitting, tearing.

पदालेति – क्रि॰ – (प्रदारयति) चिपटता है, चीरता है, फाड़ता है। cleaves, splits, tears.

पदालेतु – पु॰ – (प्रदारयिता) चीरने वाला, तोड़ने वाला। one who splits or breaks open.

पदिक – वि॰ – (पदिक) (1) काव्य-पंक्तियों से युक्त (2) पैदल यात्री। (1) consist of poetical lines, (2) pedestrian.

पदिप्पति – क्रि॰ – (प्रदीप्यते) जलता है। blazes, flames forth.

पदिस्सति – क्रि॰ – (प्रदृश्यते) दिखाई देता है। becomes visible, appears.

पदिट्ठ – कृ॰ – (प्रदृष्ट) देखा गया। seen.

पदिस्समान – कृ॰ – (प्रदृश्यमान) देखा जाता हुआ। being seen.

पदीप-काल – पु॰ – (प्रदीप-काल) दीप (लैम्प) जलाने का समय। the time of lighting the lamp.

पदीपिय – न॰ – (प्रदीप्य) प्रदीप-सामग्री। material for lighting.

पदीपेति – क्रि॰ – (प्रदीपयति) दीप जलाता है, प्रदीप्त करता है, समझाता है। lights a lamp, explains, makes bright, enlightens.

पदीपेय्य – कृ॰ – (प्रदीप्य) देखें पदीपिय। see Padīpiya.

पदीयति – क्रि॰ – (प्रदीप्यते) दिया जाता है, प्रदान किया जाता है। is given out or presented.

पदुट्ठ – कृ॰ – (प्रदुष्ट) प्रदुष्ट, विकृत, खराब। wicked, defiled, mutilated.

पदुब्भति – क्रि॰ – (प्र $\sqrt{दभ्}$ = प्रदम्नोति / प्रदमति) षडयन्त्र करता है, धोखा देता है, दबाता है, सताता है। conspires, deceives, oppresses.

पदुम – न॰ – (पद्म) (1) कमल (2) नरक विशेष, (3) एक बहुत बड़ी संख्या। (1) lotus (2) name of a purgatory (3) an enormous number.

पदुम-कण्णिका – स्त्री॰ – (पद्म-कर्णिका) कमल का बीज-कोष। the pericarp of a lotus.

पदुम-कलाप – पु॰ – (पद्म-कलाप) कमल-समूह। a bundle of lotuses.

पदुम-गब्भ – पु॰ – (पद्म-गर्भ) कमल का भीतरी भाग। inside of a lotus.

पदुम-पत्त – न॰ – (पद्म-पत्र) कमल का पत्ता। a petal of lotus.

पदुम-राग – पु॰ – (पद्मराग) लाल रंग की मणि। a ruby.

पदुम-सर – पु॰ / न॰ – (पद्मसर) कमल का तालाब। a lotus pond or lake.

पदुम-जातक – (जा॰ सं॰ 261) – बोधिसत्व को तालाब से कमल गुच्छ लाने में किस प्रकार सफलता मिली उसका रोचक

वर्णन। a story (No. 261) full of wisdom how Bodhisattva got success in obtaining the bunch of lotus flowers from the pond.

पदुमिनी – स्त्री० – (**पद्मिनी**) (1) कमल का पौधा (2) कमल का तालाब। (1) a lotus plant (2) a lotus pond.

पदुमिनी-पत्त – न० – (**पद्मिनी-पत्र**) कमल का पत्ता, पुरइन। leaf of a lotus plant.

पदुमी – वि० – (**पद्मी**) कमल वाला पदुमी (हाथी)। having lotuses, spotted (elephant).

पदुस्सति – क्रि० – (**प्रदुष्यति**) दुष्कृत करता है, क्रोधित करता है, भ्रष्ट करता है। does wrong, offends, makes corrupt.

पदुस्सन – न० – (**प्रदुष्यन**) विरोधी कार्य, षड्यन्त्र, साजिश। offending or plotting against, conspiracy.

पदूसेति – क्रि० – (**प्रदूषयति**) भ्रष्ट करता है, दुष्कृत करता है। defiles, pollutes, does wrong deeds.

पदेस – पु० – (**प्रदेश**) प्रदेश, स्थान। state, region, place, location.

पदेस-ञाण – न० – (**प्रदेश-ज्ञान**) सीमित ज्ञान। limited knowledge.

पदेस-रज्ज – न० – (**प्रदेश-राज्य**) प्रदेश राज्य। principality, a district.

पदेस-राजा – पु० – (**प्रदेश-राजा**) अनु-राजा। a sub-king.

पदेसन – न० – (**प्रदेशन**) भेंट या परित्याग। gift or sacrifice.

पदोस – पु० – (**प्रदोष**) (1) प्रदोष (रात्रि का आगमन काल) (2) क्रोध (3) दोष। (1) the night-fall, (2) anger, (3) defect.

पदोसेति – क्रिया – (**प्रदूषयति**) देखें पदूसेति। see Padūseti.

पद्म – पु० – (**पद्म**) लाल कमल। red lotus.

पधंस – पु० – (**प्रध्वंस**) प्रध्वंस, विनाश। destruction, devastation.

पधंसन – न० – (**प्रध्वंसन**) लूट-मार। plunder, dacoity.

पधंसित – कृ० – (**प्रध्वंसित**) लूट-पाट की गयी। plundered, devastated.

पधंसिय – वि० – (**प्रध्वंसीय**) लूट-पाट किये जाने की सम्भावना वाला। liable to be plundered or devastated.

पधंसेति – क्रि० – (**प्रध्वंसयति**) लूट-पाट करता है, आक्रमण करता है। plunders ravages, assaults.

पधान (1) – न० – (प्र √चा - ल्युट् = प्रदहन) प्रयत्न करना, संघर्ष करना। striving, energetic effort.

पधान (2) – वि० – (**प्रधान**) प्रधान, मुख्य (न), प्रयास, प्रयत्न। chief, foremost.

पधान-घर – न० – (**प्रधान-गृह**) योगाभ्यास करने का स्थान। a house prepared for meditation.

पधानिक – वि० – (**प्रधानिक**) योगाभ्यास के लिए प्रयत्न करने वाला। attempting to meditate.

पधावति – क्रि० – (**प्रधावति**) दौड़ता है। runs out, runs forth.

पधावन – न० – (**प्रधावन**) दौड़। running out, race.

पधूपेति – कि० – (**प्रधूपयति**) धुआं देता है, धुआँ फेंकता है, भोजन सुगन्धित करने हेतु छौंक लगाता है। fumigates, causes smoke, fries to add flavour to food.

पधोत – कृ॰ – (प्रधौत) अच्छी तरह धोया गया या तेज किया गया। well washed, sharpened.

पन – अव्यय – (पन/पुनः) और, अभी, लेकिन, इसके विरुद्ध, अब, इसके अतिरिक्त। and, yet, but, on the contrary, and now, moreover.

पनस – पु॰ – (पनस) (1) कटहल का पेड़ (न॰) (2) कटहल का फल। (1) jack tree (2) jack fruit.

पनस्सति – क्रि॰ – (प्रणश्यति) विनाश को प्राप्त होता है, गायब हो जाता है। goes to ruins, becoems lost, vanishes.

पनालिका – स्त्री॰ – (प्रणालिका) नाली, पाइप, नली। a pipe, tube, channel.

पनुदति – कि॰ – (प्रणुदति) दूर करता है, हटा लेता है, धकेल देता है। dispells, removes, pushes away.

पनुदन/पनूदन – न॰ – (प्रणोदन) हटाना, दूर करना, अस्वीकृत कर देना। removal, dispelling, rejection.

पन्त – वि॰ – (प्रान्त/उपान्त) दूर, एकान्त। distant remote, solitary.

पन्त-सेनासनं – न॰ – (उपान्त-शयनासन) विश्राम-स्थल, एकान्त। a secluded resting place.

पन्थ – पु॰ – (पन्थ) मार्ग, सड़क। a path, road.

पन्थक – पु॰ – (पन्थक) पन्थी, पथिक, यात्री, राही। traveller, passenger.

पन्थ-घात – पु॰ – (पथ-घात) बटमारी। waylaying, robbery.

पन्थ-घातक – पु॰ – (पन्थ-घातक) रास्ता चलते डाका डालने वाला। a waylayer, a dacoit.

पन्थ-दूहन – न॰ – (पन्थ-दोहन) रास्ता चलते डाका डालना। way-laying.

पन्थिक – पु॰ – (पन्थिक) पथिक, देखें पन्थक। see Panthaka.

पन्न – कृदन्त – (पत् + क्त = पन्न) गिरा हुआ, पतित। fallen, gone down.

पन्नक्खन्ध – (पत्र-स्कन्ध) देखें – पत्तक्खन्ध। see Pattakkhandha.

पन्न-भार – वि॰ – (पन्न-भार) जिसने अपना भार नीचे उतारकर रख दिया। one who has put down his burden.

पन्नलोम – वि॰ – (लोम) जिसके बाल झड़ गये हों। one whose hairs have fallen.

पन्नग – पु॰ – (पन्नग) सांप। snake.

पप – न॰ – (पप/पय) जल, पानी। water.

पपञ्च – पु॰ – (प्रपञ्च) प्रपंच, रुकावट, झगड़ा, झंझट, विलम्ब, भ्रम, वहम। an obstacle, impediment, delay, illusion, hindrance in spiritual progress.

पपञ्चेति – क्रि॰ – (प्रपञ्चयति/प्रपञ्चयेते) व्याख्या करता है, विलम्ब करता है। explains, delays.

पपटिका – स्त्री॰ – (प्रपटिका) पेड़ की छाल, पपड़ी। the outer dry bark or crust of a tree.

पपतति – क्रि॰ – (प्रपतति) गिर जाता है। falls down.

पपतन – न॰ – (प्रयतन) गिरना, गिरावट। falling down, lowering down.

पपद – पु॰ – (प्रपद/प्रपाद) पांव का पंजा। tip of the foot.

पपा – स्त्री॰ – (प्रपा) प्याऊ, कुआँ। well.

पपात – पु॰ – (प्रपात) निर्झर, झरना। a
precipice, spring, a waterfall.

पपितामह – पु॰ – (प्रपितामह) दादा के
पिता। paternal great-grand-
father.

पपुत्त – पु॰ – (पौत्र) पौत्र, पोता। grandson.

पपुन्नात – पु॰ – (फल्गु/अर्जुन) फल्गु,
अर्जुन वृक्ष। the tree Terminalia
Alatagabra.

पप्पटक (1) – पु॰ – पत्थर की गिट्टी। a
broken splinter, small stone.

पप्पटक (2) – पु॰ – कुकुरमुत्ता, इन्द्रछत्र।
a mushroom.

पप्पोठेति – क्रि॰ – (प्रस्फोटयति/ताडयति)
पीटता है। slaps, beats.

पप्पोति – क्रि॰ – (प्राप्नोति) प्राप्त होता है,
पहुँचाता है। reaches, arrives.

पप्फास – न॰ – (फुप्फुस) फेफडे। the
lungs.

पबन्ध – पु॰ – (प्रबन्ध) साहित्यिक रचना
जिसकी समूची विषय-वस्तु क्रमबद्ध हो।
a connected narrative or poetical
compositon.

पबळ – वि॰ – (प्रबल) प्रबल। mighty,
powerful.

पबुज्झति – क्रि॰ – (प्रबुध्यति) जागता है,
समझता है। awakes, understands.

पबुज्झि – अतीत क्रि॰ – (प्र √ बुध + लुङ्
= प्रबिधि) जागा, समझा। awakened,
understood.

पबुद्ध – कृदन्त – (प्रबुद्ध) प्रबुद्ध, जागृत।
awakened, enlightened.

पबोधन – न॰ – (प्रबोधन) जागरण।
awakening, arousing.

पबोधेति – क्रि॰ – (प्रबोधयति) जगाता है,
प्रबुद्ध करता है। arouses, awakens,
enlightens.

पब्ब – न॰ – (पर्व) गांठ, उँगली की पोर,
विभाग, हिस्सा। knot of a stalk, joint,
section, division.

पब्बजति – क्रि॰ – (प्रव्रजति) प्रव्रजित होता
है, निकल पड़ता है, संन्यास के लिए घर
छोड़ता है। goes forth, becomes a
monk, leaves household life.

पब्बजन – नपु॰ – (प्रव्रजन) प्रव्रज्या, गृहस्थ-
जीवन का त्याग। renunciation,
giving up of household life.

पब्बज्जा – स्त्री॰ – (प्रव्रज्या) प्रव्रज्या,
संन्यास। abandonment of worldly
ties.

पब्बजित – कृदन्त – (प्रव्रजित) प्रव्रजित
हुआ, (पु॰) प्रव्रजित, साधु। exiled,
banished (m.) a monk.

पब्बत – पु॰ – (पर्वत) पहाड़। a
mountain.

पब्बत-कूट – न॰ – (पर्वत-कूट) पर्वत शिखर,
पहाड़ की चोटी। peak of a mountain.

पब्बत-गहन – न॰ – (पर्वत-गहन) पर्वत
भरा प्रदेश। a region full of
mountains.

पब्बतट्ठ – वि॰ – (पर्वतस्थ) पर्वत स्थित।
standing or situated on a
mountain.

पब्बत-पाद – पु॰ – (पर्वत-पाद) पर्वत की
तराई (उपत्यका)। the foot of a
mountain.

पब्बत-शिखर – न॰ – (पर्वत शिखर) पर्वत
की चोटी। mountain, crest.

पब्बतु-पत्थर-जातक – (जा॰ सं॰ 195) –
एक राजदरबारी द्वारा राजा के रनिवास

को दूषित करने पर भी उसके अपराध की राजा द्वारा उपेक्षा करने की कथा। it is the story (No. 195) of a king who knowing that his courtier had polluted the harm or seraglio, took no action against him.

पब्बतेय्य – वि॰ – (**पर्वतीय**) पर्वत पर रहने वाला। one who lives in mountain.

पब्बाजन – न॰ – (**प्रव्रजन**) प्रव्रजन, देश निकाला। exile, banishment.

पब्बाजनिय – वि॰ – (**प्रव्रजनीय**) प्रव्रजित या बहिष्कृत करने योग्य। deserving to be expelled.

पब्बाजेति – क्रि॰ – (प्र √ व्रज + णिच् = **प्रव्राजयति**) निकाल बाहर करता है, प्रव्रजित करता है। to exile, to banish.

पब्भार – पु॰ – (**प्राग् + भार**) उपत्यका, पर्वत की ढलान। the incline of a mountain.

पभग्ग – कृदन्त – (**प्रभग्न**) नष्ट हुआ, टूटा हुआ। broken up, destroyed.

पभङ्कर – पु॰ – (**प्रभङ्कर**) प्रभाकर, सूर्य। light bringer, the sun.

पभङ्ग – वि॰ – (**प्रभङ्गुर**) अनित्य, नाशवान। impermanent, brittle, frail, perishable.

पभङ्गुर – वि॰ – (**प्रभङ्गुर**) देखें पभङ्ग। see Pabhaṅgu.

पभव – पु॰ – (**प्रभव**) उत्पत्ति, मूल स्रोत। origin, source of origin.

पभवति – क्रि॰ – (**प्रभवति**) उत्पन्न होता है, देखें पहोति। originates. See Pahoti.

पभस्सर – वि॰ – (**प्रभास्वर**) प्रभास्वर, अत्यन्त चमकदार। very bright, resplendent.

पभा – स्त्री॰ – (**प्रभा**) प्रभा, प्रकाश। light, radiance.

पभात – कृदन्त – (**प्रभात**) स्पष्ट हुआ, चमकता हुआ, (न॰) प्रभात, सवेरा। dawn, daybreak, shining.

पभाव – पु॰ – (**प्रभाव**) प्रभाव, सामर्थ्य, तेजस्विता। brilliance, splendour.

पभावित – कृदन्त – (**प्रभावित**) प्रभावित। influenced.

पभावेति – क्रि॰ – (**प्रभावयति**) प्रभावित करता है। influences.

पभास – पु॰ – (**प्रभास**) चमक, प्रकाश। light, flash, splendour.

पभासति – क्रि॰ – (**प्रभासते**) चमकता है। shines.

पभासेति – क्रि॰ – (**प्रभासयति**) प्रकाशित कराता है। illumines.

पभिज्जति – क्रि॰ – (प्र √ भिद् + णिच = **प्रभिद्यते**) टूटता है, टुकड़े-टुकड़े हो जाता है। becomes broken.

पभिज्जन – न॰ – (प्र √ भिद् - ल्युट् = प्रभ दन) पृथक्-पृथक् होना, टूटना। separation, cleavage.

पभिन्न – कृ॰ – (प्र √ भिद् + क्त = **प्रभिन्न**) टूटा हुआ, भिन्न हुआ, टुकड़े-टुकड़े हुआ। broken, shattered.

पभु/पभू – पु॰ – (**प्रभु**) मालिक, स्वामी, प्रभु। overlord, ruler.

पभुति – अव्यय – (**प्रभृति**) प्रभृति, इत्यादि (ततो–पभुति = तब से)। beginning from, thence.

पभुत्त – न॰ – (**प्रभुत्व**) प्रभुत्व। dominance, authority.

पभेद – पु॰ – (**प्रभेद**) प्रभेद, प्रकार। variety, cleavage.

पभेदन – न० – (प्रभेदन) बंटवारा, (वि०) विनाश करने वाला। breaking up, dividing, (adj.) destructive.

पमज्जति (1) – क्रि० – (प्र √ मद् = प्रमाद्यति) लापरवाही करता है, प्रमाद करता है, नशे में होता है। becomes intoxicated, remains careless, slothful.

पमज्जति (2) – क्रि० – (प्रमार्जयति) साफ कर देता है। cleanses.

पमज्जना – स्त्री० – (प्रमाद) प्रमाद, बिलम्ब। delay, negligence.

पमत्त – कृ० – (प्रमत्त) प्रमादी, आलसी। slothful, lazy, a negligent person, idle.

पमत्त – कृ० पु० – (प्रमत्त-बन्धु) प्रमादियों का मित्र, अर्थात् मार। friend of careless or idle persons, i.e., Māra.

पमथति – क्रि० – (प्र √ मथ् = प्रमथति) अधीन करता है। crushes, subdues.

पमदा – स्त्री० – (प्रमदा) औरत। woman.

पमदा-वन – न० – (प्रमद-वन) महल के समीप का उद्यान। garden near a royal palace.

पमद्दति – क्रि० – (प्र √ मृद् = प्रमृद्नाति) मर्दन करता है, नष्ट करता है, पराजित करता है। crushes down, defeats, overcomes.

पमद्दन – न० – (प्रमर्दन) मर्दन, जीत लेना। crushing, overcoming.

पमद्दी – पु० – (प्रमर्दक) मर्दन करने वाला, विजयी होने वाला। one who crushes or defeats.

पमा – स्त्री० – (प्रमा) माप। measure, size.

पमाण – न० – (प्रमाण) माप। measure.

पमाणक – वि० – (प्रमाता) मापने वाला। one who measures, measuring by.

पमाणिक – वि० – (प्रमाणिक) प्रमाणिक माप के अनुसार। according to measurement.

पमाद – पु० – (प्रमाद) प्रमाद, लापरवाही। negligence, indolence.

पमाद-पाठ – न० – (प्रमाद-पाठ) पुस्तक का सदोष पाठ। a corrupt text in a book.

पमिणाति – क्रि० – (प्र √ मा = मिमीते ∕ याति) मापता है, अन्दाजा लगाता है। measures, estimates, defines.

पमुख – वि० – (प्रमुख) मुख्य, प्रमुख – (न०) (घर के) आगे का भाग। foremost, chief, prominent, a house front.

पमुच्चति – क्रि० – (प्रयुञ्चति) मुक्त करता है। releases, sets free.

पमुच्छति – क्रि० – (प्र √ मूच्छ् = प्रमूर्च्छति) मूर्छित होता है। swoons, faints.

पमुञ्चति – क्रि० – (प्रयुञ्चति) छोड़ता है, मुक्त करता है। sets free, emits, liberates.

पमुट्ठ – कृदन्त – (प्र √ मृज + क्त = प्रमृष्ट) भूला हुआ। forgotten.

पमुत्त – कृदन्त – (प्रमुक्त) मुक्त। released, freed.

पमुत्ति – स्त्री० – (प्रमुक्ति) मोक्ष, मुक्ति। liberation, release.

पमुदित – कृदन्त – (प्रमुदित) प्रमुदित, अति प्रसन्न। full of joy, glad, greatly delighted.

पमुह्हति – क्रि॰ – (प्र √युह = प्रयुह्यति) मोह को प्राप्त होता है, चकित होता है। becomes bewildered or infatuated.

पमुस्सति – क्रि॰ – (प्र √मृज् = प्रमार्ष्टि) भूल जाता है। forgets.

पमूल्ह – कृदन्त – (प्रमूढ) मोह को प्राप्त हुआ। bewildered.

पमेय्य – वि॰ – (प्रमेय) मापा जा सके, सीमित किया जा सके। measurable, limitable.

पमोक्ख – पु॰ – (प्रमोक्ष) मोक्ष, मुक्ति। liberation, deliverance.

पमोचन – न॰ – (प्रमोचन) मुक्त करना। setting free, loosening, deliverance.

पमोचेति – क्रि॰ – (प्र √युच् = प्रमोचयति/ते) मुक्त करता है। set free releases.

पमोद – पु॰ – (प्रमोद) आनन्द, प्रीति, खुशी। delight, joy.

पमोदति – क्रि॰ – (प्र √युंद् = प्रमोदते) आनन्दित होता है, खुश होता है। rejoices, becomes glad.

पमोदना – स्त्री॰ – (प्रमोदना) देखें पमोद। see Pamoda.

पमोहन – न॰ – (प्रमोहन) धोखा। deception, delusion.

पमोहेति – क्रि॰ – (प्र √मुह + णिच् = प्रमोहयति) धोखा देता है। deceives, bewilders, fascinates.

पम्पक – पु॰ – (पम्पक) सिन्दूरी मुख वाले लजाकु बन्दर की एक प्रजाति। a loris a species of bashful monkey.

पम्पटक – पु॰ – (पम्पटक) कच्ची फर्श की दरार में रहने वाली बभनी नामक छिपकनी। a kind of lizard.

पम्ह – न॰ – (पक्ष्म) बरौनी। the eyelash.

√पय – (भू॰) – (गमनार्थे) जाना। to go.

पय – पु॰ – (पय) दूध, पानी। milk, water.

पयत – क्रि॰ – (प्रयत) प्रयत, संयत। purified, restrained.

पयतन – न॰ – (प्रयतन) प्रयत्न, कोशिश। striving, effort, endeavour.

पयाग – पु॰ – (प्रयाग) गंगा-यमुना के संगम पर स्थित प्रयाग तीर्थ, आधुनिक इलाहाबाद। meeting place of Gaṅgā-Jamunā, now called Allahabad.

पयाग-तित्थ – पु॰ – (प्रयाग-तीर्थ) देखें – पयाग। see Payāga.

पयाग-पतिट्ठान – न॰ – (प्रयाग प्रतिष्ठान) प्रयाग-तीर्थ। Prayāga - Allahabad.

पयाति – क्रि॰ – (प्र √झ = प्रयाति) आगे बढ़ता है। moves forward, proceeds.

पयिरूपासति – स्त्री॰ – (पर्युपासते) संगति करता है, सेवा में रहता है। attends on, associates, honours.

पयिरूपासना – स्त्री॰ – (पर्युपासना) सेवा में रहना, संगति करना। attending on, associating.

पयुञ्जति – क्रि॰ – (प्र √युज = प्रयुङ्क्ते) नियुक्त करता है, लगाता है। employs, appoints.

पयुत्तक – वि॰ – (प्रयुक्तक) चर-पुरुष। one who is put to a task.

पयोग – पु॰ – (प्रयोग) प्रयोग, साधन क्रिया। means, practice, action.

पयोग-करण – न॰ – (प्रयोग करण) प्रयास, प्रयत्न। effort, practice.

पयोग-विपत्ति – स्त्री॰ – (प्रयोग विपत्ति) असफलता। failure of means.

पयोग-सम्पत्ति – स्त्री॰ – सफलता। success.

पयोजक – पु॰ – (प्रयोजक) व्यवस्थापक, निर्देशक। manager, director.

पयोजन – न॰ – (प्रयोजन) प्रयोजन, कार्य। purpose.

पयोजेति – क्रि॰ – (प्र √पुज + णिच् = प्रयोजयति) कार्य में लगाता है। engages in, undertakes, takes into service.

पयोजेतु – पु॰ – (प्रयोक्ता) देखें पयोजक। see Payojaka.

पयोधर – पु॰ – (पयोधर) बादल, स्तन। a rain cloud, breast of a woman.

पय्यक – पु॰ – (प्रपितामह) प्रपितामह। paternal great grandfather.

पर – वि॰ – (पर) दूसरा। of other, another.

पर-कत – वि॰ – (पर-कृत) परकृत, दूसरे का किया हुआ। done by other.

पर-कर – (परङ्कार) – पु॰ – परायापन। strangeness, alienation.

पर-जन – पु॰ – (पर-जन) पराया व्यक्ति, अपरिचित जन, बाहर का आदमी। a stranger, an alien.

परत्थ – पु॰ – (परार्थ) परोपकार। the welfare of others, beneficience.

परदत्तूपजीवी – वि॰ – (परदत्तोपजीवी) दूसरों के दान पर जीने वाला। living on what is given by others.

पर-दार – पु॰ – (परदारा) दूसरे की स्त्री। other than one's wife.

पर-दार-कम्म – न॰ – (परदारकर्म) पर-स्त्री-गमन करने वाला। intercourse with others' wives, adultery.

पर-दारिक – पु॰ – (परदारिन्) पर-स्त्री-गमन करने वाला। an adulterer.

परनेय्य – वि॰ – (पर + नेय) दूसरे द्वारा ले जाया जाने वाला। to be led by others, influenced by others.

पर-जातक – (जा॰ सं॰ 416) – रानी द्वारा राजा तथा पुरोहित की अनुपस्थिति में पर-तप नौकर से सहवास करने की कथा। the story (No. 416) gof a queen who had an intercourse with her servant in the absence of the king and the chaplain.

पर-पच्चय – वि॰ – (परप्रत्यय) दूसरे पर निर्भर। relying or dependent on someone else.

पर-पाटिय – वि॰ – (पराश्रित) दूसरे पर आश्रित। relying on somebody else.

पर-पुत्त – वि॰ – (पर-पुष्ठ) दूसरे द्वारा पोषित। brought up by another.

पर-पेस्स – वि॰ – (परप्रेष्य) दूसरों की सेवा करने वाला। serving others.

पर-भाग – पु॰ – (पर-भाग) दूसरा हिस्सा। other portion.

परम्मुखा – अव्यय – (पराङ्मुख) पीछे की ओर पर-लोक – पु॰ (परलोक) मरणान्तर लोक। the world beyond, heaven.

पर-बम्भन – न॰ – (पर-वम्भन) दूसरों को नीची नजर से देखना। contempt for others.

पर-वाद – पु॰ – (पर-वाद) विरोधी मत, प्रतिकूल मन्तव्य। a contrary view, opposite view.

पर-वादी – पु॰ – (पर-वादी) प्रतिकूल वादी, विरोधी मत रखने वाला। of a contrary view.

पर-विसय – पु॰ – (पर-विषय) दूसरे का राज्य, विदेश। a foreign country, abroad, overseas.

परसुवे – अव्यय – (परश्वः) परसों। day after tomorrow.

पर-सेना – स्त्री॰ – (पर-सेन) शत्रु सैन्य, विरोधी सेना। a hostile army, enemy.

पर-हत्थगत – वि॰ – (पर-हस्तगत) शत्रु-गृहीत। seized by the enemy, prisoner of war.

पर-हित – पु॰ – (परहित) दूसरों का उपकार। welfare of others.

पर-हेतु – वि॰ – (पर हेतु) दूसरों के निमित्त। for the sake of others.

परक्कम – पु॰ – (पराक्रम) पराक्रम, प्रयत्न। endeavour, effort, exertion.

परक्कमन – न॰ – (परक्रमण) प्रयास। effort.

परक्कमति – क्रि॰ – (पर √क्रम = परक्रामति) पराक्रम करता है, साहस दिखाता है। exerts, shows courage, dares.

परम – वि॰ – (परम) श्रेष्ठतम। excellent, the best.

परमता – स्त्री॰ – (परमता) श्रेष्ठत्व, पराकाष्ठा का भाव। excellence.

परमत्थ – पु॰ – (परमार्थ) परमार्थ, उच्चतम आदर्श। the highest idea, truth in the ultimate sense.

परमत्थ-जोतिका – स्त्री॰ – (परमार्थ-द्योतिका) खुद्दक पाठ, धम्मपद, सुत्तनिपात तथा जातक पर बुद्धों की अट्ठकथा। commentary on Khuddaka Pāṭha, Dhammapada, Sutta Nipāta and Jātaka by Buddhaghoṣa.

परमत्थ-दीपनी – स्त्री॰ – (परमार्थ-दीपनी) उदान, इतिवुत्तक, विमानवत्थु, पेतवत्थु थेरगाथा तथा थेरीगाथा पर धम्मपाल की उट्ठकथा। commentary on Udāna, Itivuttaka, Vimāna-vatthus, Petavatthu, Theragāthā and Therīgāthā by Dhammapāla.

परमाणु – पु॰ – (परमाणु) अणु (कण) का छत्तीसवां हिस्सा। the 36th part of atom molecule (aṇu).

परमायु – न॰ – (परमायु) आयु की सीमा। age limit.

परम्परा – स्त्री॰ – (परम्परा) (वंश) परम्परा, सिलसिला। lineage, succession, series, tradition.

परम्मुख – वि॰ – (पराङ्मुख) विमुख, मुँह दूसरी ओर। disinclined, indifference.

परम्मुखा – क्रि॰ वि॰ – (पराङ्मुखा) अनुपस्थिति में। in one's absence.

परं – क्रि॰ वि॰ – (परम्) बाद में, मरणान्तर। afterwards, beyond death.

परमरणा – क्रि॰ वि॰ – (परामरण) मरने के बाद। after death.

परसुवे – अव्यय – (परश्वः) आनेवाला परसों। day after tomorrow

परा – उपसर्ग – (परा) परिहानि व पराजय आदि अर्थों में। in the sense of defeat, loss, etc.

पराग – पु॰ – (**पराग**) पुष्प-धूलि, पुष्प-रेणु। pollen.

पराजय – पु॰ – (**पराजय**) हार। defeat.

पराजियति – क्रि॰ – (**पराजयति／पराजयते**) पराजित होता है। suffers defeat.

पराजेति – क्रि॰ – (**पराजयति**) हराता है। defeats, conquers.

पराधीन – वि॰ – (**पराधीन**) दूसरे के अधीन। dependent on others.

पराभव – पु॰ – (**पराभव**) अवनति, अपमान। downfall, disgrace.

पराभवति – क्रि॰ – (**पराभवति**) अवनत होता है, पतित होता है। falls, declines.

पराभट्ठ – कृदन्त – (**पराभृष्ट**) छुआ हुआ। touched.

पराभसति – क्रि॰ – (**पराभृषति**) स्पर्श करता है, पकड़े रहता है। touches, holds on to, becomes attached.

पराभसन – न॰ – (**पराभृशन**) स्पर्श करना, हाथ में लेना। touching, handling.

पराभास – पु॰ – (**पराभर्श**) स्पर्श। touch.

परायण／गरायन – न॰ – (**परायण**) आधार, सहारा, (वि॰) परायण। support, rest, relief, the final end.

परायत्त – वि॰ – (**परायत्त**) दूसरों का (माल)। belonging to others.

परि – उपसर्ग – (**परि**) चारों ओर से, सम्पूर्ण रूप से। a prefix, denoting completion, alround, altogether.

परिकड्ढति – क्रि॰ – (**परि + कर्षति**) खींचता है। pulls, draws, drags.

परिकड्ढन – न॰ – (**परिकर्षण**) खींचना। pulling, dragging.

परिकथा – स्त्री॰ – (**परिकथा**) व्याख्या, भूमिका। exposition, an introduction.

परिकन्तति – क्रि॰ – (**परि + √कृन्त – परिकृन्तति**) काट डालता है। cuts open, or cuts through.

परिकप्प – पु॰ – (**परिकल्प**) इरादा, संकल्प। intention, assumption.

परिकप्पेति – क्रि॰ – (**परिकल्पयति**) इरादा करता है, सार निकालता है, कल्पना करता है। intends, surmises, supposes, chalks out, imagines.

परिकम्म – न॰ – (**परिकर्म**) व्यवस्था, तैयारी। arrangement, preparation.

परिकम्म-कत – वि॰ – (**परिकर्म-कृत**) लीपा गया। plastered with, covered with.

परिकम्म-कारक – पु॰ – (**परिकर्म-कारक**) मरम्मत करने वाला, तैयारी करने वाला। repairer, one who makes preparation.

परिकस्सति – क्रि॰ – (**परिकर्षति**) खींचता है। drags about.

परिकिण्ण – कृदन्त – (**परिकीर्ण**) बिखरा हुआ। scattered.

परिकित्तेति – क्रि॰ – (**परिकीर्त्तयति**) व्याख्या करता है। expounds, publicizes.

परिकिरति – क्रि॰ – (**परि–किरति**) बिखेरता है, घेरता है। scatters about, surrounds.

परिकिलन्त – कृदन्त – (**परि √क्लम् + क्त = परिक्लान्त**) थका हुआ। tired, wearied.

परिकिलमति – क्रि॰ – (**परि + √क्लम् = परिक्लमति**) थकता है। gets tired out, becomes fatigued.

परिकिलिट्ठ – कृदन्त – (परिक्लिष्ट) धब्बा लगा हुआ, दाग लगा हुआ। dirtied, stained.

परिकिलिन्न – कृदन्त – (परि √क्लिद् + क्त = परिक्लिन्न) दागदार, मैला। stained, dirty, soiled.

परिकिलिस्सति – क्रि॰ – (परिक्लिश्यते) धब्बा लगता है, मैला हो जाता है। gets stained or soiled.

परिकिलिस्सन – न॰ – (परिक्लिश्यन) गन्दगी। dirtiness, impurity.

परिकुप्पति – क्रि॰ – (परि √कुप् = परिकुप्यति) उत्तेजित होता है। becomes excited or much agitated.

परिकोपेति – क्रि॰ – (परि √कुप् + णिच् = परिकोपयति) कुपित करता है। enrages, make angry.

परिक्कमन – न॰ – (परिक्रमण) परिक्रमा। the space around, going around.

परिक्खक – पु॰ – (परीक्षक) परखने वाला, परीक्षक, परीक्षा लेने वाला, खोज करने वाला। examiner, interviewer, investigator.

परिक्खण – न॰ – (परीक्षण) परीक्षण, जांच। examination, test, enquiry.

परिक्खत (1) – कृदन्त – (परिष्कृत) खोदा हुआ, तैयार किया हुआ। prepared, dug out.

परिक्खत (2) – कृदन्त – (परिक्षत) घायल, जख्मी। injured.

परिक्खति – क्रि॰ – (परि √ईक्ष = परीक्षते) परीक्षा लेता है, देखभाल करता है। tests, inspects, looks after.

परिक्खय – पु॰ – (परिक्षय) क्षय, हानि,

ह्रास। decay, deterioration, exhaustion.

परिक्खा – स्त्री॰ – (परीक्षा) देखें परिक्खण। see Parikkhaṇa.

परिक्खार (1) – न॰ – (परिष्कार) परिष्कार। refinement, purification.

परिक्खार (2) – पु॰ – (परिष्कार) प्रसाधन, सजावट। decoration, ornament.

परिक्खित्त – कृदन्त – (परिक्षिप्त) घेरा हुआ। surrounded, encircled.

परिक्खिपति – क्रि॰ – (परिक्षिपति) घेरता है। encircles, surrounds.

परिक्खिपापेति – क्रि॰ – (परिक्षेपयति) घिरवाता है। gets surrounded.

परिक्खीण – कृदन्त – (परिक्षीण) क्षीण हुआ, नष्ट हुआ, समाप्त हुआ। wasted, exhausted.

परिक्खेप – पु॰ – (परिक्षेप) घेरा, परिधि। circle, circumference.

परिक्किलेस – पु॰ – (परिक्लेश) कठिनाई, बाधा, अपवित्रता। hardship, obstacle, impurity.

परिखणति/पलिखणति – क्रि॰ – (परिखनति) चारों ओर खोदता है। digs around.

परिखा – स्त्री॰ – (परिखा) खाई। a ditch, a moat.

परिगण्हन – न॰ – (परिग्रहण) खोजबीन, ग्रहण करना। investigation, comprehension.

परिगण्हाति – क्रि॰ – (परिगृह्णाति) खोजबीन करता है, परीक्षा करता है, ग्रहण करता है। explores, examines, takes possession of.

परिगिलति – क्रि॰ – (परि √गृ = परिगिरति) निगलता है। swallows.

परिगूहति – क्रि॰ – (परि √ गुह = परिगूहति) छिपाता है। hides, conceals.

परिगूहना – स्त्री॰ – (परिगूहन) छिपाना। hiding, concealment.

परिग्गह – पु॰ – (परिग्रह) परिग्रह, अधि-ग्रहण, सम्पत्ति। taking up, acquisition, belongings.

परिग्गाहित – कृ॰ – (परिगृहीत) अधिगृहीत। owned, acquired.

परिचय – पु॰ – (परिचय) अभ्यास, पहचान। practice, familiarity, acquaintance.

परिचरण – न॰ – (परिचरण) देख-भाल करना, भोग-भोगना। attending to, looking after, enjoyment.

परिचरति – क्रि॰ – (परिचरति) घूमता-फिरता है, देख-भाल करता है, भोग भोगता है। enjoys, moves about, attends, looks after.

परिचारक – पु॰ – (परिचारक) परिचर्या करने वाला, सेवा करने वाला, नौकर, सेवक। server, a servant, an attendant.

परिचारणा – स्त्री॰ – (परिचारणा) देखभाल करना, खाना-पीना। looking after, enjoying.

परिचारिका – स्त्री॰ – (परिचारिका) सेविका, पत्नी। a maid-servant, a wife.

परिचारेति – क्रि॰ – (परिचारयति) सेवा कराता है। serves, waits on.

परिचिण्ण – कृदन्त – (परिचीर्ण) अभ्यस्त, संगृहीत, पहचाना हुआ। practised, attended, acquainted with, accustomed.

परिचित – कृदन्त – (परिचित) देखें परिचिण्ण। see Paricinna.

परिचुम्बति – क्रि॰ – (परिचुम्बति) चूमता है, चुम्बन लेता है। kisses, receives kisses.

परिच्च – पू॰ क्रि॰ – (परि √ इ + ल्यप् = परीत्य) समझकर। having understood.

परिच्चजति – क्रि॰ – (परित्यजति) परित्याग करता है। gives up, leaves behind.

परिच्चजन – न॰ – (परित्यजन) परित्याग। giving up, abandonment.

परिच्चाग – पु॰ – (परित्याग) परित्याग। giving up, abandonment.

परिच्छन्न – कृदन्त – (परिच्छन्न) छिपा हुआ। covered over.

परिच्छादना – स्त्री॰ – (परिच्छादना) ओढ़ना। covering all over.

परिच्छिन्दन – न॰ – (परिच्छिन्दन) सीमा, निशान, विश्लेषण। limit, mark analysis.

परिच्छेद – पु॰ – (परिच्छेद) माप, सीमा, सर्ग। measure, limit, division, a chapter.

परिजन – पु॰ – (परिजन) अनुयायी-गण। retinue, followers.

परिजानन – न॰ – (परिज्ञान) अभिज्ञान, पहचान, परिचय। knowledge, cognition.

परिजानना – स्त्री॰ – (परिज्ञान) ज्ञान, परिचय। knowledge, cognition.

परिजानाति – क्रि॰ – (परिजानाति) निश्चयात्मक रूप से जानता है। knows with certainty, knows accurately.

परिजिण्ण – कृदन्त – (परिजीर्ण) ह्रास को प्राप्त हुआ, जीर्ण हो गया। worn out, decayed.

परिञ्ञा – स्त्री॰ – (परिज्ञान) स्थिर ज्ञान। exact knowledge, full understanding.

परिञ्ञात – कृ॰ – (परिज्ञात) देखें परिजानाति। see Parijānāti.

परिञ्ञाय – पू॰ क्रि॰ – (परिज्ञाय) पूर्ण रुप से जानकर। having full knowledge.

परिञ्ञेय – वि॰ – (परिज्ञेय) ठीक से जानने योग्य। what should be known accurately.

परिडय्हति – क्रि॰ – (परि √दह् + णिच् = परिदहयते) जलता है।becomes burnt, in flames.

परिडय्हन – न॰ – (परिदहन) जलना। burning.

परिणमति – क्रि॰ – (परिणमति) पकता है, परिवर्तित होता है। gets transformed into, ripens.

परिणय – पु॰ – (परिणय) शादी, विवाह। marriage.

परिणाम – पु॰ – (परिणाम) पकना, परिवर्तन, विकास। ripening, change, development.

परिणामन – न॰ – (परिणामन) किसी के उपयोग में आना। diverting to somebody's use.

परिणामेति – क्रि॰ – (परि √नम् + णिच् = परिणामयति) परिवर्तित करता है। changes into.

परिणायक – पु॰ – (परिणायक) मार्ग-दर्शक, परामर्श-दाता। a guide, a leader, an adviser.

परिणायकरतन – (परिणायकरत्न) चक्रवर्ती नरेश का सेनापति। the chief of the army of a monarch.

परिणायिका – स्त्री॰ – (परिणायिका) अन्तर्दृष्टि। insight.

परिणाह – पु॰ – (परिणाह) परिधि, लम्बाई, चौड़ाई। girth, dimension, breadth.

परितप्पति – क्रि॰ – (परितप्यते) अनुतप्त होता है, चिन्ता करता है। worries, repents, feels remorse.

परितस्सति – क्रि॰ – (परि √त्रस् = परित्रस्यति) उत्तेजित होता है, चिन्तित होता है। becomes excited or worried.

परितस्सना – स्त्री॰ – (परित्रास) चिन्तित होना, उत्तेजना। worry, excitement.

परिताप – पु॰ – (परिताप) अनुताप, पश्चात्ताप। torment, affliction.

परितापन – न॰ – (परितापन) अनुताप, पश्चात्ताप। repentance, remorsefulness.

परितापेति – क्रि॰ – (परितापयति) त्रास देता है। scorches, torments, tortures.

परितुलेति – क्रि॰ – (परि √तुल = परितोलयति) तोलता है, विचार करता है। weighs, considers.

परितो – अव्यय – (परितः) चारों ओर से। on every side, all round.

परितोसेति – क्रि॰ – (परितोषयति) प्रसन्न करता है, संतोष देता है। pleases, makes happy.

परित्त/परित्ता (1) – नाम - (परित्रा) – खुद्दक पाठ, अंगुत्तर निकाय, मज्झिम निकाय, सुत्तनिपात के कुछ सूत्रों का संग्रह, जिनका विशेष अवसरों पर पाठ किया जाता है। 'परित्त' शब्द का अर्थ है संरक्षण। पाठ का उद्देश्य रोग आदि से संरक्षण माना जाता है। a collection of texts taken from the Khuddakapāṭha, the Aṅguttara Nikāya, and the Sutta-Nipāta, and recited on special occasions to ward off illness and danger. The word *paritta* means protection.

परित्त (2) – (परित्त) थोड़ा, स्वल्प, तुच्छ। a little, small, insignificant.

परित्तक – वि॰ – (परित्तक) थोड़ा, अल्पमात्र, तुच्छ। small, insignificant, little, trifling.

परित्त-सुत्त – न॰ – (परित्त-सूत्र) अभिमंत्रित धागा। enchanted thread.

परित्ताण – न॰ – (परित्राण) संरक्षण, शरण, सुरक्षा। protection, refuge, safety.

परित्तायक – वि॰ – (परित्रायक) संरक्षक। protector, conservator.

परिदहति – क्रि॰ – (परिधत्ते) परिधान ग्रहण करता है, वस्त्र पहनता है। puts on, clothes, dresses oneself.

परिदहन – न॰ – (परि √धा - ल्युट् = परिधानम्) वस्त्र धारण करना। dressing oneself.

परिदीपक – वि॰ – (परिदीपक) व्याख्यात्मक, प्रकाश डालने वाला। explanatory, illuminating.

परिदीपन – न॰ – (परिदीपन) व्याख्या, उदाहरण। explanation, illustration.

परिदीपेति – क्रि॰ – (परिदीपयति) स्पष्ट करता है, व्याख्या करता है, प्रकाशित करता है। makes clear, explains, illumines.

परिदूसेति – क्रि॰ – (परिदूषयति) दूषित करता है। spoils altogether, contaminates.

परिदेव – पु॰ – (परि √दिवु + ल्युट् = परिदेवन) रोना-पीटना, बिलखना। waiting, lamentation.

परिदेवना – स्त्री॰ – (परिदेवना) देखें परिदेव। see Parideva.

परिदेवति – क्रि॰ – (परिदेवयति) रोता-पीटता है, विलाप करता है। wails, laments.

परिदेवित – न॰ – (परिदेवित) परिदेवन, विलाप, रोना-पीटना। lamentation.

परिधंसक – वि॰ – (परिध्वंसक) विध्वंसक, नष्ट करने वाला। destructive, ruinous.

परिधावति – क्रि॰ – (परिधावति) इधर-उधर दौड़ता है। runs about.

परिधि – पु॰ – (परिधि) सूर्य-चन्द्र का परिवेश, सूर्य-चन्द्र मंडल। circle round the sun or moon.

परिधोत – कृदन्त – (परिधौत) धोया हुआ। washed, clear.

परिधोवति – क्रि॰ – (परिधावति) सम्पूर्ण रूप से धोता है, अच्छी तरह साफ करता है। washes completely.

परिनिट्ठान – न॰ – (परिनिष्ठान) अन्तिम सिरा, परिसमाप्ति। the end, accomplishment, conclusion.

परिनिट्ठापेति – क्रि॰ – (परिनिष्ठापयति) समाप्त करता है। brings to an end, concludes.

परिनिब्बान – न॰ – (परिनिर्वाण) जन्म-मरण के बन्धन से मुक्ति, अर्हत् की अन्तिम मृत्यु। final release from transmigration, final death of *arhant.*

परिनिब्बापन – न॰ – (परिनिर्वापन) राग-द्वेषाग्नि का सम्पूर्ण रूप से बुझ जाना। final extinguishment of longing and enmity.

परिनिब्बाति – क्रि॰ – (परिनिर्वाणं गच्छति) परिनिर्वाण को प्राप्त होता है। gets finally freed from rebirth.

परिनिब्बायी – वि॰ – (परिनिर्वृत्त) परिनिर्वाण प्राप्त। one who has attained the final release.

परिपक्क – क्रि॰ – (परिपक्व) अच्छी तरह पका हुआ, प्रौढ़। well-matured, quite ripe.

परिपतति – क्रि॰ – (परिपतति) गिर पड़ता है, विनाश को प्राप्त होता है। falls down, goes to ruin.

परिपन्थ – पु॰ – (परिपन्थ) खतरा, बाधा, किनारा। danger, obstacle, side.

परिपन्थिक – वि॰ – (परिपन्थक) बाधक। obstructing, opposing.

परिपाक – पु॰ – (परिपाक) पका होना, प्रौढ़ होना, हाज़मा। ripeness, maturity, digestion.

परिपाचन – न॰ – (परिपाचन) पकना, प्रौढ़ होना, विकसित होना, हज़म होना। ripening, maturing, digestion, developing.

परिपाचेति – क्रि॰ – (परिपाचयति) पकाता है, प्रौढ़ बनाता है, विकसित करता है। brings maturity, ripens, develops.

परिपातेति – क्रि॰ – (परिपातयति) आक्रमण करता है, गिराता है, नाश कर डालता है। attacks, causes fall, destroys.

परिपालेति – क्रि॰ – (परिपालयति) पालन करता है, पहरा देता है, संरक्षण करता है। protects, guards, watches.

परिपीलेति – क्रि॰ – (परिपीडयति) पीड़ित करता है। oppresses.

परिपुच्छक – वि॰ – (परिपृच्छक) प्रश्न पूछने वाला। one who asks a question or investigates.

परिपुच्छति – क्रि॰ – (परिपृच्छति) पूछ-ताछ करता है। interrogates, inquires.

परिपुच्छा – स्त्री॰ – (परिपृच्छा) पूछताछ, प्रश्न। a question, interrogation, enquiry.

परिपुण्ण – कृ॰ – (परिपूर्ण) सम्पूर्ण। full, complete.

परिपुण्णता – स्त्री॰ – (परिपूर्णता) सम्पूर्णता। fullness, perfection.

परिपूर – वि॰ – (परिपूर्ण) सम्पूर्ण। full, complete.

परिपूरक – वि॰ – (परिपूरक) पूर्ति करने वाला। one who fills or fulfils.

परिपूरकारिता – स्त्री॰ – (परिपूरकारिता) पूर्ति का भाव। state of completion, fullness.

परिपूरकारी – पु॰ – (परिपूरकारी) पूरा करने वाला। one who completes or fulfils.

परिपूरण – न॰ – (परिपूरण) पूर्ति। fulfilment, completion.

परिपूरति – क्रि॰ – (परिपूरयति) पूरा करता है। completes, makes full or perfect.

परिपूरेति – क्रि॰ – (परिपूरयति) पूरा कराता है। fulfils, completes, accomplishes.

परिप्फुट – कृ॰ – (परिस्फुट/परिपूर्ण) भरा हुआ, व्याप्त। filled, pervaded.

परिप्लव – वि॰ – (परिप्लव) चंचल, अस्थिर। unsteady, wavering, swerving.

परिप्लवति – क्रि॰ – (परि + प्लु – परिप्लवते) कांपता है, इधर-उधर घूमता है। quivers, swerves, roams about.

परिफन्दति – क्रि॰ – (परि √स्पन्द् = परिस्पन्दते) कांपता है, धड़कता है। trembles, throbs.

परिवाहिर – वि॰ – (परि + बाह्य) बाह्य, बाहरी। external, alien to, an outsider.

परिब्बजति – क्रि॰ – (परि √व्रज = परिव्रजति) घूमता है। wanders about.

परिब्बय – पु॰ – (परित्यय) खर्च। expenses.

परिब्बाजक – पु॰ – (परिव्राजक) परिव्राजक, घूमने-फिरने वाला साधु। a wandering mendicant.

परिब्बाजिका – स्त्री॰ – (परिव्राजिका) परिव्राजिका, घूमने-फिरने वाली साध्वी। a wandering nun.

परिब्बूल्ह – कृ॰ – (परिव्यूढ) घिरा हुआ। surrounded.

परिब्भमति – क्रि॰ – (परिभ्रमित) इधर-उधर भटकता है, भ्रमण करता है। roams about.

परिब्भमन – न॰ – (परिभ्रमण) परिभ्रमण। roaming or reeling about.

परिब्भमेति – क्रि॰ – (परिभ्रामयति) परिभ्रमण कराता है। makes reel round, makes roam about.

परिभट्ठ – कृ॰ – (परिभ्रष्ट) परिभ्रष्ट, पतित। faltered, dropped.

परिभण्ड – पु॰ – (परिलिम्पन) लीपना, घेरना। plastered flooring, an encircling.

परिभण्ड-कत – वि॰ – (परिलिम्पित) लीपा हुआ। plastered.

परिभव – पु॰ – (परिभव) घृणा, अपशब्द। contempt, abuse.

परिभवन – न॰ – (परिभवन) घृणा, निंदा, अपमान। contempt, abuse, humiliation.

परिभवति – क्रि॰ – (परिभवति) घृणा करता है, अपशब्द कहता है, निन्दा करता है। beats with contempt, despises, abuses, reviles.

परिभावित – क्रि॰ – (परिभावित) शिक्षित, दीक्षित। trained, practised.

परिभास – पु॰ – (परिभाष) निंदापूर्वक उलाहना, दोषारोपण। expression of contempt, blaming.

परिभासक – वि॰ – (परिभाषक) निंदा करने वाला, अपशब्द कहने वाला। one who abuses, abusive.

परिभासति – क्रि॰ – (परिभाषते) अपशब्द कहता है, बुरा-भला कहता है। abuses, scolds, defames.

परिभासन – न॰ – (परिभाषण) अपकथन, निन्दा, उपहास। contempt, derision, ridicule.

परिभिन्न – कृ॰ – (परिभिन्न) टूटा हुआ, गिरा हुआ, विरुद्ध हुआ। broken, split, set at variance.

परिभुञ्जति – कृ॰ – (परिभुञ्जति) खाता है, उपयोग में लाता है, भोग भोगता है। eats, uses, enjoys, consumes.

परिभुत्त – कृ॰ – (परिभुक्त) खाया हुआ, भोगा हुआ। eaten, used, consumed.

परिभूत – कृ॰ – (परिभूत) निन्दा-कृत। condemned, censured.

परिभोग – पु० – (**परिभोग**) उपयोग, भोग, भोग-सामग्री। use, enjoyment, feeding, material for enjoyment.

परिभोग-चेतिय – न० – (**परिभोग-चित्तिता**) तथागत द्वारा उपभुक्त होने के कारण पवित्रता प्राप्त। something used by the Buddha and consequently sacred.

परिभोजनीय – वि० – (**परिभोग्य**) उपयोग में लाने योग्य। fit to be used.

परिमञ्जक – पु० – (**परिमार्जक**) रगड़ने वाला या थपथपाने वाला। one who rubs or strokes.

परिमञ्जति – क्रि० – (**परिमार्जयति/ते**) रगड़ता है, थपथपाता है, पोंछता है, साफ करता है। strikes, rubs, polishes, cleans.

परिमञ्जन – न० – (**परिमार्जन**) रगड़ना, पोंछना, मालिश करना, साफ करना। rubbing, wiping off, massaging, cleaning.

परिमण्डल – वि० – (**परिमण्डल**) मण्डलाकार, गोलाकार, घेरा। round, circular.

परिमण्डलं – क्रि० वि० – (**परिमण्डलम्**) चारों ओर से ढककर। all-around.

परिमद्दति – क्रि० – (**परिमर्दति**) रगड़ता है, मर्दन करता है, मालिश करता है। rubs, crushes, massages.

परिमाण – न० – (**परिमाण**) माप, सीमा, मात्रा। measure, extent, quantity.

परिमित – कृ० – (**परिमित**) मापा गया, सीमा निर्धारित कर दी गई। measured, limited, restricted, finite.

परिमुखं – क्रि०वि० – (**परिमुखम्**) सामने। in front of.

परिमुच्चति – क्रि० – (**परिमुच्यते**) मुक्त होता है, बच निकलता है। becomes released, gets escaped.

परिमुच्चन – न० – (**परिमुञ्चन**) मुक्ति, बच निकलना। release, escape.

परिमुत्त – कृ० – (**परिमुक्त**) मुक्त, बच निकला हुआ। released, escaped.

परिमुत्ति – स्त्री० – (**परिमुक्ति**) मुक्ति, बचाव। release, deliverance.

परिमोचेति – क्रि० – (**परिमोचयति**) मुक्त करता है। releases, sets free.

परियत्त – न० – (**पर्याप्त = परि + आप्त**) कण्ठस्थ। kept in mind, learnt by heart.

परियत्ति – स्त्री० – (**पर्याप्ति**) धार्मिक ग्रन्थों को याद करना, धर्म-ग्रन्थों के अध्ययन में उपलब्धि। to memorize scriptures.

परियत्ति-धर – वि० – (**त्रिपिटक-धर**) तिपिटक को कण्ठस्थ करने वाला। who has learnt the scriptures (Tipiṭaka) by heart.

परियत्ति-धम्म – पु० – (**त्रिपिटक-धर्म**) तिपिटक में वर्णित धर्म। code of the holy texts (Tipiṭaka).

परियत्ति-सासन – न० – (**त्रिपिटक-शासन**) तिपिटक और उसकी अट्ठ कथाएं। code of the holy texts (the Tipiṭaka and its Aṭṭhakathās).

परियन्त – पु० – (**पर्यन्त**) आखिरी सिरा, सीमा। last point, extent, extreme end.

परियन्त-कत – वि० – (**पर्यन्त-कृत**) सीमित, बाधित। limited, restricted.

परियन्तिक – वि० – (**पर्यन्तिक**) समाप्त, सीमाबद्ध। ending in, bounded by.

परियाति – क्रि॰ – (परि + याति) चारों ओर घूमता है। goes round.

परियाददाति – क्रि॰ – (परि+आ √दा = पर्याददाति/पर्यादत्ते) अधिक मात्रा में ग्रहण करता है, खाली कर देता है। exhausts, takes up in an excessive degree.

परियादियति – क्रि॰ – (परि+आ √दा + णिच् = पर्यादापयति) काबू कराता है, खाली करा देता है। enables to control, overpowers, causes to exhaust.

परियापन्न – कृ॰ – (पर्यापन्न) सम्मिलित, सम्बन्धित। included in, belonging to, related to.

परियापुणन – न॰ – (पर्यापुणन) अध्ययन करना। learning, studying.

परियापुणाति – क्रि॰ – (पर्यापुणाति) भली-भांति अध्ययन करता है। learns thoroughly, masters, gets skilled into.

परियापुत – कृ॰ – (परि+आप्त) कण्ठस्थ किया हुआ, जाना हुआ। mastered, well known.

परियाय – पु॰ – (पर्याय) क्रम, गुण, आदत, कारण, समानार्थी। order, quality, course, method, cause, a synonym.

परियाय-कथा – स्त्री॰ – (पर्याय-कथा) गोल-मोल बातचीत। a round-about talk, ambiguous talk.

परियाहत – कृ॰ – (परि + आहत) चोट खाया हुआ। hurt, stricken, wounded.

परियाहनति – क्रि॰ – (परि + आ + हन्ति) चोट करता है, खटखटाता है। strikes, knocks against.

परियुट्ठाति – क्रि॰ – (परि + उत् + तिष्ठति) उठती है, सब जगह फैल जाता है, छा जाता है। arises, pervades, prevails.

परियुट्ठान – न॰ – (पर्युत्थान) उदान, पूर्व-संकल्प। outburst, pre-possession, pre-pledge, standing up.

परियेट्ठि – स्त्री॰ – (पर्येष्टि) खोज। search for, discovery.

परियेसति – क्रि॰ – (पर्येषति) खोजता है। searches for, discovers.

परियेसना – स्त्री॰ – (पर्येषणा) खोज। search, quest.

परियोग – पु॰ – (पिठरः) भाजन, देग, हण्डा। a vessel to keep curry.

परियोगाळ्ह – कृ॰ – (परि + अवगाढ = पर्यवगाढ) कसा हुआ, गहरे गया हुआ। tightened, immersed, plunged into.

परियोगाहति – क्रि॰ – (परि + अवगाहते) डुबकी मारता है, पानी की गहराई तक जाता है। dives, plunges into, bottom.

परियोगाहन – न॰ – (पर्यवगाहन) डुबकी मारना, भीतर जाना। plunging into, penetration.

परियोदपना/परियोदपना – क्रि॰ – (पर्यवदापना) शुद्धि, साफ करना। purification.

परियोदपेति – क्रि॰ – (पर्यवदापति) शुद्ध करता है, साफ करता है। cleanses, purifies.

परियोदात – वि॰ – (पर्यवदात) शुद्ध, परिशुद्ध। very clean, pure.

परियोनद्ध – कृ॰ – (आ √नह् + क्त = आनद्ध) बंधा हुआ, ढका हुआ। tied, bound, covered.

परियोनन्धति – क्रि॰ – (आ √नह् = आनह्यति) बांधता है, ढकता है। ties down, envelops, covers up.

परियोनन्धन – न॰ – (अवनन्धन) ढकना। covering, enveloping.

परियोनाह – पु॰ – (पिधान) ढकना। covering.

परियोसान – न॰ – (पर्यवसान) समाप्ति, उपसंहार। the end, conclusion.

परियोसापेति – क्रि॰ – (परि + अवसायपति) समाप्त करता है। brings to an end.

परियोसित – कृ॰ – (परि + अव √सो + क्त = पर्यवसित) finished, concluded, satisfied.

परिक्खति – क्रि॰ – (परिरक्षति) रक्षा करता है, संरक्षण करता है। defends, protects.

परिरक्खण – न॰ – (परिरक्षण) रक्षा करना, संरक्षण। defending, protection.

परिवच्छ – न॰ – (परितृत्यम्) तैयारी। preparation.

परिवज्जन – न॰ – (परिवर्जन) बचाव, टरकाना। avoidance, defence.

परिवज्जेति – क्रि॰ – (परिवर्जयति) हटाता है, दूर-दूर रखता है, टरकाता है। shuns, avoids, keeps away from.

परिवड्ड – न॰ – (परिवृत्त) घेरा। a circle.

परिवत्त – कृ॰ – (परिवर्त्त) लोटता-पोटता। turned round, rolled about.

परिवत्तक – वि॰ – (परिवर्त्तक) लोटता-पोटता हुआ, (पु॰) गोला, अनुवादक। rolling, turning, twisting (m.) ball of thread, translator.

परिवत्तति – क्रि॰ – (परिवर्त्तते) लोटता-पोटता है। turns round, rolls.

परिवत्तन – न॰ – (परिवर्तन) परिवर्तन, उलटना-पलटना, अनुवाद। change, turning round, translation.

परिवत्तेति – क्रि॰ – (परि √वृत् + णिच् = परिवर्त्तयति) उलटता है। turns round, rolls.

परिवसति – क्रि॰ – (परिवसति) शागिर्द बनकर रहता है। lives under probation.

परिवार – पु॰ – (परिवार) अनुयायी, अनुगामी, नौकर-चाकर। retinue, followers, servants.

परिवारक – वि॰ – (परिवारक) अनुचर, साथी। follower, companion.

परिवारण – न॰ – (परिवारण) घेर लेना। the act of surrounding.

परिवार-पालि – (परिवार-पालि ग्रन्थ) विनय पिटक का उपसंहारात्मक भाग। the concluding part of Vinaya Piṭaka.

परिवारेति – क्रि॰ – (परिवारयति) घेर लेता है। surrounds, follows.

परिवासित – कृ॰ – (परि + वासित) सुगन्धित। perfumed, scented.

परिवितक्क – पु॰ – (परिवितर्क) विचार-विमर्श। reflection, consideration, exchange of ideas.

परिवितक्केति – क्रि॰ – (परिवितर्कयति) तर्कपूर्ण विचार करता है, मनन करता है। considers, thinks over, ascertains by reasoning.

परिविसति – क्रि॰ – (परिविशति) भोजन कराता है, सेवा में रहता है। serves with food, waits upon.

परिवीमंसति – क्रि॰ – (परि + वि √मृश =

परिविमर्शयति) विचार करता है, मनन करता है। considers, thinks over.

परिवुत – कृ॰ – (**परिवृत्त**) घिरा हुआ। surrounded by, encircled.

परिवेण – न॰ – (**परिवेण**) भिक्षुओं का निवास-स्थान, भिक्षुओं का विद्यालय। a separated residence of monks, a place for religious learning for monks.

परिवेसक – वि॰ – (**परिवेशक**) भोजन परोसने वाला। server, one who serves meals.

परिवेसना – स्त्री॰ – (**परि √ विष् + ल्युट् + टाप् = परिवेषणा**) भोजन परोसना। feeding, serving meals.

परिसक्कति – क्रि॰ – (**परिशक्नोति**) सहन करता है, कोशिश करता है, प्रयत्न करता है। endeavours, tries.

परिस-गत – वि॰ – (**परिषद् गत**) परिषद में सम्मिलित, मण्डली के अन्तर्गत। having entered a company.

परिसङ्कति – क्रि॰ – (**परिशङ्कते**) सन्देह करता है। suspects.

परिसङ्का स्त्री॰ (**परिशङ्का**) सन्देह। suspicion, doubt.

परिस-दूसक – पु॰ – (**परिषद्-दूषक**) परिषद को दूषित करने वाला। a black sheep in an assembly.

परिसप्पति – क्रि॰ – (**परिसर्पति**) रेंगता है। creeps, crawls about.

परिसप्पना – स्त्री॰ – (**परिसर्पण**) रेंगना, कांपना, सन्देह, हिचकिचाहट। crawling about, trembling, doubt, hesitation.

परिसमन्ततो – क्रि॰ वि॰ – (**परिसमन्ततः**) चारों ओर से। from all sides, all-round.

परिसहति – क्रि॰ – (**परि √ सह् = परिसहते**) जीत लेता है। overcomes, masters, wins.

परिसा – स्त्री॰ – (**परिषद्**) परिषद्। an assembly, a company.

परिसावचर – वि॰ – (**परिषदावचर**) सभा-समिति में विचरने वाला। one who moves in society.

परिसिञ्चति – क्रि॰ – (**परिसिञ्चति**) सर्वत्र छिड़कता है। sprinkles all over.

परिसुज्झति – क्रि॰ – (**परिशुध्यति**) परिशुद्ध होता है। becomes clean, becomes purified.

परिसुद्ध – कृ॰ – (**परिशुद्ध**) साफ, पवित्र। pure, clean, sacred.

परिसुद्धि – स्त्री॰ – (**परिशुद्धि**) सफाई, पवित्रता। purity, sacredness.

परिसुद्धि सील – स्त्री॰ – (**परिशीलम्**) जीवन के साधनों की शुद्धि। purity of livelihood.

परिसज्ज – वि॰ – (**परिषद्यः**) किसी परिषद का सदस्य। belonging to an assembly.

परिसुस्सति – क्रि॰ – (**परिशुष्यति**) सूख जाता है, व्यर्थ जाता है। becomes dried up, is wasted.

परिसुस्सन – न॰ – (**परिशुष्यन**) पूर्ण रूप से सूख जाना। drying up completely.

परिसेदित – कृ॰ – (**परिस्वेदित**) वाष्प से उबाला गया। heated with steam.

परिसेदेति – क्रि॰ – (**परिस्वेदयति**) वाष्प स्नान करता है, सेंकता है, (अण्डे) सेता है। hatches, bathes with steam, heats with steam.

परिसोधन – न॰ – (**परिशोधन**) शुद्धि। purification, cleansing.

परिसोधेति – क्रि० – (परिशोधयति) शुद्ध करता है, साफ करता है। cleanses, purifies.

परिसोसेति – क्रि० – (परिशोषयति) सुखाता है। dries up, evaporates.

परिस्सजति – क्रि० – (परिष्वजति) गले मिलता है। embraces.

परिस्सजन – न० – (परिष्वजन) गले मिलना। embracing.

परिसन्त – कृ० – (परिश्रान्त) परिश्रान्त, थका हुआ। tired, fatigued, weary.

परिस्सय – पु० – (परिक्षय) खतरा, परेशानी। danger, trouble.

नोट – संस्कृत में परिश्रय (परि √ श्रि + अच्) का अर्थ होता है सभा, आश्रय, वेष्टन। पाली में परिस्सय (परिश्रय) का प्रयोग सर्वथा विपरीत अर्थों में हुआ है।

परिस्सावन – न० – (परिस्रवण) पानी छानने का साधन। a water strainer, a filter.

परिस्सावेति – क्रि० – (परिस्रावयति) पानी छानता है। strains, filters.

परिहरण – न० – (परिहरण) ले जाना, संरक्षण। keeping on, protection.

परिहरणा – स्त्री० – (परिहरणा) रखना, ले जाना, संरक्षण। keeping on, protection, attention.

परिहरति – क्रि० – (परि √ हृ = परिहरति) संभालता है, रक्षा करता है, ले जाता है। keeps up, to protects, carries about.

परिहसति – क्रि० – (परिहसति) हंसी उड़ाता है, चिढ़ाता है। laughs at, mocks.

परिहानि – स्त्री० – (परिहानि) हानि। loss, decrease.

परिहानिय – वि० – (हानिकर) हानिकार। causing loss or ruin.

परिहापेति – क्रि० – (परिहाययति) क्षीण होता है, उपेक्षा करता है, लापरवाही करता है। deteriorates, neglects, omits.

परिहायति – क्रि० – (परिहीयते) क्षीण या अवनत होता है, नुकसान उठाता है। deteriorates, declines, suffers loss.

परिहार – पु० – (परिहार) संरक्षण, बचाव। care, attention, protection.

परिहारक – वि० – (परिहारक) संरक्षक, पहरेदार। one who protects or guards, watchman.

परिहार-पथ – पु० – (परिहार-पथ) घुमावदार रास्ता। a round about way, circular road.

परिहारिक – वि० – (पारिहारिक) (जीवित) रखने वाला। keeping up (alive).

परिहास – पु० – (परिहास) हंसी-मजाक। joke, jest, fun.

परिहीन – कृ० – (परिहीण) हानिग्रस्त, अनाथ। slacken with loss, destitute, emanciated, abandoned.

परूपक्कम – पु० – (पर + उपक्रम) शत्रु का आक्रमण। aggression of an enemy, violence.

परूपघात – पु० – (परोपघात) दूसरों का घात। injuring others, cruelty.

परूपवाद – पु० – (परापवाद) दूसरों द्वारा किया गया दोषारोपण। censuring by others, reproach of others.

परूळ्ह – कृ० – (प्ररूढ) उगकर परिपुष्ट। grown long.

परूळ्ह-केस – वि० – (प्ररूढ केश) लम्बे बालों वाला। with hair grown long.

परेत – वि॰ – (पर √इ + क्त = परेत) युक्त, संयुक्त। combined, gone to, affected by, overcome by.

परो – अव्यय – (पर) मरणान्तर, आगे, ऊपर। beyond death, further, above.

परोक्ख – वि॰ – (परोक्ष) परोक्ष, आंख से ओझल। beyond the eye, out of sight.

परोक्खे – अव्यय – (परोक्ष) परोक्ष में, अनुपस्थिति में। in the absence, behind one's back.

परोदति – क्रि॰ – (प्र √रूद् = प्रोदिति) विलाप करता है, क्रन्दन करता है। wails, cries out.

परोवर – वि॰ – (परावर = पर + अवर) ऊंच-नीच। high and low.

परोवरिय – वि॰ – (परावरे) ऊंचे-नीचे। high and low.

परोसत – वि॰ – (परः + शतम्) सौ से अधिक। more than a hundred.

परोसहस्स – वि॰ – (परः + सहस्रम्) हजार से अधिक। more than a thousand.

परोसहस्स-जातक – (जा॰ सं॰ 99) – तपस्वी के हजार शिष्य, 'आकिञ्चञ्ञायतन' का यथार्थ भावार्थ नहीं समझ सके। कथा का सारांश है कि अकेला बुद्धिमान व्यक्ति हजारों मूर्खों से श्रेष्ठ है। the story (No. 99) concludes that "far better than a thousand fools is one who is intelligent."

पळ – न॰ – (पल) तोल की माप-विशेष, 16 माषक = 1 सुवर्ण, 4 सुवर्ण = 1 पल, 10 पल = 1 धरण। a certain weight (of about 4 ounces) 16 *maṣaka* = 1 *suvarṇa*, 4 *suvarṇa* = 1 *pala*, 4 *palas* = 1 *dharaṇa*.

पल-गण्ड – पु॰ – (पलगण्ड) राज, मकान बनाने वाला, कारीगर। a mason, a brick-layer, a worker.

पलण्डु – पु॰ – (पलाण्डु) प्याज। onion.

पलण्डुक – पु॰ – (पलाण्डु) देखें पलण्डु। see Palaṇḍu.

पलपति – क्रि॰ – (प्र + लपति) बकवास करता है। talks nonsense.

पलपन – न॰ – (प्रलपन) व्यर्थ की बातचीत। nonsense talk.

पलपित – न॰ – (प्रलपित) देखें पलपन। see Palapana.

पलय – पु॰ – (प्रलय) प्रलय, विनाश। dissolution.

पलपङ्ग – पु॰ – (प्लवङ्ग/प्लवङ्गय) काला मुंह व लम्बी पूंछ वाला बन्दर, लंगूर। a kind of monkey with black face and long tail, a baboon.

पलात – कृ॰ – (पलायित) भगोड़ा, भागा हुआ। one who runs away, fugitive.

पलाप (1) – पु॰ – (पलाल) पयाल, पैरा, धान का डंठल (तना)। chaff (of corn), straw.

पलाप (2) – पु॰ – (प्रलाप) व्यर्थ की बकवास। nonsense talk, prattle.

पलापी – पु॰ – (प्रलापी) बकवास करने वाला। one who talks nonsense.

पलापेति (1) – क्रि॰ – (पलाययति) भगा देता है। forces to escape.

पलापेति (2) – क्रि॰ – (प्रलपति) बकवास करता है। talk nonsense.

पलायति – क्रि॰ – (पलायते) भागता है, बच निकलता है। runs away, escapes.

पलायन – न॰ – (पलायन) भाग जाना। escape, running away.

पलायनक – वि॰ – (पलायनक) भागता हुआ। fleeing.

पलायी – पु॰ – (पलायी) पलायन करने वाला। one who escapes.

पलायी-जातक – (जा॰ सं॰ 229) – बनारस नरेश तक्षशिला पर आक्रमण करने गया किन्तु नगर की अटारियों के शिखरों को ही देखकर वापिस भाग गया। (story No. 229) the king of Varanasi had marched to capture Takṣaśilā but on seeing the towers of the city gate, he took fright and fled.

पलाल – न॰ – (पलाल) पुआल (पैरा) धान का, सूखा डँठल, फूस। straw.

पलाल-पुञ्ज – (पलाल-पुञ्ज) पुआल का ढेर। a heap of straw.

पलास – पु॰ न॰ – (पलाश) (1) पत्ता (2) ढाक का पेड़। (1) leaf, (2) a kind of tree Butea Frondosa.

पलास-साद – वि॰ – (पलाशाद) पत्तों का भोजन करने वाला। one who subsists on foliage.

पलास-जातक – (जा॰ सं॰ 307) – एक ब्राह्मण को पलाश वृक्ष के नीचे गड़ा धन मिलने की कथा। the story (No. 307) of how a brāhmaṇa got wealth under a palāśa tree which was buried.

पलास-जातक – (जा॰ सं॰ 370) – पलाश वृक्ष में उगे वट-वृक्ष ने धीरे-धीरे पलाश-वृक्ष को ही नष्ट कर दिया। the story (No. 370) tells how the sapling of a banyan seed sprang in the fork of a palāśa tree and destroyed the latter.

पलासाद – पु॰ – (पलाशाद) गैंडा। rhinoceros.

पलासी – वि॰ – (पल + अशिन, पल = मांस अशिन = खाने वाला) जो ईर्ष्या करके अपना ही मांस गला देता (खाता) है अर्थात् ईर्ष्यालु। spiteful, malicious.

पलिघ – पु॰ – (परिघ) अर्गला, बाधा, रुकावट। hurdle, obstacle, interruption.

पलित – वि॰ – (पलित) प्रौढ़, सफेद बाल। matured, grey hair, old.

पलिप – पु॰ – (पलिप) दलदल। marsh, sloppiness.

पलिपथ – पु॰ – (परिपथ) खतरनाक रास्ता। a dangerous or difficult path.

पलिपन्न – क्रि॰ – (परिपन्न) गिरा, डूबा हुआ। fallen or sunk into.

पलुग्ग – कृदन्त – (पतित) नीचे गिरा हुआ, टूटा हुआ। to be dissolved, fell down.

पलुज्जति – (पतति) नीचे गिरता है, टूट जाता है। fell or sinks into.

पलुज्जन – न॰ – (पलुज्जन) लड़खड़ाना। staggering, trembling, crumbling.

पलुद्ध – कृ॰ – (प्रलुब्ध) अत्यन्त आसक्त। much attached, enticed.

पलेति – क्रि॰ – (पलायते) चला जाता है। goes, walks away, escapes.

पलोभन – न॰ – (प्रलोभन) प्रलोभन, लालच। enticement, temptation, seduction.

पलोभेति – क्रि॰ – (प्र √ लुभ = प्रलुभ्यति) लालच देता है। entices, seduces.

पल्लङ्क – पु॰ – (पल्य्ङ्क्) (1) पर्यङ्क, पलंग, पल्लंङ्क, दीवान (2) पालथी मारकर बैठा हुआ। (1) sofa, a couch, (2) sitting cross-legged.

पल्लत्थिका – स्त्री॰ – (पल्यङ्की) शिविका, छोटी पालकी जिसमें बैठने भर की जगह हो। a palanquin with sitting space.

पल्लल – न॰ – (पल्वल) छोटा तालाब, दलदली भूमि। a small pond, marshy land.

पल्लव – पु॰ – (पल्लव) किसलय, कोंपल। a young leaf, sprout.

पवक्खति – क्रि॰ – (प्र + वक्ष्यति) कहेगा, बता देगा। (he) will tell.

पवड्ढ/पवड्ढ – वि॰ – (प्रवृद्ध) वर्धित, शक्तिशाली। grown up, strong.

पवड्ढति – क्रि॰ – (प्रवर्धते) बढ़ता है। grows, increases.

पवड्ढन – न॰ – (प्रवर्द्धन) वृद्धि। growth, increase.

पवत्त – वि॰ – (प्रवृत्त) (1) चालू रहा, नीचे गिरा (2) (न) वह जो चालू रहे, यानी भवचक्र (जन्म-मरण) का चक्कर। (1) going on, fallen down (2) (n.) the cycle of life and death.

पवत्तति – क्रि॰ – (प्रवर्तते) चालू रहता है, विद्यमान रहता है। exists, moves on, proceeds.

पवत्तन – न॰ – (प्रवर्त्तन) अस्तित्व, चालू रखना। existence, carrying out, moving forward.

पवत्तापन – न॰ – (प्रवर्त्तयन) लगातार चालू रखना। continue, to keep running.

पवत्ति – स्त्री॰ – (प्रवृत्ति) प्रवृत्ति, घटना। happening, incident, tendency.

पवत्तेति – क्रि॰ – (प्रवर्त्तयति) चालू करता है। gets going, keeps on.

पवत्तेतु – पु॰ – (प्रवर्त्तयिता) चालू करने वाला। one who keeps on or continues.

पवड्ढ – कृ॰ – (प्रवृद्ध) देखें पवड्ढ। see Pavaḍḍha.

पवन – न॰ – (पवन) (1) वायु (2) अनाज पछोरना। (1) the wind, (2) winnowing.

पवर – वि॰ – (प्रवर) श्रेष्ठ। noble, excellent.

पवसति – क्रि॰ – (प्रवसति) विदेश में रहता है, प्रवास करता है। dwells abroad, resides away from home.

पवस्सति – क्रि॰ – (प्रवर्षति) जोर से बरसता है। rains heavily.

पवस्सन – न॰ – (प्रवर्षण) वर्षा। raining.

पवात – न॰ – (प्रवात) हवादार जगह। an airy place.

पवाति – क्रि॰ – (प्र + वाति) सुगन्धि फैलती है, हवा चलती है। diffuses a scent, blows forth.

पवायति – क्रि॰ – (प्रवाति) हवा चलती है, बहती है, सुगन्धि फैलाती है। blows forth, diffuses.

पवारणा – स्त्री॰ – (प्रवारणा) निमंत्रण, वर्षावास के बाद किया जाने वाला एक धार्मिक संस्कार, सन्तोष। invitation, a ceremony at the end of rainy season, happiness.

पवारित – कृ॰ – (प्रवारित) निमंत्रित, पवारणा सम्पादित। invited, one who has celebrated 'Pavāraṇā' (see Pavāraṇā).

पवारेति – क्रि॰ – (प्रवारयति) निमंत्रण देता है, सौंपता है, पवारणा करता है। invites, hands over, observes 'Pavāraṇa'

पवाल – पु॰ – (प्रवाल) प्रवाल, मूंगा, कोंपल। coral, sprout.

पवास – पु॰ – (प्रवास) प्रवास, घर से दूर रहना। sojourning abroad.

पवासी – पु॰ – (प्रवासी) पैतृक गृह से दूरस्थ स्थान पर रहने वाला, प्रवासी। one who lives abroad.

पवाह – पु॰ – (प्रवाह) प्रवाह, बहाव। continuous flowing.

पवाहक – वि॰ – (प्रवाहक) ले जाने वाला। carrier, one who carries away.

पवाहेति – क्रि॰ – (प्रवाहयति) प्रवाहित करता है, बहा देता है। makes to flow, causes to be carried away.

पवाळ – पु॰ – (प्रवाल) देखें पवाल। see 'Pavāla'.

पवाळह – कृ॰ – (प्र √बाध् + क्त = प्रबाधित) रद्द कर दिया गया। cancelled.

पविज्झति – क्रि॰ – (प्र + विध्यति) बींधता है। throws forth, shoots, pierces, पविज्झि – भू॰ क॰ कृ॰ (प्रविद्ध) डाला हुआ। aorist, प्रविद्ध – (प्रविध्य) past participle, पविज्झित्वा (प्रविध्यित्वा) डालकर। absolutive.

पविट्ठ – कृ॰ – (प्रविष्ट) भीतर गया हुआ, घुसा हुआ। entered, gone into, pierced.

पविवित्त – वि॰ – (प्र + विवृत) पृथक् कृत एकान्त (स्थान)। separated, secluded.

पविवेक – पु॰ – (प्रविवेक) एकान्त। solitude, seclusion.

पविसति – क्रि॰ – (प्रविशति) प्रवेश करता है। goes in, enters.

पवीण – वि॰ – (प्रवीण) प्रवीण, होशियार। clever, skillful.

पवुच्चति – क्रि॰ – (प्र + उच्यते) कहलाता है, कहा जाता है। it is said.

प्रवुत्त – कृ॰ – (प्र + उक्त = प्रोक्त) कहा गया। said, to be called.

पवुत्थ – कृ॰ – (प्र √वस् + क्त = प्र + उषित/प्रवसित) बसा रहा। lived abroad, dwelled overseas.

पवेणि – स्त्री॰ – (प्रवेणी) (1) परम्परा, उत्तरा-धिकार (2) (सिर के बालों की) वेणी। (1) tradition, succession (2) a braid of hair.

पवेदन – न॰ – (प्रवेदन) घोषणा, प्रज्ञप्ति। announcement.

पवेदियमान – कृ॰ – (प्रवेद्यमान) घोषित किया जाता हुआ। being announced.

पवेदेति – क्रि॰ – (प्रवेदयति) विज्ञापित करता है, प्रकट करता है। manifests, declares.

पवेधति – क्रि॰ – (√एज् = राजते) काँपता है। trembles, becomes agitated.

पवेस – पु॰ – (प्रवेश) प्रवेश। entrance, entering.

पवेसन – न॰ – (प्रवेशनम्) दाखिला, घुसना। entrance, entry.

पवेसक – वि॰ – (प्रवेशक) प्रवेश करने वाला या कराने वाला। one who enters, who makes one enter.

पवेसेति – क्रि॰ – (प्रवेशयति) प्रवेश कराता है, परिचय कराता है। makes enter, introduces.

पवेसेसि – क्रि. सं – (प्रवेशति) प्रवेश करता है। to usher in, aorist.

पवेसित – सं – (प्रवेशित) अन्दर पहुँचाया हुआ। past participle.

पवेसेत्वा – सं – (प्रविश्य) प्रवेश करके। absolutive.

पवेसेन्त – (प्रवेष्टः) पहुँचा हुआ। potential participle.

पवेसेतुं – पु. – (प्रवेशकः) प्रवेश कराने वाला। an user, one who allows to enter.

पसंसक – पु. – (प्रशंसक) प्रशंसा करने वाला या खुशामद करने वाला। one who praises or flatters.

पसंसति – क्रि. – (प्रशंसति) प्रशंसा करता है। praises, commends.

पसंसन – न. – (प्रशंसन) प्रशंसा। praise, commendation.

पसंसा – स्त्री. – (प्रशंसा) स्तुति, संस्तुति। commendation, recommen-dation.

पसङ्ग – पु. – (प्रसङ्ग) प्रसङ्ग, अवस्था, आसक्ति। inclination, attachment, event, occasion.

पसट – कृ. – (प्रशस्त) प्रशस्त, फैला हुआ। expanded, strewn with.

पसट्ठ – कृ. – (प्रशस्त) देखें पसत्थ। see Pasattha.

पसत – पु. – (प्रसृत) प्रसर, गहरी की हुई अंजली। a handful, as a measure (= 2 palas) intense, respect.

पसत्थ/पसट्ठ – कृ. – (प्रशस्त) सराहा हुआ, प्रशस्त। extolled, commended.

पसद – पु. – (वि.- प्रशान्त / पृथ्यति = पसत / पसद) चीतल मृग। spotted deer.

पसन्न – कृ. – (प्रसन्न) प्रसन्न, स्पष्ट, तेजयुक्त। clear, bright, pleased.

पसन्न-चित्त – वि. – (प्रसन्न-चित्त) प्रसन्नचित्त। gladdened.

पसन्न-मानस – वि. – (प्रसन्न-मानस) प्रसन्न-मग। having a gladdened mind.

पसय्ह – पू. क्रि. – (प्रसह्य) बलपूर्वक, जबर्दस्ती। forcibly, by force.

पसव – पु. – (प्रसव) सन्तान, (बच्चा) पैदा करना। offspring, bringing forth.

पसवति – क्रि. – (प्र √ सू = प्रसूते) उत्पन्न करती है। brings forth, gives birth to.

पसहति – क्रि. – (प्रसहते) दबाता है, जीत लेता है, मर्दन करता है। uses force, subdues, oppresses.

पसहन – न. – (प्रसहन) अधिकार करना, अधीन करना। overcoming, mastering.

पसहय – अव्यय – (प्रसह्य) हठात्, बलात्। by force.

पसाख – न. – (प्रशाख) शाखाऐं फूट निकलने का स्थान। the spot on the tree from where the branches grow.

पसाखा – स्त्री. – (प्रशाखा) प्रशाखिका, मोटी शाखा में से निकली छोटी पतली शाखा। a small branch or twig.

पसाद – पु. – (प्रसाद) प्रसन्नता, श्रद्धा, स्पष्टता, (इन्द्रिय) प्रसाद-इन्द्रियों का कार्य। joy, faith, clearness, the faculty of senses.

पसादनिय – वि. – (प्रसादनीय) विश्वासोत्पादक। inspiring confidence.

पसादेति – क्रि॰ – (प्रसादयति) प्रसन्न करता है, पवित्र करता है, श्रद्धावान बना लेता है। to gladden, to purify, to make one faithful.

पसाधन – न॰ -- (प्रसाधन) गहना, सजावट। an ornament, decoration.

पसाधेति – न॰ – (प्रसाधयति) गहना पहनता है, सजता है। adorns, decorates, arrays.

पसारण – न॰ – (प्रसारण) फैलाव, प्रसारण। stretching out, spreading.

पसारित – कृ॰ – (प्रसारित) प्रसारित, फैलाया गया। stretched out.

पसारेति – क्रि॰ – (प्रसारयति) फैलाता है। streches out.

पसासति – क्रि॰ – (प्र √ शास् = प्रशास्ति) अनुशासन करता है, शिक्षा देता है, राज्य करता है। instructs, rules, governs.

पसिति – स्त्री॰ – (प्रसृति) बन्धन। पसर, एक हथेली में जितना अनाज भरा जा सके, सीमित मात्रा। measure equal to one handful of grain, (= 2 palas) the palm of the hollowed hand, limited measure.

पसिद्ध – वि॰ – (प्रसिद्ध) प्रसिद्ध। famous.

पसिब्बक – पु॰ – (प्रसेवनी/प्रसेव) रूपयों की बासनी, थैली। a purse, sack, bag.

पसीदति – क्रि॰ – (प्रसीदति) प्रसन्न होता है, श्रद्धावान् होता है। becomes pleased, becomes bright, becomes devoted.

पसीदन – न॰ – (प्रसीदन) श्रद्धा, प्रसन्नता। devotion, gratification.

पसीदना – स्त्री॰ – (प्रसीदना) श्रद्धा, संतोष। devotion, satisfaction.

पसु – पु॰ – (पशु) पशु, चौपाया। animal, quadruped, four-legged.

पसुत – वि॰ – (प्रसित) लगा हुआ, आसक्त। attached to, enticed with.

पसूत – कृ॰ – (प्रसूत) प्रसूत, बच्चा दिया, जन्मा। produced, delivered, born.

पसूति – स्त्री॰ – (प्रसूति) प्रसूति, जन्म। bringing forth, birth.

पसूतिका – स्त्री॰ – (प्रसूतिका) प्रसूतिका, वह स्त्री जिसने किसी बच्चे को जन्म दिया हो। a woman who has delivered a child.

पसूतिका-घर – न॰ – (प्रसूति-गृह) प्रसूतिका-गृह। labour-room, lying-in-home.

पसेनदि – पु॰ – (प्रसेनजित) बुद्ध का समकालीन कोसल नरेश। the king of Kosala, contemporary of Buddha.

पस्स (1) – पु॰ – (पार्श्व) बगल, पास। aside, near.

पस्स (2) – पु॰ – (पाश/पाशक) द्यूत क्रीडा का पांसा। a dice.

पस्सति – क्रि॰ – (√ दृश = पश्यति) देखना, पता लगाना, समझना। to see, to trace, to find out, to understand.

पस्सद्ध – कृदन्त – (प्रशान्त) शान्त। calm, quiet.

परसद्धि – स्त्री॰ – (प्रशान्ति) शान्ति गाम्भीर्य। calmness; tranquility, serenity.

पस्सम्मति – क्रि॰ – (प्रशाम्ति) शान्त होना। to calm down; to be quiet.

पस्सम्मना – स्त्री॰ – (प्रशमन) शान्ति। allayment; calmness.

पस्सम्मेति – क्रिया – (प्रशमित) शान्त करना। to make calm or allayed.

पस्समति – क्रिया – (प्रश्वासति) प्रश्वास लेना। to breathe out.

पस्साव – पु॰ – (प्रस्रावः) पेशाब। urine.

पस्साव – पु॰ – (प्रश्वासः) सांस निकालना। exhalation.

पस्सासी – पु॰ – (प्रश्वासी) सांस निकालने वाला। one who exhales.

पहट – कृदन्त – (प्रहत) चोट खाया हुआ। wounded.

पहट्ठ – कृदन्त – (प्रहस्य) अत्यन्त प्रसन्न-चित्त। delighted; very cheerful.

पहरण – नपु॰ – (प्रहरणम्) पीटना, प्रहार करना। beating; a weapon to strike with.

पहरति – क्रिया – (प्रहरति) पीटना। to beat; to strike; to hit.

पहाण – नपु॰ – (प्रहाणम्) हटाना, छोड़ना, त्यागना। removal; giving up; abandoning.

पहाय – पूर्व॰ – (प्रहीण) छोड़कर। having left or giving up.

पहायी – पु॰ – (प्रहायी) छोड़ने वाला। one who gives up or abandons.

पहार – पु॰ – (प्रहारः) प्रहार, चोट। a blow, a stroke.

पहार-दान – नपु॰ – (प्रहार-दान) चोट पहुँचाना। giving a blow.

पहास – पु॰ – (प्रहसनम्) अत्यन्त प्रीति। great joy, mirth.

पहिणन – नपु॰ – (प्रहसति) हँसाना, आनन्दित करना। to make one laugh, to gladden.

पहिणन – नपु॰ – (प्रेषण) भेजना। sending; dispatch.

पहिण – नपु॰ – (प्रेषः) दूत की तरह जाना, प्रेषण करना। going as a messenger.

पहिणति – क्रिया – (प्रेषयति) भेजता है। to send.

पहित – कृदन्त – (प्रेषित) प्रेषित, भेजा गया। sent.

पहीन – कृदन्त – (प्रहीण) प्रहीण, रहित, व्यक्त, नष्ट। eliminated, abandoned, destroyed.

पहीयति – क्रिया – (प्रहीणति) प्रहीण होना, नहीं रहना, त्यागा जाना। to vanish, to pass away, to be abandoned.

पहू – वि॰ – (प्राणाव्य) योग्य। able.

पहूत – वि॰ – (प्रभूत) बहुत अधिक। abundant; broad.

पहूत-जिण्ह – वि॰ – (प्रभूत-जिण्हा) बड़ी जीभ वाला। having a broad tongue.

पहूत-भक्ख – वि॰ – (प्रभूत-भक्ष) प्रचुर खाद्य-पदार्थ वाला या प्रचुर खाने वाला। having much to eat or eating much.

पहेणक – नपु॰ – (प्रेष्य) किसी को भेजने योग्य भेंट। a present fit to be given to someone.

पहोति – क्रिया – (प्रभूतिः) समर्थ होना। to be able; sufficient, adequate.

पहोनक – वि॰ – (पर्याप्त) उपलब्ध, पूर्ण। sufficient; enough.

पलिगुण्ठेति – क्रिया – (प्रतिच्छन्नति) उलझाना, ढंकना। to entangle; to envelop.

पलिघ – पु॰ – (प्रतिघः) अरगल, बाधाएँ। cross-bar, an obstacle.

पलिबुज्झति – क्रि॰ – (प्रतिवद्धति) प्रमाद करना, मैला होना, बाधित होना। to be delayed or spoiled; to be obstructed.

पलिबुज्झन – नपु॰ – (प्रतिवद्धन) मैला होना। becoming dirty.

पलिबोध – नपु॰ – (प्रबद्ध) बाधा, अवरुद्ध। obstruction; hindrance; impediment.

पलिवेठन – नपु॰ – (प्रतिच्छदनम्) लपेटना, घेर लेना। wrapping; encircling.

पहलवेठेति – क्रिया – (प्रतिच्छेदति) लपेटना, घेर लेना। to wrap up; to entwine; to encircle.

पंसु – पु॰ – (पांसुः, पांशु) धूल। soil, dust.

पंसु-कूल – नपु॰ – (पांसु कूलम्) चेल का ढेर। a dust heap.

पंसुकूल-चीवर – नपु॰ – (पांशुकूल वस्त्रम्) कूड़े-करकट के ढेर पर से इकट्ठे किए हुए चीथड़ों का चीवर। a robe made of rags taken from dustbins.

पंसुकूलित – वि॰ – (पांसुल) चीथड़ों का चीवर पहननेवाला। one who wears such robes.

पाक – पु॰ – (पाकः) पकाना, पकाया हुआ। cooking; that which is cooked.

पाकट्ठान – नपु॰ – (पाकस्थानम्) रसोईघर। kitchen.

पाकतिक – नपु॰ – प्राकृतिक, कुदरती, नैसर्गिकी। natural, original.

पाकार – पु॰ – (प्रकारः) चारदीवारी। encircling wall; a rampart.

पाकार-परिक्खित्त – वि॰ – (प्राकार प्रकृष्टः) दीवार से घिरा। surrounded by a wall.

पागब्भिय – नपु॰ – (प्रगल्भ) वाचालता, वाक्पटुता, हिम्मत। boldness; eloquence in speech; impudence; forwardness.

पागुञ्ञता – स्त्री॰ – (प्रगुणता) प्रगुणी, कुशल, प्रवीण, चतुर। experience; cleverness.

पाचक – वि॰ – (पन्चेलुकः) पकाने वाला, रसोईया। one who cooks.

पाचन – नपु॰ – (पाचन) पचन, पकाना, पशु हाँकने की छड़ी, पकाने वाला, पकने वाला। a goad.

पाचरिय – नपु॰ – (प्राचार्यः) प्राचार्य। teacher's teacher.

पाचापेति – क्रिया – (पक्वेति) बकवाना। to cause to cook.

पाचिका – स्त्री॰ – (पाचिका) पकाने वाली। female cook.

पाचित्तिय – (प्राचित्तिय) विनयपिटक का एक ग्रन्थ। a book of Vinaya Piṭaka.

पाचीन – वि॰ – (प्राचीन) पूर्वीय। eastern.

पाचीन-दिसा – स्त्री॰ – (प्राचीन दिशा) पूर्व दिशा। the east.

पाचीन-मुखा – वि॰ – (प्राची-मुखम्) पूर्वदिशा विमुख। facing the east.

पाचेति – क्रिया – (पक्वेति) पकवाता है। to cause to cook.

पाजन – नपु॰ – (प्राजनः) हाँकना, driving.

पाजेति – क्रिया – (प्राजेतिः) हाँकना। to drive, to lead.

पाटल – वि॰ – (पाटलम्) गुलाबी। pale and red, pink.

पाटलिपुत्र – (पाटलिपुत्रम्) मगध की प्राचीन राजधानी (पटना)। name of a city in Magadha (present Patna).

पाटली – पु॰ – (**पाटलिः**) पृक्ष विशेष, पादर का फूल। the trumpet and flower tree.

पाटव – पु॰ तथा नपु॰ – (**पाटवम्**) पटु-भाव, दक्षता, कौशल। skill.

पाटिकङ्ख – वि॰ – (**प्रतिक्षणम्**) आशान्वित। to be desired or expected.

पाटिकङ्खी – वि॰ – (**प्रतिक्षित**) आशा करने वाला। one who desires or expects.

पाटिका – स्त्री॰ – (**पातिका**) अर्धगोलाकार, चन्द्रप्रस्तर। half-moon stone at the entrance of a building or at the base of a flight of steps.

पाटिकुल्य – नपु॰ – (**प्रतिकूल**) प्रतिकूलत। loathsomeness.

पाटिपद – पु॰ – (**प्रतिपदा**) चन्द्रमास के शुक्ल पक्ष का प्रथम दिन। the first day of a lunar fortnight.

पाटिभोग – पु॰ – (**प्रतिभूः**) प्रतिभूति जिम्मेदार, जमानत देने वाला। a sponsor; a surety; bail security.

पाटियेक्क – वि॰ – (**प्रत्येक**) पृथक्-पृथक्, separate; single.

पाटिहार – नपु॰ – (**प्रतिहारः**) करिश्मा, ऐन्द्रजालिक, जादूगरी-चाल। miracle; an extraordinary event.

पाटेक्क – प्रत्येक, single.

पाठ – पु॰ – (**पाठः**) ग्रन्थ-विशेष का अनुच्छेद, पाठ। a passage; text reading.

पाठक – वि॰ – (**पाठकः**) पाठ करने वाला। reciter, one who reads.

पाठीन – पु॰ – (**पाठीनः**) मछली का एक प्रकार। a kind of fish.

पाण – पु॰ – (**प्रणः**) जीवन, साँस, प्राणी। life; breath; a living being.

पाण-घात – पु॰ – (**प्राण-घातः**) प्राणी-हत्या। killing; slaying life.

पाण-घाती – पु॰ – (**प्राण-घाती**) जीव हत्या करने वाला। one who destroys life.

पाणद – वि॰ – (**प्राणप्रद**) प्राण-रक्षक, जीवन देने वाला। one who preserves life.

पाण-भूत – पु॰ – (**प्राणधारः**) जीवित प्राणी। a living being.

पाण-वध – पु॰ – (**प्राण-आघातः**) जीव-हत्या। destruction of life.

पाण-सम – वि॰ – (**प्राण-प्रिय**) प्राण के समान। dear as life.

पाण-हर – वि॰ – (**प्राणहर**) प्राण हरण करने वाला। one who takes away life.

पाणक – पु॰ – (**प्राणकः**) जीवनधारी जन्तुय कीड़ा। an insect.

पाणि – पु॰ – (**पाणिः**) हाथ, हथेली। the hand; the palm.

पाणि-तल – नपु॰ – (**पाणिः**) तलमय, हाथ की हथेली। the palm of the hand.

पाणिग्गह – पु॰ – (**पाणिः ग्रहणम्**) विवाह करना। marriage.

पाणिका – स्त्री॰ – (**पाणिका**) हाथ जैसी वस्तु, तौलिया। a hand-like thing; a towel.

पाणी – पु॰ – (**प्राणीः**) प्राणी। living being.

पातु – पु॰ – (**पातः**) गिरना, फेंकना। a fall, a throw.

पातन – नपु॰ – (**पातनम्**) गिराना, फेंकना। bringing to fall; throwing down; killing.

पातब्ब – कृदन्त – (**पानकम्**) पीने योग्य। fit to drink.

पातरास – पु० – (प्रतराशः) कलेवा, सुबह का नाश्ता। morning meal.

पाताल – पु० – (पातालम्) पृथ्वी के नीचे का भाग, पाताललोक। an abyss; proclivity; the other side of the earth.

पाति – स्त्री० – (पात्रम्) थाली। a bowl; a dish.

पातिक – नपु० – (पात्रिकम्) तश्तरी। a small dish.

पाती – वि० – (पातिन्) फेंकने वाला, छोड़ने वाला। one who throws or shoots.

पातु – अव्यय – (पातुः) सामने, दिखाई देने वाला, प्रकट। visible, in front, manifest.

पातुकम्म – नपु० – (प्रतिकमन्) प्रकट करना। making visible.

पातुकरण – नपु० – (प्रतिकर्मन्) प्रकट करना। making visible.

पातुमाव – पु० – (प्रादुर्भाव) प्रकट होना। appearance, coming into manifestation.

पातुमूत – कृदन्त – (प्रादुमूर्त) प्रकट हुआ। appeared.

पातुकम्यता – वि० – (पिपासति) पीने की इच्छा। desire to drink.

पातुकरोति – क्रिया – (प्रादुर्भवति) प्रकट होना। to manifest.

पातुकरि – (प्रादुष्करणं) प्रकट किया। to manifest.

पातुकाम – वि० – (पिपासु) पीने की इच्छा वाला। desirous of drinking.

पातुभवति – क्रिया – (प्रादुर्भवति) प्रादुर्भूत होता है, प्रकट होता है। to appear.

पातुं – (पातुम्) पीने के लिए जल। drinking water.

पातेति – क्रिया – (पातेतिख) गिराना, फेंकना। to fall; to throw off.

पातो – अव्यय – (प्रातःकालः) प्रातःकाल। in the morning.

पातोव – अव्यय – (प्रतार) सुबह, सवेरे, तड़के। right early.

पाथेय्य – नपु० – (पाथेयम्) रास्ते के लिए खुराकी। provision for a journey.

पाद – पु०, नपु० – (पादः) पाँव, टाँग, पैर, किसी लम्बाई का चौथा हिस्सा, किसी छन्द की चार पंक्तियों में से एक। the foot; leg; one fourth of any measure or of a stanza.

पादक – वि० – (पादक्) आधार-सहित, नींव वाला। having feet or a basis.

पादकञ्भवन – नपु० – (पादकः ध्यान) साधार ध्यान-भावना। meditation forming a basis.

पाद-कठलिका – स्त्री० – (पाद-कष्टिका) पैर रगड़ने के लिए लकड़ी। a wooden block to wash feet on.

पादङ्गुट्ठ – नपु० – (पादङ्गुष्ठः) अंगूठा। the big toe.

पादङ्गुलि – स्त्री० – (पादङ्गुलि) पंजा। a toe.

पाद-तल – (पादतलम्) पाँव का तल्ला, तलवा। the sole of the foot.

पाद-परिचारिका – स्त्री० – (पाद-परिचारिका) पत्नी। a wife.

पाद-पीठ – नपु० – (पाद-प्रतिष्ठानम्) पाँव रखने की चौकी। a foot-stool.

पाद-पुंछन – नपु० – (पाद-पुंछकम्) पाँव पोंछने का कपड़ा। a matting for wiping feet.

पाद-मूले – (पाद-मूले) चरणों में। at the feet.

पाद-मूलिक – पु॰ – (पाद-मूलिकः) नौकर। a servant; one who sits at one's feet.

पाद-सम्बाहन – नपु॰ – (पाद-सम्बाहनम्) पैरों का दबाना। massaging of feet.

पादप – पु॰ – (पादपः) वृक्ष। a tree.

पादुका – स्त्री॰ – (पादुकः) खड़ाऊँ। a slipper or shoe.

पाददूर – पु॰ – (पादूदरः) साँप। a snake.

पादोदक – पु॰ – (पादोदकम्) पाँव धोने का जल। water for washing feet.

पान – नपु॰ – (पानम्) पीना, पेय पदार्थ। drinking, a drink.

पानक – नपु॰ – (पानागारः) सुरापान करने का स्थान (पानागार)। a drinking booth.

पानीय – नपु॰ – (पानीयम्) पानी, पेय पदार्थ। water; beverage.

पानीय-घट – पु॰ – (पानीय-घटम्) पानी का घड़ा। water pot; pitcher.

पानीय-थालिका – स्त्री॰ – (पानिलम्) पीने का प्याला। drinking cup.

पानीय-भाजन – नपु॰ – (पानीय भाजनम्) पीने का बर्तन। drinking vessel.

पानी-साला – स्त्री॰ – (पानीय) शालिका, प्याऊ। a hall where drinking water is kept.

पाप – नपु॰ – (पाप) अकुशल-कर्मय। sin; evil.

पाप-कम्म – नपु॰ – (पाप-कर्म) अपराध। पाप-कर्म, crime, evil action.

पाप-कम्मन्त – वि॰ – (पापिन्) पापी। an evil-doer; a villain.

पापकर (पापकारी) – वि॰ – (पापकारिन्) पापी। sinful; wicked.

पापक-करण – नपु॰ – (पापकृत) दुष्कर्म करना। committing sin.

पाप-धम्म – वि॰ – (पापअधम) पापी, अत्यन्त दुष्ट। of evil character or habits.

पाप-मित्र – पु॰ – (पाप मित्रः) बुरा दोस्त। bad companion.

पाप-मित्रता – स्त्री॰ – (पाप मित्रता) कुसंगति। association with wicked people.

पाप-सङ्कप्प – पृ॰ – (पाप-सङ्कल्प) बुरे विचार। evil thought.

पाप-सुपिन – नपु॰ – (पाप-स्वपनः) बुरा सपना। an evil dream.

पापक – वि॰ – (पापिन्) पापी। wicked; sinful.

पापणिक – पु॰ – (प्रापणिकः) दुकानदार। a shopkeeper.

पापिका – स्त्री॰ – (पापिनी) पापिन। feminine of *pāpaka* (पापक)।

पापित – कृदन्त – (पापिन्) जिसने बुरा किया हो। sinful.

पापिमन्तु – वि॰ – (पापमति) पाप करने वाला। a sinner, the wicked one.

पापियो – वि॰ – (पापीयस्) तुलनात्मक रूप से बड़ा पापी। comparatively bigger sinner.

पापुणन – नपु॰ – (प्रापणम्) प्राप्ति, पहुँच। attainment; arrival.

पापुणाति – क्रिया – (प्रापणाति) पहुँचाता है। to reach; to attain.

पापुरण – नपु॰ – (प्रच्छादनम्) ओढ़ना, कम्बल। a cover; blanket.

पापुरति – क्रिया – (प्रच्छेदति) लपेटना, ओढ़ना। to cover, to wrap with.

पापेति – क्रिया – (प्राप्णोति) पहुँचाना, प्राप्त करना। to let go to; to cause to reach or attain.

पामत – नपुं॰ – (प्राभृतम्) भेंट, उपहार। a present.

पाम – नपुं॰ – (पामन्) खुजली। a skin disease.

पामगङ् – नपुं॰ – (प्रालम्बम्) छाती पर बांधने की पट्टी। waistband.

पामुज्ज – नपुं॰ – (प्रमुद) प्रसन्नता, आनन्द। delight; joy.

पामेति – क्रिया – (प्रमित) तुलना करना। to compare with.

पामोक्ख – वि॰ – (प्रमुख) मुख्य, प्रधान। chief; first.

पाय – वि॰ – (प्रायः) भरा हुआ (समास में)। for the most part, mostly.

पायक – वि॰ – (पायकः) चुसनेवाला या पीने वाला। one who sucks or drink.

पायास – पु॰ – (पायस्) दूध की खीर। rice cooked in milk.

पायेति – क्रिया – (पायेति) चुसवाना, पिलाना। to make one suck or drink.

पार – नपुं॰ – (पार) (नदी के) पार, दूसरा तट। the opposite shore; the other side.

पार-गत – वि॰ – (पारगामिन्) पार पहुँचा हुआ। one who has gone to the end or the other shore.

पार-गवेसी – वि॰ – (पारगवेषी) उस पार जाने का इच्छुक। looking for the final end or the other shore.

पार-गामी – पु॰ – (पारगामिन् (पारणू)) उस पार जाने वाला। one going to the other shore.

पारग् – वि॰ – (पारग्ङत) उस पार पहुँचा हुआ। gone beyond.

पारलौकिक – वि॰ – (पारलौकिक) परलोक सम्बन्धी। connected with the other world.

पारद – पु॰ – (पारदः) पारा। quick-silver.

पारदारिक – पु॰ – (पारदारिकः) व्यभिचारी, परायी स्त्री के पास जाने वाला। adulterer.

पारमिता – स्त्री॰ – (पारमिता) पूर्णता, पार पहुँचा हुआ। completeness, perfection.

पारम्परिय – नपुं॰ – (पारम्परीय) परम्परा, tradition.

पाराजिक – वि॰ – भिक्षुओं द्वारा किये जा सकने वाले चार प्रधान दोषों में से किसी एक का दोषी। one who has committed the gravest transgression of the rules for bhikshus.

पारापत (पारावत भी) – पु॰ – (पारावतः) कबूतर। a pigeon.

पारायन – नपुं॰ – (परिचर्या) प्रधान उद्देश्य। chief object.

पारिचरिया – स्त्री॰ – (परिचर्या) सेवा-सुश्रूषा। service.

पारिच्छत्तक – (पारिजातः) त्रयोत्रिंश देवलोक के नन्दनवन में उगा हुआ वृक्ष, मूँगे का पेड़। the coral tree.

पारिपन्थिक – वि॰ – (पारिपंथिकः) खतरनाक लुटेरा, डाकू। threatening; a highwayman.

पारिपूरि – स्त्री॰ – (**परिपूर्तिः**) पूर्ति, सम्पूर्णता। fulfilment; completion.

पारिम – वि॰ – (**परिसारः**) इधर-उधर, आगे। yonder; farther.

पारिभोगिक – वि॰ – (**परिमुक्त**) उपयोग में लाने योग्य या लाया हुआ। fit for use; used.

पारन्त – कृदन्त – (**परिवृत्त**) ओढ़ा हुआ। of to cover up.

पारूपति – क्रिया – (**परिवेष्ठति**) ओढ़ाता है, पहनता है। to wrap in; to veil.

पारोह – पु॰ – (**परोहः**) वट-वृक्ष की भाँति किसी पेड़ की शाखा से लटकाने वाली दाढ़ी। fork of a tree, a root descending from a branch (like that of a banyan tree).

पाल – पु॰ – (**पालक**) संरक्षक। guard; keeper; protector.

पालक – नपुं॰ – (**पालकः**) पालनेवाला। संरक्षक, protector.

पालन – नपुं॰ – (**पालनम्**) संरक्षण। protection; guarding.

पालि – स्त्री॰ – (**पालिः**) पंक्ति, बौद्ध त्रिपिटक अथवा त्रिपिटक की भाषा। a line; the canon of the Buddhist writings or the language in which it is written.

पालिच्च – नपुं॰ – (**पालित्यम्**) सिर के बालों की सफेदी। greyness of hair.

पालेतु – पु॰ – (**पालयित**), पालनेवाला, संरक्षक। protector.

पावक – पु॰ – (**पावकः**) अग्नि, fire.

पावचन – नपुं॰ – (**प्रवचन**), बुद्धोपदेश। the scriptures.

पावस्सि – स्त्री॰ – (**प्रावृष्**) वर्षा। rain.

पावार – पु॰ – (**प्रावरः**) चोगा, उत्तरीय वस्त्र। a cloak; mantle.

पावारिक – पु॰ – (**प्रावारिकः**) चोगा बेचने वाला। cloak-seller.

पावुस – पु॰ – (**प्रावृषः**) वर्षा ऋतु। rainy season.

पावुस्सक – वि॰ – (**प्रावृषिक**) वर्षा ऋतु सम्बन्धी। belonging to the rainy season.

पास – पु॰ – (**पाशः**) फंदा, जाल। a sling; a snare.

पासक – पु॰ – (**पाशकः**) पासा। a die; a throw.

पासण्ड – नपुं॰ – (**पाषंडः**) मिथ्या दृष्टि। heresy.

पासण्डिक – पु॰ – (**पाषंडः**) मिथ्या-दृष्टिवाला, पाखण्डी। a heretic; sectarian.

पासाण – पु॰ – (**पाषाण**) पत्थर, चट्टान। a stone; rock.

पासाण-चेतिय – नपुं॰ – (**पाषाण चैत्यः**) पत्थर का देवालय या चैत्य। a shrine made of stone.

पासाण-लेखा – स्त्री॰ – (**पाषाण-लेखः**) चट्टान पर उत्कीर्ण लेख। rock inscription.

पासाद – पु॰ – (**प्रासादः**) महल। a mansion; palace.

पासाद-तल – नपुं॰ – (प्रासाद-तलम्) महल का ऊपरी तल्ला। an upper storey or floor (of a mansion).

पासादिक – वि॰ – (प्रेयस) प्रिय, प्रियकर, अच्छा लगनेवाला। pleasing; lovely.

पि – अव्यय – पि, अपि, भी। also; and also; even so.

पिक – पु॰ – (पिकः), कोयल। a cuckoo.

पिङ्गल – वि॰ – (पिंगल) ताम्र-वर्ण। brown; tawny.

पिङ्गल-नेत्र – वि॰ – (पिंगल अक्षः) पिंगल-वर्ण नेत्रोंवाला। having red eyes.

पिङ्गल-मक्खिका – स्त्री॰ – (पिङ्गल-मक्षिका) गोमक्खी। gadfly.

पिचु – नपुं॰ – (पिचुः) कपास, रूई। cotton.

पिचु-पटल – (पिचु-तलम्) कपास की तह। a film of cotton.

पिच्छ – नपुं॰ – (पिच्छम्) मोर का पिछला पंख। tail-feather of peacock.

पिच्छिल – वि॰ – (पिन्छिल) फिसलने वाला। slippery.

पिञ्ज – नपुं॰ – (पिञ्जः) पक्षियों का पिछला भाग। tail of a bird.

पिञ्जर – वि॰ – (पिञ्जरकम्) रक्त वर्ण। of a reddish colour.

पिटक – नपुं॰ – (पिटकः) पिटारी, सन्दूक, पालि त्रिपिटक में से कोई एक पिटक। a basket; a container; one of the three main divisions of Pāli canon.

पिटकधर – वि॰ – (पिटकधरः) जिसे समस्त पिटक कण्ठस्थ हों। one who knows the Piṭakas by heart.

पिट्ठ – नपुं॰ – (पृष्ठकम्) पीठ, पीछे का हिस्सा। the back.

पिट्ठ-खादनीय – नपुं॰ – (पिष्टिक) आटे की मिठाई। sweets made of flour.

पिट्ठ-पिण्डी – स्त्री॰ – (पिष्ट-पिण्डः) आटे की पिण्डी। a lump or ball of flour.

पिटिठ – स्त्री॰ – (पृष्ठकम्) पीठ। the back.

पिटिठ-कण्टक – नपुं॰ – (पृष्ठमास्थि) रीढ़ की हड्डी। the backbone.

पिटिठ-गत – वि॰ – (पृष्ठतोगम्) किसी पशु या अन्य की पीठ पर चढ़ना। riding on an animal or on someone's back.

पिटिठ-पस्स – नपुं॰ – (पृष्ठतस्) पिछला हिस्सा। the hind part.

पिटिठ-मंसिक – वि॰ – (पृष्ठमदन्) चुगलखोर। backbiter.

पिटिठ-वंस – (पृष्ठ-वंशः) पीठ की हड्डी, इमारत की कोई शहतीर। a back verandah.

पिठर – पु॰ – (पिठरः) मिट्टी का बड़ा मटका। a big jar.

पिण्ड – पु॰ – (पिंडम्) आधर-पिंड। a lump; a lump of food.

पिण्ड-चारिका – वि॰ – (पिण्ड-पातिकः) भिक्षाटन करने वाला। one who goes to collect alms.

पिणिड – स्त्री॰ – (पिंडि) गुच्छा। a cluster; bunch.

पिणिडयालोप-भोजन – नपुं॰ – (पिण्डकः) भिक्षाटन से प्राप्त भोजन। food received through collecting alms.

पितामह – पु॰ – (पितामहः) पितामह, दादा। grandfather.

पितिक – वि॰ – (पितृक) जिसका पिता है। having a father.

पिति-पक्ख – पु॰ – (पितृ-पक्षः) पिता की ओर से। father's side.

पितु – पु॰ – (पितृ) पिता। father.

पितु-किच्च – नपुं॰ – (पितृ-कार्यम्) पिता का कर्त्तव्य। duty of a father.

पितु-घात – नपुं॰ – (पितृ-द्रव्यम्) पिता की सम्पत्ति। father's possession.

पितुच्छा – स्त्री॰ – (पितृष्वसृ) पिता की बहन, बुआ, फूफी। father's sister.

पितुच्छा-पुत्त – पु॰ – (ष्वस्त्रीय) फूफी का लड़का। aunt's son.

पित्त – नपुं॰ – (पित्तम्) पित्त, पित्तदोष। the bile.

पित्ताधिक – वि॰ – (पित्तल) जिसमें पित्त का बाहुल्य हो। bilious.

पिदहन – नपुं॰ – (पिधानम्) बन्द करना, ढँकना। to be closed.

पिघान – नपुं॰ – (विधानम्) ढक्कन। a lid, a cover

पिपासा – स्त्री॰ – (पिपासा) प्यास। thirst.

पिपासित – कृदन्त – प्यासा। thirsty.

पिपिल्लिका (पिपीलिका) – स्त्री॰ – (पिपीलः) चींटी। an ant.

पिप्फुली – स्त्री॰ – (पिप्पलः) पिप्पली। long pepper.

पिय – वि॰ – (प्रिय) प्यारा। dear.

पियकम्मता – स्त्री॰ – (प्रियकर्मन्) प्रिय वस्तुओं की या स्वयं प्रिय बनने की इच्छा। desire for dear things or to become dear.

पियतर – वि॰ – (प्रियतर) अधिक प्रिय, more dear.

पियतम – वि॰ – (प्रियतम्) सर्वाधिक प्रिय। most dear.

पिय-दस्सन – वि॰ – (प्रियदर्शन) देखने में प्यारा। good-looking.

पिय-रूप – नं॰ – (प्रियरूप) आकर्षक रूप। an enticing object of sight.

पिय-वचन – नपुं॰ – (प्रिय-वचन) मीठी बोली। a term of endearment.

प्रिय-भाणी – वि॰ – (प्रिय-वादिन्) मधुर वचन भापी। speaking pleasantly.

पियवादी – वि॰ – (प्रियंवाद) मीठा बोलने वाला। sweet spoken.

पिययिपपयोग – पु॰ – (प्रिय-विप्रयोग) प्रिय से विछोह। separation from the beloved.

पियङ्गु – पु॰ – (पियङ्गु) दवाई में काम आने वाला पौधा-विशेष। medicinal plant.

पियता – स्त्री॰ – (प्रियता) प्रियभाव। belovedness.

पिया – स्त्री॰ – (प्रिया) पत्नी। the wife.

पंललक्ख – पु॰ – (प्रियालः) अंजीर फग पेड़। wave-leaved big tree.

पिलवति – क्रिया – (प्लवति) तैरना। to float; to swim.

पिवन – नपुं॰ – (पी) पीना। to drink.

पिसति – क्रिया – (पिषति) पीसना। to grind, to crush.

पिसन – नपु – (पिष्) पीसना। grinding.

पिसाच, पिसाचक – पु॰ – (पिशाचः) भूत। पिशाच, a goblin or spirit.

पिसित – नपुं॰ – (पिशितम्) मांस। flesh.

पिसुण – नपुं॰ – (पिशुण) चुगली। slander, malicious speech.

पिसुणावाचा – स्त्री॰ – (पिशुण-वचनम्) चुगलीखोरी। malicious speech.

पिहक – नपु॰ – (प्लीहा) तिल्ली। the spleen.

पिहयति – क्रिया – (स्पृह्यति) इच्छा करना। desire.

पिहायना – स्त्री॰ – (स्पृहणम्) प्रिय करना, desire.

पिहित – कृदन्त – (पिहित) ढँका हुआ। covered.

पिंसति – (पिसति) पिष्टति, पीसना। to grind.

पीठ – नपु॰ – (पीठम्) आसन्। a small chair, a seat.

पीठक – न॰ – (पीठ/पीठक) बैठने का पीढ़ा या आसन। a small chair, a seat, a small bench.

पीठ-जातक – (जा॰ सं॰ 337) – कथा बतलाती है कि उपयुक्त अवसर पर किया गया कार्य ही फलदायी होता है, समय से पहले या समय के बीत जाने पर किया गया कार्य नहीं। the story (No. 337) tells that only the action done at the proper time is fruitful and neither the early nor the late performance.

पीठ-सप्पी – पु॰ – (पीठ-सर्पी) कुर्सी के सहारे सरकने-पहुँचने वाला, लूला-लँगड़ा। a cripple.

पीठिका – स्त्री॰ – (पीठिका) बैठने का पीढा या आसन। a small chair or bench.

पीणन – पु॰ – (प्रीणन) संतोष। satisfaction.

पीणेति – क्रिया – (√ प्री = प्रीणति/प्रीणेति) प्रसन्न करता है, सन्तुष्ट करता है। gladdens, pleases.

पीत – कृदन्त – (√ पा + क्त = पीत) पिया हुआ। drunk.

पीत – वि॰ – (पीत) पीला, पीला रंग। yellow, yellow colour.

पीतक – वि॰ – (पीतक) पीत वर्ण वाला, पीले रंग का। of yellow colour.

पीतन – न॰ – (पीतन) पीत रंजक। yellow pigment.

पीति – स्त्री॰ – (प्रीति) प्रसन्नता, आनन्द। joy, delight, emotion.

पीति-पामोज्ज – न॰ – (प्रीति-प्रामोद्य) प्रसन्नता तथा आनन्द। joy, pleasure.

पीति-भक्ख – वि॰ – (प्रीति-भक्ष्य) प्रीति ही आहार हो जिसका। love-seeking.

पीति-मन – वि॰ – (प्रीति-मन) प्रसन्नचित्त। of glad heart, exhilarated.

पीति-रस – पु॰ – (प्रीति-रस) प्रीति-रस। taste or emotion of joy.

पीति-सम्बोझङ्ग – पु॰ – (प्रीति-सम्बोध्यङ्ग) प्रीति-सम्बोधिका (प्रीति) अङ्ग। the joy constituent of enlightenment.

पीति-सहगत – वि॰ – (प्रीति-सहगत) accompanied by joy.

पीण – वि॰ – (पीन) मोटा, फूला हुआ। fat, swollen, bloated.

पील – (चु॰) – (बाधाय) पीड़ा देना। to oppress, to harm.

पीळक – वि॰ – (पीडक) पीड़ा देने वाला। (न॰) फोड़ा-फुन्सी, फफोला। oppressing, one who oppresses, (n.) a boil.

पीळन – न॰ – (पीडन) पीड़न, त्रास, पीड़ा। injury, damage.

पीळा – स्त्री॰ – (पीडा) पीड़ा। oppression.

पीळेति – क्रि॰ – (√पीड् = पीड्यति) पीड़ित करता है। oppresses.

पुक्कस/पुक्कुस – पु॰ – (पुक्कुष/पुरषिक) बुद्धकालीन एक निम्न जाति के लोग जो कूड़ा और मैला साफ करते थे। a lower caste which was called to remove dirty or waste material at the time of Buddha.

पुग्गल – पु॰ – (पुद्गल) पुद्गल व्यक्ति, व्यष्टि। an individual.

पुग्गलपञ्ञत्ति – स्त्री॰ – (पुद्गल-प्रज्ञप्ति) पुद्गलों का वर्गीकरण (नाम) अभिधम्म पिटक के सात प्रकरणों में से चौथा प्रकरण। classification of individuals, the fourth amongst the seven chapters of Abhidhamma Piṭaka.

पुग्गलिक – वि॰ – (पुद्गालिक) व्यक्तिगत। individual, personal.

पुङ्ख – न॰ – (पुडाख) तीर का पंख वाला हिस्सा। the feathered part of an arrow.

पुङ्गव – पु॰ – (पुडाशव) वृषभ, श्रेष्ठ पुरुष। a bull, a noble person.

पुचिमन्द – पु॰ – (निम्ब-तरु) नीम का वृक्ष। the margosa tree, anadirachta Indica.

पुचिमन्द-जातक – (जा॰ सं॰ 311) – नीम के वृक्ष पर रहने वाले वृक्ष-देवता द्वारा लूट का माल लाए चोरों को भगा देने की कथा। a story relates to tree-god who drove away the thieves who had brought the stolen goods.

पुच्चण्ड – न॰ – (पूति + अण्ड = पूत्यण्डम्) सड़ा हुआ अण्डा। a rotten egg.

पुच्चण्डता – स्त्री॰ – (पूति + अण्डता –

पूत्यण्डता) अण्डे की सड़ाँध। staleness of rotten egg.

पुच्छ – न॰ – (पुच्छ) पूँछ। a tail.

√पुच्छ – (भू॰) – (पृच्छने) पूछना। to ask.

पुच्छक – पु॰ – (पृच्छक) प्रश्न पूछने वाला। one who asks question, questioner.

पुच्छति – क्रि॰ – (पृच्छति) पूछता है, प्रश्न करता है। asks question.

पुच्छन – न॰ – (पृच्छन) पृच्छा, पूछना। the act of questioning.

पुच्छा – स्त्री॰ – (पृच्छा) प्रश्न। question.

पुज्ज – वि॰ – (पूज्य) पूज्य, गौरवाह। adorable, respectful.

√पुञ्छ – (भू॰) – प्रोक्षणे, पोंछना। to wipe, to clean.

पुञ्छति – क्रि॰ – (प्र √उक्ष = प्रोक्षते) पोंछता है, साफ कर देता है। wipes off, cleans.

पुञ्छन – न॰ – (प्रोक्षणम्) झाड़न, पोंछने का वस्त्र। duster, a cloth for wiping.

पुञ्छनी – स्त्री॰ – (प्रोक्षणी) पोंछने का छोटा वस्त्र, तौलिया। a towel, a small cloth for washing.

पुञ्ज – पु॰ – (पुञ्ज) ढेर। a heap, pile.

पुञ्जकत – वि॰ – (पुञ्जीकृत) ढेरी लगाई हुई। piled, heaped.

पुञ्ञ – न॰ – (पुण्य) शुभ कृत्य, पुण्य। merit, righteousness.

पुञ्ञ-कम्म – न॰ – (पुण्य-कर्म) शुभ कार्य, पुनीत कार्य। meritorious act.

पुञ्ञ-काम – वि॰ – (पुण्य-काम) पुण्य चाहने वाला। desirous of merit.

पुञ्ज-किरिया – स्त्री॰ – (पुण्य-क्रिया) पुनीत क्रिया, पवित्र कर्म। good action, pious deeds.

पुञ्जक्खन्ध – पु॰ – (पुण्य-स्कन्ध) पुण्य-स्कन्ध, पुण्यों का ढेर। a mass of merit.

पुञ्जक्खय – पु॰ – (पुण्य-क्षय) पुण्य का क्षय, पुण्य की हानि। decrease or reduction of merit.

पुञ्जपेक्ख – वि॰ – (पुण्य पेक्षी) पुण्य की अपेक्षा रखने वाला। expecting merit, aspiring for merit.

पुञ्ज-फल – न॰ – (पुण्य-फल) पुण्य का फल। the result of meritorious action.

पुञ्ज-भाग – पु॰ – (पुण्य-भाग) पुण्य का भाग। share of merit.

पुञ्ज-भागी – वि॰ – (पुण्य-भागी) पुण्य भाजन, पुण्य का भागीदार। sharer of merit.

पुञ्ज-वन्त – पु॰ – (पुण्यवान) पुण्यकर्मी, पुण्यवान। possessing merit.

पुञ्जानुभाव – पु॰ – (पुण्यानुभाव) पुण्य का प्रताप। the power of merit.

पुञ्जामिसन्द – पु॰ – (पुण्य + अभिष्यन्द) पुण्यों का राशिकरण। accumulation of merit.

√पुट – (चु॰) – (भेदने) तोड़ना। to break.

पुट – पु॰न॰ – (पुट) पत्तों का दोना। a container (usually made of leaves).

पुटबद्ध – वि॰ – (पुट-बद्ध) दोने में बँधा हुआ। bound as a parcel.

पुट-भत्त – न॰ – (पुट-भक्त) भात का दोना, रास्ते के लिए खाने का पैकेट। a parcel of boiled rice, a lunch packet.

पुट-भेदन – न॰ – (पुट-भेदन) दोनों का खोलना। opening of packages.

पुटक – न॰ – (पुटक) पत्तों का दोना। a basket made of leaves.

पुटदूसक-जातक – (जा॰ सं॰ 280) – पत्तों के दोनों को नष्ट करने वाले बन्दर की कथा। the story (No. 280) of a monkey who destroyed the lunch packets.

पुट-भत्त-जातक – (जा॰ सं॰ 219) – एक राजकुमार की कथा जिसने अपने भात के दोने में से अपनी भार्या को भात नहीं दिया। the story (No. 219) of a prince who did not give food from his lunch packet to his wife.

पुट्ठ – कृदन्त – (√पृच्छ + त = पुष्ट) पूछा गया। asked or questioned by.

पुण – (तु॰) – (शुभ कर्मणि) धर्म-कृत्य करना। to observe righteous deeds.

पुणाति – क्रि॰ – (√पू = पुनाति) शुद्ध करता है, साफ करता है। purifies, cleans.

पुण्डरीक – न॰ – (पुण्डरीक) श्वेत-कमल। white lotus, lily.

पुण्ण – कृदन्त – (पूर्ण) सम्पूर्ण। complete, full.

पुण्ण-घट – पु॰ – (पूर्ण घट) पूरा भरा हुआ घड़ा। a full pitcher.

पुण्ण-चन्द – पु॰ – (पूर्ण-चन्द्र) पूर्णमासी का चन्द्रमा। the full moon.

पुण्ण-पत्त – न॰ – (पूर्ण पात्र) उपहार, पूर्ण-पात्र, भेंट। a gift or present.

पुण्ण-भासी – स्त्री॰ – (पूर्णमासी) पूर्णिमा। full moon.

पुण्णनदी-जातक – (जा॰ सं॰ 241) – शत्रुओं द्वारा कान भरे जाने पर राजा द्वारा निष्कासित निर्दोष पुरोहित को पुनः अभिमंत्रित किए जाने की कथा। the story (No. 241) is related to the recall of a brāhmaṇa who was exiled by the king listening to his enemies.

पुण्ण पाति-जातक – (जा॰ सं॰ 53) – शराब के भरे रहने की कथा। astonishing story (No. 53) of wine-pitchers which remained always full.

पुण्णता – स्त्री॰ – (पूर्णता) पूर्णत्व, पूर्णता। fullness, perfection.

पुण्णमी – स्त्री॰ – (पूर्णिमा) पूर्णमासी। full-moon day.

पुत्त – पु॰ – (पुत्र) पुत्र, बेटा। a son, a child.

पुत्तक – पु॰ – (पुत्रक) छोटा बेटा। little son, younger son.

पुत्त-दार – पु॰ – (पुत्र-दार) पुत्र तथा पत्नी। wife and son.

पुत्त-धीतु – स्त्री॰ – (दुहिता पुत्री) बेटा-बेटी। son and daughter.

पुत्तिम – वि॰ – (पुत्रमान) पुत्रवाला। having children.

√पुथ – (तु॰) – (विस्तारे) फैलाना। to spread.

पुथु – अव्यय – (पृथक) पृथक-पृथक, व्यक्तिगत, दूर-दूर। separated in individual capacity.

पुथुज्जन – पु॰ – (पृथक्-जन) नीच, पामर। people of low class.

पुथु – वि॰ – (पृथु) विपुल, विस्तृत, प्रभूत। broad, wide spread.

पुथु-भूत – वि॰ – (पृथु-भूत) सर्वत्र फैला हुआ। widely spread.

पुथु-लोम – पु॰ – (पृथु-लोम) मछली की एक विशेष जाति। a kind of fish having broad fins.

पुथुक – न॰ – (पृथुक) (1) चिउड़ा (2) जानवर का बच्चा। (1) flattened rice (2) young of an animal.

पुथुल – वि॰ – (पृथुल) चौड़ा, विशाल। broad, large, wide.

पुथुवी – स्त्री॰ – (पृथिवी) पृथ्वी। the earth.

पुथुसो – क्रि॰ वि॰ – (पृथुशः) उल्टी तरह से अलग-अलग। diversely separated.

पुन – अव्यय – (पुनः) फिर। again.

पुन-दिवस – पु॰ – (पुनर्दिवस) अगले दिन। the following day.

पुनप्पुनं – अव्यय – (पुनः पुनः) बार-बार। again and again.

पुनब्भव – पु॰ – (पुनर्भव) पुनर्जन्म। birth in a new existence, re-incarnation.

पुनवचन – न॰ – (पुनर्वाचन) दोहराना। repeating, reiterate.

पुनरुत्ति – स्त्री॰ – (पुनरुक्ति) दुहराना, पुनरुक्ति। repetition.

पुनागमन – न॰ – (पुनरागमन) फिर आना। coming again.

पुनाति – (पुनाति) देखें – पुणाती। see Punāti.

पुनेति – क्रि॰ – (पुनः + एति = पुनरेति) फिर आना। comes again.

पुन्नाग – पु॰ – (पुन्नाग) जायफल का पेड़। nutmeg tree.

√पुफ्फ – (भू॰) – (विकसने) फूलना। to blossom.

पुप्फ – न॰ – (पुष्प) (1) पुष्प (2) मासिक धर्म, अर्त्तव। (1) flower, (2) the menstrual flux.

पुप्फ-गच्छ – पु॰ – (पुष्प-गच्छ) फूलने वाला पौधा। a flowering plant.

पुप्फ-गन्ध – पु॰ – (पुष्प-गन्ध) फूलों की सुगन्धि। fragrance of flowers.

पुप्फ-चुम्बटक – न॰ – (पुष्प-स्तबक) फूलों का गुच्छा। a bouquet of flowers.

पुप्फ-छड्डक – वि॰ – (पुष्प-क्षेपक) कुम्हलाए फूलों को फेंकनेवाला, पाखाना साफ करने वाला। remover of withered flowers or rubbish.

पुप्फ-दाम – पु॰ – (पुष्प-दाम) पुष्प-माला, फूलों की माला। a garland of flowers, a chaplet.

पुप्फ-धर – (पुष्प-धर) फूलदार। bearing flowers.

पुप्फ-पट – पु॰ न॰ – (पुष्प-पट) बेल-बूटेदार कपड़ा। a cloth embroidered with flowers.

पुप्फ-मुट्ठि – पु॰ – (पुष्प-मुष्टि) फूलों की मूठी। a handful of flowers.

पुप्फ-रासि – पु॰ – (पुष्प-राशि) फूलों का ढेर। a heap of flowers.

पुप्फवती – स्त्री॰ – (पुष्पवती) रजस्वला, पुष्पवती, मासिक धर्मवाली स्त्री। a woman during her menstruation.

पुप्फ-रत्त-जातक – (जा॰ सं॰ 147) – स्वामी ने स्त्री की इच्छा पूरी करने के लिए राजा के केसर-बाग में से केसर चुराने का प्रयत्न किया, पकड़ा गया। the story tells (No. 147) how a husband was arrested when trying to steal saffron from the royal garden to fulfil the desires of his wife.

पुप्फति – क्रि॰ – (पुष्पायते) पुष्पित होता है, फूलता है। flowers, blossoms.

पुब्ब (1) – पु॰ – (पूय/पूति) घाव में पड़ने वाली पीप। pus, viscid, matter from an abscess.

पुब्ब (2) – वि॰ – (पूर्व) (1) पहला (2) पूरब (दिशा)। (1) former, (2) the east.

पुब्बन्त – पु॰ – (पूर्वान्त) (1) अतीत काल (2) पूर्व का सिरा (छोर)। (1) the past (2) the former or earlier end.

पुब्ब-कम्म – न॰ – (पूर्व-कर्म) पूर्व जन्म का कर्म। a deed done in a former existence.

पुब्ब-किच्च – न॰ – (पूर्व-कृत्य) पहले या पूर्व जन्म में किए गए कर्म। the former deeds.

पुब्ब-किच्च – न॰ – (पूर्व-कृत्य) आरम्भिक कार्य। preliminary function.

पुब्बङ्गम – वि॰ – (पूर्वङ्गम) पूर्वगामी। going at the head, preceding.

पुब्ब-चरित – न॰ – (पूर्व-चरित) पूर्व-चरित (जीवन)। former life story.

पुब्ब-देव – पु॰ – (पूर्व-देव) प्राचीन देवता-गण। ancient gods.

पुब्ब-निमित्त – न॰ – (पूर्व निमित्त) पूर्व-लक्षण। preliminary symptoms.

पुब्ब-पुरिस – पु॰ – (पूर्व पुरुष) पूर्व-पुरुष, पुरखा। the ancestor.

पुब्ब-पेत – पु॰ – (पूर्व प्रेत) पूर्व प्रेत। a deceased spirit.

पुब्बङ्ग – पु॰ – (पूर्वाङ्ग) पहला हिस्सा। former part.

पुब्ब-योग – पु॰ – (पूर्व योग) पूर्व सम्बन्ध। a former connection.

पुब्ब-विदेह – पु॰ – (पूर्व-विदेह) पूर्वीय महाद्वीप का नाम। the name of the eastern continent.

पुब्बण्ह – पु॰ – (पूर्वाह्ण) पूर्वाह्ण, दोपहर से पहले। fore-noon.

पुब्बन्न – न॰ – (पूर्वान्न) चावल, गेहूं आदि सात प्रकार के धान। the name given to seven kinds of cereals such as rice, wheat, etc.

पुब्बा – स्त्री॰ – (पूर्वा) पूर्व। the east.

पुब्बा-चरिय – पु॰ – (पूर्वाचार्य) पूर्वाचार्य, प्रथमाचार्य। the first teacher.

पुब्बापर – वि॰ – (पूर्वापर) पहले का और बाद का। former and latter.

पुब्बाराम – पु॰ – (पूर्वाराम) श्रावस्ती के पूर्व ओर स्थित उद्यान। अनाथपिंडिक के घर पर भोजन कर चुकने के अनन्तर भगवान बुद्ध इसी उद्यान में विश्राम किया करते थे। a park outside the eastern-gate of Śrāvastī, in which the Buddha used to take rest after taking meals at the house of Anāthapiṇḍika.

पुब्बुट्ठायी – वि॰ – (पूर्व + उत्थायी) किसी दूसरे से पहले उठने वाला। getting up beofe anyone else.

पुब्बे – अव्यय – (पूर्वे) पहले, पूर्व काल में। formerly, in the past.

पुब्बेकत – वि॰ – (पूर्वकृत) पूर्वकृत, पिछले जन्म में किए गए कर्म। deeds formerly done.

पुब्बे-निवास – पु॰ – (पूर्व-निवास) पूर्व जन्म, पूर्व योनि। one's former state of existence.

पुब्बे-निवास-आण – न॰ – (पूर्व-निवास-ज्ञान) पूर्वजन्म का ज्ञान। knowledge of one's former state of existence.

पुब्बे-निवासानुस्सति – स्त्री॰ – (पूर्व-निवास अनुस्मृति) पूर्व जन्म की स्मृति। memory of one's former state of existence.

पुम – पु॰ – (पुमान्) पुरुष। a male, a man.

पुर – न॰ – (पुर) नगर या शहर। a town or city.

पुरक्खत – कृदन्त – (पुरस्कृत) पुरस्कृत, सम्मानित। rewarded, honoured, esteemed.

पुरक्खरोति – क्रि॰ – (पुरस्करोति) पुरस्कृत करता है, सम्मानित करता है। rewards, honours.

पुरतो – अव्यय – (पुरतः) आगे, सामने। in front of, before.

पुरत्था – अव्यय – (पुरत्र) पूर्व दिशा। the east.

पुरत्थाभिमुख – वि॰ – (पूर्वाभिमुख) पूर्वाभिमुख। looking eastward.

पुरत्थिम – वि॰ – (पुरश्चिम) पूर्व दिशा। eastern.

पुरा – अव्यय – (पुरा) पहले, अतीत काल में। formerly, in the past.

पुराण – वि॰ – (पुराण) प्राचीन। the ancient.

पुराण-दुतियिका – स्त्री॰ – (पुराण द्वितीयका) जो पहले पत्नी रही हो (खासकर किसी भिक्षु की)। former wife (chiefly of a Bhikkhu).

पुराण-सालोहित – वि॰ – (पुराण-सलोहित) पूर्व का रक्त-सम्बन्धी। former blood relation.

पुरातन – वि॰ – (पुरातन) प्राचीन । ancient.

पुरिन्दद – पु॰ – (पुरन्दर) इन्द्र । an epithet for the king of Devas.

पुरिम – वि॰ – (पुरिय) पूर्व का, पहला । former, earlier.

पुरिम जाति – स्त्री॰ – (पूर्व/प्रथम जाति) पूर्वजन्म । previous birth.

पुरिमतर – वि॰ – (पुरिमतर) प्रथमतर, पूर्वतर । before formerly.

पुरिमत्तभाव – पु॰ – (पुरिमत्तभाव) पूर्व जन्म । previous birth.

पुरिस – पु॰ – (पुरुष) पुरुष, आदमी । a male, a man.

पुरिसकार – पु॰ – (पुरषकार) पुरषत्व । manliness.

पुरिस-थाम – पु॰ – (पुरुष सत्व) पुरुष-सामर्थ्य । manly strength.

पुरिस-दम्म – पु॰ – (दम्य पुरुष) शैक्ष्य मनुष्य । a person to be trained or converted.

पुरिस-दम्म-सारथी – पु॰ – (दम्य पुरुष सारथी) शैक्ष्य मनुष्यों का सारथी, बुद्ध । a guide of men the Buddha.

पुरिस-परक्कम – पु॰ – (पुरुष-पराक्रम) पौरुष, पुरुष पराक्रम । manly effort.

पुरिस-मेध – पु॰ – (पुरुष-मेध) नरबलि, मानव बलि । human sacrifice.

पुरिस-लिङ्ग – पु॰ – (पुरुष-लिङ्ग) पुरुष का द्यौतक, पुरुषेन्द्रिय । the male organ.

पुरिस-व्यञ्जन – (पुरुष-व्यञ्जन) पुरुषेन्द्रिय । the male organ.

पुरिसाजञ्ञ – पु॰ – (पुरुष श्रेष्ठ) a remarkable man.

पुरिसादक – पु॰ – (पुरुषादक) नरभक्षी, मनुजाद, आदमखोर । a cannibal, a man-eater.

पुरिसाधम – पु॰ – (पुरुषाधम) अधम पुरुष, नीच आदमी । a wretched-man, a person of mean mentality.

पुरिसिन्द्रिय – न॰ – (पुरुषेन्द्रिय) पुरुष-भाव । male faculty, masculinity.

पुरिसुत्तम – पु॰ – (पुरुषोत्तम) श्रेष्ठतम पुरुष । the highest of men.

पुरे – क्रि॰ वि॰ – (पुरे) पूर्व, पूर्वतर । before, formerly.

पुरेचारिक – वि॰ – (पुरोगामी) आगे-आगे चलने वाला । front runner.

पुरेजव – वि॰ – (पुरोजब) आगे-आगे दौड़ने वाला । running ahead.

पुरेतरं – क्रि॰ वि॰ – (पूर्वतरम्) अन्य सबसे आगे या पहले । before anyone else, most early.

पुरेभत्त – न॰ – (कल्यवर्त्त) सबेरे का नाश्ता, कलेवा । breakfast.

पुरेक्खार – पु॰ – (पुरस्कार) पुरस्कार, आगे बढ़ाना, आदर करना, भक्ति करना । honour, pushing forward, devotion.

पुरेजात – वि॰ – (पूर्वजात) पूर्वोत्पन्न । born before hand.

पुरोगामी – पु॰ – (पुरोगामी) आगे चलने वाला । one who is marching ahead.

पुरोहित – पु॰ – (पुरोहित) पुरोहित । a king's religious adviser, chaplain, family priest.

√पुल – चु॰ – (महत्तायाम) ऊँचा होना । to rise, to go high.

√पुल – चु० – (समुञ्चये) ढेर करना। to heap.

पुलवक – पु० – कीड़ा। a worm.

पुलिन – न० – (पुलिन) रेतीला तट, रेत। sand, a sandy bank.

√पुस – (भू०) – (पोषणे) पालन-पोषण करना। to nourish, to look after.

√पुस – चु० – (पोषणे) पालन-पोषण करना। to bring up, to take care of.

√पू – भि० – (पवित्रकरणे) पवित्र करना। to purify.

√पू – भू० – (पावनकरणे) पवित्र करना। to purify.

पूग – पु० – (पूग) व्यावसायिक परिषद, (न) ढेर। a guild, corporation.

पूग-रुक्ख – पु० – (पूगवृक्ष) सुपारी का पेड़। the arecanut palm.

√पूज – चु० – (पूजायाम) पूजना। to worship.

पूजना – स्त्री० – (पूजा) पूजा, भक्तिपूर्ण, भेंट। veneration, homage, devotion, offering.

पूजनेय्य – वि० – (पूजनीय) पूजा योग्य। entitled to homage.

पूजिय – वि० – (पूज्य) पूज्य। adorable.

पूजिय-मान – कृदन्त – (पूज्यमान) सम्मानित या पूजित किया जाता हुआ। being adored.

पूजित – कृदन्त – (पूजित) सम्मानित, गौरवान्वित। adored, honoured esteemed.

पूजेति – क्रि० – (√पूज = पूजयति ⁄ ते) पूजा करता है। (पूजेन्त, पूजियमान, पूजेत्वा)। honours, respects.

पूति – वि० – (पूति) पीब, सड़ा हुआ, दुर्गन्ध-युक्त। (f) pus, (a) rotten, putrid, stinking.

पूति-काय – पु० – (पूति-काय) पबीयुक्त, गन्दा शरीर। a body which contains foul substances.

पूति-गन्ध – पु० – (पूति-गन्ध) पीब की दुर्गन्ध, गन्दगी। smell of a stinking object.

पूति-मच्छ – पु० – (पूति-मत्स्य) सड़ी मछली। rotten fish.

पूति-मुख – वि० – (पूति-मुख) दुर्गन्ध-युक्त। मुँह वाला। having a putrid mouth.

पूति-मुत्त – न० – (पूति-मूत्र) गो-मूत्र। urine of a cow.

पूति-लता – स्त्री० – (पूति-लता) पोय नामक लता, जिसका साग खाया जाता है। a kind of creeper.

पूतिक – वि० – (पूतिक) सड़ा हुआ। rotten.

पूति-मंस-जातक – (जा० सं० 437) – एक शृगाल द्वारा बकरियों को साजिश से मारकर खाने की कथा। the story of a jackal who performed a device for killing the goats one by one and eating them.

पूय – न० – (पूय) अपूय, पुआ। a sweet cake.

पूपिय – पु० – (पूप-विक्रेता) पुए बेचने वाला। cake-seller.

पूय – पु० – (पूय) पीब, पीप। pus.

√पूर – भू० – (पूरणे) पूरा करना, भरना। to fill up.

पूर – वि० – (पूर) पूर्ण। full, full of.

पूरक – वि० – (पूरक) पूर्ति करने वाला। one who fills, supplier.

पूरा-पेति – क्रि॰ – ($\sqrt{}$ पूर + णिच = पूरयति) पूर्ण करता है। (पूरायेसि, पूरापित, पूरा-पेत्वा)। causes to make full.

पूरेति – क्रि॰ – ($\sqrt{}$ पूर = पूरयति) पूर्ति करता है। makes full.

पूव – पु॰ न॰ – (पूव) अपूप, पुआ। sweet cake.

पूविक – पु॰ – (थूप-विक्रेता) पुए बेचने वाला। dealer in cake.

पेक्खक – वि॰ – (प्रेक्षक) देखने वाला। one who is looking, observer.

पेक्खण – न॰ – (प्रेक्षण) दृश्य देखना। seeing sight.

पेक्खति – क्रि॰ – (प्रेक्षते) देखता है। sees, looks at.

पेखुण – न॰ – (मयूर-पुच्छ) कलाय, मोर-पंख। a peacock's tail feather.

पेच्च – अव्यय – (प्रेत्य) मरणान्तर। after death.

पेटक – न॰ – (पिटक) टोकरी, पिटारी (वि) पिटक सम्बन्धी। (1) basket (2) relating to Piṭaka.

पेत – वि॰ – (प्रेत) मृत (पु) भूत-प्रेत। dead, departed, a ghost.

पेत-किच्च – न॰ – (प्रेत-कृत्य) अन्त्येष्टि। funeral, rites.

पेत-योनि – स्त्री॰ – (प्रेत-योनि) प्रेत योनि। in ghost form, in the state of ghost.

पेत-लोक – पु॰ – (प्रेत-लोक) प्रेत-लोक। realm of goblins.

पेत-वत्थु – न॰ – (प्रेत-वस्तु) (1) प्रेत-कथा (2) खुद्दक निकाय का सातवाँ ग्रन्थ जो प्रेत लोक की कथाओं से सम्बन्धित

है। (1) ghost story (2) the seventh booklet of the Khuddaka-Nikāya which contains the story of ghosts.

पेत्तिक – वि॰ – (पैतृक) पैतृक। paternal.

पेत्तणिक – वि॰ – पिता की सम्पत्ति पर जीने वाला। one who lives on father's property.

पेत्ति-विसय – पु॰ – (पितर-लोक) पितरलोक। the world of dead creatures.

पेत्तेय्य – वि॰ – (पितृ-भक्त) पिता का सम्मान करने वाला। respecting one's father.

पेत्तेय्यता – स्त्री॰ – (पितृ-भक्ति) पितृ-भक्ति। devotion towards father.

पेम – न॰ – (प्रेम) प्रेम। love, affection.

पेमनीय – वि॰ – (प्रेम-पात्र) प्रेम-पात्र। affectionate, amiable.

पेय्य – वि॰ – (पेय) पीने योग्य (न) पेय पदार्थ। drinkable, a drink.

पेय्यवज्ज – न॰ – (प्रिय वचन) प्रिय वाणी। loving speech.

पेय्याल – न॰ – (पेय्याल) बीच में से वाक्यांश छोड़ दिये रहने का संकेत। 'पेय्याल' शब्द 'पर्याय' का मागधी रूप है। यह निर्देश करता है कि पूर्वोक्त अंश की पुनः आवृत्ति की जाय। an indication to show that a passage has been omitted, here (follows) the formula (paryāya).

$\sqrt{}$ पेल – भू॰ – (चलने) चलता है। to walk, to move.

पेलक – पु॰ – (शशक) खरगोश। a hare, a rabbit.

पेलव – न॰ – (पेलव) कोमल, बारीक। slender, soft, thin.

पेसक – पु॰ – (प्रेषक) प्रेषक, भेजने वाला, नौकर। sender, one who attends.

पेसकार – पु॰ – (पेशस्कार √पिंश – पिंशति) वस्त्रों पर कढ़ाई या जरदोजी करने वाला, सजावट करता है। an embroider, skill in embroidery.

पेसन – न॰ – (प्रेषयाम) भेजना। sending out.

पेसन-कारक – पु॰ – (प्रेषणक) नौकर। a servant.

पेसल – वि॰ – (पेशल) सदाचरण-युक्त, कुशल। well behaved, skilful.

पेसि/पेसिका – स्त्री॰ – (पेशि) मांस-पेशी। muscle, the foetus in the third stage.

पेसित – कृदन्त – (प्रेषित) प्रेषित, भेजा गया। sent out.

पेसीयति – क्रि॰ – (प्रेष्यते) भेजा जाता है। is being sent.

पेसुण – न॰ – (पिशुन) चुगलखोरी, चुगली खाना। backbiting, slandering.

पेसुण-कारक – वि॰ – (पिशुन कारक) चुगलखोर। a backbiter, a slanderer.

पेसुणिक – पु॰ – (पैशुनिक) चुगलखोर, निन्दक। slanderer, backbiter.

पेसुञ्ञ – न॰ – (पैशुन्य) पिशुनता, चुगली, निन्दा। slander, calumny, backbiting.

पेसेति – क्रि॰ – (प्रेषयति) भेजता है। sends out, sends forth, sends for.

पेस्स – पु॰ – (प्रेष्य) नौकर अथवा दूत। a servant or a messenger.

पेसिक/पेसिय – पु॰ – (प्रेष्य) भेजे जाने योग्य व्यक्ति, नौकर, दूत। a servant, a messenger.

पेत्ठा – स्त्री॰ – (पेटा, पेड़ा) पेटी, पेटिका, बाक्स। a box, a container.

पोक्खर – न॰ – (पुरष्कार) इन्दीवर, नीलकमल। blue lotus.

पोक्खरता – पु॰ – (पुष्करता) सौन्दर्य। beauty.

पोक्खर-पत्त – न॰ – (पुष्कर पत्र) कमल-पत्र। lotus leaf.

पोक्खर-मधु – न॰ – (पुष्कर-मधु) कमल-मधु। the honey sap of lotus.

पोक्खर-बस्स – न॰ – (पुष्कर-वर्षा) ओलों की वृष्टि, पुष्प-वर्षा। rain of flowers, snowfall, a snow rain.

पोक्खरणी – स्त्री॰ – (पुष्करिणी) तालाब। a pond, an artificial pool.

पोङ्ख – (पुङ्ख) देखें पुङ्ख। see Puṅkha.

पोटगल – पु॰ – (काश) काश नामक घास और उसका फूल। यह घास वर्षा ऋतु की समाप्ति पर फूलती है। a kind of grass flowering at the end of the rainy season.

पोट्ठ-पाद – पु॰ – (प्रोष्ठपाद) भाद्रपद मास, भादौं का महीना। भगवान् बुद्ध के साथ आत्म-विषयक प्रश्न पूछने वाला परिब्राजक। (1) name of a month, (August/September) (2) a hermit who had a discussion with the Buddha about the soul.

पोठन – न॰ – (स्फोटन) पीटता है, चोट पहुँचाता है। ऊँगलियाँ चटखाता है। (पोठेसि, पोठित, पोठेत्वा)। beats, strikes, snaps.

पोठेति – क्रि॰ – (पीडयति) पीटता है, चोट पहुँचाता है। beats, strikes.

पोण (1) – वि॰ – (दान्त) दन्त खोदनी। a toothpick.

पोण (2) – वि॰ – (प्र + अव + नमित) झुका हुआ। sloping down, bent.

पोत – पु॰ – (पोत) (1) जानवर का बच्चा (2) कोपँल (3) नौका। (1) the young of an animal (2) a sprout or offshoot (3) a ship, a boat.

पोतक – पु॰ – (पोतक) जानवर का बच्चा। the young of an animal.

पोतिका – स्त्री॰ – (पोतिका) जानवर का मादा बच्चा। the female young of an animal.

पोतवाह – पु॰ – (पोतवाह) नाविक। a sailor.

पोत्थक – पु॰ न॰ – (पुस्तक) पुस्तक, फलक, जिस पर चित्र बनाया जाय। a book, a canvas for painting on.

पोत्थनिका – स्त्री॰ – (छुरिका) कटारी, बर्छी। a dagger.

पोत्थलिका – स्त्री॰ – (पुत्तलिका) गुड़िया। a doll made of canvas.

पोत्थुज्जनिक – वि॰ – (पृथुजनिक) सामान्य आदमी से सम्बन्धित। relating to ordinary man.

पोथियमान – कृदन्त – (ताड्मान) पिटता हुआ। having been beaten.

पोथेति – क्रि॰ – (स्फोटयति) देखें पोठेति। see Potheti.

पोनोभविक – वि॰ – (पौनर्भविक) पुनर्भव का कारण। cause leading to rebirth.

पोराण – वि॰ – (पुराण) प्राचीन, पुराकालिक, पुराना। ancient, old, former.

पोराणक – वि॰ – (पौराणिक) (1) प्राचीन, पुराकालिक (2) पुराण ग्रन्थों से सम्बन्धित। (1) ancient, of ancient age (2) relating to or belonging to Purāṇas.

पोरिस – न॰ – (पौरुष) पुरुषत्व, पुरुष से सम्बन्धित। manliness belonging to a man.

पोरिसाद – वि॰ – (पुरुषाद) मनुजाद, मानव-भक्षी, आदमखोर। a man-eater.

पोरी – पु॰ – (पौर) नागर, नागरिक, शहरी, शिष्ट। urban, polite.

पोरोहिच्च – न॰ – (पौरोहित्य) पुरोहित, कर्म। duties or deeds of a purohita.

पोस – वि॰ – (पोष्य) जिसका पोषण किया जाए। worthy of being nourished, one who deserves nourishment.

पोसक – वि॰ – (पोषक) पोषण करने वाला। one who brings up, nourishes or feeds.

पोसिका – स्त्री॰ – (पोषिका) पोषण करने वाली, दायी। a nurse, the woman by whom a child is looked after, fed and brought up.

पोसथ – (व्रतोपवास) देखें उपोसथ। see Uposatha.

पोसथिक – पु॰ – (व्रतोपवासी) उपोसथ व्रत करने वाला। one who observes fasting.

पोसन – न॰ – (पोषण) पालन-पोषण। nourishing, feeding.

पोसावनिक – न॰ – (पोषण पारिश्रमिक) पालने-पोसने का खर्चा। fee for bringing somebody up, allowance.

पोसित – कृदन्त – (पुष + क्त = पोषित) पोषण किया गया, पाला गया। brought up, nourished.

पोसेति – क्रि॰ – (√पुष = पुष्यति/ पुष्णाति) पोसता है, पोषण करता है। nourishes, brings up, takes care of.

प्लव – पु॰ – (प्लव) बेड़ा, डोंगी, उड़ुप। a sheep, a raft, a small boat, asnare to catch fish.

प्लवन – न॰ – (प्लवन) कूदना, तैरना। jumping, floating.

प्लवङ्गम – पु॰ – (प्लवङ्गम) बन्दर। a monkey.

√प्लु – (भू॰) – (गमनार्थे) जाना। to go.

फ

फ – पालि वर्णमाला का बाइसवाँ व्यञ्जन। the 22nd consonant of Pāli alphabet.

फग्गव – पु॰ – (**फाल्गव**) गूलर के पेड़ में उत्पन्न होने वाली गोदिया (फली), शाक का एक प्रकार। the unripe fruits of a fig tree used as a vegetable.

फग्गु – पु॰ – (**वै॰ फल्गु**) व्रत-काल, निराहार रहने का समय। a period of fasting.

फग्गुण – पु॰ – (**फाल्गुन**) महीने का नाम, फाल्गुण, फागुन। name of a month (February-March).

फग्गुणी – स्त्री॰ – (**फाल्गुनी**) फाल्गुनी नक्षत्र दो हैं (1) पूर्वा फाल्गुनी (2) उत्तरा फाल्गुनी। name of a constellation.

√ **फण** – (**भू॰**) – (**पसरणे**) व्याप्त होना। to pervade.

फण – पु॰ – (**फण**) साँप का फन। the hood of a snake.

फणक/फनक – न॰ – (**फणक**) साँप के फन जैसा। shaped like a snake's hood.

फणिज्जक – न॰ – (**समीरण**) उशीर नामक घास जिसे अवधी में गँड़रा कहते हैं। a fragrant, grass named anaropogon nuricatum.

फणिज्जक – पु॰ – (**फणिज्जक**) (1) समीरण (2) जम्बीर विशेष। a kind of lemon.

फणी/फनी – पु॰ – (**फणिन**) सर्प। snake.

फन्द – (**भू॰**) – (**स्पन्दने/किञ्चित चलने/स्फुरणे**) धड़कना-हिलना। to tremble, to throb.

फन्दति – क्रि॰ – (**स्पन्दति**) काँपता है, धड़कता है। trembles, throbs, beats (heart).

फन्दन – न॰ – (**स्पन्दन**) धड़कन, स्पन्दन, हिलना-डुलना। throbbing, motion, agitation, beating.

फन्दना – स्त्री॰ – (**स्पन्दन**) स्पन्दन। throbbing.

फन्दन-जातक – (जा॰ सं॰ 475) – वृक्ष के नीचे पड़े शेर पर शाखा टूट पड़ने से उसके आहत होने की कथा। the story (No. 475) of lion who got injured by the falling of a branch of a tree under which he was lying.

फन्दित – न॰ – (**स्पन्दित**) प्रकम्पित, क्षुब्ध। trembled, agitated.

√ **फर** – भू॰ – (**प्रसरणे**) व्याप्त होना। to pervade.

फरण – न॰ – (**प्रसरण**) व्याप्ति। pervading, suffusion.

फरणक – न॰ – (**प्रसरणक**) व्याप्त। suffusing, filling with.

फरति – क्रि॰ – (प्र √ सृ = प्रसरति) व्याप्त होता है, पूरा करता है। pervades, suffuses, fills.

फरसु – पु॰ – (**परशु**) कुल्हाड़ी, फरसा। axe, hatchet.

फरुस – वि॰ – (**परुष**) परुष, कठोर। rough, harsh.

फरुस-वचन – न॰ – (**परुष-वचन**) कठोर वचन। harsh speech, rough talk.

फरुसा-वाचा – स्त्री॰ – **(परुषा–वाचा)** कठोर वचन। a harsh talk, rough speech.

√**फल** – भू॰ – **(फलने)** फल आना। to bear fruits.

फल – न॰ – **(फल)** (1) फल, परिणाम। (2) चाकू आदि का फलक। (1) fruit, nut, result, consequence (2) the blade of knife or weapon.

फल-चित्त – न॰ – **(फल-चित्त)** मार्ग आदि का फल। the fruits or benefit of following the path.

फलट्ठ – वि॰ – **(फलस्थ)** फल स्थित। steadfast in the enjoyment of the path.

फलत्थिक – वि॰ – **(फलार्थी)** फलार्थी। looking for fruit.

फलदायी – वि॰ – **(फलदायी)** फल देने वाला, लाभप्रद। fruitful, advantageous.

फलरुह – वि॰ – **(फल वृक्ष)** फल देने वाला पेड़। fruit-giving tree.

फलवन्तु – वि॰ – **(फलवान)** फलदार। bearing or having fruits.

फला-फल – न॰ – **(फलाफल)** नाना प्रकार के फल। various kinds of fruits.

फलासव – पु॰ – **(फलासव)** फलों का आसव। extract of fruits.

फल-जातक – (जा॰ सं॰ 54) – जंगल में से गुजरते हुए सार्थवाह द्वारा अपने कारवाँ को उसकी अनुमति बिना किसी फल-फूल को न खाने का निर्देश देने की कथा। the story (No. 54) of a troop leader who, when passing through a jungle with his caravan forbade his companions not to eat any fruit or flower without his permission.

फलक – न॰ – **(फलक)** बख्ता, ढाल। a board, a plank, a shield.

फलति (1) – क्रि॰ – **(फलति)** फल देता है। bears fruit.

फलति (2) – क्रि॰ – **(√दृ = तृणाति)** फाड़ता है। splits, tears.

फली – पु॰ – **(फलिन)** फलदार वृक्ष। bearing fruit, fruit producing plant, tree with fruit.

फलु – न॰ – **(वै॰ परु)** सरकण्डे की गाँठ। a knot or a joint in a reed.

फलु-बीज – न॰ – **(बीज-फल)** गाँठ। knot.

फस्स – पु॰ – **(स्पर्श)** स्पर्श। touch, contact.

फस्सेति – क्रि॰ – **(√स्पर्श = स्पृशति)** स्पर्श करता है, प्राप्त करता है। touches, obtains, attains.

फलु – न॰ – **(पादप-ग्रन्थि)** बाँस आदि की गाँठ। a node produced in a plant (like bamboo tree).

फटिक्कम – न॰ – **(प्राति कम्मं)** देखें पाटिकम्म। see Pātikamma (restoration).

फाणित – न॰ – **(फाणित)** शीरा से बना, सिरका। vinegar.

फाणित-पुट – पु॰ – **(फाणित-पुट)** सिरका का पात्र। a container of vinegar.

फाति – स्त्री॰ – **(स्फीति)** बढ़त, समृद्धि, बढ़ोतरी। growth, increase, prosperity.

फत्थ – (भू॰) – **(स्फीतर्थे)** बढ़ना। to prosper, to grow.

फारुसक – न॰ – **(फारुसक/पारुषक)** गिरि पीलु, फालसा नामक पौधा और उसका फल। a small fruit of *Grewie Asiatica* tree.

फाल – पु॰ – **(फाल)** हल का फाल। a ploughshare.

फालक – पु॰ – (फालक) फाड़ने वाला या तोड़ने वाला । one who splits or breaks.

फालन – न॰ – (फालन) फाड़ना । splitting.

फालेति – क्रि॰ – (फालयति) फाड़ता है, तोड़ता है । breaks, splits.

फासु – पु॰ – (वै. प्राशु) सुवास, आसानी, आराम, वि॰ आरामदेह । comfort, ease, (adj) comfortable.

फासुक – वि॰ – (वै. प्राशुक) सुखद, आसान । pleasant, convenient.

फासुका/फासुलिका – स्त्री॰ – (वै. पाशुका) पसली । ribs.

फासु-पाश – (प्राशु-प्राशु) जाल । a snare, a sling, a net.

फीत – वि॰ – (स्फीत) स्फीत, समृद्ध । opulent, prosperous.

फिथ – न॰ – (नौ दण्ड/क्षेपणी) चप्पू पतवार । oar, fishing net, sling for hurling stones.

फुट – (स्पृष्ट) व्याप्त । pervaded, spread.

फुटन – न॰ – (स्फुटन) चीरना, फाड़ना । splitting, tearing off.

फुट्ठ – कृदन्त – (स्पृष्ट) स्पृष्ट । touched, attained.

फुल्ल – कृदन्त – (फुल्लित) पूर्ण रूप से खिला हुआ । fully blossomed.

फुसति – क्रि॰ – (√ स्पृश = स्पृशति) स्पर्श करता है, पहुँचता है, प्राप्त करता है । touches, reaches, attains.

फुसन – न॰ – (स्पृशन) स्पर्श करना । touching.

फुसना – स्त्री॰ – (स्पर्शना) स्पर्श, छुवन । touching.

फुसित/फुसितक – न॰ – (पृशित) बुन्दीदार, चित्तीदार । spotted, with dots.

फुर – (तु॰) – (स्फुरणे) चलने, फडकना । to tremble.

फुल्ल – (भू॰) – (विकसने) फूलना । to flower, to blossom.

फुसीयति – क्रि॰ – स्पर्श किया जाता है । is being touched.

√ फुस – तु॰ – (संस्पर्शे) छूना । to touch.

फुस्स – पु॰ – (पुष्य/पोष) नक्षत्र विशेष, पौष-मास । name of a month December-January, name of constellation.

फुस्स-रथ – पु॰ – (पुष्य-रथ) राज्यरथ, राज्य का उत्तराधिकारी खोज निकालने के लिए छोड़ा गया रथ । a state carriage running on its own accord in order to find an heir.

फुस्स-राग – पु॰ – (पुष्पराज) पुष्पराज, पुखराज । topaz.

फेगु – न॰ – (फल्गु) बल्कल, बक्कल, छाल । bark, wood surrounding the pith of a tree.

फेण – न॰ – (फेन) झाग । foam.

फेण-पिन्ड – पु॰ – (फेन-पिण्ड) झाग-पिण्ड । a lump of foam.

फेणुद्देहक – वि॰ – (फेनोद्धेजक) झाग उठाता हुआ । raising up foam.

फेणिल – पु॰ – (फेनिल) झाग देने वाला वृक्ष अर्थात् रीठा का पौधा । soap-nut tree.

फोट – पु॰ – (स्फोट) फोड़ा, फफोला । boil, blister.

फोट्ठब्ब – न॰ – (प्रष्टव्य) स्पर्श का विषय । object of touch or contact.

फोसित – क्रि॰ – (प्र + अक्षित) छिड़का हुआ । sprinkle, sprayed.

ब

ब — पालि वर्णमाला का तेइसवाँ अक्षर (व्यञ्जन) the 23rd consonant of Pāli alphabet.

बक — पु॰ — (बक) बगुला। a crane.

बक-जातक — (जा॰ सं॰ 388) — धोखा देकर बगुला मछलियों को खाता रहा। अन्त में एक केकड़े ने उसकी जान ली। the story (No. 388) of a wily crane who ate all the fish with his deceitful tactic but at last was killed by a crab.

बक-जातक — (जा॰ सं॰ 236) — यह कथा एक धूर्त बगुले की बगुला-भक्ति का आख्यान करती है। the story (No. 236) tells about the deceitful demeanour of a wily crane.

बक-ब्रह्म-जातक — (जा॰ सं॰ 405) — बुद्ध भगवान की बक-ब्रह्म से भेंट का आख्यान। the story (No. 405) relates to the Buddha's visit to Baka Brahma.

बज्झति — क्रि॰ — (√ बन्ध + णिच् = बन्धयति) बँधवाता है। gets captured or caught.

बत्तिंसति — स्त्री॰ — (द्वात्रिंशस्) बत्तीस। thirty-two.

बदर — न॰ — (बदर) बेर का फल। jujube fruit.

बदरमिस्स — वि॰ — (बदरी मिश्रित) mixed with jujube.

बदरा — स्त्री॰ — (बदरा) कपास। cotton.

बदरी — स्त्री॰ — (बदरी) बेर का पेड़। jujube tree (Ziziphus Jujuba).

बदालता — स्त्री॰ — (बदालता) मधुर स्वाद वाली एक लता। a particular creeper of sweet taste.

बद्ध — कृदन्त — (√ बन्ध + क्त = बद्ध) बँधा हुआ, फँसा हुआ, दृढ़। bound, trapped, fastened.

बद्धञ्जलिक — वि॰ — (बद्धाञ्जलिक) हाथ जोड़े हुए। keeping two hollowed palms put together in salutation.

बद्ध-राव — पु॰ — (बद्ध-राव) पकड़े गए या फँसे जानवर की चिल्लाहट। the cry of the trapped or caught animal.

बद्ध-वेर — न॰ — (बद्ध-वैर) दृढ़ वैर। confirmed enmity.

√ बधा — (अ॰) — (बन्धने) बँधाना। to get tied.

√ बधा — (भू॰) — (बन्धने) बाँधना। to tie, to fasten.

बधिर — वि॰ — (बधिर) बहरा। deaf person.

बन्ध — पु॰ — (बन्ध) बन्धन, आसक्ति। bond, fetter, attachment.

बन्धति — क्रि॰ — (√ बन्ध = बध्नाति) बाँधता है। ties, combines, captures.

बन्धन — न॰ — (बन्धन) बन्धन। fetter.

बन्ध-मोक्ख-जातक — (जा॰ सं॰ 120) — राजा ने रानी का कुशल समाचार जानने के लिए युद्ध-भूमि से दूत भेजे। रानी ने सभी दूतों के साथ सहवास किया। This story (No. 120) tells about a queen who sinned with all the messengers sent by the king from battle-field to enquire after her welfare.

बन्धनागार – न॰ – (बन्धनागार) कारागार, जेलखाना। a prison.

बन्धनागार-जातक – (जा॰ सं॰ 201) – दो बच्चों की माता को छोड़ तपस्या करने चले गए पति की कथा। this *Jātaka* tale (No. 201) concludes that no chains are stronger than those of passion.

बन्धनागरिक – पु॰ – (बन्धनागरिक) कैदी। a prisoner.

बन्धव – पु॰ – (बान्धव) सगे-सम्बन्धी, भाई-बन्द। relative, kinsmen.

बन्धापेति – क्रि॰ – ($\sqrt{}$ बन्ध + णिच् = बन्धयति) बँधवाता है। causes to be fettered.

बन्धु – पु॰ – (बन्ध) देखें बन्धव। see Bandhava.

बन्धु-जीवक – पु॰ – (बन्धु-जीवक) बन्धु-जीव, बन्धूक गुल दूपहरिया नामक फूल का पौधा। the china-rose plant (pentapetes phoenicea, a plant with a red flower which opens at mid-day)

बन्धुमन्तु – वि॰ – (बन्धुवान्) रिश्तेदारों वाला। having kinsmen.

बन्धुल – पु॰ – (बन्धुल) कुशीनगर के मल्लों के सेनापति का पुत्र। son of a chieftain of the Mallas in Kuśīnagara.

बप्प – पु॰ – (वाष्प) भाप। steam, tears.

बब्बज – न॰ – (वै॰ बल्बज) यज्ञीय तृणास्तरण (चटाई) बनाई जाने वाली बनकस नामक घास जिससे रस्सी बंटी जाती है। ballaja coarse grass (*Eleusine Indica*) locally called *bankasa* not liked by cattle and used for making strings.

बब्बु-बब्बुक – पु॰ – (बभ्रु) बिलार, बिल्ली। a cat.

बब्बु-जातक – (जा॰ सं॰ 137) – धन की लोभी पत्नी के मरकर चुहिया के रूप में जन्म पाने वाली स्त्री की कथा। story (No. 137) of a wife who, because of her lust for money was reborn as a mouse to enjoy the family treasure.

बरिह – न॰ – (बर्हि) मोर की पूँछ, कलाप। the peacock's tail.

बरिहिस – न॰ – (बर्हिष) दर्भ, कुश नामक घास। *kuśa* grass.

बल – न॰ – (बल) शक्ति, सैनिक शक्ति। strength, power, force.

बलक्कार – पु॰ – (बलात्कार) जबरदस्ती शील भंग, दूसरे की इच्छा के विरुद्ध बलपूर्वक कार्य करना। application of force, doing anything by force, violation of chastity.

बलट्ठ (बलत्थमी) – पु॰ (बलस्थ) सैनिक, सिपाही। a soldier, member of an army.

$\sqrt{}$ बल – (भू) – (प्राणने) श्वास लेना। to breath.

बलन्यास – पु॰ – (बलन्यास) सेना की कतार। the array of an army.

बलवै – अव्यय – (बलात्) प्रबल रूप से। forcefully.

बलाका – स्त्री॰ – (बलाका) सारस, सारस-पंक्ति। a brown crane, a row of cranes.

बलिकम्म – पु॰ – (यज्ञकर्म, बलिकर्म) यज्ञकर्म, आहुति । an oblation.

बलि-पटिग्गाहक – वि॰ – (बलिप्रतिवाहक) आहुति ग्रहण करने वाला । receiving oblation or revenues.

बलिपुट्ठ – पु॰ – (बलि-पुष्ट) कौआ । a crow.

बलिवद्ध – पु॰ – (बलिवर्द) बलीवर्द, वृषभ, बैल । an ox.

बलि-हरण – न॰ – (बलिहरण) कर (टैक्स) उगाहना । tax-collection.

बली – वि॰ – (बली) बलवान, शक्तिशाली । powerful.

बळिटास – (बालश) मछली पकड़ने का काँस । the hook for catching fish.

बव्हाबाध – वि॰ – (बट्वाबाध) रोग-बहुलता । plenty of diseases, full of sickness.

√बह – (भू॰) – (वृद्धौ) बढ़ना । to grow, to increase.

बहल – वि॰ – (बहुल) गाढ़ा, घना, सख्त । dense, thick, hard.

बहलत्ता – न॰ – (बहुलत्त्व) घनत्व, गाढ़ापन । thickness, density, hardness.

बहि – अव्यय – (बहिः) बाह्य, बाहर । outer, external, outside.

बहिगत – वि॰ – (बहिर्मंत) बाहर गया । gone outside.

बहिद्धा – अव्यय – (बहिर्धी) बाहर । outside, outer.

बहि-नगर – पु॰ – (बहिर्नगर) नगर के बाहर, या नगर के बाहर या बाहर का नगर । the outer city or outside the city.

बहि-निक्खमन – न॰ – (बहिःनिष्क्रमण) अभिनिष्क्रमण, बाहर जाना । go out.

बही – अव्यय – (बहिः) बाहर । outside.

बहु – वि॰ – (बहु) बहुत, अनेक । much, many, plenty.

बहुक – वि॰ – (बहुक) अनेक । many, several.

बहुकरणीय – वि॰ – (बहुकरणीय) कार्या-धिक्य ग्रस्त । having much to do.

बहुकार – वि॰ – (बहुकार) बहुत उपयोगी । very useful.

बहुकिच्च – वि॰ – (बहु-कृत्य) कार्या-धिक्य ग्रस्त । extremely busy, too much engaged.

बहुक्खत्तु – वि॰ – (बहु-कृत्वा) अनेक बार । many times.

बहु-जन – पु॰ – (बहुजन) जन समूह । a mass of people.

बहुजागर – वि॰ – (बहु-जागृतिशील) बहुत जागृत । very wakeful.

बहु-धन – वि॰ – (बहुधन) धनी । rich.

बहु-पद – वि॰ – (बहु-पद, बहु-पाद) अनेक पैरों वाला । many footed.

बहु-बीहि – वि॰ – (बहु-ब्रीही) समास का एक भेद, बहुब्रीहि नामक समास । the relative compound.

बहु-भण्ड – वि॰ – (बहु-भाण्ड) बहुत सामान वाला । having abundance of goods.

बहु-भाणी – वि॰ – (बहु-भाषी) मुखर, वाचाल, बहुत बोलने वाला । talkative, garrulous, loquacious.

बहु-भाव – पु॰ – (बहुभाव) बहुत्व का भाव, विपुलता, आधिक्य, प्रचुरता । abundance.

बहु-मत – वि॰ – (बहुमत) बहु मान्य। accepted by many.

बहु-मान – पु॰ – (बहुमान) सम्मान। respect, veneration.

बहु-मानन – न॰ – (बहुमानन) सम्मान, गौरव। respect, veneration.

बहुमानित – वि॰ – (बहु-मानित) सम्मानित। much esteemed.

बहु-वचन – न॰ – (बहुवचन) अनेक वचन। the plural number.

बहु-विध – वि॰ – (बहुविध) अनेक प्रकार का। manifold, multiform.

बहुस्सुत – वि॰ – (बहुश्रुत) बहुश्रुत, पण्डित। very learned, widely known.

बहुत्त – न॰ – (बहुत्व) बहुत्व। multiplicity, manifoldness.

बहुधा – क्रि॰ वि॰ – (बहुधा) नाना प्रकार से। in many ways.

बहुल – वि॰ – (बहुल) विपुल। abundant, frequent.

बहुलता – स्त्री॰ –(बहुलता) बहुत्व। in abundance, in larger quantity.

बहुलत्व – न॰ – (बहुलत्व) बहुत्व। abundance.

बहुलीकत – वि॰ – (बहुलीकृत) अभ्यस्त, प्राय: करके। accustomed, frequently.

बहुलीकरण – न॰ – (बहुलीकरण) लगातार-अभ्यास। continuous practice.

बहुलीकम्म – न॰ – (बहुलीकर्म) सतत् अभ्यास। constant practice.

बहुलीकार – पु॰ – (बहुलीकार) निरन्तर अभ्यास। uninterruptive exercise.

बहुलीकरोति – क्रि॰ – (बहुली करोति) बढ़ाता है। increases.

बहुसो – क्रि॰ वि॰ – (बहुशः) अधिक करके, प्रायः। after, mostly, repeatedly.

बहूपकार – वि॰ – (बहूपकार) बहुत उपकार करने वाला। a very helpful.

बाकुची – स्त्री॰ – (बाकुची) सुवल्ली, सोमराजी नामक पौधा। the plant *Vernonia Anthelminthica*.

बाण – पु॰ – (बाण) बाण, तीर। arrow.

बाणधि – पु॰ – (बाणधि) तूणीर, तरकश। quiver for arrouse.

$\sqrt{}$ बाध – भू॰ – (बाधायां) पीड़ा देना। to obstruct, to oppress.

बाधक – वि॰ – (बाधक) रोकने वाला। obstructionist.

बाधकत्त – न॰ – (बाधकत्व) बाधकता, बाधकत्व। obstructiveness.

बाधति – क्रि॰ – ($\sqrt{}$ बाध = बाधते) बाधक होता है। obstructs, hinders.

बाधन – न॰ – (बाधन) बाधा, रुकावट। obstacle, impediment.

बाधित – कृदन्त – (बाधित) बाधा-युक्त। one who is obstructed, hindered.

बाधेति – क्रि॰ – (बाधयति) बाधा डालता है, दबाता है। obstructs, oppresses.

बारस – वि॰ – (द्वादश) बारह। twelve.

बाराणसी – स्त्री॰ – (वाराणसी) वाराणसी, काशी जनपद की राजधानी। Varanasi was the capital town of Kāśī *mahājanpada* (state) at the time of the Buddha.

बाराणसेय्यक – वि॰ – (वाराणसेय) वाराणसी का वासी, वाराणसी निर्मित। an inhabitant of Varanasi, made in or coming from Varanasi.

बाल – वि॰ – (बाल) आयु में कम, अज्ञानी, अबोध, (पु॰) बच्चा, मूर्ख। (1) young in years, ignorant, foolish (2) (m.) a child, a fool.

बालक – पु॰ – (बालक) बच्चा। a child.

बालता – स्त्री॰ – (बालता) बालत्व, मूर्खता। foolishness, childishness.

बाला – स्त्री॰ – (बाला) लड़की। a girl.

बालिका – स्त्री॰ – (बालिका) बालिका। a girl.

बालिसिक – पु॰ – (बालिशिक) मछली मारने वाला। a fish hunter.

बाल्य – न॰ – (बाल्य) बचपन, मूर्खता। childhood, folly.

बावीसति – स्त्री॰ – (द्वा+विंशति) बाईस। twenty-two.

बावेरु-जातक – (जा॰ सं॰ 331) – वाराणसी से बावेरु (बेबीलोनिया) गए व्यापारियों की कथा। the story (No. 331) of merchants of Varanasi who had gone to Bāveru (Babylonia) in connection with their trade.

बाहा – स्त्री॰ – (बाहु) बाजू खम्भा, मूठ। arms, a post, handle.

बाह-बल – न॰ – (बाहु–बल) बाहुबल। power of the arms, muscle power.

बाहित – कृदन्त – (बाह्यकृत/बाहिष्कृत) बाहर रखा, दूर रखा। kept out, kept at a distance.

बाहिर – वि॰ – (बाह्य) बाहरी। external, outer.

बाहिर – अव्यय – (बाहिर) बाहर की ओर, वि॰ बाहर वाला। outside.

बाहिरे – अव्यय – (बहिर) बाहर। outside.

बाहिरक – वि॰ – (बहिरक) दूसरे मत का। of another faith, outsider.

बाहिरक-पब्बज्जा – स्त्री॰ – (बाह्य प्रव्रज्या) दूसरे मतों के अनुसार प्रव्रज्या। ceremony according to another faith.

बाहिरत्त – न॰ – (बाह्यत्त्व) बाहर का भाव। exteriority.

बाहिय-जातक – (जा॰ सं॰ 108) – अपनी प्रकृति कौशल से एक गँवारु महिला के पटरानी पद पर पहुँचने की कथा। the story (No. 108) relates to a rustic woman who by her natural skill became the chief queen of the king.

बाहु – पु॰ – (बाहु) बाँह, बाजू। arms.

बाहुज – पु॰ – (बाहुज) क्षत्रीय। a kṣatriya, a warrior race.

बाहुजञ्ञ – वि॰ – (बाहुजन्य) सार्वजनिक। belonging to the public.

बाहुमूल – न॰ – (बाहुमूल) काँख, बगल। arm-pit.

बाहुलिक – वि॰ – (बाहुलिक) विपुलता में निवास करने वाला। living in abundance.

बाहुल्ल – न॰ – (बाहुल्य) प्रचुरता, कामोपभोगी जीवन। luxurious living.

बाहु-सच्च – न॰ – (बाहु-सत्य) अधिक विद्वता। great learning.

बाहेति – क्रि॰ – दूर रखता है, दूर करता है। keeps away, wards off, removes.

बाल्ह – वि॰ – (बाढ़) दृढ़, मजबूत। loud, strong.

बाल्हं – क्रि॰वि॰ – (बाढम) भली प्रकार, निश्चय ही। certainly, indeed.

बिदल – न० – (द्विदल ∕ विदना) मूँग। a kind of pulse, split-pea (*mudga*) (*Phaseolus Mungo*).

बिदल – न० – (विदल) बाँस की चिरी हुई कमची या फट्टी। a split bamboo cane.

बिदलकारी – स्त्री० – (वै. बिदलकारी) बाँस फाड़ने वाली स्त्रियाँ। woman making splits of bamboo.

बिन्दु – न० – (बिन्दु) बिन्दु, बूँद। a drop.

बिन्दुमत्त – वि० – (बिन्दुमात्र) बिन्दुमात्र। as much as a drop.

बिन्दुमत्तं – क्रि० वि० – (बिन्दु मात्रम्) मात्र एक बूंद। only a drop.

बिन्दुसार – पु० – (बिन्दुसार) अशोक के पिता, मगध नरेश। the father of Aśoka, the king of Magadha.

बिम्ब – न० – (बिम्ब) छाया, आकृति (सूर्य अथवा चन्द्र-मण्डल)। an image, figure, the disc of (sun or moon).

बिम्बा – स्त्री० – (बिम्बा) सिद्धार्थ गौतम की पत्नी (यशोधरा)। the wife of Siddhārtha Gautama also known as Yaśodharā.

बिम्बिका – बिम्बी – स्त्री० – (बिम्बिका) कुँदरु, कुँदरु की लता और उसका फल, कुँदरु का फल अपने चटक लाल रंग के लिए प्रसिद्ध है। the creeper *Brayonia Grandis*, which produces red oval fruits.

बिम्बसार – पु० – (बिम्बिसार) मगध नरेश बिम्बिसार। Bimbisāra, the king of Magadha and the father of Aśoka.

बिम्बोहन – न० – (उपधान) तकिया। a pillow.

बिल – न० – (बिल) गुहा, सूराख (चूहे का) बिल। a hole, a den.

बिलङ्ग – पु० – सिर का। vinegar.

बिलङ्ग-थालिका – स्त्री० – एक प्रकार की यन्त्रणा। a kind of torture.

बिलसो – क्रि० वि० – (पुञ्जशः) पृथक्-पृथक् करके। having split, having heaped.

बिल्ल – पु० – (बिल्व) बिल्व का पेड़ और उसका फल। the *Aegle Marmelos* (wood-apple or *bel*) tree and the fruit.

बिळार – पु० – (बिडाल) बिल्ला, नर बिल्ली। a cat, a male cat.

बिळार-भस्ता – स्त्री० – (बिडालभस्त्रा) (लोहार की) भाथी। (a bag of cat skin), the bellows.

बिळार-जातक – (जा० सं० 128) – प्रतिदिन एक-एक चूहा मारकर खा जाने वाले गीदड़ को मूषक-राज द्वारा मार डालने की कथा। the story (No. 128) is related to a fraudulent jackal who used to eat up one rat daily but was at last killed by the king of rats.

बिळारिकोसिय-जातक – (जा० सं० 450) – विलारकोसिय सेठ की कथा जिसने अपने कंजूसपन के कारण परम्परागत दानशाला नष्ट करा दी थी। the story (No. 450) related to a miser merchant who burnt the almonry established by his ancestors.

बिलाली – स्त्री० – (बिडाली) बिल्ली। a she cat.

बीज – न० – (बीज) बीज। seed.

बीजकोस – पु० – (बीजकोश) पौधे में बीज-भरी पोटली। seed vessel of flowers.

बीज-गाम – पु० – (बीज ग्राम) बीजों का समूह। seed kingdom.

बीज-जात – न० – (बीज-जात) बीजों की भिन्न प्रजाति। species of seed.

बीज-बीज – न० – (बीज-बीज) भोजन के उपयोग में आने वाले धान्य केन्द्र, शाक, आदि प्रमुख पाँच वर्ग। one of the five groups of edible or useful plants falling under Bīja-Gāma.

बीभच्च – वि० – (बीभत्स) वीभत्स, जुगुप्सित। awful, horrible.

बीरण – न० – (बीरण) वीरणी मूल, उशीर अथवा खस। a fragrant grass Anaropogon Nuricatum.

बीरण-थम्भ – पु० – (बीरण-स्तम्भ) बीरण घास का खम्भा। a pool of bīraṇa grass.

बुज्झति – क्रि० – (√ बुध = बुध्यते) जानता है, समझता है, बूझता है। knows, understands, perceives.

बुज्झन – न० – (बोधन) बूझना, ज्ञान प्राप्त करना। attaining knowledge, understanding, working up.

बुज्झनक – वि० – (बोद्धा / बोधनक) समझदार। prudent, intelligent.

बुज्झतु – पु० – (बोद्धा) जागने वाला, बूझने वाला, ज्ञानी। one who wakes up or becomes enlightened.

बुड्ढ – वि० – (वृद्ध) वृद्ध। aged, old.

बुड्ढतर – वि० – (वृद्धतर) वृद्धतर। older.

बुद्ध – पु० – (बुद्ध) जिसने बोधि प्राप्त कर लिया है। one who has attained enlightenment.

बुद्धकारक-धम्म – पु० – (बुद्धकारक धर्म) बुद्धत्व प्राप्ति में सहायक चर्या। the practices bringing about Buddhahood.

बुद्ध-काल – पु० – (बुद्धकाल) बुद्धोत्पत्ति का काल। the time when a Buddha appears.

बुद्ध-कोलाहल – पु० – (बुद्धकोलाहल) बुद्ध के आगमन की पूर्व सूचना। the prediction about coming of a Buddha.

बुद्धक्खेत्त – न० – (बुद्ध-क्षेत्र) बुद्ध की शक्ति का सीमा क्षेत्र। the sphere where a Buddha's power exist.

बुद्ध-गुण – पु० – (बुद्ध-गुण) बुद्ध के गुण। virtues of a Buddha.

बुद्धंकुर – पु० – (बुद्धाङ्कुर) जिसमें बुद्धत्व प्राप्ति के अङ्कुर विद्यमान हैं। one who is destined to be a Buddha.

बुद्ध-चक्खु – न० – (बुद्ध-चक्षु) बुद्ध की अन्तर्दृष्टि। the faculty of complete intuition.

बुद्ध-आण – न० – (बुद्ध-ज्ञान) अनन्त ज्ञान। the boundless knowledge.

बुद्धन्तर – न० – (बुद्धान्तर) एक बुद्ध और दूसरे बुद्ध के बीच का काल। the intermission between the appearance of one Buddha and the next.

बुद्ध-पुत्त – पु० – (बुद्ध-पुत्र) बुद्ध-पुत्र। the disciple of a Buddha.

बुद्ध-बल – न० – (बुद्ध-बल) बुद्ध की शक्ति। the power of Buddha.

बुद्ध-भाव – पु० – (बुद्ध-भाव) बुद्ध भाव, बुद्धत्व। the Buddhahood.

बेलुव

बुद्ध-भूमि – स्त्री॰ – (बुद्ध-भूमि) बुद्ध-भूमि का। the ground of Buddhahood.

बुद्ध-भामक – वि॰ – (बुद्ध-भामक) बुद्ध-भक्त। attached to Buddha.

बुद्ध-रस्मि/बुद्धरसि – स्त्री॰ – (बुद्ध-रश्मि) बुद्ध के शरीर से निकलने वाली रश्मियाँ। the rays rising from the person of the Buddha.

बुद्ध-लीलाहा – स्त्री॰ – (बुद्ध-लीला) बुद्ध-लीला। performance or life of Buddha.

बुद्ध-वचन – न॰ – (बुद्ध-वचन) बुद्ध की शिक्षा। the teaching of the Buddha.

बुद्ध-विसय – न॰ – (बुद्ध-विषय) बुद्ध-क्षेत्र। scope of a Buddha.

बुद्ध-वेनेय्य – वि॰ – (बुद्ध-वेनेय्य) बुद्ध के द्वारा विनीत, बनाया जा सकने वाला। to be converted by a Buddha.

बुद्ध-सासन – न॰ – (बुद्ध-शासन) बुद्धों की शिक्षा। the teaching of Buddha.

बुद्धानुभाव – पु॰ – (बुद्धानुभाव) बुद्धों का प्रताप। the majestic power of the Buddha.

बुद्धानुस्सति – स्त्री॰ – (बुद्धानुस्मृति) बुद्ध का अनुस्मरण। mindfulness of the Buddha's virtues.

बुद्धारम्मण – न॰ – (बुद्धलम्बन) बुद्ध के गुणों का ध्यान। meditation on the virtues of the Buddha.

बुद्धपट्ठाक – वि॰ – (बुद्ध + उपस्थाक) बुद्ध सेवक। attending upon the Buddha.

बुद्धप्पाद – पु॰ – (बुद्ध + उत्पाद) बुद्ध युग। age in which a Buddha is born.

बुद्ध-घोस – पु॰ – (बुद्ध-घोष) त्रिपिटक का सर्वश्रेष्ठ, व्याख्याकार अट्ठकथाचार्य। the best and renowned commentator of Tripiṭaka.

बुद्धघोसुप्पति – स्त्री॰ – (बुद्धघोषोत्पत्ति) इस नाम का ग्रन्थ जिसमें अट्ठकथाकार बुद्धघोष का आख्यानपरक जीवनवृत्त है। a very late account of the life of Buddhaghoṣa, it is more a romance than a historical chronicle.

बुद्धत्त – न॰ – (बुद्धत्व) बुद्धत्व प्राप्ति की अवस्था। the state of a Buddha.

बुद्ध-वंस – पु॰ – (बुद्ध-वंश) खुद्दक निकाय का चौदहवाँ ग्रन्थ। the fourteenth epic of Khuddaka Nikāya.

बुद्धि – स्त्री॰ – (बुद्धि) प्रज्ञा। wisdom, intelligence.

बुद्धिमन्तु – वि॰ – (बुद्धिमान) मतिमान (बुद्धिमान)। a wise, an intelligent man.

बुद्धिसम्पन्न – वि॰ – (बुद्धि-सम्पन्न) मतिमान, बुद्धिमान। wise, intelligent.

बुध – वि॰ – (अवगमने) जानना, समझना। to understand.

बुध – पु॰ – (बुध) बुद्धिमान आदमी, बुध ग्रह, बुध (वार)। the wise man, the planet, Mercury, Wednesday.

बुब्बुल/बुब्बुलक – न॰ – (बुद बुद) बुलबुला। a bubble.

बुभुक्खति – क्रि॰ – (बुभुक्षते) खाने की इच्छा करता है। desires to eat.

बुन्द – पु॰ – (वै. बुघन) जड़। root.

बेलुव – पु॰ – (बिल्व) बिल्व, बेल का पेड़। the tree *Aegle Marmelo*s.

बेलुव-पक्क – वि॰ – (बिल्व-पक्व) पका बेल। a ripe *Marmelos* or *bel*.

बेलुव-लट्ठि – स्त्री॰ – (बिल्व-यष्टि) बेल का गाछ। a young *Marmelos* tree.

बेलुव-सलाटुक – न॰ – (बिल्व / शद:) बेल का कच्चा फल। the unripe fruit of *Marmelos* or *bel*.

बोज्झङ्ग – न॰ – (बोध्यङ्ग) बोधि प्राप्ति के लिए आवश्यक सहायक गुण। a helping factor, essential knowledge, or wisdom.

बोध – पु॰ – (बोध) बुद्धत्व, ज्ञान। enlightenment, knowledge.

बोधनीय/बोधनेय – वि॰ – (बोधनीय) बुद्धत्व लाभ कर सकने वाला। capable of being enlightened.

बोधि – स्त्री॰ – (बोधि) श्रेष्ठतम ज्ञान। supreme knowledge.

बोधिअङ्गण – न॰ – (बोधि अङ्गण) बोधि वृक्ष का आँगन। a courtyard in which a *bodhi* tree stands.

बोधि-पक्खिक – वि॰ – (बोधि-पाक्षिक) बोधिपक्षीय धर्म। belonging to enlightenment.

बोधि-पादप/बोधिरुक्ख – पु॰ – (बोधि-वृक्ष) पीपल। the *bodhi* tree the *Ficus Religiosia*.

बोधि-पूजा – स्त्री॰ – (बोधि-पूजा) बोधि-वृक्ष की पूजा। offering to a *bodhitree*.

बोधि-मण्ड – पु॰ – (बोधि-मण्डप) बोधि-वृक्ष के नीचे का वह स्थान जहाँ सिद्धार्थ गौतम वज्रासन लगाकर बुद्ध प्राप्ति के लिए कृतसंकल्प होकर बैठे थे। the ground under *bodhi* tree where the Buddha sat at the time of his enlightenment.

बोधिमह – पु॰ – (बोधि-महोत्सव) बोधिवृक्ष के सम्मान में उत्सव। offering to a *bodhi* tree.

बोधि-मूल – न॰ – (बोधि-मूल) बोधि वृक्ष की जड़। the root of the *bodhi* tree.

बोधि-सत्त – पु॰ – (बोधिसत्त्व) बुद्धत्व प्राप्ति के लिए कृतसंकल्प प्राणी, बुद्धत्व प्राप्ति से पूर्व का सिद्धार्थ गौतम बुद्ध का परिचायक नाम। the name given to one who aspires for *bodh* or enlightenment, it is an introductory name of Siddhārtha Gautama Buddha before attaining enlightenment.

बोधेति – क्रि॰ – (बोधयति) ज्ञान प्राप्त कराता है। awakes enlightenment.

बोधेतु – पु॰ – (बोद्धा) जागृत होने वाला, ज्ञानलाभी। to be awakened one, beneficiary of knowledge.

बोन्दि – पु॰ – (बोन्दि, प्राकृत में बोन्दी अपि) शरीर। body.

ब्यग्ध – पु॰ – (व्याघ्र) बाघ, व्याघ्र। a tiger.

ब्यञ्जन – न॰ – (व्यञ्जन) (1) स्वरों के अतिरिक्त वर्णमाला के शेष अक्षर (2) सालन, कढ़ी, पकवान। (1) a syllable, a consonant, a sign or a mark (2) a curry, a dish for meal.

ब्यापाद – पु॰ – (व्यापाद) पर द्राह चिन्तन, द्वेष। malevolence.

ब्याम – पु॰ – (वै. व्याम) वयस्क व्यक्ति द्वारा क्षैतिज स्थिति में सीधे फैलाए गए हाथ के दोनों मध्यमा उँगलियों के बीच की दूरी का माप, एक व्याम = 6 फीट। a measurement equal to six feet.

व्यामप्पभा – स्त्री॰ – (व्याम-प्रभा) बुद्ध के शरीर से निकलने वाली प्रभा। the lustre rising from the person of the Buddha.

ब्यूह – पु॰ – (व्यूह) सेना की रचना-पद्धति। the method of arranging the troop.

√ ब्रह – (भू॰) – (बृहणे) बढ़ना। to prosper, to grow or increase.

ब्रहन्त – वि॰ – (वृहत्) विशाल। vast, lofty.

ब्रह्म-ब्रह्मा – पु॰ – (ब्रह्मा) सृष्टिकर्ता। the creator.

ब्रह्मकायिक – वि॰ – (ब्रह्म-कायिक) ब्रह्माओं की मण्डली का। belonging to company of Brahmās.

ब्रह्म-घोस – वि॰ – (ब्रह्म-घोष) ब्रह्मा सदृश आवाज। having sound similar to that of Brahmā.

ब्रह्मचर्या – स्त्री॰ – (ब्रह्मचर्या) श्रेष्ठ जीवन। complete chastity.

ब्रह्मचारी – पु॰ – (ब्रह्मचारी) मैथुन धर्म से विरत रहने वाला। leading a chaste life.

ब्रह्मजच्च – वि॰ – (ब्रह्मजात्य) ब्राह्मणजन्मा। belonging to the brāhmaṇa caste.

ब्रह्मञ्ञ – न॰ – (ब्रह्मण्यता) ब्राह्मणत्व, श्रेष्ठ जीवन। brahmaṇahood, a pure life.

ब्रह्मण्यता – स्त्री॰ – (ब्रह्मण्यता) ब्राह्मणत्व, श्रेष्ठ जीवन। Brāhmaṇahood, a pure life.

ब्रह्म-दण्ड – पु॰ – (ब्रह्म-दण्ड) दण्ड विशेष जिसमें अपराधी से संवाद और सम्पर्क से पूर्णतया निषिद्ध कर दिया जाता है। a kind of punishment by stopping all conversation and communications with the criminal.

ब्रह्म-देय्य – न॰ – (ब्रह्म-देय) राजकीय-भेंट। a royal gift.

ब्रह्मप्पत्त – वि॰ – (ब्रह्मत्व-प्राप्त) श्रेष्ठतम अवस्था को प्राप्त। arrived at the highest state.

ब्रह्म-बन्धु – पु॰ – (ब्रह्म-बन्धु) ब्रह्म का सम्बंधी ब्राह्मण। a relative of a Brahma, i.e., a brāhmaṇa.

ब्रह्मभूत – वि॰ – (ब्रह्म-भूत) सर्वश्रेष्ठ। most excellent.

ब्रह्मलोक – पु॰ – (ब्रह्मलोक) ब्रह्म-लोक। Brahma-world.

ब्रह्म-विमान – न॰ – (ब्रह्म-विमान) ब्रह्मा का निवास-स्थान। the mansion of a Brahma-god.

ब्रह्म-विहार – पु॰ – (ब्रह्म-विहार) चित्त की वाञ्छनीय स्थिति-मैत्री, करुणा, मुदिता तथा उपेक्षा का सम्मिलित नाम। divine state of mind, a name collectively given to *maitrī*, *karuṇā*, *muditā* and *upekṣa*.

ब्रह्म-जातक – (जा॰ सं 323) – ऐसे तापस की कथा जिसने बारह वर्षों बाद राजा से विदा लेते समय केवल पत्तों का बना एक छाता और खड़ाऊँ की जोड़ी की इच्छा की। the story (No. 323) of an ascetic who at the time of his departure from the king after twelve years asked only a pair of single-soled wooden chappals and a leaf parasol.

ब्राह्मण – पु॰ – (ब्राह्मण) ब्राह्मण वर्ण का व्यक्ति। a man of the brāhmaṇa caste.

ब्रह्म-कञ्ञा – स्त्री॰ – (ब्राह्मण-कन्या) ब्राह्मण-कन्या । a brāhmaṇa maiden.

ब्रह्म-वाचनक – पु॰ – (ब्रह्म-वाचनक) ब्राह्मणों द्वारा किया जाने वाला वेद-पाठ । recitation of Vedas by brāhmaṇas.

ब्राह्मण-वाटक – पु॰ – (ब्राह्मण-वाटक) ब्राह्मणों के एकत्र होने का स्थान । place where brāhmaṇas assemble.

ब्रूति – क्रि॰ – (ब्रूते/वदति) बोलता है । says, speaks.

बू – (भू॰) – (वचने) बोलना । to speak.

बृह – भू॰ – (बृद्धणे) बढ़ना । to grow.

बृहने – न॰ – (बृंहण) वृद्धि । development, increment.

बृहेति – क्रि॰ – (बृहति) बढ़ाता है, वृद्धि करता है । increases, develops.

बृहेतु – पु॰ – (वृहंयिता) बढ़ाने वाला । one who increases.

भ

भ – पालि वर्णमाला का चौबीसवाँ व्यञ्जन the 24th consonant of Pāli alphabet.

भक्ख – (भू०) – (अदने) खाना। to eat.

भक्खक – पु० – (भक्ष्य) खाने वाला। fit to be eaten (n.) food, prey, edible.

भक्ख – वि० – (भक्ष्य) खाने योग्य (न०) भोजन, खाद्य पदार्थ। fit to be eaten, (n.) food, prey, edible.

भक्खक – पु० – (भक्षक) खाने वाला। one who eats.

भक्खति – क्रि० – (भक्षयति) खाता है। eats, feeds upon.

भक्खन – न० – (भक्षण) खाना। eating.

भक्खेति – क्रि० – (भक्षयते) खाता है। eats, feeds upon.

भग (1) – न० – (भाग्य) भाग्य। luck, fortune.

भग (2) – न० – (भग) योनि, स्त्री इन्द्रिय। female organ.

भगन्दला – स्त्री० – (भगन्दर) भगन्दर नामक रोग। fistula.

भगवन्तु – वि० – (भाग्यवान) भाग्यवान (पु०) भगवान् (बुद्ध)। fortunate, (m.) Buddha.

भगिनी – स्त्री० – (भगिनी) बहन। sister.

भगु – पु० – (भृगु) भृगु नामक ऋषि। a famous sage named Bhṛgu.

भग्ग – कृदन्त – (√ भञ्ज + ल = भग्न) टूटा हुआ। broken.

भङ्ग (1) – पु० – (भङ्ग) टूटना। dissolution, breaking up.

भङ्ग (2) – न० – (भङ्ग) पटसन। the jute or hemp cloth.

भङ्ग-खण – न० – (भङ्ग-क्षण) टूटने का क्षण। the moment of dissolution.

भङ्गानुपस्सना – स्त्री० – (भङ्गानुपश्यना) वस्तुओं के विनाश के सम्बन्ध में अन्तर्दृष्टि। insight into disruption.

भच्च – पु० – (भृत्य) मृत्यु, नौकर, (वि०) पालित, पोषित। servant, a dependant (adj.) to be nourished or brought up.

भजति – क्रि० – (√ भज् = भजति) संगति करता है। associates.

भजन – न० – (भजन) संगति। association with.

√ भज्ज – (भू०) – (पाके) भूनना। to roast, to fry.

भज्ज – (भू०) – (अवमर्दने) नष्ट करना। to destroy.

भज्जति – क्रि० – (भुज्जति) भूजता है। roasts, gets roasted.

भज्जक – वि० – (भज्जक) तोड़ने वाला, नष्ट करने वाला। one who breaks or spoils.

भञ्जति – क्रि० – (√ भञ्ज् = भञ्जति) तोड़ता है, नष्ट करता है। breaks, destroys.

भञ्जन – न० – (भञ्जन) तोड़, विनाश। breakage, destruction.

भञ्जनक – न॰ – (भञ्जन) तोड़ना, नष्ट करना। to break, to destroy.

√भट – (भू॰) – (भृत्य कर्मे) नौकरी करना। to remain in service.

भट – पु॰ – (भट) सैनिक, सिपाही, नौकर। a soldier, a constable, a hireling, a servant.

भट-सेना – स्त्री॰ – (भट-सेना) पैदल सेना। infantry.

भट्ठ (1) – कृदन्त – (भ्रष्ट) गिरा हुआ। dropped, fallen.

भट्ठ (2) – कृदन्त – (भृष्ट) भुना हुआ। parched, roasted.

√भण – (भू॰) – (भजने) स्पष्ट कहना। speak frankly.

भणे – अव्यय – (भणे) राजाओं द्वारा प्रजा के लिए सम्बोधन विशेष "अच्छा"। a term used for addressing inferiors to mean "be sure", "look here."

भण्ड – न॰ – (भाण्ड) सामान। goods, wares.

√भण्ड – (भू॰) – (परिहास्ने) परिहास करना। to mock.

भण्डक – न॰ – (भाण्डक) सामान, चीजें। goods, wares.

भण्डागार – न॰ – (भाण्डागार) भण्डार, खजाना। a storehouse, treasury.

भण्डागारिक – पु॰ – (भाण्डागारिक) भण्डारी, खजानची। a storekeeper, treasurer.

भण्डति – क्रि॰ – (√भड् - परिभाषणे = भण्डते) झगड़ा करता है। quarrels.

भण्डन – न॰ – (√भड्ड् + ल्युट् = भण्डन) उपद्रव, कलह, झगड़ा। a quarrel, dispute.

भण्डिका – स्त्री॰ – (भण्डिका) बण्डल, गठरी। bundle, package.

भण्डु – पु॰ – (भुण्डित) मुण्डित शिर वाला व्यक्ति। a person of shaven head.

भण्डु-कम्म – न॰ – (मुण्डन कर्म) हजामत बनाना। shaving.

भत – कृदन्त – (√भृ + क्त = भृत) पालित, पोषित पु॰ (नौकर)। supported, fed, maintained.

भतक – पु॰ – (भृतक) भृत्य, कुली। a hired servant.

भति – स्त्री॰ – (भृति) मजदूरी। wages.

भत्त – न॰ – (भक्त) भात, भोजन। boiled rice, food.

भत्त-कारक – पु॰ – (भक्तकार) खाना बनाने वाला। a cook, butler.

भत्त-किच्च – न॰ – (भक्त-कृत्य) आहार कर्म, भात खाना, भोजन करना। taking meal, eating food.

भत्त-किलमथ – पु॰ – (आहार-बलात्ति) भोजनान्तर आलस्य। fatigue after eating.

भत्त-सम्मद – पु॰ – (आहार-तन्द्रा) भोजनान्तर तन्द्रा। drowsiness after a meal.

भत्त-गाम – पु॰ – (भक्त-ग्राम) भेंट या सेवा देने वाला ग्राम। a village giving tribute or service.

भत्तग्ग – न॰ – (भोजनालय) भोजन-कक्ष, भोजनालय। a refectory, a kitchen.

भत्त-पुट – न॰ – (भक्त-पुटम्) भात का ढोना। a parcel of food.

भत्त-विसग्ग – पु॰ – (भक्त-विसर्ग-परिवेषणम्) भोजन, भोजन परोसना। serving a meal.

भक्त-वेतन – न॰ – (भक्त-वेतनम्) भोजन और तनख्वाह। food, salary or charges.

भक्त-वेला – स्त्री॰ – (भक्त-वेला) आहार-समय, भोजन का समय। meal times.

भक्ति – स्त्री॰ – (भक्ति) भक्ति। devotion.

भत्तिक/भत्तिमन्तु – वि॰ – (भक्तिमान) भक्त। devotee.

भत्तु – पु॰ – (भर्तृ) भर्ता, स्वामी, पति। husband, one who supports or looks after his wife.

भदन्त – वि.पु॰ – (भदन्त, भद्रम + ते) थैरवार्ट, पूज्य (बौद्ध जनों के लिए)। venerable, reverend (used for Buddhists).

√ भद्द – पु॰ – (कल्याणे) श्रम कर्म करना, साकी होना। to perform.

√ भद्द – भू॰ – (कल्याणे) उपरिवत। as above.

भद्द – वि॰ – (भद्र) शुभ (मूहूर्त)। auspicious, lucky.

भद्दक – न॰ – (भद्रक) भाग्य-सम्पन्न (वि॰) भाग्य-सम्पन्न (वस्तु)। favoured by luck, lucky.

भद्द-कच्चाना – स्त्री॰ – (भद्र-कात्यायनी) यशोधरा (राहुल-माता) का एक और नाम। another name of Yaśodharā, the mother of Rāhul.

भद्द-कुम्भ – पु॰ – (भद्र-कुम्भ) पानी भरा घड़ा जिसे शुभ शकुन माना जाता है। sacred pitcher.

भद्द-दारु – पु॰ – (भद्र-दारु) देव-दारु के जाति का एक वृक्ष। *Pinus Devadāru*, *devadāru* tree, cidae, fir.

भद्द-पदा – स्त्री॰ – (भाद्र-पद) भाद्र-पद नक्षत्र। name of a constellation.

भद्द-पीठ – न॰ – (भद्र-पीठ) रत्नासन, भद्रासन। a royal chair, throne.

भद्द-मुख – वि॰ – (भद्र-मुख) भद्र-मुख, सुन्दर मुख (एक शिष्ट सम्बोधन)। a handsome face (a complimentary address).

भद्द-युग – न॰ – (भद्र-युगल) श्रेष्ठ-जोड़ा। a noble pair.

भद्द-साल-जातक – (जा॰ सं॰ 465) – राजा के उद्यान के श्रेष्ठ भद्रशाल वृक्ष के काटे जाने की कथा। the story (No. 465) related to the cutting of the fine *śāla* tree in the king's garden.

भद्द-घट-जातक – (जा॰ सं॰ 291) – एक शराबी लड़के की कथा जिसने इन्द्र-प्रदत्त भद्रघट भी फोड़ डाला। the story (No. 291) of a drunken youth who broke the noble vessel gifted by Indra.

भद्दा/भद्दिका – स्त्री॰ – (भद्रा) एक शिष्ट स्त्री। a noble woman.

भद्दिय – पु॰ – (भद्रिय) अङ्ग जनपद का का एक नगर, भगवान् बुद्ध वहाँ अनेक बार पधारे थे। a town in Aṅga *janapada* (state), the Buddha visited it many times.

भन्त – कृदन्त – (भ्रान्त) भान्त, भ्रमित। confused under an illusion.

भन्तत्त – न॰ – (भ्रान्ति, भ्रान्त्वा) भ्रान्त-भाव, गड़बड़ी। confusion, disruption.

भन्ते-सम्बोधन – (भन्ते!) भदन्त का सम्बोधन रूप। Reverened Sir! O Lord (respectful address).

भब्ब – वि॰ – (भव्य) भव्य, योग्य। fine, able, capable.

भब्बता – स्त्री॰ – (भव्यता) सामर्थ्य, भव्यता, योग्यता। splendour, grandeur, ability, capability.

√ भम – (भू॰) – (अनवस्थाने) घूमना। to revolve.

भम – पु॰ – (भ्रम) घूमने वाली चीज। a revolving thing.

भमकार – पु॰ – (भ्रमकार) घुमाने वाला। a turner.

भमति – क्रि॰ – (√ भ्रम = भ्रमति) घूमता है। whirls about, roams.

भमर – पु॰ – (भ्रमर) भ्रमर, भौंरा। a humming-bee.

भमरिका – स्त्री॰ – (भ्रमरिका) लट्टू। a humming top (a top).

भमु-भमुका – स्त्री॰ – (भ्रू) भौंह eye-brow.

भय – न॰ – (भय) डर। fear.

भयङ्कर – वि॰ – (भयङ्कर) भयंकर। horrible.

भय-दस्सावी – वि॰ – (भय-दर्शी) भय की प्रतीति करने वाला। one realizing the danger.

भय-दस्सी – वि॰ – (भयदर्शी) देखें भय दस्सावी। see Bhayadassāvī.

भयानक – वि॰ – (भयानक) भयानक। frightful, horrible.

भयावह – वि॰ – (भयावह) भयानक। horrible.

√ भर – (भू॰) – (भरणे) पालना। to bring up.

भर – वि॰ – (भर) (समास में) पोषण करने वाला। (in compounds) supporting.

माता-पेत्ति-भर – वि॰ – (मातृ, पितृ, भर) माता-पिता का पोषण करने वाला। one who supports his parents.

भरण – न॰ – (भरण) भरण-पोषण। maintenance.

भरत-कुमार – दशरथ पुत्र राम का सौतेला भाई। the son of Daśaratha the step-brother of Rāma.

भरति – क्रि॰ – (√ भृ – भरति) भरण-पोषण करता हैं। supports, maintains.

भरति – कृदन्त – (भरित) भरा हुआ। filled up, full of, maintained.

भरिया – स्त्री॰ – (भार्या) भार्या, पत्नी। wife.

भरुकच्छ – पु॰ – (भृगु-कच्छ) भड़ौंच, मरु प्रदेश का बन्दरगाह। an ancient sea-port named Bharu-Kaccha.

भरु-जातक – (जा॰ सं॰ 213) – कथानुसार भरु देश के राजा ने तपस्वियों के मुकदमे में गलत निर्णय देकर विनाश को प्राप्त किया। the story (No. 213) tells how the king of Bharu invited disaster by passing a wrong judgement against the ascetics.

भल्लटिक – लोध्र नामक वृक्ष, भिलावाँ का पेड़। the soap-tree, the marking-nut tree.

भल्लाटिक-जातक – (जा॰ सं॰ 504) – इसमें भल्लाटिय नरेश के रोमांचक शिकार की कथा वर्णित है। this tale describes an astonishing hunting expedition of a king.

भल्ली – स्त्री॰ – (भल्ली) भल्लातक, भिलावाँ। the marking-nut, the soap nut tree.

भव – (पु॰) – (भव) अस्तित्व, संसार। the estate of existence.

भवग्ग – पु॰ – (भवाग्र) संसार का उच्चतम शिखर। the highest point of existence.

भवङ्ग – न॰ – (भवाङ्ग) अचेतन मन। the sub-conscious mind.

भव-चक्क – न॰ – (भव-चक्र) भव-चक्र। पुनर्जन्म का चक्र। the wheel of re-birth.

भवतण्हा – स्त्री॰ – (भव-तृष्णा) भव-तृष्णा, पुनर्जन्म की लालसा। the craving for rebirth.

भवन्तग – वि॰ – (भवान्तग) भव के अन्त तक पहुँचा हुआ। gone to the end of existence.

भवन्तग् – वि॰ – (भवन्तग) देखें भवन्तग। see Bhavantaga.

भव-संयोजन – न॰ – (भव-संयोजन) पुनर्जन्म का बन्धन। fetter of re-birth.

भवा-भव – पु॰ – (भवा-भव) यह या वह जीवन। this or that life.

भवेसना – स्त्री॰ – (भवेषणा) भवेषणा, भवेच्छा। longing for re-birth.

भवोध – पु॰ – (भवौघ) पुनर्जन्म रूपी बाढ़। the flood of re-birth.

भवति – क्रि॰ – (√ भू = भवति) होता है। becomes, exists.

भवन – न॰ – (भवन) (1) होना (2) निवास-स्थान। (1) becoming (2) dwelling place.

भस्तारू – स्त्री॰ – (भस्त्रा) धौंकनी। the bellows, a leather bag.

भस्म – न॰ – (भस्म) राख। ashes.

भसमच्छन्न – वि॰ – (भस्माच्छन्न) राख से ढका हुआ। covered with ashes.

भस्स – न॰ – गप-शप, बेकार बातचीत। useless talk.

भस्सारामता – स्त्री॰ – गप-शप में रूचि। or interested in, fond of, useless talk.

भस्सति – क्रि॰ – (√ भ्रंश = भंशते) गिर पड़ता है। falls down.

भस्सर – वि॰ – (भास्वर) दीप्त, कान्तिमान, प्रकाशमान। bright, shining, resplendent.

√भा – (भू॰) – (दीप्त्यर्थे) चमकना। to shining, to shine.

√भा – (भू॰) – (अवबोधते) समझना, प्रकाशित करना। to make under-stand, to light.

भा – स्त्री॰ – (भा) कान्ति, प्रकाश की चमक। the light, splendour.

भाकुटिक – वि॰ – (भ्राकुटिक) भृकुटि टेढ़ी करने वाला। knitting the brows, frowning.

भाग – पु॰ – (भाग) हिस्सा। share, part.

भागवन्तु – पु॰ – (भागवान्) हिस्से वाला, हिस्सेदार। sharer, partner.

भागदेय्य – न॰ – (भागधेय) भाग्य। luck.

भागसो – क्रि॰ वि॰ – (भागशः) हिस्सों के अनुसार। according to shares.

भागिनेय्य – पु॰ – (भागिनेय) भानजी। sister's daughter.

भागिनेय्या – स्त्री॰ – (भागिनेया) भानजी। sister's daughter.

भागीय – वि॰ – (भागी) (समास में) सम्बन्धित। (in compounds) connected with.

भागी – वि॰ – (भागी) हिस्सेदार। sharer, shareholder.

भागीरथी – स्त्री॰ – (भागीरथी) गंगा नदी का एक नाम। the Gaṅgā river.

भाग्य – न॰ – (भाग्य) सौभाग्य। good luck, fortune.

भाजक – वि॰ – (भाजक) बाँटने वाला। one who divides or distributes.

भाजन – न॰ – (भाजन) विभाजन / बँटवारा। distribution, partition.

भाजन – न॰ – (भाजन) बर्त्तन, पात्र। a vessel, a container.

भाजन-विकति – स्त्री॰ – (भाजन-विकृति) नाना प्रकार के बर्त्तन। various kinds of vessels.

भाजेति – क्रि॰ वि॰ – (वि √ भज् = विभाजति) बाँटता है। divides or distributes.

भाणक – पु॰ – (भाणक) (1) धर्म ग्रन्थों का पाठ करने वाला (2) बड़ा मटका। (1) a reciter of the scriptures (2) a big jar.

भाणवार – पु॰ – (भाणवार) त्रिपिटक के अनेक भागों में से एक। एक भाणवार आठ सहस्र अक्षरों से समन्वित माना जाता है। one of the several divisions of Tipiṭaka, each Bhāṇavāra consists of eight thousand letters.

भाणी – वि॰ – (भाणी / भाषी) भाषी, बोलने वाला। reciter, speaker.

भाति – क्रि॰ – (√ भा = भाति) चमकता है। shines.

भातिकभातु – पु॰ – (भ्राता) भाई। brother.

भानु – पु॰ – (भानु) (1) प्रकाश (2) सूर्य। (1) light (2) the sun.

भानमन्तु – वि॰ – (भानुमान) (1) प्रकाशवान (2) – (पु॰) सूर्य। (1) luminous (2) the sun.

भायति – क्रि॰ – (√ भी = विभेति) डरता है। fears, afraid.

भायापेति – क्रि॰ – (भाययति) डराता है। frightens.

भार – पु॰ – (भार) बोझा। a weight, load, burden.

भार-निक्खेपन – न॰ – (भार-निक्षेपण) भार उतारकर रख देना। the laying down of burden or charge.

भार-मोचन – न॰ – (भार-मोचन) भार-मुक्ति। deliverance of a burden.

भार-वाही – पु॰ – (भार-वाही) भार ढोने वाला, पदभार ग्रहण करने वाला। bearing the burden, one who holds an office.

भारहार – पु॰ – (भारहार) बोझा ढोने वाला। a load carrier.

भारिक – वि॰ – (भारिक) भार-युक्त। loaded.

भारिय – वि॰ – (भारिय) भारी। weighty.

भाव – पु॰ – (भाव) प्रकृति, स्थिति, स्वभाव। nature, condition.

भावना – स्त्री॰ – (भावना) चिन्तन-विकास, योगाभ्यास। developement by means of thought, meditation.

भावनानुयोग – पु॰ – (भावनानुयोग) योगाभ्यास में लगना। engages in meditation.

भावनामय – वि॰ – (भावनामय) भावना-युक्त। accomplished by meditation.

भावना-विधान – न॰ – (भावना-विधान) योगाभ्यास की पद्धति। process of meditation.

भावनीय – वि॰ – (भावनीय) अभ्यास करने योग्य, सम्माननीय। fit to be cultivated, deserving respect.

भावित – कृदन्त – (भावित) अभ्यस्त, विकसित। cultivated, developed.

भावित्तत्त – वि॰ – (सुभावित) विशेष अभ्यासी, संयत। a well-trained, self-compared.

भावी – वि॰ – (भावी) होने वाला, अनिवार्य। going to be, inevitable.

भावेति – क्रि॰ – (भावयति) वृद्धि करता है, अभ्यास करता है। increases, cultivates.

√ भास – (भू॰) – (वचने) बोलना। to speak.

भासीते – क्रि॰ – (√ भाष = भाषते) बोलता है। speaks.

भासति – क्रि॰ – (√ भास = भासते) चमकता है। shines.

भासन – न॰ – (भाषण) भाषण। speech, talk.

भासन्तर – न॰ – (भाषान्तर) अन्य भाषा। different language.

भासा – स्त्री॰ – (भाषा) भाषा, बोली। language, dialect.

भासित – न॰ – (भाषित) कथन। saying, statement.

भासितु-भासी – पु॰ – (भाषी) बोलने वाला, कहने वाला। one who says.

भासुर – वि॰ – (भास्वर) दीप्त, चमकदार। bright, shining.

√ भिक्ख – (भू॰) – (याचने) माँगना। to beg.

भिक्खक – वि॰ – (भिक्षक) भिखमंगा। a beggar.

भिक्खति – क्रि॰ – (√ भिक्ष = भिक्षते) भीख मांगता है, याचना करता है। begs, asks for alms.

भिक्खन – न॰ – (भिक्षण) भीख माँगना। begging.

भिक्खा – स्त्री॰ – (भिक्षा) भिक्षा। alms.

भिक्खाचरिया – स्त्री॰ – (भिक्षाचर्या) भिक्षाटन। going about for alms.

भिक्खाचार – पु॰ – (भिक्षाचार) भिक्षाटन। going about for alms.

भिक्खाहार – वि॰ – (भिक्षाहार) भिक्षा द्वारा प्राप्त आहार। food received by begging.

भिक्खा-परम्पर-जातक – (जा॰ सं॰ 496) – कथा बतलाती है कि कैसे राजा को प्राप्त भोजन क्रमशः प्रत्येक बुद्ध को प्राप्त हुआ। the story (No. 496) tells how the food offered to the king, satisfied Pacceka-Buddha.

भिक्खु – पु॰ – (भिक्षु) बौद्ध भिक्षु। a Buddhist monk.

भिक्खुणी – स्त्री॰ – (भिक्षुणी) बौद्ध भिक्षुणी। a Buddhist nun.

भिक्खु-भाव – पु॰ – (भिक्षु-भाव) भिक्षुत्व। monkhood.

भिक्खु-भेद – पु॰ – (भिक्षु-भेद) भिक्षु विशेष। a particular *bhikṣu.*

भिक्खु-संघ – पु॰ – (भिक्षु-संघ) भिक्षुओं का संघ। congregation of monks.

भिङ्क – पु॰ – (करि-पोवक) गज-शावक, हाथी का बच्चा। a young elephant.

भिङ्कार – पु॰ – पानी की झारी। a water jug.

भिज्जति – क्रि॰ – (√ भिद् = भिद्यते) टूट जाता है, नष्ट हो जाता है। becomes broken or destroyed.

भिज्जन – न॰ – (भिद्यन) टूटना। breaking itself.

भिज्जन-धम्म – वि॰ – (भिद्यन-धर्म) टूटने के स्वभाव वाला, भंगुर। brittle, falling into ruin.

भित्ति – स्त्री॰ – (भित्ति) दीवार। a wall.

भित्ति-पाद – पु॰ – (भित्ति-पाद) दीवार की नींव। foundation of a wall.

√ भिद – (रु॰) – (विदारणे) तोड़ना-फोड़ना, चीरना। to break, to split.

√ भिद – (दि॰) – (विदारणे) तोड़ना-फोड़ना, चीरना। to break, to tear, to split.

भिन्दति – क्रि॰ – (√ भिद = भिनत्ति) तोड़ता है, फाड़ता है, पृथक्-पृथक् करता है। breaks, splits.

भिन्दन – न॰ (भिन्दन) टूटना। breaking up.

भिन्न – कृदन्त – (√ भिद + क्त = भिन्न) टूटा हुआ। broken, separated.

भिन्नत्त – न॰ – (भिन्नत्व/भिन्नता) भिन्नत्व। diversity.

भिन्न-भाव – पु॰ – (भिन्न-भाव) पार्थक्य। diversity.

भिन्न-नाव – वि॰ – (भिन्न नौका) टूटी नाव। a wrecked ship.

भिन्न-पट – न॰ – (भिन्न-पट) फटा-वस्त्र। a torn cloth.

भिन्न-मरियाद – वि॰ – (भिन्न-मर्याद) सीमोल्लंघित। gone beyond limits.

भिन्न-सील – वि॰ – (भिन्न-शील) शील-भ्रष्ट। one who has broken some precepts.

भिय्यो – अव्यय – (भूयः) और अधिक, अत्यधिक। still more, further.

भिय्योसो – अव्यय – (भूयशः) पुनः-पुनः, अधिकाधिक। more, much, again and again.

भिय्यसो-मत्ताय – क्रि॰ वि॰ – (भूयशः मत्या) अत्यधिक, अपनी योग्यता से अधिक। exceedingly, more than one's ability.

भिस – न॰ – (विस/बिस) कमल-नाल तन्तु, कमल-नाल के भीतर का तन्तु या सूत्र। fibre of a lotus, stem or stalk.

भिस-पुप्फ – न॰ – (विस-पुष्प) कमल-पुष्प। lotus flower.

भिस-मुटठाल – न॰ – (बिस-मृणाल) कमल-नाल, कमल का डंठल जिसमें फूल लगा रहता है। lotus-stalk.

भिस-जातक – (जा॰ सं॰ 488) – पिता के मरने पर सभी भाई द्वारा सम्पदा छोड़कर बहनों के साथ हिमालयाभिमुख होने की कथा। the story (No. 488) of a family in which on the father's death all the brothers and sisters left the entire property and look their abode in the Himālayas as ascetics.

भिसक्क – पु॰ – (भिषक) वैद्य, चिकित्सक। a physician.

भिस-पुप्फ-जातक – (जा॰ सं॰ 392) – देवी ने बोधिसत्व को दूसरे व्यक्ति के स्वामित्व वाले फूल की गन्ध मात्र सूँघने के लिए उसे गन्ध चोर बतलाया। the story (No. 392) tells how the goddess called Bodhisattva a thief for smelling a lotus which did not belong to him.

भिसि – स्त्री॰ – (वै. बृशी ⁄ वृशी ⁄ वृसी) घास या पुआल का गद्दा। a cushion or a pad made of grass.

भिंसन-भिंसनक – वि॰ – (भीषण) भयानक। a horrible, dreadful.

√भी – (भू॰) – (भये) डरना। to fear.

भीत – कृदन्त – (भीत) डरा हुआ। frightened.

भीति – स्त्री॰ – (भीति) भय। fear.

भीम – वि॰ – (भीम) भयानक। dreadful, horrible.

भीमसेन-जातक – (जा॰ सं॰ 80) – कथा बताती है कि किस प्रकार भीमसेन का उपयोग कर बौने धनुषधारी ने यश प्राप्त किया। the story (No. 80) tells how an incapable dwarf earned fame using the skill of the able one.

भीयो – वि॰ – (भूयः) बहुत। much.

भीरु – वि॰ – (भीरु) कायर, डरपोक। timid, fearful.

भीरुक – वि॰ – (भीरु) डरपोक, कायर। fearful, timid.

भीरुत्तान – न॰ – (भीरु-त्राण) डरपोक का संरक्षक। refuge for the fearful.

भुक्करण – न॰ – (बुक्कनम्) कुत्ते का भौंकना। barking (of a dog).

भुंकार ⁄ भुक्कार – पु॰ – (बुक्कार) (कुत्ते का) भौंकना। barking (of a dog).

भुंकरोति – क्रि॰ – (√बुक्क = बुक्कति) भौंकता है। barks.

√भुज – (तु॰) – (कौटिल्ये) टेढ़ा होना। to be zig-zag.

√भुज – (रु॰) – (पालनाहरेषु) पालना, खाना। to bring up, to eat.

भुज – पु॰ – (भुज) भुजा, बाहु, कुटिलता। the arm, hand, curve.

भुज-पत्त – पु॰ – (भूर्ज-पत्र) भोज-पत्र का वृक्ष। a kind of birch (-tree).

भुजग – पु॰ – (भुजग) साँप। snake.

भुजझ –पु॰ – (भुजझ) सर्प। snake.

भुजिस्स – पु॰ – (भुजिष्य = √भुज + किष्यन) (स्वामि उच्छिष्टं भुक्क्ते) दास, गुलाम, पालि में दासता से मुक्त हुए व्यक्ति के लिए भी प्रयुक्त। a slave, in Pāli it is used for a freed slave also.

भुज्जक – पु॰ – (भोक्ता) खाने वाला या भागने वाला। one who eats or enjoys.

भुज्जति – क्रि॰ – (√भुज = भुनक्ति = भुङ्क्ते) खाता है, भोगता है। eats, enjoys.

भुज्जन – न॰ – (भुज्जन) खाना, उपयोग करना। eating, enjoying.

भुज्जन-काल – पु॰ – (भोजन-काल) भोजन का समय। meal time.

भुत्त – कृदन्त – (√भुज + क्त = भुक्त) खाया हुआ, सोया हुआ। eaten, enjoyed.

भुत्तावी – वि॰ – (भुक्ताविन) खाने वाला। one who has had a meal, one who has eaten.

भुम्म – वि॰ – (भौमिक) भूमि से सम्बन्धित, (समास में) 'तलों वाला', अर्थ में प्रयुक्त। terrestrial, (in compounds) having stages or stories.

भुम्मट्ठ – वि॰ – (भूमिष्ठ) भूमि स्थित। situated on earth.

भुम्मत्थरण – न॰ – (भूम्यास्तरण) दर्रा, बिछावन । earpot, ground covering.

भुम्मन्तर – न॰ – (भूम्यन्तर) भिन्न भूमियाँ । different stages or planes.

भुवन – न॰ – (भुवन) संसार । the world.

भुस (1) – न॰ – (बुस) भूसा । chaff.

भुस (2) – न॰ – (मृश) बहुत अधिक । much, abundant.

भुसं – क्रि॰ वि॰ – (भृशम्) अधिकांशतः । exceedingly, frequently.

भुसति – क्रि॰ – (√ बुक्क् = बुक्कति) भौंकता है । barks.

भुसत्थ – पु॰ – (भृशत्व) आधिक्य का अर्थ । the excess.

√ भू – (भू) – (सताया) होना । to be or exist.

भू – स्त्री॰ – (भू) पृथ्वी । the earth.

भूत – कृदन्त – (√ भू + क्त = भूत) हुआ, उत्पन्न हुआ । become, born, produced, what has happened.

भूत-पुन – (भूत) पञ्च-तत्त्व, कल्पित भूतयोनि । an element, a ghost.

भूत-काय – पु॰ – (भूत-काय) महाभूतों से उत्पन्न शरीर । body produced by elements.

भूत-गाम – पु॰ – (भूत-ग्राम) जीवधारी मात्र की समष्टि, वनस्पति । vegetation.

भूत-गाह – पु॰ – (भूत-ग्राह) भूत-प्रेत द्वारा ग्रसित । possession by a demon.

भूतणक – न॰ – (भूतृणक) फणिज्जक, उसीर नामक सुगन्धित घास । a fragrant grass, *Andropogon Schoenanthus.*

भूत-वादी – वि॰ – (भूतवादी) यथार्थवादी । truthful.

भूत-वेज्ज – पु॰ – (भूत-वैद्य) भूत उतारने वाला, ओझा । an exorcist.

भूतत्त – न॰ – (भूतत्व) होने का भाव । the fact of having become.

भूतिक – वि॰ – (भौतिक) भौतिक । composite, of elements.

भूतिण – न॰ – (भू-तृणक) फणिज्जक या समीरण नामक भूतृण, उशीर । a fragrant grass, *Andropogon schoenanthus.*

भूधर – पु॰ – (भूधर) पहाड़ । mountain.

भू-नाथ – पु॰ – (भू-नाथ) राजा । a king.

भू-भुज – पु॰ – (भू-भुज) भूपति । king.

भूमक – वि॰ – (भूमिक) समासान्त में प्रयुक्त तल्लों वाला (मकान) जैसे पञ्चभूमिक पाँच मंजिल वाला । having five floors or storeys.

भूमि – स्त्री॰ – (भूमि) पृथ्वी । the earth.

भूमि-कम्पा – स्त्री॰ – (भू-कम्प) भू-कम्प । an earthquake.

भूमि-गत – वि॰ – (भूमि-गत) जमीन पर या जमीन के भीतर स्थित । situated on the ground or stored away in the ground.

भूमि-तल – न॰ – (भूमि-तल) पृथ्वी तल । ground surface.

भूमिप्पदेस – पु॰ – (भूमि-प्रदेश) जमीन का टुकड़ा । a piece of land.

भूमि-भाग – पु॰ – (भूमि-भाग) भू-भाग, जमीन का टुकड़ा । a piece of land.

भूरि – स्त्री॰ – (भूरि) प्रज्ञा । wisdom.

भूरि – वि॰ – (भूरि) विपुल, प्रचुर । abundant.

भूरि-दत्त-जातक – (जा॰ सं॰ 543) – एक नागकन्या द्वारा एक तापस के लुभाए जाने की कथा । story (No. 543) of an ascetic enticed by a Nāga maiden.

भूरि-पञ्ञ – वि॰ – (भूरि-प्रज्ञ) बहुत प्रज्ञा वाला । of extensive wisdom.

भूरि-पञ्ह-जातक – (जा॰ सं॰ 452) – महाउम्मग्ग जातक का एक अंश । it is a (story No. 452) part of the Mahā-umagga Jātaka.

भूरि-मेध – वि॰ – (भूरि-मेध) बहुत मेधावी । of much wisdom.

√ **भूस** – (चु॰) – (अलङ्कार) सजाना । to decorate, to adorn.

√ **भूस** – (भू॰) – (अलङ्कार) सजाना । to decorate, to adorn.

भूसन – न॰ – (भूषण) आभूषण, अलंकार । an ornament, decoration.

भूसा – स्त्री॰ – (भूषा) सजावट । decoration.

भूसापेति – (√ भूष + णिच् = भूषयति) सजवाता है । causes to adorn of decorate.

भूसेति – क्रि॰ – (√ भूष = भूषयति) सजाता है । decorates.

भेक – पु॰ – (भेक) मेंढक । frog.

भेज्ज – वि॰ – (भेद्य) भुरभुरा, जो टूट सके (न॰) टूटना या काटना । brittle, breakable, (n.) breaking or cutting off.

भेण्डिवाल – पु॰ – एक प्रक्षेपास्त्र । a kind of missile.

भेण्डुक – पु॰ – (गेन्दुक) कन्दुक, खेलने की गेंद । a ball for playing.

भेत्तु – पु॰ – (भेदक) तोड़ने वाला । one who breaks.

भेद – पु॰ – (भेद) मेल का अभाव, अनेकता । breach, disunion.

भेदक – वि॰ – (भेदक) एकता नष्ट करने वाला । one who causes disunion.

भेदकर – वि॰ – (भेदकर) भेद पैदा करने वाला । bringing disunion.

भेदन – न॰ – (भेदन) टूटना । breaking, break.

भेदनक – वि॰ – (भेदनीय) तोड़ डालने योग्य, फूटने योग्य । fit to be broken, fit for disunion.

भेदन-धम्म – वि॰ – (भेदन-धर्मी) टूटने के स्वभाव वाला, भंगुर । perishable.

भेदित – कृदन्त – (√ भिद् + क्त = भिन्न) टूटा हुआ । broken.

भेदति – (√ भिद् = भिनत्ति) तोड़ता है । breaks.

भेरण्ड – पु॰ – (भेरुण्ड) गीदड़ । a jackal.

भेरण्डक – न॰ – (भेरुण्डक) गीदड़ की आवाज । howling of jackal.

भेरव – वि॰ – (भैरव) भयानक । frightful.

भेरि – स्त्री॰ – (भेरी) दुन्दुभि, बड़ी ढोल । a drum (musical instrument).

भेरि-चरण – न॰ – (भेरी-चरण) ढोल बजाकर मुनादी कराना । proclamation through sounding a drum.

भेरि-तल – न॰ – (भेरी-तल) ढोल का तल्ला । the surface of a drum.

भेरि-वादक – पु॰ – (भेरी-वादक) ढोल बजाने वाला । a drummer.

भेरि-वादन – न॰ – (भेरी-वादन) ढोल का बजाना । sounding of a drum.

भेरि-सद्द – पु॰ – (भेरी-शब्द) ढोल की आवाज । sound of drum.

भेरि-वाद-जातक – (जा॰ सं॰ 59) – लड़के ने पिता का कहना न मानकर ढोल को बार-बार बजाया जिससे डाकुओं ने आकर पिता-पुत्र दोनों को लूट लिया। the story (No. 59) tells how a disobedient son with his foolish action (dacoits to rob caused) both the son and father.

भेसज्ज – न॰ – (भैषज्य) भेषजम्, औषधि। medicine.

भेसज्ज-कपाल – न॰ – (भैषज्य-कपाल) औषधि-पात्र। medicine bowl.

भो – अव्यय – (भो!) श्रीमन्!, जैसा सम्बोधन का बहुप्रचलित शब्द। a familiar term of address, o, ae, my dear.

भोग – पु॰ – (भोग) धन-सम्पदा, आनन्द। possession, wealth, enjoyment.

भोगक्खन्ध – पु॰ – (भोग स्कन्ध) धन का ढेर। a mass of wealth.

भोग-गाम – पु॰ – (भोग-ग्राम) करदाता, गाँव। a tributary village.

भोग-मद – पु॰ – (भोग-मद) धन का अभिमान। pride of wealth.

भोगवन्तु – वि॰ – (भोगवत) धनी। a wealthy person.

भोगी – पु॰ – (भोगी) (1) सर्प (2) धनी व्यक्ति। (1) a serpent, (2) wealthy person.

भोग्ग – वि॰ – (भोग्य) उपयोग की वस्तु, भोग्य। thing to be enjoyed.

भोजक – पु॰ – (भोजक) खिलाने वाला, कर उगाहने वाला। one who feeds, a collector of revenues.

भोजन – न॰ – (भोजन) खाद्य-सामग्री। food, meal.

भोजनिय – वि॰ – (भोजनीय) खाने योग्य, स्वादिष्ट खाद्य-सामग्री। fit to be eaten, soft edible food.

भोनाजानीय-जातक – (जा॰ सं॰ 23) – श्रेष्ठ घोड़े की कथा जिसने जख्मी होने पर भी शत्रु पर आक्रमण किया। the story (No. 23) of a faithful horse which, even after being wounded, attacked, its masters enemies.

भोजापेति – क्रि॰ – (भोजयति) खिलाता है। feeds, serves at meals.

भोजी – वि॰ – (भोजी) समास में प्रयुक्त, भोजन करने वाला। feeding on, one who eats.

भोजेति – वि॰ – (भोजयति) खिलाता है। feeds.

भोज्ज – न॰ – (भोज्य) खाने योग्य वस्तु। an edible thing.

भोज्ज – कृदन्त – (भोज्य) खाने योग्य। fit to be eaten.

भोति-सम्बोधन – (भवति!) महिला के लिए आदरयुक्त सम्बोधन। Madam (respectful address).

भोतब्ब – न॰ – (भोक्तव्य) देखें भोज्ज। see Bhojja.

भोत्तु – कृदन्त – (√ भुज + तुमुन = भोक्तुम्) खाने के लिए। to eat, for eating.

भोवादी – पु॰ – (भो-वादी) ब्राह्मण। a brāhmaṇa.

म

म – पालि वर्णमाला का पच्चीसवाँ व्यञ्जन । The 25th consonant of Pāli alphabet.

मंस – न॰ – (मांस) मांस, गोश्त । flesh, meat.

मंस-चक्खु – न॰ – (चर्म-चक्षु) दिव्य-चक्षु आदि से भिन्न भौतिक आँखें । the eye.

मंस-जातक – (जा॰ सं॰ 315) – कथा बतलाती है कि मधुर वाणी और विनम्र निवेदन सफलता का रहस्य है । the story (No. 315) concludes that sweet voice and humble behaviour is the key to success.

मंस-पुञ्ज – पु॰ – (मांस-पुञ्ज) मांस का ढेर । heap of flesh.

मंस-पेसि – स्त्री॰ – (मांस-पेशी) पट्ठा, मांस-पेशी । muscle.

मंसोदन – न॰ – (मांसौदन) मांस मिला पुलाव, बिरियानी । rice mixed with meat.

मकचि – पु॰ – (शण) पटसन, पटुआ का पौधा जिसके सन से धनुष की डोरी बनाई जाती है । the jute, hemp, the plant *Pentaptera Tomentosa*.

मकचि-वाक – न॰ – (शण-त्वक्) पटुए का छिलका जिसे बटकर रस्सी बनाई जाती है । the fibres of hemp.

मकचि-वत्थ – न॰ – (शण-वस्त्र) पटुए का बुना वस्त्र । a canvas.

मकर – पु॰ – (मकर) मगरमच्छ । a crocodile.

मकर-दन्तक – न॰ – (मकर-दन्तक) मगरमच्छ के दाँतों के समान । a design like that of a crocodile's teeth.

मकरन्द – पु॰ – (मकरन्द) पुष्प रस । the nectar of a flower.

मकस – पु॰ – (मशक) मच्छर । a mosquito.

मकस-वारण – न॰ – (मशक-वारण) मसहरी । mosquito-net.

मकस-जातक – (जा॰ सं॰ 44) – बाप के सिर पर बैठे मच्छर को हटाने के लिए बेटे ने कुल्हाड़ी से प्रहार कर बाप का सिर ही फाड़ दिया । this story (No. 44) concludes that, an enemy with sense is better than a stupid friend.

मुकुट – पु॰ तथा न॰ – (मुकुट) मुकुट, ताज । crest, crown, a coronet.

मुकुल – न॰ – (मुकुल) कलिका, फूल की कली । bud, a knob.

मक्कट – पु॰ – (मर्कट) बन्दर । a monkey.

मक्कटक – पु॰ – (मर्कटक) मकड़ी । a spider.

मक्कटक-सुत्त – न॰ – (मर्कटक-सूत्र) मकड़ी के जाले का धागे । the thread of a spider-net.

मक्कट-जातक – (जा॰ सं 173) – एक बन्दर की कथा जिसने तपस्वी का बल्कल चीर धारण करके एक तपस्वी की कुटी में प्रवेश करना चाहा, किन्तु सफल न हुआ । it is a story (No. 173) of a monkey who wearing the bark-dress of a dead ascetic wished to enter another ascetic's hut but was driven away.

मक्कटी – स्त्री॰ – (**मर्कटी**) बन्दरी। a female monkey.

√ **मक्ख** – (भू॰) – (**प्रक्षणे**) माखना। to smear.

मक्ख – पु॰ – (**प्रक्ष**) दूसरे के गुण का मूल्य घटाना। concealment of one's voice.

मक्खण – न॰ – (**प्रक्षण**) (तेल) चुपड़ना। smearing, anointing.

मक्खली-गोसाल – पु॰ – (**मक्खलि-गोशाल**) बुद्ध के समकालीन छः भिन्न मतावलम्बी आचार्यों में से एक जो आजीवक पंथ के प्रवर्तक थे। इनका सिद्धान्त अक्रियवाद के नाम से जाना जाता है। one of the heretical teachers at the time of the Buddha. According to his doctrine the attainment of any benefits does not depend either on one's own actions or of other's and also not on human efforts.

मक्खिका – स्त्री॰ – (**मक्षिका**) मक्खी। a fly.

मक्खित – कृदन्त – (**मक्षित**) चुपड़ा हुआ। माखा हुआ। smeared, anointed with.

मक्खी – पु॰ – (**प्रक्षी**) दूसरे के गुणों का मूल्य घटाने वाला। one who devaluates the merit of others.

मक्खेति – क्रि॰ – (**प्रक्षति**) माखता है, चुपड़ता है। smears, anoints with.

माखादेव-जातक – (जा॰ सं॰ 9) – एक राजा की कथा जिसने सिर में उगे सफेद बाल को देवदूत समझकर प्रव्रज्या ग्रहण की। finding a grey-hair the king handed over his kingdom to his son and renounced the world as he thought he had seen the death's messenger.

मग – पु॰ – (**मृग**) पशु, चौपाया। a quadruped, an animal.

मगसिर – पु॰ – (**मृगशिर**) मृगशिरा नामक नक्षत्र विशेष। name of a constellation.

मगध – पु॰ – (**मगध**) बुद्धकालीन 16 महाजनपदों में से एक जिसका विस्तार आधुनिक बिहार और उड़ीसा तक था। Magadha which was one of 16 states during Buddha's time, includes present Bihar and Orissa.

मग्ग – पु॰ – (**मार्ग**) रास्ता, सड़क, पथ। path, road, way.

√ **मग्ग** – (भू॰) – (**अन्वेषण**) खोजना। to search.

√ **मग्ग** – (चु॰) – (**अन्वेषणे**) खोजना। to search.

मग्ग-किलन्त – (**मार्ग-क्लिन्न**) चलने से थका हुआ। wearied by walking.

मग्ग-कुसल – वि॰ – (**मार्ग-कुशल**) रास्ते का जानकार। one who knows the road well.

मग्गक्खायी – वि॰ – (**मार्गख्यायी**) रास्ता बताने वाला। preacher, one who shows the path.

मग्गङ्ग – न॰ – (**मार्ग + अङ्ग**) सम्यक् दृष्टि आदि आर्य-मार्ग के आठ अङ्ग। यथा सम्यक् दृष्टि, सम्यक् संकल्प, सम्यक् वाचा, सम्यक् कर्मान्त, सम्यक् आजीविका,

सम्यक् व्यायाम, सम्यक् स्मृति और सम्यक् समाधि। the eight constituents of the path—viz., right view, right aspiration, right speech, right-conduct, right livelihood, right effort, right mindfulness, and right rapture.

मग्ग-ञाण – न॰ – (**मार्ग-ज्ञान**) मार्ग के बारे में ज्ञान। knowledge of path.

मग्गञ्जू – वि॰ – (**मार्गज्ञ**) मार्ग का जानकार। one who knows the path.

मग्गट्ठ – वि॰ – (**मार्गस्थ**) मार्ग पर स्थित। one who is on the path, or who has attained the path.

मग्ग-दूसी – पु॰ – (**मार्ग-दूषक**) मुसाफिरों को लूटने वाला डाकू। a highway robber.

मग्ग-देसक – वि॰ – (**मार्ग-दर्शक**) मार्ग-दर्शक। one who points out the way.

मग्ग-पटिपन्न – वि॰ – (**मार्ग-प्रतिपन्न**) यात्री, मार्गारुढ़। one who has entered the path.

मग्ग-भावना – स्त्री॰ – (**मार्ग-भावना**) आर्य-मार्ग का अभ्यास। cultivation of the path, following the path.

मग्ग-मूलह – वि॰ – (**मार्ग-मूढ़**) मार्ग-भ्रष्ट, रास्ता भूला हुआ। one who has lost the path.

मग्ग-सच्च – न॰ – (**मार्ग-सत्य**) आर्य-मार्ग नामक सत्य, बुद्ध द्वारा उपदिष्ट चार आर्य सत्य। the truth concerning the path, four noble paths preached by Buddha.

मग्गति – क्रि॰ – (**मार्गति**) खोजता है, पता लगाता है। seeks, traces out.

मग्गन – न॰ – (**मार्गण**) खोज, तलाश। search, tracing out.

मग्गना – स्त्री॰ – (**मार्गणा**) खोज, तलाश। search, tracing out.

मग्गिक – पु॰ – (**मार्गिक**) पथारुढ़, मार्गारुढ़। a wayfarer.

मग्गित – कृदन्त – (**मार्गित**) खोज लिया गया मार्ग। sought way, traced path.

मग्गुर – पु॰ – (**मङ्गुर/मङ्गूर**) माँगुर या मंगूर नामक मछली की जाति विशेष। a kind of river fish.

मग्गेति – क्रि॰ – (**मार्गयति**) देखें मग्गति। see Maggati.

मघवन्तु – पु॰ – (**मघवा**) शक्र (इन्द्र) का एक और नाम। another name of Indra.

मघा – स्त्री॰ – (**मघा**) मघा नक्षत्र। name of the tenth lunar mansion containing five stars.

मङ्कु – वि॰ – (**मङ्कु**) उत्साहहीन। down cast.

मङ्कु-भाव – पु॰ – (**मङ्कु-भाव**) नैतिक दौर्बल्य, उत्साहहीनता। moral weakness.

मङ्कु-भुत – वि॰ – (**मङ्कु-भूत**) मन्दोत्साह। downcast.

√ **मङ्ग** – (भू॰) – (**माङ्गल्ये**) मङ्गल होना। to be auspicious.

मङ्गल – वि॰ – (**मङ्गल**) (1) शुभ (2) राजकीय। (1) auspicious, (2) royal.

मङ्गल-किच्च – न॰ – (**मङ्गल-कृत्य**) माङ्गलिक कार्य, उत्सव। festivity, auspicious act.

मङ्गल-कोलाहल – पु॰ – (**मङ्गल-कोलाहल**)

शुभ मुहूर्त्त आदि के सम्बन्ध में विवाद। dispute about auspicious things or acts.

मङ्गल-दिवस – पु० – (मङ्गल-दिवस) उत्सव का दिन, शादी का दिन। a festival day, a marriage day.

मङ्गल-अस्स – पु० – (मङ्गल-अश्व) राजकीय अश्व। the royal horse.

मङ्गल-सिन्धव – पु० – (मङ्गल-सैन्धव) राजकीय घोड़ा। the royal horse.

मङ्गल-पोक्खरणी – स्त्री० – (मङ्गल-पुष्करणी) मङ्गल-पुष्करणी। royal bathing-pond.

मङ्गल-सिलापट्ट – न० – (मङ्गल-शिलापट) राजा के बैठने का शिलासन। a slab used by a king to sit on.

मङ्गल-सुपिन – न० – (मङ्गल-स्वप्ने) शुभ स्वप्न। a lucky dream.

मङ्गल-हत्थी – पु० – (मङ्गल-हस्ती) राजकीय हाथी। the royal elephant.

मङ्गल-जातक – (जा० सं० 87) – चूहे द्वारा काट डाले गए कपड़ो को घर मे रखना अशुभ समझकर अन्धविश्वासी ब्राह्मण के द्वारा श्मशान भूमि में फिंकवाने की कथा। this story (No. 87) relates to a brāhmaṇa who believed in omens.

मङ्गुर – पु० – (मङ्गुर) (1) नदी की मछली विशेष (2) (वि०) पीत-वर्णी। (1) a kind of river-fish (2) (adj.) of dark-yellow colour.

मच्च – पु० – (मर्त्य) मरण-धर्मी अर्थात् मनुष्य। a man.

मच्चु – पु० – (मृत्यु) मृत्यु, मौत। death.

मच्चु-तर – वि० – (मृत्युतर) मृत्युजयी। one who overcomes death.

मच्चु-धेय्य – न० – (मृत्यु-क्षेत्र) मृत्यु के अधिकार में स्थित। the sphere of death.

मच्चु-परायण – वि० – (मृत्यु-परायण) मरणाधीन। subject to death.

मच्चु-पास – न० – (मृत्यु-पाश) मृत्यु-पाश, मृत्यु-बन्धन। snare of death.

मच्चु-मुख – न० – (मृत्यु-मुख) मृत्यु का सामना। facing death.

मच्चु-राज – पु० – (मृत्यु-राज) यमराज। the king of death.

मच्चु-वस – पु० – (मृत्यु-वश) मृत्यु की सामर्थ्य। the power of death.

मच्चु-हायी – वि० – (मृत्युञ्जयी) मृत्यु को जीतने वाला। victorious over death.

मच्छ – न० – (मत्स्य) मछली। a fish.

मच्छण्ड – न० – (मत्स्याण्ड) मछली का अण्डा। fish egg.

मच्छण्डि – स्त्री० – (मत्स्याण्डिका) भेली, गुड़, गन्ने के रस को पकाकर बनाया गया गोल पिण्ड। treacle, molasses ball like form of boiled sugarcane juice.

मत्स्य-भस – न० – (मत्स्य-मांस) मत्स्य-मांस। fish and flesh.

मच्छ-बन्ध – पु० – (मत्स्य-बन्ध) मछुआ। fisherman.

मच्छ-जातक – (जा० सं० 75) – इस जातक कथा में मछली की सत्य क्रिया से वर्षा होने का वर्णन है। the story (No. 75) tells how drought-hit public got a heavy rain by a noble act of a fish.

मच्छ-चरिया – न० – (मात्सर्य) ईर्ष्या, असूया, डाह। envy, jealousy, malice.

मच्छरचारी – पु॰ – (मत्सर-चारी) कृपण, कंजूस। a miser.

मच्छरायति – क्रि॰ – (मत्सरायते) कंजूसी करता है। acts miserly.

मच्छरिय – न॰ – (मात्सर्य) मात्सर्य, कंजूसपन। partiality, jealousy, miserliness.

मच्छा – पु॰ – (मत्स्य महाजनपद) बुद्ध-कालीन (1) सोलह महाजनपदों में से एक जनपद (2) मत्स्य के वासी। (1) one of the sixteen *mahā janapada*s (states) of north India at the time of the Buddha (2) the inhabitants of Matsya.

मच्छिक – पु॰ – (मात्स्यिक) मछलीमार, मछुआरा। fisherman.

मच्छी – स्त्री॰ – (मत्स्य) मछली। fish.

मच्छुद्दान-जातक – (जा॰ सं॰ 288) – मछली के पेट में से रुपयों की थैली वापस मिलने की कथा। the story (No. 288) tells how the stolen money was recovered from the stomach of a fish.

मच्छेर – न॰ – (मात्सर्य) देखें मच्छरिय। see Machariya.

मज्ज – न॰ – (मद्य) मद्य। an intoxicant.

√ मज्ज – (भू॰) – (मार्जने) साफ करना। to clean.

मज्जन – न॰ – (मद्यन) नशा। intoxication.

मज्जप – वि॰ – (मद्यप) मदिरापायी, शराबी। one who a drunkard drinks liquor.

मज्जपान – न॰ – (मद्यपान) मदिरापान, शराब पीना। taking liquor or wine.

मज्जपायी – वि॰ – (मद्यपायी) देखें मज्जप। see Majjapa.

मज्ज-विक्कयी – पु॰ – (मद्य-विक्रयी) मद्य विक्रेता। wine-seller.

मज्जति – क्रि॰ – (√ मृज् = मार्जयति) माँजता है, साफ करता है, पालिश करता है। cleans, wipes, polishes.

मज्जना – स्त्री॰ – (मार्जना) माँजना। wiping, polishing.

मज्जार – पु॰ – (मार्जार) विडाल, बिल्ला। a cat.

मज्जारी – स्त्री॰ – (मार्जारी) विडाली, बिल्ली। she-cat.

मज्झ – पु॰ – (मध्य) मध्य भाग, बीचका। the middle.

मज्झट्ठ-मज्झत्त – वि॰ – (मध्यस्थ) मध्यस्थ, पक्षपात-रहित। neutral, impartial.

मज्झत्त – वि॰ – (मध्यत्त्व) मध्यस्थता। impartiality.

मज्झण्ह – पु॰ – (मध्याह्न) दुपहर, मध्याह्न। the noon, mid-day.

मज्झत्तता – स्त्री॰ – (मध्यस्थता) पक्षपात रहित, मध्यस्थता। impartiality, equanimity.

मज्झ-देस – पु॰ – (मध्य-देश) मध्य देश जो बौद्ध धर्म का उद्भव विकास क्षेत्र और प्राचीन काल का सर्वाधिक जाग्रत् एवं समुन्नत क्षेत्र रहा है। पालि वाङ्मय के अनुसार इसकी लम्बाई तीन सौ योजन, चौड़ाई ढाई सौ योजन और परिधि नौ सौ योजन थी। वर्तमान उत्तर प्रदेश इसी के अन्तर्गत था। the country of middle India which was the birthplace of Buddhism and the region of early activities, according to Pāli scriptures, it was three hundred *yojana*s in length, two-and-a-half hundred in breadth and nine hundred in circumference. The present day Uttar Pradesh was within this area. An *yojana* equals 2.5, 5 or 9 miles according to different calculations.

मज्झान्तिक-समय – (मध्याह्) मध्याह्, दोपहर। the noon, the mid-day.

मज्झान्तिक-थेर – पु॰ – (मध्यान्तिक-स्थविर) अशोक पुत्र महेन्द्र स्थविर को उपसम्पदा देने वाला महास्थविर जो धर्म-प्रचारार्थ काश्मीर-गान्धार की ओर गए थे। the Mahāthera by whom Thera Mahendra the son of Emperor Aśoka was preached. He was sent to Kashmir and Gāndhāra for preaching Buddhism.

मज्झिम – वि॰ – (मध्यम) मध्यम, केन्द्रीय। middle, central.

मज्झिम-पुरिस – पु॰ – (मध्यम-पुरुष) औसत आदमी व्याकरणिक मध्यम पुरुष। a man of moderate height, the second person in grammar.

मज्झिम-याम – पु॰ – (मध्यम-याम) अर्धरात्रि। the middle portion of the night.

मज्झिम-वय – पु॰ – (मध्यम-वय) अधेड़ उम्र। the middle age.

मज्झिम-निकाय – पु॰ – (मध्यम-निकाय) सुत्तपिटक के पाँच निकायों में से मध्या-कार के सूत्रों का संग्रह। one of the five Nikāyas of Sutta-Piṭaka, it is a collection of the middle Nikāya.

मज्झिम-देस – पु॰ – (मध्यम / मध्य-देश) प्राचीन भारत का मध्य-मण्डल जिसकी पूर्वी सीमा वर्तमान कंकजोल मानी जा सकती है, जिसके दक्षिण-पूर्व में वर्तमान सलिलवती नदी थी, जिसके दक्षिण-पश्चिम भाग में हजारी बाग जिले का सुतकण्णिक नाम का प्राचीन कस्बा था और पश्चिम भाग में हरियाणा जिले का थानेसर नाम का कस्बा था और जिसकी उत्तरी सीमा उशीरध्वज नाम का हिमालय का कोई पर्वत भाग रही होगी। the country of central India at the time of Buddha. It extended to the town of Kankjola, on the north-east, the river Salilavatī on the south-east, the town Sutakaṇṇika on the south-west, on the west Thanesar of Harayana and on the north was Uśiradhvaja mountain.

मञ्च – पु॰ – (मञ्च) चारपायी। a bed.

मञ्चक – पु॰ – (मञ्चक) मचिया, छोटी चारपाई। a small bed.

मञ्च-परायण – वि॰ – (मञ्च-गारागण) चारपाई पर पड़ा रहने वाला। confined to bed.

मञ्च-पीठ – न॰ – (मञ्च-पीठ) चारपाई तथा कुर्सी, आदि। beds, chairs and furniture.

मञ्चवान – न॰ – (मञ्च-वान) चारपाई का बुनना। netting of a bed.

मञ्जरी – स्त्री॰ – (मञ्जरी) बौर, गुच्छा। a bunch or cluster.

मञ्जिट्ठ/मञ्जेट्ठ – वि॰ – (मञ्जिष्ठ) मजीठिया रंग। a bright redcolour.

मञ्जिट्ठा – स्त्री॰ – (मञ्जिष्ठा) मजीठ का वृक्ष। the red sanders tree, its seeds are used as a weight, by jewellers.

मञ्जिर – न॰ – (**मञ्जीर**) पाजेब, नूपुर, पाँव का आभरण। anklet, foot-ornament.

मञ्जु – वि॰ – (**मञ्जु**) रमणीय, रूचिकर। lovely, charming.

मञ्जु-भाषक – (**मञ्जु-भाषी**) प्रियंवद। speaking sweetly.

मञ्जुस्सर – वि॰ – (**मञ्जु-स्वर**) मधुर-भाषी, प्रिय-भाषी। a sweet voiced.

मञ्जूसक – पु॰ – (**मञ्जूषक**) देवताओं का वृक्ष। a celestial tree.

मञ्जूसा – स्त्री॰ – (**मञ्जूषा**) पिटक, पिटारी, पेटी। chest, box.

मञ्जेट्ठी – स्त्री॰ – (**मञ्जिष्ठा**) मजीठ (लता)। the Bengal madder.

मञ्ञति – क्रि॰ – (√**मन्** = **मन्यते**) कल्पना करता है, संकल्प करता है, विचार करता है। imagines, deems, ponders over.

मञ्ञना – स्त्री॰ – (**मन्यना**) मान्यता, कल्पना। imagination, illusion.

मञ्ञे – अव्यय – (**मन्ये**) मैं कल्पना करता हूँ। I am imagining.

मट्ठ – वि॰ – (**मृज + क्त = मृष्ट**) परिष्कृत, संस्कृत, घिसा हुआ, पालिश किया हुआ। smoothed, polished, rubbed.

मट्ट-साटक – न॰ – (**मृष्ट-शाटक**) चिकना वस्त्र। fine cloth.

मट्ठकुण्डलि-जातक – (जा॰ सं॰ 449) – ब्राह्मण के पुत्र की शोक से मुक्ति होने की कथा। the story (No. 449) tells how the brāhmaṇa overcame his grief caused by his son's death.

√**मण** – (भू॰) – (**शब्द करणे**) शब्द करना। to sound.

मणि – पु॰ – (**मणि**) रत्न, जवाहर। a gem, jewel.

मणिकार – पु॰ – (**मणिकार**) रत्नशिल्पी। a gem-cutter.

मणि-कुण्डल – न॰ – (**मणि-कुण्डल**) मणियों का कुण्डल। jewelled-earring.

मणिक्खन्ध – पु॰ – (**मणि-स्कन्ध**) अतिशय मूल्यवान मणि। precious jewel.

मणि-पल्लङ्क – पु॰ – (**मणि-पर्यन्क**) मणि-जडित पलँग या सिंहासन। a jewelled seat, a throne.

मणि-बन्ध – पु॰ – (**मणि-बन्ध**) कलाई। the wrist.

मणि-मय – पु॰ – (**मणिमय**) मणि-निर्मित। made of precious stones.

मणि-रतन – न॰ – (**मणि-रत्न**) मूल्यवान मणि। great valuable gem.

मणि-वण्ण – वि॰ – (**मणि-वर्ण**) मणि के रंग का। of the colour of crystal.

मणि-सप्प – पु॰ – (**मणि-सर्प**) मणि वाला सर्प। a kind of green snake.

मणिक – पु॰ – (**मणिक**) कूड़ा, मटका, बड़ा बर्तन। a large water vessel.

मणि-कण्ठ-जातक – (जा॰ सं॰ 253) – मणिकण्ठ नाम के सर्प ने उसकी मणि माँगने पर तपस्वी को हैरान करना छोड़ दिया। the Jātaka (No. 253) tells how an ascetic got rid of his snake friend (Nāga king) by asking the jewel, the Nāga-king was wearing round his neck.

मणि-कुण्डल-जातक – (जा॰ सं॰ 351) – कथा बतलाती है कि एक राजा ने अपना रनिवास दूषित करने वाले मन्त्री को

किस प्रकार देश से बाहर निकाल दिया। the Jātaka (No. 351) tells how a king exiled his minister who had intruded his harem.

मणि-चोर-जातक – (जा॰ सं॰ 194) – कथा बताती है कि कैसे एक राजा ने अपनी मणि गृहस्थ की गाड़ी में छिपा उसे चोर घोषित करा, उसकी रूपवती पत्नी को हथियाने की कुचेष्टा की। the Jātaka (No. 194) tells how a king with an intention of possessing a farmer's extra-ordinarily beautiful wife wrongly blamed the farmer to be a thief, by hiding the gem in his cart.

मणि-सूकर-जातक – (जा॰ सं॰ 285) – कथा बतलाती है कि कीचड़ से रगड़ने पर भी मणि अधिकाधिक चमकती है। the tale (No. 285) concludes that crystal cannot be sullied.

√ मण्ड – (चु॰) – (भूषायां) सजाना। to adorn.

√ मण्ड – (भू॰) – (भूषायां) विभूषित करना। to decorate.

मण्ड – पु॰ – (मण्ड) माँड (वि॰) अति स्पष्ट। scum of boiled rice (adj.) very clear.

मण्डन – न॰ – (मण्डन) सजावट। adornment, decoration.

मण्डन-जातिक – वि॰ – (मण्डनप्रिय) सजने-सजाने का शौकीन। one who is fond of decoration.

मण्डप – पु॰ – (मण्डप) मण्डप। temporary shed, pavilion.

मण्डल – न॰ – (मण्डल) घेरा, गोल वेदिका। a circle, a round flat platform.

मण्डल-माल – पु॰ – (मण्डल-माल) गोलाकार मण्डप। a circular pavilion.

मण्डलिक – वि॰ – (मण्डलिक) प्रदेश (मण्डल) से सम्बन्धित। belonging to a region.

मण्डलिस्सर – पु॰ – (मण्डलेश्वर) मण्डल का शासक। governor of a province.

मण्डली – वि॰ – (मण्डली) मण्डल वाला। having a disc, circular.

मण्डित – क्रि॰ – (√ मण्ड + क्त = मंडित) सज्जित, विभूषित। adorned, decorated.

मण्डूक – पु॰ – (मण्डूक) मेंढक। a frog.

मण्डेति – क्रि॰ – (√ मण्ड = मण्डति/ मण्डयति) सजाता है। adorns, decorates.

मत (1) – न॰ – (मत) राय, सम्मति, विचार। a view.

मत (2) – कृदन्त – (√ मृ + क्त = मृत) मृत। dead.

मत-किच्च – न॰ – (मृत-कृत्य) मृत व्यक्ति के सम्बन्ध में सम्पादनीय कृत्य। rites for the dead, to be performed for dead.

मतक – पु॰ – (मृतक) मृतक, मरा हुआ। the deceased.

मतक-भत्त – न॰ – (मृतक-भोज) मृतक व्यक्ति के श्राद्ध में दिया जाने वाला भोज। feast offered for the dead.

मतक-वत्थ – न॰ – (मृतक-वस्त्र) मृतक व्यक्ति के नाम पर सम्बन्धियों द्वारा दिया गया वस्त्र-दान। clothes offered for the dead.

मतक-भत्त-जातक – (जा॰ सं॰ 18) – इस कथा में एक मृतक भोज में बलि के पूर्व बलि के बकरे ने हँसने का रहस्य वर्णित किया। the Jātaka (No. 18) unveils the laughing of a goat when it was to be slain by Mataka Bhatta.

मतरोदन-जातक – (जा॰ सं॰ 317) – कथा में उल्लेख है कि भाई तथा पिता के मरने पर भी अनित्यता का स्मरण कर बोधिसत्व ने एक बूँद भी आँसू नहीं गिराया। the Jātaka tells that Bodhisattva at the death of his father and brother shed not a drop of tear, remembering that all things are transient.

मति – स्त्री॰ – (मति) प्रज्ञा, विचार। wisdom, idea.

मति-मन्तु – वि॰ – (मतिमान्) बुद्धिमान। wise.

मति-विप्पहीन – वि॰ – (मति-विप्रहीण) क्षीणमति, मूर्ख। a foolish, imprudent.

मत्त – कृदन्त – (मत्त) नशे में चूर, गर्व में चूर। intoxicated, arrogant.

मत्त – अव्यय – (मात्र) समासान्त में मात्रा-बोध के लिए। in compounds of the size as much as.

मत्त-हत्थी – पु॰ – (मस्त-हस्ती) मत्त गज, नशें में चूर हाथी। a rutted elephant.

मत्तञ्ञू – वि॰ – (मात्रज्ञ) परिमाणविद, मात्रा का जानकार। knowing the measure or limit.

मत्तञ्ञुता – स्त्री॰ – (मात्रज्ञता) मात्रज्ञ होना। moderation.

मत्ता – स्त्री॰ – (मात्रा) परिमाण, मात्रा। measure, quantity.

मत्तासुख – न॰ – (मात्रा-सुख) समुचित परिमाण, मात्रा या सीमा के भीतर मिलने वाला सुख। happiness arising from limited consumption.

मत्तिका – स्त्री॰ – (मृत्तिका) मिट्टी। clay, soil.

मत्तिका-पिण्ड – पु॰ – (मृत्तिका-पिण्ड) मिट्टी का पिण्ड। a lump of clay.

मत्तिका-भाजन – न॰ – (मृत्तिका-भाजन) मिट्टी का बर्तन। earthenware.

मत्तिघ – पु॰ – (मातृघ्न) मातृ-हन्ता। a matricide.

मत्तेय्य – वि॰ – (मातृ-भक्त) माता की सेवा करने वाला। respecting one's mother.

मत्तेय्यता – स्त्री॰ – (मातृ-भक्ति) मातृ-भक्ति। filial love towards one's mother.

मत्थक – पु॰ – (मस्तक) मस्तक, शिखर। the head, forehead, top, summit.

मत्थ-लुङ – न॰ – (मस्तिष्क) दिमाग। the brain.

मत्थु – न॰ – (मस्तु) दही का निस्तार, मथने के बाद दही से पृथक् हुआ जल। whey, butter milk.

मथ – (भू) – (विलोडने) मथना। to churn.

मथति – क्रि॰ – (√ मथ = मथ्नाति) मथता है। churns, shakes.

मथन – न॰ – (मथन) मथ देना, मथना। churning, destroying.

√ मद – क्रि॰ – (उन्मादे) नशे में होना। to get intoxicated.

मद – पु॰ – (मद) अभिमान, अहंकार। pride, egoism.

मदन – पु॰ – (मदन) कामदेव (न॰) नशा। god of love (n.) intoxication.

मदनीय – वि॰ – (मदनीय) मादक, मदकारी, नशीला। intoxicating.

मदिरा – स्त्री॰ – (मदिरा) दारु, शराब। wine, liquour.

मद्र – पु॰ – (मद्र) देश विशेष, मद्र। a province named Madra.

√मद्द – (भू॰) – (मर्दने) मसलना। to crash, to trample.

मर्दति – क्रि॰ – (√मृद् = मर्दति) दबाता है, निचोड़ता है, रौंदता है। crushes, tramples on.

मद्दन – न॰ – (मर्दन) मर्दन करना, रौंदना। crushing, trampling, threshing.

मद्दल – पु॰ – (मर्दल) मादल, मृदङ्ग। a kind of drum.

मद्दव – न॰ – (मार्दव) मार्दव, कोमलता। softness, mildness.

मर्दित – कृदन्त – (मर्दित) मर्दन किया गया, रौंदा गया। crushed, subjugated.

मधु – न॰ – (मधु) (1) शहद (2) महुए के फूल से बनी शराब या दारु। (1) honey (2) spirituous liquor made from blossom of *Bassia latifolia*.

मधुक – पु॰ – (मधूक) महुआ नामक पेड़। a Mahuwa tree (*Bassia latifolia*).

मधुकर – पु॰ – (मधुकर) मधुमक्खी, भौंरा। a bee, a large black-bee.

मधु-गन्ध – पु॰ – (मधु-कोश) शहद का छत्ता, मधुपटल। a bee-hive.

मधु-पटल – पु॰ – (मधु-पटल) मधु-कोश, शहद का छत्ता। bee-hive.

मधुप – पु॰ – (मधुप) मधुमक्खी, भ्रमर। sucker of honey, a bee.

मधु-पिण्डिका – स्त्री॰ – (मधु-पिण्डिका) शहद में सने-भुने आटे का पिण्ड। a ball of flour mixed with honey.

मधुव्ब्रत – पु॰ – (मधु + ब्रत) शहद की मक्खी। a bee.

मधुमक्खित – वि॰ – (मधु-म्रक्षित) शहद से भरा हुआ, या चुपड़ा हुआ। smeared with honey.

मधु-मेह – पु॰ – (मधुमेह) मधुमेह, बहुमूत्र रोग। diabetes.

मधु-लट्ठिका – स्त्री॰ – (मधु-यष्टिका) मुलहठी। liquorice.

मधु-लाज – पु॰ – (मधु-लाजा) शहद मिश्रित खील, भुने चावल के लड्डू। fried corn mixed with honey.

मधु-लीह – पु॰ – (मधु-लिह) मधुमक्खी। a honey bee.

मधुस्सव – वि॰ – (मधु-स्राव) टपकता हुआ मधु। dripping honey.

मधुका – स्त्री॰ – (मधुका) मुलहठी, औषधि विशेष। liquorice.

मधुर – वि॰ – (मधुर) मीठा (न॰) मीठी चीज। sweet, sweet things.

मधुरत्त – न॰ – (मधुरत्त्व) मधुरता। sweetness.

मधुरस्सर – पु॰ – (मधुर स्वर) मधुर-स्वर, मधुर भाषी। sweet voice (adj.) having a sweet voice.

मधुरा – (मधुरा/मथुरा) मथुरा नगर, यमुना तट पर स्थित प्राचीन शूरसेन जनपद की राजधानी। Mathurā the capital of ancient Śūrasena *mahā-janapada*, situated on the bank of Yamunā river.

मध्वासव – पु॰ – (मधु-आसव) महुए की शराब। wine made from the flowers of *Bassia lotifolia*.

√ मन – (तु॰) – (बोधने) विचार करना। to think over.

√ मन – पु॰ तथा न॰ – (मन) चित्त, विज्ञान। mind, consciousness.

√ मन – (दि॰) – (ज्ञाने) जानना। to know.

मनक्कार – पु॰ – (मनस्कार) मन का संकल्प। ideation, mental resolve.

मनता – स्त्री॰ – (मनोभाव) समा-सान्त में प्रयुक्त मनोभाव जैसे (अत्तमनता = आनन्द-पूर्ण मनोभाव)। mentality, used in compounds as *attamanatā* joyful-mood.

मनन – न॰ – (मनन) विचार करना। thinking.

मनसि करोति – क्रि॰ – (मनस्करोति) मन में रखता है, विचार करता है। keeps in mind, thinks over.

मनसिकार – पु॰ – (मनस्कार) मन का संकल्प। mental resolve.

मन – अव्यय – (मनाक) थोड़ा, लगभग। a little, nearly, almost, somewhat.

मनाप/मनापिक – वि॰ – (मनाप) मनोनुकूल, आकर्षक। desirable, attractive.

मनुज – पु॰ – (मनुज) मनु का वंशज, मनुष्य। man, mankind.

मनुजाधिप – पु॰ – (मनुजाधिप) राजा। king.

मनुजिन्द – पु॰ – (मनुजेन्द्र) नरेन्द्र, राजा। king.

मनुञ्ञ – वि॰ – (मनोज्ञ) रमणीक, सुन्दर। delightful, pleasant.

मनुस्स – पु॰ – (मनुष्य) मनुष्य। man, human being.

मनुस्सत्त – न॰ – (मनुष्यत्व) मानवता। humanness, humanity.

मनुस्स-भाव – पु॰ – (मनुष्य-भाव) मनुज भाव, मनुष्यता, मानवता। feeling of humanity.

मनुस्स-भूत – वि॰ – (मनुष्य-भूत) मनुष्य योनि में उत्पन्न। born in human race.

मनुस्स-लोक – पु॰ – (मनुष्य-लोक) मनुष्य लोक। human world.

मनेसिका – स्त्री॰ – दूसरे के विचार की जानकारी। knowledge of others' thought.

मनो – पु॰/वि॰ – (मन) (समास में) मन। used in compound — for *mana*.

मनोकम्म – न॰ – (मनोकर्म) मानसिक कर्म। mental action.

मनोजव – वि॰ – (मनोजव) मन के समान तीव्र गति। fast as thought.

मनोदुच्चरित – न॰ – (मनोदुश्चरित) मानसिक दुष्कर्म। mental evil.

मनोद्वार – न॰ – (मनोद्वार) मन रूपी द्वार। the gate of consciousness.

मनोधातु – स्त्री॰ – (मनोधातु) चित्त। the ideational faculty.

मनोपदोस – पु॰ – (मनःप्रदोष) द्वेष। ill-will.

मनोपसाद – पु॰ – (मनःप्रसाद) भक्ति। devotional feeling.

मनोपुब्बङ्गम् – वि॰ – (मनोपूर्वङ्ग्रामः) जिसका पूर्वगामी मन हो। directed by mind.

मनोमय – वि॰ – (मनोमय) मन से उत्पन्न। mind-made.

मनोरथ – पु॰ – (मनोरथ) अभिलाषा, कामना, इच्छा, संकल्प। wish, desire, resolve.

मनोरम – वि॰ – (मनोरम) मनोहर, आनन्द-दायक। delightful.

मनोविज्ञाण – न॰ – (**मनो-विज्ञान**) मनोविज्ञान, मन की एकाग्रता। psychology, cognition of the mind.

मनोविज्ञेय – वि॰ – (**मनो-विज्ञेय**) मन के द्वारा जानने योग्य। to be comprehended by the mind.

मनोवितक्क – पु॰ – (**मनो-वितर्क**) विचार। thought.

मनोहर – वि॰ – (**मनोहर**) सुन्दर, आकर्षक। charming, captivating.

मनोज-जातक – (जा॰ सं॰ 397) – कथा बताती है कि किस प्रकार गीदड़ के उकसाने पर राजकीय अश्वों पर आक्रमण करने वाला शेर, राजा के धनुर्धारियों द्वारा मार डाला गया। the Jātaka (No. 397) tells how a lion inspired by a jackal attacked the royal horse and was shot dead by the king's archers.

मनोसिला – स्त्री॰ – (**मनःशिला**) मैनसिल, संखिया। red arsenic.

मन्त – (चु॰) – (**गुप्त संभाषणे**) सलाह करना। to counsel.

मन्त – न॰ – (**मन्त्र**) मन्त्र। a charm, a spell.

मन्तज्झायक – वि॰ – (**मन्त्र + अध्यायी**) मन्त्रों का अध्ययन करने वाला। one who studies the holy incantation.

मन्तन – न॰ – (**मन्त्रण / मन्त्रणा**) मन्त्रणा, विचार-विमर्श। consultation, discussion.

मन्तना – स्त्री॰ – (**मन्त्रणा**) मन्त्रणा, विचार-विमर्श करना। consultation, discussion.

मन्ता – स्त्री॰ – (**प्रज्ञा**) प्रज्ञा। intelligence.

मन्ती – पु॰ – (**मन्त्री**) मन्त्री, सलाहकार, सचिव। a counsellor, a minister, an adviser.

मन्तिणी – स्त्री॰ – (**मन्त्रिणी**) मन्त्रिणी। a woman counsellor.

मन्तु – पु॰ – कल्पना करने वाला। one who imagines.

मन्तेति – क्रि॰ – ($\sqrt{}$ **मन्त्र = मन्त्रयते**) मन्त्रणा करता है, विचार-विमर्श करता है। consults, takes counsel, discusses.

$\sqrt{}$ **मन्थ** – (भू॰) – (**विलोडने**) मथना। to churn.

मन्थ – पु॰ – (**मन्थ**) (1) मथानी, (2) चिउड़ा। churning stick, parched corn.

मन्थ – पु॰ – (**मन्थर**) कच्छप, कछुआ। a tortoise.

मन्द – वि॰ – (**मन्द**) शिथिल, आलसी, मूर्ख, फिसड्डी। slow, dull, foolish.

मन्दता – स्त्री॰ – (**मन्दता**) मन्द-भाव, मूर्खता। stupidity, dullness.

मन्दत्त – न॰ – (**मन्दत्त्व**) मन्द-भाव, जड़ता। inanimation, insensitivity, flaccidity.

मन्दं/मन्द-मन्द – क्रि॰ वि॰ – (**मन्दं-मन्दम्**) धीरे-धीरे। slowly, little by little.

मन्दाकिनी – स्त्री॰ – (**मन्दाकिनी**) झील विशेष, एक नदी का नाम जो चित्रकूट में स्थित है। name of a lake, a river in Citrakūṭa.

मन्दामुखी – स्त्री॰ – अँगीठी। grate, portable oven.

मन्दार – पु॰ – (**मन्दार**) मन्दार नामक पर्वत विशेष। the Mandāra mountain.

मन्दिय – न॰ – (**मन्द्य**) मूर्खता, आलस्य। stupidity, laziness, idleness.

मन्दिर – न॰ – (मन्दिर) भवन, महल, मन्दिर। mansion, dwelling place, temple.

मन्धातु-जातक – (जा॰ सं॰ 258) – इस जातक में मान्धाता नरेश की कथा वर्णित है। the Jātaka (No. 258) describes the story of the king Māndhātā.

ममङ्कार – पु॰ – (ममङ्कार) ममकार, ममत्व। extreme self-interest.

ममायना – स्त्री॰ – (ममायना) स्वार्थपरता, आसक्ति। selfishness, attachment.

ममायति – क्रि॰ – (ममायते) आसक्त होता है। becomes deeply attached.

मम्म – न॰ – (मर्म) मर्म स्थान जहां आघात लगने पर मृत्यु हो जाती है। a vital spot of the body, a nerve centre.

मम्मट्ठान – न॰ – (मर्म स्थान) देखें मम्म। see Mamma.

मम्मच्छेदक – वि॰ – (मर्मच्छेदक) घातक, मर्म स्थान को चोट पहुँचानेवाला। wounding vital spot, fatal.

मम्मन – वि॰ – (मम्मक) हकलाने वाला। one who stammers.

√ मय – (भू॰) – (गमनार्थे) जाना। to go.

मयं – सर्वनाम – (वयम्) हम सब। we (all of us).

मय्हक-जातक – (जा॰ सं॰ 390) – धन के लिए भाई द्वारा भतीजे को नदी में डुबा कर मार डालने की कथा। the Jātaka (No. 390) tells how a brother drowned his nephew lest he could not share the property.

मयूख – पु॰ – (मयूख) प्रकाश की किरण। the ray of light.

मयूर – पु॰ – (मयूर) मोर। a peacock.

√ मर – (भू॰) – (प्रायात्यारो) मरना। to die.

मरण – न॰ – (मरण) मृत्यु, मौत। death.

मरण-काल – पु॰ – (मरण-काल) मरने का समय। time of death.

मरणचेतना – स्त्री॰ – (मरण-चेतना) मार डालने का इरादा। intention to kill.

मरण-धम्म – वि॰ – (मरण-धर्म) मरण-स्वभाव। subject to death.

मरणान्त – वि॰ – (मरणान्त) जीवन, जिसका अन्त मृत्यु हो। having death as end.

मरण-परियोसान – वि॰ – (मरण-पर्यवसान) देखें मरणान्त। see Maraṇānta.

मरण-भय – न॰ – (मरण-भय) मृत्युभय। fear of death.

मरण-मञ्चक – पु॰ – (मरण-मञ्च) मरण शैय्या। death-bed.

मरण-मुख – न॰ – (मरण-मुख) मृत्यु का मुँह। the mouth of death, door of death.

मरण-लिङ्ग – न॰ – (मरण-लक्षण) मृत्यु के चिह्न। the signs of death.

मरण-सति – स्त्री॰ – (मरण-स्मृति) मरणानुस्मृति, मृत्यु का स्मरण। meditation on death.

मरण-समय – पु॰ – (मरण-समय) मृत्यु का समय। the death time.

मरति – क्रि॰ – (√ मृ = म्रियते) मरता है। dies.

मरिच – न॰ – (मरिच) काली मिर्च का पौधा। pepper-shrub.

मरिच – न॰ – (मरिचम्) काली मिर्च। pepper corn.

मरियादा – स्त्री॰ – (मर्यादा) सीमा, नियम। boundary, limit.

मरीचि – स्त्री॰ – (मरीचि) प्रकाश-किरण। ray of light.

मरीचिका – स्त्री० – (मरीचिका) मृग-तृष्णा। mirage.

मरीचि-धम्म – वि० – (मरीचि-धर्म) मृग-तृष्णा-सदृश। equal to mirage, unsubstantial.

मरु – स्त्री० – (मरु) निर्जल-प्रदेश, कान्तार। a sandy waste, desert.

मरुम्ब – न० – (स्फटिक) बिल्लौर-मापी। a quartz, pebble.

मल – न० – (मल) मैल, मैला। impurtiy, dust, dung.

मलतर – वि० – (मलतर) अधिक मैला। more dirty, or impure.

मलय – पु० – (मलय) मलय-पर्वत। name of a mountain.

मलयज – पु० – (मलयज) चन्दन। sandal.

मलिन – वि० – (मलिन) धब्बेदार, मैला। stained, dirty.

मल्ल – पु० – (मल्ल) (1) पहलवान (2) मल्ल जाति से सम्बन्धित। (1) a wrestler, (2) a man of the Malla class.

मल्ल-युद्ध – न० – (मल्ल-युद्ध) कुश्ती। wrestling.

मल्लक – पु० – (मल्लक) बर्तन, थैला। a vessel, a receiver.

मल्लिका – स्त्री० – (चमेली) the (Arabian) jasmine.

√**मस** – (भू०) – (आमर्षणे) माफ करना। to excuse.

मसार-गल्ल – न० – (मसार) इन्द्र नीलमणि, मरकत-मणि। emerald.

मसि – पु० – (मषी) मसिः, मसी, लेखन की स्याही। ink used in Bharat since fourth century BC onwards.

मस्सु – न० – (श्मश्रु) दाढ़ी-मूँछ। beard.

मस्सुक – वि० – (श्मश्रुक) दाढ़ी वाला। having beard.

मस्सु-कम्म – न० – (श्मश्रु-कर्म) हजामत। shaving beard, dressing.

मस्सु-करण – न० – (श्मश्रु-करण) हजामत बनाना। beard dressing.

√**मह** – (चु०) – (अन्वेषणे) खोजना। to search.

√**मह** – (भू०) – (पूजायाम्) पूजना। to respect, to honour, to worship.

मह – पु० – (मह्) धार्मिक उत्सव। a religious festival.

महग्गत – वि० – (उत्तुंग) बहुत ऊँचा। lofty.

महग्घ – वि० – (महार्घ) अत्यन्त मूल्यवान। very costly.

महग्घता – स्त्री० – (महार्घता) कीमतीपन। costliness.

महग्घस – वि० – (महग्घस) बहुत खाने वाला, भुलक्कड़। eating much, gluttonous.

महण्णव – पु० – (महार्णव) महासागर, विशाल समुद्र। a great ocean.

महति – क्रि० – (√मह = महति) आदर करता है, सम्मान करता है, गौरव प्रदान करता है। honours, reveres, enriches.

महत्त – न० – (महत्त्व) महत्त्व। effluent.

महद्धन – वि० – (महद्धन) अत्यन्त धनवान। having great riches.

महनीय – वि० – (महनीय) आदरणीय। respectable.

महन्त – वि० – (महन्त) महान्, बड़ा। great, big.

महफ्फल – वि॰ – (महाफल, महत्फल) महान फल वाला। rich in result.

महब्बल – वि॰ – महान् बलशाली (न॰) बड़ी भारी सेना। having enormous power.

महब्भय – न॰ – (महाभय) बहुत डरना। great fear.

महल्लक – वि॰ – (महल्लक) पहरे पर नियुक्त खोझा क्लीव। eunuch in a king's palace.

महल्लकतर – वि॰ – (महल्लकतर) ज्येष्ठ प्रतिहारी। the senior door-keeper.

महल्लिका – स्त्री॰ – (महल्लिका) प्रतिहार, रक्षिका, प्रतिहार पालिका। a female door-keeper.

महा – वि॰ – (महान्) महन्त, महान्। great.

महाउपासक – पु॰ – (महा + उपासक) बुद्ध का श्रद्धा-सम्पन्न अनुयायी। a great follower of the Buddha.

महाउपासिका – स्त्री॰ – (महा + उपासिका) a great female devotee.

महाकरुणा – स्त्री॰ – (महा + करुणा) महान् दया। great compassion.

महाकाय – वि॰ – (महाकाय) बड़े शरीर वाला। having a giant body.

महागण – पु॰ – (महा + गण) बड़ी मण्डली, बड़ा समूह। a great community.

महागणी – पु॰ – (महागणी) अनेक अनुयायियों सहित। having many followers.

महाजन – पु॰ – (महाजन) जनता। the public.

महातण्ह – वि॰ – (महाकृपणः) बहुत लोभी, कंजूस, very greedy, miser.

महाधन – नपु॰ – (महाधनम्) विशाल धन, immense wealth.

महानरक – पु॰ – (महानरकः) भयानक नरक, the great hell.

महानुभाव – वि॰ – (महानुभावः) महान प्रतापी of great majesty.

महापञ्ञ – वि॰ – (महाप्रज्ञः) अत्यन्त प्रज्ञावान, very wise.

महापथ – पु॰ – (महापथम्) महामार्ग, high road.

महापितु – पु॰ – (महापितु) पिता का बड़ा भाई / ताऊ। father's elder brother.

महापुरिस – पु॰ – (महापुरुष) महापुरुष। a great person.

महाभूत – न॰ – (महाभूत) पृथ्वी, जल, पावक, वायु, आदि महाभूत। five great elements.

महाभोग – वि॰ – (महाभोग) प्रचुर ऐश्वर्य। having great wealth.

महामत्त – पु॰ – (महामात्य) प्रधानमन्त्री। the prime-minister.

महामति – पु॰ – (महामति) महान, बुद्धिमान। great wise man.

महामत्त – पु॰ – (महामात्य) प्रधानमन्त्री। the prime minister.

महामुनि – पु॰ – (महामुनि) महान् मुनि। great sage.

महामेघ – पु॰ – (महावृष्टि) वर्षा की तेज बौछार। torrential rain.

महायञ्ञ – पु॰ – (महायज्ञ) महान् यज्ञ। a great sacrifice.

महायस – वि॰ – (महायश) महान यशस्वी। a great fame.

महायोग – पु॰ – (महायज्ञ) महान् यज्ञ। a great sacrifice.

महारह – वि॰ – (**महार्ह**) अत्यन्त मूल्यवान्। very precious.

महाराजा – पु॰ – (**महाराजा**) महान नरेश। a great king.

महालताप-साधन – न॰ – (**महालताप साधन**) स्त्रियों के श्रृंगार में सहायक होनेवाली लता। a creeper used to make a cosmetic product for a woman.

महासत्त – पु॰ – (**महासत्त्व**) महान् सत्त्वशाली। the great being.

महासमुद्र – पु॰ – (**महासमुद्र**) महासमुद्र। the ocean.

महासर – न॰ – (**महासर**) सरोवर, एक बड़ी झील। a great lake.

महासार – वि॰ – (**महासार**) विशाल धन के स्वामी। having immense wealth.

महासाल – वि॰ – (**महाशाल**) महाधनपति। having immense wealth.

महासावक – पु॰ – (**महा श्रावक**) ज्येष्ठ-शिष्य। a senior disciple.

महाअस्सारोह-जातक – (जा॰ सं॰ 302) – कथा शिक्षा देती है कि विपत्ति का साथी सच्चा मित्र ही परम सम्मान का पात्र है। the Jātaka (No. 302) tells that only the real friend who helps in adversity deserves honour.

महाउक्कस-जातक – (जा॰ सं॰ 486) – कथा बताती है कि मित्रों की सहायता से कठिन संकट भी दूर हो जाते हैं। the Jātaka (No. 486) tells that great dangers are averted with the help of an intimate friend.

महाउम्मग्ग-जातक – (जा॰ सं॰ 546) – इस कथा में महोषध पण्डित के पाण्डित्य की अनेक कथाएँ वर्णित हैं। this Jātaka tale (No. 546) consists of many stories of wisdom.

महाकण्ह-जातक – (जा॰ सं॰ 469) – महाकर्ण नाम के अपने कुत्ते को साथ ले जाकर, इन्द्र द्वारा दुराचारी मनुष्यों को बुरी तरह भयभीत करने की कथा। the story (No. 469) tells how the dog of Sakka terrified the people indulged in immoral activities.

महाकपि-जातक – (जा॰ सं॰ 407) – कथा बताती है कि किस प्रकार एक बन्दर ने अपने शरीर का पुल बना, अपनी सारी जाति को अपने शरीर पर से गुजरने देकर यथार्थ नेता का धर्म निभाया। the story (No. 407) describes the virtues of a true leader.

महाकपि-जातक – (जा॰ सं॰ 576) – कृतघ्न, आदमी ने बन्दर का सिर फोड़ दिया किन्तु परहित-कामी बन्दर ने ऐसे आदमी की भी जान बचाई। it is a story (No. 576) of a generous monkey who saved the life of a wood-cutter though the latter had broken its head.

महाकस्सप-थेर – भगवान बुद्ध के प्रधान शिष्यों में से एक प्रमुख शिष्य। one of the chief disciples of the Buddha.

महाजनक-जातक – (जा॰ सं॰ 539) – मिथिला के महाजनक नाम के राजा के दो पुत्रों के संघर्ष की कथा। the tale (No. 539) describes the conflict between two sons of Mahājanaka the king of Mithilā.

महाजनपद – पु॰ – (**महाजनपद**) बुद्धकालीन उत्तर भारत के सोलह महाजनपद (राज्य), वे थे – कासी, कोसल, अङ्ग, मगध, बज्जि, मल्ल, चेतिय, वंस, कुरु, पञ्चाल, मच्छ, सूरसेन, अस्सक, अवन्ति, गन्धार तथा कम्बोज। इसमें प्रथम चौदह मज्झिम-

देस (मध्यमण्डल) में हैं, अन्त के दो उत्तरा- पथ में। the sixteen *mahājanapada*s of north India at the time of Buddha, viz., Kāśī, Kosal, Aṅga, Magadha, Vajji, Malla, Cetiya, Vansa, Kuru, Pañcāla Machha, Surasena, Assaka, Avanti, Gandhāra and Kamboja. Of these the first fourteen were situated in Majjhima maṇḍala (middle regien) and the rest two in Uttarāpatha (in the north).

महातक्कारि-जातक – देखें तक्कारि-जातक। see Takkāri Jataka.

महाथूप – पु॰ – (**महा-स्तूप**) राजा दुट्ठगामणी द्वारा निर्मित अनुराधपुर स्थित महान् चैत्य। the great Thūpa in Anurādhapura (Ceylon) which was built by king Duṭṭhagāmaṇī.

महाधम्मपाल-जातक – (जा॰ सं॰ 447) – चिरंजीव होने का रहस्य इस जातक कथा में वर्णित है। this tale (No. 447) describes the secret of longevity.

महाधम्मरक्खित-थेर – पु॰ – (**महाधर्मरक्षित स्थविर**) तृतीय संगीति के बाद महाराष्ट्र में धर्म-प्रचारक के रूप में भेजे गए महास्थविर। he was sent as a preacher of Buddhism to Mahārāṣṭra.

महानारदकस्स्य-जातक – (जा॰ सं॰ 544) – बलि कर्म द्वारा स्वर्गलोक की प्राप्ति का खण्डन करने वाली कथा। the tale (No. 544) dispels the doubts about *svarga-loka* by describing the folly of sacrifices.

महानेरु/महामिरु – (**महामिरन**) सुमेर पर्वत का एक और नाम। it is another name of Sumeru mountain.

महापजापति-गौतमी – स्त्री॰ – (**महाप्रजापति गौतमी**) सिद्धार्थ गौतम की माता महामाया का देहान्त होने पर, मौसी महाप्रजापति गौतमी ने ही सिद्धार्थ को दूध पिलाकर पाला था तथा भिक्षुणी संघ की स्थापना का सारा श्रेय महाप्रजापति गौतमी को ही है। when mother Mahāmāyā died seven days after birth of the Buddha, her sister Pajāpati Gautamī looked after him, and nursed him. The credit goes to her for the establishment of Bhikṣuṇī Saṅghas.

महापुदुम-जातक – (जा॰ सं॰ 472) – एक विमाता द्वारा पुत्र पर झूठा लांछन लगाने की कथा। the tale (No. 472) tells about a woman who falsely accused her step-son of ill-treatment.

महापनाद-जातक – (जा॰ सं॰ 264) – इसकी कथा सुरुचि जातक में आई है। for the text see Mahāpanāda Jātaka.

महालोभन-जातक – (जा॰ सं॰ 507) – इसकी कथा चुल्ल-पलोभन-जातक की कथा के ही समान है। the text of this Jātaka tale is same as of Cullapalobhana-Jātaka.

महापिङ्गल-जातक – (जा॰ सं॰ 240) – कथा के अनुसार दुष्ट महापिङ्गल नरेश के मरने पर उसकी प्रजा ने खुशियाँ मनाई। the story (No. 240) of a wicked and quite pitiless king on whose death the people were delighted and burnt his body amidst great festivity.

महाबोधि-जातक – (जा॰ सं॰ 528) – राजा द्वारा बोधि की न्यायप्रियता के कारण उसे न्यायाधीश नियुक्त करने की कथा। the tale (No. 528) describes how a superceded justice-loving wise person superceded the unjust judges and was appointed as chief justice by the king.

महामङ्गल-जातक – (जा॰ सं॰ 453) कथा बतलाती है कि मनुष्य के लिए वास्तविक महामङ्गल कौन-कौन से हैं। the tale (No. 453) described the virtues that constitute auspiciousness.

महामाया – (महामाया) सिद्धार्थ गौतम बुद्ध की जननी। the mother of Siddhārtha Gautama Buddha.

महामोग्गल्लान-थेर – (महा मौद्ग्लायन स्थविर) भगवान् बुद्ध के दो प्रधान शिष्यों में से एक दूसरे थे, धर्म-सेनापति-सारिपुत्र। one of the two chief disciples of the Buddha, the other was Dharma Senāpati-Sariputra.

महारक्खित-थेर – पु॰ – (महाराक्षित-स्थविर) तृतीय संगीत के अनन्तर यवन-देश में धर्म प्रचारार्थ जाने वाले महास्थविर। he was sent to preach Buddhism in Yavan country after the third council of the monks.

महारट्ठ – पु॰ – (महाराष्ट्र) वह प्रदेश जहाँ तृतीय संगीति के अनन्तर महाधम्म रक्खित धर्म-प्रचारार्थ भेजे गए थे। the country where Mahādhamma-rakkhita was sent to preach Buddhism after the third council.

महावंस – पु॰ – (महावंश) सिंहलद्वीप का प्रसिद्ध ऐतिहासिक महाकाव्य। the famous historical epic related to Singhala (Ceylon).

महावग्ग – पु॰ – (महावर्ग) विनय पिटक के पाँच ग्रन्थों में से एक, जो आगे खन्धकों में विभक्त है। one of the five books of Vinayapiṭaka, it is further divided into *khandhaka*s.

महावाणिज-जातक – (जा॰ सं॰ 493) – इस जातक कथा के अनुसार वट-वृक्ष की एक शाखा से व्यापारियों को पानी मिला, दूसरी से भोजन, तीसरी से सुन्दर लड़कियाँ, और चौथी से अनेक दूसरी मूल्यवान वस्तुएँ। the tale (No. 493) says how from a banyan tree merchants obtained water from one branch, food from the second, charming girls from the third and precious things from its fourth branch.

महाविहार – पु॰ – (महाविहार) अनुराधपुर (सिंहलद्वीप) का प्रसिद्ध विहार। शताब्दियों तक यही बौद्ध-धर्म का प्रधान केन्द्र बना रहा। the great monastry at Anurādhapura, for many years it had been the chief seat of Buddhism in Ceylon.

महावेसन्तर-जातक – देखें वेस्सन्तर जातक। see Vessantara Jataka.

महासंघिक – द्वितीय संगीति के ही समय स्थविरवाद से पृथक् हो जाने वाला एक बौद्ध सम्प्रदाय। one of the Buddhist cults which broke away from the Theravādins at the Second Council.

महासार-जातक – (जा॰ सं॰ 92) – रानी की मोतियों की माला उठा ले जाने वाली एक बन्दरिया की कथा। the story (No. 92) of a female monkey who stole away the pearl necklace of the queen.

महासीलव-जातक – (जा॰ सं॰ 51) – राजा के रनिवास को दूषित करने वाले मन्त्री के राजा द्वारा देश निकाला दिए जाने की कथा। the story (No. 51) of a minister who was exiled for spoiling a female member of the king's harem.

महासुक-जातक – (जा॰ सं॰ 429) – गूलर-वृक्ष के फलरहित हो जाने पर भी उसका परित्याग न करने वाले तोते की कथा। the story (No. 429) of a parrot who did not leave his fig-tree in the odd season even when there were no fruits.

महासुतसोम-जातक – (जा॰ सं॰ 537) – एक मानव-मांसभक्षी राजा की कथा। the story (No. 537) of a cannibal king who ate the meat cut from a recently dead human body and cooked.

महासुदस्सन-जातक – (जा॰ सं॰ 95) – महासुदस्सन, राजा की विलक्षण मृत्यु का रोचक वृत्तान्त। it is an interesting story (No. 95) related to the peculiar death of king Sudarśana.

महा-सुपिन-जातक – (जा॰ सं॰ 77) – कोसल नरेश प्रसेनजित द्वारा देखे गए सोलह महान् स्वप्नों की व्याख्या की कथा। Prasenjit the king of Kosala was anxious to know about the meanings of the sixteen dreams he had the previous night. The explanation of Buddha-sattva is given in the tale (No. 77).

महा-हंस-जातक – (जा॰ सं॰ 534) – स्वर्ण वर्ण राजहंस द्वारा सिंहासन पर बैठ, रानी को धर्मोपदेश देने की कथा। the story (No. 534) of a golden rājahansa (royal swan), who preached the Dhamma to the queen.

महिंसासक – स्थविरवाद से पृथक् हो जाने वाला एक और बौद्ध सम्प्रदाय। another heretical sect which broke off from the Therāvādins.

महिका – स्त्री॰ – (महिका) तुषार, पाला, निहारिका। the frost, mist.

महिच्छ – वि॰ – (महेच्छ) अत्यन्त लोभी। avaricious man.

महिच्छता – स्त्री॰ – (महेच्छता) अत्यधिक लोभ। greediness.

महित – कृदन्त – (महित) पूजित, उत्कृष्ट। revered, excellent.

महिद्धिक – वि॰ – (महा-ऋद्धिक) महा-ऋद्धिवान, प्रचुर समृद्धिशाली। of extreme riches, very contented man.

महिन्द – पु॰ – (महेन्द्र) सम्राट् अशोक के सुपुत्र, जो महामोग्गलिपुत्ततिस्स की प्रेरणा से धर्म-प्रचारार्थ अपनी बहन संघमित्रा के साथ सिंहल गए थे। the son of emperer Aśoka, who had gone to Ceylon with his sister Sanghamitra for preaching Buddhism.

महिला – स्त्री॰ – (महिला) स्त्री। a woman.

महिला-मुख-जातक – (जा॰ सं॰ 26) – महिलामुख नामक राजकीय हाथी की कथा। it is a story (No. 26) of the royal elephant, named Mahilamukh.

महिस – पु॰ – (महिष) भैंस। a buffalo.

महिस-जातक – (जा॰ सं॰ 278) – बन्दर द्वारा की गई सभी शरारतों को एक भैंसा

सहन करता रहा किन्तु वह बन्दर एक दूसरे भैंसे द्वारा अंततः मार ही डाला गया। it is a story (No. 278) of a monkey who used to foul a buffalo and remained unhurt as the buffalo showed no resentment. One day the monkey tried to play his mischief on another bufalo who killed him.

महिस-मण्डल – पु॰ – (**महिष-मण्डल**) महादेव स्थविर का धर्म-प्रचार क्षेत्र। वर्तमान "मैसूर"। the modern Mysore where Mahādeva Thera had gone to preach Buddhism.

महिस्सर – पु॰ – (**महेश्वर**) महेश्वर, महादेव। a great lord, the god Śiva.

मही – स्त्री॰ – (**मही**) (1) पृथ्वी, (2) नदी विशेष। (1) earth (2) name of a river.

मही-तल – न॰ – (**महीतल**) जमीन की सतह। the surface of the earth.

महीधर – पु॰ – (**महीधर**) पर्वत। mountain.

महीपति – पु॰ – (**महीपति**) राजा। a king.

महीपाल – पु॰ – (**महीपाल**) राजा। a king.

महीभाग – पु॰ – (**महीभाग**) कान्तार। a desert.

महीरूह – पु॰ – (**महीरुह**) वृक्ष। a tree.

महेसक्ख – वि॰ – महाप्रतापशाली। one possessing great valour and power.

महेसि – स्त्री॰ – (**महर्षि**) महर्षि। the great sage.

महेसि – पु॰ – (**महिषी**) रानी। a queen.

महोघ – पु॰ – (**महौघ**) महान बाढ़। immense river flood.

महोदधि – वि॰ – (**महोदधि**) समुद्र। ocean.

महोदर – वि॰ – (**महोदर**) बड़े पेट वाला। having a big belly, pot bellied.

महोग्ग – पु॰ – (**महोरगी**) साँपों (नागों) का राजा। a king of Nāgas.

महोसध – न॰ – (**महौषध**) अचूक दवा, लहसुन, सोंठ। very efficacious drug, garlic, dried ginger.

मा – अव्यय – (**मा**) निषेधार्थक, मत, नहीं। (a prohibitive particle) do not.

मागध – वि॰ – (**मागध**) मगध सम्बन्धी। belonging to Magadha.

मागधिक – वि॰ – (**मागध**) मगध सम्बन्धी। belonging to Magadha.

मागधी – स्त्री॰ – (**मागधी**) मगध की बोली। the dialect of Magadha.

मागविक – पु॰ – (**मार्गिक**) व्याध, शिकारी। a man engaged in hunting, a hunter.

मागसिर – पु॰ – (**मार्गशीर्ष**) मार्गशीर्ष, अगहन मास। month of November-December.

माघ – पु॰ – (**माघ**) माघ का महीना। month of Januray-February.

माघात – पु॰ – (**माघात**) हत्या विरत रहने की आज्ञा। command not to kill.

माणव – पु॰ – (**माण्णव**) तरुण। a young man.

माणवक – पु॰ – (**माणवक**) तरुण। a young man.

माणविका – स्त्री॰ – (**माणविका**) तरुणी। a maiden.

मातङ्ग – पु॰ – (**मातङ्ग**) (1) हाथी का नाम (2) नीची मानी जाने वाली जाति। (1) an elephant (2) low-caste man.

मातली – पु॰ – (मातलि) इन्द्र के सारथी का नाम। name of Indra's charioteer.

मातापितु – पु॰ – (मातापितु) माता-पिता। parents, the mother and the father.

मातापेत्तिक – वि॰ – (मातृ-पैतृक) माता-पिता से आगत। come from father and mother.

मातपेत्ति-भार – पु॰ – (मातृ-पितृ-भार) माता-पिता की सेवा में रहना। supporting or serving one's parents.

मातामह – पु॰ – (मातामह) नाना। mother's father.

मातामही – स्त्री॰ – (मातामही) नानी। mother's mother.

मातिक – वि॰ – (मातृक) माता सम्बन्धी। connected with mother.

मातिका – स्त्री॰ – (मात्रिका) जलमार्ग, अभि-धर्म सम्बन्धी विषयों के शीर्ष स्थान, प्राति मोक्ष नियमावलि। the water course, table of contents, the code of Pāttmokṣa.

माति-पक्ख – पु॰ – (मातृ-पक्ष) मातृ-पक्ष। mother's side.

मातु – स्त्री॰ – (मातृ) मां। the mother.

मातु-कुच्छि – पु॰ – (मातृ-कुक्षि) माता की कोख। mother's womb.

मातु-गाम – पु॰ – (मातृ-ग्राम) माताएं, माता जैसे स्थान रखने वाली स्त्रियाँ जैसे काकी, चाची, मामी, मौसी। of mother's status as aunt, mother-in-law, etc.

मातु-घात – पु॰ – (मातृ-घातक) मातृघावी, मातृ-हत्यारा। mother's murderer.

मातुच्छा – स्त्री॰ – (मातृष्वसा) मौसी। mother's sister.

मातु-पट्ठान – न॰ – (मातृ + उपस्थान) माता की सेवा। looking after one's mother.

मातुपोसक – वि॰ – (मातृ-पोषक) माता का पोषक। supporting one's mother.

मातु-पोसक-जातक – (जा॰ सं॰ 455) – एक हाथी की कथा जिसने अपनी अन्धी माता की सेवा की। the story (No. 455) of an elephant who looked after his blind mother.

मातु-भगिनी – स्त्री॰ – (मातृ-भगिनी) मौसी, मातृष्वसा। mother's sister.

मातु-भातु – पु॰ – (मातुला, मातुली) मामी। mother's brother's wife.

मातुल – पु॰ – (मातुल) मामा। maternal uncle.

मातुलानी – स्त्री॰ – (मातुलानी) मामी। maternal uncle's wife.

मातुलुङ्ग – पु॰ – (मातुलुङ्ग) चकोतरा। the citron a kind of large sweet lemon.

मादिस – वि॰ – (मादृश) मेरे जैसा। one who is like me, alike myself, one who resembles me.

√ मान – (चु॰) – (पूजायां) पूजना। to honour, to worship.

मान (1) – न॰ – (मान) माप। measurement.

मान (2) – (मान) अहंकार, अभिमान। ego.

मानकूट – पु॰ – (मानकूट) खोटा माप। a false measure.

मानत्थद्ध – वि॰ – (मानस्तब्ध) अहंकार से जड़ीभूत। stubborn in pride.

मानद – वि॰ – (**मानद**) मानप्रद, मान बढ़ाने वाला, प्रेरक । inspiring, respect.

मानन – न॰ – (**मानन**) आदर करना, सम्मान करना । paying respect or honour.

मानव – पु॰ – (**मानव**) मनुष्य । mankind.

मानस – न॰ – (**मानस**) मन, चित्त, विज्ञान (समास में) संकल्प लिए हुए । mind, intention (in compound) having the intention of.

मानित – कृदन्त – (**मानित**) सम्मानित । respected, honoured.

मानी – पु॰ – (**मानी**) अभिमानी । one who is proud.

मानुस – वि॰ – (**मानुष**) मनु का अपत्य, मनुष्य सम्बन्धी (पु॰) मनुष्य । of human race. (m.) a man.

मानुसक – वि॰ – (**मानुषक**) मनुष्य सम्बन्धी । belonging to man.

मानुसी – स्त्री॰ – (**मानुषी**) मानव जाति की स्त्री । female member of the human race.

मानेति – क्रि॰ – (√ मान = **मानयति** / **मानति**) आदर करता है, सत्कार करता है । honours, pays respects, reveres.

मापक – पु॰ – (**मापक**) नापने वाला स्वायिता, निर्माण करने वाला । one who measures, the creator, construction.

मापित – कृदन्त – (**मापित**) रचित, निर्मापित । constructed.

मापेति – क्रि॰ – (**मापयति**) निर्माण करता है । constructs.

मामक – वि॰ – (**मामक**) श्रद्धावान, प्रेमी, ममत्वयुक्त । devoted to, loving.

माया – स्त्री॰ – (**माया**) ठगी, जादू । deceit, magic, jugglery.

माया-महामाया – स्त्री॰ – (**माया देवी**) सिद्धार्थ गौतम (बुद्ध) की माता, उसका पिता था 'अञ्जन शाक्य', और उसकी माता थी 'जयसेन' की लड़की यशोधरा । the mother of Siddhārtha Gautama, her father was Añjana Śākya of Devdaha and mother Yaśodharā the daughter of Jayasena.

मायाकार – पु॰ – (**मायाकार**) मायावी, जादूगर । a juggler, magician.

मायावी – वि॰ – (**मायावी**) माया करने वाला, ढोंगी, जादूगर । hypocrite, a juggler, a magician.

मायु – पु॰ – (**मायु**) पित्त । bile.

मार – पु॰ – (**मार**) चित्त की अकुशल वृत्तियों की मूर्ति, लुभाने वाला यमराज, मारक । the evil one, the tempter, the killer, the death personified.

मारकायिक – वि॰ – (**मार–कायिक**) मार-लोक सम्बन्धी । belonging to the group of Mara deities (connected with death).

मार-धेय्य – न॰ – (**मार-क्षेत्र**) मार का क्षेत्र । the realm of Māra.

मार-बन्धन – न॰ – (**मार-बन्धन**) मृत्यु का बन्धन । fetter of death.

मार-सेना – स्त्री॰ – (**मार-सेना**) the army of Māra.

मारक – वि॰ – (**मारक**) मारने वाला । a killer.

मारण – न॰ – (**मारण**) वध, मार डालना । killing.

मारापित – कृदन्त – मरवाया । contrived the killing.

मारापेति – क्रि॰ – मरवाता है। contrives the killing.

मारित – वि॰ – (मारित) मारा गया। killed.

मारिस – वि॰ – (मारिष) (सम्बोधन विशेष), मित्र! मान्यवर! । (found only in vocative) sir, sirs.

मारुत्त – पु॰ – (मारुत) हवा। the wind.

मारेति – क्रि॰ – (मारयति) मारता है। kills.

माल – पु॰ – (माल) घेरेदार जगह, आँगन। the circular enclosure, a round yard.

माळ – पु॰ – (माल) मकान की मंजिल, एक तल्ला (माळ)। single storey building.

मालती – स्त्री॰ – (मालती) मालती लता। *Jasminum grandiflorum.*

माला – स्त्री॰ – (माला) (फूलों की) माला। a garland.

माला-कम्म – न॰ – (माला-कर्म) (1) माला गूँथने का काम (2) दीवार पर बेल-बूटे की पच्चीकारी। (1) the act of stringing or wreathing (2) a mural drawing.

मालाकार – पु॰ – (मालाकार) माली। a garland maker, a gardener.

माला-गच्छ – पु॰ – (माला) माला बनाने लायक फूल देने वाला पौधा। a plant whose flowers are usable.

माला-गुण – पु॰ – (माला-शुत्र) माला-सूत्र, माला गूँथने वाला धागा। a string of a garland.

मालागुल – न॰ – (माला-राशि) फूलों का ढेर। a cluster of a heap of flowers.

माला-चुम्बटक – पु॰ – फूलों का गजरा। a chaplet of flowers.

माला-दाम – पु॰ – (माला-दाम) माला-सूत्र, माला गूँथने का धागा। a string of flowers.

मालाधर – वि॰ – (मालाधारी) wearing a garland of flowers.

मालाधारी – वि॰ – (मालाधारी) पुष्पमाला धारण करने वाला। wearing a garland.

माला-भारी – वि॰ – (माला-भारी) पुष्पमाल से लदा हुआ व्यक्ति। a person garlanded with flowers.

मालावच्छ – न॰ – पुष्पोद्यान, पुष्प शैय्या। garden of flowers, bed of flowers.

मालिक/माली – वि॰ – (मालाकार) माली। a garland maker, gardener.

मालिनी – स्त्री॰ – (मालिनी) मालाधारिणी। a woman wearing a garland.

मालुत – पु॰ – (मारुत) हवा। the wind.

मालुत-जातक – (जा॰ सं॰ 17) – सिंह और बाघ के इस विवाद पर कि कृष्ण-पक्ष की रात अधिक ठंडी होती है या शुक्ल-पक्ष की। तापस ने समाधान दिया कि ठंडक हवा के तीव्र या मन्द बहने पर निर्भर है, प्रकाश पर नहीं। in this story (No. 17) a hermit gives his decision that the cold is caused by wind and not by light.

मालुवा – स्त्री॰ – (मालु-लता) आकाश-बेल। parasite creeper *Casytha elifomis.*

मालूस – पु॰ – (मालूर) कपित्थ वृक्ष, कैथे का पेड़। the *kapittha* tree, wood apple tree (*fernia elephantum*).

माल्य – न॰ – (माल्य) पुष्प-माला, पुष्प-समूह। garland, wreath, mass of flowers.

मास (1) – पु॰ – (मास) महीना। a month.

मास (2) – पु॰ – (माष) उड़द। a particular bean.

मासिक – वि॰ – (मासिक) माहवार। monthly.

मासक – पु॰ – (माषक) माषा भर तोल का एक सिक्का। a small coin.

मिग – पु॰ – (मृग) (1) पशु, चौपाया (2) – हिरण। (1) a beast, quadruped, an animal (2) a deer.

मिगछापक – पु॰ – (मृगशावक) मृग छौना। the young of a deer.

मिगतण्हिका – स्त्री॰ – (मृग–तृष्णा) मृग-तृष्णा। mirage.

मिग-दाय – पु॰ – (मृग–दाव) हरिण उद्यान, मृगोद्यान। a deer-park.

मिग-मद – पु॰ – (मृग–मद) कस्तूरी। musk.

मिग-मातुका – स्त्री॰ – (मृग–मातुका) मृग विशेष। a hoofed animal of the size of a cat.

मिग-लुद्दक – पु॰ – (मृग–लुब्धक) शिकारी। a hunter.

मिग-पोतक-जातक – (जा॰ सं॰ 372) – तपस्वी ने बड़े स्नेह से हरिण के बच्चे का पालन पोषण किया, फलतः उसके मरने पर तपस्वी बहुत संतप्त हुआ। the story (No, 372) of a hermit and his tamed deer concludes that the attachment causes great suffering.

मिगव – न॰ – (मृगया) शिकार। hunting.

मिगार-मातु-पासाद – पु॰ – (मृगारमाताप्रसाद) श्रावस्ती के पूर्वी द्वार पर पूर्वाराम में विसाखा मृगार माता द्वारा बनवाए गए विहार का नाम। name of the monastery constructed by Viśākhā Migāramātā in Pūrvārāma garden situated at the eastern gate of Śrāvastī.

मिगालोप-जातक – (जा॰ सं॰ 381) – अपने पिता का कहना न मानकर जान गँवाने वाले एक तरुण गृद्ध की कथा। it is a story (No. 381) of a young vulture who met miserable death due to disregarding his father's advice.

मिगिन्द – पु॰ – (मृगेन्द्र) पशुओं का राजा, सिंह। The king of animals, a lion.

मिगी – स्त्री॰ – (मृगी) हरिणी। a hind, a doe.

मिच्छत्त – न॰ – (मिथ्यात्व) मिथ्यात्व। falsehood.

मिच्छा – अव्यय – (मिथ्या) झूठ। false.

मिच्छा-कम्मन्त – पु॰ – (मिथ्या-कर्मान्त) मिथ्याचरण, दुराचरण। wrong conduct or action.

मिच्छा-गहण – न॰ – (मिथ्या-ग्रहण) गलत समझ। wrong conception, misunderstanding.

मिच्छाचार – पु॰ – (मिथ्याचार) कदाचार, मिथ्याचरण। wrong behaviour.

मिच्छाचारी – कदाचारी, दुराचारी। one who behaves wrongly.

मिथ्या-दिट्ठि – स्त्री॰ – (मिथ्या-दृष्टि) मिथ्या-दृष्टि, मिथ्या-मतधारी। false view, a hearsay.

मिच्छा-पणिहित – वि॰ -- (मिथ्या-प्रणिहिति) गलत ओर झुका हुआ। wrongly directed.

मिच्छा-वाचा – स्त्री॰ – (मिथ्या-वाक्) मिथ्या वाणी । false speech.

मिच्छा-वायाम – पु॰ – (मिथ्या-आयास) मिथ्या प्रयत्न । vain effort.

मिच्छा-सङ्कप्प – पु॰ – (मिथ्या-संकल्प) मिथ्या संकल्प । false resolve.

मिज्ज – न॰ – (मेद्य) मज्जा । kernel, marrow, pith.

मिणन – न॰ – माप । measurement.

मिणति – क्रि॰ – (√ मा = माति) मापता है, तोलता है । measures, weights.

मितभाषी – पु॰ – (मितभाषी) संयतभाषी । one with restrained or controlled speech.

मितचिन्ती-जातक – (जा॰ सं॰ 114) – बहुचिन्ती, अप्पचिन्ती, मितचिन्ती मछलियों की कथा । the story (No. 114) describes three categories of fish, i.e., one thought much, the other thought wrong, and third thought a little, thus the story concludes that by mere thinking one cannot achieve the goal.

मित्त – पु॰ तथा न॰ – (मित्र) मित्र । friend.

मित्त-दुब्भि – पु॰ – (मित्र-द्रोही) मित्रघाती, मित्रद्रोही । one who betrays his friend.

मित्त-दूभी – वि॰ – (मित्र-द्रोही) मित्र से द्रोह करने वाला । one who betrays his friend.

मित्तद्दु – वि॰ – (मित्र-द्रोही) मित्र से छल करने वाला । one who betrays his friend.

मित्त-पतिरुपक – वि॰ – (मित्र-प्रतिरुपक) झूठा मित्र । a false friend.

मित्त-भेद – पु॰ – (मित्र-भेद) मैत्री-विच्छेद । breach of alliance.

मित्त-सन्थव – पु॰ – (मित्र-सन्धि) मैत्री-सम्बन्ध । association with a friend, friendly relations.

मित्त-विन्दक-जातक – (जा॰ सं॰ 82) – चतुर्द्वार जातक में वर्णित मित्तविन्द-जातक-कथा का एक अंश । it (story No. 82) is an additional fragment of Catudvāra Jātaka.

मित्त-विन्दक-जातक – (जा॰ सं॰ 104) – चतुर्द्वार जातक का ही एक और अतिरिक्त अंश । it (story No. 104) is also an additional fragment of the Catudvāra Jātaka.

मित्त-विन्द-जातक – (जा॰ सं॰ 369) – चतुर्द्वार जातक का ही एक तीसरा अतिरिक्त अंश । (story No. 369) the third additional fragment of Catudvāra Jātaka.

मित्तामित्त-जातक – (जा॰ सं॰ 197) – तपस्वी ने हाथी के बच्चे का पोषण किया किन्तु उसी ने बड़े होने पर तपस्वी को मार डाला । it is a story (No. 197) of a hermit who adopted young elephant whose dam was dead, the elephant grew up and killed his master.

मित्तामित्त-जातक – (जा॰ सं॰ 473) – सच्चे मित्र के लक्षण । the story (No. 473) describes the characteristics of a true friend.

मिथिला – स्त्री॰ – (मिथिला) विदेह जनपद की राजधानी, नेपाल की सीमा के अन्दर वर्तमान जनकपुर । the capital town of ancient Videha *janapada* now known as Janakapura situated in Nepal.

मिथु – अव्यय – (मिथस / मिथो) (1) परस्पर अदल-बदलकर (2) एकान्त में । (1) mutual among each other (2) secretly.

मिथु-भेद – पु॰ – (मित्र-भेद) मैत्री-विच्छेद । breach of alliance.

मिथुन – न॰ – (मिथुन) स्त्री-पुरुष का जोड़ा, मिथुन, युगल । a pair of male and female.

मिथु – (भू॰) – (सङ्गमे) युक्त करना । to unite, to couple.

मिथो – अव्यय – (मिथो) परस्पर । among each other.

√ मिद – भू॰ – (मिद्) स्नेहयुक्त होना । to be soaked with affection.

√ मिद – (दि॰) – (स्नेहने) स्नेहयुक्त होना । to fall in love.

मिद्ध – न॰ – (मिद्धम्) आलस्य । laziness, dullness.

मिद्धी – वि॰ – आलसी । lazy, dull.

√ मिध – (दि॰) – (अभिकांक्षायाम्) चाहना । to wish, to desire.

मिय्यति – क्रि॰ – (√ मृ = म्रियते) मरता है । dies.

मियमान – कृदन्त – (म्रियमाण) मरता हुआ । already dead.

मिलक्ख – पु॰ – (म्लेक्ष) बर्बर जाति का । a barbarian.

मिलक्ख-देस – पु॰ – (म्लेक्ष-देश) बर्बर-देश । country of barbarians.

√ मिला – (दि॰) – (म्लान होना) to fade.

मिलात – कृदन्त – (म्लान) म्लान हुआ । withered, faded.

मिलातता – स्त्री॰ – (म्लानता) म्लान भाव, कुम्हलायापन । vein of fading, faded posture.

मिलायति – क्रि॰ – (म्लायते) कुम्हलाता है । fades, gets faded.

मिलिन्द – पु॰ – (मिलिन्द) सागल का राजा मिनाण्डरा । उसका जन्म अलसन्दा (अलैक्जेण्ड्रया) के समीप कलसी में हुआ था । मिलिन्द-पञ्ह में उसी के साथ नागसेन स्थविर का हुआ शास्त्रार्थ दर्ज है । king of Sāgala where discussion with Buddhist elder Nāgasena are recorded in the Milindapañha.

मिलिन्द-पञ्ह – न॰ – (मिलिन्द-प्रश्न) भिक्षु नागसेन तथा राजा मिलिन्द के प्रश्नोत्तरों से समन्वित ग्रन्थ । book containing dialogue between Buddhist elder Nāgasena and Milinda.

√ मिस्स – चु॰ – (सम्मिश्रणे) मिश्रित करना । to mix.

मिस्स – वि॰ – (मिश्र) मिश्रित । mixed, combined.

मिस्सेति – क्रि॰ – (मिश्र / मिश्रयति) मिश्रित करता है । mixes.

√ मिह – (भू॰) – (ईषत्-हसने) मुस्कुराना । to smile.

√ मिह – (भू॰) – (सेचने) गीला करना । to water, to make wet.

√ मिह – (चु॰) – (पूजायां) पूजना । to honour, to worship.

मिहित – न॰ – (स्मित) मुस्कराहट । a smile.

√ मी – क्रि॰ – (हिंसायां) हिंसा करना । to cause violence, to cause injure.

मीन – पु॰ – (मीन) मछली । fish.

√ मील – (भू॰) – (निमीलने) मूँदना । to shut.

√ **मील** – (चु॰) – (**निमीलने**) मूंदना। to shut.

मीळह – न॰ – (**गूँह**) विष्ठा, मल। excrement.

मुकुल – न॰ – (**मुकुल**) कली। a bud.

मुख – न॰ – (**मुख**) मुँह, चेहरा, प्रवेशद्वार, (वि॰) प्रमुख। face, entrance (Adj.) chief.

मुख-तुण्ड – न॰ – (**मुख-तुण्ड**) चञ्चु, चोंच। a beak.

मुख-द्वार – न॰ – (**मुख-द्वार**) मुँह। mouth.

मुख-धोवन – न॰ – (**मुख-क्षालनम्**) मुँह का धोना। mouth washing.

मुख-पुञ्छन – न॰ – (**मुख-प्रोक्षणम्**) मुँह पोंछने का वस्त्र। towel for wiping the face.

मुख-पूर – न॰ – (**मुख-पूर**) मुँह भरना, वि॰ मुँह भरने वाला। a mouthful, filling the mouth.

मुख-वट्टि – स्त्री॰ – (**मुख-वर्ति**) किनारा। brim, rim, edge.

मुख-वण्ण – पु॰ – (**मुख-वर्ण**) चेहरे का रंग। the features.

मुख-विकार – पु॰ – (**मुख-विकार**) चेहरे का रंग-ढंग। gesture of the face.

मुख-संकोचन – न॰ – (**मुख-संकोचन**) चेहरे की विकृति, मुँह बनाना। distortion of the face (as a sign of displeasure).

मुख-संयत – स्त्री॰ – (**मुख-संयत**) वाणी का संयमी। controlling one's tongue.

मुखर – वि॰ – (**मुखर**) वाचाल। talkative, garrulous.

मुखरता – स्त्री॰ – (**मुखरता**) वाचालता। talkativeness.

मुखाधान – न॰ – (**मुखाधान**) लगाम। a bridle, bit and reins.

मुखुल्लोकक – वि॰ – (**मुखावलोकक**) आदमी के चेहरे की ओर देखने वाला। looking into a person's face.

मुखोदक – न॰ – (**मुखोदक**) मुँह धोने का जल। water for washing the face.

मुख्य – वि॰ – (**मुख्य**) प्रमुख, प्रधान, अति महत्त्वपूर्ण। chief, foremost, significant.

मुग्ग – पु॰ – (**मुद्ग**) मूँग। green peas.

मुग्गर – पु॰ – (**मुद्गर**) मुगदर। a club, mallet.

मंगुस – न॰ – (**अङ्कुष**) नेवला। a mongoose.

√ **मुच** – (रु॰) – (**मोचने**) छुड़ाना, मुक्त करना। to get released, to get freed.

√ **मुच** – (चु॰) – (**प्रमोचने**) छुड़ाना, मुक्त करना। to set free, to untie.

मुचलिन्द – पु॰ – (**मुचलिन्द**) नारंगी का पेड़ (नाम) उरुवेला में अजपाल न्यग्रोध के पास का एक वृक्ष, जिसके नीचे बुद्धत्व प्राप्ति के अनन्तर भगवान बुद्ध ने तीसरा सप्ताह मनाया। orange tree *Barringtonia Acutangula*, the Buddha had spent the third week after the enlightenment under the Mucalinda tree situated near the Ajapāl *nyagrodha* in Uruvelā.

मुच्चति – क्रि॰ – (√ **मुच** = मुञ्चति) स्वतन्त्र होता है, मुक्त होता है। becomes free or liberated.

√ **मुच्छ** – (भू॰) – (**मोहे**) मूर्छित होना। to faint.

मुच्छति – क्रि॰ – (√ **मुर्च्छ** = मूर्च्छति) मूर्च्छित होता है। faints.

मुच्छन – न॰ – (**मूर्च्छन**) मूर्छा। fainting, unconciousness.

मुच्छना – स्त्री॰ – (**मूर्च्छना**) मूर्छा। fainting unconsciousness.

√ **मुज्ज** – (भू॰) – (**मज्जने**) गोता लगाना। to dive.

मुञ्चक – वि॰ – (**मुञ्चक**) मुक्त करने वाला। one who liberates.

मुञ्चति – क्रि॰ – (√ **मुच्** = मुञ्चति) मुक्त करता है, ढीला करता है। releases, loosens.

मुञ्चन – न॰ – (**मुञ्चन**) छोड़ना, मुक्त करना। liberating, releasing.

मुञ्ज – न॰ – (**मुञ्ज**) मूँज, तृण का एक प्रकार। reed-grass.

मुट्ठ – कृदन्त – विस्मृत। forgetfulness.

मुट्ठस्सती – वि॰ – विस्मृत करने वाला। forgetful, oblivious.

मुट्ठि – पु॰ तथा स्त्री॰ – (**मुष्टि**) मुट्ठी, मूठ। fist, clenched hand.

मुट्ठिक – पु॰ – (**मुष्टिक**) घूँसे से प्रहार करने वाला, पहलवान। a boxer, a wrestler.

मुट्ठि-मल्ल – पु॰ – (**मुष्टि-मल्ल**) मुक्केबाज। a boxer.

मुट्ठि-युद्ध – न॰ – (**मुष्टि-युद्ध**) मुक्का-मुक्की। boxing.

√ **मुण्ड** – (भू॰) – (**मुण्डने / वपने**) मूंडना। to shave.

मुण्ड – वि॰ – (**मुण्ड**) मुण्डित, बालरहित, गंजा। man with shaved head, bald.

मुण्डक – पु॰ – (**मुण्डक**) (1) बालरहित (मुण्डित) सिर वाला (2) सिर के बाल बनाने वाला। (1) shaven headed, (2) barber.

मुण्डच्छद – पु॰ – (**मुण्डच्छद**) चौड़ी छत वाला मकान। a building with a flat-roof.

मुण्डत्त – न॰ – (**मुण्डत्त्व**) मुण्डित होने का भाव, मुण्डित होने की स्थिति। the state of being shaven.

मुण्डेति – क्रि॰ – (√ **मुण्ड** – मुण्डति) शिर मूँडता है। shaves.

मुणिक-जातक – (जा॰ सं॰ 30) – इस जातक कथा की शिक्षा है कि वैभव की प्रचुरता प्रायः आसन्न विपदा का कारण बनती है। the story (No. 30) tells that luxury often causes suffering.

मुत – न॰ – नाक, जीभ तथा स्पर्शेन्द्रिय द्वारा होने वाला इन्द्रियानुभव। sense perceptions through nose, tongue and skin.

मुतिङ्ग-मुदिङ्ग – पु॰ – (**मृदङ्ग**) मर्दल, पखावज। a kind of small drum.

मुतिमन्तु – वि॰ – (**मतिमान्**) बुद्धिमान। sensible, intelligent.

मुत्त – न॰ – (**मूत्र**) पेशाब। urine.

मुत्त – कृदन्त – (√ **मुच** + **क्त** = **मुक्त**) स्वतन्त्र किया हुआ, आजाद छोड़ा हुआ। released, liberated, freed.

मुत्ताचार – वि॰ – (**मुक्ताचार**) आचारहीन, शिथिलाचार। of loose habit.

मुत्तकरण – न॰ – (मूत्र-करण) मूत्रेन्द्रिय। urinary organ.

मुत्तवत्थि – स्त्री॰ – (मूत्र-वस्ति) मूत्राशय। the bladder, urine bladder.

मुत्ता – स्त्री॰ – (मुक्ता) मौक्तिक, मोती। a pearl.

मुत्तावलि – स्त्री॰ – (मुक्तावली) मोती की लड़ी। a string of pearls.

मुत्ताहार – पु॰ – (मुक्ता-हार) मोतियों का हार। pearl necklace.

मुत्ताजाल – न॰ – (मुक्ता-जाल) मोतियों का जाल। a net or zone of pearls.

मुत्ति – स्त्री॰ – (मुक्ति) मुक्ति। release, freedom.

√ मुद – (भू॰) – (तोषे) संतुष्ट होना, प्रसन्न होना। to be glad.

मुदा – स्त्री॰ – (मुद) मोद, प्रसन्नता। gladness, joy.

मुदित – वि॰ – (मुदित) प्रसन्न। glad, happy.

मुदित-मन – वि॰ – (मुदित-मन) प्रसन्नचित्त। with happy heart.

मुदिता – स्त्री॰ – (मुदिता) दूसरों की समृद्धि देखकर आनन्दित होना। joy in seeing others' prosperity.

मुदु – वि॰ – (मृदु) मुलायम, कोमल। soft, tender, mild.

मुदुक – वि॰ – (मृदु) नर्म, कोमल। soft, mild.

मुदु-चित्त – वि॰ – (मृदु-चित्त) कोमल चित्त वाला। of a tender heart.

मुदु-जातिक – वि॰ – (मृदु-जातिक) मृदु स्वभाव वाला। of tender nature.

मुदुता – स्त्री॰ – (मृदुता) कोमलता, मार्दव। softness.

मुदुत्त – न॰ – (मृदुत्त्व) कोमलता, सरलता। softness, simplicity.

मुदु-भूत – वि॰ – (मृदु-भूत) मृदुलीकृत, सरलीकृत। softened.

मुदुल – वि॰ – (मृदुल) कोमल, सरल। soft.

मुदुलक्खण-जातक – (जा॰ सं॰ 66) – राजा के आश्रय में पल रहा तपस्वी जो राजा की पत्नी पर ही मोहित हो गया। the story of an ascetic depending on the king who subsequently fell in love with the queen and lost all his *siddhi* powers.

मुदु-हृदय – वि॰ – (मृदु-हृदय) कोमल मन वाला। soft-hearted, kind-hearted.

मुद्दङ्कन – न॰ – (मुद्राङ्कन) छपाई। printing.

मुद्दा – स्त्री॰ – (मुद्रा) मुद्रा, संकेत (हस्त-मुद्रा) छपाई। a seal, a gesture, printing.

मुद्दापक – पु॰ – (मुद्रक) मुद्रण-कर्त्ता, मुद्रक। printer.

मुद्दापन – न॰ – (मुद्रण) छपाई, मुद्रण। printing.

मुद्दायन्त – न॰ – (मुद्रण-यन्त्र) छापाखाना, मुद्रणालय। a printing press.

मुद्दापेति – क्रि॰ – छपाता है, मुद्रित करता है। gets printed.

मुद्दिका – स्त्री॰ – (मुद्रिका) अँगूठी, नामांकित अँगूठी। a ring, signet.

मुद्दिकासव – पु॰ – (द्राक्षासव) अँगूरी आसव। grape-wine.

मुद्ध – वि॰ – (मुग्ध) मूर्ख, चकित। idiot, of confused mind, swerved.

मुद्धातुक – वि॰ – मूर्ख स्वभाव। foolish nature.

मुद्धता – स्त्री॰ – (मुग्धता) मूर्खता। foolishness.

मुद्धा – पु॰ – (मूर्धा) शीर्ष, शिखर। the head, summit.

मुद्धज – पु॰ – (मूर्धज) (1) शिर (मूर्धा) से उत्पन्न केश (2) मूर्धन्य वर्ण-टवर्ग, षकार। (1) hair, (2) cerebrals, ṭ ṭh etc.

मुद्धाधिपात – पु॰ – (मूर्धाधिपात) सिर का गिरना। falling or splitting of the head.

मुद्धावसित्त – वि॰ – (मूर्धाभिषिक्त) राज-तिलक किया हुआ नरेश। a properly anointed king.

मुधा – अव्यय – (मुधा) व्यर्थ, वृथा। in vain, to no purpose.

मुनाति – क्रि॰ – (√ मन - मन्यते) मानता है, जानता है। accepts, thinks, believes, reflects.

मुनि – पु॰ – (मुनि) मुनि, मनन करने वाला साधु। meditator, a sage.

मुनिन्द – पु॰ – (मुनीन्द्र) मुनियों में प्रधान (बुद्ध)। the great sage (the Buddha).

मुह्हति – क्रि॰ – (√ मुह - मुह्यति) भूल जाता है, मन्द बुद्धि होता है। forgets, becomes dull-minded.

√ मुह – (दि॰) – (विचेतने) मोहित होना, संज्ञा-शून्य होना। to faint, to loose senses.

√ मुह – (भू॰) – (मूर्छायां) मूर्छित होना। to faint, to become unconscious.

मुह्हन – न॰ – (मोह) भूल, विस्मृति। infatuation, forgetfulness.

मुरज – पु॰ – (मुरुज) क्षुद्र मर्दल, चंग या झाँझ नामक वाद्य। a tambourine.

मुरमुरायति – क्रि॰ –(मुर्मुरायते) मुर-मुर शब्द करके काट डालता है। cuts off with a craking sound.

√ मुस – (तु॰) – स्तेये – चोरी करना। to steal, to cheat.

मुसल – पु॰ – (मुसल) मूसल। a pestle.

मुसली – वि॰ – (मुसली) मूसल वाला। one having a pestle in his hand.

मुसा – अव्यय – (मृषा) झूठ। falsehood, lie.

मुसाबाद – पु॰ – (मृषावाद) झूठ। lying.

मुस्सति – क्रि॰ – (मुञ्चति) भूल जाता है, अन्तर्ध्यान हो जाता है। to forget; to pass into oblivion.

मुहुत्त – पु॰ – (मुहुत्तं; मुहुत्तम्) मुहूर्त। a moment; a minute.

मुहुत्तेन – क्रि॰ वि॰ – (मुहुर्त्तेन) क्षण-भर में। in a moment.

मुहुत्तिक – वि॰ – (मुहूर्त्तकः) मुहूर्त्त भर रहने वाला। existing only for a moment, an astrologer.

मुलाल – नपुं॰ – (मृनाल) कमल नाल। lotus root.

मुलाल-पुप्फ – नपुं॰ – (मृनाल-पुष्प) कमल का फूल। lotus flower.

√ मू – (भि॰) – (बन्धने) बाँधना। to fasten.

√ मू – (भू॰) – (बन्धने) बाँधना। to fasten.

मूग – पु॰ वि॰ – (मूक) मूक व्यक्ति, गूँगा। dumb, a dumb person.

मूग-प्रकख-जातक – (जा॰ सं॰ 538) – देखें तमीय जातक। see Tamīya Jātaka.

मूल – न॰ – (मूल) जड़, उत्पत्ति, तल्ला, कारण, नींव, आरम्भ। root, origin, cause.

मूल-कन्द – पु॰ – (मूल-कन्द) प्याज। onion.

मूल-धन – न॰ – (मूलधन) जमा धन। capital, deposit money.

मूल-बीज – न॰ – (मूलबीज) अंकुरित होने वाला आधार बीज। germinative or basic root.

मूलपरियाय-जातक – (जा॰ सं॰ 245) – काल सबको खाता है, अपने आप को भी सभी को खाने वाले काल को कौन खा सकता है? प्रश्न का समाधान इस कथा में प्रस्तुत है। the tale (No. 245) solves the riddle: "Time consumes all, even itself, but who can consume all-consumer".

मूलक (1) – पु॰ – (मूलक) (प्रायः समासान्त में प्रयुक्त) हेतुक कारणीभूत जैसे प्रयोजन-मूलक। (used in compounds) originating in.

मूलक (2) – पु॰ – (मूलक) मूली। The radish.

मूलिक – क्रि॰ – (मौलिक) मुख्य, आप्त, प्राथमिक। fundamental, elementary.

मूल्य – न॰ – (मूल्य) कीमत, मजदूरी। price, wages.

मूसा – स्त्री॰ – (मूषा) धातु पिघलाने की धरिया। a crucible.

मूसिक – पु॰ – (मूषक) चूहा। mouse.

मूसिका – स्त्री॰ – (मूषिक) चुहिया। female mouse.

मूसिक-छिन्न – वि॰ – (मूषिका-छिन्न) चूहों द्वारा कुतरा गया। gnawed by mice.

मूसिक-बच्च – न॰ – (मूषिकला) चूहे की मेंगनी। mice-dung.

मूसिक-जातक – (जा॰ सं॰ 377) – पिता की हत्या करने की चेष्टा करने वाले पुत्र की कथा। the story (No. 377) of a son trying to kill his father.

मूल्ह – कृदन्त – ($\sqrt{}$ मुह् + क्त = मूढ) मूर्ख, मूढ, भ्रान्त। foolish, confused, gone astray.

मे – सर्वनाम – (मे) मुझे, मेरा। to me, mine.

मेखला – स्त्री॰ – (मेखला) करधनी। a girdle for woman.

$\sqrt{}$ मेघ – (भू॰) – (संग्रामे) लड़ाई करना। to fight.

मेघ – पु॰ – (मेघ) जलधर, बादल। rain, cloud.

मेघनाद – पु॰ – (मेघनाद) मेघ-गर्जन। thunder.

मेघ-पासाण – पु॰ – (मेघ-पाषाण) ओले, करका। hail-shower.

मेघ-वण्ण – वि॰ – (मेघ-वर्ण) मेघ-घटा के वर्ण का। of cloud colour.

मेचक – वि॰ – (मेचक) काला या गहरा नीला। black, dark blue.

मेज्झ – वि॰ – (मेध्य) पवित्र। holy, pure.

मेण्ड-मेण्डक – पु॰ – (मेढ) मेंढा या भेंड। a ram.

मेण्डक – पु॰ – (मेण्डक) प्रसिद्ध धनपति धनञ्जय का पिता, विशाखा मिगार माता का पितामह। father of the famous rich merchant Dhanañjaya and grandfather of Visākha.

मेत्त-चित्त – (मैल-चित्त) मैत्रीपूर्ण चित्त। having a benevolent heart.

मेत्ता – स्त्री॰ – (मैत्री) मैत्री-भावना, उदारता। amity, benevolence.

मेत्त-भावना – स्त्री॰ – (मैत्री-भावना) मैत्री का अभ्यास करना। cultivating of benevolence.

मेत्तायना – स्त्री॰ – (मैत्रीभाव) मैत्रीभाव। friendly feeling.

मेत्ता-विहारी – वि॰ – (मैत्री-विहारी) मैत्री-भाव में रमता हुआ। moving forward in friendly behaviour.

मेत्तायति – क्रि॰ – (मैत्रीयति) मैत्री करता है। establishes friendly relations.

मेत्तेय्य-नाथ – पु॰ – (मैत्रेय-नाथ) भावी बुद्ध, मैत्रेय। would be or the coming Buddha, Metteyya.

मेथुन – न॰ – (मैथुन) सम्भोग, मैथुन। coupling, sexual intercourse.

मेथुन-धम्म – न॰ – (मैथुन-धर्म) मैथुन-क्रिया। coupling, sexual intercourse.

मेद – पु॰ – (मेद) चर्बी। the fat.

मेदक-थालिका – स्त्री॰ – (मेदस्थालिका) चर्बी भूनने का भाजन। the pan for frying fat.

मेद-वण्ण – वि॰ – (मेद-वर्ण) चर्बी के रंग का। of the colour of fat.

मेदिनी – स्त्री॰ – (मेदिनी) पृथ्वी। the earth.

मेध – पु॰ – (मेध) यज्ञ। sacrifice.

मेधग – पु॰ – (मेधग) झगड़ा। a quarrel.

मेधा – स्त्री॰ – (मेधा) बुद्धि, प्रज्ञा। wisdom, intellect.

मेधाविनी – स्त्री॰ – (मेधाविनी) प्रज्ञावती स्त्री। an intellectual lady.

मेधावी – वि॰ – (मेधावी) प्रज्ञावान। the intellectual.

मेरय – न॰ – (मेरय) सुरा, मदिरा। liquor, wine.

मेरु – पु॰ – (मेरु) उच्चतम पर्वत का नाम। name of the highest mountain.

मेलक – न॰ – (मेलक) सभा, संगत, समूह। assemblage, multitude.

मेलन – न॰ – (मेलनम्) मिलना, सम्मिलन। a gathering, meeting.

मेस – पु॰ – (मेष) भेंड़ा। a ram.

मेह – पु॰ – (मेह) मूत्ररोग। urinary affliction.

मेहन – न॰ – (मेहन) मूत्रेन्द्रिय। urinary organ.

√ मोक्ख – (चु॰) – (मोचने) छुड़ाना। to release, to set free.

मोक्ख – पु॰ – (मोक्ष) मोक्ष, मुक्ति। salvation, liberation, emancipation.

मोक्खक – वि॰ – (मोक्षक) मोक्षदाता। one who grants release.

मोक्ख-मग्ग – पु॰ – (मोक्ष-मार्ग) मोक्ष का मार्ग। the path leading to salvation.

मोक्खति – क्रि॰ – (√ मोक्ष - मोक्षयति) मुक्त होता है, दुःखों से आत्यन्तिक निवृत्ति प्राप्त करता है। gets freedom from worldly sufferings.

मोग्गल्लान – पु॰ – (मोद्गल्लान) भगवान् बुद्ध के दो प्रधान शिष्यों में से एक। इनका जन्म राजगृह के कोलित ग्राम में हुआ था। पालि ग्रन्थों में इन्हें महामोगलान

कहा गया है। one of the two chief disciples of the Buddha, he was born in Kolita-grāma near Rājgṛha. In Pāli texts, he has been called Mahā Moggalāna.

मोग्गलिपुत्त-तिस्स-थेर – पु॰ – (**मोद्गलि-पुत्र तिष्य**) ये तृतीय बौद्ध संगीति के प्रधान तथा सम्राट् अशोक के गुरु थे। he was the president of the third assembly of the Buddhist monks and had been the teacher of emperor Aśoka.

मोघ – वि॰ – (**मोघ**) निष्फल, व्यर्थ। vain, useless.

मोघपुरिस – पु॰ – (**मोघ-पुरुष**) बेकार आदमी, मूर्ख। stupid person, useless person.

मोच – पु॰ – (**मोचा**) कदली, केला। plantain.

मोचन (1) – न॰ – (**मोचन**) छुड़ाना, मुक्त करना। releasing.

मोचन (2) – पु॰ – (**मोचन**) छुड़ाने वाला। one who causes release.

मोचापन – न॰ – मुक्त करना। getting released.

मोचेति – क्रि॰ – (**मुञ्चति**) मुक्त करता है। releases.

मोदक – पु॰ – (**मोदक**) लड्डू। a sugar-ball sweet-meat.

मोदति – क्रि॰ – (√**मुद्**- **मोदते**) आनन्दित होता है। becomes delighted.

मोदन – न॰ – (**मोदन**) आनन्दित होना। causing delight.

मोदना – स्त्री॰ – (**मोदन**) प्रमुदित होना। rejoicing, revelling.

मोन – न॰ – (**मौन**) मुनि-भाव, मौन। self-possession, silence.

मोनेय्य – न॰ – नैतिक सम्पूर्णता। moral perfection.

मोमुह – वि॰ – (**मुमुग्ध**) जड़बुद्धि, मूर्ख। silly, blunt-minded.

मोर – पु॰ – (**मोर / मयूर**) मोर पक्षी। a peacock.

मोर-पिञ्ज – न॰ – (**मयूर-पिच्छ**) मोर की पूँछ। peacock's tail.

मोर-जातक – (जा॰ सं॰ 159) – एक मोर की कथा जो सूर्य तथा बुद्ध की प्रशंसा में स्तोत्र गाते हुए हर तरह सुरक्षित रहा। the story (No. 159) of a peacock who remained safe in every respect as it used to recite the hymn in honour of the sun and another in praise of the Buddha.

मोस – पु॰ – (**मोष**) चोर, चौर्य, चुराई वस्तु। thief, theft, things taken in theft.

मोसन – न॰ – (**मोषण**) चौर्य, चोरी। theft.

मोसवज्ज – न॰ – (**मोष-वचन**) असत्य। untruth.

मोह – पु॰ – (**मोह**) मोह, मूर्खता। stupidity, delusion.

मोहक्खय – पु॰ – (**मोहक्षय**) अविद्या का नाश। annihilation, ignorance.

मोह-चरित – वि॰ – (**मोह-चरित**) मूढ़-चरित। of foolish habits.

मोहतम – पु॰ – (**मोहतम**) मोहान्धकार, अविद्यान्धकार। the gloom of ignorance.

मोहनीय – वि॰ – (**मोहनीय**) मोहने वाला, मूर्ख बनाने वाला। leading to attachment or infatuation.

मोहन – न॰ – (**मोहन**) मुग्ध करना, मोहना। enticement.

मोहक – वि॰ – (**मोहक**) मोह उत्पन्न करने वाला। charming, infatuating.

मोहेति – क्रि॰ – ($\sqrt{}$ **मुह - मुह्यति**) मोह उत्पन्न करता है, मुग्ध कर देता है। deludes, enchants, infatuates.

मोलि – पु॰ तथा स्त्री॰ – (**मौलि**) चूड़ा, सिर का उच्चतम भाग। topknot of hair, top of the head.

य

य – पालि वर्णमाला का छब्बीसवाँ व्यञ्जन। the 26th consonant of Pāli alphabet.

य – सर्वनाम – (यद्) जो, कौन, क्या, जो कुछ भी। who, which, what, whatsoever.

यकन – न॰ – (यकृत) यकृत, जिगर। the liver.

यक्ख – पु॰ – (यक्ष) कल्पित देव योनि विशेष। a presumed class of demi-gods, attendant of Kuvera to guard his gardens.

यक्ख-गण – पु॰ – (यक्ष-गण) यक्ष-गण। a multitude of demi-gods.

यक्ख-गाह – पु॰ – (यक्ष-गृह) यक्षाधिकृत। acquisition by a demi-god.

यक्खत्त – न॰ – (यक्षत्व) यक्षत्व। state of a demi-god.

यक्खभूत – वि॰ – (यक्ष-भूत) यक्ष होकर पैदा हुआ। born as a demi-god.

यक्ख-समागम – पु॰ – (यक्ष-समागम) यक्षों का सम्मेलन। conference or gathering of yakṣas, an epithet of Kuvera.

यक्खाधिप – पु॰ – (यक्षाधिप) यक्षों का राजा। the king of the yakṣas.

यक्खिनी – स्त्री॰ – (यक्षिणी) यक्षिणी। a wife of yakṣa, a fairy, wife of Kuvera.

यक्खी – स्त्री॰ – (यक्षिणी) देखें यक्खिनी। see Yakkhinī.

यग्घे – वि॰ – आदर-सूचक शब्द, आदर-सूचक सम्बोधन। respectful address, calling alone with affection.

√ यज् – (भू॰) – (सङ्गतिकरण) द्यनेषु। यक्ष करना, पूजन-भजन। to sacrifice, to pay oblation.

यजति – क्रि॰ – (√ यज् - यजति, यजते) यज्ञ करता है, दान करता है। sacrifices, offers gifts, worships gods with oblation.

यजन – न॰ – (यजन) यज्ञ करना, दान देना। sacrifice, worship, offers gifts.

यजु – न॰ – (यजुर्वेद) यजुर्वेद। the *Yajurveda.*

यञ्ञ – पु॰ – (यज्ञ) यज्ञ, यजन - कर्म। sacrifice.

यञ्ञ-सामी – पु॰ – (यज्ञ-स्वामी) यज्ञ-स्वामी। organiser of a sacrifice, in whose name the sacrifice is done.

यञ्ञावाट – पु॰ – (यज्ञ-वाट) यज्ञ-कुण्ड, यज्ञ-वेदिका (यज्ञगर्त)। the sacrificial pit, altar.

यञ्ञ-उपनीत – वि॰ – (यज्ञोपनीत) यज्ञ के निमित्त लाई गई सामग्री। the things brought for sacrifice.

यट्ठि – पु॰ तथा स्त्री॰ – (यष्टि) लाठी, लकड़ी का डंडा। stick, staff.

यट्ठि-कोटि – स्त्री॰ – (यष्टि-कोटि) लाठी का सिरा। the end of a staff.

यटि्ठ-मुधका – स्त्री० – (यष्टि-मधुका) मुलहठी । liquorice.

√यत – (चु०) – (नियतिने) बाहर भेजना । sending out.

यत – कृदन्त – (यत) यमित, नियन्त्रित, रोका गया, संयत । controlled, restrained.

√यत – (चु०) – (नियन्त्रणे, संकोचने) संयत रखना, संकोच करना । to control, to hesitate.

यतति – क्रि० – (यतते) प्रयत्न करता है । exerts oneself, strives.

यतन – न० – (यत्न) प्रयत्न । endeavour.

यति – पु० – (यति) भिक्षु, साधु, ब्रह्मचारी । a monk, a sage.

यतो – अव्यय – (यतः) जहाँ से, जब से, क्योंकि, चूंकि । from where, whence, since, because, on account of which.

यत्तक – वि० – (यावत) यावन्मात्र, जितना । whatever much.

यत्थ/यत्र – क्रि० वि० – (यत्र-क्वच) जहाँ कहीं । wherever.

यत्थ – अव्यय – (यत्र) जहाँ । where.

यथत्त – अव्यय – (यथात्वम्) ऐसा, ही, यथार्थ में । in reality, as such.

यथरिय – अव्यय – (यथैव) जैसा । just as.

यथा – अव्यय – (यथा) जैसे । as, like.

यथाकम्मं – क्रि० वि० – (यथा-कर्म) यथाकर्म । according to one's action.

यथा-कामं – क्रि० वि० – (यथाकामम्) यथेच्छ । according to one's wish, at random.

यथाकारी – वि० – (यथाकारी) अपनी मर्जी से करने वाला । one who acts according to his wishes.

यथाकाल – क्रि० वि० – (यथाकाल) योग्य समय, उपयुक्त समय । proper time.

यथाकाल – क्रि० वि० – (यथाकालम्) उपयुक्त समय । appropriate time.

यथाकम्मं – क्रि० वि० – (यथाक्रम) क्रमानुसार । in order, in succession.

यथाच – अव्यय – (यथाच) जैसे । as.

यथाठित – वि० – (यथास्थित) जैसा पहले था, यथास्थित, पूर्ववत् । as it was, just as it stood.

यथातथ – अव्यय – (यथातथ्य) तथ्य के अनुसार, यथा-तथ्य, सत्य । true, real.

यथातथं – क्रि० वि० – (यथा-तथ्यम्) तथ्य के अनुसार, यथासत्य । according to truth.

यथाधम्मं – क्रि० वि० – (यथाधर्म) धर्म के मुताबिक, नियमानुसार । according to the law.

यथाधोत – वि० – (यथाधौत) ठीक से धुला, जैसे धुला हो । well-washed, as if it were washed.

यथानुसिट्ठं – क्रि० वि० – (यथा + अनुशिष्टम्) उपदेशानुसार, अनुशासन के अनुरूप । in accordance with the advice.

यथानुभावं – क्रि० वि० – (यथा + अनुभावम्) योग्यतानुसार । according to one's authority or belief.

यथापसादं – क्रि० वि० – (यथा + प्रसादम्) प्रसन्नता के अनुसार । according to one's gratification.

यथापि – अव्यय – (यथापि) जैसे। as.

यथापूरित – वि॰ – (यथापूरित) पूरी तरह भरा हुआ। as full as could be, completely filled.

यथाफासुक – वि॰ – (यथा + स्पर्शक) सुविधाजनक। comfortable.

यथाबलं – क्रि॰ वि॰ – (यथावलम्) यथासक्ति, शक्ति के अनुसार। according to one's strength, within one's capacity.

यथाभतं – क्रि॰ वि॰ – (यथाभृतम्) जैसे लाया गया। as it was brought.

यथाभिरतं – क्रि॰ वि॰ – (यथा + अभिरतम्) जब तक (जैसी कि) रूचि हो। as long as one likes.

यथाभूत – वि॰ – (यथाभूत) तथ्य, यथार्थ। a real, evident.

यथाभूतं – क्रि॰ वि॰ – (यथाभूतम्) यथार्थ रूप से। in its real sense.

यथारहं – क्रि॰ वि॰ – (यथा + अर्हम्) यथाई योग्यतानुसार। according to one's ability.

यथारूचिं – क्रि॰ वि॰ – (यथारूचिम्) रूचि के अनुसार। according to one's liking.

यथावतो – क्रि॰ वि॰ – (यथावत्) यथावत। according to established system.

यथाविधिं – क्रि॰ वि॰ – (यथाविधिम्) यथा-विधि, विधि के अनुसार। according to rules.

यथाविहितं – क्रि॰ वि॰ – (यथाविहितम्) व्यवस्था के अनुसार। as arranged.

यथावुद्धं – क्रि॰ वि॰ – (यथा + वृद्धम्) ज्येष्ठानुक्रम, ज्येष्ठपन के अनुसार। according to seniority.

यथावुत्तं – क्रि॰ वि॰ – (यथा + उक्तम्) यथोक्त। a staled before.

यथासकं – क्रि॰ वि॰ – (यथा + स्वकम्) स्वत्वानुसार, अपनी मिल्कियत के अनुसार। according to one's status.

यथासत्तिं – क्रि॰ वि॰ – (यथा + शक्तिम्) भरसक शक्ति के अनुसार। according to one's power.

यथासद्धं – क्रि॰ वि॰ – (यथाश्रद्धम्) श्रद्धा के अनुसार। according to one's devotion.

यथासुखं – क्रि॰ वि॰ – (यथासुखम्) सुखपूर्वक। comfortably.

यथाहि – अव्यय – (यथाहि) जैसे की। as.

यथिच्छितं – क्रि॰ वि॰ – (यथेच्छ) इच्छानुसार। according to one's liking or desire.

यथेव – अव्यय – (यथेव) जैसे। as.

यदा – क्रि॰ वि॰ – (यदा) जब। when.

यदि – अव्यय – (यदि) अगर। if, however.

यदिच्छा – स्त्री॰ – इच्छा, प्रवृत्ति। wish, desire.

यदीदं – अव्यय – (यदीदम्)। whatever, whichever is this.

यन्त – न॰ – (यन्त्र) यन्त्र, मशीन। a machine.

यन्त-नालि – स्त्री॰ – (यन्त्र-नलिका) पाइप। mechanical pipe.

यन्त-मुत्त – वि॰ – (यन्त्र-मुक्त) मशीन द्वारा फेंका गया। thrown or discharged by a machine.

यन्त-युत्त – वि॰ – (यन्त्र-युक्त) मशीन से जुड़ा हुआ। connected with a machine.

यन्तिक – पु॰ – (यान्त्रिक) मशीन बनाने या सुधारने वाला, टेकनीशियन। a mechanic.

√ यम – (भू॰) – (परिणये) विवाहित होना। be married.

√ यम – (चु॰) – (उपरमे) रुकना। stop.

यम – पु॰ – (यम) यमराज। god of death.

यम-दूत – पु॰ – (यम - दूत) यमराज का दूत। the messenger of Yama — the god of death.

यम-पुरिस – पु॰ – (यम-पुरुष) नरक में यन्त्रणा देने वाले। those who torture in the hell.

यम-लोक – पु॰ – (यमलोक) प्रेत-लोक। the world of the ghost.

यमक (1) – वि॰ – (यमक) यमज, सहोदर, जुड़वाँ, दुहरा। a twin, a pair, double.

यमक (2) – (यमक) अभिधम्म पिटक का छठा प्रकरण (ग्रन्थ)। the sixth book of the Abhidhamma Piṭaka.

यमक-साल – पु॰ – (यमक-शाल) शाल-वृक्षों की जोड़ी, साखू के जुड़वाँ। twin of śāla tree.

यमुना – स्त्री॰ – (यमुना) प्रसिद्ध यमुना नदी, जिसके तट पर मथुरा बसी है। the famous Yamunā river, on the bank of which Mathurā city is situated.

यव – पु॰ – (यव) जौ। barley.

यव-सूक – पु॰ – (यव-शूक) जौ का टूड़। the stalk of barley.

यवस – पु॰ – (यवस) घास विशेष। a kind of grass.

√ यस – (दि॰) – (प्रयत्ने) प्रयत्न करना। to make effort.

यस – पु॰ तथा न॰ – (यश) यश, प्रसिद्धि। fame, glory.

यसदायक – वि॰ – (यशदायक) यशप्रद। fame-giving.

यसमहत्त – न॰ – (यशमहत्त्व) यशमाहात्म्य। magnanimity or sublimity of fame.

यस-लाभ – पु॰ – (यशोलाभ) यशोप्राप्ति। attainment of glory.

यस-थेर – पु॰ – (यशथेर) वाराणसी सेठ का पुत्र, यश, जिसके सन्तप्त हृदय को बुद्ध की अमृत वाणी ने शान्ति प्रदान की। the story of the son of a wealthy merchant in Varanasi, the nectar-like voice of Buddha had given peace to his grieved heart.

यसोधर – वि॰ – (यशोधर) कीर्त्तिधर, यशस्वी। reputed, glorious.

यसोलद्ध – वि॰ – (यशोलब्ध) (1) यश प्राप्त, (2) यश के द्वारा अर्जित। (1) reputed, (2) earned by fame.

यहिं – अव्यय – (यत्र) जहाँ, जहाँ कहीं। where, wherever.

यं – अव्यय – (यद्) जो, जो कुछ (वस्तु)। which, whatever (thing).

√ या – (भू॰) – (प्राप्तकरणे) प्राप्त करना। to obtain.

याग – पु॰ – (यज्ञ) यज्ञ, दान। sacrifice, donation, charity.

यागु – स्त्री॰ – (यवागू) जौ अथवा तण्डुल कणों से दूध में पकायी गयी मीठी लस्सी। a dish prepared with sugar, milk and barley or rice gruels.

√ याच – (भू॰) – (याचने) मांगना। to beg.

याचक – पु॰ – (याचक) याचना करने

वाला, माँगने वाला। one who begs or requests.

याचति – क्रि॰ – ($\sqrt{}$ याच - याचते) माँगता है, याचना करता है। begs, asks, entreats.

याचन – न॰ – (याचन) याचना। begging, entreaty.

याचनक – वि॰ – (याचक) देखें याचक। see Yācaka.

याचयोग – वि॰ – (याचनयोग्य) जिससे याचना करना उचित है। suitable for begging from.

याचित – कृ॰ – ($\sqrt{}$ याच् + क्त = याचित) याचित, माँगा गया। begged.

याचितक – न॰ – (याचितक) माँगी हुई वस्तु। a begged thing.

याजक – पु॰ – (याजक) यज्ञ कराने वाला। the instructor under whose directions the sacrifice is performed.

यात – कृ॰ – ($\sqrt{}$ इ + क्त = यात) चला गया। gone.

याति – क्रि॰ – (याति) जाता है। goes.

यात्रा – स्त्री॰ – (यात्रा) गमन, सफर। travel, voyage.

याथाव – वि॰ – (यथावत) ठीक-ठीक। exact, the same.

याथावतो – वि॰ – (यथावत) ठीक-ठीक। exactly.

यादिस – वि॰ – (यादृश) जिसके समान, जिससा। like which.

यान – न॰ – (यान) वाहन, गाड़ी, रथ। a carriage, chariot.

यानक – न॰ – (यानक) लघु वाहन, छोटी गाड़ी। a small carriage, a light vehicle.

यानगत – वि॰ – (यानगत) गाड़ी में स्थित। seated in a carriage.

यान-भूमि – स्त्री॰ – (यान-भूमि) गाड़ी जा सकने लायक भूमि। road accessible to a carriage.

यानी – पु॰ – (यानी) (1) वाहन का स्वामी (2) गाड़ी हाँकने वाला। (1) owner of the vehicle, (2) a person who drives the carriage.

यानीकत – वि॰ – (यानीकृत) अभ्यस्त, पटुता प्राप्त। accustomed, skilled, mastered.

यापन – न॰ – (यापन) (समासान्त में प्रयुक्त) गुजारा, बिताना जैसे जीवन-यापन, जीवन-निर्वाह। (used in compounds) subsistence, e.g. *jīvana-yāpana*, subsistence of life.

यापनीय – वि॰ – (यापनीय) यापन के योग्य, जीवन-आधार, निर्वाह-क्षय। sufficient for supporting one's life.

यापेति – क्रि॰ – ($\sqrt{}$ यापि - या + णिच् = यापयति) गुजारा करता है, व्यतीत करता है। subsists, keeps up.

याम (1) – पु॰ – (यामा) रात्रि। night.

याम (2) – पु॰ – (याम) रात्रि का पहर। one quarter of the night.

याम-कालिक – वि॰ – (यामकालिक) भिक्षु द्वारा अपराह्न तथा रात के समय ग्रहण की जा सकने वाली वस्तु। the thing allowed to be taken by a monk in afternoon and in the night.

यायी – वि॰ – (यायी) जाते हुए (समासान्त में प्रयुक्त) जैसे अनुयायी – पीछे चलने

वाला । (used in compounds) one who follows or goes behind, an alherent.

याव – अव्यय – (**यावत्**) जब तक । up to, so far as.

याव-कालिक – वि॰ – (**यावत् + कालिक**) अस्थायी । temporary.

याव-जीवं – वि॰ – (**यावत् + जीवन**) यावज्जीवन, जीवन-पर्यन्त । life-long.

याव-जीवं – क्रि॰ वि॰ – (**यावज्जीवम्**) जीवन भर । for the whole life.

याव-जीविक – वि॰ – (**यावत् + जीविक**) जीवन पर्यन्त बने रहने वाला । existing as long as one's life lasts.

यावतक – अव्यय – (**यावतक**) जितना । as much as.

यावता – अव्यय – (**यावत्**) जहाँ तक । as far as.

यावतायुकं – क्रि॰ वि॰ – (**यावतायुकम्**) जीवन बना रहने तक । as long as life lasts.

यावतावतिहं – क्रि॰ वि॰ – (**यावतावतीहम्**) जितने दिनों तक । for as many days as.

यावत्ततियम – अव्यय – (**यावत + तृतीयम्**) तीसरी बार तक । up to the third time.

यावदत्थं – अव्यय – (**यावदर्थम्**) आवश्यकतानुसार । as far as need be.

यिट्ठ – कृदन्त – (√**यज् + क्त = इष्टः**) यजनकृत, आहुति, अर्पित, अभीष्ट । offered, dedicated, desired, cherished bestowed, sacrificed.

युग – न॰ – (**युग**) जोड़ा, जुआ, युग, जमाना । a pair, a yoke, an age or generation.

युगन्त – पु॰ – (**युगान्त**) युग का अन्त । the end of an age or generation.

युगाह – पु॰ – ईर्ष्या, काबू । jealously, control, hold.

युगच्छिद – न॰ – (**युग + छिद्र = युगच्छिद्र**) जुए का छेद । the hole of a yoke.

युगनद्ध – वि॰ – (**युगनद्ध**) जुए में जुता । connected to a yoke.

युगनन्ध – वि॰ – (**युगनद्ध**) देखें युगनद्ध । see Yuganaddha.

युगमत्त – वि॰ – (**युगमात्र**) युग-मात्र, जुए की लम्बाई भर की दूरी । an iota of an age, the distance upto the length of a yoke.

युगन्धर – पु॰ – (**युगन्धर**) हिमालय के पर्वतों में से एक । one of the Himālayan mountains.

युगल – न॰ – (**युगल**) जोड़ी । a pair.

युगलक – न॰ – (**युगलक**) युगल, जोड़ा । a pair.

√**युज** – (दि॰) – (**समाधिकरणे**) ध्यान लगाना । to meditate.

√**युज** – (चु॰) – (**संयमे**) संयम करना । to practise, to restraint.

√**युज** – (ए॰) – (**योगे**) जोड़ना । to accumulate.

युञ्झति – क्रि॰ – (√**युध् - युध्यति**) युद्ध करता है । fights, makes war.

युञ्झन – न॰ – (√**युध् + ल्युट् = योधन**) युद्ध करना । fighting.

युञ्जति – क्रि॰ – (√**युज् - युनक्ति**) मिलाता है, शामिल होता है, प्रयत्न करता है । joins with, engages in, makes effort.

युञ्जन – न॰ – (√ युज् + ल्युट् = योजन) जोड़ना, सम्मिलित होना । engaging in, joining with.

युत्त – कृदन्त – (युक्त) संयुक्त, जुड़ा हुआ, संलग्न । connected with, engaged in.

युत्ति – स्त्री॰ – (युक्ति) न्याय, उपाय, करतब । justice, trick, skill.

युध् – (दि॰) – (सम्प्रहारे) लड़ना, जूझना । to fight.

युद्ध – न॰ – (युद्ध) संग्राम, लड़ाई । fight, war.

युद्ध-भूमि – स्त्री॰ – (युद्ध-भूमि) संग्राम-भूमि । battle-field.

युद्ध-मण्डल – न॰ – (युद्ध-मण्डल) संग्राम-भूमि । battle-field.

युव – पु॰ – (युव) युवा, तरुण, नौजवान । a youth.

युवती – स्त्री॰ – (युवती) तरुणी । a young woman.

युवञ्जय-जातक – (जा॰ सं॰ 460) – ओस की बूँदों का सूख जाना देख राजकुमार को संसार की अनित्यता का बोध हुआ । Seeing that dew drops had evaporated the prince realised that the world was transient, not permanent.

युथ – पु॰ – (यूथ) समूह, पशु-समूह । a flock, a herd of animals.

यूथ-जेट्ठ – पु॰ – (यूथ-ज्येष्ठ) पशुओं के झुण्ड का मुखिया । leader of a herd of cattle.

यूथप – पु॰ – (यूथप) यूथपति, सरदार । leader of a herd.

यूप – पु॰ – (यूप) यज्ञ-स्तम्भ । a sacrificial post.

यूस – पु॰ – (यूष) सूप, मांड, जूस । juice, soup.

येन – अव्यय – (येन) जिसके कारण, जिसके द्वारा । because of.

येव – अव्यय – (एव) ही । even, also, just.

यो – सर्वनाम – (यः) जो, जो कोई (पुरुष) । who, any (man), whoever.

योग – पु॰ – (योग) सम्बन्ध । attachment, mixture.

योगक्खेम – पु॰ – (योगक्षेम) आसक्ति से मुक्ति । freedom from attachments.

योग-युत्त – वि॰ – (योग + युक्त) आसक्ति से बँधा । bound by attachments.

योगावचर – पु॰ – (योगावचर) योगी । one who practises spiritual exercise.

योगातिम – वि॰ – (योगातिम) पुनर्जन्म के बंधन से मुक्त । one who has conquered the bond of rebirth.

योग्ग – वि॰ – (योग्य) समर्थ, निपुण, उपयुक्त । capable, suitable.

योजक – पु॰ – (योजक) जोड़ने वाला । one who joints, connects or yokes.

योजन – न॰ – (योजन) दूरी का माप (चार कोस या लगभग 13 किलोमीटर की दूरी) । a measure of length which is four kosa or about 13 kms.

योजना – स्त्री॰ – (योजना) कार्य प्रारूप । planning, action plan.

योजनिक – वि॰ – (योजनिक) योजना बनाने वाला । planner.

योजित – कृदन्त – (योजित) जुड़ा हुआ, संलग्न, मिला हुआ । combined, yoked, mixed with.

योजेति – क्रि॰ – (√ युज् - योजयति ∕ ते) जोड़ता है (योजेसि, योजेन्त, योजेत्वा, योजिय)। connects, adds.

योत्त – न॰ – (योवत्र) धागा, रस्सी, पगहा। a string, a twine.

योध – पु॰ – (योद्धा) योधा। a warrior.

योधाजीव – पु॰ – (युद्धजीवी) सैनिक। a soldier.

योधेति – क्रि॰ – (√ युध् - युध्यति) लड़ता है, युद्ध करता है। fights, combats.

योना – (यवन) यूनान देशवासी, ग्रीक। a Roman, a Greek.

योनि – स्त्री॰ – (योनि) मूल (मनुष्य) योनि, (स्त्री) योनि। origin, realm of existence, the female organ.

योनिसो – क्रि॰ वि॰ – यथार्थ ढंग से, बुद्धिपूर्वक। judiciously, wisely, properly.

योनिसो-मनसिकार – पु॰ – (यथार्थ-चिन्तने) यथार्थ विचार। real consideration.

योब्बन – न॰ – (यौवन) यौवन, जवानी। youth.

योब्बन-मद – पु॰ – (यौवन-मद) यौवन-मद, जोशे जवानी। the pride of youth.

र

र – पालि वर्णमाला का सत्ताइसवाँ व्यञ्जन । the 27th consonant of Pāli alphabet.

रक्खक – पु॰ – (**रक्षक**) रक्षक, पहरेदार । a guard, one who keeps.

√ **रक्ख** – (भू॰) – (**पालने**) पालना । to take care of.

रक्खति – क्रि॰ – (√ **रक्ष् - रक्षति**) रक्षा करता है । protects, guards.

रक्खन – न॰ – (**रक्षण**) रक्षण । protection, observance.

रक्खनक – वि॰ – (**रक्षणक**) रक्षण करता हुआ । observing, guarding.

रक्खस – पु॰ – (**राक्षस**) राक्षस । a demon.

रक्खा – स्त्री॰ – (**रक्षा**) सुरक्षा, आरक्षा । protection, safety, security.

रक्खित – कृदन्त – (√ **रक्ष् + त = रक्षित**) संरक्षित । protected, guarded.

रक्खित-थेर – पु॰ – (**रक्षित - स्थविर**) तृतीय संगति की समाप्ति पर वनवासी प्रदेश में भेजे गये स्थविर । name of the revered Ther who was sent to preach Buddhism in Vanvāsī region at the end of the Third Council.

रक्खिय – वि॰ – (**रक्ष्य**) रक्षण करने योग्य । to be protected, defensible.

रमा – स्त्री॰ – (**रमा**) मार की तीन कन्याओं में से एक, जिसने बुद्ध को प्रलोभित करने की चेष्टा की थी । one of the three daughters of Māra who had tried to entice the Buddha.

√ **रह्ब** – (भू॰) – (**रिङ्घणे**) रेंगना । to crawl.

रङ्कु – पु॰ – (**रङ्कु**) मृगों की एक प्रजाति । a species of deer.

रङ्ग – पु॰ – (**रङ्ग**) (1) रंग (2) अभिनय । (1) colour, paint (2) theatre, a play.

रङ्गकार – पु॰ – (**रङ्गकार**) (1) रँगने वाला, (2) रंगकर्मी (नाटक का पात्र) । (1) a dyer, (2) an actor.

रङ्गजात – न॰ – (**रङ्गजात**) नाना प्रकार के रंग । various kinds of dye, or colour.

रङ्गरत्त – वि॰ – (**रङ्गरक्त**) रंग में रंगा । dyed with.

रङ्गाजीव – पु॰ – (**रङ्गाजीव**) चित्रकार या रंग-साज । a painter or dyer.

रचयति – क्रि॰ – (√ **रच् - रचयति**) रचता है, व्यवस्था करता है, तैयार करता है । arranges, composes, prepares.

√ **रच** – (चु॰) – (**रचनायां**) रचना । to compose, arrange.

रचना – स्त्री॰ – (**रचना**) व्यवस्था । arrangement, a treatise.

रच्छा – स्त्री॰ – (**रथ्या**) गली, बाजार की सँकरी गली । a street, a lane, alley.

रज – पु॰ तथा न॰ – (**रज**) रेणु, धूलि । dust, pollen.

रजक्ख – वि॰ – रज (= चित्त-मैल से युक्त । soaked with or full of menstruum.

रजक्खन्ध – पु॰ – (रजस्कन्ध) धूल का अंबार । a heap of dust.

रजक – पु॰ – (रजक) धोबी । washerman.

रजत – न॰ – (रजत) चाँदी । silver.

रजति – क्रि॰ – (√ रज् - रजयति) रँगता है । dyes, colours.

रजन – न॰ – (रजनम्) रँगना । colouring, dyeing.

रजन-कम्म – न॰ – (रजन-कर्म) रँगना । colouring, dyeing.

रजनी – स्त्री॰ – (रजनी) रात्रि । night.

रजनीय – वि॰ – (कमनीय) मोहक, आकर्षक । enticing, charming.

रजस्सला – स्त्री॰ – (रजस्वला) मासिक धर्म वाली स्त्री । a woman in menses.

रजोजल्ल – न॰ – कीचड़ । muddy dirt.

रजोहरण – न॰ – (रजोहरण) धूल का हटाना, धूल का पोंछना । removal of dirt.

रज्ज – न॰ – (राज्य) राज्य । empire.

रज्ज-सिरि – स्त्री॰ – (राज्यश्री) राज्यश्री । sovereignty.

रज्ज-सीमा – स्त्री॰ – (राज्य-सीमा) राज्य-सीमा । the boundary of a kingdom.

रज्जति – क्रि॰ – (√ रञ्ज - रज्यति / रज्यते) आनन्दित होता है, प्रसन्न होता है । finds pleasure in, rejoices in, recreation, amusement.

रज्जन – न॰ – (रञ्जन) अनुरंजन । defilement.

रज्जु – स्त्री॰ – (रज्जु) रस्सी । a rope, a cord.

रज्जुगाहक – पु॰ – (रज्जु-ग्राहक) जमीन मापने वाला । a land surveyor.

√ रञ्ज – (भू॰) – (रंगने) रंगना । to colour, to paint.

√ रञ्ज – (दि॰) – (रंगने) रंगना । to colour, to paint.

रञ्जति – क्रि॰ – (√ रञ्ज् - रज्यति / रज्यते) आनन्दित होता है । is amused, becomes delighted.

रञ्जेति – क्रि॰ – (रञ्जयति) (रञ्जेसि-रञ्जित-रञ्जेन्त) आनन्द देता है, रँगता है । gives pleasure, colours.

√ रट – (भू॰) – (कीत्तने) रटना । gets at heart, mutters.

रट्ठ – न॰ – (राष्ट्र) राष्ट्र । a nation, a country.

रट्ठ-पिण्ड – न॰ – (राष्ट्र-पिण्ड) राष्ट्र-पिण्ड, लोगों का दिया हुआ भोजन । food obtained or grains or collected from the people.

रट्ठवासी – पु॰ – (राष्ट्रवासी) राष्ट्र का अधिवासी । an inhabitant of a country, a citizen.

रट्ठवासिक – पु॰ – (राष्ट्रवासिक) राष्ट्र का अधिवासी । an inhabitant of a country.

रट्ठिक – वि॰ – (राष्ट्रिक) राष्ट्र विशेष, सरकारी अफसर, राष्ट्र विशेष से सम्बन्धित । an official.

√ रण – (भू॰) – (ध्वनि करणे) आवाज करना । to sound.

रण – न॰ – (रण) (1) युद्ध, लड़ाई (2) पाप, अपराध । (1) war, battle, (2) sin, fault.

रणञ्जह – वि॰ – (रणञ्जह) वासनाओं के उद्वेग को विदलित करने वाला । one avoiding the tumult of passion.

रत – कृदन्त – (रत) अनुरक्त, आनन्द लेता हुआ, तल्लीन। delighting in, absorbed, rapt in.

रतन – न॰ – (रत्न) रत्न, बहुमूल्यवती वस्तु, लम्बाई का माप एक हाथ (लगभग 18 इंच)। (1) a gem, precious thing (2) a cubit (about 18 inches).

रतनत्तय – न॰ – (रत्नत्रय) रत्न-त्रय-बुद्ध, धर्म तथा संघ। three gems, viz. the Buddha, his doctrine and his organization.

रतनवर – न॰ – (रत्नवर) उत्तम रत्न, श्रेष्ठ रत्न। fine gems.

रतनाकर – पु॰ – (रत्नाकर) समुद्र। an ocean.

रतनिक – वि॰ – (रत्निक) (इतने) रतन लम्बा, चौड़ा (समासान्त में प्रयुक्त)। having so many cubits in length and breadth.

रति – स्त्री॰ – (रति) अनुरक्ति, आसक्ति, प्रेम। attachment, love.

रति-क्रीडा – स्त्री॰ – (रति-क्रीडा) मैथुन-क्रीड़ा। sexual intercourse.

रती – (रति/रती) मार की कन्याओं में से एक। one of the daughters of Māra.

रत्त – वि॰ – (रक्त) (1) लाल (2) रक्त, खून। (1) red, gory (2) blood.

रत्तक्ख – वि॰ – (रक्ताक्ष) लाल आँख वाला। with red eyes.

रत्त-चन्दन – न॰ – (रक्त-चन्दन) लाल चंदन। red sandal-wood.

रत्त-फला – स्त्री॰ – (रक्त फला) लाल फलों वाली लता। a creeper having red oval fruits.

रत्त-पदुम – न॰ – (रक्त-पद्म) लाल कमल। red lotus.

रत्त-मणि – पु॰ – (रक्त-मणि) माणिक्य लाल मणि। a ruby.

रत्त-अतिसार – पु॰ – (रक्त-अतिसार) खूनी पेचिश। the bloody dysentery.

रत्तञ्ञू – वि॰ – दीर्घकालीन। lasting for long, long-living, of long term.

रत्तन्धकार – पु॰ – (रात्रान्धकार) रात का अँधेरा। darkness of the night.

रत्तपा – स्त्री॰ – (रक्तपा) जोंक। a leech.

रत्तं – अव्यय – (रात्रम्/रात्रौ) रात में। in the night.

रत्ति – स्त्री॰ – (रात्रि) रात्रि। night.

रत्तिक्खय – पु॰ – (रात्रिक्षय) रात्रि-क्षय। the decay of night.

रत्तिक्खित्त – वि॰ – (रात्रि-क्षिप्त) रात्रि में फेंका गया। thrown in the night.

रत्ति-भाग – पु॰ – (रात्रि-भाग) रात्रि का समय। night time.

रत्ति-भोजन – न॰ – (रात्रि-भोजन) रात्रि का भोजन। dinner.

रत्तूपरत – वि॰ – (नत्तोपरत) रात्रि-भोजन से विरत। abstaining from night-meal.

रथ – पु॰ – (रथ) रथ, गाड़ी। a carriage, a chariot.

रथकार – पु॰ – (रथकार) रथ बनाने वाला। chariot-maker, carpenter.

रथङ्ग – न॰ – (रथाङ्ग) रथ के अङ्ग। parts of a chariot.

रथ-गुत्ति – स्त्री॰ – (रथ-गुप्ति) रथ के बचाव हेतु छत्र। fender of a chariot.

रथ-चक्क – न॰ – (रथ-चक्र) रथ का पहिया। chariot-wheel.

रथ-पञ्जर – पु॰ – (रथ-पञ्जर) रथ का ढाँचा। the structure of a chariot.

रथ-युग – न॰ – (रथ-युग) रथ की हरीस (बल्ली, जुआ)। shaft of a chariat.

रथ-रेणु – पु॰ – (रथ-धूलि) रथ से उठने वाली रेणु। a mole of dusts caused by a chariot.

रथाचरिय – पु॰ – (रथाचार्य) रथ हाँकने वाला। a charioteer, driver.

रथानीक – न॰ – (रथानीक) युद्ध-रथों का समूह। a group of war chariots.

रथारोह – पु॰ – (रथारूढ) रथ में बैठा योद्धा। a warrior in a chariot.

रथ-लट्ठि-जातक – (जा॰ सं॰ 332) – पुरोहित की चाबुक से उसके अपने सिर में चोट लग गयी। (story No. 332) the charioteer himself got struck with his own good or whip.

रथिक – पु॰ – (रथी) रथ में बैठकर युद्ध करने वाला। one who fights from a chariot.

रथिका – स्त्री॰ – (रथिका/रथ्या) देखें रच्छा। see Racchā.

√रद – (भू॰) – (विलेखने) खोदना। to dig out.

रद – पु॰ – (रद) गजदन्त, (हाथी) दाँत। a tusk, of an elephant.

रदन – न॰ – (रदन) दाँत। tooth.

रन्ध – न॰ – (रन्ध्र) रन्ध, छेद, दोष, दुर्बलता का हेतु। an opening, cleft, fault, a weak point.

रन्ध-गवेसी – पु॰ – (रन्ध्र-गवेषी) छिद्रान्वेषी। one who finds fault or weak points.

रन्धक – पु॰ – (रन्धक) राँधने वाला, रसोईया। a cook.

रन्धन – न॰ – (रन्धन) राँधना, पकाना। cooking, boiling.

रन्धेति – क्रि॰ – (√रन्धू - रन्धयति) घकाता है, उबालता है, राँधता है। boils, cooks.

√रण – (भू॰) – (वचने) बोलना। to utter, to speak.

√रम – भू॰ – (शीघ्रतार्थे) जल्दी में होना। to hurry.

√रम – भू॰ – (क्रीडायाम्) खेलना। to play.

√रम – भू॰ – (गमनार्थे) जाना। to go.

रमण – (न॰) – (रमण) स्त्री सुख। sexual union.

रमणी – स्त्री॰ – (रमणी) कामिनी, केलिप्रिया। lustful woman.

रमणीय – वि॰ – (रमणीय) रमण के योग्य, मनोरम। pleasant, enjoyable.

रमन – न॰ – केलि-विलास, मजा लेना। to revel, to enjoy.

रमनी – स्त्री॰ – (रमणी) विलासिनी, कामिनी। a charming woman, lustful woman.

रमनीय – वि॰ – (रमणीय) आकर्षक। attractive, enjoyable.

रमति – क्रि॰ – (√रम् - रमते) आनन्दित होता है। delights in.

√रम – (भू॰) – (आरम्भे) शुरु करना। to begin, to start.

√रम्ब – (भू॰) – (अवशेषणे) बचाना। to save.

रम्भा – स्त्री० – (रम्भा) केले का गाछ। bunch of bananas, plantain tree.

रम्म – वि० – (रम्य) रमणीक, मनोरम, सुन्दर। charming, enjoyable.

रम्मक – पु० – (रम्यक) चैत्र मास का नाम। the name of a month Chaitra (March-April).

रय – पु० – (रथ) वेग। speed.

रव – पु० – (रव) आवाज। sound.

रवन – न० – (रवनम्) चिल्लाना। scream, squall.

रवति – क्रि० – (√ रु - रौति) शोर करता है, ऊँची आवाज निकालता है। makes loud noise.

रवि – पु० – (रवि) सूर्य। sun.

रवि-हंस – पु० – (रवि-हंस) कलहंस पक्षी-विशेष। the mallard, common wild duck.

√ रस – (चु०) – (आस्वाद-स्नेहेषु) स्वाद लेना, प्यार करना। to taste, to enjoy, to pave.

√ रस – (भू०) – (आस्वादने) स्वाद लेना। to taste.

रस – पु० – (रस) स्वाद, सार, जूस। taste, juice, essence.

रसक – पु० – (रसक) रसोइया। a cook.

रसग्ग – न० – (रसाग्र) अत्यन्त स्वादिष्ट। excessively tasteful.

रसञ्जन – न० – (रसाञ्जन) आँख में लगाने का एक प्रकार का अंजन। a sort of collyrium.

रस-तण्हा – स्त्री० – (रस-तृष्णा) रस-तृष्णा, स्वाद-तृष्णा। the thirst for taste.

रसना – स्त्री० – (रशना) करधनी या कमरबन्द नामक स्त्रियों का आभूषण। a woman's girdle.

रसवती – स्त्री० – (रसवती) रसोईघर। kitchen.

रसवाहिनी – स्त्री० – (रस-वाहिनी) वेदेह नाम के एक भिक्षु द्वारा संगृहीत पालि कथा-ग्रन्थ। a Pāli story book compiled by Vedeha-Thera.

रसातल – न० – (रसातल) पाताल लोक। nether world.

रसाल – पु० – (रसाल) आम्र वृक्ष एवं फल, इक्षु, ऊख। mango tree and fruit, sugarcane.

रसित – न० – (रशन) मेघ-ध्वनि, गर्जन। thunder.

रस्मि – स्त्री० – (रश्मि) (1) (घोड़े की मुँह की) लगााम, (2) सूर्य की किरण। (1) a cord, a rein (2) ray of light.

रस्स – वि० – (ह्रस्व) खर्व, ह्रस्व, बौना। dwarf, short, stunted.

रस्सत्त – न० – (ह्रस्वत्व) बौनापन। dwarfism, shortness.

√ रह – (भू०) – (त्यागे) त्यागना। to leave, to sacrifice.

√ रह – (चु०) – (परित्यागे) छोड़ देना। to vacate.

रह – न० – (रहः) निर्जन, विजन, एकान्त स्थान। solitude, alone, privacy.

रहद – पु० – (ह्रद) तालाब। tank, pond.

रहस्स – न० – (रहस्य) गोप्य, गूढ़चरित, रहस्य। secret, mystery, concealment.

रहाभाव – पु॰ – (**रहस्य + अभाव**) रहस्य के अभाव की स्थिति। the state of not being secret.

रहित – वि॰ – (**रहित**) वञ्चित, बिना। without, devoid of.

रहो – अव्यय – (**रहः**) विजन क्षेत्र, गुप्त, एकान्त जनशून्य क्षेत्र। a lonely place.

रहो-गत – वि॰ – (**रहस्-गत**) एकान्त जगह पर स्थित। setted at a lonely place.

रंसि – स्त्री॰ – (**रश्मि**) देखें रस्मि। see Rasmi.

रंसिमन्तु – पु॰ – (**रश्मिवान्**) सूर्य, (वि॰) प्रकाशमान। sun (adj.) radiant.

√ रा – (भू॰) – (**आदाने**) लेना। to take.

राग – पु॰ – (**राग**) (1) रंग (2) आसक्ति। (1) colour, a dye (2) attachment.

रागक्खय – पु॰ – (**रागक्षय**) आसक्ति का नाश। decay of lust.

रागग्गि – पु॰ – (**रगाग्नि**) वासना-दाह, वासना-ज्वर। the fire of lust.

राग-चरित – वि॰ – (**राग-चरित**) राग-प्रवृत्त, वासनाजन्य कृत्य। of lustful behaviour.

राग-रत्त – वि॰ – (**रागरक्त**) राग में अनुरक्त। infatuated with lust, engrossed in lust.

रागी – वि॰ – (**रागी**) अनुरागी, कामुक। lustful, amorous, salacious, libidinous.

√ राज – (भू॰) – (**दीप्त्यर्थे**) शोभा देना। add splendour.

राज – पु॰ – (**राजा**) राजा। king.

राजककुधभण्ड – न॰ – (**राजककुद् भाण्ड**) राजचिह्न, राजकीय चिह्न। ensign of kingship, regalia.

राजकथा – स्त्री॰ – (**राजकथा**) राजाओं के बारे में कथा-वार्ता। talk about kings.

राज-कम्मिक – पु॰ – (**राजकर्मिक**) सरकारी अफसर, राजकर्मी। a government official.

राजकुमार – पु॰ – (**राजकुमार**) राजपुत्र। a prince.

राजकुमारी – स्त्री॰ – (**राजकुमारी**) राजकन्या। a princess.

राज-कुल – न॰ – (**राज-कुल**) राज्य कुल, महल। a royal family, king's palace.

राज-गेह – न॰ – (**राज-गृह**) राजा का महल। king's palace.

राजङ्गण – न॰ – (**राजाङ्गण**) राजमहल का आंगन। the courtyard of a palace.

राज-दण्ड – पु॰ – (**राजदण्ड**) राजा द्वारा दिया गया दण्ड। punishment given by a king.

राज-दाय – पु॰ – (**राजदाय**) राजा द्वारा दी गई भेंट। a royal gift.

राज-दूत – पु॰ – (**राजदूत**) राजा का दूत। a king's messenger, envoy.

राज-देवी – स्त्री॰ – (**राजदेवी**) राजा की रानी। a consort of a king, queen.

राज-धम्म – पु॰ – (**राजधर्म**) राजा का कर्तव्य। duty of a king.

राजधानी – स्त्री॰ – (**राजधानी**) राजकीय नगर। the royal city, capital.

राज-धीतु/राजपुत्ती – स्त्री॰ – (**राजपुत्री**) राज-पुत्री। princess.

राज-निवेसन – न॰ – (**राजनिवेशन**) राजभवन, राज-प्रासाद। king's abode, palace.

राजन्तेपुर – न॰ – (**राज + अन्तःपुर**) रनिवास। royal harem.

राज-परिसा – स्त्री॰ – (राज-परिषद्) राज्य परिषद् । king's advisory council.

राज-पुत्त – पु॰ – (राजकुमार) राजपुत्र, राजकुमार । prince.

राज-पुरिस – पु॰ – (राजपुरुष) सरकारी नौकर । a government official.

राज-बलि – पु॰ – (राजबलि) राज्य-कर, टैक्स । a government tax.

राज-भट – पु॰ – (राजभट) राजा के सैनिक । king's soldier.

राज-भय – न॰ – (राज-भय) राजा का भय, सरकार का डर । fear of a king or government.

राज-भवन – न॰ – (राज-भवन) राजमहल । king's palace.

राज-भोग्ग – वि॰ – (राज-भोग्य) राजा के लिए योग्य । fit to be used by a king.

राज मन्दिर – पु॰ – (राज मन्दिर) राजमहल । king's palace.

राज-महामत्त – पु॰ – (राज महामात्य) प्रधानमंत्री । the prime minister.

राज-महेसी – स्त्री॰ – (राज महिषी) पटरानी । principal queen.

राज-मुद्दा – स्त्री॰ – (राज-मुद्रा) राजकीय मुद्रा । the royal seal.

राजवर – पु॰ – (राजवर) नृपतिवर, श्रेष्ठ राजा । a noble king.

राज-वल्लभ – वि॰ – (राज-वल्लभ) राजा का प्रिय पात्र, प्रेम-भाजन । a king's favourite.

राज-सम्पत्ति – स्त्री॰ – (राज-सम्पत्ति) सरकारी ठाट-बाट, राजकीय ऐश्वर्य । splendour of a king.

राजगह – न॰ – (राजगृह) मगध जनपद की राजधानी, आधुनिक राजगीर । the capital town of ancient Magadha, the modern Rājagīr.

राजञ्ञ – पु॰ – (राजन्य) क्षत्रिय-जन । of kṣatriya caste.

राजति – क्रि॰ – (√ राज् - राजते / राजति) चमकता है । shines.

राजत्त – न॰ – (राजत्व) राजत्व । kingship.

राजहंस – पु॰ – (राजहंस) हंस की एक प्रजाति जिसकी चोंच और चरण लाल होते हैं । a species of swan having red beak and red claws.

राजाणा – स्त्री॰ – (राजाज्ञा) राजाज्ञा । king's command.

राजानुभाव – पु॰ – (राजानुभाव) राजा का प्रताप या ठाट-बाट । the pomp or majesty of a king.

राजामच्च – पु॰ – (राजामात्य) राजामात्य । a royal minister.

राजायतन – पु॰ – (राजादन) खिरनी नामक वृक्ष । the tree Buchanarie latifolia, also Mimusops kauli and its fruit.

राजि – स्त्री॰ – (राजि) पंक्ति । a row, line or range.

राजित – कृदन्त – (√ राज् + क्त = राजित) दीप्त, चमक वाला । resplendent, shining.

राजिद्धि – स्त्री॰ – (राजर्द्धि) राजकीय शक्ति, राज-ऋद्धि । royal power.

राजिनी – स्त्री॰ – (राज्ञी) महिसी, रानी । queen.

राजिसि – पु॰ – (राजर्षि) राजर्षि । a kṣatriya seer.

राजुपट्ठान – न॰ – **(राजोपस्थान)** राजा की सेवा में रहना। attendance on a king.

राजुय्यान – न॰ – **(राजोद्यान)** राजकीय उद्यान। a royal garden.

राजुल – पु॰ – **(राजिल)** मजगिधण या रजिल नामक पनिहा साँप। a poisonless water snake.

राजोरोध – पु॰ – **(राजावरोध)** राजा का रनिवास। the harem of a king.

राजोवाद-जातक – (जा॰ सं॰ 151) – यह कथा उस घटना का निर्देश करती है जब काशी तथा कोसल नरेश अपने-अपने राज्यों की सीमा बाँधकर अपने अवगुणों का पता लगाने चले। the Jātaka (No. 151) describes the incident when the kings of Kāśī and Kosala went out of their country to discover their own faults if any.

राजोवाद-जातक – (जा॰ सं॰ 334) – कथा बताती है कि निरंकुश राजा का अन्यायपूर्ण शासन फलों में भी कड़नाहट भर देता है। the story (No. 334) tells that the kingdom misruled by a tyrant pours bitterness even in fruits.

√ **राध** – (दि॰) – **(संसिद्धि अर्थे)** सिद्ध होना। to get perfection.

√ **राध** – (दि॰) – **(हिंसायां)** हिंसा करना। to kill, to torture.

राध-जातक – (जा॰ सं॰ 145 / 198) – पोट्ठपाद तथा राध नाम के दो तोतों की कथा। it is the story (No. 145/198) of two wise parrots.

राधित – कृदन्त – (√ रध्‍ + क्त = राधित) तैयार किया गया। cooked, boiled, prepared.

राम – पु॰ – **(राम)** राजा दशरथ का ज्येष्ठ पुत्र राम का ही दूसरा नाम राम पण्डित था। Rāma the eldest son of king Daśaratha. Rāma was also called Rāma Pandita.

राम-गाम – पु॰ – **(राम ग्राम)** गंगा के तट पर बसा हुआ एक कोलिय ग्राम। इसके बाशिन्दों ने भी बुद्ध के शरीर की पवित्र धातु का एक अंश प्राप्त कर उस पर चैत्य बनवाया था। the Koliyan village on the bank of the Gaṅgā. Its inhabitants had shared the Buddha's relics over which they erected a thūpa.

रामञ्ज – न॰ – **(रामण्य)** बर्मा देश का पालि नाम। the Pāli name of Burma.

रामणेय्यक – वि॰ – **(रमणीय)** मनोहर, आकर्षक। pleasant, lovely.

राव – पु॰ – **(रव)** चिल्लाहट, शोर। a squeal, a cry, howling noise.

रासि – पु॰ – **(राशि)** ढेर, मात्रा। a heap, quantity.

रासि-वड्ढक – पु॰ – **(राशि-वर्धक)** राज्य-कर का व्यवस्थापक। the revenue controller.

राहसेय्यक – वि॰ – **(रहस्यक)** रहस्य या एकान्त में रहने वाला। secluded, secret, aloof.

राहु – पु॰ – **(राहु)** एक असुर राजा, चाँद को ग्रसने वाला राहु। an *asura* chieftain which causes lunar eclipse, one of the nine planets, the mythological dragon-head.

राहु-मुख – न॰ – **(राहु-मुख)** राहु का मुँह, दण्ड विशेष। the mouth of Rāhu, a kind of punishment.

राहुल-थेर – पु॰ – (राहुल स्थविर) गौतम बुद्ध के एकमात्र पुत्र, जिनका जन्म सिद्धार्थ गौतम के गृह-त्याग करने के दिन ही हुआ था। the only son of Siddhārtha Gautama Buddha, he was born on the day his father left the household life.

राहुल-माता – स्त्री॰ – (राहुल माता) सिद्धार्थ गौतम की पत्नी तथा राहुल-जननी। उसके दूसरे नाम हैं भद्दकच्चाना, यशोधरा, बिम्बा देवी और सम्भवतः बिम्बासुन्दरी भी। the wife of Siddhārtha Gautama and the mother of Rāhula, she was also called Yaśodharā, Bimbā Devī, Bhaddakaccānā and probably Bimbāsundarī.

रिञ्चति – क्रि॰ – छोड़ देता है, खाली कर देता है। neglects, abandons.

√ रिच – (क॰) – (विरेचने) दस्त आना। to purgate.

√ रिच – (दि॰) – (विरेचने) दस्त आना। to purgate.

√ रिञ्च – (भू॰) – (रिञ्चने) खाली होना। to be empty.

रिते – अव्यय – (महते) बिना। without.

रित्त – कृदन्त – (√ रिच् + क्त = रित्त) रीता, खाली, अकिंचन। empty, poor.

रित्त-मुट्ठि – वि॰ – (रिक्त-मुष्टि) खाली मुट्ठी, अकिञ्चन। destitute, poor.

रित्त-हत्थ – वि॰ – (रिक्त-हस्त) अकिंचन, खाली हाथ (आदमी)। destitute, poor, empty handed.

रिपु – पु॰ – (रिपु) शत्रु। enemy.

√ रु – (भू॰) – (शब्दे) शब्द करना। to utter.

रुक्ख – पु॰ – (वृक्ष) वृक्ष। a tree.

रुक्ख-गहण – न॰ – (वृक्षावलिः) सघन वृक्ष, वृक्षों का झुण्ड। a thicket of trees.

रुक्ख-देवता – स्त्री॰ – (वृक्ष देवता) वृक्ष-देवता। a tree sprite.

रुक्ख-मूल – न॰ – (वृक्ष-मूल) वृक्ष की जड़। the root or foot of a tree.

रुक्ख-मूलिक – वि॰ – (वृक्ष-मूलिक) वृक्ष के नीचे रहने वाला। one who lives at the root of tree.

रुक्ख-सुसिर – न॰ – (वृक्ष सुसिर) पेड़ का खोडर (खोखला)। a hollow in a tree.

रुक्खधम्म-जातक – (जा॰ सं॰ 74) – वृक्ष देवताओं से सम्बन्धित कथा। a story (No. 74) related to tree sprites.

√ रुच – (चु॰/दि॰) – (रोचने) पसन्द आना। to be of one's liking or choice.

√ रुच – (भू॰ दि॰ चु॰) – (दीप्त्यर्थे) आसमान, चमकना। to shine.

रुचि – स्त्री॰ – (रूचि) पसन्द, पसन्दगी। liking, choice.

रुचिर – वि॰ – (रूचिर) सुन्दर, रुचिकर, अनुकूल। pleasant, agreeable, beautiful.

रुच्चति – क्रि॰ – (√ रुच् - रोचते) अच्छा लगता है। finds delight in.

रुच्चन – न॰ – (√ रुच् - रोचन) रुचि, आनन्द। interest, joy.

रुच्चनक – वि॰ – (रोचक) अच्छा लगने वाला। pleasing, satisfying.

√ रुज – (तु॰) – (भङ्गे) टूटना, पीड़ित होना। to break, to get pains.

रुजति – क्रि॰ – (√**रुज्** - **रुजति**) दर्द होता है, पीड़ा देता है। the pain is felt, gives pain.

रुजन – न॰ – (**रोजन**) पीड़ा। pain.

रुजा – स्त्री॰ – (**रुजा**) पीड़ा। pain.

रुजक – वि॰ – (**रुजक**) दुःखता हुआ। pinching, aching.

रुज्झति – क्रि॰ – (√**रुध्** - **रुणद्धि**) रुँधता है, रुकावट पैदा होती है। obstructs, prevents.

रुट्ठ – कृदन्त – (**रुष्ट**) क्रुध, अप्रसन्न, असन्तुष्ट। enraged, vexed, dissatisfied.

√**रुठ** – (तु॰) – (**उपसंघाते**) मारना। to beat.

रुण्ण – कृदन्त – (√**रुद्** + **शतृ** = **रुदन्**) रोता हुआ, चिल्लाता हुआ। crying, lamenting.

रुत – न॰ – (**रुत**) किसी जानवर का शब्द। cry of an animal.

√**रुद** – (भू॰) – (**रोदने**) रोना। to weep.

रुदति – क्रि॰ – (√**रुद्** - **रुदति**) रोना। to weep.

रुदम्मुख – वि॰ – (**रुद-न्मुख**) अश्रुमुख। with the face covered with tears.

रुद्ध – कृदन्त – (√**रुध्** + **क्त** = **रुद्ध**) अवरुद्ध, रुका हुआ। prevented, obstructed.

√**रुध** – (दि॰) – (**आवरणे**) रोकना, घेर लेना। to obstruct, to imprison, to surround.

रुधिर – न॰ – (**रुधिर**) रक्त, खून। blood.

रुन्धति – क्रि॰ – (√**रुध** - **रुणद्धि**) रोकता है, बाधा डालता है, जेल में डालता है। prevents, obstructs, imprisons.

रुन्धन – न॰ – (**रुन्धन**) रोक, जेल में डालना। prevention, imprisonment.

रुप्पति – क्रि॰ – (√**रूप** - **रूपयति**) परिवर्तित होता है। gets vexed or changed.

रुप्पन – न॰ – लगातार परिवर्तन। constant change.

रुरु – कृष्ण मृग, काला हिरण। a kind of black deer.

रुरु-मिग-जातक – (जा॰ सं॰ 482) – अयोग्य पुत्र ने माता-पिता की सारी सम्पत्ति नष्ट कर दी और संन्यासी बन गया। the story (No. 482) of an unworthy son who after spending and wasting the inherited wealth adopted the garb of a *sādhu*.

√**रुस** – (दि॰/भू॰) – (**रोषे**) रूठना, नाराज होना। to be angry.

√**रुष** – (चु॰) – (**पारुष्ये**) कठोर होना। to be harsh.

√**रुह** – (भू॰) – (**जनने**) उगना। to grow.

रुह – वि॰ – (**रुह**) (समासान्त में) उगने वाला, वृद्धि को प्राप्त होने वाला जैसे शिरोरुह = बाल। (used in compounds) growing, rising up, ascending.

रुहक-जातक – (जा॰ सं॰ 191) – रुहक की पत्नी ने अपने पुरोहित पति को उल्लू बनाया। (story No. 191) it describes the act of *purohita*'s wife who befooled her own husband and concludes that the whole womenfolk is beguiling.

रूहिर – न॰ – (रुधिर) रूधिर, रक्त, खून। blood.

रूप – न॰ – (रूप) चक्षुरेन्द्रिय का विषय, भौतिक पदार्थ, आकार, मूर्ति। form, figure, image, object of the eye.

रूपक – न॰ – (रूपक) एक छोटा आकार प्रकार, (अर्थालङ्कार का एक भेद)। a small figure, a metaphor.

रूप-तण्हा – स्त्री॰ – (रूप-तृष्णा) रूप-तृष्णा। craving after form.

रूप-दस्सन – न॰ – (रूप-दर्शन) रूप-दर्शन। seeing an object.

रूप-भव – पु॰ – (रूप-भव) रूप-लोक, ब्रह्म-लोक। the Brahma-loka.

रूप-राग – पु॰ – (रूप-राग) रूप-लोक में उत्पन्न होने की इच्छा। desire to be born in the world of form.

रूपवन्तु – वि॰ – (रूपवान) सुन्दर। handsome, beautiful.

रूप-सम्पत्ति – स्त्री॰ – (रूप-सम्पत्ति) सौन्दर्य। beauty.

रूप-सिरि – स्त्री॰ – (रूप-श्री) लावण्य। personal splendour, loveliness.

रूपारम्मण – न॰ – (रुप-आरम्भण) चक्षुरेन्द्रिय का विषय। an object of visual sense.

रूपावचर – वि॰ – (रूपावचर) रूप-लोक से सम्बन्धित। belonging to the world of form.

रूपिय – न॰ – (रूप्य) चाँदी। silver.

रूपियमय – वि॰ – (रूप्यमय) रजतमय। made of silver.

रूपिनी – स्त्री॰ – (रूपिणी) रूपवती, सुन्दरी। a beautiful woman.

रूपी – वि॰ – (रूपी) रूप वाला। having the qualities of loveliness.

रूपूपजीविनी – स्त्री॰ – (रूपोपजीविनी) वेश्या। a harlot, prostitute.

रूळ्ह – कृदन्त – (√रुह् + क्त = रूढ) उगा हुआ। grown, ascended.

रूहति – क्रि॰ – (√रुह-रोहति) उगता है, चढ़ता है, (जख्म) अच्छा करता है। grows, ascends, heals (a wound).

रूहन – न॰ – (√रुह + ल्युट् = रोहण) उगना, चढ़ना, वृद्धि (जख्म का भरना)। growing, ascending, rising, healing (a wound).

रेचन – न॰ – (रेचन) बाहर निकलना, पेट साफ होना। emission, clearning of the stomach.

रेणु – पु॰ तथा न॰ – (रेणु) धूलि, रेणु। dust, pollen.

रेणुक – पु॰ – (रेणुक) रेणुक नाम का सुगन्धित द्रव्य। a kind of perfume.

रेवती – स्त्री॰ – (रेवती) सत्ताइस नक्षत्रों में से के एक। one amongst the twenty-seven *nakṣatra*s.

रोग – पु॰ – (रोग) रोग, बीमारी। disease, illness.

रोग-निड्ड – न॰ – (रोगनीड) रोग-स्थान। the seat of disease.

रोग-नीळ – न॰ – (रोगनीड) देखें रोग-निड्ड। see Roga-niḍḍa.

रोग-हारी – पु॰ – (रोग-हारी) वैद्य। a physician.

रोगातुर – वि॰ – (रोगातुर) रोगी। a sick person, patient.

रोगी – पु॰ – (रोगी) बीमार। a patient.

रोचति – क्रि॰ – (√रुच्-रोचते) चमकता है। shines.

रोचन – न॰ – (रोचन) चुनाव, पसन्द, चमक। liking, choice, shining.

रोचेति – क्रि॰ – (√ रुच् - रोचते) अच्छा लगता है (रोचेसि, रोचित, रोचेत्वा)। looks charming.

रोदति – क्रि॰ – (√ रुद् = रुदति) चिल्लाता है, रोता है। cries, laments.

रोदन – न॰ – (रुदन/रोदन) रोना। the act of cyring.

रोध – पु॰ – (रोध) रुकावट। obstruction, prevention.

रोधन – न॰ – (रोधन) रोक। obstruction, prevention.

रोप – पु॰ – (रोपण-कर्त्ता) पौधे लगाने वाला। a planter, cultivator, gardener.

रोपित – कृदन्त – (रोपित) रोपा हुआ। planted.

रोपेति – क्रि॰ – (रोपयति) रोपता है। plants, cultivated.

रोम – न॰ – (रोम) रोयाँ, शरीर के बाल। hair on the body.

रोमक – वि॰ – (रोमक) रोम-निवासी। a Roman.

रोमञ्च – न॰ – (रोमाञ्च) रोम-हर्ष, रोमाञ्च, रोम का उठ खड़े होना। bristling of hair.

रोमन्थति – क्रि॰ – (रोमन्थति) जुगाली करता है। munches, chews (the cud).

रोमन्थन – न॰ – (रोमन्थन) जुगाली। ruminating, munching.

रोरुव – पु॰ – (रौरव) रौरव नामक नरक। name of a hell.

रोस – पु॰ – (रोष) क्रोध। anger.

रोसक – वि॰ – (रोषक) क्रुद्ध करने वाला। making anger.

रोसना – स्त्री॰ – (रोषणा) रोष का भाव। enragement.

रोसेति – क्रि॰ – (√ रुष् = रोषति/रुष्यति) क्रोधित करता है। makes angry, irritates.

रोहति – क्रि॰ – (√ रुह् - रोहति) देखें रुहति। see Rūhati.

रोहन – न॰ – (रोहण) उठना, उगना। rising up, growing up.

रोहिणी – स्त्री॰ – (रोहिणी) रोहिणी नक्षत्र। one amongst the 27 nakṣatras (lunar mansions).

रोहित – नि॰ – (रोहित) लाल, (पु॰) मृग-विशेष। a kind of deer.

रोहित-मच्छ – पु॰ – (रोहित-मत्स्य) रोहित या रोहू नामक प्रजाति की मछली। a kind of fish, a salmon.

ल

ल – पालि वर्णमाला का 28वाँ व्यञ्जन the 28th consonant of Pāli alphabet.

लकार – पु॰ – (लकार) (नाव की) पाल । a sail.

लकुण्टक – वि॰ – (लकुण्टक) बौना । a dwarf.

√ लक्ख – (चु॰) – (दर्शने) देखना । to see.

लक्ख (1) – न॰ – (लक्ष्य) निशान, लक्ष्य । a mark, a target.

लक्ख (2) – न॰ – (लक्ष) लाख । a hundred thousand.

लक्खण – न॰ – (लक्षण) निशान, लक्षण, गुण । signs, mark, characteristic.

लक्खण-पाठक – पु॰ – (लक्षण-पाठक) ज्योतिषी, सामुद्रिक । a palmist, astrologer.

लक्खण-सम्पत्ति – स्त्री॰ – (लक्षण-सम्पत्ति) अच्छे लक्षण । auspicious marks.

लक्खण-सम्पन्न – वि॰ – (लक्षण-सम्पन्न) अच्छे लक्षणों वाला । endowed with auspicious signs.

लक्खण-जातक – (जा॰ सं॰ 11) – लक्खण तथा काल मृगों की कथा । the story (No. 11) of two deers named Kāla and Lakkhaṇa.

लक्खिक – वि॰ – (लाक्षिक) भाग्यवान । a fortunate, a lucky man.

लक्खित – कृदन्त॰ – (लक्षित) लक्षित, चिह्नित । marked, distinguished.

लक्खी – स्त्री॰ – (लक्ष्मी) लक्ष्मी, भाग्य, ऐश्वर्य । (1) the goddess of wealth (2) prosperity, good luck.

लक्खेति – क्रि॰ – चिह्न लगाता है । distinguishes, stamps, marks.

लगुळ – पु॰ – (लगुड) डण्डा । a cudgel, a stick.

लग्ग – वि॰ – (लग्न) लगा हुआ, जुड़ा हुआ । stuck, attached.

लग्गकेस – पु॰ – (लग्नकेश) जटाएँ, उलझे बाल । entangled hair.

लग्गति – क्रि॰ – (लग्नाति) लगता है, जुड़ता है, लटकता है । sticks, attaches, hangs from.

लङ्घी – स्त्री॰ – (अर्गला) द्वार-दण्ड । a rod, a bar, a pole for fastening a door.

लङ्गुल – न॰ – (लाङ्गूल) पूँछ । a tail.

√ लङ्घ – (भू॰) – (लाङ्घने) लाँघना । to step across, to cross, to leap over.

√ लङ्घ – (भू॰) – (गति शोषणेसु) जाना, सूखना । go, dry up.

लङ्घक – पु॰ – (लङ्घक) लाँघने वाला, बाजीगर । who jumps, an acrobat.

लङ्घति – क्रि॰ – (√ लङ्घ - लङ्घयति ⁄ ते) लाँघता है, कूदता है । jumps over, hops.

लङ्घन – न॰ – (लङ्घन) लाँघना, कूदना । jumping, hopping.

लङ्घापेति – क्रि॰ – (लङ्घयति) लँघाता है, कुदवाता है । causes jumping or hopping.

लङ्घी – पु॰ – (लङ्घी) लाँघने वाला, कूदने वाला, बाजीगर। a jumper, a threshold acrobat.

लङ्घेति – क्रि॰ – (लङ्घयति) कूदता है, छलाँग मारता है, उल्लंघन करता है। jumps over, transgresses.

√लज्ज – (भू॰) – (लज्जने) लजाना। to feel shy.

लज्जति – क्रि॰ – (√लज्ज - लज्जते) लज्जा करता है। becomes ashamed or abashed.

लज्जन – न॰ – (लज्जन) लज्जा। modesty, shame.

लज्जितब्बक – वि॰ – (लज्जितव्यक) (1) लज्जा करने योग्य, (2) वह जिसके कारण लज्जित होना पड़े। (1) humiliating (2) one who humiliates.

लज्जी – वि॰ – (लज्जी) लज्जा अनुभव करने वाला, शर्मीला। feeling shame, modest, conscientious.

लच्छति – क्रि॰ – (√लभ् + लृट = लप्स्यति) प्राप्त करेगा। shall get, shall obtain.

लञ्च – पु॰ – (लञ्चा) भेंट, धूँस, उत्कोच। a gift, bribe.

लञ्च-खादक – वि॰ – (लञ्चखादक) रिश्वतखोर, घूसखोर। one who receives bribe.

लञ्च-दान – न॰ – (लञ्चदान) घूस देना। bribery.

√लञ्छ – (भू॰) – (लक्षणे) निशान करना। to mark.

लञ्छ – पु॰ – (लाञ्छन) चिह्न, निशान। a mark, an imprint.

लञ्छन – न॰ – (लाञ्छन) चिह्न, निशान। a mark, an imprint.

लञ्छक – पु॰ – (लाञ्छक) निशान लगाने वाला। one who marks or stamps.

लञ्छति – क्रि॰ – (√लच्छ् = लच्छति) निशान लगाता है, चिह्नित करता है, मुहर लगाता है। marks, seals, stamps.

लञ्छित – कृदन्त – (लञ्छित) चिह्नित। marked, stamped.

लञ्छेति – क्रि॰ – (√लच्छ् - लच्छति) चिह्नित करता है। marks.

लटुकिक-जातक – (जा॰ सं॰ 357) – कथा बतलाती है कि साहसी बटेरनी ने उसके बच्चों को रौंद डालने वाले हाथी से किस प्रकार बदला लिया। the story (No. 357) ftells how a she quail took revenge for her young ones who were crushed by an elephant.

लटुकिका – स्त्री॰ – (लटुटिका) बटेरनी। a she quail.

लट्ठि – स्त्री॰ – (यष्टि) लाठी। a staff.

लट्ठिका – स्त्री॰ – (यष्टिका) लाठी। a staff.

लण्ड – पु॰ – (लेण्ड) लेड़ी। dung of animals.

लण्डिका – स्त्री॰ – (लेण्डिका) लेंड़ी। dung of animals.

लता – स्त्री॰ – (लता) बेल। a creeper.

लता-कम्म – न॰ – (लताकर्म) बेल-बूटे का काम। creeper work (in painting), embroidery.

लद्ध – कृदन्त – (√लय् + क्त = लब्ध) प्राप्त। obtained, received, achieved.

लद्धक – वि॰ – (लब्धक) आकर्षक, अच्छा लगने वाला। charming, pleasant.

लद्धतब्ब – कृदन्त – (लभ्य) प्राप्तव्य। what should be received, what is due.

लद्ध-भाव – पु॰ – (लब्ध-भाव) प्राप्ति। the fact of receiving or attainment, receipt.

लद्धस्साद – वि॰ – (लब्धाश्वास) दुःख से मुक्त। liberated or released from a trouble, relieved.

लद्धा – पू॰ क्रि॰ – (√लभ् + त्वा = लब्ध्वा) प्राप्त करके। having got, having attained.

लद्धि – स्त्री॰ – (लब्धि) लब्धि, दृष्टिकोण, मत। attainment, a view or theory.

लद्धिक – वि॰ – (लब्धिक) जिसका मत हो, सम्प्रदाय वाला। having a certain view.

लद्धुं – कृदन्त – (√लभ् + तुमुन् = लब्धुम्) प्राप्त करने के लिए। to get, to attain.

लपति – क्रि॰ – (√लप् - लपति) बोलता है। speaks, talks.

√लप – (भू॰) – (वचने) बात करना। to talk.

लपन – न॰ – (लपन) बोलना, बकना, मुँह। speech, mouth, prattle.

लपनज – पु॰ – (लपनज) दाँत। a tooth.

लपना – स्त्री॰ – (लपना) जबान की लपलप, खुशामद। prattling, flattering.

लब्भति – क्रि॰ – (√लभ् + णिच् = लभ्यते) प्राप्त करता है, प्राप्त होता है। gets, obtains, attains.

लब्भा – अव्यय – (लभ्य) पाने योग्य, प्राप्य, सम्भव। obtainable, possible.

√लभ – (भू॰) – (सङ्गे) आसक्त होना। to cling.

लभ – (भू॰) – (लाभे) पाना। for obtaining, for attaining.

लभति – क्रि॰ – (√लभ् - लभति) प्राप्त करता है। gets, obtains, attains.

√लम्ब – (भू॰) – (लम्बने) लटकना। to hang.

लम्ब – वि॰ – (लम्ब) लटकता हुआ। hanging from.

लम्बक – न॰ – (लम्बक) लटकने वाला। which is hanging down, a pendulum.

लम्बति – क्रि॰ – (√लम्ब - लम्बते) लटकता है। hangs down.

लय – पु॰ – (लव) छत्तीस निमेस का समय, समय का बहुत ही छोटा भाग। a brief measure of time, a fraction of time.

√लल – (चु॰) – (उपसेवायां) पालना-पोसना। to nourish.

√लल – (भू॰) – (विलासे) ऐश करना। to revel in pleasure.

√लल – (चु॰) – (इच्छायां) चाहना। to desire, to like.

ललना – स्त्री॰ – (ललना) स्त्री। a woman.

ललित – वि॰ – (ललित) सुन्दर, कोमल, आकर्षक। graceful, charming, soft.

लव – पु॰ – (लव) बूँद। a drop, a particle the clove, a son of Rama.

लवङ्ग – न॰ – (लवङ्ग) लौंग। the cloves.

लवण – न॰ – (लवण) नमक। salt.

लवन – न॰ – (लवन) कटनी, कटाई। mowing, reaping.

√लस – (भू॰) – (कान्त्यर्थे) शोभा देना। to give beauty, grace or charm, looking beautiful, graceful, or charming.

लसति – क्रि॰ – (√लस - लसति) चमकता है, खेलता है। shines, plays.

लसिका – स्त्री॰ – (लसिका) शरीर के जोड़ों को तर रखने वाला पदार्थ। lymph.

लसी – स्त्री॰ – मस्तिष्क। brain, drink made of curd, water and sugar mixed together.

लसुण – न॰ – (लशुन) रसोन-लहसुन। garlic.

लहु – अव्यय – (लघु) जनयी। light.

लहु – वि॰ – (लघु) हल्का, शीघ्र (न॰) ह्रस्व स्वर। light, quick, (n.) a short-vowel.

लहुक – वि॰ – (लघुक) हल्का। light, triffling.

लहुकं – क्रि॰ वि॰ – (लघुकम्) शीघ्रता से। quickly.

लहुता – स्त्री॰ – (लघुता) हलकापन। lightness, buoyancy.

लहु-परिवत्त – वि॰ – (लघु-परिवर्त्य) शीघ्र बदलने वाला। quickly changing.

लहु-लहुसो – क्रि॰ वि॰ – (लघु/लघुशः) जल्दी से। quickly.

√ला – (भू॰) – (आदाने) ग्रहण करना। to acquire, to possess.

लाखा – स्त्री॰ – (लाक्षा) चपड़ा, लाख (मुहर लगाने की लाख)। lac, sealing wax.

लाखा-रस – पु॰ – (लाक्षा–रस) लाख का सार, जो रँगने के काम आता है। essence of lac which is used in colouring.

लाज – पु॰ – (लाज) धान का लावा, खील। parched paddy.

लाजपञ्चभक – वि॰ – (लाजपञ्चभक) अन्य चार वस्तुओं सहित पाँचवीं चीज खील। having parched paddy as the fifth.

लाप – पु॰ – (वर्त्तकी) बटेर। a sort of quail.

लापु – स्त्री॰ – (अलाबु) लौकी। bottle-gourd, pumpkin.

लाबु – स्त्री॰ – (अलाबु) लौकी। a boltle-gourd.

लाबु-कटाह – पु॰ – (अलाबु-कटाह) तूम्बा। the outer crest of a gourd used as a vessel.

लाभ – पु॰ – (लाभ) फायदा, प्राप्ति। gain, acquisition.

लाभ-कम्यता – स्त्री॰ – (लाभ-काम्यता) लाभ की इच्छा। desire for gain.

लाभगग – पु॰ – (लाभाग्र) श्रेष्ठतम लाभ। the highest gain.

लाभ-मच्छरिय – न॰ – (लाभ-मात्सर्य) लाभ-मात्सर्य। selfishness in gain.

लाभ-सक्कार – पु॰ – (लाभ–सत्कार) लाभ और सत्कार। gain and honour.

लाभगरह-जातक – (जा॰ सं॰ 287) – बिना परिश्रम रातों-रात सम्पन्न बन जाने का तरीका उन्हें पसन्द नहीं जो परिश्रमी और नैतिकता सम्पन्न हैं। the story (No. 287) tells that those, who believe in labour and morality, reject the unlawful means for becoming prosperous.

लाभा – अव्यय – (लाभा) 'यह लाभ की बात है', 'यह फायदे की बात है', इन अर्थों में प्रयुक्त होता है। an interjection used in the sense of : 'it is profitable', 'it is a gain'.

लाभी – पु० – (लाभी) जिसे बहुत लाभ होता है। one who gains much.

लामक – वि० – (लामक) पापक, निकृष्ट। inferior, sinful.

लायक – पु० – (लवक) काटने वाला। a reaper, a mower.

लायति – क्रि० – (√लू - लुनाति) काटता है। reaps.

लालन – न० – (लालन) पोषण, दुलार, लाड। lulling, dalliance.

लालपति – क्रि० – (प्रलपति) अधिक बोलता है, प्रलाप करता है। talks much, prattles.

लालसा – स्त्री० – (लालसा) ललक, बलवती इच्छा। longing, desire (strong desires).

लालेति – क्रि० – (लालयति) लाड करता है। lulls, soothes, earesses.

लाळ – (लाट देश) विजय राजकुमार का जन्म प्रदेश, वर्तमान गुजरात। Lāṭa is the birth place of prince Rajkumar, now known as Gujarat state.

लास – पु० – (लास) नृत्य। dance.

लासन – न० – (लास) नृत्य, वास (विलास)। dancing.

लिकुच – पु० – (लकुच) बड़हल का फल और उसका वृक्ष। acid and sweet fruit of Artocarpus laucha tree.

लिक्खा – स्त्री० – (लीक्षा) जूँ का अण्डा, लीख, माप विशेष। an egg of a louse, a measure named after it.

लिखति – क्रि० – (√लिखू - लिखति) लिखता है। writes.

√लिख – (तु०) – (लेखने) उत्कीर्ण करना, खुरचकर चिह्न बनाना, लिखना। to write, to scratch.

लिखन – न० – (लेखन) लिखावट, चित्रण, फाड़ना। writing, painting, tearing up.

लिखापेति – क्रि० – (√लिखू + णिच् = लेखयति) लिखवाता है। makes one to write.

लिखितक – पु० – जिसे विद्रोही घोषित कर दिया गया। one who has been declared an outlaw.

लिङ्ग – न० – (लिङ्ग) चिह्न, निशान, जननेन्द्रिय। sign, mark, generative organ.

लिङ्ग-विपल्लास – पु० – (लिङ्ग-विपर्यास) लिङ्ग परिवर्तन। change of the gender or sex.

लिङ्गिक – वि० – (लैङ्गिक) लिङ्ग सम्बन्धी अथवा स्त्री-पुरुष लिङ्ग सम्बन्धी। pertaining to a gender or a generative organ.

लिच्छवि – स्त्री० – (लिच्छवि) बुद्ध की समकालीन, वैशाली जनपद की लिच्छवि जाति। a renowned kṣatriya tribe of Vaiśālī at the time of the Buddha.

लित्त – कृदन्त – (√लिप् + क्त = लिप्त) लेप किया गया, लेपित। smeared, anointed.

लित्त-जातक – (जा॰ सं॰ 91) – एक ऐसे छली जुआरी की कथा जो मुँह में गोटी छिपा लेता था। the story (No. 91) of a dice player who suffered a lot for his cunning tactics.

लिपि – स्त्री॰ – (लिपि) लेखाक्षर। a writing, script.

लिपि-कार – पु॰ – (लिपिकार) लेखक। writer.

√ लिप – (ए.) – (लिम्पने) लीपना। to smear, to plaster.

लिम्पति – क्रि॰ – (√ लिम्प् - लिम्पति) लेप करता है, लेपन करता है। smears, plasters.

लिम्पन – न॰ – (लिम्पन) लेप करना। smearing with.

लिम्पेति – क्रि॰ – (लिम्पति) लेप करता है। anoints, smears.

लिम्पापेति – क्रि॰ – (लिम्पाययति) लिपवाता है। gets anointed, causes plastering.

√ लिस – (दि.) – (अलिङ्गने) आलिंगन करना। to embrace.

√ लिह – (भू॰) – (आस्वादने) चाटना। to lick.

लिहति – क्रि॰ – (√ लिह् - लेढि) चाटता है। licks.

√ ली – (दि.) – (द्रवीकरणे / श्लेषणे) पिघलाना, चिपकाना। to stick.

लीन – कृदन्त – (√ ली + क्त = लीन) संकोची, शर्मीला। hesitant, shy, reserved.

लीनता – स्त्री॰ – (शालीनता) संकोच, लज्जा। hesitation, shyness.

लीनत्त – न॰ – (शालीनत्त्व) संकोच, लज्जा। hesitation, shyness.

लीयति – क्रि॰ – (√ ली - लीयते) संकोच करता है। hesitates.

लीयन – न॰ – (लीयन) संकुचित होना, बिखरना। shrinking, to be seathered, to be strewn, dispersed.

लीला – स्त्री॰ – (लीला) हाव-भाव। grace, charm, sportiveness, gesture.

√ लुज – (दि.) – (विनाशे) विनाश, नाश। to destroy.

लुज्जति – क्रि॰ – (√ रुज् कर्मवा॰ रुज्यते) तोड़ा जाता है। is broken.

लुज्जन – न॰ – गिरना। to fall.

√ लुञ्च – (भू॰) – (अपनयने) बाल उखाड़ना। to uproot.

लुञ्चति – क्रि॰ – (√ लुञ्च - लुञ्चति) लुचन करता है, बाल नोचता है। pulls out, uproots (the hair).

√ लुठ – (तु॰) – (उपसंघाते) मारना, लूटना। to rob, to plunder, to beat and loot.

लुत – कृदन्त – (लूत / लून) काटा। mowed.

लुत्त – कृदन्त – (लूत / लून) टूटा हुआ, कटा हुआ। cut-off.

लुद्द – वि॰ – (रुद्र) निर्दयी। cruel, merciless.

लुद्दक – पु॰ – (लुब्धक) शिकारी। a hunter.

लुब्ध – कृदन्त – (लुब्ध) लोभी। a greedy.

लुनाति – क्रि॰ – (√ लू - लुनाति) काटता है। reaps, cuts.

लुप – (ए॰ दि॰) – (छेदने) काटना। to cut.

लुब्भति – क्रि॰ – (√लुभ् - लुभ्यति) लोभ करता है। covets, becomes greedy, hankers after.

लुब्भन – न॰ – (लोभन) लोभ, लोभ करना। greediness.

√लुभ – (दि॰) – (लोभे) लोभ करना। to greed, to covet, to hanker after.

लुम्पति – क्रि॰ – (√लुप् - लुम्पति/ते) लूटता है, खा डालता है। plunders, eats out, devours.

लुम्पन – न॰ – (लुम्पन) लूटना। plundering, eating.

लुम्बिनी – स्त्री॰ – (लुम्बिनी) कपिलवस्तु तथा देवदह के मध्य स्थित लुम्बिनी नाम का उद्यान, जहाँ गौतम बुद्ध का जन्म हुआ था। a park situated between Kapilavastu and Devadaha, it was there that the Buddha was born.

लुळित – कृदन्त – (आ√लुड् + क्त = आलोडित) हिलाया गया, क्षुब्ध। stirred, disturbed, shaken.

√लू – (जि॰) – (छेदने) काटना। to cut.

लूख – वि॰ – (रुक्ष) रुखा। rough, coarse, dry.

लूख-चीवर – वि॰ – (रुक्ष-चीवर) मोटा-झोटा चीवर। coarse robe of a Bhikhu.

लूखता – स्त्री॰ – (रुक्षता) रुक्षता, मोटा-झोटापन। coarseness, dryness.

लूखप्पसन – वि॰ – (रुक्षप्रसन्न) मोटा-झोटा पहनने वाले के प्रति श्रद्धावान। devoted to a person who is shabby.

लूण – कृदन्त – (लून) काटा गया। reaped, mowed.

लेखक – पु॰ – (लेखक) लिपि-कारक। a scribe, writer, a clerk.

लेखिका – स्त्री॰ – (लेखिका) लिखने वाली। a female clerk or writer.

लेखन – न॰ – (लेखन) लिखना। writing.

लेखनी – स्त्री॰ – (लेखनी) कलम। a pen.

लेखनी-मुख – न॰ – (लेखनीमुख / लेखनी-जिह्वा) निब। a nib.

लेखा – स्त्री॰ – (लेखा) रेखा, लेखन-कला। a line, art of writing.

लेड्डु – पु॰ – (लेष्टु) मिट्टी का ढेला। a clod of earth.

लेड्डु-पात – पु॰ – (लेष्टु-पात) ढेला फेंक सकने भर की दूरी। a stone's throw, short distance.

लेण – न॰ – संरक्षण, गुफा। safety, a cave, a rock-cell.

लेप – पु॰ – (लेप) लेप। coating, plastering.

लेपन – न॰ – (लेपन) लेप करना। smearing, coating.

लेपेति – क्रि॰ – (√लिप् - लिम्पति) लेप करता है। plasters, smears.

लेय्य – वि॰ – (लेह्य) जो चाटा जा सके। fit to be licked or sipped.

लेस – पु॰ – (लेश) नगण्य, लेश (= मात्र)। a trifle.

√लोक – (चु॰) – (अवलोकने) देखना। to look.

लोक – पु॰ – (लोक) दुनिया, लोग। the world, the population.

लोकग्ग – पु॰ – (लोकाग्र) लोक-श्रेष्ठ बुद्ध। the chief of the world, i.e. the Buddha.

लोकनायक – पु॰ – (लोक-नायक) लोक-स्वामी, यानी बुद्ध। the lord of the world, the Buddha.

लोकन्त – पु॰ – (लोकान्त) लोक का अन्त। the end of the world.

लोकन्तगू – पु॰ – (लोकान्तगामी) लोक के अन्त को पहुँचा हुआ। one who has reached the end of worldly things, one who has no more desires.

लोकन्तर – न॰ – (लोकान्तर) लोकों के बीच का अन्तराल, अन्य लोक। a different world, the space between two worlds.

लोकन्तरिक – वि॰ – (लोकान्तरिक) दो लोकों के बीच स्थित। situated between two worlds.

लोक-निरोध – पु॰ – (लोक-निरोध) लोक-विनाश। destruction of the world.

लोक-पाल – पु॰ – (लोकपाल) लोक-संरक्षक। a guardian of the world.

लोक-वज्ज – न॰ – (लोक-वद्य) दुनिया की दृष्टि में सदोष। a common sin, a sin in the eyes of the world.

लोक-विवरण – न॰ – (लोक-विवरण) लोक-उद्घाटन। unveiling, of the universe.

लोक-वोहार – पु॰ – (लोक-व्यवहार) सामान्य व्यवहार। common behaviour.

लोकाधिपच्च – न॰ – (लोकाधिपत्य) लोक पर अधिकार। domination over/in the world.

लोकानुकम्पा – स्त्री॰ – (लोकानुकम्पा) लोगों पर दया। sympathy with the people.

लोकायतिक – वि॰ – (लोकायतिक) लोकायत-दृष्टि वाला, भौतिकवादी। one who holds the materialistic view, atheistical philosophy, a nihilist.

लोकिक – वि॰ – (लौकिक) सांसारिक, दुनियावी, लोक-सम्बन्धी। worldly, mundane.

लोकिय – वि॰ – (लौकिक) देखें लोकिक। see Lokika.

लोकुत्तर – वि॰ – (लोकोत्तर) लोकोत्तर। transcendental, super-mundane.

√लोच – (चु॰) – (दर्शने) देखना। to look.

लोचक – वि॰ – (लुञ्चक) बालों को नोचने वाला, जड़ से उखाड़ने वाला। one who pulls out or uproots the hair.

लोचन – न॰ – (लोचन) आँख। the eye.

लोण – न॰ – (लवण) नमक, वि॰, नमकीन, खारा। salt, (adj.) salty.

लोणकार – पु॰ – (लवणकार) नमक बनाने वाला। salt-maker.

लोण-धूपन – न॰ – (लवण-धूपन) नमक से बघारना। flavouring with salt.

लोण-सक्खरा – स्त्री॰ – (लवण-शर्करा) दरदरा नमक। a crystal of salt.

लोणिक – वि॰ – (लवणिक) क्षार। alkaline, salty.

लोणी – स्त्री॰ – (लवण पटल) लोनी, नमक की परत। a salt-pan, a lagoon.

लोप – पु॰ – (लोप) लुप्त होना, काटना। disappearing, cutting off.

लोभ – पु॰ – (लोभ) लालच। greed.

लोभनीय – वि॰ – (लोभनीय) लोभ करने योग्य। to be coveted, desirable.

लोभ-मूलक – वि॰ – (लोभ-मूलक) जिसके मूल में लोभ हो। having greed as its root.

लोम – न॰ – (लोम) रोयाँ, बदन का बाल। the hair on the body.

लोम-कूप – पु॰ – (रोम-कूप) रोम-छिद्र। a pore of the skin.

लोम-हट्ठ – (लोम-हृष्ट) (रोमाञ्च) जिसे लोमहर्ष हुआ हो, रोमांचित। having hair standing on the end, titillated, horripilated.

लोम-हंस – पु॰ तथा न॰ – (लोम-हर्ष) रोम-हर्ष, रोमाञ्च। horripilation.

लोमस – वि॰ – (लोमश) रोमिल, रोयेंदार। hairy, covered with hair.

लोमस-पाणक – पु॰ – (लोमश-कीट) रोयेंदार, सूँड़ी, सूँड़ी नामक कीट। a caterpillar.

लोमहंस-जातक – (जा॰ सं॰ 94) – कथा बताती है कि कैसे एक आजीवक ने सभी प्रकार के काय-क्लेश सहन कर देवलोक में जन्म पाया। the story (No. 94) tells how Ājīvaka practised intense austerities and was reborn in deva-world.

लोल-जातक – (जा॰ सं॰ 274) – कबूतर तथा लोभी कौवे की कथा। it is a story (No. 274) of a pigeon and greedy crow.

लोल – वि॰ – (लोल) लोभी, चंचल। greedy, unsteady.

लोलता – स्त्री॰ – (लोलता) उत्सुकता, लोभ, चंचलता। curiosity, greed, unsteadiness.

लोलुप – वि॰ – (लोलुप) लोभी, लालची। covetous, greedy.

लोलुप्प – न॰ – (लोलुप्य) लोभ, लालच। lust, greed.

लोलेति – क्रि॰ – (लोलुयति) हिलाता है। stirs, shakes, agitates.

लोसक-जातक – (जा॰ सं॰ 41) – आगन्तुक भिक्षु के प्रति ईर्ष्यालु हुए ज्येष्ठ भिक्षु के सन्तप्त जीवन की कथा। the story (No. 41) of the miserable life of an old monk who grew jealous of a newcomer.

लोह – न॰ – (लौह) ताँबा, लोहा। copper, iron.

लोह-कटाह – पु॰ – (लौह-कटाह) लोहे का कड़ाहा। an iron receptacle.

लोहकार – पु॰ – (लौहकार) लोहार। an iron-smith.

लोह-कुम्भी – स्त्री॰ – (लौह-कुम्भ) लोहे की गागर, लौहघट। a copper vessel.

लोह-पिट्ठ – पु॰ तथा न॰ – (लौह-पृष्ठ) सारस, बगुला। a heron, a crane.

लोह-पिण्ड – पु॰ – (लौह-पिण्ड) लोहे का गोला। a lump of iron.

लोह-जाल – न॰ – (लौह-जाल) लोहे की जाली। brass or iron netting.

लोह-थालक – पु॰ – (लौह-स्थालिका) ताँबे की थाली। a brass plate or bowl.

लोह-पासाद – (ताम्र-प्रासाद/लौह-प्रासाद) श्रीलंका के अनुराधपुर का प्रसिद्ध विहार जो ताम्र पत्र से आच्छादित था। name of the palatial house in Anurādhapura which was covered with copper-tiles.

लोह-भण्ड – न॰ – (लौह-भाण्ड) लोहे का सामान। iron-ware.

लोह-मासक – पु॰ – (लौह-माषक) ताँबे का सिक्का। a copper coin.

लोह-सलाका – स्त्री॰ – (जा॰ सं॰ 314) – (लौह-शलाका) ताँबे/लोहे की सलाई। an iron or brass wire or pin.

लोह-कुम्भि-जातक – (जा॰ सं॰ 314) – पुरोहित के शिष्य ने यज्ञ में बलि दिये जाने वाले पशुओं की जान बचाई। the story (No. 314) tells how the disciple of a priest saved the life of animals who were taken to be killed at the place of sacrifice.

लोहित – न॰ – (लोहित, रक्तिम) रक्त, (वि॰)॰, रक्त वर्ण, रक्तिम। sanguine, ruddy blood (adj.) red colour, of red colour.

लोहितक्ख – वि॰ – (लोहिताक्ष) लाल आँखों वाला। having red eyes.

लोहित-चन्दन – न॰ – (लोहित-चन्दन) रक्त चन्दन, लाल चन्दन। red sandal-wood.

लोहित-पक्खन्दिका – स्त्री॰ – (लोहित-प्रस्कन्दिका) रक्तातिसार। bloody diarrhoea.

लोहित-भक्ख – वि॰ – (लोहितभक्षी) रक्त-भक्षक, रक्तपायी। feeding on blood.

लोहितुप्पादक – पु॰ – (बुद्ध के) शरीर का रक्त बहाने वाला। one who sheds the blood.

लोहितक – न॰ – (माणिक्य) लाल वर्ण मणि वि॰ लाल वर्ण। a ruby.

व

व – पालि वर्णमाला का 29वाँ व्यञ्जन। 29th consonant of Pāli alphabet.

व – (इव) इव (जैसा) या एव (ही) का संक्षिप्त रूप। a shortened form of Pāli *iva*.

√ वक – (भू॰) – (अदाने) लेना। to take.

वक – पु॰ – (वृक) भेड़िया। a wolf.

वक-जातक – (जा॰ सं॰ 300) – फिसल पड़े तो हरगंगा वाली कहावत चरितार्थ करने वाली बकरे भेड़िये की कथा। the story of a wolf, who being unsuccessful in catching the prey consoles himself by observing a fast-day (holyday).

वकुल – वि॰ – (वकुल) मौलिश्री, मौलसिरी का वृक्ष। the tree *Mimusops elengi*.

वक्क – न॰ – (वृक्क) गुर्दा। the kidney.

वक्कल – न॰ – (वल्कल) वल्कल-चीर, पेड़ की छाल का बना वस्त्र। a garment made of bark.

वक्कली – वि॰ – (वल्कली) वल्कल-चीर पहनने वाला। wearing a bark garment.

वक्खति – क्रि॰ – (√ वच् + लूट् = वक्ष्यति) कहेगा। will say.

वग्ग – पु॰ – (वर्ग) समूह, पुस्तक का परिच्छेद, पृथक् इकाई वाला। a group, chapter of a book, (adj.) of separate identity.

वग्ग-बन्धन – न॰ – (वर्ग बन्धन) वर्ग में संगठित करना। formation of a group or a gang, a guild.

वग्गिय – वि॰ – (वर्गीय) (समास में) वर्ग से सम्बन्धित। (in compounds) belonging to a group.

वग्गु – वि॰ – (वल्गु) प्रिय, मनोहर। lovely, pleasant.

वग्गु-वद – वि॰ – (वग्गु-वद) प्रिय-वद, मधुर-भाषी। of lovely speech.

वग्गुलि – पु॰ तथा स्त्री॰ – (वल्गुलि) चमगादड़। a bat.

√ वङ्क – (भू॰) – (कौटिल्ये) टेढ़ा होना। crookedness, curvature.

वङ्क – वि॰ (वङ्क्क/वक्र) टेढ़ा, बेईमान (न॰), मछली पकड़ने का काँटा। curved crooked, dishonest, a fishing hook.

वङ्क-घस्त – वि॰ – (वङ्क-ग्रस्त) जो काँटा निगल गयी हो (मछली)। the hook which has been swallowed by the fish.

वङ्कता – स्त्री॰ – (वक्रता) टेढ़ापन। crookedness.

√ वङ्ग – (भू॰) – (गमनार्थे) जाना। to go.

वङ्ग – पु॰ – (वङ्ग) वङ्ग-प्रदेश, बंगाल। the province of Bengal.

√ वच – (चु॰) – (भाषणे) बोलना। to speak.

वच – पु॰ तथा न॰ – (सूक्ति) कहावत। a saying.

√ **वच** – (भू०) – (व्यक्तवचने) बोलना। to speak.

वचन – न० – (वचन) शब्द, वाणी, व्याख्या। utterance, word, an expression.

वचन-कर – वि० – (वचनकर) आज्ञाकारी। obedient.

वचनक्खम – वि० – (वचनक्षम) कहने के अनुसार चलने वाला। willing to do what others bid.

वचनत्थ – पु० – (शब्दार्थ) शब्द का अर्थ। meaning of a word.

वचनीय – वि० – (वचनीय) कहने योग्य। fit to be spoken.

वचन-पथ – पु०– (वचन-पथ) वचनमार्ग। the way of saying.

वचा – स्त्री० – (वच) वच नाम की औषधि । orris-root.

वची – स्त्री० – (वाक्) वचन वाणी। speech, word.

वची-कम्म – न० – (वचस् कर्म) वाणी का कर्म। verbal action.

वची-गुत्त – वि० – (वचोगुप्त) वाणी का संयत। controlled in speech, good mannered speech.

वची-दुच्चरित – न० – (वचो-दुश्चरित) वाणी का असंयम। non-restrainment of speech.

वची-परम – वि० – (वाक् + शूरः) डींगें मारने वाला, शेखीबाज। boastful.

वची-भेद – पु० – (वचो-भेद) मुँह से निकले शब्द। an utterance.

वची-विञ्ञत्ति – (वचो-विज्ञप्ति) वाणी द्वारा सूचना। intimation by language.

वची-संङ्ख्कार – पु० – (वाक्-संस्कार) वाणी का संस्कार (चेतसिक)। antecedent for speech.

वची-समाचार – पु० – (शुभवाचनिक) शुभ कथन। auspicious speech, good conduct in speech.

वची-सुचरित – न० – (वाक्-सुचरित) वाणी का संयम। good mannered speech.

वचो – न० – (वाक्) वाणी, शब्द, कथन। speech, word, saying.

वच्च – न० – (विष्ठा) मल, गूह, तलछट। excrement, faeces, dung.

√ **वच्च** – (चु०) – (अध्ययने) पढ़ना। to read.

वच्च-कुटि – स्त्री० – (शौचगृह) शौचालय, शौचघर। lavatory, privy.

वच्च-कूप – (शौच-कूप) पाखाना करने का कुएँ जैसा गड्ढा। a privy-pit.

वच्च-मग्ग – पु० – (मल-द्वार) गुदा। the anus.

वच्च-सोधक – पु० – (मल-शोधक) भंगी, मेहतर। a privy cleaner.

वच्छ – पु० – (वत्स) वत्स, बछड़ा। a calf, the young one of an animal.

वच्छक – पु० – (वत्सक) छोटा बछड़ा। a small calf.

वच्छगिद्धिनी – स्त्री० – (वत्सगृद्धा) बछड़े के लिए लालायित। a cow longing for her calf.

वच्छतर – पु० – (वत्सतर) बड़ा बछड़ा। a big calf.

वच्छनख-जातक – (जा० सं० 235) – एक तापस की दृष्टि में गृहस्थ जीवन के दोषों का वर्णन इस कथा में हुआ है। in this story (No. 235) the disadvantages of a household life are narrated by a hermit.

वच्छर – न॰ – (वत्सर) वत्सर, वर्ष। a year.

वच्छल – वि॰ – (वत्सल) वत्सल, स्नेह-पात्र। affectionate.

√ वज – (भू॰) – (गमने) जाना। to go.

वज – पु॰ – (व्रज) व्रज, पशुओं का अड्डा। a cow-pen, cattle-fold.

वजति – क्रि॰ – (√ व्रज - व्रजति) जाता है। goes, proceeds.

वजिर – न॰ – (वज्र) वज्र। a diamond, a thunderbolt.

वजिर-पाणी – पु॰ – (वज्र-पाणि) देवराज, शक्र। king of God, Śakra, Indra.

वजिर-हत्थ – पु॰ – (वज्र-हस्त) इन्द्र। having a *vajra* in his hand, i.e., Indra.

वज्ज – (चु॰) – (वर्जने) मना करना। to forbade.

वज्ज (1) – न॰ – (वद्य) दोष, अकरणीय। fault, (adj.) which should be avoided.

वज्ज (2) – न॰ – (वाद्य) बाजा। a musical instrument.

वज्जनीय – वि॰ – (√ वृज् + उनीयर = वर्जनीय) वर्जनीय, न करने योग्य, त्याज्य। fit to be avoided or shunned.

वज्जन – न॰ – (वर्जन) वर्जन, निषेध। avoidance, shunning.

वज्जिय – पू॰ क्रि॰ – (वर्जयित्वा) छोड़कर, वर्जित करके। having avoided or shunned.

वज्जी – पु॰ – (वज्जि जनपद) बुद्ध के समय के सोलह जनपदों में से एक वज्जी जनपद। one of the sixteen *mahājanapada*s of India in the Buddhist period.

वज्जेति – क्रि॰ – (√ वृज - वर्जयति) मना करता है, त्याग देता है, बचता है, बचाता है। avoids, abstains from, renounces.

वज्झं – वि॰ – (वध्य) वध्य, मारणीय, मार डालने योग्य। fit to be killed or punished.

वज्झप्पत्त – वि॰ – (वध्यत्त्व प्राप्त) वध्य, जिसको प्राण-दण्ड दिया गया। sentenced to death.

वज्झभेरि – स्त्री॰ – (वध्य-भेरी) प्राण-दण्ड की डौण्डी या मुनादी। the drum beaten at time of excution.

√ वञ्च – (चु॰) – (प्रलम्भने) ठगना। to cheat.

√ वञ्च – (भू॰) – (गमने) जाना। to go.

वञ्चक – पु॰ – (वञ्चक) ठग, धूर्त। a cheater, an imposter.

वञ्चन – न॰ – (वञ्चन) ठगी, धूर्तता। cheating, fraud.

वञ्चना – स्त्री॰ – (वञ्चना) धूर्तता, ठगी। cheating, fraud.

वञ्चनिक – वि॰ – (वञ्चनिक / वञ्चक) धूर्त, ठग। fraudulent.

वञ्चेति – क्रि॰ – (√ वञ्च् - वञ्चयते) ठगता है। cheats.

वञ्जु – पु॰ – (वञ्जु) बेंत, अशोक वृक्ष। cane, reed, Aśoka tree (Jonesia Asoka).

वञ्झ – वि॰ – (वन्ध्य) बाँझ। barren.

वञ्झा – स्त्री॰ – (वन्ध्या) बाँझ स्त्री। a barren woman.

वट – पु॰ – (वट) वट-वृक्ष, बरगद का पेड़। a banyan tree, *Ficus Bengalensis.*

वटंसक – पु॰ – सिर के लिए पुष्प-माला। a garland for the head.

वटुम – न॰ – (वर्त्म) (√ वृत् + मनिन्) रास्ता, सड़क। a road, path.

वट्ट – वि॰ – (वृत्त) गोल, (न॰) चक्कर, घेरा, जन्म-मरण का चक्कर। circular, round, (n.) a circle, the cycle of re-birth.

वट्टक-जातक – (जा॰ सं॰ 35) – एक तुच्छ बटेर की सत्य क्रिया से भयंकर आग बुझ जाने की कथा। the story (No. 35) tells how owing to the noble and true act of a quail the spot could not be harmed by flames.

वट्टक-जातक – (जा॰ सं॰ 118) – कहानी बताती है कि एक बटेर ने किस प्रकार अपने आपको भूखा रखकर बहेलिए से मुक्ति प्राप्त की। the story (No. 118) tells how by starving himself a quail freed itself from the fowler.

वट्टक-जातक – (जा॰ सं॰ 394) – बटेर ने कौवे को बताया कि उसके मोटापे का रहस्य उत्तम पौष्टिक भोजन नहीं अपितु चिन्तामुक्त जीवन है। (story No. 394) the quail told a greedy crow that the cause of its beautiful body is not the nutritious food but the freedom from worry.

वट्टक-जातक – (जा॰ सं॰ 33) – देखें सम्मोदमान जातक। see Sammodamāna Jataka.

वट्टका – स्त्री॰ – (वर्त्तका) – मादा बटेर। a female quail.

वट्टति – क्रि॰ – (√ वृत्त = वत्तैते) घुमाना, उचित होना, वाजिब होना, उचित होना। turns round, becomes proper, fit or sight.

वट्टन – न॰ – (√ वृत्त + ल्युट् = वत्तैने) घूमना, चक्कर खाना। making rounds, rotation, revolution.

वट्टि/वट्टिका – स्त्री॰ – (वर्त्तिका) बत्ती, किनारा। a wick, a brim.

वट्टुल – वि॰ – (वर्त्तुल) वर्तुल, गोलाकार। circular, of round shape.

वट्टेति – क्रि॰ – (वर्त्तयति) घुमाता है। causes to turn or move.

वट्ठ – कृदन्त – (वृष्ट) वृष्टि से भीगा हुआ। wet with rain.

वठर – वि॰ – स्थूल, मोटा। bulky, fat.

वड्ढ/वड्ढक – वि॰ – (वर्द्धक) बढ़ता हुआ, वर्द्धमान। increasing, growing.

वड्ढन – न॰ – (वर्द्धन) वर्धन। growth, increase, increment.

वड्ढनक – वि॰ – (वर्द्धनक) वर्धित होता हुआ, बढ़ता हुआ। increasing, growing.

√ वड्ढ – (भू॰) – (वृद्धयर्थे) बढ़ना। to increase, to grow.

√ वड्ढ – (भू॰) – (वर्द्धने) बढ़ाना। to grow, to increase.

वड्ढकी – पु॰ – (वर्द्धकिन्) तक्षक, बढई। a carpenter.

वड्ढकी-सूकर-जातक – (जा॰ सं॰ 283) – एक बुद्धिमान नेता के निर्देशों में संगठित सुअरों द्वारा शेर को मार डालने की यह कथा संगठन और बुद्धिबल की महत्ता दर्शाती है। this story (No. 283) states the importance of unity and intelligence.

वड्ढति – क्रि॰ – ($\sqrt{}$वृद्ध = वद्धते) बढ़ता है। increases, grows.

वड्डि – स्त्री॰ – (वृद्धि) वृद्धि, सूद, increase; growth; profit; welfare; interest on money.

वड्ढेति – क्रिया – (वर्धेति) बढ़ाता है, to increase, to cultivate; to rear or bring up; to serve in; to set into motion.

वण – न॰ – (व्रण) व्रण, जख्म। a wound, a sore, an injury.

वण-चोलक – न॰ – (व्रण-चोल) जख्म पर बाँधन की पट्टी। a bandage or gauze for dressing wound.

वण-पटिकम्म – न॰ – (व्रण-प्रतिकर्म) घाव की चिकित्सा। treatment or healing of a wound.

वण-बन्धन – न॰ – (व्रण-बन्धन) जख्म के लिए पट्टी। bandage for a wound.

वणिज्जा – स्त्री॰ – (वाणिज्य) वाणिज्य, व्यापार, तिजारत। trade, commerce.

वणित – कृदन्त – (व्रणित) व्रणयुक्त, जख्मी। wounded, injured.

वणिप्पथ – पु॰ – (वणिक्-पथ) वह स्थान या देश जहाँ से व्यापार चल रहा है। a place or a country where trade is going on.

वणिब्बक – पु॰ – दरिद्र, याचक। a pauper, a beggar.

$\sqrt{}$वण्ट – (चु॰) – (विभाजने) बांटना। to divide.

वण्ट/वण्टक – न॰ – (वृत्त/वृत्तक) फल या पत्र का डंठल। a stalk, a petiole.

वण्टिक – वि॰ – (वृत्तिक) डंठल वाला। having a stalk, having a petiole.

$\sqrt{}$वण्ण – (चु॰) – (वर्णने) वर्णन करना। to describe.

वण्ण – पु॰ – (वर्ण) वर्ण, रंग, चमड़ी का रंग। colour, appearance, colour of the skin.

वण्णक – न॰ – (वर्णक) रंग (कपड़े रँगने का)। a dye.

वण्ण-कसिण – न॰ – (वर्ण-चक्र) चित्त की एकाग्रता का अभ्यास करने के लिए रंगीन चक्कर। a colour circle for the practice of meditation, concentration.

वण्णद – वि॰ – (वर्णद) वर्ण दान करने वाली/वाला, सौन्दर्य प्रदान करने वाला। imparting colour or beauty.

वण्णदद – वि॰ – (वर्णन) देखें वण्णद। see Vaṇṇada.

वण्ण-धातु – स्त्री॰ – (वर्ण-धातु) रंग। colour.

वण्ण-पोक्खरता – स्त्री॰ – (वर्ण-पुष्करता) वर्ण कर निखार। beauty of complexion.

वण्णवन्तु – वि॰ – (वर्णमान) वर्णमान। colourful.

वण्णवादी – पु॰ – (वर्णवादी) आत्म-प्रशंसक। self-praiser.

वण्ण-सम्पन्न – वि॰ – (वर्ण-सम्पन्न) वर्ण-युक्त, सुन्दर। endowed with beauty.

वण्ण-दासी – स्त्री॰ – (वर्णदासी) वेश्या, नगर-वधू। a courtesan.

वण्णना – स्त्री॰ – (वर्णना) व्याख्या। explanation; a commentary; praising.

वण्णनीय – वि॰ – (वर्णनीय) प्रशंसनीय। fit to be praised/praise, worth appreciation, deserving.

वण्णारोह-जातक – (जा॰ सं॰ 361) – गीदड़ ने शेर और चीते में मनमुटाव पैदा करने की कोशिश की लेकिन शेर और चीते की सदबुद्धि से उनमें मनमुटाव पैदा करने की गीदड़ की चाल विफल हो जाने पर दुष्ट गीदड़ को जंगल छोड़ना पड़ा। the story (No. 361) tells how a jackal living on the leavings of a tiger and a lion tried to antagonise one against the other but due to their mutual understanding his plot failed and the wicked jackal had to leave the jungle.

वण्णित्त – कृदन्त – (वर्णित) व्याख्यात, प्रशंसित। described, praised.

वण्णी – वि॰ – (वर्णी) (समासांत में प्रयुक्त) वर्ण का, शक्ल का जैसे रक्तवर्णी, लाल रंग का। (in compounds) having the appearance of.

वण्णु – स्त्री॰ – (बालुका) बालू, रेत। sand.

वण्णु-पथ – (बालुका-पथ) बालू की जमीन। a sandy path or passage.

वण्णपथ-जातक – (जा॰ सं॰ 2) – कथा बताती है कि किस प्रकार एक सार्थवाह के अप्रमाद से सभी साथियों के प्राण बच गए। the story (No. 2) tells how the alertness of a caravan leader saved the lives of his companions.

वण्णेति – क्रि॰ – (वर्णयति) वर्णन करता है। describes.

वत – अव्यय – (बत!) निश्चय ही, निश्चय से, ओह। (an exclamation) surely, certainly.

वत – न॰ – (व्रत/व्रतम्) व्रत, किसी बात का पक्का संकल्प। a religious duty or observance.

वत-पद – न॰ – (व्रत पद) व्रत-कृत्य। an item of good practice, vow, resolution, or determintion.

वतवन्तु – वि॰ – (व्रतमान) व्रती। observant of religious duties, practices.

वत-समादान – न॰ – (व्रत-समादान) व्रत, ग्रहण करना। taking up of a religious vow.

वति – स्त्री॰ – (वाट) वप्र, प्राकार, बाड़, चारदीवारी। a fence, rampart, surrounding wall.

वतिक – वि॰ – (वर्तिन्/वर्त्ती) (समासान्त में प्रयुक्त) अभ्यासी। (in compounds) having the habit of acting like.

√वत्त – (भू॰) – (वर्त्तने) होना। to exist.

वत्त – न॰ – कर्तव्य, सेवा-कार्य। duty, service.

वत्त-पटिवत्त – न॰ – सभी कर्तव्य। all kinds of practices or duties.

वत्त-सम्पन्न – वि॰ – (कर्त्तव्यनिष्ठ) कर्तव्य का पालन करने वाला। dutiful, sincere.

वत्तक – पु॰ – (वर्त्तक) बरतने वाला। exercising, observing, keeping on.

वत्तति – क्रि॰ – (वर्त्तते) घटित होता है। exists, happens, takes place.

वत्तन – न॰ – (वर्त्तने) वर्तन, आचरण। conduct.

वत्तना – स्त्री॰ – (वर्त्तना) बर्तना, व्यवहार, आचरण। conduct.

वत्तनी – स्त्री॰ – (वर्त्मनि) सड़क, रास्ता। a road, a path.

वत्तब्ब – कृदन्त – (वक्तव्य) कहने योग्य। fit to be told.

वत्तमान – वि॰ – (वर्त्तमान) विद्यमान, (पु॰) वर्तमान काल। existing, (m.) the present period.

वत्तमानक – वि॰ – (वर्त्तमानक) विद्यमान। existing, going on.

वत्तमाना – स्त्री॰ – (वर्त्तमान) वर्तमान काल। the present tense.

वत्तिका – स्त्री॰ – (वर्त्तिका) बत्ती। a thong, a wick.

वत्तितब्ब – कृदन्त – (वर्त्तितव्य) जारी रखने योग्य। fit to be continued.

वत्ती – वि॰ – (वर्त्ती) (समासान्त में प्रयुक्त) अभ्यासी। (in compounds) one who keeps up, practises.

वत्तु – पु॰ – (वक्ता) बोलने वाला। one who speaks.

वत्तुं – कृदन्त – (वक्तुम्) कहने के लिए, कहने को। to say, for saying.

वत्तेति – क्रि॰ – (वर्त्तयति) जारी रखता है। keeps on, makes go on, continues.

वत्थ – न॰ – (वस्त्र) वस्त्र। cloth, garment.

वत्थ-गुह्य – न॰ – (वस्त्र-गुह्य) गुप्त-स्थान। that which is concealed by clothes, private part.

वत्थन्तर – न॰ – (वस्त्रान्तर) वस्त्र का नमूना। specimen of some clothes.

वत्थ-युग – न॰ – (वस्त्रयुग्म) कपड़ों का जोड़ा। a pair of suit or clothes.

वत्थि – स्त्री॰ – (वस्ति) वस्ति, मूत्राशय। lower belly, bladder, pelvis.

वत्थि-कम्म – न॰ – (वस्ति-कर्म) वस्ति-क्रिया, पेट की सफाई। a technique to purge the stomach.

वत्थु – न॰ – (वस्तु) वस्तु, स्थान, भूमि। object, field, ground.

वत्थुक – वि॰ – (वस्तुक) (समासान्त में) स्थानीय। (in compounds) founded on, having its ground in.

वत्थु-कत – वि॰ – (वस्तु-कृत) आधार-कृत। made a basis of, practised thoroughly.

वत्थु-गाथा – स्त्री॰ – (वस्तु-गाथा) भूमिका के पद। the introductory stanzas.

वत्थु-देवता – स्त्री॰ – (वास्तु-देवता) स्थानीय देवता। a deity haunting a certain place, a local deity.

वत्थु-विज्जा – स्त्री॰ – (वास्तु-विद्या) गृह-निर्माण-शिल्प। the science of building, architecture.

वत्थु-विसद-किरिया – स्त्री॰ – (वस्तु-विशद- क्रिया) महत्त्वपूर्ण भाग की शुद्धि। cleansing of the fundamentals.

वत्वा – पू॰ क्रि॰ – (उक्त्वा) कहकर। having told or said.

√ वद् – (भू॰) – (वचने) बोलना। to speak.

वदञ्ञू – वि॰ – (वदान्य) प्रियवादी, उदार। liberal, bountiful, generous.

वदञ्ञुता – स्त्री॰ – (वदान्यता) उदारता। liberality, generosity.

वदति – क्रि॰ – (वदति) बोलता है। speaks, tells.

वदन – न॰ – (वदन) चेहरा, वाणी। countenance, face, speech.

वदानिय – वि॰ – (वदान्य) त्यागी, दान-वीर, उदार। renouncing, munificent, liberal.

वदापन – न॰ – (वादनम्) बुलवाना। causing to speak.

वदापेति – क्रि॰ – (√ वद् + णिच् = वादयति) बुलवाता है, कहलवाता है। makes somebody speak or say.

वदेति – क्रि॰ – (वदति) कहता है। speaks.

वद्दलिका – स्त्री॰ – (कादम्बिनी) मेघमाला, घने बादल। dense layers of clouds, concentration of rain clouds.

वद्धापचायन – न॰ – (वृद्धोपचर्या) बड़ों का सम्मान, वृद्ध जनों की सेवा। the respect or attendance to the elders.

√ वध – (भू॰) – (हिंसायाम्) हिंसा करना। to kill, to torture.

वध – पु॰ – (वध) हनन, दण्ड, प्राण-दण्ड। punishment, killing, execution.

वधक – पु॰ – (वधिक) जल्लाद। an executioner, one who inflicts punishment.

वधुका – स्त्री॰ – (वधुका) तरुण पत्नी, पुत्र-वधू। a young wife, a daughter-in-law.

वधू – स्त्री॰ – (वधू) स्त्री, पत्नी। a woman, wife.

वधेति – क्रि॰ – (√ हन् - हन्ति √ वध - वधति) जान से मार डालता है, सताता है, कष्ट पहुँचाता है। kills, teases or hurts, tortures.

√ वन – (तु॰) – (याचने) माँगना। to beg.

वन – न॰ – (वन) जंगल। a wood, a forest.

वन-कम्मिक – पु॰ – (वन-कर्मी) वन-कर्मी, वन-सम्बन्धी कार्य करने वाला। a forester, forest worker.

वन-गहन – न॰ – (वन-गहन) घना जंगल। a dense forest.

वन-गुम्ब – पु॰ – (वन-गुल्म) झुरमुट घने पेड़। a cluster of trees.

वन-चर – वि॰ – (वन-चर) वनवासी। a forest dweller.

वन-चरक – वि॰ – (वन-चर) वनेचर, वन में रहने वाला। person dwelling in a forest.

वन-चारी – वि॰ – (वन-चारी) वन में विचरने वाला। person roaming about or dwelling in a forest.

वनथ – पु॰ – (वनथ) तृष्णा। craving, intense desire.

वन-दुग्ग – न॰ – (वन दुर्ग) कान्तार, वनों से घिरा अगम दुर्ग। made inaccessible due to forest.

वन-देवता – स्त्री॰ – वन का देवता। god or goddess of forest.

वनप्पति – पु॰ – (वनस्पति / महावृक्ष) बिना फूलों के फल देने वाला वृक्ष। a big tree, the tree bearing fruit without flowers.

वनप्पथ – पु॰ – (वनप्रस्थ) जंगल से ढका पठार। wounded table land.

वनवास – पु॰ – (वनवास) दक्षिण भारत का उत्तर कन्नड़ जिला जहां तीसरी संगीति के बाद रक्खित स्थविर को धर्म प्रचारार्थ भेजा गया था। a place in south India presumably North Kannaḍa where Rakkhita Sthavira was sent to preach Buddhism after the third council.

वनवासी – न॰ – (वनवासी) वनचर, जंगल में रहने वाला। a person dwelling in forest, a forest dweller.

वन-सण्ड – पु॰ – (वन-षण्ड) वन-खण्ड। a patch of forest.

वनिक – वि॰ – (वनिक) (समाासान्त में) वन सम्बन्धी। (in compounds) pertaining to a forest.

वनिता – स्त्री॰ – (वनिता) नारी। a woman.

वनिब्बक – पु॰ – (√वन - याचने/वनीयक) भिखारी, याचक। a beggar.

वन्त – कृदन्त – (वान्त) वमन किया गया, परित्यक्त। vomited out, renounced.

वन्त-कसाव – वि॰ – (वान्त-कषाय) त्यक्त दुरित, दोष-विरहित। one who is purged of all fault.

वन्त-मल – वि॰ – (वान्त-मल) निर्मल। stainless, spotless, unblemished.

√वन्द – (चु॰) – (अभिवादने, स्तुतौ) नमस्कार करना, प्रशंसा करना। to salute, to praise.

वन्दक – वि॰ – (वन्दक) वन्दना करने वाला। one who venerates.

वन्दति – क्रि॰ – (√वन्द् - वन्दते) नमस्कार करता है, वन्दना करता है। praises, salutes with respect.

वन्दन – न॰ – (वन्दन) नमस्कार, स्तोत्र, प्रणति। praise, salutation, prayer.

वन्दना – स्त्री॰ – (वन्दना) स्तुति, नमस्कार। praise, salutation, prayer.

वन्दापन – क्रि॰ – (वन्द्यन) वन्दना कराना। causing one to pay homage, or to offer prayer.

वन्दापेति – क्रि॰ – (√वन्द् + णिच् = वन्द्यति) वंदना करता है। causes one to pay homage.

√वन्ध – (भू॰) – (अभिवादने/स्तुतौ) नमस्कार, प्रशंसा करना। to salute, to praise.

वपति – क्रि॰ – (√वप् - वपति/वपते) बोता है, मुण्डन करता है। sows, shaves.

√वप – (भू॰) – (बीजनिक्षेपे) बीज बोना। to sow.

वपन – न॰ – (√वप् + ल्युट् = वपन) बोना। sowing.

वपु – न॰ – (वपुष) शरीर। the body.

वप्प – पु॰ – (वपन) बोना, कार्त्तिक मास। sowing, the lunar month of Kārttika.

वप्प-काल – पु॰ – (वपन-काल) बीज बोने का समय। the time for sowing.

वप्प-मङ्गल – न॰ – (वप्र-मङ्गल) हल चलाने का उत्सव। ploughing festival.

वप्प-थेर – पु॰ – (वप्प-स्थविर) पंचवर्गीय स्थविरों में से एक। one of the Pañca-vaggīya Bhikṣus.

√वम – (भू॰) – (उद्गिरणे) उल्टी करना। to vomit.

वमति – क्रि॰ – (√वम् - वमति) वमन करता है।

वमथु – न॰ – (वान्त) वमन, वमित पदार्थ। vomiting, discharged food.

वम्भन – पु॰ – (वम्हन/वम्मन) घृणा। hate, dislike.

वम्भी – पु॰ – (वम्ही/वम्भी) घृणा करने वाला। one who treats with contempt, one who hates or condemns.

वम्भेति – क्रि॰ – (वम्हेति) घृणा करता है, वम्भित । despises, treats with contempt.

वम्म – न॰ – (वर्म) कवच । an armour.

वम्मी – पु॰ – (वर्मिन् / वर्मी) कवचधारी । wearing armour, armoured.

वम्मिक – पु॰ – (वाल्मीक) दीमक की बाँबी । an ant-hill.

वम्मित – कृदन्त – (वर्मित) कवच धारण किया हुआ । clad in armour, equipped with armoured.

वम्मेति – क्रि॰ – (√ वृ - आवरणे) कवच-धारण करता है । equips or gets armour.

√ वम्ह – (चु॰) – (गर्हणे) निन्दा करना । to condemn, to scandalise.

वय – (भू॰) – (गमनार्थे) जाना । to pass, to go.

वय (1) – पु॰ तथा न॰ – (वयः) आयु । age.

वय (2) – पु॰ – (व्यय) क्षय (न॰) खर्च । loss (n.) expenditure.

वय-करण – न॰ – (व्यय-करणम्) खर्च । expenditure, act of expending.

वय-कल्याण – न॰ – (वयस्+कल्याण) तरुणाई का आकर्षण । charm of youth.

वयट्ठ – वि॰ – (वयस्थ) प्रौढ़, प्रौढ़त्व । grown up, full-grown.

वयप्पत्त – वि॰ – (वयःप्राप्त) तरुण, आयु-प्राप्त, विवाह करने के योग्य । of marriageable age, come of age, a youth.

वयस्स – पु॰ – (व्यस्य) मित्र । a friend, of similar age.

वयोवुद्ध – वि॰ – (वयोवृद्ध) वयोवृद्ध । of advanced age, senior.

वयोहर – वि॰ – (वयोहर) आयु का हरण । snatching one's life or longevity.

वय्ह – न॰ – (वाह्यम्) वाहन, गाड़ी । carriage, transport.

√ वर – (चु॰) – (आवरणेच्छासु) छिपाना, चाहना । to hide, to desire.

√ वर – (भू॰) – (वारण / विभाजने) मना करना, बाँटना । to prevent, to divide.

वर – सं॰ वि॰ – (वर) श्रेष्ठ, वरदान । excellent, a boon.

वरङ्गना – स्त्री॰ – (वराङ्गना) वरांगना, विदुषी । a lady with attractive features, a noble lady, an erudite woman.

वरद – वि॰ – (वरद) वर देने वाला, श्रेष्ठ वस्तु प्रदाता । boon-giver, giver of the best things.

वरदान – न॰ – (वरदान) वर देना । grant of a boon or priviledge.

वर-पञ्ञ – वि॰ – (वर-प्रज्ञ) श्रेष्ठ-प्रज्ञ । having excellent knowledge.

वर-लक्खण – न॰ – (वर लक्षण) श्रेष्ठ चिह्न (शरीर पर) । an excellent sign or mark (on the body).

वर – पु॰ – (वर) प्रेमी, पति । husband, suitor.

वरक – वि॰ – (वरक) अँगरखा, चोगा, गाउन । cloak, mantle.

वरण – पु॰ – (वरण) एक वृक्ष-विशेष । the tree *ctrataeva Roxburghii*, also called varume and setu, used in medicine.

वरण-जातक (जा॰ सं॰ 71) – आलसी लड़का जलाने के लिये गीली लकड़ी ले आया, जिसके कारण आग न जल सकी। आलस्य बहुत बड़ा शत्रु है इस उक्ति को चरितार्थ करने वाले एक आलसी शिष्य की कथा। the story (No. 71) tells how idleness causes ruin.

वरत्ता – स्त्री॰ – (वरत्रा) चमड़े की पट्टी। a thong, a leather strap.

वराक – वि॰ – (वराक) बेचारी या बेचारा, दया करने लायक व्यक्ति। a pitiable person, a miserable person.

वरारोहा – स्त्री॰ – (वरारोहा) सुन्दर स्त्री, आकर्षक आरोह-अवरोह शात्रयष्टिवाली स्त्री। a woman with attractive curves and contour, a beautiful woman.

वराह – पु॰ – (वराह) वन्यशूकर, सुअर। hog, boar, swine.

वराही – स्त्री॰ – (वराही) शूकरी, सुअरी। a female hog.

√वल – (भू॰) – (संवरणे) छिपाना। to hide, to conceal.

वलञ्ज – न॰ – (अवलञ्ज) मार्ग, उपयोग, मल-त्याग। a track, use.

वलञ्जनक – वि॰ – (अवलञ्जनक) उपयोग में लाने योग्य। fit to be used or spent, usable.

वलञ्जियमान – वि॰ – (अवलञ्ज्यमान) उपयोग में लाया जाता हुआ। being used.

वलञ्जेति – क्रि॰ – (अव+लञ्जयति) उपयोग में लाता है, खर्च करता है। uses, spends.

वलय – न॰ – (वलय) कङ्कण, कंगन। a bracelet, a bangle.

वलयाकार – वि॰ – (वलयाकार) गोलाकार। circular.

वलाहक – पु॰ – (बलाहक) जनाधर, मेघ। a rain cloud.

वलाहस्स-जातक – (जा॰ सं॰ 196) – रूपवती स्त्री के रूप में अपने सौन्दर्य पाश में व्यक्तियों को फंसाकर उनका भक्षण करने वाली यक्षिणी की कथा। the story (No. 196) of a Yakṣiṇī in the guise of beautiful damsel who used to entice the traders in the way and eat them in the night.

वलि – स्त्री॰ – (वलि) सिकुड़न, झुर्री। a fold, a wrinkle.

वलिक – वि॰ – (वलिक) जिसके बदन पर झुर्री पड़ी हों। having wrinkles on the face or body.

वलित – कृदन्त – (वलित) झुर्री पड़ा हुआ। wrinkled.

वलित्तच – वि॰ – (वलित्त्वम्) झुर्री पड़ी चमड़ी। wrinkled skin.

वलिर – वि॰ – (√वल् + किरच् = वलिर) ऐंचा-ताना, ऐंची आँख वाला, भेंगा। squint-eyed.

वली – वि॰ – (वलिन् / वली) झुर्रीदार, झुर्रियों वाला। having wrinkles.

वलीमुख – पु॰ – (वलीमुख) बन्दर। monkey.

√वल्ल – (भू॰) – (संवरणे) छिपाना। to cover, to conceal.

वल्लकी – स्त्री॰ – (वल्लकी) वीणा। a lute.

वल्लभ – वि॰ – (वल्लभ) प्रिय। favourite.

वल्लभत्त – न॰ – (वल्लभत्व) प्रिय होना। the state of being a favourite.

वल्लरी – स्त्री॰ – (**वल्लरी**) लता, गुच्छा, मञ्जरी । a creeper, a bunch, a cluster.

वल्लि – स्त्री॰ – (**वल्लि/वल्ली**) लता । a creeper.

वल्लि-हारक – पु॰ – (**वल्लिहारक**) लताओं का संग्राहक । a collector of creepers.

वल्लिभ – पु॰ – (**कूष्माण्ड**) कद्दू । a pumpkin.

वल्ली – स्त्री॰ – (**वल्लि/वल्ली**) लता । a creeper.

वल्लुर – न॰ – (**वल्लुर**) लताकुञ्ज, सूखी मछली । a grove of creepers, dried fish.

ववत्थपेति – क्रि॰ – (**व्यवस्थापयति**) व्यवस्था करता है, निश्चित् करता है, तय करता है । settles, defines, fixes, designates, establishes.

ववत्थापन – न॰ – (**व्यवस्थापन**) स्थिर करना, निश्चित् करना । definition, determination, establishment, the act of defining or settlement.

ववत्थेति – क्रि॰ – विश्लेषण करता है । analyses, defines.

√ **वस** – (**चु॰**) – (**आच्छादने**) ढकना । to cover.

√ **वस** – (**भू॰**) – (**निवासे**) रहना । to reside.

वस – पु॰ – (**वश**) निमन्त्रण, अधिकार, प्रभाव । control, influence, authority.

वसग – वि॰ – (**वशाग्र**) जो किसी के अधिकार में हो । that which is within someone's powers.

वसंगत – वि॰ – (**वशङ्गत**) नियन्त्रणाधीन । under control.

वसति – क्रि॰ – (√ **वस् - वसति**) बसता है, ठहरता है, निवास करता है । resides, lives, stays.

वसन – न॰ – (**वसन**) वस्त्र, रहना, रहने का स्थान । dwelling, living, an act of dwelling or living.

वसनक – वि॰ – (**वसनक**) रहते हुए । living, residing.

वसनट्ठान – न॰ – (**वसनस्थान**) वास-स्थान । residence, dwelling place.

वसन्त – पु॰ – (**वसन्त**) वसन्त-ऋतु । the spring season.

वसवत्तक – वि॰ – (**वशवर्त्तक**) शक्तिशाली, प्रभावशाली । dominating.

वसवत्तन – न॰ – (**वशवर्त्तन**) वशवर्ती होना । the state of being under control.

वसवत्ती – वि॰ – (**वशवर्त्ती**) नियन्त्रणाधीन । under control.

वसानुवत्ती – वि॰ – (**वशानुवर्त्ती**) आज्ञाकारी । obedient.

वसल – पु॰ – (**वृषल**) वृषल, अन्त्यज । an outcaste, a person of lowly-birth.

वसा – स्त्री॰ – (**वसा**) मेद, चर्बी । the fat.

वसानुग – वि॰ – (**वशानुग**) वशवर्ती, नियन्त्रणाधीन, आज्ञाकारी । under control, obedient.

वसापेति – क्रि॰ – (√ **वस् + णिच् - वासयति**) बसाता है । causes to dwell.

वसिता – स्त्री॰ – (वशित्व) वश में होना, दक्षता। mastery, cleverness.

वसितुं – कृदन्त – ($\sqrt{}$ वस् +तुमुन्) रहने के लिए। for living.

वसिप्पत्त – वि॰ – (वशप्राप्त) जिसने वश में कर लिया। one who has mastered subjugated (someone).

वसी – वि॰ – (वशी) वश वाला, शक्तिशाली। mastering, powerful.

वसीकत – वि॰ – (वशीकृत) वशीकृत। subjugated, brought under one's authority.

वसीभाव – पु॰ – (वशीभाव) वश में होना। masterly, the state of being subjugated.

वसीभूत – वि॰ – (वशीभूत) वश में हुआ। having become a master over, under control, subjugated.

वसु – न॰ – (वसु) धन। wealth.

वसुधा – स्त्री॰ – (वसुधा) पृथ्वी। the earth.

वसुन्धरा – स्त्री॰ – (वसन् धारयति) वसुन्धरा, पृथ्वी the earth.

वसुमति – स्त्री॰ – (वसुमती) धारित्री, पृथ्वी। the earth.

$\sqrt{}$ वस्स – (भू॰) – (सेवने) सेवन करना। to use.

वस्स – न॰ तथा पु॰ – (वर्ष) (1) वर्ष, साल, (2) वर्षा। (1) the year (2) the rains.

वस्स-काल – पु॰ – (वर्षाकाल) पावस, वर्षाकाल। rainy season.

वस्सग्ग – न॰ – (वर्षाग्रत) भिक्षुओं का ज्येष्ठपन। the seniority of monks.

वस्सवर – पु॰ – (वर्षतर) हिजड़ा, नपुंसक। eunuch.

वस्सति – क्रि॰ – (वृष् - वर्षति) बरसता है। rains.

वस्सति – क्रि॰ – (कूजति) कूजता है। utters a cry (by some bird or animal).

वस्सन (1) – न॰ – (वर्षण) बरसना। raining.

वस्सन (2) – न॰ – (कूजन) पश-पक्षी का कूजन। warbling (of a bird), uttering of a bird or animal.

वस्साटिका – स्त्री॰ – (वर्षशाटकम्) भिक्षुओं का वर्षाकालीन अतिरिक्त वस्त्र। the additional garment of Bhikṣus for rainy season.

वस्सान – पु॰ – (वर्षा) पावस, वर्षा-ऋतु। the rainy season.

वस्सापनक – वि॰ – (वर्षापक) बरसाने वाला। causing rain.

वस्सापेति – क्रि॰ – ($\sqrt{}$ वृष णिच् - वर्षयति) बरसाता है। causes to rain.

वस्सिक – वि॰ – (वार्षिक) (1) वर्षा ऋतु सम्बन्धी (2) वर्ष से सम्बन्धित। (1) belonging to the rainy season (2) related to a year.

वस्सिका – स्त्री॰ – (वार्षिका) उत्फुल्ल चमेली का पौधा। great-flowered, jasmine, a flowering jasmine plant.

वस्सित – कृदन्त – (वृष्ट/वर्षित) वर्षा से भीगा हुआ। wet with rain, moist.

$\sqrt{}$ वह – (भू॰) – (वहने) ढोना। to carry.

$\sqrt{}$ वह – (भू॰) – (प्राप्तकरणे) पाना। to get, to receive.

वहति – क्रि॰ – (वह् - वहति) धारण करता है, सहन करता है, बहता है। bears, carries, flows.

वहन – न० – **(वहन)** ढोना, ले जाना, बहना । carrying, bearing, flowing.

वहनक – वि० – **(वहनक)** लाता हुआ । bringing forth.

वहितु – पु० – **(वोढा)** धारण करने वाला, ले जाने वाला, सहन करने वाला । one who retains, holds, possesses, wields, bearer.

वळवा – स्त्री० – **(बडवा)** घोड़ी । a mare.

वळवा-मुख – न० – **(वाडवाग्नि)** समुद्र के भीतर की आग । a submarine fire.

वंस – पु० – **(वंश)** (1) जाति, नस्ल, वंश-परम्परा, (2) बाँस (3) बाँस की बंशी । (1) a race, lineage (2) a bamboo tree (3) a bamboo flute, or a fishing rod made of bamboo.

वं – अव्यय – **(एवं हि)** निश्चय से । surely, certainly.

वंस-कळीर – पु० – **(वंश-करील)** बाँस की कोंपल । the sprout of a bamboo, the young shoot of a bamboo.

वंसज – वि० – **(वंशज)** वंश-विशेष में उत्पन्न । born in a certain clan or race.

वंस-वण्ण – पु० – **(वंश वर्ण)** वैदूर्य, बहुमूल्य नीला रत्न । a sapphire, the lapislazuli.

वंसागत – वि० – **(वंशागत)** पैतृक, वंश-परम्परा से प्राप्त । hereditary.

वंसानुपालक – वि० – **(वंशानुपालक)** वंश-परम्परा का रक्षक । preserving the lineage.

वंसिक – वि० – **(वंशिक)** वंश-सम्बन्धी (प्रायः समासान्त में प्रयुक्त) । belonging to a clan or race.

√वा – (दि०) – **(गति बन्धनेसु)** जाना, बाँधना । to blow, or go, to fasten.

वा – अव्यय – **(वा)** या, अथवा । or, either this or that .

वाक – न० – **(वर्क/वल्क)** पेड़ की छाल । bark of a tree.

वाक-चीर – न० – **(वल्क-चीर)** वल्कल-चीर, वल्कल-वस्त्र । a bark garment, a garment made of bark.

वाकमय – वि० – **(वल्कल-मय)** वल्कल-छाल से निर्मित । made of barkstrips.

वाकरा – स्त्री० – **(वागुरा)** हिरण पकड़ने का जाल । a net for trapping the deer or wild animals.

वाक-करण – न० – **(संवाद)** बात-चीत । conversation, interaction.

वाक्य – न० – **(वाक्य)** शब्दों का सार्थक समूह । a sentence (in grammar).

वागुरिक – पु० – **(वागुरिक)** जाल का उपयोग करने वाला, व्याध । a hunter.

वाचक – पु० – **(वाचक)** बाँचने वाला, शिक्षक अथवा पाठक । one who teaches or recites.

वाचनक – न० – **(वाचनक)** पाठ करने का उत्सव अथवा स्थान । a ceremony or place of recitation.

वाचना-मग्ग – पु० – **(वाचना-मार्ग)** पाठ करने की पद्धति । the way or technique of recitation.

वाचसिक – वि० – **(वाचसिक)** वाणी से सम्बन्धित । connected with speech, pertaining to speech.

वाचा – स्त्री० – **(वाचा, वाक्)** शब्द, वाणी । word, speech.

वाचानुरक्खी – वि० – **(वाचानुरक्षी)** वाणी का संयमी । guarding one's speech, restraint, moderation check in speech.

वाचाल – वि॰ – (वाचाल) मुखर, व्यर्थ बातचीत करने वाले, बकवासी। garrulous, talkative, verbose.

वाचुगत – वि॰ – (वाच्युद्गत) कण्ठस्थ। learned by heart.

वाचेति – क्रि॰ – (√ वच् - वाचयति) पढ़ता है, पढ़ाता है, पाठ करता है। reads, teaches, recites.

वाचेतु – पु॰ – (वक्तृ - वक्ता) पढ़ने वाला या पढ़ाने वाला। one who reads or teaches.

वाज – पु॰ – (वाज) (1) तीर का पंख, (2) पेय-पदार्थ विशेष। (1) the feather of an arrow (2) a kind of drink.

वाजपेय्य – न॰ – (वाजपेय) यज्ञ-विशेष। a kind of sacrifice (*yajña*).

वाजी – पु॰ – (वाजि) अश्व, घोड़ा। a horse.

वाट – पु॰ – बाड़, घेरा। an enclosure.

वाटक – पु॰ – (बाड़) घेरा। an enclosure.

वाणिज – पु॰ – (वणिक) व्यापारी। a merchant, a trader.

वाणिजक – (वणिक) व्यापारी। a merchant, a trader.

वाणिज्ज – न॰ – (वाणिज्य) व्यापार। trade, commerce.

वाणी – स्त्री॰ – (वाणी) शब्द। word, speech.

वात – पु॰ – (वात) हवा। the wind, air.

वात/वातक – पु॰ – वृक्ष विशेष शीतल, अपराजिता, शतपर्मी पटसन अमलतास 1. आरग्वैध 2. कृत्मान। a creeper (elitoria termatea), a purgative medicinal plant (cassia fistula).

वात-जव – वि॰ – (वातजव) वायु-वेग। as surfi, as the wind.

वातपान – न॰ – (वातायन) खिड़की, झरोखा, गवाक्ष। a window.

वात-मण्डलिका – स्त्री॰ – (वात-मण्डलिका) झंझावात। a whirlwind.

वात-रोग – पु॰ – (वातज-रोग) गठिया, व्याधि। gout, rheumatism.

वाता-बाध – पु॰ – (वात-बाधा) वातज रोग। gout, rheumatism, etc.

वात-बुट्ठि – स्त्री॰ – (वात-वृष्टि) हवा तथा वर्षा। wind and rain.

वात-वेग – पु॰ – (वात-वेग) हवा का जोर, वायु- वेग। velocity of speed or force of the wind.

वातग्ग-सिन्धव-जातक – (जा॰ सं॰ 266) – गधी ने अपने प्रेम-पात्र को लतियाया और बाद में उसके वियोग में मर गयी। the story (No. 266) of a she-ass who kicked her lover horse when he made advances. The horse went away never to return and the she-ass died of separation.

वातमिग्ग – (जा॰ सं॰ 14) – विषय-तृष्णा का दुष्परिणाम बताने वाली कथा बताती है कि कैसे वातमृग रस तृष्णा के कारण बन्धन में जकड़ा गया। (story No. 14) an animal suffered bondage on account of lust or intense longing.

वातातप – पु॰ – (वातातप) हवा तथा धूप। wind and heat.

वाताभिहत – वि॰ – (वाताहत) वायु से हिलाया हुआ, वायु ताड़ित। shaken by the wind.

वातायन – न॰ – (**वातायन**) गवाक्ष, झरोखा। a window, ventilator.

वाताहत – वि॰ – (**वाताहत**) वायु द्वारा लाया गया। brought by the wind.

वाति – क्रि॰ – ($\sqrt{}$ **वा - वाति**) बहता है, चलता है। blows, flows.

वातिक – वि॰ – (**वातिक**) वायु से सम्बन्धित। caused by the wind, related to wind.

वातिंगण – पु॰ – (**वृन्ताक्**) बैंगन, भाटा। brinjal.

वातेरित – वि॰ – (**वात+ईरित**) वायु-विकम्पित, वायु द्वारा झकझोरा हुआ। shaken by the wind.

वाद – पु॰ – (**वाद**) सिद्धान्त। theory, principle, doctrine.

वाद-काम – वि॰ – (**वाद-कामी**) वाद-विवाद का इच्छुक, शास्त्रार्थ-कामी। desirous of debate or discussion or dispute.

वादक्षिक्त – वि॰ – (**वादक्षिप्त**) वाद-विवाद में उखड़ा हुआ। upset in a debate or discussion or dispute.

वाद-पथ – (**वाद-पथ**) वाद-विवाद का कारण, वाद-विवाद का आधार। ground for a dispute.

वादक – पु॰ – (**वादक**) किसी वाद्य-यन्त्र को बजाने वाला। player of a musical instrument.

वादित्त – न॰ – (**वादित्र**) बजाना। to blow, a play.

वादी – पु॰ – (**वादी**) मत विशेष की स्थापना करने वाला। one who disputes or preaches some other doctrine.

वादेति – क्रि॰ – (**वादयति**) वाद्य यन्त्र को बजाता है। plays a musical instrument.

वान – न॰ – (1) तृष्णा (2) चारपाई का बुनना। (1) craving (2) netting or strings of a bed.

वानर – पु॰ – (**वानर**) बन्दर। a monkey.

वानर-जातक – (जा॰ सं॰ 342) – चतुर बन्दर द्वारा मगरमच्छ को बेवकूफ बनाने की कथा। the story (No. 342) of an innocent monkey who befooled a crocodile.

वानरी – स्त्री॰ – (**वानरी**) बन्दरी। female monkey.

वानरिन्द – पु॰ – (**वानरेन्द्र**) बन्दरों का राजा। monkey king.

वानरिन्द-जातक – (जा॰ सं॰ 57) – एक चतुर बन्दर द्वारा मगरमच्छ को छकाने की कथा। the story (No. 57) of a monkey befooling or dodging a crocodile.

वापी – स्त्री॰ – (**वापी**) तालाब, पुष्पकरणी। pond, a tank, a reservoir of water.

वापित – कृ॰ – ($\sqrt{}$ **वप्** + **क्त** = **उप्त**) बोया गया। sown.

वाम – वि॰ – (**वाम**) बायाँ। the left.

वाम-पस्स – न॰ – (**वाम-पार्श्व**) बाई ओर। the left side.

वामन – पु॰ – (**वामन**) बौना (वि॰) बौना। (m.) a dwarf, (adj.) dwarfish.

वामनक – वि॰ – (**वामनक**) देखें वामन। see Vāmana.

वाय – पु॰ तथा न॰ – ($\sqrt{}$ **व** + **धञ्** = **वाय**) बुनावट, बुनना। netting, weaving.

वायति – क्रि॰ – ($\sqrt{}$ वा = वाति) बहता है, चलता है, सुगन्ध फैलाता है। blows, moves, scatters, spreads fragrance.

वायति – क्रि॰ – ($\sqrt{}$ वे = वयति) बुनता है। weaves.

वायन – न॰ – (वायन) (हवा का) चलना, सुगन्ध का फैलाना। blowing (of the wind), dissemination of fragrance.

वायन-दण्डक – पु॰ – (वाय-दण्ड) जुलाहे का करघा। a loom.

वायमति – क्रि॰ – प्रयास करता है, कोशिश करता है। attempts, strives.

वायस – पु॰ – (वायस्) काक, कौवा। a crow.

वायसारि – न॰ – (वायसारि) उलूक, उल्लू। an owl.

वायाम – पु॰ – (व्यायाम/प्रयास) प्रयास, प्रयत्न। exertion, striving, exercise.

वायित – कृदन्त – ($\sqrt{}$ वे + त = उत) बुना गया, (हवा) चला हुआ। woven, blown (wind).

वायिम – वि॰ – बुना हुआ। woven.

वायेति – क्रि॰ – ($\sqrt{}$ वे + णिच् = वाययति) बुनवाता है। causes to weave.

वायु – न॰ – (वायु) हवा। wind.

वायो – (वायो) समास में वायु का ही रूपान्तर। the form taken by *vāyu* (wind), (in compounds, transformation of *vāyu* in combination).

वायो-कसिण – न॰ – चित्ताग्रता के लिए वायु को ध्यान का विषय बनाना। wind taken as an object of concentration in the course of meditation.

वायो-धातु – स्त्री॰ – (वायु-तत्त्व) वायु तत्त्व। the mobile principle, wind element.

वार – पु॰ – (वारम्) बारी, मौका। a turn, occasion.

वारक – पु॰ – (वारक) मटका, बड़ा बर्तन। a jar.

वारण – पु॰ – (वारण) हाथी, गरूड़, उकाब की एक जाति। an elephant, a hawk.

वारण – न॰ – (वारण) निवारण, रोकना। warding off, obstruction, resistance.

वारि – न॰ – (वारि) जल। water.

वारि-गोचर – वि॰ – (वारि-चर) पानी में रहने वाला। living in water, aquatic.

वारिज – वि॰ – (वारिज) पानी में उत्पन्न, (पु॰) मछली (न॰) कमल। water-born (m) fish (n.) lotus.

वारि-मग्ग – पु॰ – (जलमार्ग) नाली। drains, a conduit, water channel, watercouse.

वारित – कृदन्त – (वारित) निवारित, हटाया गया, रोका गया। prevented, obstructed.

वारित्त – न॰ – (वारणीय) न करना, न करने योग्य। avoidance, preventable, an act that should not be done.

वारिद – पु॰ – (वारिद) जलधर, बादल। rain, cloud.

वारिधर – पु॰ – (वारिधर) मेघ, बादल। rain, cloud.

वारिवाह – पु॰ – (वारिवाह) मेघ, बादल। rain, cloud.

वारियमान – वि॰ – (वार्यमाण) रोका जाता हुआ, बाधा डाली जाती हुई, मना किया जाता हुआ। being hindered, obstructed or prevented.

वारुणी – स्त्री॰ – (वारुणी) शराब। spirituous liquor.

वारूणी-जातक – (जा॰ सं॰ 47) – मधु विक्रेता के शिष्य द्वारा शराब में नमक मिलाकर, पिलाने की मूर्खता की कथा। (story No. 47) the folly of a tavern keeper's apprentice to mix salt in liquor.

वारेति – क्रि॰ – ($\sqrt{}$ वृ - वारयति) मना करता है, बाधा डालता है, रोकता है। prevents, obstructs, hinders.

वाल (1) – पु॰ – (बाल) पूँछ के बाल। the hair of the tail.

वाल (2) – वि॰ – भयानक, ईष्यालु। fierce, malicious.

वाल-कम्बल – न॰ – (केश–कम्बल) (घोड़े के) बालों का कम्बल। a blanket made of horse-hair.

वालग्ग – न॰ – (केशाग्र) बाल का सिरा। the tip of a hair.

वालण्डुपक – पु॰ तना नं॰ – (बाल–कूर्चिका) घोड़े के बालों की बनी कूँची या ब्रश। a brush made of horse-tail.

वाल-बीजनी – स्त्री॰ – (चमर व्यजन) चँवरी। a whisk or flapper made of yak's tail.

वाल-वेधी – पु॰ – (वाल–वेधी) बाल को बींध सकने वाला धनुर्धारी। an archer who can hit a hair.

वालधी – पु॰ – (बालधी) पूँछ। tail.

वालिका – स्त्री॰ – (बालुका) बालू। sand.

वालुका – स्त्री॰ – (बालुका) बालू-रेत। sand.

वालुका-कन्तार – पु॰ – (मरु कान्तार) बालू का रेगिस्तान। a sandy wasteland.

वालुका-कुञ्च – पु॰ – (बालुका पुञ्ज) बालू का ढेर। a heap of sand.

वालुका-पुलिन – न॰ – (बालुका–पुलिन) बालू-तट, रेतीला तट। a sandy bank.

वालोदक-जातक – (जा॰ सं॰ 183) – यह कथा बताती है कि तुच्छ कुलोत्पन्न लोगों में छिछोरापन की प्रवृत्ति होती है। the story (No. 183) tells that the low-born lacks self-control or has tendency to be mean.

वास – पु॰ – (वास) (1) रहना, प्रवास (2) वस्त्र (3) सुगन्धित। (1) living, habitation, (2) clothes, (3) perfume/fragrance.

वास-चुण्ण – न॰ – (वास–चूर्ण) सुगन्धित चूर्ण। perfumed powder, fragrant.

वासट्ठान – न॰ – (वास स्थान) रहने का स्थान। dwelling place.

वासन – न॰ – ($\sqrt{}$ वास् + ल्युट् = वासन) (1) सुगन्धित करना (2) वसाना। perfuming.

वासना – स्त्री॰ – (वासना) पूर्व-संस्कार, पूर्व-स्मृति। past impression, recollection of the past, to remove bad odour, to inhabit, to rehabilitale.

वास-योग – पु॰ – (वास–योग) स्नान-चूर्ण। bathing powder.

वासर – पु॰ – (वासर) वार, दिन। a day.

वासव – पु० – (वासव) देवराज, शक्र, इन्द्र। the king of the gods, Indra.

वासि – स्त्री० – (वासिः) तक्षणी (बढ़ई का) बसूला या बसूली। an adze, a hatchet, an axe.

वासि-जट – न० – (वसि-जट) बसूले की मूठ। the handle of an adze.

वासि-फल – न० – (वासि-फलक) बसूले का लोह-अंश। the blade of an adze.

वासिक (वासी भी) – पु० – (वासिक/वासी) रहने वाला (समासान्त में प्रयुक्त)। one who lives, in (used in compounds).

वासितक – न० – (सुगन्ध-चूर्ण) सुगन्धित चूर्ण। fragrant powder.

वासेति – क्रि० – (वस् + णिच् = वासयति) बसाता है, (सुगन्धित) बसाता है। makes dwell, perfumes, inhabits, rehabilitates, makes (something), perfumed, (to make something small).

वाह – वि० – (वाह) (1) वाहक, पथदर्शक, (2) नेता, (3) गाड़ी, गाड़ी का भार, (4) माल ढोने वाला पशु, (5) जल-धारा। (1) carrier (2) leader, (3) a cart, a cartload, (4) a beast of burden, (5) a waterstream, water flow.

वाहक – पु० – (वाहक) भार ढोने या ले जाने वाला। one who bears or carries (something).

वाहन – न० – (वाहन) गाड़ी। a vehicle, carriage.

वाहसा – अव्यय – कारण से। an account of.

वाहिनी – स्त्री० – (वाहिनी) सेना, नदी। an army, a river.

वाही – वि० – (वाही) ले जाता हुआ (प्रायः समासान्त में प्रयुक्त)। carrying, conveying, transporting.

वाहेति – क्रि० – (√ वह + णिच् = वाहयति) ढुला ले जाता है, वहन कराता है। conveys, leads to, carries.

विकच – वि० – (विकच) विकसित, खिला हुआ। blown, blossoming, blossomed.

विकट – वि० – (विकृत) परिवर्तित, बदला हुआ, (न०), गन्दगी। changed, altered, (n.) filth, dirt, polluted, corrupted.

विकण्णक-जातक – (जा० सं० 233) – राजा को जब यह मालूम हुआ कि मछलियाँ और कछुवे उसके संगीत पर मोहित हैं, तो उसने उनको रोज खाना खिलाये जाने की व्यवस्था की। तृष्णा विपदा का मूल है इस तथ्य को प्रमाणित करने वाली एक कथा। the story (No. 233) tells that desire or longing or attachment always leads to suffering.

विकति – स्त्री० – (विकृति) प्रकृति, प्रकार, विकृति। a sort or kind, made of a shape formation.

विकतिक – वि० – (विकृतिक) नाना आकार-प्रकार के (प्रायः समासान्त में प्रयुक्त)। of many sorts or shapes (used in compounds).

विकत्थक – पु० – (विकत्थक) शेखी बघारने वाला। one who boasts, brags, a boaster, a bragger.

विकत्थति – क्रि॰ – (वि + √कत्थ् = विवादयति) शेखी बघारता है। boasts, brags.

विकत्थन – न॰ – (विकत्थन) शेखी बघारना। boasting.

विकन्तति – क्रि॰ – (वि + √कृत = विकृन्तति) काटता है। gnaws.

विकन्तन – न॰ – (विकृन्तन) काटना, काटने का चाकू। cutting, a knife for cutting.

विकप्प – पु॰ – (विकल्प) विचार, विकल्प, अनिश्चय। thought, consideration, alternatives, indecision.

विकप्पन – न॰ – (विकल्पन) अस्थिरता। indefiniteness, not steady, changing.

विकप्पेति – क्रि॰ – (विकल्पयति) संकल्प करता है, व्यवस्था करता है, इरादा करता है, परिवर्तित करता है। resolves, intends, assigns, arranges.

विकम्पति – क्रि॰ – (वि + √कम्प् = विकम्पति/ते) काँपता है। trembles, becomes unsettled.

विकम्पन – न॰ – (विकम्पन) काँपना। trembling, tremor, shivering.

विकरोति – क्रि॰ – (विकरोति) परिवर्तन करता है। alters.

विकल – वि॰ – (विकल) सदोष, अभावपूर्ण। defective, lacking or devoid of (something).

विकलक – वि॰ – (विकलक) जो अभावपूर्ण हो, जो कम हो। being short of.

विकसति – क्रि॰ – (वि + √कस् = विकसति) विकसित होता है। opens out, becomes blown, blossom, develops.

विकार – पु॰ – (विकार) परिवर्तन, तब्दीली, विकृति। alternatives, deformity, deformation.

विकाल – पु॰ – (विकाल) अनुचित समय, मध्याह्नोत्तर तथा रात्रि। inappropriate or unsuitable time, afternoon and the night.

विकाल-भोजन – न॰ – (विकाल-भोजन) मध्याह्नोत्तर तथा रात्रि का भोजन। taking food in the afternoon and night, the afternoon and night meals.

विकास – पु॰ – (विकास) फैलाव। expansion.

विकासेति – क्रि॰ – (वि √काश् = विकाशते) चमकता है। shines.

विकिण्ण – कृदन्त – (वि √कृ + क्त = विकीर्ण) विकीर्ण, बिखेरा हुआ। scattered, strewn.

विकेसिक – वि॰ – (विकेशिक/न) बिखरे हुए बाल वाला। having uncombed hair.

विकिरण – न॰ – (विकिरण) बिखराव, बिखराता हुआ। scattering, disperson, diffusion.

विकिरति – क्रि॰ – (वि √कृ = विकिरति) बिखेरता है, छिड़कता है, फैलाता है। scatters, spreads, sprinkles.

विकिरीयति – क्रि॰ – (विकीर्यते) बिखेरा जाता है। falls into pieces, is scattered or strewn.

विकुणित – कृदन्त – (विकृत) विकृत। deformed.

विकुब्बति – क्रि॰ – (वि √ कृ = विकुरुते) परिवर्तन करता है, प्रातिहार्य (= करिश्मे) करता है। transforms, performs, miracles, charms.

विकुब्बन – न॰ – (विकरणम्) ऋद्धि-बल का प्रदर्शन। miraculous transformation, show of force.

विकूजति – क्रि॰ – (वि √ कूज् = विकूजति) कूजता है, शब्द करता है, चहचहाता है। chirps, warbles.

विकूजन – न॰ – (विकूजन) पक्षियों का कूजना, चहचहाना। cooing of a bird.

विकूल – वि॰ – (विकूल) ढलान। sloping down, slope.

विकोपन – न॰ – (विकोपन) कुपित करना, हानि पहुँचाना। offending, upsetting, injuring.

विकोपेति – क्रि॰ – (वि √ कुप् + णिच् = विकोपयति) कुपित करता है, हानि पहुँचाता है। upsets, injures, destroys, damages, offends.

विक्कन्त – न॰ – (विक्रान्त) विक्रान्त-भाव, वीरता। heroism, bravery.

विक्कन्दति – क्रि॰ – (विक्रन्दति) चिल्लाता है, चीखता है। cries loudly, makes a great noise.

विक्कम – पु॰ – (विक्रम) विक्रम, शक्ति। strength, heroism.

विक्कमन – पु॰ – (विक्रमण) प्रयास, गमन। exertion, stepping, striving, marching.

विक्कय – पु॰ – (विक्रय) बिक्री। sale.

विक्कय-भण्ड – न॰ – (विक्रय-भाण्ड) बिक्री का सामान। sale material.

विक्कयिक – पु॰ – (विक्कयिक) बिक्री करने वाला। a seller, salesman.

विक्किणाति – क्रि॰ – (वि + √ क्री = विक्रीणाति) बेचता है। sells.

विक्केतु – (विक्रेता) बेचने वाला। a seller, a sales man.

विक्खम्भ – पु॰ – (विष्कम्भ) वृत्त का व्यास। a diameter of a circle.

विखम्भन – न॰ – (विष्कम्भन) रोकना, त्यागना, मथना, दबाना। elimination, suppression.

विक्खम्भेति – क्रि॰ – (वि + √ स्कम्भ् = विष्कम्भोति) पृथक् करता है, रोकता है, अलग-अलग थामता है। separates, impedes, obstructs, holds asunder.

विक्खालेति – क्रि॰ – (प्रक्षालयति) धोता है। washes.

विक्खित्त – कृदन्त – (विक्षिप्त) विक्षिप्त। upset, perplexed.

विक्खित्त-चित्त – वि॰ – (विक्षिप्त-चित्त) अस्वस्थ-चित्त, पागल। a confused or upset mind of unhealthy disposition.

विक्खित्तक – वि॰ – (विक्षिप्तक) सर्वत्र बिखरा हुआ, (न॰), सर्वत्र बिखरा हुआ मृतक शरीर। scattered all over a corpse.

विक्खिपति – क्रि॰ – (विक्षिपति) विक्षेप उत्पन्न करता है। disturbs, confuses.

विक्खिपन – न॰ – (विक्षेपण) गड़बड़ी। disturbance, act of causing disturbance.

विक्खेप – पु॰ – (विक्षेप) विक्षेप, गड़बड़ी। disturbance, deflection.

विक्खेपक – वि॰ – (विक्षेपक) गड़बड़ी उत्पन्न करने वाला। one who disturbs.

विक्खोभन – न॰ – (विक्षोभन) विक्षोभ, गड़बड़ी। a great disturbance.

विक्खोभेति – क्रि॰ – (विक्षोभयति) हिलाता-डुलाता है, क्षुब्ध करता है। shakes, or disturbs thoroughly.

विगच्छति – क्रि॰ – (विगच्छति) विदा होता है। departs.

विगत – कृदन्त – (विगत) चला गया, विरहित हो गया। gone away, deprived of.

विगत-खिल – वि॰ – (विगत-खिल) दोष-रहित। free from flaw.

विगत-रज – वि॰ – (विगत-रज) रज-रहित। free from defilement.

विगास – वि॰ – (विगास) तृष्णा-रहित। free from desire.

विगासव – वि॰ – (विगतास्रव) चित्तमैल-रहित, अर्हत। free from depravity, a saint.

विगम – पु॰ – (विगम) विदा, प्रस्थान। departure, going away.

विगमन – न॰ – (विगमन) विदा, प्रस्थान। departure, going away.

विगह्व – पु॰ क्रि॰ – (वि √गाह् + ल्यप्/ विगाह्य) प्रविष्ट होकर, गोता लगाकर। having entered or plunged into.

विगरहति – क्रि॰ – (वि √गर्ह - विगर्हते/ विगर्हयति) निन्दा करता है, गाली देता है। condemns, abuses, calls names, censures.

विगलित – कृदन्त – (विगलित) स्थान से च्युत, पतित। displaced, dropped down.

विगाहति – क्रि॰ – (वि √गाह - विगाहते) प्रविष्ट होता है, डुबकी लगाता है। enters, dives, submerges.

विगाहन – न॰ – (वि √गाह + ल्युट् = विगाहन्) डुबकी मारना, प्रविष्ट होना। plunging, getting into, diving.

विगग्ह – पू॰ क्रि॰ – (वि √ग्रह + ल्युट् = विग्रह्य) विग्रह करके, विश्लेषण करके। having quarrelled or analysed.

विग्गह – पु॰ – (विग्रह) (1) झगड़ा, विवाद (2) शरीर (3) शब्द-व्युत्पत्ति। (1) dispute, quarrel (2) body (images or idol) (3) etymology.

विग्गाहिक-कथा – स्त्री॰ – (विग्राहिक कथा) झगड़े की बात-चीत। altereation, quarrelsome speech.

विघट्टन – न॰ – (विघट्टन) प्रहार देना। knock, stroke, blow.

विघाटन – न॰ – (विघाटन) उद्घाटन, विवृत करना, ढीला करना। opening, unfastening, unveiling, uncovering.

विघाटेति – क्रि॰ – (वि √घट्ट् - विघट्टयति) खोलता है, तोड़ता है। puts asunder, destroys, opens, breaks, exposes.

विघात – पु॰ – (विघात) विनाश, दुरावस्था, विद्वेष। destruction, distress, misery, miserable or sad plight.

विघातेति – क्रि॰ – (वि √घात् - विघातयति) हत्या करता है, नष्ट करता है। kills, destroys.

विघास – पु॰ – अवशिष्ट या बचा हुआ भोजन। remainder of food, residual food.

विघासाद – पु॰ – अवशिष्ट भोजन खाने वाला। one who eats the residual food.

विघास-जातक – (जा॰ सं॰ 393) – तपस्वी ने तपस्वी-जीवन का स्वरूप स्पष्ट किया। (story No. 393) the ascetic who elucidate the true character or nature of ascetic life.

विचक्खण – वि॰ – (विचक्षण) चतुर, (पु॰) (बुद्धिमान) व्यक्ति। sagacious, wise, farsighted.

विचय – पु॰ – (विचय) धर्म-विवेचन, धर्म-विचार। investigation (religious), critical appreciation, evaluation.

विचरण – न॰ – (विचरण) विचरना, घूमना, आना-जाना। walking, going about wandering, loitering.

विचरति – क्रि॰ – (वि √चर् = विचरति) घूमता है, आता-जाता है। goes about, wanders.

विचार – पु॰ – (विचार) विचार, चिन्तन, व्यवस्था करना, योजना बनाना। idea, reflection, investigation, planning, idea, concept.

विचारक – पु॰ – (विचारक) विचार करने वाला, खोज-बीन करने वाला, व्यवस्थापक। thinker, investigator, manager.

विचारेति – क्रि॰ – (विचारयति) सोचता है, व्यवस्था करता है, योजना बनाता है। thinks over, manages, plans.

विचिकिच्छति – क्रि॰ – (विचिकित्सति) सन्देह करता है, हिचकिचाता है, आगा-पीछा करता है। doubts, hesitates, wavers.

विचिकिच्छा – स्त्री॰ – (विचिकित्सा) सन्देह। doubt, uncertainty.

विचिण्ण – कृदन्त – (विचीर्ण) चयनित, चुना हुआ। related, collected, discriminated.

विचित – कृदन्त – (विचित) चुना गया। selected, collected.

विचित्त – वि॰ – (विचित्र) विचित्र, अलंकृत सजाया गया। variegated, ornamented, decorated, adorned.

विचिनन – न॰ – (विचयन / विवेचन) विवेचन करना, चुनाव करना। discrimination, selection, distinction, act of distinguishing.

विचिनाति – क्रि॰ – (विचिनोति) विचार करता है, चुनाव करता है, संग्रह करता है। considers, discriminates, selects, collects.

विचिन्तिय – पू॰ क्रि॰ – (वि √चित् + ल्यप् = विचिन्त्ये) विचार करके। having thought of, having reflected.

विचिन्तेति – क्रि॰ – (विचिन्तयति) विचार करता है, मनन करता है। thinks over, considers, reflect.

विचुण्ण – वि॰ – (विचूर्ण) चूर्ण किया गया, टुकड़े-टुकड़े किया गया। crushed, powdered, broken into pieces.

विचुण्णेति – क्रि॰ – (विचूर्णयति) पीसता है, चूर्ण बनाता है, टुकड़े-टुकड़े करता है। crushes up, powders, breaks into pieces.

विच्छिक – पु॰ – (वृश्चिक) बिच्छू। scorpion.

विच्छिद्दक – वि॰ – (विच्छिद्रक) छिद्रों से भरा हुआ। full of holes, porous.

विच्छिन्दति – क्रि॰ – (वि + √छिम्द् = विच्छिन्दति) काटता है, रोकता है, बाधक होता है। cuts off, interrupts, prevents.

विच्छिन्न – कृदन्त – (विच्छिन्न) कटा हुआ, पृथक् किया हुआ। cut off, interrupted.

विच्छेद – पु॰ – (विच्छेद) काट, पार्थक्य। interruption, cutting off, separation.

√विज – (तु॰) – (भय चलनेसु) डरना-काँपना। to fear, to tremble.

विजटन – न॰ – (वि √जट् + ल्युट् = विजटन) सुलझावट। the act of disentangling, the act of solving.

विजटेति – क्रि॰ – (वि √जट् = विजटति) सुलझाता है। disentangles, solves.

विजन – वि॰ – (विजन) जन-रहित, शून्य-स्थान। deserted of people, solitude.

विजन-वात – वि॰ – (विजन-वात) एकान्त, सूनापन लिये। an atmoshphere of loneliness.

विजृम्भति – क्रि॰ – (विजृम्भति) अँगड़ाई लेता है। rouses oneself, yawns, stretches the limbs or body to relax.

विजृम्भना – स्त्री॰ – (विजृम्भणा) अँगड़ाई लेना। arousing, the act of stretching the body for relaxation.

विजम्भिका – स्त्री॰ – (विजृम्भिका) जंभाई, उबासी। yawn.

विजय – पु॰ – (विजय) जीत। victory, triumph.

विजय – पु॰ – (विजय) सिंहल-द्वीप का प्रथम आर्य-नरेश, सिंह-बाहु तथा सिंह-सीवली की सन्तान। the first Āryan king of Sri Lanka, he was the son of the king Siṁhabāhu and Siṁhasīvalī.

विजयति – क्रि॰ – (वि √जि = विजयते) जीतता है। conquers.

विजहति – क्रि॰ – (वि √हा = विजहाति) छोड़ता है, त्याग देता है। abandons, leaves, gives up.

विजहन – न॰ – (विजहन) परित्याग। the act of giving up, leaving aside.

विजहित – कृदन्त – (विजहित) परित्यक्त। left off, abandoned, given up.

विजाता – स्त्री॰ – (विजाता) प्रसूता, जननी, जच्चा। a woman who has given birth to a child, mother.

विजातिक – वि॰ – (विजातिक) विदेशी, दूसरी जाति का। of a different nation, an outsider.

विजानन – न॰ – (विजानन) ज्ञान, पहचान। knowledge, recognition, identification.

विजानाति – क्रि॰ – (वि √ज्ञा = विजानाति) जानता है, पहचानता है। knows, understands, recognies.

विजायति – क्रि॰ – (वि √जन् = विजायते) जन्म देती है। gives birth, brings forth, produces, yields.

विजायन – न॰ – (विजायन) जन्म देना। bringing forth, giving birth to.

विजायन्ती – स्त्री॰ – (विजायन्ती) जन्म देती हुई। woman giving birth to a child.

विजायमाना – स्त्री॰ – (विजायमाना) बच्चे को जन्म देती हुई। a woman having given birth to a child.

विजायिनि – स्त्री॰ – (विजायिनी) बच्चे को जन्म दे सकने वाली। able to bear a child.

विजित – कृदन्त – (विजित) जीत लिया गया, (न॰) राज्य। conquered, subdued, (n.) a kingdom.

विजित-सङ्ग्राम – वि॰ – (विजित-संग्राम) विजयी, जिसने संग्राम जीत लिया है। by whom the battle has been won, who has won the battle.

विजिनाति – (विजिनाति) देखें जिनाति। see Jināti.

विजितावी – पु॰ – (विजितावी) विजयी। victorious.

विज्ज-ट्ठान – न॰ – (विद्यास्थान) अध्ययन का विषय। branch of study, a subject or a topic of study.

विज्जति – क्रि॰ – (विद्यते) विद्यमान होता है। exists.

विज्जन्तरिका – स्त्री॰ – (विद्युत + अन्तराल) बिजली कड़कने के बीच का समय। an interval of lightning, duration of a flash of lightning.

विज्जा – स्त्री॰ – (विद्या) विद्या। higher knowledge, science, wisdom.

विज्जाचरण – न॰ – (विद्याचरण) विद्या तथा आचरण। special wisdom and virtue.

विज्जाधर – वि॰ – (विद्याधर) ओझा, जादू-टोना करने वाला। a knower of charms, exorcist, a juggler, a magician, a charmer.

विज्जा-विमुत्ति – स्त्री॰ – (विद्या-विमुक्ति) विद्या द्वारा विमुक्ति ज्ञान-मुक्ति। emancipation through wisdom.

विज्जु – स्त्री॰ – (विद्युत) बिजली। lightning.

विज्जुता – स्त्री॰ – (विद्युत) तड़ित, बिजली। lightning.

विज्जुलता – स्त्री॰ – (विद्युल्लता) दामिनी, बिजली। lightning

विज्जोतेति – क्रि॰ – (वि √ द्युत = विद्योतते) चमकता है। shines.

विज्झति – क्रि॰ – (√ विध् - विध्यति) बींधता है, छेद करता है। pierces, stings, perforates.

विज्झन – न॰ – (विध्यन) बींधना, निशाना लगाना। shooting, piercing, targeting, stinging.

विज्झायति – क्रि॰ – (वि √ ध्मा = विध्माति) बुझता है। extinguishes (V.I.).

विज्झापेति – क्रि॰ – (वि √ ध्या + णिच् = विध्यापयति) (आग) बुझाता है। extinguishes (V.T.).

विञ्ञत्त – कृदन्त – (विज्ञप्त) सूचित। one who is informed, instructed.

विञ्ञत्ति – स्त्री॰ – (विज्ञप्ति) सूचना। notification, information.

विञ्ञाण – न॰ – (विज्ञान) विज्ञान, चेतना। animation, consciousness.

विञ्ञाणक – वि॰ – (विज्ञानक) सचेतन। endowed with vitality.

विञ्ञाणक्खन्ध – पु॰ – (विज्ञान-स्कन्ध) विज्ञान-स्कन्ध। the aggregate of life force.

विञ्ञाणट्ठिति – स्त्री॰ – (विज्ञान – स्थिति) विज्ञान-स्थिति, चेतना की अवस्था। state of consciousness.

विञ्ञाण-धातु – स्त्री॰ – (विज्ञान-धातु) विज्ञान-चेतना, चित्त-मन। mind element.

विञ्ञात – कृदन्त – (विज्ञात) विज्ञात, ज्ञात, जाना गया। understood, perceived, known.

विञ्ञातब्ब – कृदन्त – (विज्ञातव्य) जानने योग्य, समझने योग्य। that which should be understood, worth knowing.

विञ्ञातु – पु॰ – (विज्ञाता) जानने वाला। perceiver, one who knows, knower.

विञ्ञापक – पु॰ – (विज्ञापक) शिक्षणपटु, जानने वाला। adept in teaching or instruction.

विञ्ञापन – न॰ – (विज्ञापन) विज्ञापन, जानकारी। information, advertisement.

विञ्ञापय – वि॰ – (विज्ञाप्य) शिशिक्षु, शैक्ष्य, जिसे सिखाया जा सके। accessible to instruction, able to comprehend instruction.

विञ्ञापित – कृदन्त – (विज्ञापित) सूचित किया हुआ। instructed, informed.

विञ्ञापेति – क्रि॰ – (विज्ञापयति) सूचित करता है, शिक्षा देता है। intimates, informs, teaches.

विञ्ञापेतु – पु॰ – (विज्ञापक) सूचना देने वाला शिक्षक। an instructor, informer.

विञ्ञाय – पू॰ क्रि॰ – (वि √ ज्ञा + ल्यप् =

विज्ञाय) जानकर, सीखकर। having known or learnt.

विञ्ञायति – क्रि॰ – (विज्ञायते) जाना जाता है। becomes known.

विञ्ञू – वि॰ – (विज्ञ) बुद्धिमान, ज्ञाता, विज्ञ, (पु॰) बुद्धिमान आदमी। wise, learned.

विञ्ञुता – स्त्री॰ – (विज्ञाता) विज्ञता, विवेक। discretion, power of discrimination, wisdom, learning, knowledge clearness.

विञ्ञुप्पसत्थ – वि॰ – (विज्ञ-प्रशस्त) बुद्धिमानों द्वारा प्रशंसित। extolled by the wise.

विञ्ञेय्य – वि॰ – (विज्ञेय) जानने योग्य। worth knowing.

विटङ्क – पु॰ तथा न॰ – (विटङ्क) गृहकपोत पालिका, कबूतर का दरबा। highest point of palace, a pigeon hole, top of a palace.

विटप – पु॰ – (विटप) बहुशाखी, वृक्ष। a tree.

विटपी – पु॰ – (विटपी) बहु शाखा वाला, वृक्ष। a tree.

विडूडभ – पु॰ – (विदूडभ) प्रसेनजित तथा वासभ खत्तिया का पुत्र, प्रसिद्ध सेनापति। the son of Prasenajit and Vāsabha Khattiya, the famous army commander.

विडोज – पु॰ – (विडौजा) इन्द्र। the king of gods, Indra.

वितक्क – पु॰ – (वितर्क) तर्क-वितर्क। reflexion, argumentation, discussion.

वितक्कन – न॰ – (वितर्कण) दलील, विचार, मनन। contemplation, reasoning.

वितक्केति – क्रि॰ – (वितर्कयति) विचार करता है, मनन करता है। reflects, considers.

वितच्छिका – स्त्री॰ – (विचर्चिका) खुजली। scabies, itch.

वितच्छेति – क्रि॰ – (वि √ तक्षू = वितक्षति) छिलका उतारता है, चिकना करता है। peels, makes smooth, smooens.

वितण्ड-वाद – पु॰ – (वितण्डा-वाद) व्यर्थ का वाद-विवाद। sophistry.

वितत – कृदन्त – (वि √ तनू + क्त = वितत) फैलाया हुआ, विस्तृत किया गया। stretched, extended.

वितथ – वि॰ – (वितथ) तथ्य-रहित, मिथ्या, अयथार्थ (न॰) झूठ। false, untrue (n.) untruth.

वितनोति – क्रि॰ – (वितनोति) फैलाता है। stretches, spreads out.

वितरण – न॰ – (वितरण) बाँटना। distribution.

वितरति – क्रि॰ – (वितरति) बाँटता है। distributes.

वितान – न॰ – (वितान) चँदवा, चँदोवा। a canopy.

वितुदति – क्रि॰ – (वि √ तुद् = वितुदति) चुभोता है। nudges, pricks, pierces.

वितुदन – न॰ – (वितुदन) चुभोना। pricking, piercing.

वित्त – न॰ – (वित्त) धन, सम्पत्ति। wealth, property.

वित्ति – स्त्री॰ – (वित्ति) ज्ञान-प्राप्ति। knowledge, acquisition.

वित्थ – न॰ – (चषक) शराब पीने का पात्र। a bowl for drinking liquor.

वित्थत – कृदन्त – (विस्तृत) फैलाया हुआ। expanded.

वित्थम्भन – न॰ – (विस्तम्भन) विस्तार। expansion.

वित्थम्भेति – क्रि॰ – (वि √ स्तम्भ = विस्तम्भते विस्तम्भाति) फैलाता है। expands, inflates.

वित्थार – पु॰ – (विस्तार) व्याख्या, विस्तार। explanation, elucidation, elaboration.

वित्थार-कथा – स्त्री॰ – (विस्तार-कथा) टीका। a commentary.

वित्थारतो – क्रि॰ वि॰ – (विस्तारतः) विस्तार से। in detail.

वित्थारिक – वि॰ – (विस्तारित) विस्तारित, जिसका नाम दूर तक फैला हो। widespread, widely known.

वित्थारेति – क्रि॰ – (विस्तारयति) विस्तार करता है, फैलाता है। spreads out, expands.

वित्थिन्न – कृदन्त – (विस्तीर्ण) फैलाया हुआ, विस्तृत। expanded.

√ विद – (दि॰) – (सत्तायाम्) होना। to be.

√ विद – (चु॰ तु॰) – (ज्ञाने) जानना। to know.

√ विद – (स॰) – (लाये) पाना। to get or obtain.

विदत्थि – स्त्री॰ – (वितस्ति) बालिश्त। a span.

विदहति – क्रि॰ – (विदधाति) व्यवस्था करता है। arranges, manages.

विदारण – न॰ – (वि √ दृ + ल्युट् = विदारण) चीरना-फाड़ना। rending, splitting, cutting, tearing.

विदारेति – क्रि॰ – (वि √दृ = विदृणाति) चीरता है, फाड़ता है। splits.

विदालन – न॰ – (विदारण) चीरना-फाड़ना। rending, splitting.

विदालित – कृदन्त – (विदारित) चीरा गया, फाड़ा गया। rent, split.

विदालेति – (विदृणाति) देखें Vidāreti। see Vidāreti.

विदित – कृदन्त – (विदित) ज्ञात। known, found out.

विदित्त – न॰ – (विदितत्व) जान लिये जाने का भाव। the act of having known, or being known.

विदिसा – स्त्री॰ – (विदिशा) दिक्कोण, चार उपदिशाएं – आग्नेयी, आदि। the middle point between the two directions, i.e., the north-east, south-east, etc.

विदुग्ग – न॰ – (वि + दुर्ग) अगम स्थल, कठिनाई से पहुँचा जा सकने वाला, किला। a difficult passage, a fortress, that which is inaccessible.

विदू – वि॰ – (विदुस) ज्ञानी, निपुण, बुद्धिमान, (पु॰) बुद्धिमान व्यक्ति। learned, wise, skilled.

विदूर – वि॰ – (वि + दूर) अति दूर। far away, very distant.

विदूर-जातक – (आदित्य) देखें आदित्य (आदिच्च जातक)। see Ādica-Jātaka.

विदूसित – कृदन्त – (वि + दूषित) दूषित, भ्रष्ट। corrupted, depraved, polluted.

विदूसेति – (विदुषयति) देखें दूसेति। see Dūseti.

विदेस – पु॰ – (विदेश) विदेश। a foreign country.

विदेसिक – वि॰ – (वैदेशिक) वैदेशिक। a foreigner.

विदेसी – वि॰ – (विदेशी) विदेशी। a foreigner.

विदेह – पु॰ – (विदेह) वज्जि जनपद का एक भाग विदेह था, जिसकी राजधानी थी मिथिला नगरी। a part of Vajji Janapada with Mithilā as its capital.

विद्दसु – वि॰ – (विद्रस) बुद्धिमान। wise.

विद्देस – पु॰ – (विद्वेष) शत्रुता। enmity.

विद्ध – कृदन्त – (√विध + त = विद्ध) बींधा गया। pierced, struck, shot, stung.

विद्धंसक – वि॰ – (विध्वंसक) विध्वंस करने वाला। one who destroys, a destroyer.

विद्धंसन – न॰ – (विध्वंसक) विध्वंस करना, विनष्ट करना। destruction, demolition.

विद्धंसेति – क्रि॰ – (वि √ध्वंस = विध्वंसते) विध्वंस करता है, विनष्ट करता है। demolishes, destroys.

√विध – (भू॰ दि॰) – (वेधने) बींधना। to pierce.

विध – अव्यय – (विध) सदृश। alike, like.

विध – वि॰ – (विध) (समासान्त में) प्रकार (नाना) जैसे नानाविध, अनेक प्रकार से। (in compounds) of a kind.

विधमक – वि॰ – (विध्वंसक / विधमक) विध्वंस करने वाला। destroyer.

विधमति – क्रि॰ – (वि √ध्या = विधयति) विध्वंस करता है। destroys, ruins.

विधमन – न॰ – (विधमन) विनाश। destruction.

विधमेति – (विधमति) देखें विधमति। see Vidhamati.

विधवा – स्त्री॰ – (विधवा) जिसके पति का देहान्त हो गया हो। a widow.

विधा – स्त्री॰ – (विधा) रीति, विभाग, प्रकार, ढंग। sort, manner, division, kind.

विधातु – पु॰ – (विधाता) विधाता, सृष्टि, रचयिता। arranger, dispenser, creator Brahmā.

विधान – न॰ – (विधान) व्यवस्था, आज्ञा, पद्धति। arrangement, command, process.

विधायक – वि॰ – (विधायक) व्यवस्था करने वाला। one who arranges or performs.

विधावति – क्रि॰ – (वि + धावति) दौड़ता-भागता है। runs about, roams.

विधावन – न॰ – (वि + धावन) दौड़ना-भागना। running about.

विधि – पु॰ – (विधि) ढंग, भाग्य, प्रकार। method, way, destiny, form.

विधिना – क्रि॰ वि॰ – (विधिना) विधिपूर्वक। methodically.

विधुनाति – क्रि॰ – (वि √धू = विधूनोति) धुनता है। cards or combs.

विधुर – वि॰ – (विधुर) जिसकी पत्नी मर चुकी है, एकाकी। a widower, a solitary.

विधुर-पंडित-जातक – (जा॰ सं॰ 545) – विधुर पण्डित नामक प्रत्युत्पन्नमति के आचरण भरे कार्यों का वृतान्त। the story

(No. 545) relates the astonishing acts of wisdom.

विधूत – कृदन्त – (वि √धू + क्त = विधूत) धुना गया। to card or comb.

विधूपन – न॰ – (विधूपन) बघारना, धुँआ से सुवासित करना। flavouring, fumigation.

विधूपेति – क्रि॰ – (विधूपयति) धुआँ देता है, विखेरता है। flavours, fumigates.

विधूम – वि॰ – (विधूम) धूम्र-रहित, राग-रहित। smokeless, passionless.

विधेय्य – वि॰ – (विधेय्य) आज्ञाकारी। obedient.

विनट्ठ – कृदन्त – (विनष्ट) विनष्ट। destroyed.

विनत – कृदन्त – (विनत) झुका हुआ। bent.

विनता – स्त्री॰ – (विनता) गरुड़ों की माता का नाम। the mother of the Garuḍa race.

विनद्ध – कृदन्त – (विनद्ध) घेरा हुआ, लपेटा हुआ। encircled, twisted round.

विनन्धति – क्रि॰ – घेरता है, लपेटता है। encircles, twists round.

विनन्धन – न॰ – लपेटना। twisting round, wrapping over.

विनय – पु॰ – (विनय) बौद्ध भिक्षु का आचार-शास्त्र। the code of monastic discipline.

विनयन – न॰ – (विनयन) नियमबद्ध करना, शिक्षित करना। taming, instructing the act of regularization.

विनय-धर – वि॰ – (विनयघर) विनय का विशेषज्ञ। an expert in Vinaya code.

विनय-पिटक – पु॰ – (विनय-पिटक) त्रिपिटक का द्वितीय खण्ड जो बौद्ध भिक्षुओं के आचार-शास्त्र के रूप में निबद्ध है। the code of discipline for the Buddhist monks.

विनय-वादी – पु॰ – (विनय-वादी) विनय के नियमों के समर्थन में बोलने वाला। one who speaks in accordance with the rules or conduct.

विनळीकत – कृदन्त – (विनष्टीकृत) नष्ट किया हुआ। destroyed, rendered useless.

विनस्सति – क्रि॰ – (विनश्यति) नष्ट होता है। perishes, becomes destroyed.

विनस्सन – न॰ – (विनश्यन) नष्ट होना। the act of perishing.

विना – अव्यय – (विना) रहित। without.

विना-भाव – पु॰ – (विना-भाव) पार्थक्य। separation.

विनाति – क्रि॰ – (√वे - वयति) बुनता है। weaves.

विनामन – न॰ – (विनमन) शरीर का झुकाना। bending the body or limbs.

विनामेति – क्रि॰ – (वि √नम् = विनमयति) झुकाता है। bends.

विनायक – पु॰ – (विनायक) महान् नेता, बुद्ध। a great leader, the Buddha.

विनास – पु॰ – (विनाश) विनाश। destruction.

विनासक – वि॰ – (विनाशक) विनाश करने वाला। destroying, causing ruin.

विनासन – न॰ – (विनाशन) विनाश करना। perishing.

विनासेति – क्रि॰ – (वि √नश् + णिच् = विनाशयति) नष्ट करता है। causes ruin, destroys.

विनिग्गत – कृदन्त – (विनिर्गत) बाहर निकला हुआ। came out from, emerged.

विनिच्छय – पु॰ – (विनिश्चय) विनिश्चय, फैसला। decision, judgement.

विनिच्छय-कथा – स्त्री॰ – (विनिश्चय-कथा) विश्लेषणात्मक वार्ता। analytical discussion.

विनिच्छयटठान – न॰ – (विनिश्चय-स्थान) न्यायालय, कचहरी। law-courts.

विनिच्छय-साला – स्त्री॰ – (विनिश्चय-शाला) न्याय कक्ष। the hall of judgement.

विनिच्छित – कृदन्त – (विनिश्चित्) निर्णीत, निश्चय हुआ, फैसला हुआ। decided, judged.

विनिच्छिनन – न॰ – (विनिश्चिनन) निर्णय, फैसला। judgement, decision.

विनिच्छिनाति – क्रि॰ – (विनिश्चिनोति) खोज-बीन करता है। investigates, decides.

विनिच्छेति – क्रि॰ – (विनिश्चिनोति) खोज-बीन करता है, फैसला देता है। investigates, decides.

विनिधाय – पु॰ क्रि॰ – (विनिधाय) अनुचित व्यवस्था करके, अनुचित स्थापना करके। having misplaced, ascertaining wrongly.

विनिपात – पु॰ – (विनिपात) दुष्टतन, दुःख भोगने का स्थान। a place of suffering.

विनिपातिक – वि॰ – (विनिपातिक) नरक में गिरने वाला। destined to suffer in hell.

विनिपातेति – क्रि॰ – (विनिपातयति) नाश का कारण होता है। brings to ruin.

विनिबद्ध – कृदन्त – (विनिबद्ध) सम्बन्धित। bound to, connected with.

विनिबन्ध – पु॰ – (विनिबन्ध) बन्धन, आसक्ति। bondage, attachment.

विनिब्भुजति – क्रि॰ – (वि + निर् + भजति) पृथक्-पृथक् करता है, बाँटता है। separates, discriminates.

विनिब्भोग – पु॰ – (वि + निर् + भाग) पृथक् करण। separation, discrimination.

विनिमय – पु॰ – (विनिमय) अदला-बदली। reciprocity, exchange.

विनिमोचेति – क्रि॰ – (वि + निर + √ मुञ्च = विनिमुञ्चति) अपने-आपको मुक्त करता है। gets rid of, frees oneself.

विनिम्मुत्त – कृदन्त – (विनिर्मुक्त) विमुक्त। released, freed from.

विनिवट्टेति – क्रि॰ – (विनिवर्त्तयति) लोट-पोट होता है, फिसलता है। turns or rolls over.

विनिविज्झ – कृदन्त – (विनिर्विद्ध) बींधा गया। pierced through.

विनिविज्झति – क्रि॰ – (वि + निर् √ विधृ = विनिर्विध्यति) बींध डालता है। pierces through.

विनिविज्झन – न॰ – (विनिर्विध्यन) बींधना। piercing through.

विनिविद्ध – कृदन्त – (विनिर्विद्ध) बींधा गया। pierced through.

विनिवेठेति – क्रि॰ – बन्धन-मुक्त करता है। unwraps, frees oneself from.

विनिवेठन – न॰ – बन्धन-मुक्त होना या करना। disentangling.

विनीत – कृदन्त – (विनीत) नियमित जीवन का अभ्यस्त। trained to a cultured life, accustomed to a regular life.

विनीलक-जातक – (जा॰ सं॰ 160) – हंस और कौवे के मेल से विनीलक का जन्म हुआ। (story No. 160) Vinīlaka was born of a swan and a crow by cross-breeding.

विनीवरण – वि॰ – चित्त मलों से मुक्त। free from mental turbidity, free from the obstructions to the progress of mind.

विनेति – क्रि॰ – (वि √ नी - विनेति) शिक्षित करता है। trains for a cultured life.

विनेतु – पु॰ – (विनेतृ - विनेता) शिक्षक। a trainer, an instructor.

विनेय-जन – पु॰ – (विनेय–जन) बुद्ध द्वारा विनीत किये जाने वाले लोग। people who are to be trained by Buddha.

विनेय्य – पू॰ क्रि॰ – (विनेय्य) (1) हटाकर (2) (वि॰) शिक्षित किये जाने योग्य। (1) having removed, (2) (adj.) fit to be trained.

विनोद – पु॰ – (विनोद) प्रीति, आनन्द। joy, pleasure.

विनोदन – न॰ – (विनोदन) भ्रान्ति को हटाना या दूर करना, मन बहलाव। eliminating fatigue by way of entertainment.

विनोदेति – क्रि॰ – (वि √ नुद् = विनुदति ⁄ ते) मनबहलाव करता है। entertains.

विन्दक – पु॰ – (विन्दक) अनुभव करने वाला। one who experiences (joy or suffering).

विन्दति – क्रि॰ – (विन्दति) अनुभव करता है। experience (joy or sorrow).

विन्दियमान – कृदन्त – (विन्द्यमान) अनुभव किया जाता हुआ। having endured or suffered.

विन्यास – पु॰ – (विन्यास) टिकाना, विशिष्ट न्यास, व्यवस्था में रखना। composition, putting down or up, arrangement.

विपक्ख – वि॰ – (विपक्ष) यिपक्ष। of opposite side, hostile.

विपक्खिक – वि॰ – (विपक्षिक) विरोधी का पक्षपाती। siding with the enemy.

विपच्चति – क्रि॰ – (विपच्यते) पकता है, फल देता है। ripens, bears fruit.

विपज्जति – क्रि॰ – (विपद्यते) व्यर्थ सिद्ध होता है, विनष्ट होता है। fails, perishes.

विपज्जन – न॰ – (विपद्यन) व्यर्थ, सिद्ध होना, नष्ट होना। failing, perishing becoming futile.

विपत्ति – स्त्री॰ – (विपत्ति) विपदा, असफलता, मुसीबत। failure, misfortune, distress.

विपथ – पु॰ – (विपथ) कुमार्ग। wrong path.

विपन – कृदन्त – (वि √पद् + त = विपन्न) विपद्-ग्रस्त। afflicted.

विपन्न-दिट्ठि – वि॰ – (विपन्न-दृष्टि) मिथ्या-दृष्टि वाला। one who has wrong views, ill-minded.

विपन्न-सील – वि॰ – (विपन्न-शील) शील-भ्रष्ट। gone wrong in morals.

विपरिणत – कृदन्त – (विपरिणत) परिवर्तित, रागयुक्त। perverted, lustful.

विपरिणाम – पु॰ – (विपरिणाम) परिवर्तन। change.

विपरिणामेति – क्रि॰ – (विपरिणामयति) परिवर्तित करता है, बदलता है। changes, alters.

विपरियय – पु॰ – (विपर्याय) विरुद्ध भाव। wrong state, transposition, reversal of the situation.

विपरियेस – पु॰ – (विपर्यास) विपर्यय, प्रतिकूल होना। contrariety, upsetting.

विपरिवत्तति – क्रि॰ – (वि + परि √वृत = विपरिवत्तते) उलट देता है। turns away.

विपरिवत्तन – न॰ – (विपरिवर्त्तन) परिवर्तन, उलट देना। change, turning away.

विपरीत – स्त्री॰ – (विपरीत) उलटा, बदल दिया गया। reversed, opposite.

विपरीतता – स्त्री॰ – (विपरीतता) विरोधी भाव। opposition.

विपल्लत्थ – कृदन्त – (वि + पर्यस्त) परावृत्त, पलट दिया गया। inversed, reversed.

विपल्लास – पु॰ – (विपर्यास) पलटा खा जाना, स्थानान्तर होना। contrariety, to be reversed.

विपस्सक – वि॰ – (विपश्यक) अन्तर्दृष्टि वाला। gifted with introspection.

विपस्सति – क्रि॰ – (विपश्यति) देखता है, अन्तर्दृष्टि प्राप्त करता है। sees clearly, has intuition.

विपस्सना – स्त्री॰ – (विपश्यना) विपश्यना, अन्तर्दृष्टि। insight, intuition.

विपस्सना-ञाण – न॰ – (विपश्यना-ज्ञान) विपश्यना-ज्ञान। ability of attaining insight.

विपस्सना-धुर – न॰ – (विपश्यना-धुर) विपश्यना-पथ। obligation of introspection.

विपस्सी – पु॰ – (विपश्यी) विपश्यी, अन्तर्दृष्टि-युक्त। gifted with insight.

विपाक – पु॰ – (विपाक) परिणाम, फल। consequence of one's actions.

विपातिका – स्त्री॰ – (विपातिका) विपाट, बिवाई, बेवाय। foot-sore.

विपिटि्ठकत्वा – पू॰ क्रि॰ – (वि √पृष्ठकृत्वा) (किसी की ओर) पीठ करके मुँह फेरकर। having turned one's back on, having left aside, ignoring.

विपिन – न॰ – (विपिन) जंगल। jungle, forest.

विपुल – वि॰ – (विपुल) विशाल। extensive, great, large, abundant.

विपुलता – स्त्री॰ – (विपुलता) अधिकता, प्रचुरता। abundance, excessiveness.

विपुलत्त – न॰ – (विपुलत्त्व) देखें विपुलता। see Vipulatā.

विप्प – पु॰ – (विप्र) विप्र, ब्राह्मण। brāhmaṇa.

विप्प-कुल – न॰ – (विप्रकुल) ब्राह्मण-कुल। the brāhmaṇa family or lineage.

विप्पकत – वि॰ – (विप्रकृत) अधूरा। left unfinished.

विप्पकार – पु॰ – (विप्रकार) परिवर्तन, बजाय। change, alteration.

विप्पकिण्ण – कृदन्त – (विप्रकीर्ण) बिखेरा हुआ। strewn, scattered.

विप्पकिरति – क्रि॰ – (वि + प्र + √कृ = विप्रकिरति) चारों तरफ बिखेरता है, नष्ट करता है। strews all over, wastes.

विप्पजहति – क्रि॰ – (वि + प्र √जह् = विप्रजहाति) छोड़ देता है, त्याग देता है। gives up, abandons.

विप्पटिपज्जति – क्रि॰ – (विप्रतिपद्यते) गलती करता है, दोष-भागी होता है। commits, error or sin.

विप्पटिपत्ति – स्त्री॰ – (विप्रतिपत्ति) दुराचरण। transgression of rules, misconduct.

विप्पटिपन्न – कृदन्त – (विप्रतिपन्न) पथभ्रष्ट, कुपथवान। gone wrong, divergent.

विप्पटिसार – पु॰ – (विप्रतिसार) पश्चात्ताप। remorse, repentance.

विप्पटिसारी – वि॰ – (विप्रतिसारी) पश्चात्तापी। repentant.

विप्पमुत्त – कृदन्त – (विप्रमुक्त) विमुक्त। released, set free.

विप्पयुत्त – कृदन्त – (विप्रयुक्त) पृथक किया हुआ। separated.

विप्पलपति – क्रि॰ – (विप्रलपति) विलाप करता है। laments, wails.

विप्पलाप – पु॰ – (विप्रलाप) प्रलाप। confused talk, irrelevant utterance.

विप्पलुज्जति – क्रि॰ – (वि + प्र √रुण् = विप्ररुज्ते) टुकड़े-टुकड़े हो जाता है। gets broken up, becomes destroyed.

विप्पवसति – क्रि॰ – (विप्रवसति) अनुपस्थित होता है, प्रवास करता है। remains absent, dwells away from home.

विप्पवास – पु॰ – (विप्रवास) अनुपस्थिति, प्रवास। absence, living abroad.

विप्पवुत्थ – कृदन्त – (विप्रवसित) अनुपस्थित, प्रवासी। absent, being away from home.

विप्पसन्न – कृदन्त – (वि + प्रसन्न) अति स्पष्ट। very clear, very explicit.

विप्पसीदति – क्रि॰ – (विप्रसीदति) सुस्पष्ट या प्रसन्न होता है। becomes clear, bright or explicit.

विप्पहीन – न॰ – (विप्रहीण) वञ्चित, रहित। removed, deprived of.

विप्फन्दति – क्रि॰ – (विस्पन्दति) फड़फड़ाता है, हाथ-पैर मारता है। struggles, makes movements.

विप्फन्दन – न॰ – (विस्पन्दन) संघर्ष करना, या फड़फड़ाना, हाथ-पैर मारना। struggle, movement.

विप्फार – पु॰ – (विस्फार) विस्तार। expansion.

विप्फारिक – वि॰ – (विस्फारित) फैलाया हुआ। spread out.

विप्फारित – कृदन्त – (विस्फारित) फैलाया हुआ। spread out.

विप्फुरण – न॰ – (विस्फुरण) व्याप्ति। pervasion, omnipresence.

विप्फुरति – क्रि॰ – (विस्फुरति) व्याप्त होता है, हलचल मचाता है, कँपा देता है। pervades, vibrates, agitates.

विप्फुलिङ्ग – न॰ – (विस्फुलिङ्ग) स्फुलिंग, अग्निकण। a spark.

विफल – वि॰ – (विफल) व्यर्थ, निष्फल। fruitless, profitless.

विबन्ध – पु॰ – (बन्ध) बन्धन। a fetter bond.

विबाधक – वि॰ – (वि + बाधक) बाधा डालने वाला, हानि पहुँचाने वाला। causing harm, obstructing, preventing.

विबाधति – क्रि॰ – (विबाधते) बाधा डालता है, रुकावट डालता है। hinders, obstructs.

विबाधन – न॰ – (विबाधन) बाधा, रुकावट। obstruction, hurdle.

विबुध – पु॰ – (विबुध) देवतागण। gods, devas.

विब्भन्त – कृदन्त – (विभ्रान्त) विभ्रान्त। confused, perturbed, restless.

विब्भन्तक – वि॰ – (विभ्रान्तक) भिक्षु-जीवन परित्यक्त। one who has forsaken the mendicant order.

विब्भमति – क्रि॰ – (विभ्रमति) कुपथगामी होता है, भटक जाता है, भिक्षु जीवन त्याग देता है। goes astray, forsakes the mendicant order.

विभङ्ग – पु॰ – (विभङ्ग) बँटवारा, विभाग, वर्गीकरण। distribution, division, classification.

विभङ्ग – पु॰ – (विभङ्ग) विनय-पिटक के पाराजिक तथा पाचित्तिय दोनों ग्रंथों का सामूहिक नाम। the combined name of both the books Pārājika and Pācittiya related to Vinaya-Piṭaka.

विभङ्गप्पकरण – न॰ – (विभङ्ग प्रकरण) अभिधम्म पिटक के सात प्रकरणों में से दूसरा प्रकरण या ग्रन्थ। the second of the seven books of Abhidhamma Piṭaka.

विभजति – क्रि॰ – (विभजति / विभजते) बँटवारा करता है, वर्गीकरण करता है। divides, classifies.

विभज्ज – पू॰ क्रि॰ – (विभज्य) विभक्त करके अथवा विश्लेषण करके। having divided or analysed.

विभज्जवाद – पु॰ – (विभज्यवाद) युक्तिवाद। the religion of logistics.

विभज्जवादी – पु॰ – (विभज्यवादी) थेरवाद, अनुयायी। one who follows or practises the Theravāda doctrine.

विभत्त – कृदन्त – (विभक्त) विभक्त, बँटा हुआ। divided, classified, disunited, separated.

विभत्ति – स्त्री॰ – (विभक्ति) वर्गीकरण, विभक्ति (रूप)। classification, declension (in grammar).

विभव – पु॰ – (विभव) धन, ऐश्वर्य। wealth, prosperity.

विभाग – पु॰ – (विभाग) बँटवारा। distribution, division.

विभाजन – न॰ – (विभाजन) बँटवारा। distribution, division.

विभात – कृदन्त – (वि $\sqrt{}$ भा + क्त = विभात) चमका। shone.

विभाति – क्रि॰ – (विभाति) चमकता है। becomes bright, shines.

विभावन (1) – न॰ – (विभावन) व्याख्या, प्रकाशन। explanation, interpretation, commentary.

विभावना (2) – स्त्री॰ – (विभावना) भाष्य। exposition, commentary, annotation.

विभावना – स्त्री॰ – (विभावना) एक अलंकार जिसमें कारोबार के बिना कार्य की उत्पत्ति दिखाई जाती है। a figure of speech where effects arise without cause.

विभावी – पु॰ – (विभावी) प्रज्ञावान। intelligent, intellectual, a man of intellect.

विभावेति – क्रि॰ – (विभावयति) स्पष्ट करता है। makes clear, explains.

विभीतक – पु॰ – (विभीतक) बहेड़ा। the tree *Terminalia Bellerica* (belleric myrobalan), its berries.

विभीतकी – स्त्री॰ – (विभीतकी) बहेड़ा। the tree *Terminalia Bellerica* (belleric myrobalan), its berries.

विभू – वि॰ – (विभु) सर्व-व्यापक। all-pervading, omnipresent.

विभूत – कृदन्त – (विभूत) स्पष्ट। clear, distinct.

विभूति – स्त्री॰ – (विभूति) प्रताप। splendour, glory, magnificence.

विभूसन – न॰ – (विभूषण) विभूषण, गहने सजावट। an ornament, decoration.

विभूसित – कृदन्त – (विभूषित) विभूषित। decorated.

विभूसेति – क्रि॰ – (विभूषयति) सजाता है, अलंकृत करता है। adorns, embellishes.

विमति – स्त्री॰ – (विमति) सन्देह, शक। doubt, perplexity, suspicion.

विमतिच्छेदक – वि॰ – (विमतिच्छेदक) सन्देह की निवृत्ति करने वाला। one who removes doubts.

विमन – वि॰ – (विमन) असन्तुष्ट। displeased, dissatisfied.

विमल – वि॰ – (विमल) निर्मल, स्वच्छ। clean, spotless, unstained.

विमान – न॰ – (विमान) भवन। mansion, heavenly palace.

विमान-पेतु – पु॰ – (विमान-प्रेत) योनि विशेष, पुण्यफल और पापकर्म फल दोनों

का समान भागीदार । a form of spirits liable to share equally the rewards and punishment for their deeds.

विमान-वत्थु – न० – (**विमान-वस्तु**) खुद्दक निकाय का छठा ग्रन्थ जिसमें दिव्य सुखावासों की कथाएं संकलित हैं । the sixth book of the Khuddaka Nikāya, it describes the splendour of various celestial abodes belonging to different *devas*.

विमानन – न० – (**विमानन**) अपमान । disrespect, insult.

विमानेति – क्रि० – (**विमानयति**) अनादर करता है । disrespect, treats with contempt, insults .

विमुख – वि० – (**विमुख**) लापरवाह । neglectful, negligent.

विमुच्चति –क्रि० – (**विमुच्यते**) मुक्त होता है । gets released, gets absolved.

विमुञ्चति – क्रि० – (**विमुञ्चति**) मुक्त होता है । becomes released, become free.

विमुत्त – कृदन्त – (**विमुक्त**) मुक्त किया हुआ । released, freed.

विमुत्ति – स्त्री० – (**विमुक्ति**) मुक्ति, छुटकारा । release, emancipation.

विमुत्ति-रस – पु० – (**विमुक्ति-रस**) मुक्ति-रस । the essence of emancipation.

विमुत्ति-सुख – न० – (**विमुक्ति-सुख**) मुक्ति-सुख । happiness of emancipation.

विमोक्ख – पु० – (**विमोक्ष**) विमुक्ति, विमोक्ष । deliverance, emancipation.

विमोचक – पु० – (**विमोचक**) मुक्त करने वाला । one who releases.

विमोचन – न० – (**विमोचन**) मुक्ति । release from, discharging, acquittal, liberation.

विमोचेति – क्रि० – (**विमोचयति**) मुक्त करता है । releases, makes free, acquits, liberates.

विमोहेति – क्रि० – (**वि √ मुह् = विमुह्यति**) मोह में डालता है, भ्रग उत्पन्न करता है । deludes, bewilders.

विम्हय – पु० – (**वि √ स्मि + अच् = विस्मय**) आश्चर्य । astonishment.

विम्हापक – वि० – (**विस्मापक**) आश्चर्य में डालने वाला, चकित करने वाला । one who amazes or surprises.

विम्हापन – न० – (**वि √ स्मि + णिच् = विस्थापन**) आश्चर्य में डालना । an act of surprising or amazing someone.

विम्हापेति – क्रि० – (**विस्माययति**) आश्चर्य उत्पन्न करता है, चकित करता है । surprises, amazes, astonishes.

विम्हित – कृदन्त – (**विस्मित**) आश्चर्यान्वित, चकित । astonished.

विय – अव्यय – (**इव**) समान, जैसा (तुलनार्थक) । word or particle in grammar, depicting comparison e.g. like, as.

वियत्त – वि० – (**व्यक्त**) पण्डित, सुयोग्य । learned, accomplished, erudite.

वियूहति – क्रि० – (**व्यूहति**) हटाता है, बिखेरता है । scatters, removes.

वियूहन – न० – (**वि + ऊहन**) हटाना, बिखेरना । an act of scattering, removal.

वियूल्ह – (**व्यूढ**) एकत्रित । assembled.

वियोग – पु॰ – (वियोग) अलगाव, पृथक होना । separation.

विरचित – कृदन्त – (विरचित) रचा हुआ । composed, put together.

विरचयति – क्रि॰ – (विरचयति) रचना करता है, निर्माण करता है । composes, puts together.

विरज – वि॰ – (विरज) निर्मल, शुद्ध । stainless, free from defilement.

विरज्जति – क्रि॰ – (विरज्यते) वैराग्य को प्राप्त होता है, अनासक्त होता है । becomes unattached, forsakes attachment.

विरज्जन – न॰ – (विरञ्जन) विरक्त होना । becoming unattached.

विरज्झति – क्रि॰ – (विराध्यति) चूक जाता है । misses, loses (chance).

विरत – कृदन्त – (विरत) जो रत न हो । abstained from, unattached.

विरति – स्त्री॰ – (विरति) रति का अभाव, बचाव, दूर-दूर रहना । abstinence.

विरत्त – कृ॰ – (विरक्त) विरक्त, अनासक्त । dispassioned, unattached.

विरद्ध – कृ॰ – (वि √राध् + क्त = विरुद्ध) चूक गया । failed, missed.

विरमन – न॰ – (विरमण) रुकना, विरत होना । abstinence, abstaining from.

विरमति – क्रि॰ – (वि √रम् = विरमति) विरत रहता है । abstains from.

विरल – वि॰ – (विरल) बिरला, पतला, जो घना न हो । sparse, rare, thin.

विरळ – वि॰ – (विरल) देखें विरल । see Virala.

विरव – पु॰ – (वि + रव) चीख-चिल्लाहट । cry, scream.

विरवति – क्रि॰ – (वि √रु = विरौति) चीखता है, चिल्लाता है । cries, screams.

विरवन – न॰ – (विरवण) देखें विरव । see Virava.

विरह – पु॰ – (विरह) पार्थक्य, शून्यता । separation, emptiness.

विरहित – वि॰ – (विरहित) खाली, शून्य, बिना । empty, exempt from, without, devoid of.

विराग – पु॰ – (वि + राग) वैराग्य, आसक्ति का अभाव, इच्छा का न होना । dispassionateness, absence of desire.

विरागता – स्त्री॰ – (विरागता) राग का न होना । absence of lust, desire, attachment.

विरागी – वि॰ – (विरागी) राग-रहित । passionless, emancipated.

विराजति – क्रि॰ – (विराजते) चमकता है । shines.

विराजेति – क्रि॰ – (विरञ्जयति) दूर करता है, हटाता है, नष्ट करता है । removes, eliminates.

विराधना – स्त्री॰ – (विराधना) असमर्थता, चूक जाना । failure, inability, incapacity.

विराधेति – क्रि॰ – (वि √राध् = विराध्नोति) चूक जाता है । omits, fails.

विराव – पु॰ – (विराव) चीख, चिल्लाहट । scream, cry, shouting.

विरिच्यति – क्रि॰ – (वि √रिच् + णिच् विरिङ्क्त) विरेचन किया जाता है । gets purged, is purged.

विरिच्चमान – कृदन्त – (वि √ रच् + शानच् = विरिच्यमाण) विरेचन करता हुआ। being purged.

विरित्त – कृदन्त – (वि √ रिच् + क्त) विरेचन हुआ। purged.

विरिय – न॰ – (वीर्य) शक्ति, सामर्थ्य। strength, vigour.

विरिय-बल – न॰ – (वीर्य-बल) पौरुष। the power of energy, vigour, virility.

विरियवन्तु – वि॰ – (वीर्यवान्) पौरुषवान, साहसी। energetic, virile, vigorous.

विरिय-समता – स्त्री॰ – (वीर्य-समता) पौरुष सन्तुलन, वीर्य-साम्य। moderation of energy.

विरियारम्भ – पु॰ – (वीर्यारम्भ) प्रयत्न का आरम्भ। application of exertion.

विरियिन्द्रिय – न॰ – (वीर्येन्द्रिय) वीर्य, प्रयास, प्रयत्न। the faculty of energy.

विरुज्झति – क्रि॰ – (वि √ रुध् = विरुणद्धि) विरुद्ध होता है, प्रतिकूल होता है। opposes, becomes hostile.

विरुद्ध – कृदन्त – (विरुद्ध) विरोधी। opposed, hostile.

विरुद्धता – स्त्री॰ – (विरुद्धता) प्रतिकुलता, विरोधी भाव। hostility, opposition.

विरूप – वि॰ – (विरूप) कुरूप। deformed, ugly.

विरूपक्ख – पु॰ – (विरूपाक्ष) नागों का अधिपति। name of the overlord of Nāgas.

विरूपता – स्त्री॰ – (विरूपता) कुरूपता। ugliness.

विरूळह – कृदन्त – (वि √ रुह + क्त = विरूद) उगा हुआ, बढ़ा हुआ। grown, increased.

विरूळिह – स्त्री॰ – (विरूढि) वृद्धि। growth.

विरूहति – क्रि॰ – (वि √ रुह् = विरोहति) उगता है, बढ़ता है। grows, sprouts, increases, climbs.

विरेक – पु॰ – (विरेक) विरेचन, जुलाब। purging, a purgative, purgation.

विरेचेति – क्रि॰ – (विरिणक्ति) पेट की सफाई करता है। purges.

विरोचति – क्रि॰ – (वि √ रुच् = विरोचते) चमकता है। shines.

विरोचन – न॰ – (विरोचन) चमकना। shining.

विरोचन-जातक – (जा॰ सं॰ 143) – गीदड़ ने हाथी पर आक्रमण किया फलतः उसके पाँव तले रौंदा गया। (story No. 143) the foolish jackal attacked the elephant and ultimately got crushed to death under its foot.

विरोचेति – क्रि॰ – (वि √ रुच् + णिच् - विरोचयते) प्रकाशित करता है, दीप्त करता है। illumines or illuminates.

विरोध – पु॰ – (विरोध) प्रतिकूलत्व। opposition, antagonism contradiction, resistance, protest.

विरोधन – न॰ – (वि √ रुध् + ल्युट् = विरोधन) प्रतिकूल ता। opposition, contradiction, obstruction.

विरोधेति – क्रि॰ – (वि √ रुध् = विरुणद्धि) विरोध कराता है। causes obstruction, obstructs.

विलग्ग – कृदन्त – (विलग्न) चिपका हुआ, लगा हुआ। stuck, attached.

विलङ्घति – क्रि॰ – (वि √लङ्घ् = विलङ्घते) कूदता है, फाँदता है, कलाबाजी खाता है। jumps over, makes a somersault.

विलङ्घेति – क्रि॰ – (वि √लङ्घ् = विलङ्घयति) उल्लंघन करता है। violates, jumps over.

विलपति – क्रि॰ – (वि √लप् = विलपति) रूदन करता है, प्रलाप करता है। laments, wails, talks nonsense.

विलम्बति – क्रि॰ – (वि √लम्ब् = विलम्बते) बिलम्ब करता है, देर लगाता है, लटकता रहता है। hangs about, loiters, lingers, delays, puts off.

विलम्बन – न॰ – (विलम्बन) मटरगश्ती करना, देर लगाना। loitering, delaying.

विलम्बिन – वि॰ – (विलम्बिन्) विलम्बकारी, चिरकारी, लटकता हुआ। loiterer, hanging down.

विलम्बेति – क्रि॰ – (विलम्बयति) मुँह चिढ़ाता है, शक्ल बनाता है, नीची नजर से देखता है। makes faces at somebody, disgraces, teases, mocks, grimaces.

विलय – पु॰ – (विलय) विलीन हो जाना, घुल-मिल जाना। dissolution, merge.

विलसति – क्रि॰ – (विलसति) चमकता है, खेलता है, सहयोग करता है। shines, supports, dallies.

विलसित – कृदन्त – (विलसित) प्रसन्न-चित्त, शानदार। splendid, jubilant, jovial.

विलाप – पु॰ – (विलाप) रोना-पीटना, व्यर्थ की बकवास। wailing, idle talk, verbosity.

विलास – पु॰ – (विलास) सौन्दर्य (हास-) विलास, नखरा। charm, appearance, coquetry, luxury.

विलासिता – स्त्री॰ – (विलासिता) हाव-भाव, नखरा। coquetry.

विलासिनी – स्त्री॰ – (विलासिनी) विलास-युक्त स्त्री। licentious woman.

विलासी – पु॰ – (विलासी) विलास-युक्त पुरुष। licentious person.

विलिखति – क्रि॰ – (विलिखति) खुरचता है, रगड़कर चमकाता है। scratches, scrapes, rubs to brighten or to shine.

विलिखित – कृदन्त – खुरचा हुआ। scraped, scratched.

विलित्त – कृदन्त – (विलिप्त) लेप किया गया। anointed with.

विलिम्पति – क्रि॰ – (विलिम्पति) लेप करता है। smears, anoints.

विलिम्पेति – क्रि॰ – (विलिम्पति) लेप करता है, अभिषेक करता है। anoints.

विलीन – कृदन्त – (विलीन) घुल-मिल गया, लीन हो गया। dissolved, merged.

विलीयति – क्रि॰ – (वि √ली = विलीयते) पिघल जाता है, घुल जाता है, नष्ट हो जाता है। loses entity, dissolves.

विलीयन – न॰ – (विलीयन) घुलना। dissolution.

विलीव – न॰ – (तनु वंश शकलः) बाँस या सरकण्डे की खपची। a splinter of bamboo or reed.

विलीवकार – पु० – (करण्डकारः) टोकरी बनाने वाला। a basket-maker.

विलुग्ग – कृदन्त – (अवलग्न) टूटा, टुकड़ों-टुकड़ों में विभक्त। broken or split into pieces.

विलुत्त – कृदन्त – (वि √लुप् + क्त = विलुप्त) लूटा गया, नष्ट किया गया। plundered, robbed, eliminated.

विलून – कृदन्त – (वि √लू-क्त = विलून) काटा गया। cut or torn off.

विलेख – पु० – (विलेख) उलझन, काटना-पीटना, खरौंच। perplexity, searching.

विलेपन – न० – (विलेपन) उबटन, लेप, सुगन्धित चूर्ण आदि। a cosmetic (to beautify hair or skin), pefume (fragrant powder, etc.).

विलेपित – कृदन्त – (विलेपित) सुगन्धित लेप किया गया। anointed.

विलेपेति – क्रि० – (वि √लिप् = विलिम्पति/विलिम्पते) सुगन्धित लेप करता है। anoints.

विलोकन – न० – (विलोकन) देखना, खोज-बीन करना। investigation, act of observing.

विलोकेति – क्रि० – (वि √लोक् = विलोकयति) देखता है, खोज-बीन करता है। looks at, inspects.

विलोचन – न० – (विलोचन) आँख। eye.

विलोपन – न० – (विलोपन) लूट-मार। plunder, loot.

विलोपक – पु० – (विलोपक) लूटमार करने वाला। one who plunders or destroys.

विलोम – वि० – (विलोम) विरुद्ध, प्रतिकूल। opposite, reverse, contrary.

विलोमता – स्त्री० – (विलोमता) प्रतिकूलता। opposition.

विलोमेति – क्रि० – असहमत होता है, विवाद करता है। disagrees, contradicts.

विलोळन – न० – (वि √लुड् + क्त = विलोडन) बिलोना, मथना। shaking, stirring.

विलोळेति – क्रि० – (वि √लुड् = विलोडति) बिलोता है, मथता है। shakes, stirs, churns.

विवज्जन – न० – (वि √वृज् + क्त = विवर्जन) त्याग, दूर-दूर रहना। avoiding, abandonment, desisting.

विवज्जेति – क्रि० – (वि √वृज् = विवर्जयति) बचाता है, त्यागता है, छोड़ देता है। avoids, abandons.

विवट – कृदन्त – (विवृत) विवृत, खुला, नंगा, विस्पष्ट। laid bare, unveiled, explicit.

विवट्ट – न० – (विवर्त्त) उत्तरोत्तर बढ़ते हुए कल्पों के सम्बन्ध में। devolution of rebirth.

विवट्ट-कप्प – (विवर्त्त-कल्प) उत्तरोत्तर बढ़ता हुआ कल्प (समय विभाग)। an ascending aeon.

विवट्टति – क्रि० – (विवर्त्तते) पीछे की ओर हटता है, फिर से आरम्भ करता है। moves back, revolves, begins again.

विवट्टन – न० – (विवर्त्तन) परावर्तन, पीछे हटना, मुड़ जाना। turning away, going round, moving back.

विवट्टेति – क्रि॰ – (विवर्त्तयति) पीछे हटता है, दूसरी ओर पलटता है, नष्ट कर देता है। reverses, turns back, diverts, destroys.

विवण्ण – वि॰ – (विवर्ण) बदरंग, दुर्बल। of a faded colour, feeble, colourless, discolouration.

विवण्णेति – क्रि॰ – (वि॰ - वर्णयति) निन्दा करता है, बदनामी करता है। dispraises, defames, blemishes.

विवदति – क्रि॰ – (विवदति) विवाद करता है, झगड़ा करता है। disputes, quarrels.

विवदन – न॰ – (विवदन) विवाद। disputation.

विवर – न॰ – (विवर) दरार, सुराग, छिद्र। cleft, flaw, hole, cavity, clue.

विवरण – न॰ – (विवरण) उघाड़ना, खोलना, व्याख्या करना, व्याख्या। opening, unveiling, revelation, exposition, description, comment.

विवरति – क्रि॰ – (विवारयति) विवृत करता है, उघाड़ता है, स्पष्ट करता है, विश्लेषण करता है। opens, unveils, analyses.

विवस – वि॰ – (विवश) बेवश, असंयत। unrestrained, unbridged.

विवाद – पु॰ – (विवाद) कलह, झगड़ा। dispute, quarrel.

विवादी – पु॰ – (विवादी) विवाद करने वाला। one who disputes, litigant.

विवादक – पु॰ – (विवादक) झगड़ालू। disputant.

विवाह – पु॰ – (विवाह) शादी। marriage.

विवाह-मङ्गल – न॰ – (विवाह मङ्गल) विवाह कौतुक, मांगलिक सूत्र। the auspicious thread worn on the occasion of marriage.

विविच्च – अव्यय – (विविक्त) पृथक्। separated, alone, alienated.

विवित्त – वि॰ – (विविक्त) अकेला, एकान्त में। alone, lonely, secluded.

विवित्तता – स्त्री॰ – (विविक्तता) एकान्त का भाव। the state of loneliness.

विविध – वि॰ – (विविध) नाना प्रकार के। of various sorts.

विवेक – पु॰ – (विवेक) एकान्त, अकेले में, तथ्य की पहचान, प्रकृति-पुरुष के भेद का ज्ञान। discrimination, knowledge of differences between *prakṛti* and *puruṣa*.

विवेचन – न॰ – (विवेचन) आलोचना, समीक्षा। critical appreciation.

विवेचेति – क्रि॰ – पृथक्-पृथक् करता है, आलोचना करता है। separates, discrimination, criticizes.

विस – न॰ – (विष) विष। poison, venom.

√ विस – (तु॰) – (प्रवेशने) घुसना। to enter.

विस-कण्टक – न॰ – (विष कण्टक) विषैला, कण्टक। a poisonous thorn, a kind of sugar.

विस-धर – पु॰ – (विषधर) साँप। snake.

विस-पीत – वि॰ – (विषाक्त / विषपीत) विष में बुझा हुआ। toxic, poisonous, soaked in poison.

विस-रुक्ख – पु॰ – (विष–वृक्ष) विष-वृक्ष। a poisonous tree.

विस-वेज्ज – न॰ – (विष वैद्य) विष-वैद्य। a physician who removes poison.

विस-सल्ल – न॰ – (विष शल्य) विष में बुझा तीर। a poisonous dart.

विसञ्ञ – वि॰ – (विसंज्ञ) बेहोश, अचेतन। unconscious.

विसञ्ञी – वि॰ – (विसंज्ञी) बेहोश, अचेतन। unconscious.

विसट – कृदन्त – (विसत भी) (विसृत) फैला हुआ। spread, diffused.

विसति – (विशति) देखें पविसति। see Pavisati.

विसत्त – वि॰ – (विसक्त) विशेष रूप से आसक्त, उलझा हुआ। deeply attached, entangled.

विसत्तिका – स्त्री॰ – (आसक्ति) तृष्णा, आसक्ति। attachment, craving.

विसद – वि॰ – (विशद) स्पष्ट, साफ, व्यक्त। clean, pure, manifest.

विसद-किरिया –स्त्री॰ – (विशदीकरण) स्पष्ट करना। making clear, an act of elaboration.

विसदता – स्त्री॰ – (विशदता) स्पष्टता। clearness, elaboration.

विसद-भाव – पु॰ – (विशद भाव) स्पष्टता। elaboration, clearness.

विसभाग – वि॰ – (विसंभाग) भिन्न, विरोधी, असाधारण। different, contrary, uncommon, extraordinary.

विसम – वि॰ – (विषम) विषम, ऊबड़-खाबड़। uneven (odd), unequal, disharmonious.

विसय – पु॰ – (विषय) स्थान, प्रदेश, क्षेत्र (इन्द्रियों का) विषय। locality, region, object, sensual pleasure.

विसह्य – वि॰ – (वि + सह्य) जो सहन किया जा सके, सम्भव। bearable, plausible, tolerable.

विसय्ह-जातक – (जा॰ सं॰ 340) – इस कथा में एक ऐसे महादानी सेठ की उदारता का आख्यान है जिसके दानशीलता से देवराज शक्र स्वयं सिंहासनच्युत हो जाने की आशंका से दहल उठे। this story (No. 340) is about the worry of Sakra, king of the gods on learning of the charitable deeds of a philanthropist.

विसर – पु॰ – (विसर) समूह। group.

विस-वन्त-जातक – (जा॰ सं॰ 69) – सर्प-विष वैद्य ने सर्प को पुनः अपना विष चूसने को कहा। the (story No. 69) physician commanded the serpent to suck back its venom, from the victim.

विस-लित्त – वि॰ – (विषाक्त) विष में बुझा हुआ (तीर)। (an arrow) dipped in poison, poison soaked arrow.

विसल्ल – वि॰ – (विशल्य) शोक-मुक्त। free from grief, removal of the darts.

विसहति – क्रि॰ – (उत्+ सहते) समर्थ होता है, साहस करता है। becomes able, dares, ventures.

विसंयुत्त – कृदन्त – (विसंयुक्त) असंयुक्त, जो जुता नहीं, जो पृथक् किया गया हो। un-yoked, detached.

विसंयोग – पु॰ – (वि + संयोग / असंयोग) पार्थक्य। disconnection, separation, alienation.

विसंवाद – पु॰ – (विसंवाद) धोखा, झूठ। deception, a lie, a fake.

विसंवादक – वि॰ – (विसंवादक) अविश्वसनीय। untrustworthy, unreliable.

विसंवादन – न॰ – (विसंवादन) झूठ बोलना, झूठा व्यवहार करना। lying.

विसंवादेति – क्रि॰ – (विसंवादयति) वचन-भंग करता है, झूठ बोलता है। break one's words, deceives, tells a lie.

विसंसट्ठ – वि॰ – (विसंसृष्ट) पृथक् हुआ। disconnected, separated, alientated.

विसङ्कित – वि॰ – (विशङ्कित) सन्दिग्ध। suspicious, doubtful.

विसङ्खार – पु॰ – (विसंस्कार) सङ्खार-निरोध। divestment of all material things.

विसङ्खित – कृदन्त – (विसंस्कृत) नष्ट किया गया। destroyed.

विसाखा – स्त्री॰ – (विशाखा) विशाखा, नक्षत्र। name of a lunar mansion, name the 16th lunar mansion, ie. (nakṣatra consisting of two stars.

विसाखा – भगवान् बुद्ध की उदारचेतादायिका, उपासिकाओं में प्रमुख, मिगारमाता विसाखा। a female devotee of the Buddha also known as Migāra-mātā.

विसाण – न॰ – (विषाण) विषाण, सींग। a horn.

विसाणमय – वि॰ – (विषाणमय) सींग से बना। made of horn.

विसाद – पु॰ – (विषाद) विषाद, खेल, उल्लास का अभाव। dejection, depression.

विसारद – वि॰ – (विशारद) विशारद, दक्ष, संयत। self-possessed, skilled, confident.

विसाल – वि॰ – (विशाल) विशाल। large, broad.

विसालक्खी – स्त्री॰ – (विशालाक्षी) विशालाक्षी। a woman having large eyes.

विसालता – स्त्री॰ – (विशालता) विशालता। largeness, immensity.

विसालत्त – न॰ – (विशालत्त्व) विशालत्व। largeness, immensity.

विसिखा – स्त्री॰ – (विशिखा) गली, संकरी सड़क। a street.

विसिट्ठ – वि॰ – (विशिष्ट) विशिष्ट, प्रमुख, असाधारण। distinguished, eminent.

विसिट्ठतर – वि॰ – (विशिष्टतर) विशिष्टतर। more prominent.

विसिब्बेति – क्रि॰ – (वि √सीव् = विसीव्येति) उधेड़ता है, सिलाई उखाड़ता है। unsews, opens the stiches.

विसीदति – क्रि॰ – (वि √सद् = विषीदति) हतोत्साह होता है, उद्विग्न होता है। sinks down, becomes dejected, becomes agitated.

विसीदन – न॰ – (विषीदन) हतोत्साह होना। sinking, dejection.

विसीवन – न॰ – (वि + सीवन) अपने-आपको गरमाना। warming oneself.

विसीवेति – क्रि॰ – अपने-आपको गरमाता है। warms oneself.

विसुज्झति – क्रि॰ – (वि √शुध् = विशुध्यति) स्वच्छ होता है। becomes clean or pure.

विसुद्ध – कृदन्त – (विशुद्ध) विशुद्ध, परिशुद्ध। clean, pure, stainless.

विसुद्धता – स्त्री॰ – (विशुद्धता) विशुद्धि-भाव। purity, cleanliness.

विसुद्धि – स्त्री॰ – (विशुद्धि) पवित्रता। purity, holiness.

विसुद्धि-देव – पु॰ – (पूतात्मा) सच्चरित्र व्यक्ति। a holy person.

विसुद्धि-मग्ग – पु॰ – (विशुद्धि मार्ग) विशुद्धि का मार्ग। the path to obtain holiness.

विसुद्धिमग्ग – (विशुद्धिमार्ग) संघपाल स्थविर की प्रार्थना पर आचार्य बुद्धघोष द्वारा रचित बौद्ध धर्म का विश्वकोश। the encyclopaedia of the Buddha's teachings compiled by Buddhaghoṣa at the request of Sanghapāla Thera.

विसुं – क्रि॰ वि॰ – (विषु) पृथक्-पृथक्। separate, in various directions.

विसुंकरण – न॰ – (विष्वक्) पार्थक्य। separation.

विसुंकत्वा – पू॰ क्रि॰ – (विषु कृत्वा) पृथक् करके। having separated.

विसूक – न॰ – (विशूक) तमाशा। wriggling, a show.

विसूक-दस्सन – न॰ – (विशूक-दर्शन) नाटक आदि का देखना। visiting shows, viewing the theatre shows, or dramas.

विसूचिका – स्त्री॰ – (विषूचिका) हैजा। cholera.

विसेस – पु॰ – (विशेष) विशेष, भेद-प्राप्ति। distinction, attainment.

विसेसक – पु॰ – (विशेषक) विशेष चिह्न। distinguishing mark.

विसेस-गामी – वि॰ – (विशेष गामी) विशेषता की ओर अग्रसर। marching towards distinction.

विसेस-भागिय – वि॰ – (विशेष-भागी) विशेषता की ओर या उत्थान की ओर, अग्रगामी। leading to distinction or progress.

विसेसाधिगम – पु॰ – (विशेषाधिगम) विशेष पद की प्राप्ति। specific attainment.

विसेसता – स्त्री॰ – (विशेषता) विशेषता, वैशिष्ट्य, खासियत। distinction.

विसेसतो – क्रि॰ वि॰ – (विशेषतः) विशेष रूप से। distinctively.

विसेसन – न॰ – (विशेषण) विशेष्य का गुण। distinction, adjective.

विसेसिय – वि॰ – विशेष व्यवहार का पात्र, वैशिष्ट्य के योग्य। deserving distinction, worthy of special treatment.

विसेसी – वि॰ – (विशेषी) विशेषता-युक्त। possessing distinction.

विसेसेति – क्रि॰ – (विशेषं करोति) विशेष करता है। does something special.

विसोक – वि॰ – (वि + शोक) शोक-रहित। free from grief.

विसोधन – न॰ – (वि + शोधन) शुद्धिकरण। purifying, cleaning.

विसोधेति – क्रि॰ – शुद्ध करता है। purifies, corrects.

विसोसेति – क्रि॰ – सुखाता है, बिखेर देता है। dries, scatters.

विस्सगन्ध – पु॰ – (क्रव्यगन्ध) कच्चे मांस की सी गन्ध। a smell like that of raw flesh.

विस्सग्ग – पु॰ – दान। donation.

विस्सज्जक – वि॰ – (विसर्जक) देने वाला, बाँटने वाला, प्रश्न का उत्तर देने वाला। giver, distributer, one who answer a question.

विस्सज्जति – क्रि॰ – देता है, बाँटता है, प्रश्नों का उत्तर देता है। distributes, answers.

विस्सज्जन – न॰ – (विसर्जन) भेजना, प्रत्युत्तर, खर्चा। bestowing, sending off, an answer, expenditure.

विस्सज्जनक – वि॰ – प्रत्युत्तर देने वाला, दान देने वाला। one who answers, bestows or spends.

विस्सज्जनीय – (विसर्जनीय) विसर्जन करने योग्य, बाँटने योग्य, उत्तर देने योग्य। fit for distribution, competent to answer.

विस्सज्जेति – क्रि॰ – उत्तर देता है, बाँटता है, भेजता है, खर्च करता है, बाहर करता है, जाने देता है। answers, distributes, sends off, spends, gets rid of, emits, releases.

विस्सट्ठ – कृदन्त – (विसृष्ट) भेजा गया, उत्तरित। sent off, answered.

विस्सट्ठि – स्त्री॰ – (विसृष्टि) बाहर निकलना। emission, discharge.

विस्सत्थ – कृदन्त – (विश्वस्त) विश्वास करने योग्य, विश्वसनीय, भरोसेमन्द। confident, trustworthy.

विस्सन्द – पु॰ – (विस्यन्द) उमड़ना, उफान आना। overflow, oozing.

विस्सन्दन – न॰ – (विस्यन्दन) उमड़ना। overflow, oozing.

विस्सन्दति – क्रि॰ – (वि √स्यन्द = विस्यन्दति) उमड़ता है, उफन जाता है। overflows, oozes.

विस्समति – क्रि॰ – (वि √श्रम् = विश्राम्यति) विश्राम करता है। takes rest.

विस्सन्त – कृदन्त – (वि √श्रम् + क्त = विश्रान्त) विश्रान्त, विश्रान्त प्राप्त। reposed, refreshed.

विस्सर – वि॰ – (आर्त्त स्वर) दुःखपूर्ण स्वर। cry of distress.

विस्सरति – क्रि॰ – (वि √स्मृ = विस्मरति) भूल जाता है। forgets.

विस्ससति – क्रि॰ – (वि √श्वस् = विश्वसिति) विश्वास करता है। belilenes, confides in.

विस्सास – पु॰ – (विश्वास) विश्वास, घनिष्ठता। confidence, faith.

विस्सास-भोजन-जातक – (जा॰ सं॰ 93) – खाल को चाटने से मर जाने वाले एक शेर की कथा वासना के मोह के दुष्परिणाम का आख्यान करती है। the story (No. 93) tells about the distress caused by passion.

विस्सुत – वि॰ – (विश्रुत) प्रख्यात, विश्रुत, प्रसिद्ध। famous, renowned.

विहग – पु॰ – (विहग) खग, पक्षी। a bird.

विहङ्गम – (विहङ्गम) पक्षी, चिड़िया। a bird.

विहञ्ञति – क्रि॰ – (वि √हन्यते) दुःखित होता है। grieves.

विहत – कृदन्त – (वि √हम् + क्त = विहत) (1) मारा गया (2) धुनी गई (कपास)। (1) killed, (2) carded (cotton).

विहनति – क्रि॰ – (वि √हन् = विहन्ति) मारता है। kills.

विहरति – क्रि॰ – (वि √हृ = विहरति) किसी स्थान पर रहता है, जीता है। lives, abides, dwells.

विहाय – पू॰ क्रि॰ – (वि √हा + ल्यप्) छोड़कर। having left or given up.

विहार – पु॰ – (विहार) निवास-स्थान, भिक्षुओं के रहने की जगह, बौद्ध प्रतिमागृह। an abode, a dwelling place of monks, a Buddhist temple.

विहार देवी – दुट्ठगामिणी की माता, mother of Dutthagāminī.

विहारिक – वि॰ – (विहारी) रहने वाला या विचरने वाला (प्रायः समस्त पदों में प्रयुक्त)। staying or sojourning (used in compounds).

विहारी – वि॰ – (विहारी) देखें Vihārika.

विहिंसति – क्रि॰ – (वि √हिंस = विहिंसति) चोट या कष्ट पहुँचाता है। hurts, injures.

विहिंसना – स्त्री॰ – (विहिंसा) निर्दयता। cruelty.

विहित – कृदन्त – (विहित) योग्य, उचित, व्यवस्थित। fit, arranged, furnished.

विहीन – कृदन्त – (विहीन) त्यक्त, विरहित। lost, decreased.

विहेठक – वि॰ – (विहेठक) परपीड़क, कष्ट देने वाला, हानि पहुँचाने वाला। harassing, annoying.

विहेठ-जातिक – वि॰ – (विहेठक) परपीड़क, तंग करने वाला। harassing, annoying.

विहेठन – न॰ – (विहेठन) कष्ट देना। oppression.

विहेठियमान – कृदन्त – (विहेठ्यमान) दुःख पहुँचाया जाता है। being harassed or oppressed.

विहेठेति – क्रि॰ – (विहेठयति) कष्ट देता है। harasses.

विहेसक – वि॰ – (वि √हेष् + णवुल् = विहेषक) कष्टप्रद। vexing, troubling.

विहेसा – स्त्री॰ – (वि + हेषा) हैरानी। trouble.

विहेसियमान – कृदन्त – (विहेष्यमाण) देखें विहेठियमान। see Vihethiyamāna.

विहेसेति – क्रि॰ – (विहेषति) देखें विहेठेति। see Vihetheti.

√वी – (भू॰) – (गमने) जाना। to go.

√वी – (भू॰) – (तन्तु सन्ताने) बुनना। to weave.

वीचि – स्त्री॰ – (वीचि) लहर। wave.

वीच्छा – स्त्री॰ – (वीप्सा) बार-बार एक ही बात कहना। saying something again and again.

√वीज – (भू॰) – (वीजने ∕ व्यजने) हवा करना। to fan.

वीजति – क्रि॰ – (√वीज = वीजयति) पंखा फरता है, पंखा झलता है। fans.

वीजन – न॰ – (वीजन) पंखा करना। fanning.

वीजनी – स्त्री॰ – (वीजनी) पंखा। fan.

वीजयमान – कृदन्त – (वीज्यमान) पंखा किया जाता हुआ। being fanned.

वीजेति – क्रि॰ – (वीजति) पंखा करता है। fans.

वीतच्चिक – वि॰ – (वीत + अर्चिक) लौ-रहित (चमक)। (flameless) glowing.

वीत-गेध – वि॰ – (वीत-गृध्य) लोभ-रहित। without greed or craving.

वीत-तण्ह – वि॰ – (वीत-तृष्ण) तृष्णा-रहित। without craving or greed.

वीत-मल – वि॰ – (वीत-मल) निर्मल, मल-रहित। stainless.

वीत-मोह – वि॰ – (वीत-मोह) मोह-रहित, अज्ञान-रहित। without ignorance.

वीत-राग – वि॰ – (वीत-राग) राग-रहित (पु॰) अर्हत। passionless (m.) a saint.

वीतिक्कम – पु॰ – (व्यतिक्रम) व्यतिक्रम, नियम का उल्लंघन। transgression, going beyond.

वीतिक्कमति – क्रि॰ – (वि + अति √ क्रम = व्यतिक्रामति) व्यतिक्रमण करता है। transgresses, goes beyond.

वीतिच्छ-जातक – (जा॰ सं॰ 244) – ऐसे वाचाल की कथा जिसने प्रति-प्रश्न पूछकर प्रश्नकर्ता को हरा दिया। the story (No. 244) of a talkative who defeated his opponent.

वीतिनामेति – क्रि॰ – (कालंक्षेपयति) समय बिताता है। spends time, waits.

वीतिवत्त – कृदन्त – (वीतिवर्त्त) गुजर गया, खर्च हो गया, जीत लिया गया। having passed or overcome, spent, gone through.

वीतिवत्तेति – क्रि॰ – (वीति वर्त्तयति) जीत लेता है, समय व्यतीत करता है। overcomes, passes time.

वीतिहरण – न॰ – (वीतिहरण) लम्बे-लम्बे डग धरना। walking with long steps, a stride.

वीतिहार – पु॰ – (वीतिहार) डग। a stride, long steps.

वीतिहरति – क्रि॰ – (वीतिहरति) चलता है, टहलता है। walks, strides.

वीथि – स्त्री॰ – (वीथि) गली, रास्ता। street, track.

वीथि-चित्त – न॰ – (वीथि-चित्त) क्रियाशील चित्त। process of cognition.

वीमंसक – वि॰ – (विमर्शक) विमर्श करने वाला, परीक्षा करने वाला। one who investigates, tests.

वीमंसन – न॰ – (विमर्श) विमर्श करना, खोज-बीन करना। experiment, investigation.

वीमंसा – स्त्री॰ – (विमर्श) छान-बीन, परीक्षण। investigation.

वीमंसति – क्रि॰ – (वि √ मर्श = विमृशति) विमर्श करता है, खोज-बीन करता है, परीक्षण करता है। investigates, experiments.

वीमंसी – पु॰ – (विमर्शी) खोज-बीन करने वाला, परीक्षण करने वाला। investigator.

वीर – वि॰ – (वीर) बहादुर, वीर। brave, hero.

वीरक-जातक – (जा॰ सं॰ 204) – कथा बतलाती है कि कभी-कभी दूसरे की नकल करना घातक बन जाता है। the story (No. 204) tells how imitation causes distress.

वीयति – क्रि॰ – (√ वे = वयति / वयते) बुनता है। weaves.

वीरु – स्त्री॰ – (वीरुध) लता, वल्लरी। a creeper.

वीसति – स्त्री॰ – (विंशति) बीस। twenty.

वीसतिम – वि॰ – (विंशतितम) बीसवाँ। the twentieth.

वीहि – पु॰ – (ब्रीहि) धान। paddy.

√ बु – (की॰) – (संवरणे) ढकना। to cover.

√ वु – (सु॰) – (संवरणे) ढकना। to cover.

वुच्यति – क्रि॰ – (उच्यते) कहा जाता है। is said or called.

वुच्यमान – कृ॰ – (वक्ष्यमाण) कहा जाता हुआ। having been said.

वुट्ठ – कृ॰ – (वृष्टि म्लिन्न) बारिश का भीगा। wet with rain.

वुट्ठहति – क्रि॰ – (उत्तिष्ठति) उठता है। arises, gets up.

वुट्ठान – न॰ – (उत्थान) ऊपर उठना, उत्थान। rising up.

वुट्ठापेति – क्रि॰ – (उत्थापयति) उठवाता है। rouses.

वुट्ठि – स्त्री॰ – (वृष्टि) वर्षा। rain.

वुट्ठिक – वि॰ – (वृष्टिक) वर्षाकारी, वर्षा वाला। having rain.

वुड्ढ – वि॰ – (वृद्ध) वृद्ध, ज्येष्ठ। old, venerable.

वुड्ढतर – वि॰ – (वृद्धतर) वृद्धतर, ज्येष्ठतर। elder, older.

वुड्ढि – स्त्री॰ – (वृद्धि) वृद्धि, ऐश्वर्य। increase, growth, prosperity.

वुत्त (1) – कृदन्त – ($\sqrt{}$ वच् + क्त = उक्त) कहा गया, कहा गया वचन। said (n.) the thing already said.

वुत्त (2) – कृदन्त – ($\sqrt{}$ वप् + क्त = उप्त) बोया गया। sown.

वुत्तप्पकार – वि॰ – (उक्त प्रकार) कथनानुसार। as said above.

वुत्तप्पकारेन – क्रि॰ वि॰ – (उक्त प्रकारेण) उक्त कथनानुसार। in the way explained above.

वुत्त-वादी – पु॰ – (उक्तवादी) कथित बात को दुहराने वाला। one who reiterates what is said.

वुत्त-सिर – (मुण्डित शीर्ष) मुण्डित सिर। with a shaven head.

वुत्ति – स्त्री॰ – (उक्ति) व्यवहार, आचरण, जीविका। conduct, habit, livelihood.

वुत्तिक – वि॰ – (व्रती) अभ्यस्त। having the habit or practice.

वुत्तिका – स्त्री॰ – (वृत्ति, वृत्तिका) वृत्ति का भाव। stipend, livelihood.

वुती – वि॰ – (व्रती) अभ्यस्त। having the habit or practice.

वुत्थ – क्रि॰ वि॰ – (वस् = उसित्वा) रहकर, समय बिताकर। having dwelt or spent time.

वुत्थ-वस्स – वि॰ – (उसित-वर्ष) जिसने 'वर्षा-वास' किया हो। having spent the rainy season.

वुद्ध – वि॰ – (वृद्ध) देखें वुड्ढ। see Vuddha.

वुद्धि – स्त्री॰ – (वृद्धि) देखें वुड्ढि। see Vuddhi.

वुद्धिप्पत्त – वि॰ – (वृद्धि-प्राप्त) वयस्क, विवाह करने योग्य। adolescent, fit to be married.

वुद्धियुत्त – वि॰ – (वृद्धि-युक्त) समृद्ध। prosperous.

वुद्धिरोग – पु॰ – (वृद्धि रोग) अण्डकोश की वृद्धि। hydrocele (a disorder).

वुय्हति – क्रि॰ – (वह् + णिच् = उह्यते) ले जाया जाता है। is being carried away or floated.

वुय्हन – न॰ – (वहन) ढोया जाना। floating.

वुस – पु॰ – (वृष / वृषभ) बैल। an ox.

वुसित – कृ॰ – (उसित) वास किया। dwell.

वुसितत्त – न॰ – (वास) रहना । dwelling.

वुसित-भाव – पु॰ – (वास) निवास का भाव । dwelling.

वुस्सति – क्रि॰ – (वस्यते) रहा जाता है । to dwelt by.

वुपकट्ठ – वि॰ – (उपकण्ठ) समीप का, नजदीकी । near, approaching.

वूपसन्त – कृदन्त – (उपशान्त) शान्ति प्राप्त । calmed, allayed.

वूपसमन – न॰ – (उपशमन) शान्ति । calmness, relief.

वूपसमेति – क्रि॰ – (उप √शम् + णिच = उपशामयति) शान्त करता है । appeases.

वूपसम्मति – क्रि॰ – (उप √शम् = उपशाम्यति) उपशमित होता है, शान्त होता है । becomes assuaged or quiet.

वूळ्ह – कृदन्त – (√वह + क्त = ऊढः) ले जाया गया । carried away or floated.

वे – अव्यय – (वै) निश्चयबोधक अव्यय । वास्तव में, स्थिर रूप से । a particle of affirmation or emphasis, indeed, truely, surely.

वेकल्ल – न॰ – (वैकल्प) विकलता का भाव । deformity, deficiency.

वेकल्लता – स्त्री॰ – (विकलता) अंग-विकृति । deformity.

वेग – पु॰ – (वेग) शक्ति, गति, जोर । force, speed, velocity.

वेजयन्त – पु॰ – (वैजयन्त) इन्द्र के महल का नाम, इन्द्रध्वज । the name of Indra's palace, the banner of Indra.

वेज्ज – पु॰ – (वैद्य) वैद्य । a physician, doctor.

वेज्ज-कम्म – न॰ – (वैद्य-कर्म) वैद्य-कर्म, चिकित्सा । medical treatment.

√वेठ – (चु॰) – (वेष्टने) लपेटना । to wrap, to envelop, to cover.

वेठक – वि॰ – (वेष्टक) लपेटने वाला, घेरने वाला । one who covers or wraps.

वेठन – न॰ – (वेष्टन) बेठन, लपेट, पगड़ी । a wrapper, a turban.

वेठियमान – कृ॰ – (√वेष्ट + शानच् = वेष्टमान) लपेटे जाते हुए, या मरोड़े जाते हुए । being wrapped or twisted.

वेठेति – क्रि॰ – (वेष्ट = वेष्टति) लपेटता है, मरोड़ता है । wraps, twists around.

वेण – पु॰ – (वेणुकार) टोकरी बनाने वाला । a basket-maker.

वेणविक – पु॰ – (वेणुवादक) वंशी बजाने वाला । player on a pipe or flute.

वेणिक – पु॰ – (वीणावादक) वीणा बजाने वाला । a player on a lute.

वेणी – स्त्री॰ – (वेणी) केशगुच्छ, बालों की जट । a braid of hair.

वेणी-कत – वि॰ – (वेणीकृत) केश गुँथा शिर । plaited hair.

वेणी-करण – न॰ – (वेणी–करण) वेणी-गुम्फन, गट्ठर बाँधना । making plaits of hair, making sheafs.

वेणु – पु॰ – (वेणु) बाँस । bamboo.

वेणु-गुम्ब – पु॰ – (वेणु-गुल्म) बँसवाड़ी, बाँसों का झुण्ड । a bush of bamboo.

वेणु-बलि – पु॰ – (वेणु-बलि) बाँस के रूप में चुकता किया जाने वाला कर (टैक्स) ।

a tax to be paid in the form of bamboo.

वेणु-वन – न॰ – (वेणु वन) बाँसों का वन। a bamboo-grove.

वेतन – न॰ – (वेतन) मजदूरी, तनख्वाह, फीस। wages, hire, fee.

वेतनिक – न॰ – (वैतनिक) वैतनिक, वेतन पर काम करने वाला, किराये का टट्टू। one who works for wages, a hireling.

वेतरणी – स्त्री॰ – (वैतरणी) नरक की एक त्रासदायिनी कल्पित नदी। name of a mythical river in hell.

वेतस – पु॰ – (वेतस्) नरकट, सरकण्डा। a ratan, reed.

वेतालिक – पु॰ – (वैतालिक) राजदरबारी गायक। a court musician.

वेति – क्रि॰ – (√वि = व्ययति) लुप्त हो जाता है, अन्तर्धान हो जाता है। wanes, disappears.

वेत्त – न॰ – (वेत्र) वेतस् बेंत। a cane, a twig.

वेत्तग्ग – न॰ – (वेत्राग्र) बेंत का सिरा। the sprout of a cane.

वेत्त-लता – स्त्री॰ – (वेत्रलता) बेंत की लता। cane creeper.

वेद – पु॰ – (वेद) सृष्टि के आदिभूत 'स्वयं-प्रमाण' गाने जाने वाले ज्ञान के चार ग्रन्थ। the authorized religious teachings of Brāhmaṇic canon, which is the oldest book of the world.

वेदंगू – पु॰ – (वेदञ्ज) उच्चतम ज्ञान-प्राप्त। one who has attained the highest knowledge.

वेदजात – वि॰ – (वेदजात) आनन्दित। filled with joy.

वेदन्तगू – पु॰ – (वेदान्तग) ज्ञान की पराकाष्ठा पर पहुँचा हुआ। one who excels in the knowledge of the Vedas.

वेदन्त-पारगू – पु॰ – (वेदान्त पारगामी) वेदान्त ज्ञान के दूसरे छोर तक गया हुआ। one who excels in the knowledge of Vedānta.

वेदक – पु॰ – (वेदकः) अनुभव करने वाला या भोगने वाला। one who feels or suffers.

वेदनट्ट – वि॰ – (वेदनार्त्त) कष्ट से पीड़ित। afflicted with pain.

वेदना – स्त्री॰ – (वेदना) पीड़ा, इन्द्रिय-जनित अनुभूति। pain, sensation.

वेदनाक्खन्ध – पु॰ – (वेदनास्कन्ध) वेदना-स्कन्ध, वेदना-समूह। the aggregate of sensation.

वेदब्भ-जातक – (जा॰ सं॰ 48) – बेदब्भ-मन्त्र के जानकार ब्राह्मण तथा लोभी डाकुओं के प्राणान्त की कथा। the story (No. 48) tells about the massacre of greedy robbers and also of a brāhmaṇa knowing the Vedabbha charm.

वेदयित – न॰ – (अनुभूति) अनुभूति, अनुभव। feeling, experience.

वेदिका – स्त्री॰ – (वेदिका) वितर्दी, नन्हा चबूतरा, वेदी। a raised place, a platform, an altar.

वेदित – कृ॰ – (विदित) ज्ञात। felt, known.

वेदियति – क्रि॰ – (वेद्यते) अनुभव किया जाता है। is being felt or experienced.

वेदियमान – कृदन्त – (वेद्यमान) अनुभव किया जाता हुआ। being experienced or felt.

वेदेति – (√ विद् = वेत्ति) अनुभव करता है, जानता है। feels, knows.

वेदेह – वि॰ – (वैदेह्य) विदेह देश का। belonging to the Videha country.

वेदेहीपुत्त – पु॰ – (वैदेही पुत्र) विदेह की राजकुमारी का पुत्र। son of a princess from Videha.

वेध – पु॰ – (वेध) बींधना। piercing, shooting, pricking.

वेधन – न॰ – (वेधनम्) तीर मारना। arrow-shooting.

वेधति – क्रि॰ – (√ कम्प् = कम्पते) काँपता है। trembles, quakes.

वेधी – पु॰ – (वेधी) बींधने वाला। one who shoots or hits.

वेनयिक – पु॰ – (विनयविद्) विनय का विशेषज्ञ। an expert in Vinaya (good behaviour decorum, propriety of conduct).

वेनेय्य – वि॰ – (वेनेय्य) विनीत बनाया जा सकने वाला, शिक्षणीय। accessible to instruction, tractable.

√ वेप – (भू॰) – (चलने) काँपना। to tremble.

वेपुल्ल – न॰ – (वैपुल्य) विपुलता। abundance.

वेपुल्ल – पु॰ – (वैपुल्ल) राजगृह के आसपास के पाँच पर्वतों में से उच्चतम पर्वत। highest amongst the five hills situated in Rājagṛha region.

वेभञ्जिय – वि॰ – (विभज्य) विभजनीय, बाँटने योग्य। fit to be distributed.

वेभार – पु॰ – (वैभार) राजगृह के चारों ओर के पर्वत-शिखरों में से एक। one of the Rājagṛha hills.

वेम – पु॰ – (वेमन्) वायदण्ड, दरकी। shuttle.

वेमज्झ – न॰ – (वि + मध्य) बीच, मध्य। the middle, centre.

वेमतिक – वि॰ – (वैमतिक) सन्दिग्ध। doubtful.

वेमत्त – न॰ – (वैमत्य) सन्देह, भेद। difference, distinction.

वेमत्तता – स्त्री॰ – (वैमतत्त्व / विमतता) द्वैध-भाव, दुविधा। difference, distinction.

वेमातिक – वि॰ – (वैमात्रिक) विमाता पुत्र, सौतेला। the step brother or sister.

वेमानिक – वि॰ – (वैमानिक) विमान वाला, दिव्य-भवन का स्वामी। having a divine abode.

वेमानिक-पेत – पु॰ – (वैमानिक-प्रेत) विमान-पेत, पुण्य फल और पाप कर्म फल का समान भागीदार। a kind of spiritual being liable to equal share of enjoyment and suffering.

वेय्यग्घ – वि॰ – (वैयाघ्र) बाघ-सम्बन्धी, बाघ के चमड़े से ढका हुआ। belonging to tiger, covered with a tiger's skin.

वेय्यत्तिय – न॰ – (वैयत्ता) स्पष्टता। lucidity, accomplishment.

वेय्याकरण – न॰ – (वैयाकरण) व्याख्या, (पु॰), व्याकरण का जानकार, व्याख्याकार। explanation, (m.) a grammarian, one who explains.

वेय्याबाधिक – वि॰ – (आबाधिक) कष्टप्रद। causing trouble or injury.

वेय्यायिक – न॰ – (व्यय) खर्च। expenditure, money to defray expenses.

वेय्यावच्च – न॰ – (वैयावृत्य) बुद्धिस्ट संस्कृत, वैयावृत्य, सेवा, कर्तव्य। duty, service.

वेय्यावच्चकर – पु॰ – (वैयावृत्तिकर / भृत्य) सेवक, नौकर। an attendant, servant.

वेय्यावतिक – पु॰ – (वैयावृत्तिक-भृत्य) सेवक, नौकर। attendant, servant.

वेर – न॰ – (वैर) वैर। enmity.

वेरज्जक – वि॰ – (बहुराज्यक) नाना राज्यों का। belonging to many countries.

वेरञ्ञा – स्त्री॰ – (वेरञ्जा) नगर-विशेष, जहाँ भगवान् बुद्ध ने अपना एक वर्षा-वास बिताया। a township where the Buddha passed one rainy season.

वेरमणी – (विरति) अलगाव, विरति। abstinence.

वेरम्भ-वात – पु॰ – (पर्वत-वात) पर्वत प्रदेशों में चलने वाली हवा। a wind blowing in high altitudes.

वेरिक – वि॰ – (वैरी) शत्रु भाव लिये, द्वेषी। revengeful, an enemy.

वेरी – वि॰ – (वैरी) शत्रु। enemy.

वेरी-जातक – (जा॰ सं॰ 103) – डाकुओं के डर से बैलों को तेज भगाया और धनी व्यापारी सकुशल घर लौट आया। the story (No. 103) of a rich merchant who got rid of the robbers with his intelligence.

वेरोचन – पु॰ – (वैरोचन) सूर्य। son of Virocana.

√ वेल – (भू॰) – (चलने) हिलना। to tremble, to move.

वेला – स्त्री॰ – (वेला) समय, समुद्रतट, सीमा। time, shore, limit, boundary.

वेलातिक्कम – पु॰ – (वेलातिक्रमण) समय की सीमा को बाँध जाना। going out of limits.

वेल्लित – वि॰ – (वेल्लित) टेढ़ा, घुँघराले (बाल)। crooked, curly (hair).

वेल्लितग्ग – वि॰ – (वेल्लिताग्र) घुँघराले बालों का सिरा। having curly tips of hair.

वेवचन – न॰ – (समानार्थी पद) पर्याय वचन, सामानार्थी वचन। an epithet, a synonym.

वेवण्णिय – न॰ – (विवर्ण-कर्म) विवर्ण करना, बदरंग करना। disfiguration, discolouring.

वेस – पु॰ – (वेश) पहनावा, वेश, भेष। appearance, dress.

वेसम्म – न॰ – (वैषम्य) विषमता। inequality, disharmony.

वेसाख – पु॰ – (वैशाख) वैशाख महीना। बुद्ध का जन्म, ज्ञान-प्राप्ति, परिनिर्वाण-सभी वैशाख में हुए माने जाते हैं। name of a lunar month April-May, it is believed that Buddha's birth, enlightenment and parinirvan happened in this month.

वेसारज्ज – न॰ – (वैशारद्य) विशारदत्व, आत्म-विश्वास। skill, self-confidence.

वेसाली – स्त्री॰ – (वैशाली) लिच्छवियों की प्रसिद्ध राजधानी वैशाली। the famous capital town of Licchavīs.

वेसिया – स्त्री॰ – (वेश्या) वेश्या, बारवनिता। a prostitute, a harlot.

वेस्म – न॰ – (वेश्म) निवास-स्थान, घर। a dwelling place, house.

वेस्स – पु॰ – (वैश्य) वैश्य वर्ण वाला। a member of the third social grade.

वेस्सन्तर-जातक – (जा॰ सं॰ 547) – वेस्सन्तर राजा की दानशीलता की कथा। this Jātaka tale (No. 547) describes the unparalleled alms-giving habit of king Vessantara.

वेहास – पु॰ – (विहायस) आकाश। sky.

वेहास-कुटी – स्त्री॰ – (विहायस-कक्ष) ऊपर के तल्ले पर हवादार कमरा, हवामहल। an airy room upstairs.

वेहास-गमन – न॰ – (विहायस-गमन) आकाश-गमन। going through the air.

वेहासट्ठ – वि॰ – (नभस्थ) आकाश स्थित। situated in the sky.

वेळु – (वेणु) देखें वेणु। see Venu.

वेळुरिय – न॰ – (वैदूर्य) स्फटिक, वैदूर्य मणि, लाजवर्त। lapis lazuli.

वेळुक-जातक – (जा॰ सं॰ 43) – बाँस में रखे, पोषित साँप ने सपेरे को काटा। it is the story (No. 43) of a hermit who has a pet-viper which was kept in a bamboo basket. One day the viper bit the hermit and caused his death.

वेळुवन – (वेणु वन) राजगृह के समीप राजा बिम्बसार का प्रमोद-उद्यान, जो बाद में बुद्ध-प्रमुख भिक्षु-संघ को अर्पित कर दिया गया था। the pleasure garden of Bimbisāra near Rājgṛha, it was bestowed on the Buddha and the fraternity by the king.

वो – सर्वनाम – (सर्वमान) (युष्मान्, युष्माकम्, युष्भ्यम के पर्याय) तुम सबको, तुम सबका, तुम सबके द्वारा। to you, of you, by you.

वोकार – पु॰ – रुप, वेदना आदि पाँच स्कन्ध। a constituent of being.

वोकिण्ण – कृदन्त – (अव √कृ + क्त = अवकीर्ण) ढका हुआ, बिखरा हआ, मग्न। strewn, covered, violated.

वोक्कमति – क्रि॰ – (अवक्रामति) एक ओर हो जाता है, पथच्युत होता है। turns aside, deviates from.

वोच्छिज्जति – क्रि॰ – (उत् √छिद् + णिच् = उच्छिद्यते) काटता है। becomes cut-off.

वोत्थपन – न॰ – (अवस्थापन / व्यवस्थापन) परिभाषा। definition.

वोदक – वि॰ – (अव + उदक) जल-शून्य जल-रहित। free from water.

वोदापन – न॰ – (अवदापन) शुद्धि। cleansing, purification.

वोदापेति – क्रि॰ – (अवदापयति) शुद्ध करता है। cleanses, purifies.

वोदान – न॰ – (व्यवदान) शुद्धि। cleansing, purity.

वोदात – वि॰ – (अव √कृ + क्त = अवदात) शुद्ध, स्वच्छ। clean, pure.

वोमिस्सक – वि॰ – (अवमिश्रित) मिश्रित, विविध, मिला-जुला। miscellaneous, mixed.

वोरोपन – न॰ – (विरोपण) वञ्चित करना। depriving of.

वोरोपेति – क्रि॰ – (विरोपयति / व्यवरोपयति) वञ्चित करता है । deprives of, takes away.

वोलोकेति – क्रि॰ – (अविलोकयति / व्यवलोकयति) परीक्षा करता है । examines, scrutinizes.

वोसित – वि॰ – (अवसित) समाप्त, पूरा हुआ । accomplished, perfected.

वोस्सग्ग – पु॰ – (उत्सर्ग / अवोत्सर्ग) परित्याग, दान । donation, giving up.

वोस्सजन – न॰ – (अव + उत्सर्जन) परित्याग । giving up, relinquishing.

वोस्सजति – क्रि॰ – (अव + उत्सृजति) परित्याग करता है । gives up, relinquishes.

वोहरति – क्रि॰ – (व्यवहरति) व्यवहार में लाता है, व्यापार करता है । uses, expresses, trades.

वोहरियमान – कृदन्त – (व्यवहार्यमाण) बुलाया जाता हुआ । being called.

वोहार – पु॰ – (व्यवहार) बुलाना, प्रकट करना, उपयोग, व्यापार, कानून । calling, expression, use, trade, current appellation.

वोहारिक – पु॰ – (व्यावहारिक) व्यापारी, न्यायाधीश । trader, judge.

वोहारिकामच्च – पु॰ – (व्यावहारिकामात्य) मुख्य न्यायाधीश । the Chief Justice.

व्यग्घ – पु॰ – (व्याघ्र) बाघ । tiger.

व्यग्घ-जातक – (जा॰ सं॰ 272) – कथा सचेत करती है कि बाघ और सिंह के जंगल से चले जाने पर लोग जंगल के पेड़ काटने लगते हैं और जंगल नष्ट हो जाता है । the story (No. 272) warns that when frightened lion and tiger disappear from the forest people cut down the trees and destroy the jungle.

व्यञ्जन – न॰ – (व्यञ्जन) मसालेदार भोजन, चिह्न, स्वरेतर वर्ण । a spicy dish, indicating mark, a consonant.

व्यञ्जेति – क्रि॰ – (व्यञ्जयति) प्रकट करता है, संकेत करता है । indicates, denotes.

व्यत्त – वि॰ – (व्यक्त) विद्वान्, पण्डित । learned, wise, prudent.

व्यत्ततर – वि॰ – (व्यक्ततर) बड़ा पण्डित, अधिक विद्वान् । more learned or skilful.

व्यत्तता – स्त्री॰ – (व्यक्तता) पाण्डित्य, होशियारी । cleverness, learning.

√ व्यथ – (भू॰) – (दुःख भय चलनेषु) दुःखी होना, डरना, काँपना । to grieve, to bear, to tremble.

व्यथति – क्रि॰ – (व्यथते) कष्ट देता है, दबाता है । oppresses, subdues.

व्यन्तिकरोति – क्रि॰ – (नाशयति) नष्ट करता है । abolishes, gets rid of.

व्यन्तिभवति – क्रि॰ – (व्यन्तं गच्छति) रोकता है, रुकता है । stops, comes to an end.

व्यपगच्छति – क्रि॰ – (वि + अप + गच्छति) विदा होता है । departs.

व्यम्ह – न॰ – (हर्म्य) विमान, महल । a celestial mansion, a vimāna, i.e. abode for fairies, etc.

व्यत्यय – पु॰ – (व्यत्त्यत) व्यतिक्रम, उलटफेर । opposition, reversed.

व्यसन – न॰ – (व्यसन) दुर्भाग्य, विपदा,

विनाश। misfortune, ruin, destruction.

व्याकत – कृदन्त – (व्याकृत) व्याख्यात। explained, declared.

व्याकरण – न॰ – (व्याकरण) व्याकरण, व्याख्या। grammar, explanation.

व्याकरियमान – कृदन्त – (व्याक्रियमाण) व्याख्या किया जाता हुआ। being explained or declared.

व्याकरोति – क्रि॰ – (व्याकरोति) व्याख्या करता है। explains.

व्याकुल – वि॰ – (व्याकुल) परेशान, गड़बड़ाया हुआ। perplexed, confused.

व्याख्याति – क्रि॰ – (व्याख्याति) सूचित करता है। announces, explains.

व्याध – पु॰ – (व्याध) शिकारी। hunter.

व्याधि – पु॰ – (व्याधि) रोग। disease.

व्याधित – वि॰ – (व्याधि-ग्रस्त) रोगी। affected with illness.

व्यापक – वि॰ – (व्यापक) सर्वत्र व्याप्त, विभु। omnipresent.

व्यापज्जति – क्रि॰ – (व्यापद्यति) असफल होता है। fails, becomes troubled.

व्यापज्जना – स्त्री॰ – (व्यापादन) असफलता, क्रोध। failing, ill-will, anger.

व्यापन्न – कृदन्त – (व्यापन्न) विपद्ग्रस्त, मार्ग-भ्रष्ट, नष्ट। gone wrong, malevolent, vexed.

व्यापाद – पु॰ – (व्यापाद) परद्रोह चिन्तन, द्वेष। ill-will, malevolence.

व्यापदेति – क्रि॰ – (व्यापादयति) बिगाड़ता है। spoils.

व्यापार – पु॰ – (व्यापार) पेशा। occupation.

व्यापारित – कृदन्त – (व्यापारित) उत्तेजित। instigated.

व्यापित – कृदन्त – (व्यापित) पूरित। pervaded.

व्यापेति – क्रि॰ – (व्याप्नोति) व्याप्त होता है, सर्वत्र फैलता है। pervades, diffuses.

व्याबाधेति – क्रि॰ – (वि + आ + बाधते) हानि पहुँचाता है, बाधा डालता है। harms, obstructs.

व्याभङ्गी – स्त्री॰ – (व्याभङ्गी) वेणुशिम्या, स्कन्धवाहिनी, बोझा ढोने के लिए बांस की लाठी। a bamboo pole for carrying burden.

व्याम – पु॰ – (व्याम) दोनों खुली बाहों के बीच की माप। measure of the extended arms, fathom.

व्यावट्ट – वि॰ – (व्यावृत्त) उन्मृष्ट, निवृत्त। separated from, removed from.

व्यासत्त – वि॰ – (वि + आसक्त) परिगृहीत, घोर आसक्त। deeply attached, clasped tightly.

व्यासेचन – न॰ – (वि + आ + सेचन) सींचना, छिड़कना। sprinkling.

व्याहरति – क्रि॰ – (व्याहरति) बोलता है, बातचीत करता है। utters, speaks, talks.

व्यूह – पु॰ – (व्यूह) सैन्य विन्यास, सैनिक व्यवस्था, व्यूह-रचना। military array.

√व्ह – (भू॰) – (आह्वाने) पुकारना। to call.

स

स – वि॰ – (स्व) निज, स्वकीय, अपना सहित। one's own.

स – तो॰ – (सः) कर्त्ता एकवचन का पुलिंग रूप। he.

स-उपादन – वि॰ – (सोपादन) आसक्ति-सहित। showing attachment.

स-उपादिसेस – वि॰ – (सोपाधिशेष) शरीर के रहते (निर्वाण)। having the substratum of life remaining.

√ सक – (त॰, सु॰, क्या) – (सामर्थ्ये) सकना, समर्थ होना। capable of, can (do).

सक – वि॰ – (स्वक) स्वकीय, (पु॰), सम्बन्धी (न॰) अपनी निजी सम्पत्ति। one's own (m.) a relation (n.) one's own property.

सक-मन – वि॰ – (मुदित मन) आनन्दित। joyful.

सकङ्ख – वि॰ – (साकांक्ष) सन्देहयुक्त, सन्देह सहित। doubtful.

सकट – पु॰ तथा न॰ – (शकट) गाड़ी। a cart, a wagon.

सकट-भार – पु॰ – (शकट-भार) एक गाड़ी का बोझ। a cart-load.

सकट-वाह – पु॰ – (शकट-वाह्) एक गाड़ी का बोझ। a cart-load, a wagon-load.

सकट-व्यूह – पु॰ – (शकट-व्यूह) गाड़ियों की व्यूह सज्जा। an array of carts or wagons.

सकण्टक – वि॰ – (सकण्टक) कण्टकयुक्त, कंटक-सहित। thorny, having thorns.

सकदागामी – पु॰ – (सकृतागामी) धर्म-पथ का ऐसा पथिक, जिसके पुनः एक ही बार और इस संसार में जन्म लेने की संभावना हो। one who has attained the second stage of the Path and to be reborn on the earth only once.

सक-बल – वि॰ – (स्वकबलम्) अपना बल, आत्म-पौरुष। one's own strength.

सक-कवल – वि॰ – (स कवल) कवल (भोजन का कौर या ग्रास) सहित। with food in the mouth.

स-कम्म – न॰ – (स्वकर्म) स्वकीय कर्म। one's own duty.

स-कम्मक – वि॰ – (सकर्मक) सकर्मक क्रिया। transitive verb.

स-करणीय – वि॰ – (स + करणीय) जिसके लिए 'करणीय' शेष हो। one who still has something to do.

स-कल – वि॰ – (सकाल) सम्पूर्ण, तमाम। whole, entire.

स-कलिका – स्त्री॰ – (कञ्चिका) खपच्ची, कमची, खमाची। a splint.

स-कास – पु॰ – (सकाश) पड़ोस। neighbourhood.

स-किच्च – न॰ – (स्व + कृत्य) अपना कृत्य, निज का कार्य। one's own business.

स-किञ्चन – वि॰ – (सकिञ्चन) दुनियादी वस्तुओं का मालिक, आसक्तियुक्त। having worldly attachment.

सकिं – क्रि॰ वि॰ – (सकृत्) एक बार। once.

सकीय – वि॰ – (स्वकीय) स्वकीय, अपना। one's own.

सकुण – पु॰ – (शकुन) पक्षी। bird.

सकुण्घी – पु॰ – (श्येन) बाज। a hawk.

सकुणी – स्त्री॰ – (शाकुन्तिका) मादा पक्षी। a female bird.

सकुण-जातक – (जा॰ सं॰ 36) बुद्धिमान पक्षीराज द्वारा पक्षियों को पूर्व चेतावनी देकर अग्नितांडव से बचाने की कथा। the story tells how the intelligent leader bird alerted his followers and saved them from jungle fire.

सकुण्घी-जातक – (जा॰ सं॰ 160) – इस कथा में बताया गया है कि बटेर ने अपनी चतुराई से बाज की जान ली। the story (No. 160) tells how a quail overcame a falcon with his intelligence.

सकुन्त – पु॰ – (शकुन्त) पक्षी, a bird.

√ सक्क – (भू॰) – (गमनार्थे) जाना। to go.

सक्क (1) – वि॰ – (शक्य) समर्थ, संभव। able, possible.

सक्क (2) – पु॰ – (शक्र) देवराज इन्द्र। the king of devas.

सक्क (3) – पु॰ – (शाक्य) शाक्य वंश में उत्पन्न। a man of the Śākya race.

सक्कच्च – पू॰ क्रि॰ – (सा √ कृ + ल्यप् – सत्कृत्य) भली-भांति करके। having honoured well or respected.

सक्कच्चकारी – पु॰ – (सत्कृत्यकारी) सावधानी बरतने वाला। one who acts carefully.

सक्कच्चं – क्रि॰ वि॰ – (सत्कृत्यम्) सावधानी-पूर्वक। carefully.

सक्कत – कृदन्त – (सत्कृत) सत्कृत, सम्मानित। honoured, duly attended.

सक्कत्त – न॰ – (शक्रत्व) शक्रता, देवेन्द्र शक्र की सी स्थिति। state of being a king of devas or demi-gods.

सक्करोति – क्रि॰ – (सत् √ कृ = सत्करोति) सत्कार करता है, आदर करता है, आतिथ्य करता है। honours, treats with respect.

सक्किरयते – क्रि॰ – (सत्क्रियते) सत्करोति का कर्मवाच्य, सत्कृत होता है। is being honoured, is being reputed.

सक्का – अव्यय – (शक्य) शक्य, सम्भव। possible.

सक्काय – पु॰ – (सत्काय) विद्यमान शरीर, सत्-काय। the existing body.

सक्काय-दिट्ठि – स्त्री॰ – (सत्काय-दृष्टि) आत्मदृष्टि। expression of individuality.

सक्कार – पु॰ – (सत्कार) आदर-सम्मान। honour, hospitality.

सक्कुणाति – क्रि॰ – (√ शक् - शक्नोति) समर्थ होता है। becomes able.

सक्कुणेय्यत्त – न॰ – (शक्यता) योग्यता, सम्भावना। ability, possibility.

सक्कोति – क्रि॰ – (शक्नोति) समर्थ होता है। becomes able.

सक्खर – न॰ – (मुद्रिका) नाम के मुहर वाली अँगूठी। a finger-ring bearing the name.

सक्खरा – स्त्री॰ – (शर्करा) शर्करा, शक्कर। sugar.

सक्खलि – स्त्री॰ – (**शष्कुलि**) पूड़ी, मीठी पूड़ी । a sort of cake or sweetmeat.

सक्खलिका – स्त्री॰ – (**शष्कुलिका**) देखें सक्खलि । see Sakkhali, छिद्र, the orifice (of the ear); a slice; the scale of fish.

सक्खि – अव्यय – (**साक्षि**) आमने-सामने । face to face, before one's eyes.

सक्खिक – वि॰ – (**साक्षिक**) साक्षी, गवाह । an eye-witness, witness.

सक्खि-दिट्ठ – वि॰ – (**साक्षि-दृष्ट**) आमने-सामने दिखाई दिया । seen personally, happened in one's presence, before one's eyes.

सक्खि-पुट्ठ – वि॰ – (**साक्षि-पृष्ट**) गवाह के रूप में पूछा गया । asked as a witness.

सक्खी – पु॰ – (**साक्षी**) गवाह । an eye-witness, witness.

सक्क-पुत्तिय – पु॰ – (**शाक्य-पुत्रक**) शाक्य-पुत्र, बौद्ध-भिक्षुओं को दिया गया नाम । belonging to the Śākya race, the name given to Buddhist monks.

सक्क-मुनि – (**शाक्य-मुनि**) भगवान् बुद्ध का एक नाम, शाक्य मुनि । Śākya-muni, a name given to the Buddha.

सक्क-सीह – पु॰ – (**शाक्य-सिंह**) गौतम बुद्ध का एक अधिवचन । a praiseful address to Buddha.

सख – पु॰ – (**सखा**) मित्र । friend.

सखि – (**सखा**) देखें सख । see Sakha.

सखिल – वि॰ – (**मृदुभाषी**) मधुर-भाषी । pleasant or charming in speech, sweet talking.

सख्य – न॰ – (**सख्य**) सखा-भाव, मैत्री । friendship.

सगब्भ – वि॰ – (**सगर्भा**) गर्भवती । pregnant woman.

सगाह – वि॰ – (**स + ग्राह**) भयानक जन्तुओं (घड़ियालों) से युक्त । full of ferocious animals like crocodiles.

सगामेय्य – वि॰ – (**सहग्रामिक**) एक ही ग्राम के । hailing from the same village.

सगारव – वि॰ – (**सगौरव**) गौरव सहित । with honour.

सगारवं – क्रि॰ वि॰ – (**सगौरवम्**) गौरव सहित । honourably.

सगारवता – स्त्री॰ – (**सगौरव**) आदर, गौरव, सम्मान । with respect or honour.

सगोत्त – वि॰ – (**सगोत्र**) एक ही गोत्र के । of the same lineage.

सग्ग – पु॰ – (**स्वर्ग**) स्वर्ग । heaven.

सग्ग-काय – पु॰ – (**स्वर्ग काय**) दिव्य सभा, स्वर्ग सभा । the divine assembly.

सग्ग-मग्ग – पु॰ – (**स्वर्ग मार्ग**) दिव्यपथ । a way to heaven.

सग्ग-लोक – पु॰ – (**स्वर्ग लोक**) दिव्यलोक, स्वर्ग-प्रदेश । the heavenly region.

सग्ग-संवत्तनिक – वि॰ – (**स्वर्ग सवर्त्तनिक**) स्वर्गाभिमुख । leading to heaven.

सग्ग-वासी – पु॰ – (**स्वर्गवासी**) देवतागण । of heavenly abode.

सग्गुण – पु॰ – (**सद्गुण**) सद्गुण । good quality.

सङ्क – (**भू॰**) – (**शङ्कायाम्**) सन्देह करता है । to doubt, to suspect.

सङ्कट – न॰ – (**दुर्गम**) अगम्य, संकीर्ण दर्रा, तंग स्थान । impassable place, narrow space.

सङ्कटीर – न॰ – (अवस्करः) कूड़े-कचरे का ढेर। a dust heap.

सङ्ड्ढति – क्रि॰ – (सङ्गृह्णाति) एकत्र करता है। collects, accumulates.

सङ्कति – क्रि॰ – (√ शङ्का - शङ्कते) संदेह करता है, शंका करता है। doubts, becomes uncertain.

सङ्कन्तति – क्रि॰ – (सं √ कृत् - सङ्कुन्तति) चारों ओर से काटता है। cuts all round.

सङ्कन्तिक – वि॰ – (सांक्रान्तिक) संक्रान्ति की स्थिति, एक अवस्था में से दूसरी में जाना। moving from one state or stage to another.

सङ्कन्तिक-रोग – पु॰ – (साङ्क्रान्तिक व्याधि) छूत की बीमारी। an epidemic.

सङ्कप्प – पु॰ – (संकल्प) इरादा। intention, purpose.

सङ्कप्प-जातक – (जा॰ सं॰ 251) – रानी के शरीर के नग्न भाग को देखकर रानी पर आसक्त हुए तापस की कथा। the story (No. 251) of an ascetic who became indulged in lust seeing the exposed parts of a queen's body.

सङ्कप्पेति – क्रि॰ – (सम् √ क्लृप् - सङ्कल्पते) संकल्प करता है, विचार करता है। thinks about.

सङ्कमति – क्रि॰ – (सङ्क्रमति) संक्रमण करता है, कायान्तरण करता है। passes over to, transmigrates.

सङ्कमन – न॰ – (सञ्चरण पथ) पारगमन सेतु, रास्ता, पुल। a passage, a bridge.

सङ्कम्पति – क्रि॰ – (सम् √ कम्प् = सङ्कम्पति) काँपता है। trembles.

सङ्कर – वि॰ – (शङ्कर) कल्याण कारक। blissful.

सङ्कर – पु॰ – (सङ्कर) मिश्रित। hybrid.

सङ्कलन – न॰ – (सङ्कलन) संग्रह। collection.

सङ्कस्स – पु॰ – (संकिसा) स्वर्ग में अभिधम्म का उपदेश देने के बाद भगवान बुद्ध की स्वर्गावतरण भूमि। Sankisā, the place where Buddha returned after preaching the Abhidhamma Tāvatimsa.

सङ्का – स्त्री॰ – (शङ्का) शंका, सन्देह। doubt, uncertainty.

सङ्कायति – क्रि॰ – (शङ्क्यते) शंका करता है। becomes doubtful or uncertain about.

सङ्कार – पु॰ – (अवस्कर) कूड़ा-करकट। rubbish, dust.

सङ्कार-कूट – पु॰ – (अवस्कर कूट) उचिछष्ट-राशि कूड़े-करकट का ढेर। rubbish heap, dust heap.

सङ्कार-चोल – न॰ – (अवस्कर कर्पटः) कूड़े-कचरे के ढेर पर से उठाया गया चीकड़। a rag picked up from rubbish heap.

सङ्काररट्ठान – न॰ – (अवस्कर-स्थान) कूड़ा-कचरा फेंकने की जगह। a dustbin, a rubbish heap.

सङ्कास – वि॰ – (सन्निभ) अनुरूप, सदृश, एक जैसा। similar.

सङ्कासना – स्त्री॰ – (सङ्काशना) व्याख्या। explanation.

सङ्किच्च-जातक – (जा॰ सं॰ 530) – इस कथा में एक राजकुमार को पितृ-हत्या के संकल्प से विरत रखने के प्रयास का वर्णन हुआ है। this is a story (No.

530) of a prince who is desisted from carrying out his plan to murder his father.

सङ्कित्तन – न॰ – **(सङ्कीर्त्तन)** संकीर्तन, प्रचारित करना। proclamation, making known.

सङ्किलिट्ठ – कृदन्त – **(बुद्धिष्ट संस्कृत-संकिलष्ट)** दूषित, मैला हुआ। soiled, corrupt.

सङ्किलिस्सति – क्रि॰ – **(बुद्धि॰ सं॰ संकिलिश्यते)** अशुद्ध होता है, मैला होता है। becomes soiled or impure.

सङ्किलिस्सन – न॰ – **(संकिलिश्यनृ)** अशुद्धि, मैल। impurity, defilement.

सङ्किलेस – पु॰ – **(बुद्धि॰ सं॰ संकिलेश)** चित्त-मैल। impurity, defilement.

सङ्किलेसिक – वि॰ – **(बुद्धि॰ सं॰ – संकिलेशन)** प्रदूषक, हानिकारक। corrupting, baneful.

सङ्की – वि॰ – **(शङ्की)** सन्देह करने वाला। doubtful, one who doubts or suspects.

सङ्कु – पु॰ – **(शङ्कु)** मेख, खूँटा। a stake, a spike.

सङ्कु-पथ – **(शङ्कु-पथ)** खूँटों की सहायता से चलने लायक मार्ग। a path to be crossed with the help of stakes.

सङ्कुचति – क्रि॰ – **(सम् √ कुच = सङ्कुचति)** संकोच करता है। feels shy.

सङ्कुचन – न॰ – **(सङ्कुचन)** सिकुड़न। shrinkage.

सङ्कु-चित – वि॰ – **(सङ्कुचित)** सिकुड़ा। shrunk, clenched.

सङ्कुटित – वि॰ – **(सन्दिग्ध)** सन्देहमय। doubtful, suspicious.

सङ्कुपित – कृदन्त – **(सङ्कुपित)** क्रुद्ध। enraged.

सङ्कुल – वि॰ – **(सङ्कुल)** भरा हुआ, भीड़ सहित। full of, crowded.

सङ्केत (1) – पु॰ – **(सङ्केत)** निशान, चिह्न। a mark.

सङ्केत (2) – न॰ – **(सङ्केतमृ)** नायक-नायिका की मिलनस्थली, सहेट। rendezvous, meeting place of couples.

सङ्केत-कम्म – न॰ – **(सङ्केत-कर्म)** समझौता। engagement.

संकोच – पु॰ – **(सङ्कोच)** झिझक, हिचकिचाहट। hesitation, contraction.

सङ्कोचेति – क्रि॰ – **(सम् √ कुच् = सङ्कुचति)** हिचकिचाता है, झिझकता है। contracts, hesitates, distorts.

सङ्क्षोप – पु॰ – **(सङ्क्षोप)** कोप, व्यवधान, विरोध। disturbance, agitation.

सङ्ख – पु॰ – **(शङ्ख)** शंख। a conch-shell, one of the treasures of Kuvera

सङ्खट्ठी – पु॰ – **(सङ्कृष्ठी)** कुष्ट रोगी, कोढ़ी। leper.

सङ्ख-थाल – पु॰ – **(शङ्ख-स्थाल)** शंख-थाली। a vessel made of conch-shell.

सङ्ख-धम – पु॰ – **(शङ्खध्माता)** शंख बजाने वाला। a conch blower.

सङ्ख-नख – पु॰ – **(शङ्खनक)** छोटा शंख। a small conch-shell.

सङ्ख-मुण्डिक – न॰ – **(शङ्ख-मुण्डिक)** त्रास देने की विधि जिसमें अपराधी का सिर मुंडाकर घुमाया जाता है। a kind of torture.

सङ्ख-जातक – (जा॰ सं॰ 442) – यह कथा कृतज्ञता की महिमा का वर्णन करती है। the story (No. 442) describes about the reward of gratefulness.

सङ्खत – कृदन्त – **(संस्कृत)** संस्कारित, सुसंस्कृत, समुत्पन्न। cultured, conditioned, produced by a cause.

सङ्ख-धम्म-जातक – (जा॰ सं॰ 60) – कथा में पढ़िये पुत्र द्वारा पिता को बार बार शंख बजाने से रोकने का रहस्य। the story (No. 60) tells how a father was stopped from blowing the conch again and again by his son.

सङ्ख-पाल-जातक – (जा॰ सं॰ 524) – तपस्वी द्वारा शंखपाल नाग को धर्मोपदेश दे की कथा। the story (No. 524) tells about the preaching of an ascetic to Śaṅkhapāla Nāga.

सङ्खय – पु॰ – **(संक्षय)** हानि, पतन, विनाश, हानि। loss, destruction, consumption.

सङ्खरण – **(संस्करण)** मरम्मत, तैयारी। restoration, preparation.

सङ्खरोति – क्रि॰ – **(संस्करोति)** मरम्मत करता है, संस्कार करता है। restores, prepares, puts together.

सङ्खला – स्त्री॰ – **(शृङ्खला)** अर्गला, हाथी के पाँव की जंजीर। the chain on an elephant's foot.

सङ्खलिका – स्त्री॰ – **(शृङ्खलिका)** बेड़ी। a fetter, bondage.

सङ्खा – स्त्री॰ – **(संख्या)** अंक, गिनती। a number, calculation, counting.

सङ्खात – कृ॰ – **(संख्यातभी)** (संख्यात) (अमुक) नाम का, समस्त पद के रूप में प्रयुक्त। in compounds used in the sense of so-called or such named.

सङ्खादति – क्रि॰ – **(सङ्खादति / √ चर्व - चर्वति)** चबाता है। masticates.

सङ्खान/संख्यान – न॰ – **(संख्यान)** गिनती। calculation, counting.

सङ्खय – पू॰ क्रि॰ – **(सञ्चिनत्य / सङ्ख्याम)** विचार करके, मनन करके। having deep consideration.

सङ्खार – पु॰ – **(संस्कार)** परिष्करण, दीक्षा, संस्कार। culture, impressions, consecration.

सङ्खारकखन्ध – पु॰ – **(संस्कार-स्कन्ध)** संस्कार, समुच्चय। the aggregate of mental coefficients.

सङ्खार-दुक्ख – न॰ – **(संस्कार-दुःख)** भौतिकतावादी जीवन के दोष। the evil of material life.

सङ्खार-लोक – पु॰ – **(संस्कार-लोक)** सम्पूर्ण प्रकृति। the whole creation.

सङ्खित – कृदन्त – **(संक्षिप्त)** संक्षिप्त। abridged.

सङ्खिपति – क्रि॰ – **(संक्षिपति)** संक्षेप करता है। shortens, abridges, curtails.

सङ्खुभति – क्रि॰ – **(सम् √ क्षुभ् = संक्षुभति)** क्षुब्ध होता है। becomes agitated.

सङ्खुभन – न॰ – **(संक्षोभ)** क्षोभ। stirring, agitation.

सङ्खेप – पु॰ – **(संक्षेप)** संक्षेप, सारांश। abridgement, abstract.

सङ्खेय्य – वि॰ – **(संख्य)** जिसकी गिनती की जा सके। calculable, which may be counted.

सङ्ख्येय्य-परिवेण – पु॰ – (संङ्ख्येय्य परिवेण) सागल (स्यालकोट) का वह विहार, जिसमें राजा मिलिन्द के साथ शास्त्रार्थ करने वाले भिक्षु नागसेन रहते थे। a monastery in Syālkoṭa (Sāgala) where Nāgasena lived, Milinda visited the palce for discussions.

सङ्क्षोभ – पु॰ – (संक्षोभ) क्षोभ, हलचल। an agitation, a disturbance.

संख्या-भेद – पु॰ – (संख्या-भेद) संख्या-विशेष जैसे एक सहस्र। a particular number as one thousand.

सङ्ग – पु॰ – (सङ्ग) आसक्ति। attachment, clinging.

सङ्गच्छति – क्रि॰ – (सम् + गच्छति) साथ-साथ चलता है, सहयोग करता है। walks together, cooperates.

सङ्गणिका – स्त्री॰ – (सङ्गणिका) संगत, समाज। society.

सङ्गणिकाराम – वि॰ – (सङ्गणिकारत) देखें सङ्गणिकारत। see Saṅgaṇikārata.

सङ्गणिकारत – वि॰ – (सङ्गणिकारत) जिसे समाज में रहना पसन्द हो। delighting in society.

सङ्गण्हाति – क्रि॰ – (सम् √गृह् = सङ्गृह्णाति) संग्रह करता है, शालीनता का व्यवहार करता है। collects, compiles, treats kindly.

सङ्गम – पु॰ – (सङ्गम्) मेल। unity.

सङ्गर – पु॰ – (सङ्गर) युद्ध, संघर्ष, प्रतिज्ञा, विक्रय, आदि अर्थों में। battle, quarrel, transaction of sale, promise, knowledge, etc.

सङ्गह – पु॰ – (सङ्ग्रह) संग्रह, आतिथ्य। collection, compilation, kindly, treatment.

सङ्गति – स्त्री॰ – (सङ्गति) साथ रहना। association with.

√सङ्गाम – चु॰ – (युद्धे) युद्ध करना। to fight.

सङ्ग्राम – (पु॰) – (सङ्ग्राम्) संग्राम, युद्ध करना। fight, battle.

सङ्ग्रामावचर-जातक – (जा॰ सं॰ 182) – कथा बताती है कि किस प्रकार फीलवान के वचनों से उत्साहित होकर एक हताश हाथी ने विजय प्राप्त कर ली। the story (No. 182) tells how a scared elephant achieved victory by the encouragement of his trainer.

सङ्ग्रामेति – क्रि॰ – (सङ्ग्रामयति) संग्राम करता है। fights, comes into conflict.

सङ्गायति – क्रि॰ – (सङ्गायति) संगायन करता है। chants, rehearses.

सङ्गह – पु॰ – (सङ्ग्रह) संग्रह। a collection.

सङ्गहक – वि॰ – (सङ्ग्राहक) संग्रहकर्ता, संग्रह करने वाला। one who collects or holds together.

सङ्गीति – स्त्री॰ – (सङ्गीति) तिपिटक के वचनों का संगायन करने के लिए अर्हतों का सम्मेलन। a conference of the Buddhist clergy in order to settle questions of doctrine.

सङ्गीति-कारक – पु॰ – (सङ्गीति-कारक) संगीति करने वाले अर्हत् गण। the elders who held the conference or seminar.

सङ्घ – पु॰ – (सङ्घ) समूह, परिषद, भिक्षुओं की मण्डली। a multitude, an assemblage of the Buddhist clergy.

सङ्घ-कम्म – न॰ – (**सङ्घ-कर्म**) भिक्षु-संघ के सदस्यों द्वारा किया गया धार्मिक कार्य। an act performed by a chapter of Buddhist monks.

सङ्घ-गत – वि॰ – (**सङ्घ-गत**) संघ को गया (दान)। gone into or given to the community.

सङ्घ-थेर – पु॰ – (**सङ्घ-थेर**) संघ का ज्येष्ठतम भिक्षु। the senior-most monk of a congregation.

सङ्घ-भत्त – न॰ – (**सङ्घ-भत्त**) संघ को कराया गया भोजन। food given to the community.

सङ्घ-भेद – पु॰ – (**सङ्घ-भेद**) संघ में फूट। dissension among the order.

सङ्घ-भेदक – पु॰ – (**सङ्घ-भेदक**) संघ में भेद करने वाला। one who causes dissension in the community of monks.

सङ्घ-मामक – वि॰ – (**सङ्घ-मामक**) संघ के प्रति ममत्व रखने वाला। devoted to the community.

सङ्घटेति – क्रि॰ – (**सम् √घट् = सङ्घट्टते**) संघटन करता है। joins together.

सङ्घट्टन – न॰ – (**संघट्टन**) संगठन, चोट पहुँचाना। contact, collision.

सङ्घट्टेति – क्रि॰ – (**संघ्+ घट्टयति**) चोट पहुँचाता है, उत्तेजित करता है। knocks against, provokes by taunting or scoffing.

सङ्घमित्ता-थेरी – स्त्री॰ – (**सङ्घमित्रा**) अशोक पुत्री तथा महास्थविर महेन्द्र की बहन। उसका जन्म उज्जयिनी में हुआ था। वही बुद्ध गया से बोधि-वृक्ष की शाखा लेकर सिंहल द्वीप पहुँची थी। the daughter of Aśoka and sister of Mahendra, she was born in Ujjayinī, a branch of the *bodhi* tree was carried by her to Ceylon.

सङ्घाट – पु॰ – (**सङ्घात**) जोड़, मेल, बेड़ा। junction, union, a raft.

सङ्घाटी – स्त्री॰ – (**सङ्घाटी**) बौद्ध भिक्षु के तीन चीवरों में से एक, उपरला चीवर। the upper robe of a Buddhist monk.

सङ्घात – पु॰ – (**सम्यक् घात**) आक्रमण, उँगलियों का चटखाना, संग्रह। attack, snapping (of fingers), accumulation.

सङ्घिक – पु॰ – (**साङ्घिक**) संघ-सम्बन्धी, संघ की मिल्कियत। belonging to the order.

सङ्घी – वि॰ – (**सङ्घिन्**) संघ या समूह का नेता। the leader of a group or community.

सङ्घुट्ठ – कृदन्त – (**सम् √घुष + क्त = सङ्घुष्ट**) घोषित, गूँजता हुआ। resounding with, proclaimed.

सचित – न॰ – (**स्वचित्त**) अपना चित्त। one's own mind.

सचित्तक – वि॰ – (**सचित्तक**) सचेतन, चेतनायुक्त। endowed with mind.

सचित्तक – वि॰ – (**सचित्तकः**) संमनस्क, समान चित्त वाला। of the same mind.

सचिव – पु॰ – (**सचिव**) अमात्य, राजा का मन्त्री। minister.

सचे – अव्यय – (**सचे / चेत्**) यदि, अगर। if.

सचेतन – वि॰ – (सचेतन) चेतना-युक्त, प्राणवान। animate, conscious.

सच्च – न॰ – (सत्य) सत्य, सच, (वि॰) सत्य (वचन)। truth (adj.) true.

सच्च-अभिसमय – पु॰ – (सत्य + अभि समय) सत्य का ज्ञान। comprehension of the reality.

सच्चकार – पु॰ – (सत्यकार) प्रतिज्ञा। a pledge.

सच्च-किरिया – स्त्री॰ – (सत्य + क्रिया) किसी सत्य बात की बाजी लगाकर कोई कामना करना। a declaration on oath.

सच्चङ्किर-जातक – (जा॰ सं॰ 73) – एक दुष्ट तथा अकृतज्ञ राजकुमार के दुःखद अवसान की कथा। it is a story (No. 73) of an ungrateful wicked prince who met an awful end.

सच्च-पटिवेध – पु॰ – (सत्य + प्रतिवेध) सत्य का साक्षात्कार। comprehension of the reality.

सच्चबद्ध – व्यक्तिवाचक संज्ञा – (सत्यबद्ध) श्रावस्ती तथा सूनापरन्त के बीच का बुद्धयुगीन पर्वत। a hill between Śrāvastī and Sūnāparanta in Buddha's period.

सच्च-वाचा – स्त्री॰ – (सत्य वाक्) सत्य वाणी। a truthful word.

सच्चवादी – पु॰ – (सत्यवादी) सत्य बोलने वाला। one who speaks the truth.

सच्च-सन्ध – वि॰ – (सत्य-सन्ध) विश्वसनीय। reliable.

सच्चापेति – क्रि॰ – (सत्यापयति) शपथ दिलाता है। binds with an oath.

सच्छि – अव्यय – (साक्षात्) प्रत्यक्ष। apparently.

सच्छिकरण – न॰ – (साक्षात्कार) प्रत्यक्षानुभव करना, साक्षात् करना। realization, experiencing.

सच्छिकरणीय – वि॰ – (साक्षिकरणीय) साक्षात् करने योग्य। fit to be realized.

सच्छिकत – कृदन्त – (साक्षिकृत) साक्षात्-कृत। experienced by oneself.

सच्छिकरोति – क्रि॰ – (साक्षिकरोति) साक्षात करता है। realizes, experiences by oneself.

सच्छिकिरिया – स्त्री॰ – (साक्षिक्रिया) देखें सच्छिकरण। see Sacchikaraṇa.

√सज (भ्वा॰) – (अलिङ्ग्ने) गले लगाना। to embrace.

√सज – (दि॰) – (सङ्गे) आसक्त होना। to entice, to cling.

सजति – क्रि॰ – (√सञ्ज् - सजति) गले लगाता है। embraces.

सजन – पु॰ – (स्व॰जन) रिश्तेदार, स्वकीय जन। kinsman, one's own men.

सजातिक – वि॰ – (सजातिक) उसी जाति या नस्ल का। of the same race or nation.

सजीव – वि॰ – (सजीव) प्राणवान, जीवन-युक्त। endowed with life.

सजोति-भूत – वि॰ – (स + ज्योति + भूत) प्रज्वलित। ablaze, aglow.

√सज्ज – (भू॰) – (अर्जने) उपार्जन करना। to earn.

सज्जति – क्रि॰ – (√सञ्ज् - सजति) चिपटता है, आसक्त होता है। clings to, becomes attached.

सज्जन – न॰ – (√सस्ज् + णिच् + ल्युट्) आसक्ति, सजावट, तैयारी, (पु॰), सत्पुरुष।

attachment, decoration, preparation.

सज्जित – कृदन्त – (√ **सस्ज्** + **णिच्** + **क्त**) तैयार हुआ। prepared, decorated.

सज्जु – अव्यय – (**सद्यः/सपति**) तुरन्त, उसी समय। at the moment, immediately.

सज्जुकं – क्रि. वि. – (**सत्त्वर**) शीघ्रता से। quickly.

सज्जु-दुम्म – पु. – (**शाल-द्रुमः**) शाल (सेखुआ) का पेड़। the tree *Shorea Robusta* (*Vatica Robusta*) also called *sāl* or *sākhū* in Hindi.

सज्जुलस – पु. – (**शाल-रस**) राल या करायल। resin.

सज्जेति – क्रि. – (√ **सस्ज - सज्जयति**) तैयारी करता है, सजाता है। prepares, decorates.

सज्झाय – पु. – (**अधि** √ **इ = अध्याय**) अध्ययन, पाठ। study, lesson.

सज्झायति – क्रि. – (**सम्** + **अछीते**) अध्ययन करता है, दोहराता है, मिलकर पाठ करता है। recites, studies.

सज्झायना – स्त्री. – (**सहाध्ययन**) मिलकर पाठ करना, अध्ययन करना। recitation, study.

सज्झु – न. – (**रजतम्**) रुप्य, कलधौत, चाँदी। silver.

सज्झुमय – वि. – (**रजतमय**) चाँदी का बना। made of silver.

सञ्चय – पु. – (**सञ्चय**) एकत्रीकरण, इकट्ठा करना। accumulation, quantity.

सञ्चरण – न. – (**सञ्चरण**) विचरण, विचरना, घूमना-फिरना। wandering about.

सञ्चरति – क्रि. – (**सम्** √ **चर् = सञ्चरति**) विचरता है, घूमता है। goes about, wanders.

सञ्चरित्त – न. – (**सञ्चरित्व**) सन्देशों का ले जाना। communication.

सञ्चार – पु. – (**सञ्चार**) रास्ता, हलचल, संचरण। passage, movement, wandering.

सञ्चारण – न. – (**सञ्चारण**) चलने के लिए अथवा कुछ करने के लिए प्रेरित करना। causing to move or act.

सञ्चारेति – क्रि. – (**सञ्चारयति**) संचार करता है। causes to move about.

सञ्चलति – क्रि. – (**सञ्चलति**) अस्थिर होता है, उत्तेजित होता है। becomes unsteady or agitated.

सञ्चलन – न. – (**सञ्चलन**) हलचल, उत्तेजना। agitation.

सञ्चिच्च – अव्यय – (**सम्** + √ **चिन्त** + **ल्यप् = सञ्चिन्त्य**) जान-बूझकर। knowingly, after deep thinking.

सञ्चित – कृदन्त – (**सञ्चित**) एकत्रित। accumulated.

सञ्चिनन – न. – (**सञ्चयन**) एकत्रीकरण, इकट्ठा करना। accumulation.

सञ्चिनाति – क्रि. – (**सञ्चिनोति**) इकट्ठा करता है, चयन करता है। accumulates.

सञ्चिण्ण – कृदन्त – (**सम्** + √ **चि** + **क्त** = **सञ्चित**) संगृहीत, अभ्यस्त आचरित। accumulated, practised.

सञ्चूर्णेति – क्रि॰ – (सञ्चूर्णयति) पीस डालता है, चूर्ण बना देता है। crushes, powders.

सञ्चेतना – स्त्री॰ – (सञ्चेतना) चेतना, इरादा। cognition, intention.

सञ्चेतनिक – वि॰ – (सञ्चेतना पूर्वकम्) जान-बूझकर। intentional.

सञ्चेतेति – क्रि॰ – (सञ्चेतयते) सोचता है, सूझ-बूझ दिखाता है। thinks, perceives.

सञ्चोदित – कृ॰ – (सम् + √चुद् + क्त = सञ्चोदित) प्रेरित, उत्तेजित, उत्साहित। instigated, excited, stimulated.

सञ्चोपन – न॰ – (सञ्चोपन) हटाना, स्थानान्तरित करना। removal, changing of the place.

सञ्छन्न – कृदन्त – (सञ्छन्न) ढका हुआ, भरा हुआ। covered with, full of.

सञ्छादेति – क्रि॰ – (आ √छद् = आच्छादयति) ढकता है, छत डालता है। covers, thatches.

सञ्छिन्दति – क्रि॰ – (सम् √छिद् = सञ्छिन्नत्ति) काट डालता है, नष्ट कर डालता है। cuts, destroys.

√सज्ज – (भू॰) – (सङ्गे) आसक्त होना। to cling.

सज्जग्घति – क्रि॰ – (परिहसति) हँसता है, मजाक करता है। laughs, cracks jokes, makes fun of.

सज्जनन – न॰ – (सम् √जन् - ल्युट् = सज्जनन) उत्पत्ति। birth.

सज्जनेति – क्रि॰ – (सम् √जन् = सज्जजन्ति) उत्पन्न करता है, पैदा करता है। produces, gives birth to.

सञ्जय-वेलट्ठिपुत्त – पु॰ – (वेलट्ठिपुत्र सञ्जय) बुद्ध के समकालीन छह प्रमुख दार्शनिकों में से एक जो अनिश्चयवाद के प्रवर्तक आचार्य थे। one of the six famous heretical teachers of Buddha's days; his doctrine is known for evasion of problems and the suspensions of judgements.

सञ्जात – कृदन्त – (सञ्जात) उत्पन्न, उठा, पैदा हुआ। produced, born.

सञ्जाति – स्त्री॰ – (सञ्जाति) उत्पत्ति, जन्म ग्रहण करना। production, taking birth.

सञ्जानन – न॰ – (सञ्जानन) पहचानना, जानना। recognition, perception.

सञ्जानाति – क्रि॰ – (सम् + जानाति) पहचानता है, अनुभव करता है। recognizes, becomes aware of.

सञ्जानित – कृदन्त – (सञ्जानित) जान लिया गया, पहचान लिया गया। recognized.

सञ्जायति – क्रि॰ – (सञ्जायते) जन्म ग्रहण करता है, पैदा होता है, उत्पन्न होता है। takes birth, becomes born, or produced.

सञ्जीव-जातक – (जा॰ सं॰ 150) – ऐसे साधक के दुर्भाग्य की कथा जो मुर्दों को जिलाने का मन्त्र जानता था किन्तु मार पाने का नहीं। the story (No. 150) tells about the ill fate of a pupil who had learnt a spell for raising the dead but not the counter spell.

सञ्जीवन – वि॰ – (सञ्जीवन) पुनर्जीवन, प्राण-संचार। reviving.

सज्झा – स्त्री॰ – (सन्ध्या) सायं, सन्ध्या काल। the evening.

सज्झा-धन – पु॰ – (सन्ध्या-धन) शाम के बादल। evening cloud.

सज्झातप – पु॰ – (सन्ध्यातप) शाम की धूप। evening sun, light.

सञ्ञत्त – कृदन्त – (संज्ञप्त) प्रेरित, सूचित। induced, talked over, convinced.

सञ्ञत्ति – स्त्री॰ – (संज्ञप्ति) सूचना, शान्त भाव। information, pacification.

सञ्ञा – स्त्री॰ – (संज्ञा) जानने की मानसिक क्रिया, नाम, इशारा। sense, perception, name, gesture.

सञ्ञा-क्खन्ध – पु॰ – (संज्ञा-स्कन्ध) पाँच स्कन्धों में से तीसरा, संज्ञा स्कन्ध। the aggregate of perception.

सञ्ञापक – पु॰ – (संज्ञापक) ज्ञापन या सूचना देने वाला। who makes one understand.

सञ्ञापन – न॰ – (संज्ञापन) जानकारी देना, सूचित करना। convincing, making known.

सञ्ञाण – न॰ – (संज्ञान) संकेत, इशारा। a mark or sign.

सञ्ञापेति – क्रि॰ – (संज्ञापयति) प्रकट करता है, सूचित करता है। makes known, convinces.

सञ्ञित – वि॰ – (संज्ञित) संज्ञा वाला, नाम वाला। so-called, named.

सञ्ञी – वि॰ – (संज्ञी) संज्ञावान, होश में। conscious, having perception.

सट्ठि – स्त्री॰ – (षष्टि) साठ। sixty.

सट्ठिहायन – वि॰ – (षष्टि वर्षीय) साठ वर्ष का। sixty years old.

सट्टुं – कृदन्त – (√सृज्+तुमुन्=स्रष्टुम्) त्याग देने के लिए, छोड़ देने के लिए। to give up, to dismiss.

√सठ – (भू॰) – (केतवे) ठगना। to cheat.

सठ – वि॰ – (शठ) प्रवंचक, ठग। a cheat, crafty, fraudulent.

सठता – स्त्री॰ – (शठता) दुर्जनता, शठता। wickedness.

सणति – क्रि॰ – (√स्वन् - स्वनति) शोर मचाता है। makes a noise.

सण्ठपन – न॰ – (संस्थपन) स्थापित करना। adjustment, establishing.

सण्ठपेति – क्रि॰ – (संस्थापयति) स्थापित करता है। settles, adjusts, establishes.

सण्ठहन – न॰ – (पुनर्जन्म) दुबारा पैदाइश, दुबारा उत्पत्ति। re-creation, coming again into existence.

सण्ठाति – क्रि॰ – (संस्थाति) ठहरता है, स्थित होता है। remains, stands still, becomes established.

सण्ठान – स्त्री॰ – (संस्थान) आकार-प्रकार, संस्थान, स्थिति। shape, form, position.

सण्ठित – कृदन्त – (संस्थित) स्थित, संस्थापित। settled, established in.

सण्ठिति – स्त्री॰ – (संस्थिति) स्थिरता, संस्थिति। stability, firmness, settling.

सण्ड – पु॰ – (षण्ड) झुण्ड, समूह। a grove, cluster.

सण्डास – पु॰ – (सन्दश) खण्डासी, सँडसी। pincers, tweezers.

सण्ह – वि॰ – (श्लक्ष्ण) मसृण, चिकना, मृदु। smooth, soft, delicate.

सण्हकरणी – स्त्री॰ – (क्षुद् + करणी) चक्की, खरेल। grinding stone.

सण्हेति – क्रि॰ – (श्लक्ष्णयति) पीसता है, चूर्ण बनाता है। grinds, powders.

सत – वि॰ – (सत्त्व) सतोगुण। one amongst the three attributes of *prakṛti* (the other two are *rajas* and *tamas*).

सत – न॰ – (शत) सौ। a hundred.

सतक – न॰ – (शतक) सौ या सौ चीजें, सौ व्यक्तियों या वस्तुओं का समूह। group of a hundred.

सतक्ककु – वि॰ – (शत + अक्षक) सौ या सौ लकीरों वाला। having a hundred projections.

सतक्खत्तुं – क्रि॰ वि॰ – (शतकृत्त्वा) सौ बार। a hundred times.

सतधा – क्रि॰ वि॰ – (शतधा) सौ तरह से। in a hundred ways.

सत-पाक – न॰ – (शतपाक) सौ बार पकाया हुआ (तेल)। medicated oil boiled and purified hundred times.

सतपुञ्जलक्खणं – वि॰ – (शतपुण्यलक्षण) अनेक पुण्य चिह्नों वाला। having the signs of innumerable merits.

सत-पोरिस – वि॰ – (शतपुरुषकम्) सौ आदमियों की ऊँचाई जितना। of the height of a hundred men.

सत-सहस्स – न॰ – (शतसहस्रम्) लाख। a hundred thousand.

सतत – वि॰ – (सतत) लगातार, अनवरत। constant, continual.

सततं – क्रि॰ वि॰ – (सततम्) लगातार, निरन्तर, सदैव। constantly, continually.

सतधम्म-जातक – (जा॰ सं॰ 279) – क्षुधार्त ब्राह्मण द्वारा चाण्डाल की जूठन खाने की कथा। the story (No. 279) of a hungry brāhmaṇa who ate impure food of a cāṇḍāla (lowest of low caste).

सत-पत्त – न॰ – (शतपत्र) कमल, (पु॰), कठफोड़वा। a lotus (m.) a woodpecker.

सतपत्त-जातक – (जा॰ सं॰ 179) – एक ऐसे व्यक्ति की कथा जो शत्रु और मित्र की परख कर पाने में अक्षम था। the story (No. 179) of such a man who did not know how to distinguish between friend and foe.

सतपदी – पु॰ – (शतपदी) कर्णजलौका, कनखजूरा। centipede.

सत-भिसज – पु॰ – (शतभिषा) सत्ताईस नक्षत्रों में से एक। one amongst the 27 *nakṣatras* Śatabhiṣā.

सतमूली – स्त्री॰ – (शतमूली) शतावरी, इन्दीर्ण, सतावर। *Asparagus* plant — a rejuvenating herb.

सतरंसी – पु॰ – (शतरश्मि) सूर्य। the sun.

सत-वक – पु॰ – (शतवक) मछली विशेष। a kind of fish.

सतावरी – पु॰ – (शतावरी) नारायणी, बहुसुता, शतावरी। a kind of herb named *Asparagus*.

सति – स्त्री॰ – (स्मृति) स्मृति, जागरूकता। memory, mindfulness.

सतिन्द्रिय – न॰ – (स्मृतीन्द्रिय) जागरूकता। mindfulness.

सति-पट्ठान – न॰ – (स्मृति + उपस्थान) स्मृति का उपयोग। the application of mindfulness.

सतिमन्तु – वि॰ – (स्मृतिमान्) स्मृतिमान, विचारवान। thoughtful, careful.

सति-वोसग्ग – पु॰ – (स्मृति-उत्सर्ग) प्रमाद। inattention, negligence.

सति-सम्पञ्ञ – न॰ – (स्मृति + सम्पन्नता) जागरूकता। mindfulnss.

सति-सम्बोज्झङ्ग – पु॰ – (स्मृति सम्बोधि + अङ्ग) सम्बोधि-अङ्ग-स्वरूप स्मृति। self-possession as a constituent of enlightenment.

सति-सम्मोस – पु॰ – (स्मृति-लोप) विस्मृति। loss of memory, forgetfulness.

सति-सम्मोह – पु॰ – (स्मृति-सम्मोह) देखें सतिसम्मोस। see Satisammosa.

सति – स्त्री॰ – (सती) पतिव्रता स्त्री। a chaste woman.

सतेकिच्छ – पु॰ – (चिकित्स्य) जिसकी चिकित्सा हो सके, जिसे क्षमा किया जा सके। curable, pardonable.

सत्त (1) – पु॰ – (सत्त्व) सत्व, प्राणी। a creature, living being.

सत्त (2)– वि॰ – (सप्त) सात। seven.

सत्त (3) – कृदन्त – (सज् + क्त = सत्त) आसक्त। clinging to, attached.

सत्तक – न॰ – (सप्तक) सात का समूह, सप्तक। a group of seven.

सत्तक्खत्तुं – क्रि॰ वि॰ – (सप्तकृत्वा) सात बार। seven times.

सत्त-गुण – वि॰ – (सप्तगुण) सात-गुना। sevenfold.

सत्त-तन्ति – वि॰ – (सप्तन्त्री) सात तारों वाली (वीणा)। having seven strings.

सत्त-ताल-मत्त – वि॰ – (सप्त ताल मात्रक) ताड़ के सात पेड़ों की ऊँचाई जितना। about the height of seven palm trees.

सत्त-तिंसा – स्त्री॰ – (सप्तत्रिंशत्) सैंतीस। thirty-seven.

सत्तदस – वि॰ – (सप्तदश) सत्तरह, सत्रह। seventeen.

सत्त-पण्णी – पु॰ – (सप्तपर्णी) सप्तपर्णी वृक्ष। the male plant *Alstonia scholaris*, the sensitive female plant *Mimosa Pudica*.

सत्तपण्णी-गुहा – स्त्री॰ – (सत्तपर्णी-गुहा) राजगृह की प्रसिद्ध गुफा, जिसमें प्रथम बौद्ध संगीति हुई थी। a cave in Rājagṛha, the first council was held there in a hall erected by Ajātaśatru.

सत्त-भूमक – वि॰ – (सप्तसौध) सात तल्ले वाला (भवन)। consisting of seven storeys.

सत्त-महासर – पु॰ – (सप्त महासागर) अनोत्त आदि सात महान् सरोवर। seven big lakes.

सत्त-रतन – न॰ – (सप्तरत्न) सात मूल्यवान पदार्थ – सोना, चाँदी, मूँगा, मोती, हीरा, माणिक्य (लाल) और लानवर्द। seven kinds of precious things, viz., gold, silver, pearls, rubies, lapis-lazuli, coral and diamond.

सत्त-रत्त – न॰ – (सप्तरात्र / सप्ताह) सप्ताह। a week.

सत्तरस – वि॰ – (सप्तदश) सत्रह। seventeen.

सत्तला – स्त्री॰ – (सिता) नवमल्लिका, वनचन्द्रिका, सौम्या। Jasminum Sambac, a kind of jasmine.

सत्त-वंक – पु॰ – (सप्तवङ्क) मछली विशेष। a kind of fish.

सत्त-वस्सिक – वि॰ – (सप्त वार्षिक) सात वर्ष का। seven years old.

सत्त-वीसति – स्त्री॰ – (सप्तविंशति) सत्ताईस। twenty-seven.

सत्त-सट्टि – स्त्री॰ – (सप्तषष्टिः) सड़सठ। sixty-seven.

सत्त-सत्तति – स्त्री॰ – (सप्तसप्तति) सतहत्तर। seventy-seven.

सत्तसत्तति – स्त्री॰ – (सप्तसप्तति) सतहत्तर। seventy-seven.

सत्तम – वि॰ – (सप्तम) सातवाँ। seventh.

सत्तमी – स्त्री॰ – (सप्तमी) अधिकरण कारक की सप्तमी विभक्ति, सप्तमी तिथि। seventh phase of the moon from new moon and full-moon.

सत्ता – स्त्री॰ – (सत्ता) अस्तित्व। existence.

सत्ताह – न॰ – (सप्ताह) सप्ताह। a week.

सत्ति – स्त्री॰ – (शक्ति) (1) शक्ति, योग्यता, सामर्थ्य, (2) बरछी। (1) ability, power, strength, (2) a spear.

सत्ति-सूल – न॰ – (शक्ति-शूल) बरछी की नोंक। the stake of a spear.

सत्तिगुम्ब-जातक – (जा॰ सं॰ 503) – यह कथा संगति का प्रभाव बताती है कि डाकुओं के बीच पाले गए तोते ने राजा को मार डालने की बातें की जबकि तपस्वियों के बीच पले तोते ने राजा का स्वागत किया। the story (No. 503) explains how different upbringing accounts for the difference in the nature of the real brothers too.

सत्तु (1) – पु॰ – (शत्रु) शत्रु, वैरी। enemy.

सत्तु (2) – पु॰ – (सक्तुः) सत्तू, सतुआ। parched flour.

सत्तु-भस्ता – स्त्री॰ – (सक्तु – भस्त्रा) सत्तु की थैली। a leather bag full of parched flour.

सत्तुभस्ता-जातक – (जा॰ सं॰ 402) – एक साँप ब्राह्मण की सत्तुओं की थैली में घुस गया। the story (No. 402) tells how a snake enter into the parched flour bag, of a brāhmana.

सत्थ (1) – न॰ – (शस्त्र) शस्त्र, कारवाँ। weapon.

सत्थ (2) – न॰ – (सार्थ) सार्थ, काफिला, कारवाँ। a caravan, group of travellers.

सत्थ (3) – न॰ – (शास्त्र) शास्त्र। a science or an art.

सत्थक – न॰ – (शस्त्रक) छुरी, छुरिका। a pen-knife.

सत्थ-कम्म – न॰ – (शस्त्र-कर्म) शल्य क्रिया। surgical operation.

सत्थक-वात – पु॰ – (शल्यवात) तीव्र वेदना। unbearable pain.

सत्थ-गमनीय – वि॰ – (सार्थ-गम्य) कारवाँ के साथ जाने लायक रास्ता। (a path) to be passed with a caravan.

सत्थ-वाह – पु॰ – (सार्थवाह) कारवाँ का मुखिया। a caravan leader.

सत्थि – स्त्री॰ – (सक्थि) जाँघ। the thigh.

सत्थु – पु॰ – (शास्ता) सदुपदेशक, शास्ता। teacher, master, the Buddha.

सत्र – न॰ – (सत्र) नियमित दान। an act of regular donation.

सत्वादि – (सत्त्वादि) त्रिगुण, प्रकृति के तीन गुण - सत, रज, और तम। the three attributes of *prakṛti* — *sattva*, *rajasa* and *tamasa*.

√ सद – (भू॰) – (विशीर्णगति + अवसादन + आगमेषु) जीर्ण होना, जाना, नीचे गिराना, लेना। to digest, to fall down, to go, to take.

सदत्थ – पु॰ – (सद् + अर्थ = सदर्थ) सदर्थ, आत्म-कल्याण। one's own welfare.

सदन – न॰ – (सदन) घर। a house.

सदर – वि॰ – (स + दर) दुःखद, डरावना, भयानक। troublesome.

सदस – वि॰ – किनारी (गोटा) वाली (चटाई)। mat with a fringe.

सदस्स – पु॰ – (सद + अश्व) अच्छा घोड़ा, अच्छी नस्ल का घोड़ा। horse of a good bread.

सदा – अव्यय – (सदा) हमेशा। always.

सदातन – वि॰ – (सदातन) शाश्वत, सनातन, सदैव बना रहने वाला। eternal.

सदार – पु॰ – (स्वदारा) अपनी पत्नी। one's own wife.

सदार-तुट्ठि – स्त्री॰ – (स्वदार-तुष्टिः) अपनी पत्नी से ही संतुष्ट रहना। satisfaction with one's own wife.

सदिस – वि॰ – (सदृश) सदृश, समान। similar, alike.

सदिसत्त – न॰ – (सदृशत्त्व) बराबरी। similarity.

सदुम – पु॰ तथा न॰ – (सद्म) सदन, सद्म, घर। house.

सदेवक – वि॰ – (स + देवक) देवताओं सहित। including the *deva*s.

सदद – पु॰ – (शब्द) शब्द, आवाज। sound, noise.

सदद्त्थ – पु॰ – (शब्दार्थ) शब्द का अर्थ। meaning of a word.

सदद-विद् – पु॰ – (शब्द-विद्) नानाविध आवाजों को समझ सकने वाला। one who can understand various sounds.

सदद-वेधी – पु॰ – (शब्द-वेधी) शब्द-वेधी बाण चला सकने वाला। one who shoots by grasping a sound.

सदद्सत्थ – न॰ – (शब्द-शास्त्र) शब्द-शास्त्र। grammar, science of words.

सदद्ल – पु॰ – (शाद्दल) हरित घास से ढकी जगह। a place covered with new grass.

सदद्हति – क्रि॰ – (श्रद्दधाते) श्रद्धा करता है, विश्वास करता है। believes, keeps faith in.

सदद्हन – न॰ – (श्रद्धा-मयता) विश्वास करना। believing, trusting.

सदद्हना – स्त्री॰ – (श्रद्धामयत्व) विश्वास करना। believing, trusting.

सदद्हान – पु॰ – (श्रद्धालु) विश्वास करने वाला। man who keeps trust.

सद्दायति – क्रि॰ – (शब्दायते) शब्द करता है। makes a noise.

सद्दूल – पु॰ – (शार्दूल) तेन्दुआ। a leopard, panther, a tiger.

सद्धं – अव्यय – (सार्द्धम) अनुकूल, साथ। with.

सद्ध – वि॰ – (श्रद्धान) श्रद्धा करते हुए। believing, having faith in.

सद्धम्म – पु॰ – (सद्धर्म) सत्-धर्म। the true doctrine.

सद्धा – स्त्री॰ – (श्रद्धा) श्रद्धा, भक्ति। faith, devotion.

सद्धातब्ब – कृ॰ – (श्रद्धेय) श्रद्धा करने योग्य। fit to be believed with respect.

सद्धादेय्य – वि॰ – (श्रद्धोपहार) श्रद्धापूर्वक दिया हुआ (दान)। a gift in faith.

सद्धा-धन – न॰ – (श्रद्धा-धन) श्रद्धारूपी धन। the wealth of devotion.

सद्धायिक – वि॰ – (श्रद्धेय) विश्वसनीय। trustworthy.

सद्धालु – वि॰ – (श्रद्धालु) श्रद्धालु। much devoted.

सद्धि-विहारिक – पु॰ – (सार्ध-विहारी) सब्रह्मचारी। a co-resident, an attending monk.

सद्धि-विहारिक – पु॰ – (सार्धविहारिक) सब्रह्मचारी। attending monk.

सद्धिं – अव्यय – (सार्धम) साथ। with, together.

सद्धि-चर – वि॰ – (सहचर) साथी। a companion, a follower.

सधन – वि॰ – (धनिक) धनी। rich, wealthy.

सधम्मी – पु॰ – (सहधर्मी) समान धर्मी। followers of the same faith.

√सन – (तु॰) – (दाने) दान करना। to donate, give in charity.

सनति – क्रि॰ – (स्वनति) शोर करता है। shouts, makes loud noise.

सनं – अव्यय – (सर्वदा) सदा। always.

सनंतन – वि॰ – (सनातन) शाश्वत, सनातन, सदा से। primeval, eternal.

सनाभिक – वि॰ – (सनाभिक) नाभि-युक्त, नाभि सहित। having a navel.

समिकं – अव्यय – (द्रुतम्) शीघ्र। at once.

सनित – कृदन्त – (स्वनित) ध्वनित। sounded.

सन्त (1) – कृदन्त – (√श्रम् + क्त = श्रान्त) श्रान्त, थका हुआ। tired, wearied.

सन्त – (2) पु॰ – (सन्त) महात्मा, सन्त। a virtuous man.

सन्त-काय – वि॰ – (शान्त-काय) शान्त शरीर। having a calmed body, a quiet man.

सन्त-तर – वि॰ – (शान्त-तर) अपेक्षाकृत अधिक शान्त। more calmed.

सन्त-मानस – वि॰ – (शान्त-मनस) शान्त-चित्त। of tranquil mind.

सन्त-भाव – पु॰ – (शान्त-भाव) शान्त-भाव। calmness.

सन्तक – वि॰ – (स्वक) स्वकीय, अपना। one's own, personal, private.

सन्तक – वि॰ – (स + अन्तक) सीमित। limited.

सन्तज्जेति – क्रि॰ – (सं √तर्ज् = संतर्जयति) त्रास देता है, डराता है। frightness, menaces.

सन्ततं – क्रि॰ – (सन्ततम्) देखें सततं। see Satatam.

सन्तति – स्त्री॰ – (सन्तति) सन्तति, परम्परा। offspring, lineage, continuity.

सन्तत्त – कृ॰ – (संतप्त) सन्तप्त, तपा हुआ। healed, grieved.

सन्तप्पति – क्रि॰ – (सं √तुप् = संतपति) दुःखी होता है, संताप करता है। becomes grieved, gets sorrow.

सन्तप्पित – कृ॰ – (सं + तृप्त) संतुष्ट, प्रसन्न। satisfied, pleased.

सन्तप्पेति – क्रि॰ – (सं √ तृप् = संतृप्यति) सन्तुष्ट होता है, प्रसन्न होता है। gets satisfied, becomes pleased.

सन्त-बाहिर – वि॰ – (सान्तर्बाहिः) भीतर तथा बाहर। with the inner and the outer.

सन्त-बाहिरं – क्रि॰ वि॰ – (सान्तर्बाहिरकम्) भीतर-बाहर करके। within and without.

सन्तरति – क्रि॰ – (सं √ तुरण् = संतुरण्यति) शीघ्रता करता है, जल्दी करता है। makes haste, gets quickly.

सन्तसति – क्रि॰ – (सं √ त्रस् = संत्रस्यति) डरता है, भयभीत होता है। fears, becomes terrified.

सन्तसन – न॰ – (संत्रास) भय, डर। terror, fright.

सन्तान – न॰ – (सन्तान) (1) सन्तति, परम्परा, (2) मकड़ी का जाल। (1) continuity, offspring, (2) a cobweb.

सन्तानेति – क्रि॰ – (सं √ तन् = संतनोति / संतनुते) परम्परा बनाए रखता है। continues in succession.

सन्ताप – पु॰ – (सन्ताप) ताप, पश्चाताप। heat, torment, grief.

सन्तापेति – क्रि॰ – (√ स √ तप् + णिच् = संतापयति) तपाता है, जलाता है, त्रास देता है। heats, burns, torments.

सन्तास – पु॰ – (सन्त्रास) डर, त्रास, काँपना। fear, trembling, shock.

सन्तासी – वि॰ – (सन्त्रसन्) काँपता हुआ, डरता हुआ। fearing, trembling.

सन्ति – स्त्री॰ – (शान्ति) शान्ति। peace, calmness.

सन्ति-कम्म – न॰ – (शान्ति-कर्म) शान्ति स्थापित करना। pacification, an act of appeasing.

सन्ति-पद – न॰ – (शान्ति-पद) शान्तावस्था। the tranquil state.

सन्तिक – वि॰ – (सन्तिकम्) समीप, (न॰) पड़ोस। near, (n.) neighbourhood.

सन्तिका – अव्यय – (सन्तिकम्) (उसके पास) से। from.

सन्तिकावचर – वि॰ – (सन्तिक + अवचरः) नजदीक रहने वाला। intimate.

सन्तिके-निदान – न॰ – (सन्तिके-निदानम्) जातकट्ठ-कथा का वह भाग, जिसमें भगवान् बुद्ध के बुद्धत्व लाभ से लेकर परिनिर्वृत होने तक का वृतान्त संगृहीत है। the portion of the Jātakaṭṭha- kathā which gives an account of the activities of the Buddha.

सन्तिट्ठति – क्रि॰ – (सं √ स्था = संतिष्ठति) ठहरता है, निश्चल रहता है। stands still, remains.

सन्तीरण – न॰ – (अनुसन्धान) खोज-बीन करना। investigation.

सन्तुट्ठ – कृदन्त – (सन्तुष्ट) संतुष्ट, प्रसन्न- चित्त। pleased, happy.

सन्तुट्ठता – स्त्री॰ – (सन्तुष्टि) सन्तुष्ट रहने का भाव। state of contentment.

सन्तुट्ठि – स्त्री॰ – (सन्तुष्टि) सन्तोष, प्रीति, आनन्द। satisfaction, contentment, joy.

सन्तुसित – कृ॰ – (सन्तुष्ट) देखें सन्तुट्ठ। see Santuṭṭha.

सन्तुस्सक – वि॰ – (सन्तुष्ट) सन्तुष्ट, प्रसन्न। satisfied, glad.

सन्तुस्सन – न॰ – (सन्तुष्यन) सन्तोष। contentment, joy.

सन्तुस्सति – क्रि॰ – (सन्तुष्यति) सन्तुष्ट रहता है। remains pleased or happy.

सन्तोस – पु॰ – (सन्तोष) सन्तोष। satisfaction.

सन्थत – कृदन्त – (संस्थत) ढका हुआ। covered with.

सन्थम्भेति – क्रि॰ – (सं √ स्तम्भ् = संस्तम्भति) कठोर बनता है। becomes stiff or rigid, becomes numb.

सन्थम्भना – स्त्री॰ – (संस्तम्भना) कठोर होना। stiffening, rigidity.

सन्थर – पु॰ – (संस्थर / संस्तरण) चटाई, बिछावन। a mat, a covering.

सन्थरति – क्रि॰ – (संस्तृणोति) बिछाता है, चादर से ढकता है। spreads, strews, covers with.

सन्थरापेति – क्रि॰ – (संस्तारयति) बिछवाता है। gets spread, gets strewn.

सन्थव – पु॰ – (सम् √ स्तु + घञ् = संस्तव) गहरी मित्रता, संसर्ग, समागम। intimacy, acquaintance.

सन्थव-जातक – (जा॰ सं॰ 162) – यह कथा बताती है कि नादान दोस्त से अच्छा दुश्मन होता है। the Jātaka (No. 162) teaches a lesson that a good enemy is better than bad friends.

सन्थागार – पु॰ तथा न॰ – (संस्थागार) सभा-भवन। a meeting or discussion hall.

सन्थार – पु॰ – (संस्तरण) फर्श, बिछावन। a covering, flooring.

सन्थुत – कृ॰ – (बुद्धि सं॰ संस्तुत) परिचित। acquainted, familiar.

√ सन्द – (भू॰) – (प्रस्रवणे) टपकना। to drip.

सन्द (1) – वि॰ – (सान्द्र) गाढ़ा, घना। thick, dense.

सन्द (2) – पु॰ – (सान्द्र) बहाव। a flow.

सन्दच्छाय – वि॰ – (सान्द्रच्छाया) घनी छाया वाला। giving dense shade.

सन्दति – क्रि॰ – (√ स्यन्द - स्यन्दते) बहता है। flows.

सन्दन – न॰ – (स्पन्दन) बहना, (पु॰) रथ। flowing down, (m.) a chariot.

सन्दस्सक – पु॰ – (सन्दर्शक) दिखाने वाला। one who shows or instructs.

सन्दस्सन – न॰ – (सन्दर्शन) शिक्षण, मार्ग-दर्शन। instruction, pointing out.

सन्दस्सियमान – वि॰ – (सन्दृश्यमाण) शिक्षित किया जाता हुआ। being instructed or pointed out.

सन्दस्सेति – क्रि॰ – (सन्दर्शयति) समझाता है, व्याख्या करता है। points out, explains.

सन्दहति – क्रि॰ – (सन्धत्ते) मेल बिठाता है। connects, unites.

सन्दहन – न॰ – (सन्धान) मेल बिठाना। putting together.

सन्दान – न॰ – (सन्दान) दाम, पादबन्धन, रज्जु, जंजीर, परम्परा। a chain, a string, a tether.

सन्दालेति – क्रि॰ – (सं √ दृ = सन्दृणाति) तोड़ता है, चीरता है। breaks, shatters.

सन्दिट्ठ – कृदन्त – (सं √ दृश् + क्त = सन्दृष्ट) एक साथ देखे गये, (पु॰) मित्र। seen, together, (m.) a friend.

सन्दिट्ठिक – वि० – (सन्दृष्टिक) दृष्टिगोचर, दिखाई देने वाला, इहलोक सम्बन्धी। one who shows the way, a preacher, companion in this world.

सन्दित – कृ० – (√ स्यन्द् - स्यन्दित) बहा। flowed.

सन्दिद्ध – कृ० – (सन्दिग्ध) अस्पष्ट, सशंकित, (विष) मिश्रित। smeared, indistinct.

सन्दिस्सति – क्रि० – (सन्दृश्यते) दिखाई देता है। is seen, appears.

सन्दीपन – न० – (सन्दीपन) स्पष्ट करना, प्रकाशित करना। kindling, making clear.

सन्दीपेति – क्रि० – (सन्दीप्यते) प्रकाशित करता है। kindles, makes clear.

सन्देस – पु० – (सन्देश) सन्देश। a message.

सन्देस-हर – पु० – (सन्देश हर) सन्देश-वाहक। a messenger.

सन्देसागार – न० – (सन्देशागार) डाकखाना। a post office.

सन्देह – पु० – (सम्देह) शक, अपनी देह। doubt, one's own body.

सन्दोह – पु० – (सन्दोह) ढेर। a heap.

सन्धन – न० – (स्वधन) निजी सम्पत्ति। one's own property.

सन्धमति – क्रि० – (सं √ ध्या = सन्धमति) फूँकता है, बजाता है। blows.

सन्धातु – पु० – (सन्धाता) मेल मिलाने वाला। one who conciliates.

सन्धान – न० – (सन्धान) मेल, एकता। uniting, conciliation.

सन्धाय – पू० क्रि० – (सम् √ धा + ल्यप्) मेल होकर। having united.

सन्धारक – वि० – (सन्धारयन) सहन करते हुए, रोकते हुए। bearing, restraining.

सन्धारण – न० – (सन्धारण) रोकना। checking, bearing.

सन्धारेति – क्रि० – (सन्धारयति) सहन करता है। bears, endures.

सन्धावति – क्रि० – (सन्धावति) दौड़ता है। runs through.

सन्धि – स्त्री० – (सन्धि) मेल, समझौता। junction, agreement.

सन्धिच्छेदक – वि० – (सन्धि-छेदक) सेंध लगाने वाला। a burglar.

सन्धिभेद-जातक – (जा० सं० 349) – कहानी बताती है कि किस प्रकार चुगलखोर दो मित्रों में फूट डालकर उनमें शत्रुता करा देता है। the story (No. 349) tells how the habit of back-biting converts friendship into enmity.

सन्धिमुख – न० – (सन्धिमुख) सेंध का मुँह। opening of a wall made by a burglar.

सन्धीयति – क्रि० – (सन्धीयते) मेल मिलाया जाता है। becomes connected, puts together.

सन्धूपायति – क्रि० – (धूमोत्सर्जनं करोति) धुआँ बाहर निकालता है। emits smoke.

सन्धूपेति – क्रि० – (धूमायते) धुआँ देता है। fumigates.

सनन्ह्रति – क्रि० – (स √ नह् = संनह्यति) शस्त्र बाँधता है। arms oneself.

सन्नकद्दु – पु॰ – (प्रियाल) पियाल, चिरौंजी का पेड़, पियाल वृक्ष । tree *Buchanania Latifolia*, commonly called piyal.

सन्नद्ध – कृदन्त – (सन्नद्ध) बँधा हुआ, हथियारबन्द शस्त्र । fastened, armed.

सन्नाह – पु॰ – (कवच) कवच । armour.

सन्निकट्ठ – न॰ – (संनिकर्ष) पड़ोस । neighbourhood, vicinity.

सन्निकास – वि॰ – (सन्निकाश) अनुरूपता- युक्त, मेल खाता हुआ, समान । resembling, looking like.

सन्निचय – पु॰ – (निचय) संचय, संग्रह । collection, accumulation.

सन्निचित – कृदन्त – (संचित) संगृहीत । accumulated, hoarded.

सन्निट्ठान – न॰ – (सारांश) सारांश । conclusion, gist.

सन्निधान – न॰ – (सन्निकर्ष / सन्निधान) सामीप्य । vicinity, proximity.

सन्निधि – पु॰ – (सं + निधि) एकत्र करना, जमा करना । storing up, hoarding.

सन्निधि-कारक – पु॰ – (सं + निधि + कारक) जमा करके रखने वाला । one who holds large stock, hoarder.

सन्निधि-कत – वि॰ – (सं + निधि + कृत) जमा किया हुआ माल । hoarded.

सन्निपतति – क्रि॰ – (संनिपतति) सम्मेलन करता है । calls a meeting.

सन्निपात – पु॰ – (संनिपात) संगम, सम्मेलन, वात-पित्त-कफ का मेल । combination, assemblage, union of the humours of the body.

सन्निपातिक – वि॰ – (संनिपातिक) शारीरिक गुणों (वात-पित्त-कफ) का परिणाम । resulting from the union of the humours.

सन्निपातन – न॰ – (संनिपातन) इकट्ठा करना । calling together.

सन्निपातेति – क्रि॰ – (संनिपातयति) सम्मेलन बुलाता है । calls a meeting, convokes.

सन्निभ – वि॰ – (संनिभ) सदृश, मेल खाता हुआ । resembling.

सन्निय्यातन – न॰ – (संनियार्तन) सौंपना, इस्तीफा देना । handing over.

सन्निरुम्भन – न॰ – (सं √रुध् + ल्युट् = संरोधनम्) रोकना । restraining, suppression.

सन्निरुम्भेति – क्रि॰ – (सं √रुध् = संरुणद्धि) रोकता है, बाधा डालता है । restrains, blocks.

सन्निवसति – क्रि॰ – (संनिवसति) एक साथ रहता है । lives together.

सन्निवास – पु॰ – (संनिवास) संगति । living together.

सन्निवेस – पु॰ – (सहनिवास) एक साथ रहना । living together.

सन्निरीवति – क्रि॰ – (सांनिरीवति) शान्त हो जाता है, स्थिर हो जाता है । settles, subsides.

सन्निसित – वि॰ – (संनिश्रित) आश्रित सम्बन्धी । connected with, based on.

सन्निहित – कृ॰ – (संनिहित) रखा गया । put down, placed well.

सन्नेति – क्रि॰ – (सन्नयति / सम्मिश्रयति) मिश्रित करता है । mixer together mingles well.

√सप – (भू॰) – (आक्रोशे) कोसना, शाप देना । to curse.

सपच – पु॰ – (श्वपच) चण्डाल, भंगी। a man of degraded class (eaters of dogs).

सपजापतिक – वि॰ – (सप्रजपतिक) पत्नी सहित। with one's wife.

सपति – क्रि॰ – (√शप् - शपति/शपते) शपथ खाता है। swears, takes an oath.

सपत्त – पु॰ – (सपत्न) प्रतिद्वन्द्वी, बैरी। rival, enemy.

सपत्त-भार – वि॰ – (स्वपत्र-भार) अपने जैसे के भार को लिए। having one's wings as one's whole burden.

सपत्ती – स्त्री॰ – (सपत्नी) सपत्नी, सौत। a co-wife.

सपथ – पु॰ – (शपथ) शपथ। an oath.

सपदान – वि॰ – (सर्पाद्) क्षिप्र, तत्काल। immediately.

सपदानं – क्रि॰ वि॰ – (क्रमशः) अनवरत, क्रमशः। successive.

सपदान-चारिका – स्त्री॰ – (सर्पाद्-चारिका) बिना एक भी घर छोड़े, हर घर से भिक्षाटन करना। to go on alms begging not leaving a single house in his course.

सपदि – अव्यय – (सपदि) तुरन्त, तत्काल। immediately, at once.

सपरिग्गह – वि॰ – (स्वपरिग्रह) अपनी सम्पत्ति अथवा पत्नी के साथ। together with one's professions or a wife.

सपाक – पु॰ – (श्वपत्त) अन्त्यज, कुत्ते खाने वाला। a man of degraded class, dog-eater.

सोपाक – देखे सपाक। se Sapāka.

सप्प – पु॰ – (सर्प) सर्प, साँप। snake.

√सप्प – (भू॰) – (गमने/सर्पणे) जाना, रेंगना। to crawl, to creep.

सप्प-पोतक – पु॰ – (सर्प-पोतक) साँप का बच्चा। a young serpent.

सप्पच्चय – वि॰ – (सप्रत्यय) सहेतुक, सकारण। having a cause, conditioned.

सप्पञ्ञ – वि॰ – (सप्रज्ञ) प्रज्ञावान, बुद्धिमान। wise.

सप्पटिघ – वि॰ – (स + प्रतिघ) प्रतिघात-युक्त, जिससे सम्बन्ध स्थापित किया जा सके, जिससे प्रतिक्रिया हो। contactable, approachable.

सप्पटिभय – वि॰ – (सप्रतिभय) भयानक। dangerous, harmful.

सप्पति – क्रि॰ – (सर्पति) रेंगता है। crawls, creeps.

सप्पन – न॰ – (सर्पण) रेंगना। crawling, creeping.

सप्पाणक – वि॰ – (सप्राणक) प्राणिवान, प्राणी-सहित। containing animate (living) objects.

सप्पाय – वि॰ – (लाभप्रद) लाभप्रद। beneficial, suitable.

सप्पायता – स्त्री॰ – (भद्रता) कल्याणकारिता। wholesomeness.

सप्पि – न॰ – (सर्पिस्) तपाया घी। clarified butter.

सप्पिनी – स्त्री॰ – (सर्पिणी) साँपिन। female snake.

सप्पिनी – स्त्री॰ – (सप्पिणिका भी) (सर्पिणी) राजगृह के बीच से बहने वाली एक प्राचीन नदी। a river situated in Rājagṛha at the time of Buddha.

सप्पीतिक – वि॰ – (सप्रीतिक) प्रीतियुक्त। joyful.

सप्पुरिस – पु॰ – (सत्पुरुष) सत्पुरुष। righteous man.

सफरी – स्त्री॰ – (शफरी) मछली विशेष। a shell-fish.

सफल – वि॰ – (सफल) फलयुक्त। having its reward, bearing fruit.

सबल – वि॰ – (सबल) बलशाली। strong.

सबल – वि॰ – (शबल) चित्तीदार। spotted.

सब्ब – वि॰ – (सर्व) सब। all, whole.

सब्बकनिट्ठ – वि॰ – (सर्वकनिष्ठ) सबसे छोटा। the youngest of all.

सब्बकम्मिक – वि॰ – (सर्वकार्मिक) सर्वकार्मी (मंत्री)। a minister.

सब्ब-चतुप्पद – पु॰ – (सर्व चतुष्पद) सभी चौपाये, सभी चतुष्पाद प्राणी। all four-footed animals.

सब्बञ्ञू – वि॰ – (सर्वज्ञ) सब जानने वाला, (पु॰) भगवान् बुद्ध। all-knowing, the omniscient one.

सब्बञ्ञुता – स्त्री॰ – (सर्वज्ञता) सर्वज्ञ-भाव। omniscience.

सब्बट्ठक – वि॰ – (सर्वाष्टक) सभी आठ-आठ प्रकार की चीजें। eight numbers of each kind.

सब्बतो – अव्यय – (सर्वतः) चारों ओर, हर तरह से। from every side.

सब्बत्थ – क्रि॰ वि॰ – (सर्वत्र) सर्वत्र, हर जगह। everywhere.

सब्बत्र – (सर्वत्र) देखें सब्बत्थ। see Sabbattha.

सब्बथा – क्रि॰ वि॰ – (सर्वथा) हर तरह से। in every way.

सब्बदा – क्रि॰ वि॰ – (सर्वदा) सर्वदा, हमेशा। always, everyday.

सब्बदाठ-जातक – (जा॰ सं॰ 241) – कथा बतलाती है कि दूसरों को क्षति पहुँचाने की धूर्त्तता उस चालाक के ही विनाश का कारण बन जाती है। the story (No. 241) tells that the attempt to injure others causes harm to the cunning man himself.

सब्बधि – क्रि॰ वि॰ – (सर्वत्र) सर्वत्र। everywhere.

सब्बपठम – वि॰ – (सर्वप्रथम) सबसे प्रमुख। the chief among all.

सब्बपठमं – क्रि॰ वि॰ – (सर्वप्रथमम्) सबसे आगे, सबसे पहले। the foremost, the first of all.

सब्ब-विद् – वि॰ – (सर्वविद्) सर्वज्ञ, सब जानने वाला। all knowing.

सब्ब-सत – वि॰ – (सर्वशत) सभी सौ-सौ प्रकार की चीजें। hundred numbers of each kind.

सब्बसो – क्रि॰ वि॰ – (सर्वशः) सब तरह से। altogether, in every respect.

सब्ब-सोवण्ण – वि॰ – (सर्व-सौवर्ण) पूर्णतया स्वर्ण-निर्मित। entirely made of gold.

सब्बस्स – न॰ – (सर्वस्व) तमाम सम्पत्ति। the whole of one's property.

सबस्सहरण – न॰ – (सर्वस्वहरण) सारी सम्पत्ति का हरण। confiscation of one's whole property.

सब्भ – वि॰ – (सभ्य) गुणों वाला। noble person.

सब्रह्मक – वि॰ – (सब्रह्मक) ब्रह्मलोक सहित। including the Brahmaloka.

सब्रह्मचारी – पु॰ – (सब्रह्मचारी) सहपाठी, गुरु भाई। a fellow monk.

सभगत – वि॰ – (सभागत) सभास्थित, सभा में गया हुआ। come to an assembly.

सभा – स्त्री॰ – (सभा) परिषद। an assembly, a hall for meeting.

सभाग – वि॰ – (सभाग) सहभाग, समान भाग, एक ही विभाग से सम्बन्धित। common, being of the same division.

सभागट्ठान – न॰ – (सभागस्थान) अनुकूल स्थान, सुविधा का स्थान। a convenient place.

सभागवुत्ती – वि॰ – (सभागवर्ती) परस्पर शालीनतापूर्वक रहने वाला। living in mutual courtesy.

सभाय – न॰ – (सभागृह) सभामण्डप, सभा-भवन। the assembly-hall.

सभाव – पु॰ – (स्वभाव) स्वभाव, प्रकृति। nature, disposition.

सभाव-धम्म – पु॰ – (स्वभाव-धर्म) स्वभाव का सिद्धान्त। principle of nature.

सभोजन – वि॰ – (सभोजन) भोजन-सहित। with food.

√ सम – (भू॰) – (परिश्रमे) थकना। to get tired.

सम – वि॰ – (सम) समान, बराबर। equal.

सम – पु॰ – (शम) शान्ति, निश्चलता। calmness, tranquillity.

√ सम – (दि॰) – (उपशम स्वेदेसु) उपशान्ति पाना, पसीना छूटना। to attain peace, to sweat.

समक – वि॰ – (समक) समानता वाला, बराबरी करने वाला। equal, like, same.

समंक – क्रि॰ – (समम्) बराबर-बराबर। equally.

समेन – क्रि॰ वि॰ – (समेन) समदृष्टिपूर्वक, बिना पक्षपात के। impartially.

समग्ग – वि॰ – (समग्र) समग्र-भाव, एकता। being in unity.

समग्ग-करण – न॰ – (समग्रकरणम्) मेल कराना। peace-making.

समग्गत्त – न॰ – (समग्रत्व) समग्र-भाव, समझौता। agreement, state of being united.

समग्गरत – वि॰ – (समग्ररत) एकतारत, एकता में प्रसन्न। rejoicing in peace.

समग्गाराम – वि॰ – (समग्रताप्रिय) एकता में प्रसन्न। rejoicing in peace.

समङ्गिता – स्त्री॰ – (समङ्गित्व) युक्त होना। the fact of being endowed.

समङ्गी – वि॰ – (समाङ्गी) युक्त, समन्वित। endowed with.

समङ्गीभूत – वि॰ – (समाङ्गीभूत) युक्त। endowed with.

समचरिया – स्त्री॰ – (शमाचरण) शान्त चर्या। living in spiritual calm.

समचित्त – वि॰ – (शम्-चित्त) शान्त-चित्त। possessed of equanimity.

समचित्तता – स्त्री॰ – (समचित्तता) शान्त-चित्त होने का भाव। equanimity of mind, peace of mind.

समजातिक – वि॰ – (समजातिक) एक ही जाति का। of the same caste.

समज्ज – न॰ – (संमर्द) मेले की भीड़। a festive gathering.

समज्जट्ठान – न॰ – (संमर्द-स्थान) मेले की जगह। an arena.

समज्जाभिचरण – न० – (संमर्दाभिचरण) मेलों में घूमना। visiting fairs or festivals.

समज्ञा – स्त्री० – (समज्ञा) पद, नाग। designation.

समज्ञात – वि० – (समज्ञात) पद-प्राप्त, जाना हुआ। designated.

समण – न० – (श्रमण) साधु। recluse.

समण-कुत्तक – पु० – (कुत्सित श्रमण) ढोंगी श्रमण। fake hermit, fraudulent monk.

समणी –स्त्री० – (श्रमणी) साध्वी। a nun.

समणुद्देसा – पु० – (श्रमणोद्देश्यकः) श्रामणेर। a novice.

समण-धम्म – पु० – (श्रमण-धर्म) श्रमण-धर्म। duties of a monk.

समण-सारुप्प – वि० – (श्रमणोचित्त) श्रमण के योग्य। lawful for a monk.

समता – स्त्री० – (समता) बराबरी। equality.

समतिक्कन्त – कृ० – (समतिक्रान्त) लाँघ गया, सीमा पार कर गया। passed beyond, overcome.

समतिक्कम – पु० – (समतिक्रम) देखें समतिक्कमन। see Samatikkaman.

समतिक्कमन – न० – (समतिक्रमण) सीमोलंघन। passing beyond, overcoming.

समतिक्कमति – क्रि० – (सम् + अति √ क्रम् = समतिक्रामति) सीमा लाँघ जाता है। passes over, transcends.

समतित्तिक – वि० – किनारे तक भरा हुआ। brimful up to the limit.

समतिवत्तति – क्रि० – (समतिवर्त्तते) सीमा लाँघता है। overcomes, transcends.

समत्त – वि० – (समस्त) सम्पूर्ण। entire, the whole.

समत्त – न० – (समत्त्व) बराबरी का भाव, समानता। equality.

समत्थ – वि० – (समर्थ) सामर्थ्यवान। able, skillful.

समत्थता – स्त्री० – (समर्थता) दक्षता, निपुणता, योग्यता। ability, proficiency.

समथ – पु० – (शमन) चित्त की शान्ति, कानूनी झगड़ों का निबटारा। settlement of legal question, quietude of the mind.

समथ-भावना – स्त्री० – (शमन-भाव) चित्त-शान्ति का अभ्यास। exercises for concentration of the mind.

समधिगच्छति – क्रि० – (सम् + अधि + गच्छति) प्राप्त करता है, भली प्रकार समझता है। attains, understands clearly.

समनन्तर – वि० – (तदनन्तर) तुरन्त बाद का। immediate, nearest.

समनन्तरा – क्रि० वि० – (तदनन्तरम्) ठीक बाद में। just after.

समनुगाहति – क्रि० – (सम् + अनु √ गाह् = समनुगाहति) कारणों का पता लगाता है। indulges to find out the root cause.

समनुञ्ञ – वि० – (समनुज्ञय) स्वीकार्य। approving.

समनुञ्ञा – स्त्री० – (समनुज्ञा) स्वीकृति। approval.

समनुञ्ञात – वि० – (समनुज्ञात) स्वीकृत, अनुमत। approved.

समनुपस्सति – क्रि० – (समनुपश्यति) देखता है, अनुभव करता है। perceives.

समनुभासति – क्रि॰ – (सम + अनु + भ
।षते) संलाप करता है। converses
together.

समनुभासना – स्त्री॰ – (समनुभाषणा)
वार्त्तालाप, संलान, पूर्वाभ्यास।
conversation, rehearsal.

समनुथुञ्जति – क्रि॰ – (सम् + अनु +
√ युज = समनुयुङ्क्ते) प्रश्नोत्तर करता
है। raises cross-question.

समनुस्सरति – क्रि॰ – (सम् + अनु + √ स्मृ
= समनुस्मरति) अनुस्मरण करता है।
recollects.

समन्त – वि॰ – (समन्त) सब, सारा। all,
entire.

समन्त-चक्खु – वि॰ – (समन्तचक्षुः) सर्वद्रष्टा,
सब कुछ देखने वाला। all-seeing, the
omniscient one.

समन्त-पासादिक – वि॰ – (समन्त प्रासादिक)
सबको प्रसन्न रखने वाला। all
pleasing.

समन्त-पासादिका – स्त्री॰ – (समन्त
प्रासादिका) आचार्य बुद्धघोष द्वारा रचित
विनय पिटक की अट्ठकथा। the
Aṭṭhakathā of Vinaya written by
Buddhaghoṣa.

समन्त-भद्दक – वि॰ – (समन्त-भद्रक) सबके
के लिए कल्याणकारक। well-wishes,
good-doer for all.

समन्त-कूट-पब्बत – पु॰ – (समन्तकूट) सिंहल
द्वीप का पर्वत शिखर विशेष, जो भगवान्
बुद्ध के चरण-चिह्न से पूत हुआ माना जाता
है। a mountain peak in Ceylon
(Sri Lanka), it is said that it has
the foot-prints of the Buddha.

समन्ततो – क्रि॰ वि॰ – (समन्ततः) चारों
ओर से। all round.

समन्ता – क्रि॰ वि॰ – (समन्तात्) चारों ओर
से। all-round, everywhere.

समनागत – वि॰ – (समन्वागत) समन्वित,
युक्त। endowed with, possessed
of.

समनाहरति – क्रि॰ – (सम् + आहरति)
इकट्ठा करता है। collects together.

समपेक्खति – क्रि॰ – (सम् + ईक्षते) भली
प्रकार देखता है, सम्यक् विचार करता
है। considers well.

सम्पेति – क्रि॰ – (समर्पयति) समर्पित करता
है, सौंपता है। offers, hands over,
consigns.

समय – पु॰ – (समय) काल, परिषद्, ऋतु,
अवसर, धार्मिक मत। time,
congregation, season, occasion,
religious doctrines.

समयन्तर – न॰ – (समयान्तर) भिन्न-भिन्न
सम्प्रदाय। the different religious
sects.

समर – न॰ – (समर) युद्ध। battle.

समल – वि॰ – (स + मल) अपवित्र, मल-
सहित। impure, contaminated.

समलङ्कत – कृदन्त – (सम् + अलङ्कृत)
अलंकृत। decorated, adorned.

समलङ्करोति – क्रि॰ – (सम् + अलङ्करोति)
सजाता है। decorates, adorns.

समवाय – पु॰ – (समवाय) मेल, एकत्र
होना। combination, coming
together.

समवेक्खति – क्रि॰ – (सम् + वि √ ईक्ष =
संवीक्षते) भली प्रकार छान-बीन करता है,
प्रतीक्षा करता है। considers,
examines thoroughly.

समवेपाकिनी – स्त्री॰ – (समविपाकिनी) हजम करने वाली। promoting good digestion.

सम-सिप्पी – पु॰ – (सम-शिल्पी) समान शिल्प वाले, हमपेशा। of the same livelihood.

समस्सास – पु॰ – (समाश्वाश) सहायता, विश्राम। relief, refreshment.

समस्सासेति – क्रि॰ –(सम् + आ √श्वस् = समाश्वासयति) सहायता पहुँचाता है, आराम पहुँचाता है, आश्वस्त करता है। relieves, refreshes.

समं – अव्यय – (समम्) साथ-साथ। with, along with.

समा – स्त्री॰ – (समा) वर्ष। year.

समाकड्ढति – क्रि॰ – (सम् + आ √कृष् = समाकर्षति) सार निकालता है, खींचता है। extracts, pulls along.

समाकड्ढन – न॰ – (समाकर्षण) खींचना, घसीटना, सार निकालना। pulling, dragging, extracting.

समाकिण्ण – वि॰ – (सम् + आ √कृ + क्त = समाकीर्ण) विकीर्ण, भरा हुआ, बिखरा हुआ। scattered, overspread, full.

समागच्छति – क्रि॰ – (समागच्छति) आकर मिलता है, एकत्र होता है। meets together, assembles.

समागत – कृ॰ – (समागत) एकत्रित। assembled.

समागम – पु॰ – (समागम) सम्मिलन, सभा। meeting with, an assembly.

समाचरति – क्रि॰ – (समाचरति) आचरण करता है, अभ्यास करता है। behaves, practises.

समाचरण – न॰ – (समाचरण) आचरण, व्यवहार। conduct, behaviour.

√समाज – (चु॰) – (प्रीतिदर्शने) खातिर करना। to host.

समादपक – पु॰ – (समादपक) उत्साहित करने वाला, प्रेरित करने वाला। instigator, exciter.

समादपन – न॰ – (समादपन) उत्साहवर्द्धन, प्रेरित करना, उत्तेजित करना। excitation, instigation.

समादपेति – क्रि॰ – (समादपयति) उत्साहित करता है, प्रेरित करता है, उत्तेजित करता है। excites, instigates.

समादहति – क्रि॰ – (समादहति) जोड़ता है, एकाग्र करता है, (अग्नि) जलाता है। puts together, concentrates, kindles fire.

समादाति – क्रि॰ – (सम् + आदाति) ग्रहण करता है, स्वीकार करता है। takes, accepts.

समादान – न॰ – (समादान) स्वीकार करना, अंगीकार करना, आचरण करना। taking, observance, acceptance.

समादाय – पू॰ क्रि॰ – (सम् + आ √दा + ल्यप् = समादाय) ग्रहण करके, लेकर के। having accepted.

समादियति – क्रि॰ – (सम् + आदत्ते) अंगीकार करता है। accepts.

समादिसति – क्रि॰ – (सम् + आ √दिश् = समादिशति) आदेश देता है, आज्ञा देता है। indicates, commands.

समाधान – न॰ – (समाधान) एकत्र करना, एकाग्रता। putting together, concentration.

समाधि – पु॰ – (समाधि) योगाभ्यास, चित्त की एकाग्रता। meditation, concentration of the mind.

समाधिज – वि॰ – (समाधिज) समाधि से उत्पन्न। produced by concentration.

समाधि-बल – न॰ – (समाधि बल) समाधि का बल। the power of concentration.

समाधि-भावना – स्त्री॰ – (समाधि-भावना) समाधि का अभ्यास। cultivation of concentration.

समाधि-संवत्तनिक – वि॰ – (समाधि-संवर्त्तनिक) एकाग्रता में सहायक। conducive to concentration.

समाधि-सम्बोज्झङ्ग – पु॰ – (समाधि-सम्बोध्यङ्ग) सम्बोधि के अङ्ग स्वरूप समाधि। concentration as a constituent of enlightenment.

समाधियति – क्रि॰ – (समाधत्ते) समाहित होता है। becomes calmed or concentrated.

समान – वि॰ – (समान) बराबर। equal.

समान-गतिक – वि॰ – (समानगतिक) समान गति वाला। identical.

समानत्त – न॰ – (समानत्त्व) समानत्व, समानता। equality.

समानता – स्त्री॰ – (समानता) देखें समानत्त। see Samānatta.

समानत्तता – स्त्री॰ – निष्क्षपात्, शान्त भाव। impartiality, sociability.

समान-वस्सिक – वि॰ – (समान वर्षीया) आयु में समान (भिक्षु)। equal in seniority, of the same age.

समान-संवासक – वि॰ – (समान संवासक) एक ही साथ रहने वाला। belonging to the same communion.

समानेति – क्रि॰ – (सम् + आ √नी = समानयति) मेल मिलाता है, पास-पास लाता है। brings together, compares.

समापज्जति – क्रि॰ – (सम् + आपद्यते) (कार्य) में लगता है, रत होता है। engages in, enters upon.

समापज्जन – न॰ – (समापद्यन) कार्य में लगना, रत होना। entering upon, passing through.

समापत्ति – स्त्री॰ – (समापत्ति) प्राप्ति, समाधि द्वारा आनन्द की प्राप्ति। attainment, an enjoying stage of meditation.

समापन्न – कृ॰ – (समापन्न) कार्य रत। engaged in.

समापेति – क्रि॰ – (सम् √आप् = समाप्नोति) समाप्त करता है। concludes, finishes, completes.

समायाति – क्रि॰ – (समायाति) समीप आता है, एकत्र होता है। comes together, becomes united.

समायुत – वि॰ – (संयुक्त) जुड़ा हुआ। combined.

समायोग – पु॰ – (समायोग) मेल, जोड़। combination, conjunction.

समारक – वि॰ – (स+मार) मार (कामदेव) सहित। associated with cupid, the god of love.

समारद्ध – कृ॰ – (सम् + आरब्ध) आरम्भ हुआ। begun.

समारब्धति – क्रि॰ – (सम् + आ √रभ् = समारभते) आरम्भ करता है। begins, undertakes.

समारम्भ – पु॰ – (समारम्भ) आरम्भ, साहसिक कार्य। undertaking, activity.

समारम्भ – पु॰ – (समालम्भन्) बलि पशु को पकड़ना, वध करना। killing of sacrificial animal.

समारुहति – क्रि॰ – (सम् + आ √रुह् = समारोहति) ऊपर चढ़ता है। climbs up, ascends.

समारुहन – न॰ – (समारुहन्) चढ़ना। climbing, ascending.

समारोपन – न॰ – (समारोपण) चढ़ाना, ऊपर उठाना। raising up, putting on.

समारोपेति – क्रि॰ – (समारोपयति) चढ़ाता है। makes ascends, puts on.

समावहति – क्रि॰ – (सम् + आ √वह् = समावहति) लाता है। brings about.

समास – पु॰ – (समास) समास, शब्दों का संक्षिप्त गुच्छ। compound, an abridgement.

समासेति – क्रि॰ – (सम् + √आस = समास्ते) संगति या संगीति करता है। associates, combines.

समाहत – क्रि॰ – (सम् + आहत) चोट खाया हुआ। stuck, hit, hurt.

समाहनति – क्रि॰ – (सम् + आ √हन् = समाहनति) चोट पहुँचाता है, वाद्य ध्वनित करता है। hits, sounds a musical instrument.

समाहार – पु॰ – (समाहार) संग्रह। collection.

समाहित – कृ॰ – (समाहित) स्थिरचित्त, एकाग्रचित्त। concentrated.

समिज्झति – क्रि॰ – (सम् √इध् = समिध्यति) सफल होता है। succeeds, prospers.

समिज्झन – न॰ – (समिध्यन) सफलता। success.

समित – कृ॰ – (√शम् + क्त = शान्त) शमित, शान्त। calmed, appease.

समितत्त – न॰ – (शमितत्त्व) शान्त भाव। state of being calmed.

समितावी – वि॰ – (शान्त) स्थिर चित्त, शान्त (पुरुष)। one who has quietened himself.

समित – क्रि॰ वि॰ – निरन्तर, सदैव। always, eternal.

समिति – स्त्री॰ – (समिति) परिषद। assembly.

समिद्ध – कृ॰ – (समृद्ध) समृद्ध, सफल। prosperity, success.

समिद्धि-जातक – (जा॰ सं॰ 167) – इस जातक में एक तापस को अप्सरा द्वारा प्रलोभित करने की चेष्टा का उल्लेख है। this story (No. 167) describes the efforts of a heavenly damsel to entice a monk.

समीप – वि॰ – (समीप) निकट, नजदीक। near, close.

समीपग – वि॰ – (समीपग) समीप गया हुआ। got near.

समीपचारी – वि॰ – (समीपचारी) समीप रहने वाला, निकटवर्ती। being near.

समीपट्ठ – वि॰ – (समीपस्थ) निकटस्थ, समीप स्थित। standing near, standing not far.

समीपट्ठान – न॰ – (समीप-स्थान) निकट स्थान, नजदीक का स्थान। a place nearby.

समीर – पु० – (समीर) शीतल मन्द पवन। the swift cold wind.

समीरण – पु० – (समीरण) देखें समीर। see Samīra.

समीरति – क्रि० – (समीरति) (हवा) बहती है, हवा चलती है। blows, moves.

समीरेति – क्रि० – (ईरयति) कँपाता है, आवाज निकालता है, बोलता है। shakes, utters, speaks.

समुक्कन्सेति – क्रि० – (श्लाघते) बड़ाई करता है। praises, extols.

समुग – पु० – (समुद्र-गर्भम्) मंजूषा, टोकरी, बाक्स। a casket.

समुग-जातक – (जा० सं० 436) – एक असुर द्वारा अपनी सुन्दर स्त्री को सुरक्षित रखने के लिए एक डिबिया बन्द करके निगल लिए जाने की कथा। the story (No. 436) of a demon who put his beautiful wife in a box for protection and swallowed it.

समुगच्छति – क्रि० – (सम् + उद् = गच्छति) उभरता है, ऊपर उठता है। arises, comes in to existence.

समुग्गत – कृदन्त – (समुद्गत) भली प्रकार, प्रकट, उदित। well arisen.

समुगगण्हाति – क्रि० – (सम + उद् + ग्रह्णाति) पाठ को भली प्रकार ग्रहण करता है। learns well.

समुग्गम – पु० – (समुद्गम) उत्पत्ति। origin.

समुग्गिरति – क्रि० – (समुद्गिरति) बोलता है, बाहर निकालता है। utters, emits.

समुग्गिरण – न० – (समुद्गिरण) मुँह से निकले हुए शब्द। utterance.

समुग्घात – पु० – (समुद्घात) उच्छेदन, प्रताड़न। uprooting, knocking against, jostling.

समुग्घातक – वि० – (समुद्घातक) उच्छेदक, हटाने वाला, उखाड़ फेंकने वाला। abolisher, remover.

समुग्घातेति – क्रि० – (समुद्घातयति) उखाड़ फेंकता है, हटाता है, दूर करता है। abolishes, uproots.

समुचित – कृदन्त – (सञ्चित) संगृहीत, एकत्रित। accumulated.

समुच्चय – पु० – (समुच्चय/सञ्चय) संग्रह। collection, accumulation.

समुच्छिन्दति – क्रि० – (सम् + उत् √छिन्द् - समुच्छिन्दति) मूलोच्छेद करता है, नष्ट करता है। gets uprooted, destroys.

समुच्छिन्न – कृदन्त – (समुच्छिन्न) मूलोच्छेद, कृत, विनष्ट। uprooted, destroyed.

समुच्छिन्दन – न० – (समुच्छेदन) मूलोच्छेद, विनाश। extirpation, destruction.

समुज्जल – वि० – (समुज्ज्वल) अत्यन्त उज्ज्वल। resplendent, shining.

समुज्जित – वि० – (समुज्झित) फेंका गया, छोड़ दिया गया, परित्यक्त। thrown away, discarded.

समुट्ठहति/समुट्ठाति – क्रि० – (समुत्थाति) ऊपर उठता है। rises.

समुट्ठान – न० – (समुत्थान) उत्पत्ति। origination.

समुट्ठापक – वि० – (समुत्थापक) उत्पन्न करने वाला। producer.

समुट्ठापेति – क्रि० – (समुत्थापयति) ऊपर उठता है। raises, produces, originates.

समुत्तरति – क्रि० – (सम् + उत् + तरति) ऊपर से गुजरता है। passes over.

समुत्तेजक – वि० – (समुत्तेजक) उत्तेजित करने वाला। instigator, stimulator.

समुत्तेजन – न॰ – (सम् + उत्तेजनम्) उत्तेजना । instigation, stimulation.

समुत्तेजेति – क्रि॰ – (सम + उत् + तेजयति) उत्तेजित करता है । stimulates, instigates.

समुदय – पु॰ – (समुदय) उत्पत्ति । rise, origin.

समुदय-सच्च – न॰ – (समुदय-सत्य) उत्पत्ति सम्बन्धी सत्य । the truth of origination.

समुदागत – कृ॰ – (समुदागत / समुद्गत) उत्पन्न । arisen, come into existence.

समुदागम – पु॰ – (समुदागम) उत्पत्ति । rising, product.

समुदाचरति – क्रि॰ – (समुदाचरति) आचरण करता है । behaves towards, occurs to.

समुदाचरण – न॰ – (समुदाचरण) आचरण, अभ्यास, व्यवहार । behaviour, habit, practice.

समुदाचरण – पु॰ – (समुदाचरण) देखें समुदाचरण । see Samudācaraṇa.

समुदाचिण्ण – कृ॰ – (सम् + उद् + आ √ चार + क्त = समुदाचीर्ण) आचरित । behaved towards.

समुदाय – पु॰ – (समुदाय) समूह । a multitude.

समुदाहरति – क्रि॰ – (समुदाहरति) शब्द उच्चारण करता है । speaks, utters.

समुदाहरण – न॰ – (समुदाहरण) शब्दोच्चारण, बातचीत । conversation, utterance.

समुदाहार – पु॰ – (समुदाहार) शब्दोच्चारण, बातचीत । conversation, utterance.

समुदीरण – न॰ – (समुदीरण) शब्दोच्चारण । utterance, movement.

समुदीरेति – क्रि॰ – (सम् + उद् √ ईरे = समुदीरयति) हलचल करता है । utters, moves.

समुदेति – क्रि॰ – (सम् + उदयति / उदेति) ऊपर उठता है । arises.

समुद्द – पु॰ – (समुद्र) समुद्र, जलनिधि । the sea, ocean.

समुद्दट्ठक – वि॰ – (समुद्रस्थ) समुद्र में स्थित । situated in ocean.

समुद्द-जातक – (जा॰ सं॰ 296) – समुद्र देवता द्वारा अत्यन्त लोभी कौवे को उड़ाकर भगा देने की कथा । the story (No. 296) tells how a greedy water-crow was frightened away by the sea-spirit.

समुद्द-वाणिज-जातक – (जा॰ सं॰ 466) – ऋणी व्यापारियों के द्वीपान्तर में पहुँचकर धनी हो जाने की कथा । the story (No. 466) of poor merchants who became prosperous reaching a foreign fertile island.

समुद्धट – कृ॰ – (सम् + उद् √ हृ + क्त = समुद्धृत्) उद्धृत, ऊपर उठाया गया । lifted up, taken out, saved from.

समुद्धरति – क्रि॰ – (समुद्धृति) ऊपर उठाता है, बाहर निकालता है । to lift up; to take out, to save from.

समुपगच्छति – क्रि॰ – (समुपगच्छति) समीप पहुँचता है । approaches.

समुपगमन – न॰ – (समुपगमन) नजदीक पहुँचाना । approach.

समुपगम्म – पू॰ क्रि॰ – (सम् + उप √ गम् + ल्यम् = समुपगम्य) to approach.

समुपब्बूलह – वि॰ – (समुपन्यूढ) भीड़-युक्त। crowded, in full swing.

समुपसोभित – वि॰ – (समुपशोभित) शोभित, अलंकृत। adorned, endowed with.

समुपागत – वि॰ – (समुपागत) नजदीक आया। approached to.

समुपज्जति – क्रि॰ – (समुपद्यते) उत्पन्न होता है। originates.

समुब्बहति – क्रि॰ – (समुद्वहति) सहन करता है। bears, carries, endures.

समुब्भवति – क्रि॰ – (समुद्भवति) उत्पन्न होता है। arises, gets, produces.

समुल्लपति – क्रि॰ – (समुल्लपति) बातचीत करता है। converses friendly.

समुल्लपन – न॰ – (समुल्लपन) बातचीत। conversation.

समुल्लाप – पु॰ – (संलाप) बातचीत। conversation.

समुस्सय – पु॰ – (समुच्चय) जमाव, तमाम चीजों का इकट्ठा रूप। accumulation.

समुस्सापेति – क्रि॰ – (समुत्थापयति) ऊपर उठाता है। lifts, raises.

समुस्साहेति – क्रि॰ – (समुत्साहयति) उत्साहित करता है, उत्तेजित करता है। instigates, stimulates.

समुस्सित – कृ॰ – (समुत्थित) ऊपर उठाया गया। lifted, raised.

समूलक – वि॰ – (समूल) जड़ सहित। including the root.

समूह – पु॰ – (समूह) झुण्ड। multitude, a mass, aggregation.

समूहनति – क्रि॰ – (समुन्मूलयति) जड़ से उखाड़ देता है। uproots, abolishes, removes.

समेक्खति – क्रि॰ – (सम् √ ईक्षू = समीक्षते) भली प्रकार देखता है। look for, considers.

समेक्खन – न॰ – (समीक्षण) परीक्षण, ध्यानपूर्वक देखना, गहन विचार। thorough inspection.

समेत – कृ॰ – (समेत) संलग्न, सम्बन्धित, जोड़ दिया गया। endowed, connected with, combined.

समेति – क्रि॰ – (सम् + एति) पास आता है, इकट्ठा होता है। comes together, agrees with, meets.

समेरित – कृ॰ – (सम् √ ईर + क्त = समीरित) चालू किया गया। moved, set in motion.

समोकिरति – क्रि॰ – (सम् + अव √ कृ = समविकरति) छिड़कता है। sprinkles, strews.

समोकिरण – नपुं॰ – (समविकरण) छिड़कना। sprinkling; strewing.

समोतत – कृदन्त – (सम + अवं √ तन् + क्त = समावतत) सर्वत्र फैलाया गया। strewn all over, spread.

समोतरति – क्रि॰ – (समवतरति) उतरता है। descends (into water).

समोदहति – क्रि॰ – (सम् + आ √ धा = समाधत्ते) इकट्ठा करता है, समाधान करता है। puts together, applies.

समोदहन – न॰ – (सम + आ √ धा + ल्युट् = समाधान) इकट्ठा करना, एक स्थान पर रखना। collection, combination.

समोधान – न॰ – (समाधान) मेल। combination.

समोधानेति – क्रि॰ – (समाधत्ते) मेल मिलाता है। put the sequence, fits together.

समोसरण – न॰ – (सम् + अवसरण) अधिवेशन, एकत्र होना। coming together, meeting.

समोसरति – क्रि॰ – (समवसरति) एकत्र होता है, एक स्थान पर सम्मिलित होता है। assembles, comes together.

समोह – वि॰ – (स + मोह) मोह-युक्त। infatuated.

समोहित – कृदन्त – (समोदहति) अन्तर्गत ढका हुआ, एकत्र किया हुआ। (past-perfect) Samodhati-fascinated, enraptured, love-stricken.

सम्पकम्पति – क्रि॰ – (सम् + प्र √ कम्प् = प्रकम्पते) काँपता है, प्रकम्पित होता है। trembles, becomes shaken.

सम्पजञ्ञ – न॰ – (सम्प्रज्ञा) विवेक। knowledge of discrimination.

सम्पजान – वि॰ – (सम्प्रज्ञान) जानबूझकर। thoughtful.

सम्पज्जति – क्रि॰ – (सम्पद्यते) सफल होता है। succeeds, prospers.

सम्पज्जन – न॰ – (साफल्यम्) सफलता। success.

सम्पज्जलित – कृदन्त – (सम + प्र √ ज्वल + क्त = सम्प्रज्वलित) प्रज्वलित। in flames, burning, blazing.

सम्पटिच्छति – क्रि॰ – (सम् + प्रति √ इच्छ = सम्प्रतीच्छति) प्राप्त करता है, स्वीकार करता है। receives, accepts.

सम्पटिच्छन – न॰ – (सम्प्रतीच्छा) स्वीकृति, सहमति। acceptance, agreement.

सम्पति – अव्यय – (सम्प्रति) इस समय, अभी। just now, at present.

सम्पतित – कृदन्त – (सम् + पतित) पतित, गिरा। fallen, corrupt, degenerate.

सम्पत्त – कृदन्त – (सम्प्राप्त) पहुँचा। reached, arrived.

सम्पत्ति – स्त्री॰ – (सम्पत्ति) धन, सम्पत्ति। wealth, fortune, success, attainment.

सम्पदा – स्त्री॰ – (सम्पदा) देखें सम्पत्ति। see Sampatti.

सम्पदान – न॰ – (सप्रदान) (1) सदा के लिए दे देना, (2) चतुर्थी विभक्ति, सूचक कारक। (1) giving over, (2) the dative case.

सम्पदालन – न॰ – (विदरण) चीरना। tearing, splitting.

सम्पदालेति/सम्पदाळेति – क्रि॰ वि॰ – (वि √ दृ = विदृणाति) चीरता है, फाड़ता है। tears, splits.

सम्पदुस्सति – क्रि॰ – (सम् + प्र √ दुष् = सम्प्रदुष्यति) दूषित होता है। becomes corrupt, spoiled.

सम्पदुस्सन – न॰ – (सम्प्रदूषण) दूषण, प्रदूषण। corruption, pollution.

सम्पदोस – पु॰ – (सम्प्रदोष) शरारत, बदमाशी। wickedness, misdemeanour.

सम्पन्न – कृदन्त – (सम्पन्न) पूर्ण, सफल। successful, complete, endowed with.

सम्पयात – कृदन्त – (सम्प्रयात) चला गया, निकल गया। gone forth, proceeded.

सम्पयुत्त – वि॰ – (सम्प्रयुक्त) समन्वित, सम्बन्धित। associated, connected.

सम्पयोग – पु॰ – (सम्प्रयोग) मेल। union, association.

सम्पयोजेति – क्रि॰ – (सम्प्रयोजयति) मिलाता है। associates with.

सम्पराय – पु॰ – (सम्पराय) भविष्य-काल, भावी अवस्था। future state, the next world.

सम्परायिक – वि॰ – (सम्परायिक) परलोक सम्बन्धी। belonging to next world.

सम्परिकड्ढति – क्रि॰ – (सपरिकर्षति) घसीटता है। drags, pulls.

सम्परिवज्जेति – क्रि॰ – (सम + परि √ वर्ज = सम्परिवर्जयति) दूर-दूर रखता है, टाल देता है। avoids, shuns.

सम्परिवत्तति – क्रि॰ – (सम्परिवर्तते) पलटता है, लोट-पोट होता है। turns, rolls about.

सम्परिवारेति – क्रि॰ – (सम्परिवारयति) घेरता है, सेवा में उपस्थित रहता है। surrounds, waits upon, attend upon.

सम्पवत्तेति – क्रि॰ – (सम्प्रवत्तते) प्रवृत्त करता है। get going.

सम्पवायति – क्रि॰ – (सम् + प्र √ वा = सम्प्रवाति) वायु बहती है, चलती है, बाहर आती है। blows, emits.

सम्पवेधति – क्रि॰ – झकझोरी जाती है। becomes shaken violently.

सम्पसाद – पु॰ – (प्रसाद) प्रसाद, आनन्द। pleasure, serenity.

सम्पसादनिय – वि॰ – शान्तिप्रद, आनन्दप्रद, सुखद। leading to serenity, inspiring.

सम्पसादेति – क्रि॰ – (सम्प्रसादयति) प्रसन्न करता है। gladdens, purifies.

सम्पसारेति – क्रि॰ – (सम्प्रसारयति) फैलाता है। spreads, stretches out.

सम्पसीददति – क्रि॰ – (सम्प्रसीदति) प्रसन्न होता है, आनन्दित होता है। becomes pleased.

सम्पसीदन – न॰ – (सम्प्रसीदन) आनन्द, प्रीति। joy, happiness.

सम्पस्सति – वि॰ – (सम्पश्यति) भली प्रकार देखता है। goes through, considers.

सम्पहट्ठ – कृदन्त – (सम् + प्र √ हृष् + क्त = सप्रहृष्ट) आनन्दित, प्रसन्नचित्त। gladdened, joyful.

सम्पहंसक – वि॰ – (सम्प्रहर्षक) हर्षकारक, प्रसन्नतादायक। gladdening.

सम्पहंसति – क्रि॰ – (सम्प्रहृष्यति) प्रसन्न होता है। becomes happy.

सम्पहार – पु॰ – (सम्प्रहार) संघर्ष, प्रहार। strife, battle, striking.

सम्पात – पु॰ – (सम्पात) एक साथ गिरना, एक साथ आ पड़ना। falling together.

सम्पादक – वि॰ – (सम्पादक) तैयारी करने वाला, प्राप्त करने वाला। one who obtains, one who prepares.

सम्पादान – न॰ – (सम्प्रदान) प्राप्त करना, प्राप्ति। preparing, obtaining.

सम्पादियति – क्रि॰ – (कर्मवाच्य=समद्यते) उसे प्राप्त किया जाता है, उस तक (सामान) पहुँचाया जाता है। gets supplied, makes things available.

सम्पादेति – क्रि॰ – (सम्पद्यति) पूरा करने का प्रयास करता है। tries to accomplish, prepares.

सम्पापक – वि॰ – (सम् + प्रापक) लाने वाला (किसी ओर) ले जाने वाला। leading to, bringing.

सम्पापन – न॰ – (सम्प्रापण) (कहीं) पहुँचाना leading, getting to.

सम्पापुणाति – क्रि॰ – (सप्राप्नोति) पहुँचता है। reaches, attains, meets with.

सम्पिण्डन – न॰ – (सम्पिण्डन) मेल मिलाना, गोल पिण्ड बनाना। combination, addition forming lumps.

सम्पिण्डेति – क्रि॰ – मेल मिलाता है, पिण्डी बनाता है। forms combination, forms lumps.

सम्पियायति – क्रि॰ – (सम्प्रियायति) प्रेमपूर्वक स्वागत करता है। receives with joy, treats kindly.

सम्पिय्यना – स्त्री॰ – (सम्प्रीतिः) प्रेम, अत्यन्त निकट सम्बन्ध। intimate relations, great fondness.

सम्पीणेति – क्रि॰ – (सम् √ प्री = सम्प्रीयते) सन्तुष्ट करता है, खुश करता है। satisfies, gladdens.

सम्पीलेति – क्रि॰ – (सम् √ पीड् = सम्पीडयति) पीड़ा देता है। oppresses, causes worry, crushes.

सम्पुच्छति – क्रि॰ – (सम्पृच्छति) पूछता है। asks.

सम्पुट – पु॰ – (सम्पुट) पत्र-पुट, अञ्जलि, दोन, अँजुरी। leaf, shaped like a bowl, the hollowed palms put together, as a form of greeting or respect.

सम्पुट्ट – वि॰ – (सम √ स्पृश + क्त संस्पृष्ट) सम्यक् स्पृष्ट, भली-भाँति छुआ गया। thoroughly touched, come in contact with.

सम्पुण्ण – कृदन्त – (सम्पूर्ण) सम्पूर्ण। full, complete, filled.

सम्पुप्फित – कृदन्त – (सम्पुष्पित) पुष्पित। in full bloom.

सम्पूजेति – क्रि॰ – (सम् √ पूज् = सम्पूजयति / सम्पूजयते) सम्मान करता है। honours, respects.

सम्पूरेति – क्रि॰ – (सम्पूरयति) fills, accomplishes.

सम्फ – न॰ – (शाष्य) तुच्छ, व्यर्थ, निष्प्रयोजन। frivolous.

सम्फप्पलाप – पु॰ – (शाष्य-प्रलाप) व्यर्थ बकवास। frivolous talk.

सम्फस्स – पु॰ – (संस्पर्श) स्पर्श। touch, contact.

सम्फुल्ल – वि॰ – (सम्फुल्ल) उत्फुल्ल, अच्छी तरह खिला हुआ फूल। fully open flower open blossom.

सम्फुसति – क्रि॰ – (संस्पृशति) स्पर्श करता है। touches, comes in contact with.

सम्फुसना – स्त्री॰ – (संस्पर्शन / संस्पर्शना) स्पर्श। touch.

सम्फुसित – कृदन्त – (संस्पृष्ट) स्पर्शकृत। touched, well fitted.

सम्बद्ध – पू॰ क्रि॰ – (सम्बद्ध) जुड़ा हुआ, संयुक्त। connected.

सम्बन्ध – पु॰ – (सम्बन्ध) परस्पर का सम्बन्ध। mutual relation or connection.

सम्बन्धति – क्रि॰ – (सम्बध्नाति) जोड़ता है। binds together, unites.

√ सम्ब – (भू॰) – (माडने) सजाना। to decorate, to adorn.

सम्बन्धन – न॰ – (सम्बन्धन) सम्बन्ध का जोड़ना। connection.

सम्बर – पु॰ – (शाम्बर) असुरों का एक राजा जिसका नाम सम्बर था। Sambar, the name of a king of asuras or demons.

सम्बरी – स्त्री॰ – (शाम्बरी) जादूगरनी, माया-जाल। a female juggler, illusion.

सम्बल – न॰ – (शाम्बल) पाथेय, रास्ते का कलेवा। (food) provisions for the journey.

सम्बहुल – वि॰ – (सम्बहुल) अनेक, बहुत करके। many.

सम्बाध – पु॰ – (सम्बाध) बाधा, रुकावट, भीड़-भाड़। obstruction, inconve-nience, crowding.

सम्बाधेति – क्रि॰ – (सम् √ बाध = सम्बाधते) बाधित होता है, भीड़-भाड़ से घिरा रहता है। gets crowded, faces obstruction.

सम्बाहति – क्रि॰ – (संवाहति) मालिश करता है। massages, rubs.

सम्बाहन – न॰ – (संवाहन) मालिश। massage, rubbing, shampooing.

सम्बुक – पु॰ – (शाम्बूक) जल शुक्ति, सीप। oyster shell.

सम्बुज्झति – क्रि॰ – (सम्बुद्धयते) भली-भाँति समझता है। understands clearly.

सम्बुद्ध – पु॰ – (सम्बुद्ध) सम्यक् सम्बुद्ध, सम्पूर्ण ज्ञानी। the omniscient one.

सम्बुल-जातक – (जा॰ सं॰ 519) – पति परायण सम्बुला द्वारा जंगल में भी साथ जाकर अपने कोढ़ी पति की सेवा करने की कथा। the story (No. 519) of queen Sambulā who went with her leper husband and tended him with great divotion.

सम्बोज्झङ्ग – पु॰ – (सम्बोध्यङ्ग) सम्बोधि-प्राप्ति में सहायक अंग। constituent of enlightenment.

सम्बोधन – न॰ – (सम्बोधन) आमन्त्रण, प्रबोध। (1) arousing, call, (2) vocative case.

सम्बोधि – स्त्री॰ – (सम्बोधि) पूर्ण ज्ञान। enlightenment, the highest wisdom.

सम्बोधेति – क्रि॰ – (सम्बोधयति) ज्ञान देता है, शिक्षा देता है। teaches, preaches, makes understand.

सम्भ – (भू॰) – (विश्वासे) भरोसा करना। to put faith, to keep faith.

सम्भग्ग – कृदन्त – (संभग्न) टूटा हुआ। broken, split.

सम्भज्जति – क्रि॰ – (सम् √ भञ्ज = संभञ्जनति) तोड़ता है। breaks, gets split.

सम्भत – (सम्भृत) लाया गया। brought together, stored up.

सम्भत्त – वि॰ – (सम्भक्त) मित्र, समर्पित व्यक्ति। friend, a devoted person.

सम्भम – पु॰ – (सम्भ्रम) व्यग्रता, उलझन, उत्तेजना, भ्रान्ति। excitement, confusion.

सम्भमति – क्रि॰ – (सम् + भ्रमति) चक्कर खाता है। revolves.

सम्भव – पु॰ – (सम्भव) उत्पत्ति। origin, birth.

सम्भवति – क्रि॰ – (सम्भवति) उत्पन्न होता है। arises, comes in to existence.

सम्भवन – न॰ – (सम्भवन) उत्पन्न होता है। coming into existence.

सम्भवेसी – पु॰ – (सम्भवेषिन्) उत्पत्ति की इच्छा करने वाला। one who is seeking birth.

सम्भार – पु॰ – (सम्भार) सामग्री। materials.

सम्भावना – स्त्री॰ – (सम्भावना) सत्कार। honour, reverence.

सम्भावनीय – वि॰ – (सम्भावनीय) आदरणीय। a venerable.

सम्भावेति – क्रि॰ – (सम्भावयति) सत्कार करता है। esteems, honours.

सम्भिन्दति – क्रि॰ – (सम् √ भिद् = सम्भि – नक्ति) (1) मिलाता है (2) तोड़ता है। (1) mixes, (2) breaks.

सम्भिन्न – कृदन्त – (सम्भिन्न) टूटा हुआ। broken.

सम्भीत – कृदन्त – (सम्भीत) भयभीत। terrified.

√ सम्भु – क्रि॰ – (प्राप्तकरणे) प्राप्त करना। to collect.

सम्भुञ्जति – क्रि॰ – (सम् √ भुज् = सम्भुनक्ति) मिलकर खाता है। eats together.

सम्भूत – कृदन्त – (सम् √ भू + क्त = सम्भूत) उत्पन्न हुआ। arisen, come in to existence.

सम्भेद – पु॰ – (सम्भेद) मिलावट। mixing up, confusion.

सम्भोग – पु॰ – (सम्भोग) (1) सहभोज (2) सहवास (मैथुन)। (1) eating together, (2) sexual.

सम्म – अव्यय – (सौम्य) निकटस्थ व्यक्तियों के लिए सम्बोधन-पद। (used in vocative case) my dear.

सम्म – न॰ – (मञ्जीरम्) मंजीर। a cymbal.

सम्मक्खन – न॰ – (√ मुक्ष + ल्युट् = भ्रक्षण) तेल मर्दन करता है, तेल मालिश करता है। smearing.

सम्मक्खेति – क्रि॰ – (भ्रक्षयति) तेल मर्दन करता है। smears.

सम्मग्गत – वि॰ – (सम्यक्-गतः) सम्यक मार्गी। who has come to the right path.

सम्मज्जति – क्रि॰ – (सम् √ मार्ज – सम्मार्जयति / ते) झाड़ू देता है। sweeps, polishes.

सम्मज्जनी – स्त्री॰ – (सम्मार्जनी) झाड़ू। a broom.

सम्मत – कृदन्त – (सम्मत) जिसे सहमति प्राप्त हो। agreed upon.

सम्मताल – पु॰ – (मञ्जीर) मंजीरा। a cymbal.

सम्मति – क्रि॰ – (√ शम् - शाम्यति) शान्त होता है। becomes appeased, calmed.

सम्मत्त – कृदन्त – (सम्मत्त) नशे में धुत। intoxicated.

सम्मद – पु॰ – (तन्द्रा) तन्द्रा। drowsiness after a meal.

सम्मदक्खात – वि॰ – (सम्यक् + आख्यात) भली प्रकार से समझाया गया। well preached.

सम्मदञ्ञा – पू॰ क्रि॰ – (सम्यक् ज्ञात्वा) अच्छी तरह समझकर। having understood properly.

सम्मदञ्ञाय – पू॰ क्रि॰ – (सम्यक् ज्ञात्वा) भली-भाँति समझकर। having understood properly.

सम्मदेव – अव्यय – (सम्मगेव) ठीक तरह से। properly.

सम्मद – पु॰ – (सम्मर्द) भीड़। crowd.

सम्महति – क्रि॰ – (सम् √ मृद् - सम्मर्दति) कुचल देता है। tramples down, crushes.

सम्महन – न॰ – (सम्मर्दन) कुचलना। trampling, crushing.

सम्महस – वि॰ – (सम्यक्दर्शी) सम्यक् दृष्टि रखने वाला। seeing rightly, having right views.

सम्मनेति – क्रि॰ – (सम्मन्त्रयति) मंत्रणा करता है, परामर्श करता है। consults or discusses together.

सम्मनति – क्रि॰ – (सम् √ मन - सम्मन्यते) अधिकार देता है, सहमत होता है, स्वीकार करता है, चुनाव करता है। authorises, agrees, assents, selects.

सम्मपञ्ञा – स्त्री॰ – (सम्यक्-प्रज्ञा) सम्यक्-प्रज्ञा। right exertion.

सम्मसति – क्रि॰ – भली-भाँति ग्रहण करता है, छूता है, समझता है, चिन्तन करता है। grasps, touches, knows, thoroughly meditates.

सम्मा – अव्यय – (सम्यक्) सम्यक् रूप से। properly, rightly.

सम्मा-आजीव – पु॰ – (सम्यक् आजीविका) सम्यक् आजीविका। right means of livelihood.

सम्मकमन्त – पु॰ – (सम्यगाचरण) सम्यक् आचरण। right conduct.

सम्मा-दिट्ठि – स्त्री॰ – सम्यक् दृष्टि, right views.

सम्मा-दिट्ठिक – वि॰ – (सम्यक्-दृष्टा) सम्यक् दृष्टि वाला। having right views.

सम्म-पतिपत्ति – स्त्री॰ – (सम्यक-प्रतिपत्ति) सम्यक् आचरण। right mental disposition.

सम्मा-पटिपन्न – वि॰ – (सम्यक्-प्रतिपन्न) सम्यक् प्रवृत्त। rightly disposed.

सम्मा-पास – पु॰ – (सम्यक्-प्राश) व्रत विशेष। a kind of sacrifice.

सम्मा-वत्तना – स्त्री॰ – (सम्यक्-वर्त्तनम्) सम्यक् व्यवहार। proper conduct.

सम्मा-वाचा – स्त्री॰ – (सम्यक्-वाक्) सम्यक् वाणी। right speech.

सम्मा-वायामो – पु॰ – (सम्यक् + उद्योग) सम्यक् प्रयत्न। right effort.

सम्मा-विमुत्ति – स्त्री॰ – (सम्यक्-विमुक्ति) right emancipation.

सम्मा-संकप्प – पु॰ – (सम्यक् + संकल्प) सम्यक् संकल्प। right resolve, right intention.

सम्मोदमान-जातक – (जा॰ सं॰ 33) – एकता की शक्ति और विग्रह की दुर्बलता को व्यक्त करने वाला दृष्टान्त। the story (No. 33) tells the strength of unity and evils of quarrel.

सम्मोस – पु॰ – (सम्मोह) मूढ़ता, घबड़ाहट। confusion, delusion.

सम्मोह – पु॰ – घबड़ाहट, मोह। confusion, delusion.

सय – वि॰ – (स्वयम) अपना। self, by ownself.

सयति – क्रि॰ – (√ शी - शेते) सोता है, लेटता है। sleeps, lies down.

सयथु – पु॰ – (कण्डू) खुजली। itches, itching.

सयन – न॰ – **(शयन)** सोना, शयन। sleeping, a bed.

सयनघर – न॰ – **(शयनगृह)** शयनागार, सोने का कमरा। a sleeping room.

सयमभू – पु॰ – **(स्वयम्भू)** विधाता, स्वयंभू। creator, self-existent (i.e. Brahman).

सयं – अव्यय – **(स्वयम्)** अपने आप। self, by ownself.

सयंकत – वि॰ – **(स्वयम् + कृत)** स्वयंकृत। made by itself, self-done.

सयंवर – पु॰ – **(स्वयंवर)** स्वयंवर, अपने पति का चुनाव स्वयं करना। self-choice, to seek husband according to own choice.

सयान – वि॰ – **(√ शी + शतृ = शयान)** सोते हुए। sleeping, lying down.

सयापित – कृदन्त – **(शायापित)** लिटाया गया। lain down.

सयापेति – क्रि॰ – **(√ शी + णिच् = शाययति)** सुलाता है। makes one sleep or lie down.

सय्ह – वि॰ – **(सह्य)** सहन करने योग्य। bearable, able to endure.

सय्ह-जातक – (जा॰ सं॰ 310) – राजपुरोहित बनाने के आमन्त्रण को ठुकराने की कथा। the story (No. 310) tells how an ascetic refused the post of a chaplain.

सर – पु॰ तथा न॰ – **(शर)** (1) शर, बाण (2) स्वर (आवाज) (3) स्वर अक्षर (अ व्यञ्जन अक्षर)। (1) an arrow (2) sound (3) a vowel.

√ सर – (भू) – **(गति, हिंसा, चित्तासु)** आना, हिंसा करना, सोचना। to come, to torture, to think.

सरतुण्ड – न॰ – **(शरतुण्ड)** बाणाग्र, तीर की नोंक। point of an arrow.

सर-तीर – न॰ – **(सरसीतट)** सरोवर का किनारा। the bank of a lake.

सरभङ्ग – पु॰ – **(शरभङ्ग)** तीर को तोड़ डालना। the arrow breaking.

सरभञ्ज – न॰ – **(स्वर-भञ्ज)** गायन-विधि I विशेष। a particular practice of a vocal music.

सरभाणक – पु॰ – **(स्वर-भाणक)** धर्मग्रन्थों का सस्वर पाठ करने वाला। one who recites the sacred texts.

सर-मण्डल – न॰ – **(स्वर-मण्डल)** स्वर-मण्डल। a group of vowels.

सरक – पु॰ – **(चषक)** प्याला, कसोरा, सरावा, सकोरा। a drinking bowl or vessel.

सरज – वि॰ -- **(स + रज)** रजोयम, धूल सहित। dusty, impure.

सरट – पु॰ – **(सरट)** कृकलास, गिरगिट। lizard.

सरण – न॰ – **(शरण)** संरक्षण, पनाह। protection, refuge.

सरणागमन – न॰ – **(शरणागमन)** शरण-ग्रहण। taking refuge.

सरणीय – वि॰ – **(स्मरणीय)** स्मरणीय। fit to be remembered.

सरति – क्रि॰ – **(√ स्मृ - स्मरति)** याद रखता है। remembers.

सरद – पु॰ – **(शरद्)** शरद् ऋतु। the autumn.

सरभ – पु॰ – **(शरभ)** प्राचीन साहित्य तथा कोश-ग्रन्थों में एक कल्पित आठ पैरों वाला पशु जो हाथी और गैंडे को भी मार सकता था किन्तु जन्तु विज्ञानी इसे

कपोल-कल्पित बताते हैं। आज तक न उक्त पशु देखा गया न ही उसके जीवाश्म मिले हैं। संभव है कि शलभ विशेष को ही शरभ कह दिया गया है जो की वर्ग का प्राणी है कीट के छः पाद और मुखाग्र पर पाँव की शक्ल जैसे दो संसूचक अवयव होते है। it is a mythical animal described as having eight feet. Nowhere it has been traced. Salabha, may be Śalabha, an insect which has six legs and two leg-like indicators on the face.

सरभ-जातक – (शरभ-जातक) देखें सरभ-मिग-जातक। see Sarabha Mig Jātaka.

सरभ-मिग-जातक – (जा॰ सं॰ 483) – सरभ-मृग द्वारा राजा को धर्मोपदेश देने की कथा। the story (No. 483) tells how Sarabh-mṛga preached to the king.

सरभू – पु॰ – (सरदु/सरट) कृकलास, छिपकली। lizard.

सरभू – (सरयू भी) – स्त्री॰ – (सरयू) बुद्धकालीन पाँच नदियों में से एक, जिसके दाहिने तट पर अयोध्या बसी है। one of the five main during rivers the Buddhist period, the famous Ayodhyā is situated on its right bank.

सरभङ्ग-जातक – (जा॰ सं॰ 522) – अप्रतिम धनुर्धर (जोतिपाल) के अद्भुत कौशल की कथा। it is a story (No. 522) of an unparralleled archer Jotipāla's astonishing skill.

सरल – पु॰ – (सरल) देवदारु नामक वृक्ष विशेष। the tree Devadāru, a species of pine tree.

सरलद्दव – पु॰ – (सरल द्रव) देवदारु के गोंद से बना सुगन्धित द्रव्य। a fragrant preparation from the exudation of Devadāru tree.

सरलांग – पु॰ – (सरलाङ्ग) देवदारु का तेल तारपीन। turpentine.

सरव्व – न॰ – (शरव्य) शरु अर्थात् तीर से वेध्य, लक्ष्य। target of an arrow.

सरस – वि॰ – (सरस) स्वादिष्ट। tasteful.

सरसी – स्त्री॰ – (सरसी) पुष्करिणी, छोटी झील। a small lake, tank.

सरसीरुह – न॰ – (सरसीरुह) सरोरुह, कमल। a lotus.

सरस्सति – स्त्री॰ – (सरस्वती) सरस्वती नदी। the river Sarasvati.

सराग – वि॰ – (सराग) रागयुक्त, रागी। lustful.

सराजिक – वि॰ – (सराजक) राजा के साथ। including a king.

सराव – पु॰ – (शरावः) कुल्हड़, सकोरा। shallow earthen cup.

सरासन – न॰ – (शरासन) धनुष। a bow.

सरिक्खक – वि॰ – (सदृश) एक जैसा। similar.

सरितव्व – कृदन्त – (स्मृ + तव्यत् = स्मर्त्तव्य) स्मरण करने योग्य। to be remembered, memorable.

सरिता – स्त्री॰ – (सरिता) नदी। river.

सरितु – पु॰ – (स्मृतिमान) याद रखने वाला। one who remembers.

सरीर – न॰ – (शरीर) शरीर। the body.

सरीर-किच्च – न॰ – (शरीर-कृत्य) शौच कर्म। easing of the body, obsequies.

सरीरट्ठ – वि॰ – (शरीरस्थ) शरीर स्थित ।
deposited in the body.

सरीर-धातु – स्त्री॰ – (शरीर-धातु) बुद्ध के
पवित्र शरीर-धातु । a body relic of the
Buddha.

सरीर-निस्सन्द – पु॰ – (शरीर-निष्यन्द) शरीर
का मल । excretion of the body.

सरीप्पभा – स्त्री॰ – (शरीर-प्रभा) शरीर की
कान्ति । lustre of the body.

सरीर-मंस – न॰ – (शरीर-मांस) शरीर का
मांस । the flesh of the body.

सरीर-वण्ण – पु॰ – (शरीर-वर्ण) शरीर का
वर्ण । the appearance of the body.

सरीर-वलञ्ज – पु॰ – (शरीर-मल) शरीर-
मल । discharge from the body.

सरीर-वलञ्जट्ठान – न॰ – (शौच स्थान)
शौच स्थान, शौच करने का स्थान । a
toilet, a place where people ease
their bodies, where people
relieve.

सरीर-सण्ठान – न॰ – (शरीर-संस्थान)
शारीरिक आकार-प्रकार । feature of the
body.

सरीरी – पु॰ – (शरीरी) प्राणी । living being.

सरूप – वि॰ – (सरूप) समरूप, उसी रूप
का । of the same form, having a
form.

सरूपता – स्त्री॰ – (सरूपता) अनुरूपता,
समानता । similarity.

सरोज – न॰ – (सरोज) सरोरुह, कमल । lotus.

सरोरुह – न॰ – (सरोरुह) सरोज, कमल ।
lotus.

√सल – (भू॰) – (गमनार्थे) जाना । to go.

सलक्खण – वि॰ – (सलक्षण) शुभ चिह्नों से
युक्त, लक्षणों सहित । together with
the characteristics.

सलभ – पु॰ – (शलभ) पतिंगा, दीपक पर
जलने वाला । a moth, a grasshopper.

सलळवती – (सलिलवती) सलिलवती, मध्य
मण्डल की दक्षिणी सीमा । river
Salilavatī, which forms the
southern boundary of middle
India.

सललागार – (सल्लागार) जैतवन का एक
बुद्धकालीन भवन । one amongst the
famous buildings of Jetavana at
the time of Buddha.

सलाका – स्त्री॰ – (शलाका) सलाई, छतरी
की तीली, छोटी लकड़ी, घास की
धारदार पत्ती, चीड़-फाड़ का औजार ।
ribs of a parasol, a blade of
grass, a surgical instrument,
slide of wood.

सलाका-वुत्त – वि॰ – (शलाका-भुक्त)
शलाका भोजन खाकर रहने वाला ।
subsisting by means of food
tickets.

सलाकग्ग – न॰ – (शलाकाग्र) शलाका की
विधि से भोजन बाँटने का स्थान । a
room for distributing food on
tickets.

सलाका-गाह – पु॰ – (शलाका-ग्राह)
शलाकाओं का ग्रहण करना । the
collection of food tickets or votes.

सलाका-गाहापक – पु॰ – (शलाका वितरक)
शलाका बाँटने वाला । distributing of
voting tickets.

सलाका-भत्त – न॰ – (शलाका भोजन)
शलाकाओं के अनुसार बाँटा जाने वाला
भोजन । food to be distributed.

सलाटुक – वि॰ – (शद:) सलाद, बिना भूने पकाए कच्ची ताजी खाई जाने वाली शाक-सब्जी। salād, leaves and vegetables taken without roasting or cooking.

सलाभ – पु॰ – (स्वलाभ) अपना लाभ। one's own gain or advantage.

सलिल – न॰ – (सलिल) जल, पानी। water.

सलिल-धारा – स्त्री॰ – (सलिल-धारा) जल-धारा। a shower of water, waterfall.

सल्ल – पु॰ – (शल्य) बर्छी, भाला, कुन्त, तीर, कील। a dart, spike, stake.

सल्लक – पु॰ – (शल्यक) साही का तीलीनुमा काँटा। the quill of a porcupine.

सल्लकत्त – पु॰ – (शल्यकार) शल्य-कर्ता। a surgeon.

सल्ल-कत्तिय – न॰ – (शल्य-कृत्य) शल्य-कर्म। surgery.

सल्लक्खन – न॰ – (सद् + लक्षण) विवेक। right consideration.

सल्लक्खना – स्त्री॰ – (सद् + लक्षणा) विचार, मनन। right consideration.

सल्लक्खेति – क्रि॰ – ध्यान देता है। considering.

सल्लपति – क्रि॰ – (सम् √लप् = संलपति) बात-चीत करता है। talks with, converses.

संल्लपन – न॰ – (संलाप) बात-चीत, वार्तालाप। conversation, discussion.

सल्लहुक – वि॰ – (सं + लघुक) हलका। light, frugal.

सल्लाप – पु॰ – (संलाप) मैत्रीपूर्ण बातचीत। friendly talk.

सल्लिखति – क्रि॰ – (सं √लिख = संल्लिखति) टुकड़े-टुकड़े कर डालता है। cuts into slices.

सल्लीन – (सन्लीन) एकान्त-प्राप्त। secluded.

सल्लीयति – क्रि॰ – (संलीयते) एकान्तवास करता है। becomes secluded.

सल्लीयना – स्त्री॰ – (संलीयना) एकान्त। seclusion.

सल्लेख – पु॰ – (संल्लेख) कड़ी तपस्या। austere penance.

सवङ्क – वि॰ – (सवङ्क) वक्रिम, टेढ़ेपन सहित। having bend (bends).

सवण – न॰ – (श्रवण) सुनना, कान। hearing, the ear.

सवणीय – न॰ – (श्रवणीय) कर्ण-प्रिय। pleasant to hear.

सवन – न॰ – (√सु + ल्युट् - स्रवण) बहना। flowing.

सवति – क्रि॰ – (√सु = स्रवति) बहता है। flows.

सवन्ती – स्त्री॰ – (स्रवन्ती) सरित, नदी। river.

सविघात – वि॰ – (स + वि + घात) विद्वेष-युक्त, उत्पीड़न-सन्ताप सहित। bringing vexation.

सविञ्ञाणक – वि॰ – (स + विज्ञानक) चेतन प्राणी, होश वाला। animate, conscious.

सवितक्क – वि॰ – (स + वितर्क) सवितर्क, संकल्प-विकल्प-युक्त। full of reasoning.

सविभक्तिक – वि॰ – (सविभक्तिक) वर्गीकरण सहित। consisting of classification.

सवेर – वि॰ – (सवैर) वैर-सहित। connected with enemity.

सव्यञ्जन – वि॰ – (स + सव्यञ्जन) (1) सालन-सहित (2) व्यञ्जन अक्षरों सहित। (1) together with condiments, (2) including consonants.

√ सस – (भू॰) – (श्वसनम्) साँस लेना। to breath.

सस – पु॰ – (शश / शशक) खरगोश। hare.

सस-लक्खण – न॰ – (शशाङ्क) शश लाँञ्छन। चन्द्रमा में प्रतीत्य खरगोश का चिह्न। the sign of hare in the moon.

सस-विसाण – न॰ – (शशा-विषाण) शश-शृङ्ग, खरगोश की सींग (असम्भव)। a hare's horn (an impossibility).

सस-(पण्डित)-जातक – (जा॰ सं॰ 316) – शीलवान खरगोश द्वारा भूखे अतिथि को स्वमांस ही दान देने की संकल्प कथा। the story (No. 316) tells how a virtuous hare decided to give his own body to the hungry guest.

ससक्कं – क्रि॰ वि॰ – (सशक्यम्) निश्चय से, जितना हो सके उतना। certainly, as much as possible.

ससङ्क – पु॰ – (शशाङ्क) चन्द्रमा। the moon.

ससति – क्रि॰ – (√ श्वस = श्वसिति) सांस लेता है। breaths, takes breaths.

ससत्थ – वि॰ – (सशस्त्र) सशस्त्र। bearing weapons.

ससन – न॰ – (हनन) मार डालना। killing.

ससन्तान – पु॰ – स्व-चित्त-सन्तान। family, originating in or caused by self (in mind).

ससम्भार – वि॰ – (ससम्भार) उप सामग्री समेत, अचार-चटनी आदि के साथ। with the ingredients or constituents, with accompaniments.

ससी – पु॰ – (शशि) चन्द्रमा। the moon.

ससीसं – क्रि॰ वि॰ – (सशीर्ष) आशीर्ष, सिर के साथ, सिर तक। together with the head, up to the head.

ससुर – पु॰ – (श्वशुर) पत्नी अथवा पति का पिता। father-in-law.

ससेन – न॰ – (स-सैन्य) सेना सहित। accompanied by an army.

सस्स – न॰ – (शस्य) धान्य, फसल। corns, crop.

सस्स-कम्म – न॰ – (शस्य-कर्म) खेती। agriculture.

सस्स-काल – न॰ – (शस्य-काल) खेती काटने का समय। harvest time.

सस्सत – वि॰ – (शाश्वत्) शाश्वत, सदैव रहने वाला। eternal, permanent.

सस्सत-दिट्ठि – स्त्री॰ – (शाश्वत दृष्टि) शाश्वत् दृष्टि। eternal sight.

सस्सत-वाद – पु॰ – (शाश्वत-वाद) आत्मा की नित्यता का सिद्धान्त। eternalism, doctrine of eternity of soul (or ātman).

सस्सत-वादी – पु॰ – (शाश्वत्-वादी) शाश्वत सिद्धान्त वाला, आत्मा को नित्य मानने वाला। follower of eternalism.

सस्सतिक – वि॰ – (शाश्वतिक) आत्मा को अन्तकालिक मानने वाला। follower of eternalism.

सस्समण-ब्राह्मण – वि॰ – (सश्रमण-ब्राह्मण) श्रमणों तथा ब्राह्मणों सहित। including teachers and brāhmaṇas.

सससामिक – वि॰ – (सस्वामिक) स्वामि-युक्त, जिसका पति हो, जिसका मालिक हो । having a husband or a owner.

सस्सिरीक – वि॰ – (सश्रीक) श्री-सहित, ऐश्वर्य सहित । glorious, resplendent.

सस्सु – स्त्री॰ – (श्वश्रू) सास, पति अथवा पत्नी की माँ । mother-in-law.

√सह – (भू॰) – (मर्षणे) क्षमा करना । to forgive.

सह – अव्यय – (सह) एक उपसर्ग, साथ (वि॰) सहनशील । (conjunctive particle) with, together, accompanied by.

सहकार – पु॰ – (सहकार) आम्र-फल । mango.

सह-गत – वि॰ – (सहगत) युक्त, समन्वित । connected or endowed with.

सहज – वि॰ – एक साथ उत्पन्न । born together.

सहजात – वि॰ – (सहजात/सोदर) सहोदर । brother, co-uterine, born at the same time, a twin.

सहजाति – न॰ – (सहजात) गंगा के तट पर बसा नगर विशेष, जो वैशाली से थोड़ी दूर गंगा पार था । a township situated on the bank of Gaṅgā, people of Vaiśālī used to go there by boat.

सहजीवी – वि॰ – (सहजीवी) साथ रहने वाला । living together with.

सह-नन्दी – वि॰ – (सह-नन्दी) साथ-साथ आनन्द मनाने वाला । rejoicing together.

सह-धम्मिक – वि॰ – (सह-धार्मिक) सहधर्मी, अपने धर्म का सहानुयायी । co-religionist.

सह-भू – वि॰ – (सह-भू) एक साथ उत्पन्न होने वाला । arising together with.

सहयोग – पु॰ – (सहयोग) पारस्परिक सहायता, सहकारिता । co-operation.

सहवास – पु॰ – (सहवास) साथ रहना । living together.

सह-सेय्या – स्त्री॰ – (शहसय्या) साथ-साथ सोना । sharing the same bedroom.

सहति – क्रि॰ – (√सह् - सहते) सहन करता है, योग्य सिद्ध होता है, जीत लेता है । bears, endures, overcomes.

सहत्थ – पु॰ – (स्वहस्त) अपना हाथ । one's own hand.

सहन – न॰ – (सहन) तितिक्षा, सहनशक्ति, सहन करना । endurance.

सहम्पति – पु॰ – (महाब्रह्म) अनेक 'ब्रह्माओं' में ज्येष्ठ । the great Brahman, the Supreme Spirit (in Buddhism).

सहव्य – न॰ – (सहचर) मित्र । friend.

सहव्यता – स्त्री॰ – (साहचर्य) मैत्री । friendship.

सहसा – अव्यय – (सहसा) अकस्मात्, जबर्दस्ती से । suddenly, forcibly.

सहस्स – न॰ – (सहस्र) हजार । a thousand.

सहस्सक्ख – पु॰ – (सहस्राक्ष) सहस्राक्ष इन्द्र । the thousand-eyed Sakka, Indra.

सहस्सक्खत्तुं – क्रि॰ वि॰ – (सहस्र बारम्) हजार बार । a thousand times.

सहस्सग्घनक – वि॰ – (सहस्रार्घनक) हजार के मूल्य का । worth a thousand times.

सहस्सत्थविका – स्त्री॰ – (सहस्र-स्तविका) हजार अशर्फियों की थैली। a bag containing a thousand gold coins.

सहस्सधा – क्रि॰ वि॰ – (सहस्रधा) हजार तरह से। in a thousand ways.

सहस्सनेत्त – वि॰ – (सहस्रनेत्र) सहस्राक्षी, देखें सहस्सक्ख। see Sahassakkha.

सहस्स-भण्डिका – स्त्री॰ – (सहस्र-भण्डिका) देखें सहस्सत्थविका। see Sahassatthavikā.

सहस्स-रंसी – पु॰ – (सहस्र-रश्मि) भानु, सूर्य। the sun.

सहस्सार – वि॰ – (सहस्रार) सहस्र अरों वाला चक्र, हजार तीलियों वाला पहिया। having thousand spokes.

सहस्सिक – वि॰ – (साहस्रिक) हजार वाला। consisting of a thousand.

सहस्सि-लोक-धातु – स्त्री॰ – (सहस्र-लोक-धातु) सहस्र परिमाण के लोक समूह। a thousandfold world.

सहाय – पु॰ – (सहायक) सहचर, साथी, सहायक। a companion, an ally.

सहायक – वि॰ – (सहायक) सहायता करने वाला, दोस्त। a friend, an ally.

सहायता – स्त्री॰ – (सहायता) मैत्री, सहयोग। friendship, help.

सहित – वि॰ – (सहित) साथ-साथ लिए। accompanied with, consistent.

सहितब्ब – कृदन्त – (√सह् + तव्यत् = साढेव्व) सहन करने योग्य। to be endured.

सहितु – पु॰ – (सहनकर्त्ता) सहन करने वाला। one who endures.

सहेतुक – वि॰ – (सहेतुक) सकारण। having a cause.

सहोढ – वि॰ – चुराए गए माल के साथ। together with the stolen goods.

सळायतन – न॰ – (षडायतन) छः ज्ञानेन्द्रियों आँख, कान, नाक, जीभ त्वचा, मन का समूह। group of five sense organs plus mind.

संकस्स – न॰ – (संकस्स) संकिसा। बौद्ध तीर्थ-स्थल जहाँ भगवान बुद्ध अपनी माँ को उपदेश देकर स्वर्ग तावत्रिंस से उतरे हैं। फारूखाबाद, उत्तर प्रदेश, One of the Buddha's Holy places where the Buddha descended from heaven.

सं – अव्यय – प्रसन्नतापूर्वक। with joy.

संयत्त – वि॰ – (संयत) आत्म-जित। restrained, self-controlled.

संयतत्त – वि॰ – (संयतत्त्व) संयतता, आत्मनियन्त्रण का भाव, आत्मजयी। restrainment, self-controlled.

संयतचारी – वि॰ – (संयतचारी) संयमी। abstinence, living in self-control.

संयम – पु॰ – (संयम) इन्द्रियों का वश में होना। abstinence, control over senses.

संयमन – न॰ – (संयमन) देखें संयम। see Samyam.

संयमी – पु॰ – (संयमी) इन्द्रिय-जयी। restrained.

संयमेति – क्रि॰ – (संयच्छते = सम्- √ यम्) संयम करता है। restrains, practises self-control.

संयुञ्जति – क्रि॰ – (सं √ युज् = संयुङ्क्ते) जुड़ता है, सम्बन्धित होता है। becomes combined or connected.

संयुत (संयुत्त भी) – कृदन्त – **(संयुक्त)** जुड़ा हुआ, सम्बन्धित। combined, connected.

संयुत्तनिकाय – पु० – **(संयुक्त निकाय)** सुत्तपिटक के पाँच निकायों में से एक। one of the five chapters of Suttapiṭaka.

संयूहति – क्रि० – ढेरी बना देता है। accumulates piles up, makes a heap.

संयोग – पु० – **(संयोग)** बन्धन, एकता, स्वर का तालमेल। a bond, union, association.

संयोजन – न० – **(संयोजन)** सम्बन्ध, बन्धन। connection, fettering.

संयोजनीय – वि० – **(सं √ युज् + अनीयर्)** संयोजनों, (बन्धनों के अनुकूल)। fit for combination.

संयोजेति – क्रि० – **(सं √ युज् = संयोजयति)** जोड़ता है, बाँधता है। joins, combines.

संरक्खति – क्रि० – **(सं √ रक्ष = संरक्षित)** पहरा देता है, रक्षा करता है। guards, wards off.

संरक्खना – स्त्री० – **(संरक्षण)** पहरा देना, संरक्षण। guarding, protection.

संवच्छर – न० – **(संवत्सर)** वर्ष। a year.

संवट्टकप्प – क्रि० – **(सवर्त्तकल्प)** उच्छिन्न होने वाला कल्प। dissolving world.

संवट्टति – क्रि० – **(सं √ वर्त्त = सवत्तेति)** विद्यमान रहता है। remains, exists.

संवट्टन – न० – **(संवर्त्तन)** संवर्त्तन, लौटना। rolling, dissolution.

संवड्ढ – कृदन्त – **(संवृद्ध)** बढ़ा हुआ। grown up, brought up.

संवड्ढति – क्रि० – **(सम् + √ वृध् = संवर्धते)** बढ़ता है, वृद्धि को प्राप्त होता है। grows, increases.

संवड्ढित – कृदन्त – **(संवर्धित)** संवर्धित, बढ़ा हुआ। increased, grown up.

संवड्ढेति – क्रि० – **(संवर्धयति)** बढ़ाता है, पोसता है, पालन करता है। nourishes, brings up.

संवण्णना – स्त्री० – **(संवर्णना)** व्याख्या। exposition, explanation.

संवण्णेति – क्रि० – **(संवर्णयति)** व्याख्या करता है। explains, comments, praises.

संवत्तति – क्रि० – **(स √ वर्त्त = संवत्तते)** विद्यमान रहता है। exists.

संवत्तनिक – वि० – **(संवर्त्तनिक)** प्रेरक। conducive, involving.

संवत्तेति – क्रि० – **(संवर्त्तयति)** प्रवृत्त करता है। makes go on, continues.

संवर – पु० – **(संवर)** संयम। restraint.

संवर-जातक – **(जा० सं० 462)** – संवर राजकुमार ने आचार्योपदेश के अनुसार कार्य करके सभी का हृदय जीत लिया। the story (No. 462) of prince Saṁvara who, by acting on his teacher's advice, won all hearts.

संवरण – न० – **(संवरण)** रोक। restriction, obstruction.

संवरति – क्रि० – **(सं √ वृ = संवरति)** रोकता है। restrains.

संवरी – स्त्री० – **(शर्वरी)** रात्रि। night.

संवसति – क्रि० – **(सं √ वस् = संवसति)** संगति करता है। associates.

संवास – पु० – **(संवास)** साथ रहना। co-residence.

संवासक – वि॰ – (संवासक) साथ-साथ रहने वाला। co-resident.

संविग्ग – कृदन्त – (सं √विज् + क्त = संविग्न) उद्विग्न। agitated, moved by anger or fear.

संविज्जति – क्रि॰ – (सं √विद् = संविद्यते) विद्यमान रहता है। exists.

संविदहति – क्रि॰ – (सं + वि √धा = संविदधाति) व्यवस्था करता है। arranges, prepares.

सविदहन – न॰ – (संविधान) व्यवस्था। arrangement, giving orders.

संविधान – न॰ – (संविधान) देखें संविदहन। see Samvidahana.

संविधाय – पू॰ क्रि॰ – (संविधाय) व्यवस्था करके। getting arranged.

संविधायक – वि॰ – (संविधायक) व्यवस्थापक। manager, one who arranges.

संविधातु – कृदन्त – (संविधातुम्) व्यवस्था करने के लिए। to arrange.

संविभजति – क्रि॰ – (सं + वि √भज् = संविभजते) divides, shares.

संविभजन – न॰ – (संविभाजन) बाँटना। dividing, sharing.

संविभाग – पु॰ – (संविभाग) देखें संविभजन। see Samvibhajana.

संविभत्त – कृदन्त – (स + वि √भज् + क्त = संविभक्त) अच्छी तरह विभक्त। well divided.

संविभागी – पु॰ – (संविभागी) दानी / उदार। generous, open hearted.

संवुत – कृदन्त – (संवृत्त) संयत। restrained.

संवुतिन्द्रिय – वि॰ – (संवृत्तेन्द्रिय) संयतेन्द्रिय। having the senses under control.

संवेग – पु॰ – (संवेग) व्यग्रता। anxiety, agitation.

संवेजन – न॰ – (संवेजन) संवेग पैदा होना। causing of emotion or agitation.

संवेजनीय – वि॰ – (संवेदी) संवेग पैदा करने वाला। apt to cause emotion or agitation.

संवेजेति – क्रि॰ – (सं √विज् = संविजते) संवेग पैदा करता है। causes agitation or emotion.

√संस – (भू॰) – (प्रशंसने) प्रशंसा करता है। praises, applauds, eulogises.

संसग्ग – पु॰ – (संसर्ग) संगति, सम्बद्ध। union, contact.

संसट्ठ – कृदन्त – (संसृष्ट) श्लिष्ट, संलग्न, आसक्त। mixed with, associated with.

ससन्दति – क्रि॰ – अनुकूल होता है। responds, agrees, tallies.

संसन्देति – क्रि॰ – मिलान करता है। comprares, verifies.

संसप्पति – क्रि॰ – (संसर्पति) रेंगता है। creeps along.

संसप्पन – न॰ – (संसर्पण) रेंगना। crawling, writhing, struggling.

संसय – पु॰ – (संशय) संदेह। doubt.

संसरति – क्रि॰ – (सं √सृ = संसरति) चलता, फिरता है, संसरण करता है। moves about continuously, transmigrates.

संसरण – न॰ – (संसरण) संचरण। moving about, wandering.

संसादेति – एक ओर रखता है। keeps on one side.

संसग्गर – पु० – संसरण। world, a path, a road, a motion.

संसार-चक्क – न० – (संसार-चक्र) आवा-रामन, जन्म-मरण का चक्र। the wheel of rebirth.

संसार-दुक्ख – न० – (संसार-दुःख) जन्म-मरण रूपी दुःख। the ill of transmigration.

संसार-सागर – पु० – (संसार-सागर) संसार रूपी समुद्र। the ocean of rebirth.

संसिज्झति – क्रि० – (सं √सिध = ससिध्यति) सफल होता है। succeeds, becomes fulfilled.

संसित – कृदन्त – (शंसित) स्तुत, ख्यात, इष्ट। praised, desired.

संसिद्धि – स्त्री० – (संसिद्धि) सफलता। success.

संसिब्बित – कृदन्त – (सं √सिव् + त = संस्यूत) सिला, गूंथा। sewn, entwined.

संसीदति – क्रि० – (सं √सीद् = संसीदति) डूब जाता है, हिम्मत हार जाता है, दिल बैठ जाता है। sinks down, looses heart, feels depressed.

संसीदन – न० – (संसीदन) डूबना, तल में जाना। sinking down, drowns.

संसीन – कृदन्त – गिरा, नष्ट। fell, destroyed.

संसुद्ध – कृदन्त – (संशुद्ध) परिशुद्ध, पवित्र। pure, clean.

संसुद्ध-गहणिक – वि० – (शुद्ध परम्परावान्) शुद्ध वंश परम्परा का। of pure descent.

संसुद्धि – स्त्री० – (संशुद्धि) पवित्रता। purity.

संसूचक – वि० – (संसूचक) सूचक, सूचित करते हुए। indicator.

संसेदज – वि० – (स्वेदज) पसीने से उत्पन्न होने वाले जीव। born from sweat.

संसेव – पु० – (संसेव) देखें संसेवना। see Saṁsevanā.

संसेवति – क्रि० – (सं √सेव् - संसेवते) संगति करता है। associates, attends.

संसेवना – स्त्री० – (संसेवना) संगति। association.

संसेवी – वि० – (संसेवी) संगति में रहने वाला, सेवा में रहने वाला। associate, or attendant.

संहत – कृदन्त – (सं √हृ + त - संहृत) एकत्रित। collected.

संहत – वि० – (संहत) दृढ़, कसा हुआ। firm, compact.

संहरण – न० – (संहरण) एकत्र करना, तह बिठाना। gathering, folding.

संहरति – क्रि० – (संहरति) बटोरता है, सिकोड़ता है। draws together, folds up.

संहार – पु० – (संहार) संक्षेप, संग्रह। abridgement, compilation.

संहारक – वि० – (संहारक) बटोरने वाला, एकत्र करने वाला। drawing together.

संहित – वि० – (संहित) संयोजित, एकत्रित, युक्त। equipped with, possessed of.

संहिता – स्त्री० – (संहिता) मन्त्र समुच्चय, मेल, स्वरों का तालमेल। collection of

Vedic hymns, euphonic combination of letters.

√ **सा** – (दि.) – (तनूकरणे) पैना करना, स्तन धरना। to good one to act, to sharpen.

सा – पु॰ – (श्वा / श्वान) कुत्ता। dog.

सा – स्त्री॰ – (सा) वह (स्त्रीवाची)। she.

साक – पु॰ तथा न॰ – (शाक) शाक-सब्जी। vegetable.

साक-पन्न – पु॰ – (शाक-पर्ण) शाक के पत्ते। vegetable-leaf.

साकच्छा – स्त्री॰ – परामर्श, चर्चा। conversation, discussion.

साकटिक – पु॰ – (शाकटिक) शकट वाला, गाड़ीवान। a carter.

साकल्य – न॰ – (साकल्य) संकलता, सकल-भाव। totality.

साकिय – वि॰ – (शाक्य) शाक्य जाति का। belonging to Śākya race.

साकुणिक – पु॰ – (शाकुनिक) शकुन्त-बधिक, चिड़ीमार। a fowler, a bird-catcher.

साकुन्तिक – पु॰ – (शाकुन्तिक) शकुन्त-बधिक, चिड़ीमार। a fowler, a bird-catcher.

साकेत – (साकेत) कोसल जनपद का प्रसिद्ध नगर, वर्तमान फैजाबाद। a famous town of Kośala, it is identified with modern Faizabad.

साकेत-जातक – (जा॰ सं॰ 68) – ब्राह्मण द्वारा भगवान बुद्ध को अपना (पुत्र) बना घर ले जाने की कथा। the story (No. 68) of a brāhmaṇa who took the Buddha home calling him his son.

साकेत-जातक – (जा॰ सं॰ 230) – यह ऊपर की साकेत-जातक कथा का ही परिशिष्ट है, जिसके अनुसार बुद्ध द्वारा यह पूछने पर कि ब्राह्मण ने पुत्र को कैसे पहचान लिया। उसने उत्तर दिया, पूर्वजन्म में सुकृत वाले जलाशय के कमल के अनुरूप होते हैं। this story (No. 230) is related to the previous Jātaka (No. 68), it is a dialogue between the brāhmaṇa and the Buddha which concludes that for those who had loved in previous births, love springs afresh like lotus in the pond.

साखा – स्त्री॰ – (शाख) शाखा। a branch.

साखा-नगर – न॰ – (शाखा-नगर) उपनगर। a suburb.

साखा-पलास – न॰ – (शाखा-पलाश) शाखा तथा पत्ते। branch and leaves.

साखा-भङ्ग – (शाखा-भङ्ग) शाखा का टूटना। breaking of a branch.

साखा-मिग – पु॰ – (शाखा-मृग) बन्दर। monkey.

साखी – पु॰ – (शाखिन्) वृक्ष। tree.

सागतं – अव्यय – (स्वागतम्) स्वागत। hail, welcome.

सागर – पु॰ – (सागर) समुद्र। sea, ocean.

सागार – वि॰ – (स + आगार) घर में रहने वाला। living in a house.

सागल – (स्यालकोट) राजा मिलिन्द की राजधानी। the capital town of king Milinda.

साचारियक – वि॰ – (साचार्य) आचार्य सहित। together with one's teacher.

साटक – पु॰ – (शाटक) वस्त्र, चोगा। a clothe, a cloak.

साटिका – स्त्री॰ – (शाटिका) देखें साटक। see Sāṭaka.

साठेय्य – न॰ – (शठता) धूर्त्तता। craft, treachery.

साण – न॰ – (शाण) सनया सन का बना कपड़ा। hemp or hempen cloth.

साणि – स्त्री॰ – (शाणी) शण-यवनिका, सन से बना परदा। a curtain made of hemp.

साणि-पसिब्बक – पु॰ – (शाणि-प्रसेवः) सन का थैला। a hempen sack.

साणि-पाकार – पु॰ – (शाणि-प्राकार) शाणि यवनिका, सन के टाट से बनाया गया घेरा। a screen wall (made with hempen cloth).

सात – न॰ – (शात) मंगल, भद्र। welfare, pleasant, agreeable.

सातकुम्भ – न॰ – (हारक) स्वर्ण, सोना। gold.

सातच्च – न॰ – (सातत्य) निरन्तरता। continuation, continuously.

सातच्चकारी – पु॰ – (सातत्यकारी) निरन्तर या लगातार कार्यरत। acting continuously.

सातच्चकिरिया – स्त्री॰ – (सातत्य क्रिया) अध्यवसाण, दृढ़ता। perseverence.

सातातिक – वि॰ – (सातातिक) सतत् अर्थात् लगातार लगे रहने वाला। acting continuously.

साति – स्त्री॰ – (स्वाति) सत्ताइस नक्षत्रों में से एक। the Swāti nakṣatra (star).

सातोदिका – स्त्री॰ – (सातोदिका) सुरट्ठ (सूरत) में एक नदी। name of a river situated in Sūrat district.

सात्थ/सात्थक – वि॰ – (सार्थक) उपयोगी, अर्थ-सहित। useful, advantageous, meaningful.

साथलिक – वि॰ – (शिथिल) शिथिल, ढीला-ढाला। lethargic, of loose habit.

√साद – (भू॰) – (आस्वादने) स्वाद लेना। to taste.

सादर – वि॰ – (सादर) आदर-सहित। with regards, with respect.

सादरं – क्रि॰ वि॰ – (सादरम्) आदर के साथ, प्रेमपूर्वक। respectfully, affectionately.

सादियति – क्रि॰ – (√स्वद् - स्वादयति) स्वीकार करता हे, आनन्द मनाता है, अनुमति देता है। accepts, enjoys, permits.

सादियन – न॰ – (सहमति) स्वीकृति। acceptance, appropriation.

सादियना – स्त्री॰ – (सहमति) देखें सादियन। see Sādiyana.

सादिस – पु॰ – (सदृश) सदृश, समान। like, similar.

सादु – वि॰ – (स्वादु) स्वादिष्ट, जायकेदार। tasteful, pleasant.

सादुतर – वि॰ – (स्वादुतर) अधिक स्वादिष्ट, अधिक मधुर। more tasteful, more pleasant.

सादु-रस – वि॰ – (स्वादु-रस) स्वादिष्ट-रस। having a pleasant taste.

√साध – (दि॰) – (संसिद्धि करने) सिद्ध करना। to prove.

साधक – वि॰ – (साधक) जो घटित हो सके, जो प्रमाणित हो सके (न॰) प्रमाण। effecting, accomplishing, (n.) a proof.

साधन 604

साधन – न॰ – (साधन) प्रमाण, सहायक-कृति, ऋण-मुक्ति। proving, setting, clearing of a debt.

साधारण – वि॰ – (साधारण) सामान्य। common, general.

साधिक – वि॰ – (साधिकम्) आधिक्य-युक्त, अधिकता लिए। having something in excess.

साधित – कृ॰ – (साधित) प्रमाणित, घटित, ऋण-मुक्त। proved, accomplished clearance of debt.

साधिय – वि॰ – (साध्य) जो सम्पन्न किया जा सके, जो प्रमाणित किया जा सके। that which can be accomplished or proved.

साधीन-जातक – (जा॰ सं॰ 494) – मिथिला के साधीन नामक नरेश की दानशीलता का वर्णन। the story (No. 494) describes the virtues of munificent Sādhīna, the king of Mithilā.

साधु (1) – (साधु) अच्छा, लाभप्रद, शीलसम्पन्न। good, virtuous, profitable.

साधु (2) – अव्यय – (साधु) हाँ, बहुत अच्छा। well, thoroughly.

साधुक – क्रि॰ वि॰ – (साधुकम्) अच्छी तरह। well, thoroughly.

साधु-काम्यता – स्त्री॰ – (साधु-काम्यता) कार्य के भली प्रकार सम्पन्न होने की इच्छा। desire for proficiency.

साधु-कार – पु॰ – (साधुकार) 'बहुत अच्छा किया' कहने का भाव। cheering-applause.

साधु-कीळन – न॰ – (साधु-कीडनम्) एक पवित्र त्यौहार। a sacred festival.

साधु-रूप – वि॰ – (साधुरूप) अच्छे स्वभाव का। of good disposition.

साधु-सम्मत – वि॰ – (साधु-सम्मत) आदृत, भले आदमियों द्वारा प्रशंसित। highly honoured by the virtuous.

साधुसील-जातक – (जा॰ सं॰ 200) – ब्राह्मण ने आचार्य का उपदेश मानकर अपनी चारों लड़कियाँ शील सम्पन्न व्यक्ति को दीं। according to the teacher's advice the brāhmaṇa gave all his four daughters to the virtuous men (story No. 200).

साधेति – क्रि॰ – (साधयति) (किसी कार्य को) सिद्ध करता है, (किसी बात को) प्रमाणित करता है, ऋण उतारता है। accomplishes, proves, clears a debt.

सानु – पु॰ तथा न॰ – (सानु) उपत्यका, पर्वत की ढलान। a mountain slope.

सानुचर – वि॰ – (सानुचर) अनुचरों सहित। together with followers.

सानुवज्ज – वि॰ – (सानुवद्य) सदोष। blamable, faulty, sinful.

साप – पु॰ – (शाप) शाप। curse.

सापतेय्य – न॰ – (सम्पदा) सम्पत्ति, धन। property, wealth.

सापत्तिक – वि॰ – (आपत्ति-युक्त) आपत्ति-प्राप्त, जिसने विनय के नियमों का उल्लंघन किया है। one who has transgressed a Vinaya rule.

सापद – न॰ – (श्वपद) जंगली जानवर जिसका शिकार किया जाय। wild animal.

सापदेस – वि॰ – (सापदेश) कारण-सहित। with reasons.

सापेक्ख (सापेख भी) – वि॰ – (सापेक्ष) आशावान, अपेक्षा-सहित। expecting, longing for.

सा-बन्धन – न॰ – (श्वा-बन्धन) कुत्ते की जंजीर। dog's chain.

साम (1) – वि॰ – (श्याम) श्याम, काला। black, dark.

साम (2) – पु॰ – (साम) (1) शान्ति (2) सामवेद। (1) peace, (2) one of the four Vedas, Sāmaveda.

साम-जातक – (जा॰ सं॰ 540) – यह राजा दशरथ द्वारा श्रवण कुमार की हत्या की कथा से मिलती-जुलती कथा है। this story (No. 540) resembles that of the king Daśaratha and Śravaṇa Kumāra.

साम – अव्यय – (स्वयम्) स्वयं, अपने आप। oneself, by oneself.

सामग्गी – स्त्री॰ – (समैक्य) एकता, मेलजोल। unity.

सामग्गिय – न॰ – (समग्रता) एकता का भाव। unity, concord.

सामच्च – वि॰ – (स + अमात्य) मंत्रियों या मित्रों सहित। together with ministers or friends.

सामञ्ञ – न॰ – (श्रामण्य) श्रमण-भाव। the state of a monk.

सामञ्ञता – स्त्री॰ – (श्रामण्यता) श्रमणों के प्रति आदर का भाव। respect for the religious mendicants.

सामञ्ञ-फल – न॰ – (श्रामण्य-फल) श्रमण-जीवन का फल। fruit of the life of a recluse.

सामणक – वि॰ – (श्रामणक) श्रमण के लिए योग्य अथवा आवश्यक। worthy or needful for a monk.

सामणेर – पु॰ – (श्रामणेर) श्रामणेर, किसी भिक्षु का शिष्य, भिक्षु बनने से पूर्व की अवस्था वाला। a novice of a monk.

सामणेरी – स्त्री॰ – (श्रामणेरी) किसी भिक्षुणी की शिष्या, भिक्षुणी बनने से पूर्व की अवस्था वाली। a female apprentice or nun.

सामत्थिय – न॰ – (सामर्थ्य) सामर्थ्य, योग्यता। ability.

सामन्त – न॰ – (सामन्त) पास-पड़ोस, (वि॰) पड़ोस सम्बन्धी। neighbourhood (adj.) bordering, neighbouring.

सामयिक – वि॰ – (सामयिक) (1) नित्य क्रिया, (2) अस्थायी। (1) call of nature, (2) temporary.

सामल – पु॰ – (श्यामल) श्यामल रंग। dark colour.

सामा – स्त्री॰ – (श्यामा) (1) श्यामा लता, (2) काले रंग की स्त्री। (1) a medicinal plant (2) woman of black or dark colour.

सामाजिक – पु॰ – संस्था विशेष का सदस्य। socialite, leader in society.

सामिक – पु॰ – (स्वामिन्) पति, स्वामी, मालिक। the husband, master, the owner.

सामिनी – स्त्री॰ – (स्वामिनी) स्वामिनी, मालकिन। mistress, a female owner.

सामिवचन – न॰ – (स्वामि वचन) स्वामी का निर्देश। the master's instruction.

सामिस – वि॰ – (सामिष) मांस सहित, मांस-युक्त, मांसाहार। non-vegetarian, fleshy.

सामीचि (1) – स्त्री॰ – (सामीचि) प्रशंसा, स्तुति। praise.

सामीचि (2) – स्त्री॰ – (**समीचीन**) उचित, योग्य, मैत्री-पूर्ण आचरण। proper cause, friendly treatment.

सामीचि-कम्म – न॰ – (**समीचीन-कर्म**) उचित कार्य, मैत्री-पूर्ण व्यवहार। proper task, friendly treatment.

समीचि-पटिपन्न – वि॰ – (**सन्मार्गारूढ़**) उचित पथ पर आरूढ़। entered into the proper course.

सामुद्दिक – वि॰ – (**सामुद्रः**) समुद्र पर रहने वाला, समुद्र की यात्रा करने वाला। sea-faring, marine.

सायं – अव्यय – (**सायं काल**) सन्ध्या काल। evening, twilight, dusk.

√ **साय** – (भू॰) – (**लेहने**) चाटना। to lick.

सायक – वि॰ – (**आस्वादक**) चखने वाला। one who tastes.

सायण्ह – पु॰ – (**सायम्**) सन्ध्या समय, साँझ। evening, dusk.

सायण्ह-काल – पु॰ – साँझ। evening.

सायण्ह-समय – पु॰ – (**सायं काल**) सन्ध्या-काल, साँझ। evening.

सायति – क्रि॰ – (आ √स्वद् = आस्वादयति) चखता है। tastes.

सायन – न॰ – (आ + स्वादन्) चखना, स्वाद लेना। tasting.

सायनीय – वि॰ – (**आस्वाद्य**) चखने योग्य, स्वाद लेने योग्य। fit to be tasted.

सार – पु॰ – (**सार**) तत्व, वृक्ष की साल, पका हुआ भाग। essence, the pith of tree.

सार-गन्ध – पु॰ – (**सार-गन्ध**) वृक्ष के उपादेय तत्व (साल) की सुगन्ध। odour of the heart of a tree.

सार-गवेसी – वि॰ – (**सार-गवेषी**) सार तत्त्व खोजने वाला। one who seeks the essence.

सारमय – वि॰ – (**सारमय**) लकड़ी की साल से निर्मित। made of hard wood.

सार-सूचि – (**सार-सूचि**) साल (मजबूत लकड़ी) की बनी सुई। a needle made of hard wood.

सारवन्तु – वि॰ – (**सारवान**) सार तत्त्व वाला, लकड़ी का बीच का कड़ा पका भाग। valuable, having kernel or pith.

सारक्ख – वि॰ – (**सारक्षा**) आरक्षा-सहित। guarded.

सारज्जति – क्रि॰ – (अनु √रञ्ज - अनुरज्यते) आसक्त होता है। gets attached to.

सारज्जना – स्त्री॰ – (**सारञ्जना**) आसक्ति। attachment.

सारत्त – कृदन्त – (**अनुरक्त**) आसक्त, मुग्ध, अनुरक्त। enamoured, impassioned.

सारथि/सारथी – पु॰ – (**सारथिः**) रथ-वाहक, सूत, रथनियन्ता। charioteer.

सारद/सारदिक – वि॰ – (**शारदिक**) शरद-ऋतु, सम्बन्धी। autumnal.

सारद्ध – वि॰ – (**संरद्ध**) उग्र, उत्तेजित। violent, angry.

सारभेय्य – पु॰ – (**सारभेय**) कुत्ता। a dog.

सारम्भ – पु॰ – (**सारम्भ**) क्रोध, उत्तेजना, कलह, विवाद। impetuosity, anger.

सारम्भ-जातक – (जा॰ सं॰ 88) – देखें नन्दि-विसाल-जातक। see NandiVisāla-Jātaka.

सारस – पु॰ – (**सारसः**) क्रौञ्च, कुंज, कराँकुल सारस पक्षी। Indian crane.

साराणीय – वि॰ – (स्मारणीय) याद कराने योग्य। fit to be remembered.

सारिबा – स्त्री॰ – (शारिवा) सारस परिल्ला-नामक रक्त-शोधक पौधा। the *sārasa parillā* plant used in blood purification to creeping name of plants (Hemidesmus Indicus and Ichnocarfus frutescens).

सारिपुत्त – पु॰ – (सारिपुत्र) भगवान् बुद्ध के प्रमुख शिष्य अपर नाम 'उपतिस्स' से भी प्रसिद्ध हैं। सारि नाम की माता के पुत्र होन से सारिपुत्त कहे गए। the chief disciple of Buddha, who is called Uptissa. As Sāri was his mother, he was also called Sariputra.

सारी – (सारी) – (सारी) यह सामासिक पदों में उत्तर पदरूप में प्रयोग में 'विचरण करने वाला' या 'अनुसरण करने वाला' अर्थ में आता है। used in compounds only denoting the sense of wandering, following.

सारी – स्त्री॰ – (सारी) 'सारिपुत्त', की माता का नाम, पूरा नाम था (रूपसरि)। the mother of Sāriputta, her full name was Rūpa-sari.

सारीरिक – वि॰ – (शारीरिक) शरीर से सम्बन्धित। connected with the body.

सारूप्प – वि॰ – (सारूप्य) योग्य, ठीक, उचित। fit, suitable, proper.

सारेति – क्रि॰ – (√ स्मृ + णिच् = स्मारयति) याद करता है। reminds.

साल – पु॰ – (श्याला) श्यालक, साला। brother-in-law.

साल – पु॰ – (शाल) देखें साल-रुक्ख। see Sālarukkha.

साल-रुक्ख – पु॰ – (शाल-वृक्ष) साखू का पेड़, शाल वृक्ष। the tree *Shorea Robusta* (also *Vatica Robusta*).

साल-बन – न॰ – (शाल-वन) शाल-वन, साखू का जंगल। a *sāla*-grove.

साल-लट्ठि – स्त्री॰ – (शाल-यष्टि) शाल का पौधा। a young *sāla*-tree.

सालक-जातक – (जा॰ सं॰ 249) – एक सपेरे ने सालक नाम का बन्दर पाला जो साँप से खेलता था, यही सपेरे की आजीविका थी। the story of a monkey named Sālaka who used to play with the snake and thus earned the livelihood for his master the snake-charmer.

सालय – वि॰ – (आलय सहित) आसक्ति-सहित। having attachments.

साला – स्त्री॰ – (शाला) शाला, भवन। a hall, a shed.

सालाकिय – न॰ – (शालाक्य) आँख आदि का चिकित्सा-शास्त्र, आँख में सलाई डालना। ophthalmology.

सालि – पु॰ – (शालि) शालि, सुगन्धित प्रजाति का धान। a kind of fine rice.

सालिक्खेत्त – न॰ – (शालि-क्षेत्र) धान का खेत। a rice field.

सालि-गब्भ – पु॰ – (शालि-गर्भ) पकी हुई शालि धान की फसल। ripening young rice.

सालि-भत्त – न॰ – (शालि-भक्तम्) चावल का भोजन। boiled rice of śāli.

सालिका – स्त्री॰ – (सारिका) सारिका, मैना। the bird Maina.

सालि-केदार-जातक – (जा॰ सं॰ 484) – ऐसे पितृभक्त तोते की कथा जो बूढ़े माता-पिता के लिए, खेत से धान ले आया

करता था। the story (No. 484) of a parrot who took some corn daily to his old parents.

सालित्तक-जातक – (जा॰ सं॰ 107) – इसमें बातूनी पुरोहित की कथा वर्णित है। the story (No. 107) is related to a very talkative chaplain.

सालित्तक-सिप्प – न॰ – ढलवाँस, या गुलेल से पत्थर फेंकने की विद्या। the art of throwing potsherds with a catapult.

सालिय-जातक – (जा॰ सं॰ 367) – कहानी बताती है कि गाँव के वैद्य ने लड़के को साँप पकड़ने भेजा, उलटे साँप ने वैद्य को ही जा काटा। the story (No. 367) of a village doctor who sent a boy to catch a snake which, falling on the ground, bit the doctor and he died.

सालुक – न॰ – (शालूकं) भसींड, जलकमल की जड़। the root of a water-lily.

सालूक-जातक – (जा॰ सं॰ 286) – इस जातक में सालूक नामक सुअर को खिला-पिलाकर उसका वध किए जाने की कथा वर्णित है। it is a story (No. 286) of a pig, fattened for the feast.

सालोहित – पु॰ – (रक्त-सम्बन्धी) रक्त-सम्बन्धी, रिश्तेदार। having blood-relation, relative.

सावक – पु॰ – (श्रावक) सुनने वाला, शिष्य। a listener, a hearer, a disciple.

सावकत्त – न॰ – (श्रावकत्त्व) शिष्य-भाव। the state of a disciple.

सावक-सङ्घ – पु॰ – (श्रावक-सङ्घ) शिष्यों का समूह। the congregation of disciples.

साविका – स्त्री॰ – (श्राविका) शिष्या। a female disciple.

सावज्ज – वि॰ – (सावद्य) सदोष होने का भाव। guilt, blamability.

सावट्ट – वि॰ – (सावर्त्त) आवर्त्त-युक्त, भँवर सहित। containing whirl-pool.

सावण – न॰ – (श्रावण) (1) घोषणा (2) श्रावण-मास। (1) announcement, (2) month of July-August.

सावत्थी – स्त्री॰ – (श्रावस्ती) श्रावस्ती, बुद्धकालीन कोसल जनपद की राजधानी। the capital town of Kosal country at the time of Buddha.

सावसेस – वि॰ – (सावशेष) अवशेष सहित, अपूर्ण। incomplete, with a remainder.

सावेति – क्रि॰ – (श्रावयति) सुनाता है, घोषणा करता है। makes hear, announces, declare.

सावेतु – पु॰ – (श्रावयिता) सुनाने वाला। one who announces.

सास – (भू॰) – (अनुशासने) अनुशासन रखना। to discipline.

सासङ्क – वि॰ – (सशङ्क-आशङ्कित) आशंका सहित, संदिग्ध। suspicious.

सासति – क्रि॰ – (√ शास् - शास्ति) शिक्षा देता है, शासन करता है। teaches, instructs.

सासन – न॰ – (शासन) शिक्षण, आज्ञा, सन्देश, सिद्धान्त। teaching, order, message, doctrine.

सासनकर – वि॰ – (शासनकर) आज्ञाकारी, शिक्षा के अनुसार चलने वाला। Administrator, who enforces order according to teachings or low.

सासन कारक – वि० – (शासन–कारक) देखें 'सासनकर'। see Sāsanakara.

सासनकारी – वि० – (शासनकारी) देखें 'सासनकर'। see Sāsanakara.

सासनन्तरधान – न० – (शासनान्तर्धान) (बुद्ध) शासन का लोप। disappearance or loss of the teachings (of the Buddha).

सासन-हर – पु० – (शासनहर) सन्देशवाहक। a messenger.

सासनावचर – वि० – (शासनानुचर) धर्मानुयायी। observing the religious rules.

सासनिक – वि० – (शासनिक) बुद्ध शासन- सम्बन्धी। connected with Buddhism.

सासप – पु० – (सर्षप) सरसों के दाने। mustard seed.

सासव – वि० – (साश्रव) आस्रव-सहित, चित्त-मैल-युक्त। connected with depravities.

साहत्थिक – वि० – (स्वहास्तिक) अपने हाथ से किया। done with one's own hand.

साहस – न० – (साहस) हिंसा, दुस्साहस, मनमानी करना। violence, arbitrary action.

साहसिक – वि० – (साहसिक) हिंसक या असभ्य। violent, savage.

साहु – अव्यय – (साधु) अच्छा। good, well.

साळव – पु० – (शद:) सल्पद, कच्चा साक- सब्जी का भोजन। salād, leafy vegetables which are eaten raw as radish, onion, etc.

√ सि – जि० त० – (बन्धने) बाँधना। to fasten, to tie.

√ सि – (भू) – (सेवायाम्) टहल करना। to serve.

सिकता – स्त्री० – (सिकता) रेत, बालू। sand.

सिक्का – स्त्री० – (शिक्या) छींका। pingo-basket.

सिक्ख – भू – (विद्योपादाने) विद्या सीखना। to learn.

सिक्खति – क्रि० – (√ शिक्ष् - शिक्षते) सीखता है, अभ्यास करता है। learns, practises, trains oneself.

सिक्खन – न० – (शिक्षण) शिक्षण, अभ्यास। learning, training.

सिक्खमाना – स्त्री० – (शिक्षामीणा) शिक्षण प्राप्त करने वाली। a female novice undergoing a probationary course.

सिक्खा – स्त्री० – (शिक्षा) शिक्षा, नियम पालन। study, discipline.

सिक्खा-काम – वि० – (शिक्षा–काम) उपदेशानुसार चलने (वाला) का इच्छुक। anxious to observe religious rule.

सिक्खापक – पु० – (शिक्षापक) शिक्षक। teacher, trainer.

सिक्खापनक – पु० – (शिक्षापनक) देखें सिक्खापक। see Sikkhāpaka.

सिक्खापद – न० – (शिक्षापद) शील सम्बन्धी नियम। a precept, a religious code.

सिक्खापन – न० – (शिक्षापन्) शिक्षण। teaching, instruction.

सिक्खा-समादान – न० – (शिक्षा-समादान) शील ग्रहण करना। taking the precepts upon oneself.

सिक्खित – कृदन्त – (शिक्षु + क्त = शिक्षित) शिक्षित। learnt, trained.

सिखण्ड – पु० – (शिरखण्ड) मोर के सिर की कलँगी। the crest of a peacock.

सिखर – न० – (शिखर) पर्वत का शिखर। the top, summit, peak of a mountain.

सिखरी – पु० – (शिखरी) पर्वत, शिखर वाला। a mountain.

सिखा – स्त्री०० – (शिक्षा) (1) शिखा (2) दीपक की लौ। (1) top knot, (2) a flame.

सिखी – पु० – (शिखवी) (1) आग (2) – मोर। (1) fire, (1) peacock.

सिगाल – पु० – (शृगाल) गीदड़। a jackal.

सिगालक – न० – (शृगालक) गीदड़ की आवाज। jackal's howl.

सिगाल-जातक – (जा० सं० 113) – गीदड़ द्वारा एक लोभी ब्राह्मण की चादर में मल-मूत्र त्याग कर उसे मूर्ख बनाने की कथा। the story (No. 113) of a jackal befooling a greedy brāhmaṇa by fouling his robe.

सिगाल-जातक – (जा० सं० 142) – एक चतुर शृगाल ने मुर्दे का नाटक करने वाले शिकारी से किस प्रकार अपनी प्राण रक्षा की। the story (No. 142) tells how a clever jackal saved his life from a silly hunter.

सिगाल-जातक – (जा० सं० 148) – मांस के लोभ में हाथी के पेट में जाकर कैद हुए गीदड़ के पश्चाताप की कथा। the story (No. 148) of a greedy jackal who became prisoner in the dead body of an elephant.

सिगाल-जातक – (जा० सं० 152) – कहानी बताती है कि शेरनी को अपना प्रेम निवेदन करना गीदड़ के लिए किस प्रकार जानलेवा बन गया था। the story (No. 152) tells how a jackal invited his death due to his love for a lioness.

सिग्गु – पु० – (तीक्ष्ण गन्धक) शोभांजन या सहिजन नामक वृक्ष-विशेष। a horse radish tree the *Boswellid-Thurefera*.

सिङ्ग – (शृङ्ग) सींग। horn.

सिङ्गार – पु० – (शृङ्गार) सिंगार, शृंगार रस। erotic sentiment.

सिङ्गिवेर – न० – (शृङ्गवेर) आर्द्रक, अदरक। ginger.

सिङ्गी (1) – न० – (शृङ्गि) आभूषणों का स्वर्ण। gold for ornaments.

सिङ्गी – वि० – (शृङ्गिन) पहाड़, सींग वाला (2) मेष। (1) peaked, horned, mountain (2) ram.

सिङ्गी-नद – न० – (शृङ्गि कनक) आभूषण के रूप में सोना। gold in the form of ornament.

सिङ्गी-वण्ण – वि० – (शृङ्गीवर्ण) सुनहला। of gold colour.

√ **सिङ्घ** – भू० – (घ्राण) सूँघना। to smell.

सिङ्घति – क्रि० – (सिंहति) नस लेता है, सूँघता है। sniffs, smells.

सिङ्घाटक – पु० तथा न० – (शृङ्गार) चतुष्पद, चौरस्ता। cross-roads, where four roads meet, palate.

सिङ्घाणिका – स्त्री॰ – (**सिंहाण**) नासामल, नाक की सींढ। mucus of the nose, snot.

सिंच – (रु॰) – (**क्षरणे**) टपकना, सींचना। to trip, to water.

सिज्झति – क्रि॰ – (√ **सिध् - सिध्यति**) घटित होता है, सफल होता है, लाभान्वित होता है। happens, succeeds, avails.

सिज्झन – न॰ – (√ **सिध् + ल्युट् - सिध्यन**) घटना का होना, सफल होना। happening, success.

सिञ्चक – वि॰ – (√ **सिञ्च् + ण्वुल = सिञ्चक**) सींचने वाला। one who waters or sprinkles.

सिञ्चन – न॰ – (√ **सिञ्च् + ल्युट् = सिञ्चन**) सेचन, सींचना। watering, sprinkling.

सिञ्चति – क्रि॰ – (√ **सिञ्च - सिञ्चति**) सींचता है। waters, sprinkles.

सित (1) – वि॰ – (**श्रित**) निभृत, निर्भर। depending on.

सित (2) – वि॰ – (**सिक्त**) आसक्त। attached.

सित (3) – वि॰ – (**सित**) श्वेत, सफेद। white.

सित (4) – न॰ – (**स्मिति**) स्थिति, मुस्कान। smile.

सित्त – कृदन्त – (√ **सिञ्च + क्त = सिक्त**) सिञ्चित। watered, sprinkled.

सित्थ – न॰ – (**सिक्थ**) मोम, भात का कण। wax, a grain of boiled rice.

सित्थाव-कारक – क्रि॰ वि॰ – (**सिक्थाव-कारक**) भात के दाने बिखर-बिखेरकर। scattering boiled rice all over.

सित्थक – न॰ – (**सिक्थक**) मोम। bee's wax.

सिथिल – वि॰ – (**शिथिल**) ढीला-ढाला। loose, lax, yielding.

सिथिलत्त – न॰ – (**शिथिलत्त्व**) शैथिल्य, शिथिलता, ढीलापन। looseness.

सिथिल-भाव – न॰ – (**शिथिल भाव**) शैथिल्य, ढीलापन। looseness.

√ **सिद** – (भू॰ दि॰) – (**पाके**) पकाना। to cook.

सिद्ध (1) – कृदन्त – (√ **सिध् + क्त = सिद्ध**) समाप्त, पूरा हुआ, उबला हुआ, पका हुआ। ended, accomplished, happened.

सिद्ध (2) – पु॰ – (**सिद्ध**) सिद्ध-पुरुष, इन्द्रजालिक। semi-divine being, a magician.

सिद्धत्थ – वि॰ – (**सिद्धार्थ**) जिसका अर्थ सिद्ध हो गया, (पु॰) शाक्य मुनि गौतम बुद्ध का नाम। who has succeeded all the enterprises, the name of Śākyamuni Gautama Buddha.

सिद्धत्थक – न॰ – (**सर्षपि**) सरसों के दाने। the mustard.

√ **सिध** – (दि॰) – (**संसिद्धौ**) सिद्ध होना। to be accomplished.

सिद्धि – स्त्री॰ – (**सिद्धि**) सफलता। accomplishment, success.

√ **सिध** – (भू॰) – (**गमने**) जाना। to go.

√ **सिना** – (दि॰) – (**शुचौ**) स्नाने-स्नान करना। to bathe.

सिनान – न॰ – (**स्नान**) स्नान। bathing, bath.

सिनिद्ध – वि॰ – (**स्निग्ध**) चिकना, नरम। smooth, soft.

सिनेरु – पु॰ – (सुमेरु) सिनेरु या सुमेरु पर्वत । mountain Sumeru.

√**सिनिह** – (दि॰) – (स्नेहे) स्नेह करना । to love.

सिनेह (स्नेह भी) – पु॰ – (स्नेह) प्रेम, तेल, चिकनाई । affection, love, oil, fat.

सिनेहन – न॰ – (स्नेह-कर्म) चिकना करना । oiling.

सिनेह-बिन्दु – न॰ – (स्नेह-बिन्दु) तेल की बूँद । a drop of oil.

सिनेहेति – क्रि॰ – (√ स्निह् = स्निहयति) स्नेह करता है, तेल चुपड़ता है । loves, smears with oil.

सिन्दी – स्त्री॰ – (खर्जूर) खजूर । the date-palm.

सिन्दूर – पु॰ – (सिन्दूर) (माथे पर लगाने का) सिन्दूर । the red-arsenic.

सिन्धव – वि॰ – (सैन्धव) सिन्ध सम्बन्धी, (पु॰) सेंधा नमक, सिन्धव घोड़ा । belonging to Sindha, (m.) rock-salt, a Sindha-horse (a breed).

सिन्धु (1) – पु॰ – (सिन्धु) समुद्र, नद । ocean, one of the seven holy rivers of pre-independent India.

सिन्धु (2) – स्त्री॰ – (सिन्धु) हिमालय से निकलकर अरब सागर में गिरने वाली एक बड़ी नदी । a big river which originates in the Himālayas and falls into the Arabian sea.

सिन्धु-रट्ठ – न॰ – (सिन्धु राष्ट्र) सिन्धु राष्ट्र । country of Sindha.

सिन्ध-सङ्गम – पु॰ – (सिन्धु-सङ्गम) जहां नदी समुद्र में गिरती है । the mouth or confluence of a river.

सिपाटिका – स्त्री॰ – (श्री पट्टिका) फलभित्ति, फली, नन्हीं मन्जूषा । a small case, a pericarp.

सिप्प – न॰ – (शिल्प) शिल्प, हुनर, धन्धा । art, craft.

सिप्पट्ठान – न॰ – (शिलप-स्थान) शिल्पाधार, शिल्प की शाखा । a branch of craft.

सिप्प-साला – स्त्री॰ – (शिल्प-शाला) शिल्प-शाला । a school of arts and crafts.

सिप्पायतन – न॰ – (शिल्पायतन) शिल्प की शाखा या आधार । a branch of craft.

सिप्पिक – स्त्री॰ – (शिल्पिक) शिल्पी । an artist, a craftsman.

सिप्पिका – स्त्री॰ – (शुक्ति) सीपी । an oyster.

सिप्पी – पु॰ – (शिल्पियन) शिल्पी, हुनर वाला । an artist, a craftsman.

सिब्बति – क्रि॰ – (√ सिव - सीव्यति) सीता है । stitches, sews.

सिब्बन – न॰ – (सीव्यन) सिलाई, सिलना । sewing.

सिब्बनी – स्त्री॰ – (सियून) कपड़े सिलने वाली स्त्री, दर्जिन, seamstress.

सिब्बनी-मग्ग – पु॰ – (कपालास्थि - सन्धि) खोपड़ी की हड्डी का जोड़ । the suture.

सिब्बापेति – क्रि॰ – (√ सिव् + णिच् - सेवयति) सिलवाता है । gets stitched.

सिब्बेति – क्रि॰ – (सीव्यति) सिलता है, सीता है । sews, stitches.

सिम्बलि – स्त्री॰ – (शाल्मली) सेमल का पेड़ । silk-cotton tree.

सिर – पु॰ तथा न॰ – (शिर) सिर । the head.

सिरा – स्त्री॰ – (शिरा) शिरा, नस। tendon, vein.

सिरि (सिरी भी) – स्त्री॰ – (श्री) भाग्य, ऐश्वर्य, लक्ष्मी। luck, wealth, splendour, goddess of wealth.

सिरि-गब्भ – पु॰ – (श्री-गर्भ) श्रीमान जन का शयनागार। the bedroom of a noble person.

सिरिभन्तु – वि॰ – (श्रीमन्त) श्री सम्पन्न। glorious, wealthy.

सिरि-विलास – पु॰ – (श्री-विलास) ठाट-बाट। the pomp and splendour.

सिरि-सयन – न॰ – (श्री-शयन) राजकीय शय्या, विस्तार हेतु देखें काल कण्णि जातक (जा॰ सं॰ 192)। the royal-bed, for details see Śrī Kālakaṇṇi Jātaka.

सिरि-धर – वि॰ – (श्रीधर) शानदार। glorious.

सिरि-जातक – (जा॰ सं॰ 284) – कथा बताती है कि कैसे एक मुर्गे का मांस खाने वाला पीलवान राजा बन गया, उसकी पत्नी रानी बनी और तपस्वी राजपुरोहित बना। the Jātaka (No. 284) tells how by eating the flesh of a cock an elephant trainer became a king, his wife a queen and a hermit a chaplain.

सिरकालकण्णि-जातक – (जा॰ सं॰ 192) सिरिकाल कण्हि पञ्ह का ही एक और नाम। it (story No. 192) is another name of siri Kālakaṇṇi-pañha.

सिरिकाळ-कण्णि-जातक – (जा॰ सं॰ 382) – बनारस के एक व्यापारी ने एक पलंग किसी ऐसे व्यक्ति के लिए बिछवाकर रखा था, जो उसकी अपेक्षा शुद्ध–पवित्र हो। उसका अधिकारी कैसे पहचाना गया यही बतलाती है, यह कथा। the story (No. 382) of a merchant who kept an unused couch and bed for anyone who might come to his house and was purer than himself. How such a person was distinguished, is given in this tale.

सिरिमन्द-जातक – (जा॰ सं॰ 500) सिरिमन्द पण्ह का ही एक और नाम। लक्ष्मी और सरस्वती में से कौन अधिक श्रेष्ठ है, इस प्रश्न को लेकर हुआ विवाद। (story No. 500) another name of Sirmand-pañha, it deals with the debate, as to who is greater between Lakṣmī and Sarasvatī.

सिरिवास – पु॰ – (श्रीवासः) तारपीन, देवदारु का स्राव-तेल, ताड़पीन (तेल)। turpentine.

सिरीस – पु॰ – (शिरीष) शिरीषा या सिरस का पेड़। the tree Acacia Sirissa.

सिरोजाल – वि॰ – (शिरोजाल) सिर ढकने की जाली। veil for the head.

सिरोमणि – पु॰ – (शिरोमणि) सिर की मणि। a diadem, a jewelled crest.

सिरोरूह – पु॰ तथा न॰ – (शिरोरूह) बाल (सिर के)। hair.

सिरोवेठन – न॰ – (शिरोवेष्ठन) पगड़ी। a turban.

सिला – स्त्री॰ – (शिला) पत्थर। stone.

सिला-गुल – न॰ – (शिला गोलक) पत्थर का गोला। a ball of stone.

सिला-थम्भ – पु॰ – (शिला-स्तम्भ) पत्थर का खम्भा। a stone pillar.

सिलापट्ट – न॰ – (शिलापट्ट) पत्थर की पटरी। a slab of stone.

सिला-पाकार – पु॰ – (शिला-प्राकार) पत्थर की चारदीवारी। a stone wall.

सिलामय – वि॰ – (शिलामय) शिला-निर्मित। made of stone.

√ **सिलाघ** – भू॰ – (कत्थने) बखान करना। to praise.

सिलाघति – क्रि॰ – (श्लाघते) प्रशंसा करता है, डींग मारता है। extols, boasts.

सिलाघा – स्त्री॰ – (श्लाघा) प्रशंसा। praise.

सिलिस – (दि॰) – (आलिङ्गने) गले लगाना। to embrace.

सिलिट्ठ – वि॰ – (श्लिष्ट) स्निग्ध, चिकना। smooth.

सिलिट्ठता – स्त्री॰ – (श्लिष्टता) स्निग्धता, चिकनापन, चिकनाहट। smoothness.

सिलुच्चय – पु॰ – (शिलोच्चय) चट्टान। a rock.

सिलुत्त – पु॰ – (गन्धमुखी) दीर्घातुंडी, छछूँदर। a rat snake.

सिलेस – पु॰ – (श्लेष) पहेली, श्लेषालंकार, लेसदार चीज। a riddle, a rhetoric figure, an adhesive substance.

सिलेसुम – पु॰ – (श्लेष्मा) कफ, बलगम। the phlegm.

सिलोक – भू॰ – (काव्यरचनायाम्) काव्य रचना करना। to compose verses.

सिलोक – पु॰ – (श्लोक) प्रसिद्धि, श्लोक। fame, a verse.

सिव – वि॰ – (शिव) कल्याण (स्थल), सुरक्षित (स्थान) (पु॰) शिव (महादेव) (न॰) परमानन्द, खुशी। sheltering, safe, (m.) the God Śiva, (n.) the *nirvāṇa*.

√ **सिव** – (दि॰) – (तन्तु संताने) सिलना। to sew.

सिवि-जातक – (जा॰ सं॰ 499) – राजा शिवि द्वारा अपना शरीर तक दान दे देने की कथा। the story (No. 499) of king Śivi who gifted his eyes to a blind brāhmaṇa.

सिविका – स्त्री॰ – (पालकी) (शिविका) पालकी। a litter, a planquin.

√ **सिस** – च॰ – (शेषे) बचाना, शेष रखना। to save, to keep remains.

√ **सिस** – भू॰ – (इच्छायाम्) चाहना। to desire.

सिसिर – पु॰ – (शिशिर) शीत ऋतु, ठंडक, वि॰ ठंडा, या ठंडी। the winter, cold season (adj.) cool.

सिस्स – पु॰ – (शिष्य) शिष्य, विद्यार्थी। a pupil, a student.

√ **सी** – भू॰ – (शयने) सोना। to sleep.

सीकर – न॰ – (सीकर) वृष्टि कण, वर्षा की छोटी-छोटी बूँदें। the small rain-drops.

सीघ – वि॰ – (शीघ्र) शीघ्र, जल्दी। quick, rapid, swift.

सीघ-गामी – वि॰ – (शीघ्र-गामी) शीघ्रगामी। going or moving quickly.

सीघ-तरं – क्रि॰ वि॰ – (शीघ्रतर) अधिक शीघ्रता से। more quickly.

सीघ-सीघं – क्रि॰ वि॰ – (शीघ्रातिशीघ्र) बहुत जल्दी। very quickly.

सीघ-सोत – वि॰ – (शीघ्र-स्रोत) शीघ्र-स्रोत। having a running stream.

सीत – वि॰ – (शीत) ठंडा (न॰) ठंड या ठंडक। cool (n.) coolness, cold.

सीत-भीरुक – वि॰ – (शीत-भीरुक) शीत से भयभीत। afraid of cold.

सीतल – वि॰ – (शीतल) ठंडा (न) ठंड या ठंडक। cool (n.) coolness, cold.

सीता – स्त्री॰ – (सीता) हल की लकीर। a furrow.

सीति-भाव – पु॰ – (शीत-भाव) शीतलता, शान्ति। coolness, calm.

सीति-भूत – कृदन्त – (शीत-भूत) शान्ति–भाव को प्राप्त, शमथ प्राप्त। calmed, tranquilized.

सीतोदक – न॰ – (शीतोदक) ठण्डा जल। cool water.

सीदति – क्रि॰ – (सीदति) डूब जाता है, नीचे बैठ जाता है, हार मान लेता है। sinks, subsides, yields.

सीदन – न॰ – (सीदन) डूबना। sinking.

सीन – कृदन्त – (सीन) डूबा हुआ। sunk.

सीपद – न॰ – (श्लीपद) फील पाँव। elephantiasis (of leg).

सीमट्ठ – क्रि॰ – (सीमान्तर्गत) सीमागत, सीमा पर या सीमा के भीतर स्थित। situated within or on the boundary.

सीमन्तिनी – स्त्री॰ – (सीमन्तिनी) औरत। a woman.

सीमा – स्त्री॰ – (सीमा) सीमा, अन्तिम लकीर, भिक्षुओं का विनय-कर्म करने के लिए निर्धारित सीमा। a boundary, a limit, a hermitage for Buddhist monks.

सीमा-कत – वि॰ – (सीमा-कृत) सीमित। limited.

सीमातिग – वि॰ – (सीमातिग) सीमा को लाँघने वाला। gone over the limits.

सीमा-समुग्घात – पु॰ – (सीमा-समुद्घात) पहले की सीमा को तोड़ दिया जाना। removing or destroying a former boundary.

सीमा-सम्मुति – स्त्री॰ – (सीमा-सम्मति) नई सीमा की स्थापना। fixing of a new boundary, convention of a chapter house.

सीर – पु॰ – (सीर) हल। plough.

सीरङ्ग – पु॰ – (सीराङ्ग) हल का मुख्य भाग। the main part of the plough.

√ सील – भू॰ – (शील पालने) शील का पालन करना। to observe morals.

सील – न॰ – (शील) शील, सदाचार। moral practice, code of morality.

√ सील – भू॰ चु॰ – (शील / उञ्छ चयने) चुनना, शीला बीनना। to pick up, to choose, to select, to elect, to weave.

सील-कथा – स्त्री॰ – (शील-कथा) शील की व्यवस्था। exposition of the duties of morality.

सीलक्खन्ध – पु॰ – (शील-स्कन्ध) शील-स्कन्ध, शील परिच्छेद। all that relate to moral practices.

सील-गन्ध – पु॰ – (शील–गन्ध) शील की सुगन्धि। the fragrance (fame) of moral nature.

सीलब्बत – न॰ – (शील-व्रत) शील व्रत। ceremonial observances.

सीलभेद – पु॰ – (शील-भेद) शीलभङ्ग। breach of morality.

सीलमय – वि॰ – (शील-मय) शीलवान। connected with morality.

सीलवन्तु – वि॰ – (शीलवान) शील का पालन करने वाला। veituous, observing the moral practices.

सील-विपत्ति – वि॰ – (**शील-विपत्ति**) शील की मर्यादा का उल्लंघन, दुराचार। moral transgression.

सील-विपन्न – (**शील-विपन्न**) शील भङ्ग करने वाला। one who has trespassed the moral precepts.

सील-सम्पत्ति – स्त्री॰ – (**शील-सम्पत्ति**) शील–पालन, सदाचार। accomplishment of morals.

सील-सम्पन्न – वि॰ – (**शील-सम्पन्न**) शीलवान, सदाचारी। observing the moral precepts.

सीलन – न॰ – (**शीलन**) संयत रहना, विनय के अधीन रहना। practising, restraining.

सीलवनाग-जातक – (जा॰ सं॰ 72) – कृतघ्नता के दुष्परिणाम को दर्शाने वाली एक कथा। this story (No. 72) illustrates the evils of ingratitude.

सीलवीमंस-जातक – (जा॰ सं॰ 330) – तपस्वी ने शील का महत्व कैसे समझा, इसका बोध कराने वाली तीन घटनाएं इसमें वर्णित हैं। the story (No. 330) describes three incidents of morality which reformed the life of an ascetic.

सीलवीमंस-जातक – (जा॰ सं॰ 362) – इस कथा का निष्कर्ष है कि विद्या की अपेक्षा शील की अधिक प्रतिष्ठा है। the story (No. 362) concludes that virtue is more highly esteemed than learning.

सीलवीमंस-जातक – (जा॰ सं॰ 86) – कथा में वर्णित दृष्टान्त से पुरोहित ने समझा कि शील का महत्व विद्या-बल की अपेक्षा अधिक है। the story (No. 86) tells how a chaplain came to the conclusion that virtue is superior to learning.

सीलवीमंस-जातक – (जा॰ सं॰ 290) – सीलवीमंस जातक 362 के ही समान। it (story No. 290) is similar to Sīlvimansa Jātaka No. 362.

सीलवीमंस-जातक – (जा॰ सं॰ 305) – ब्राह्मण ने अपने पाँच सौ शिष्यों में से जो सचमुच शीलवान था, उसे ही अपनी कन्या प्रदान की। the story (No. 305) of a brāhmaṇa who gave his daughter in marriage to the most virtuous amongst his five hundred pupils.

सीलानिसंस-जातक – (जा॰ सं॰ 190) – यह एक ऐसे शीलवान उपासक की कथा है जिसने अपने पुण्य का कुछ हिस्सा, संकट में पड़े हत्यारे नाई को देकर उसकी भी प्राण रक्षा की। it is a story (No. 190) of such a virtuous disciple who made over the merits of his own virtues to the sinful barber and saved his life.

सीलिक – वि॰ – (**शीली / शीलक**) स्वभाव वाला, प्रकृति वाला (केवल समस्त पदों में प्रयुक्त)। having the nature of (used in compounds).

सीली – पु॰ – (**शीलः / शीलिन्**) (समास में प्रयुक्त), वि॰, शीलवाला। having the nature of (used in compounds).

सीवथिका – स्त्री॰ – (**पिशाच-भूमि**) कच्चा शमशान। a place where the dead bodies are thrown to rot away.

सीस – न॰ – (**शीश / शीर्ष**) शीर्ष, सिर, उच्चतम शिखर, धान की बाली लेख का

शीर्षक, सीसा। the head, the highest point, a year of corn, heading of an article, the lead.

सीस-कपाल – पु॰ – (शीर्ष-कपाल) खोपड़ी। the skull.

सीस-कटाह – पु॰ – (शीर्ष कटाह) खोपड़ी। the skull.

सीसच्छवि – स्त्री॰ – (शिरच्छवि) सिर की चमड़ी। the skin of the head.

सीसच्छेदन – न॰ – (शिरश्छेदन) सिर का काट डालना। behead.

सीसप्पचालन – न॰ – (शिरः प्रचालन) सिर का हिलाना-डुलाना। swaying of the heads.

सीसपम्परा – स्त्री॰ – (शीर्ष परम्परा) एक सिर पर का भार दूसरे सिर पर लेना। changing of the burden from one head to another.

सीस-बेठन – न॰ – (शिरो वेष्ठन) पगड़ी। a turban.

सीसाबाध – पु॰ – (शिरोबाधा) शिरो-पीड़ा, सिर का दर्द। headache.

सीह – (पु॰) – (सिंह) सिंह, शेर। a lion.

सीह-चम्म – न॰ – (सिंह-चर्म) सिंह की चमड़ी। lion's skin.

सीह-नाद – पु॰ – (सिंह-नाद) सिंह गर्जना। lion's hide.

सीहनादिक – वि॰ – (सिंह-नादिक) सिंह की तरह गरजने वाला। one who speaks like a lion's roar, one who roars like a lion.

सीह-पञ्जर – पु॰ – (सिंह-पञ्जर) झरोखा, सिंह का पिंजरा। a kind of window, a lion's cage.

सीह-पोतक – पु॰ – (सिंह-पोतक) सिंह-शावक, शेर का बच्चा। a young lion.

सीह-विक्कीलित – न॰ – (सिंह क्रीडा) शेर का खेल। lion's play.

सीह-सेय्या – स्त्री॰ – (सिंह-शैया) सिंह-शैया, दाहिनी करवट शयन करना। lying on the right side.

सीहस्सर – वि॰ – (सिंह-स्वर) सिंह के समान स्वर वाला। having voice like a lion.

सीह-हनु – वि॰ – (सिंह-हनु) सिंह के समान दाढ़ वाला, (पु॰) शाक्य मुनि गौतम बुद्ध के पितामह। having a jaw like that of a lion, (m.) the grandfather of Gautama Buddha.

सीह-कोट्ठक-जातक – (जा॰ सं॰ 188) – शेर और गीदड़ी के संयोग से एक सिंह शावक पैदा हुआ परन्तु उसका स्वर गीदड़ का ही रहा। the story(No. 188) tells that once a lion had a cub by a she jackal, the cub though was like his sire in appearance but like his dam in voice.

सीह-चम्म-जातक – (जा॰ सं॰ 189) – शेर की खाल ओढ़कर चरत-फिरते रहने वाले गधे को किसानों ने मार डाला। a merchant used to throw a lion's skin over his donkey and let him loose in the fields. One day the donkey frightened and heehawed, and was killed by the farmers.

सीह-बाहु – पु॰ – (सिंह-बाहु) सिंहल द्वीप पर राज्य करने वाले प्रथम आर्य-नरेश विजय का पिता। father of Vijya Singh who was the first Ārya king who ruled over Ceylon.

सीहल – पु॰ – (**सिंहल**) सिंहल द्वीप में प्रथम आर्य उपनिवेश बसाने वाले विजय तथा उसके साथियों के लिए व्यवहृत होने वाला शब्द। the name given to Vijay and his companions, founders of the Sinhalese race in Ceylon.

सीहल-दीप – पु॰ – (**सिंहल द्वीप**) जब से तम्बपण्णि द्वीप का उपनिवेश बना, तभी से यह सीहल-द्वीप कहलाने लगा। the name given to Ceylon (Tambapaṇṇi) since it became the country of the Sihala.

सीहळ – वि॰ – (**सैंहल**) सिंहल-द्वीप का। belonging to Ceylon.

सीहळ-भासा – स्त्री॰ – (**सिंहली-भाषा**) सिंहल लोगों की भाषा। Sinhalese language.

सीहासन – न॰ – (**सिंहासन**) सिंहासन। throne.

√ **सु** (सु-की) – (**श्रवणे**) सुनना। to hear.

√ **सु** – (त॰) – (**अभिस्नवे**) नहाना। to bathe.

सु – उपसर्ग – (**सु**) अच्छा। a preposition expressing the notion of well, happily and thoroughly.

संसुमार-जातक – (जा॰ सं॰ 208) – एक चतुर बन्दर द्वारा मगरमच्छ को छकाने की कथा। the story (No. 208) of a monkey who cleverly befooled the crocodile who intended to kill him.

संसुमार-गिरि – पु॰ – (**संसुमार-गिरि**) भग्ग जनपद का एक प्रसिद्ध नगर, बुद्ध ने यहाँ आठवाँ वर्षावास व्यतीत किया था। the city in the Bhagga country of which it was probably the capital, the Buddha spent eighth Vāssa there.

सुक – पु॰ – (**शुक**) तोता। a parrot.

सु – अव्यय – (**अथवा**) अथवा। or.

सुक-जातक – (जा॰ सं॰ 255) – पिता के उपदेश की अवज्ञा कर जान गँवाने वाले शुक की कथा। story No. 255 about a son who disobeys his father and wastes his life.

सुकट (सुकत भी) – वि॰ – (**सुकृत**) सुकृत (न॰) शुभ-कर्म। a well done (n.) meritorious act.

सुकर – वि॰ – (**सुकर**) आसान। easy, easily done.

सुकुमार – वि॰ – (**सुकुमार**) मृदु, कोमल। delicate.

सुकुमारता – स्त्री॰ – (**सुकुमारता**) मृदुभाव, कोमलता। delicateness.

सुकुसल – वि॰ – (**सुकुशल**) पटु, अत्यन्त-दक्ष। very skilful.

सुक्क – वि॰ – (**शुक्ल**) शुक्ल, सफेद (न॰) शुभ-कर्म। white, bright (n.) virtue.

सुक्क-पक्ख – पु॰ – (**शुक्ल-पक्ष**) महीने का शुक्ल पक्ष। the bright half of a month.

सुक्ख – वि॰ – (**शुष्क**) सूखा। dry.

सुक्खति – क्रि॰ – (√ **शुष्** - **शुष्यति**) सूखता है। becomes dried up.

सुक्खन – न॰ – (**शुष्यन**) सूखना। drying up.

सुक्खापन – न॰ – (**शोषणम्**) सुखाना। making dry.

सुक्खापेति – क्रि॰ – (√ **शुष्** + **णिच्** = **शोषयति**) सुखाता है या सुखवाता है। dries or makes dry.

सुख – न॰ – (सुख) सुख, आराम। happiness, comfort.

सुख-काम – वि॰ – (सुख-काम) सुख की इच्छा वाला। longing for happiness.

सुखत्थिक/सुखत्थी – वि॰ – (सुखार्थी) सुखार्थी। longing for happiness.

सुखद – वि॰ – (सुखद) सुखदायक। producing happiness.

सुख-निसिन्न – वि॰ – (सुख निषण्ण) सुखपूर्वक बैठा हुआ। comfortably seated.

सुख-पटिसंवेदी – वि॰ – (सुख प्रतिसंवेदी) सुख का अनुभव करने वाला। experiencing happiness.

सुखप्पत्त – वि॰ – (सुख प्राप्त) सुख प्राप्त। happy.

सुखभागीय – वि॰ – (सुखभागी) सुख में हिस्सा बँटाने वाला। participating in happiness.

सुख-यानक – न॰ – (सुखयानक) सुखद-यान, आरामदेह गाड़ी। an easy going cart, smooth-going life.

सुख-विपाक – वि॰ – (सुखविपाक) सुख-फलदायी। one who gives happiness as a reward.

सुख-विहरण – न॰ – (सुख विहरण) सुख पूर्वक रहना। comfortable living.

सुखविहारी-जातक – (जा॰ सं॰ 10) – राज्य-त्याग के अनन्तर सुखपूर्वक विचरने वाले तपस्वी की कथा। (story No. 10) about a monk wandering happily after giving-up his kindgom.

सुख-संवास – पु॰ – (सुख-संवास) सुगद-संगति। pleasant to associate with.

सुख-सम्फस्स – वि॰ – (सुख-संस्पर्श) सुखद स्पर्श। pleasant to touch.

सुख-सम्मत – वि॰ – (सुख-सम्मत) सुख माना गया। deemed a pleasure.

सुखं – क्रि॰ वि॰ – (सुखम् / सुखेन) आसानी से, आराम से। easily, comfortably.

सुखायति – क्रि॰ – (सुखमनुभवति) सुखी होता है। feels comfortable or happy.

सुखावह – वि॰ – (सुखद) सुखद। bringing happiness.

सुखित – कृदन्त – (सुखित) सुखी। happy.

सुखुम – वि॰ – (सूक्ष्म) सूक्ष्म, बारीक। minute, fine.

सुखुमतर – वि॰ – (सूक्ष्मतर) बहुत सूक्ष्म। very fine or subtle.

सुखुमत्त – न॰ – (सूक्ष्मत्व) सूक्ष्मत्व, बारीकपन। fineness, delicacy.

सुखुमता – स्त्री॰ – (सूक्ष्मता) देखें सुखमत्त। see Sukhumatta.

सुखुमाल – वि॰ – (सुकुमार) सुकुमार, कोमल-प्रकृति। tender, delicate.

सुखुमालता – स्त्री॰ – (सुकुमारता) सुकुमारता। delicacy, tenderness.

सुखेति – क्रि॰ – सुखित करता है। makes happy.

सुखेधित – वि॰ – (सुखपोषित) सुखवर्धित, सुख से पालित-पोषित। tenderly brought up.

सुगत – वि॰ – (सुगत) सुगति प्राप्त। पु॰ भगवान बुद्ध। faring well, (m.) the Buddha.

सुगतालय – पु॰ – (सुगतालय) तथागत का निवास स्थान, सुगत की नकल। dwelling place of the Buddha, imitation of the Buddha.

सुगति – स्त्री॰ – (सुगति) अच्छी अवस्था, स्वर्ग लोक। a happy state, heaven.

सुगती – वि॰ – (सुगती) सुकृति, शुभ कर्म करने वाला। righteous.

सुगन्ध – पु॰ (सुगन्ध) वि॰ (सुगन्ध) – (सुगन्ध) सुगन्ध। fragrance, pleasant odour (adj.) fragrant.

सुगन्धिक/सुगन्धी – वि॰ – (सुगन्धित) सुगन्ध सहित। fragrant.

सुगहन – न॰ – (सुग्रहण) दृढ़ता से ग्रहण करना, मजबूत पकड़। a good grip.

सुगुत्त – कृदन्त – (सुगुप्त) सुरक्षित। well guarded or protected.

सुगोपित – कृदन्त – (सुगोपित) देखें सुगत्त। see Sugatta.

सुगहित – वि॰ – (सुगृहीत) सुगृहीत, भली प्रकार धारण किया गया (पाठ)। grasped tightly, well learnt.

सुङ्क – पु॰ – (पथकर) मार्गशुल्क, राहदारी, चुंगी, कर। toll tax.

सुङ्कघात – पु॰ – (पथकर–घात) चुंगीकर से बच निकलना। evasion of customs duties.

सुंकट्ठान – न॰ – (मार्गशुल्क स्थान) पथकर शाला, चुंगीधर। taxing place, customs house.

सुङ्कित – पु॰ – (पथकर–संग्राहक) पथकर उगाहने वाला। a collector of toll taxes.

√सुच – (चु॰) – (पैशुन्ये) सूचना देना। to inform.

सुचरित – न॰ – (सुचरित) सदाचरण। right conduct.

√सुच – (भू॰) – (शोके) शोक करना। to mourn.

सुचि – वि॰ – (शुचि) पवित्र। pure, clean.

सुचिकम्म – वि॰ – (शुचि–कर्म) शुभ कर्म करने वाला। whose actions are pure.

सुचिगन्ध – वि॰ – (शुचिगन्ध) शुभ कर्मों की गन्ध वाला। having a smell (fame) of pure action, fame of righteous action.

सुचि-जातिक – वि॰ – (शुचिप्रिय) सफाई पसन्द करने वाला। one who likes cleanliness.

सुचि-वसन – वि॰ – (शुचि वसन) शुद्ध वस्त्रों वाला, साफ कपड़ों वाला। having a clean dress.

सुचित्त – वि॰ – (विचित्र) अतिविचित्र, सुचित्रित। much variegated, well-painte.

सुचित्तित – वि॰ – (सुचित्रित) देखें सुचित्त। see Sucitta.

सुच्चन-जातक – (जा॰ सं॰ 320) – इस जातक में एक राजा द्वारा अपनी उपेक्षिता रानी को मान-सम्मान प्रदान करने की चमत्कारी घटना वर्णित है। the story tells how a king becomes affectionate to his neglected queen.

सुच्छन्न – वि॰ – (सुच्छन्न) अच्छी तरह ढका या छाया हुआ। well covered or well thatched.

सुजन – पु॰ – (सुजन) भला व्यक्ति, सज्जन। virtuous person.

सुजा – स्त्री॰ – (स्रुवा) यज्ञ में कार्य आने वाली श्रुवा या लकड़ी की जलधी। a ladle used in a sacrifice.

सुजात – कृदन्त – (सुजात) सुजन्मा, (ऊँची) जाति वाला। well born, of good birth.

सुजान-जातक – (जा॰ सं॰ 269) – पुत्र द्वारा कर्कशभाषी माता को सुधारने की कथा । the story (No. 269) tells how a son admonished his harsh and ill-tongued mother.

सुजात-जातक – (जा॰ सं॰ 306) – राजा द्वारा फल बेचने वाली लड़की की मधुर वाणी सुन, उसे बुलाकर अपनी रानी बना लेने की कथा । the story (No. 306) tells how a king hearing the sweet voice of a fruit-selling girl, fell in love and made her his queen.

सुजात-जातक – (जा॰ सं॰ 352) – कथा बतलाती है कि पुत्र सुजात ने अपने शोकमग्न पिता के शोक को किस प्रकार दूर किया । the story (No. 352) tells how a wise son convinced his father of his folly and made him come out of his grief.

सुजाता – स्त्री॰ – (**सुजाता**) उरुवेला के पास के सेनानि गाँव के मुखिया की लड़की, जिसने गौतम बुद्ध को वृक्ष देवता मान खीर से संतृप्त किया था । the daughter of a landowner of the village of Senāni near Uruvelā who had offered a dish of rice boiled in milk to Buddha on the very day of Buddha's enlightenment.

सुज्झति – क्रि॰ – (√ **सुध् - शुध्यति**) शुद्ध होता है । becomes clean or pure.

सुञ्ञ – वि॰ – (**शून्य**) शून्य । empty, void.

सुञ्ञ-गाम – पु॰ – (**शून्य-ग्राम**) निर्जन ग्राम, खाली गाँव । a deserted village.

सुञ्ञता – स्त्री॰ – (**शून्यता**) शून्यता । emptiness.

सुञ्ञागार – न॰ – (**शून्यागार**) शून्य प्रकोष्ठ, एकान्त स्थल । an empty place.

सुट्ठु – (**सुष्ठु**) अव्यय, अच्छा, excellent.

सुण – पु॰ – (**श्वानः**) कुत्ता, a dog.

सुणाति – क्रिया – (**श्रृणोति**) सुनता है, to hear.

सुणिसा – स्त्री॰ – (**सूनुः वधु**) पुत्रवधु, daughter-in-law.

सुत – पु॰ – (**सुत**) पुत्र, लड़का, कृदन्त – सुना हुआ, धर्म-ग्रन्थ, a son, heard, the sacred lore; learning.

सुतत्त – कृदन्त – (**सुतप्त**) भली प्रकार गर्म किया गया । much heated.

सुतनु – वि॰ – (**सुतनु**) सुन्दर शरीर वाला । having a handsome body.

सुतनो-जातक – (जा॰ सं॰ 398) – परिवार की रक्षा के लिए सत्पुत्र ने नरभक्षी यक्ष के पास जाना स्वीकार किया । (story No. 398) for the welfare of his family the virtuous son offered himself to go to the man-eater *yakṣa*.

सुतप्पय – वि॰ – (**सुतृप्य**) आसानी से संतुष्ट हो सकने वाला । easily satisfied.

सुति – स्त्री॰ – (**श्रुति**) श्रुति, अनुश्रुति, वेद, आवाज । sound, hearing, tradition, Veda.

सुति-हीन – वि॰ – (**श्रुति-हीन**) बधिर, बहरा । deaf.

सुत्त (1) – कृदन्त – (**सुप्त**) सोया हुआ । slept.

सुत्त (2) – न॰ – (**सूत्र**) धागा । a thread.

सुत्त (3) – न॰ – (**सूत्र**) (व्याकरण) सूत्र । aphorism.

सुत्तकन्तन – न॰ – (सूत्र-कर्त्तन) सूत कातना। spinning.

सुत्तकार – पु॰ – (सूत्रकार) सूत्रों का रचयिता। a composer of grammatical aphorisms.

सुत्तगुळ – न॰ – (सूत्र-गोलकं) सूत का गोला। a ball of string.

सुत्त-निपात – पु॰ – (सुत्त-निपात) सुत्तपिटक के खुद्दक निकाय के पन्द्रह ग्रन्थों में से एक। the fifteenth book of Khuddaka Nikāya.

सुत्त-पिटक – न॰ – (सुत्त-पिटक) तीनों पिटकों में से एक। the first main, division of Tripiṭaka containing discourses.

सुत्त-मय – वि॰ – (सत्र-मय) सूत्र-निर्मित। made of thread.

सुत्तन्त – पु॰ तथा न॰ – (सुत्तन्त) बुद्धोपदेश या प्रवचन। a discourse related to Buddha.

सुत्तन्त-पिटक – (सुत्तन्त-पिटक) पाँच निकायों से समन्वित सुत्तपिटक, वे पाँचों निकाय हैं : – (1) दीघ-निकाय (2) मज्झिम-निकाय (3) संयुत्त निकाय (4) अङ्गुत्तर-निकाय (5) खुद्दक-निकाय। the whole of the Sutta-piṭaka which contains five sub-divisions, i.e.,(1) Dīgha Nikāya, (2) Majjhima Nikāya (3) Sanyutta Nikāya, (4) Aṅguttara Nikāya, (5) Khuddaka Nikāya.

सुत्तन्तिक – वि॰ – (सुत्तान्तिक) सुत्तन्त पाठी, सारे सुत्तपिटक या उसके एक हिस्से को कण्ठाग्र किए रहने वाला। one who has learnt a portion or the whole of the Sutta-piṭaka.

सुत्ति – स्त्री॰ – (शुक्ति) सीप। a pearl oyster.

सुदन्त – वि॰ – (सुदान्त) सुष्ठुनियन्त्रित, वशीकृत, सुशिक्षित। well tamed.

सुदस्स – वि॰ – (सुदर्श) आसानी से देखा गया। easily seen.

सुदस्सन – वि॰ – (सुदर्शन) सुदर्शन, सुन्दर रूप वाला। having a charming appearance.

सुदं – अव्यय – (सुदम्) निरर्थक शब्द-प्रयोग। pleonastic particle.

सुदिट्ठ – वि॰ – (सुदृष्ट) भली प्रकार देखा गया। well seen.

सुदिन्न – वि॰ – (सुदत्त) भली प्रकार दिया गया। well given.

सुदुत्तर – वि॰ – (सु-दुस्तर) जिसे बड़ी कठिनाई से पार किया जा सके। very difficult to escape from.

सुदुक्कर – वि॰ – (सुदुष्कर) जो बड़ी कठिनाई से किया जा सके। very difficult to do.

सुदुद्दस – वि॰ – (सुदुर्दर्श) जो बड़ी कठिनाई से देखा जा सके। very difficult to be seen.

सुदुब्बल – वि॰ – (सुदुर्बल) अत्यन्त दुर्बल। very weak.

सुदुल्लभ – वि॰ – (सुदुर्लभ) अत्यन्त दुर्लभ। very difficult to obtain.

सुदेसित – वि॰ – (सुदेशित) भली प्रकार उपदिष्ट। well preached.

सुद – पु॰ – (शूद्र) शूद्र वर्ण का व्यक्ति। a person of the sūdra caste.

सुद्ध – वि॰ – (शुद्ध) शुद्ध, पवित्र, साफ। clean, pure.

सुद्धता – स्त्री॰ – (शुद्धता) शुद्धता । purity.

सुद्धत्त – न॰ – (शुद्धत्व) शुद्धता । purity.

सुद्धाजीव – वि॰ – (शुद्धाजीवी) शुद्ध आजीविका वाला । having righteous livelihood.

सुद्धावास – पु॰ – (शुद्ध + आवास) शुद्ध निवास-स्थल, तात्पर्य ब्रह्मलोक । the pure abode (in Brahma-heaven).

सुद्धावासिक – वि॰ – (शुद्धावासिक) ब्रह्म-लोक (शुद्धावास) में रहने वाला । living in the pure abode.

सुद्धि – स्त्री॰ – (शुद्धि) शुद्धि, पवित्रता । purity, purification.

सुद्धि-मग्ग – पु॰ – (शुद्धि-मार्ग) पवित्रता का मार्ग । the path of purification.

सुद्धोदन – पु॰ – (शुद्धोदन) कपिलवस्तु के शाक्य नरेश तथा शाक्यमुनि गौतम बुद्ध के पिता । the Śākya king of Kapila-vastu and the father of Gautama Buddha.

सुधन्त – कृदन्त – (सु + √ ध्मा + क्त = सुध्मातः) अच्छी तरह फूँका गया या साफ किया गया । well blown or purified.

√ सुध – (दि॰) – (शुचितायाम्) शोधन करना, पवित्र, करना । to purify.

सुधम्मता – स्त्री॰ – (सुधर्मता) अच्छा स्वभाव । fine nature, good natured.

सुधा – स्त्री॰ – (सुधा) अमृत, चूना । (1) nectar (2) lime.

सुधाकम्म – न॰ – (सुधाकर्म) चूना पोतना । white washing with lime.

सुधाकर – पु॰ – (सुधाकर) चन्द्रमा । the moon.

सुधाभोजन-जातक – (जा॰ सं॰ 535) – इन्द्र द्वारा 'सुधा-भोजन' के माध्यम से अतिकृपण 'मच्छरीकोसीय' नामक राजा को दानशील और अर्हत् पद योग्य बनाने की कथा । the story (No. 535) tale relates how Sakka achieved success in converting the miser king Macchari Kosīya into a hermit.

सुधी – पु॰ – (सुधी) धीमान, बुद्धिमान आदमी । wise man.

सुधोत – कृदन्त – (सु + धौत) अच्छी तरह धोया गया । well washed, thoroughly cleaned.

सुनख – पु॰ – (सुनख) श्वान, कुत्ता । a dog.

सुनखी – स्त्री॰ – (सुनखी) कुतिया, कुत्ती । a bitch.

सुनख-जातक – (जा॰ सं॰ 242) – मालिक के सो जाते ही चम्पत हो जाने वाले एक चालाक कुत्ते की कथा । it is a story (No. 242) of a cunning dog who escaped when the master was in deep sleep.

सुनहात – कृदन्त – (सु + स्नात) अच्छी तरह नहाया हुआ । well bathed.

सुनिसित – कृदन्त – (सु + निशित) भली प्रकार तेज किया गया । well whetted or sharpened.

सुन्दर – वि॰ – (सुन्दर) रमणीय, आकर्षक । nice, beautiful.

सुन्दरतर – वि॰ – (सुन्दरतर) रम्यतर, अधिक सुन्दर । more beautiful.

सुन्दरिका – स्त्री॰ – (सुन्दरिका) पाप नाशन के लिए प्रसिद्ध कोसल जनपद की एक नदी । a river in Kosala reputed to be efficacious in washing away sins.

सुनापरन्त – (सुप्पारक पुत्तन) शूपरिक बन्दरगाह के आस-पास का क्षेत्र जहाँ 'पुण्ण थेर' का जन्म हुआ था । a country in which was the part of Suppāraka, birth place of Puṇṇa Thera.

सुपक्क – वि॰ – (सुपक्व) भली प्रकार पका हुआ । thoroughly ripe.

√ **सुप** – तु॰ – (शयने) सोना । to sleep.

सुपटिपन्न – वि॰ – (सुप्रतिपन्न) सुप्रतिपन्न, सुमार्ग पर आरुढ़ । entered the right path.

सुपण्ण – पु॰ – (सुपर्ण) गरुड़ । a kind of battle array, a large vulture, eagle.

सुपत्त-जातक – (जा॰ सं॰ 292) – सुपत्त नामक वायस-राज की सदाशयता की कथा । the story (No. 292) of the crow-king Supatta's goodness.

सुपति – क्रि॰ – (स्वपिति) सोता है । sleeps.

सुपरिकम्म बत नि॰ – (सु + परिकम्म + कृत) सुपरिमार्जित, अच्छी तरह से भाँजा हुआ या पालिश किया हुआ । well prepared or polished.

सुपरिहीन – वि॰ – (सुपरिक्षीण) अत्यन्त दुबला-पतला । lean, weak.

सुपिन (सुपिनक - सपिनन्त भी) – न॰ – स्वप्न । a dream.

सुपिन-पाठक – पु॰ – (स्वप्नज्ञ) स्वप्न-वेत्ता, स्वप्नों की व्याख्या करने वाला । explainer of a dream, reader of a dream.

सुपुप्फित – वि॰ – (सुपुष्पित) फूलों से लदा हुआ, पूरी तरह से खिला हुआ । covered with flowers, fully blown.

सुपीठित – कृदन्त – भली प्रकार पीटा गया । well-beaten.

सुपोत्थित – देखें सुपोठित । see Supoṭhita.

सुप्प – पु॰ तथा न॰ – (शूर्प) सूप या छाज । a winnowing basket.

सुपटिविध – कृदन्त – (सुप्रतिविद्ध) भली प्रकार समझ लिया गया । thoroughly understood.

सुप्पतिट्ठित – कृदन्त – (सु + प्रतिष्ठित) भली प्रकार प्रतिष्ठित । firmly established.

सुप्पत्तीत – वि॰ – (सुप्रतीत) हृष्ट मनः, अच्छी तरह प्रसन्न । well pleased.

सुप्पधंसिय – वि॰ – (सुप्रध्वंसित) सुविध्वंसित, आसानी से दबा दिया गया । easily assaulted or overpowered.

सुप्पबुद्ध – पु॰ – (सुप्रबुद्ध) माया तथा गौतमी प्रजापति का भाई । the brother of Māyādevī and Prajāpati Gautamī.

सुप्पभात – न॰ – (सुप्रभात) सुप्रभात । good morning.

सुप्पवेदित – वि॰ – (सुप्रवेदित) भली प्रकार प्रबोधित । well preached.

सुप्पसन्न – वि॰ – (सुप्रसन्न) सुस्पष्ट, भली प्रकार प्रसन्न, श्रद्धावान । fully pleased, full of faith, very clear.

सुप्पार-सुप्पारक – पु॰ – (शूपरि-शूपरिक) बुद्धकालीन भारत 'सुप्पारक' बन्दरगाह । a sea port of Buddhist India.

सुप्पारक-जातक – (जा॰ सं॰ 463) – अन्धे नाविक के मार्गदर्शन की कथा । the story of a blind master-mariner of Bharukaccha.

सुफ्फसित – वि॰ – (**सुस्पष्ट**) ठीक तरह से लगा हुआ। well fitted.

सुबहु – वि॰ – (**सुबहु**) बहु मात्रिक, अत्यन्त। a vast quantity.

सुब्बच – वि॰ – आज्ञाकरी, विनम्र। obedient, humble.

सुब्बत – क्रि॰ – (**सुव्रत**) सदाचरण, परायण। of noble conduct.

सुब्बुट्ठि – स्त्री॰ – (**सुवृष्टि**) अनुकूल तथा पर्याप्त वर्षा। abundant and useful rain.

√ **सुभ** – (भू॰) – (**शोभने**) शोभा देना। give beauty, add lustre.

सुभ – वि॰ – (**शुभ**) शुभ, शुभ (मुहूर्त्त), अच्छा लगने वाला। auspicious, lucky.

सुभकिण्ण – पु॰ – देवताओं की एक जाति। one sect of demi-gods.

सुभनिमित्त – न॰ – (**शुभनिमित्त**) शुभंकर, शुभ शकुन, सुन्दर वस्तु। an auspicious sign.

सुभग – वि॰ – (**सुभग**) सौभाग्यपूर्ण। lucky, fortunate.

सुभद्दथेर – पु॰ – (**सुभद्र स्थविर**) भगवान बुद्ध परिनिर्वृत्त होने को थे उस समय उन्होनें समुद्र परिव्राजक को आदेश दिया। यह भगवान् बुद्ध के जीवन-काल में उन्हीं के द्वारा दीक्षित उनका अन्तिम शिष्य था। Subhadda was the last disciple to be converted by the Buddha; he was preached a few hours before Buddha's *parinirvāṇa*.

सुभर – वि॰ – (**सुभर**) जिसका आसानी से भरण-पोषण किया जा सके, जिसका किसी पर अधिक भार न हो। easily supported or satisfied.

सुभिक्ख – वि॰ – (**सुभिक्ष**) जहाँ आहार की कमी न हो। having plenty of food, prosperous.

सुमङ्गल-जातक – (जा॰ सं॰ 420) – इस जातक कथा की शिक्षा है कि राजा अपराधी को दण्डज्ञा तब तक न दे, जब तक अभियुक्त के प्रति राज्य का क्रोध-भाव शान्त न हो जाय। the story (No. 420) reveals that for a king it is wrong to act hastily in his anger.

सुमति – पु॰ – (**सुमति**) मतिमान व्यक्ति। a wise man.

सुमन – वि॰ – (**सुमन**) प्रसन्न। glad.

सुमन-पुप्फ – न॰ – (**सुमन पुष्प**) चमेली का फूल। jasmine flower.

सुमन-मुकुल – न॰ – (**सुमन-मुकुल**) चमेली की कलिका। a jasmine-bud.

सुमन-माला – स्त्री॰ – (**सुमन-माला**) चमेली की माला। garland of jasmine.

सुमन-सामणेर – (**सुमन-सामणेर**) भिक्षुणी संघमित्रा का पुत्र सुमन श्रामणेर महास्थविर महिन्द के साथ यह भी सिंहल-द्वीप गया था। son of Sanghamitra, at the age of seven he became a Sāmaṇera and accompanied Mahendra to Ceylon.

सुमना – स्त्री॰ – (**सुमना**) चमेली, प्रसन्न-वदना स्त्री। jasmine, a pleasant woman.

सुमनोहर – वि॰ – (**सुमनोहर**) अत्यन्त आकर्षक। very charming.

सुमानस – वि॰ – (**सुमानस**) प्रसन्न-चित्त। joyful.

सुमापित – कृदन्त – (**सुमापित**) सुनिर्मित।
well built.

सुमुत्त – कृदन्त – (**सुमुत्त**) सुविमुक्त, अच्छी
तरह से विमुक्त। well released.

सुमेध – (सुमेधस भी) वि॰ – (**सुमेधस**)
बुद्धिमान। wise.

सुमेरु – पु॰ – (**सुमेरु**) सुमेरु पर्वत, मैनाक।
mountain Sumeru.

सुयिट्ठ – वि॰ – (**सुहुत**) अच्छी तरह से
आहुति दी गई। oblation given in
plenty and in the right way.

सुयुत्त – वि॰ – (**सुयुक्त**) अच्छी तरह से
नियुक्त किया गया। well arranged
or suited.

सुर – पु॰ – (**सुर**) देवता। a god, deity.

सुरनदी – स्त्री॰ – (**सुरनदी**) देवताओं की
नदी। the celestial river.

सुरनाथ – पु॰ – (**सुरनाथ**) देवताओं का
राजा। the king of devas.

सुरपथ – पु॰ – (**सुरपथ**) व्योम, आकाश।
the sky.

सुरगिपु – पु॰ – (**सूररिपु**) देवताओं का शत्रु,
असुरा। the enemy of gods, i.e. an
asura.

सुरत – वि॰ – (**सुरत**) भक्त, आसक्त, प्रेमी।
a well loving, devoted, attached.

सुरत्त – वि॰ – (**सुरक्त**) अच्छी तरह से रँगा
हुआ, अत्यन्त लाल। well-dyed, deep
red.

सुरसेन – पु॰ – (**शूरसेन**) बुद्धकालीन भारत
के सोलह महाजनपदों में से एक। one
of the sixteen *mahājanapada*s of
Buddha's India.

सुरभि – वि॰ – (**सुरभि**) सुगन्धित।
fragrant.

सुरभि-गन्ध – वि॰ – (**सुरभिगन्ध**) सौम्य-
गन्ध, सुवास, सुगन्ध। a fragrance.

सुर सुरा – स्त्री॰ – (**सुरा**) नशीली शराब।
intoxicating liquor.

सुरा-घट – पु॰ – (**सुराघट**) शराब का घड़ा।
a pitcher of liquor.

सुरा-धुत्त – पु॰ – (**सुराधुत्त**) शराब के नशे
में मस्त। a drunkard.

सुरा-पान – न॰ – (**सुरापान**) मदिरा-पान,
सुरा का पीना। drinking a strong
liquor.

सुरा-पायिका – स्त्री॰ – (**सुरापायिका**) शराबी
औरत। a drunkard woman.

सुरा-पीत – वि॰ – (**सुरापीत**) जिसने शराब
पी ली हो। one who has drunk.

सुरा-मद – पु॰ – (**सुरामद**) शराब का नशा।
tipsiness, drunkenness.

सुरा-मेरय – न॰ – (**सुरामेरय**) सुरा आसव,
सुरा तथा अन्य नशीले पदार्थ। alcohol
and spirits.

सुरा-सोण्ड/सुरा-सोण्डक – पु॰ – (**सुरा
सौण्डिक**) शराबी। addicted to strong
drink, an alcoholic.

सुरापान-जातक – (जा॰ सं॰ 81) – यह
कथा कुछ तपस्वियों के शराब पीकर
निर्लज्जतापूर्वक नाचने की घटना का
वर्णन करता है। the tale (No. 81)
describes how hermits got
durnk and behaved with undue
hilarity.

सुरिय – पु॰ – (**सूर्य**) सूर्य। the sun.

सुरियग्गाह – पु॰ – (**सूर्य-ग्रहण**) सूर्य-ग्रहण।
eclipse of the sun.

सुरिय-मण्डल – न॰ – (**सूर्य-मण्डल**) सूर्य
के गिर्द का चक्कर। the orb of the
sun.

सुरियत्थङ्गम – पु॰ – (सूर्यास्तः गमन) सूर्यास्त। the sunset, dusk.

सुरिय-रंसि – (सूर्य-रश्मि) सूर्य की किरण। rays of the sun.

सुरिय-रस्मि – (सूर्य-रश्मि) देखें सुरियरंसि। see Suriya-ransi.

सुरियुग्गमन – न॰ – (सूर्योद्गमन) सूर्योदय। the sun-rise.

सुरुचि-जातक – (जा॰ सं॰ 489) – सुरुचि कुमार तथा सुमेधा के गृहस्थ जीवन को दर्शाने वाली कथा। tale No. 489 on the family life of Suruchi Kumar and Sumedhā.

सुरुङ्ग – स्त्री॰ – (सुरुङ्गा) कारा, जेलखाना। a prison.

सुरुसुरु-कारकं – क्रि॰ वि॰ – (सुरसुरायनम्) खाते समय सुरसुर की आवाज करना। making hissing sound while eating.

सुरूप/सुरूपी – वि॰ – (सुरुप) सुन्दर, रूपवान। handsome.

सुरूपिनी – स्त्री॰ – (सुरुपिणी) सुन्दर, रूपवती। beautiful.

सुलब्ध (1) – कृदन्त – (सुलब्ध) सुगमता से प्राप्त। easily gained.

सुलब्ध (2) – वि॰ – (सुलब्ध) सुष्ठु-लाभ, सुलाभ। well-gained.

सुलभ – वि॰ – (सुलभ) जो आसानी से मिल सके। easily to be obtained.

सुलसा-जातक – (जा॰ सं॰ 419) – इस जातक में सुलसा वेश्या द्वारा कृतघ्न सत्तक डाकू को चट्टान से गिराकर मार डालने की कथा वर्णित है। the Jātaka tells (No. 419) how courtesan Sulasā crushed the ungrateful robber Sattaka to death.

सुव – पु॰ – (शुकः) तोता। a parrot.

सुवच – क्रि॰ वि॰ – (सुवच) देखें सुब्बच। see Subbaca.

सुवण्ण – न॰ – (सुवर्ण) स्वर्ण, सोना (वि॰) अच्छे रंग का। gold, (adj.) of good colour.

सुवण्णकार – पु॰ – (स्वर्णकार) सोनार। goldsmith.

सुवण्ण-गब्भ – पु॰ – (स्वर्ण-गर्भ) सोना रखने के लिए सुरक्षित कमरा। a strong room for gold.

सुवण्ण-गुहा – स्त्री॰ – (स्वर्ण-गुहा) सुनहरी गुफा। a golden cave.

सुवण्णता – स्त्री॰ – (सुवर्णता) सुरूपता, सुवर्णता। beauty of complexion.

सुवण्ण-पट्ट – न॰ – (स्वर्ण-पट्ट) स्वर्ण-पट्ट। a sheet of gold, gold bar.

सुवण्ण-पीठक – न॰ – (स्वर्ण-पीठिका) स्वर्ण-पीठिका। a golden chair, a throne.

सुवण्ण-मय – वि॰ – (स्वर्णमय) स्वर्णिम, कनकमय, सोने का बना। made of gold.

सुवण्ण-भिङ्गार – पु॰ – (स्वर्ण-घर) सोने की झारी। a golden pitcher.

सुवण्ण-वण्ण – वि॰ – (स्वर्ण-वर्ण) सुनहरे रंग का। gold-coloured.

सुवण्ण-हंस – पु॰ – (स्वर्ण-हंस) सुनहरा हंस। a golden swan.

सुवण्णकट्टुक-जातक – (जा॰ सं॰ 389) – केकड़े द्वारा साँप तथा कौवे की हत्या कर किसान के प्राणों की रक्षा करने से सम्बन्धित कथा। the story (No. 389) tells how a crab protected the life of a farmer by killing the snake and the crow.

सुवण्ण-भूमि – स्त्री॰ – (स्वर्ण-भूमि) तृतीय संगीति के बाद सोण तथा उत्तर स्थविरों की प्रचार भूमि, वर्तमान समय का म्याँमार देश। Suvaṇṇabhumi is identified with lower Burma where Soṇa and Uttara had gone to preach Buddhism after the third council.

सुवण्णमिग-जातक – (जा॰ सं॰ 359) – व्याध द्वारा हिरणी के आत्मत्याग की भावना से प्रभावित हो, बन्दी हिरण तथा हिरणी दोनों को मुक्त कर दिए जाने की कथा। the story (No. 359) tells how a hunter was so amazed with sacrifice of the act of the doe that he set both the stag and doe free.

सुवत्थापित – वि॰ – (सुस्थापित) सुनिश्चित। well defined or ascertained.

सुवात्थि – अव्यय – (स्वस्ति) स्वस्ति, कल्याण हो। a benediction, may you be happy.

सुवम्मित – कृदन्त – (सुवर्मित) भली प्रकार कवच पहने। well harnessed or armoured.

सुवाण – पु॰ – (श्वान) कुत्ता। a dog.

सुवाण-दोणि – स्त्री॰ – (श्वान-द्रोणिः) कुत्ते की नाँद या कठौती। a dog's trough.

सुविजान – वि॰ – (सुविद्य/सुवेद्य) आसानी से समझ में आने वाला। easily understood.

सुविञ्ञापय – वि॰ – (सुविज्ञाप्य) सुविज्ञापनीय, जिसे आसानी से शिक्षित किया जा सके। easy to instruct.

सुविभत्त – कृदन्त – (सुविभक्त) भली प्रकार विभक्त या व्यवस्थित। well divided or arranged.

सुविलित्त – कृदन्त – (सुविलिप्त) भली प्रकार लेप किया गया, सुगन्धित। well coated, perfumed.

सुविम्हित – कृदन्त – (सुविस्मित) अत्यन्त-चकित। much astonished.

सुविसद – वि॰ – (सुविशद) साफ-साफ, अत्यन्त स्पष्ट। very clear.

सुवीर – पु॰ – (सुवीर) पुत्र। son.

सुवुट्ठिक – वि॰ – (सुवृष्टिक) पर्याप्त वर्षायुक्त। having abundant rain.

सुवे – अव्यय – (श्वः) कल (आने वाला कल)। tomorrow.

सुस – (दि॰) – (शोषणे) सूखना। to dry.

सुसङ्खत – कृदन्त – (सुसंस्कृत) सुसंस्कृत, अच्छी तरह तैयार किया गया। well prepared.

सुसञ्ञत – वि॰ – (सुसंयत) पूर्ण रूप से संयत। thoroughly restrained.

सुसण्ठान – वि॰ – (सुसंस्थान) भले आकार-प्रकार का। well featured.

सुसमारद्ध – कृदन्त – (सुसमारब्ध) अच्छी प्रकार से आरम्भ किया गया। well-begun.

सुसमाहित – कृदन्त – (सुसमाहित) पूर्ण रूप से संयमित। well restrained.

सुसमुच्छिन्न – कृदन्त – (सुसमुच्छिन्न) पूर्ण रूप से उखाड़ दिया गया। completely eradicated.

सुसान – न॰ – (श्मशान) श्मशान। cemetery.

सुसान-गोपक – न॰ – (श्मशान-गोपक) श्मशान-रक्षक, श्मशान-पालक। a cemetery keeper.

सुसिक्खित – कृदन्त – (सुशिक्षित) पूर्ण रुप से शिक्षित। well trained, thoroughly learnt.

सुसिर – न॰ – (सुषिर) खोंडर (वि.) पोलवाला, छिद्रयुक्त । hollow, (adj.) perforated, having a hole.

सुसीम-जातक – (जा॰ सं॰ 163) – सुसीम-राजा के पुरोहित-पुत्र द्वारा तीन दिन में बनारस से तक्षशिला आ-जाकर हस्ति विद्या सीख लेने का अचरज । the Jātaka (No. 163) tells how king Susīma's chaplain's son learnt the elephant-lore within three days time by reaching Takṣaśīla from Benaras.

सुसीम-जातक (जा॰ सं॰ 411) – जातक कथा बतलाती है कि वैभव एवं काम सुखों के भोज स्थिर चित्त व्यक्ति को आकर्षित नहीं कर पाते । the story (no. 411) tells that worldly charms fail to attract the enlightened.

सुसील – वि॰ – (सुशील) सुशील । virtuous.

सुसु – पु॰ – (शिशु) शिशु (वि.) शिशु-स्वभाव वाला । a baby, (adj.) young.

सुसुका – स्त्री॰ – (सुसुका) एक प्रकार की मछली । a kind of fish.

सुसुक्क – वि॰ – (सुश्वेत) अत्यन्त सफेद । very white.

सुसुनाग – पु॰ – (शिशुनाग) कालाशोक का पिता तथा मगध नरेश । the king of Magadha and the father of Kālāśoka.

सुसुद्ध – वि॰ – (सुशुद्ध/विशुद्ध) अत्यन्त शुद्ध, परिशुद्ध । very clean.

सुस्सति – क्रि॰ – (√ शुष - शुष्यति) बिखर जाता है, सूख जाता है । withers, becomes dried.

सुस्सरता – स्त्री॰ – (सुस्वरता) स्वर-माधुर्य, मधुर स्वर होना । having a sweet voice.

सुस्सूसति – (शृणोति) सुनता है । listens.

सुस्सूसा – स्त्री॰ – (शुश्रूषा) सुनने की इच्छा, आज्ञाकारिता । wish to hear, commands, orders.

सुस्सोन्दी-जातक – (जा॰ सं॰ 360) – रानी सुस्सोन्दी तथा गरुड़ की प्रेम-कथा जो कामान्धता का दृष्टान्त प्रस्तुत करती है । the tale (no. 360) reveals how lust makes a person blind.

सुहज्ज – न॰ – (सुहृद्/सौहार्दि) सुहृदयता, मैत्री । amity, friendship,.

सुहद – पु॰ – (सुहृद्) मित्र । friend.

सुहनु-जातक – (जा॰ सं॰ 158) – महासोष तथा सुहनु अश्वों के बीच मित्रता स्थापित हुई । मित्रता के सुपरिणाम की कथा । the story (No. 158) of two horses tells that the likeness in nature removes the hate.

सुहित – वि॰ – (सन्तुष्ट) सन्तुष्ट । satisfied.

√सू – (भू) – (प्रसवे) पैदा करना । to give birth.

सूक – पु॰ – (शूक) जौ, गेहूँ आदि का टूँड़, जौ की सींक । the awn of the barley etc.

सूकर – पु॰ – (शूकर) सुअर । a pig, a hog.

सूकर-पोतक – पु॰ – (शूकर-पोसक) सुअर का बच्चा । the young of a pig.

सूकर-मंस – न॰ – (शूकर-मांस) सुअर का मांस । pork.

सूकर-जातक – (जा॰ सं॰ 153) – सुअर द्वारा शेर को युद्ध के लिए चुनौती देने और उसके दुष्परिणाम से भयभीत होकर बचाव का नायाब तरीका अपनाने की

कथा। once a bear challenged a lion to fight, the lion fixed the date after a week, the boar moistened his body with dew and rolled in the hermit's dunghill, when the lion arrived at the fixed time, he smelt the filth and allowed the boar to go away uninjured.

सूकरिक – पु॰ – (शूक-वधिक) कसाई। a dealer in swine, pork-butcher.

सूचक – वि॰ – (सूचक) सूचना देने वाला। informer, indicator.

सूचन – न॰ – (सूचन) सूचना। indication.

सूचि – स्त्री॰ – (सूची) तालिका, सुई, बालों में लगाने का काँटा, बन्द दरवाजे के पीछे लगाई जाने वाली लकड़ी। list, a needle, a hairpin, a small door-bolt.

सूचिका – स्त्री॰ – (सूचिका) सूची, सुई, अर्गला। a list, a needle, a door bolt.

सूचिकार – पु॰ – (सूचीकार) सुई बनाने वाला, कब्जा। a bolt holder.

सूचि-घर – न॰ – (सूची-पिटक) सुई रखने की डिबिया। a needle case.

सूचि-मुख – पु॰ – (सूची-मुख) मशक, मच्छर। mosquito.

सूचि-लोम – वि॰ – (सूची-लोम) सुई जैसे कड़े बालों वाला। having hair like needles.

सूचि-विज्झन – न॰ – (सूची-विद्धन) सूजा, मोची का टेकुआ। an awl.

सूचि-जातक – (जा॰ सं॰ 387) – निपुण सुनार ने एक ऐसी सुई बनाई जिसके एक के बाद सात घर (खोल) बनाए, जो कान को भेद सकती थी और उसे अपनी पुत्री को देकर गौरवान्वित किया। it is the story of a goldsmith who made a delicate needle that could pierce dice and float on water as well, the royal smith honoured his skill and gave his daughter to him in marriage.

सूजु – वि॰ – (ऋजु) सीधा। upright.

सूत – पु॰ – (सूत) रथ हाँकने वाला। a charioteer.

सूति-घर – (प्रसूति घर) प्रसूति-घर। labour room.

√ **सूद** – (भू॰) – (क्षरणे) टपकना। to drip.

सूद/सूदक – पु॰ – (सूद) सूदकार, रसोइया। a cook.

सून – वि॰ – (सून) उच्छून, सूजा हुआ, फूला हुआ। swollen, blossomed.

सूना – स्त्री॰ – (सूना) वध-स्थान, कसाई का थड़ा (ठीहा)। slaughter house, place of slaughter butcher's block.

सूना-घर – न॰ – (सूना-गृह) वध-शाला, कसाई-खाना। slaughter-house.

सूनु – पु॰ – (सूनु) पुत्र। son.

सूप – पु॰ – (सूप) कढ़ी। curry.

सूपकार – पु॰ – (सूपकार) रसोइया। a cook.

सूपतित्थ – वि॰ – (सु + उप + तिष्ठ = सूपतिष्ठ) अच्छे पतन या अच्छे घाट वाला। with good fall or incline leading to a river bank.

सूपधारित – कृदन्त – (सु + उपधारित = सूपधारित) सुअवधारित, सुविचारित। well considered.

सूपिक – पु॰ – (सूपकार) रसोइया। a cook.

सूपेय्य – वि॰ – (सूपोचित) सूप (कढ़ी) के लिए योग्य। suitable for curry.

सुपेय्य-पण्ण – न॰ – (सूपेय्य-पर्ण) कढ़ी बनाने में प्रयुक्त, 'कढ़ी नीम' का पत्ता। leaf used in food prepared from flour of gram with spices and sour curd.

सुयति – क्रि॰ – (श्रूयते) सुना जाता है। (it is) heard.

सूर (1) – वि॰ – (शूर) शूर, बहादुर। valiant, a hero.

सूर (2) – पु॰ – (सूर्य) भानु, सूर्य। the sun.

सूरत – वि॰ – (सूरत) शान्त, सौम्य, मृदु, करुणा करने वाला। tranquil, kind-hearted.

सूरता – स्त्री॰ – (शूरता) शौर्य, बहादुरी, पराक्रम। valour, heroism.

सूरत्त – न॰ – (शूरत्व) शौर्य, पराक्रम, साहस, शूरता का भाव। valour, might, heroic dead.

सूर-भाव – पु॰ – (शौर्य) पराक्रम, साहस, शूरता का भाव। valour, strength, prowess.

सूरिय – पु॰ – (सूर्य) सूरज, सूर्य। the sun.

√**सूल** – (भू) – (वेदनायम्) दर्द होना। to pain.

सूल – न॰ – (शूल) शूल, भाला, बर्छी। stake, pike.

सूलारोपण – न॰ – (शूलारोपण) सूली पर चढ़ाना। impalement.

सेक – (पु॰) – (सेक) छिड़काव। sprinkling.

सेख/सेक्ख – पु॰ – (शैक्ष्य) शिशिक्षु, सीखने वाला, उन्नति-पथ पर आरूढ़, वह जो अभी अर्हत् नहीं बना। a learner, one who is in the course of perfection.

सेखर – न॰ – (शेखर) सिर पर धारण की जाने वाली पुष्प-माला। a garland for the head or crown or crest.

सेखिय – वि॰ – (शैक्ष्य) धार्मिक जीवन में अभ्यास-क्रम से सम्बन्धित। connected with spiritual training.

सेग्गु-जातक – (जा॰ सं॰ 217) – पिता द्वारा सेग्गु नामक अपनी बेटी के शील की परीक्षा की कथा। the story (No. 217) of a father who in order to test his daughter, Seggu, took her to the woods and made it appear as if he was going to reduce her.

सेचन – न॰ – (सेचन) छिड़कना। sprinkling.

सेट्ठ – वि॰ – (श्रेष्ठ) श्रेष्ठ। foremost, superb, superior, great.

सेट्ठतर – वि॰ – (श्रेष्ठतर) श्रेष्ठतर। most excellent, supreme.

सेट्ठ-सम्मत – वि॰ – (श्रेष्ठ सम्मत) श्रेष्ठ माना गया। considered the best.

सेट्ठि/सेट्ठी – पु॰ – (श्रेष्ठी) सेठ। a leading and rich merchant, trader.

सेट्ठिट्ठान – न॰ – (श्रेष्ठि स्थान) सेठ का पद। the position of a Setthi.

सेट्ठि-जाया – स्त्री॰ – (श्रेष्ठि-जाया) सेठ की पत्नी, सेठानी। wife of a rich merchant.

सेट्ठि-भरिया – स्त्री॰ – (श्रेष्ठि-भार्या) सेठानी। wife of a rich merchant.

सेणि – स्त्री॰ – (श्रेणी) श्रेणी, एक-एक पेशा करने वालों की पृथक्-पृथक् परिषद्। a guild, a category, a business concern.

सेणिय – पु० – (श्रेणिय) एक जाति का चौधरी, श्रेणी का मुखिया। a guild master.

सेत – वि० – (श्वेत) श्वेत, सफेद, (पु०) सफेद रंग। white, pure (m.) the white colour.

सेत-कुट्ठ – न० – (श्वेत-कुष्ठ) सफेद कोढ़। white leprosy.

सेतच्छत्त – न० – (श्वेत-छत्र) श्वेत-छत्र, सामन्त पद परिचायक। a white parasol which is an emblem of royalty.

सेत-पच्छाद – वि० – (श्वेत-प्रच्छाद) श्वेत ओढ़ावन। white covering.

सेतकेतु-जातक – (जा० सं० 377) – जाति अभिमानी श्वेतकेतु को एक चाण्डाल ने नीचा दिखाया। the story (No. 377) tells how Śvetaketu, a brāhmaṇa who prided himself on his high-caste, was defeated by a cāṇḍāla (lower-caste man) in a spiritual debate.

सेतट्ठिका – स्त्री० – (श्वेतिष्ठिका) तुलासिता, पौधों पर एक सफेद फफूँदी-जनित रोग। the mildew.

सेति – क्रि० – (√ शी - शेते) सोता है। sleeps.

सेतु – पु० – (सेतु) पुल। a bridge.

सेद – पु० – (√ स्विद् - स्वेद) पसीना। sweat, perspiration.

सेदक – वि० – (स्वेदक) पसीना पाते हुए। sweating.

सेदन – न० – (स्वेदन) भाप से उबालना। boiling by steam.

सेदावक्खित्त – वि० – (स्वेदावक्षिप्त) स्वेदक्लिन्न, पसीने से तर। sweat-covered.

सेदेति – क्रि० – (√ स्विद् - स्विद्यति) पसीना या भाप उत्पन्न कराता है। causes to sweat or seethe or perspire.

सेन/सेनक – पु० – (श्येन) चील, बाज। a hawk.

सेना – स्त्री० – (सेना) फौज। an army.

सेना-नायक – पु० – (सेनानायक) सेना का संचालक, सेनानी, सेनापति। a general.

सेनानी – न० – (सेनापत्य) देखें सेनानायक। see Senānāyaka.

सेना-पच्च – न० – (सेनापत्य) सेनापति का कार्यालय। the office of a general.

सेनापति – पु० – (सेनापति) देखें सेनानायक। see Senānāyaka.

सेना-व्यूह – पु० – (सेना-व्यूह) सेना का चक्रव्यूह। an array of troops.

सेनासन – न० – (शयनासन) शयनासन, सोने के लिए स्थान, सोने की व्यवस्था। lodging, sleeping place.

सेनासन-गाहापक – पु० – (शयनागार-व्यवस्थापक) सोने के स्थानों की व्यवस्था करने वाला। one who allots lodging place.

सेनासन-चारिका – स्त्री० – (शयनासन चारिक) एक शयनासन से दूसरे शयनासन तक भटकना। wandering from lodging to lodging.

सेनासन-पञ्ञापक – पु० – (शयनासन-प्रज्ञापक) शयन आसनों का व्यवस्थापक। regulator of lodging places.

सेफालिका – स्त्री० – (शेफालिका) नेवारी नामक पुष्प-वृक्ष, नील सिंधुवार, निर्गुंडी। a kind of jasmine plant.

सेम्ह – न० – (श्लेष्मा) श्लेष्मा, कफ। phlegm.

सेम्हिक – वि॰ – (श्लेष्मिक) श्लेष्मा-पीड़ित, कफ प्रकृति वाला। a man of phlegmatic humour.

सेय्य – न॰ – (श्रेय) श्रेष्ठतर। better, excellent.

सेय्य-जातक – (जा॰ सं॰ 282) – दुश्चरित मन्त्री द्वारा राजा के रनिवास में गड़बड़ी करने पर उसे देश निकाला देने की कथा। the story (No. 282) of a minister who was found guilty of an intrigue in the harem and was banished.

सेय्यथापि – अव्यय – (स यथापि) जैसाकि, जैसे। just as.

सेय्यथीदं – अव्यय – (स यथा + इदम्) निम्नोक्त के अनुसार। as follows.

सेय्या – स्त्री॰ – (शय्या) सेज, शयन, शय्या। a bed, sleep, bedding.

सेय्यो – अव्यय – (श्रेयस्) श्रेष्ठ, श्रेयस्कर। better.

सेरिचारी – वि॰ – (स्वैराचारी) स्वेच्छाचारी, यथा-रूचि, विचरने वाला। acting according to one's liking.

सेरिता – स्त्री॰ – (स्वैरिता) स्वच्छन्दता, स्वैरी-भाव। self-willedness.

सेरिवाणिज-जातक – (जा॰ सं॰ 3) – इस जातक में एक लोभी बनिए के पश्चाताप की कथा है। this Jātaka (No. 3) tells the sorrow tale of a greedy merchant.

सेरिविहारि – वि॰ – (स्वैरी-विहारी) स्वच्छन्द-विहारी, स्वच्छन्द विचरण करने वाला। living at one's own choice.

सेल – पु॰ – (शैल) शैल, पर्वत। a rock, stone, hill.

सेलमय – वि॰ – (शैलमय) पत्थर का बना। made of stone.

सेलेय्य – न॰ – (शैलेय) शिलाजीत। mineral pitch, bitumen, Anethum Graveolens.

√सेव – (भू॰) – (सेवने) सेवा करना। to serve.

सेवक – पु॰ – (सेवक) नौकर, सेवा करने वाला। a servant, an attendant.

सेवक – वि॰ – (सेवक) सेवा करता हुआ, संगति में रहता हुआ। serving, associating.

सेवति – क्रि॰ – (√सेव् - सेवते) सेवा करता हुआ, संगति करता है, उपयोग करता है, अभ्यास करता है। serves, associates with, makes use of, practises.

सेवन – न॰ – (सेवनम्) सेवन, संगति, सेवा, उपयोग। association with, service, use of.

सेवना – स्त्री॰ – (सेवना) देखें सेवन। see Sevana.

सेवा – स्त्री॰ – (सेवा) सेवा-टहल। service.

सेवाल – पु॰ – (शैवाल) शैवाल, सेवार, काई। moss, slime, the aquatic plant, Vallisnaria Octandra.

सेवित – कृदन्त – (√सेव् + त = सेवित) उपयोग में लाया गया, अभ्यस्त संगति में रहा। used, practised, associated.

सेवी – पु॰ – (सेवी) संगति करने वाला, अभ्यास करने वाला। one who associates or practises.

सेस – वि॰ – (शेष) शेष, बचा हुआ। remaining, left.

सेसेति – क्रि॰ – (√ शिष - शेषयति) शेष छोड़ता है। leaves over.

सो – सर्वनाम – (सः) वह। he.

सोक – पु॰ – (शोक) विषाद, शोक। grief.

सोकग्गि – पु॰ – (शोकाग्नि) विषादाग्नि, शोकाग्नि। the fire of sorrow.

सोक-परेत – वि॰ – (शोकाकुल) सन्तापकर्षित, शोकाभिभूत। overcome with grief.

सोक-विनोदन – न॰ – (शोक-विनोदन) शोक को दूर करना। dispelling grief.

सोक-सल्ल – न॰ – (शोक-शल्य) शोक-शल्य। the dart of sorrow.

सोकी – वि॰ – (शोकी / शोकिन) शोक करने वाला। aggrieved.

सोख्य – न॰ – (सौख्य) स्वास्थ्य, सुख। health, happiness.

सोखुम्म – न॰ – (सौक्षुम्य) सूक्ष्मता, बारीकी। fineness.

सोगन्धिक – न॰ – (सौगन्धिकम्) पद्म की एक विशिष्ट प्रजाति, श्वेत कमल। white waterlily.

सोचति – क्रि॰ – (√ शुच् - शोचति) सोचता है, चिन्ता करता है, पश्चाताप करता है। mourns, grieves.

सोचना – स्त्री॰ – (शोचना) चिन्ता करना, अफसोस करना। sorrowing.

सोचेय्य – न॰ – (शुचिता) पवित्रता। purity.

सोण – पु॰ – (श्वान) शुनक, कुत्ता। dog.

सोणित – न॰ – (शोणित) शोणित, रक्त। blood.

सोणी (1) – स्त्री॰ – (शुनका) कुतिया, कुत्ती। bitch.

सोणी (2) – स्त्री॰ – (श्रोणी / श्रोणि) कटि या जघन-प्रदेश। waist, hip and loins, buttock.

सोण्ड – वि॰ – (शौण्ड) मद्यप, नशेबाज। addicted to.

सोण्डक – वि॰ – (शौण्डिक) देखें सोण्ड। see Soṇḍa.

सोण्डा – स्त्री॰ – (शुण्डा / शौण्डा) हाथी की सूँड, (वि॰) नशेबाज औरत। trunk of an elephant, (adj.) a woman addicted to.

सोण्डिक – वि॰ – (शौण्डिक) सुरा-विक्रेता, शराब बेचने वाला। spirit-seller, wine-seller.

सोण्डिका-सोण्डी – स्त्री॰ – (1) लता का प्रतान, (2) ह्रद (पर्वतों से घिरा जलाशय)। (1) tendril of a creeper, (2) water tank amongst the hills.

सोण्ण – न॰ – (स्वर्ण) स्वर्ण, सोना। gold.

सोण्णमय – वि॰ – (स्वर्णमय) स्वर्ण-निर्मित। made of gold.

सोत (1) – न॰ – (श्रोत) कर्ण, कान। ear.

सोत (2) – पु॰ – (स्रोत) घास, स्रोत। stream, torrent.

सोत-द्वार – न॰ – (श्रोत्र-द्वार) कर्णेन्द्रिय। the auditory organ.

सोतु-विल – न॰ – (श्रोत्र-विल) श्रोत्र-रन्ध्र, कान का छेद। the orifice of the ear.

सोतवन्तु – वि॰ – (श्रोत्रमान) कान वाला। one who has ear.

सोत-विञ्ञाण – वि॰ – (श्रोत्र-विज्ञान) श्रोत्र-विज्ञान। auditory cognition.

सोत-विञ्ञेय्य – वि॰ – (श्रोत्र-विज्ञेय) कान द्वारा ग्रहण किया जाने वाला विज्ञान। cognizable by hearing.

सोतायतन – न॰ – (श्रोत्रायतन) कर्णेन्द्रिय। the sense of hearing.

सोतब्ब – कृदन्त – (श्रोतव्य) सुना जाने योग्य। fit to be heard.

सोतापत्ति – स्त्री॰ – (श्रोतापत्ति) धर्म-पथ रूपी स्रोत में आ पड़ना, धर्मपथ की पहली मंजिल। entering the noble path.

सोतापन्न – वि॰ – (श्रोतापन्न) धर्म-पथ रूपी स्रोत में आ पड़ा व्यक्ति। one who has entered the stream of noble path.

सोतिन्द्रिय – न॰ – (श्रोत्रेन्द्रिय) श्रवणेन्द्रिय, कान। the ear.

सोतु – पु॰ – (श्रोतृ) श्रोता, सुनने वाला। listener, hearer.

सोतु-काम – वि॰ – (श्रोतु-कामः) सुनने की इच्छा वाला। willing to hear.

सोतुं – कृदन्त – (√ श्रु + तुमुन = श्रोतुम्) सुनने के लिए। to hear, for hearing.

सोत्थि – स्त्री॰ – (स्वास्ति) स्वास्ति, कल्याण, सुरक्षा, आशीर्वचन। well-being, safety, blessing.

सोत्थि-कम्म – न॰ – (स्वस्ति-कर्म) आशीर्वचन। blessing.

सोत्थि-भाव – पु॰ – (स्वस्ति-भाव) स्वस्तिभाव, कुशलता। safety.

सोत्थि-साला – स्त्री॰ – (स्वस्ति-शाला) आरोग्यधाम, आरोग्य-मन्दिर। hospital, sanatorium.

सोदक – वि॰ – (स + उदक) आर्द्र, भीगा हुआ, जल टपकाता हुआ। wet dripping.

सोदरिय – वि॰ – (सोदर) एक ही माता की सन्तान, सहोदर। born of the same mother.

सोधक – वि॰ – (शोधक) सफाई करने वाला, शुद्ध करने वाला। one who cleans, corrects or purifies.

सोधन – न॰ – (शोधन) सफाई, शुद्धि। cleansing, correcting.

सोधापेति – क्रि॰ – (शोधाययति) सफाई कराता है, शुद्धि कराता है। causes to clean or correct, makes someone to clean.

सोधित – कृदन्त – (√ शुध् + क्त - शोधित) साफ किया गया, शुद्ध किया गया। cleaned, corrected, makes someone to clean.

सोधेति – क्रि॰ – (√ शुध् = शुध्यति) साफ करता है, शुद्ध करता है। makes clean, purifies.

सोनक-जातक – (जा॰ सं॰ 529) – अरिन्दम रूप में जन्म लेने की कथा। the story (No. 529) of Bodhisattva in his birth as Arindama.

सोन-नन्द-जातक – (जा॰ सं॰ 532) – नन्द, द्वारा माता-पिता को कच्चा फल ला देने के कारण उसके भाई 'सोन' के रोष, तत्पश्चात् उसके समाहार की कथा। the story (no. 532) of two brothers anger and forgiveness.

सोपाक – पु॰ – (श्वपाक) चाण्डाल। cāṇḍāla (a low caste).

सोपान – पु॰ तथा न॰ – (सोपान) सीढ़ी। stairs, a ladder.

सोपान-पन्ति – स्त्री॰ – (सोपान-पंक्ति) सीढ़ियों की कतार। a flight of steps.

सोपान-पाद – पु॰ – (सोपान-पाद) सीढ़ियों का आरम्भ। the foot of the stairs.

सोपान-फलक – न॰ – (सोपान-फलक) जीने का एक डंडा, एक सीढ़ी। a step of staircase.

सोपान-सीस – न॰ – (सोपान-शीर्ष) ऊपर की सीढ़ी। the top of a staircase.

सोप्प – न॰ – (स्वप्न) सुप्ति, निद्रा, नींद। sleep.

सोब्भ – न॰ – (श्वभ्रं / स्वभ्रम) गड्ढा, जलाशय। a pit, a pool of water.

सोभग्ग – न॰ – (सौभाग्य) सौभाग्य, सौन्दर्य। splendour, beauty.

सोभग्ग-पत्त – वि॰ – (सौभाग्य-प्राप्त) सौभाग्यशाली, सौभाग्यवान, सुन्दर। endowed with beauty or splendour.

सोभण/सोभन – वि॰ – (शोभन) कान्तिमान, शोभन, सुन्दर। shining, beautiful.

सोभति – क्रि॰ – (√ शुभ् - शोभते) चमकता है, सुन्दर लगता है। shines, looks beautiful.

सोभा – स्त्री॰ – (शोभा) शोभा, सौन्दर्य। splendour, beauty.

सोभित – कृदन्त – (√ शुभ + णिच् = शोभयति) चमकता है, सजाता है। makes resplendent, adorns.

सोम – पु॰ – (सोम) चन्द्रमा। the moon.

सोमदत्त-जातक – (जा॰ सं॰ 211) – अग्निदत्त-पुत्र सोमदत्त की कथा। it is the story (No. 211) of Somadatta, son of Agnidatta.

सोमदत्त-जातक – (जा॰ सं॰ 410) – अपने पोषित सोमदत्त गज शावक की मृत्यु पर दुःखी तपस्वी को बोधिसत्व का उपदेश। (tale No. 410) preaching of *bodhisattva* to the hermit who was in grief caused by the death of his adopted elephant-calf Somadatta.

सोमनस्स – न॰ – (सौमनस्य) सौमनस्य, प्रसन्नता, सुख। delight, joy, happiness.

सोमनस्स-जातक – (जा॰ सं॰ 505) – इस जातक में ठग तपस्वी द्वारा राजकुमार सोमनस्स को दण्डित करने का दुष्प्रयत्न वर्णित है। the story (No. 505) tells how the Somanassa exposed the cheat-hermit's knavery.

सोम्म – वि॰ – (सौम्य) सौम्य, अनुकूल। gentle, pleasing.

सोरच्च – न॰ – (सौरत्व) सुखपना, विनम्रता। gentleness, meakness.

सोलस – वि॰ – (षोडश) सोलह। sixteen.

सोलसम – वि॰ – (षोडशः) सोलहवाँ। the sixteenth.

सोवग्गिक – वि॰ – (स्वर्गिक) स्वर्ग-सम्बन्धी। connected with heaven.

सोवचस्सता – स्त्री॰ – (सुवर्चस्वता) आज्ञा, कारिता, विनम्रता। suavity, obedience.

सोवण्ण – न॰ – (सुवर्ण / स्वर्ण) कनक, हिरण्य, सोना। gold.

सोवण्णमय – वि॰ – (स्वर्णमय / सुवर्णमय) कनकमय, स्वर्ण, निर्मित, सोने का बना हुआ। golden, made of gold.

सोवत्थिक – न॰ – (स्वस्तिक) एक मांगलिक चिह्न, स्वस्तिक, स्वास्तिक चिह्न ·ᚦ·। a mark like ·ᚦ· as on the hood of a cobra.

सोवीरक – पु॰ – (सौविरि + कन) सुवीर का वासी, खट्टी काँजी, सिरका। sour gruel, vinegar.

सोस – पु० – (√ शुष् + घञ) शोषण, सूखना। drying up, consumption.

सोसन – न० – (√ शुष + णिच् + ल्यु) सोखना, चूसना, सुखाना। causing to dry.

सोसानिक – वि० – (श्मशानिक) शमशान में रहने वाला। one who lives in a cemetery.

सोसेति – क्रि० – (शोषयति) सुखा देता है, सुखवाता है। causes to dry or wither.

सोस्सति – क्रि० – (√ श्रु - श्रवणे - लृट् लकार - श्रोष्यति) will/shall hear or listen.

सोहज्ज – न० – (सौहार्द/सौहृद/सौहृदय) मैत्री, मित्रता, बन्धुता। friendship.

√ स्निह – (दि०) – (प्रीणने) प्रेम करना। to love.

स्नेह – पु० – (स्नेह) बड़ों का छोटों के प्रति प्रेम, चिकनाहट, तेल। affection, oil.

स्वाकार – वि० – (सु + आकार) अनुकूल प्रकृतिवाला, भली प्रकृति वाला। being of good disposition.

स्वाक्खात – वि० – (सु + आख्यात) सुष्ठु व्याख्यायित, भली प्रकार व्याख्या किया गया, उपदेश किया गया। well explained, well preached.

स्वागत – वि० – (सु + आगत) स्वागत, कण्ठस्थ। welcome, learnt, by heart.

स्वागतं – क्रि० वि० – (स्वागतम्) स्वागतम्, शुभागमन। welcome to you.

स्वातन – वि० – (श्वः + तन = श्वस्तन) श्वस्त्य (आने वाले) कल से सम्बन्धित। relating to tomorrow.

स्वातनाय – क्रि० वि० – (श्वस्तनका चतुर्थी विभक्ति एकवचन) आने वाले कल के लिए। for tomorrow.

स्वे – क्रि० वि० – (श्वः) आने वाला कल। tomorrow.

ह

ह – पालि वर्णमाला का इकत्तीसवाँ व्यञ्जन the 31st consonant of Pāli alphabet.

हज्ज – वि० – (हृदय) हृदय को रुचने वाला, सुन्दर, प्रियतम। pleasing or dear to the heart, beloved, cherished.

हञ्ञति – क्रि० – (हन्यते) मारा जाता है, नष्ट किया जाता है। is being killed or destroyed.

हञ्ञन – (√हन् + ल्युट) हनन, यातना देना, जान से मार डालना। torture, distress, killing.

हट – कृदन्त – ले जाया गया। removed.

हट्ठ – कृदन्त – (√हृष् + क्त = हृष्ट) हर्षित, संतुष्ट, आनन्दित। joyful, bristling.

हट्ठ-तुट्ठ – वि० – (हृष्ट-तुष्ट) प्रसन्न-चित्त। full of mirth.

हट्ठ-लोम – वि० – (हृष्ट-रोमन) हृष्ट-लोग, रोमाञ्चित। with bristling hair, horripilant.

√हठ – (भू०) – (बलात्कारे) हठ करना। to force.

हठ – पु० – (हठ) अत्याचार, दुराग्रह। deviation from moral rules, outrage, aggression.

हत – कृदन्त – (√हन + क्त) हत, आहत, मारा गया, जख्मी हुआ, नष्ट कर दिया गया। struck, killed, destroyed.

हत-भाव – पु० – (हत-भाव) नष्ट किए जाने का भाव। the fact of being destroyed.

हतन्तराय – वि० – (हस्तान्तराय) जिसने विघ्न बाधाएँ दूर कर दी हैं, बाधा-रहित। one who has removed obstacles.

हतावकासो – वि० – (हतावकाशः) शुभाशुभ की सीमा से परे। cut off every occasion of good and evil.

हत्थ – पु० – (हस्त) हाथ, हत्था, हाथ भर का माप। the hand, a handle, a cubit.

हत्थक – पु० – (हस्तक) हत्था, (वि०) हाथ वाला। a hand-like thing.

हत्थ-कम्म – न० – (हस्त-कर्म) शारीरिक-श्रम। manual labour.

हत्थ-गत – वि० – (हस्त-गत) हस्तगत, जिस पर अपना अधिकार हो। come into possession.

हत्थ-गहण – न० – (हस्त-ग्रहण) हाथ से पकड़ना। seizing by the hand.

हत्थ-गाह – पु० – (हस्त-ग्राह) हाथ से धरना। seizing by the hand.

हत्थच्छिन्न – वि० – (छिन्न-हस्त) जिसके हाथ कटे हों। whose hand is cut off.

हत्थ-छेद – पु० – (हस्तच्छेद) देखें हत्थ-छेदन। see Hatha-Chedana.

हत्थ-छेदन – न० – (हस्त-छेदन) हाथों का काटा जाना। cutting of the hand.

हत्थ-तल – न० – (हस्त-तल) करतल, हथेली। the palm of the hand.

हत्थ-पसारण – न॰ – (हस्त-प्रसारण) हाथ फैलाना । stretching out one's hand.

हत्थ-पास – पु॰ – (हस्त-परिमाण) हाथ की लम्बाई । a hand's length.

हत्थ-बट्टक – पु॰ – (हस्त-शकटिका) हाथ की गाड़ी । a hand cart.

हत्थ-विकार – पु॰ – (हस्त-सञ्चालन) हाथ का सञ्चालन । motion of the hand.

हत्थ-सार – पु॰ – (हस्त-सार) मूल्यवान वस्तु, चल सम्पत्ति । the most valuable thing.

हत्थापलेखन – न॰ – (हस्तापलेहन) भोजनान्तर हाथ चाटना । licking the hand after taking meals.

हत्थाभरण – न॰ – (हत्थाभरण) अंगद, बाजूबन्द, केयूर । an arm bracelet.

हत्थत्थर – पु॰ – (हस्ति-कुन्था) हाथी की झूल, हाथी का चोगा । elephant's cover or rug.

हत्थाचरिय – पु॰ – (हस्ति-प्रशिक्षक) हस्तिक, हस्ति-प्रशिक्षक, हाथी को सिखाने वाला । elephant trainer.

हत्थारोह – पु॰ – (हस्तियक) आधोरण, पीलवान, महावत । an elephant driver.

हत्थि – पु॰ – (हस्ति) हाथी । elephant.

हत्थि-कन्त-वीणा – स्त्री॰ – (हस्ति मोहिनी वीणा) हाथियों को बेझाने की वीणा । a lute inticing elephants.

हत्थि-कलभ – पु॰ – (हस्ति-कलभ) गज-शावक, हाथी का बच्चा । the young of an elephant.

हत्थि-कुम्भ – पु॰ – (हस्ति-कुम्भ) गज-कुम्भ, हाथी का मस्तक । the frontal globe of an elephant.

हत्थि-कुल – न॰ – (हस्ति-कुल) गज-यूथ, गजता, हाथियों का परिवार अथवा झुण्ड । herd of elephants, multitude of elephants.

हत्थिक्खन्ध – पु॰ – (हस्ति-स्कन्ध) गज-स्कन्ध, हाथी की पीठ । the back of an elephant.

हत्थि-गोपक – पु॰ – (हस्ति-गोपक) हस्ति-पाल, महावत । an elephant keeper.

हत्थि-दन्त – पु॰ न॰ – (हस्ति-दन्त) गज-दन्त, हाथी का दाँत । the tusk of an elephant, ivory.

हत्थि-दमक – पु॰ – (हस्ति-दमनक) हस्ति-प्रशिक्षक, हाथी को संयत करने वाला । an elephant tamer.

हत्थि-दम्म – पु॰ – (हस्ति-दम्य) प्रशिक्षु-गज, प्रशिक्षित किया जाता हुआ हाथी । an elephant in training.

हत्थि-पद – न॰ – (हस्ति-पाद) हस्ति-पद, हाथी का पाँव या कदम । an elephant foot or step.

हत्थि-पाकार – पु॰ – (हस्ति-प्राकार) गज-प्राचीर, वह परकोटा जिस पर हाथियों की शक्ल उत्कीर्ण की गयी हो । a surrounding wall with figures of elephants in relief.

हत्थिप्पभिन्न – वि॰ – (मत्त गज) गन्ध गज, मदमस्त हाथी, सात स्थानों से मद चूता हुआ हाथी, मदोन्मत्त हाथी । an elephant in rut, a furious elephant.

हत्थि-बन्ध – पु॰ – (हस्तिपकः) महावत, हाथी-रखवाला । an elephant-keeper.

हत्थि-मेण्ड – पु॰ – (गजपाल) फीलवान, गजाजीन, महावत, हाथी रखवाला । an elephant-keeper.

हत्थि-मत्त – वि॰ – (हस्ति-मात्र) हस्ति-मात्रक, हाथी जितना बड़ा। as big as an elephant.

हत्थि-मारक – पु॰ – (हस्ति-मारक) गज-मारक, हाथियों का शिकारी। elephant-hunter.

हत्थि-यान – न॰ – (हस्ति-यानम्) गज-यान, हाथी की सवारी। elephant carriage, or riding elephant.

हत्थि-युद्ध – न॰ – (हस्ति-युद्ध) गज-युद्ध, हाथियों की लड़ाई। combat of elephants.

हत्थि-रूपक – न॰ – (हस्ति-रूपकम्) गजाकृति, हाथी की आकृति अथवा हस्ति-चित्र। figure of an elephant.

हत्थि-लेण्ड – पु॰ – (गज-विष्ठा) हाथी की लीद। elephant-dung.

हत्थि-लिङ्ग-सकुण – (गज-शुण्ड-शकुन्त) हाथी की सूँड जैसी चोंच वाला गीध। a vulture with a bill like an elephant's trunk.

हत्थि-साला – स्त्री॰ – (हस्ति-शाला) हथिसार, हस्ति शाला। elephant-stable.

हत्थि-सिप्प – न॰ – (हस्ति-शिल्प) गज-विद्या, हस्ति – शिल्प। art of taming an elephant.

हत्थि-सोण्डा – स्त्री॰ – (हस्ति-शुण्ड) गज-शुण्ड, हाथी की सूँड। the trunk of an elephant.

हत्थिनी – स्त्री॰ – (हस्तिनी) हथिनी। female elephant.

हत्थी – पु॰ – (हस्तिन्) द्विरद, वारण, गज, हाथी। elephant.

हदय – न॰ – (हृदय) दिल, हृदय। the heart.

हृदयङ्गम – (हृदयङ्गम) हृदि-स्पर्श, अनुकूल, आकर्षक। pleasant, caring, agreeable.

हृदय-मंस – न॰ – (हृदय-मांस) हृदय का मांस। the flesh of the heart.

हृदय-वत्थु – न॰ – (हृदय-वस्तु) हृदय का सार। the substance of the heart.

हृदय-संताप – पु॰ – (हृदय-सन्ताप) मनो-व्यथा, हृदय का संताप या पश्चाताप, मनस्ताप। grief.

हृदयस्सित – वि॰ – (हृदयाश्रित) हृदय-सम्बन्धी, हृदय-आश्रित। connected with the heart.

हृदय-निस्सित – वि॰ – (हृदय-निश्रित) हृदय-आश्रित। connected with the heart.

√हन – (दि॰) – (हिंसायाम्) हिंसा करना। to kill, to torture.

हनति – (हन्तिभी) क्रि॰ (√हन - हन्ति) मारता है, चोट पहुँचाता है, जख्मी करता है। kills, strikes, injures.

हनन – न॰ – (√हन् + ल्युट = हनन) मारना, चोट पहुँचाना। killing, striking.

√हनु – (भु॰) – (अपनयने) छिपाना। to hide, to conceal.

हनु/हनुका – स्त्री॰ – (हनु/हनुका) जबड़ा, दाढ़। the jaw.

हन्तु – पु॰ – (हन्तृ/हन्ता) जान से मारने वाला, चोट पहुँचाने वाला। killer, striker.

हन्त्वा – पू॰ क्रि॰ – (√हन् + त्वा = हत्वा) मार डालकर। absolutive form of 'Hanati'.

हन्द – अव्यय – (हन्त) अच्छा, अब मेरी बात पर ध्यान दो, इस अर्थ में प्रयुक्त।

an interjection used in the sense of "well, then," now come along.

हम्भो – अव्यय – (भोः, हंहोः, हम्भोः) अपने समान लोगों को सम्बोधित करने का ढंग। a particle used in addressing equals.

हम्मिय – न॰ – (हम्र्य) प्रसाद, अट्टालिका, अनेक तल्लों का मकान। multistoreyed building.

हय – पु॰ – (हय) अश्व, घोड़ा। a horse.

हय-पोतक – पु॰ – (हय-पोतक) अश्वशावक, बछेड़ा। a colt.

हय-वाही – वि॰ – (हय-वाही / हय-वाहक) अश्व-शकटी, घोड़ो द्वारा खींची जाने वाली गाड़ी, अश्वयान। chariot drawn by horses.

हयानीक – न॰ – (अश्व सेना) घुड़सवार दस्ता, घुड़सवार सेना। a cavalry.

हर – (दि॰) – (लज्जायाम्) शरमाना। to feel shy.

√हरँ – (भू॰) – (हरणे) चुराना। to steal.

हर (1) – वि॰ – (√हृ-हर) हरने वाला। taking away, removing or depriving of.

हर (2) – पु॰ – (हरः) शिव, महादेव। God Śaṅkara.

हरण – न॰ – (√हृ + ल्युट् - हरण) ले जाना। taking away.

हरणक – वि॰ – (हरणक) हरणकर्त्ता, ले जाता हुआ, ले जाया जा सकने वाला (पदार्थ)। carrying, movable.

हरति – क्रि॰ – (√हृ - हरति) ले जाता है, चुरा लेता है, लूट लेता है। carries, steals, plunders.

हरायति – क्रि॰ – (√ह्री - जिहेति) लज्जित होता है, चिन्तित होता है। becomes ashamed, depressed, worried or vexed.

हरापेति – क्रि॰ – (√हृ + णिच् - हारयति) लिवा जाता है। makes one carry, taken away.

हरि – पु॰ – (हरिः) विष्णु। the God Viṣṇu.

हरिण – पु॰ – (हरिण) मृग। a deer.

हरित – वि॰ – (हरित) हरा, ताजा (न॰) साग-सब्जी। green, tawny, fresh (n.) vegetable, greens.

हरितत्त – न॰ – (हरितत्त्व) हरितपन, हरियाली। the greenness, freshness.

हरितब्ब – कृदन्त – (हर्त्तव्य) हरण किए जाने अथवा ले जाए जाने योग्य। fit to be carried or removed.

हरिताल – न॰ – (हरितास्र) हरिताल, पीली हड़ताल। orpiment, yellow mineral, trisulphide of arsenic.

हरितु – पु॰ – (हर्त्तृ-हर्त्ता) ले जाने वाला। one who carries away.

हरित्तव – वि॰ – (हरित्त्वक) हरिताभ, सुनहरे रंग का। gold-coloured.

हरिस्सवण्ण – वि॰ – (हरिद्वर्णः) सुनहरी झलक वाला। having a golden hue.

हरीतक – स्त्री॰ – (हरीतिकी) हर्रे, हरड़। yellow myrobalan, *terminalia-chebula*.

हरीतकी – न॰ – (हरीतकी) देखें हरीतक। see Harītaka.

हरे – अव्यय – (हरे!) अपने से छोटों को पुकारने के लिए सम्बोधन शब्द। a particle used in addressing inferiors.

हल – न॰ – (हल) (खेत जोतने का) हल।
plough.

हलं – अव्यय – (अलम्) अथकिम्, पर्याप्त।
enough, why should.

हला-हल – न॰ – (हला-हल) कालकूट,
हला-हल, विष। a deadly poison.

हलिद्रा – स्त्री॰ – (हरिद्रा) हल्दी। turmeric.

हलिद्री – स्त्री॰ – (हरिद्रा) हल्दी। turmeric.

हवे – अव्यय – (खलु-हंहो) निश्चय से।
surely, indeed.

हव्य – न॰ – (हव्य) आज्य, आहुति। an
oblation offered to god.

√ हस – (भू॰) – (हसने) हँसना। to laugh.

√ हस – (भू॰) – (आलिग्ये) मजाक करना।
to laugh, to mock.

हसति – क्रि॰ – (√ हस् - हसति) मुसकराता
है, हँसता है। smiles, laughs.

हसन – न॰ – (√ हस् + ल्युट्) हसन, हास,
हँसी। laughter.

हसित – कृदन्त – (√ हस् + क्त = हसित)
मुसकराया, हँसी। laughed, past
participle of Hasati.

हसितुप्पाद – पु॰ – (स्मिति) मुस्कान,
मुस्कराहट। smile.

हस्स – न॰ – (हास / हास्य) हास-परिहास,
हँसी, मजाक। joke, jest.

हंस – पु॰ – (हंस) हंस। a swan.

हंस-पोतक – पु॰ – (हंस-पोतक) हंस का
बच्चा। a young of swan.

हँसति – क्रि॰ – (हर्षति) रोमाञ्चित होता
है। bristles with joy, the hairs of
the body stand erect on the end.

हंसन – न॰ – (हर्षण) रोमाञ्चित होना।
delighting, bristling.

हंसी – स्त्री॰ – (हँसी / हंसिनी) मादा हंस,
हंसिनी। female swan.

हंसेति – क्रि॰ – (√ हृष् + णिच् = हर्षयति)
हँसता है। causative of Hansati.

√ हा – (भू॰) – (त्यागे) त्यागना। to leave,
to give up.

√ हा – (भू॰) – (हानौ) हानि होना। to
loose.

हा – अव्यय – (हा!) विषादबोधक अव्यय,
हन्त, अफसोस। alas!

हाटक – न॰ – (हाटक) सोना, स्वर्ण। a
kind of gold.

हातब्ब – कृदन्त – (√ हा + तव्यत =
हातव्य) त्याज्य। fit to be given up.

हातुं – कृदन्त – (√ हा + तुमुन् = हातुम्)
त्याग देने के लिए। to give up, to
remove.

हानभागिय – वि॰ – (हात / हान + भागीय)
छोड़ने के अनुकूल। conducive to
relinquishment.

हानि – स्त्री॰ – (हानि) क्षति, नुकसान।
loss, decrease.

हापक – वि॰ – (√ हा + णिच् + ण्वुल =
हापक) हानि का कारण, हानि पहुँचाने
वाला। causing decrease or loss.

हापन – न॰ – (हापन) क्षति, हानि। loss,
reduction.

हापेति – क्रि॰ – (हापेति) उपेक्षा करता है,
विलम्ब करता है, कम कर देता है।
omits, neglects, reduces, delays.

हायति – क्रि॰ – (√ हा - त्यागे = हायति)
घटाता है, व्यर्थ नष्ट करता है।
diminishes, dwindles, wastes
away.

हायन (1) – न॰ – (हायनम्) क्षीणता, कमी, ह्रास । decay, decrease.

हायन (2)– पु॰ – (हायन) वर्ष । a year.

हायी – वि॰ – (हायी) छोड़ देने वाला (प्रायः समस्त पद में प्रयुक्त) । one who gives up or leaves behind.

हार – पु॰ – (हार) फूलों या मोतियों अदि की माला । necklace, a string of pearls, or flowers.

हारक – वि॰ – (√ हृ + ण्वुल = हारक) हरने या ले जाने वाला । carrying, removing, ravishing, abducting.

हारिका – स्त्री॰ – (हारिका) हारक का स्त्री लिंग रूप । feminine of Hāraka.

हारिय – वि॰ – (√ हृ + ल्यप = हार्य) हरने योग्य, ले जाने योग्य । capable of being carried.

हास – पु॰ – (हास) हास, हँसी । laughter, mirth.

हासकर – वि॰ – (हासकर) आनन्दप्रद । giving pleasure.

हासेति – क्रि॰ – (हासयति) प्रसन्न करता है, हँसाता है । makes laugh.

√ हि – (तु॰) – (गत्याम्) जाना । to go.

हि – अव्यय – (हि) निश्चय से, वास्तव में । because, indeed.

हिक्का – स्त्री॰ – (हिक्का) हिचकी । hiccup.

हिड्गु – न॰ – (हिड्गु) हींग । the exudation of asafoetida plant.

हिड्गुसक – न॰ – (हिड्ड्गुल) सिन्दूर । vermilion.

हित – न॰ – (हित) भलाई (वि॰) उपयोगी (पु॰) मित्र । beneficial, suitable, friend.

हितकर – वि॰ – (हितकर) हित करने वाला । beneficial.

हितावह – वि॰ – (हितावह) हितकर । beneficial.

हितेसी – पु॰ – (हितैषी) हितैषी, हित चाहने वाला । well-wisher.

हिंताल – पु॰ – (हिन्ताल) ताल, खजूर । marshy date tree.

हिम – न॰ – (हिम) बर्फ । snow.

हिमवन्तु – वि॰ – (हिमवान) हिमालय पर्वत । the Himālaya mountain.

हियो – क्रि॰ वि॰ – (ह्यः) बीता हुआ कल । yesterday.

हिरञ्ञ – न॰ – (हिरण्य) स्वर्ण, सोना । gold.

√ हिरि – (दि॰) – (लज्जायाम्) शरमाना । feel shy.

हिरि – स्त्री॰ – (ही) त्रया, शर्म, लज्जा । shame, modesty.

हिरि-कोपीन – न॰ – (ही-कौपीनम्) लँगोटी । a strip of that passes in between the legs and covers private parts.

हिरिमन्तु – वि॰ – (ही-मान) शर्मीला । modest, bashful.

हिरियति – क्रि॰ – (ही-जिहेति) लज्ज करता है । blushes, feels shy, becomes ashamed.

हरीयना – स्त्री॰ – (ही) त्रया, लज्जा । shame, modesty.

हिरोत्तप्प – न॰ – (ही-तापन) लज्जा-भय, (पाप से) । shame or fear for sin.

√ हिलाद – (भू॰ चु॰) – (सुखे) सुखी होना । to be happy.

हिंसति – क्रि॰ – (√ हिंस - हिंसति) हिंसा करता है, चोट पहुँचाता है, चिढ़ाता है। hurts, injures, teases.

√ हिंस – (रु॰) – (हिंसा याम्) मारना, हिंसा करना। to kill.

हिंसन – न॰ – (हन् हिंसन) हिंसा करना, चोट पहुँचाना, चिढ़ाना। hurting, injury, teasing.

हिंसना – स्त्री॰ – (हन्) हिंसा, देखें हिंसन। violence, see Hinsana.

हिंसापेति – क्रि॰ – (√ हिंस + णिच = हिंसयति, हनति) कष्ट पहुँचाता है। causes to hurt or injure.

हीन – वि॰ – (हीन) तुच्छ, अधम, नीच। low, inferior, despicable.

हीन-जच्च – वि॰ – (हीन-जात्य) हीन-जन्मा। having a low birth.

हीन-विरिय – वि॰ – (हीन-वीर्य) पौरुषहीन, साहसहीन, हिम्मत हारे हुए। lacking in energy.

हीनाधि-मुत्तिक – वि॰ – (हीन लक्षणः) मन्द पौरुष, मन्दोत्साह। having low or poor vigour or enthusiasm.

हीयति – क्रि॰ – (हायति-क्षीयते) हानि को प्राप्त होता है, त्याग दिया जाता है। gets decreased or dwindled, decays in giving up.

हीयो – अव्यय – (ह्यः) बीता हुआ कल। yesterday.

हीर/हीरक – न॰ – (हरीम्) खमाची। a splinter, a stripe.

√ हील – (चु॰) – (निन्दायाम्) निन्दा करना। to insult, to condemn, to blame, to censure.

हीलन – न॰ – (हेलनम्) अवमानना, उपेक्षा, घृणा करना। disdain, contempt.

हीलमा – स्त्री॰ – (हेलना) देखें हीलन। see Hīlana.

हीलेति – क्रि॰ – घृणा करता है। hates, dislikes, to mock at.

हुत – न॰ – (√ हु + क्त = हुत) आहुति। the thing sacrificed, an oblation.

हुतासन – न॰ – (हुतासन) पावक, अग्नि। fire.

हुत्त – न॰ – (हुत) होम किया गया। sacrificed.

हुत्वा – पू॰ क्रि॰ – (भूत्वा) होकर। having been.

हुर – क्रि॰ वि॰ – दूसरे लोक में। in the other world, in the next birth.

हुंक – (भू॰) – (गमनार्थे) जाना। to go.

हुङ्कार – पु॰ – (हुङ्कार) हुङ्कति, हुंकार, 'हुं' शब्द। the sound *hum*.

√ हूं – (भू॰) – (सत्तयाम्) होना। exist.

हे – अव्यय – (हे) हे, हो आदि, सम्बोधन के लिए शब्द। a vocative particle hey, oh!.

हेट्ठतो – (हेटठतो भी) – क्रि॰ वि॰ – (अधस्तात्) नीचे से from below.

हेट्ठा – अव्यय – (अधस्तन) नीचे। below, down, under.

हेट्ठा-भाग – पु॰ – (अधोभाग) नीचे का भाग। lower portion.

हेट्ठा-मञ्चे – क्रि॰ वि॰ – (अधोमञ्चे) मंच, मचान, या चारपाई के नीचे। under the bed.

हेट्ठिम – वि॰ – (अधस्तम्) सबसे नीचे। lowest.

हेट्ठक – वि॰ – (पीडक) कष्टदायक । one who troubles.

हेठना – स्त्री॰ – (पीडनम्) कष्ट पहुँचाना । harassing.

हेठेति – क्रि॰ – (पीडयति, हत) व्यथित करता है, कष्ट पहुँचाता है । harasses, troubles, injures.

हेति – स्त्री॰ – (√ हन् + क्तिन् = हेति) हथियार । weapon.

हेतु – पु॰ – (हेतु) कारण । cause, reason.

हेतुक – वि॰ – (हेतुक) कारण से सम्बन्धित । connected with a cause.

हेतुप्प-भव – वि॰ – (हेतु प्रभव) एक कारण से हुआ । arising from a cause.

हेतुवाद – पु॰ – (हेतुवाद) कारण-कार्य अथवा हेतु-फल का सिद्धान्त । the theory of cause.

हेम – न॰ – (हेमन्) सोना । gold.

हेम-जाल – न॰ – (हेमजालम्) स्वर्ण-जाल । a golden netting.

हेमन्त – पु॰ – (हेमन्त) हेमन्त ऋतु, शीत काल, अगहन-पौष । winter season from mid-November to mid-January.

हेमन्तिक – पु॰ – (हेमन्तिक) हेमन्त ऋतु सम्बन्धी । belonging to winter.

हेम-वण्ण – वि॰ – (हेमवर्णः) सुनहरे रंग वाला । golden coloured.

हेम-वतक – वि॰ – (हिमि-गिरिवासी = हेमवतः) हिमालय में रहने वाला । dwelling in the Himālaya.

हेरञ्ञिक – पु॰ – (हिरण्यकर्मी) स्वर्णकार, सुनार । goldsmith.

हेला – स्त्री॰ – (हेला) आमोदमयी क्रीडा, हाव-भाव । keen sexual desire.

हेसा – स्त्री॰ – (हेषा) घोड़े का हिनहिनाना । the neighing of a horse.

हेसा-रव – पु॰ – (हेषा-रव) घोड़े के हिनहिनाने की आवाज । the neighing of a horse.

होति – क्रि॰ – (भवति) होता है । exists.

होम – न॰ – (होम) आहुति । oblation.

होम-दब्बि – स्त्री॰ – (होम-दर्वि) यज्ञ-स्रुवा, यज्ञ करने की कड़छी । the ladle used in pouring oblation.

होरा – स्त्री॰ – (होरा) घंटा । hour.

होरा-पाठक – पु॰ – (होरा-पाठक) ज्योतिषी । an astrologer.

होरा-यन्त – न॰ – (होरा-यन्त्र) कालबोधक यन्त्र, बड़ी घड़ी । any device showing the time, a clock.

होरा-लोचन – न॰ – (होरा-लोचन) होरा-दर्शक, घड़ी । a clock.